International
Encyclopedia of the
SOCIAL
SCIENCES

International Encyclopedia of the SOCIAL SCIENCES

DAVID L. SILLS EDITOR

VOLUME 1

The Macmillan Company & The Free Press

Production Staff

Walter W. Wriggins, *Administrative Editor*
Jean Paradise, *Managing Editor, Copy Department*
Judith S. Levey, *Senior Editor*
Sheila Meyer, *Production Coordinator*
Jane Rogers Tonero, *Director of Indexing*

Donna M. Smith, *Assistant Editor*
Barbara J. Westergaard, *Assistant Editor*

BIBLIOGRAPHY DEPARTMENT
Eizenija B. Shera, *Assistant Editor*
Hunter M. Wilson, *Bibliographer*
Karen Greenberg, *Editorial Assistant*
Gisele J. Juhasz, *Editorial Assistant*
Nancy T. Manson, *Editorial Assistant*

COPY DEPARTMENT
Pearl Greenberger, *Associate Editor*
George Shriver, *Associate Editor*
Susan H. Arensberg, *Assistant Editor*
Marshall De Bruhl, *Assistant Editor*
Bernard J. Johnston, *Assistant Editor*
Paule H. Jones, *Assistant Editor*
Susan J. Levinsohn, *Assistant Editor*
Leland S. Lowther, *Assistant Editor*
Martha R. Neufeld, *Assistant Editor*
Pauline Piekarz, *Assistant Editor*
Francine Pollner, *Assistant Editor*
Joyce D. Portnoy, *Assistant Editor*
Claire Sotnick, *Assistant Editor*
Doris Anne Sullivan, *Assistant Editor*
John F. Thornton, *Assistant Editor*
Elizabeth I. Wilson, *Assistant Editor*
Alice H. Klein, *Editorial Assistant*
Kendra C. Lifschutz, *Editorial Assistant*

SIDNEY SOLOMON
DIRECTOR OF DESIGN

Editorial Advisory Board

Foreword

AT THE CLOSE of World War I, many scholars throughout the United States felt the need for an encyclopedia of the social sciences. There were a number of reasons for this concern. First, at that time the graduate student majoring in any one of the social sciences was expected to be at home in all of them, and the chances were against his achieving this end through his courses alone. Often a graduate student would choose for his thesis a subject that had been handled adequately in some other thesis or in some treatise not known to him or his academic adviser. One could cite instances of students losing half a year in their progress toward a degree because of this lack of information. Some professors were indifferent to this situation. A student should expect that a given project would prove illusory. Following a false track was a part of education. But most teachers held the view that an encyclopedia was as essential for the graduate student of the social sciences as a general laboratory was for the student of the physical sciences.

Second, even at that time economists and social psychologists were drifting off into corporate jobs or public office. It was hard for these nonacademic scholars to use university libraries; for them, an encyclopedia of the social sciences would be a life saver.

Third, the academic scholars themselves were in need of a reference work to consult, and it was increasingly expected that a scholar be at home in adjacent fields. An encyclopedia of all the social sciences seemed to be one important solution to this problem.

Further, it was argued, such an encyclopedia was needed for the lay scholar of the social sciences. The contributions of nonacademic scholars to the social sciences have been notable. In economics, David Ricardo and John Stuart Mill made great contributions without claiming the title of professional economist. Alexander Hamilton and Thomas Jefferson made overwhelmingly important contributions to political science. In our own day there have been many able minds outside of the academic realm whose writings are worth reading. In most cases they would have been helped to come to sound conclusions by a competent encyclopedia.

But there were two grave objections. The world had not settled down after the war, and all the social sciences were in the process of change. It was alleged that an encyclopedia would be out of date on the day of its publication. And as matters stood at the time, the social sciences were ridden by cliques grouped around leading authorities. Economists lined up behind E. R. A. Seligman, John Bates Clark, Frank W. Taussig, Jacob Hollander, Richard T. Ely, and J. Lawrence Laughlin. Sociologists formed cliques around Franklin H. Giddings and Albion W. Small. Anthropologists gathered around Franz Boas and Bronislaw Malinowski; students of jurisprudence followed Roscoe Pound and Karl Llewellyn. Now, if we undertook to put out an encyclopedia, what clique would run it, and what would be the attitude of other cliques?

We who ardently wanted an encyclopedia agreed that the social sciences were undergoing rapid change, but they had always been undergoing change and would continue to do so. An encyclopedia could summarize the achievements of the outgoing generation. In twenty or thirty years we would need an entirely new encyclopedia, and another in twenty or thirty years after that. We pictured to ourselves the fortunate position of the future scholar with a series of encyclopedias to enlighten him on the progress of ideas.

And as for cliques, those of us who had had experience on popular encyclopedias thought we knew very well how to deal with them in such a way as to draw all of them into our common project.

We formed committees, solicited foundation support, and got nowhere. But finally a committee organized at the New School for Social Research by Alexander Goldenweiser, a most talented but erratic general scholar of the social sciences, although officially an anthropologist, succeeded in enlisting Professor E. R. A. Seligman of Columbia. Professor Seligman was known as a scholar of far-reaching competence in the social sciences who had a widespread acquaintance among scholars at home and abroad. He was highly visible to the foundations and the publishers, as none of the rest of us had ever been. In a few meetings he brought together the Rockefeller, Carnegie, and Russell Sage foundations and The Macmillan Company in order to launch an encyclopedia under his editorship.

Professor Seligman knew nearly everything, but not how to make an encyclopedia. He had been my teacher and a warm friend through my early years as a professor of economics in various universities. I had been an encyclopedist in a small way. Beginning as an emergency contributor, I had soon become the office editor for economics on the *New International Encyclopaedia*, under Frank Moore Colby. Soon I had to take over sociology, and not long after that political science. And I learned how to walk barefoot among the hot embers of mistaken commitments.

It was not unnatural that Professor Seligman should ask me to examine the great commission he had undertaken as editor of the *Encyclopaedia of the Social Sciences*. He unfolded his plan—himself as editor, an associate editor, a copy editor (probably a depressed lady scholar), three or four secretaries, and a far-flung farming out of articles.

I loved E. R. A., and I hated to throw cold water on his ideas, but I had to say that this is no way to make a real encyclopedia. In the first place, articles should not be farmed out. Every article should be assigned to the man who is to sign it. In the second place, there should be a staff of eight or ten young PH.D.s, who are still used to running around to libraries, laboratories, anywhere. No professors out of a job; professors want to sit, but encyclopedia work is not a sitting job. And, I added, although reluctantly, that he had agreements with the foundations for support that would supply only half the amount needed to put out a respectable encyclopedia. Professor Seligman thanked me with all the ardor you expect from a man whose project you have criticized. It was weeks before I saw him again.

When I did, he said, "Alvin, I tried to get A. A. Young to be associate editor, and I have tried six other people. I had been warned not to try you, because you are bent on your own way."

"Yes," I said, "I've been warned not to go in with you if I am asked, because you are bent on your own way. But maybe we can put our own ways together and do a job."

"All right, let's try it," said E. R. A. At this point, let me say that in seven years our opinions never once conflicted and never did the slightest cloud obscure our personal friendship.

I specified that there would be no farming out of articles. Every article, big or small, would be assigned directly to the contributor. Every topic would be dissected into constituent elements for separate articles and there would be no assignment of more than 5,000 words. Furthermore, no scholar would be asked for more than one article for each volume. This rule, we believed, would ban the cliques. Every article would first be read by the associate editor and then put in the hands of one competent assistant editor for fact checking and another for bibliographical checking. If an article needed revision, the associate editor would revise it and send the revised copy to the author, with appropriate apologies. This was agreed to.

It was our practice to make lists of related topics, perhaps twenty of them, and send them out to scholars competent in the field with the request, "If any of these topics are worthless, please strike them out. If any topic appeals to you, will you write on it for us? If you know anyone who could handle another topic, will you let us have his name?"

We sent out four hundred such letters. Two brought no replies. We found out later that these correspondents were dead. The rest replied in a most cooperative spirit, except one, a socialist, who felt that if we wanted to pick his brains we should offer him a fee!

We never met that bogey of cliques. We asked scholars independently of clique position, and they responded as scholars. No review of the encyclopedia ever charged us with favoring one clique or another.

In 1950, at the request of my associates and the publisher, I made a survey of the encyclopedia volumes to decide how far a revision would need to go. I found that roughly one-third of the articles could stand; one-third could go with more or less extensive revision; and the last third would need to be replaced with new articles. I might have added to my report that even the articles that could stand would contain vestiges of the past in proportion, emphasis, and objectives.

I was willing to work on such a revision, but I had never believed in the practice of revising encyclopedias; I have always held that an encyclopedia, particularly one of the social sciences, should remain a historical document of its time and that each generation should have an encyclopedia —new from the ground up. And I am very happy that this is what we now have: an encyclopedia that is entirely new, entirely expressive of the times.

ALVIN JOHNSON

Preface

THIS ENCYCLOPEDIA is, first and foremost, the work of social scientists. It is part of the fabric of their professional literature—their journals, annals, proceedings, monographs, treatises, textbooks, and expository writings. It has been planned by social scientists, directed by social scientists, and edited by social scientists. The writers, with a number of important exceptions, are social scientists. Social scientists will be the most frequent users, although undoubtedly they will be a minority among students, journalists, lawyers, legislators, administrators, educators, other professional people, and all the other users.

Recognition of those responsible for the creation of the encyclopedia must, therefore, start with the social scientists themselves. Many—perhaps even most—of the leading social scientists of this generation have written it. Their work has been admirable, not only in its excellence but in its accommodation to the encyclopedia's needs in content, exposition, and schedule. Credit for the quality of the articles belongs to the authors.

The influence of the associate editors, each responsible for one of the major social sciences, and of the special editors, each responsible for an important specialty, has been considerably greater than is the case for a professional journal. Their work required not only evaluating articles after submission and suggesting improvements, but planning the articles to be included, ascertaining who could best write each article, and persuading him to write it. Even though the associate and special editors could not have done what the authors did, the value to the encyclopedia of what the authors did was dependent on the associate and special editors. We were fortunate indeed in securing the dedication of so able a group of editors.

Above all, it is to the editor, David L. Sills, that the character and quality of the encyclopedia must be credited. While he could not have done what the associate and special editors did, they could not have made their contributions without his participation in their work, his coordination of the various fields that they represented, his direction of the editorial staff that supported them, his management of the procedures for assigning, scheduling, editing, verifying, cross-referencing, indexing, and proofreading the articles, and especially his intellectual leadership and standards.

Several people were responsible for the launching of this undertaking, but principally Alvin Johnson, Bernard Berelson, and Jeremiah Kaplan.

Johnson recognized the need and attempted to interest those who could fulfill it. Berelson picked up Johnson's idea, had it thoroughly studied and evaluated, and had a plan prepared for a new encyclopedia of the social sciences. Kaplan secured a commitment from the publishers and played a leading role in selecting the editors.

Johnson had, with E. R. A. Seligman, edited the *Encyclopaedia of the Social Sciences*, which was prepared between 1927 and 1933 and published between 1930 and 1935. This had been financed by three foundations. Twenty years after its publication, Johnson tried to interest these foundations and others in supporting a revision of that encyclopedia. His words fell on deaf ears until January 1954, when they reached Berelson, then an officer of the Ford Foundation. Berelson and his associate, Francis X. Sutton, solicited advice from about twenty social scientists and a similar number of librarians. This advice was generally positive, and in March 1955 Berelson held a conference that also found much merit in the idea.

At Berelson's suggestion, and with Ford Foundation funds, a special group was formed to study the matter; it met during the summer of 1955 under my chairmanship. The other members were Kingsley Davis (sociology), Clyde Kluckhohn (anthropology), Lyle H. Lanier (psychology), Charles McKinley (political science), Frederick Mosteller (statistics), Arthur M. Schlesinger, Sr. (history), and Jacob Viner (economics). A small staff worked under the direction of Bert F. Hoselitz, who in 1951 had independently proposed the preparation of a new or revised encyclopedia of the social sciences.

The study group, with major assistance from Hoselitz, prepared a report of 65 pages—supported by 193 pages of appendix materials by the staff and by consultants—entitled *A Study of the Need for a New Cyclopedic Treatment of the Social Sciences*, dated August 25, 1955. Of its recommendations, which were submitted "unanimously and without reservations," the principal ones were as follows:

> . . . what is needed is a completely new social science cyclopedia of the highest quality. . . . The new cyclopedia should, in our opinion, be both narrower and broader in scope than [the *Encyclopaedia of the Social Sciences*]. On the one hand, we recommend reducing the amount of purely descriptive matter and eliminating articles upon certain topics competently and more appropriately treated in general cyclopedias. On the other hand, we urge inclusion of considerably more material upon methods, empirical regularities, and such subjects as human biology, linguistics, and the interrelations between the social sciences and various other disciplines. A new cyclopedia of the scope we propose would contain about eight million words. . . . Virtually all of the cyclopedia would be written by contributors chosen according to professional qualifications, not only from the United States, but from any part of the world.

These and most other recommendations of the study group are carried out in this encyclopedia.

While the study was in progress, arrangements were made with Pendleton Herring to hold at a number of universities—under the auspices of the Social Science Research Council—discussions of the possibility of a new encyclopedia and to devote two sessions of the council's meeting in the fall of 1955 to the subject.

The matter was then dormant—indeed, apparently dead—for five years until it was brought to life in December 1960 by Jeremiah Kaplan, who had followed the proposals closely and with great sympathy and had assisted the study group. Late in 1960 he arranged to merge his publishing firm, The Free Press of Glencoe, with the Crowell-Collier Publishing Company, which shortly before had acquired The Macmillan Company, publishers of the *Encyclopaedia of the Social Sciences*. Almost immediately after the merger was arranged, Raymond C. Hagel, president of Crowell-Collier (now Crowell Collier and Macmillan, Inc.), committed that firm to invest two million dollars in the preparation and publication of this new encyclopedia, and I became chairman of the Editorial Advisory Board. (On the early history of this encyclopedia, see Francis X. Sutton, "Developing the Idea of a New Social Science Encyclopedia," *American Behavioral Scientist*, September 1962, pp. 27–30.)

The initial members of the Editorial Advisory Board were selected by Kaplan, Edward Shils, Morris Janowitz, and me. The initial members and the editors then nominated other members of the board, and others were added as preparation of the encyclopedia proceeded. The members of the Editorial Advisory Board reviewed the preliminary table of contents; they made suggestions on articles and contributors; and they advised on a variety of questions during the work. It is a pleasure to acknowledge our debt to this distinguished international Editorial Advisory Board.

Shils, Kaplan, Janowitz, and I also selected the editor and, with his advice, the associate editors. Initially, Bert F. Hoselitz was editor. In the fall of 1961 the editorial offices were moved from Chicago to New York; an entirely new group of editors and staff was appointed, with Hoselitz becoming special editor for economic development; and preparation of the encyclopedia as it stands today got under way.

Janowitz, Kaplan, Shils, and I have continued as an executive committee under my chairmanship, joined part of the time by W. D. Halsey and Martin Kessler, but our administrative activities have been minimal since the first few months of Sills' editorship. To him belongs the credit for planning, organizing, and executing what will prove to be, I am confident, one of the proudest and most enduring works of our generation of social scientists—the "important historical and cultural event" called for by the 1955 study group.

W. Allen Wallis

Introduction

THE *International Encyclopedia of the Social Sciences* is a completely new reference work, designed to complement, not to supplant, its predecessor, the *Encyclopaedia of the Social Sciences*. That 15-volume set was edited by Edwin R. A. Seligman and Alvin Johnson and published by The Macmillan Company between 1930 and 1935. It has never been revised, and the original edition remains in print.

The major aims of this encyclopedia are to reflect and encourage the rapid development of the social sciences throughout the world. It consists entirely of articles prepared expressly for it at the invitation of the editors; no articles have been reprinted from the earlier encyclopedia or from any other publication.

The expansion of the social sciences in recent years has been remarkable from many points of view. The growth in the number of social scientists in the world and the annual increase in the number of new social science publications of all kinds are, of course, a part of the general explosion of science that characterizes our age. A consequence of this explosion is the growth in public awareness, acceptance, and use of the social sciences. The widespread use of both social scientists and social science by government agencies; business and industry; schools, colleges, and universities; philanthropic foundations; religious bodies; and voluntary associations of many kinds provides abundant evidence of this growth. There is hardly a social, economic, or political problem in the world that social scientists are not asked to study, and many programs undertaken to alleviate such problems are subject to social scientific scrutiny and evaluation. Particularly in industrialized countries, but increasingly in others, the social sciences have become an indispensable source of guidance for administrators and professionals of all kinds.

Further evidence of this growth is the extent to which the social sciences have permeated society itself. It is not just that the vocabulary of the social sciences has infiltrated everyday speech, although it is common for persons with no formal training in the social sciences to use such terms as "IQ," "subculture," "power structure," "GNP," and "the unconscious" in their daily conversation. More important, many people today perceive the world differently because they have been exposed to the perspective of the social sciences: they raise their children differently; they have different attitudes toward government borrowing and spending; they make different judgments of their friends, neighbors, and family members;

they view both local and national politics differently; they place a different and more sympathetic interpretation upon the guilt of criminals, drug addicts, and deviants of all kinds; and they make different judgments of their own successes and failures. Whether people are aware of it or not, whether they like it or not, the social sciences have influenced, if not determined, the assumptions about reality upon which their daily lives are based.

The rapid development of any branch of science always creates problems, and the social sciences are no exception. There is concern in some quarters that social science research often entails the invasion of individual privacy—a concern that many social scientists have come to share. There are critics who assert that the scientific study of social and political life diminishes the wonder and mystery that for them constitute the essence of human experience. There is no answer to this criticism: the social sciences do explain aspects of human behavior that were previously mysterious. Insofar as they have contributed to rational understanding, the social sciences have fostered the secular trend toward the "disenchantment (*Entzauberung*) of the world," to use the phrase of Schiller's that Max Weber made famous. Yet it should be pointed out that in explaining behavior the social sciences do not explain away man's ultimate need for mystery.

Regardless of what we may think about the quality of life in the prescientific era (and the evidence suggests that for most people life was more brutal and brutalizing a century ago than it is today), the ethos of that time cannot be restored; and the satisfactions and material advantages that derive from understanding and from some measure of control seem in the 1960s to be mankind's best hope for a measure of contentment. It is perhaps relevant to note that in recent decades the leaders of the churches of all the major faiths have become sympathetic supporters and users of the social sciences.

Expansion of the social science curriculum in universities, professional schools, colleges, and even secondary schools has placed great demands upon the available supply of teachers. Terminology and research procedures are far from standardized, both within and between the various disciplines. The availability of funds and the opportunities for participation in large-scale empirical research projects have led many young social scientists to neglect the study of the history of their disciplines, with unfortunate consequences for the systematic cumulation of knowledge. Specialization, normally a mark of scientific maturity, has often been achieved by ignoring related avenues of approach to the same problems. Since it is impossible to read more than a fraction of the relevant new books and articles, many social scientists are less informed than they should be about new developments, even in their own fields. Finally, the emergence of new nations, which have more than their share of old problems, has dramatized the need for both understanding and remedial action based to some extent upon social scientific knowledge.

This is a formidable set of problems, but it is the hope of the editors that the encyclopedia may in some ways serve to mitigate them. We think that the articles and attached bibliographies will be helpful to teachers and students throughout the world by providing summaries of what is known about many hundreds of topics. The encyclopedia should help in the standardization of terminology and research procedures, largely through example but also through articles that have been included expressly for this purpose, for example, the articles on EXPERIMENTAL DESIGN; GRAPHIC

PRESENTATION; SAMPLE SURVEYS; SCALING; SURVEY ANALYSIS; and TABULAR PRESENTATION. The biographies and the articles on the individual disciplines will provide many social scientists with an introduction to the history of their field of specialization.

We have sought to counteract some of the unfortunate consequences of specialization by deliberately placing two or more articles from different fields under one entry. The problem of keeping abreast of relevant new developments is discussed—but certainly not solved—in a number of articles. The article on CONFERENCES, the articles under the heading INFORMATION STORAGE AND RETRIEVAL, and the article on SCIENTIFIC COMMUNICATION under the heading SCIENCE are specifically related to this problem. The issue of privacy is discussed in the article entitled PRIVACY and in the article on ETHICAL ISSUES IN THE SOCIAL SCIENCES under the heading ETHICS.

The encyclopedia has been prepared for social scientists themselves, for students of the social sciences, and for professionals from other fields who seek information about a topic in the social sciences; we believe that it will also find many readers among the public at large. We have not attempted to make every article useful to the reader without prior knowledge of the subject, but we have tried to make the exposition in each case as clear as the content permits. Moreover, by inserting guides to the reader and appropriate cross references to other articles, we have attempted to direct the reader to the articles that are most suited to his needs.

Scope of the Encyclopedia

The question "What Are the Social Sciences?" is the title of Edwin R. A. Seligman's opening chapter in the Introduction to the earlier *Encyclopaedia of the Social Sciences*. Professor Seligman's first answer was to define the social sciences as "those mental or cultural sciences which deal with the activities of the individual as a member of a group." His second answer was to list the disciplines that were included in the encyclopedia. In so doing, he made a distinction between the social sciences (which he defined as politics, economics, law, anthropology, sociology, penology, and social work); the semi-social sciences (ethics, education, philosophy, and psychology); and the sciences with social implications (biology, geography, medicine, linguistics, and art).

It is apparent from this definition that the question "What are the social sciences?" is one to which no final answer can be given, since—like other groupings of scientific and academic fields—the social sciences differ in their scope from one generation to another. There are also within-generation differences: witness the continuing controversies over whether history should be considered as one of the social sciences or as a humanistic discipline; whether geography is an independent social science or a synthetic discipline that draws upon both the social sciences and the earth sciences; whether law is a social science or a body of professional knowledge; whether psychology belongs with the social or the natural sciences; and whether psychiatry is a social science or a branch of medicine.

These controversies will not soon be resolved, nor need they be. In fact, it can be argued that a certain amount of controversy and diversity is beneficial. Universities throughout the world follow different practices in assigning social science departments to graduate faculties and professional schools, and it cannot be demonstrated that the absence of a universal system of classification has impeded the progress of either teaching or research. What is required is only that whoever uses the term "social sciences" make clear what he includes under this heading.

The scope of the present encyclopedia has been determined in part by the scope of the earlier encyclopedia and in part by the recommendations of the Ford Foundation-sponsored study group at the University of Chicago described by W. Allen Wallis in the Preface to this encyclopedia. For the most part, however, it has been determined by the editors themselves. The majority of the topical articles are devoted to the concepts, theories, and methods of the following disciplines:

Anthropology—includes cultural, economic, physical, political, social, and applied anthropology, as well as archeology, ethnography, ethnology, and linguistics.

Economics—includes econometrics, economic history, the history of economic thought, economic development, agricultural economics, industrial organization, international economics, labor economics, money and banking, public finance, and certain aspects of business management.

Geography—includes cultural, economic, political, and social geography, but not physical geography.

History—includes the traditional subject-matter fields of history and the scope and methods of historiography.

Law—includes jurisprudence, the major legal systems, legal theory, and the relationship of law to the other social sciences.

Political science—includes public administration, public law, international relations, comparative politics, political theory, and the study of policy making and political behavior.

Psychiatry—includes theories and descriptions of the principal mental disorders and methods of diagnosis and treatment.

Psychology—includes clinical, counseling, educational, experimental, personality, physiological, social, and applied psychology.

Sociology—includes economic, organizational, political, rural, and urban sociology; the sociologies of knowledge, law, religion, and medicine; human ecology; the history of social thought; sociometry and other small-group research; survey research; and such special fields as criminology and demography.

Statistics—includes theoretical statistics, the design of experiments, nonsampling errors, sample surveys, government statistics, and the use of statistical methods in social science research.

The reader who consults the entry for each of these ten fields of study will find a guide or cross references to the major topical and biographical articles related to the discipline. In addition, a large number of articles present modern social thought about the arts, the major religions, and many of the professions. The encyclopedia also includes articles on the major societies of the world; the article Societal analysis provides a discussion of these articles. The articles Area studies; Behavioral sciences; and Regional science are examples of new fields or new groupings of old fields that we have included.

The inclusion of statistics in this encyclopedia deserves special discussion, since today statistics is not generally considered to be one of the social sciences. Some of its main origins, however, were in the social sciences, and it has always had a close and mutually fruitful relationship with the social sciences. All the social sciences today depend increasingly upon statistical methods for the gathering and interpretation of their data; accordingly, we have treated statistics as a critical auxiliary discipline and have included both articles on a wide range of statistical topics and biographies of statisticians whose work is of continuing importance.

Contents of the Encyclopedia

The goal of the editors has been to make the new encyclopedia as much a distinctive product of the current generation of social scientists as the earlier encyclopedia was of its generation. We have sought to make available to readers throughout the world the concepts, principles, theories, methods, and empirical regularities that characterize the social sciences today. Contributors were advised that the major emphasis of their articles should be on the analytical and comparative aspects of the topic and that historical and descriptive material should be included primarily to illustrate concepts and theories. The international audience of the encyclopedia was also stressed, and contributors were urged to use research and illustrative material from as many societies as possible.

TOPICAL ARTICLES

The selection and arrangement of topics for a multidisciplinary encyclopedia require the satisfactory resolution of a number of dilemmas: some of these must be resolved by the editors of any encyclopedia; others are peculiar to an encyclopedia that stresses concepts and theories.

The major dilemma can be expressed as "alphabetization versus systematization." It was decided very early in the planning that an alphabetical arrangement would be most useful to readers. The subject matter of the social sciences, however, does not easily lend itself to alphabetical treatment.

We have tried to resolve this dilemma in three ways. First, many specific articles that share a general subject matter are grouped under one title. The entry DIFFUSION, for example, is made up of an article by an anthropologist on cultural diffusion, an article by a geographer on the diffusion of innovations, and an article by a sociologist on the role of interpersonal influence in the process of diffusion.

Second, we have provided as many guides as possible to the location of articles in the encyclopedia. Articles are located in an alphabetical position that we hope will be consulted by most readers, and alternative entries give a cross reference to the actual location. The reader who consults the entry SOCIAL STRATIFICATION, for example, is directed to STRATIFICATION, SOCIAL. When several articles are grouped under one entry, alternative entries are provided with a cross reference to this entry. For example, the reader who looks under "R" for an article on the Rorschach test is told to consult the entry PROJECTIVE METHODS. An extensive system of cross references within articles has also been developed to guide the reader with specialized interests.

Third, there is an exhaustive index. It is a commonplace for editors of reference books to urge readers to consult the index first; it is also the common practice of users of reference books to search under an alphabetical heading in the text *before* consulting the index. Accordingly, as far as possible the encyclopedia has been made self-indexing; that is, the articles themselves and the cross references that lead to them constitute a partial index. Although entries have been included in the body of the encyclopedia for the majority of topics that readers might consult, these entries cannot be a true substitute for an index, and readers are advised to follow the traditional advice if they have difficulty in locating a topic. The volume and page location of many names and specific topics can of course be obtained only by consulting the index.

Another dilemma has involved coping with the changing vocabulary and mode of organization of the social sciences. Topics are constantly being regrouped along analytical, substantive, and methodological lines. In the early stages of the preparation of the encyclopedia the editors considered whether it was possible to develop a conceptual outline of all the social sciences, from which article titles could then be derived.

It became apparent that this was not possible, although each disciplinary editor used a system of his own for ensuring optimal coverage. As a result, the encyclopedia reflects the diversity in modes of organizing knowledge that characterizes the social sciences today. The titles of articles are on many analytical levels: social processes (acculturation, cooperation, socialization) and social pathologies (crime, poverty, war); individual faculties (hearing, reasoning, thinking) and individual pathologies (blindness, drug addiction, paranoia); economic processes (competition, decision making, economic growth) and economic institutions (cartels and trade associations, central banks, cooperatives); political doctrines (anarchism, conservatism, liberalism) and forms of government (democracy, dictatorship, monarchy); cultural expressions (architecture, film, language) and forms of settlement (city, neighborhood, village); stages in the life cycle (infancy, adolescence, aging) and forms of social life (friendship, marriage, family); methods of empirical research (index numbers, sampling, interviewing) and methods of presenting research results (graphs, tables). In brief, the articles reveal the social sciences in all their diversity and complexity; the editors, for their part, have attempted to provide as many editorial guides to this complexity as they deemed necessary.

BIOGRAPHICAL ARTICLES

The encyclopedia includes biographies of some six hundred persons whose research and writings have had an impact upon the social sciences. This is many fewer than the four thousand biographies in the earlier encyclopedia—for reasons described below. However, the biographical articles in this encyclopedia are considerably longer; the median length is approximately 1,500 words, and 100 of them are over 2,500 words.

The editors had no clear mandate in making decisions about the people whose biographies they should include, what proportion of the total text should be devoted to biographies, the proper length of a biography, or what relationship the biographies should have to the topical articles. The Ford Foundation study group report contained suggestions that ranged from including only biographies of "major" figures to preparing a separate "dictionary of social science biography"—a work that would devote some two million words to 3,500 individuals. Members of the Editorial Advisory Board also gave contradictory advice: the advice of one distinguished scholar was to include no biographies at all, on the grounds that they are out of place in a topically and conceptually oriented reference work; another thought that there should be *only* biographical articles in the encyclopedia, on the grounds that these are the only articles in the earlier encyclopedia that he ever reads!

The notion of excluding biographies entirely was never seriously considered, partly because of tradition, partly because of the widespread interest in the individuals who developed the social science disciplines.

But most important, it was felt that the majority of the contributors would not be able to include much material on the history of their topics in the space assigned to them and that the biographies would serve to complement the topical articles by providing some measure of intellectual history. For this reason, the editors have tried to tie the biographies to the topical articles with two-way cross references; where they have not done this, the relevant entries in the index will often indicate the topical articles or biographies that should be consulted.

We did briefly consider having biographies only of major figures, but this possible course of action was rejected for two reasons. First, biographies and critical works about many major figures—for example, Sigmund Freud, John Maynard Keynes, Rousseau, Adam Smith, or Max Weber—are widely available. Second, we believed that the development of a science cannot be described or explained adequately by the contributions of the major figures in its history; the original, if smaller-scale, work of others is perhaps cumulatively of equal importance.

But we also rejected the suggestion that the encyclopedia have 3,000 to 4,000 biographies, and again for two reasons. First, it seemed likely that the readership of many of these biographies would be very small. Second, it seemed unlikely that contributors could be found who could write interesting and useful articles about many minor figures. The social science disciplines have for the most part neglected their histories, and biographical source material even about fairly well-known people is often hard to find.

The biographical subjects were selected in a variety of ways. Lists of obvious candidates were drawn up and circulated among the editors, members of the Editorial Advisory Board, and consultants. Names were added to and deleted from these lists as a consensus developed; fashioning the list was a continuous process right up to the time when the printing schedule made further additions impossible. We cannot claim that we used a systematic selection procedure; rather, we relied on the informed judgment of the editors and other scholars.

One further departure from the practice followed by the editors of the earlier encyclopedia should be mentioned: biographies of living persons are included in this encyclopedia. We felt that readers should not be deprived of information about a man because he happened to live a long time; however, we felt that in order to be included a person should have completed most of his scientific work. Accordingly, a rule was established that no living person could be included who was born after 1890.

The list that was finally established contains essentially three types of persons. First, there are the key figures in the development of each discipline: Franz Boas, Alfred L. Kroeber, and Bronislaw Malinowski in anthropology; John Maynard Keynes, Adam Smith, and Léon Walras in economics; Aristotle, Machiavelli, and Charles E. Merriam in political science; Sigmund Freud, Clark L. Hull, and Pavlov in psychology; Émile Durkheim, Karl Marx, and Max Weber in sociology; and R. A. Fisher, Karl Pearson, and Abraham Wald in statistics. We believe that the encyclopedia contains articles on all persons of this stature.

Second, there are the important figures who are below this level of eminence: Leo Frobenius, Marcel Granet, or Earnest A. Hooton in anthropology; Jules Dupuit, Gustav Schmoller, or Joseph A. Schumpeter in economics; Walter Bagehot, A. D. Lindsay, or Gaetano Mosca in political science; C. E. Spearman, Edward L. Thorndike, or Edward C. Tolman in psychology; Charles H. Cooley, L. T. Hobhouse, or Georg Simmel in sociology; Ladislaus von Bortkiewicz, Adolphe Quetelet, or G. Udny Yule in statistics. We think that we cover at least three-fourths of the persons of this level of achievement, biased toward contemporary figures, since it is often difficult for readers to find information about twentieth-century social scientists, and biased toward those who have written in English, because these are generally the people who have had the most impact upon the social sciences as they are described by the contributors to this encyclopedia. (This does not mean that the biographical subjects are mainly Anglo–Americans; most are not, and many more became American or British only through the massive migration of scholars from continental Europe in the 1930s.)

Third, there is a widely divergent group of biographical subjects that was selected to provide an indication of the range of persons whose ideas have contributed significantly to the social sciences. Plato, Shang Yang, and Kautilya are examples of persons from antiquity whose ideas remain important. Historians who had what would today be called a social science orientation are represented by, for example, Karl Lamprecht, James Harvey Robinson, Frederick Jackson Turner, and Giovanni Battista Vico; legal theorists by Eugen Ehrlich, Hermann Kantorowicz, and Hans Kelsen. Philosophers whose relevance for the social sciences is great, even if it has not been fully appreciated, include Edmund Husserl, Moritz Schlick, and Alfred North Whitehead. Major figures from geography, law, education, and the history of science are also represented. From the social sciences themselves this group includes people whose influence has been important but limited in scope—Ernst Engel because of Engel's law; Patrick Geddes because of his influence upon city planning; Ziya Gökalp, Harold J. Laski, and D. N. Majumdar because they influenced an entire generation of scholars in their countries. Finally, we have also included a few biographies of "has beens," persons whose influence was once wide but who have almost been forgotten, and a few "might have beens," or "should have beens," scholars who were never fully appreciated during their lifetimes and are perhaps little known even today.

Of the approximately six hundred scholars who have biographies in this encyclopedia, more than half were not included in the earlier encyclopedia, despite the fact that it contained nearly seven times as many biographies. Most of the biographies that are new to this encyclopedia are of persons who were alive during the early 1930s and thus ineligible for inclusion in the earlier work. In fact, more than one hundred of the scholars who have biographies in this encyclopedia were contributors to the previous one, which attests to the skill of its editors in marshaling the significant scholars of the generation. A number of biographies that are new to this encyclopedia, however, are of persons who were eligible by the criteria of the earlier work. We cannot determine why they were not included, but some of their characteristics are interesting. Approximately half were physiologists, experimental psychologists, mathematicians, and statisticians—scientists whose relevance for the social sciences is undoubtedly better appreciated today than it was thirty-five years ago. A few are persons whose contributions were virtually unknown thirty-five years ago but who have since been discovered or rediscovered. Nearly all of these new biographical subjects are Europeans, which suggests that the European contribution to the social sciences is widely appreciated today—despite occasional allegations to the contrary. There are undoubtedly some whom the editors of the earlier encyclopedia would have liked to include but did not because they could not find a qualified contributor.

BIBLIOGRAPHIES

The selected bibliographies that follow each article serve two purposes. First, they contain the relevant information about works cited in the text; the entries in the bibliographies thus constitute the documentation of the article. Second, the bibliographies contain suggestions for further reading, sources for further bibliography, sources for historical and current data, and the titles of journals concerned more or less exclusively with the topic of the article.

The entries in the bibliographies were for the most part selected by the contributors. The bibliographical staff has verified the accuracy of each entry and has often provided additional bibliographical information about it. In a few instances the editors have added new items that came to their attention after the contributor had submitted the article; in other instances, considerations of space made it necessary to shorten the bibliography provided by the contributor. The entries listed under the heading WORKS BY in the bibliographies of the biographical articles are selected bibliographies of the subject's writings; whenever possible, publications giving more extensive bibliographies are included.

When a specific work is mentioned in the text of an article, the date given as a citation to the bibliography of the article is the date (or dates) when the work was first published; or, in the occasional instance of works that remained in manuscript form for many years, when it was written. (We have followed this practice because this date is important information if the chronological development of ideas is not to be distorted.)

The date of first publication is usually given in parentheses both in the text of articles and in the bibliographies; when it is given in the text, the context distinguishes it from dates in parentheses that signify biographical data. If pages from a subsequent edition are given in a citation in the text, the date of first publication is given in brackets, followed by the date of the edition used for the page references.

The following examples, from the text and the bibliography of the article on BUREAUCRACY, illustrate several of these bibliographical details:

> In sum, these ideal types of administration and the rule of law are more fully realized "the more completely [they] succeed in achieving the exclusion of love, hatred, and every purely personal, especially irrational and incalculable, feeling from the execution of official tasks" (Weber [1922*b*] 1954, p. 351).

> WEBER, MAX (1922*b*) 1954 *Max Weber on Law in Economy and Society.* Edited, with an introduction and annotations, by Max Rheinstein. Cambridge, Mass.: Harvard Univ. Press. → First published as Chapter 7 of Max Weber's *Wirtschaft und Gesellschaft.*

The goal of the bibliographical staff has been to make it possible for readers in libraries to find the works listed with a minimum of effort. The cataloguing procedures of libraries throughout the world vary widely; as a rule, the practices of the U.S. Library of Congress have been followed in determining whether an entry should be alphabetized and cited by title, by the name of the author, or by the organization that published or sponsored the work.

The bibliographies include some works described as unpublished manuscripts. These are of two kinds. A few are documents that exist in typescript or in mimeographed form and that for one reason or another have not been published. Most, however, are manuscripts that were in press at the time the bibliography was printed.

Contributors

We endeavored to select for each article the most qualified scholar we could locate; at the same time, we tried to achieve as much institutional and geographical representation as possible. The contributors are from more than thirty countries, and we are deeply indebted to them all. They took their assignments seriously, they performed admirably, and nearly all were conscientious about meeting the delivery dates we imposed. Their articles were reviewed by the editors, primarily for clarity and standardization of usage, but also for the appropriateness of content; virtually all of the consequent suggestions for revisions were agreed upon, and each contributor was sent a final version of his article for his review and correction.

It must be recorded, however, that not all the articles that were commissioned were delivered, and not all the articles delivered met the standards set by the editors. We are particularly grateful to those contributors who responded to our last-minute appeals for articles to replace those that never arrived or could not be accepted; thanks to them, we feel that no essential topic has been omitted.

Our requests to contributors for revisions of their articles must have seemed at times to be unreasonable; our urgent pleas to them to submit overdue manuscripts must at times have seemed shrill. Perspective on this aspect of editor–contributor relationships can be gained from the words of the nineteenth-century English mathematician Augustus De Morgan. In the course of writing a review of new editions of the *English Cyclopaedia* and the *Encyclopaedia Britannica*, De Morgan complimented the editors upon their success in obtaining contributions in these words:

If any one should imagine that a mixed mass of contributors is a punctual piece of machinery, let him take to editing upon that hypothesis, and he shall see what he shall see and learn what he shall learn.

(*Athenaeum*, October 19, 1861)

The names and affiliations of all contributors are listed in a directory adjacent to the index, together with the titles of the articles they wrote. Since the encyclopedia has been planned to represent the social sciences of the 1960s, most contributors belong to the generation that is in midcareer. However, the continuity between this encyclopedia and the earlier one is reflected in the fact that the 60 scholars in the list that follows have spanned the generations by contributing to both encyclopedias:

Georg Andrén	Maurice Dobb	R. F. Harrod
Thurman Arnold	Merle Fainsod	Friedrich A. von Hayek
Harry Elmer Barnes	Frank W. Fetter	Rudolf Heberle
Edwin G. Boring	P. Sargant Florence	Pendleton Herring
Marian Bowley	Maurice Fréchet	Harold Hotelling
Crane Brinton	Carl J. Friedrich	Otto Klineberg
Ruth Bunzel	Morris Ginsberg	Hans Kohn
Lester V. Chandler	Harold F. Gosnell	Jürgen Kuczynski
John Maurice Clark	C. W. Guillebaud	Harold D. Lasswell
Jesse D. Clarkson	Earl J. Hamilton	William C. Lehmann
Gerhard Colm	Frank H. Hankins	Max Lerner

Acknowledgments

The encyclopedia is the product of an unusual collaboration between the academic community and several subsidiaries of Crowell Collier and Macmillan, Inc. The impetus and organization of this work originated in an arrangement between The Macmillan Company and The Free Press, who are the publishers. The encyclopedia subsequently became a special project of the Crowell-Collier Educational Corporation, the reference book subsidiary, which provided professional production and technical personnel as well as administrative services. The editors, however, have had full responsibility for the assignment of articles to contributors, for the substantive editing of articles, and for all other matters relating to the encyclopedia's content.

Before the editorial offices were moved to New York from Chicago late in 1961, Bert F. Hoselitz served as editor and as editor for economics. He was ably assisted by Gail Kelly (anthropology), Clare Munro (psychology), Martin Taitel (statistics), and Ann Ruth Willner (political science), and the present editorial staff is grateful for the impetus provided by the preliminary work of this group of editors.

An undertaking of this scope and magnitude requires the active support of a large group of people, and I am deeply grateful to them all. The members of the Editorial Advisory Board are listed elsewhere in these introductory pages; I would like to express my gratitude to those members who responded to my requests for advice with detailed and helpful letters. I am, of course, deeply indebted to W. Allen Wallis, chairman of the Editorial Advisory Board, who has been intimately associated with the plans for a new encyclopedia since the spring of 1955. We are all beneficiaries of his advice, judgment, and vision.

Alvin Johnson not only consented to serve as honorary editor, but he also provided all of us who have been fortunate enough to know him with a portrait of the model nonagenarian scholar: hard-headed, yet understanding; wise, but not condescending; interested, but not interfering. Never has the post of honorary editor been so well filled.

The editorial policies of the encyclopedia were determined by the editor, the associate editors, and the special editors. Although each editor was primarily responsible for the articles in his own discipline, there was frequent exchange of information and opinions among all the editors.

The part played by the associate and special editors was an extensive one. They were initially responsible for nominating the articles for their disciplines and for selecting a contributor for each. With the passage of time the responsibilities of the editor, the associate and special editors, and the staff editors developed some degree of overlap, but each editor retained responsibility for the articles within his discipline.

The selection of biographical subjects and the editing of the biographical articles presented special problems. Each associate and field editor was asked to nominate subjects and contributors in his field, and each was consulted during the editing phase. Editorial responsibility, however, remained with me and with the biographies editor, who consulted the disciplinary editors about the substantive aspects of the biographies. The biographies editor served both as a special editor and as a member of the editorial staff.

The work of the editorial staff—whose members are listed on the title page—permeates the entire encyclopedia. It was difficult to find young social scientists who were willing to interrupt their careers for the period of time necessary to create an encyclopedia, and I am fortunate to have had such talented colleagues. Each worked closely with me and with the editor in his or her discipline, and each contributed both specialized knowledge and editorial skills. They brought wisdom and humor to the assignment, and the quality of the encyclopedia is a direct reflection of their work.

I am indebted to my colleagues in ways that only each can fully appreciate. I am also indebted to four staff editors who worked during the early stages of the encyclopedia's preparation for varying lengths of time before returning to academic positions: Lawrence Casler (psychology), Sidney M. Greenfield (anthropology and sociology), Mary Peter Mack (political science), and J. Arthur Greenwood (statistics).

The work of the editors was immensely facilitated by the supporting services provided by the bibliographical, copy, indexing, and production staffs. The task of converting manuscript copy into printed pages is one that requires patience, skill, and tact, and we were furnished these in abundance.

The sponsors of the research projects upon which some articles are based and the publishers who kindly gave permission to use quoted and tabular matter from their publications are gratefully acknowledged in a special section of the index volume.

The preparation of the bibliographies in the encyclopedia and the verification of all quotations from other publications required library facilities far in excess of those available from the publishers. These facilities were provided by a number of libraries in New York City, but particularly by the Columbia University Library. Without the assistance of Dr. Richard H. Logsdon, director of the university libraries, and his helpful staff, the bibliographies in the encyclopedia could never have been verified.

Although the stimulus for a new encyclopedia of the social sciences came from many sources, the present encyclopedia became a reality through the initiative of Jeremiah Kaplan, president of The Macmillan Company. I am grateful to him for asking me to undertake this assignment, and I am deeply appreciative of his restraint in giving me the freedom to carry it out to the best of my ability.

DAVID L. SILLS

International
Encyclopedia of the
SOCIAL
SCIENCES

ABILITY

ABNORMAL PSYCHOLOGY

ABORTION

ABRAHAM, KARL

Karl Abraham (1877–1925) was a psychoanalyst who made important theoretical contributions to the psychology of sexuality, character development, manic–depressive disorders, and symbolism. He was born into a Jewish family in Bremen, Germany. From 1896 to 1901 he pursued a medical curriculum at Würzburg, Berlin, and Freiburg. His major interest was biology and his dissertation topic was the anatomical development of parrots. This early biological orientation was reflected later in his absorption in the infantile development of the sexual instincts and its effects on the adult organism. After completing his medical studies he became deeply interested in philology and linguistics. He spoke five languages, read several others, and even psychoanalyzed some patients in English. His interests in philology were mirrored in his writings on symbolism and myths and in a paper that related psychoanalytic concepts to the rise of monotheism in Egypt.

From 1901 to 1904 Abraham was an assistant at the Berlin Municipal Asylum, where he investigated various aspects of aphasia, apraxia, paresis, and drug-induced deliria. His psychiatric interests changed completely when he became an assistant to the famous Eugen Bleuler at the Burghölzli Mental Hospital in Zurich in 1904. Here Abraham met Jung and became acquainted with Freud's writings. His first psychoanalytic paper, presented in 1907, was entitled "Über die Bedeutung sexueller Jugendträumen für die Symptomatologie der Dementia Praecox" ("On the Significance of Sexual Trauma in Childhood for the Symptomatology of Dementia Praecox") and began with the phrase, "According to Freud. . . ." The beginning was prophetic: Abraham, uniquely among Freud's disciples, never deviated from either personal loyalty to Freud or the classical principles of psychoanalysis. A deep friendship with Freud began in 1907 and lasted until Abraham's death.

In 1907 Abraham left Zurich to start the first psychoanalytic practice in Berlin; except for the war years this practice occupied him for the rest of his life. He presented his views at medical gatherings in Germany and met with much opposition, as did Freud in Vienna. By 1909 he had one colleague, Max Eitingon, and by 1910 there were eight others, with whom he formed the Berlin Psychoanalytic Society, the first branch of the International Psychoanalytic Association. Abraham was president of the Berlin Society for the rest of his life and of the International Association in 1924 and 1925. Among his pupils in training analyses were Edward and James Glover, Helene

Deutsch, Melanie Klein, Sandor Rado, and Theodor Reik.

During World War I he was chief psychiatrist at a German army hospital in East Prussia. His experiences led to a joint publication on war neuroses with Freud, Ferenczi, Ernst Simmel, and Jones. During the war years Abraham contracted dysentery and never fully recovered. In 1925 he became ill with pneumonia and attendant complications and died seven months later.

Those who knew Abraham during his early years as a psychoanalyst repeatedly commented on the tenacity, courage, and cheerfulness with which he faced opposition. He was dedicated to his work, self-confident, and seemed completely free from ambivalence and hatred. Ernest Jones described him as "cheerfully reasoning with someone who was glowering with anger and resentment, apparently blandly ignoring the emotion and full of hope that a quiet exposition would change the situation" (Jones [1926] 1953, p. 39).

Abraham was an organizer, a practitioner who pioneered in treating psychoses psychoanalytically, and a theorist who kept closer to clinical observations than did most of his colleagues. He was one of the less prolific writers among the psychoanalysts of his generation: he wrote 49 papers, many very brief, and 4 quite short books, a total output of less than 700 pages. All but the first 8 papers dealt with psychoanalytic problems. Three of the books were on dreams and myths (1909), the libido and manic–depressive disorders (1924), and character formation (1925). The second of these is usually considered his most important contribution. His fourth book was a collection of clinical papers originally written between 1907 and 1920.

Contributions to psychoanalysis

Abraham's analysis of the libido and its relation to character formation was based on the hypothesis that the libido develops through six stages: the first two are oral, the next two anal, and the last two genital. In the earlier oral stage, that of sucking, the infant does not distinguish between himself and the objects he incorporates. He is objectless and free of ambivalence. The later oral stage is one of biting, or sadistic "cannibalism," in which the infant incorporates objects in order to destroy them. He becomes ambivalent and remains so throughout the ensuing anal and phallic stages. The anal periods include a hostile, anal-expulsive stage followed by a more controlled, anal-retentive stage. The phallic stage, or first stage of genitality, is marked by the emergence of object-

love in a clearer form than in the anal phases. Finally, the adult genital stage, reached only by individuals who are able to avoid psychotic or neurotic fixations in earlier stages, is distinguished by postambivalent object-love. This schema of development was not completely original, for Freud's "Three Essays on the Theory of Sexuality" had hinted at the basic ideas in 1905. Abraham worked out the stages more fully than Freud, and he also tied the oral and anal stages closer to later character development.

At any stage of development the infant may be either gratified and move on to the next developmental stage, or frustrated or deprived and remain in the one stage developmentally. In the latter case, he may manifest a fixation, the defensive persistence of a pattern of behavior or stage of development, or a reaction formation, the defensive reinforcement of a repression by behavior directly opposed to the unconscious trend (for example, the display of outward kindness in place of the unconsciously felt cruelty).

Thus, depending on the events that occur during the oral period—indulgent gratification of the infant by the mother, frustration by the mother or by infantile intestinal difficulties, or deprivation during weaning—the individual may develop such traits as lasting optimism, a leechlike dependency, an impatient restlessness, a compulsive loquacity, or a sarcastic, "biting" envy. Gratification in the earlier stage of orality leads to sociability, curiosity, and accessibility to new ideas. Fixation at the oral-sadistic stage is indicated by maliciousness and hostility.

Anal fixations are represented in the traits of moroseness, reticence, inaccessibility to new ideas, conservative resistance to innovation, perseverance, procrastination, and hesitation—in short, the reverse of many of the oral traits. Anal expulsiveness is present in sadism; anal retentiveness in stinginess, orderliness, pleasure in material possessions, stubborn defiance (or a reaction formation resulting in submissiveness), inability to delegate responsibilities to others or share activities with them, and underestimation of others. The pleasure that an anal individual takes in contemplating his own mental products, e.g., letters and manuscripts, has as its prototype the infantile pleasure of looking at one's own feces. The anal individual may collect useless bits and pieces of objects and then on some occasion get rid of the lot in one expulsive gesture. Anal eroticism of the retentive type provides the characterological basis for neurotic obsessions and compulsions.

Abraham's theory of manic–depressive disorders

centered on the twin concepts of libidinal fixation and ambivalence to a love object. In a paper written in 1911 and published in 1912 he asserted that depression or melancholia (the terms are interchangeable in the present context) is a reaction comparable to grief at the loss of a love object. Depression is to grief as anxiety is to fear. Just as anxiety occurs when the individual strives for impulse gratification but is prevented from reaching it by repression, so depression occurs when a sexual aim must be renounced. The depressive's libido is narcissistically withdrawn from the external world. He loses the ability to love and therefore feels hated in return. His self-abasement gives him a masochistic gratification and a hostile revenge on those who care for him.

As Freud developed this formulation by Abraham, in publications between 1911 and 1923, in melancholia the lost or renounced object is again set up in the ego, so that the melancholic's self-reproaches are really aggressive attacks on the incorporated object. The individual is unconsciously ambivalent, hating as well as loving the lost object. Abraham in turn went further than Freud in his 1924 book on the libido and manic–depressive disorders and theorized that orality was the basis of both incorporation and ambivalence. The incorporation of the lost love object is an unconscious, cannibalistic fantasy that arouses guilt, and guilt in turn leads to depression. As always, Abraham cited a number of cases in support of his views. For example, the depression of a patient who delusively accused herself of being a thief had been precipitated by the arrest of her father for theft. She had loved her father, but on his arrest she was estranged from him psychologically as well as physically. She then introjected his image and began to experience delusional reproaches against herself.

Abraham hypothesized that an adult depression is preceded by a primal depression in the phallic stage. The primal depression is a response to repeated disappointments of love for a parent, the predecessor of the love object lost at a later time. The primal depression is itself a regression to orality, and the later depression is a repetition of this regression. Abraham believed that for constitutional reasons orality is particularly strong in depressives. In summary, his theory viewed depression as a re-enactment of past conflicts between oral-receptive and aggressive impulses. There are two types of depression: either the introjected image of the object is the recipient of reproaches (the type stressed by Freud), or the introjected image directs reproaches against the self. Abra-

ham considered that manic–depressive patients exhibit, during their lucid intervals, the same characteristics as patients with obsessional neuroses that are under control. These character traits were evidence, to him, that the two pathological conditions have a common psychological relation to the anal-sadistic organization of the libido. The obsessive regresses to the anal-retentive stage and the depressive to an earlier one, a combination of orality and anal expulsiveness; the latter is indicated by the depressive's "expulsion" of the external world.

Although Abraham worked more with depression than with schizophrenia, or dementia praecox as it was then called, he believed that the concept of a withdrawal of libido from external reality and a concomitant turning back of the libido upon the ego was as applicable to schizophrenia as to depression. In *A General Introduction to Psychoanalysis* Freud stated that Abraham's concept of libido withdrawal was the basis of the psychoanalytic position regarding all the psychoses.

The psychology of myths and symbols was enriched by two contributions from Abraham. First, he attributed to various objects symbolic meanings that have since been widely accepted in analytic circles. A house represents the mother, a spider a feared mother, and so forth. Second, he tied myths to dreams by considering both to be wish-fulfilling fantasies that result from processes of repression, condensation, displacement, and secondary elaboration. "Thus the myth," he wrote, "is a surviving fragment of the psychic life of the infancy of the race whilst the dream is the myth of the individual" ([1909] 1955, p. 208). This conclusion would be accepted by some, but by no means all, anthropologists and other persons concerned with myths. The originality of Abraham's analysis of myths may be disputed, for its basis was Freud's discussion of the Oedipus myth in *The Interpretation of Dreams*. However, the details of Abraham's exposition were quite original.

Abraham also made a number of minor contributions to a variety of topics. In a paper entitled "Manifestations of the Female Castration Complex" (1921), he presented material to justify the application of the term "castration complex" to women as well as men, and he elaborated its manifestations in women's ideas, fantasies, and wishes. He was the first analyst to call much attention to the now familiar concept of the castrating female. He described her as a "revenge type" and hypothesized that her attempts to dominate males, reduce their potency, and then blame them for her own sexual disappointments were a cover for her unconscious masochistic tendencies. The self-destructive behavior of various other types of individuals was also explained as due to unconscious masochism. Finally, he had some original comments to make on ejaculatio praecox. It resulted from a dread of hurting women, he believed, which originated in repressed sadism; this in turn was due to disappointment in love for the mother and consequent hostility to her. The parallel to the explanation offered for depression is noticeable.

Although Abraham's original work had a relatively restricted scope, it continues to arouse considerable interest many years after his death. There are several reasons for this interest. In recent decades there has been an apparent increase in the number of psychiatric patients without a clear-cut neurotic or psychotic symptomatology, who suffer from instability of personality and unsatisfying interpersonal relationships. Abraham's discussions of character as it is influenced by early development are helpful in understanding these patients. Second, his developmental theories are relevant to longitudinal studies of human and animal behavior. In the past two decades, there have been many objective investigations of the effects on later behavior of infantile oral deprivation, early discipline, toilet-training practices, isolation, and other variables; in future years, more and more research of this type may be expected. Third, his theory of the genesis of depression has been widely accepted and also developed further, for example, by Sandor Rado. Last, his writings on infantile sexuality and other highly controversial topics have a level-headed reasonableness, cautiousness, and respect for clinical data that make him more acceptable to skeptical readers than some of his psychoanalytic contemporaries.

EPHRAIM ROSEN

[*For the historical context of Abraham's work, see the biographies* BLEULER; FERENCZI; FREUD; JONES. *For discussion of the subsequent development of his ideas, see* DEPRESSIVE DISORDERS.]

WORKS BY ABRAHAM

(1907) 1955 On the Significance of Sexual Trauma in Childhood for the Symptomatology of Dementia Praecox. Pages 13–20 in Karl Abraham, *Selected Papers*. Volume 2: Clinical Papers and Essays on Psychoanalysis. New York: Basic Books. → First published in German.

(1907–1925) 1953–1955 *Selected Papers*. 2 vols. New York: Basic Books. → Volume 1: *Selected Papers on Psychoanalysis*. Volume 2: *Clinical Papers and Essays on Psychoanalysis*.

(1907–1926) 1966 FREUD, SIGMUND; and ABRAHAM, KARL. *A Psycho-analytic Dialogue: The Letters of Sigmund Freud and Karl Abraham, 1907–1926*. Edited by Hilda C. Abraham and Ernst L. Freud. New York: Basic Books.

(1909) 1955 Dreams and Myths: A Study in Folk-psychology. Pages 151–209 in Karl Abraham, *Selected Papers*. Volume 2: Clinical Papers and Essays on Psychoanalysis. New York: Basic Books. → First published in German.

(1912) 1953 Notes on the Psycho-analytical Investigation and Treatment of Manic–Depressive Insanity and Allied Conditions. Pages 137–156 in Karl Abraham, *Selected Papers*. Volume 1: Selected Papers on Psychoanalysis. New York: Basic Books. → First published in German.

(1921) 1953 Manifestations of the Female Castration Complex. Pages 338–369 in Karl Abraham, *Selected Papers*. Volume 1: Selected Papers on Psychoanalysis. New York: Basic Books. → First published as "Äusserungsformen des weiblichen Kastrationskomplexes."

(1924) 1953 A Short Study of the Development of the Libido, Viewed in the Light of Mental Disorders. Pages 418–501 in Karl Abraham, *Selected Papers*. Volume 1: Selected Papers on Psychoanalysis. New York: Basic Books. → First published as *Versuch einer Entwicklungsgeschichte des Libido auf Grund der Psychoanalyse seelischer Störungen*.

(1925) 1953 Character-formation on the Genital Level of Libido-development. Pages 407–417 in Karl Abraham, *Selected Papers*. Volume 1: Selected Papers on Psychoanalysis. New York: Basic Books. → First published in German in Volume 7 of the *International Journal of Psycho-analysis*.

SUPPLEMENTARY BIBLIOGRAPHY

JONES, ERNEST (1926) 1953 Introductory Memoir. Pages 9–41 in Karl Abraham, *Selected Papers*. Volume 1: Selected Papers on Psychoanalysis. New York: Basic Books.

ABSOLUTISM
See AUTOCRACY.

ABSTRACTING SERVICES
See INFORMATION STORAGE AND RETRIEVAL, *article on* INFORMATION SERVICES.

ACADEMIC FREEDOM

Academic freedom, in its primary sense, is the freedom claimed by a college or university professor to write or speak the truth as he sees it, without fear of dismissal by his academic superiors or by authorities outside his college or university. In a secondary sense, the term denotes the corporate freedom claimed by an institution of higher learning to determine its policies and practices, without restraint from outside agencies. This latter usage is clearly distinct and derivative; for such corporate autonomy derives its justification ultimately from the services performed by the scholars whose activity it exists to foster and protect, while, on the other hand, the freedom of the individual scholar often requires protection from the pressures of his own institution, as well as from outside forces. Finally, the term is coming to be used, in a much looser sense, to denote the freedom claimed by a teacher, in any school and of any grade, to perform his function without unreasonable restrictions from public law, institutional regulations, or public opinion. The freedom to learn has traditionally been regarded, particularly in German universities, as an inseparable accompaniment of the freedom to teach, but it has only recently received explicit attention in the United States as an element of academic freedom representing the student's right to be as free of external pressures in his learning as the professor is in his teaching.

History

The idea of academic freedom is an offshoot of the root idea of freedom of thought. Thinking arises as a questioning of accepted beliefs and ways of acting, and it is thus always a potential enemy of reigning ideas; but the consciousness of the need for intellectual freedom does not arise until the thinker encounters opposition from religious tradition or political authority. In the Western world, the earliest clear statement of such opposition appeared in Socrates' famous defense of himself, at Athens in 399 B.C., against the charge of impiety. Socrates' claim of freedom of thought implies the freedom to teach, and Socrates justified this claim both as a duty that he owed the gods and a benefit that he conferred upon the state. These are, in germ, the themes that recur in all later discussions of the issue in Western history. Freedom of thought and expression is now generally recognized in the liberal states of modern times as a fundamental civic right, indeed as the chief trait that distinguishes liberal societies from totalitarian or despotic ones.

As a special form of intellectual freedom, academic freedom implies the existence of a corporate body of teachers, organized as a college, university, or other institution of higher learning, exercising some control over its individual members and itself subject to control by the agencies, private or public, that support it. In their early days, the medieval universities successfully maintained their corporate autonomy, supported as it was by the great prestige that they enjoyed as centers of intellectual life, by their capacity for unity and self-discipline, and by the loyalty of the important persons in church and state who had studied in them. With the hardening of church doctrine in the thirteenth century and the establishment of the Inquisition for suppressing heresy, the proponents of novel ideas in philosophy and theology began to be subject to more than academic disapproval; and the universities lost much of their autonomy and their professors much of their individual freedom. In the three succeed-

ing centuries, the recovery of ancient learning and the revival of scientific inquiry enlarged the area of possible conflict between the scholar and the church; and when the spiritual unity of Christendom was split by the Reformation and the Counter Reformation and the political power of both church and empire dissolved before the rising nation-states, the universities lost even the semblance of autonomy, and their professors had to bow to, or at least refrain from openly opposing, the sect or sovereign that controlled them.

Out of these religious and political conflicts of the early modern period, the idea of academic freedom was born. It first appeared as an announced policy in the new universities of Leiden (in 1575), Helmstädt (in 1574), and Heidelberg (in 1652), although its life was at first precarious. The claim to *libertas philosophandi* received powerful support, however, from the growing prestige of the new science and the increasing recognition of its utility. Francis Bacon, in his *Advancement of Learning* (1605), sounded an eloquent call for a rebirth of experimental inquiry, freed from the shackles of personal prejudice, religious and scholastic dogma, and the spirit of faction and dedicated to "the glory of God and the relief of man's estate." This vision of science as the mother of inventions that increase man's power, enlarge the range of his activity, and aid him against his ancient enemies, hunger, poverty, and disease, has exercised an increasing fascination upon the modern mind. Scientific research, which in the seventeenth and eighteenth centuries tended to take refuge in nonuniversity organizations—such as the Royal Society in England (in 1660), the Academy of Sciences in Germany (in 1700), and the American Philosophical Society (in 1743)—was brought back, in the nineteenth century, into the colleges and universities, together with the freedom of inquiry that such pursuit demands.

A second powerful influence leading to the acceptance of freedom of inquiry was the prolonged wrestling of modern philosophy with the problem of knowledge. Reflection upon the methods of scientific inquiry has shown that the attainment of truth requires professional competence of a high order; any claim to truth, however plausible, needs to be persistently questioned and has to be verified by objective procedures that become ever more complex and technical as knowledge advances. Even after prolonged examination and testing, the claim can be accorded only a high degree of probability; and its status is never immune to later criticism. These conditions imply a community of scholars and scientists cooperating with one another through mutual criticism and selecting and recruiting new members through disciplined and systematic training. These very requirements tended to produce such a community, animated by a professional spirit and resentful of any attempts by incompetent outside authorities to control its activities or judge its results.

Finally, the movement toward academic freedom received powerful support from the general liberalizing tendency of the modern age, intent upon removing the restraints of older institutions and customs and upon opening the way for diversity and freedom of enterprise in increasingly pluralistic nation-states. Economic liberalism supplied the suggestive metaphor of a free market in ideas, and the give-and-take of scholarly controversy is regarded as the academic parallel to a principle taken as essential in a modern economy. These are the chief traits of the climate of opinion within which academic freedom has developed and in which it lives today.

Justification and guarantee

The justification of academic freedom cannot be based merely on the right to freedom of thought and expression enjoyed by all citizens of a liberal society, for academic freedom implies immunity to some natural consequences of free speech that the ordinary citizen does not enjoy. An ordinary citizen who expresses unpopular opinions may lose customers if he is a merchant, clients if he is a lawyer, patients if he is a physician, advertisers or subscribers if he is the editor of a newspaper, or suffer other forms of social or economic penalty resulting from disapproval of his expressed opinions. The university professor, in some degree, suffers similar consequences; but where academic freedom is recognized, he is protected from the gravest of them, namely, the loss of his position. The justification of academic freedom must therefore be sought in the peculiar character and function of the university scholar. The scholar's function is to lead in the discovery and promulgation of knowledge; and the multiplication of universities in modern times and the expansion of their activities testify to the importance attached to this function. But the professor's performance of this function is hampered or frustrated and his usefulness diminished if his inquiry is restricted in its range by religious, political, or economic pressures, if he is not allowed to communicate his results freely to others, or if he has to color or qualify his honest opinion through deference to powerful prejudices or special interests outside the world of science and scholarship. Hence, a society that believes that its stability, prosperity, and progress are dependent upon the advance of knowledge and establishes universities for this purpose is patently inconsistent if it denies to these universities the freedom that they must have if they are to fulfill their nature and function. Academic freedom exists, then, not to serve the interests of the professor but for the benefit of the society in which he functions, ultimately the community of mankind.

This does not imply that the scholar should be uncontrolled by any authority above him. He may make a mistake, like any other man; but his errors as a teacher or research worker can properly be corrected only by other scholars and scientists of similar competence and possessing the same academic freedom that he enjoys. His method and his results are always subject to their approval or disapproval; indeed, it is only by the freedom of other scholars to criticize his methods, to present evidence that he has overlooked, and to suggest alternative explanatory theories that his own results can safely be accepted. Such freedom to examine, to object, to amend, and to enlarge—in short, as Socrates put it long ago, "to follow the argument wherever it may lead"—is the indispensable condition for the proper performance of the scholar's function, and it must be subject to no authority other than that which is inherent in its own operations.

Academic tenure. The chief means of assuring academic freedom is security of tenure. This is enjoyed as a legal right by professors in German universities and in the older universities of the United Kingdom. Under French law, a university professor may not be deprived of his chair except by a judgment pronounced by his peers. A similar principle holds in Italy, in Belgium, and in most other countries of western Europe. It has been adopted also by Japan and by some of the new nations in the Near East and in Africa. In the United States, Canada, and Australia, and in some of the new universities in the United Kingdom, legal control is usually vested in a nonacademic board, council, or court, distinct from the faculties of the institutions. Although their control is legally unlimited, these boards are subject to the restraint of public opinion, of academic custom and precedent, and of accrediting bodies and professional organizations. The better universities and colleges provide in their statutes that certain grades of the academic staff—usually professors, or professors and associate professors—shall have continuous or indefinite tenure; and those institutions that do not have such provisions in their governing law are under pressure to conform in practice to the example set by the ones that do.

Academic freedom in the United States

Certain conditions peculiar to higher education in the United States have hampered the growth of the tradition of tenure so firmly established in western Europe. The typical form of college and university government in the United States, i.e., government by a nonacademic board of trustees, has often been taken erroneously to imply that the faculty of a college or university are employees whom the trustees, at their discretion, have a right to hire or fire, as is usually the case in business organizations of similar structure. Moreover, the private institutions of higher education in the United States have always been largely supported by private benefactors, and it is natural for those who provide support for an institution to feel that they have a right to control the teaching that goes on in it and the opinions that emanate from it. After the establishment of state-supported universities, administered usually by politically appointed boards of trustees, the same reasoning was frequently used to demand that teaching in these institutions conform to the religious, political, and economic views of the citizens whose taxes supported them, or of the politicians who claimed to speak for the citizens. Finally, the princely benefactions that became available to universities and colleges at the turn of the century, from men who had acquired great fortunes during the period of economic expansion after the Civil War, placed additional pressure upon presidents and faculties to avoid antagonizing these sources of support. But this was precisely the period when the social scientists were becoming conscious of their scientific competence and were proposing reforms in the unregulated economic enterprise that had hitherto prevailed. In 1900, the forced resignation of the eminent sociologist E. A. Ross from Stanford University, at the insistence of Mrs. Stanford and contrary to the judgment of President David Starr Jordan and his faculty, focused national attention upon the danger to freedom of thought latent in the economic power of benefactors and trustees. But although there were numerous and grave instances of their abuse of this power, the trustees and presidents of these institutions were not, in general, indifferent to the public interest or unaware of the importance of academic freedom; they needed mainly to be reminded of the nature and limits of their responsibilities and to be provided with patterns of acceptable procedure for their guidance.

In the United States, the leading professional organization concerned with the clarification and defense of academic freedom is the American Association of University Professors, which, since its founding in 1915, has devoted itself to the formulation of acceptable principles of freedom and tenure and to the investigation of alleged violations. The careful and judicious inquiries that have preceded its published reports, plus the intrinsic justice of the principles asserted and the unfavorable publicity attending a vote of censure by this association, have made administrators and boards of trustees increasingly aware of the principles of academic practice that an institution of higher learning is expected to observe. The most basic of these principles is that teachers or investigators should have permanent or continuous tenure after the expiration of a probationary period, and their services should be terminated only for adequate cause. This principle recognizes the right and duty of an institution to assure itself of the quality of its members by keeping them on probation for a certain period after initial appointment, but it also sets a reasonable time limit for determining whether an appointee is qualified for tenure. The association recognizes that the dismissal of a professor on tenure is sometimes justified, for example, because of academic incompetence or gross personal misconduct. Here it insists, however, that the decision to terminate an appointment should not be made arbitrarily by the president or governing board; it must be arrived at by what is known in Anglo-American tradition as "due process." This means that the case should be considered by both a faculty committee and the governing board of the institution; the accused should be informed in writing of the charges made against him; he should have the opportunity to be heard and to introduce evidence in his own defense; and if it is a charge of incompetence, the testimony should include that of other scholars, either from his own institution or from other institutions. These procedures are analogous to the elaborate provisions in French and Italian law covering the hearing of charges against a professor who has tenure.

The years immediately following World War II were difficult ones for academic freedom in the United States. The sudden public realization of the insidious methods of infiltration and subversion advocated by communist propagandists and the discovery of pockets of communism within a few American institutions of higher education caused much alarm, and suspicion was directed against all colleges and universities. This suspicion, exploited and inflamed by demagogues, led to a demand for extra-academic controls to assure the loyalty of the professors. State legislatures passed laws requiring loyalty oaths of all state employees, including teachers in colleges and universities, and some boards of independent institutions imposed similar requirements on their faculties. Legislative committees conducted public inquisitions of distinguished scholars; unsupported accusations against others were given wide publicity in newspapers; and some boards of trustees took arbitrary action to dismiss without a hearing professors against whom charges of communist affiliation had been publicly made. These individual incidents were tragic in their consequences for the persons concerned and filled the academic world with foreboding. But what is most remarkable is the extent and vigor of the resistance these procedures aroused. Despite what was said at the time by pessimistic commentators, the professors were not cowed; nor were the universities, for most of them defended their prerogatives and their professors, some with exemplary force and wisdom. Above all, the academic profession acquired from this experience a new consciousness of its unity and importance.

Thus, upon balance, it appears that the principles of academic freedom, as a result of the crisis just described, are more firmly than ever accepted as guides to policy and practice in the colleges and universities of the United States. With the improvement, which has occurred since then, in the economic status of the academic profession, and with the prospect of ever-increasing demands upon it for staffing the enlarged programs of higher education that are planned by both state and federal governments, it can be said that the prestige of the profession is greater than it has ever been in this century; and its newfound unity and determination should make it better able to resist any future attacks that threaten the proper performance of its function. In such future contests, it can rely upon the increased public understanding of the importance of academic freedom that has resulted from the books and articles called forth by the crisis of the 1950s. Even more hopeful is the fact that recent decisions of the United States Supreme Court have shown that academic freedom is beginning to be recognized as a principle of public law, thus opening up the possibility of its receiving, as a constitutional right, a substantial measure of judicial protection.

World status of academic freedom

In most countries of western Europe, academic freedom and tenure are well established by law and tradition. The main exception is Spain, where the universities are included in the national syndi-

calist system and are subjected to a rigorous ideological control that effectively stifles any free philosophical, religious, or social expression. In the communist countries of eastern Europe, there is a great deal of institutional autonomy and vigorous academic activity in mathematics, the natural sciences, linguistics, and archeology; but in the social sciences, freedom of thought is restricted by the official ideology. Thus, in Yugoslavia, every faculty has a special professor for the social sciences whose function is to expound the principles of Marxism and Leninism; and academic freedom is explicitly restricted to those who do not, by their ideas or actions, threaten the existing socialist regime. In Poland, the officially declared purpose of higher education is to develop "cadres of people's intelligentsia," and scholarship is secondary to the building of a socialist society. There is evidence that professors do speak their minds in lecture rooms, but all published material is subjected to strict academic and political censorship. In Czechoslovakia, the impatience of the students with intellectual control was signalized in Prague, in 1956, by a mass demonstration, in the guise of a student festival, in which they demanded freedom of the press, an end to compulsory attendance at lectures on Marxism and Leninism, and an opportunity to hear presentations of non-Marxist theory. The government's reaction was to reassert that the educational function of the state is to assure a Marxist–Leninist orientation in all studies. In the Soviet Union, there is an elaborate and efficient system of higher education, providing considerable autonomy for individual academies, universities, and institutes; but the whole is controlled from above, by the Communist party and its ideology. It is characteristic of all the communist countries that they claim adherence to the principle of academic freedom, as they conceive it; they regard the principles accepted in western Europe as only an ideological camouflage of economic interests, who will, according to the communists, inevitably interpret and apply them to their own advantage.

In China, the universities are apparently flourishing as never before, but they have lost their former status of neutral critics and have been made an integral part of the state's apparatus. All teachers are subject to influence from the police and departments of government, and all communications with scholars in other parts of the world have been severed. But the incident of the "Hundred Flowers" shows that the tradition of independent thought is still alive, and it is said that the strength of this tradition has kept the government from using the most extreme measures against university professors. Yet Ma Yin-Chu, the eminent professor of economics, was dismissed as rector of Peking University in 1960 because he questioned certain fundamental assumptions of communist doctrine and published articles critical of the government's economic policies.

It is encouraging to note that, in the plans for reorganizing university life in Egypt, Syria, Iran, and Pakistan, the principle of academic freedom, in the Western sense, is declared to be fundamental. Likewise, in the recently established universities in Africa—in Nigeria, Ghana, Rhodesia, and elsewhere—the statutes usually contain a guarantee of academic freedom. These countries, however, face almost insuperable difficulties in their attempts to develop systems of higher education and, at the same time, to raise the general level of literacy among their peoples; while their political inexperience and the resulting instability make the principle of academic freedom particularly liable to subversion, through the personal ambitions and rivalries of politicians. In South Africa, the commitment of the government to its policy of apartheid and the bringing of all the universities under government control have effectively stifled all freedom of thought in the area of race relations.

Thus, the status of academic freedom today is by no means assured. Even those countries in which it is well established in doctrine and custom, where its principles and their applications have been carefully formulated, and where its connection with fundamental needs of a progressive society has been amply demonstrated are not safe from waves of public opinion, the machinations of political reactionaries, vested religious and economic interests, or the jealousies of politicians, all of which may, in critical times, play havoc with established principles and practices. Whoever reflects soberly on the events of the past half century, and recalls what happened in the 1930s in Germany, the land in which academic freedom was most strongly rooted in law and custom, and in the United States during the 1950s, will not feel unduly confident of the future. Yet academic freedom does now have a long tradition behind it, a tradition that steadily gains in prestige from the material prosperity and political stability of those countries in which it thrives.

GLENN R. MORROW

[See also FREEDOM; UNIVERSITIES. Other relevant material may be found under CONSTITUTIONAL LAW; EDUCATION; ETHICS.]

BIBLIOGRAPHY

Academic Freedom. 1963 *Law and Contemporary Problems* 28:429–671.
AMERICAN ASSOCIATION OF UNIVERSITY PROFESSORS 1954 The 1915 Declaration of Principles: Academic Freedom and Tenure. American Association of University Professors, *Bulletin* 40:90–112.
AMERICAN ASSOCIATION OF UNIVERSITY PROFESSORS 1958 Statement on Procedural Standards in Faculty Dismissal Proceedings. American Association of University Professors, *Bulletin* 44:270–274.
AMERICAN ASSOCIATION OF UNIVERSITY PROFESSORS 1960 Academic Freedom and Tenure, 1940 Statement of Principles. American Association of University Professors, *Bulletin* 46:410–411.
AMERICAN CIVIL LIBERTIES UNION 1956a Academic Due Process: A Statement of Desirable Procedures Applicable Within Educational Institutions in Cases Involving Academic Freedom. American Association of University Professors, *Bulletin* 42:655–661.
AMERICAN CIVIL LIBERTIES UNION 1956b Academic Freedom and Academic Responsibility: Their Meaning to Students, Teachers, Administrators and the Community. American Association of University Professors, *Bulletin* 42:517–529.
AMERICAN CIVIL LIBERTIES UNION 1962 Academic Freedom and Civil Liberties in Colleges and Universities. American Association of University Professors, *Bulletin* 48:111–115.
BACON, FRANCIS (1605) 1958 *The Advancement of Learning.* Edited with an introduction by G. W. Kitchin. London: Dent; New York: Dutton.
BYSE, CLARK; and JOUGHIN, LOUIS 1959 *Tenure in American Higher Education: Plans, Practices and the Law.* Ithaca, N.Y.: Cornell Univ. Press.
CONGRESS FOR CULTURAL FREEDOM, HAMBURG, *1953* 1955 *Science and Freedom.* London: Secker & Warburg.
FELLMAN, DAVID 1961 Academic Freedom in American Law. *Wisconsin Law Review* [1961]: 3–46.
Freedom and Restriction in Science and Its Aspects in Society. 1955 The Hague: Nijhoff.
HOFSTADTER, RICHARD; and METZGER, WALTER P. 1955 *The Development of Academic Freedom in the United States.* New York: Columbia Univ. Press.
HOOK, SIDNEY 1953 *Heresy, Yes–Conspiracy, No!* New York: Day.
IRSAY, STEPHEN D' 1933–1935 *Histoire des universités: Françaises et étrangères des origines à nos jours.* 2 vols. Paris: Picard. → Volume 1: *Moyen âge et renaissance.* Volume 2: *Du XVI siècle à 1860.* Supplemented by René Aigrain, *Les universités catholiques,* published by Picard, Paris, 1935.
KIRK, RUSSELL 1955 *Academic Freedom; An Essay in Definition.* Chicago: Regnery.
LAZARSFELD, PAUL F.; and THIELENS, WAGNER, JR. 1958 *The Academic Mind: Social Scientists in a Time of Crisis.* A report of the Bureau of Applied Social Research, Columbia University. Glencoe, Ill.: Free Press.
LOVEJOY, ARTHUR O. 1930 Academic Freedom. Volume 1, pages 384–388 in *Encyclopaedia of the Social Sciences.* New York: Macmillan.
MacIVER, ROBERT M. 1955 *Academic Freedom in Our Time.* New York: Columbia Univ. Press.
MURPHY, WILLIAM P. 1963 Educational Freedom in the Courts. American Association of University Professors, *Bulletin* 49:309–327.
POLANYI, MICHAEL 1962 The Republic of Science: Its

Political and Economic Theory. *Minerva: A Review of Science, Learning and Policy.* 1:54–73.

Science and Freedom: A Bulletin of the Committee on Science and Freedom. No. 1–19. 1954–1961. Manchester (England): The Committee.

SHRYOCK, RICHARD H. (editor) 1961 *The Status of University Teachers.* Reports from sixteen countries prepared with the assistance of UNESCO. Ghent (Belgium): International Association of University Professors and Lecturers.

ACCELERATION PRINCIPLE

See INVESTMENT, *article on* THE AGGREGATE INVESTMENT FUNCTION.

ACCEPTANCE SAMPLING

See under QUALITY CONTROL, STATISTICAL.

ACCESS TO POLITICS

The goal of group theory is to describe the distribution of power within a political system in terms of the group concept. In this effort, "power" and "influence" are used synonymously; and political power may be defined as the probability that the claims of the group will be incorporated as the basis of policy by governmental decision makers (Truman 1960). Group theory is a special rather than a general theory of politics, appropriate to the United States, the Anglo-Saxon democracies, and—more recently—western European nations. It presupposes considerable differentiation among individuals according to interest, some definite aggregation of like-interests through interpersonal interaction or identification, and considerable separation of the institutions of the polity from those of the society and economy. [*See* POLITICAL GROUP ANALYSIS.] Within this context, political access is posited as follows: "power of any kind cannot be reached by a political interest group, or its leaders, without access to one or more key points of decision in the government" (Truman 1951, p. 264). This definition of access is basic to all interest group approaches, but it is essentially an illustration rather than an explicit definition.

To be meaningful and useful for systematic research, the concept of political access must be clearly distinguished from the concept of power. Access should be regarded as the measurable (in principle) probability that if the members of a group or its leaders perceive an interest affected by a future authoritative decision, the group can obtain the *attentive interest* of the relevant decision makers. Access thus describes a continuum of behavioral situations: at one end, the group has no access (and no power) regardless of whether it perceives an interest or not; in the middle, if the group perceives an interest, it can act—it has effective access; at the other end—the maximum preferred goal of all interest groups—the group has privileged access. Privileged access can be defined as the probability that authoritative decision makers automatically take a group's interests into account as the basis of decision.

Group theory posits that all groups seek privileged access, that some groups may indeed achieve this, but that all groups would be willing to settle for effective access. Thus, groups without access have no political power, but groups with effective access *may*, but need not, have political power. For power also depends upon the internal characteristics of the group and upon the tactics, techniques, and skills that can be mobilized by the group.

Finally, the concept of access is the abstraction in group theory that defines the bridging relationship between society and governmental structure.

The determinants of access

The political power of a group may be viewed as a dependent variable that is the function of three broad intervening variables: effective access; internal characteristics of the group; and mobilized tactics, techniques, and skills. Effective access is, in turn, a function of three clustered independent variables: (1) the strategic position of the group in the society; (2) the internal characteristics of the group (again); and (3) the nature of governmental institutions. Each of *these* may also be subdivided, at least logically, into discrete subvariables.

Strategic position. The strategic position of the group is a composite of (*a*) the social status of the group membership; (*b*) the conformity of the group to the rules of the game; (*c*) the extent of membership overlap with governmental personnel; and (*d*) the technical and political information which the group possesses. However, no research exists which satisfactorily operationalizes and measures these discrete (sub-)variables.

For example, presumably group theory refers to the *perceived* mean social status of a group's membership—as perceived by formal decision makers relative to *their* status. But this raises questions of the definition of membership, which clearly ranges from sympathetic fellow travelers, through nominal members, to committed "true believers."

Similar problems exist with regard to "conformity to the rules" [*see* RULES OF THE GAME]. Yet even if there existed accurate description and measurement of adherence to the various rules—general and specific, unwritten and written—one would still face the problem of specifying the relevance of this variable. Again, group theorists presumably intend to refer to the measurable extent to which the leaders and/or the average members of the group are perceived as conforming to democratic norms. But almost no research can be cited (see Stouffer 1955; Trow 1957).

Overlap with governmental personnel, which is a restricted definition of the term "multiple-membership," presents the same problem. Most research remains at the level of simple, objective, demographic variables; yet the group theorists probably intend to produce research on overlapping *subjective* identifications.

The analyst reaches the same conclusion about the fourth element, technical and political information: instead of sophisticated research, there is much ex post facto speculation. The subjective factor is neglected—yet the extent to which the authoritative decision maker perceives *himself* dependent on the monopolized control of technical or political data is probably the significant factor. A beginning effort, in the area of role structures in legislative systems, indicates that much more can and should be done.

Internal characteristics.   According to Truman, four characteristics "internal" to the group can have an influence on access: (*a*) appropriateness of organization; (*b*) leadership skills; (*c*) resources; and (*d*) cohesion.

First, how appropriate is the group's organization to its purposes? This does *not* refer to the relatively sterile classification of formal structures but rather to the question of the "degree and appropriateness" of group organization as a functioning communications system which is designed to gather information about threatening social and political change, including new public policies, and to mobilize members, fellow travelers, and potential allies. This variable has been "measured" largely in a historical, deductive manner: groups have been analyzed with regard to imputed objective interest, and where no access or influence was observed, one of the conclusions drawn is lack of appropriateness of organization. A more systematic, direct test requires efficient application of the techniques for assessing the direct impact of mass communication (see Klapper 1960). Equally needed is research on political intelligence functions themselves and on the extent to which the techniques and the substantive findings of modern social science are used by political activists. [*See* LEADERSHIP.]

Leadership skills, the second discrete independent variable, overlaps to a large extent with the previous variable. Here, anecdotal descriptions

abound, and the state of research may be broadly characterized as an attempt to locate allegedly powerful groups, from which leadership skills are then deduced. However, the study of political leadership has hardly benefited from the large body of experimental studies of leadership in small groups which now exists in sociology and psychology (but see Verba 1961). The relative importance of self-selection as against experience in development of skillful leadership, the importance of variables other than the most obvious demographic factors —these and other aspects currently remain unresearched.

A group's resources—its membership and/or its financial status—constitute the third variable. Analysis of resource potential for politics has not advanced far. The study conducted by Dahl (1961) provides a model for what can and should be done with groups as the unit of analysis. However, most available work has been done in a backward fashion: the designated winner in a policy outcome is tentatively identified, and then analysis proceeds backwards to the hypothesized independent variables that *might* have played an influential role. Such analysis must overcome the problem that policy beneficiaries, politically active persons, and influentials may not be identical. If investigation does not permit this empirical possibility, theoretical conclusions will be tautological.

Traditionally, the analysis of membership or money has been undertaken in the crudest numerical terms. Quantity alone may be irrelevant. For many decades political scientists have known that the power of an idea in politics is a function not only of the number of persons holding that idea but also of their rate of activity in advancing it. We are only beginning to face the measurement problems entailed in this deceptively simple idea (Monypenny 1954).

According to group theorists, the fourth internal characteristic, cohesion, probably has the greatest impact. However, here too, group theory is deficient. For example, Truman (1951, chapter 6) merely equates cohesion with "unity," offering various examples. There is no definition. Unity begs the further question, With regard to what? Certainly one must investigate several successively narrowed levels of unity: on the saliency of the interest; on the importance of a particular group to that interest; on the leadership of the group in directing goal achievement; on the strategy, tactics, and timing as developed by the leadership of the group.

Governmental institutions.   Governmental institutions were identified as the third broad clustered variable determining effective access. This area is most familiar to political scientists. It refers, first, to the formal operating structure of government, which both reflects and sustains past distributions of power. Analyses of the consequences of federalism, bicameralism, etc., are so prevalent as to require no further reference. The fact that the flesh-and-blood actors of any social entity identified as an institution themselves develop norms and all the accouterments of group life has been known for some centuries. But systematic observation in this area is very new and has been directed chiefly to legislative systems (Matthews 1960; Wahlke et al. 1962).

Some scholars (Eckstein 1960) would add extant public policy as a determining influence of political access. However, the concrete examples used to illustrate this abstract definition all fall within the categories already provided by Truman. Therefore, it seems preferable to continue with the most widely known interest group approach.

It is certainly true that groups struggle to perfect their own access and to reduce or eliminate the effective access of opponents or potential enemies. The Buchanan committee hearings of 1950; Title III of the 1946 Legislative Reorganization Act; the Hatch Acts of the late 1930s and early 1940s; the Federal Corrupt Practices Act of 1925—these are but contemporary examples of the residue of the group struggle. In this sense it is also accurate to say that the newer type of electoral interest group, such as the National Committee for an Effective Congress, concerns itself primarily with access. Even though this type of group has no specific policy goals, its goals in elections may be interpreted as the quest for access for the interests its members share and, contrariwise, control of the access of all other potential actors in the system. In conclusion, these examples all reduce themselves either to the most generalized elements of "fairness" or to more specific policy statements of procedure and/or value. Thus they are incorporated in our meaning of "the rules of the game."

Patterns of access

Patterns of access are a shorthand way of discussing a continuum that describes the possible relationships between political interest groups and governmental institutions. The continuum extends from "a loose pattern" of access to "a taut pattern." The loose pattern describes a situation in which there is a multiplicity of points of access to the governmental decision makers and in which the authoritative position holder is or can be a relatively autonomous decision maker. The taut pattern describes a situation in which the institution is a recognized effective leadership to which interest groups make their "pitch," with which groups attempt to bargain, and from which groups derive policy or patronage.

Most research—primarily American but increasingly also British—has focused on the manner and degree to which a political interest group establishes, especially through party mechanisms, access to the legislative system. And this pattern has been generalized frequently to the entire political system. While it is useful to describe and compare, say, the British legislative system with the American one, we should be aware that we have largely ignored other contexts—institutional, policy-scope, systemic, and historical—within which the study of "patterns" should take place. In the United States, for example, the judicial pattern seems similar to the legislative in that the initiatives come primarily from the interest groups. In the executive–bureaucratic pattern, however, it is the policy makers who establish access to clientele groups (see Selznick 1949). At the same time, the judicial institutional pattern seems quite distinctive from the other two in that Anglo–American traditions of judicial independence and the uniquely American expectation that courts will grant privileged access to all social interests, provide insulation against group activities prevalent in the other two patterns. This suggests the need to discuss patterns along a continuum ranging from direct to indirect access as well as in the context of the now conventional taut–loose continuum. If one were to array the American institutions along both continua, available evidence suggests that: the judicial is tautest and most indirect; the executive–bureaucratic falls at the midrange on both; and the legislative is loosest and most direct.

It would be desirable for research to break away from institutional patterns, however. Future research may usefully direct itself to the question of patterns of access in the context of particular policy scopes or generalized functions of the political system. For example, one may usefully divide governmental output into three broad categories of domestic economic policy, domestic social policy, and foreign policy. Perhaps because of the intellectual impact of the 1930s depression, research has been overconcentrated on the economic scope. We cannot now say whether patterns of access which are appropriate to economic policy are equally accurate in describing patterns for other major areas.

Political analysts have also ignored the pattern of access along the dimension of stability–change.

As is evident in the next section, the broad American pattern of access may be characterized over time as inherently unstable—in contrast to the British pattern which may explicitly yet impressionistically be characterized as quite stable. What are the dynamics of change? Of stability? At present we do not know why it is that a system will evolve in the direction of a stable, or indeed a taut, pattern of access in which the interest group must offer as its *quid pro quo* political services of use to a political party or legislative majority rather than to individual entrepreneurs. What conditions created and now maintain the stability of the British pattern? What factors contributed to the breakup of the American party and interest group system in the Civil War and now contribute to the inherent instability of the American pattern?

Historical trends in access

In very broad terms it can be said that in the evolution of American politics (as in post-World War II western Europe), the trend in access has been twofold: from party to pressure group and from direct to indirect. Available evidence suggests that politically active individuals in most democratic systems have turned from the political party to the pressure group as the primary instrument of access in these systems. This would seem a function both of the complexity of modern industrial, urbanized, bureaucratic society and of the decline of enthusiasm for mathematical schemes of representation, such as proportional representation.

Group leaders have turned from direct to indirect access to government. This is the transition in American politics from the direct lobby to the attempt to concern oneself with the effective sociopolitical environment within which the decision maker acts—that is, the environment, which if effectively manipulated, sets the limits of the range within which *any* decision maker may act. This shift in techniques of access, most noticeable since World War II, represents a tendency toward direct, "grass roots" lobbying—congruent with the manipulative intent of modern public relations techniques.

However, two additional historical aspects of American politics require separate mention. First, it has become fashionable to note a parallelism between the American political model and what is occurring in the postwar integration of western Europe. Despite the apparent parallelism, it is appropriate to note a contradictory tendency now occurring in American politics which may set a distinctive pattern for the future (see Eldersveld 1958; Key 1961). Since World War II, political interest groups have increasingly tended to issue formal enunciations of their stands on a wide variety of political issues and have moved toward a more thorough integration of the group within one of the two major political parties. This American countertendency seems important.

Second, as hinted earlier, the instability in the historical pattern of access makes the American political system quite distinctive. Since the Civil War "taut" and "loose" patterns have alternated. If descriptions of the operation of the American party system between the 1870s and 1910 are accurate, then it would seem appropriate to characterize that era as one of "responsible two-party government." It would seem more necessary than ever to go back to that era to determine both the conditions that created a taut pattern of access and the conditions which led to its degeneration. And the very loose pattern by which we now traditionally characterize the 1938 to 1960 era should be similarly reexamined. The evidence since 1960 points to the potential emergence of a new period of competitive, responsible, integrated party performance.

Problems of measurement

Most research has been done on access to legislative bodies, describing techniques of access rather than evaluating the effectiveness of alternative actions: Why was one technique selected rather than others? What factors condition the utility of alternative techniques? Work on the evaluation of planned social action is relevant here (see Hyman et al. 1962).

There is also very little evidence on how official decision makers establish effective access to the individuals and groups necessary in the carrying out of policy. This direction of flow would seem to be especially appropriate for the study of interest groups and foreign policy (see Cohen 1959; Bauer et al. 1963).

Such research needs are relatively simple in that they can be efficiently met by existing personnel and research methodologies. When we turn to the critique by Easton (1953; 1956), we will be forced into areas of new research techniques. For Easton gloomily concludes that political analysts cannot even rank interest groups for their relative power, much less for their absolute power. Group theorists must directly face this challenge and attempt to quantify the power of the groups in the system. This need not take place *in vacuo*, but it will force them into the current polemical and often muddy debate on operationalizing the concept of power. By assigning ordinal or numerical values to the power of various interest groups operating in the system, the analyst could then work back to hypothesized independent causes. Using this approach, one might find close correlations among certain of the presently hypothesized independent variables. For example, high status, strategic position, access, and money resources, perhaps also numerical membership, seem closely related. And some of the logically possible relationships that can be deduced from Truman's theory probably do not exist in reality.

As group theory makes efficient use of the ferment now occurring in political systems analysis, it could also turn more directly to problems of quantifying the determinants of power. This type of needed research would take the list of possible determinants, summarize them in a single quantitative measure, predict future policy outcomes, observe the actual outcomes in the various political arenas, and then reassess the original catalogue of possibilities. This suggestion would entail use of vector analysis (see Monypenny 1954), which in principle is applicable but remains untried. If Truman's catalogue of possible variables presents too complex an array, it would still be possible to take a reduced number, perhaps successive pairs, and test them in systematic fashion. It would require more data than we now have; it would require creative adaptation of the sample survey methodology to deliberately inefficient cross-sectional samples or some manner of purposive oversampling to obtain data, for instance, on the saliency of interest, the multiple levels of cohesion, and the rate of political activity of group memberships. Finally, the obvious place to test much of group theory is at the state, provincial, and municipal systemic levels, for then truly comparative analysis can be undertaken.

HARRY M. SCOBLE

[See also POLITICAL EFFICACY and POLITICAL GROUP ANALYSIS. Other relevant material may be found in POLITICAL BEHAVIOR; POLITICAL SCIENCE.]

BIBLIOGRAPHY

BAUER, RAYMOND A.; POOL, ITHIEL DE SOLA; and DEXTER, L. A. 1963 *American Business and Public Policy: The Politics of Foreign Trade.* New York: Atherton.

BRYCE, JAMES (1888) 1909 *The American Commonwealth.* 2 vols., 3d ed. New York and London: Macmillan. → An abridged edition was published in 1959 by Putnam.

COHEN, BERNARD C. 1959 *The Influence of Non-governmental Groups on Foreign Policy-making.* Boston: World Peace Foundation.

DAHL, ROBERT A. (1961) 1963 *Who Governs? Democracy and Power in an American City.* New Haven: Yale Univ. Press.

EASTON, DAVID 1953 *The Political System: An Inquiry Into the State of Political Science.* New York: Knopf.

EASTON, DAVID 1956 Limits of the Equilibrium Model in Social Research. Pages 397–404 in Heinz Eulau et al. (editors), *Political Behavior: A Reader in Theory and Research.* Glencoe, Ill.: Free Press.

ECKSTEIN, HARRY H. 1960 *Pressure Group Politics: The Case of the British Medical Association.* London: Allen & Unwin; Stanford (Calif.) Univ. Press.

ELDERSVELD, SAMUEL J. 1958 American Interest Groups: A Survey of Research and Some Implications for Theory and Method. Pages 173–196 in International Political Science Association, *Interest Groups on Four Continents.* Edited by Henry W. Ehrmann. Univ. of Pittsburgh Press.

HYMAN, HERBERT H.; WRIGHT, CHARLES R.; and HOPKINS, TERENCE K. 1962 *Applications of Methods of Evaluation: Four Studies of the Encampment for Citizenship.* Berkeley and Los Angeles: Univ. of California Press.

KEY, VALDIMER O. 1961 *Public Opinion and American Democracy.* New York: Knopf.

KLAPPER, JOSEPH T. 1960 *The Effects of Mass Communication.* Glencoe, Ill.: Free Press.

MATTHEWS, DONALD R. 1960 *U.S. Senators and Their World.* Chapel Hill: Univ. of North Carolina Press.

MONYPENNY, PHILLIP 1954 Political Science and the Study of Groups: Notes to Guide a Research Project. *Western Political Quarterly* 7:183–201.

SELZNICK, PHILIP 1949 *TVA and the Grass Roots: A Study in the Sociology of Formal Organization.* University of California Publications in Culture and Society, Vol. 3. Berkeley: Univ. of California Press.

STOUFFER, SAMUEL A. (1955) 1963 *Communism, Conformity, and Civil Liberties: A Cross-section of the Nation Speaks Its Mind.* Gloucester, Mass.: Smith.

TROW, MARTIN A. 1957 Right Wing Radicalism and Political Intolerance: A Study of Support for McCarthy in a New England Town. Ph.D. dissertation, Columbia Univ.

TRUMAN, DAVID B. (1951) 1962 *The Governmental Process: Political Interests and Public Opinion.* New York: Knopf.

TRUMAN, DAVID B. (1960) 1961 Organized Interest Groups in American National Politics. Pages 126–141 in Alfred J. Junz (editor), *Present Trends in American National Government: A Symposium.* New York: Praeger.

VERBA, SIDNEY 1961 *Small Groups and Political Behavior: A Study of Leadership.* Princeton Univ. Press.

WAHLKE, JOHN et al. 1962 *The Legislative System: Explorations in Legislative Behavior.* New York: Wiley.

ACCOUNTING

Accounting is an information system. More precisely, it is the measurement methodology and communication system designed to produce selected quantitative data (usually in monetary terms) about an entity engaged in economic activity. Alternatively, accounting has been described as the art of classifying, recording, and reporting significant financial events to facilitate effective economic activity. The accounting entity (the focus of attention) may be a profit-seeking business enterprise, a governmental unit or activity, an eleemosynary institution, or any other organization for which financial data will be useful in determining the proper conduct of its economic affairs.

The major functions of accounting are (1) to provide summarized reports of the financial position and progress of the firm to a variety of groups who are not part of management, including those who furnish capital, and (2) to furnish detailed data that will facilitate the effective control and planning of operations by management. To fulfill the first function, a statement of financial position (balance sheet), a statement of operations (income statement or profit and loss statement), and a statement of fund flows (sources and applications of funds) are usually furnished. These statements are designed to indicate the current status and the changes during the period of the entity's resources and of the relative position of the various claimants—owners (stockholders), creditors, employees, and the government in its regulatory and taxing role. The second function includes all the appurtenances of cost accounting that are useful in the efficient administration of an entity's resources—for example, standard costs, flexible budgets, cost–profit volume analysis, and responsibility accounting.

Historical development. From the very earliest times, the levying and collection of taxes by government has called for record keeping and reports. Governmental reporting requirements have served since antiquity to reinforce business needs for accounting systems and controls. Clay tablets used by Babylonian businessmen to record their sales and money lending some four thousand years ago are still in existence. Egyptian papyri describing tax collections before 1000 B.C. are on exhibit in museums. The Greeks and Romans had well-developed record-keeping systems, especially for government affairs. The Emperor Augustus is said to have instituted a governmental budget in A.D. 5. Somewhat later, inspectors from the central government in Rome were sent out to examine the accounts of provincial governors.

During the Middle Ages, accounting, in company with most other elements of learning and trade, languished. With a barter, manorial economy, the financial transactions that are the lifeblood of accounting tended to disappear. Only the church and strong monarchs maintained and occasionally pushed forward the earlier systems of record keeping and control. Conspicuous developments during the medieval era included the annual inventory of property instituted by Charlemagne in the year 800 and the pipe rolls of various English rulers, which recorded the taxes and other obligations due the monarch. The pipe roll of Henry I in 1131 may be the most complete of these records.

The revival of Italian commerce in the thirteenth and fourteenth centuries created a need for rec-

ords: to help merchants control their dealings with customers and employees, to indicate the relative interests of creditors and owners, and to apportion profits among partners. The first double-entry systems of bookkeeping evolved during this period; there are extant sets of double-entry records prepared in Genoa in 1340. The earliest systematic description of the double-entry procedure was provided by the Franciscan friar Luca da Bargo Pacioli in 1494 in his book *Summa de arithmetica, geometria proportioni et proportionalita* (which was, incidentally, the first published work on algebra). The system outlined by Pacioli in the section entitled "De computes et scriptures" ("Of Reckonings and Writings") was a surprisingly complete one, and for four centuries almost all texts on accounting were closely patterned after it.

As it has developed in the more than four and a half centuries since Pacioli, the term "double entry" has probably referred to the two-sided nature of transactions, to the debit and credit aspects of each event. Some writers, however, have chosen to emphasize the dual steps in recording, i.e., the use of a book of original entry (the journal) and a classified record by accounts (the ledger). A more refined requirement of double-entry record keeping is the provision of separate accounts for the recording and analyzing of gains and losses, with a periodic reckoning of income and closing of these accounts into ownership capital. Pacioli's treatise dealt with all these attributes of double entry, and it still serves as the basis for the far more complex accounting systems of today. The many modifications and elaborations that have been introduced have largely resulted from the desire for periodic financial statements of publicly held corporations and the need for additional financial data to facilitate the control and planning of operations of the large-scale firm.

Financial statements. Commencing in the nineteenth century, increasing emphasis was placed on the preparation of annual financial statements. The position statement (or balance sheet) was originally viewed as the most significant financial report and frequently was the only statement prepared. More recently, interest has shifted to the operating data of the income statement, and this now usually commands major attention.

The income statement is a systematic array of revenues, expenses (including depreciation), income taxes, and interest charges, culminating in the net income. The disposition of net income between dividends and reinvested earnings is usually shown either at the bottom of the income statement or in a separate statement of retained earnings (surplus). One major problem of income statement presentation is the treatment to be accorded unusual gains and losses, especially where the event giving rise to the gain or loss relates to a different or longer time period than that of the income statement. Many accountants feel that these items should be treated as adjustments of capital, but the more common view is to include them in the income statement, segregating them in a nonoperating category.

The balance sheet is a schedule of financial position or financial condition; and one of these two terms is being increasingly used as the title of the statement. The balance sheet contains a list of the entity's assets (economic resources), divided into current and long-term categories. Cash, marketable securities, receivables, and inventories are the major current asset items. Land, buildings, and equipment are usually the major items in the long-term (fixed) asset section. Intangible assets, such as patents, copyrights, and purchased goodwill, are often accorded a separate classification. Like other assets, they are valued at cost. The "going value" of the entity is not listed as an asset and must be judged by the ability of the firm to earn a higher than normal rate of return.

Total assets are equal to the total liabilities (the rights and claims of all creditors) plus the ownership equity. The ownership equity indicates the interest of the proprietor or partners of an unincorporated entity or the equity of the stockholders of a corporation. If there are several classes of stockholders, it is customary to show the interests of each group separately. It is common to stress the distinction between contributed capital and reinvested earnings portions of the stockholders' equity.

A recent development is an alternative form of balance sheet presentation that emphasizes the entity's current position. This is accomplished by deducting current liabilities from current assets and labeling the difference net working capital; to this subtotal, long-term assets are added and other liabilities deducted. The resulting figure is the excess of all assets over all liabilities. The components of the ownership equity are then listed, and their summation is equal to this total net asset figure.

The most recent of the three major accounting reports is the statement of fund flows (sources and applications of funds statement). Its general nature is well described by the title originally applied to it by Cole—a "where got, where gone" statement. The major sources of fund inflows for the period covered are shown (operating transactions with customers and clients, proceeds of the issuance of securities and debt instruments, and occasional sales of noninventory assets), and these are compared with the major uses of funds (distributions to investors, reduction of long-term debt, retirement of stock, and investment in plant and equipment). Funds are usually defined as net working capital (current assets minus current liabilities). An alternative definition that would exclude inventories from the funds total has been suggested. If this suggestion were adopted, change in inventories during the period under consideration would be shown explicitly as a source, or use, of funds. Other alternatives, such as defining funds as cash (or cash plus marketable securities), are occasionally used. The result, practically speaking, is to trace the flows of cash of the business.

Income determination. The usual economic concept of income relates it to the enhancement of wealth. Focusing on the business entity, periodic income can be described as the amount of wealth that can be distributed to the owners during a certain period without making the entity's prospects less than they were at the start of the period. To make such a concept operational, it would be necessary to have well-defined rules for measuring the firm's prospects or wealth at the start and close of the period. This requires a measure of the discounted value of the entity's anticipated net cash inflows. Such a measure would be highly subjective, depending wholly on the measurer's current prognosis of the likely amount, and timing, of future inflows and on the appropriate discount rate to employ.

A more restricted definition of wealth would limit it to the sum of the values of individual tangible assets, rather than the worth of the firm as a whole. With this definition of wealth, income would be determined by intertemporal differences in total asset values (adjusted for changes in liabilities and capital contributions and withdrawals). This view of income was widely accepted in accounting until the end of the first decade of the twentieth century. About that time, it became more and more apparent that there would be continuing increases in the significance of specialized long-lived assets that would be difficult to value; also, and perhaps more important, a graduated income tax was imposed in the United Kingdom in 1909, and the sixteenth (income tax) amendment and related legislation were adopted in the United States in 1913. These developments led to the gradual displacement of the increase in value view of income by one that emphasized market transactions. Early tax decisions of the U.S. Supreme Court that held that there was no income without "severance" of property from the firm added support to the newer view. This was reinforced by the unhappy experience of many firms with appraisal values during the late 1920s and early 1930s.

For several decades now, the emphasis has been shifted toward evaluation of enterprise operating performance and a more restricted view of income measurement that focuses on the matching of asset inflows (revenues) and asset outflows (expenses) in the rendering of services. The following four concepts play central roles in the income reporting process:

(1) *Realization.* Reflects accounting's preference for objectivity. Only events that have come to fruition by a market transaction or some ascertainable change in an asset or liability are recorded in the accounts.

(2) *Consistency.* Indicates that comparable events are treated in similar fashion from period to period. Although some alternative procedures may be acceptable, consistency minimizes the year-to-year effects of different procedures by requiring that the same alternative be selected each period.

(3) *Conservatism.* Relates to the feeling that where a choice exists it is better to understate, rather than overstate, income and ownership equity.

(4) *Disclosure.* Emphasizes the need to furnish all relevant information about the firm's financial position and operations. It accepts the fact that some financial events are difficult to express adequately in the formal reports; footnotes are integral parts of the reports, and significant information that is not indicated in the body of the report is disclosed by footnote.

In considering when to recognize revenue, there is controversy among experts about how liquid the asset received in a sales transaction must be. In some cases, especially for income tax reporting, it is held that revenue recognition should be deferred until the cash is in hand (the installment method). Usually, however, revenue is recognized when a bona fide sale results in a legally enforceable receivable. Neither the receipt of orders nor activity in the productive process is normally accepted as a basis for recognizing revenue; instead, the realization concept suggests that all revenue from a transaction should be recorded at the time of sale.

The measurement of expense is largely a matter of recognizing the expiration of the economic usefulness of assets. All purchases are made to acquire services that will benefit the production of revenue; in fact, the most operational definition of an asset is simply that of a service potential or an unutilized service that will render a future benefit to the firm. As services are utilized, assets become expenses.

Determining when, or what portion of, service potential has expired is the difficult practical problem. Conservatism has long been a guiding principle in external financial reporting; in doubtful cases, accountants have tended to minimize recognition of anticipated future benefits. Under a conservative approach, costs of such items as research and development, advertising, and employee training are charged to expense in the period during which they are incurred. The extreme form of this view results in recording assets only when their physical presence makes it embarrassing to ignore them.

In the income determination process, the cost of purchased merchandise must be divided between expense (cost of goods sold) and asset (inventory); the operational rule for measuring remaining service potential (asset) in this area is the acquisition cost of units physically present in final inventory. Costs of long-lived assets, like plant, must similarly be apportioned between depreciation expense and asset valuation. Operating procedures for handling assets in this category stress a systematic apportionment of plant costs, based to some extent on the relative expiration of service potential during this period compared to estimated total service potential available from the asset.

At the time of acquisition, the present value of anticipated services from an asset must be at least equal to its acquisition cost, or the purchase would not be made. Thus minimum initial value is established by acquisition cost, and acquisition cost remains the basis for the accounting valuation of the asset as long as the asset retains its power of rendering services. As service expirations occur, the original cost valuations are charged to expense. In periods of rapidly changing prices, some expense figures may lag significantly behind current values. Since revenues tend to adjust to changing prices more rapidly, the matching process may result in the comparison of revenues stated in current price terms with expenses stated in prices of a different vintage.

To cope with this problem, some accountants have recommended that expenses be recognized on a replacement cost basis. This view has not received general acceptance, but partial approaches to the same goal have received some approval. The last-in, first-out (LIFO) inventory procedure has come to be generally accepted in the United States. By charging the cost of the most recent purchases to expense, it results in an expense figure that approximates current costs in most cases. The first-in, first-out procedure (FIFO) is based, in most cases, on a more realistic assumption about inventory flows, but the expense amount is stated in less current terms. In the late 1940s, efforts by a few American firms to base depreciation on replacement cost failed to win general approval, and advocacy of this method has waned. However, acceleration of depreciation charges based on acquisition cost, by recognition of a faster rate of service expiration, has won acceptance both in financial reporting and in the income tax laws; this may offset, in part, the effect of price level changes.

The use of replacement costs for expenses implies a concept of wealth measured by physical resources or productive capacity; income emerges only after resources or capacity are maintained. An alternative correction for price changes would apply an index of general price level change to all assets and then charge these restated costs to expense in the traditional fashion. This approach implies a purchasing power concept of wealth.

All measurements of income for periods shorter than the life of the entity are tentative. The shorter the time period of the income statement, the more difficult the measurement of income. Many asset acquisitions represent joint costs of long periods of service, and there is no known logical way of allocating their costs to shorter periods of income reporting. The date of expiration of service benefits of many other assets cannot be determined exactly. There are alternative, acceptable procedures in many areas. Reported income for relatively short periods is, at best, a rough indicator of enterprise performance. The seeming accuracy indicated by reporting income to the nearest dollar (or in larger firms to the nearest thousand dollars) gives an improper impression of precision. Since the income data have their greatest significance in guiding investment decisions and facilitating evaluation of management, a knowledge that income of a firm falls within a relatively narrow range may be virtually as satisfactory as knowing its exact amount. The effort of the accounting profession to reduce the number of permissible alternative procedures reflects the desire to narrow this range and increase the usefulness of income reporting.

Cost accounting. Cost accounting (managerial accounting) is chiefly concerned with measuring, analyzing, and reporting the operating costs of specific centers of activity. Early developments in cost accounting were associated almost exclusively with manufacturing operations. They focused on measuring the cost of products, processes, and departments for inventory valuation and pricing purposes. Since about 1930, there has been an enormous expansion in cost-accounting activity. It has been extended to administrative and distributive activities, and it has become clear that the more significant uses of cost accounting are found in the areas of cost control and cost planning, rather than in product costing for purposes of inventory valuation and income determination.

Cost accounting operates as a branch of the general financial accounting system. It provides a detailed analysis of the costs associated with specific products or processes that are important enough to warrant such attention. If costs are accumulated by departments or operating centers, the system is described as a process-cost system; if accumulated by jobs or products, it is known as a job-order system. Most existing systems, however, are hybrids that contain some aspects of both the process-cost system and the job-order system.

Certain costs, like production labor and raw materials, can be assigned directly to jobs or processes with little question. These costs usually vary with the level of operations. The jobs or processes responsible for the incurring of these costs can be identified, and they receive all of the benefits of the services used. However, there frequently are many costs that are not directly associated with individual jobs or processes but, instead, are joint to several activities. For the most part, these costs are fixed. Under a "full-costing" procedure, these common costs (fixed overhead) are also assigned, somewhat arbitrarily, to jobs or processes. The basis for assignment is usually some subjective estimate of relative benefit as measured by labor cost, labor hours, machine hours, or some other measure of activity.

There is a growing tendency to question the desirability of assigning indirect fixed costs to jobs and activities. The advocates of the direct-costing (variable-costing) view argue that the assignment serves no useful decision-making purpose and may distort the data that are relevant for short-run price, and output, decisions. They stress that in making short-period decisions the significant figure is the excess of additional revenues over variable costs, rather than over "full costs." They describe the excess of revenue over variable costs as the "contribution" to the meeting of fixed costs and the earning of profit.

The control aspect of cost accounting is based upon the use of operating budgets and performance standards. Budgets have been used in government finance for many years, but their major purpose has been to place a limit on authority to spend. In contrast, managerial accounting views the budget as a financial plan and a control over future operations, a means whereby it is determined whether operations are proceeding in accord with management's plans and policies. Recently some government budget practice has come closer to this view [*see* BUDGETING]. By combining performance standards (standard costs) with estimates of physical activity, the budget spells out the position that the firm should achieve at the end of the budget period. Comparison of the results of operations with budgeted figures indicates the areas where managerial attention and action may be needed.

To be effective as a control device, the budget must be prepared in sufficient detail for estimated and actual costs to be assigned to those areas specifically responsible for their incurrence. To prevent individual managers being charged with responsibility for costs that are not under their control, careful preliminary studies and even modification of organizational structure may be necessary before the installation of a budget and a standard-cost system.

Standard costs for units of performance are a central part of the control process. Standard costs have connotations of normative behavior and indicate what the effort expended (assets given up) to attain the entity's production objectives *should be*. The development of appropriate standards is a complex task, which may require the cooperative effort of industrial engineers, psychologists, statisticians, personnel men, and accountants. Standards are usually expressed in terms of both prices and usage, and they frequently contain more detail than is found in the budget.

In a standard-cost system, actual costs are recorded for each activity, and differences between actual and standard costs are isolated in variance accounts; separate variance accounts for the cost of materials, materials usage, labor wage rates, labor effectiveness, idle capacity, and overhead expenditures are commonly provided. These are usually expressed in monetary units, although a minority view holds that the conversion of physical variances, that is, materials usage and labor effectiveness, to dollar terms serves no useful purpose. The investigation and analysis of major variances is a prime task of the internal accounting staff.

Cost accounting contributes to cost control in other ways as well. The timekeeping and payroll systems that are required for cost assignments help to assure management that workers are actually on the job and being paid according to wage agreements. Control of issuance of materials is usually built into the cost-accounting system, as are detailed records of machine and tool availability and maintenance costs.

Special studies utilizing data produced by the cost-accounting system play a central role in many planning decisions of management. Decisions on equipment replacement, size of production runs or quantities ordered, discontinuance of "unprofitable" products or territories, as well as make-or-buy decisions, are frequently guided by reports relying on cost-accounting information. The analysis underlying management decisions in these areas is based on incremental cost data rather than full costs. Proper classification of costs into fixed and variable categories for cost-measurement and cost-control purposes ensures that much of the needed information will be available for these special studies. Not all costs that are significant for measurement and control purposes are relevant for management planning. An effective cost-accounting system will have the capability of providing the data that are needed for all three purposes.

Auditing and public accounting. Auditing is concerned with the independent verification of the statement of financial position and the results of operations of an entity. An audit is an outside expert's professional attestation that the financial reports have been prepared in conformity with generally accepted accounting principles on a basis consistent with that of the preceding period. This independent appraisal of the fairness of the financial statements has traditionally been the major function of the public accounting profession. The growth of large-scale enterprise, with its separation of ownership and management, emphasizes the need for an external verification so that present and potential investors may rely on the published financial statements.

Since 100 per cent checking of records would be prohibitively expensive, auditing necessarily uses sampling procedures. In the analysis of a firm's activities and records, the independent public accountant examines selected documents and transactions until he is satisfied professionally that the financial statements prepared by management "present fairly" the position and results of operation of the firm. (The quoted words are from the standard auditor's report in the United States; the British wording is a "true and fair view.") In recent years, professional accountants have often relied on probability theory and formal statistical sampling techniques in deciding on how much testing and evidence is needed before an opinion on the financial statements can be rendered.

Public accounting and auditing have a long history in the commercial and industrial world, but the dramatic growth of the public accounting profession has been a fairly recent phenomenon. The first *New York Directory*, compiled in 1786, listed only three accountants in public practice in New

York. At about the same time, similar directories prepared in Great Britain showed 14 public accountants in Edinburgh, 10 in Glasgow, and 5 each in London and Liverpool. The substantial growth of corporations in the nineteenth century demanded expanded and improved public accounting services for the protection of investors and the effective operation of securities markets. In order to improve standards, professional organizations evolved in most industrialized nations. Accreditation for public identification of professional competence and status developed somewhat later. Accreditation procedures take one of two general forms—acceptance to membership in a government-approved professional society, as in Great Britain; or state designation under an applicable statutory enactment, as in the United States.

The first British accounting society was founded in Edinburgh in 1854, followed in the next year by a similar society in Glasgow. These two societies form the basis of the Institute of Chartered Accountants of Scotland. The Institute of Accountants was formed in London in 1870 and ten years later was incorporated by royal charter as The Institute of Chartered Accountants in England and Wales. The Society of Incorporated Accountants was formed five years later and merged into the English and Scottish Institutes in 1957. The Association of Certified and Corporate Accountants came into being shortly after the turn of the century.

The Companies Act and various other legal enactments in the United Kingdom list certain responsibilities that may be discharged only by members of one of the institutes or societies. Each of the groups imposes an experience requirement for membership. To become a member of a chartered institute the experience must be acquired in an articled clerkship under the direction of an accountant who is a member of the group. In addition, satisfactory written examinations in accounting theory and practice, as well as related subjects, are required by each of the groups. By 1965, membership in these British organizations totaled more than fifty thousand.

In the United States, the title of certified public accountant (CPA) is conferred by each of the states. In 1896 New York became the first state to provide for such certification, followed in 1899 by Pennsylvania. By 1923, all the states provided for the legal designation of CPA's. Each state has its own education and experience requirements for the certificate; many states require some college education and a small, but growing, number require a college degree as a prerequisite for certification. All the states use a uniform CPA examination, prepared and graded by the American

Institute of Certified Public Accountants. In 1965 the number of CPA's in the United States was approximately 90,000, compared with 38,000 in 1950, 13,000 in 1930, and 250 in 1900.

Most of the nations of the British Commonwealth and many European nations follow the English lead of having government-chartered organizations prescribe their own rules for membership and thus admission to the public accounting profession. A smaller number of countries use the American plan of licensing of qualified accounting practitioners.

The professional groups in each country have developed roughly comparable codes of ethics and standards of conduct. All emphasize the concept of independence, which intends that the auditor be able to give an unbiased evaluation of management's representation about financial position and progress. Other rules stress maintenance of high levels of professional competence and integrity. The American Institute of Certified Public Accountants has, in addition, been active in seeking to define generally accepted accounting principles and to narrow the areas where alternative treatments are acceptable. The Opinions of the Accounting Principles Board, established by the American Institute, are widely accepted as authoritative statements on accounting concepts.

In addition to their auditing function, accountants have traditionally played an important role in the preparation of business and individual income tax returns. Although the statutory definition of taxable income differs to some extent from accounting formulations of income, the accountant's familiarity with a firm's financial records and the income measurement process makes him the natural person to perform this service.

More recently, many public accounting firms have extended their activities in the management services area, where they render consulting service on a wide range of management problems. When these problems are financial in nature or relate to information or control systems, the public accountant's management services work is comparable to that performed by the internal accounting staff of many large industrial firms. All signs indicate that the management services function is likely to be the public accounting activity that will grow most rapidly in the years to come.

SIDNEY DAVIDSON

[See also Cost.]

BIBLIOGRAPHY

BOOKS AND HANDBOOKS

Accountants' Handbook. 4th ed.   (1923) 1956   New York: Ronald Press.

AMERICAN INSTITUTE OF CERTIFIED PUBLIC ACCOUNTANTS

1921 *Accountants' Index: A Bibliography of Accounting Literature to December, 1920.* New York: The Institute. → The Index is kept up-to-date by supplements.

DICKEY, ROBERT I. (editor) (1944) 1960 *Accountants' Cost Handbook.* 2d ed. New York: Ronald Press. → The first edition, edited by Theodore Lang, was published under the title *Cost Accountants' Handbook.*

EDWARDS, EDGAR O.; and BELL, PHILIP W. 1961 *The Theory and Measurement of Business Income.* Berkeley: Univ. of California Press.

HORNGREN, CHARLES T. 1962 *Cost Accounting: A Managerial Emphasis.* Englewood Cliffs, N.J.: Prentice-Hall.

KOHLER, ERIC L. (1952) 1963 *A Dictionary for Accountants.* 3d ed. Englewood Cliffs, N.J.: Prentice-Hall.

LITTLETON, ANANIAS C. 1933 *Accounting Evolution to 1900.* New York: American Institute Publishing Company.

MAUTZ, ROBERT K.; and SHARAF, HUSSEIN A. 1961 *The Philosophy of Auditing.* Madison, Wis.: American Accounting Association.

PATON, WILLIAM A. 1952 *Asset Accounting: An Intermediate Course.* New York: Macmillan.

PATON, WILLIAM A. 1955 *Corporation Accounts and Statements: An Advanced Course.* New York: Macmillan.

PATON, WILLIAM A.; and LITTLETON, ANANIAS C. 1940 *An Introduction to Corporate Accounting Standards.* Chicago: American Accounting Association.

PERIODICALS

The Accountant (London). → Published weekly since 1874.

The Accounting Review. → Published quarterly with annual volume numbers since 1926.

Journal of Accountancy. → Published monthly (volume numbers semiannually) since 1905.

Journal of Accounting Research. → Published semiannually since 1963.

N.A.A. Bulletin. → Published by the National Association of Accountants from 1919. Title changed to *Management Accounting* in October 1965.

ACCULTURATION

The term "acculturation" is widely accepted among American anthropologists as referring to those changes set in motion by the coming together of societies with different cultural traditions. This field of investigation is generally referred to by British anthropologists (and by British-influenced students in Africa, Oceania, and Asia) as "culture contact." In contrast with this straightforward phrase focused on the conditions under which the changes take place, the term "acculturation" and its derivatives remain somewhat ambiguous. A persistent usage gives it the meaning of cultural assimilation, or replacement of one set of cultural traits by another, as in references to individuals in contact situations as more or less "acculturated"; inconsistency is often apparent in the writings of American anthropologists with regard to whether the term is applied to results or to processes of change.

Early studies in acculturation

The emergence of acculturation as a significant field of study in social science may be readily traced. First glimpsed as an area of anthropological inquiry in the 1880s, it became a major focus of investigation during the subsequent eighty years. The term appears first in the writings of North Americans—for instance, W. H. Holmes (1886), Franz Boas (1896), and W. J. McGee (1898)—but they did not use it to name the same phenomena. McGee spoke of "piratical acculturation" and "amicable acculturation," meaning transfer and adjustment of customs under conditions of contact between peoples of "lower grades" and "higher grades" respectively, a distinction that was not very clear in his essay. Boas used the term in a more general way to refer to an inferred process of change as a result of which the cultures of a region become similar to one another. Boas' usage gained some currency among German ethnologists, notably Ehrenreich (1905) and Krickeberg (1910). However, the current, widely accepted usage is much closer to that advanced by McGee, even though his two "types" have never been regarded as useful.

Ethnographic observation. From the 1880s on, North American anthropologists concerned themselves increasingly with studying the phenomena of cultural change resulting from contacts between peoples. It is notable, however, that their interest was so directed toward the reconstruction of dead cultures, as in Lowie's (1935) intensive studies of Crow Indian culture of the buffalo period, that they very rarely described what they saw before them. They applied themselves to gathering data for tracing the extent of diffusion of cultural elements in the past, but they did not make direct observation of the process of diffusion among the people with whom they were working.

In the 1930s, almost simultaneously among anthropologists working in North America and in Africa, a new focus of field studies developed. Attention turned to firsthand observation of the contacts between Indians and Anglo-Americans and between native Africans and Europeans, and some attempt was made at relating present conditions among the native peoples to current and recent conditions of contact. One early study of this type, made by Margaret Mead (1932), was reported as *The Changing Culture of an Indian Tribe*; another of greater historical depth and wider scope, but with the same focus of interest, was *Reaction to Conquest,* by Monica Hunter Wilson (1936), which reported the great variety of results of contact among the Pondo and other natives of

South Africa. Studies of this sort increased steadily during the following decade, North American and British anthropologists being the chief contributors, although one German, Richard Thurnwald (1935), was active. The shifting focus of interest among anthropologists was indicated in 1936, in a question raised at the annual meeting of the American Anthropological Association. The editor of the influential *American Anthropologist*, Leslie Spier, asked for instructions as to whether he should accept for publication papers dealing with "the culture of natives who participate in civilized life . . . the so-called acculturation studies . . . of . . . hybrid cultures . . ." (American Anthropological Association 1937).

Contemporary developments

By 1936, however, studies by Herskovits (1927), Lesser (1933), Redfield (1929), Schapera (1934), and Spier himself (1935) were making it clear that acculturation studies had become an important interest of anthropologists. This fact gave rise to an action in 1935 by the Social Science Research Council aimed at the better coordination of research in acculturation. The foundation appointed a committee of three prominent anthropologists and instructed them to attempt the formulation of a more systematic approach. Under the chairmanship of Robert Redfield, the committee prepared a short memorandum called "Outline for the Study of Acculturation" (Redfield et al. 1935). It sought to define the field of study that was coming to be called "acculturation" and to provide a check list of topics concerning which field data should be gathered if the phenomena defined were to be systematically investigated.

Definition.   Modest in scope and severely practical in aim, the memorandum turned out to have an extremely important effect. The definition of acculturation delimited a field of observation consistent with much previous anthropological research: "Acculturation comprehends those phenomena which result when groups of individuals having different cultures come into continuous first-hand contact, with subsequent changes in the original cultural patterns of either or both groups" (Redfield et al. [1935] 1936, p. 149).

This definition was epoch-making, or perhaps better said, epoch-marking, for it immediately established a conceptual framework for both the long-standing interest in diffusion that had characterized anthropological work in culture history and the newer interest in directly observable processes of cultural change. The concept of diffusion had not been associated with any clear conception of cultural mechanisms.

The memorandum identified types and situations of contact, processes, psychological mechanisms, and results. The processes of "determination," "selection," and "integration" were identified as, respectively, those resulting in the presentation of traits by a "donor group" in contact situations, the accepting of traits by a receiving group, and the modification of accepted traits by a receiving group. The use of the terms "acceptance," "adaptation," and "reaction" recognized the replacement of cultural elements, combination of elements into new wholes, and rejection of elements. These features became the basis of much later analysis of acculturation phenomena.

Contemporary British efforts (Methods . . . 1938; Malinowski 1945) called attention to the importance of establishing a "zero point" from which the nature and extent of change could be measured, pointed to the utility of detailed census data in connection with the determination of trends in cultural change, and introduced the concept of intermediating or contact social structures as a recurrent part of every contact situation.

Herskovits and Linton.   During the next 25 years an increasing number of field studies in acculturation gave occasion for the development and sharpening of concepts. Herskovits (1937a; 1937b) in his studies of New World Negro cultures provided numerous analyses of what he called "syncretism," or recombinations of cultural elements from different societies into new wholes. He also introduced the concept of cultural focus, the area of greatest awareness and elaboration of cultural elements, which he held is the area of most rapid change but, under certain contact conditions, may be the area of greatest resistance to change. Linton (1940) emphasized the distinction between two major classes of conditions under which contact changes take place. He designated one of these "directed culture change," calling attention to circumstances under which a dominant society may induce or force changes in the way of life of a subordinated society. These circumstances, he held, have consequences very different from those in which members of a society are able to choose cultural elements freely. Linton (1943) recognized a class of "reactions" as nativistic movements and proceeded to classify these into some six different types, ranging from "magical–revivalistic" to "rational–perpetuative" movements, a useful beginning at the classification of very complex recurrent phenomena of culture contact. Ralph Beals (1951) pointed out similarities in the processes that anthropologists were referring to as acculturation and those that had long been studied by sociologists as urbanization. He also suggested (1953) the applicability of concepts and research approaches derived from acculturation studies to the study of ethnic and class relations in large, complex political units. Another Social Science Research Council committee (Social Science Research Council 1954) made notable advances toward sharper conceptualization of results of contact and of types of contact situations in terms of role networks. Although Kroeber's characterization of the field of acculturation as a passing fad ([1923] 1948, p. 426) was belied, it was still true by 1960 that generally accepted propositions about the nature of change under contact conditions were lacking. The 1935 memorandum had ventured no generalizations, nor did the 1954 committee report.

One of the early criticisms of acculturation studies had been that they were ethnocentric. They were almost exclusively limited to situations in which societies of Western culture were dominant. Kroeber, Herskovits, and others felt that this led to serious bias because there was inadequate basis for comparative analysis. This criticism came before anthropologists were led to attempt acculturation analyses outside the Western framework. Actually, the great variety of Western cultures provided considerable basis for broad comparative study. Studies of the contact conditions set up under the dominance of Spain during the period from 1500 to 1800 in Mexico, the Philippines, and South America began to be made in great detail (for instance, Foster 1960; Phelan 1959). The processes and results of Hispanization during the colonial phase and Mexicanization during a later phase were very different, just as were the sharp differences between Anglicization of North American Indians on reservations and Anglicization of Ghanaians on the Guinea coast of Africa. In short, a wide variety of historical acculturation situations were fairly well known by 1960. These differed according to the dominant European nations, according to the historic periods as the European nations changed, and according to the cultures that were subordinated. Students of acculturation were beginning to bring into the same framework with Westernization those instances of acculturation called Hinduization (Bose 1929), Sinification, and Japanization; it also seemed likely that Romanization and Hellenization were on the point of being included in the same framework of investigation.

The main line of development of acculturation studies continued to be descriptive. Studies seemed to aim at determining what kinds of cultural elements changed readily and what kinds were resistant to change. Most studies took their direction from the circumstances of acculturation in the parts of the world where they were carried out.

Thus the North American investigators learned about many instances of cultural loss and disintegration and about cultural assimilation as they conducted research on the Indian reservations of the United States and Canada. Similarly, Mexican and other students, as they worked in the cultures of Middle America, became familiar with examples of syncretism, or cultural fusion, in the Indian religious, economic, and social systems of that region.

It was apparent that some half-dozen foci of interest had developed that were leading to the formulation of general problems. These foci of investigation were the following: (a) nativistic movements, (b) cultural fusion, (c) personality and acculturation, (d) biculturism, (e) social scale and cultural change, and (f) techniques in directed change.

Nativistic movements. Detailed information concerning nativistic movements among non-Western peoples began to accumulate before the concept of acculturation had taken form. One of the earliest careful studies was that of James Mooney (1896), who in the 1890s studied the Ghost Dance among Indians of the western United States for the Bureau of American Ethnology. He combined this with less detailed comparative studies of other nativistic movements among Indians north of Mexico. Variant forms of the Ghost Dance continued to be described (Spier 1935; Suttles 1957), as well as other North American Indian movements, such as the Native American Church and the Handsome Lake Religion (Wallace 1961a).

A similar abundant body of data regarding the nativistic movements characteristic of Melanesia, usually collectively called "cargo cults," steadily developed, beginning with early studies of the Vailala Madness (Williams 1923) and continuing to the present in the study of the Paliau movement in the Admiralty Islands (Schwartz 1962). These were summarized at some length by Worsley (1957) and by Hogbin (1958). The Hau Hau movement of the Maoris of New Zealand and the Mau Mau movement of the Kikuyu of East Africa, as well as numerous other nativistic movements in South Africa, Siberia, South America, and Middle America were intensively described. Notable efforts to explain these recurrent contact phenomena in terms of a general theory have been those by Nash (1937), Worsley (1957), and Wallace (1961b). Nash's analysis of Klamath and Modoc nativistic movements in the western United States and Worsley's study of cargo cults opened the way to consideration of the relation between deprivation of groups and individuals in contact situations and their participation in movements focused by symbols expressing basic attitudes of acceptance and rejection of the dominant culture. This approach has been carried farther and made more systematic on a comparative basis by Wallace, whose studies of the Iroquois Handsome Lake Religion have led to the formulation of hypothetical stages in what he calls the revitalization process under conditions of dominant–subordinate relations in culture contact. The immense variety in nativistic movements, now known in great detail for most areas of the world under Western dominance and less well for some other conditions, is being reduced to some kind of systematic classification and general interpretation. It is at the same time being related to theories of nationalism and religious revivalism in complex states.

Cultural fusion. As soon as the pioneer students of acculturation turned their attention to firsthand studies of contact, they became aware of emergent cultural forms stimulated by contact situations. In some instances, very circumscribed portions of the cultures combined under new circumstances to give rise to new culture complexes or traits. This was the case of the New World Negro supernatural figures described by Herskovits, which were a combination of elements taken from both European Christianity and African religions. In other instances, large segments of cultures were transformed into something which could be matched in neither the receiving nor the donor society prior to contact. This was the case of the institution of "potlatch" among Northwest Coast American Indians. In still other instances, it was clear that the process of recombination could result in the creation of whole new cultures, a process that appeared to characterize many of the Indian cultures of Middle America following the period of extensive innovation from Spanish culture in the sixteenth and seventeenth centuries. Such instances of cultural fusion gained the special attention of anthropologists, who presented descriptions of them from all over the world in all aspects of culture, including technology, language, economy, social organization, religion, and art. It became clear that fusion characterized all instances of contact change and that results of contact varied in respect to the degree to which fusion took place, rather than as to whether or not it occurred to the exclusion of replacement or other processes. For example, revitalization movements characteristically employed fusions of various cultural elements available in the contact situation. This was true even though such movements (in the minds of their participants) might stand for rejection of everything from a dominant society.

Furthermore, there appeared to be certain conditions that were recurrently associated with fusion (e.g., Interuniversity Summer Research Seminar . . . 1961; Firth 1959).

Biculturism. The contact phenomenon known originally as "acceptance," or replacement by borrowed elements, was studied rather intensively, although perhaps not so much so as cultural fusion. It was studied especially among North American Indians, but also to some extent among Polynesians and Africans. Studies of Navaho veterans of World War II made it possible to identify stages in the process of individual acceptance of new modes of living (Vogt 1952), and studies of what was called biculturation by Polgar (1960) made clear that individuals in contact situations that stimulated replacement were not restricted to a single type of response. As in bilingualism, two or more ways of behavior could be learned by an individual and employed under different circumstances where appropriate. Bicultural response was found to be a recurrent phenomenon under the conditions set up on Indian reservations in the United States. Its implications in terms of integration of the individual personally and as a participant in culture were obvious. Distinction was made between acculturation processes as they affect individuals and as they affect groups.

Acculturation and personality. A. I. Hallowell (1945) made a series of studies among Indians of Canada that pointed to the conclusion that personality configuration remained relatively stable as compared with cultural behavior. These studies among Ojibwa and Salteaux Indians seemed to disagree with studies by the Beagleholes (1941) of Polynesians in New Zealand and elsewhere, which led them to the conclusion that personality structure must change before cultural systems could change. Wallace (1961b) held that the personalities of peoples in contact acted as screens that selected elements from the cultures of neighboring societies with which they were in contact, a viewpoint consistent with Hallowell's interpretations. Studies by George Spindler (1955) of Indians in the same region as those studied by Hallowell attempted to relate changing sociocultural variables to changing personality variables. These studies pointed more and more to an interest in the types of individual response and adjustment correlated with types of contact situations. As such they constituted investigations very closely related to the studies of biculturalism.

Social scale. In Africa and in Middle America there was an interesting convergence of research approaches represented by Godfrey and Monica

Wilson (1945) and Robert Redfield (1941) respectively. This consisted in the study of the relationship between social scale and cultural change. Redfield's studies of acculturation in Middle American communities led him to the formulation of a general theory of cultural change that related changes in degree of secularization, individuation, and cultural disorganization to change in "isolation." In general, he held that decreasing isolation was associated with increases in the other three variables. This was not presented by Redfield as "acculturation theory," but it is obvious that by decrease in isolation of a community or group of communities, he could only mean increase of contacts. This aspect of his "folk–urban" theory is therefore to be considered as concerned with conditions of contact. Employing different phraseology, but obviously proceeding from the observation of phenomena very similar to those observed by Redfield, the Wilsons developed a similar body of theory. They did not employ the term "isolation," but identified a variable that they called "social scale." This in general means the extent of the area of social interaction of a given set of individuals and appears, therefore, to be more easily measurable than Redfield's isolation. However, the Wilsons insisted that intensity as well as numbers of persons in interaction had to be considered in social scale. This introduced complications but still seemed to promise better possibility of precise statement of relationships than did Redfield's propositions. The propositions that the Wilsons advanced were very similar to those of Redfield. They suggested, for example, that increase of social scale is correlated with decrease of magicality. This was close to the proposition that decrease of isolation is correlated with increase in secularization. Both these efforts at formulation of theories of contact change were important as offering a common, broad framework for acculturation studies within the general theory of cultural and social change.

Applied anthropology. After World War II, one of the most active areas in acculturation study was one often spoken of as applied anthropology. Attention was focused on practical programs aimed at specific changes in societies or subsocieties dominated by others. Programs of colonial administrations in Africa and Oceania, of Latin American governments in areas of high Indian density, and on Indian reservations in the United States were all studied intensively by such investigators as Keesing (1953), Hogbin (1958), Erasmus (1961), Aguirre Beltrán (1957), and many others. These programs of directed cultural change were analyzed with respect to the techniques employed for bringing about change, the objectives, and the results achieved. The work of Keesing (1953) and Foster (1962) was increasingly directed toward establishing a comparative framework within which propositions concerned with the dynamics of directed culture change could be tested.

EDWARD H. SPICER

[See also CULTURE AND PERSONALITY; DIFFUSION; NATIVISM AND REVIVALISM. *Directly related are the entries* ANTHROPOLOGY, *article on* APPLIED ANTHROPOLOGY; CULTURE, *article on* CULTURE CHANGE; EVOLUTION, *article on* CULTURAL EVOLUTION.]

BIBLIOGRAPHY

AGUIRRE BELTRÁN, GONZALO 1957 *El proceso de aculturación.* Mexico City: Universidad Nacional Autónoma de Mexico.

AMERICAN ANTHROPOLOGICAL ASSOCIATION 1937 Proceedings of the Annual Meeting for 1936. *American Anthropologist* New Series 39:316–327.

BARNETT, HOMER G. 1940 Culture Processes. *American Anthropologist* New Series 42:21–48.

BEAGLEHOLE, ERNEST; and BEAGLEHOLE, PEARL 1941 *Pangai, Village in Tonga.* Polynesian Society Memoirs, Vol. 18. Wellington (New Zealand): The Society.

BEALS, RALPH L. 1951 Urbanism, Urbanization and Acculturation. *American Anthropologist* New Series 53: 1–10.

BEALS, RALPH L. 1953 Acculturation. Pages 621–641 in International Symposium on Anthropology, New York, 1952. *Anthropology Today: An Encyclopedic Inventory.* Univ. of Chicago Press.

BOAS, FRANZ 1896 The Growth of Indian Mythologies: A Study Based Upon the Growth of the Mythologies of the North Pacific Coast. *Journal of American Folklore* 9:1–11.

BOSE, NIRMAL KUMAR (1929) 1961 *Cultural Anthropology.* Rev. ed. New York: Asia Pub. House.

EHRENREICH, PAUL 1905 *Die Mythen und Legenden der südamerikanischen Urvölker und ihre Beziehungen zu denen Nordamerikas und der alten Welt.* Zeitschrift für Ethnologie, Vol. 37, Supplement. Berlin: Asher.

ERASMUS, CHARLES J. 1961 *Man Takes Control: Cultural Development and American Aid.* Minneapolis: Univ. of Minnesota Press.

FIRTH, RAYMOND W. 1959 *Social Change in Tikopia: Restudy of a Polynesian Community After a Generation.* New York: Macmillan; London: Allen & Unwin.

FOSTER, GEORGE M. 1960 *Culture and Conquest: America's Spanish Heritage.* Viking Fund Publications in Anthropology, Vol. 27. New York: Wenner-Gren Foundation.

FOSTER, GEORGE M. 1962 *Traditional Cultures, and the Impact of Technological Change.* New York: Harper.

HALLOWELL, A. IRVING (1945) 1957 Sociopsychological Aspects of Acculturation. Pages 171–200 in Ralph Linton (editor), *The Science of Man in the World Crisis.* New York: Columbia Univ. Press.

HERSKOVITS, MELVILLE J. 1927 Acculturation and the American Negro. *Southwestern Political and Social Science Quarterly* 8:211–224. → Now called the *Southwestern Social Science Quarterly.*

HERSKOVITS, MELVILLE J. (1937a) 1965 African Gods and Catholic Saints in New World Negro Belief.

Pages 541–547 in William A. Lessa and Evon J. Vogt (editors), *Reader in Comparative Religion: An Anthropological Approach.* 2d ed. New York: Harper. → First published in Volume 39 of the *American Anthropologist* New Series.

HERSKOVITS, MELVILLE J. (1937b) 1964 *Life in a Haitian Valley.* New York: Octagon Books.

HOGBIN, HERBERT I. 1958 *Social Change.* London: Watts.

HOLMES, WILLIAM H. 1886 Pottery of the Ancient Pueblos. Pages 257–360 in U.S. Bureau of American Ethnology, *Fourth Annual Report, 1882–1883.* Washington: Smithsonian Institution.

INTERUNIVERSITY SUMMER RESEARCH SEMINAR, UNIVERSITY OF NEW MEXICO, 1956 1961 *Perspectives in American Indian Culture Change.* Edited by Edward H. Spicer. Univ. of Chicago Press.

KEESING, FELIX M. (1941) 1945 *The South Seas in the Modern World.* New York: Day.

KEESING, FELIX M. 1953 Cultural Dynamics and Administration. Pages 102–117 in Pacific Science Congress, Seventh, 1949, *Proceedings.* Volume 7: Anthropology, Public Health and Nutrition, and Social Sciences. Christchurch (New Zealand): Pegasus Press.

KRICKEBERG, WALTER (1910) 1922 Die Völker des Ostens und Südostens. Volume 1, pages 97–112 in Georg Buschan (editor), *Illustrierte Völkerkunde.* Stuttgart (Germany): Strecker.

KROEBER, ALFRED L. (1923) 1948 *Anthropology: Race, Language, Culture, Psychology, Prehistory.* New rev. ed. New York: Harcourt.

LESSER, ALEXANDER 1933 *The Pawnee Ghost Dance Hand Game: A Study of Cultural Change.* Columbia University Contributions to Anthropology, Vol. 16. New York: Columbia Univ. Press.

LINTON, RALPH (editor) 1940 *Acculturation in Seven American Indian Tribes.* New York: Appleton.

LINTON, RALPH (1943) 1965 Nativistic Movements. Pages 499–506 in William A. Lessa and Evon Z. Vogt (editors), *Reader in Comparative Religion: An Anthropological Approach.* 2d ed. New York: Harper. → First published in Volume 45 of the *American Anthropologist* New Series.

LOWIE, ROBERT H. (1935) 1956 *The Crow Indians.* New York: Rinehart.

McGEE, W. J. (1898) 1960 Piratical Acculturation. Pages 793–799 in American Anthropologist, *Selected Papers from the American Anthropologist, 1888–1920.* Evanston, Ill.: Row, Peterson. → First published in Volume 11 of the *American Anthropologist* New Series.

MALINOWSKI, BRONISLAW 1945 *The Dynamics of Culture Change: An Inquiry Into Race Relations in Africa.* New Haven: Yale Univ. Press. → A paperback edition was published in 1961 by Yale University Press.

MEAD, MARGARET 1932 *The Changing Culture of an Indian Tribe.* Columbia University Contributions to Anthropology, Vol. 15. New York: Columbia Univ. Press.

Methods of Study of Culture Contact in Africa. International Institute of African Languages and Cultures, Memorandum No. 15 (1938) 1959. London: Oxford Univ. Press.

MOONEY, JAMES 1896 The Ghost-dance Religion and the Sioux Outbreak of 1890. Part 2, pages 641–1110 in U.S. Bureau of American Ethnology, *Fourteenth Annual Report, 1892–1893.* Washington: Smithsonian Institution. → An abridged edition, with an introduction by Anthony F. C. Wallace, was published by the University of Chicago Press in 1965.

NASH, PHILLEO (1937) 1955 The Place of Religious Re-vivalism in the Formation of the Intercultural Community on Klamath Reservation. Pages 375–442 in *Social Anthropology of North American Tribes.* 2d ed. Univ. of Chicago Press.

PHELAN, JOHN LEDDY 1959 *The Hispanization of the Philippines: Spanish Aims and Filipino Responses, 1565–1700.* Madison: Univ. of Wisconsin Press.

POLGAR, STEVEN 1960 Biculturation of Mesquakie Teenage Boys. *American Anthropologist* New Series 62: 217–235.

REDFIELD, ROBERT 1929 The Material Culture of Spanish–Indian Mexico. *American Anthropologist* New Series 31:602–618.

REDFIELD, ROBERT 1941 *The Folk Culture of Yucatan.* Univ. of Chicago Press.

REDFIELD, ROBERT 1953 *The Primitive World and Its Transformations.* Ithaca, N.Y.: Cornell Univ. Press. → A paperback edition was published in 1957.

REDFIELD, ROBERT; LINTON, RALPH; and HERSKOVITS, MELVILLE J. (1935) 1936 Outline for the Study of Acculturation. *American Anthropologist* New Series 38: 149–152. → First published in *Man.*

SCHAPERA, ISAAC (editor) 1934 *Western Civilization and the Natives of South Africa: Studies in Culture Contact.* London: Routledge.

SCHWARTZ, THEODORE 1962 The Paliau Movement in the Admiralty Islands, 1946–1954. Volume 49, part 2 in American Museum of Natural History, New York, *Anthropological Papers.* New York: The Museum.

SOCIAL SCIENCE RESEARCH COUNCIL, SUMMER SEMINAR ON ACCULTURATION, 1953 1954 Acculturation: An Exploratory Formulation. *American Anthropologist* New Series 56:973–1002.

SPIER, LESLIE 1935 *The Prophet Dance of the Northwest and Its Derivatives: The Source of the Ghost Dance.* Menasha, Wis.: Banta.

SPINDLER, GEORGE D. 1955 *Sociocultural and Psychological Processes in Menomini Acculturation.* University of California Publications in Culture and Society, Vol. 5. Berkeley: Univ. of California Press.

SUTTLES, WAYNE 1957 The Plateau Prophet Dance Among the Coast Salish. *Southwestern Journal of Anthropology* 13:352–396.

THURNWALD, RICHARD 1935 *Black and White in East Africa; The Fabric of a New Civilization: A Study of Social Contact and Adaptation of Life in East Africa.* With a chapter on women by Hilde Thurnwald. London: Routledge.

VOGT, EVON Z. 1951 *Navaho Veterans: A Study of Changing Values.* Harvard University, Peabody Museum of American Archaeology and Ethnology, Papers, Vol. 41, No. 1. Cambridge, Mass.: The Museum.

WALLACE, ANTHONY F. C. 1961a Cultural Composition of the Handsome Lake Religion. Pages 139–151 in Symposium on Cherokee and Iroquois Culture, Washington, D.C. 1958, *Symposium on Cherokee and Iroquois Culture.* Edited by William N. Fenton and John Gulick. U.S. Bureau of American Ethnology Bulletin No. 180. Washington: Government Printing Office.

WALLACE, ANTHONY F. C. 1961b *Culture and Personality.* New York: Random House.

WILLIAMS, FRANCIS EDGAR 1923 *The Vailala Madness and the Destruction of Native Ceremonies in the Gulf Division.* Territory of Papua Anthropology Report, No. 4. Port Moresby (New Guinea): Baker.

WILSON, GODFREY; and WILSON, MONICA H. (1945) 1965 *The Analysis of Social Change, Based on Observations in Central Africa.* Cambridge Univ. Press.

WILSON, MONICA (HUNTER) (1936) 1961 *Reaction to*

Conquest: Effects of Contact with Europeans on the Pondo of South Africa. 2d ed. London: Oxford Univ. Press. → The first edition was published under author's maiden name, i.e., Hunter.

WORSLEY, PETER 1957 *The Trumpet Shall Sound: A Study of "Cargo" Cults in Melanesia.* London: Mac-Gibbon & Kee.

ACHIEVEMENT MOTIVATION

Achievement motivation, also referred to as the need for achievement (and abbreviated *n* Achievement), is an important determinant of aspiration, effort, and persistence when an individual expects that his performance will be evaluated in relation to some standard of excellence. Such behavior is called achievement-oriented.

Motivation to achieve is instigated when an individual knows that he is responsible for the outcome of some venture, when he anticipates explicit knowledge of results that will define his success or failure, and when there is some degree of risk, i.e., some uncertainty about the outcome of his effort. The goal of achievement-oriented activity is to succeed, to perform well in relation to a standard of excellence or in comparison with others who are competitors (McClelland 1961, chapter 6; Atkinson 1964).

The topic is obviously of practical importance in education and industry. It is related to traditional sociological interest in the determinants of mobility; and through McClelland's (1961) study of its relationship to entrepreneurial activity, it has become a matter of considerable interest to economists, historians, and others concerned with economic development.

Individuals differ in their strength of motive to achieve, and various activities differ in the challenge they pose and the opportunity they offer for expression of this motive. Thus, both personality and environmental factors must be considered in accounting for the strength of motivation to achieve in a particular person facing a particular challenge in a particular situation. The very same person may be more strongly motivated at one time than at another time, even though in most situations he may generally tend to be more interested in achieving than other people.

Basic problems. The basic psychological problems are (*a*) the dynamics of achievement motivation, i.e., the nature of the joint influence of personality and environmental challenge on the strength of motivation and the consequent effects on behavior; (*b*) the refinement of diagnostic tests of achievement motivation; and (*c*) the development of individual differences in achievement motive. Of more general interest is the analysis of social origins and social consequences of achievement motivation.

History of study. The concept of achievement motivation has its antecedents in earlier psychological studies conducted under a variety of different rubrics, particularly "success and failure" (Sears 1942), "ego-involvement" (Allport 1943), and "level of aspiration" (Lewin et al. 1944). At that time, there was little basis for a meaningful integration of knowledge because research findings were not anchored by the use of a common method for assessment of motivation. This is less true today as a result of a methodological innovation shortly after World War II: namely, the experimental validation of a method of measuring achievement motivation, followed by systematic use of this new tool in behavioral and societal studies (McClelland et al. 1953). McClelland and his co-workers combined the traditional clinical assumption that human motives are freely expressed in imagination with procedures developed within experimental psychology for manipulation of strength of motivation. It was demonstrated, first with hunger, then with concern over achievement and other human motives, that the motivational state of an individual can be diagnosed by means of content analysis of his fantasy or imaginative behavior (Atkinson 1958) as revealed, for example, in the thematic apperception test [*see* PROJECTIVE METHODS, *article on* THE THEMATIC APPERCEPTION TEST].

Achievement imagery in fantasy takes the form of thoughts about performing some task well, of sometimes being blocked, of trying various means of achieving, and of experiencing joy or sadness contingent upon the outcome of the effort. The particular diagnostic signs of achievement motivation were identified by experimental fact. The results of validating experiments have been replicated in other social groups and societies. Together these experimental findings specify what is counted in an imaginative protocol to yield the *n* Achievement score, an assessment of the strength of achievement motivation (McClelland et al. 1953, chapter 4; McClelland et al. 1958).

To study antecedents or effects of individual differences, the method of content analysis is applied to analysis of imaginative stories written by different persons under standard conditions. The same method has been successfully applied to stories obtained in a national survey study (Veroff et al. 1960), to folk tales, to children's readers, and to other samples of the imaginative behavior of whole societies (McClelland 1961).

Individuals who produce the most achievement imagery in a standard assessment situation are assumed to be the most highly motivated to achieve. Societies whose literary documents are saturated with achievement imagery are likewise assumed to be more concerned about achievement than those in which this type of imagery is less prevalent.

Dynamics

Current theory, which is an elaboration, with greater specification, of an earlier theory of level of aspiration (Lewin et al. 1944), provides the simplest organization of facts about achievement-oriented activity and an explicit guide for further study (Atkinson 1957; 1964; Atkinson & Feather 1966).

Achievement-oriented behavior is conceived as invariably influenced by the strength of an individual's tendency to achieve success and, in addition, by his tendency to avoid failure, which is also inherent in situations involving evaluation of performance. Attention is also drawn to the determinative role of extrinsic motivational tendencies on what appear to be achievement-oriented activities. An extrinsic tendency is one produced by some motive or incentive other than achievement per se (e.g., money, social approval, compliance with authority) and that is not inherent in an achievement-related situation.

The tendency to achieve success in a particular activity (T_s) is conceived as jointly determined by the strength of a general motive to achieve success (M_s), considered a relatively stable characteristic of an individual's personality, and two factors that define the challenge of the immediate task and situation; namely, the strength of expectancy or subjective probability of success in the activity (P_s) and the relative attractiveness or incentive value of success in that particular activity (I_s). It is assumed that the three variables combine multiplicatively to determine the strength of the tendency to achieve, i.e., $T_s = M_s \times P_s \times I_s$.

The earlier generalization that the attractiveness of success is directly proportional to the difficulty of a task (Lewin et al. 1944) is now specified more exactly: $I_s = 1 - P_s$. Following from the two assumptions are the general implications shown graphically in Figure 1. The tendency to achieve, which determines interest and the impetus to undertake an activity with the intention of doing well, is generally stronger when the motive to achieve (M_s) is strong and when the task is one of intermediate difficulty or risk. Persons who score high in n Achievement normally perform at a higher level in achievement-oriented activities, tend to prefer intermediate degree of risk (or difficulty) and/or to have a moderately high, i.e., realistic, level of aspiration, and tend to be more persistent in achievement-oriented activity when confronted with opportunities to undertake other kinds of activity instead (Atkinson 1964; Atkinson & Feather 1966; McClelland 1961, chapter 6).

A further assumption is that success increases and failure decreases the expectancy of success (P_s) at the same and similar activities; this helps to account for effects of success and failure on changes in motivation that are expressed in subsequent aspiration and persistence. Typically, individuals who are strongly motivated to achieve set a moderately high level of aspiration (or prefer an intermediate risk), raising the aspiration level somewhat following success and lowering it somewhat after failure. Since success increases P_s at the same and similar activities, and $I_s = 1 - P_s$, the effect of success at a moderately difficult task is a change in subsequent motivation so that the tendency to undertake the same activity again is weakened and the tendency to undertake an activity that initially appeared a little more difficult is strengthened. The point at which $P_s = .50$ shifts upward at the next most difficult task. A change in the opposite direction occurs following failure at the initial activity. Hence a moderately high aspiration is lowered following failure.

As is suggested in Figure 1, continual success or continual failure will ultimately produce loss of achievement interest in an activity without implying any change, however, in the strength of the individual's general motive to achieve (M_s). The immediate effect of failure at a task that is considered relatively easy to begin with is a heighten-

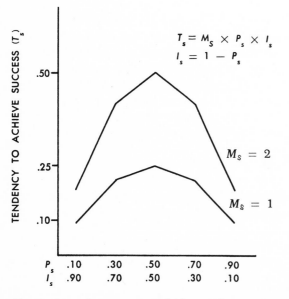

Figure 1 — Components of the tendency to achieve success

ing of interest before the gradual decline. Men who are strong in n Achievement are considerably more persistent in the face of repeated failure when their initial expectation of success (P_s) is quite high than when it is initially very low (Feather 1961). Often, because he has more of a history of success behind him, the person who is strongly motivated to achieve approaches a novel or somewhat ambiguous situation more optimistically than others (Atkinson & Feather 1966).

The occupational ladder, which gives one measure of a man's success in life, is a hierarchy of achievement-oriented activities that represent potential goals for most people, ordered in terms of the difficulty of attainment. The principle $I_s = 1 - P_s$ applies to the prestige normally accorded persons in different occupations. Vocational aspiration, effort, and persistence displayed in the instrumental activities of getting an education and work are expressions of achievement motivation. Men who are highly motivated to achieve set moderate, realistic vocational aspirations; often perform better in school; attain a higher level of education; and—if they come from a low-status background—are more upwardly mobile than men who are weak in n Achievement (Crockett 1962). Men who are motivated to achieve may be especially attracted to careers in business because they offer opportunity to take calculated risks with explicit knowledge of results (i.e., profits and losses) and provide one of the few channels that an individual of low-status background can enter without higher education and still have a realistic chance of moving up to a higher status. Available evidence supports the view that business leaders and managers, particularly in sales and marketing, are relatively strong in n Achievement (McClelland 1961, chapter 7).

Avoidance of failure. The analysis of determinants of achievement-oriented activity is more complete when effects of the tendency to avoid failure and the role of extrinsic sources of motivation are also taken into account. The motive to avoid failure (M_{AF}), conceived as a disposition to be anxious about failure, has been reliably assessed by tests that require a person to report the symptoms of anxiety he normally experiences in test situations and, more recently, by thematic content analysis (Heckhausen 1963). This motive, combining multiplicatively with the subjective probability of failure (P_f) and the negative incentive value of failure (I_f), produces a tendency to avoid undertaking an activity when there is an expectancy of failure. The easier the task the greater is the pain of an expected failure, i.e., $I_f = -P_s$. Hence

the implications concerning determinants of the strength of the tendency to avoid failure parallel those shown in Figure 1 for the positive tendency. But the behavioral implications are diametrically opposite. The tendency to avoid failure produces a resistance to achievement-oriented activity that must be overcome, if not by a stronger tendency to achieve then by some extrinsic motivational tendency. When an individual's motive to achieve exceeds his motive to avoid failure ($M_S > M_{AF}$), then the tendency to achieve will dominate in the assumed algebraic summation of the conflicting tendencies and the patterns of achievement-oriented activity already described will occur. When the motive to avoid failure is stronger ($M_{AF} > M_S$), as is more likely when n Achievement is weak, all interest in achievement-oriented activity should be inhibited and resistance should be greatest for tasks that represent moderate risks where P_s is near .50. The resistance is often overcome by extrinsic sources of positive motivation, e.g., the tendency to gain approval by doing what is expected. This is more easily accomplished where resistance is weakest, namely, where the probability of success is either very high or very low. Thus both a very high level of aspiration (corresponding to preference for an activity where P_s is very low) and a very low level of aspiration are construed as symptomatic of a relatively strong motive to avoid failure and not of a strong motive to achieve. These extreme levels of aspiration occur most frequently among men who are weak in n Achievement and strong in anxiety. Nonadaptive behavioral trends, including atypical changes in aspiration following success and failure and dogged persistence when there is little obvious chance to succeed (Feather 1961), are among the other empirically confirmed consequences of a strong tendency to avoid failure that follow from the logic of the theory (Atkinson & Feather 1966; Moulton 1965).

Diagnostic tests

Several other methods yield results comparable to those obtained with the imaginative n Achievement score. One method requires an individual to explain the actions of another person, which have been described to him in a short statement. The explanations impute feelings and intentions to the person and are coded as if they were imaginative stories. To avoid some limitations of verbal measures a technique for analysis of characteristics of an individual's graphic expression has been developed. It discriminates reliably between persons who score high and low on imaginative n Achievement in the United States, and it has been employed with meaningful results in studies of children's designs and in inferring achievement motivation from designs on artifacts of ancient civilizations (Atkinson 1958; McClelland 1961).

The current theory and evidence also suggest that the slope of an individual's ratings of the attractiveness of occupations in relation to increasing level of status (difficulty) may be developed as a useful measure of achievement motivation (Atkinson 1964; Atkinson & Feather 1966).

There has been a series of efforts to develop a simpler and more direct test of the strength of achievement motive by employing an individual's self-descriptive statements or endorsements of particular beliefs and attitudes implying strong achievement motivation; but none has produced an adequate substitute for the indirect, projective method of assessing motivation. This is partly because self-descriptive activities are much more complexly determined social actions than is commonly imagined and partly because intuitive misconceptions of how an achievement motive should be expressed in behavior have influenced the content of test items that have been tried (Atkinson 1958; McClelland 1961, p. 331).

The peculiar advantage of imaginative behavior seems to lie in the fact that the individual is less constrained than in his other actions and is able to spell out the nature of his inner concerns in his spontaneous imagery without being aware that he is doing it.

Social origins and consequences

McClelland's hypothesis that "achievement motivation is in part responsible for economic growth" (1961, p. 36) has provided the main impetus and conceptual framework for studies concerning development and social consequences of *n* Achievement. Preliminary evidence that *n* Achievement in middle-class American boys is related to parental encouragement of self-reliance and mastery early in childhood (Winterbottom 1958) suggested that Max Weber's hypothesis concerning the influence on the development of capitalism of the Protestant ethic, which encouraged this kind of training, might be considered a specific instance of the more general hypothesis. McClelland's view is that innovating and risk-taking activities of entrepreneurs are to be viewed as expressions of a strong motive to achieve and not merely a profit motive as traditionally assumed [1961, pp. 233–237; *see* TAWNEY; WEBER, MAX].

Of the several kinds of evidence he presents, the most novel and impressive, particularly as a meth-

odological innovation, are studies that relate societal indexes of *n* Achievement obtained from content analysis of folk tales, children's readers, and other literary documents to indexes of the society's economic development. This illustrates how psychological techniques that have undergone considerable experimental validation can be applied in comparative studies of society and in the analysis of historical trends (McClelland 1961, chapters 3–4).

The *n* Achievement scores obtained from content analysis of folk tales from preliterate societies are positively correlated with early achievement training (p. 343) and with presence of some full-time entrepreneurs in the society (p. 66). Similar *n* Achievement scores obtained from readers employed to teach children in 21 different societies in 1925 are positively correlated with an index of economic growth in those societies between 1929 and 1950 (p. 92). Another set of *n* Achievement scores obtained from readers in 39 societies in 1950 does not relate to the economic gain between 1929 and 1950 but does predict the gain by those societies between 1952 and 1958 (p. 100). Furthermore, the average *n* Achievement scores obtained from children's readers is significantly higher in 1950.

The amount of achievement imagery in children's readers is considered a sensitive barometer of the concern felt in the country for economic development. Since this imagery is correlated with economic growth in the very near future, it would appear that it is mostly a reflection of the mood and motivation of the adult population at the time (pp. 101–102).

The question of whether a rise in *n* Achievement precedes economic growth and a fall in *n* Achievement precedes a decline of a society is treated by motivational content analysis of representative samples of imaginative literature from the same society at critical periods in its history. David Berlew selected samples of the literature of ancient Greece from the periods of growth (900–475 B.C.), climax (475–362 B.C.), and decline (362–100 B.C.) and analyzed them for achievement imagery. The level of *n* Achievement was highest in the period preceding the rise in Greek civilization, lower during the period of climax, and lower still after the decline. An index of *n* Achievement obtained from analysis of graphic expression in designs on Grecian vases during the same time periods yielded equivalent results (pp. 108–129). A similar analysis of the economic growth and decline of Spain between 1200 and 1730 produced the same general findings.

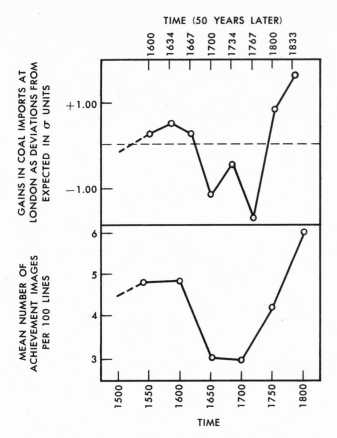

Figure 2 — Achievement imagery in English literature (1550–1880) compared with rates of gain in coal imports at London 50 years later

Source: McClelland 1961, p. 139.

A study of England from Tudor times to the industrial revolution (1500–1833) included a more complete sampling of time periods. It produced the remarkable result that "motivational changes *precede* the economic ones by 30–50 years" (McClelland 1961, p. 138), as shown in Figure 2. An even closer relationship is shown between *n* Achievement level in children's readers in the United States from 1800 to 1950 and a measure of technological innovation. Both level of *n* Achievement in readers and number of patents granted (relative to population) rise steadily from 1800 to 1890 and decline thereafter (p. 150). McClelland believes that facts of this sort should serve to direct the attention of social scientists "away from an exclusive concern with the external events in history to the 'internal' psychological concerns that in the long run determine what happens in history" (p. 105).

Developmental factors

Individual differences in *n* Achievement have been detected as early as the age of five, and the evidence, although very sparse, is nevertheless consistent with the prevailing view that strength of achievement motive is probably relatively stable from childhood to adulthood (Kagan & Moss 1962; Crandall 1963). Studies of how parents rear their children—based on reports of parents, ethnographic data, observational studies of parent–child interactions, and longitudinal studies—have begun to identify some key factors in development of the achievement motive.

The weight of evidence suggests that in child rearing early emphasis on self-reliant mastery tends to promote the development of *n* Achievement, provided it is not merely an expression of authoritarianism or rejection of the child by parents who are pushing it to look out for itself so that it will be less burdensome to them. Exposure to high standards of excellence, accompanied by warmth and encouragement of independent effort, should occur neither too early for the child's abilities nor too late in childhood for him to internalize the standards as his own (McClelland 1961, p. 345; Veroff 1965). Equally important is the opportunity given a child to practice self-reliant behavior and to exercise his talents without domination by his father (Strodtbeck 1958; Rosen & D'Andrade 1959). Also important is opportunity for practice in mechanical and constructional activities. This provides early practice in independent mastery with very explicit knowledge of results (Kagan & Moss 1962, chapter 5).

Major political, economic, social, and other environmental forces—even climate—may have an important impact on motivation insofar as they tend to modify one or another of these key factors (or others yet to be discovered). McClelland stresses this point with conjectures about the indirect and unintended effects of slavery and war on *n* Achievement in a society. The institution of slavery (e.g., in ancient Greece) means that children will be very dependent upon the slave responsible for their early training and will not be exposed to the high standards and demands for self-reliant mastery that might have been transmitted directly by early parental supervision. Thus a society's *n* Achievement may be lost in the process of training the next generation. And war, by taking a potentially domineering father out of the home during the critical years, may contribute to the growth of *n* Achievement by giving the child an opportunity for self-reliant mastery.

In American society, *n* Achievement is strongest in the middle class and among Jews. The social values of these groups tend to encourage some favorable combination of the key factors early in life. A representative survey of the United States showed that high n Achievement is more prevalent among Catholics than Protestants (Veroff et al. 1962); but this result, like most other comparisons between ethnic, religious, and racial groups, must be qualified in terms of what social classes are being compared, the degree of assimilation to the culture, whether religious orientation is strong, and other factors (McClelland 1961, chapter 9; Veroff et al. 1962).

Problems and unresolved issues

Growth in knowledge depends more upon coherence than mere accumulation of empirical facts. Studies that employ *ad hoc* tests and methods of unproven validity to assess achievement motivation still evade systematic discussion. Future study must combine substantial effort to improve valid methods and to develop better ones with awareness that common use of the best available tools holds greater promise than the use of unproven techniques.

Future study must include systematic assessment of individual differences in anxiety and its effects and must identify the effects of so-called extrinsic motivational tendencies and the conditions under which they operate (Atkinson & Feather 1966). At issue is the question of whether the characteristics of behavior referred to as "entrepreneurial" necessarily require a strong motive to achieve, rooted in a particular kind of early background, or whether manipulation of incentives that appeal to other motives (e.g., money or social approval) might, under specified conditions, produce equivalent behavioral effects.

The major unresolved interpretive issue concerning different levels of n Achievement in various individuals, social groups, and historical periods is that of disentangling the effects of basic personality structure from effects of the immediate environment. McClelland (1961) has emphasized that changes in the societal level of n Achievement are mediated by changes in the way children are reared in the family, that is, by changes in basic personality. But theory concerning the dynamics of achievement motivation gives equal emphasis—not the disproportionate emphasis of the traditional environmentalist but *equal* emphasis—to the immediate environmental challenge (P_s) as a determinant of the level of n Achievement in stressing the interaction of personality and environmental influences (Atkinson & Feather 1966). This perplexing issue is treated candidly by Veroff et al. (1960) in relation to national survey results in the United States showing that the level of n

Achievement is higher among more educated people, among professionals and managers, and among men aged 21–24 and 35–50 than among others. Do these results, and others like them, refer to differences in the strength of general and enduring dispositions of personality that are rooted in differences in early childhood training? Their answer:

Facing frankly the paucity of evidence concerning dispositional versus situational factors in motivation, and their interactions, we can see that any one of the following arguments might be pursued in the interpretation of obtained differences between certain social groups. (1) The obtained difference is attributable to differences in enduring personality dispositions acquired early in life. (2) The obtained difference is the consequence of a change in personality disposition induced by important situational factors later in life. (3) The obtained difference is a consequence of exposure to differential temporary situational pressures affecting the level of aroused motivation regardless of equivalence in underlying personality disposition. (Veroff et al. 1960, p. 22)

This basic theoretical issue is tied to one of more immediate practical importance: Can an individual's need for achievement be strengthened? McClelland (1965) has begun to mobilize the whole armament of psychological techniques for producing a change in behavior or attitude in an effort to devise a program for training a willing adult to be more highly motivated to achieve. His approach leaves open the question of what, in current theoretical terms, is being changed: the motive, the perception of the achievement-relatedness of some activities not previously viewed in that light (see also Veroff 1965), the extent to which other motives will be engaged in achievement-oriented behavior, or, perhaps, the strength of an individual's expectancy of success in certain activities.

From the viewpoint of current theory, the strength of an individual's subjective probability of success in some activity deserves special emphasis and systematic study as a manipulable motivational variable. It approximates what Arnold Toynbee has called "environmental challenge." Motivational effects of homogeneous ability grouping of children in schools have been meaningfully treated as the result of changing the strength of a student's subjective probability of success in schoolwork, relative to his peers, from what it would normally be in a more heterogeneous classroom situation. In the traditional, heterogeneous classroom in the United States, the very bright child often faces a prospect that is too easy to be challenging to him, and the very dull child often faces one that is so hopelessly difficult for him that he cannot become either enthusiastically or anxiously involved. When students are grouped according to ability, everybody faces an intermediate achievement risk (Atkinson & Feather 1966).

Perhaps the revolution of rising expectations in underdeveloped countries and among American Negroes, for whom opportunity has finally arrived, should be conceived in terms of a change in the environment from one that had previously defined any effort to achieve as a relatively hopeless prospect to one that now presents a moderate, realistic challenge to whatever latent motives to achieve there are in people who answer its call.

JOHN W. ATKINSON

[*Other relevant material may be found in* DRIVES, *article on* ACQUIRED DRIVES; ENTREPRENEURSHIP; FANTASY; MOTIVATION; SOCIAL MOBILITY.]

BIBLIOGRAPHY

ALLPORT, GORDON W. 1943 The Ego in Contemporary Psychology. *Psychological Review* 50:451–478.

ATKINSON, JOHN W. (1957) 1958 Motivational Determinants of Risk-taking Behavior. Pages 322–339 in John W. Atkinson (editor), *Motives in Fantasy, Action, and Society: A Method of Assessment and Study.* Princeton, N.J.: Van Nostrand. → First published in volume 64 of the *Psychological Review*.

ATKINSON, JOHN W. (editor) 1958 *Motives in Fantasy, Action, and Society: A Method of Assessment and Study.* Princeton, N.J.: Van Nostrand.

ATKINSON, JOHN W. 1964 *An Introduction to Motivation.* Princeton, N.J.: Van Nostrand. → See especially pages 240–268, "A Theory of Achievement Motivation."

ATKINSON, JOHN W.; and FEATHER, N. T. (editors) 1966 *A Theory of Achievement Motivation.* New York: Wiley.

CRANDALL, VAUGHAN 1963 Achievement. Volume 62, pages 416–459 in National Society for the Study of Education, *Yearbook.* Part 1: Child Psychology. Univ. of Chicago Press.

CROCKETT, HARRY J. 1962 Achievement Motive and Differential Occupational Mobility in the United States. *American Sociological Review* 27:191–204.

FEATHER, NORMAN T. 1961 The Relationship of Persistence at a Task to Expectation of Success and Achievement Related Motives. *Journal of Abnormal and Social Psychology* 63:552–561.

HECKHAUSEN, HEINZ 1963 *Hoffnung und Furcht in der Leistungsmotivation.* Meisenheim am Glan (Germany): Hain.

KAGAN, JEROME; and MOSS, HOWARD A. 1962 *Birth to Maturity: A Study in Psychological Development.* New York: Wiley.

LEWIN, KURT et al. 1944 Level of Aspiration. Volume 1, pages 333–378 in Joseph McV. Hunt (editor), *Personality and the Behavior Disorders.* New York: Ronald Press.

McCLELLAND, DAVID C. 1961 *The Achieving Society.* Princeton, N.J.: Van Nostrand.

McCLELLAND, DAVID C. 1965 Toward a Theory of Motive Acquisition. *American Psychologist* 20:321–333.

McCLELLAND, DAVID C. et al. 1953 *The Achievement Motive.* New York: Appleton. → See especially pages 107–138, "Analysis of Imaginative Stories for Motivational Content."

McCLELLAND, DAVID C. et al. 1958 A Scoring Manual for the Achievement Motive. Pages 179–204 in John W. Atkinson (editor), *Motives in Fantasy, Action, and Society: A Method of Assessment and Study.* Princeton, N.J.: Van Nostrand.

MOULTON, R. 1965 Effects of Success and Failure on Level of Aspirations as Related to Achievement Motives. *Journal of Personality and Social Psychology* 1:399–406.

ROSEN, BERNARD C.; and D'ANDRADE, ROY C. 1959 The Psychosocial Origins of Achievement Motivation. *Sociometry* 22:185–218.

SEARS, ROBERT R. 1942 Success and Failure: A Study of Motility. Pages 235–258 in *Studies in Personality, Contributed in Honor of Lewis M. Terman.* New York: McGraw-Hill.

STRODTBECK, FRED L. 1958 Family Interaction, Values and Achievement. Pages 135–194 in David C. McClelland et al., *Talent and Society.* Princeton, N.J.: Van Nostrand.

VEROFF, JOSEPH 1965 Theoretical Background for Studying the Origins of Human Motivational Dispositions. *Merrill–Palmer Quarterly of Behavior and Development* 11:3–18.

VEROFF, JOSEPH et al. 1960 The Use of Thematic Apperception to Assess Motivation in a Nationwide Interview Study. *Psychological Monographs* 74, no. 12.

VEROFF, JOSEPH et al. 1962 Achievement Motivation and Religious Background. *American Sociological Review* 27:205–217.

WINTERBOTTOM, MARIAN 1958 The Relation of Need for Achievement to Learning Experiences in Independence and Mastery. Pages 453–478 in John W. Atkinson (editor), *Motives in Fantasy, Action, and Society: A Method of Assessment and Study.* Princeton, N.J.: Van Nostrand.

ACHIEVEMENT TESTING

The purpose of achievement testing is to measure some aspect of the intellectual competence of human beings: what a person has learned to know or to do. Teachers use achievement tests to measure the attainments of their students. Employers use achievement tests to measure the competence of prospective employees. Professional associations use achievement tests to exclude unqualified applicants from the practice of the profession. In any circumstances where it is necessary or useful to distinguish persons of higher from those of lower competence or attainments, achievement testing is likely to occur.

The varieties of intellectual competence that may be developed by formal education, self-study, or other types of experience are numerous and diverse. There is a corresponding number and diversity of types of tests used to measure achievement. In this article attention will be directed mainly toward the measurement of cognitive achievements by means of paper and pencil tests. The justifications for this limitation are (1) that cognitive achievements are of central importance to effective human behavior, (2) that the use of paper and pencil tests to measure these achievements is a comparatively well-developed and effective technique, and (3) that other aspects of intellectual competence will be discussed in other articles, such as those on motivation, learning, attitudes, leadership, aesthetics, and personality.

Measurability of achievement. Despite the complexity, intangibility, and delayed fruition of many educational achievements and despite the relative imprecision of many of the techniques of educational measurement, there are logical grounds for believing that all important educational achievements can be measured. To be important, an educational achievement must lead to a difference in behavior. The person who has achieved more must in some circumstances behave differently from the person who has achieved less. If such a difference cannot be observed and verified no grounds exist for believing that the achievement is important.

Measurement, in its most fundamental form, requires nothing more than the verifiable observation of such a difference. If person A exhibits to any qualified observer more of a particular trait than person B, then that trait is measurable. By definition, then, any important achievement is potentially measurable.

Many important educational achievements can be measured quite satisfactorily by means of paper and pencil tests. But in some cases the achievement is so complex, variable, and conditional that the measurements obtained are only rough approximations. In other cases the difficulty lies in the attempt to measure something that has been alleged to exist but that has never been defined specifically. Thus, to say that all important achievements are potentially measurable is not to say that all those achievements have been clearly identified or that satisfactory techniques for measuring all of them have been developed.

Achievement, aptitude, and intelligence tests. Achievement tests are often distinguished from aptitude tests that purport to predict what a person is able to learn or from intelligence tests intended to measure his capacity for learning. But the distinction between aptitude and achievement is more apparent than real, more a difference in the use made of the measurements, than in what is being measured. In a very real sense, tests of aptitude and intelligence are also tests of achievement.

The tasks used to measure a child's mental age may differ from those used to measure his knowledge of the facts of addition. The tasks used to assess a youth's aptitude for the study of a foreign language may differ from those used to assess his knowledge of English literature. But all of these tasks test achievement; they measure what a person has learned to know or to do. All learning except the very earliest builds on prior learning. Thus, what is regarded as achievement in retrospect is regarded as aptitude when looking to the future.

There may well be differences in genetically determined biological equipment for learning among normal human beings. But no method has yet been discovered for measuring these differences directly. Only if one is willing to assume that several persons have had identical opportunities, incentives, and other favorable circumstances for learning (and that is quite an assumption) is it reasonable to use present differences in achievements as a basis for dependable estimates of corresponding differences in native ability to learn.

Types of tests. Although some achievement testing is done orally, with examinee and examiner face to face, most of it makes use of written tests. Of these written tests there are two main types: essay and objective. If the test consists of a relatively small number of questions or directions in response to which the examinee writes a sentence, a paragraph, or a longer essay of his own composition, the test is usually referred to as an essay test. Alternatively, if the test consists of a relatively large number of questions or incomplete statements in response to which the examinee chooses one of several suggested answers, the test is ordinarily referred to as an objective test.

Objective tests can be scored by clerks or scoring machines. Essay tests must be scored by judges who have special qualifications and who sometimes are specially trained for the particular scoring process. The scores obtained from objective tests tend to be more reliable than those obtained from essay tests. That is, independent scorings of the same answers, or of the same person's answers to equivalent sets of questions, tend to agree more closely in the case of objective tests than in the case of essay tests.

There are four major steps in achievement testing: (1) the preparation or selection of the test, (2) the administration of the test to the examinees, (3) the scoring of the answers given, and (4) the interpretation of the resulting scores.

Test development. In the United States, and to a lesser extent in other countries, achievement tests have been developed and are offered for sale by commercial test publishers. Buros (1961) has provided a list of tests in print and has indicated where they may be obtained. Recent catalogs of tests are available from most of the publishers listed in that volume.

Most achievement tests, however, are prepared for limited, specific use by teachers, professors, test committees, or test specialists. These test constructors usually start with some fairly well-defined notions of the reasons for testing. Their purposes, and their acquaintance with the theory and principles of achievement testing, lead them to select certain abilities and areas of knowledge to test, certain types of test items, and certain procedures for test administration and scoring.

Mental abilities.   Too little is known about the mind and how it works to permit clear identification of distinct and relatively independent mental abilities or mental processes. Thus, while it is easy to say that a good achievement test should sample in due proportions all the mental abilities related to that achievement, it is much more difficult to speak clearly about the nature and unique characteristics of these supposedly distinct mental abilities. Terms like *recognition, recall, problem solving, critical thinking,* and *evaluative judgment* have been used in referring to such abilities or mental processes. But although these terms obviously refer to somewhat different kinds of tasks, the evidence that they involve independent and distinct mental processes is practically nonexistent. Hence, the test constructor may be well advised to avoid claims or speculations about the mental abilities he is testing.

Among specialists in test construction there is general preference for test questions that require more than the recall of factual details: for test questions that require thought. This has led many test constructors to avoid simple true–false or completion types of test items in favor of more complex test situations that call for problem solving, critical interpretation, or evaluative judgment. Sometimes the test constructor supplies as background information much of the factual information the examinee is likely to need to answer the questions successfully. Then, presumably, a student's score depends more on his ability to use knowledge than on his ability to recall it.

It is easier to specify areas of knowledge than mental abilities, but test constructors often face problems in determining just which areas a particular achievement test ought to sample, and with what relative weights. Sometimes textbooks, courses of study, and other sources are studied for guidance as to which areas of content deserve inclusion or emphasis. But in the last analysis, problems of this sort must be resolved on the basis of the judgments of the test constructor or test construc-

tion committee. Since different test constructors may not agree on these judgments, two achievement tests bearing the same titles may cover somewhat different areas of content.

Types of questions.   A wide variety of different types of questions may be used in essay tests of achievement. Here are some examples.

List the similarities and differences of the eye and the camera.

What is the relation between the boiling point of water and the atmospheric pressure on the surface of the water?

Explain the electrolysis of water.

What is meant by the term "cultural lag"?

What internal weaknesses and external forces led to the fall of the Roman Empire?

Objective test items also differ widely. Two of the more common types are illustrated here.

True–False. Weather systems affecting the State of Illinois usually approach from the southeast rather than from the northwest. (False)

Multiple-choice. Why is chlorine sometimes added to water in city water supply systems?
  1. To clarify the water (dissolve sediment).
* 2. To kill bacteria.
  3. To protect the pipes from corrosion.
  4. To remove objectionable odors.

Other types of objective test items are illustrated and discussed in various books on achievement test construction. Some of these are listed at the end of this article.

The choice between essay or objective tests, or among different types of objective test items, is often made on the assumption that each of these types is particularly well adapted, or poorly adapted, to the measurement of a particular ability or mental process. But available evidence does more to question this assumption than to support it. It is true that certain questions or tasks used in achievement testing fall more naturally into one type of test or test item than into another. But on the whole, types of test items appear to be general rather than specific in function. Whatever educational achievement that can be measured well using one type of test item can probably also be measured quite well using some other types. How well the achievement is measured seems to depend less on the type of item chosen than on the skill with which it is used.

Test administration.   Most tests of educational achievement are given to groups rather than individuals. In either case, effective administration requires (1) that examinees be motivated to do as well as they can, (2) that they understand clearly what the test requires them to do, (3) that the environment in which they work allows and encourages their best efforts, and (4) that each examinee has an equal chance to demonstrate his achievement.

Examinees are usually motivated to do their best on an achievement test because of the present rewards and future opportunities that depend on the quality of their performance. It is possible for an examinee to be so highly motivated that his anxiety actually interferes with his best performance on a test. Some examinees report that they never do themselves justice on a written examination because of the emotional upset they suffer or because of some deficiency in test-taking skills. But the evidence suggests that these problems afflict persons of low achievement far more often than those of high achievement.

Cheating.   Cheating is a perennial problem in achievement testing. The problem could be alleviated, as some have suggested, by reducing emphasis on, and rewards for, achievement; but there are obvious disadvantages in this solution. A better solution, in general, is to provide sufficient supervision during the test administration to discourage attempts to cheat and to deal with those who do cheat firmly enough to make cheating quite unattractive. In some cases cheating on school and college achievement tests has been discouraged effectively by cultivation of honor systems, in which the students themselves take responsibility for honest examination behavior and for reporting any instances of cheating.

Time limits.   The current trend in achievement testing is to avoid "speed tests." Examinees differ widely in their rates of work, so that the slowest may require twice as long as the fastest to complete a test to his satisfaction. There is usually a positive correlation between rate of work and correctness of response, that is, examinees who know the most answers tend to give them the most quickly. But the correlation is not high enough to allow rate-of-work scores to add appreciable valid information to correct-answer scores as measures of achievement. Even among the most capable examinees there may be wide differences in rate of work. Hence, the most accurate predictions of subsequent achievement can usually be made when tests have time limits generous enough to allow most examinees to finish.

Scoring.   Each type of test presents unique problems of scoring.

Essay test scoring.   Essay test scoring calls for higher degrees of competence, and ordinarily takes considerably more time, than the scoring of objective tests. In addition to this, essay test scoring presents two special problems. The first is that of providing a basis for judgment that is sufficiently definite, and of sufficiently general validity, to give the scores assigned by a particular reader some objective meaning. To be useful, his scores should not represent purely subjective opinions and personal biases that equally competent readers might or might not share. The second problem is that of discounting irrelevant factors, such as quality of handwriting, verbal fluency, or gamesmanship, in appealing to the scorer's interests and biases. The reader's scores should reflect unbiased estimates of the essential achievements of the examinee.

One means of improving objectivity and relevancy in scoring essay tests is to prepare an ideal answer to each essay question and to base the scoring on relations between examinee answers and the ideal answer. Another is to defer assignment of scores until the examinee answers have been sorted and resorted into three to nine sets at different levels of quality. Scoring the test question by question through the entire set of papers, rather than paper by paper (marking all questions on one paper before considering the next) improves the accuracy of scoring. If several scorers will be marking the same questions in a set of papers, it is usually helpful to plan a training and practice session in which the scorers mark the same papers, compare their marks and strive to reach a common basis for marking.

Objective test scoring.   Answers to true–false, multiple-choice, and other objective-item types can be marked directly on the test copy. But scoring is facilitated if the answers are indicated by position marking a separate answer sheet. For example, the examinee may be directed to indicate his choice of the first, second, third, fourth, or fifth alternative to a multiple-choice test item by blackening the first, second, third, fourth, or fifth position following the item number on his answer sheet.

Answers so marked can be scored by clerks with the aid of a stencil key on which the correct answer positions have been punched. To get the number of correct answers, the clerk simply counts the number of marks appearing through the holes on the stencil key. Or the answers can be scored, usually much more quickly and accurately, by electrical scoring machines. Some of these machines, which "count" correct answers by cumulating the current flowing through correctly placed pencil marks, require the examinee to use special graphite pencils; others, which use photoelectric cells to scan the answer sheet, require only marks black enough to contrast sharply with the lightly printed guide lines. High-speed photoelectric test scoring machines usually incorporate, or are connected to, electronic data processing and print-out equipment.

Correction for guessing. One question that often arises is whether or not objective test scores should be corrected for guessing. Differences of opinion on this question are much greater and more easily observable than differences in the accuracy of the scores produced by the two methods of scoring. If well-motivated examinees take a test that is appropriate to their abilities, little *blind* guessing is likely to occur. There may be many *considered* guesses, if every answer given with less than complete certainty is called a guess. But the examinee's success in guessing right after thoughtful consideration is usually a good measure of his achievement.

Since the meaning of most achievement test scores is relative, not absolute—the scores serve only to indicate how the achievement of a particular examinee compares with that of other examinees—the argument that scores uncorrected for guessing will be too high carries little weight. Indeed, one method of correcting for guessing results in scores higher than the uncorrected scores.

The logical objective of most guessing correction procedures is to eliminate the expected advantage of the examinee who guesses blindly in preference to omitting an item. This can be done by subtracting a fraction of the number of wrong answers from the number of right answers, using the formula $S = R - W/(k - 1)$ where S is the score corrected for guessing, R is the number of right answers, W is the number of wrong answers, and k is the number of choices available to the examinee in each item. An alternative formula is $S = R + O/k$ where O is the number of items omitted, and the other symbols have the same meaning as before. Both formulas rank any set of examinee answer sheets in exactly the same relative positions, although the second formula yields a higher score for the same answers than does the first.

Logical arguments for and against correction for guessing on objective tests are complex and elaborate. But both these arguments and the experimental data point to one general conclusion. In most circumstances a correction for guessing is not likely to yield scores that are appreciably more or less accurate than the uncorrected scores.

Score interpretation. It is possible to prepare an achievement test on which the scores have absolute meaning. For example, scores on a test of ability to add pairs of single-digit numbers can be used to estimate how many of the 100 addition

facts an examinee knows. Or, if a test of word meanings is built by systematically sampling the words in a particular dictionary and systematically mixing words and definitions to produce test items, the test can be used to estimate what portion of the words in that dictionary an examinee understands, in one sense of that term.

But most achievement tests are not constructed so systematically nor based on such clearly defined universes of knowledge. Scores on most achievement tests, therefore, are interpreted in relative terms. Whether an examinee's score on such a test is regarded as good or poor depends on whether most of his presumed peers scored lower or higher on the same test.

Several statistical techniques may be used to aid in score interpretation on a relative basis. One of these is the *frequency distribution* of a set of test scores. Each score in the set is tallied on a scale extending from the highest to the lowest scores. One can then tell by visual inspection whether a particular score is high, medium, or low relative to other scores in this distribution.

Percentile ranks. The information contained in a frequency distribution of scores can be quantified by calculating a corresponding *percentile rank* for each possible score in the total range of scores. The percentile rank of a particular score indicates what percentage of the scores in the given set (or in a hypothetical population of which the given set is a sample) are lower than the particular score. Percentile ranks can range from 0 to 100. They are easy to interpret, but they do not preserve all of the information on relative achievements available in the original set of scores, nor do they reflect these relative achievements with perfect fidelity.

Standard score systems. Measures of the average score value and of score dispersion are often used as aids to score interpretation. The measure of average value most commonly used in the *arithmetic mean,* defined as the sum of all scores divided by the number of scores. The measure of dispersion most commonly used is the *standard deviation,* the square root of the arithmetic mean of the squared deviations of the scores from their own mean. In the set of scores 1, 2, 3, 4, and 5, the mean score is 3 and the standard deviation is 1.414.

The mean and standard deviation can be used to transform the scores in any set into *standard scores* having a predetermined mean and standard deviation. One type of standard score is the *z* score. If the mean of a set of scores is subtracted from a particular score, and if the resulting difference is divided by the standard deviation, a *z* score is obtained. When *z* scores are obtained for an entire set of scores, the new z distribution has a mean of 0, a standard deviation of 1, and most of the scores fall within the range −3 to +3. The z scores corresponding to the scores 1, 2, 3, 4, and 5 are −1.4, −0.7, 0, +0.7, and +1.4.

To avoid negative scores and decimals, z scores may be multiplied by 10 and added to 50. This set of operations provides another type of standard score whose mean is 50 and whose standard deviation is 10. Single-digit standard scores, ranging from 1 to 9, with a mean of 5 and a standard deviation of 2 are called *stanines* (*standard nines*). Various other types of standard scores are in use. In stanines and some other standard score systems, the distribution of raw scores is not only converted to a standard scale but is also transformed into a normal distribution.

The special value of standard scores of the types just discussed is that each of them has a clearly defined relative meaning. Standard scores of a particular type for different tests are comparable when based on scores from the same group of examinees. That is, a particular standard score value indicates the same degree of relative excellence or deficiency in the group of examinees, regardless of the test to which it applies.

Reliability. Proper interpretation of an achievement test score requires, in addition to knowledge of its absolute and relative meanings, some perception of its precision and of its relations to other significant measurements. Achievement test specialists use *coefficients of reliability* as measures of precision.

A reliability coefficient is a coefficient of correlation between two sets of test scores. Often this is obtained when a particular group of examinees provides scores on two equivalent tests. If equivalent tests are not available, or cannot be administered conveniently, reliability may be estimated by readministering the same test after an interval of time. Alternatively, and preferably in most circumstances, a test may be split into two or more parts that are more or less equivalent. The correlations obtained between scores on the parts may be used as a basis for calculating the reliability coefficient. Reliability coefficients obtained from equivalent forms of a test are sometimes referred to as *coefficients of equivalence*. Those obtained by splitting a single test are known as coefficients of *internal consistency*. Equivalence or internal consistency in tests is often referred to as "homogeneity." Correlations obtained by readministering the same test are called *coefficients of stability*.

In most situations a good achievement test will have a reliability coefficient of .90 or higher. The reliability coefficient of a test depends on a number of factors. Reliability tends to be high if (1) the range of achievements in the group tested is broad, (2) the area of achievement covered by the test is narrow, (3) the discriminating power of the individual items is high, and (4) the number of items included in the test is large. Only the last two of these factors are ordinarily subject to control by the test constructor.

Discriminating power. The discriminating power of a test item can be measured by the difference between scores on that item for examinees of high and low achievement. To obtain the clearest contrast between these two levels of achievement, examinees whose test scores place them among the top 27 per cent are placed in the high group and those whose scores fall in the bottom 27 per cent are placed in the low group. Extreme groups of upper and lower quarters, or upper and lower thirds, are almost equally satisfactory. The difference between the two groups' total scores on the item, divided by the maximum possible value of that difference, yields an *index of discrimination*.

Good achievement test items have indexes of discrimination of .40 or higher. Items having indexes of .20 or lower are of questionable value. If the discrimination index is near zero, or even negative, as it sometimes may be, the test can be improved by omitting the item, even though this means shortening the test. Sometimes it is possible to revise items that are low in discrimination to remove errors or ambiguities or to make the level of difficulty more appropriate. Items that nearly everyone answers correctly, or nearly everyone misses, are certain to be low in discrimination. Discrimination indexes based on small groups of examinees are likely to be quite unreliable, but even unreliable data provide some basis for test improvement.

Standard error of measurement. Another measure of precision or accuracy in test scores is the standard error of measurement. The standard error of measurement depends on the standard deviation of the test scores and on their reliability. It may be calculated from the formula

$$\sigma_{\text{meas}} = \sigma_t \sqrt{1 - r_{tt}},$$

in which σ_{meas} indicates the standard error of measurement, σ_t indicates the standard deviation of the test scores, and r_{tt} represents the reliability coefficient of the test scores. About two-thirds of the scores in a given set differ from the ideal true score values by less than one standard error of measurement. The other one-third, of course, differ from the corresponding true scores by more than one standard error of measurement. A true score is defined as the mean of the scores that would be obtained in an infinite number of samples of tests equivalent to the given test.

The test having the smallest standard error of measurement is not necessarily the best test, since good tests yield large score standard deviations and this, in turn, tends to be associated with large standard errors of measurement. Hence, it is better to use the standard error of measurement as an indication of the degree of accuracy of a particular test score, rather than as a measure of the ability of the test to differentiate among various levels of achievement.

Validity. The reliability coefficient of a test shows how precisely it measures whatever it does measure. In contrast, the *validity coefficient* is sometimes said to show how precisely it measures what it ought to measure, or what it purports to measure. But since good criterion scores, i.e., actual measures of that which the test ought to measure, are seldom available to the constructor of an achievement test, the practical value of this concept of *predictive validity* is limited.

Knowledge of what other measures the test scores are related to, that is, what they correlate with, adds to the test constructor's knowledge of what the test is measuring. In this sense these correlations contribute to understanding of the *concurrent validity* of the test. But for most achievement tests, validity is primarily a matter of operational definition, or *content* or *face validity*, and only secondarily, if at all, a matter of empirical demonstration. Validity must be built into most achievement tests. The content to be covered by an achievement test and the tasks to be used to indicate achievement are best determined by a consensus of experts. Experience and experiments shed light on some of the issues that these experts may debate, but there is no good substitute for their expertness, their values, and their experience as bases for valid achievement test construction.

Importance and limitations. Achievement tests play important roles in education, in government, in business and industry, and in the professions. If they were constructed more carefully and more expertly, and used more consistently and more wisely, they could do even more to improve the effectiveness of these enterprises.

But achievement tests also have limitations beyond those attributable to hasty, inexpert construction or improper use. In the first place, they are limited to measuring a person's command of the knowledge that can be expressed in verbal or sym-

bolic terms. This is a very large area of knowledge, and command of it constitutes a very important human achievement; but it does not include all knowledge, and it does not represent the whole of human achievement. There is, for example, the unverbalized knowledge obtained by direct perceptions of objects, events, feelings, relationships, etc. There are also physical skills and behavioral skills, such as leadership and friendship, that are not highly dependent on command of verbal knowledge. A paper and pencil test of achievement can measure what a person knows about these achievements but not necessarily how effectively he uses them in practice.

In the second place, while command of knowledge may be a necessary condition for success in modern human activities, it is by no means a sufficient condition. Energy, persistence, and plain good fortune, among other things, combine to determine how successfully he uses the knowledge he possesses. A person with high achievement scores is a better bet to succeed than one with low achievement scores, but high scores cannot guarantee success.

ROBERT L. EBEL

[*Directly related are the entries* APTITUDE TESTING; INTELLIGENCE AND INTELLIGENCE TESTING. *Other relevant material may be found in* PSYCHOMETRICS; VOCATIONAL INTEREST TESTING.]

BIBLIOGRAPHY

ADKINS, DOROTHY C. 1948 *Construction and Analysis of Achievement Tests: The Development of Written and Performance Tests of Achievement for Predicting Job Performance of Public Personnel.* Washington: Government Printing Office.

AMERICAN EDUCATIONAL RESEARCH ASSOCIATION, COMMITTEE ON TEST STANDARDS 1955 *Technical Recommendations for Achievement Tests.* New York: The Association.

AMERICAN PSYCHOLOGICAL ASSOCIATION 1954 *Technical Recommendations for Psychological Tests and Diagnostic Techniques.* Washington: The Association.

BUROS, OSCAR K. (editor) 1961 *Tests in Print: A Comprehensive Bibliography of Tests for Use in Education, Psychology, and Industry.* Highland Park, N.J.: Gryphon.

EBEL, ROBERT L. 1965 *Measuring Educational Achievement.* Englewood Cliffs, N.J.: Prentice-Hall.

FURST, EDWARD J. 1958 *Constructing Evaluation Instruments.* New York: Longmans.

GERBERICH, JOSEPH R. 1956 *Specimen Objective Test Items: A Guide to Achievement Test Construction.* New York: Longmans.

LINDQUIST, EVERET F. (editor) 1951 *Educational Measurement.* Washington: American Council on Education.

TRAVERS, ROBERT M. W. 1950 *How to Make Achievement Tests.* New York: Odyssey.

WOOD, DOROTHY A. 1960 *Test Construction: Development and Interpretation of Achievement Tests.* Columbus, Ohio: Merrill.

ACTON, J. E. E. D.

Born in Naples in 1834, John Emerich Edward Dalberg-Acton, historian, was a cosmopolitan by inheritance, education, and temperament. From early childhood he spoke several languages fluently and traveled extensively. His paternal ancestors had been English baronets for centuries, and the Dalbergs on the maternal side belonged to the aristocracy of the Holy Roman Empire. Acton also had close ties to the Whig aristocracy of nineteenth-century England, through his mother's second marriage to Lord Leveson, later the earl of Granville, foreign minister under Russell and Gladstone.

The Dalbergs had always been Roman Catholic, and the Actons had been converted to Catholicism in the eighteenth century. John Acton's education was supervised by some of the most prominent Catholics of the time: Monsignor Félix Dupanloup in Paris, Bishop Nicholas Wiseman at Oscott College in England, and Professor Johann Döllinger at the University of Munich. Dupanloup and Döllinger were liberal Catholics, in contrast to Wiseman, who was known as an ultramontanist—a supporter of the papal authority in church affairs and of the authority of the church in secular affairs. It was Döllinger who exerted the strongest influence on Acton, inspiring him with a deep passion not only for religious liberalism but also for historical scholarship.

Conflict with the church. When Acton became editor of the *Rambler*, an English liberal Catholic periodical, in 1859, he sought to put into effect Döllinger's principles. Almost every issue found occasion to point out these morals: that faith and knowledge, religion and science, have to be pursued independently and fearlessly; that the church and the state have to respect each other's province and interest. The journal (later known as the *Home and Foreign Review*) was under constant attack from the ultramontane English hierarchy, and in 1864 Acton suspended publication, announcing that he wished neither to change his views nor to flout the church.

This conflict with the Roman Catholic church in England was the prelude to a more serious conflict with Rome. Döllinger and Acton were publicly opposed to the proclamation of papal infallibility, which was the avowed purpose of the ecumenical council convoked by Pope Pius IX in 1869. Although a layman, Acton was the virtual leader of the "minority," as the anti-infallibilists in the Vatican Council were called. Even after the passage of the decrees of infallibility in 1870, he continued to denounce them, intimating that they were

not legitimate and therefore not binding on members of the church. When challenged by Archbishop Manning, however, Acton avoided a direct denial of orthodoxy and was thus spared excommunication.

Conception of liberty. After the crisis in his relations with the church—perhaps provoked by this crisis—Acton turned his attention to his projected chef-d'œuvre, the "History of Liberty." Two essays, "History of Freedom in Antiquity" and "History of Freedom in Christianity," were delivered as lectures in 1877. Other essays, book reviews, hundreds of boxes of notes, and a vast library of annotated volumes and rare manuscripts testify to the devotion and scholarship that he brought to the subject. Yet, as early as 1880 he began to suspect that the "History of Liberty" would become another "Madonna of the Future"—the story, by Henry James, of an artist who dedicated his life to a single, divinely inspired picture, which after his death was revealed to be a blank canvas.

If the "History of Liberty" was indeed the "greatest book that never was written," as has been suggested, the reasons for its nonbeing lie deep in Acton's sense of both history and liberty. For Acton, all history, at least all significant history, was part of the history of liberty. And not only history in its conventional sense—diplomatic, political, military, institutional, and social history—but intellectual, cultural, religious, and even scientific history. There was little that was irrelevant. There was also little that was not vastly more complicated than was supposed, so that an infinite expenditure of scholarship was required to elicit the truth about every detail. Acton's remarks about Döllinger might be taken to apply to himself: "He knew too much to write" ([1858–1895] 1907, p. 434); "he would not write with imperfect materials, and to him the materials were always imperfect" ([1858–1895] 1907, p. 432). The editor of the *English Historical Review* described Acton as probably the most erudite Englishman of his generation; but no amount of erudition, no single lifetime, was sufficient for the task he had set himself.

Acton's conception of liberty was equally frustrating, for it embraced two contradictory ideas. The first, which particularly dominated his early years, was liberty in the Burkean sense—as a product of history and tradition, of compromise and expediency, of checks, balances, and countervailing forces. It was this view of liberty that made Macaulay appear to be a "violent liberal," respecting no principle but the will of the people and willing to subordinate the whole of the past to the interests of the present. And it was the same view that made the Northern abolitionists, during the American Civil War, seem to be acting "without consideration of policy or expediency," and thus reflecting an "abstract, ideal absolutism" ([1861–1910] 1948, p. 246).

Later, the very terms in which he had once denounced this "violent" species of liberalism became the terms in which he was to defend it. Abstract, absolute liberty pursued without consideration of policy, expediency, or history became his ideal. His experiences during and after the Vatican Council were largely responsible for this shift. He had discovered that even those who had joined him in opposing the dogma of infallibility—even Döllinger, who permitted himself to be excommunicated rather than submit to it—did not share his conviction of its absolute sinfulness. They did not take their stand on the clear and absolute precepts of morality; instead, he charged, they allowed the claims of extenuating circumstances, of differing customs and temperaments, of sins committed in good causes, and of errors that were not sins. And this moral laxity applied to secular as well as religious affairs. "Have you not discovered," he wrote to Mary Gladstone, "what a narrow doctrinaire I am, under a thin disguise of levity? . . . Politics come nearer religion with me, a party is more like a church, error more like heresy, prejudice more like sin, than I find it to be with better men" (1904*a*, p. 314). Burke, he now complained (but it was probably Döllinger he really had in mind), thought that politics was an empirical subject teaching what is likely to do good or harm, not what is right and wrong, innocent or sinful. Acton himself adhered to the principle of the Stoics: "That which we must obey, that to which we are bound to reduce all civil authorities, and to sacrifice every earthly interest, is that immutable law which is perfect and eternal as God Himself" ([1861–1910] 1948, p. 52).

Politics.   That Acton did not think of this principle as utopian or inappropriate to politics is apparent from his strong political ambitions. Oddly enough, it was while he was still an ardent Burkean that he had had the opportunity to realize such ambitions and had failed to take advantage of it. In 1859 his stepfather, Lord Granville, had obtained a seat for him in the House of Commons, and although Acton sat in Parliament for six years and twice afterward tried unsuccessfully to be re-elected, he had little respect for the Liberal party and apparently little interest in political affairs. He became an ardent Liberal and supporter of Gladstone only after his elevation to the peerage in 1869. But even then, instead of trying to distin-

guish himself in the House of Lords, Acton sought a political career in diplomacy, with the same lack of success. Several times he entertained hope for important ambassadorial appointments, but each time he was passed over. In 1892, when Gladstone became prime minister for the fourth time, Acton was indiscreet enough to confide his expectation of a cabinet position. Instead, he was offered the trivial and, as it seemed to his friends, demeaning post of lord-in-waiting to the queen. Perhaps because he did not want to embarrass Gladstone, Acton surprisingly accepted, making the best of the situation by exploring the royal libraries and cultivating what he called the "backstairs" history of the court. At the same time, he ably, if unenthusiastically, represented the Irish Office in the House of Lords.

Conception of history.   A more fitting position for Acton was found by Gladstone's successor, Lord Rosebery, who in 1895 appointed him regius professor of modern history at Cambridge. Acton's inaugural lecture, the "Study of History," expressed all the themes and passions that had long engaged him. The essence of history, he said, was the history of ideas, since it was ideas that ultimately moved men and determined events. And the essence of modern history was to be found in those ideas that have "subverted the notions of the world," revolutionizing government, law, and authority, production, wealth, and power. Indeed, the very idea that men should be ruled by ideas was both uniquely modern and intrinsically revolutionary. The most important idea ushering in modern history and inaugurating the "revolution in permanence" was the doctrine of rights. "Laden with storm and havoc," the idea of inalienable, God-given rights was the "indestructible soul of Revolution" ([1861–1910] 1948, p. 15).

Acton was aware of the irony of his role—the role of the historian as revolutionist. "What is to become of us, docile and attentive students of the absorbing past? The triumph of the revolutionist annuls the historian" ([1861–1910] 1948, p. 15). Or would annul the historian, if it were not for the existence of an absolute moral code that redeemed him. The truly objective historian, Acton held, the truly attentive student of the past, was not dispassionate and disinterested on the model of Ranke, who pretended to pass no judgments while, in fact, justifying and legitimizing everything that succeeded. In an earlier controversy with Bishop Creighton, Acton had argued that objectivity required the historian to judge the leading actors in history more, not less, severely than ordinary men: "Historic responsibility has to make up for the want of legal responsibility. Power tends to corrupt and absolute power corrupts absolutely. Great men are almost always bad men . . ." ([1861–1910] 1948, p. 364). In the inaugural lecture, he returned to the theme: "The weight of opinion is against me when I exhort you never to debase the moral currency or to lower the standard of rectitude, but to try others by the final maxim that governs your own lives, and to suffer no man and no cause to escape the undying penalty which history has the power to inflict on wrong. . . . Opinions alter, manners change, creeds rise and fall, but the moral law is written on the tablets of eternity" ([1861–1910] 1948, pp. 25, 28).

Yet the ambiguities of Acton's position—of the revolution that annuls history, of the historian as a "hanging judge," and of liberty as an absolute ideal—were not entirely resolved by the invocation of moral law. In his later lectures at Cambridge (a series on modern history and another on the French Revolution), these ambiguities came to a focus in his discussion of the American and French revolutions. The American Revolution, he said, introduced a new phase of political history because it was fought not against tyranny but purely out of principle, and not in the name of historic rights and liberties but in the name of abstract rights and liberties. In a letter to a friend, he put the issue even more boldly. He wrote that the Americans had posed the ultimate problem of politics: Should a man or a nation be prepared to risk everything for a purely speculative idea sanctioned by no law or religion? "The affirmative response," he declared, "is the Revolution, or as we say, Liberalism" (1917, p. 278).

Toward the French Revolution, however, his attitude was more ambivalent. He agreed that the French had been inspired by the same devotion to principle as the Americans, that like the Americans they were rebelling not against this or that abuse but against the whole of the "unburied past." Yet, whereas the Americans consolidated their revolution with a pacific, conservative settlement, the French permitted their revolution to degenerate into a new tyranny, so that France was given over to "bare cupidity and vengeance, to brutal instinct and hideous passion" (1910, p. 226). The new tyranny, he maintained, was brought about by the conjunction of violence and democracy, each perilous to liberty and together fatal. Liberty could only have been secured by following the example of the American constitution, with its checks and balances, or the British system, with its respect for tradition, compromise, and expediency; both of these examples the French repudiated. At the same

time, however, Acton conceded that the very logic of the French Revolution—the idea of rebelling against the whole of the unburied past—required the French to reject the American and British patterns and to embrace both violence and democracy.

This ambivalence toward revolution implied an ambivalence toward ideals and ideas. Acton's private notes express this more candidly than his lectures:

Government by idea tends to take in everything, to make the whole of society obedient to the idea. Spaces not so governed are unconquered, beyond the border, unconverted, unconvinced, a future danger.

Government that is natural, habitual, works more easily. It remains in the hands of average men, who do not live by ideas. Therefore there is less strain by making government adapt itself to custom. An ideal government, much better, perhaps, would have to be maintained by effort, and imposed by force. (Acton as quoted in Himmelfarb 1952, p. 219)

In place of the "History of Liberty," which was vitiated as much by internal contradiction as by difficulties of research, Acton devoted his last years to the editing of the *Cambridge Modern History*. By a "judicious division of labour," he sought to accomplish part of the task that he could not accomplish alone. This collective effort, utilizing the combined resources of the most distinguished historians of the world, would, he hoped, produce a universal history in which ideas rather than nations were the governing motifs. In this project, as in the other, he was finally thwarted. After issuing an ambitious prospectus and writing countless letters to contributors, the *History* was only beginning to take shape when he suffered the paralytic stroke that caused his retirement and finally his death.

Acton died in 1902, leaving behind scores of essays, reviews, lectures, and notes, but not a single sustained book. Yet his fragmentary work has earned him a higher reputation than that enjoyed by far more prolific historians, and his ambiguities and dilemmas are more instructive today than the certainties of others. Toynbee is not alone in praising him as one of the greatest minds among modern Western historians.

GERTRUDE HIMMELFARB

[*For the historical context of Acton's work, see* FREEDOM; POWER *and the biographies of* BURKE *and* MACAULAY.]

WORKS BY ACTON

(1855–1871) 1953 *Essays on Church and State*. Edited and with an introduction by Douglas Woodruff. New York: Viking.

(1858–1895) 1907 *The History of Freedom and Other Essays.* London: Macmillan.

(1858–1899) 1907 *Historical Essays and Studies.* London: Macmillan.

(1861–1910) 1948 *Essays on Freedom and Power.* Selected and with an introduction by Gertrude Himmelfarb. Boston: Beacon.

1904a *Letters of Lord Acton to Mary Gladstone.* London: Allen.

(1904b) 1913 *Letters of Lord Acton to Mary, Daughter of the Right Hon. W. E. Gladstone.* 2d ed. London: Macmillan.

1906a *Lectures on Modern History.* London: Macmillan. → A paperback edition entitled *Renaissance to Revolution; the Rise of the Free State: Lectures on Modern History* was published in 1961 by Schocken Books.

1906b *Lord Acton and His Circle.* Edited by Francis Gasquet. London: Burns & Oates.

1910 *Lectures on the French Revolution.* London: Macmillan.

1917 *Selections From the Correspondence of the First Lord Acton.* Edited with an introduction by John Neville Figgis and Reginald V. Laurence. London: Longmans. → Volume 1: *Correspondence With Cardinal Newman, Lady Blennerhassett, W. E. Gladstone and Others.* Only Volume 1 has been published.

WORKS ABOUT ACTON

HIMMELFARB, GERTRUDE 1952 *Lord Acton: A Study in Conscience and Politics.* Univ. of Chicago Press.

KOCHAN, LIONEL 1954 *Acton on History.* London: Deutsch.

MATHEW, DAVID 1946 *Acton: The Formative Years.* London: Eyre & Spottiswoode.

ADDICTION

See the entries DRINKING AND ALCOHOLISM; DRUGS; SMOKING.

ADJUDICATION

The articles under this heading deal with the role and processes of national and international judicial institutions. Further discussion of the relations between judicial and other political institutions is found under JUDICIAL PROCESS *and* JUDICIARY. *For more general themes see under* INTERNATIONAL LAW *and* LAW.

I
DOMESTIC ADJUDICATION

Adjudication is a method of settling controversies or disputes. Characteristically, it gives assurances that the parties involved will be able to participate by presenting proofs and reasoned argument. The function of adjudication is normally regarded as belonging to the law courts; although not all adjudication takes place in the courts, and not everything the courts do can be called adjudication.

Society has many methods available for the resolution of disputes. In a democratic system of government, many important issues are resolved by the people through voting. Individuals and groups often settle their disputes by negotiation and contractual agreement. Parents adjudicate disputes among their children. Legislative bodies occasionally exercise adjudicatory functions when they sit as courts of impeachment, and, in a larger sense, legislation is concerned with the resolution of controversies all the time. Many disputes are resolved through arbitration, as in the fields of labor relations, commerce, and, occasionally, in international relations. A vast amount of adjudication takes place in the regulatory administrative agencies. In the American system of government, such agencies handle far more adjudication, in sheer bulk, than do the courts. For example, the number of hearings in appeals cases held by the U.S. Veterans Administration Board of Veteran Appeals exceeds the total number of civil cases disposed of by all the federal district courts [*see* ADMINISTRATION, *article on* THE ADMINISTRATIVE PROCESS].

Functions of the courts

Although adjudication is characteristically a judicial function, courts are often involved in other types of activity. They perform managerial functions, for example, when administering bankruptcy laws, or probating wills, or supervising the enforcement of antitrust decrees. Such matters as the naturalization of aliens and the handling of divorces and other domestic relations questions involve mainly administrative responsibilities. In the United States, state judges often have the power of appointment to certain public offices or exercise licensing functions. State courts are obliged to assume whatever functions are assigned to them by the state constitutions. The federal courts, on the other hand, are authorized by article III of the United States constitution to hear "cases" or "controversies," and this directive has been construed strictly by the Supreme Court to exclude other than adjudicative functions.

The disputes that courts resolve through adjudication arise between private parties, between private parties and public officials, and between public officials or public bodies. Characteristically, the disputes are adjudicated according to some general principle, or rule of law, and with settled and distinctive procedures that involve the presentation of proofs and reasoned arguments by the parties. Participation by the parties in this fashion is insured by formal rules embedded in an institutional framework, and the objective is to attain a result that will meet the test of reason. The judge to whom reasoned argument is made must be impartial, that is to say, free of bias or corruption, if there is to be any confidence in his decision. The issues that are tried by the judges in civil cases are claims of right resting upon some general principle, or rule of law; and in criminal cases the issues involve accusations of fault that also rest upon general rules.

Normally, courts lack the power to take the initiative; they must wait for parties to bring controversies to them, and thus their role is essentially passive. Since the judge must be impartial, it is preferable to leave the initiation of litigation to the interested parties. In an ultimate sense, courts even lack the power to enforce their decrees, for when a powerful group intransigently refuses to obey a judicial decree, the courts must depend upon the executive branch of the government for the muscle of enforcement. In addition, the courts depend upon the legislature for financial support and for most organizational matters.

Adjudication by courts involves several different functions: the establishment of the facts in controversy, the definition and interpretation of relevant rules of law, and the fashioning, if necessary, of rules of law. The establishment of the facts is controlled by the complex rules of evidence, which often vary among different jurisdictions in respect to such matters as the style of pleading or the admission of various types of evidence, such as hearsay. In the Anglo-American system of "accusatorial" justice, the facts in criminal cases are brought out through the presentation of evidence and through cross-examination by opposing counsel. In civil law countries, where the methods of "inquisitorial" justice prevail, the determination of the essential facts is largely in the hands of the presiding judge.

The discovery of the relevant rule of law that will control the resolution of the dispute is not always a simple or automatic process. Many statutes are ambiguous and permit judges to exercise a wide latitude of judgment. They must look into such matters as legislative intent, available precedents, and the reasonable meaning of words. Rules of construction may vary a great deal. Thus, courts tend to construe social legislation broadly, whereas it is customary to construe penal statutes strictly, since human liberty is involved. Nor are judges indifferent, in construing statutes, to the practical consequences that will flow from one interpretation or another.

Judicial lawmaking

Anglo-American common law, built up over centuries of experience on the basis of *stare decisis*, or following precedents, was developed by the judges in the course of deciding numberless cases. When an American court exercises the power of judicial review and declares a statute to be contrary to the constitution, it is obviously legislating. Thus, the Supreme Court made a legislative judgment, that is to say, it fashioned a new rule of law, when in *Brown* v. *Board of Education of Topeka* (347 U.S. 483, 1954) it decided that the equal protection clause of the fourteenth amendment forbade racial discrimination by force of state law in the public schools. The courts of other countries, for example, West Germany, Italy, France, Australia, and Canada, have similar judicial review powers. Furthermore, courts must occasionally decide what is usually known as the unprovided case, that is, a case for which there seems to be no established, or known, rule of law. In such instances, the courts will not shrink from deciding the case and will find a way of deducing some rule from existing rules or from a consideration of the facts of life and their social ends and purposes. Similarly, courts will find a way to deal with hardship cases, although often at the cost of legal uncertainty.

Whether judges actually make law, or merely discover and apply the law, is the subject of an old and lively controversy in Anglo-American jurisprudence. According to one point of view, courts do not make law but merely find and declare what the law is. Coke taught that the common law of England was the common custom of the realm, and Lord Hale took the position that judicial decisions were not law but only "evidences" of the common law. Based on these views, Sir William Blackstone maintained in his *Commentaries on the Laws of England* (1765–1769) that judicial decisions are not the common law, but only "the principal and most authoritative evidence that can be given, of the existence of such a custom as shall form a part of the common law." He insisted that judges do not decide cases on the basis of private views; they are "not delegated to pronounce a new law, but to maintain and expound the old one" (*Com.*, I, 69 in the 1811 edition).

This declaratory theory concerning the nature of the judge's function has been rejected by the great weight of modern jurisprudential opinion. Jeremy Bentham argued that every judicial decision is lawmaking, even if the judge is merely following precedents, since even then his course of decision is one that he chooses to follow. John Austin believed that judges make law, and he ridiculed Blackstone for accepting "the childish fiction employed by our judges, that judiciary or common law is not made by them, but is a miraculous something made by nobody, existing, I suppose, from eternity, and merely declared from time to time by the judges" ([1861] 1873, II, §655). Sir Henry Maine also took this position. In *The Nature and Sources of the Law* ([1909] 1921, p. 283), John Chipman Gray argued that the "true view . . . is that the Law is what the judges declare"; and that statutes, precedents, the opinions of learned experts, custom, and morality are merely sources of law. This was the view of Oliver Wendell Holmes, who once said that "the prophecies of what the courts will do in fact, and nothing more pretentious, are what I mean . . . by the law" ([1897] 1952, p. 173). At a much later date, however, Justice Holmes declared: "I recognize without hesitation that judges do and must legislate, but they can do so only interstitially; they are confined from molar to molecular motions" (*Southern Pacific Co.* v. *Jensen*, 244 U.S. 205, 221, 1917). President Theodore Roosevelt flatly asserted, in a message to Congress on December 8, 1908 (43 Cong. Rec., part I, p. 21), that "the chief lawmakers in our country may be, and often are, the judges, because they are the final seat of authority. Every time they interpret contract, property, vested rights, due process of law, liberty, they necessarily enact into law parts of a system of social philosophy; and as such interpretation is fundamental, they give direction to all law-making." Justice Cardozo maintained in *The Nature of the Judicial Process* ([1921] 1960, pp. 26–28) that it is not true that judges only give effect to law, but that the judge makes law in an evolutionary, rather than a revolutionary, manner and has limited powers of innovation, considering "the bulk and pressure of the rules that hedge him on every side."

While the declaratory theory has been rejected philosophically, there is plenty of evidence that it still commands considerable support. English and American judges still assert that judges do not make law. When a new question is decided by a court, the judge will usually try to establish analogies with existing precedents, statutes, or constitutional provisions. He is apt to be very reluctant to admit to very much innovation. Similarly, when courts are authorized to exercise discretion, judges will often describe it as "judicial" discretion, meaning to suggest that they are not merely following a personal sense of right.

The assertion of the notion that judges do not make law may well have practical consequences. What, for example, is the effect of an overruled decision? If judges do not make law, but only discover and declare it, then it seems to follow that the newly announced rule of law was always the proper rule, thus giving a retrospective effect to the last decision. Similarly, a judicial decision declaring an act to be criminal, which was not so regarded in the light of decisions prevailing at the time it occurred, is not regarded as *ex post facto*, unlike a comparable statutory change, since judges only find or declare the law but do not make it. On the other hand, a judicial decision that affects the validity of a contract previously made is regarded as impairing the obligation of the contract, but this can be so only on the theory that judges do make law. It follows that the debate as to whether or not judges make law is not altogether academic in nature, and in many circumstances the theory prevails that gives the best result.

Sources of law

Where does the judge find the law for his case? What are his sources? Sometimes, of course, the answer is clear and obvious: the judge may find a plain and unequivocal rule to follow in a statute or in a constitution. But statutes and constitutions are often highly ambiguous, and in such cases the judge must fashion rules of law through a process of interpretation. Furthermore, there are vast areas of human activity that are untouched by statute or formal constitutional documents. Clearly, the process of decision by a judge involves the subtle interplay of many influences. He will consider the precedents, if such are available, or reason by analogy from previous decisions. He will take into account the customs of the community, considerations of social welfare, ideals of justice and morality, the usages of the trades, markets, and professions, and the course of historical experience. On some points, "a page of history," Justice Holmes declared, "is worth a volume of logic" (*New York Trust Co.* v. *Eisner*, 256 U.S. 345, 349, 1921). Back of the precedents and basic juridical conceptions, Justice Cardozo said, "are the habits of life, the institutions of society" ([1921] 1960, p. 19). Basically, Justice Holmes maintained, "the secret root from which the law draws all the juices of life" is a conviction as to what is expedient for the community; every important principle developed by litigation "is in fact and at bottom the result of more or less definitely understood views of public policy" ([1881] 1963, p. 35). Similarly, Justice Cardozo thought that the greatest single force behind the law is "the power of social justice." He asserted that "the final cause of law is the welfare of society" (p. 66). But Justice Cardozo also recognized that "deep below consciousness are other forces, the likes and the dislikes, the predilections and the prejudices, the complex of instincts and emotions and habits and convictions, which make the man, whether he be litigant or judge" (p. 167). Furthermore, he emphasized that everyone has an underlying philosophy of life, "which gives coherence and direction to thought and action. Judges cannot escape that current any more than other mortals" (p. 12).

In short, judges are influenced by many forces: the customs of the community, prevailing ethical principles, the dictates of logic, the push of history, and considerations of utility and expediency. They are also influenced by professional factors: the habits of mind of lawyers, the criticisms of a learned profession, and the nature of law, such as its concern for uniformity, impartiality, logical consistency, and stability.

The role of precedents

The place of precedents in the adjudicatory scheme of things involves a number of important considerations. Normally, judges feel obliged to follow precedents. Clearly, *stare decisis* gives to the law needed elements of certainty and predictability. It adds reliability to the administration of law and offers assurances of equality and uniformity of treatment to litigants. It also preserves the values inherent in the judicial experience of the past. Furthermore, as Sir Frederick Pollock once pointed out, where a line of decisions has been accepted as law for a long time, and has been acted on by many persons, reversal of the rule, even though it may have been originally founded on a mistake, "might well produce an amount of inconvenience greater than any advantage that could be expected from the restoration or establishment of a rule more correct in itself" (Pollock [1896] 1918, p. 327).

Sir William Holdsworth has explained that the modern theory of *stare decisis* began to develop at the end of the fifteenth century, when changes in the system of pleading shifted attention from oral debate in court to the formulation of decisions on the basis of written pleadings studied by the judge before the case came to court (1934, p. 180). The rule that judges are bound to follow precedents has always had a high place in English law and practice. Accordingly, precedents are strictly followed in Britain, and the House of Lords will not overrule previous decisions.

On the other hand, a more flexible attitude toward *stare decisis* prevails in the United States. "Whether it shall be followed or departed from," the Supreme Court once observed, "is a question entirely within the discretion of the court, which is again called upon to consider a question once decided." And it said to the lower court where the

decision was being reviewed: "The Circuit Court of Appeals was obviously not bound to follow its own prior decision" (*Hertz* v. *Woodman*, 218 U.S. 205, 212, 1910). Justice Holmes declared that "it is revolting to have no better reason for a rule of law than that so it was laid down in the time of Henry IV. It is still more revolting if the grounds upon which it was laid down have vanished long since, and the rule simply persists from blind imitation of the past" ([1897] 1952, p. 187).

Of course, a U.S. Supreme Court decision on a federal question is binding upon all federal and state courts, but American legal doctrine has been fully sensitive to social, political, and economic change; and the Supreme Court has never regarded itself as being rigidly bound by its own decisions, particularly in the field of constitutional law, where large policy questions are likely to be dominant considerations. Thus, in a considerable number of great constitutional law cases, the Supreme Court has consciously rejected former precedents. (See, for example, *The Legal Tender Cases*, 79 U.S. 457, 1870; *Brown* v. *Board of Education of Topeka*, 347 U.S. 483–496, 1954.)

Adherence to precedent is, however, the rule in the other American courts. To be sure, only the reasoning bearing directly upon judgment carries weight, and judges do not feel bound to follow mere dictum. But precedents not only command respect; they also have a tendency to extend themselves along lines of logical development. They develop continuities, permit prediction, and by helping to insure fair and equal treatment they tend to create restraints upon arbitrariness. Since a judge must follow relevant precedents, for which good reasons have been advanced, he is obliged to give new and persuasive reasons to justify a different outcome.

Since even in English law it is recognized that some exceptions to the rule of *stare decisis* exist, we may conclude that the authority of a decision is not attached to the words used but to the principle necessary for the decision; it is only the *ratio decidendi* that really matters.

Hearings

The essence of adjudication is a hearing at which parties present proofs and reasoned argument. The sort of facts that are the object of inquiry at a hearing are facts about specific parties. In contrast, legislative facts are general facts relating to broad questions of policy and law affecting the general population or very large segments of it.

Legal necessity. No hearing is necessary, as a matter of legal right, for the determination of legislative facts, whether by a legislature or by an administrative agency, since legislators, administrators, and their staffs may have their own adequate knowledge concerning the facts. On the other hand, since parties are in the best position to know the facts of their particular situations, the determination of adjudicative facts requires a hearing. The hearing may be conducted either by a court or by an administrative agency, depending upon whether the proceeding involves mainly private or public interests.

The place of the hearing in adjudication is reflected in the holding of a New York court: "The act of an administrative or ministerial officer does not become judicial simply because it is necessary to use discretion and judgment in its performance. It becomes judicial only when there is opportunity to be heard, evidence presented and a weighing of the evidence and a decision thereon" (*People* ex. rel. *Argus Co.* v. *Hugo,* 101 Misc. 481, 168 N.Y.S. 25, 27 Sup. Ct. Albany Co. 1917).

The difference between adjudicative and legislative facts is reflected in two famous decisions of the Supreme Court of the United States dealing with taxation. In *Londoner* v. *City and County of Denver* (210 U.S. 373, 386, 1908), the Court ruled that when a state board of equalization raises the property assessment of a single taxpayer, he has a right to a hearing, and merely allowing him to file written objections will not suffice. The Court said that "a hearing in its very essence demands that he who is entitled to it shall have the right to support his allegations by argument however brief, and, if need be, by proof, however informal," since the facts are adjudicative in nature. On the other hand, the same Court held that a hearing was not necessary where a city increases the valuation of all taxable property within its borders, since this is a general policy decision based on general information and ideas (*Bi-Metalic Investment Co.* v. *State Board of Equalization of Colorado,* 239 U.S. 441–446, 1915). In other words, the facts were legislative in character.

But even where the facts to be determined are adjudicative, a legal right to a hearing is not always recognized. Thus, a hearing may be dispensed with, at least for a period of time, where emergency action is necessary, or where inspection, or testing, or examination are suitable substitutes for hearings, as in the case of the inspection of an airplane. In addition, a hearing is often denied in cases involving certain types of privilege. Thus, the Supreme Court has ruled that an entering alien has no right to a trial-like hearing on the issue of whether his admission would be prejudicial to the

best interests of the United States, since at best his entry is a matter of privilege and not of right (*U.S.* ex rel. *Knauff* v. *Shaughnessy,* 338 U.S. 537, 1950; *Shaughnessy* v. *U.S.* ex rel. *Mazei,* 345 U.S. 206, 1953). Similarly, state courts generally hold that licenses to operate liquor stores, dance halls, pool halls, theaters, and the like, where the public interest in safety and morality is apt to be very great, may be revoked without notice of hearing, on the basis of the privilege doctrine.

On the other hand, the revocation of professional licenses, such as those of doctors and lawyers, must as a matter of law be preceded by a hearing following due notice.

Adjudication by administrative agencies tends to resemble adjudication by the courts. There are differences, of course, particularly in respect to the rules of evidence and in the degree of formality, but the resemblances are great; and as the administrative agencies mature, they tend to approximate more and more the procedures of the courts, partly as a result of legislation and partly as a result of pressures from the legal profession. Adjudication by arbitration is still another matter. Here the source of the power of the arbiter is generally the consent of the litigants, whereas the judge derives his power from government. Adjudication by a court has the advantage that the judge is less tempted to compromise, and his decision may be more acceptable because he seems to apply general rules he did not make and because he is surrounded by a powerful mystique. On the other hand, the arbitrator may exert greater effort than the judge in order to secure acceptance of the award, and the arbitrator is less bound by technical rules of procedure. In addition, he is often guided by the actual terms in the agreement to arbitrate.

Types of hearings. There are, in the courts, two different types of hearings. One takes the form of a trial, where evidence is presented, witnesses are cross-examined, and the tribunal makes its determination on the record. The other type of hearing essentially involves the presentation of arguments, as in appellate courts. The trial is designed to resolve fact issues, to assign facts to legal categories, and to apply rules of law to the facts. A hearing involving only argument is designed to resolve issues of law, policy, or discretion. Although a judge must limit his findings to the facts in the trial record, judges inevitably take judicial notice of some facts of general public knowledge; and they may make some decisions, not bearing on the immediate issues of the trial, on the basis of knowledge derived out of court, as in the collection of information bearing on the problem of the sentence (*Williams* v. *New York*, 337 U.S. 241, 1949).

Adversary proceedings. The rule prevailing in most American courts is that adjudication must involve a real controversy between adversary parties. An American Bar Association report has noted that "in whatever form adjudication may appear, the experienced judge or arbitrator desires and actively seeks to obtain an adversary presentation of the issues. Only when he has had the benefit of intelligent and vigorous advocacy on both sides can he feel fully confident of his decision" (Report 1958, p. 1161). This means that courts will not give advisory opinions (*United States* v. *Evans*, 213 U.S. 297, 1909), although state courts are obliged to do so if their state constitutions so provide. Furthermore, it should be noted that courts often give judgment for plaintiffs by default, where the defendant makes no appearance and offers no defense. This often happens in cases involving the collection of small retail debts, or the recovery of goods sold on conditional sales contracts, or the recovery of unpaid rents. These are not truly adversary proceedings, although that is the result of the defendant's choice. Here the court is used to help in making collections by coercing defendants who make no defense and generally have no defense, either in fact or in law.

In addition, since courts deal only with real controversies between adverse parties, they decline to hear cases where the issues are moot, or premature, or too speculative and abstract to be ruled upon intelligently, or where the suit is collusive in character. Test cases are not necessarily improper, provided real issues are asserted by adverse parties; and American courts are willing to give declaratory judgments, since they include every element of a traditional case except for the appendage of a coercive decree (*Nashville, C. & St. L. Ry.* v. *Wallace*, 288 U.S. 249, 1933).

The judge who presides over an adjudication should be properly qualified, and he should be impartial, which, among other things, means that he should have no direct, pecuniary interest in the outcome (*Tumey* v. *Ohio*, 273 U.S. 510, 1927). Although it is not always possible, as a general proposition it is desirable for the judge to rest his decision on the grounds argued by the parties. If the decision is completely outside the framework of argument and proofs presented by the parties, then their participation in the decision loses its meaning. This is least likely to occur where the relevant rules of law are fairly certain and well settled. There are some devices that help to achieve desirable results in this respect, such as oral argument, reargument, and the tentative decree accompanied by an order to show cause why it should not be made final. Furthermore, while a decision need not necessarily be accompanied by a statement of supporting reasons, reasoned opinions, generally speaking, are desirable and to be preferred, since they reassure the parties that their views were given attention.

Rules of procedure. While adjudication in courts is conducted according to rather complex and technical rules of procedure, the tendency in modern courts is toward simplicity and directness and away from technicality. Speaking of the Federal Rules of Civil Procedure, the Supreme Court said in *Conley* v. *Gibson* (355 U.S. 41, 48, 1957): "The Federal Rules reject the approach that pleading is a game of skill in which one misstep by counsel may be decisive to the outcome and accept the principle that the purpose of pleading is to facilitate a proper decision on the merits." Indeed, Rule 1 of the Federal Rules of Civil Procedure provides that the rules are to be construed "to secure the just, speedy, and inexpensive determination of every action."

Karl N. Llewellyn, in *The Common Law Tradition* (1960), listed a considerable number of factors that exert a steadying influence upon courts: law-conditioned judges, legal doctrine, known doctrinal techniques, the responsibility for justice, the tradition of the single right answer, opinion writing, review on a record made below, limited issues sharpened and phrased in advance, adversary argument by counsel, group decision making, judicial security and honesty, a known bench, general period style, and professional judicial office. The last he regarded as the most important of all. "The place to begin," he wrote, "is with the fact that the men of our appellate bench are human beings. I have never understood why the cynics talk and think as if this were not so. For it is so. And one of the more obvious and obstinate facts about human beings is that they operate in and respond to traditions, and especially to such traditions as are offered to them by the crafts . . . they follow" (p. 53).

The limits of adjudication

Adjudication has its appropriate limits. It is not suited for the handling of problems that involve very many parties in a fluid state of affairs. Such problems are best settled in some other way. For example, problems involved in the allocation of economic resources are generally dealt with by methods other than adjudication, as in the case of the processes of collective bargaining or legislation. Courts are not equipped to exercise licensing functions, as in the awarding of transportation certificates or the allocation of radio and television wave lengths; nor are they equipped to undertake the affirmative direction of complex economic affairs, although they do get involved, on occasion, in connection with such matters as bankruptcy administration and the probate of wills. Adjudication is limited to the declaring of rights and duties and does not extend to situations and problems, such as the operation of the railroads, where analysis in terms of rights and duties is inadequate.

Adjudication is often subjected to many criticisms. It is said that the law is too uncertain, that the rules of evidence are too complex, that procedures seem mysterious to laymen, that legal rules are too intricate, that litigation is too expensive and too slow, that the courts are chronically congested, that newspaper publicity corrupts judicial processes, and that in criminal cases defendants are treated either too harshly or too leniently. While there is some truth in all these criticisms, at least at some times and in some places, nevertheless it can hardly be denied that there is a great deal of popular confidence in the judiciary as being honest, impartial, and objective. The predominance of case law as the main form of law has influenced legal education and has tended to emphasize the pragmatic qualities of the law. Judicial review has tended to focus attention upon underlying ethical, social, and economic values. The growth of administrative tribunals has given a broader scope and usefulness to the processes of adjudication.

DAVID FELLMAN

[*See also* LEGAL REASONING; LEGAL SYSTEMS.]

BIBLIOGRAPHY

ALLEN, CARLETON K. (1927) 1964 *Law in the Making.* 7th ed. Oxford: Clarendon Press.

AMERICAN BAR ASSOCIATION; and the ASSOCIATION OF AMERICAN LAW SCHOOLS 1958 Professional Responsibility: Report of the Joint Conference. *American Bar Association Journal* 44:1159–1162; 1216–1218.

AUSTIN, JOHN (1861) 1873 *Lectures on Jurisprudence or the Philosophy of Positive Law.* Edited by Robert Campbell. 2 vols., 4th ed., rev. London: Murray.

BLACKSTONE, WILLIAM (1765–1769) 1922 *Commentaries on the Laws of England.* 4 books in 2 vols. Edited by William Draper Lewis. Philadelphia: Bisel.

CARDOZO, BENJAMIN N. (1921) 1960 *The Nature of the Judicial Process.* New Haven: Yale Univ. Press.

DAVIS, KENNETH CULP 1960 *Administrative Law and Government.* St. Paul, Minn.: West.

FRANK, JEROME (1930) 1949 *Law and the Modern Mind.* New York: Coward.

FRANKFURTER, FELIX 1939 *Law and Politics: Occasional Papers, 1913–1938.* Edited by A. MacLeish and E. F. Prichard, Jr. New York: Harcourt. → A paperback edition was published in 1962 by Putnam.

GRAY, JOHN C. (1909) 1921 *The Nature and Sources of the Law.* 2d ed. New York: Macmillan.

HART, HERBERT L. A. 1961 *The Concept of Law.* Oxford: Clarendon.

HOLDSWORTH, WILLIAM S. 1934 Case Law. *Law Quarterly Review* 50:180–195.

HOLMES, OLIVER WENDELL (1881) 1963 *The Common Law.* Cambridge, Mass.: Harvard Univ. Press.

HOLMES, OLIVER WENDELL (1885–1918) 1952 *Collected Legal Papers.* Edited by Harold J. Laski. New York: Smith.

HOLMES, OLIVER W. (1897) 1952 The Path of the Law. Pages 167–202 in Oliver W. Holmes, *Collected Legal Papers.* New York: Peter Smith. → First published in Volume 10 of the *Harvard Law Review.*

LAWSON, FREDERICK H. 1953 *A Common Lawyer Looks at the Civil Law.* Ann Arbor: Univ. of Michigan Law School.

LLEWELLYN, KARL N. 1960 *The Common Law Tradition: Deciding Appeals.* Boston: Little.

MURPHY, WALTER F. 1964 *Elements of Judicial Strategy.* Univ. of Chicago Press.

PATTERSON, EDWIN W. 1953 *Jurisprudence: Men and Ideas of the Law.* New York: Foundation Press.

POLLOCK, FREDERICK (1896) 1918 *A First Book of Jurisprudence for Students of the Common Law.* 4th ed. London: Macmillan.

SCIGLIANO, ROBERT G. 1962 *The Courts: A Reader in the Judicial Process.* Boston: Little.

II

INTERNATIONAL ADJUDICATION

The term "adjudication," in the vocabulary of international lawyers, is only partly a term of art. It is used loosely to cover many different forms of third-party decision concerning international disputes which have developed in the course of the ages. When the term is used in this sense, a distinction is sometimes drawn between "arbitration" before *ad hoc* bodies and "judicial settlement" by permanent tribunals (see League of Nations, Covenant 1919, art. 12, 13, and 15, as amended in 1921, and United Nations, Charter 1945, art. 33). In a more precise sense, "international adjudication" is used to describe the settlement of disputes by permanent international tribunals, a new development of the twentieth century, and is, in effect, a synonym for "judicial settlement."

In both senses the concept includes three elements: an impartial judge or judges, who may, without a change in the nature of their function, be described as arbitrators, commissioners, or umpires; a procedure (which may or may not include oral hearings) that enables the parties to present fully and on a footing of equality their views on the questions submitted for decision; and a decision "on the basis of respect for law," which, given with all the solemnity of judicial process after a full and fair hearing before impartial judges, is binding in substance, even though it may not always be technically binding in form.

While international adjudication has a recognized place in the United Nations system, its progress continues to be retarded by four factors: jurisdiction remains voluntary in principle rather than compulsory; the margin of uncertainty in the law is substantially wider than in mature systems of municipal law; there is no legislature to give the judiciary new law to apply and to change the law when its decisions are unacceptable; and there is no organized procedure for the execution of international decisions and awards. All of these factors reflect the sociology, political structure, and temper of international society. Their combined result is that while international adjudication represents a vital element in the progress of world organization, its future remains precarious.

Origins and growth

The history of international adjudication starts with the origins of international arbitration. The law and practice of permanent international tribunals have grown out of the much longer history of international arbitration. Even today the distinction between judicial settlement and arbitration remains much less clear than in municipal law by reason of the voluntary basis of the jurisdiction of international courts.

International arbitration.   The origins of international arbitration have been traced back, with doubtful justification, to the Amphyctionic Council of ancient Greece. Arbitration was, however, a recognized practice among the Greeks, mentioned as such by both Herodotus and Thucydides. The Roman Senate and later the Roman emperor arbitrated between subject peoples, and in medieval times both pope and emperor acted as arbitrators. From the thirteenth century on, there was a gradual process of development from arbitration in feudal quarrels, like the Mise of Amiens, the award of St. Louis between Henry III of England and the barons in 1264, to arbitration in international disputes, one of the most famous antecedents of which was the bull *Intercoetera* of Pope Alexander VI, dividing the New World between Spain and Portugal in 1493. It is rarely appreciated that the Treaty of Vervins of 1598, the Peace of Westphalia of 1648, the Treaty of Westminster of 1655, the Treaty of the Pyrenees of 1659, the Treaty of Ryswick of 1697, and the Treaty of Utrecht of 1713 all provided for arbitration in specified disputes.

However, the modern history of international arbitration is generally dated from the Jay Treaty of 1795, which inaugurated the tradition of recourse to arbitration as the recognized method of settling disputes between Great Britain and the United States not adjusted by negotiation.

In the nineteenth century the practice of arbitration became widespread. International boundaries in sparsely settled areas, particularly in the Americas, were determined by arbitration in a wide range of cases. Complaints of belligerent interference with neutral rights and failures to discharge neutral duties were frequently referred to arbitration. Allegations of state responsibility for injury to persons and property were the staple business of an important series of claims commissions, culminating in the Venezuelan arbitrations of 1903–1904 (which involved 12 states), the Anglo-American tribunal of 1910 (which liquidated outstanding claims, some of which were almost a century old), and the Mexican claims commissions, 1923–1934 (which involved seven states). Much of this activity attracted little or no public interest, but the settlement by arbitration in 1871–1872 of the Alabama claims controversy focused attention upon the possibility of recourse to international arbitration in disputes of political importance. The effect was the more dramatic because the arbitration proceedings followed immediately after the Franco-Prussian War. The British Guiana–Venezuela boundary arbitration of 1899 between Great Britain and Venezuela, which again followed a period of acute diplomatic strain between Great Britain and the United States, revived this interest in arbitration as an alternative to war.

It was in these circumstances that the First Hague Peace Conference of 1899 discussed the desirability of compulsory arbitration and the possibility of creating a permanent international tribunal. It succeeded in creating the Permanent Court of Arbitration, which is not a permanent court, but a standing panel from which *ad hoc* tribunals can be drawn. The conference made an important advance by codifying international arbitral procedure, and the establishment of the Permanent Court of Arbitration gave a significant stimulus to international arbitration. An increasing number of *ad hoc* tribunals were constituted from its membership in the following years.

But neither the 1899 conference nor the Second Hague Peace Conference of 1907, which proclaimed, in an anodyne manner, the principle of compulsory jurisdiction, was successful in securing the acceptance of any firm obligation to arbitrate or in establishing a permanent tribunal. Progress was made in drafting a statute for a proposed Court of Arbitral Justice, but it proved impossible to secure agreement upon a method of electing the judges acceptable to both the larger and the smaller states. A considerable number of bilateral arbitration treaties were negotiated in the following years, but many of these failed to be ratified and others had little practical effect.

Permanent Court of International Justice. The decisive step forward was taken in 1920 when the Assembly of the League of Nations approved the Statute of the Permanent Court of International Justice. The Court, whose judges were elected by an absolute majority of votes in independent elections in both the Assembly and the Council, held its first session in 1922. During the period from 1922 to 1940 it gave 33 judgments and 27 advisory opinions.

Neither the United States nor the Soviet Union became parties to the statute; nevertheless, the Court played a significant part in the international life of the League of Nations period. A substantial proportion of its cases related to the interpretation and application of the 1919 peace settlement, but the principles formulated in its decisions were frequently more important and permanent than the contexts in which they were enunciated. Three examples should be mentioned. The first is the principle that the conclusion of a treaty is to be construed as an exercise rather than a restriction of sovereignty; consequently, the treaty must be interpreted so as to give effect to its terms rather than preserve the sovereignty of the parties (*The S.S. Wimbledon,* 1923 P.C.I.J. Series A, No. 1). The second principle is that "domestic jurisdiction" is "an essentially relative" concept, the content of which at any particular time "depends on the development of international relations" (*Nationality Decrees in Tunis and Morocco,* 1923 P.C.I.J. Series B, No. 4). Third is the "well-known rule that no-one can be judge in his own suit" (art. 3, paragraph 2 of the interpretation of *Treaty of Lausanne [Frontier Between Turkey and Iraq]* 1925 P.C.I.J. Series B, No. 12). Of these principles the first two have done much to shape the whole subsequent development of international law; failure to acknowledge the implications of the third principle remains the crucial weakness of contemporary international organization.

Nominally, there was a considerable widening of the scope of the Court's compulsory jurisdiction from 1929 on, chiefly through the acceptance by France, the British Commonwealth countries, and other states of the "optional clause" of its statute, which conferred such jurisdiction in certain classes of disputes. But in the course of the 1930s an increasing proportion of the questions actually submitted to the Court consisted of claims cases rather than larger issues, partly because of the general political climate of the times, partly as the result of what was widely regarded as a political alignment in the Court in the *Austro-German Customs Union Case* (1931 P.C.I.J. Series A/B, No. 41).

Throughout the interwar period a considerable number of cases continued to be referred to *ad hoc* tribunals, sometimes drawn from the Permanent Court of Arbitration, and mixed arbitral tribunals handled a large volume of business arising out of the World War I.

International Court of Justice. On the founding of the United Nations in 1945 the Permanent Court was reconstituted as the International Court of Justice by a statute annexed to the UN Charter which forms an integral part thereof and is binding on all UN members. The Court consists of 15 judges, elected by the General Assembly and the Security Council for terms of nine years. Only states may be parties in cases before the Court, but public international organizations may furnish information (Statute, art. 34), and advisory opinions may be requested by the General Assembly, by the Security Council, and by other organs of the United Nations and specialized agencies which may at any time be so authorized by the General Assembly (Statute, art. 65; Charter, art. 96).

The function of the Court is to decide in accordance with international law such disputes as are submitted to it. It is to apply international conventions, whether general or particular, that establish rules expressly recognized by the contesting states; international custom as evidence of a general practice accepted as law; the general principles of law accepted by civilized nations; and, subject to the rule that a decision had no binding force except between the parties and in respect of the particular case, judicial decisions and the teachings of the most highly qualified publicists of the various nations as subsidiary means for the determination of the law (Statute, art. 38).

The jurisdiction of the Court comprises all cases that the parties refer to it and all matters specially provided for in the Charter of the United Nations or in treaties and conventions in force.

The states party to the statute may at any time declare that they recognize as compulsory *ipso facto* and without special agreement, in relation to any other state accepting the same obligation, the jurisdiction of the Court in all legal disputes concerning: (*a*) the interpretation of a treaty;

(*b*) a question of international law; (*c*) the existence of any fact that, if established, would constitute a breach of an international obligation; or (*d*) the nature or extent of the reparation to be made for any such breach. Thirty-seven states have made such declarations. Many of these declarations are, however, subject to time limits or other provisions that make the obligations created by them precarious, and five declarations, including that of the United States, exclude matters of domestic jurisdiction as determined by the state concerned. No communist state has made such a declaration; few of the new Asian, Middle Eastern, and African states have made declarations; and an important group of Latin American states are no longer bound by such declarations.

The Court has an extensive compulsory jurisdiction under other instruments, such as the European Convention for the Peaceful Settlement of Disputes; the constituent instruments of a number of international organizations (e.g., the International Labour Organisation, the International Civil Aviation Organization, and others); a widespread but uneven network of bilateral arbitration conventions; and clauses providing for compulsory jurisdiction contained in a large number of general treaties on a wide range of subjects. In recent years, however, there has been a marked decline in the practice of including such clauses in newly negotiated general international conventions, chiefly because the inclusion is normally opposed by the Soviet Union.

Activities of the International Court. The rhythm of business in the International Court of Justice has been slow, but a number of cases referred to it have been important either because of the questions of law at issue or because of their political context. In the *Reparation for Injuries Suffered in the Service of the United Nations Case* (1949 I.C.J. 174) the Court recognized the objective international personality of the United Nations and its capacity to protect those in its service by a diplomatic claim. In the *Barcelona Traction, Light and Power Company, Limited, Case* (1964 I.C.J. 168) some of the fundamentals of the scope of diplomatic protection of corporate bodies are involved. The *Certain Expenses of the United Nations Case* (1962 I.C.J. 151) deals with an issue that has since paralyzed the UN General Assembly. The South-West Africa cases (1950 I.C.J. 128; 1955 I.C.J. 67; 1956 I.C.J. 23; 1962 I.C.J. 319) deal with one of the most explosive issues in contemporary international politics.

The value of the part played by the Court in these cases remains a matter of debate, and there has been increasing concern over the fact that a number of decisions, opinions, and orders of the Court have remained ineffective in practice. The judgment of the Court in the *Corfu Channel Case* (1949 I.C.J. 237) was ignored by Albania; a number of advisory opinions have remained ineffective; and no effect was given to the order made by the Court in the *Anglo-Iranian Oil Co. Case* (1951 I.C.J. 89) indicating provisional measures for the protection of the rights of the parties.

Moreover, compliance for a certain time with the Court's decision in a case does not furnish any continuing guarantee that the problem out of which the case arose has been solved or that the decision will not be frustrated or negated by further developments. The opinion of the Permanent Court of International Justice in the *Austro-German Customs Union Case* did not prevent the *Anschluss*; the decision of the International Court of Justice in the *Right of Passage Over Indian Territory Case* (1960 I.C.J. 6) was followed, after an interval, by the Indian occupation of Goa.

These difficulties inevitably prompt serious questions concerning both the appropriateness of the decisions given in the cases in which they have arisen and the long-range problem of what measures can be taken to ensure compliance with international decisions and awards; it nevertheless remains true that the general standard of compliance with international decisions and awards is high.

Meanwhile, there has been a significant increase in the proportion of cases submitted to the Court originating from Latin America, Asia, and Africa; and in the *Certain Expenses of the United Nations Case* the Soviet Union appeared before the Court for the first time.

In these circumstances it is still premature to attempt to strike a balance between the encouraging and the discouraging elements in the record of the Court. A valid appraisal must await further developments, and the answer will be determined by a combination of three factors: (1) the degree of confidence in the Court that governments are prepared to show by referring important matters to it; (2) the degree to which the Court justifies such confidence by resolving the issues submitted to it with creative imagination; and (3) the extent to which the United Nations can make a reality of the obligation of compliance with international decisions and awards.

Specialized tribunals. While the International Court of Justice is the principal judicial organ of the United Nations, a substantial proportion of international judicial business continues to be entrusted to *ad hoc* or specialized tribunals. Model rules on arbitral procedure, designed for the guidance of *ad hoc* tribunals, were approved by the

International Law Commission of the United Nations in 1958. Among specialized tribunals the Arbitral Commission on Property Rights and Interests in Germany and the Arbitral Tribunal and Mixed Commission for the Agreement on German External Debts have been of particular importance.

Important arbitrations have been conducted between governments and international commercial interests, such as the Alsing case, involving the Alsing Trading Company, Limited, and the Swedish Match Trust versus the Greek state (1956 *International Law Reports* 633), and the Aramco Case, involving Saudi Arabia versus Aramco and the Onassis interests (1963 *International Law Reports* 117). The International Bank for Reconstruction and Development has established the Centre for the Settlement of Investment Disputes. The International Labour Organisation has conducted judicial inquiries into charges of forced labor in violation of international conventions brought by Ghana against Portugal (International Labor Office, *Official Bulletin*, vol. 45, no. 2, supplement 2, April 1962) and by Portugal against Liberia (vol. 46, no. 2, supplement 2, April 1963).

There have been exceptionally important regional developments in Europe, where the Court of Justice of the European Communities has a general mandate to "ensure the observance of law and justice" in the operation of the six-nation communities (Bebr 1962). The European Court of Human Rights hears complaints referred to it by the European Commission of Human Rights or submitted by governments that allege violations of the European Convention for the Protection of Human Rights and Fundamental Freedoms (Robertson 1963). These regional developments may at some stage furnish a model for further international developments. The United Nations and the International Labour Organisation maintain administrative tribunals that are making a significant contribution to international administrative law (Jenks 1962).

These varied developments illustrate the extent to which international adjudication is increasingly including in its scope matters lying beyond the traditional purview of international law.

Problems of international adjudication

Compulsory jurisdiction. Proposals for extending the compulsory jurisdiction of the Court have attracted widespread attention. They take varied forms. Some of them envisage a far-reaching reconstruction of world organization on the basis of an amended Charter of the United Nations (Clark & Sohn 1958). Under such a scheme compulsory jurisdiction might include not only disputes between states but also disputes between states and international organizations and disputes relating to the constitutionality of action taken by international organizations. Disputes between states would be referred to the Court if the General Assembly decided that their continuance would be likely to endanger the maintenance of international peace and security. It has been argued that compulsory jurisdiction would have made it possible to secure a prompt determination of the legal issues involved in such matters as the Berlin crisis of 1961, the nationalization of the Suez Canal, the Sino–Indian border dispute, the Gulf of Aqaba dispute, the *U-2* and *RB-47* aerial incidents, and the Cuban and Indonesian expropriations (Larson 1961). Such proposals raise important questions of judgment concerning the breadth of support they are likely to secure, the measure in which the acceptance of jurisdiction will be honored when a concrete case arises, and the extent to which it will be practicable to secure compliance with the decisions given.

More modest proposals envisage a gradual approach, consisting essentially of (*a*) the abandonment of the automatic or self-judging reservation, which excludes from the compulsory jurisdiction of the Court questions of domestic jurisdiction as determined by the state concerned; and (*b*) making further provision for compulsory jurisdiction when negotiating international arrangements on particular political or economic questions.

The Institute of International Law has outlined a series of recommendations to implement this kind of approach: (1) In an international community the members of which have renounced the right of war, recourse to international adjudication constitutes a normal method of settlement of legal disputes and should therefore never be regarded as an unfriendly act toward a respondent state. (2) Obligations of compulsory jurisdiction should not be illusory; they should therefore be undertaken in terms that respect the right of the Court to settle any dispute concerning its own jurisdiction. (3) Obligations of compulsory jurisdiction should not be precarious; declarations accepting the jurisdiction of the International Court should therefore be valid for periods of not less than five years. (4) General conventions should contain a jurisdiction clause permitting the institution of proceedings by unilateral application. (5) Economic and financial agreements concerning development schemes should include a jurisdiction clause. (6) Certain economic and financial agreements between states could usefully contain a general provision for compulsory jurisdiction in respect of claims brought by one of the states concerned (either acting on its own behalf or espousing a claim on behalf of one of its nationals) against the other state concerned (Institute of International Law 1959).

The potential effectiveness of the gradual approach presupposes a sustained continuity of action. Great advances might be possible if public opinion were sufficiently informed and farsighted to sanction initiatives even if they are unlikely to be reciprocated by all states in the foreseeable future. As compulsory jurisdiction always rests on a reciprocal basis, such initiatives do not expose the state taking them to any liability; if not reciprocated, they are ineffective rather than dangerous. However, what risks should be taken in the matter is basically a question of practical statesmanship, going beyond legal analysis.

Scope and limits of justiciability.   Throughout the history of international adjudication there has been recurrent controversy concerning the potential scope of the international judicial function and the limits of justiciability. John Westlake was the first major writer to discuss the question in terms that remain relevant today (1904–1907). Since the publication of his work most of the leading treatises and textbooks have discussed the matter at some length. The leading American and British treatises (Hyde 1922; Oppenheim 1905) deal with it particularly fully, and the current Soviet textbook of international law available in English does so more briefly (Akademiia Nauk S.S.S.R. 1947).

Four main conceptions of limited justiciability may be distinguished in the literature: (a) that the scope for international judicial settlement as a matter of binding obligation accepted in advance is limited by the existence of gaps and deficiencies in international law; (b) that disputes of high political importance are unsuitable for judicial settlement; (c) that judicial settlement is appropriate only when application of the existing rules of law is consistent with right and justice; and (d) that a distinction must be drawn between disputes over rights and conflicts of interests. These conceptions exercised for many years a far-reaching influence on the policy of governments and the drafting of arbitration treaties as well as on legal doctrine, but the life has now gone out of the whole controversy. Sir Hersch Lauterpacht's *The Function of Law in the International Community* (1933) established beyond any possibility of refutation that there are no technical limitations to the possibility of determining judicially every international controversy.

It is, however, now widely and generally conceded that this is not the heart of the matter. The essence of the problem is that a judicial determination on the basis of the existing law may, according to circumstances, resolve the problem, circumscribe it without resolving it, create a new situation in which the solution of the problem by negotiation becomes less difficult, or aggravate rather than eliminate the difficulty. Whether or not it is wise to seek a judicial decision in a particular situation is a question of political judgment, but the fact that it may not always be wise to go to law does not imply that it should not be possible to go to law unless all concerned are agreed that it is wise and desirable to do so. The question of the usefulness or desirability of proceedings in given circumstances, therefore, has little bearing on that of the balance of advantage in accepting or declining compulsory jurisdiction. This latter question must be decided on the basis of the effect of the decision taken on the strength and stability of the international legal order as a whole.

Present role and future potential

The present role and future potential of international adjudication in world affairs remain controversial. Adjudication is no longer thought of as it was a century ago, in the early days of the modern movement for the promotion of international arbitration, as the alternative to war. It is generally recognized that it must take its place with other processes of peaceful settlement (including negotiation, inquiry, mediation, conciliation, resort to regional agencies or arrangements, and other peaceful means) within a wider framework of world organization in which diplomacy, economic policy, the protection of human rights, the promotion of social progress and better standards of life in larger freedom, international cooperation in science and technology, the progressive development of international law, and effective collective measures for the prevention and removal of threats to the peace all have essential parts to play. The question has become, How large a part can and should adjudication play within such a framework? The answer will depend partly on the future of national attitudes toward such adjudication, partly on the extent to which the procedures of international adjudication are satisfactorily adapted to changed needs and partly on the measure in which the future decisions of the International Court and other international tribunals achieve a balance between the conflicting claims of stability and change.

A number of convergent but essentially different factors have tended to retard the development of international adjudication during the middle years of the twentieth century.

National attitudes. Great differences exist among the attitudes of the United States, the Soviet Union and states sharing her general approach, and the Asian and African states that have during these years won or recovered their independence. None of these attitudes is necessarily permanent.

The United States has, with the significant exception of its nonparticipation during the League of Nations period in the Permanent Court of International Justice, played a leading part in the development of international adjudication since the Jay Treaty of 1795, but it has shown a continuing reluctance to accept a binding obligation to adjudicate in advance of the emergence and definition of the issue to be adjudicated. The United States qualified this attitude in 1946 by accepting in principle the compulsory jurisdiction of the International Court, but subject to the exclusion of matters of domestic jurisdiction as determined by the United States. The Connally amendment, embodying this reservation, has been much criticized and its repeal sought by successive governments, but the issue remains in doubt.

The Soviet opposition to compulsory jurisdiction is widely regarded as a transposition to the international scene of the Marxist concept that matters of state lie beyond the frontiers of the law and is assumed, on this basis, to be of a more unyielding character. While this opposition has been relaxed in a limited number of special contexts, there has been no indication that any more general modification is under consideration.

The reserved attitude of many of the new states reflects a general distrust of the traditional content of international law but may well change rapidly if the decisions of the International Court and of other tribunals during the coming years command their respect.

These attitudes differ widely in their historical background, present significance, and susceptibility to change, but they nevertheless influence one another. All of them will be influenced by the future vitality of the concept of the rule of law in national and international society alike.

The range of judicial procedures. The Statute of the International Court of Justice, in its present form, allows only two types of proceedings: contested cases between states and requests for an advisory opinion by an authorized United Nations organ or specialized agency. In the Court of Justice of the European Communities and other European regional tribunals a much wider range of procedures and remedies is available. These include proceedings by the communities against their member states, against decisions of the communities, and proceedings by and against corporate bodies and individuals. The scope of such proceedings includes the interpretation and application of treaties and community regulations and decisions, questions of administrative law, and matters of tort and contract. The remedies available include, in addition to damages and penalties, the annulment of decisions, the equivalent of a decree of specific performance, and a ruling on a question of law raised before a municipal tribunal designed as a directive to that tribunal. The future importance of international adjudication may depend in substantial measure on the extent to which it develops a comparable range of procedures and remedies.

International change and stability. In every growing and changing society the significance of judicial process depends on its relationship to the rhythm of growth and change. The future significance of international adjudication will depend on the extent to which it becomes a recognized part of orderly processes of growth and change in international society. If we are prepared to accept the twin facts that a substantial margin of uncertainty is an inherent characteristic of every legal system that is in process of rapid growth but that the margin cannot be so wide that the hard core of accepted law dissolves, adjudication can be a major creative influence in the development of a new world of law.

As was convincingly demonstrated by Sir Hersch Lauterpacht (1927), the general principles of law recognized by civilized nations have been a major fertilizing influence and source of decision throughout the modern history of international arbitration and adjudication. Such recourse to general principles must now, in view of the changed political structure of the world, draw upon a wider range of legal systems (Jenks 1958, pp. 62–172). The scope is limited only by the extent to which judicial agreement can be secured on the principles and their application and the measure in which the resulting decisions command general confidence and acceptance. The authority to use such principles, specifically conferred upon the International Court of Justice by the terms of its statute (art. 38, 1, c), would justify its assuming a dynamic role in the development of the law.

Recourse to principles of equity by international courts and tribunals has likewise been widespread throughout the modern history of international arbitration, and there is a solid body of established precedent and well-tested experience from which it is clear that equitable concepts can and should play an important part in adapting principles to circumstances in a world in which the law is constantly confronted with new problems and needs. There are significant indications that general concepts of international policy may play an increasingly important part in the international adjudication of the future (Jenks 1964, pp. 316–546). These concepts will entail: recognizing the full implications of the changed legal status of violence; testing the claims of sovereignty by the public interest; securing the effectiveness of international organization; developing a law of contract and tort adequate to contemporary needs; and evolving rules concerning prescription, acquiescence, and estoppel that would secure a necessary minimum of stability in a world of cataclysmic change.

International adjudication has played no significant part in the most far-reaching developments in the international life of our time: the accession of some thousand million people to political independence in less than 20 years (primarily by peaceful means) and the acceptance by economically advanced countries of a recognized responsibility for disinterested cooperation in the economic development of the whole world. Adjudication will not serve to bridge the still widening gap between affluent and underdeveloped societies or ensure that advanced technology becomes the servant rather than the master of man. It can make little immediate contribution to the relaxation of political tension between rival ideologies. But in a world in which appropriate action is being taken in respect of all these matters it remains as necessary as a sound judicial system is in a well-governed state.

In brief, adjudication fulfills much the same function in international as in national life, namely, the settlement of disputes by recourse to law. It can fulfill this function satisfactorily only as an element in a comprehensive approach to world organization in which the restraint of violence by collective action, diplomacy, economic policy, and other measures all play mutually complementary parts. Within such a framework it represents an indispensable element in ensuring that justice is not sacrificed in the hope that through this sacrifice peace and security can be maintained.

C. WILFRED JENKS

[*See also* INTERNATIONAL LAW. *Other relevant material may be found in* CONFLICT OF LAWS; INTERNATIONAL LEGISLATION; *and under* INTERNATIONAL ORGANIZATION; LAW.]

BIBLIOGRAPHY

The growth, development, and problems of international adjudication have been one of the major themes of the literature of international law for the last half-century. A bibliography of the subject appears annually in International Court of Justice, Yearbook. This includes 6,875 items for the period 1946–1965. In this immense literature a choice of authorities inevitably involves an element of preference.

Ralston 1929, Hudson 1944, Politis 1924 are standard general accounts of the historical development of international adjudication. Moore 1898 remains the outstanding authoritative work, there being nothing comparable for the later period. Hudson 1943 is the leading work on the Permanent Court; Rosenne 1957, the leading general account of the International Court as reconstituted in 1945; Jessup 1959, the best short account of the Court's current position. Lauterpacht 1933 provides the outstanding theoretical study of peaceful settlement and the concept of justiciability. Lauterpacht 1934 gives the most illuminating evaluation of the methodological and other intellectual problems inherent in the international judicial process. Simpson & Fox 1959 is the most comprehensive recent account of international arbitral procedure. Jenks 1964 is a study of the measures necessary to consolidate and improve the process of international adjudication to enable it to play its proper part in promoting and securing the rule of law in world affairs.

The leading collections of international decisions and awards are: Moore 1898; Lapradelle et al. 1905–1954; Hague, Permanent Court of Arbitration 1916; League of Nations, Permanent Court of International Justice 1922–1940; International Court of Justice 1947–1964; International Court of Justice, Registry; International Law Reports. International Court of Justice 1952–1963 is a digest of the decisions of the International Court; Hague, Permanent Court of Justice 1961 is designed to be a comprehensive digest of the pleadings before the Court.

AKADEMIIA NAUK S.S.S.R., INSTITUT GOSUDARSTVA I PRAVA (1947) 1960 *International Law: A Textbook for Use in Law Schools.* Moscow: Foreign Languages Publishing House. → First published as *Mezhdunarodnoe pravo.* See especially pages 377–400.

BEBR, GERHARD 1962 *Judicial Control of the European Communities.* London: Stevens; New York: Praeger.

CLARK, GRENVILLE; and SOHN, LOUIS B. (1958) 1960 *World Peace Through World Law.* 2d ed., rev. Cambridge, Mass.: Harvard Univ. Press.

HAGUE, PERMANENT COURT OF ARBITRATION 1916 *The Hague Court Reports.* New York: Oxford Univ. Press.

HAGUE, PERMANENT COURT OF JUSTICE 1961 *Répertoire des décisions et des documents de la procédure écrite et orale de la cour permanente de justice internationale . . . Serie 1: Cour Permanente de Justice Internationale, 1922–1945.* Published under the direction of Paul Guggenheim. Paris, Université de, Institut des Hautes Études Internationales, Publication No. 38. Geneva: Droz.

HUDSON, MANLEY O. 1943 *The Permanent Court of International Justice 1920–1942: A Treatise.* New York: Macmillan.

HUDSON, MANLEY O. 1944 *International Tribunals: Past and Future.* Washington: Carnegie Endowment for International Peace and Brookings Institution.

HYDE, CHARLES CHENEY (1922) 1945 *International Law, Chiefly as Interpreted and Applied by the United States.* 3 vols., 2d ed., rev. Boston: Little. → See especially pages 1559–1653 on "Differences Between States: Modes of Redress Other Than War. Title A: Amicable Modes."

INSTITUTE OF INTERNATIONAL LAW 1959 Resolutions and Vœu Adopted by the Institute at its Session at Neuchâtel, 3–12 September 1959; Compulsory Jurisdiction of International Courts and Tribunals. Institute of International Law, *Annuaire de l'Institut de Droit International* 48, no. 2:380–388.

INTERNATIONAL COURT OF JUSTICE, REGISTRY, *Reports of International Arbitral Awards.* → Published since 1948.

INTERNATIONAL COURT OF JUSTICE, THE HAGUE, *Yearbook.* → Published since 1945/1947. Supersedes: Permanent Court of International Justice, The Hague, *Publications*, Series E: Annual Report.

INTERNATIONAL COURT OF JUSTICE, THE HAGUE 1947–1964 *Reports of Judgments, Advisory Opinions and Orders.* Leiden (Netherlands): Sijthoff.

INTERNATIONAL COURT OF JUSTICE, THE HAGUE 1952–1963 *The Case Law of the International Court: A Repertoire of the Judgements, Advisory Opinions and Orders.* Vols. 1–3. Leiden (Netherlands): Sijthoff.

International Law Reports (London). → Published since 1919/1922. See especially 1950 and onwards.

JENKS, C. WILFRED 1958 *The Common Law of Mankind.* London: Stevens; New York: Praeger.

JENKS, C. WILFRED 1962 *The Proper Law of International Organisations.* London: Stevens; Dobbs Ferry, N.Y.: Oceana.

JENKS, C. WILFRED 1964 *The Prospects of International Adjudication.* London: Stevens; Dobbs Ferry, N.Y.: Oceana.

JESSUP, PHILIP C. 1956 *Transnational Law.* New Haven: Yale Univ. Press.

JESSUP, PHILIP C. 1959 *The Use of International Law.* Ann Arbor: Univ. of Michigan Law School.

LAPRADELLE, ALBERT G. DE et al. (editors) (1905–1954) 1954–1957 *Recueil des arbitrages internationaux.* 3 vols. Paris: Éditions internationales. → Volumes 1 and 2 are second editions.

LARSON, ARTHUR 1961 *When Nations Disagree: A Handbook on Peace Through Law.* Baton Rouge: Louisiana State Univ. Press.

LAUTERPACHT, HERSCH 1927 *Private Law Sources and Analogies of International Law: (With Special Reference to International Arbitration).* New York: Longmans.

LAUTERPACHT, HERSCH 1933 *The Function of Law in the International Community.* Oxford: Clarendon.

LAUTERPACHT, HERSCH (1934) 1958 *The Development of International Law by the International Court.* Rev. ed. London: Stevens. → First published as *The Development of International Law by the Permanent Court of International Justice.*

LEAGUE OF NATIONS, COVENANT (1919) 1938 *The Covenant of the League of Nations: Including Amendments in Force, February 1, 1938.* London: H. M. Stationery Office.

LEAGUE OF NATIONS, PERMANENT COURT OF INTERNATIONAL JUSTICE 1922–1940 *Publications de la Cour Permanente de Justice Internationale.* Serie A/B: Arrêts, ordonnances et avis consultatifs, No. 1–80. Leiden (Netherlands): Sijthoff.

MOORE, JOHN B. 1898 *History and Digest of the International Arbitrations to Which the United States Has Been a Party.* 6 vols. Washington: Government Printing Office.

OPPENHEIM, LASSA F. L. (1905) 1955 *International Law: A Treatise.* Volume 1: Peace. 8th ed. Edited by Hersch Lauterpacht. New York: Longmans. → See especially the Introduction and Chapter 1.

POLITIS, NICOLAS S. 1924 *La justice internationale.* Paris: Hachette.

RALSTON, JACKSON H. 1929 *International Arbitration, From Athens to Locarno.* Stanford (Calif.) Univ. Press; Oxford Univ. Press.

ROBERTSON, ARTHUR H. 1963 *Human Rights in Europe.* Dobbs Ferry, N.Y.: Oceana.

ROSENNE, SHABTAI 1957 *The International Court of Justice: An Essay in Political and Legal Theory.* Leiden (Netherlands): Sijthoff.

SIMPSON, JOHN L.; and FOX, HAZEL 1959 *International Arbitration: Law and Practice.* London: Stevens.

UNITED NATIONS, CHARTER 1945 *Charter of the United Nations and Statute of the International Court of Justice.* New York: United Nations.

WESTLAKE, JOHN (1904–1907) 1910–1913 *International Law.* 2 vols. 2d ed. Cambridge Univ. Press. → See especially pages 300–326 on "The Political Action of States" and pages 350–368 on "International Arbitration."

ADJUSTMENT

See CONFORMITY; GROUPS, *article on* GROUP FORMATION; MENTAL HEALTH.

ADLER, ALFRED

Alfred Adler (1870–1937) was the second of six children. His father, Leopold Adler, had come to Vienna from the Burgenland and was a grain merchant; his mother was from Moravia.

Adler was graduated from the University of Vienna Medical School in 1895. Three years later he wrote his first book (1898), in which he indicated the health hazards to which tailors were exposed, stressing the principle that human beings could not be considered in isolation but only in relation to their total environment. Thus, even as a young man of 28, his approach to human problems was holistic, foreshadowing his later basic conceptual approach.

Around 1900, Adler's chief interest was the study of psychopathological symptoms within the field of general medicine. In 1902, when he wrote a review of Freud's book on dream interpretation, Freud sent him a postcard inviting him to join his discussion circle. Upon Freud's assurance that many different views, including Adler's own, would be discussed, Adler accepted the invitation.

Adler had never agreed with Freud's theory that early sexual trauma caused mental disease, and he persistently opposed Freud's method of dream interpretation. The differences between the two men became even more marked after Adler had published, in 1907, his *Study of Organ Inferiority and Its Psychical Compensation.* In 1911, Adler and nine of his followers left Freud's circle and developed their own school of thought. The two men never met again. In 1912, Adler named his system *Individualpsychologie,* and that same year he published *The Neurotic Constitution,* a book that outlined his main concepts in both their theoretical and practical aspects. In the following years, he lectured extensively, and one of his books, *Understanding Human Nature* (1927), commonly referred to as a classic and still on the required reading list of several colleges in the United States, is based on the notes of one of his listeners.

After his return from military service during World War I, Adler opened the first child guidance clinic in Vienna. Soon there were about thirty such clinics in the city, conducted under his supervision, staffed by his pupils, and affiliated with parent–teacher associations and private institutions. These clinics functioned until 1934, when they were ordered closed by the fascist regime, which favored an authoritarian approach in the field of education, as elsewhere.

In 1926 Adler was appointed visiting professor at Columbia University in New York; and in 1932, he also began teaching at the Long Island College of Medicine, where he held the title of visiting professor of medical psychology. From then on, he spent only the summer months in Vienna.

Adler was an excellent lecturer, and he established contact with his audience as easily in English as in his native German. His public lectures were always crowded. In 1937, while giving a series of lectures at the University of Aberdeen, he collapsed on the street and died of heart failure within a few minutes.

Adler was married to Raissa Timofeyevna Epstein in 1897. Of his four children, his daughter Alexandra and his son Kurt are psychiatrists.

Organ inferiority and its compensation. In 1907, in his book *Study of Organ Inferiority and Its Psychical Compensation*, Adler described the process of compensation for physical disabilities. The results of compensation may be satisfactory or unsatisfactory. As an example of so-called overcompensation, a term denoting extreme forms of compensation, he pointed to Demosthenes, who stuttered as a boy but trained his speech by placing pebbles in his mouth and trying to shout down the roar of the waves. Adler explained that the symptoms of a neurosis similarly represent the compensation of inferiority feelings but compensation in an unsatisfactory direction.

Occasionally it is alleged that Adler considered all mental disturbance to be caused by *physical* disability. However, his study of the influence of physical disability represents only the beginning of his investigations of the sources of inferiority feelings. It was not until 1925 that he used the term "inferiority complex."

Goal orientation. In 1912, in his book *The Neurotic Constitution*, Adler pointed out that all

our thinking is goal-directed and forms a unified "style of life," particularly well revealed in mental aberrations. His psychological system is, therefore, teleological, whereas Freud's is causalistic; and he used a teleological approach to explore mental illness, in particular the neuroses. He often illustrated the goal-directedness and "logic" of neurotic symptoms by the following example: If one spots a man at the foot of a scaffold, making strange gestures, one may think that he is confused. On finding out, however, that his aim is to sit on top of the scaffold, the observer may consider the man's actions to be rational enough. Even if his goal is useless, his behavior is reasonable.

Today, teleological concepts are guiding principles in the fields of psychology, psychiatry, sociology, and the biological sciences. They form the basis of the so-called holistic–organismic approach, as opposed to the mechanistic approach. At present, all personality theories recognize purposiveness or teleology, with the exception of the theories of the behaviorists and factor analysts. These developments show that Adler's emphasis upon the concept of purpose in the life sciences, which earlier was rejected by other schools of thought, has been widely accepted.

Social interest. In 1919, in the Preface to the second edition of *The Neurotic Constitution*, Adler outlined, for the first time, his concept of "social interest" (*Gemeinschaftsgefühl*), which has become one of the basic principles of individual psychology. (What he meant by social interest is something like identification with society.) World War I was for Adler the demoniacal work of unleashed drives that betray and strangle the inherent social interest of humanity ([1912] Preface to 1919 edition; 1928). He voiced his belief that a better understanding of human nature would reduce the striving for power and guide man's energies toward constructive social interest. He later asserted that social interest cannot be expected from the severely mentally defective, since intelligence and creativity are necessary for its development (1928). In persons with neuroses, psychoses, or in the criminal, social interest is always diminished, if not completely absent.

As additional evidence of the nature of social interest, Adler cited the mutual dependence of mother and child: both are in need of love, and while the infant satisfies its hunger, it relieves the milk-filled breasts of the mother—an example of the way in which social interest may originate. Adler's concept of the mother–child relationship was opposed to that of Freud, who described the relation of infant to mother as based, in part, on oral, cannibalistic drives.

Style of life. In his writings after 1920, Adler used the terms "style of life," or "pattern of life," "life plan," "life scheme," and "line of movements" interchangeably. In the normally developing child, initial errors will be gradually corrected until the life style becomes adjusted to the standards of his community and, in a wider sense, serves the progress of mankind. The basic pattern changes only when awareness develops of disturbing discrepancies between a particular style and the logic of everyday life. Such discrepancies become manifest most clearly when a challenge is faced. If through psychotherapy a patient can be encouraged to become aware of these discrepancies to increase his self-understanding and use his common sense, his erroneous style of life may change.

The three main problems of life. Adler divided the main problems of life into three categories: occupational, social, and sexual. This division was first drawn in 1917, in a series of lectures, and later published in *Understanding Human Nature* (1927). He showed that a child's choice of what he wanted to be later revealed who and what had influenced him the most so far. He considered it a danger signal if an adolescent after the age of thirteen continued to insist that he had no idea of what he wanted to be. This, he pointed out, may mean a disinclination to become a useful member of society.

Because a second main problem is social, individual psychology is included among the "social psychologies." Adler emphasized, all through his writings, that human functions develop in relation to, and as an expression of, our relation to our fellow men. Speech, for instance, develops as an expression of our striving to communicate with one another in the best possible way. Consequently, in children and in adults, disturbances of speech often expressed a blocking of human relations.

Finally, there is the sexual problem. In 1910, Adler coined the term "masculine protest" (1909–1920), denoting a striving to be powerful, to describe an overcompensation for feeling unmanly, in men as well as in women. In his later writings, this term was limited to women who protest against their sexual role through frigidity and other sexual difficulties, on the one hand, or through tomboy activities, on the other. Such girls usually grow up feeling less appreciated than boys and, consequently, feel inferior both as human beings and in their role as women.

In his later writings, Adler also always stressed that sexuality symbolically expresses the individual's relation to the whole of mankind and can be understood only when seen in the total context, rather than as a problem of the single individual.

For instance, he pointed out that seemingly insurmountable difficulties of marital adjustment or sexual deviations develop whenever an individual aims to gratify only himself through sex activities. On the other hand, if he considers the gratification of his partner first, neither he nor his partner will feel abused. This will create the desire to perpetuate married life unconditionally.

Family constellation. Between the years 1918 and 1928, Adler made his original observations on the influence that birth order exerts in siblings. He stressed the fact that siblings are usually very different from one another, in spite of their similar physical inheritance. The second-born, for instance, often behaves as if he always had to outdo someone; he may be very ambitious, is often of the "me too" type, and may constantly feel slighted. Unless he learns to adjust to reality, he may perpetuate his exaggerated struggle for equality, which repeats his childhood competition with his older sibling. He then may experience marked difficulties in cooperating with any group. On the other hand, his ambitiousness may result in positive achievements and, if he learns to adjust realistically, may stand him in good stead. He often, however, discourages an older sibling through his overactivity. This is particularly true if the older sibling is a boy followed by a rapidly maturing sister. Adler described the youngest in a family to seem often to be cast from a different mold. If his older siblings are intellectually inclined the youngest may decide to become a dancer, actor, or musician. Thus, he may often be able to earn his living earlier than his siblings. He may, however, attach himself too closely to his mother who, in turn, seeks to keep him as her baby, preventing him from developing independence.

Dreams. Adler's interest in the manifestations of the unconscious had originally been aroused by Freud's investigation of dream material. In his book on the inferiority of organs (1907), he first examined dreams that are related to physical difficulties, for instance, when patients with enuresis and malformations of the urinary tract dream about swimming. Adler never accepted Freud's theory that dreams represent the fulfillment of infantile sexual wishes, and he emphasized the limitation this theory placed upon the understanding of dreams. He did accept Freud's distinction between the manifest and the latent content of dreams (Adler 1936), and he also used Freud's method of free association for the understanding of dreams, although with modification and restriction.

Adler himself made many original contributions to the theory of dreams. He showed that dreaming is in itself an indication that the dreamer feels inadequate to solve his problems while awake. He suggested that this is why courageous, well-adjusted people dream but rarely. He added the original thought that a dreamer may becloud certain issues in the same way that an orator or writer may use metaphors and symbols if he does not understand his subject well. Adler also stressed the necessity of integrating the interpretation of dreams with the endeavor to understand the whole personality and not to look for symbols with over-all applicability. This approach again differentiates his method of dream interpretation from Freud's, particularly from the latter's early method.

Adler showed how some of the meaning of dreams can be revealed by studying directions and movements expressed in them. For instance, dreams of falling occur to people who are afraid of losing prestige after having achieved a certain standing. On the other hand, dreams of flying may occur to ambitious people who strive for superiority but who are afraid that they may not achieve it. Dreams about dead people suggest that the dreamer is still closely attached to a deceased person, as if the person were still alive. Dreams of missing a train or a boat indicate fear of losing opportunities but may also denote a tendency to avoid exposing oneself to the possibility of defeat by coming late. Dreams of examination indicate an exaggerated fear of being put to a test. The common dream of being improperly clothed is found to spring from a fear that imperfections may be discovered.

A complete absence of dreams may have various significance. For instance, a patient may for a long period have no dreams at the beginning of or during psychotherapy. This suggests that the patient hesitates to cooperate and, therefore, forgets his dreams, knowing that dream interpretation constitutes an important part of therapy. The therapist is usually justified in assuring the patient that he will dream again when he becomes less resistant. Adler also pointed out that the mentally deficient usually do not have dreams. Since the dream represents the result of a creative, imaginative struggle to overcome conflicts, of which the mentally deficient are not capable, the absence of dreaming is understandable.

The neuroses. In 1913 and 1914, Adler enlarged his original description of the neurotic pattern (1912). He defined the neurotic symptom as a safeguard behind which the patient retreated in order to be protected from the firing line of life. Later (1931) he described and explained the "yes, but" pattern underlying the neuroses: the "yes" standing for the neurotic's apparent acceptance of his obligations, the "but" for his actual retreat behind neurotic symptoms in order to be excused from his responsibilities and to try to avoid the possibility of failure.

Criminality. Criminality may develop in anyone who feels that the world is against him and that fighting is his only hope of success (1931). The style of the criminal, he wrote, is to say "no" to the demands of society. Adler suggested various ways of trying to induce the criminal to change his pattern of destructive behavior.

Adler made another important contribution by describing the childhood patterns of the later neurotic and later criminal. He observed (1931) that the potentially neurotic child is usually shy, obedient, and easily deterred from what may lead to defeat. He may stay away from other children's play, excusing himself on the ground of being too tired. He thus gives an early indication of the "yes, but" style of the adult neurotic. The potentially criminal child, on the other hand, is destructive and rebellious. Like the adult criminal, he says No to the demands of society, and he fights. Such patterns may be found, temporarily, in many children but are normally rejected after a trying-out period. In the adult neurotic or criminal, they represent, however, life-long patterns.

Organization of the school of individual psychology. In 1914, Adler founded the *Internationale Zeitschrift für Individualpsychologie*, which, after several interruptions caused by political upheavals, terminated publication in 1951. The English-language *International Journal of Individual Psychology* was started in 1935, with Adler as editor. It has steadily increased its scope and, at present, it appears semiannually, with Heinz Ansbacher as editor.

At the time of Adler's death, there were 23 individual psychologic groups in various cities in Europe and the United States. Several of them conducted mental hygiene clinics and training institutes. Adler visited most of the groups while on lecture tours, thus adding periodically to the training of the members.

Between 1922 and 1930 five international congresses were held under Adler's chairmanship. After World War II, the International Association of Individual Psychology continued to hold congresses.

ALEXANDRA ADLER

[*For the historical context of Adler's work, see* PSYCHOANALYSIS, *article on* CLASSICAL THEORY; PSYCHIATRY; *and the biography of* FREUD. *For further discussion of Adler's ideas see* INDIVIDUAL PSYCHOLOGY. *Other relevant material may be found in* SYMPATHY AND EMPATHY.]

WORKS BY ADLER

1898   *Gesundheitsbuch für das Schneidergewerbe.* Wegweiser der Gewerbehygiene, Vol. 5. Berlin: Heymann.

(1907) 1917   *Study of Organ Inferiority and Its Psychical Compensation: A Contribution to Clinical Medicine.* Nervous and Mental Disease Monograph Series, No. 24. New York: Nervous and Mental Diseases Pub. → First published in German.

(1909–1920) 1964   *Practice and Theory of Individual Psychology.* Rev. ed. New York: Harcourt. → First published in German. Contains 28 papers originally published in medical journals between 1909 and 1920. A paperback edition was published in 1959 by Littlefield.

(1912) 1930   *The Neurotic Constitution: Outlines of a Comparative Individualistic Psychology and Psychotherapy.* New York: Dodd. → First published as *Über den nervösen Charakter.*

(1927) 1946   *Understanding Human Nature.* New York: Greenberg. → First published as *Menschenkenntnis.* A paperback edition was published in 1957 by Premier Books.

1928   *Kurze Bemerkungen über Vernunft, Intelligenz und Schwachsinn. Internationale Zeitschrift für Individualpsychologie* 6:267–272.

(1930) 1963   *The Problem Child: The Life Style of the Difficult Child as Analyzed in Specific Cases.* With an introduction by Kurt A. Adler. New York: Putnam. → First published as *Die Technik der Individualpsychologie.* Volume 2: Die Seele der schwererziehbaren Schulkinder. Twenty case-study chapters of interviews with children, their parents, and teachers in Adler's open community child guidance center.

(1931) 1960   *What Life Should Mean to You.* London: Allen & Unwin. → A paperback edition was published in 1958 by Capricorn Books.

(1933) 1939   *Social Interest: A Challenge to Mankind.* New York: Putnam. → First published as *Der Sinn des Lebens.* A paperback edition was published in 1964 by Capricorn Books.

1936   On the Interpretation of Dreams. *International Journal of Individual Psychology* 2, no. 1:3–16.

1956   *The Individual Psychology of Alfred Adler.* Edited by Heinz L. Ansbacher and Rowena R. Ansbacher. New York: Basic Books. → A paperback edition was published in 1964 by Harper.

SUPPLEMENTARY BIBLIOGRAPHY

ADLER, ALEXANDRA (1938) 1948   *Guiding Human Misfits: A Practical Application of Individual Psychology.* New ed., rev. New York: Philosophical Library.

ADLER, KURT A.; and DEUTSCH, DANICA (editors)   1959   *Essays in Individual Psychology: Contemporary Application of Alfred Adler's Theories.* New York: Grove Press.

BOTTOME, PHYLLIS (1939) 1957   *Alfred Adler: Apostle of Freedom.* 3d ed. London: Faber.

DREIKURS, RUDOLF (1933) 1950   *Fundamentals of Adlerian Psychology.* New York: Greenberg. → First published as *Einführung in die Individual–Psychologie.*

International Journal of Individual Psychology. → Published since 1935; title varies.

ORGLER, HERTHA (1939) 1963   *Alfred Adler; The Man and His Work: Triumph Over the Inferiority Complex.*
3d ed. rev. and enl. London: Daniel. → A paperback edition was published in 1965 by Putnam.

PAPANEK, HELENE; and PAPANEK, ERNST   1961   Individual Psychology Today. *American Journal of Psychotherapy* 15:4–26.

ADMINISTERED PRICES

See the entries OLIGOPOLY; PRICES, *article on* PRICING POLICIES.

ADMINISTRATION

The articles under this heading deal primarily with the political aspects of administrative structures, processes, and behavior, as do also BUREAUCRACY; CENTRALIZATION AND DECENTRALIZATION; *and* INTERNATIONAL ORGANIZATION, *article on* ADMINISTRATION. *The academic study of these subjects is discussed in* PUBLIC ADMINISTRATION. *Relevant materials going beyond but not excluding the political sphere will be found in* BUDGETING; BUSINESS MANAGEMENT; DECISION MAKING; INDUSTRIAL RELATIONS; ORGANIZATIONS; *and* PLANNING, SOCIAL.

I
THE ADMINISTRATIVE FUNCTION

One way to define the "function" of administration is to state the objective that administrative action is expected to attain. Thus, it is often said that the function of administration is to "carry out" or "execute" or "implement" policy decisions, or to coordinate activity in order to accomplish some common purpose, or simply to achieve cooperation in the pursuit of a shared goal.

Another way is to describe what administrators do and to determine the consequences and the implications of their activities. This has the advantage of avoiding an unresolvable argument about what they ought to do and what their purposes should be. It seeks to discover function, not to prescribe it.

Of course, even a description contains within itself many implicit assumptions about what is worth describing and what may be ignored. One cannot describe everything about any phenomenon, and the process of selection is an expression of convictions or guesses about what is significant for the purposes at hand. The convictions underlying this discussion of the function of administration are that administration is a process of arriving at decisions operationally homologous to other decision-making processes in large-scale organizations, and that the importance of administration lies not in the uniqueness of its function but in the increasing prominence of administrators as compared to other participants in the making of decisions. For the purposes of this discussion, "administrators" will refer to appointed officers who supervise others and will be confined, for the sake of simplicity, to administrators in governmental service, even though much that follows is applicable to nongovernmental administrators as well.

Functions of public administrators

The function of public administration is quite similar to the functions of other political institutions: legislative bodies, chief executives, courts, and special interest groups.

Administrative legislation. Administrative agencies produce large quantities of legislation, and knowing "the law" on a subject often means mastering the body of relevant administrative regulations and decisions, as well as constitutional provisions, statutes, and judicial decisions and opinions. Even in the United States, where the constitution of the nation and the individual constitutions of the 50 states specify that legislative powers are vested in the respective legislative bodies, a vast collection of administrative legislation has accumulated. To avoid violation of constitutional provisions, this product of administrative agencies, which has been called "sublegislation" or "quasi legislation," may be invalidated by the courts if there is no specific statute authorizing its issuance and generally defining its scope. The Code of Federal Regulations, a codification of the regulations of all the federal administrative agencies in the United States, is longer than the United States Code, the codification of all federal statutes in force. In countries in which a separation of governmental powers has not been adopted, or in which legislative institutions are not strongly developed, administrative legislation may assume even larger proportions.

Administrative agencies often parallel the procedures of legislative bodies in the way they formulate and promulgate legislation. They may hold hearings, conduct investigations and commission studies, and consult informally with interested persons and organizations. Their hearings usually furnish opportunities for the ventilation of conflicting views, and their deliberations offer opportunities for reconciliation of differences. Their policy pronouncements are legitimated according to prescribed procedures and are publicized in prescribed fashion. In the U.S. government these proceedings are now mandated upon the administrators by statute. But the proceedings were much the same before the adoption of the statutory mandate, and they are commonly followed in state and local administrative agencies even when not absolutely required. One "function" of administration, then, is legislation.

Executive duties. Administrative officers appoint, supervise, discipline, remove, and direct subordinates. They prepare and defend programs for their agencies. They draw up and justify budgetary requests and make or authorize expenditures under the terms of appropriations made to them. They issue contracts and make purchases. They represent their agencies to the outside world, especially to protect their areas of jurisdiction. They find ways to appoint personal staff assistants in addition to their formally designated aides so as to assure themselves of loyal help in planning strategies and acting on plans. Collectively these activities constitute the executive function of administration.

Administrative adjudication. Administrative personnel dispose of a great deal of business essentially judicial in character. The bulk consists of rulings on appeals from administrative actions, including complaints by private citizens and pleas by public officers and employees against acts of their superiors. More of these are handled within administrative hierarchies than in the courts. In addition, administrative agencies conduct and decide proceedings by private parties against one another, including complaints by employees against employers, tenants against landlords, shippers against common carriers, competitors for licenses, and many others. Indeed, France and countries employing the French system of jurisprudence have established a hierarchy of administrative courts separate from the ordinary courts to hear cases against the government and review grievances of public personnel. In the United States the initial hearings are held within the regular administrative establishment (increasingly by specialized hearing examiners), and actions proceed up a ladder of administrative appeals until all administrative remedies are exhausted, whereupon they may usually be carried to the ordinary courts, which now tend to review the fairness of the procedures and the reasonableness of the judgments instead of trying the cases anew. Even in the United States influential sources have proposed the creation of a separate system of administrative courts. These proposals have not been adopted, however, and the judicial proceedings of administrative agencies (referred to as "quasi-judicial" or "administrative adjudication" to avoid conflict with the doctrine of separation of powers) remain reviewable by ordinary courts. On the whole, adjudicative procedures in administrative bodies are deliberately kept less formal than the procedures in courts of law, but there has been a tendency toward "judicialization" in recent years, and the distinctions are sometimes less pronounced than one might anticipate. So the conduct of judicial proceedings is another function of administration.

Administrators as interest groups. Public administrative officials behave much like nongovernmental interest groups. They draft and propose legislation to legislatures, testify at legislative hearings and inquiries, rally support for bills they favor, and mobilize opposition against bills they oppose. Many of them assign specialists to lobby with legislators ("legislative liaison officer" is the American euphemism) and maintain advertising and public relations ("information and education") staffs. They enter into alliances with other public agencies and with interest groups, particularly groups representing the clienteles that the public administrators serve or regulate. Their representatives even appear as witnesses at hearings conducted by other agencies. Since administrative officers are clothed with official powers in a way that interest groups are not, they have a weapon for bargaining that distinguishes them from private groups. But this is only one of their weapons; the others are the same as those of private groups. In this respect, exerting political pressure is an administrative function.

In fact, since some administrators owe their appointments to political party connections and occasionally use their discretion over employment and over decisions for partisan ends, they must be regarded as involved in the affairs of the parties. And since administrative agencies often include advisory committees made up of spokesmen for interests regulated or served, or are headed by boards comprising members of the interests affected, and generally consult extensively with these interests before taking official action (the U.S. Department of Agriculture goes so far as to conduct referenda on crop quotas), the agencies may even be said to perform the function of representation. In other words, the functions of administration may be considered virtually as broad as the functions of government.

The development of administration

The performance of all the above functions by administrators is not a new phenomenon. It had counterparts in ancient China, for example, and in ancient Rome. Its analogue was to be found in the Ottoman Empire and in medieval Europe even under feudalism. It was a source of papal leadership in the Holy Roman Empire. It was the instrument of royal power in the emergence of many national states. The distinctive feature of parliamentary democracy was the legislature's acquisition of control over the royal ministers and functionaries whose jurisdiction encompassed most of the activities of government. In the United States both Congress and the president have historically recognized the breadth of administrative functions, and a good part of the rivalry between the legislative and executive branches turns on the determination of each to hold administrators responsible to itself rather than to its competitor. In short, administration has never been a single, limited set of activities; rather, it has had a variety of functions so broad as to constitute the means by which most of the business of large governments has been conducted throughout history.

The broad powers of administrators have always presented problems to the formally designated leaders of every governmental system, for administrators tend to develop vested interests in the territories or activities over which they have jurisdiction and to exercise their authority with growing disregard for the formal rulers, and even in defiance of them. Rulers in all ages have faced the problem of preventing the reins of government from slipping out of their hands and into the hands of their administrative officials.

The problem was relatively easily solved in societies that were simple in comparison to the modern industrial state. The tasks of government were relatively uncomplicated, so the formal rulers could keep themselves well informed, even about details. The size of bureaucracies was comparatively modest, so the rulers could maintain personal contact with many of their subordinates. The duties of administrators were not highly specialized, so an untrained and inexperienced but obedient man could easily replace an official of long experience who showed signs of contumacy. Even so, many rulers lost effective command of many of their administrators. But at least they were in a position to reassert their leadership if they had the will and skill to try.

The rise of industrialism dramatically altered the position of the formal rulers. The kinds and the volume of services that governments of industrial states are called upon to provide multiplied rapidly. The varieties, intensity, and techniques of governmental regulation of economic and social relations increased abruptly. Even the traditional activities of government—defense, maintenance of internal order, administration of justice, and collection of taxes—grew more complicated and technical. Administrative departments and bureaus burgeoned profusely. Bureaucracies expanded quickly. And the urgency of specialization, technical training, and thorough mastery of procedure, as well as of substantive information, mounted correspondingly. No longer could officials be transferred casually from one office to another, or individuals plucked from unrelated nongovernmental functions and assigned successfully to government posts. No longer would obedience and loyalty to the ruler be the principal test of fitness for public administration; technical competence would have to get a higher priority if governments were to operate effectively.

By the end of the nineteenth century most industrial states had adopted some form of merit system for selecting administrative officials in the service of the national governments, and many extended the practice to subnational governments as well (although the state and local governments of the United States have on the whole been slow to follow the lead of the federal government). Most such administrators are now appointed on the basis of performance on examinations and of educational qualifications and experience and are protected against arbitrary removal. In Europe young people enter the public service at an early age and spend their lives in it, advancing as they accumulate seniority and demonstrate proficiency. In the United States people are recruited at all levels of administration and at all ages to fill specific jobs. In either case, expertise and aptitude are the qualities sought.

For the formal rulers of industrial states, consequently, the power of administrators has been especially unsettling. Not only do administrative agencies serve as governmental decision-making organs alternative (and even rival) to all other organs of government, but administrative officials are less and less vulnerable to the influences of the formal leaders. Too much goes on, too many people are involved, and the activities are much too technical for the rulers to keep track; the system has almost outrun their capacity to monitor it. Moreover, the administrators are quite firmly entrenched —by virtue of their expertise, even when their tenure enjoys no legal guarantees and safeguards— and immune to many of the sanctions in the hands of the rulers. Indeed, since it is from the administrators that the rulers get much of their information about governmental needs and performance,

and since the administrators are so much better informed and so expert, the rulers are often compelled to accept and support judgments and recommendations of their nominal subordinates. More than ever before, administrators have become a political power to be reckoned with.

The traditional organs of government did not welcome into the governmental arena the specialized, increasingly autonomous, and ever more numerous administrators. Chief executives fostered reorganization after reorganization to reduce the autonomy of administrative agencies and fought against the extension of merit system procedures to the top administrative levels. Legislative bodies delegated authority reluctantly and often hedged the authority with detailed restrictions on the substance and procedure of its exercise. Judges insisted on the right to examine administrative decisions and to reverse decisions that seemed unreasonable or unfairly reached. Political parties often opposed merit system requirements. Regulated interest groups fought the establishment of the regulatory agencies affecting them unless and until the interests managed to "capture" the agencies and obtain more sympathetic decisions. The administrators did not have a smooth road to political influence.

Yet they had to be accepted because no one could think of any other institution to assume the new burdens and responsibilities of government in the industrial era. The times called for more legislation than the legislature could possibly furnish, more management and direction of work forces than the chief executive could hope to provide, more adjudication than the courts could accommodate, more skilled personnel than the parties could present, broader social perspectives than special interests typically exhibited. Every older participant in the governmental process viewed the new development uneasily, sometimes voiced protest, and occasionally resisted it. In the end, however, out of necessity, they all acquiesced.

So the function of administration is now to share, and to share importantly, in governing. Administrators are powerful partners in governing coalitions and are significant factors in the shaping of governmental policies and practices.

Administrative powers and influence

The other organs of government are well endowed with means of influencing the behavior of administrators. Legislatures possess the powers of appropriation, of legislation (with which they can theoretically alter or abolish administrative agencies), of investigation, and of immunity to legal action for opinions and charges voiced on the floors of their chambers. Power over budgets and appointments and removals from high office, personal influence growing out of party and popular support, and the majesty and legitimacy of executive office lend great authority to chief executives. Courts have their power to review. Interest groups are as expert in their fields as the administrators they deal with. Parties have access to legislators and executives by virtue of their control of nominations for elective office and their influence on voters. Administrators must come to terms with all these participants in government and politics in order to survive.

Administrative discretion. When administrators act in their legislative, executive, judicial, interest group, or partisan capacities, they enjoy wide discretion for several reasons. First, the directives they receive from the other participants often express abstract principles in highly general terms; it is frequently not clear what kinds of specific actions would be in accord with the directives and what kinds would violate them. These crucial specifics the administrators must announce, and their own views and the positions of their agencies inevitably play a large part in the character of the decisions. However strenuously other participants seek to expand and elaborate directives to administrators, such directives are limited because they have to provide for extremely broad categories of events; they are inevitably expressed in generalities. And it is in the ambiguities of the generalities that administrators find the opportunity (if not the mandate) to exercise discretion about what concrete acts are indicated.

Second, as efforts are made to expand and elaborate instructions to administrators, the volume of communication reaches such a level that conflicts and contradictions are certain to appear. In these internal inconsistencies, administrators may find plausible justifications for any course of action they elect to pursue.

Third, even when they receive unambiguous communiqués, administrators may choose to act either vigorously and imaginatively or cautiously and ploddingly. They may move quickly and forcefully or hesitantly and fearfully. They may work enthusiastically or make evident their reluctance. The effects of a policy are determined in larger measure by these administrative choices than by the text of the directives that presumably govern the actions.

Fourth, should other participants in the political process attempt to impose their own ideas of appropriate action on administrators, the administrators generally prove capable of defending their positions. They may retreat into the labyrinths of law, or mobilize their clienteles and their friends in other organs of government, or assemble masses of expert opinion to support their contentions. They may appeal to the general public through public relations techniques. They may even engender crises to prove their points. Whatever their strategies, they are rarely passive or docile, even when the highest formal rulers are involved.

Influence in dictatorships. The influence of administrators is not equally great in all systems of government. Under totalitarian governments, for example, the opportunities for administrators to employ their strategies are restricted by the suppression of groupings with which they might join forces in order to maximize autonomy and by the rulers' use of a single party to maintain close surveillance and ensure loyalty and obedience—even to the extent of assigning political officials to military units. Yet reports from the Soviet Union suggest that political leaders have been disappointed over the interpretations placed on political directives by administrative officers and that administrators have sometimes falsified records in order to conceal their deviations from official policy pronouncements. Like Western countries, the Soviet Union has had recourse to relatively frequent reorganization of its administrative machinery to secure full compliance. Even under dictatorship, then, administrators have acquired political influence—limited, it is true, but not insignificant.

Influence in developing countries. At the other extreme from dictatorships, administrators in underdeveloped countries whose governments are attempting to industrialize enjoy unusually great influence. The small reservoirs of trained and technically expert personnel in these nations tend to concentrate in key administrative posts. Administrative careers are often more highly prized and respected than political or business careers, and the weakness of political, commercial, and industrial institutions often puts administrators in the strongest position in the political process. In Japan, for example, it was the administrators who organized the industrialization of the economy, and administrators or former administrators are leaders in every phase of Japanese political life. Nevertheless, Japan has also developed strong representative institutions, whereas in many less advanced states politics consists largely of rivalries among wings of the bureaucracy (including the armed forces). Administrative discretion is probably broadest in such situations, the only effective check on administrators being other administrators.

Influence in industrial democracies. Somewhere between the powerful bureaucracies of the underdeveloped countries and the subservient bureaucracies of the industrialized dictatorships stand the administrators of the governmental agencies of the Western democracies. On the one hand, they must contend with strong centers of power throughout their societies. Business, labor, agriculture, the professions, competitive political parties, elected officials, ethnic groups, and many other segments of the population are organized, alert, aggressive, well financed, vocal, respected, and politically sophisticated; they can be neither suppressed nor ignored, and thus they impose on the administrators' freedom of action restraints almost unknown to administrators in developing nations. On the other hand, the pluralism of the democratic system and its emphasis on law and legalism offer administrators in the democracies many chances to broaden their discretion and intensify their autonomy that their counterparts in totalitarian systems never enjoy.

In short, wherever administrators have acquired discretionary powers, administrative agencies have become centers of political decision. In the dictatorships these centers are still overshadowed by the single parties permitted in such states. In the developing nations they tend to overshadow much weaker decision-making institutions. In the Western democracies they are parallel to the alternative institutions and provide an additional arena for the peaceful resolution of controversies. But in all cases people turn with ever greater frequency to administrative agencies for service, for assistance, for redress of grievances, and for relief from policies that affect them adversely.

Research trends and needs

The rise of administrators to political prominence generated a spate of literature on administrative theory, chiefly in the twentieth century. Three scholarly approaches to the subject have emerged. One may be described as an engineering approach; it is concerned with the techniques of arranging work forces and their activities in order to achieve the maximum output at the lowest cost. The second views administration from the standpoint of political analysis, describing the characteristics of bureaucracies, the place of bureaucracies in the political systems in which they develop and the consequences of their development in terms of the shifting distribution of political influence, the

impact on policy formation, and the philosophy of government. The third approach is sociological, treating organizations as a class of phenomena moved by a common dynamics and displaying regularities of behavior (i.e., governed by "laws" of organizational behavior) that can be discovered by empirical research and formulated systematically in a body of theory roughly analogous to theories in the life sciences and the physical sciences. All three approaches overlap and affect one another, but most writing on administration emphasizes one or another sufficiently to distinguish them.

Engineering approach. The engineering viewpoint found its earliest expression in the work of Frederick W. Taylor (1911–1912), which blossomed into the "scientific management" movement. The theoretical assumption of this movement was that the speed, cost, and quality of goods and services are dependent variables that can be maximized by adjustments of a number of independent variables, including division of labor, patterns of supervision, financial incentives, flow of materials, and physical methods and conditions of work performance. "Human factors in management" were added to the roster of independent variables after the famous Hawthorne Experiment (Mayo 1933, *The Human Problems of an Industrial Civilization;* Roethlisberger & Dickson 1939, *Management and the Worker*) disclosed that social interaction among workers and between workers and management had a profound effect on output. Study of the variables has been steadily refined over the years, particularly as high-speed computers, social interaction laboratories, and other devices are brought to bear on the analysis. Nevertheless, the theoretical foundations have remained substantially unaltered; the efficiency of organizations is related in specified ways to designated factors and can be increased by deliberate manipulation of those factors on the basis of scientific investigation. It appears that some very substantial improvements in operations have in fact been achieved by this means. At any rate, much of the writing in business management, industrial engineering, public administration, industrial psychology, and industrial sociology rests on this theoretical base.

Political analysis approach. For writers of the engineering orientation, and for some concerned with the politics of administration (Finer 1932), administrative organizations are largely neutral instruments that do the bidding of others. But many writers who approach administration from the standpoint of political analysis see bureaucracies as active participants in politics. Max Weber (1906–1924) and Carl J. Friedrich (1937; *see also* Friedrich & Cole 1932) were among the first to treat administrators as the key to governmental control in any modern state; the rationality and expertise of the bureaucracy are now required for rulership, they argued, and whoever controls the administrators can govern the state. Indeed, they suggested, the expertise of the administrators may make it virtually impossible for any outside influence to control them. Some later theorists (Burnham 1941, *The Managerial Revolution*) did in fact take the position that administrators have attained dominance in politics and every other phase of organized life in industrial societies. A host of polemicists, writing denunciatory tracts rather than scholarly analyses, also seized upon this theme to indict "the new despotism" of administrators and the "dead hand of bureaucracy," but their outcries seldom added much to an understanding of the phenomenon against which they inveighed without restraint. Others regarded administrators as outriders of a ruling class (Kingsley 1944, *Representative Bureaucracy*). Many treated administrators as independent and highly important, but not dominant, elements in the process of government (Neumann 1942, *Behemoth*; Truman 1951, *The Governmental Process*), a view reflected in expressions of anxiety in both the United States and England and in proposals for increased executive control (U.S. President's Committee on Administrative Management 1937) or increased legislative control (e.g., U.S. Congress, Senate 1937; Great Britain, Ministry of Reconstruction 1918; Great Britain, Committee on Ministers' Powers 1932). Increasing attention is now given also to the growing political influence of the rank and file of governmental bureaucracies as they organize in trade unions and professional associations (Sayre & Kaufman 1960). Dwight Waldo (1948) undertook to demonstrate that writers on administration, as well as administrators, have an implicit political theory about who should govern. The expanding power of administrators and bureaucrats is thus engendering a re-examination and modification of philosophies of government, traditional and contemporary, democratic and totalitarian. Research and writing on the problem will doubtless multiply in the years ahead, for the problem, from all present indications, seems likely to grow more pressing with the passage of time.

Sociological approach. The sociological approach is increasingly being used in work on organization theory, bureaucracy, and administrative behavior. It differs from the work of political analysts in that it is more concerned with the internal structure and operation of organizations than with the political consequences of growing bureaucratic influence. Yet, unlike the engineering orientation, it is not focused exclusively on factors related to output, and therefore it tends to be more comprehensive; it aims at a complete, systematic description of organizational behavior. Much of the research is experimental, and most of the reports of findings or statements of theory are studiously rigorous. There have even been a number of attempts to present mathematical models of organizations. (An excellent summation of much of the relevant literature will be found in March & Simon 1958.) Most researchers prefer striking out in their own directions and devising their own experiments to duplicating the experiments of others, so the level of theorizing is still very modest and the accumulation of evidence very slow.

The literature on administration has been enriched by a large number of case studies and case histories, especially in the field of public administration since the beginning of World War II. The cases have not been mobilized around any common theoretical statements and have therefore been employed for illustrative and teaching purposes rather than for the testing of generalizations. Nevertheless, they constitute a large reservoir of experience and observation upon which theorists may find a way to draw profitably.

The function of administration has both stimulated and challenged theories about administration. The expansion of the role of administrators in government has been especially rapid, but similar observations could be made about administrators in commerce, industry, charitable associations, universities, trade unions, and other forms of organized activity. As more and more decision making of all kinds gravitates toward administrative officers, and as these officers come to rival and perhaps even to overshadow the other decision-making institutions in governments and other organizations, we can anticipate an intensification of study, experimentation, and theorizing in all three approaches to administration. What the fruit of this activity will be—whether, indeed, it will be truly fruitful at all—remains to be seen.

HERBERT KAUFMAN

BIBLIOGRAPHY

BARKER, ERNEST (1937) 1944 *The Development of Public Services in Western Europe, 1660–1930.* New York and London: Oxford Univ. Press.
BURNHAM, JAMES 1941 *The Managerial Revolution: What Is Happening in the World.* New York: Day.

→ A paperback edition was published in 1960 by Indiana Univ. Press.

FINER, HERMAN (1932) 1949 *The Theory and Practice of Modern Government.* Rev. ed. New York: Holt.

FRIEDRICH, CARL J. (1937) 1950 *Constitutional Government and Democracy: Theory and Practice in Europe and America.* Rev. ed. Boston: Ginn. → First published as *Constitutional Government and Politics: Nature and Development.*

FRIEDRICH, CARL J.; and COLE, TAYLOR 1932 *Responsible Bureaucracy: A Study of the Swiss Civil Service.* Cambridge, Mass.: Harvard Univ. Press.

GREAT BRITAIN, COMMITTEE ON MINISTERS' POWERS 1932 *Report.* Papers by Command, Cmd. 4060. London: H.M. Stationery Office.

GREAT BRITAIN, MINISTRY OF RECONSTRUCTION, MACHINERY OF GOVERNMENT COMMITTEE (1918) 1938 *Report.* Papers by Command, Cd. 9230. London: H.M. Stationery Office.

KINGSLEY, JOHN D. 1944 *Representative Bureaucracy: An Interpretation of the British Civil Service.* Yellow Springs, Ohio: Antioch Press.

MARCH, JAMES G.; and SIMON, HERBERT A. 1958 *Organizations.* New York: Wiley.

MAYO, ELTON (1933) 1946 *The Human Problems of an Industrial Civilization.* 2d ed. Boston: Division of Research, Graduate School of Business Administration, Harvard University.

MICHIGAN, UNIVERSITY OF, INSTITUTE OF PUBLIC ADMINISTRATION (1957) 1960 *Comparative Public Administration: A Selective Annotated Bibliography.* By Ferrel Heady and Sybil L. Stokes. 2d ed. Ann Arbor, Mich.: The Institute.

MORNSTEIN MARX, FRITZ 1957 *The Administrative State: An Introduction to Bureaucracy.* Univ. of Chicago Press.

NEUMANN, FRANZ LEOPOLD (1942) 1963 *Behemoth: The Structure and Practice of National Socialism 1933–1944.* 2d ed. New York: Octagon Books.

ROETHLISBERGER, FRITZ J.; and DICKSON, WILLIAM J. (1939) 1961 *Management and the Worker.* Cambridge, Mass.: Harvard Univ. Press. → A paperback edition was published in 1964 by Wiley.

SAYRE, WALLACE S.; and KAUFMAN, HERBERT 1960 *Governing New York City: Politics in the Metropolis.* New York: Russell Sage Foundation.

STEIN, HAROLD (editor) 1952 *Public Administration and Policy Development: A Case Book.* New York: Harcourt.

TAYLOR, FREDERICK W. (1911–1912) 1947 *Scientific Management.* 3 vols. in 1. New York: Harper. → Volume 1: *Scientific Management, Comprising Shop Management.* Volume 2: *The Principles of Scientific Management.* Volume 3: *Testimony Before the Special House Committee.*

TRUMAN, DAVID B. (1951) 1962 *The Governmental Process: Political Interests and Public Opinion.* New York: Knopf.

U.S. CONGRESS, SENATE, SELECT COMMITTEE ON INVESTIGATION OF EXECUTIVE AGENCIES 1937 *Investigation of Executive Agencies of the Government.* Senate Report 1275. 75th Congress, 1st Session.

U.S. PRESIDENT'S COMMITTEE ON ADMINISTRATIVE MANAGEMENT 1937 *Report of the Committee, With Studies of Administrative Management in the Federal Government.* Submitted to the President and to Congress in Accordance with Public Law No. 739, 74th Congress, 2d Session. Washington: U.S. Government Printing Office.

WALDO, DWIGHT 1948 *The Administrative State: A Study of the Political Theory of American Public Administration.* New York: Ronald Press.

WEBER, MAX (1906–1924) 1946 *From Max Weber: Essays in Sociology.* Translated and edited by Hans H. Gerth and C. Wright Mills. New York: Oxford Univ. Press.

YANAGA, CHITOSHI 1949 *Japan Since Perry.* New York: McGraw-Hill.

II

THE ADMINISTRATIVE PROCESS

The administrative process is, in essence, the making of rules, the adjudicating of cases, and the issuance of orders affecting the rights and obligations of private citizens and parties by public officials other than judges or legislators. It is the exercise of undifferentiated governmental power—that power which simultaneously encompasses making the law, deciding its application in particular cases, and commanding that specific acts be or not be performed. The history of constitutionalism in the West has been largely concerned with the differentiation of governmental power and the elaboration of procedures for its exercise and control. Although this development has never gone so far as to inhibit the concentration of governmental powers in the same hands in all fields of governmental action, it has given rise to a widely accepted set of political ideas that oppose such concentration.

These ideas are roughly expressed in the conceptions associated with "the rule of law" and "the separation of powers."

Rule of law. The meaning of the rule of law was given classic formulation by A. V. Dicey: "We mean, in the first place, that no man is punishable or can lawfully be made to suffer in body or goods except for a distinct breach of law established in the ordinary legal manner before the ordinary courts of the land. In this sense the rule of law is contrasted with every system of government based on the exercise by persons in authority of wide, arbitrary, or discretionary powers of constraint" ([1885] 1964, p. 188). Dicey's formulation places each person, regardless of his official position and no matter under whose authority he is acting, under the ordinary law and amenable to the ordinary courts for any violation of that law. Of course, even in Britain this has represented more of an ideal than an actuality. As an ideal, however, it has powerfully influenced the legal profession in both England and the United States and through that profession has conditioned the thinking of important sectors of public opinion. The amenability of the officials of government to the ordinary courts to account for the legality of their acts symbolizes both the independence of the judiciary and the supremacy of Parliament.

Separation of powers.   The doctrine of the rule of law has been powerfully reinforced in the United States by that of the separation of powers. These doctrines together form the simple model of government, widely held as the correct ideal, where one branch of government makes the law, another branch carries out the law, and a third branch decides cases arising under the law. It is this model of constitutional propriety that the administrative process violates in some measure. To accomplish an increasing range of objectives it has been found expedient and even necessary to invest the same hands with the power to make rules having the force of law, to adjudicate cases falling under these rules, and to issue binding orders.

For several centuries governments in England and the United States have been taking administrative action in such fields as public health, public safety, taxation, customs, immigration and other areas, in which powers were mingled and the vaunted supremacy of the rule of law itself avoided. However, a truly luxuriant growth of the administrative process has accompanied the development of complex, urban industrial society. In the United States the flowering of the administrative process dates from the creation of the Interstate Commerce Commission (ICC) in 1887. Its full maturity came with the New Deal and is most typically embodied in such agencies as the National Labor Relations Board (NLRB) and the Securities and Exchange Commission (SEC). In the states the growth came earlier and, indeed, the inability of state jurisdictions to cope with a transportation industry increasingly regional and even national in scope accounts in large part for federal action. But at a more fundamental level the states as the holders of the police power have always been in the habit of investing certain officials in the fields of health and safety with broad regulatory authority that could not be squared with any strict adherence to the separation-of-powers principle. Courts and public alike have found these exceptions so familiar that they have never forced reconsideration of the scope and validity of the principle violated.

The model of government that requires separate bodies to make the law, to enforce it, and to adjudicate cases arising under it breaks down in areas where expertness of knowledge, speed of action,

number of cases, need for prevention, and rapid change render its operation cumbersome and ineffective. In theory, the legislature might know enough and have time enough to enact and keep up to date a code of public-health laws adequate for the citizens' protection. In theory, aggrieved private citizens and zealous district attorneys might adequately police violations. And in theory, courts of general jurisdiction might know enough about public health to decide cases in such a fashion as to implement public policy adequately. In fact, however, in field after field the conditions requisite to the theory do not obtain. If rules are needed that reflect expert knowledge in a dynamic field, experts and not the legislature must make and remake them. If these rules are to be effectively enforced, preventive rather than remedial action must be available. A suit for damages, or even a criminal prosecution, is no substitute for preventive public-health measures to remove the potential cause of an epidemic. Knowledge, interest, and the vigor to ensure forceful action in developing and applying a concept in the public interest in any area is heavily dependent on program emphasis in organization structure and objective. Finally, the adjudication of cases by courts of general jurisdiction puts policy objectives at the mercy of judges who may not understand the subject matter or have a strong sense of urgency in policy fulfillment.

Administrative tribunals and values

The history of workmen's-compensation legislation exhibits the frustration of legislative policy in courts whose judges, trained in the common law, were unsympathetic to objectives that seemed to them to conflict with traditional property rights. Ultimately, administrative tribunals were resorted to as a means of circumventing judicial hostility and placing the development and enforcement of policy in sympathetic hands. In effect, the legislature gave to an administrative body plenary authority to effect a public policy the legislature could only formulate after a fashion but could not itself bring into detailed existence or continuously push and superintend. The administrative body was charged with the responsibility of developing a body of rules, almost a body of law, governing an area of public policy and ensuring that these rules and their enforcement kept pace with relevant new developments and the policy mandate.

Initially, there was much naive faith that administrative tribunals or commissions would provide an effective means of turning pressing public problems over to bodies of experts, who would develop, through the application of their expertise, impartial nonpolitical solutions to the problems—thus taking hot issues out of politics and creating agreement that had previously proved impossible. Faith in experts and the quest for policy without politics were common to the credo of nineteenth-century reform and have died hard.

Irritation with the courts and their tenderness for private property, together with a contempt for the separation-of-powers doctrine as political metaphysics designed to hamstring effective and prompt governmental action, converted many liberals to a belief in a more or less unfettered administrative process. Judicial misgivings and reluctance to abandon a detailed superintendence of administrative action, especially where significant property and other rights were involved, occasioned a long-drawn-out struggle to delineate the roles of courts and administrative bodies. The result has been a continuous judicial retreat from earlier positions, in which proceedings before an administrative body could be all but ignored and matters started from scratch in the court, to one where the record of the agency is accepted and the agency's finding upheld if supported by "substantial evidence." The scope of review became narrowed to one of the law, with great weight, on occasion, given to administrative interpretation of it. Courts have found that the price of overzealous superintendence of administrative bodies is either substituting themselves for the agencies whose work they are supposed to review or hamstringing the agencies—in effect paralyzing the public policy to which they were intended to give life. Gradually, there came to be an acceptance that the agencies' findings of fact were well nigh as conclusive as those of a jury.

The struggle over the roles of courts and agencies in the administrative process can be understood in terms of groups seeking expression through rival and competing institutions and in terms of differing sets of values whose realization is accentuated or diminished by the emphasis the rival institutions place on them. Whereas group analysis would concentrate on the differing group pressures and their modes of influence in administrative bodies, courts, legislatures, and executives, attention should also be paid to the procedures and values embedded in the different institutions. Liberals who at one time could see no ill in the untrammeled sway of the administrative process now have second thoughts regarding the fields of immigration and loyalty and security proceedings, where results are sometimes painful. In these cases they see real virtues in the courts. On the other hand, conservatives who at other times are vehe-

ment in their advocacy of judicial restraint on administrative action see little use for it in such instances. If the protection of the individual is highly valued the courts are in order. If policy is to be forwarded without hindrance the courts are an obstacle. The anguish of prosecutors and police before judicial safeguards increasing the difficulty of their task is paralleled by the rejoicing of the civil libertarian, who zealously seeks the protection of the individual with little concern for the problems of law enforcement.

The contrast between administrative concern with policy and court concern with individual rights is of course not nearly so black and white. Courts are concerned with the policy outcomes of their decisions and administrative agencies are concerned with the values of individual justice. The contrast, however, is justified in terms of emphasis. The courts have a general sphere of concern (although it is true the nonconstitutional courts are specialized); agencies, on the other hand, have a particular policy area to oversee and a public interest to promote; they cannot, therefore, be neutral toward the policy they are set up to effectuate. Again, however, the contrast may be too stark. The neutrality between state and individual in the courts is based on a commitment to the value of individual justice. This commitment is supposed to be not just the predilection of the court but also an overarching value of the political community. The conflict between the requirements of particular public policies and the demands of individual justice is unending. Neither value can be treated as an absolute without unacceptable loss. The dialectic of the resolution of the conflict is a constant process within agencies and between agencies, courts, legislatures, executives, and publics. However policy-bent, even in time of war, agencies can never, without danger, completely neglect the value of individual justice. And courts, however concerned that individual justice be done, still must reckon the cost to the political community.

Contrary and sometimes even contradictory value emphases are structured into political institutions and into the training and recruitment of their staffs. Thus, protagonists of differing value positions clash and interact in the ordinary processes of government. These value positions characteristically attract the support of the interests in the society who feel furthered by their action consequences. That this implies no necessary permanent commitment to particular institutions and the values expressed through them is well illustrated by the shifting attitudes of conservatives and liberals in the United States toward the Supreme Court.

Administrative agencies

The continuum between an administrative body and a court and the value conflict or disparity involved in the two kinds of governmental activity are well brought out in the critical connotations of the term "judicialized" administration. In many quarters this assumption of the judicial posture is regarded as the abandonment of the protective and fostering role appropriate to an administrative body in its policy area. Sitting back and waiting for the parties to present their case is frequently viewed as a retreat from the positive formulation and assertion of the public interest that is the appropriate function and use of the administrative process. In addition, the almost inevitable inequality in the resources of the parties at interest means that the adoption of the judicial role favors the regulated over those whom the regulations are designed to protect.

But while the judicialization of administration is criticized as a retreat from the positive role appropriate to the administrative process, it would be incorrect not to recognize that the administrative process implies concern of a judicial nature that differentiates it from simple executive action. Whereas a space agency or a department of defense may formulate rules of procedure to assure fairness in its procurement policies and even provide some review for decisions affecting those who do business with it, this is a long way from what is expected of administrative bodies in formulating rules and deciding cases.

A comparison of the ICC and the Civilian Aeronautics Board with the Department of Defense and the National Aeronautics and Space Administration is suggestive of the differing roles and what is appropriate to them. The clearest difference is that in the one case the ground and air transport are predominantly in private hands and in the other the responsibility for achieving the defense or space objectives belongs to government agencies. Much of the criticism of the regulatory agencies stems from the ambiguity of their responsibility. This responsibility calls for them to make rules and adjudicate cases in such a way that the self-interested action of private parties within the governmentally provided ground rules will produce results approximately in the public interest. Indeed, what is wanted is a positive program for a limited and public-goal-oriented form of laissez-faire.

Critics of the commissions frequently seem to suppose that there is a way to achieve the virtues of both government and private enterprise while avoiding the vices of either. A frequent result is to weaken the mechanism of competition in the allocation of resources without replacing it with a superior form of political decision making. The major task of regulation is the search for a means to produce a body of rules and an adjudication of their application such that the private interests of the regulated parties will produce a publicly desirable result. The most serious weakness is the almost inevitable belief in the sovereign efficacy of more rather than less regulation on the part of the regulators. Witness the unwillingness of the ICC to allow the no longer monopolistic railroads to compete for survival with the unregulated private carriage lest the competition jeopardize the vulnerable common carrier trucking and inland waterways transport.

Indeed, the sense of paternal responsibility on the part of the regulatory body may lead to a sincere belief that its charges, unless prevented, will do themselves harm. Such a view stems readily enough from the depression-born concept of destructive competition. The identification of the regulators with the regulated frequently leads to the charge that the agencies are industry-minded.

Given a sense of responsibility for the running of the railroad, even though lacking full power to do the actual running, it is scarcely surprising that regulators share many of the preoccupations of management. And since the success of management in the regulated enterprise may well depend on managing the regulators, it is scarcely surprising that this should occur. While the regulated must be concerned with the viability of their enterprise, the consumers of their product can scarcely be expected to rise to a statesmanlike concern over the profits needed to maintain the services they enjoy. Selfish interests weigh more heavily than theoretic concern with the health of a system for which individuals feel small responsibility and which they feel unable to affect.

The adversary balance of interests that pressure-group analysts have seen as providing a basis for freedom of regulators to pursue an independent course is important in providing political freedom of maneuver. But even when agencies can play off the contending parties against each other, a long-term concern with the efficient operation of the regulated activity must give an appearance of industry-mindedness. Few agencies with the political strength to act would have faith that a neutral judicial posture between the parties is likely to produce a desirable result. The attitude of the agency is more like that of the nurse to a child than of a servant to an acknowledged master, though an occasional commission member may have the latter perspective.

The charge of industry-mindedness that is leveled against some commissions oddly enough is rarely raised with such concern about government bureaus and departments. The departments of Agriculture and Labor or the Army Corps of Engineers scarcely need apologize for championing their constituencies. Doubtless the judicial aura of an administrative agency makes any such open partisanship offensive. Yet the duty to foster a national transportation system is scarcely less compelling or markedly different from fostering the nation's agriculture.

The administrative process has been utilized in agencies and within departments to secure needed reform where the formulation of rules and their development were the preferred means of action. It thus represents an approach to a desired result through regulatory alteration of the behavior of private parties rather than government production of the result through its own primary agency. The force behind the regulatory action is initially the political impetus behind the reform. This impetus is seldom long sustained, and the ebbing of the tide is apt to leave the agency in the shallows of day-to-day routine. Critics of the administrative process frequently complain of stagnation and the loss of creativity. This criticism often seems to suppose the existence of some organizational means to secure sustained administrative drive. The facts of political life seem to be that president, Congress, and public alike have the energy to press vigorously for only a few objectives at a time. In the absence of this kind of concern the currents of political action must run at a low voltage and their results be in measure to the strength of the current.

The fairest way to measure administrative agencies is to examine their product and compare it with the output of alternatives here and elsewhere. By any reasonable standard, such agencies as the NLRB and the SEC have taken difficult fields and reduced them to a satisfactory state of order, the interests of the private parties subordinated, without excessive harshness, to a broader public interest. While the CAB has been guilty of seeming gross inconsistencies in the nationalization of its decisions, the aviation network that has developed compares favorably with networks in other countries. Meaningful alternatives must suggest—and specify the criteria for determining—who or what would do a better job. Despite the real difficulties in the nation's ground transport system it is doubtful that the record of the Department of Agriculture in its field is better than that of the ICC.

Executive action and administrative process

The power of presidential direction and coordination of administrative agencies seems to assure efficiency until it is scrutinized in the light of the operations of the constituents of the executive branch.

The administrative process although usually associated with the independent commissions and other regulatory tribunals is not confined to them. In one way or another it is utilized in areas as varied as the Treasury, the Post Office, and Agriculture departments. (Although the administrative process is usually associated with government it characterizes all organizations that desire to proceduralize their administration in such a way as to make their decisions conform to rules and secure uniformity of justice in the individual cases falling under their jurisdiction.) Once it is accepted that objectives cannot be satisfactorily attained through a governmental mechanism of separated powers, it becomes important to see how the values that mechanism is designed to implement can be given effective recognition in the administrative system. Granted the limited control of the legislature through statutory definition of purpose and through budgetary control, the limited power of the courts through their necessarily limited review, and the limited control of the executive through the exercise of the power of selection and retention, how are bodies possessing powers of decision and rule making in important policy areas to be kept from becoming tyrannous?

The administrative process is most appropriately contrasted not with the ideal of the separation of powers but with the actuality of the executive process. A functioning system of separated powers should, theoretically, provide adequate protection for individuals. In practice, however, it is likely to do considerably less for the individual than does the administrative process, which openly unites the powers.

The procedures or lack of procedures characteristic of the immigration and loyalty and security areas illustrate this point. In both cases—the one dealing with aliens, the other with government employees—privileges, not rights, are supposed to be involved. Accordingly, the concern of the courts is less tender and the processes permitted more rough and ready. The commitment to individual justice takes a back seat to particular public policy and even to administrative convenience. What is involved is basically the relative position of two values—the protection of the individual and his legitimate interests and the effective and economical attainment of a public purpose. The civil libertarian might wish to deny that there is any ultimate conflict between the two, but the hard-pressed administrator and the defense counsel know otherwise, though from differing perspectives.

Another example is provided by the most fundamental governmental activity in political society, that of the police. Here, for the protection of the society the activity is supposed to be purely executive. The policeman is not supposed to make the rules or to decide their application in particular cases. In fact, however, both policeman and district attorney decide which rules to enforce and against whom and frequently with what degree of severity. Given the factual discretion of the police within the general mandate of law enforcement, their activity might seem an excellent example of the administrative process. They, in effect, make rules, decide particular cases, and issue binding orders. The reason for their doing so is much the same as that which occasions resort to the administrative process in other areas, need for speed and preventive action, multitude of cases, and presumptively expert knowledge. Yet, it would be a travesty on the administrative process to regard police administration as more than a parody upon it.

The essence of the administrative process is contained in the debate as old as Plato's *Republic* and Aristotle's *Politics* whether government by the unfettered judgment of the expert is preferable to government by law, by rule, and by procedure. Aristotle's claim that government by law was indeed government by reason unaffected by desire and was alone compatible with human dignity and freedom has been the generally held ideal of the West, even though the Platonic claim for the philosopher-king, the businesslike expert, has had powerful appeal.

The administrative process, unlike purely executive action, aspires to act through known, intellectually defensible rules and procedures. It aspires further to defend its decisions and orders in terms of these rules and claims that these decisions and orders implement a concept of the public interest in the policy area in question. The administrative process is government by procedure rather than government by fiat. While it combines the powers of rule making and deciding in one area in the same hands, it subjects the use of these powers to an obligation to act in a regular fashion and to give a rational account of the relation of the means to the public end in view. The minimal procedures of notice and hearing, written opinions, publication of rules, and the like are the historic devices for encouraging, if not compelling, rational action.

The proceduralized duty to state the grounds of action in terms of a concept of the public interest may produce no more than rationalizations; however, even the acceptance of this duty admits in principle the duty to do justice.

NORTON LONG

[*See also* JUDICIAL PROCESS; LEADERSHIP; POLITICAL PROCESS; PUBLIC LAW. *Other relevant material may be found in* JUSTICE *and* PRESIDENTIAL GOVERNMENT.]

BIBLIOGRAPHY

AMERICAN BAR ASSOCIATION, SPECIAL COMMITTEE ON ADMINISTRATIVE LAW 1944 *Legislative Proposal on Federal Administrative Procedure.* Chicago: The Association.

BLACHLY, FREDERICK F.; and OATMAN, MIRIAM E. 1934 *Administrative Legislation and Adjudication.* Washington: The Brookings Institution.

CARR, CECIL T. 1941 *Concerning English Administrative Law.* New York: Columbia Univ. Press.

DAVIS, KENNETH C. 1958 *Administrative Law Treatise.* St. Paul, Minn.: West.

DICEY, ALBERT V. (1885) 1964 *Introduction to the Study of the Law of the Constitution.* 10th ed. London: Macmillan; New York: St. Martins.

DICKINSON, JOHN 1927 *Administrative Justice and the Supremacy of Law in the United States.* Cambridge, Mass.: Harvard Univ. Press.

FREUND, ERNST 1928 *Administrative Powers Over Persons and Property.* Univ. of Chicago Press.

GELLHORN, WALTER (1940) 1960 *Administrative Law: Cases and Comments.* 4th ed. New York: Fountain Press.

GELLHORN, WALTER 1941 *Federal Administrative Proceedings.* Baltimore: Johns Hopkins Press.

GOODNOW, FRANK J. (1893) 1903 *Comparative Administrative Law: An Analysis of the Administrative Systems, National and Local, of the United States, England, France and Germany.* 2 vols. New York: Putnam.

GREAT BRITAIN, COMMITTEE ON MINISTERS' POWERS 1932a *Minutes of Evidence.* London: H.M. Stationery Office.

GREAT BRITAIN, COMMITTEE ON MINISTERS' POWERS 1932b *Report.* Papers by Command, Cmd. 4060. London: H.M. Stationery Office.

GREAT BRITAIN, MINISTRY OF RECONSTRUCTION, MACHINERY OF GOVERNMENT COMMITTEE (1918) 1938 *Report.* Papers by Command, Cd. 9230. London: H.M. Stationery Office. → Known as the Haldane Committee Report.

HART, JAMES (1940) 1950 *An Introduction to Administrative Law.* 2d ed. New York: Appleton.

HEWART, GORDON 1929 *The New Despotism.* New York: Cosmopolitan.

LANDIS, JAMES M. 1938 *The Administrative Process.* New Haven: Yale Univ. Press.

NEW YORK (STATE) COMMISSIONER TO STUDY, EXAMINE AND INVESTIGATE THE EXERCISE OF QUASI-JUDICIAL FUNCTIONS BY ANY BOARD, COMMISSION OR DEPARTMENT OF THE STATE 1942 *Administrative Adjudication in the State of New York: Report to Honorable Herbert H. Lehman, Governor of the State of New York.* 6 vols. Albany, N.Y.: The Commissioner.

PENNOCK, JAMES R. 1941 *Administration and the Rule of Law*. New York: Farrar.

ROBSON, WILLIAM A. (1928) 1951 *Justice and Administrative Law: A Study of the British Constitution*. 3d ed., rev. & enl. London: Stevens.

SCHWARTZ, BERNARD 1949 *Law and the Executive in Britain: A Comparative Study*. New York Univ. Press.

U.S. ATTORNEY GENERAL'S COMMITTEE ON ADMINISTRATIVE PROCEDURE 1941a *Administrative Procedure in Government Agencies: Report*. 77th Congress, 1st Session, Senate Document No. 8. Washington: Government Printing Office.

U.S. ATTORNEY GENERAL'S COMMITTEE ON ADMINISTRATIVE PROCEDURE 1941b *Administrative Procedure in Government Agencies*. 77th Congress, 1st Session, Senate Document No. 10, in 14 parts. Washington: Government Printing Office.

U.S. COMMISSION ON ORGANIZATION OF THE EXECUTIVE BRANCH OF THE GOVERNMENT 1949 *Concluding Report*. 81st Congress, 1st Session, House Document No. 197. Washington: Government Printing Office.

U.S. PRESIDENT'S COMMITTEE ON ADMINISTRATIVE MANAGEMENT 1937 *Report of the Committee: With Studies of Administrative Management in the Federal Government*. Washington: Government Printing Office.

III
ADMINISTRATIVE BEHAVIOR

The phrase "administrative behavior" is used to designate human behavior in an organizational setting, particularly behavior that involves making decisions or influencing the behavior of others. The phrase is most often employed by scientists and scholars who are concerned with administration as a species of social behavior. The study of administrative behavior has thus been part of the wider development that is generally labeled "behavioral science."

The work in administrative theory to which the phrase is applied tends, first, to be descriptive rather than normative—to explain what is rather than prescribe what ought to be. The literature that deals particularly with motivation, however, is a partial exception, being often concerned with applications advising, for example, how to secure greater worker productivity or acceptance of change.

Second, the behavioral approach to administration has emphasized operational definition of terms and empirical study: the observation of organizations in the field, controlled field experiments on organizations, and laboratory studies of organization-like groups. Third, this work is largely, but not exclusively, concerned with quantification, mathematization, and formal theory construction. For example, the mathematical theories of games and of graphs have been applied to organizational phenomena.

The study of administrative behavior thus is

distinguishable from the other behavioral sciences only in the particular phenomena it takes as its subject matter. It makes much use of propositions drawn from psychology, sociology, and economics. It applies these propositions to the prediction of organizational phenomena and uses empirical data on administrative behavior to test them in an organizational context.

It is only since World War II that there has been any considerable body of research and writing on administration employing a behavioral approach. Most of this writing, which is fast becoming a torrent, can be traced back to four prewar sources. The work of sociologists in this field generally shows most strongly the influence of Max Weber (1922), whose approach has been adopted and developed by Robert K. Merton (1949) and his students (Blau 1955; Blau & Scott 1962). In public and business administration, the behavioral approach can largely be traced back to Chester I. Barnard's *The Functions of the Executive* (1938) and to the Hawthorne experiments reported by Roethlisberger and Dickson (1939). The attention of social psychologists was attracted to administrative phenomena by the Hawthorne studies and the experiments on leadership by Kurt Lewin and his associates (Likert 1961).

The phrase "administrative behavior" gained currency with the book by Simon (1947) that developed and extended Barnard's work. Along with this general acceleration of activity in the behavioral sciences after World War II, the study of administrative behavior became inextricably interwoven with the human relations movement (McGregor 1960) and with the study by sociologists and social psychologists of small groups (Homans 1950) and leadership. There has also been much borrowing between research on administrative behavior and work in industrial sociology and the economic theory of the firm (Chapple & Sayles 1961; Cyert & March 1963).

The convergence of so many social science disciplines upon human behavior in organizations has led to great diversity in approach and vocabulary (Foundation for Research on Human Behavior 1959). A few strategic frameworks for organizing the study of administrative behavior are beginning to emerge, and it is clear that far fewer concepts are needed than there have been distinct technical terms for labeling them. As a consensus on vocabulary develops, the area of administrative behavior, comprising phenomena of great interest to all the social sciences, is becoming a major channel of communication among the various social science disciplines. An attempt to provide some common frameworks for a wide range of approaches is found in March and Simon (1958).

Contemporary research on administrative behavior can generally be classified in one of four major categories:

(1) research on bureaucracy, belonging to the Weberian stream;

(2) human relations research focused on motivations and concerned with increasing job satisfactions and productivity;

(3) research, employing the Barnard–Simon model of organizational equilibrium, aimed at explaining survival and growth of organizations in terms of the interrelations of motivations of their participants;

(4) research on the decision-making process, with primary emphasis on cognitive processes and the rational components in administrative behavior.

The study of bureaucracy

The notion of studying organizations as bureaucracies and the construction of the ideal type of that social institution are due to Max Weber. For Weber, the rise of bureaucracies was an integral part of the development of modern Western social institutions. He was interested in identifying the characteristics of bureaucracy and explaining the manner of, and reasons for, its growth; identifying accompanying social changes; and stating the consequences of bureaucratic organization for the achievement of bureaucratic goals. In assuming, as he does, that employees will generally be willing and able to perform their bureaucratic roles, Weber's postulates about motivation are closer to the views of the scientific management movement than to those set forth in more recent writings on human relations [see WEBER, MAX].

American sociologists, who, led by Robert K. Merton, have taken Weber's ideal type as the starting point for their analyses, have been primarily interested in the consequences of bureaucratization for the bureaucracy and its employees and, in particular, in the unanticipated consequences of action based on rational calculation within the bureaucratic framework. For example, the need for control by those in authority leads to an emphasis on reliability, to the elaboration of rules, to overrigid behavior, and, hence, to inappropriateness of organizational action in individual cases; again, the division of labor leads to specialization, to the development of independent or antagonistic goals in specialized subgroups, and finally to conflict among the subgroups.

Thus, the bureaucracy framework has provided not so much a comprehensive system of theory as

a way of investigating the critical boundary between the rational and intended, and the irrational and unintended, in administrative behavior. It has been a fruitful approach in accounting for peculiarly organizational species of behavior. It has shown how to explain administrative phenomena that appear irrational or nonfunctional by deriving them from simple psychological mechanisms combined with the postulate that in complex systems the indirect consequences of action are not generally foreseen or calculated. In this respect it has much in common with the theories of bounded rationality discussed below.

Motivation: human relations research

By far the greatest part of the research and writing on administrative behavior comes under the general rubric of human relations, arising out of an interest in discovering how employees could be motivated to higher productivity and how their satisfactions could be increased. Surveys of such research and its empirical findings are provided by the recent books of McGregor (1960), Argyris (1960), Chapple and Sayles (1961), and Likert (1961).

Some human relations research has used the case study as its primary source of empirical data and has been content with informal and intuitive methods for interpreting and drawing inferences from the data. A considerable body of work, however, is based on laboratory experiments or field studies that devote considerable attention to defining variables operationally, devising scales and other measuring instruments for objectifying observations, and testing hypotheses systematically. In these studies, the methodological framework is characteristically borrowed from applied experimental psychology: One or more dependent variables, or "criterion variables," measure such aspects of organizational output as productivity or employee satisfaction; the independent variables measure amounts and kinds of rewards, style of management or supervision, pattern of communication, etc. A typical finding from such studies is that of Likert: "Employees who feel more free to set their own work pace prove to be more productive than those who lack this sense of freedom" (1961, p. 20).

Two central themes are prominent in the findings of this research. First, noneconomic motivations, especially those arising out of interpersonal relations in the primary work group, are found to be far more important determinants of behavior than economists and writers on scientific management had believed. Second, under a wide range of circumstances, shifts in management styles in a nonauthoritarian and egalitarian direction have been shown to increase productivity, acceptance of change, and worker satisfactions.

Most of the empirical studies of human relations have been restricted to the blue-collar and lower supervisory levels of organizations. The attention paid to motivation in the research is not unrelated to the fact that at these levels identification with organizational objectives is characteristically, and understandably, lower than at executive levels. Hence, the research and its interpretations have had much more to say about the use of motivations *by* executives than about the motivation *of* executives or about the relation between personal and organizational goals in the behavior of executives.

Motivation: organizational equilibrium

One of Barnard's major contributions to administrative behavior was a theory of the growth and survival of organizations based on the interaction of individual motivational mechanisms; the theory has been further developed and formalized by Simon. According to Barnard, each participant in an organization is both positively and negatively motivated to remain in the system. Barnard calls the positive motivations the "inducements" provided by the organization to the participant; and the negative motivations he refers to as the "contributions" provided by the participant to the organization. (As a simplified example, an employee's inducements are his wages and, perhaps, pleasant associates; his contribution is the work he performs.) Each participant will remain in the organization as long as his inducements outweigh his contributions, on his personal utility scale.

The contributions made by the several participants are transformed by the organization into the inducements, which it then redistributes. The organization can survive and grow (is "efficient," in Barnard's use of the term) as long as it can distribute enough inducements, manufactured out of the contributions it receives, to maintain the stream of contributions; that is, it must receive enough money from its customers to pay its employees and suppliers, and it must receive enough work and raw materials from employees and suppliers to produce output adequate to maintain the flow of money from customers. It is convenient, in applying this theory, to include customers and suppliers among the participants along with the groups, such as employees, who are more usually thought of as members of the organization.

The conditions under which Barnard's theory becomes testable and not merely a tautology are discussed by March and Simon (1958, pp. 84–88).

To date, its main value has been not in stimulating empirical research but in showing how the psychologist's conceptions of organization can be correlated with the economist's conceptions of organization. Description of administrative behavior in terms of individual motivations relates that behavior to one of the main streams of psychological research; and the *quid pro quo* dissection of motivations into inducements and contributions is a generalization of the economist's concept of a demand function or a supply function. The labor supply function, for Barnard, is a schedule showing the number of persons willing to participate as employees and contribute labor for varying amounts of wage inducements. The other supply and demand functions in the markets surrounding the firm can be interpreted similarly. The accountant's profit-and-loss statement records those portions of the system of inducements and contributions that, for reasons of convenience or history, are customarily put down in money terms.

Thus the inducements–contributions schema provides a common meeting place for, say, the economist of consumption behavior, the marketing specialist, and the psychologist, who want to understand the product purchases, brand preferences, or response to advertising of consumers. It directs the economist's attention to the noneconomic components in the total motivational structure, while at the same time giving the psychologist a means for tracing the indirect systems effects of the individual motivational mechanisms [*see* BARNARD].

Decision making

Until very recently, motivational variables have received the lion's share of attention in empirical research on administrative behavior, as they have in many areas of study within psychology—for example, in research on learning and in research on perception. But as Weber emphasized in his descriptions of bureaucracy, one of the salient characteristics of administrative behavior, as compared with human behavior in other institutional settings, is its large rationalistic component. Because organizations are goal-oriented systems, administrative behavior is largely concerned with finding effective patterns of activity directed toward the goals and with influencing subordinates to adopt these patterns. The theory of this large cognitive component of administrative behavior is closely tied to the theory of thinking and problem solving.

Thinking and problem solving that is directed toward the discovery and selection of courses of action is usually called decision making. If the term is used to describe what takes place in organizations, it must be interpreted broadly (Simon

1960). Only a small fraction of the time of administrators is spent in actually choosing among courses of action once they have been presented for selection. A larger fraction is spent in what the military calls "intelligence activities": searching for situations and problems that call for attention, and filtering and interpreting incoming information about the changing environment that might signal such situations and problems. An even larger fraction is spent in designing action alternatives, that is, sharpening the formulation of problems to which attention has been drawn by intelligence activities, specifying possible courses of action, and elaborating and evaluating them. Approval of an action, the final act of choice, takes place in administration only within this larger context of intelligence and design activities. Administrative decision making involves all three processes.

Theories of rational decision. A considerable body of formal theory of rational decision making has accumulated in economics and mathematical statistics [see DECISION THEORY]. The theory can be interpreted either normatively or descriptively—either as a theory of how a man should choose in order to behave rationally or as a theory of how a man does choose (e.g., the rational economic man). The normative interpretation, which we shall not be concerned with here, has been of primary interest in statistics and management science; the descriptive interpretation has played a central role in the economic theory of the firm.

The formal theory of rational decision making has been enormously important in clarifying the concept of rationality and the associated concepts of utility and expectations. It has been less successful in explaining the real-world facts of administrative decision making, because of (1) its preoccupation with choice behaviors, to the near exclusion of intelligence activities and design activities, and (2) its assumptions of the chooser's omniscience. Typically, formal decision models assume that all the alternatives of choice are known, that all the consequences attached to each alternative are known, and that each set of consequences has attached to it a known utility, i.e., a magnitude by which it can be ordered relative to the other sets. Rationality (optimization) then consists in choosing the alternative whose consequences have the greatest utility (Simon [1947] 1961, chapter 4; March & Simon 1958, chapter 6).

In recent years there have been some efforts to extend the theory to take account of uncertainty of consequences (statistical decision theory), of time and cost involved in obtaining information (sequential sampling, search theory, theory of teams), and of opposition of interest among ra-

tional actors [see OLIGOPOLY; GAME THEORY]. Nevertheless, limitations on the information available to the chooser about alternatives, consequences, or utilities, and limitations on his ability to perform the computations presupposed by the theory, enter the theory, if at all, as boundary conditions rather than phenomena of central interest.

Theories of bounded rationality. An alternative approach to administrative decision making takes as its starting point the very limitations upon omniscient rationality that formal decision theory tends to de-emphasize. In real life, human beings exhibit only *bounded rationality* (Simon [1947] 1961, chapter 5). The central phenomenon to be explained is how organisms are able to behave in a relatively adaptive, goal-oriented fashion in an environment whose complexity is grossly disproportionate to their information-processing and computational powers. How does the organism notice and attend to those aspects of the environment calling for action (intelligence processes); how does it discover and integrate adaptive responses (design activities); and how does it select action alternatives (choice activities)?

These questions about administrative behavior are, of course, also central questions in the psychology of cognition—in learning, perception, and problem solving. Research on administrative decision making based on the concept of bounded rationality has drawn heavily upon, and contributed to, research in individual and social psychology of cognition. Several generalizations have emerged:

First, intelligence processes in organizations, as in individual behavior, are governed by laws of selective perception. In particular, specialization will cause different administrators to be exposed to different environments, to have different sensitivities to particular events in their environments, and to internalize different subgoals (identification).

Second, the processes of design in administration are largely identical with the processes that have been identified in individual problem solving in the psychological laboratory. A reasoned account has been given of design activity as an organized system of means–end analysis (Simon 1960).

Third, *satisficing*—choosing good alternatives rather than searching for an unattainable "best"—is a central means used by decision makers for matching the choice process to their information-processing limitations. Moreover, satisficing provides an important connection between cognitive and motivational systems. The satisficing criterion is familiar to psychologists as the aspiration level, which adjusts upward or downward, over time, as a function of the ease or difficulty that the decision maker encounters in finding satisfactory alternatives.

There is not complete agreement that the phenomena that have been treated in terms of bounded rationality and satisficing cannot be handled by an expansion of classical formal decision theory. The chief difficulty is to account for the observed dependence of behavior upon the sequence in which action alternatives are presented by the environment or are discovered by design activities. Whatever the possibilities of reconciling the two viewpoints, the emphasis upon the limits of rationality has directed attention in research on administrative decision making to new variables and processes.

Describing the decision process. Until quite recently theories of decision making had far outgrown the means available for testing them empirically. The relatively few studies of administrative behavior that focused specifically upon decision making were mostly case studies; and no matter how competently executed, they tended to suffer from subjectivity and did not easily lend themselves to empirical hypothesis testing. Laboratory experiments with small groups, particularly the work of Freed Bales, Alex Bavelas, and Harold Guetzkow brought some methodological advance. Category systems were developed, for example, that allowed at least some aspects of decision-making behavior in different situations to be objectively recorded and compared. Most of these systems, however, retained only a small part of the information in the raw data and ignored a great deal of the structure and organization of the decision-making process.

The prospects for testing theories of decision making changed radically with the invention of the electronic digital computer and the discovery that computer programs could be written to simulate human cognitive processes. These new techniques have led to the development and partial testing of some fairly general theories of human problem solving and of specific applications of these theories to the administrative behavior of middle managers. For example, we now have a fairly well-substantiated picture of some of the decision-making processes of a bank trust officer and of a department store buyer (Cyert & March 1963).

Computer simulation techniques have also led to improvement in our less formal methods for handling data. Central to simulation and independent of computer technology is the idea that an effective and parsimonious way to explain a segment of human decision-making behavior is to prescribe a program that would generate such a behavior segment—or a highly similar one. A program can be prescribed at the level of detail necessary to instruct a computer; but it can also be described much more generally and approximately. Thus, the concept of "program" provides a means for formalizing and analyzing case-study of historical data in whatever detail and structure the data will support. The components of programs are themselves smaller programs called *subroutines*, which may be equated with the *decision premises* in an earlier nomenclature of decision making.

Organization structure

The behavioral study of administration has brought about a substantial change in theories of organization structure—of the consequences of arranging systems of specialization, authority relations, and communication patterns in one way rather than another. A first contribution has been operational definitions of some of the key variables.

The concept of *authority* provides an example [*see* AUTHORITY]. In traditional administrative theory, authority was generally defined in quasi-legal terms. Barnard pointed out that authority is significant for administration to the extent that it has behavioral consequences. He proposed that we speak of an authority relation between two persons only when the commands of the superior are generally obeyed by the subordinate. If this definition is accepted, then the way is open for empirical research to discover what conditions have to be satisfied for an authority relation to be maintained, i.e., what the motivational bases are for the acceptance of authority. The question of whether legitimacy buttresses authority, whose answer is tautological in a legal theory of authority, thus becomes an empirical question; and research on attitudes toward legitimacy can be related to other psychological research on superego formation, the authoritarian personality, and so on.

A few samples can be given here of the generalizations that have been formulated and tested when organization structure has been approached as a behavioral phenomenon (Simon, Smithburg, & Thompson 1950). A unit within an organization is said to be *self-contained*, to the extent that its work is carried on without coordination or communication with other units; such units will be self-contained to the extent that the division of work among units parallels the division of the goal of the organization into subgoals. Further, conflict among units will vary inversely with their degree of self-containment.

Goals are called *operational* insofar as their attainment can be evaluated objectively and insofar as the connections between actions and attainment can be determined. Then, organizational conflict will be settled by analytic techniques when there is a set of common operational goals that apply to the disputing units, and by bargaining techniques when there is not.

The phenomena examined in classical organization theory remain—the division of work, the processes of coordination, the hierarchy of authority, and the hierarchy of status relations. But with a behavioral approach, the task of understanding these phenomena becomes a task of explaining them in terms of social and psychological mechanisms that are familiar from research in other areas of sociology and psychology. From this point of view, administrative behavior is examined as human behavior in a particular kind of social setting. An organization is thus a relatively stable pattern of human behaviors, which is maintained by motivational forces. When analyzed in terms of the inducements and contributions of its participants, it is at, or near, equilibrium. The individual behaviors are components in a complex decision-making process comprising intelligence, design, and choice activities. The behavioral "outputs" of the decision-making individual administrators are information and decision premises that serve as "inputs" to the processes of other participants. These interpersonal relations derive in part from a formal and legitimized plan of authority and status relations and decision procedures and in part from informal and social processes. The study of administrative behavior becomes a study of basic psychological mechanisms—motivational and cognitive—under conditions where these mechanisms are linked together in a complex, formalized, goal-oriented social system.

HERBERT A. SIMON

BIBLIOGRAPHY

ARGYRIS, CHRIS 1960 *Understanding Organizational Behavior.* Homewood, Ill.: Dorsey.

BARNARD, CHESTER I. (1938) 1962 *The Functions of the Executive.* Cambridge, Mass.: Harvard Univ. Press.

BASS, BERNARD M. 1960 *Leadership, Psychology, and Organizational Behavior.* New York: Harper.

BLAU, PETER M. (1955) 1963 *The Dynamics of Bureaucracy: A Study of Interpersonal Relations in Two Government Agencies.* Rev. ed. Univ. of Chicago Press.

BLAU, PETER M.; and SCOTT, W. RICHARD 1962 *Formal Organizations: A Comparative Approach.* San Francisco: Chandler. → Contains an extensive bibliography.

CAPLOW, THEODORE 1964 *Principles of Organization.* New York: Harcourt.

CHAPPLE, ELIOT D.; and SAYLES, LEONARD R. 1961 *The Measure of Management: Designing Organizations for Human Effectiveness.* New York: Macmillan.

COLLINS, BARRY E.; and GUETZKOW, HAROLD S. 1964 *A Social Psychology of Group Processes for Decision-making.* New York: Wiley.

CYERT, RICHARD M.; and MARCH, JAMES G. 1963 *A Behavioral Theory of the Firm.* Englewood Cliffs, N.J.: Prentice-Hall.

FOUNDATION FOR RESEARCH ON HUMAN BEHAVIOR 1959 *Modern Organization Theory: A Symposium.* Edited by Mason Haire. New York: Wiley.

HOMANS, GEORGE C. 1950 *The Human Group.* New York: Harcourt.

LIKERT, RENSIS 1961 *New Patterns of Management.* New York: McGraw-Hill.

McGREGOR, DOUGLAS 1960 *The Human Side of Enterprise.* New York: McGraw-Hill.

MARCH, JAMES G. (editor) 1965 *Handbook of Organizations.* Chicago: Rand McNally.

MARCH, JAMES G.; and SIMON, HERBERT A. 1958 *Organizations.* New York: Wiley.

MERTON, ROBERT K. (1949) 1957 *Social Theory and Social Structure.* Rev. & enl. ed. Glencoe, Ill.: Free Press.

ROETHLISBERGER, FRITZ J.; and DICKSON, WILLIAM J. (1939) 1961 *Management and the Worker: An Account of a Research Program Conducted by the Western Electric Company, Hawthorne Works, Chicago.* Cambridge, Mass.: Harvard Univ. Press. → A paperback edition was published in 1964 by Wiley.

SIMON, HERBERT A. (1947) 1961 *Administrative Behavior: A Study of Decision-making Processes in Administrative Organization.* 2d ed. New York: Macmillan. → See especially chapters 4 and 5.

SIMON, HERBERT A. 1960 *The New Science of Management Decision.* New York: Harper.

SIMON, HERBERT A.; SMITHBURG, DONALD W.; and THOMPSON, VICTOR A. 1950 *Public Administration.* New York: Knopf.

WEBER, MAX (1922) 1957 *The Theory of Social and Economic Organization.* Edited by Talcott Parsons. Glencoe, Ill.: Free Press. → First published as Part 1 of *Wirtschaft und Gesellschaft.*

ADMINISTRATIVE LAW

Definition and scope. Administrative law is that branch of the law which determines the organization, powers, and duties of administrative authorities, the legal requirements governing their operation, and the remedies available to those adversely affected by administrative action.

There is a basic difference in approach between the Anglo–American conception of administrative law and that which prevails in civil-law countries. In the Anglo–American legal system administrative law tends to be narrower than the above definition and is essentially divided into three parts: (1) the delegation of legislative and judicial powers to the administration; (2) the manner in which such powers must be exercised (emphasizing primarily the procedural requirements imposed by the law); and (3) judicial control of administrative authority. In a civil-law country like France, the conception of administrative law is broader. In addition to covering the topics just referred to, French works on the subject describe the various forms of administrative agencies (what they term "the subjects of rights" in administrative law); the exercise of and limitations upon administrative regulatory power; civil service law; the acquisition and management of property by the administration; public works; and the obligations of the administration (subdivided into contracts, quasi contracts, and tort liability).

In the Anglo–American view much that is included in the civil-law approach to administrative law involves matters within the domain of public administration, not of administrative law. The Anglo–American administrative lawyer is not concerned with administrative powers as such; only when administrative power is turned outward against the person or property of private citizens does he deem it a proper subject of administrative law. Hence the Anglo–American emphasis upon powers of delegated legislation and adjudication, for it is through exercise of these substantive powers that administrative authorities are able to determine private rights and obligations.

Basic systems. Even more important than the difference in approach to the scope of the subject is the basic difference between common-law and civil-law systems of jurisprudence in the very structure of administrative law. Civil-law countries tend to make a sharp distinction between administrative law and private law and to have a separate set of courts for each. The model in this respect has been the French system, which since the revolution has been based upon such a distinction, with an autonomous body of administrative courts (headed by the Conseil d'État), wholly separate from the ordinary law courts. The latter have, since 1790, been barred from exercising jurisdiction in other than private-law cases.

In the common-law countries there has been no sharp dichotomy between administrative law and private law and no separate system of administrative courts. Questions of administrative law have been determined by the ordinary law courts on the basis of principles worked out by analogy with those developed in private-law cases.

The difference in this respect has not been merely a structural one. The law fashioned by the administrative courts in France has been an autonomous system, developed independently of the direct influence of private-law principles. This separation has been established since 1873, when the celebrated decision in the Blanco case eliminated the notion of fault, on which the French private law of torts was grounded, from the law of administrative tort liability. The French administrative courts have regarded the Blanco case as a mandate to develop the whole system of adminis-

trative law as a body distinct from the ordinary private law, proceeding from wholly different principles. French administrative law has, as a consequence, come to be based on the existence of a special law for cases involving the administration, as well as of special courts to decide such cases.

In the Anglo–American system this French conception of the autonomy of administrative law has been rejected. Administrative-law cases and those arising between private citizens are decided by the same law courts, and the judges have refused to accept the notion that wholly different rules must be applied in their decision. If anything, indeed, the outstanding feature of the common-law legal system has been the primacy of private, as compared to public, law. Anglo–American courts have tended to conceive of the state as only a collective person and then to resolve cases involving the state by analogy with the private law of persons. The result has been that many of the most important doctrines and conceptions of Anglo–American administrative law have been drawn from the different branches of private law. These include: the maxim against the delegation of legislative power (derived from the law of agency); the doctrine of *ultra vires* (imported from the law of corporations); the rule of personal tort liability of public officers (based on the treatment of administrative wrongful acts as private torts); and the concept of government employment as only a privilege (based on the treatment of the state employer as an ordinary private employer).

Most countries have adopted either the French or the Anglo–American type of administrative-law system as a model, although often with significant variations. Thus, many South American countries have accepted the formal structure of the Anglo–American systems (with control by the ordinary courts) but have tended to follow the substantive doctrines (and especially the basic division between administrative law and private law) espoused by French and other civil-law jurisprudence. In Japan, the administrative-law system was first set up on the civil-law pattern (modeled upon the German system); but since 1945, the structure has been remodeled and patterned on that of the United States. Such drastic change in the basic system has been very rare, although suggestions as to its desirability have been made in other countries, even in Britain and France themselves.

Historical background. Administrative law, in its broad sense as the law relating to administration, is as old as government itself. In its modern connotation, however, it was not recognized as a separate branch of the law until the nineteenth century. In the Anglo–American countries, indeed, such recognition was not widespread until the twentieth century. This delay stemmed in large part from the dominance of private law. In Blackstone, administrative law is essentially part of the private law of persons, with officials treated as persons governed by the same law as everyone else. The great Victorian public lawyer A. V. Dicey asserted that in England and the United States administrative law was unknown.

Today such a statement could not be made, for administrative law exists as a recognized rubric of both British and American law. The change in this respect has resulted largely from the drastic transformation in the role of the state during the twentieth century which has led it to play an increasingly positive role in the life of the people. Such a role has been manifested in two principal ways: through regulation and operation of various aspects of the economy and through the dispensation of benefits connected with state social-service plans.

In the United States the rise of administrative law is contemporaneous with the need for governmental regulation of industry. Such a need led to the creation in 1887 of the Interstate Commerce Commission (ICC). That body, set up to regulate the railroads (then of crucial importance to the national economy), became the prototype of the American regulatory agency. The industrial abuses that called forth the ICC were to be dealt with by an independent commission vested with authority over the most significant aspects of railroading, from the prescription of rates to the control of discriminatory practices and the supervision of financial operations. The ICC has been well characterized as a super-board of directors of the railroad industry and was given jurisdiction over other forms of surface transportation as well—over oil pipelines in 1906, interstate motor carriers in 1935, and domestic water carriers in 1940.

In the years that followed the creation of the ICC the same need for regulation was felt in other parts of the American economic scene. This was especially true during the period following the economic crisis of 1929. The result has been the establishment of a host of regulatory agencies modeled on the ICC. The most important are the Federal Trade Commission, established in 1914, regulating unfair trade practices; the Federal Power Commission, 1930, regulating water, electric, and gas power; the Federal Communications Commission, 1934, regulating broadcasting and wire communications; the Securities and Exchange Commission, 1934, regulating dealings in securi-

ties; the National Labor Relations Board, 1935, regulating labor practices; and the Civil Aeronautics Board, 1938, regulating aviation.

American administrative law developed from the operation of these different regulatory agencies, vested with significant powers to determine, by rule or by decision, private rights and obligations. As the regulations and orders promulgated by these organs impinged more and more upon the community and the bar that counseled it, the development of legal rules to ensure the subordination of agency activities to law became of concern to jurists. During the 1920s courses on administrative law began to be offered in law schools, the American Bar Association set up a special committee on the subject, and it came increasingly to occupy the attention of courts and lawyers.

In Britain the development of administrative law is intimately connected with the modern growth of the social-service functions of the state. In the first part of the nineteenth century, spurred on by Bentham's philippics, Parliament swept aside the archaisms that had become encrusted in the common law. Toward the end of the century it was seen that negative reform of this type was not enough; public opinion required the state to bring ever-increasing parts of the population under its guardianship. In particular, a vast system of social insurance has been established, designed to protect the individual against the hazards of employment and of life in general in the modern industrial society. The continuous tasks involved in the operation of this system have been delegated to various ministries, although the tendency has been to assign the cases arising to specific executive tribunals, and not to the one relevant minister.

The growth of social-service agencies of the type just referred to, as well as of significant administrative powers over private rights (particularly those involving authority to acquire land compulsorily), led British jurists of the twentieth century to reject Dicey's denial of the existence of administrative law. Lord Chief Justice Hewart's attack on what he termed "administrative lawlessness" in *The New Despotism* (1929), the consequent appointment by the lord chancellor of the Committee on Ministers' Powers, which reported in 1932 (Great Britain 1932), and the 1957 report of the Franks Committee on Administrative Tribunals and Enquiries (Great Britain 1957) have served to make administrative law an accepted branch of English jurisprudence.

In Continental countries administrative law as a recognized branch of the law has a much longer history. In France the subject has its beginnings in the postrevolutionary era, with the setting up of the Conseil d'État at the end of 1799 and the creation within it in 1806 of a separate section to decide cases touching on the validity of administrative action, a function performed by the law courts in Anglo–American countries. The existence of a separate administrative court and its development of autonomous legal principles focused the attention of French jurists upon administrative law as a distinct subject worthy of doctrinal attention. Treatises on the subject began to appear during the course of the nineteenth century; the classics of modern French administrative law made their first appearance toward the end of the century.

Delegation of power. The question of which powers may be delegated to administrative agencies is of importance in all systems of administrative law; but it is of particular moment in a system like the American one, which is dominated by a judicially enforceable written constitution. Relying upon the separation-of-powers doctrine and the maxim (derived from the law of agency) against the further delegation of a delegated power, the American courts have required delegations of power to be limited by defined standards. This has not barred wide grants of legislative and judicial types of power to administrative agencies, although it has prevented such extreme delegations as those granted under the "Henry VIII clause" and the decree-law power. Although since 1935 no delegation has been held unconstitutional by the United States Supreme Court, the mere existence of judicial control has served to restrain delegations so broad as to constitute abdications of the legislative function.

British public law rests on the doctrine of parliamentary supremacy, which is inconsistent with the notion of restrictions on the power that may be delegated to the administration. There are no limitations on Parliament to restrain it from assigning authority when and as it will. Hence, the so-called Henry VIII clause (named in disrespectful commemoration of that monarch's tendency to absolutism), which goes so far as to delegate the authority to amend acts of Parliament. Since the Committee on Ministers' Powers strongly criticized this type of clause in 1932, it has virtually disappeared from British legislation.

In France, a civil-law country, the existence of a written constitution has led jurists to deny that the legislature may delegate power without limitations. But the absence of effective judicial review has meant that, in practice, there are no legal restrictions on delegation. Since World War I the executive has often been given the broadest power to govern by so-called decree laws. These might override any existing laws and could include any measures deemed necessary to cope with the economic or political exigency that called them forth. The delegation of the decree-law power continued under the Fourth Republic despite an express prohibition against such delegation in the 1946 constitution. Under the Fifth Republic the power to promulgate decree laws is an essential part of the augmented executive authority which is that republic's chief characteristic. Similar power has existed under other Continental constitutions, notably the Weimar constitution and, to a lesser extent, that of the German Federal Republic. [*See* DELEGATION OF POWERS.]

Administrative procedure. Works on American administrative law devote what may seem to be inordinate attention to the subject of administrative procedure, but this is a natural reflection of the country's preoccupation with the adjective aspects of the subject. Earlier American works were concerned mainly with the delegation of authority and judicial control. More recently has come the realization that the exercise of administrative power is of equal, if not greater, importance. This has led to an emphasis on procedural safeguards to ensure the proper exercise of administrative authority— an emphasis that found articulation in the Federal Administrative Procedure Act of 1946, which lays down the basic procedures to be followed by American administrative agencies.

It is fair to say that American administrative law is the most developed system in existence, insofar as the procedural requirements that must be followed prior to the taking of administrative action are concerned. In the main, this results from the fact that the due-process clause of the American constitution is construed as a demand of notice and hearing. This means that before an administrative decision which adversely affects the personal or property rights of a particular individual may be made, that individual is entitled, as a matter of constitutional right, to notice and a full and fair hearing. Such a hearing must conform to the essential adjudicatory requirements of the courtroom, which means that the individual has the right to an adversary trial, with the right of oral evidence and argument, cross-examination, counsel, and the like, before an administrative decision can be made against him. Above all, he has the right to have the decision based only upon known evidence presented at the hearing (the principle of "exclusiveness of the record," as it is termed) and to be given the reasons for an adverse decision.

In Britain and other countries the law of administrative procedure is not so fully developed. The British courts have imposed the rule of *audi alteram partem* as a principle of natural justice; but this is far from a requirement of a full adversary-trial type of hearing. It is common for English statutes to require a public local inquiry in many cases or an opportunity to appear before a tribunal; yet these, too, are far more informal than their American counterparts. In France the concept of a full hearing as a legal requirement for administrative action has been virtually unknown, although, starting in 1944, the Conseil d'État has held that an individual has a right to present a defense before an administrative penalty may be imposed upon him—a right demanded by the "general principles" of French administrative law.

Judicial review. It is essential in a developed system of administrative law that the citizen aggrieved by an administrative decision have the right to have the legality of such a decision reviewed by an independent judge. In the Anglo–American system, as already indicated, such judicial review is afforded by the ordinary law courts. In the French system and those modeled upon it, it is provided for in a separate set of administrative courts, headed by a supreme administrative court (in France, the Conseil d'État: in Germany, the Bundesverwaltungsgericht).

The subject of judicial review is divided into two parts: (1) availability of review and (2) scope of review. In both the Anglo–American and French systems the general rule is that one adversely affected by an administrative act may obtain judicial review of its legality. This is true regardless of whether a statute provides for such review and even in the face of legislative provisions that appear to preclude review. The plaintiff in the review action must show that the challenged administrative action is "final" in that it has adverse effect (mere preliminary or procedural action not being "ripe" for review) and that he has standing to sue (in that he is personally affected by the act which he challenges). In the Anglo–American system the review action is one for an injunction, declaratory judgment, or certiorari, mandamus, or prohibition. In the French system the normal action is a nontechnical proceeding to annul an *ultra vires* administrative act (*recours pour excès de pouvoir*), normally brought without counsel.

As far as the scope of judicial review is concerned, all systems of administrative law make a basic distinction between questions of law and questions of fact. The former are for the judge, the latter for the administrator. Hence, there is full review of questions of law, but only limited review of questions of fact. In America the scope of review of facts is limited by the so-called substantial-evidence rule. Under it, the reviewing court looks only to see whether the administrative finding of fact is supported by substantial evidence, i.e., such evidence as a reasonable mind might accept as adequate to support a conclusion. Other systems reach a comparable result, although they do not articulate a similar theory. [*See* JUDICIAL PROCESS, *article on* JUDICIAL REVIEW.]

Tort liability. Closely connected with judicial review is the subject of the responsibility of the administration and its agents for damages caused by wrongful administrative acts. Anglo–American law starts with the principle of strict personal liability of administrative officers. Although this principle is still followed in British countries, in the United States it has been departed from during the twentieth century. In American law the public officer may no longer be sued personally where he exercises adjudicative authority or discretionary power. Such personal liability is now limited to officers exercising ministerial functions. In other systems there has been a different development. Most Continental countries started with a rule of immunity for officers. During the nineteenth century such immunity was withdrawn in cases of serious faults. Thus, in the French system the public officer is now personally liable for so-called *fautes personelles*, which involve willfulness, malice, gross negligence, or action outside the scope of official functions.

So far as the tort liability of the state is concerned, Anglo–American law starts with the doctrine of sovereign immunity, which bars suits against the state without its consent. Such consent has now been given both in Britain, in the Crown Proceedings Act of 1947, and in America, in the Federal Tort Claims Act of 1946. Under these laws the state is liable in tort on the same basis as a private person. There are, however, important exceptions in the American act which preserve governmental immunity from liability for intentional torts, nonnegligent action under a statute or regulation, and exercises of discretionary power. In Continental countries like France and Germany, state immunity from tort suits was done away with during the nineteenth century. An ever-widening principle of governmental liability has taken its place. The state is now responsible for damage caused not only by the faults (such as negligence) of its officers but also by their failure to act and, more recently, by a risk theory of absolute liability. Such state liability even without fault is evolving into what is really a scheme of social insurance far removed from the normal operation of the law of torts.

BERNARD SCHWARTZ

[*See also* ADMINISTRATION; JUDICIAL PROCESS; LEGAL SYSTEMS. *Other relevant material may be found under* ADJUDICATION; LAW.]

BIBLIOGRAPHY

Works dealing with administrative law in the United States are Davis 1958 *and* Schwartz 1950, 1952, 1958. *The British viewpoint is presented by* Great Britain 1932, 1957; Griffith 1951; Hewart 1929; Schwartz 1949; *and* Wade 1961. *France is represented by the works of* Waline 1944; Laubadère 1953; *and* Schwartz 1954. *German treatments are to be found in* Forsthoff 1950 *and* Jellinek 1948–1950.

DAVIS, KENNETH C. 1958 *Administrative Law Treatise.* St. Paul, Minn.: West.

FORSTHOFF, ERNST (1950) 1961 *Lehrbuch des Verwaltungsrechts.* 8th ed. Munich: Beck.

GREAT BRITAIN, PARLIAMENT, COMMITTEE ON ADMINISTRATIVE TRIBUNALS AND ENQUIRIES 1957 *Report.* Papers by Command, Cmd. 218. London: H.M. Stationery Office.

GREAT BRITAIN, PARLIAMENT, COMMITTEE ON MINISTERS' POWERS 1932 *Report.* Papers by Command, Cmd. 4060. London: H.M. Stationery Office.

GRIFFITH, J. A. G.; and STREET, HARRY (1951) 1957 *Principles of Administrative Law.* 2d ed. New York and London: Pitman.

HEWART, GORDON 1929 *The New Despotism.* New York: Cosmopolitan.

JELLINEK, WALTER (1928) 1948–1950 *Verwaltungsrecht.* 3d ed. rev. Offenburg (Germany): Lehrmittel. → This is a reprint of the third edition, which appeared in 1931, together with a supplement published in 1950.

LAUBADÈRE, ANDRÉ DE (1953) 1963 *Traité élémentaire de droit administratif.* 3d ed. Paris: Librairie Générale de Droit et de Jurisprudence.

SCHWARTZ, BERNARD 1949 *Law and the Executive in Britain: A Comparative Study.* New York Univ. Press.

SCHWARTZ, BERNARD 1950 *American Administrative Law.* London and New York: Pitman.

SCHWARTZ, BERNARD 1952 *Le droit administratif américain: Notions générales.* Paris: Sirey.

SCHWARTZ, BERNARD 1954 *French Administrative Law and the Common-law World.* New York Univ. Press.

SCHWARTZ, BERNARD (1958) 1962 *An Introduction to American Administrative Law.* 2d ed. Dobbs Ferry, N.Y.: Oceana; London: Pitman.

WADE, HENRY W. R. 1961 *Administrative Law.* Oxford: Clarendon.

WALINE, MARCEL (1944) 1963 *Droit administratif.* 9th ed. Paris: Sirey. → The titles of different editions vary slightly.

ADOLESCENCE

Adolescence is an era in the historical sense. A dictionary defines "era" as "a period extending from an epoch and characterized especially by a new order of things." Here the epoch, defined as "the starting point of a new period, especially as marked by striking events," is puberty, marked by striking biological events that signal the initiation of the sequence of biochemical, physiological, and physical transformations of child into adult. Whether during behavioral development there is a concomitant or analogous transitional period, set apart by distinctive psychological properties and processes, has been a major issue in developmental psychology. Around this proposition and its corollaries—identification of the psychological features and transitions, their antecedents and consequents, their specificity or generality, and the mode (gradual or saltatory) and tenor of their development—have centered the theoretical controversies and empirical problems of the psychology of adolescence.

Disciplines, too, have developmental phases, defined by significant events. Psychology emerged as a separate discipline about 1860 and was only 22 years old when child psychology made its appearance in Germany and comparative psychology in England, and the psychology of adolescence emerged as the first branch of psychology native to the United States (Hall 1882). Not until the 1890s, however, did Hall and others, primarily his students, begin to publish a series of papers on the interests, abilities, problems, and fantasies of adolescents. About the turn of the century Hall was working on a companion set of textbooks on childhood and adolescence. The text on adolescence actually appeared first, and with its publication the psychology of adolescence may be said to have entered adulthood. Furthermore, epitomized in the title—*Adolescence: Its Psychology and Its Relations to Physiology, Anthropology, Sociology, Sex, Crime, Religion and Education* (1904)—are the multidisciplinary affinities that continue to characterize the psychology of adolescence. The capacities, interests, attitudes, and roles of the young and the way they are influenced by the structure and training techniques of the family and other social institutions are of concern to a wide range of social scientists. As the individual becomes able to reproduce his kind and approaches the time when he will become the bearer, and perhaps molder, of his culture, the import of these factors grows ever more apparent. But no single discipline can encompass them; thus many sciences—biological and social, basic and applied—contribute to and draw upon developmental theories, methods, and data. So also do most domains of psychology, and these intradisciplinary affiliations are reflected in the range of behaviors with which Hall dealt:

sensation, perception, motor skills, motivation, emotion, socialization, cognition, learning, and vocational training—all topics of current concern.

Hall's ontogenic approach to the data and his phylogenetic theoretical structure served to establish the psychology of adolescence as a branch of developmental psychology. From this affiliation are derived its definitions, methods, and theories, for none of these are peculiar to the psychology of adolescence; rather, they are shared with all of developmental psychology.

Terminology. "Adolescence" is derived from *adolescens*, the present participle of *adolescere*, to grow up or to grow from childhood to maturity. Developmental psychologists prefer this term because its etymology is most consistent with the physical and behavioral characteristics of this era. In contrast to the developmental significance of adolescence are the chronological implications of a number of synonyms in current usage among social scientists. For Gesell (Gesell et al. 1956) "youth" refers to the years from 10 to 16; to some it refers to biological adolescence and to others to a combination of late adolescence and young adulthood; and, as our historical survey will show, it has meant middle age or the entire interval from early childhood to old age. "Juvenile," too, is applied to a wide range of ages. It has acquired further connotations in legal usage and in primate anthropology, where it refers to a stage between the infant and the adult or subadult. "Teen-ager" labels an age group, regardless of developmental status, and "junior or senior high-school age" an educational group of disparate chronological and developmental ages. All terms other than adolescence suggest status rather than change, product not process, an approach that is more descriptive than conceptual, and a more limited temporal and situational view toward antecedents and consequents of behavior.

Concepts of adolescence

Historical. For many thousands of years man has been aware of certain adolescent phenomena and of variations in human behavior with age. Aristotle, however, is usually cited as the first source of detailed records of adolescent development. He described voice changes in both sexes, breast development and menarche in the female, the appearance of pubic hair and seminal emissions in the male; he gave average ages at which these phenomena occurred and presented evidence for a period of adolescent sterility in the male. Aristotle is also sometimes credited with a psycho-

logical characterization of adolescence because he noticed a number of traits which in more recent times have been attributed to the adolescent in industrialized societies. But Aristotle's characterization was only that of a tripartite age continuum—childhood, youth, and old age—and in his account the term "young" could have included any age from about seven to forty years. Nor did the Romans of the pre-Christian era clearly differentiate between infancy, childhood, adolescence, and young adulthood. An *infans* was not only one who did not speak but also a child up to the age of seven; yet *puerilis* also meant childish. *Puerilis* and *adolescens* were often used synonymously and applied to young males without reference to any particular age; Octavianus at 19 was called *puer* and Caesar at about 38, *adolescentulus*.

Expanded divisions of the life span and more restricted definitions had evolved by the beginning of the fourth century; writers of the golden age of the Byzantine Empire refer to Constantine as the authority for some definitions that delimit six or seven age periods. The third age was called adolescence: during this age the person grows "to the size allotted to him by Nature." Adolescence is followed by youth, the age of greatest strength (Ariès [1960] 1962, p. 21). These definitions are taken from a sixteenth-century French translation of a thirteenth-century Latin encyclopedia; it was noted that the translator had difficulties because the French language of the time had only three words to signify age periods—childhood, youth, and old age. The finer distinctions had been lost to popular speech during the Dark Ages and, despite being exhumed by thirteenth-century scholars, disappeared again for several centuries.

During the Dark Ages the child moved into the adult world between the ages of five and seven. This pattern persisted for many centuries among the lower classes. Ariès (1960) gives a fascinating account of factors that prompted or retarded the reappearance of contrasts, first between infancy and childhood and later between childhood, adolescence, and young adulthood. For example, the establishment of schools for a larger proportion of the population helped to extend childhood but tended to obscure distinctions between child, adolescent, and young adult, because in the early medieval school neither attendance nor grade level was based on age. Indeed, after the sixteenth century discrimination was further reduced by adopting for all students, some of whom were over 20, a disciplinary method—the rod—originally reserved for the youngest pupils. A variety of synonyms for "child" or "youth" was used during the Middle Ages, but they all applied to a wide range of ages. A lowly person was a "child" regardless of his age. This usage continued into the seventeenth century, for one left childhood only by achieving superior economic or social position. Among the upper classes, however, dependency came to be primarily a function of physical ability, and the word "child" took on its modern connotations.

According to Ariès, a popular concept of adolescence began to take shape during the eighteenth century in "two characters—one literary, as represented by Cherubin, and the other social, the conscript." Cherubin represented "the ambiguity of puberty" and stressed "the effeminate side of a boy just emerging from childhood; . . . it expressed a condition . . . the period of budding love." In contrast, the character of the conscript stressed manly strength as the expression of the idea of adolescence.

Several reasons for the slow evolution of a truly developmental concept of the life span and the late recognition of adolescence may be deduced. First, the average life span was so short that the continuum of ages noted by scholars was not readily apparent to the general populace. Second, until the advent of a relatively high standard of living for a major segment of the population, the labor of all was needed. Fine distinctions between physical or mental abilities could not be afforded, and indeed, when complex skills were not required, they were not necessary. Third, the existence of quite rigid social and economic hierarchies made a large part of the population dependent upon the rich and noble minority. Dependency, whether physical, social, or economic, plays a prominent role even in current definitions of developmental status. The first two factors, at least, may also account for the lesser distinctions drawn between age groups in primitive societies in more recent times.

Biological. While laymen were rediscovering a concept of adolescence, biologists had returned to the ancient usage, adopting the term "adolescence" for the period between puberty and the termination of physical growth. In 1795 the first systematic study of an adolescent phenomenon appeared (Osiander 1795), antedating by about a century objective research on the behavior of adolescents. The volume and breadth of the literature grew, so that by the time Hall published his *Adolescence* he drew on more than sixty studies of physical growth alone, conducted in a number of different countries.

Puberty and reproduction. In the early studies, puberty sometimes meant the age of menarche in females and the age of the first seminal emission in males and sometimes the age of the first appearance of pubic hair in either sex. Termination of growth was equated with the end of growth in height. As more data became available, qualifications and refinements became necessary. Definitions of puberty are particularly difficult, and those given in most dictionaries—for example, "the period when sexual maturity is reached"—simply do not fit the facts. There is considerable evidence to indicate that nubility, the capacity to beget or bear offspring, may not be acquired until some time after menarche or first ejaculation. Furthermore, the first externally visible sign of sexual maturation is usually growth of the testes in the male and the beginning of breast development in the female, not the appearance of pubic hair. However, the order of appearance of secondary characteristics is not always the same. Some biologists prefer to consider pubescence as beginning when the levels of androgen and estrogen secretion start to rise (at about five to eight years). Defining adolescence as beginning at puberty is probably defensible if puberty means the first external sign of sexual maturation and if this development is interpreted as meaning that the complex series of processes involved in sexual maturation are already under way.

Termination of growth. It is also now clear that termination of growth in height should not be used as the sole criterion for the termination of adolescence. The anatomical and physiological changes are pervasive in quantity and quality; almost all tissues and organ systems are involved; and the length of the period of growth and change differs for different dimensions and functions. Because physical growth and changes in physiological processes arise from the hormonal changes producing reproductive maturation and are highly correlated with sexual development, a definition in which reproductive maturity is the primary referent is most satisfactory. One of the best current definitions is that of Ford and Beach: "Adolescence is the period extending from puberty to the attainment of full reproductive maturity. . . . Different parts of the reproductive system reach their maximal efficiency at different stages in the life cycle; and, strictly speaking, adolescence is not completed until all the structures and processes necessary to fertilization, conception, gestation, and lactation have become mature" (1951, pp. 171–172). This definition takes into account the fact that many physical structures and metabolic processes not directly classifiable as sexual affect reproductive maturity.

Theories of adolescence

To speak of theories of adolescence is misleading. No theory deals simply with adolescence. Each theoretical conception of adolescence is a part of a broader view of the developmental continuum, whether this be biological, psychological, or social. Some behavioral, developmental schema are an integral part of a theory of personality (for example, that of Freud) or of a theory of a certain class of behavior (for instance, Piaget's cognitive theory). Others are derived from the constructs of a general theory of behavior, such as Lewin's, but are not essential to the system. Furthermore, most of these parent formulations are closer to being descriptions or master plans than to being systems that admit of testable predications. However, convenience is served by retaining the conventional label of theory.

The following account is directed primarily toward tracing the origin and relationships of the more influential hypotheses and concepts about adolescence. Only the initial or most typical forms can be reviewed, and extremely abbreviated summaries of the theories from which they came will be given.

A year after Hall's *Adolescence* appeared, Freud published his first essay on adolescence (1905). There is little to suggest that either man drew on the other, yet in addition to being the first theorists specifically to consider adolescence, they had many ideas in common. Both postulated an innate sequence of stages in which affective development is primary and much of behavior instinctually determined. Reproductive maturation gives rise to a certain discontinuity in development and to many psychological problems. Behaviorally, adolescence is a period of emotional upheaval, behavioral contradictions, and particular vulnerability to regression and psychopathology. Only one line of Hall's massive two volumes can be interpreted as a definition of adolescence—he mentions the years from 14 to 24. His discussion indicates, however, an acceptance of the then current biological definition of adolescence as beginning at puberty and ending with the cessation of physical growth, and these ages fit the range of those landmarks at the time. It is possible to infer a more behavioral conception from Freud. Adolescence is initiated by puberty but presumably terminates with attainment of genital maturity in a psychological sense.

Hall—recapitulation theory. In Hall's amplification of recapitulation theory—the doctrine that during ontogenesis man recapitulates the phylogeny of the species and the evolution of human society—adolescence corresponds to a stressful, transitional period in cultural evolution. Its last phase, paralleling the formation of civilized societies, is not reached by all. At adolescence, the rule of instinct and self-concern is broken and, given proper environmental circumstances, the individual becomes able to further the advance of civilization. Although several other theorists incorporate modifications of the concept, literal recapitulation theory was short-lived. Stripped of biogenetic theory and Victorian phraseology, however, Hall's portrait of adolescence constitutes the major part of many current descriptions, and the core of some later theories lies in certain of his observations. His characterization of adolescence as a time of *Sturm und Drang* is always cited. Less often recognized are his observations on the shift of patterns of affectional attachment from same-sex peers to older members of the opposite sex and finally to opposite-sex age mates, the prevalence of hero worship, and the importance of peer-group affiliations for socialization. He saw a relationship between sexually based affectional patterns and developing capacities for logical thinking and abstraction and a reflection of heterosexual interests in recreational choices, dress, and the like.

Gesell—the maturation process. The subsequent character of adolescent psychology was also imprinted with Hall's concern for the normative course of all aspects of behavior. This orientation is exemplified by the work of Arnold Gesell (Gesell et al. 1956). Gesell's central concept is maturation—innate, universal processes of development modified by individual genetic inheritance. The influence of "acculturation" is acknowledged but not examined. Unique to Gesell are his year-by-year descriptions of classes of behavior, which carry stage analysis to its ultimate conclusion. Thus, he objects to speaking of adolescence as a whole and finds not general contradictions in behavior but yearly oscillations between positive and negative characteristics. The limits of adolescence are defined in physical terms, and innate processes bring about concomitant progress in reasoning ability and preferences in interpersonal relationships. Psychologically, the adolescent must come to terms with his assets and liabilities [*see* GESELL].

Freud—psychosexual development. Freud's libidinal genetic model places less emphasis on adolescence as a formative period than does Hall's phylogenetic theory. Nevertheless, resolution of the psychosexual conflicts of adolescence, the last phase of the genital stage, are necessary for complete, healthy adult functioning. Puberty reactivates and intensifies both genital and pregenital impulses. If genital maturity is to be achieved, the individual must free himself of the heterosexual attachments appropriate to early stages and the homosexual attachments of latency and early pubescence. Altruistic relationships to the love object must substantially replace narcissism. In the need for the adolescent to become emotionally independent of his parents Freud saw the source of adolescent rebellion. Emotional instability, anxiety, moodiness, and aggressiveness stem from feelings of inadequacy to meet the conflicting demands of powerful motivational forces and the societal restrictions on their expression that by this time have been quite well internalized. To Freud belongs the credit for germinating two concepts that currently enjoy widespread, nonpartisan popularity. The first is the effect of bodily changes on the self-image, both through self-perception and the influence of social interactions. The second is the developmental task, foreshadowed in libidinal forces and attachments to be overcome. Stemming also from Freud is the substitution of the principle of the coexistence and integration of phases for a simple succession of stages.

The revisionists and separatists. Psychoanalytic theory diverged into two camps—the revisionists, who elaborated the classic system, and the separatists, who defected and promulgated their own theories.

Rank. Otto Rank, an early separatist, organized his stages around the development of the "will," a creative, conscious force shaping the self. In his sequence, adolescence assumes importance because at puberty the continuing struggle to become independent is complicated by the need to resist one's own physiological drives. Rank also posited that in seeking independence the adolescent may use two defense mechanisms—asceticism and promiscuity. This apposition is similar to Spranger's "pure love" versus sexuality (1925), Bühler's spiritual and sensual aspects of sexuality (1935), and Sullivan's intimacy versus lust (1940–1945) [*see* RANK].

Sullivan. Sullivan (1940–1945) is a more recent separatist and the most resolute in stage analysis. His interpersonal theory of psychiatry is usually classified with social-psychological or social learning theories, because anxiety acquired in social interactions replaces instinctive sources of motivation, and developmental stages characterized by particular types of personal interactions supplant the libidinal genetic model. The development of cognitive processes—ways of experiencing interactions with the environment—is included in his system. Biological maturation, in the form of

capacities for perceiving and performing, underlies Sullivan's developmental sequence, but, with the exception of Piaget, no one has gone so far as he in making definitions of stages independent of physical attributes. For Western societies (the pattern in others may vary), he describes seven stages of interpersonal relationships ([1940–1945] 1953, pp. 33–34). The third, or *juvenile*, era ends and *preadolescence* begins with "the eruption, due to maturation, of a need for an intimate relation with another person of comparable status." To the juvenile stage are attributed capacities that others reserve to adolescence, for example, ability to think about and evaluate one's typical interpersonal reactions, awareness of the conditions that promote freedom from anxiety, and awareness of the goals for which one is willing to delay immediate gratification. Similarly, where Freud held that adolescence is the time when altruism begins to replace narcissism, Sullivan found less selfish, more mutual relations arising during preadolescence. This brief but important period is usually terminated, and *adolescence* initiated, by "the eruption of genital sexuality and puberty, but psychologically or psychiatrically" by "the movement of strong interest from a person of one's own sex to a person of the other sex." Physiological manifestations of puberty are accompanied by lustful sensations, which develop into the "lust dynamism." The heterosexual need is strong, but so also are needs for intimacy and security. Attempts to achieve a balance in the reduction of tensions arising from all three are the source of many adolescent conflicts. Until a pattern of behavior for satisfying the lust dynamism has been adopted, adolescence continues. *Late adolescence* encompasses a rather lengthy period of initiation into the range of adult roles, prerogatives, and obligations, the strengthening and equilibration of the self-system, and the broadening of symbolic capacities. *Adulthood* is achieved when one is able to form a love relationship in which "the other person is as significant or nearly as significant as one's self" [*see* SULLIVAN].

Anna Freud. In extending ego psychology, Anna Freud (1936) gave more attention and importance to adolescence. At least with respect to this period, she used a stage framework already established (and still prevalent) among non-Freudian European developmental psychologists. This sequence consists of three major stages, each subdivided into three phases. The first phase of the last two stages is marked by negativism and a "loosening" and instability of psychic organization. Thus, prepubescence becomes the time of greatest emotional upheaval; at puberty the turmoil subsides. Anna Freud attributed the prepuberal disturbance to a rise in diffuse libidinal energy. Alleviation results from the focusing of impulses and the utilization of two defense mechanisms particularly characteristic of adolescence—asceticism (similar to Rank's postulation) and intellectualization.

Erikson—identity. Of the Neo-Freudians drawing on variables from the social sciences, Erikson (1950) has detailed the developmental sequence most explicitly. His eight psychosocial crises in ego development cover the span from infancy through old age, the first five paralleling Freud's libidinal crises. The series is universal, but each person works out individual solutions within those offered by the institutions of his culture and their representation through significant caretakers. How successfully each conflict is resolved depends upon ego strength developed during earlier crises and the meaningfulness of the reinforcements provided by the environmental context for the current one. Although earlier stages contribute to the formation of ego identity, it is the adolescent crisis that integrates the previous ones and is defined as a conflict of identity versus role diffusion. Marked physical changes and sexual awareness and the reactions of a larger group of significant persons to these threaten the continuity of self. The adolescent is called upon to create a constructive "I" consistent with his earlier self-concept and competencies and with the "me" seen by his culture and companions, of which he is certain and with which he is comfortable. The primary problem within an industrialized society is selecting a vocational identity; clear sexual identity is established later in adolescence. In this process, the adolescent attempts to maintain himself by plunging into the peer group and overidentifying with its heroes. Then he begins to fall in love. The relationship is not primarily sexual, unless the culture so requires. It serves rather to clarify identity through the projection and reflection of diffused images. During late adolescence and early adulthood conflicts center upon relationships that demand an abandonment of self.

Erikson points to loss of the clear and limited role definitions that are provided by autocracies and agrarian societies as the major source of identity problems in most freer and urbanized societies today. He contrasts particularly the difficulties, supports, and solutions of American and German adolescents. Among middle-class and upper-class Americans a long social adolescence provides a "psychosocial moratorium" in which to establish identity. A typical adolescent male with well-defined ego identity is basically at peace with himself. His greatest concerns are those of sexuality; ego restriction is his dominant defense mechanism, occasionally relieved by delinquencies. He is anti-intellectual and cannot, as can his German counterpart, become an uncompromising idealist. Rebellion and superego conflicts present fewer problems in the United States for a number of reasons—a heritage of contrasts and experience with individual revolution, diffusion of the father ideal, fraternal relationship with the father, early independence from the mother, democratic consideration of individual interests within the family, and focusing of conflicts on peers. German adolescence, on the other hand, is the prototype of "storm and stress." The older rural and regional value systems have not yet been replaced with others that integrate societal ideals and educational methods and give meaning to the father's behavior. Furthermore, institutionalized outlets, such as the *Wanderschaft*, are no longer available. The most common solution under these conditions is to rebel and then submit [*see* IDENTITY, PSYCHOSOCIAL].

Blos. Blos, another revisionist, refers to "the physical manifestations of sexual maturation" as puberty and to the "psychological processes of adaptation to the condition of pubescence" as adolescence (1962, p. 2). He has further delineated the phases of adolescence and their associated processes, capitalizing upon the work of Anna Freud and Erikson, among others. The psychological basis of these definitions is made clear by pointing out that an individual may remain preadolescent despite the progress of sexual maturation. *Latency* is defined by the "lack of new sexual aim . . . rather than the complete lack of sexual activity." The adolescent phases have different major components and problems for males and females. For both sexes *preadolescence* brings a quantitative increase of instinctual forces and a resurgence of "all libidinal and aggressive modes of gratification which served during the early years," accompanied by intractability and compensatory behavior. For boys, however, the phase is one of diffuse homosexual defense against castration anxiety. Among girls the primary problem is preoedipal attachment to the mother.

Early adolescence and *adolescence proper* bring qualitative changes. During early adolescence boys form idealized friendships. Same-sex friendships are also important for girls, but they tend toward "crushes" on members of either sex and greater preoccupation with questions of sexual identity. Adolescence proper is characterized by reactivation of oedipal conflicts, detachment from primary love objects, and heterosexual object choice. Mental organization becomes more complex, emotions deeper and more intense, and there is a sense of finality in choices. Narcissism and overestimation of capacities are common. Unique to this period is "tender love," which later becomes fused with sexuality. Asceticism and intellectualization are seen as defenses of adolescence proper, not earlier phases. However, Blos states, as does Erikson, that these defenses are typical only of upper-class and middle-class European adolescents. American adolescents experience "conformism," a compound of such defense mechanisms as identification, denial, isolation, and counterphobia. During adolescence proper hierarchical organization begins; pregenital satisfactions become subordinated in an initial role rather than maintaining a consummatory one. If this restructuring does not occur, ego development is delayed. "Adolescence proper comes to a close with the delineation of an idiosyncratic conflict and drive constellation, which during *late adolescence* is transformed into a unified and integrated system" (Blos 1962, p. 127; italics added). Late adolescence is a period of consolidation and decisive crisis—sexual identity is irreversibly established. A transitional phase—*postadolescence*—intervenes before adulthood, during which further integration occurs, even if adult occupational and familial roles have already been assumed.

Spranger—mental structures. Soon after Hall and Freud set forth their positions, Spranger introduced a third trend that has prevailed in European thinking about development to date—the study of "mental structures" (organization of psychological processes). Only recently, with a revival of interest in Piaget's work, has this approach become familiar to American psychologists. They know the typological theories of adult personality in which some of this work is set, but not their developmental forms. Few, for example, are aware of Spranger's textbook on adolescence (1925), although it has been through 24 editions and established Spranger as Hall's counterpart, the European "father of adolescent psychology." Spranger frequently mentions instincts, and both his theory of adult personality and his developmental theory contain more emphasis on innate than on environmental determinants; however, his adult typologies are based on values rather than somatotypes, and he finds physiological factors of no help in understanding behavior. He does recognize societal influences, stating that his formulations apply directly only to middle-class German males and predicting greater differences between urban and rural youth than between those in the lower and middle classes.

Spranger conceptualizes adolescence as a period during which the undifferentiated psychological structure of the child is reorganized through self-discovery, emergence of his own value hierarchy, and development of a life plan. Concern about the self leads to feelings of isolation, greater need for social interaction and approval, experimentation with identities (including hero-worship), and rebellion against societal and familial traditions. Choosing a vocation is only one aspect of the general expansion of time perspective and of activity directed toward the integration of a value system, all phases of which may temporarily involve exaggerated estimates of ability. In adolescence reality becomes separated from fantasy, self from the world, and sexuality from pure love. The conscious distinction and different objects of sexuality and pure love help in the definition of the ego, but fusion of these two aspects of sexuality, which develop independently during adolescence, must occur if sexual maturity is to be attained. Spranger proposed that the "storm and stress" mode was one of three possible types of adolescent development; the others are gradual, continuous change and self-initiated, active participation. This idea recurs among the constitutional typologists, who see the degree of adolescent disturbance as influenced by the basic personality type. Many of Spranger's ideas have subsequently been widely adopted.

Piaget—cognitive structures. Piaget, an epistemologist who has concentrated on qualitative changes in cognitive structures, uses a biological model of organism–environment interaction; intelligence is a form of biological adaptation. Cognitive content, but not process, varies with the culture, and some individuals and societal groups never develop the most advanced intellective structures. Stages are regarded as abstractions, not entities, relevant only when the behavior in question has certain properties. Cognitive development does fit a stage format. Piaget distinguishes three major periods, each with a number of subdivisions, beginning with the infant's undifferentiated world of reflexes and terminating, during adolescence, in a formal, logical system of combinatorial operations. With the exception of studies of moral judgment, none of Piaget's research has involved personal and social behavior. On occasion, however, Piaget has discussed the relationship between cognitive and affective development. The latter is parallel to, and interdependent with, cognitive organization, another perspective on the same structural system. In particular (Inhelder & Piaget 1955), it is pointed out that the intellectual transformations of adolescence imply concomitant social transformations and a complete reorganization of the personality.

The adolescent becomes capable of hypothetico-deductive and inductive reasoning. He can conceptualize and operate not only upon present reality, but also upon abstract and remote possibilities. These abilities provide the intellectual framework for taking up adult roles, assimilating social values, and arriving at an individualized value system and life plan. Social interactions are no longer simply of a direct, interpersonal sort; they involve relationships to social institutions and ethical and political codes. Abstractions rather than persons now represent ideals and values. Even when he falls in love, the adolescent shows his inclination for theory by constructing a romance.

Neither the cognitive nor affective changes of adolescence are related to puberty. Neural maturation and experience underlie the former. The latter is initiated when the child begins to assume adult roles; thus adolescence is defined as a social transition. Instead of accepting adults as superior and dominant, the adolescent sees them as equals and sees the adult world as one he may enter and change. Whenever a new cognitive structure is evolving, thought is egocentric, i.e., subjective and undifferentiated. The adolescent tries as much to adapt the world to himself as the converse. His self-assertion, plans to reform society, and imitation of heroes do not include an understanding of the views of others. He fails to recognize that some adult activities are not yet possible for him. Such lack of differentiation necessarily produces conflicts and what appears to be deliberate rebellion. Experience within the peer group and in an occupation brings about the "decentering" prerequisite to objectivity and multiple perspective [see Developmental psychology, *article on* A theory of development].

Remplein—a synthesis of structures. Where Piaget represents a specialization of interests in mental structures, Remplein (1949) coalesces a more general structural orientation with several theoretical forms prominent in European psychology: (1) "three stages with three phases" developmental theory, (2) personality theory based on constitutional typologies, and (3) stratification theory of personality (after World War II "layer" theories of personality became popular in Germany). Specifically, he adapted and combined Kroh's developmental theory (1928), which includes a view of cognitive development much like Piaget's and a description of personality changes, the developmental adaptations of Kretschmer's constitutional typology devised by Conrad (1941)

and Stratz (1903), and Lersch's (1938) three-layer theory of personality. By adding a neuroanatomical substructure to the last he gives his amalgam an evolutionary flavor and provides a neural basis for a pattern of mental development ranging from reflex action and physiognomic perception to deduction and creativity. The psychological processes in the lowest layer, the vital-needs stratum, are associated with basic physiological functions and stem from the old brain. Attitudes, interests, and nonvital emotions come from the middle, or endothymic, stratum. For example, sex is a vital need; love is endothymic; the two are integrated and directed toward a mate during the last phase of adolescence. Self-control and cognition are neocortical functions associated with the upper, or personal, stratum. Intellectual and volitional control is acquired very gradually and is never complete: the lower strata retain some autonomy [see Psychology, *article on* constitutional psychology; Kretschmer].

The pattern of personality development Remplein outlines is in large measure typical of German theories. Prepuberty is the last phase of the childhood stage. Just prior to puberty the formerly active, aggressive, capable, reality-oriented child becomes introverted. In the first phase of adolescence (the second negativistic phase), aggressiveness and activity are augmented, and desires for adventure and groups of companions appear. As sexual drives emerge and physical maturation begins, the self-image is disturbed, and "storm and stress" ensues. A person whose basic personality type is schizoid will be particularly disturbed because adolescence is a "schizoid" period. A cycloid personality, on the other hand, will balance the developmentally determined schizoid characteristics, and adolescent turmoil will be minimal. As the new and increased needs penetrate the personal stratum, where capacities for abstraction and logical thinking are continuing to develop, the adolescent becomes reflective and seeks autonomy and greater knowledge. The need for independence increases further during the second phase, fusing with more thoughtful planning, identity experimentation, and desire for self-improvement. This combination produces a re-evaluation, and perhaps rejection, of previously acquired attitudes and values. During the last phase the self-concept and value system are harmonized; heterosexual adjustments and relationships to persons and to society are established; goal-directed activity increases; and a philosophy of life is sought.

Anthropological influences. Having traced European psychological concepts of adolescence, we return to an advance in cultural anthropology that had a major impact on developmental theory. Both Hall and Freud were familiar with the anthropological data of their time. Hall, for example, devoted three chapters of his *Adolescence* to early cultures and to contemporary primitive cultures. But these data had not been collected with a view to relating culture and personality development. Late in the 1920s, Malinowski, Benedict, Margaret Mead and others set out in a more systematic fashion to bring anthropological methods to bear on this question. Their data forcefully challenged the assumptions of universality explicit or implicit in recapitulation and Freudian theory. A great range of practices in dealing with puberty were reported—prolonged, complicated puberal rites; brief, simple ceremonies; no recognition. In some groups, the ceremonies entirely missed the period for many initiates, because they were held only every four years. Adolescent rebellion, behavioral contradictions, and patterns of peer-group affiliations were not invariant. Adults had different expectations of the adolescent. In Samoa adolescents were expected to work well, be loyal to the family, and not to be presumptuous or troublesome; Hawaiian Chinese parents assume children will present fewer problems as they get older. Benedict has provided the only attempt to formalize the implications of these observations. She proposed that the apparent discontinuities in behavioral development arise from discontinuities in social conditions and expectancies and pointed to three particular dimensions in social roles and interpersonal relationships that produce behavioral disruptions—responsible versus nonresponsible status, dominance versus submission, and contrasted sex role (Benedict 1938, p. 143). Gradual induction into adult patterns is postulated to prevent psychological distress and behavioral disturbance. More recently the cultural anthropologists have moved away from their early position of extreme cultural relativism. Indeed, at times there seems to be an embarrassing eclecticism. Cross-cultural data—once used to deny innate maturational patterns and the psychoanalytic oedipal and latency stages and to establish group differences in personality—now are used as evidence of Gesell's stages, Freud's stages, and constitutional types. However, a healthy antidote had been introduced that is reflected in empirical research and almost all textbooks and contemporary theory in developmental psychology. In combination with a growing interest among sociologists in the effect of intracultural institutions on development, the anthropological data drew greater attention to subgroup differences within societies as well [see ANTHROPOLOGY, *especially the article on* CULTURAL ANTHROPOLOGY; CULTURE].

Social learning theory. At about the same time that the anthropologists were producing their first data, learning theorists began to resist biological theories, largely on conjectural, theoretical grounds (Hollingworth 1928). Data have substantiated the validity of their resistance. Social learning theory actually combines reinforcement learning theory with psychoanalytic concepts and some of the insights of cultural anthropology and sociology. No one person can be taken as representative of this position, particularly in all its aspects. In general, social learning theorists have not been concerned with distinguishing stages. When they use labels for a group under study they tend to assume some biological definition of adolescence or else they simply use age or school-grade groups. Because learning is a continuous process, development is expected to be continuous unless societal expectations change. Those who concentrate on the reinforcement aspects of social learning observe how far the child or adolescent has progressed in learning a particular task in relation to the system of rewards and punishments that have been used, for instance, the parental child-rearing practices.

Most of the research has centered on five areas of socialization—feeding, elimination, sex, aggression, and dependency—and the development of identification and self-concepts, particularly sexual identity. Three conceptualizations of the way in which identification develops are currently under study—the Freudian model of identification with a feared and powerful father, a learning theory model of imitation of a nurturant parent, and a sociological combination of these two, i.e., identification with a powerful parent who both rewards and punishes. Learning theorists, as do the Freudians, emphasize early learning, so the major proportion of research has been conducted with infants and young children. However, considerable attention has been given to adolescents in studies of aggression (Bandura & Walters 1959) and of the role of peer groups in the development of self-esteem and attitudes.

Other research within social learning theory has focused on analyzing what persons at various points in the developmental continuum are expected to learn. This approach has given rise to lists of developmental tasks, of which Havighurst's is most frequently cited. His list is based on Western, complex cultures, but it is assumed that lists could be made for any culture or subgroup and that certain tasks, e.g., those with large biological components, will vary less from group to group. Among the adolescent's tasks are accepting one's physique and sex role, emotional independence from parents and other adults, choosing and preparing for a vocation, and preparing for marriage and parenthood (Havighurst [1948] 1951, pp. 30–55). [*See* Aggression; Imitation; Learning, *article on* reinforcement; Learning theory; Self concept; Socialization.]

Lewin—field theory. Lewin's application of field theory to adolescence provides a model for predicting the data of the cultural anthropologists and for explaining the effect of physical changes on the self-image (1939). Lewin represented behavior as a function of the "life space," which consists of the person within his "psychological environment" (the environment as he sees it). The life space is described by dimensions of reality and time perspective and the number, kind, and organization of its regions. There are individual, developmental, and cultural differences in these parameters. In general, the scope, differentiation, and hierarchical organization of the life space increase during development. When changes in the life space are rapid and thoroughgoing, the period is said to be one of transition. At least in Western societies, adolescence is such a period. The extent and kinds of behavior of the "storm and stress" variety are a function of the degree to which these three conditions prevail—(1) movement away from familiar territory (the child group), some of which is now blocked against return, to strange territory (the adult group), parts of which are not yet open; (2) marked expansion of time perspective under difficult circumstances, i.e., in regions about which one has little or contradictory information; and (3) bodily changes that render unfamiliar a once familiar region. The source of difficulties in the first condition is not the abruptness of the shift (as in puberal rites), but the clear separation between child and adult groups. An adolescent is in the position of a "marginal man," who does not fully belong to either of two distinct groups. His behavior is similar to that of the person from a minority group who is "passing the line"—tense, unstable, contradictory (boisterous or shy, sensitive and aggressive), and intolerant. The second characteristic makes it difficult to formulate life plans and leads to a tendency to follow persons or groups that offer a structured value system.

Lack of differentiation and of cognitive structure typify all "locomotion" into unknown regions. Conditions (1) and (3) intensify these factors, and in conjunction with the greater impact of new regions during rapid changes, produce tension, instability, and uncertain behavior. Increased plasticity also accompanies transitions because the individual has no anchor in either old or new regions. Together with the lack of differentiation this characteristic facilitates the emergence of radicalism [*see* Field theory; Lewin].

Empirical data

How do the data of adolescence compare with these theories? How do those who are not committed to a particular theoretical viewpoint interpret the data? Limitations on references make it impossible to cite the original sources contributing to the composite empirical adolescent, but a broad and balanced sampling of the documentation can be found in Kuhlen (1952) and in Zubek and Solberg (1954). These texts present data and conclusions that have not been controverted by later evidence and provide the advantage of a developmental orientation. The developmental approach is essential, for aside from cultural bias, the major source of misconceptions about adolescence is failure to consider trends over the total developmental span. Attributes assigned to adolescence when only that group is assessed are often, in fact, more characteristic of children or adults or equally applicable to all ages.

Intellectual development.   Many theorists refer to the adolescent's increased capacities for abstraction and logic, "theoretical world views," expansion of time perspective, intellectualization, and greater differentiation of mental abilities. Relevant data cannot be obtained directly from performance curves, because standardized intelligence tests are constructed to yield a regular increase in mental age over a considerable chronological age span, and cognitive tasks of the type used by Piaget are not scored quantitatively. However, when absolute scaling techniques are applied to standardized tests, the resulting growth curve is steady and continuous, gradually decelerating during adolescence. Factor analyses do suggest greater differentiation of abilities among adolescents than among children, but, again, there is no indication of sudden changes. Examination of individual mental test curves and comparison of mean curves for the sexes and for groups of either sex maturing physically at different rates show no consistent inflections or relationship to puberty. Another sort of influence of rate of physical maturation is, however, suggested by research on the mode of expression of intellectual competency. Among early and late maturing boys of equal IQ, the former tend to achieve through conformity, the latter through independence (Jones 1965). Piaget asserts that certain experiences affect the level or timing of acquisition of cognitive structures, e.g., that entering a vocation promotes "decentering," but research designed to test such inferences is not available.

Physical development. The effects of biological adolescence are seen most clearly in physical development—strength as well as size and shape— and in sexual behaviors, broadly defined. Acceleration of growth begins later for strength than for height and other physical dimensions, and in males marked increments continue longer, but the timing of muscular development is highly correlated with rate of physiological maturing. A considerable body of data on the psychological and social correlates of maturation rate has accumulated. Adults see the physiologically advanced as socially more mature than their slower maturing chronological age-mates and are willing to grant them greater autonomy and responsibility (Barker et al. 1946). Physiological maturity is positively related to status within the peer group, to self-concepts, and to affectionate feelings and lack of rebelliousness toward parents (Eichorn 1963; Jones 1965). Recent analyses point to strength and general physiological maturity as more important than sheer size (Jones 1965). The findings with respect to self-concepts and attitudes toward parents have been cross-validated in part in Italy as well as in the United States (Mussen & Bouterline-Young 1964). Motor skills in general improve with age, but their relationship to physical maturity is less definitive. Moreover, adolescent awkwardness, a characteristic mentioned by many writers, is not supported by objective measurement. The most plausible explanation for instances of assumed lack of coordination—and other than anecdotal evidence on this point is lacking—is social discomfort and inexperience.

Sexual development. Cross-culturally, increasing heterosexual interest—expressed directly or indirectly—is the most distinctive characteristic of adolescence. In the United States the trend, as represented, for example, by concern for personal appearance, ability to make a good impression, sexual morality, continues through the twenties. None of the techniques devised by restrictive societies has succeeded in completely eliminating intercourse among adolescents (Ford & Beach 1951). Even in those cultures that allow sex play and copulation among the young, pubescence brings a more directed, intense quality to the behavior and is accompanied by interest in adornment, acquisition of skills valued in marriage, and whatever behaviors the society links with mature

sexuality. In calm, permissive Samoa, the girls "flutter" and become self-conscious (Mead 1928). One of the earliest relationships to be documented in the United States was that between physical maturation and maturity of interests, particularly those involving culturally patterned heterosexuality. The shifts are not abrupt, nor would they be predicted to be. The hormonal and physical changes are not abrupt; some of the interests and activities included in scales of maturity of interests are culturally appropriate over a wide age range, e.g., fishing, for males; and well-established habits are extinguished gradually. Nevertheless, the curves for interests and behaviors tied to heterosexuality, such as dancing and dress, rise more steeply during adolescence than those for many other attitudes and performances. Some observers have speculated that youngsters might take up these behaviors under social pressure, without concomitant physical maturation or real involvement. The few studies that speak to this question (e.g., More 1955) indicate that extremely late maturers do not. Some less markedly slow in physical development do go through the motions, but psychological assessment shows that emotional investment is absent, and often the social overtures are not treated as meaningful by peers.

Vocational and economic concerns. Among industrialized societies, increasing preoccupation with economic or vocational concerns, particularly in males, looms next in prominence in the data on adolescence. Again, the pattern persists well into adulthood. Reports from less complex cultures are not sufficiently detailed to permit comparative statements. Graded contributions to the economy according to age or size are more common, but in many groups, puberal ceremonies signal not complete adult status, but the initiation of a more systematic training in adult economic and civic roles.

Emotional development and personal maturity. The anthropological data on the "storm and stress" aspects of adolescence have already been touched upon. Within the United States, the evidence for such phenomena ranges from negative to equivocal, as do many of the data bearing on the assumed sources, such as discontinuities in responsibility and autonomy (Barker & Wright 1954; Bandura & Walters 1959). Put very baldly, without qualifications for sex, class, or caste, the average American adolescent is not anxious, emotionally unstable, unhappy, aggressive, or rebellious. Fears and worries decrease with age and become less concrete and more socially oriented. In this process, the adolescent is intermediate between the child and the adult. Only a small proportion of adolescents report symptoms of anxiety and emotionality, and across the span from 15 years to old age, adolescents have the lowest index of emotionality. By teacher and parent report and observations in school, adolescents show fewer behavior problems than younger children. Late childhood or prepubescence, rather than adolescence, are reported as periods of increase in behavioral problems. Incidence of crime and mental illness rises gradually from early childhood through young adulthood; delinquency rates then drop, while mental illness rates continue to increase. Furthermore, a large proportion of those who become delinquent or disturbed during adolescence began showing symptoms much earlier. Elderly adults rate adolescence second only to young adulthood as the period of greatest happiness, and the majority of adolescents state they are happy most of the time. Both overt and fantasy aggression decrease with age. Socially directed aggression and internalized aggression (depression) increase. The latter appears particularly during early adulthood. The few studies that report greater aggressive fantasy during puberty are characterized by methodological errors, such as failure to obtain data on younger subjects and inadequate knowledge of the subjects' maturity status. Attachments to peers appear early in the United States, but relations with parents improve with age, and the peer group never outweighs the parents for the majority of adolescents. Parental values are more often chosen over those peers if the two are opposed. Between infancy and adolescence the sources of parent–child conflict do, however, change [see PERSONALITY].

Data on a few specific behaviors frequently mentioned in theories are also available. Crushes occur with high frequency among girls. Diary-keeping (frequently mentioned in psychoanalytic discussions) is also a female activity, but at peak incidence only about one-third of samples of girls are so engaged. Daydreaming becomes common during adolescence and is another behavior for which the frequency continues to increase into young adulthood, staying high until about age thirty. Hero-worship—if contemporary "glamorous adults" are included in the definition—is a characteristic of childhood trailing into early adolescence. True hero-worship may be more common in other Western nations, for instance, Germany.

Overview

With certain exceptions, theorists have not been active in producing evidence for their hypotheses, particularly with respect to adolescence. The rea-

sons are several. Many of the formulations are essentially unverifiable. The proponents of theories have not, in the main, been interested in development or adolescence per se, but rather in personality, therapy, cognition, or the like. Finally, the observations that many seek to account for are drawn from small, atypical samples. On the other hand, the developmentalists, who have collected most of the data, have tended to be atheoretical. Textbooks on adolescence, which reflect this orientation almost entirely, typically contain summaries of large numbers of empirical studies and only cursory references to theory. The greatest deficiency in the body of empirical data is information needed to link theory to data—definitive studies of the variables influencing the emergence or extinction of interests, attitudes, emotions, and behaviors. Certain relationships to biological maturation are reasonably well-documented, but comparable and qualifying evidence for other parameters is markedly lacking. Those interested in interpersonal and societal variables have not capitalized on methods used in the longer established biological tradition. For example, feelings of independence, extent of rebellion, or self-concepts have not been compared among adolescents completely dependent on parents, partially employed, and fully employed. Multiple-factor designs, permitting assessment of the interaction between physiological, intellectual, emotional, and social variables, are extremely rare. Anthropological data now available do not permit separation of variables such as responsibility and dominance, nor the extraction of their influence from the total cultural context.

Harbingers of *rapprochement* are appearing from both sides. If one looks beyond the particular terminologies and disciplinary frames of reference, represented in the numerous conceptual views of the developmental continuum and of adolescence in particular, communalities and lines of cleavage emerge that narrow the task of verification. Current textbooks and review volumes are beginning to reflect some integration of data collection and theory and greater ingenuity in the use of both experimental and correlational designs.

DOROTHY H. EICHORN

[See also DEVELOPMENTAL PSYCHOLOGY. Other relevant material may be found in AGING; DELINQUENCY, articles on PSYCHOLOGICAL ASPECTS and DELINQUENT GANGS; IDENTITY, PSYCHOSOCIAL; INFANCY; LIFE CYCLE; and in the biography of HALL.]

BIBLIOGRAPHY

ARIÈS, PHILIPPE (1960) 1962 *Centuries of Childhood: A Social History of Family Life.* New York: Knopf. →

First published as *L'enfant et la vie familiale sous l'ancien régime.*

BANDURA, ALBERT; and WALTERS, RICHARD H. 1959 *Adolescent Aggression.* New York: Ronald Press.

BARKER, ROGER G.; and WRIGHT, HERBERT F. 1954 *Midwest and Its Children.* Evanston, Ill.: Row.

BARKER, ROGER G. et al. (1946) 1953 *Adjustment to Physical Handicap and Illness.* 2d ed. New York: Social Science Research Council.

BENEDICT, RUTH 1938 Continuities and Discontinuities in Cultural Conditioning. *Psychiatry* 1:161–167.

BLOS, PETER 1962 *On Adolescence: A Psychoanalytic Interpretation.* New York: Free Press.

BÜHLER, CHARLOTTE 1935 *From Birth to Maturity.* London: Routledge.

CONRAD, KLAUS 1941 *Der Konstitutionstypus als genetisches Problem.* Berlin: Springer.

DENNIS, WAYNE 1946 The Adolescent. Pages 633–666 in Leonard Carmichael (editor), *Manual of Child Psychology.* New York: Wiley.

EICHORN, DOROTHY H. 1963 Biological Correlates of Behavior. Volume 62, pages 4–61 in National Society for the Study of Education, *Yearbook.* Part 1: Child Psychology. Univ. of Chicago Press.

ERIKSON, ERIK H. (1950) 1964 *Childhood and Society.* 2d ed., rev. & enl. New York: Norton.

FORD, CLELLAN S.; and BEACH, FRANK A. 1951 *Patterns of Sexual Behavior.* New York: Harper.

FREUD, ANNA (1936) 1957 *The Ego and the Mechanisms of Defense.* New York: International Universities Press. → First published as *Das Ich und die Abwehrmechanismen.*

FREUD, SIGMUND (1905) 1953 Three Essays on the Theory of Sexuality. Volume 7, pages 123–245 in *The Standard Edition of the Complete Psychological Works of Sigmund Freud.* New York: Macmillan; London: Hogarth. → First published as *Drei Abhandlungen zur Sexualtheorie.*

GESELL, ARNOLD; ILG, FRANCES L.; and AMES, LOUIS B. 1956 *Youth: The Years From Ten to Sixteen.* New York: Harper.

GOTTLIEB, DAVID; and RAMSEY, CHARLES 1964 *The American Adolescent.* Homewood, Ill.: Dorsey. → Sociological considerations.

HALL, CALVIN S.; and LINDZEY, GARDNER 1957 *Theories of Personality.* New York: Wiley; London: Chapman.

HALL, G. STANLEY 1882 The Moral and Religious Training of Children. *Princeton Review* New Series 9: 26–48.

HALL, G. STANLEY 1904 *Adolescence: Its Psychology and Its Relations to Physiology, Anthropology, Sociology, Sex, Crime, Religion and Education.* 2 vols. New York: Appleton.

HAVIGHURST, ROBERT J. (1948) 1952 *Developmental Tasks and Education.* 2d ed. New York: Longmans.

HOLLINGWORTH, LETA 1928 *The Psychology of the Adolescent.* New York: Appleton.

INHELDER, BÄRBEL; and PIAGET, JEAN (1955) 1958 *The Growth of Logical Thinking From Childhood to Adolescence.* New York: Basic Books. → First published as *De la logique de l'enfant à la logique de l'adolescent.*

JAENSCH, ERICH R.; and HENTZE, RUDOLF 1939 Grundgesetze der Jugendentwicklung. *Zeitschrift für angewandte Psychologie und Charakterkunde,* Beihefte 80: 1–217.

JONES, MARY C. 1965 Psychological Correlates of Somatic Development. *Child Development* 36:899–911.

KROH, OSWALD (1928) 1944 *Entwicklungspsychologie des Grundschulkindes.* 19th ed. Langensalza (Ger-

many): Beyer. → First published as *Die Psychologie des Grundschulkindes in ihrer Beziehung zur kindlichen Gesamtentwicklung.*

KUHLEN, RAYMOND G. 1952 *Psychology of Adolescent Development.* New York: Harper.

LERSCH, PHILIPP (1938) 1951 *Aufbau der Person.* 4th ed. Munich: Barth. → First published as *Aufbau des Charakters.*

LEWIN, KURT 1939 Field Theory and Experiment in Social Psychology: Concepts and Methods. *American Journal of Sociology* 44:868–896.

MEAD, MARGARET (1928) 1961 *Coming of Age in Samoa: A Psychological Study of Primitive Youth for Western Civilization.* New York: Morrow.

MORE, DOUGLAS M. 1955 Developmental Concordance and Discordance During Puberty and Early Adolescence. Society for Research in Child Development, *Monographs* 18, no. 1, Serial no. 56.

MUSSEN, PAUL; and BOUTERLINE-YOUNG, H. 1964 Relationships Between Rate of Physical Maturing and Personality Among Boys of Italian Descent. *Vita humana* 7:186–200.

MUUSS, ROLF E. 1962 *Theories of Adolescence.* New York: Random House. → Includes a review of the developmental aspects of central European typological and stratification theories of personality.

OSIANDER, FRIEDRICH B. 1795 Resultate von Beobachtungen und Nachrichten über die erste Erscheinung des Monatlichen. *Denkwürdigkeiten für die Heilkunde und Geburtshülfe* 2:380–388.

REMPLEIN, HEINZ (1949) 1958 *Die seelische Entwicklung des Menschen im Kindes- und Jugendalter: Grundlagen, Erkenntnisse und pädagogische Folgerungen der Kindes- und Jugendpsychologie.* 7th ed. Munich: Reinhard. → First published as *Die seelische Entwicklung in der Kindheit und Reifezeit.*

SPRANGER, EDUARD (1925) 1955 *Psychologie des Jugendalters.* 24th ed. Heidelberg (Germany): Quelle & Meyer.

STRATZ, C. H. (1903) 1923 *Der Koerper des Kindes und seine Pflege.* 10th ed. Stuttgart (Germany): Enke.

SULLIVAN, HARRY STACK (1940–1945) 1953 *Conceptions of Modern Psychiatry.* With a critical appraisal of the theory by Patrick Mullahy. 2d ed. New York: Norton. → First published in the February 1940 and May 1945 issues of *Psychiatry.*

ZUBEK, JOHN P.; and SOLBERG, P. A. 1954 *Human Development.* New York: McGraw-Hill.

ADOPTION

Adoption is the institutionalized practice through which an individual belonging by birth to one kinship group acquires new kinship ties that are socially defined as equivalent to the congenital ties. These new ties supersede the old ones either wholly or in part. Belonging by birth to a particular kinship group does not imply that all the ties are necessarily biological. For example, in many nonliterate societies biological paternity is of minimal social significance; both paternal status and responsibilities are assumed by other male adults, such as a maternal uncle in matrilineal societies. Such arrangements fall outside the scope of the above definition. However, the drawing of hard and

fast lines between what does and does not constitute adoption is an extremely difficult task. Some
formal arrangements that are legally defined as
adoption establish kinship ties only in relation to
the transmission of property. On the other hand,
some informal arrangements involve a child intensively in a new family of orientation, while at the
same time legally maintaining the separateness of
his identity.

Although adoption practices vary widely around
the world and through time, in one form or another
they appear to approach cultural universality. A
number of motives for adoption have been discussed by Lowie, who ascribed its commonness in
primitive societies to a "generic love of children
that is in no way dependent on a sense of con-
sanguinity" (1930, p. 460). However, both the
universality and the variability of adoption practices can be explained in terms of their *social
functions*.

Promotion of child welfare.   In contemporary
Western societies the chief function served by
adoption is to provide for the care and welfare of
children within a permanent family group. The
child-centeredness of Western adoption practices
is reflected in statutory law. A comparative review
of the adoption statutes of 15 Western nations
(United Nations 1956) found that they all made
some kind of provision for prohibiting any adoption that would not be in the adopted person's
interest. In a review of the origin and development
of American adoption laws, Witmer and others
noted: ". . . most laws (at least as interpreted
judicially) have had the welfare of children as
their main purpose. As a means of promoting the
children's well-being, the laws seek to assure that
adoption is in the children's interest and that they
are adopted by persons who are able and willing
to provide adequately for their care" (Witmer et al.
1963, p. 43).

There are two major ways in which these values
are implemented in American practice. In the first,
the placement of the child is arranged through the
services of a state-licensed child placement agency.
The agency assumes guardianship of the child and
may place the child in a temporary foster home
until adoptive parents meeting agency standards
(often more stringent than those of the courts)
are found. In recent years temporary foster placement has been dispensed with more frequently,
and the child is placed with adoptive parents as
soon as it leaves the hospital where it was born.
This trend reflects a change in how important
adoption agencies regard an assessment of the
child's physical status, temperament, and especially his intellectual capacity in finding the proper

home for him; there is less emphasis in recent
years on "perfect matching."

Placement through a licensed agency is legally
mandatory in only two states. Thus, roughly half
of all nonrelative adoptions are arranged without
the intermediary services of licensed agencies
("independent adoptions"). In such cases, however, the adoptive home is investigated by the court
(or some agency designated by the court) having
the responsibility of determining whether the
adoption is in the best interests of the parties concerned. The focus is on prospects for the child's
social and psychological development, and the
suitability of the adoptive parents is usually the
chief concern in the investigation.

Concern for child welfare is also evident in the
adoption practices of nonliterate societies; however, there is less emphasis on psychological development and more on the physical survival of
the child. Lowie (1930) described cases of maternal mortality in which the surviving infant died
of starvation unless a tribeswoman capable of
nursing was willing to adopt and suckle the child.
He also noted that the high incidence of orphanage
among Plains Indians, as a result of war raids,
was alleviated by adoption. Usually close relatives
adopted the child, but it was not uncommon for
a stranger who had lost a child resembling the
orphan to adopt it as a substitute.

Legitimization.   Birth into a family serves the
function of conferring upon the child a set of
ascribed social positions that define his relationship to other members of the society. When a child
is born outside the family, a problem exists as to
where to locate the child within the society's network of social positions (Winch 1952). While it is
usually easy to identify the child's biological relationship to its mother, there may be a question as
to the child's paternity. According to Malinowski
(1929), in all societies a father (although not
necessarily the biological one) is considered to be
indispensable to the child as a guardian and as a
male link between the child and the rest of society.
This "principle of legitimacy" appears to be culturally universal.

For the child without parents or the child born
outside the family adoption establishes the links
to the larger society by placing him within a family setting. With few exceptions, statuses that would
be ascribed to any natural child of the adopting
family are assumed by the adoptee. The adoptee
is granted legitimacy by being linked to a male
adult. In most societies in which birth out of wed-
lock is stigmatizing to the child, the stigma is
removed through adoption. The adopted child is
treated as if he had belonged to the family all

along. Although there may be some surreptitious gossip about the specialness of the child's status (as in the contemporary United States), the fact of adopted status is rarely concealed by the adoptive parents from either the child or their social acquaintances (Kirk 1964).

The existence of the biological parents may affect both adoptive parents and adoptive children in a variety of ways. In almost all agency adoptions, as well as in most independent arrangements, the identity of the biological parents is unknown to the adopters. A few relevant facts, such as educational level and condition of health, may be all the adoptive parents know. There is a broad range of reactions to this situation, both in the attitudes held by the adoptive parents and in the mode of their describing the natural parents to the child. The adoptive parents may be relatively unconcerned about the child's background, which is most commonly the case, or may seek further and more detailed information. Themes used in telling the child about his adoption may range from presenting his natural parents as "bad" and rejecting to simply indicating that they were unable to take care of him and wanted him to have a good home (Witmer et al. 1963). The degree to which the adoptive parents are able to accept the existence of the child's natural parents without developing rejecting attitudes toward them appears to be positively associated with their satisfaction with the adoption (Kirk 1964). It should be noted that the complete separation of natural and adoptive parents that is common in American society is not universally the case. In some Polynesian groups, although the child is given full kinship status in his adoptive family, he knows and maintains a relationship with his natural parents; this is also the case, of course, in the many societies in which children—or even adults—are adopted in order to secure an inheritance (see below).

Parental status. While it is common to think of adoption as serving to confer certain statuses on the child, it also confers the status of parenthood on adults. In societies in which nonparenthood is somewhat stigmatized and the desire for children is great, there may even be competition for adoptable children. Currently this is the case in the United States; over the last two decades applicants for adoption have outnumbered available children by an approximate ratio of seven to one (nonrelative adoptions only). This shortage in the supply of infants has led to the development of a lively black market in adoptable children. High fees are paid by prospective adopters to persons who can arrange for the placement of a child.

Similar tendencies are found in nonliterate societies, especially in Oceania. Among some East Torres Islanders, children are adopted even prior to birth and often grow up without learning the identity of their natural parents. In the Banks Islands payment of the midwife's fee is sufficient to establish adoptive claim to a child. If the husband of the natural mother cannot afford the fee or happens to be away at the time, another man is likely to arrogate paternity (Lowie 1948, p. 57). This practice of paying the medical expenses of the natural mother in return for custody of the child is remarkably similar to practice in nonagency adoptions in the United States.

In addition to satisfying the desire for children or providing adults with an honorific status, adoption may convey the prerogatives of parental authority to the adopter, thus providing a means of social control. Such is the case in the Japanese system of *oyabun–kobun* (Ishino 1953): a leader, such as a work-gang foreman, becomes a symbolic parent, "adopting" his adult followers ritually.

The transmission of property. Systems of descent and the institution of private property are closely intertwined. In many societies the principal function of the family is to provide lines for the transmission of property. When natural heirs are not available, this function may be served by means of adoption. For example, among upper-class Chinese who lacked male heirs legal rules specified which boys were to be adopted in order to fill the male line of descent, the boys usually being sought first from the closest collateral kin (Freedman 1958). The *yoshi* system in Japan provides for the acquisition, by a person having an economic relationship to a family, such as a tenant, of kinship status through adoption, with the adoptee's descendants forming a branch of the adoptive family [see KINSHIP, *article on* PSEUDO-KINSHIP].

Similar patterns are found in Western society. Both the Greeks and Romans utilized adoption to insure continuation of the family line. Similarly, the Napoleonic Code was concerned primarily with the inheritance aspects of adoption and provided only for the adoption of adults. Up until the early twentieth century the transmission of property by acquiring legal descendants when none were available was probably the principal function of adoption. Thus, adoption was largely an upper-class phenomenon. In the lower classes, when adoption occurred, it served as a form of indenture; the "property" that was acquired was the right to the labor of the adoptive child.

Most societies that practice adoption to any considerable extent have well-articulated norms specifying the property rights involved. There are four sets of relationships to be considered. In many Western societies, the inheritance rights of the adopted child are equivalent to those of a legitimate natural child of the adoptive parents. In some countries, however, restrictions safeguard the inheritance rights of specific relatives. Since adoption may involve sharing an estate with natural children, some societies prohibit adoption by those who have natural heirs except in special cases where the adoptee has saved the life of the adopter. In most jurisdictions the adopters have little, if any, right to inherit from the adoptee. And while adoption theoretically creates a binding substitute for the biological relationship, in most cases the adopted child retains his rights of inheritance from his natural parents, and they from him (United Nations 1956). These patterns probably reflect the high value attributed to blood relationships in Western culture.

Much of the early legal concern over adoption focused on property transmission. However, in the early 1900s, and particularly during the period following World War I, many Western nations passed their first adoption laws or revised existing laws. The new laws sought to regularize numerous *de facto* situations and to protect the adopted child. Analysis of their content indicates a clear ascendancy of the child-welfare function over the heir-providing function.

Adoption research.   Research in adoption can be divided into two areas. The first consists of studies of the adoption process and the practices of adoption agencies. For example, Maas and Engler (1959) explored the barriers to the adoption of the large numbers of children in foster homes and institutions (particularly older children) who could benefit from permanent adoptive homes (see also Child Welfare League 1958). Other studies have focused on the criteria used in the selection of adoptive parents (Child Welfare League 1956–1957).

The second principal area of adoption research is the study of adoption outcome, particularly the outcome for the child. Of special concern has been the evaluation of the chief modes of arranging adoptive placements: independently or through a child welfare agency (Amatruda & Baldwin 1951; Child Welfare League 1951; Simon 1953; Theis 1924; Witmer et al. 1963). Most of the studies use some measure or judgment of the "quality" of the adoptive home as the criterion of success or failure; home quality is conceived in terms of those social and psychological characteristics thought to be most conducive to the child's physical and emotional development. These studies show that a substantial majority of adopted children are placed in acceptable homes through either placement system, with the percentage of highly evaluated homes running somewhat higher in favor of agency placement.

It must be noted, however, that the characteristics of adoptive homes thought to be related to children's adjustment by professional practitioners have shown only low correlation with actual measures of adjustment in follow-up studies. For example, studies have shown that the age of the adoptive parents is not significantly related to either measures of the child's adjustment or evaluations of the quality of parental care; moreover, there is no evidence that postadoptive fertility is detrimental to the adoption outcome. The more subtle and elusive assessments of the personalities of adoptive parents made by agencies in the course of selection have yet to be correlated with systematic measures of child adjustment made after a substantial follow-up interval. Thus, the results of the scattered research evaluating adoption outcome in terms of home quality are far from definitive at this point.

The adjustment of the respective parties to adoption has been the focus of another research strategy in the study of outcome. It has been found that children adopted independently score lower, on the average, on a battery of adjustment measures than a matched sample of natural children. The differences, while small, are statistically significant; however, they tend to disappear altogether when the comparison is limited to children placed in early infancy (Weinstein 1965). The adjustment of the adoptive parents has been the concern of an extended series of studies by Kirk (1964). His central thesis is that adoptive parents suffer from "role handicap" stemming from the romanticization of natural parenthood and the view of adoption as an acceptable but inferior alternative; he concluded that acknowledgment of, and coping with, the differences involved in being an adoptive parent are adjustive, both in terms of parental satisfaction and relations with the adoptive child.

Eugene A. Weinstein

[*See also* Kinship.]

BIBLIOGRAPHY

Amatruda, Catherine S.; and Baldwin, Joseph V.   1951 Current Adoption Practices. *Journal of Pediatrics* 38: 208–212.

Befu, Harumi   1963 Patrilineal Descent and Personal Kindred in Japan. *American Anthropologist* 65:1328–1341.

BOEHM, BERNICE R. 1965 Adoption. Pages 63–68 in *Encyclopedia of Social Work*. New York: National Association of Social Workers.

CHILD WELFARE LEAGUE OF AMERICA 1956–1957 *A Study of Adoption Practice*. By Michael Shapiro. 3 vols. New York: The League.

CHILD WELFARE LEAGUE OF AMERICA 1958 *Deterrents to the Adoption of Children in Foster Care*. New York: The League.

CHILD WELFARE LEAGUE OF AMERICA, COMMITTEE ON STANDARDS FOR ADOPTION SERVICE 1951 *A Follow-up Study of Adoptive Families*. New York: The League.

CHILD WELFARE LEAGUE OF AMERICA, COMMITTEE ON STANDARDS FOR ADOPTION SERVICE 1959 *Child Welfare League of America Standards for Adoption Service*. New York: The League.

COUNCIL OF STATE GOVERNMENTS 1954 *Summaries of State Laws Pertaining to the Adoption of Children*. Chicago: The Council.

FREEDMAN, MAURICE (1958) 1965 *Lineage Organization in Southeastern China*. New York: Humanities Press.

ISHINO, IWAO 1953 The *oyabun–kobun*: A Japanese Ritual Kinship Institution. *American Anthropologist* New Series 55:695–707.

KIRK, HENRY D. 1964 *Shared Fate: A Theory of Adoption and Mental Health*. New York: Free Press.

KORNITZER, MARGARET 1952 *Child Adoption in the Modern World*. New York: Philosophical Library.

LOWIE, ROBERT H. 1930 Adoption, Primitive. Volume 1, pages 459–460 in *Encyclopaedia of the Social Sciences*. New York: Macmillan.

LOWIE, ROBERT H. (1948) 1960 *Social Organization*. New York: Holt.

MAAS, HENRY S.; and ENGLER, RICHARD E. 1959 *Children in Need of Parents*. New York: Columbia Univ. Press.

MALINOWSKI, BRONISLAW 1929 Marriage. Volume 14, pages 940–950 in *Encyclopaedia Britannica*. 14th ed. Chicago: Benton.

REID, JOSEPH 1957 Principles, Values, and Assumptions Underlying Adoption Practice. *Social Work* 2:22–29.

SIMON, ABRAHAM 1953 Social Agency Adoption: A Psycho–Sociological Study in Prediction. Ph.D. dissertation, Washington Univ.

SMITH, I. EVELYN (editor) 1963 *Readings in Adoption*. New York: Philosophical Library.

THEIS, SOPHIE 1924 *How Foster Children Turn Out*. New York: State Charities Aid Association.

UNITED NATIONS, DEPARTMENT OF ECONOMIC AND SOCIAL AFFAIRS 1956 *Comparative Analysis of Adoption Laws*. New York: United Nations.

WEINSTEIN, EUGENE 1965 Adoption and the Social Psychology of Infant Development. Pages 88–108 in Conference on the Research and Teaching of Infant Development, 1964, *Papers*. Unpublished manuscript, Merrill-Palmer Institute, Detroit.

WINCH, ROBERT F. (1952) 1963 *The Modern Family*. Rev. ed. New York: Holt.

WITMER, HELEN et al. 1963 *Independent Adoptions: A Follow-up Study*. New York: Russell Sage Foundation.

ADULT EDUCATION

The term "adult education" has come into general use within the last half century to identify two different but related phenomena: a field of social activity and an emerging discipline in social science. Although different, these phenomena are interdependent. The discipline finds its subject of study in the field, which is, in turn, dependent upon the discipline for its development.

The field of adult education has been identified and defined in various ways. Most definitions include all learning by adults, from the casual incidental learning that may occur in the natural societal setting to the systematic learning accomplished in a formal instructional setting. Thus, the field of adult education may include "all the activities with an educational purpose that are carried on by people engaged in the ordinary business of life" (Bryson 1936, pp. 3–4). This aspect of adult education may be designated by several alternate synonyms: continuous learning, adult schools, education of adults, lifelong learning, night schools, further education, extension, and continuing education.

The discipline of adult education is concerned with the study of those educational activities for adults that occur in the formal instructional setting. Consequently, it can be defined more precisely: "Adult education is the action of an external educational agent in purposefully ordering behavior into planned systematic experiences that can result in learning for those for whom such activity is supplemental to their primary role in society, and which involves some continuity in an exchange relationship between the agent and the learner so that the educational process is under constant supervision and direction" (Verner 1962, pp. 2–3).

Forms and methods

Educational activities specifically for adults, while found in all societies, have assumed different forms as a result of differing needs for learning in different cultural situations. Consequently, there are no specific forms of adult education common to all cultures. The various forms that develop in differing cultures are the methods whereby a society provides for the education of adults. Methods that come into existence within a specific culture cannot be transferred readily to a dissimilar culture, nor will they survive long in their original setting unless the method is adapted to changes in the culture. This condition explains the extensive diversity encountered in adult education from one place to another and from one era to another. The forms of adult education common to Western society grew out of English culture, and many methods that originated in England in the eighteenth century spread elsewhere in Western society as

English culture was diffused. Even in Western society, however, certain methods have developed that have not been transferred successfully from one place to another.

The earliest systematic education of adults in England concentrated on literacy. It was thought that the poor were sinful because they were illiterate and that by learning to read the Bible they could save themselves from sin. In Wales, Griffith Jones operated his peripatetic Welsh charity schools from 1740 to 1770 to teach adults to read the Bible; Robert Raikes organized Sunday schools in 1780 for secular and moral education; and Robert Owen included adult education in his model villages (Kelly 1962). The volume of such activity was sufficient for the American Quaker Thomas Pole to publish his history of adult schools in 1814 and to revise and reprint it in 1816.

It was in the United States that the concept of adult literacy became utilitarian rather than moralistic. Literacy education was accepted as a public responsibility with the extension of the function of the public school to include night schools for illiterate adults, both native and foreign born (Grattan 1955). Such night schools are now found in virtually every community; however, the original concept has been expanded to include every subject of study. Night schools have become respectable middle-class institutions, no longer associated solely with the poor and ignorant in the public mind.

As a result of the changing needs of the nineteenth century, different forms of adult education arose in different cultural settings. Adult education has flourished in the Scandinavian countries, England, and the United States more than elsewhere. In Denmark originated the predominantly cultural folk schools, which spread throughout northern Europe but did not take root successfully in other countries (Lund 1949).

The industrial revolution in England emphasized the need for education for workingmen. Mechanics institutes were established in the early nineteenth century, but after a period of intensive growth in major population centers both in England and the United States they began to decline. Very few now survive and none in their original form (Kelly 1957).

Several distinctive methods of adult education originated in the United States—some of which have survived and spread elsewhere, while some have not. Among those now virtually extinct are the lyceum, founded by Josiah Holbrook in New England in 1826, and the chautauqua, which started in New York State in 1874. The lyceum lasted some twenty years and was generally limited to the northeastern states (Bode 1956). The chautauqua, on the other hand, survived until 1930, flourishing in a number of local centers across the country (Gould 1961). The traveling or tent chautauqua was the leading source of culture and education for rural America for at least a quarter of a century (Harrison 1958). In both instances the inability of the method to adapt to changing conditions in the culture resulted in its abandonment, and although some remnants may have survived, they have no real similarity to the original idea.

University extension is an administrative pattern of adult education that originated in England in 1873 and has spread everywhere that the English university concept has been diffused (Peers 1958). It was introduced in the United States in the 1890s and has developed more extensively in that country than elsewhere. University extension employs a variety of methods, including correspondence study, extension classes, short courses, workshops, and any other method that will extend educational opportunities to adults on a university level.

A by-product of university extension, the evening college, has spread throughout the United States in urban centers (McMahon 1959). Both university-extension and evening-college concepts are being adapted to conditions in newly developing nations.

Individual study by correspondence is one of the older forms of adult education. The idea originated in Berlin in 1856 but had its greatest development in the United States after William Rainey Harper organized the first university-sponsored correspondence study in 1890 at the University of Chicago. As a method for adult study, correspondence has many advantages, for adults are not excluded from learning by reasons of geographical isolation or physical disability. It is difficult, however, and requires a high degree of motivation that few adults can sustain for the time required to complete a correspondence course. In the United States the armed forces use correspondence instruction, and there are a number of private proprietary correspondence schools. Because of the exceedingly low rate of successful course completions many universities are discontinuing this phase of their adult-education programs.

The Cooperative Agricultural and Home Economics Extension Service of the United States is another method of adult education that has spread elsewhere in the world. It began officially in 1914 after its feasibility had been amply demonstrated by unofficial organizations (Brunner & Yang 1949). Originally its efforts were confined exclusively to teaching and demonstrating improved agricultural and homemaking processes that had been attested by the research of state colleges of agriculture, through which the service operated. As it gained the confidence of rural people and as rural living conditions changed, the Extension Service was urged to broaden the program. First steps in this direction were the inclusion of instruction in marketing and the formation of cooperatives. Today, most states include community development, health, recreation, public affairs, and liberal-arts studies as part of the program of the Cooperative Extension Service. No single pattern of adult education anywhere has produced the phenomenal changes that the Extension Service has brought about in rural America since its inception.

Radio and television have been used extensively for the diffusion of information, but less successfully, on the whole, for adult education. Formal courses in some subjects have been broadcast over both media by university instructors, as in the surprisingly popular "sunrise semester" shows on television. Such courses are usually combined with correspondence study. The Canadian Farm Radio Forum enjoyed many successful years by combining group listening and discussion. Some universities operate their own broadcasting stations, and some communities operate nonprofit educational television stations. State-owned systems, such as the British Broadcasting Corporation and the Canadian Broadcasting Corporation, have developed extensive programs of high quality aimed at adult audiences, as well as daytime school broadcasts.

Adult education is spreading rapidly to the underdeveloped nations, and many of the methods of adult education developed in Western society are being adapted to different cultures. Some kinds of activity for adults in fundamental and literacy education, in agriculture, health, vocational training, and community development are appearing in these newer nations through the assistance of world organizations and aid programs of developed nations.

Institutions. The first adult-education association on record was established in England in 1903 as a student organization designed to promote educational activities for adults (Stocks 1953). In the United States a general national association was organized in 1926 as an outgrowth of earlier, more specialized professional organizations (Knowles 1962). At present there are numerous voluntary associations in the United States and other countries, which both serve specialized groups and act as general coordinating bodies in adult education.

Adult education does not fit properly into any one system, theory, or institutional structure because it is found in all institutions and systems; however, the degree of involvement varies. In rare cases, adult education is the primary function of the institution. Often, as in the case of schools and universities, adult education is an extension of the primary function of the institution. The most common form of adult education, however, is found in those institutions for which it serves as a means of accomplishing some primary function, as in the case of public or private agencies for health, welfare, business, or industry (Verner 1964, pp. 11–17).

The peripheral nature of adult education is a persuasive factor explaining its episodic history. The origin, evolution, and extinction of adult-education programs provide fertile ground for a study of institutions.

Participation

For actual participants adult education is a socializing experience, even though motivation may vary. For some, adult education compensates for basic deficiencies in their equipment for functioning in their environment. Thus, immigrants may enroll in language courses that will help them adapt to their new society.

A growing number of adults enlist in a wide variety of educational activities designed to enrich their lives through art, music, or literature or to improve their competence as citizens through a better understanding of world affairs. Many activities are designed to enhance the use and enjoyment of leisure (*Handbook . . .* 1960). Most adult educational effort, however, could be characterized as vocational or technical.

What may be called the liberal-arts, sociopolitical, and recreational aspects of adult education, as distinguished from the vocational, are chiefly found in the developed and more affluent societies. In the newly developing countries emphasis is placed on fundamental and vocational education.

The process of socialization within adult education is conditioned to some extent by its marginal character. Since it is not institutionalized in a single system, it is less bound by tradition and can be related more quickly to social and technological changes than the more formalized educational programs. The main contribution of adult education to socialization comes through the interaction among people within its groups and between them and the knowledge they study.

A recent American study estimates that about 25 million adults engage in educational activities listed under 60 different categories of subjects;

two-thirds of the participants attend formal courses, and the rest engage in independent study, frequently by correspondence (Johnstone 1964). The enrollment figure is twice as high in other considered estimates, based on organizational reports, many of which may be guesses or liberal estimates and few if any of which take account of duplications in enrollment. It is doubtful that any precise measure of participation in adult education can be achieved because of the dispersion of the activity throughout the society.

There appears to be little difference between the sexes in their enlistment in adult education, although women are in a very slight majority. By age, the largest number of adult-education participants are in the third and fourth decades of life, with those between 40 and 59 years of age close behind. Only one in 12 of the sample of participants was over 60 years of age, though that age group constitutes more than one-seventh of the population. The increasing numbers and proportion of the aged in the population are often used as an argument to gain support for adult education, but the ways of overcoming the handicaps of age have clearly not been found. Marriage appears to be no bar. Over one-fifth of the participants had three or more children. The same proportion were childless. Unemployed and retired persons made up only 3 per cent of the total registered in courses. Full-time workers accounted for 60 per cent, and another tenth were working part-time. Almost 25 per cent of the participants were in the professional and technical occupational categories, with 18 per cent listed as craftsmen and foremen. Industrial operatives and service workers each accounted for 10 per cent of the enrollees.

As might be expected, vocational subjects were the most favored by men of all ages, especially those under 35 years of age. For women, courses in home and family life were in first or second place for all age groups, especially those under 35, with recreational, academic, and vocational courses following closely in that order. The first two of these three subjects were in either second or third place among men under 55, but with sharply lower proportions than among women.

The largest proportion of participants, 36 per cent, had had no formal education after high-school graduation. Twenty per cent had had some college experience but had not graduated. Eighteen per cent were graduates or had had graduate-school experience. It follows that adult education was reaching barely one-fourth of the educationally disadvantaged. Socioeconomic status may be one explanation for this result, since the higher the

income category above $6,000 per year, the larger the proportion participating in adult education. Below the $4,000 level the proportions were in reverse order.

In one sense, the primary objective of adult education is to reduce the cultural lag. This lag has resulted from the rapid changes of the last two centuries affecting the philosophies and conduct of government, the improvements in technologies with the attendant instabilities in age-old occupations, the intensity of specialization through science and—especially in developed countries—the opportunities for more leisure, and finally, a growing complexity of human relationships.

Adult educators try desperately to meet needs arising from these phenomena, but the needs outstrip both the resources and personnel required. Furthermore, adult education has become a middle-class activity, attracting those with more, rather than less, education; consequently it tends to widen the gap between the two groups (London et al. 1963). This tendency is reinforced by those institutions involved in adult education, since they are unintentionally selective of their clientele and eliminate those from the lower socioeconomic levels. University-extension programs are directed toward those with some college or better, and public night schools appeal primarily to those with some high school or better. The Cooperative Extension Service works with higher-status farmers and only occasionally with those on the bottom. Thus, although adult education in Western civilization originated as a medium for reducing the gap between the higher and lower strata, it now tends to widen it. Those in society with the greatest need for the kinds of educational opportunities adult education can provide are least served by it (Brunner et al. 1959, pp. 89–118).

Research and theory

As an emerging field of social science research, adult education has not yet established any considerable body of research literature. The practitioners in the field are so pressed by public demands for education that they have little inclination to accomplish more than essential service studies. Thus, much of the research extant is concerned with localized surveys of needs and resources or status surveys to indicate what is going on in an area. The fundamental research in adult education is supplied largely by other disciplines—particularly by sociology and psychology. Such research, however, is usually peripheral to the central concerns of adult education and is of value to it only as a by-product not always foreseen in the original design of the study. This can be seen, for example, in much of the diffusion research produced by rural sociology. The absence of any neatly defined universe that can be identified as adult-education research is inevitable in a field that is as young as adult education and is so heterogeneous in its interests, programs, and practices.

Although certain aspects of adult education have been studied in some depth, it has not always been to the extent that permits valid generalizations; nor has adult education been adequately conceptualized so as to indicate fruitful lines of investigation. Most of the existing research is descriptive and consists largely of surveys. The earliest known survey was published in 1814 (Pole 1814) and revised in 1851 (Hudson 1851). Since then there have been literally thousands of local surveys of one kind or another involving one or another institution, but this material has never been used to show any trends or general development in the field.

Local historical studies are almost as numerous as local status surveys. Such studies are particularly popular as subjects of graduate research (Little 1961). These treat the history of adult education within an area or an institution, but there are too few historical studies that integrate, analyze, and interpret the historical evolution of adult education as a persistent social activity. In this respect adult education offers a wealth of data for a historian or a historical sociologist to investigate.

Case studies are another common form of research utilized in adult education. The earliest such study was a report of an experiment in teaching adults to read, published in England in 1816 (*Account . . .* 1816). This might also be considered the earliest experimental study. Numerous similar studies were made in the early development of adult education, but few case studies are produced now.

The major concerns of adult education include participation, organization, adult learning, program planning, instructional processes, and evaluation. These are also the major areas of research, and while some studies have been made in each area, by and large they tend to stand in isolation. Participation has been studied more than any other area of interest, and such research is closely related to similar sociological studies. These studies are sufficiently extensive to provide some valid generalizations about the characteristics of active participants in adult-education programs. The generalizations produced through research in adult education are generally consistent with the ones resulting from social participation studies; how-

ever, different institutions providing adult-education activities tend to attract different kinds of people to their programs. In spite of its scope, participation research does not yet answer some crucial adult-education questions: why do adults participate? why do they select the kinds of educational activities they do? and why do certain kinds of adults fail to participate in any further education? Answers to questions of this sort are necessary in order to plan educational programs suited to all kinds of adult learners (Brunner et al. 1959, chapter 6).

There is very little research that helps understand the structure and organization of adult education. Carefully designed historical studies could contribute much knowledge to this area. Similarly, studies of institutions designed to include adult education are needed. The most significant recent study in the latter category was made by Clark (1956); this produced his theory of marginality, which goes a long way toward explaining the episodic nature of adult education. This marginality is a function of several factors. Adult education has become an additional responsibility of established educational institutions quite recently and lacks both controls and compulsions. Because it is viewed as peripheral, neither administrators nor their boards fully accept it as a normal function of the institution, and it is a part-time, hence a secondary, activity, both for instructors and instructed. Adult education is thus handicapped in building normal institutional loyalties or institutionalized power to resist budget cutting or to answer criticisms. Among private organizations adult education is just one of many tools useful in achieving organizational objectives and is not considered an end in itself, justifying the expenditure of resources.

Since adult education is a social phenomenon that does not fit established theories of social organization and since it is a massive and persistent form of social activity, it warrants the serious attention of sociologists.

The instructional processes used in educating adults have been studied extensively by sociology, psychology, and pedagogy. Because of the numerous uncontrolled variables in an instructional situation each study is virtually an independent entity, with few generalizations resulting. This is due, in part, to the lack of precise conceptualization of the instructional situation and processes; so that different studies have employed differing concepts. It is noticeable in diffusion research, where the effectiveness of processes is measured by the rates of adoption of new practices. This research indicates that a higher rate of adoption occurs with an increase in the number of processes used, but it does not say precisely which processes are clearly the most effective (Rogers 1962).

Certain specific educational processes have been studied more thoroughly than others. Lewin (1942) made a major contribution in his pioneer study comparing the effectiveness of lecture and discussion in changing food habits. Such comparative studies have become numerous since then (Brunner et al. 1959, chapter 10). In particular, the studies by Hill (1960) and Kaplan (1960) have identified the relationship between certain socioeconomic characteristics and the effective use of educational processes. Other educational processes have also been studied, but not as extensively as lecture and discussion (Brunner et al. 1959, chapter 9).

One barrier to effective research in this area of educational processes is the confusion between the diffusion of information and education [see DIFFUSION, *article on* INTERPERSONAL INFLUENCE]. This is especially obvious in the acceptance and adoption studies by rural sociologists, where such a differentiation is implied but not clearly conceptualized in the research design (Wilson & Gallup 1955). Verner (1963) has drawn a sharp distinction between diffusion and education in developing his theory of adult educational processes. Diffusion involves the dissemination of information, such as research on proven practices, without specific concern for learning or the understanding of the theory behind the research. Thus, such learning as may result from diffusion occurs largely by chance and is rarely complete or transferable. Education, on the other hand, is primarily concerned with learning and the learning process through the management of specific instructional situations. Both diffusion and education are used by institutions and organizations concerned with introducing change, but adult education involves only the latter. This distinction permits a more precise research design by providing a needed conceptual differentiation between diffusion and education and among the instructional processes utilized, so that adoption rates can be related specifically to the process that brought about adult education (Verner 1962).

Since adult education is largely an activity involving groups, group research is of the utmost importance to the field. Some research in this area has been done by adult educators; however, most of the research pertinent to adult education is done by sociologists and social psychologists. From such research—which often uses adult-education groups for study—the dynamics of the instructional group are beginning to emerge and such factors as group size and interpersonal interaction are becoming clarified (Brunner et al. 1959, chapter 12). Jensen (1963) has developed a set of sociopsychological principles for guiding adult instruction that are derived from group research.

Although research in adult education is largely descriptive and widely dispersed, it offers more fundamental knowledge than is generally recognized owing to the lack of any really adequate systematic analysis and the paucity of theory. Brunner and others (1959) have made the only attempt at systematic integration, but this is by no means inclusive or adequate. There are numerous bibliographies of adult-education literature that list a wide variety of works, but there is no single source for research literature (*Handbook . . .* 1960, chapter 14). With the slow and persistent development of adult education in the graduate curriculum the future growth of research and theory seems assured.

EDMUND deS. BRUNNER and COOLIE VERNER

[*Other relevant material may be found in* EDUCATION; SOCIALIZATION; UNIVERSITIES.]

BIBLIOGRAPHY

Account of the Origin, Principles, Proceedings and Results of an Institution for Teaching Adults to Read, Established in the Contiguous Parts of Bucks and Berks in 1814. 1816 Windsor (England): Knight.

Adult Education. 1950–1959 *Review of Educational Research* 20:161–250; 23:191–283; 29:221–234.

AKER, GEORGE F. 1965 *Adult Education Procedures, Methods and Techniques; A Classified and Annotated Bibliography: 1953–1963.* Syracuse Univ., The Library of Continuing Education and Univ. College of Syracuse Univ.

BODE, CARL 1956 *The American Lyceum: Town Meeting of the Mind.* New York: Oxford Univ. Press.

BRUNNER, EDMUND DES.; and YANG, HSIN-PAO 1949 *Rural America and the Extension Service: A History and Critique of the Cooperative Agricultural and Home Economics Extension Service.* New York: Teachers College, Columbia University.

BRUNNER, EDMUND DES. et al. 1959 *An Overview of Adult Education Research.* Chicago: Adult Education Association.

BRYSON, LYMAN 1936 *Adult Education.* New York: American Book.

CLARK, BURTON R. 1956 *Adult Education in Transition: A Study of Institutional Security.* University of California Publications in Sociology and Social Institutions, Vol. 1, No. 2. Berkeley: Univ. of California Press.

GOULD, JOSEPH E. 1961 *The Chautauqua Movement: An Episode in the Continuing American Revolution.* New York: State Univ. of New York.

GRATTAN, CLINTON H. 1955 *In Quest of Knowledge: A Historical Perspective on Adult Education.* New York: Association Press.

Handbook of Adult Education in the United States. 1960 New York: American Association for Adult Education. → See especially Chapter 14, "The Literature of Adult Education," by Coolie Verner.

HARRISON, HARRY P. 1958 *Culture Under Canvas: The Story of Tent Chautauqua.* New York: Hastings House.

HILL, RICHARD 1960 *A Comparative Study of Lecture and Discussion Methods.* White Plains, N.Y.: Fund for Adult Education.

HOULE, CYRIL D. 1962 The Doctorate in Adult Education 1961. *Adult Education* 12:131–135.

HUDSON, JAMES W. 1851 *The History of Adult Education.* London: Longmans.

JENSEN, GALE E. 1963 Socio–Psychological Foundations of Adult Learning. Pages 20–30 in Irving Lorge et al., *Psychology of Adults.* Chicago: Adult Education Association.

JENSEN, GALE; LIVERIGHT, A. A.; and HALLENBECK, WILBUR (editors) 1964 *Adult Education: Outlines of an Emerging Field of University Study.* Washington: Adult Education Association.

JOHNSTONE, JOHN W. C. 1964 *Volunteers for Learning.* Chicago: Aldine.

KAPLAN, ABRAHAM A. 1960 *Study Discussion in the Liberal Arts.* White Plains, N.Y.: Fund for Adult Education.

KARBE, WALTHER; and RICHTER, ERNST 1962 *Bibliographie zur Erwachsenenbildung im deutschen Sprachgebiet.* Braunschweig (Germany): Westermann.

KELLY, THOMAS (1952) 1962 *A Select Bibliography of Adult Education in Great Britain.* 2d ed. London: National Institute of Adult Education.

KELLY, THOMAS 1957 *George Birkbeck: Pioneer of Adult Education.* Liverpool Univ. Press.

KELLY, THOMAS 1962 *A History of Adult Education in Great Britain.* Liverpool Univ. Press.

KNOWLES, MALCOLM 1962 *The Adult Education Movement in the United States.* New York: Holt.

LEWIN, KURT 1942 The Relative Effectiveness of a Method of Group Discussion for Changing Food Habits. Unpublished report. National Research Council.

LITTLE, LAWRENCE C. (1961) 1963 *A Bibliography of Doctoral Dissertations on Adults and Adult Education.* Rev. ed. Univ. of Pittsburgh Press.

LONDON, JACK; WENKERT, ROBERT; and HAGSTROM, WARREN D. 1963 *Adult Education and Social Class.* Berkeley: Survey Research Center, Univ. of California.

LUND, RAGNAR (editor) (1949) 1952 *Scandinavian Adult Education: Denmark, Finland, Norway, Sweden.* 2d ed. Copenhagen: Danske forlag.

MCMAHON, ERNEST E. (1959) 1960 *The Emerging Evening College.* New York: Teachers College, Columbia University.

MEZIROW, JACK D.; and BERRY, DOROTHEA 1960 *The Literature of Liberal Adult Education: 1945–1957.* New York: Scarecrow.

MILLER, HARRY L. 1964 *Teaching and Learning in Adult Education.* New York: Macmillan.

NATIONAL UNIVERSITY EXTENSION ASSOCIATION 1953 *University Extension in the United States.* University: Univ. of Alabama Press.

PEERS, ROBERT 1958 *Adult Education: A Comparative Study.* London: Routledge; New York: Humanities.

POLE, THOMAS (1814) 1816 *History of the Origin and Progress of Adult Schools: With an Account of Some of the Beneficial Effects Already Produced on the Moral Character of the Labouring Poor.* 2d ed. Bristol (England): The Author.

RANGANATHAN, SHIYALI R. 1952 *Social Education Literature for Authors, Artists, Publishers, Teachers, Librarians and Governments.* Delhi: Atma Ram.

ROGERS, EVERETT M. 1962 *Diffusion of Innovations.* New York: Free Press.

STOCKS, MARY DANVERS 1953 *The Workers' Educational Association: The First Fifty Years.* London: Allen & Unwin.

UNESCO 1952 *Universities in Adult Education.* Problems in Education, No. 4. Paris: UNESCO.

VERNER, COOLIE 1962 *A Conceptual Scheme for the Identification and Classification of Processes for Adult Education.* Chicago: Adult Education Association.

VERNER, COOLIE 1963 Concepts and Limitations. Pages 229–240 in James R. Kidd (editor), *Learning and Society: Readings in Canadian Adult Education.* Toronto: Canadian Association for Adult Education.

VERNER, COOLIE 1964 *Adult Education.* Washington: Center for Applied Research in Education.

WILSON, MEREDITH C.; and GALLUP, GLADYS 1955 *Extension Teaching Methods and Other Factors That Influence Adoption of Agricultural and Home Economic Practices.* Washington: Government Printing Office.

ADVERTISING

I. ECONOMIC ASPECTS   *Lester G. Telser*
II. ADVERTISING RESEARCH   *Charles K. Ramond*

I
ECONOMIC ASPECTS

As more resources are spent on advertising, there is increasing controversy about its consequences. Only the economic aspects of advertising, however, are within the scope of this article. First, we will give some facts about the use and importance of advertising as a means of promotion; the data relate mainly to the United States, but we will also cite some figures for the United Kingdom and Canada. Second, we will show why firms use advertising. We will then discuss how advertising affects price competition and the size of firms and why advertising is used in the Soviet Union. Finally, we will consider those communications media that depend on advertising as their major source of revenue and discuss the relation between advertising and consumer sovereignty.

Scope of advertising. In 1960 total advertising outlays in the United States were estimated to be about $12,000 million, which was 2.3 per cent of gross national product (GNP). Since in 1947 advertising was 1.8 per cent of GNP, there is a slight upward trend in the post-World War II period. However, too much should not be made of this evidence. It covers a short period of time, advertising figures prior to 1935 are unreliable, and the figures just preceding World War II show that the relation between advertising and GNP was about the same as in the late 1950s (Blank 1963).

In 1954 Canadian advertising outlays were 1.6 per cent of GNP, and comparable figures for the United Kingdom are of the same order. In both of these countries advertising outlays constitute a smaller percentage of either GNP or national income than they do in the United States. So far as can be judged from the limited data available, advertising is a less important means of promotion in most other countries than it is in the United States.

There are four major channels of advertising. The printed media, such as magazines and newspapers, contain both advertising and editorial material and are sold directly to the public. The audio–visual media, such as television and radio, are supported primarily by advertising receipts. These media do not, in many countries, collect fees directly from the public. Instead, they aim to attract an audience for advertisers by providing the public with free entertainment. Direct-mail and outdoor advertising attempt to attract the public's attention and make direct sales appeals. In the United States in 1959, advertising in the printed media accounted for between 45 and 50 per cent of total estimated advertising expenditures. Television and radio received about 14 per cent and 6 per cent, respectively, of advertising expenditures. Direct mail accounted for 14 per cent of the advertising bill, and outdoor advertising was about 2 per cent. The remaining expenditures were on sale display, advertising departments, and the like.

Modern advertising began during the early part of the nineteenth century, after the cheap daily newspaper and the national magazine were introduced. Radio in the 1920s and television in the 1950s caused major changes in the composition of advertising outlays. As a result of these innovations, the cost per advertising message has sharply decreased and the number of advertising messages has risen more than would be implied by the increased dollar expenditures.

The ratio of advertising to sales differs considerably among products. Industrial products, which are purchased primarily by a relatively small number of firms, have a much lower ratio of advertising to dollar sales than do consumer products. Promotion of industrial products depends primarily on salesmen. The products advertised most heavily in relation to dollar sales in the United States in 1957 were toilet preparations (14.7 per cent of sales), drugs and medicines (10.3 per cent), and soaps (7.9 per cent).

Canadian figures that give advertising as a percentage of sales by product category are roughly the same as the U.S. figures. Moreover, a study of advertising relative to sales in 1940 and 1941 by the U.S. Federal Trade Commission (1944) shows that the ratios by product category in the United States are quite close to comparable figures for the year 1935 in the United Kingdom as shown by the Kaldor and Silverman study (1948). That the pattern of advertising outlay with respect to commodity is similar in all three countries is an important finding and deserves a fuller explanation than has so far appeared. Equally important would be an explanation for the differences among the advertising intensities of various products.

Why firms advertise. A correct but unilluminating explanation of advertising is that firms find it profitable. Advertising, however, is only one, and not even the most important, method of sales promotion. Although some products are promoted mainly by advertising, personal selling still accounts for the largest share of promotional outlays. Advertising is a much less labor-intensive method of promotion than are many alternatives for accomplishing the same end. Therefore, it is a technique well suited to sell those products that are, or can be, widely used and for which potential customers are not readily distinguished from the rest of the population. A firm deliberates over the same kinds of factors in allocating its funds to different advertising media as in allocating funds to other methods of sales promotion.

For an understanding of why firms advertise, it is helpful to see how advertising affects sales. Advertising affects sales in two stages. In the first stage a firm buys space in the press or time on television in order to convey advertising messages that create awareness in potential customers. In the second stage these advertising messages induce sales with varying degrees of effectiveness. In order to determine its advertising budget a firm must both decide how many advertising messages of each type it should buy and estimate their effectiveness.

The audience of an advertising medium approximates the number of advertising messages that can be received via that medium. For printed media, such as magazines or newspapers, the paid circulation gives a first approximation of the audience. However, the readership of a newspaper or magazine may exceed the circulation, and, conversely, the number of readers who take note of the advertising may fall short of the circulation. Thus, paid circulation is at best only an approximation to the number of advertising messages received via a printed medium. The audience of a television or radio program is harder to estimate, and special research techniques have been devised for this purpose. Audience size (along with composition) is one of the key determinants of advertising rates. Given this information about an advertising medium, a company can calculate the cost and estimate the effectiveness of advertising messages conveyed by that medium.

The number of advertising messages is the relevant physical measure of the quantity of advertising. This is why advertising per dollar of sales is not always a reliable measure of the quantity of advertising. The absolute advertising outlay and the number of messages transmitted may be very large although the ratio between advertising expenditure and sales is very low. For example, advertising as a percentage of sales is very low for automobiles. However, in 1957 U.S. consumers received nearly $400 million of automobile advertising messages, half from auto manufacturers and half from auto dealers.

Advertising messages can be effective indirectly. Thus, potential customers can learn about products, even though not directly exposed to advertising messages, by hearing about these products from others. By a chain reaction, advertising messages can stimulate transmission of a sizable volume of information (Katz & Lazarsfeld 1955; Ozga 1960).

The preceding analysis explains some dynamic aspects of advertising. There is typically a delayed response to advertising for several reasons. First, many of the advertised products are not of great importance to consumers; thus, a certain amount of repetition or redundancy is necessary to create awareness of the product. Advertising in smaller amounts is not likely to pass the threshold of awareness and, therefore, is likely to be ineffectual. Second, in addition to the problem of making consumers aware of the product, there is the further problem of overcoming their inertia. Although inertia increases the delay between advertising messages and sales, it also makes the effects of advertising persist beyond the time the messages are disseminated. Thus, advertising expenditure can be thought of as an investment to create an asset—sometimes called good will. This asset yields a return for some period of time, it depreciates like a capital good, and it requires maintenance. The marginal rate of return on advertising, as well as the rate of depreciation, can be calculated. Nerlove and Arrow (1962) provide theoretical analysis and Telser (1962) shows empirical results along these lines.

This approach to advertising has several implications. First, we can expect new products to be more heavily advertised than established products. Second, continuous advertising of established products is necessary because new consumers enter the market and others either leave it or forget about the product. Third, in an expanding economy there will be relatively more advertising than in one that is stable or declining.

Advertising versus price competition. One of the criticisms of advertising is that it is wasteful. If firms compete by offering to sell at low prices, then buyers benefit. Such competition among sellers results in products of given quality being sold at the lowest price. However, it is argued, if sellers compete for customers by advertising, then buyers do not benefit by obtaining a lower price; on the contrary, they pay a higher price to reimburse the sellers' advertising expenses. In its crude form this argument has little merit; if some buyers do not wish to purchase advertised goods, there will generally be sellers who find it profitable to cater to their demand. Then some buyers will seek out the low-priced sellers who do not advertise, whereas other buyers will choose to pay higher prices for well-known goods.

A more sophisticated version of the argument that advertising may increase prices assumes that by advertising, a company can reduce the elasticity of demand for its product [see ELASTICITY]. Advertising can change the character of the demand so that customers become less sensitive to price and the advertiser obtains a loyal clientele. This makes possible higher prices and larger profits. Whether advertising can as a matter of fact create brand loyalty is not known with certainty although it is a possibility. There is some evidence worth bringing to bear on this question. We noted above that toilet preparations are the most intensively advertised consumer articles. If advertising tends to create brand loyalty, market shares of cosmetics and similar products should be more stable than market shares of less advertised items, such as branded food products. However, a study of the four leading brands of each of a number of articles in these two product classes over a 13-year period showed that market shares of toilet preparations were markedly less stable than were shares of branded foods. There was, in addition, a substantial turnover of brands in the toilet-preparation class. Because new brands are advertised much more intensively than are established brands, the high ratio, among toilet preparations, of advertising to sales may reflect the short life and high turnover of brands rather than brand loyalty. If this is true, the high intensity of cosmetics advertising results from the lack of brand loyalty to such products as compared with branded food items.

It is by no means obvious that advertising necessarily reduces the price elasticity of demand. Increased advertising may bring a firm new customers whose preferences for the product are weaker than those of the old customers. The new customers are consequently more sensitive to price, and the increased advertising thus increases the price elasticity. Although advertising by a given firm may reduce the price elasticity for its goods by strengthening preferences, competitive advertising has the opposite effect. On balance, increased advertising may increase price elasticity.

Advertising can intensify competition among retailers, thereby reducing retail prices. Since shoppers can compare the various retail prices of a well-known brand at different stores more easily than they can those of a nonstandard item, competition is keener among retailers selling the well-known item. This forces the retail prices of advertised articles closer to invoice costs. Retailers' advice influences consumer choice of nonstandard items more than the choice of advertised articles. Hence, advertised goods need less promotion at the point of purchase. As a result, the character of both retailing and wholesaling has changed markedly. Sales personnel can be less skilled, and discount houses and self-service stores have become feasible.

Advertising and the size of firms. Defenders of advertising often claim that advertising, by creating mass markets, makes it possible to produce goods at lower unit costs. It is doubtful that this claim is supported by the evidence available. First, many companies that rely heavily on advertising operate plants of different sizes; this is inconsistent with production economies of scale. Second, there are many industries in which a few firms are quite large but which use little advertising; examples of these are to be found primarily among producers of industrial goods. Third, as was noted above, there are some heavily advertised commodities manufactured primarily by small firms; the leading examples are toilet preparations.

There are, however, certain important producers of consumer goods who are heavily dependent on advertising and account for sizable fractions of their industry sales. Examples are producers of breakfast cereals, soaps, automobiles, cigarettes, razors and razor blades, soft drinks, canned soups, baby foods, and distilled liquor. To sum up, there is considerable evidence against the general proposition that advertising, by expanding the market, makes it possible to lower unit costs, and some evidence to support the idea that in some industries, high concentration of output is associated with considerable advertising.

An understanding of the association between advertising and concentration in the industries just cited begins with an examination of the advertising rate schedule. Advertising rates rise as audience increases, but less rapidly. This can give the national advertiser of a given product an advantage over the local advertiser, because the former has a lower promotional cost. The cost advantage to the large firm makes the growth of the small firm more difficult. In addition, sales may rise more rapidly in response to advertising expenditures over some range. If this is true, it reinforces the tendency brought into play by the structure of the advertising rates. For these reasons some firms will make and advertise a large number of consumer goods in order to obtain the savings of large-scale advertising. Certain large firms in the food and drug industries owe their size in part to these economies.

Advertising in the Soviet Union. Many of the effects of advertising stand out more clearly in the light of the Soviet Union's experience with forgoing the use of both trademarks and advertising. Because of adverse experience with this policy, the Soviet Union has come to encouragé advertising and the use of brand names. Its reasons for abandoning the old policy and adopting the new are very instructive. First, anonymous producers had less incentive to maintain quality because shoddy goods were not so easily identified by consumers. The government can now shift some of the burden of quality control to factories that are forced to trademark their products and can lose customers if their goods prove unsatisfactory. Second, when advertising is encouraged, information about new goods is disseminated more rapidly, and innovations are stimulated. Because in the past it was not possible to use advertising to generate demand for new products, the incentive to contrive new products was discouraged. Third, a more efficient marketing system, which conserves scarce resources of the state as well as saving the consumer's time and trouble, is made possible by the use of advertising. Thus, the Soviet Union can now use self-service stores and distribute a given volume of goods with a smaller amount of labor. Goldman (1960) contains a careful account of Soviet advertising experience.

Advertising and the communications industry. In the United States, the broadcasting industry receives virtually all of its revenue from advertisers. Newspapers and periodicals obtain some two-thirds of their revenue from advertising and the balance from sales and subscriptions. Clearly, a substantial part of the entertainment and news provided the public in the United States is paid for directly by advertisers and only indirectly by the public. This creates concern about the quality of the entertainment and the degree to which it reflects the public's taste. There is, in addition, the question of whether advertising affects freedom of the press. Finally, because most television advertising in the United States is purchased by relatively few companies and only three national networks exist, there are some special problems of economic policy with regard to regulation of the industry.

The public registers its taste for drama and motion pictures directly, by the purchase of tickets to those it likes. Producers have a direct financial incentive to cater to public taste. Although viewers and listeners do not pay directly for radio and television programs, it cannot be doubted that similar considerations guide the producers of these programs. Since advertisers desire large audiences and are willing to pay more for them, producers of radio and television shows have strong incentives to provide what they expect will be popular. The reason the cost of radio and television entertainment is not collected directly from the audience is the economic fact that it is cheaper to collect this cost from advertisers. If certain experiments with closed-circuit television prove successful, direct collection from viewers will make subscription television a profitable enterprise. Yet it is by no means obvious that advertising would be absent from subscription television. People buy magazines and newspapers directly, and both these media contain advertising. Newspapers that did not include advertising have either changed their policy or failed. Aside from the absence of advertising revenue, this suggests that people demand certain kinds of advertising.

There is still more direct evidence that people want certain kinds of advertising. Newspaper advertising rates have always been lower for local advertisers than for national advertisers. Since the cost to a newspaper of local advertising is, if anything, higher than the cost of national advertising, and since national advertisers have several alternatives not available to local advertisers, this phenomenon has mystified students of advertising for a long time. Ferguson (1962) provides an explanation. Most of the local advertising gives newspaper readers information about goods available from local retailers and about the terms of sale. Newspaper readers are as eager to learn about these matters as about news. Hence the more advertising of this kind a newspaper contains, the larger its circulation. Therefore, local advertising rates are lower than those for national advertising, which generally does not have the same stimulus on circulation. Perhaps the communications media would freely carry items as news about consumer goods and services if there were no advertising, just as they now review books and motion pictures.

Partly for these reasons, the more sophisticated critics of advertising take the position that advertisers and television producers cater unduly to popular taste and do not experiment boldly enough with higher art forms. Because there are only three major television networks in the United States and few television channels per city, these critics maintain that the desire to reach a maximum audience leads television producers to undue similarity and slavish imitation of what has proved to be popular. Minority audiences are ignored, and the television fare is reduced to a low, vulgar common denominator. It is one thing to argue that intellectuals cannot find suitable fare on television because it never pays an advertiser to try to attract this audience, an extreme position without empirical support; it is another to argue that serious intellectual programs should be provided during the evening hours and on the days when the potential audience is largest. It would be profitable for advertisers to cater more to minority tastes than they now do if there were more commercial television stations per city and if subscription television became a profitable enterprise. Nevertheless, even if both of these developments occurred and increased variety became possible, it would be naive to expect too much. Since there are fashions in novels and in movies, we should not expect less conformity of television programs.

Both radio and television depend on a relatively small number of firms for a substantial part of their advertising revenue. The 20 largest network television advertisers account for more than 22 per cent of network advertising receipts, and the 20 largest spot television advertisers account for nearly 14 per cent. By way of comparison, the 20 largest newspaper advertisers contribute less than 6 per cent of newspaper advertising revenue. Since there are only three national networks, it is safe to conclude that advertising rates for the largest firms are not arrived at by a purely competitive process. The Federal Communications Commission licenses all television and radio stations and limits the number of stations any one company, or network, may own. The public would benefit more from a larger number of television stations per city than it would from regulation of advertising rates. The development of ultrahigh-frequency (UHF) television, for example, would, by increasing competition, lead to a greater variety of television fare, just as the advent of frequency modulation (FM) radio and the consequent opening up of more radio stations gave listeners a wider range of choice.

Defenders of advertising have claimed as one of its benefits that it makes possible a free press. There can be little doubt that if there could not be advertising in newspapers, the price of newspapers would rise considerably and the circulation would fall—not only for this reason, but also because an important kind of news, advertising, could not be published. Without advertising, broadcasting companies could not survive unless subscription radio and television became profitable. When there is a free press the public can hear a greater variety of views than when the press is controlled by the government. Truth is less easily concealed when conflicting views can be presented to the public. A government that supports and controls the news media, no matter how benevolent it is, cannot be trusted to give as much free expression as would unfettered competition among companies in the news industry, which depend on the public and advertisers for revenue.

Advertising and consumer sovereignty. A convenient assumption in textbooks is that consumers have given, and possibly sacrosanct, tastes and that firms cater to these. As a practical matter this is a myth. People are molded by the opinions and pressures of others from the moment of birth. Our role as consumers begins with what we learn from our parents and continues throughout our lives. Of course, advertisers serve their own interests when they try to get us to buy their wares. However, most people attempting to persuade others are often serving their own interests, and we must learn to be discriminating. A free society requires freedom of persuasion, including attempts to influence how people spend their money. Critics who claim that advertisers lie or induce people to buy things they do not need or to discard goods that are still serviceable overlook the fact that sales clerks can do all this just as effectively; these critics certainly exaggerate the power of advertising. Moreover, they ignore certain mundane but nevertheless important facts about advertising. For every advertiser who tries to persuade consumers to do a particular thing or to buy a particular item, there are others trying to persuade consumers to buy a rival product. In modern industrial society consumers can choose from an ever-increasing and ever-changing array of goods. Wise consumption is difficult under these conditions and de-

mands a degree of skill not required of shoppers in a simpler economy. Efficient distribution in a society of rising real wages requires greater reliance on such labor-saving devices as the self-service store. Advertising is one of the promotional techniques that meets the requirements of efficient distribution. We can expect it to play an ever-increasing role in the developing economies of the world.

LESTER G. TELSER

[*Other relevant material may be found in* COMMUNICATION, MASS; MARKET RESEARCH.]

BIBLIOGRAPHY

Advertising Age: The National Newspaper of Marketing. → Published weekly since 1930.

BLANK, DAVID M. 1963 A Note on the Golden Age of Advertising. *Journal of Business* 36:33–38.

BORDEN, NEIL H. 1942 *The Economic Effects of Advertising.* Chicago: Irwin.

CANADA, DOMINION BUREAU OF STATISTICS 1956 *Advertising Expenditures in Canada, 1954.* Reference Paper No. 67. Prepared by the Merchandising and Services Section, Industry and Merchandising Division, Department of Trade and Commerce. Ottawa: Department of Public Printing and Stationery.

FERGUSON, JAMES M. 1962 The Advertising Rate Structure in the Daily Newspaper Industry. Ph.D. dissertation, Univ. of Chicago.

GOLDMAN, MARSHALL I. 1960 Product Differentiation and Advertising: Some Lessons From Soviet Experience. *Journal of Political Economy* 68:346–357.

HARRIS, RALPH; and SELDON, ARTHUR 1962 *Advertising and the Public.* London: Institute of Economic Affairs.

KALDOR, NICHOLAS 1950 The Economic Aspects of Advertising. *Review of Economic Studies* 18:1–27.

KALDOR, NICHOLAS; and SILVERMAN, RODNEY 1948 *A Statistical Analysis of Advertising Expenditure and of the Revenue of the Press.* Cambridge Univ. Press.

KATZ, ELIHU; and LAZARSFELD, PAUL F. 1955 *Personal Influence: The Part Played by People in the Flow of Mass Communications.* Glencoe, Ill.: Free Press.

NERLOVE, MARC; and ARROW, KENNETH J. 1962 Optimal Advertising Policy Under Dynamic Conditions. *Economica* New Series 29:129–142.

OZGA, S. A. 1960 Imperfect Markets Through Lack of Knowledge. *Quarterly Journal of Economics* 74:29–52.

Printers' Ink: The Weekly Magazine of Advertising, Selling, and Marketing. → First published in 1888. Since 1954 one issue each year is a guide to marketing.

STIGLER, GEORGE J. 1961 The Economics of Information. *Journal of Political Economy* 69:213–225.

TELSER, LESTER G. 1962 Advertising and Cigarettes. *Journal of Political Economy* 70:471–499.

U.S. FEDERAL TRADE COMMISSION 1944 Advertising as a Factor in Distribution. Part 5 of *Report on Distribution Methods and Costs.* Washington: Government Printing Office.

II

ADVERTISING RESEARCH

Advertising research is here defined as the study of that part of human behavior attributable to overtly paid-for communications. It is thus distinguished not only from the broader discipline of marketing research but also from kindred studies of aggregate purchasing behavior, economic concomitants of advertising, and communications not always or not overtly paid for. [*For discussion of these fields, see* Communication, mass; Consumers, *article on* consumer behavior; Market research; Propaganda.]

As subject matter for the social sciences, advertising remains curiously neglected. Advertising has long been of importance and today accounts for at least one per cent of the national income of most highly industrialized countries (*International Advertiser* 1965), but it had no important place in economic theory until the 1930s. Advertising accounts for a major share of the promotional expenses of most firms but has not been extensively treated in any but the most recent microeconomic theories of the firm (Ramond 1964c, pp. 662–675). Advertising accounts for an undeniably larger and larger visible and audible part of world culture but as a sociological phenomenon has been described mainly by journalists. Advertising is a much-discussed influence on individual behavior but has interested psychologists only insofar as it can be studied in the experimental laboratory or used to illustrate the clinician's theories of unconscious motivation. It is hardly surprising that there is no accepted theory of advertising.

The little known about how advertising works comes largely from research done since World War II by advertisers and advertising agencies in the United States, western Europe, and Japan. Most early studies remained unpublished. Until the establishment in 1960 of the *Journal of Advertising Research* (*JAR*), there was no means for exchange of ideas among all gatherers or users of this work. Since then some fifty or sixty reports of advertising research are published each year, mainly in the *JAR*.

Not all this research is beyond criticism. Much of it is done by practitioners whose training in the social sciences and ancillary disciplines has been acquired on the job. In the face of time and cost limitations, methodological standards relax. When this happens, advertising research often merits the charge (Forrester 1958) that it is itself nothing more than advertising.

The primary basis for these political considerations is the organizational structure of the advertising industry. Nowhere in business, perhaps, has accurate evaluation been so inhibited by the organizational structure of the process to be evaluated. Advertising is bought for a manufacturer by an agent, and this agency has usually been responsible for the evaluation of advertising effectiveness.

Someone has remarked that this is like having the fuel salesman evaluate the furnace. The fact remains that it has not always been in the best interest of the advertising agency to institute adequate research designed to evaluate advertising effectiveness. The agency has little to gain and much to lose. Instead of such evaluative research, it typically performs only those studies which are necessary to aid its own current decision making and that of the client. Such research is done only when needed and can rarely be accumulated for future guidance. Thus, the ultimate promise of any type of research—its self-liquidation through accumulation of permanent knowledge—is almost by definition denied in the advertising realm.

As most advertising research is designed to aid some decision, it is possible to classify the types of research according to the decision each is designed to help make. For example, decisions about what to say come under the heading of motivation research; decisions about how to say it, under copy research; where, when, and how often to say it, media research; and how much to spend, sales research.

Motivation research. The postwar transition from a war production economy to a consumer economy heightened advertisers' interest in the motives of their target audiences. By the early 1950s the business community had learned from clinical psychologists that consumers were governed in part by unconscious motives, or at least by motives they had trouble expressing to ordinary interviewers. Depth interviews, projective tests, and the other paraphernalia of the clinical psychologist became popular tools in advertising research. By 1955 the public became interested in whether it was in fact being sold by advertising against its will. Popular books exploited this fear on the part of the book-buying public and ultimately received a quiet rejoinder from more realistic students of human behavior. John Dollard, at the second annual conference of the Advertising Research Foundation, in a frequently anthologized paper entitled "Fear of Advertising," said:

Nor do I fear research into unconscious motives, sometimes called motivation research, as an important factor in mass subversion by advertising. My reasons are as follows: many unconscious motives are stark and ugly and cannot be used in advertising appeals. Furthermore, unconscious motives are tricky; they are likely to come in conflicting pairs of desire and disgust, and one cannot evoke the desirable member of the pair without also evoking its linked opposite. It should be noted also that people are not immediately prone to carry out the unconscious motives which they do have. There are strong forces built into the personality which operate against most unconscious motives. Looking at the matter from a quite different standpoint, it has yet to be proved that unconscious motives can be steadily identified or that, if this were done, they are of superior effect in devising advertising themes. At the moment, the notion of using hidden factors in motivation to influence behavior on a mass scale is still in the status of a bright idea or a horrible fantasy, however you prefer to look at it; but it is not a reliable and valid instrument available to advertisers. (Dollard 1956, p. 7)

As public and professional expectations grew more realistic, motivation research gradually ceased to be regarded as the search for exploitable unconscious motives. Instead it became redefined more modestly as the study of those psychological variables which might be related to the consumer's purchase of products or services. Put another way, motivation research became the study of relationships between the psychological attributes of a brand or product (its "image") and the psychological attributes of the consumer (his "personality"). If markets can be segmented, so the argument runs, according to psychological as well as demographic variables, then it should be possible to fashion advertising appeals which are unusually effective in causing sales among the appropriate population segments.

Perhaps the largest body of data on which these hypotheses have ever been tested became available at the J. Walter Thompson advertising agency in 1959, when the Edwards Personal Preference Test was administered to a sample of over three thousand households (Koponen 1960). The Edwards test provided scores on 15 personality traits for the male and female head of each household, while a purchase diary indicated amounts and brands of various products purchased. A prior experiment had shown that a subgroup selected for its scores on certain traits bought more of a mail-order product than did an unselected control group, in response to a direct-mail advertisement using appeals designed specifically to satisfy that particular subgroup's psychological needs. Neither group bought very much, however, and the results were deemed statistically significant but practically unimportant.

So, in fact, were the relationships found between personality variables and purchase behavior using the J. Walter Thompson data on beer, coffee, tea, and toilet tissue. Although brand loyalty, store loyalty, and amount purchased do correlate significantly with certain demographic and personality traits of the 8,900 subjects in the sample, these correlations are too small to give practical guidance. It seems safe to conclude that until more discriminating personality scales are developed, perhaps for the specific purpose of predicting purchase behavior, psychological market segments

will not be significantly more useful to the advertiser than demographic market segments.

Copy research. Having learned the needs of his prospects and chosen general appeals or themes by which to reach them, the advertiser must then determine how best to execute those themes. Which copy, headlines, illustrations, music, etc., will best communicate his message? Studies answering questions of this sort have traditionally made up the bulk of advertising research and are still called —even in the age of television—copy research.

Reviews and collections of recent copy research appear elsewhere (Lucas & Britt 1963; National Industrial Conference Board 1963; Twedt 1965). The common implication of many of these studies is that the respondent's verbal testimony about exposure to advertising cannot be taken at face value. Commercial services report the proportion of a sample who on being shown an advertisement claim to have noted it (the recognition method) or who, on being shown a brand advertised in a magazine they have read, can "play back" enough of the advertisement to indicate convincingly that they have in fact seen it (the aided recall method). The simultaneous popularity and questionability of these techniques led to the largest purely methodological investigation ever conducted in copy research, the five-volume Printed Advertising Rating Methods Study, or PARM (Advertising Research Foundation 1956–1957). The PARM study found, among other things, that recognition scores did not decrease as the time since reading increased, as one would expect if memory loss were occurring. This suggests not that the respondent was "recognizing" the advertisement he had actually seen but the likelihood that this was the kind of advertisement he *would have noted*, given the opportunity. Other studies find that respondents claim to recognize control advertisements that they could not have seen. The extent of misclaiming was directly related to the respondent's reports of past reading behavior, his interest in the product advertised, and other personal characteristics. It may be concluded that while these claims perhaps have some value as projective data describing the respondent, they are substantially useless as reports of prior exposure.

They may also be useless as predictors of future behavior. Haskins (1964), in a review of 28 studies, has shown that factual recall of advertising can change without corresponding changes in behavior or other attitudes. He concludes that what is retained by respondents may have nothing to do with their subsequent purchases. Ramond (1965) has shown that such failure of attitude change to predict or coincide with behavioral change may be an artifact of the methods commonly used to measure these changes.

As verbal behavior became increasingly suspect, nonverbal behavior became increasingly popular as a measure of copy effectiveness. Laboratory methods, themselves suspect for their artificiality, found increasing favor as they began to measure relatively *involuntary* responses to advertising. These included visual recognition, skin moisture, pupillary dilation, and even the rate at which someone would press a pedal to maintain a television picture and sound. No measure has been found completely free from conscious cognitive influences, but the trend of current copy research seems to indicate that such is the goal.

Media research.   Having decided what to say and how to say it, the advertiser must then decide where, when, and how often to say it. Surveys and analyses that guide these decisions are known as media research and have as their aim the selection of the audiences for advertising placed in media. They should not be confused with studies that are intended to determine the audiences of only the media themselves.

A comprehensive bibliography of U.S. media research may be found elsewhere (Ramond 1964*a*), along with a comparison of U.S. and European approaches. For example, there is much variety and controversy in U.S. media research. In the United States no single method has been hammered out for use in an industry-wide study, whereas this has been done in France, Britain, and Sweden (Ramond 1964*b*). All of these studies have been influenced by the work of the Advertising Research Foundation's (ARF) Audience Concepts Committee as expressed in its booklet, *Toward Better Media Comparisons* (Advertising Research Foundation . . . 1961). The committee maintains that to understand the transmission of advertising through media one must count or measure at six stages: vehicle distribution, vehicle exposure, advertising exposure, advertising perception, advertising communication, and consumer response—usually sales.

Vehicle distribution is a count of things, namely, the number of physical units through which advertising is distributed. In broadcast media these are receiving sets in use; in print media, number of copies sold.

Vehicle exposure is a count of people, those whose open eyes or ears were confronted by the vehicle: for broadcast media, by the ongoing program; for print media, by the open page.

Advertising exposure is a count, not of things or people, but of events. These events are also confrontations of open eyes or ears by a turned-on set or an open page, but only where the set or page is carrying a commercial or advertisement.

The fourth, fifth, and sixth stages of the model are *perception*, *communication*, and *response*. There is both a conceptual and an operational difference between these stages and the previous three.

Distribution and exposure measures can in principle be—and have in practice been—objectively defined to the satisfaction of many if not all. In dealing with perception and communication of advertising, however, we face the problem of separating the effect of the medium from the effect of the advertising message itself. So far no research supplier has come forward with any measure of these stages which is as objective, repeatable, and intuitively compelling as those of distribution and exposure.

Actually, perception and communication may be defined by an infinite number of responses. Though a perception may be defined as that which is seen, heard, or in some way received by a sense organ, our knowledge of whether it has been received must be derived from the response of the receiving person. He must somehow translate his private observation into a public gesture. Reports of recognition, recall, or attitudes are possible classes of responses which might define perception or communication of advertising. But note that whatever definition is used, it will require not only that the consumer see or hear the advertising but also that he remember something about it until he is asked to report it. Thus the number of possible definitions is further multiplied by the number of cues or aids to memory which could be used.

While the ARF Audience Concepts Committee made no recommendations concerning operational definitions of perception and communication, it did suggest a conceptual distinction. Perception is defined as an all-or-none phenomenon: it either occurs or does not occur. There are no degrees of perception.

But communication involves more than merely seeing an advertisement. For example, an advertisement can add to the consumer's knowledge, change his attitude, or make him resolve to purchase the product advertised. It may change his beliefs, make some more prominent than others, or even evoke moods in which his judgments operate differently. Thus one must recognize degrees of communication. One may merely count perceptions, but one must measure communication in a more complex way. The goal in counting perceptions is to extract from each the effect of memory, but the goal in measuring communication is to learn the degree of remembering. Thus, although perception and communication differ conceptually, in practice they both require measures that isolate and distinguish the effect of advertisement-plus-medium from memory, and the effect of the advertisement from that of the medium.

We now come to the final stage of response to advertising, and from the advertiser's point of view by far the most important. Response at this stage is necessary to justify any advertising at all. Other measures are satisfactory only insofar as they are related in some way to sales. However, sales are the outcome of a great many factors other than advertising. Not only are the personal factors, the attitudes, beliefs, perceptions, and so forth of each individual important, but external factors such as price, market conditions, changing tastes, etc., are also operative.

Theoretically, the way to estimate the sales response to an advertising unit is to arrange for tests with all factors that could possibly influence sales—except for advertising—held equal or randomized. In one area the advertising unit would be displayed, in the other it would not, and the difference in sales in the two areas would be measured. Practically, experiments of this kind turn out to be very difficult. In the first place, if we try to choose markets that are identical in all the relevant characteristics, we usually find some discrepancy between the markets on a variable which we feel sure will affect the outcome of the experiment decisively. Again, we may list what we think are the relevant variables in order to account for their effects, but we never know whether we have been able to identify them all. Even with an exhaustive list of market variables, we may find that the nature of our advertising unit is such that it may act differently in the two markets because of the different psychological characteristics of their inhabitants, or the differing media habits in the two markets. Perhaps the ultimate objection to research designed to attribute sales gains to single advertising units is the very small effect which any one advertising unit may have. Sales tests have been applied mainly to the evaluation of campaigns, not of individual messages.

Sales research. No amount of research into motivation, copy, or media will tell the advertiser what, if anything, his advertising has done to influence the sales of his product. For this information he must conduct sales research, wherein he isolates the contribution to sales of his advertising expenditures. Many advertisers have done so, in the United States and elsewhere, despite the difficulties enumerated in the previous section. The most comprehensive recent review and bibliography is Martin Mayer's booklet for ARF, *The Intel-ligent Man's Guide to Sales Measures of Advertising* (Mayer 1965). Others include Dominick (1960), the National Industrial Conference Board (1962), Palda (1963) and Ramond (1965).

Properly designed marketing experiments are used to avoid many of the above difficulties (Banks 1965). Proper design requires, among other things, that extraneous influences on sales be dealt with: controllable factors should be controlled; uncontrollable but measurable factors should be measured and accounted for statistically in the analysis; and enough experimental units should be used in each treatment to permit accurate estimates of their variability. From experiments published, we may conclude that when the following conditions are met the sales effects of advertising can be estimated with accuracy, speed, and economy:

(1) The product or the brand has no substitute now or in the foreseeable future. The number of competing products or brands is small, and it is unlikely to be made obsolete by technology during the period of experimentation.

(2) The buyers of the product or brand (*a*) can be unambiguously defined; (*b*) can be easily reached by advertising and interviewers; (*c*) are geographically concentrated; (*d*) are temporally concentrated—the shorter the selling season the better; (*e*) spend little time "in the market."

(3) The lot size of the purchase is constant from purchase to purchase by the same buyer and the same from buyer to buyer.

(4) Price is constant over time, markets, amount purchased, etc.

(5) Channels of distribution are many. The more channels of distribution to the consumer the less likely he will be frustrated in an advertising-induced attempt to buy.

(6) Levels of distribution are few. The more wholesalers, dealers, and distributors there are between producer and consumer, the more individuals who must decide before purchase can occur, and the more individuals who must be influenced by advertising.

(7) The influence of personal selling is constant over time and over markets.

(8) Technical services provided by competitors do not differ.

(9) The copy platform is constant and unambiguous. The fewer the copy points, the easier it is to tell if communication has occurred.

(10) Special promotions are not undertaken.

(11) Packaging is distinctive and constant.

(12) The producer is the only advertiser of the brand, i.e., there is no cooperative or local advertising.

(13) Competitors are slow to respond to changes

in marketing strategy and maintain more or less the same marketing policies.

(14) Competitors' advertising and marketing policies are relatively constant over markets.

(15) Potential sales can be accurately estimated for small geographical units, e.g., counties or census tracts, and during short time periods such as weeks or months. This follows from several of the previous desiderata.

(16) Government controls over product design, price, competition, and advertising are minimal or at least unchanging.

Clearly not all of these conditions can be met by most advertisers. Meeting them, moreover, does not guarantee a conclusive experiment but only the avoidance of certain common errors. Experimentation is increasingly popular, not because it always works, but because in many cases it is the *only* way to have a chance of getting unambiguous measures. In marketing as elsewhere in business, chance plays its inevitable role. Part of this role, however, can be made manifest by the experiment itself.

As published experiments accumulate, the conditions under which the sales effects of advertising can be accurately estimated will become clearer. Until then the prudent advertiser will determine for himself whether his own circumstances augur well or ill for this valuable form of marketing control.

CHARLES K. RAMOND

[*Directly related are the entries* CONSUMERS; MARKET RESEARCH. *Other relevant material may be found in* ATTITUDES, *article on* ATTITUDE CHANGE; COMMUNICATION, MASS; PERSUASION; PROPAGANDA.]

BIBLIOGRAPHY

ADVERTISING RESEARCH FOUNDATION 1956–1957 *A Study of Printed Advertising Rating Methods.* 5 vols. New York: The Foundation.

ADVERTISING RESEARCH FOUNDATION, AUDIENCE CONCEPTS COMMITTEE 1961 *Toward Better Media Comparisons.* New York: The Foundation.

ADVERTISING RESEARCH FOUNDATION 1965 *Are There Consumer Types?* New York: The Foundation.

BANKS, SEYMOUR 1965 *Experimentation in Marketing.* New York: McGraw-Hill.

DOLLARD, JOHN 1956 Fear of Advertising. Pages 1–9 in Advertising Research Foundation, *Proceedings of the Second Annual Conference.* New York: The Foundation.

DOMINICK, BENNET A. 1960 *Research in Retail Merchandising of Farm Products: Appraisal of Methods and Annotated Bibliography.* Washington: U.S. Department of Agriculture, Market Development Research Division, Agricultural Marketing Service.

FORRESTER, JAY W. 1958 The Relationship of Advertising to Corporate Management. Pages 75–92 in Advertising Research Foundation, *Proceedings of the Fourth Annual Conference.* New York: The Foundation.

HASKINS, JACK B. 1964 Factual Recall as a Measure of Advertising Effectiveness. *Journal of Advertising Research* 4, no. 1:2–8.

HRB-SINGER, INC., STATE COLLEGE, PENNSYLVANIA 1962 *The Measurement and Control of the Visual Efficiency of Advertisements.* New York: Advertising Research Foundation.

International Advertiser. → See especially 1965, Volume 6, no. 10.

KOPONEN, ARTHUR 1960 Personality Characteristics of Purchasers. *Journal of Advertising Research* 1:6–12.

LUCAS, DARRELL B.; and BRITT, STEUART H. 1963 *Measuring Advertising Effectiveness.* New York: McGraw-Hill.

MAYER, MARTIN 1961 *The Intelligent Man's Guide to Broadcast Ratings.* New York: Advertising Research Foundation.

MAYER, MARTIN 1965 *The Intelligent Man's Guide to Sales Measures of Advertising.* New York: Advertising Research Foundation.

NATIONAL INDUSTRIAL CONFERENCE BOARD 1962 *Measuring Advertising Results.* By Harry D. Wolfe et al. New York: The Board.

NATIONAL INDUSTRIAL CONFERENCE BOARD 1963 *Pretesting Advertising.* By Harry D. Wolfe et al. New York: The Board.

PALDA, KRISTIAN S. 1963 Sales Effects of Advertising: A Review of the Literature. *Journal of Advertising Research* 4, no. 3:12–16.

RAMOND, CHARLES K. 1964a Operations Research in European Marketing. *Journal of Marketing Research* 1, no. 1:17–24.

RAMOND, CHARLES K. 1964b Trends in U.S. Media Research. European Society for Opinion Surveys and Market Research, *Commentary* (Special Supplement): 35–43.

RAMOND, CHARLES K. 1964c Marketing Science: Stepchild of Economics. Pages 662–675 in Stephen Greyser (editor), *The Marketing Concept in Action.* Chicago: American Marketing Association.

RAMOND, CHARLES K. 1965 Must Advertising Communicate to Sell? *Harvard Business Review* 43, no. 5:148–158.

TWEDT, DIK WARREN 1965 Consumer Psychology. *Annual Review of Psychology* 16:265–294.

AESTHETICS

Although the term *aesthetics* has other special meanings, it has come to refer, in the context of social science, to the whole body of generalized inquiry especially relevant to the arts. Aesthetics is the study of man's behavior and experience in creating art, in perceiving and understanding art, and in being influenced by art. Work in aesthetics thus far has been principally concerned with music, literature, and the visual arts, paying little attention to the performance aspect of even these arts. The scope of the subject is greater, however.

The creation of art

In common with other human activities, art raises many questions about motives, skills, and other conditions leading to novel and socially valuable creations. These questions have been broadly investigated; and results show that creativity, whether in the arts or elsewhere, has some common origins in personality and environmental circumstances and that there are also distinctive influences on creativity in distinct areas.

Another set of problems or questions deals with whether, and in what ways, a work of art embodies the manner in which the artist perceives or understands the world. Visual representational art, for example, could be claimed to embody the way the artist perceives that which is represented; if less persuasively, the same argument could be applied to nonrepresentational art. A closely reasoned case for this view is presented by Arnheim in his book *Art and Visual Perception* (1954), which emphasizes the influence of the medium (and the artist's manner of using it) on the interaction between the perception of the world and the making and perception of objects. Going beyond the work of artists, he applies his reasoning to the visual productions of children, making sense of developmental sequences in children's art by demonstrating that what children produce is in a very real sense a portrayal of what they see. At a more complex level, it is often assumed that works of art embody the artist's understanding of the world. There has, as yet, been little attempt to examine this common critical assumption with the methods of psychology or social science.

The artist's personality. The argument that a close relationship exists between motivational themes in an artist's personality and the themes in his work has been made in a number of psychoanalytically oriented interpretations. Because there are fuller and more explicit statements of motivational themes in literary works of art, such interpretations have been more commonly made of the work of poets, novelists, and dramatists than of composers or visual artists. To the person trained in scientific criteria of evidence, such work is necessarily lacking in conviction, but it is replete with hypotheses that might be tested in other ways.

The effort to read an artist's personality in his work is parallel to the clinical psychologist's effort to read a patient's personality in his responses to projective tests. Indeed, some projective tests require the patient to be an amateur artist, producing stories or pictures. If it be useful to consider under aesthetics amateur as well as professional art, the interpretation of these tests is a problem in aesthetics. In any event, the two efforts—penetrating to the personality of both artist and nonartist—face the same uncertainties. The very scoring of the document may be excessively subjective; once scored, the method of interpretation may be ob-

scure and controversial. Attempts to objectify the scoring of projective tests have been many. A similar attempt has been made to render explicit and objective the analysis of works of art for purposes of inference about the personality of the artist. Notable work of this sort has been done by McCurdy in analyses of work by Shakespeare, D. H. Lawrence, the Brontës, and others, which he has summarized briefly in a recent publication (1961, pp. 413–427).

An even more basic problem becomes evident here: What assumptions are to be made about how characteristics of the artist are reflected in his work, and under what circumstances? The psychoanalytic "case studies" of artists and more controlled analyses, such as those by McCurdy, depend upon such assumptions; but these assumptions are not always the same and are not adequately tested in these single case studies. A major problem is to distinguish or determine when the artist's manifest characteristics will be expressed and when his latent characteristics will be expressed.

Empirical studies of personality factors. In research on productions by nonartists, the aforementioned problems have been studied. For example, in a study of graphic productions by college women, Wallach and Gahm (1960) have found that in those women who have little conscious anxiety the amount of expansiveness, as opposed to contraction, in their work is directly related to the extent to which they are socially extroverted, as opposed to introverted; whereas in those who have a great deal of such anxiety, expansiveness and extroversion are negatively related. A variety of similar findings justify a tentative generalization: For personality characteristics not subject to great interference by anxiety, guilt, or other sources of conflict, simple consistency between manifest behavior and characteristics of imaginative production tends to be the most conspicuous relationship; for those personality characteristics present to some degree in everyone, but inhibited from normal, direct expression by anxiety, guilt, or other sources of conflict, a compensatory or inverse relationship is more likely.

This generalization surely provides a better guide to thinking about probable relationships between the personality of artists and the characteristics of their productions than is provided by the vague idea that there is some kind of consistency. Yet knowledge has not advanced to the point where even such a generalization can be stated with perfect confidence, but clarification is to be expected in coming years from continuing work with projected techniques.

Simultaneously, comparable techniques may

come to be applied to the work of genuine artists. No amount of study of nonartists will tell us for certain what relations are to be found between the personality and work of artists themselves. Perhaps the secret of successful artistry lies partly in the ability to sever the usual motivational connections between self and imaginative product.

Societal factors in art. The questions considered about the individual artist in relation to his work can be extended to the societal level. Are variations in modal personality to be found among the determinants of variations in artistic creativity from one people or one epoch to another? Do the artistic productions of a society express the ways of perceiving and understanding that characterize its typical member? Can important motives in the personality of a typical member of the society be inferred from inspection of its works of art? These and similar questions are posed by many humanistic scholars. There have, as yet, been few attempts to apply to them the comparative and systematic approach of social science, except that very useful beginnings have been made in answering the third question.

Empirical studies of societal determinants. The most convincing beginning, because it includes several parallel studies of sequences of change, covering different societies and different centuries but yielding similar findings, is a set of studies reported by McClelland (1961, chapter 4). A single theme is investigated here, that of concern with achievement. McClelland and his associates have systematically sampled bodies of literature and graphic art from several societies at periods of economic growth, peak, and decline. These samples have been scored by methods developed for measuring concern with achievement as an individual personality variable. Although the findings are not perfectly uniform, they tend to show that there is an increase in achievement themes during periods of economic growth and a decrease in achievement themes in advance of a decline in economic growth. This relationship between long-term economic change and the expression in art of a motivational theme that is obviously relevant to economic productivity supports the view that the art produced in a society at a given time is expressive of themes that occupy members of the society.

Art productions of preliterate societies also permit quantitative study. A pioneer effort in this direction is that of Barry (1957), who found evidence that complexity of style in the visual art of preliterate societies was positively related to a motivational characteristic, the degree of anxiety likely to be produced by traditional child training practices. His analysis of features of style has been used by Fischer (1961) to demonstrate several relationships between structural characteristics of societies and stylistic features of their art, relationships that support the assumption that art gives symbolic expression to the thoughts and wishes of members of a society. For example, the relative predominance of curved versus straight lines may be thought of as possibly symbolizing femininity versus masculinity. Fischer provides intriguing hypotheses about personality as mediating a relationship between this variation and social structure. In a society offering solidarity and security to a particular sex (for example, men in a patrilocal society), that sex might be free to enjoy artistic symbolization of the opposite sex as objects of erotic fantasy; when, on the other hand, a particular sex is placed in a relatively insecure position (for example, men in a matrilocal society), it might be interested in artistic fantasy that provides a model or ideal pattern of its own sex. The correlations obtained between features of social structure and of art support this hypothesis.

Meaning and understanding in art

What do works of art mean? Philosophical aestheticians have offered a variety of answers to this perennial question. Modern psychological theory offers new constructs to use in its exploration, and psychological research permits an observational test of any resulting hypotheses that have clear empirical meaning.

For most of the verbal and visual arts, meaning is not an obvious problem. Referential meaning (by linguistic convention in the case of literature and by similarity to the person or place represented in the case of some visual art) and the meaning derived from practical use, most conspicuous in architecture, provide a ready commonsense answer to the question of what these arts mean.

Music. The meaning of music is more obviously a problem, and it has been examined psychologically. Pratt (1931), for example, has argued that an important element in the meaning of music (although he did not use the word *meaning* in this way) derives from the similarity between musical structure and human emotional experience: "Music sounds the way an emotion feels" is the way he summarized his view at a later time. Thus music is in part iconic, like visual art, but without specific reference. The iconic quality of music might be likened to the iconic quality of the color, lines, and forms in an abstract painting, insofar as they aptly symbolize a state of emotion.

A later treatise by Meyer (1956) on the meaning of music, drawing upon modern developments in psychology and communication theory, describes the emotional portion of the meaning of music as simply one way of viewing the structure of the music. A musical composition arouses in the listener a series of expectations that are either fulfilled or delayed or frustrated. Emotional terms are one way of describing such a series of arousals, delays, and resolutions.

Discussions of what is *the* meaning of music must be viewed as prescriptive as well as descriptive. They are concerned with what music means to some hypothetical ideal. But when one at least momentarily tries to take a purely descriptive approach, it is of course apparent that different listeners or viewers bring to the experience diverse kinds of meaning.

Empirical studies of inherent meaning.   A survey of research based on a specific formulation of this diversity has been provided by Valentine (1962, pp. 54–58, 85, 130–135, 196–209). It shows clearly that people find differing meaning both in a complete work of art and in its simplest elements. It also shows, not surprisingly, that the kinds of meaning inherent in the work itself are more prominent in the experience of people who seem most appreciative of the given art and that extraneous kinds of meaning are more prominent in the experience of those less appreciative.

In the face of such diversity is there any constancy in the meaning of works of art and in their elements, except for conventional meanings one learns in becoming expert in a particular artistic tradition? This problem, too, is considered in psychological research—most notably and persistently that of Hevner—summarized by Valentine (1962, chapters 3, 4, 10, 13). That part dealing with music also is described by Farnsworth (1958, chapter 5). This research shows, for the general student population from which the subjects were drawn, that variations in hue, brightness, and saturation of color; in pitch, rhythm, and other features of music; and in metrical pattern, choice of phonemes, etc., in poetry produce reasonably dependable variations in connotative meaning. Several of these studies compare students especially knowledgeable in a particular art with those possessing little background in it. The general finding is that there is somewhat greater agreement among those most expert in an art than among those least expert, but that the difference is surprisingly small; there is clearly a tendency toward agreement on connotative meaning even among people with relatively little experience with a particular art. All the subjects necessarily have had some exposure to the artistic traditions of our society, and these studies leave open the question of whether the agreed-upon connotative meanings are conventional, dependent upon only this minimum of experience, or whether they are instead based on a natural appropriateness of various colors, rhythms, etc. as metaphorical expression of varying human emotions, accessible to any observant person regardless of his cultural background.

Universality or cultural relativity?   It is to be hoped that with new concepts and techniques available there will be a real attack on the problem of universality versus cultural relativity in meaning. Already in some studies of connotative meaning of concepts (cf. Osgood 1960), evidence is available that some (and decidedly not all) connotative meanings are remarkably constant from one culture to another. This work has not been oriented toward aesthetics, and as yet it provides no knowledge about cross-cultural variation in connotative meaning of works of art and little about their elements. The problem of cultural relativity versus universality even applies to the elements of literature, despite the conventionality of language. The fact that it does may be illustrated by the lively controversy about whether the connotative meaning of various phonemic contrasts has transcultural validity. The same kind of question may be asked about more complicated aspects of the linguistic materials of literature, for example, features of metrical pattern such as may be incorporated in any system of meter, the difference between repetitive use of sounds and highly varied use of sounds, etc.

Perception and art.   Understanding a work of art must, whatever its meaning may be, begin with the act of perceiving. The psychology of perception, principally developed in connection with momentary experience, has been mainly applied thus far to the visual arts. The most notable application of the psychology of perception is Arnheim's (1954). His book provides an invaluable treatment of one after another aspect of perceptual processes as they relate to the artist's vision, to what he is representing in his work, and to how it is perceived and understood by others. Throughout the book, Arnheim struggles against the naive assumption that what is perceived is simply an automatic representation of an objective reality. Instead, he emphasizes that perceiving is an active process, complex in character and diverse in outcome, although understandable in terms of general principles.

There has been no comparable thorough attempt to apply knowledge of perception to the understanding of the other arts. Pratt, however, in his book on music (1931), made effective use of the knowledge of hearing. The gestalt psychology of perception may have strengthened his assurance— at a time when atomism predominated in psychology—that each musical interval has a distinctive perceived quality and that to treat auditory experience simply as a series of discrete events would be fatal.

The understanding of a work of art goes, of course, beyond perception. In the past, aestheticians have had relatively little assistance from the psychological study of higher mental processes in their attack upon further problems in understanding the arts. Some years ago Ivor A. Richards (1929), using techniques but few conceptual tools from psychology, reported a brilliant study of how readers understand poems. The psychology of cognition has now advanced to a point where it may help in subsequent research.

Effects of art on viewer or audience

The effects claimed for art are many, and sometimes contradictory. Dramatic presentation of human violence has been thought by some to purge the viewer of latent aggression and by others to incite him to similar violence. Cultivation of fine artistic appreciation has been claimed to awaken fine sensitivity to the nuances of human feeling and thus develop useful participants in society, or, on the other hand, to produce an effete withdrawal. The establishment of the long-range effects of art, social and moral, may be assisted by social science. Indeed a contribution has already been made, although to date extensive investigation has been confined to the immediate effects of art.

The immediate effects principally studied are two: liking versus disliking and aesthetic evaluation or judgment.

Research on likes and dislikes. Research on likes and dislikes is the oldest kind of quantitative research in aesthetics. In the early days of experimental psychology, much work was done on the extent to which different colors, different forms, etc. were liked or disliked. This work has continued and has revealed that there are some remarkable uniformities, as well as interesting differences, among people responding to these simple stimuli. The uniformities may in time be convincingly shown to have a significance for response to works of art, but they have not as yet.

Likes and dislikes in response to works of art have also been directly investigated, mostly among the general or the school population rather than among experts. Such studies suggest that liking or disliking is often determined by relations between personality characteristics of the viewer and the thematic structure or style of the work of art. These studies have not been highly unified in their attack on the underlying theoretical problem of exactly how a person's impulses or emotions are changed through interaction with works of art. This research, like the research on expression of the artist's personality in his work, needs clarification in relation to basic psychological processes.

Personality factors in liking and disliking. Thus far, research on likes and dislikes has dealt mainly with general aspects of personality in relation to general type or style of art preferred. This research illuminates old questions and concepts, as shown by Knapp's work (1964) on personality characteristics associated with preference for each of three types of visual art. Among the college students he studied, Knapp found liking for realistic representational paintings associated with practicality and worldliness. Geometric abstract paintings tended to be liked by intellectual and inhibited students. Expressionist abstract paintings tended to be liked by those who might be described as imaginative, impractical, and sensitive. Knapp suggests that the orientation of these three kinds of person is extremely reminiscent of the classical definitions of Apollonian, Pythagorean, and Dionysian orientations. Here is confirmation of the importance on the contemporary scene of a traditional classification of value orientation and a promise of relating it to psychological understanding of relevant personality characteristics.

A similar inquiry, by quite different methods, is found in psychoanalytically oriented writing on the gratifications people obtain from the arts. In these discussions, the quality of the work of art as such is rarely mentioned and has little relation to what is said; the work of art is treated as though it were the viewer's own fantasy and is supposed to offer him the same gratifications as a spontaneously produced fantasy of his own.

Aesthetic evaluation. A contrasting kind of inquiry has been directed at studying some sort of distinctively aesthetic appreciation of works of art. Indeed, some of the early research on likes and dislikes had this orientation; it was supposed that through some method of averaging, variable personal reactions would be eliminated and a universal and genuine aesthetic tendency would be revealed (Eysenck 1957, chapter 8). But the likes and dislikes of experts in an art, or their evaluative judgments, provide a more reasonable criterion for aesthetic quality; and, as Peel (1945) has shown, the stimulus correlates of such judgments may differ greatly from the stimulus correlates of the general likes and dislikes of nonexperts. Child (1962) found, moreover, that college students who agree with student consensus about works of art are not the same students as those who agree with expert consensus and that the personality correlates of these two kinds of agreement are not at all the same. In this and subsequent research among college men, Child found that those who agree with expert evaluation of visual art tend to show an active, inquiring orientation to the world; tolerance of, or even liking for, complexity, ambivalence, and unrealistic experience; and independence of judgment rather than conformity.

Recent advances in the psychology of knowing increase chances that the complexities involved in genuine aesthetic experience may come to be usefully analyzed with the concepts of general psychology. Berlyne's treatment (1960) of interest-arousing variables in experience illustrates the beginning of such a movement. Here seems to lie the special promise of future work in aesthetics— improved understanding of aesthetic experience through application not merely of the methods of social science but also of basic concepts and principles adequate to the complexities of the task.

IRVIN L. CHILD

[*Other relevant material may be found in the articles listed under* ART.]

BIBLIOGRAPHY

ARNHEIM, RUDOLF 1954 *Art and Visual Perception.* Berkeley: Univ. of California Press.

BARRY, HERBERT 1957 Relationships Between Child Training and the Pictorial Arts. *Journal of Abnormal and Social Psychology* 54:380–383.

BERLYNE, D. E. 1960 *Conflict, Arousal, and Curiosity.* New York: McGraw-Hill.

CHILD, IRVIN L. 1962 Personal Preferences as an Expression of Aesthetic Sensitivity. *Journal of Personality* 30:496–512.

EYSENCK, HANS J. 1957 *Sense and Nonsense in Psychology.* Baltimore: Penguin.

FARNSWORTH, PAUL R. 1958 *The Social Psychology of Music.* New York: Dryden.

FISCHER, J. L. 1961 Art Styles as Cultural Cognitive Maps. *American Anthropologist* New Series 63:79–93.

KNAPP, ROBERT H. 1964 An Experimental Study of a Triadic Hypothesis Concerning the Sources of Aesthetic Imagery. *Journal of Projective Techniques and Personality Assessment* 28:49–54.

McCLELLAND, DAVID C. 1961 *The Achieving Society.* Princeton, N.J.: Van Nostrand.

McCURDY, HAROLD G. 1961 *The Personal World: An Introduction to the Study of Personality.* New York: Harcourt.

MEYER, LEONARD B. 1956 *Emotion and Meaning in Music.* Univ. of Chicago Press.

OSGOOD, CHARLES E. 1960 The Cross-cultural Generality of Visual–Verbal Synesthetic Tendencies. *Behavioral Science* 5:146–169.

PEEL, E. A. 1945 On Identifying Aesthetic Types. *British Journal of Psychology* 35:61–69.

PRATT, CARROLL C. 1931 *The Meaning of Music.* New York: McGraw-Hill.

RICHARDS, IVOR A. (1929) 1956 *Practical Criticism: A Study of Literary Judgment.* New York: Harcourt.

VALENTINE, CHARLES W. 1962 *The Experimental Psychology of Beauty.* London: Methuen.

WALLACH, MICHAEL A.; and GAHM, RUTHELLEN C. 1960 Personality Functions of Graphic Constriction and Expansiveness. *Journal of Personality* 28:73–88.

AFFECT

See EMOTION; EXPRESSIVE BEHAVIOR.

AFFECTION

As a rule, "love" and "affection" are words used more or less interchangeably to designate warm, positive feelings directed to individuals; but they may encompass attachments to pets, institutions, things, activities, and ideas. Where differentiation is made, love usually implies more intense feeling than affection, or love may be restricted to feelings with a strong sexual component and affection to those supposedly free of it.

Instincts and behaviorism. Early psychologists, including William James (1890) and William McDougall (1908), recognized the existence of love as an emotion or sentiment and accepted it as instinctually based and consequently demanding little more than that its emergence and expression be observed. Sigmund Freud (1905) also approached love as a derivative of instinct, but he elevated it to a central position in his theory. This was the status of love in psychology about 1915, when instincts began to give way to the behavioristic approach and emotions became a problem for experimental study.

The laboratory investigation of love had a brief life, beginning with John B. Watson (1924–1925), who reported that three primary emotions—love, fear, and rage—were arousable in the newborn infant. Stroking or patting the lips, nipples, and genitals produced stretching, cooing, and extension of the arms, and these responses were considered to constitute love. Through care of the infant, the mother became a conditioned love stimulus, and by generalization and conditioning, the infant developed a broadened range of conditioned love stimuli. Consequently, Watson advised parents to handle infants objectively to avoid overly strong conditioning of love to themselves.

The subsequent flood of laboratory studies questioned the specificity of emotions in the neonate and concluded that it starts life with only vague emotional responses, which gradually differentiate by three months of age into general patterns similar to those reported by Watson. Delight, pleasure, and contentment replaced love for the three-month-old. Love, or affection, was ascribed to the second half of the first year, and love for parents and love for children were attributed to the second year (Bridges 1931). Further specificity evolved during childhood, adolescence, and adulthood. These observations were generally accepted by experimental psychologists, and for 35 years love was absent from the laboratory and from most psychology textbooks. Meanwhile, investigations of emotion centered on the negative states of fear, anger, jealousy, and the like.

Psychoanalytic theory. Psychoanalytic theory originated before instincts came into disrepute, and Freud, persevering despite criticism, continued to develop, elaborate, and amend his theory throughout the behavioristic and into the neobehavioristic periods. Freud's theory deals with love, or affection, by postulating the concept of the libido, first described as an all-inclusive sexual drive and, later, as a broad life force combining all of the positive, life-sustaining drives. The libido is, then, the basic tension-producing force leading the individual to seek relief. The objects providing relief are "love" objects, and the attachments to these objects are affectional. Thus, in simplest terms, love is the product of relieving libidinal strivings, and all attachments in life have this common origin.

Freud traced the libido from the cradle to maturity (1905), dividing development into pregenital and genital periods. The pregenital period begins at birth with the oral phase, in which satisfaction comes from stimulation of the erogenous mouth by nursing and such substitute activities as thumbsucking. The anal phase is next, initiated by the emergence of the anal area as a second erogenous zone, and is satisfied by elimination. The third pregenital phase, the phallic stage, begins with awakening of the penis and clitoris as erogenous zones in males and females, respectively, and is satisfied by urination and masturbation. A latency period follows, lasting from about five years of age to puberty. The oral, anal, and phallic satisfactions are then normally in abeyance in whole or part, and the libido finds satisfaction through sublimation—a period of great importance for education. The genital period starts at puberty with reawakening of the genital erogenous zone, this time with more intensity and, in the female, with arousal of internal as well as external genitalia. Satisfaction of the libido now comes normally through coitus, but cultural restrictions may limit satisfactions to substitute activities.

In the pregenital period, the self is a main love object because the individual can satisfy erogenous needs through self-stimulation. The mother is the primary external love object because she feeds, trains, and fondles the infant; for similar reasons the father may be an additional one. Love for the mother is enhanced in the phallic phase in boys, leading to the Oedipus complex, when the mother is an incestuous object and the father an object of hostility, followed by a resolution, usually resulting in identification and love for both parents. The girl develops a parallel complex in which the father becomes an incestuous love object and the mother a hostile object, and this is similarly resolved. The disappearance of the Oedipus complex launches the latency period. In the genital period, unrelated persons of the opposite sex become the primary love objects.

Freud's theory has had especially great impact on professional people working with children. The "institutionalized child syndrome" has been noted by many and has been a stimulus to research and theory (Spitz 1945). It has been repeatedly observed that infants reared in impersonal institutions lack interest in their environment and show inferior physical and mental development. In extreme cases they die of marasmus, a wasting away of the body, or they may develop autism, a psychological withdrawal. The basis is usually attributed to lack of mothering, although some autistic cases suggest additional or alternative causation. Similarly, many children reared by rejecting or indifferent mothers have been observed to develop early physical and psychological problems, even marasmus and autism (Ribble 1944). In the decade after Watson's advice to rear children objectively, clinicians reported many "Watsonian" problem children. Consequently, mothers today are counseled to provide abundant love to their infants and children, and whenever possible efforts are made to place motherless infants in loving foster homes [*see* INFANCY, *article on* THE EFFECTS OF EARLY EXPERIENCE].

A negative by-product of psychoanalytic theory has been the singling out of mother–child relationships as the primary cause of behavior problems, neuroses, and psychoses, to the neglect of subsequent events. The resumption of psychological laboratory studies of love promises, however, to amend both theory and practice by focusing attention on additional affectional relationships.

Affectional systems

In a series of experimental studies on the affectional development of rhesus monkeys, Harry Harlow (1959; Harlow & Harlow 1965; 1966) has advanced a theory holding that love must be treated not as a unitary function but as multiple functions served by at least five distinct but interacting affectional systems, each aroused by its own stimulus conditions and expressed through its own response patterns. Each system develops in a series of orderly stages, characterized by different underlying variables and mechanisms. These systems, in order of development, are (1) infant–mother affectional system; (2) infant–infant, or peer, affectional system; (3) heterosexual affectional system; (4) mother–infant, or maternal, affectional system; and (5) father–infant, or paternal, affectional system.

Infant–mother affectional system. The infant–mother affectional system is initiated at birth through reflex sucking and clinging, in which bodily contact plays at least as important a role as nursing. With development, attachment to the mother, whether monkey or human, comes under voluntary control, and sight and sound of the mother as well as contact provide comfort and security, enabling the infant to be away from the mother for increasingly long periods in order to explore its physical and social environment.

Infant–infant affectional system. Contact with other infants launches the infant–infant, or peer, affectional system. The monkey comes to play closely with age-mates and develops strong affectional ties for them. The human mother, and often the father and older children, may bridge the gap between mothering and early peer relationships by playing with the infant at its own level until it is physically mature enough to play actively with peers. While peer relationships strengthen, maternal ties weaken, for the infant's needs change as it matures, and the changing infant calls forth altering maternal responses. The monkey mother actively abets the process of separating her infant through gradually increasing rejection when the infant makes demands on her. The human mother normally also discourages her infant from too great attachment to her, consciously or unconsciously, by leaving it alone for increasingly long periods, by diverting its attention to toys, by restraining it when it becomes too active, and, eventually, by encouraging it to play with others.

The peer affectional system is the basis of friendship and continues to function throughout childhood, adolescence, and adult life. Affectional systems that develop later do not replace the peer system. The expression of affection may change as individuals mature, and specific friendships may change, but affectional relationships continue between like-sexed and opposite-sexed individuals.

Heterosexual affectional system. The foundation of the heterosexual affectional system is laid in the peer affectional development period. Bodily contact with peers becomes accepted and desired, a basic necessity for heterosexual affection. In monkeys, play comes increasingly to show components of the adult sexual act so that the postures and activities are well organized long before puberty, lacking only intromission and ejaculation. Anthropologists have reported similar play patterns in human cultures permitting juvenile sexual activities (Benedict 1938). Another base of monkey heterosexual behavior in the peer period lies in the development of diverse nonsexual behaviors tending to separate the sexes in their play. The male becomes progressively rougher and more aggressive in play and the female more passive and submissive. The sign of submission in monkeys is turning away from the aggressor, assuming a rigid posture, and averting the face, a pattern closely approximating the female's role in copulation. This differentiation in play is also present in human children, for boys tend to prefer physical activity and girls less active pastimes. It is likely that this is the basis for affectional preferences of girls for girls and boys for boys in middle childhood—Freud's latency period.

At puberty, the monkey is prepared for the complete sexual act, limited only by the receptivity of the female, which is restricted to estrus. Generally, the female initiates mating, and the pair shows close ties for no longer than the duration of estrus. Because pregnant or lactating females do not show estrus, opportunities for copulation may be very limited; but the group holds together because of its many and varied affectional attachments. Culture so controls heterosexual activities in human societies, even in those permissive to children, that human heterosexual relationships after puberty follow no universal patterns.

Maternal affectional system. The maternal affectional system in monkeys is initiated with the appearance of the first infant and is reinstated with each subsequent infant. Like the heterosexual affectional system, its basis is laid in the peer affectional system, when infants develop affection for others of their species. Before puberty the female shows interest in babies and may pat or hold them, but even without this experience she can minister to her first infant; monkeys captured at one year, after peer experience, and raised without seeing infants after that time, show tender care at first parturition.

The initial maternal stage is one of continuous physical care, providing nursing, contact, support, grooming, and protection. As the baby gains bodily control, the mother lets the baby leave her, first only briefly and at a short distance, then for longer periods and distances. Eventually she begins to discipline the baby for transgressions, the start of the ambivalent period, which is characterized by increasing negative responses, albeit the predominant behavior is positive, and lasts until the mother has a new infant. Bodily separation is then achieved, but psychological attachment persists long after.

Paternal affectional system. In most subhuman primates, the paternal affectional system is confined to protecting and comforting all young within the troop, for most monkeys and apes live in groups organized around adult male leaders. Females with infants cluster about the male leader or leaders, surrounded by juveniles and by childless and adolescent females. On the periphery are the other males—adolescents, young adults, and outcasts. Adult males are tolerant of infants, occasionally "mothering" abandoned older infants, and they stop uneven squabbles. The paternal affectional system is stronger in human males, doubtless enhanced by culture. It is not uncommon for older boys to protect younger children or for adolescent or childless adult males to assume a paternal role toward youngsters; but for most males in Western cultures the paternal affectional system comes into full operation only with paternity. The helpless infant elicits sympathy and tenderness, and the bonds are strengthened by the infant's responsiveness. The paternal system, like the maternal one, depends upon the prior establishment of affectional ties to others of the species. It differs from the maternal system, however, in that it lacks the underlying endocrinal changes that accompany parturition in the female and doubtless help shape maternal behavior.

Deprivation studies

The concept of multiple, interdependent affectional systems with roots in varying physical and psychological needs and elaborated by learning explains the sequential development of affectional objects and is consistent with scientific findings on subhuman and human primates, both normal and abnormal ones. Deprivation studies (Harlow & Harlow 1962) point to the importance of both mothering and early peer experience, and especially to peer affection, for later heterosexual and maternal normality, thus removing the compulsion to trace all psychological ills to maternal inadequacy.

Monkeys raised individually from birth to 12 or 24 months of age, with or without a dummy mother, become socially inadequate adolescents and adults. Deprived of both mothering and play with peers, they show abnormal behavior, such as chewing on their bodies or engaging in repetitive stereotyped movements, and they are hyperaggressive when permitted to associate with other monkeys. No male thus raised has ever shown normal sex behavior, even after repeated exposures to breeding-stock females in estrus. Some females have gradually adapted to their heterosexual role, although rarely achieving the fully normal female posture, and 20 of them have produced infants. All but 2 of these "motherless mothers" have been cruel or indifferent to their first-born. Apparently, however, they became socialized by their experience with first babies, because 6 of the 7 mothers producing additional infants were either adequate or overprotective to their later offspring.

On the other hand, monkeys raised with dummy mothers and peer experience from the first month of life, or as groups of 4 in a large cage without any mothering, developed into normal adolescents and adults. Similarly, 4 first-born infants of abusive motherless mothers were given daily experience with each other from birth to 6 months and were normal adolescents. Monkeys raised with their mothers until 8 months old and then given peer experience were hyperaggressive and fearful of intimate contact. Their social adjustment was adequate but inferior to that of mothered monkeys given earlier peer experience. Thus, it would appear that in the protected laboratory situation, monkeys can develop normally without mothering or with inadequate mothering if they can form early affectional ties with peers. Real mothers can substitute for peers somewhat, but mother-raised offspring deprived of early peer affection are less socialized as adolescents.

The Harlow theory is not antithetical to Freud's and in many aspects parallels it. It may even provide a framework for unifying the findings of psychoanalysis and learning theories of social behavior and personality.

Margaret K. Harlow

[*Directly related are the entries* FRIENDSHIP *and* SYM-PATHY AND EMPATHY. *Other relevant material may be found in* EMOTION *and* PSYCHOANALYSIS.]

BIBLIOGRAPHY

BENEDICT, RUTH 1938 Continuities and Discontinuities in Cultural Conditioning. *Psychiatry* 1:161–167.

BRIDGES, KATHERINE M. B. 1931 *Social and Emotional Development of the Preschool Child.* London: Routledge.

FREUD, SIGMUND (1905) 1953 Three Essays on the Theory of Sexuality. Volume 7, pages 123–245, in *The Standard Edition of the Complete Psychological Works of Sigmund Freud.* New York: Macmillan; London: Hogarth. → First published as *Drei Abhandlungen zur Sexualtheorie.*

HALL, CALVIN S. 1954 *A Primer of Freudian Psychology.* Cleveland: World.

HARLOW, HARRY F. 1959 Love in Infant Monkeys. *Scientific American* 200, no. 6:68–74.

HARLOW, HARRY F.; and HARLOW, MARGARET K. 1962 Social Deprivation in Monkeys. *Scientific American* 207, no. 5:136–146.

HARLOW, HARRY F.; and HARLOW, MARGARET K. 1965 The Affectional Systems. Volume 2, pages 287–334 in Allan M. Schrier, Harry F. Harlow, and F. Stollnitz (editors), *Behavior of Nonhuman Primates.* New York: Academic Press.

HARLOW, MARGARET K.; and HARLOW, HARRY F. 1966 Affection in Primates. *Discovery* 27, no. 1:11–17.

JAMES, WILLIAM (1890) 1962 *The Principles of Psychology.* 2 vols. New York: Smith.

McDOUGALL, WILLIAM (1908) 1936 *An Introduction to Social Psychology.* 23d ed., enl. London: Methuen. → A paperback edition was published in 1960 by Barnes and Noble.

RIBBLE, MARGARET A. 1944 Infantile Experience in Relation to Personality Development. Volume 2, pages 621–651 in J. McV. Hunt (editor), *Personality and the Behavior Disorders.* New York: Ronald.

SPITZ, RENÉ A. 1945 Hospitalism: An Inquiry Into the Genesis of Psychiatric Conditions in Early Childhood. *Psychoanalytic Study of the Child* 1:53–74.

WATSON, JOHN B. (1924–1925) 1962 *Behaviorism.* Rev. ed. Univ. of Chicago Press.

AFFILIATION

See AFFECTION; FAMILY; FRIENDSHIP; GROUPS; KINSHIP; MARRIAGE; VOLUNTARY ASSOCIATIONS.

AFRICAN SOCIETY

I. NORTH AFRICA   *Jacques Berque*
II. SUB-SAHARAN AFRICA   *Jacques Maquet*

I

NORTH AFRICA

It would be rash to venture upon the study of a society scarcely emerged from the crisis that brought it to independence if it were not that the rupture itself embodies a rejection of the spirit of the colonial period and harks back beyond it to older continuities. Certain cultural constants previously hidden from view by colonial conditions have clearly emerged. From another point of view, the modernization to which the Maghreb aspires points up its principal problem: the relationship of the collective personality, anxious to protect itself, to the worldliness by which it is besieged. Decolonization in our days, like colonization formerly, represents a certain stage in this dual relationship which the Maghreb is attempting to conceptualize and absorb into its own order.

To scholars of the colonial period the Maghreb prior to the European occupation had only a prehistory; because of archaism and exoticism, this prehistory aroused their curiosity. The accent, however, was on Western intervention and on the cultural disturbances, adaptations, and replacements it had provoked. Maghrebi society was seen as a social field with varying orthodoxies and survivals possessed of greater or lesser degrees of interest but scarcely as a system capable of an evolution of its own. Since independence, on the other hand, the three Maghrebi nations, Morocco, Algeria, and Tunisia, have viewed the colonial period as a transitory state, less a point of arrival than one of departure for a social organism that has already passed through many stages. In this evolution colonization is only one stage; in order to maintain its identity in the face of ever-increasing pressures of adaptation to the rest of the world, the structure of Maghreb culture must undergo radical revision (e.g., see Doutté 1908; Maunier 1932; Gautier 1931).

The Maghrebi system

In the past decade, and by a coincidence that is not devoid of irony, several partial discoveries have enabled the historian and sociologist to reassemble the elements of what might be called the Maghrebi system. With a certain regularity these elements have been found in ethnological milieus as different from each other as Berber-speaking sedentary mountaineers and Arabic-speaking bedouins, traditional Islamic towns (*madīna*'s) and modern urban working-class quarters.

It was observed among the Chleuhs of the Haut-Atlas in Morocco that the division of the elementary political group, *taqbilt*, into agnatic subgroups, *ikh*'s, corresponds to the astonishingly minute and painstaking division of the land into toponymic agricultural patches and also to the cyclical allotment of irrigation periods. The integration of technique, knowledge, and social organization—with an astonishingly permanent structure—was the governing principle for the allocation of human energies. Even inequities in wealth based upon the mortgaging of the land to a lender and the subsequent departure of the borrower, which combined a small-scale nascent capitalism, procedural astuteness, and individual initiative, remained within the collective framework. Characteristic cultural traits—such as collective and legislative group festivals; poetry, hagiology, and historicity; and the mobilization of labor for maintenance of the irrigation system—are assembled in a configuration of great continuity (J. Berque 1955).

For example, in an Arabic-speaking Tunisian group, which with its extensive economy survives in the midst of the most heavily colonized sub-littoral hills and plains and which has maintained a determined adherence to bedouin life, there appeared a matrimonial organization capable of graphic representation and numerical computation. Here the permanence of the group was based upon a balance—previously unsuspected—between exogamy and endogamy, on a dual rhythm in the collective life. A circular configuration corresponding curiously to the shape of numerous bedouin encampments, *duwār*, best depicted these regularities (Cuisenier 1963).

At the opposite pole, in the large coastal cities, where the proletarization of the uprooted masses had progressed for at least a generation in the *casbah, bidonville,* and *gourbiville* quarters (Berque 1958*b*), the urbanization of new arrivals was effected in progressive hierarchical stages. What was observable in the casbah or other quarters of Algiers differed little except for time factors from what was observable in the *rabd* of Tunis or the outer neighborhoods of Fez. In spite of its reduction in status as a result of industrial impact, the old *madīna* had to a certain degree persisted. Alongside the intrusions of the modern era it preserved its pedagogical role. In Fez, Tunis, Rabat, Salé, Constantine, Tétouan, and even Algiers there persisted a pattern of life that centered on the *khutba* (weekly sermon) mosque, whose minaret was usually adjacent to the purifying *hammām* and the *sūq* of the artisan and shopkeeper. The Islamic city in some ways continued to influence the shape of modern cities, thus compensating at the symbolic level for what it had lost in fact. The struggle for emancipation could be defined as an attempt at readjustment between the two orders, emphasizing certain fundamental cultural complementarities that functioned above and beyond conscious ideologies.

A basic alternation. One of the fundamental complementarities of the Maghreb concerns the two habitats, the town, *madīna*, and the country, *bādīya*, along with the two types of men and kinds of life, the town-dwelling and the bedouin. Even in the traditional system this was not a strict dualism, but rather a case of overlapping structures. The bedouin doubled as sedentary and as nomad or transhumant. Between the country and the town certain regions, e.g., the Sahel of Tunisia and the Yebala of Morocco, contained a villager type who was recognizable by his speech (Marçais 1902). But at times the village was only a hamlet or temporary winter camp. Bedouinism affected these middle segments of the continuum with its economic precariousness and its instability of behavior. Transhumance produced an annual confrontation of the zone of extensive exploitative economy with the more active coastal zones of arboriculture and cereal culture (Nouschi 1961). The traditional town was characteristically the center for the ideal type, the pious and the learned. This ideal was modified by the legacy of the Bani Hilal, the poetic and warlike shepherds. Economic complementarity was thus paralleled by cultural polarity.

This structure underwent profound change during the century of colonization and foreign rule, whose civil institutions were accompanied by economic stagnation. Land development and the process of giant urbanization supplanted—sometimes even eliminated—the sedentary element, with the result that the bedouins suffered a probably irreversible loss of status. The pastoral rhythm that united the life of the interior with that of the littoral was broken. The exodus toward the cities and the emigration of workers to the *métropole*, a kind of proletarian transhumance, had become substitutes for bedouinism. The contrast between a prosperity monopolized by a small number and the indigence of the masses became sharper.

The modern economy developed a structure in which the fundamental alternation of the country, though partially modified, transposed, or conserved, was still discernible (see Figure 1).

The labor requirements of the principal crops grown in north Africa are known fairly exactly. If for a given group we describe these labor requirements on the circumference of a circle whose radius is proportional to the disposable time, that is, to the number of people in the group, we are struck by the relatively small amount of time spent in production. Even if we add to the sum of necessary intensive labor (e.g., arboriculture and irrigation) the sum of the extensive labor (e.g., traditional tillage and guardianship), an interior sphere remains. This sphere corresponds to infraeconomic

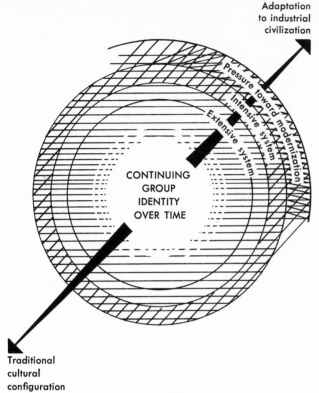

Adaptation
to industrial
civilization

Pressure toward modernization

Intensive system

Extensive system

CONTINUING
GROUP
IDENTITY
OVER TIME

Traditional
cultural
configuration

Figure 1

activities (e.g., searching for and gathering windfalls) and to ritualistic, sexual, cultural, vegetative, and amusement activities. It contrasts sharply with the peripheral belt of productive activity.

This internal sphere, with its overabundance of unproductiveness, is considered of little value by the economist and is even seen as an obstacle to progress. But its importance is nevertheless considerable. Inaccessibility and resistance to change make of this sphere the seat of collective continuity and identity par excellence. While the sensitive circumference responds to external stimuli by action and reaction, the internal sphere allows the group what I shall call the use and enjoyment of itself. Historical activation resides on the one side, and anthropological immanence on the other.

Figure 1 has more than the advantage of reproducing the shape of the bedouin campground, or *duwār*, which was once so widespread. On a Maghreb-wide scale it represents the alternation of an extensive system, tied to bedouinism, and an intensive system, which in turn supports the two variations, traditional peasantry and town dwellers. The Western impact dislocates the intensive system both in its urban and peasant forms. It rejects the extensive in every field. It breaks the former complementarity by downgrading the two old types with relation to the imported types, agricultural colonization and urbanization. Its action, furthermore, co-

incides in time with the growth of industrial technology and its social relationships: the wage appeal of commercial enterprise; growing proletarization of the masses; disruption of tribal affiliations and stratification of classes; and an alienation and depersonalization that are more and more strongly felt.

Beginning steps of the independent Maghreb. The Maghrebi system, never self-aware, was shattered by foreign domination and disfigured by industrial civilization. Still it survived. It has persisted as a structure of individual and collective behavioral patterns, a symbolic reference but with altered content. Westernization largely dislocated, modified, and disintegrated the dual patterning of extensive–intensive alternation of lifeways. And when the new nations were faced with the responsibility of reconstructing Maghrebi culture on this side of the colonial impact, there was great uncertainty, not at all limited to the difficult problems of modernization.

But if this is the trial of new nations in general, and not only of the Maghreb, it is also their strength. They appear, both to the observer and to themselves, to be in a searching and potent phase. The restructuring of their disintegrated parts and the redefinition of value systems can today build on a technology and way of thinking inherited, as it were, from the colonizers but increasingly assimilated. Their apprenticeship to modernity endows them with a sense of possessing an effective instrumentality, both in tools and in concepts. Their collective will and motivation, hardened by the struggle, strive to make the necessary adaptations to the surrounding world. The steps they take, which are both instinctive and deliberate, carry them to all the thresholds of historical creativity, from the most elementary to the most complex.

The king of Morocco, Mohammed v, perched on a tractor a short time after independence, himself inaugurated "operation tillage." Thus mechanization was given solemn approval in an agricultural setting that up to then was dependent upon an archaic set of tools. This also struck at the traditional system of land allocation, which, especially in the limited size of the cultivated plots, was a major obstacle to agrarian reform. The way was thus simultaneously opened to technical advance and to a redistribution of land parcels, perhaps even to collective working of the soil. All this would have been impossible to accomplish without the *élan* of unanimity which swept the people forward toward modernization in agriculture. Similarly, when an independent Tunisia systematically cut down the cactus that hedged in its fields, eliminated the wheeled carts from its roads, and drowned the old site of Kairouan in a forest of eucalyptus, it accelerated the disappearance of the colonial countryside and the creation of new relationships between man and the soil. In a similar manner, the building of a cellulose factory in the steppes of Frashish at Kasserine inaugurated an effective new relationship between the people and their fields and crops. In Algeria "volunteer days" are organized to accomplish land projects in an atmosphere of social service combined with collective jollity. This was the case with the 18 hectares of terraces dug by 10,000 young volunteers in four hours on September 20, 1963, on the slopes above the dam of Oued-Fodda.

Almost everywhere in north Africa there is a well-popularized emphasis on improving soils, forests, and grazing land. Seen from the air, the newly terraced hills, spotted with nascent green and slashed with concentric curves, seem marked with the fingerprints of history in process.

These activities are all the more instructive in that they spill over from the agricultural sectors into the still uncultivated and too often neglected areas which, in an excess characteristic of the Maghreb, surround them on all sides. Only one-third of the land in Morocco is cultivated; a third is in forests, and a third in grazing land. The steppes, *maquis*, and rocky areas increase as one climbs the slope of the mountains or the Hauts-Plateaux and moves toward the desert. They constitute the region of extensive economy, which becomes more and more diluted as one moves away from the coast. This geographic contrast is easily interpreted in terms of underdevelopment and development or as an irremediable dualism between the traditional and the modern. The present period of reconstruction will direct attention to these regions of extensive economy and their unique balance of man and land.

Effort and obstacle

In attempting to understand the restructuring of relations between Maghreb man and his land, we must use both ethnological and ecological information.

A tautological underemployment. The turbulent and impoverished city dweller of the postcolonial period is none other than a transplanted country person. But the dimension of time availability that characterizes the *bidonville*, although it is the lineal descendant of bedouinism, has acquired a pejorative meaning. The "dormant" time of the country dweller, so favorable to the development of the cult of the self, is now "lost time," the

wasting of human resources, degradation in every sense. Gone is the old cultural polarity between city dweller and bedouin. Its disappearance is all the more pronounced because the end of the colonial order, against which the Maghrebi personality so forcefully hurled itself, created new social relationships as a new structure emerged. Functionally centered upon collective efficiency, the new order is paralyzed by all kinds of "brakes" and "complications"; the vigorous and sometimes total denunciation of both the immediate and the distant past is unnecessarily destructive.

It is with these factors in mind that one must attempt to place north African underemployment in perspective.

In Kabylia, a particularly industrious Algerian region of 800,000 people, which furnishes a large contingent to the worker emigration, the number of unemployed is 30,000, or one-fifth of the heads of families. Of the 400,000 inhabitants of Oran, of whom nearly one-half represent a massive migration from the *bled*, one-third of the heads of families are said to be unemployed. The total number of persons affected by partial employment is estimated at two million. The situation is no more favorable in Tunisia and Morocco, where one-fifth of the men of working age are said to be without employment.

Beyond the degree of unemployment and its disastrous consequences, the problems it poses interest not only the economist and the politician but also the sociologist because of the kind of strategic change it effects in the relationships between these people and their dependence on the land. The massive tide of uprooted country people which tended to "ruralize" the Maghreb's cities also urbanized the country in the sense that it not only increased the number of communities but also introduced into them the same kind of competition between human numbers and available space that had until then been peculiar to the cities (Descloitres 1961).

The colonial economy suffered from contradictions that in the end were fatal; thus, the contradiction between social values and the profit motive led to the pauperization of local masses, permanently removing them from the sphere of consumption. The national economy that has succeeded the colonial one in the Maghreb must, as in other parts of the world, face the problems of a growing population and increasing settlement density, juxtaposed with the need for conservation of the natural resources. It also enters into a contradiction which is peculiar to our times: that between the natural setting on the one hand and culture on the other. The contradiction will not be resolved with formulas, indispensable as they may be, but rather through a fundamental reclassification involving both technological invention and a revolutionary change in qualifications.

Research against hunger. The government work project, such as road grading or eucalyptus planting, is becoming a familiar sight in north Africa. It can probably contribute in an appreciable way to substructural work and make a substantial contribution to peasant welfare in the agricultural season. But it also presents serious difficulties. It is aid from above, not a creative investment. In Morocco, where such government projects have been more or less institutionalized under the name *promotion nationale*, they have been the subject of vehement criticism (Tiano 1963). Some of these criticisms are most certainly justified. In all three countries the attraction the projects have for a peasantry living on tiny plots of land is quite understandable, but it diverts them in large numbers from their agricultural work. If the tendency were to become aggravated, a well-intentioned work project could act as a drain upon basic vitality and diversity.

This characteristic combines with others, either peculiar to the Maghreb or more generalized, to emphasize a phenomenon that is already observable in numerous areas: the waning of local spontaneity and national identification.

While the work project is a makeshift solution, the governments of the three Maghreb states are conducting substantive research into the sociology of agriculture, and statistical material is being gathered on such matters as the caloric values and labor costs of a given crop, the correlation between man-hours and the area of their employment, between investment and labor costs, and so on. Although this research is in general of a highly technical nature, it has given rise to numerous practical applications in agriculture and industry. Thus, whether or not the Maghreb becomes in certain respects a gigantic experimental laboratory is not a matter for theoretical concern only. The deliberate and scientifically deduced passing—undoubtedly incomplete and very tenuous—of large social units out of the area of traditional or imputed formulas into that of reasoned judgments is already observable. At the very least, this transition is the objective of certain long-range and short-range plans—for land improvement, creation of "industrial complexes," and so on.

The effect of this transformation on the morphology of the society, its values and attitudes, manifests itself in theoretical research, political debate, and public opinion. The data are not always encouraging; this is the case with the anticipated relationship between progressive exploitation of resources and demographic growth. It is not the function of the present study, however, to inquire into the success or failure of these plans. What must be realized is that in a society until recently disrupted by a traditionalist archaism and colonial dependency something new and irreversible has been introduced: the need for reason in things and for things in reason.

Rationalization of fields. One of the first areas in which the need for rationalization will work itself out is that of the agrarian regime (Colloque sur les conditions . . . 1963). At the time of independence foreign interests owned more than four million hectares of the best lands. Whatever the technical or financial successes, these only benefited an outlander minority and, secondarily, a native bourgeoisie. The seizure of these lands dislocated previous internal patterns: the drainage of labor and profits overseas, foreign control of bank credit and of the agricultural societies, the contrast between the magnitude of the operations undertaken and the narrow individualism of those responsible for them, the paralyzing influences brought to bear upon the state. The average area held by these entrepreneurs exceeded one hundred hectares, while the average for the fellah barely reached ten, the minimum threshold of subsistence. In a manner more tolerable politically but less defensible economically, the native latifundia bore with the same weight upon a rural world gripped by the evils of precarious climate, technical stagnation, and fragmentation of the land, without reconciling the fundamental opposition of the extensive and the intensive (Charnay 1965).

The Tunisian three-year plan for the coastal area north of the mountain ranges has estimated that the area a peasant family needs in order to produce a decent income is roughly 8 hectares of wheatland, 6 hectares of unirrigated orchards, 10 of enriched grazing land, and 27 of natural grazing land. These facts, which are, unfortunately, incontestable from a technical point of view and probably valid for the rest of the Maghreb, make the maintenance of the peasantry in its present numbers problematical, considering the saturation of the agricultural lands.

To the vividly felt need of the dispossessed masses to repossess were added, in Algeria's case, ideological presuppositions that were either implicit or formulated in the Tripoli charter. In Morocco and Tunisia, by contrast, tendencies more respectful of private property have held sway—at least up to this time. Even in Algeria it was the pressure of circumstances, beginning in the autumn of 1962, that placed upon the state the responsibility for more than one million hectares of "vacant lands" and brought on, at first empirically and later systematically (decree of March 29, 1963), collective management. Self-management committees were set up on the abandoned farms, sometimes at the initiative of the party, sometimes of the union, sometimes of the workers themselves. These committees guided the work of the agricultural season in such a way that with the aid of a good harvest the results appeared generally encouraging to the Congrès National de l'Autogestion Agricole, which met at Algiers on October 25–27, 1963. But serious questions of both a practical (division of profits) and a theoretical (devolution of the property right upon groups of workers or upon the whole society) nature nevertheless arose. The orientation of the regime will depend upon the answers given to these questions.

While Algeria has set up its self-management committees, Morocco and Tunisia have for the moment nothing that resembles this machine for building the new Maghreb. This doctrinal prudence, employed by choice by these regimes, will perhaps give way to the same collectivist motivations that have inspired Algeria. In the meantime, however, prudence has not delayed the implementation of several interesting technical ideas which are more or less colored with cooperativism. In two large bureaus, those for irrigation and for rural modernization, Morocco possesses an effective administrative apparatus which itself generates studies and local projects. However, instead of local land-improvement projects (*cellules de mise en valeur*) Tunisia has created a structure (*unités économiques*) that combines the technical cooperation of the participants with the maintenance of private rights.

Finally, there persists the problem of the economic and social dualism created by the contrast between a sector of modern economy (even "self-managed") and the traditional peasantry on the poor lands of the south. Here we find again the decongestion of the countryside. But the rural exodus, which is already massive, only transfers to the urban *faubourgs* and the edges of industrial complexes a large part of the Maghrebi difficulties, hopes, and potential.

Petroleum and trade unionism. The Maghreb countries, especially Algeria, contemplate with optimism the petroleum and natural gas resources of the Sahara, which have the capacity to supply the energy and finances for a radical modernization. It is not our place here to consider either the complex international influences or the strictly economic aspects of this anticipated qualitative and quantitative change. Nevertheless, the exploitation of these resources, which was already underway at the end of the colonial period, furnishes the north African nations with the means for an industrial "take-off" similar, except for its proportions, to those which produced the industrial rise of the Western nations at the beginning of the nineteenth century. It is comforting, moreover, to note how determined the Maghreb is to make the exploitation of petroleum the instrument of an integrated development rather than a source of royalties—a European "coal," rather than an Oriental "black gold."

Together with the acceleration of industrialization, resulting from the reinvestment of cash income, north Africa will, with the exception of Algeria, draw on increasing amounts of electrical power in the years to come. The quotient of available energy per inhabitant grew in Tunisia from 388,000 therms in 1938 to 632,000 in 1958 and 773,000 in 1962. Thus, a slight decline during the independence crisis of 1954–1958 has been largely overcome. In Morocco the consumption of energy between 1956 and 1961 increased from 2,013,000 to 2,303,000 therms.

The systematic attention the question of economic development has received in the different governmental plans should be emphasized. The degree of radicality of these plans or the energy with which they have been applied is of little importance. These political variations and the controversies that variously mirror them show how strongly the goal of planned development has entered into governmental thinking. The plans are already much more than administrative programs. They aspire to become schemes for total rebuilding; hence the kind of primacy enjoyed in Tunisia, for instance, by the ministerial organs related to them. The years to come will show to what extent this effort, up to now centralized, is balanced by popular support. Government conflict with a rejuvenated merchant bourgeoisie in Morocco or an improvised bourgeoisie in Tunisia is clearly perceived, but interference with popular sentiment is not so clearly seen. This confrontation of government with collective representation at the local level is a critical threshold of Maghrebi insight and action.

The modernization of the productive forces will without doubt bring correlative modifications of the social structure. In addition to a French-speaking or bilingual intelligentsia expressive of the new values, a group of technicians is growing up in apposition to what could be the beginning of an entrepreneurial class; its chances of success grow as the state-controlled sector increases sharply at the expense of the private sector. A small middle class of functionaries is taking over the place of the colonizers in the bureaucracy and, in so doing, at times arouses bitter rancor from the less favored levels of the population. Finally, the growing importance of the working class springs from the progress of technical modernization in both industrial and agrarian sectors. This importance is reflected in the growth and strength of trade unionism in the three north African countries.

In 1956–1957 the Union Marocaine du Travail (UMT) obtained through collective bargaining in the agricultural arena a daily wage per worker of 300 francs, which amounted to a great innovation in the country. At the same time in Tunisia the Union Générale des Travailleurs Tunisiens (UGTT), which, besides having an already long tradition, had benefited from the prestigious leadership of Ferhat Hached, set forth a remarkably lucid economic plan. In Algeria the Union Générale des Travailleurs Algériens (UGTA), which was separating at this moment from the French Confédération Générale du Travail (CGT) already had 300,000 members, and in August 1962 in an article in its newspaper, *Ouvrier algérien*, it proclaimed itself not only an organ for workers' demands and betterment but also a vehicle for social transformation. When independence came, this ideology led the unions to take over public services such as power and communications deserted by European personnel. Naturally, Algerian trade unionism is obliged to take into account the present conditions of the country. These include the single-party system, the need for organized building, cooperation with the ruling power, which is sometimes more delicate a situation than opposition, and so on. These same conditions variously affect the two other north African union confederations, but not to the same degree. Worker management, affecting a certain number of factories, for example, remains the distinguishing trait of Algerian trade unionism.

It is also from this country that the emigration of workers to Europe reaches its largest proportions. There exists, in effect, a veritable overseas Algeria. Drawn from the bedouin country and the mountain fastnesses, this emigration acquires from its contacts with a more developed industrial milieu new attitudes which the worker, when he returns to the country, carries into the farthest reaches of the *bled*. Except for its proportions, this is a kind of urbanization similar to that which affects many Maghrebis at home (Chleuhs, for ex-

ample), when they become concentrated in a city such as Casablanca, but it is what might be called a second-degree urbanization. The psychological changes of these mass influences, directly affecting the interior populations, bring about an acculturation the exact importance of whose effects has yet to be evaluated.

New debates on integration. We thus come back again to a problem we have already met. This problem concerns the relation between basic spontaneities, which are stimulated by wide-ranging experiences, and the organization with which a renovated Maghrebi society must imbue them if it is to keep control of that which affects it and avoid losing its identity once again. Recovered nationhood is one of the forms of this response, trade unionism is another, and so too are the "new" cities created by the influx of the native element into the mold left by the outlander, while the militants and those in charge worry about the new inequalities and try to save for the national history the pauperized masses of the *faubourgs*.

The interrelating of the north African countryside with the new economic and social life with which it is experimenting; the educative role exercised by function, habitat, and in a general way by the sort of container which is the modernized state; concerted and total revamping through economic development plans; the resistances encountered in these efforts; disappointments and faltering in the fight—such is the tumultuous climate of north African life. But these ups and downs operate for the most part at a level of modernity, technology, and decision making very far removed from the levels at which the major part of the country's realities remain. Undoubtedly, general enthusiasm, coupled with the prestige of the leaders or parties, is producing a certain juncture of the levels. But the problem of everything that remains outside, below, or behind still arises, and this problem concerns especially the *bled*, the "flat country," the opposite of the city.

Bedouin life is in many respects the anthropological immanence of the Maghreb. Although avoided and downgraded by contemporary history, it remains a reserve of interiority and a mistress of values. Almost everywhere, however, these traditional structures seem ruined or discredited. In Morocco, for example, the tribe, on which the government of the protectorate had leaned for support, is crumbling. In Tunisia, where the tribal structure has remained strong only in the south, the cumulative effect of economic precariousness and social erosion is bringing about an irreversible dispersion. Will the same occur in Algeria, where a communal organization that is juridically analogous to the tribe has been developed, at least in legal form? In general, is the spontaneous, albeit oligarchical and old-fashioned, democracy that attended the life of the *jamāʿa* as recently as twenty years ago salvageable in a modern system, or will it crumble before new kinds of entities?

Government projects, such as the *commune rurale* of Morocco in 1959, did not carry conviction on this point. More promising appear to be the Algerian self-management committees, to the extent that they succeed in linking large numbers and homogeneous modes of life to the unit of production in the broad sense. This development would be deprived of much of its impact if the agronomists were to fail to incorporate within the intensive production cells the vast segments of land and population still devoted to extensive systems such as grazing. Colonization, even when it is national, is still colonization. If it be defined according to the scheme outlined earlier as a cleavage between the activated periphery and the internal sphere of the Maghrebi being, an effort will have to be made in the future to select modes of action that will bring these latencies into play. Only very active research in the matter, however, both at the economic and the sociological levels will determine what is desirable and what can be achieved. Undoubtedly, certain aspects of the social structure will be radically transformed in the future, even those which were formerly made imperative by the constants of the country. Utopias such as the "*jamāʿa* on a tractor" would in this case have had their day.

At the time of the preliminary studies for the establishment of the *communes rurales* in Morocco, which broke up the tribal unit in favor of cantonal districts, it appeared that the suggested figure of ten thousand inhabitants for each administrative unit corresponded to the number of customers at a rural market—the open country *sūq*, which weekly assembled the neighboring populations around piles of grain, harness animals, and improvised displays of goods. The administrative program in this field agreed with what one might call the crude quotient of human concentration of the countryside.

There is nothing surprising in this. Even in Algeria, where the atrocious wartime *regroupements* (Planhol 1961) changed the rural habitat in a way that one might have thought permanent, an observer flying over Kabylia just at the time of the cease-fire was surprised "to see rebuilding by an almost independent reflex, in the most impossible corners and on desert peaks, the lost *mashta*

alongside the former destroyed one. Seen from the sky, the rectangle of these establishments kept exactly the same shape as the destroyed one, and the material, piled nearby by men and women at work, was the same." Another observer compared this self-building society "to those olive trees of the Temouchent region, which were cut down in 1956 by the FLN [Front de Libération Nationale], and which by 1960 had sprouted new branches from their cleanly cut-off trunks."

In the Maghreb, as elsewhere, history is both innovation and continuity. But history's appraisals of its own successive stages vary widely. Every decolonization appeals to its own history for the sources of its dynamism. Thus, Maghrebi society charts its course from its own reality. But to have validity its plans must proceed from its deepest reality.

Values and devaluations

The search for cultural identity in the Maghreb goes beyond political combat, economic competition, and appeals for social justice. Decolonization has fostered new values—formerly imposed through colonial manipulation of the technology but now intensified and "original" as the Maghreb adapts to the industrial world.

The structural role of violence. There is no reason to be surprised at the vehemence accompanying the transformation of the Maghreb. Beyond the epithets such as "revolutionary," beyond emotional enthusiasm, with its demands for political and social justice, the present phase of the Maghreb, as of other decolonized countries, is one of reintegration. A great release of anger, enthusiasm, and diffuse violence characterizes the process and makes it possible (Fanon 1961). The collectivity is not content with acclaiming or inveighing against its present. Retroactively it does the same with its past; everything is re-evaluated. But the affective polarity which opposed foreign usurpation to native emancipation gradually changes as internal rivals emerge: the "bourgeoisie" and the "people," the "conservatives" and the "progressives," the "patriots" and the "traitors." These antitheses are rich in moral judgments and affective *élan*. Going beyond their historical framework, they take from the unity of enthusiasm that bathes them, and also perhaps from the habits of religious belief, something of the absolute. Decolonization has made the Maghreb a paradise for culpabilities.

But this fact tends to hide another, more constructive phase of the transformation. Although the presence of violence is certainly a question of resentment, it is even more a question of anger.

Violence characterized the reaction against a situation of dependency and loss of identity; however, as the colonial period recedes farther and farther into time and the people of the Maghreb learn to feel through action their new responsibility, a positive affirmation of "self" replaces imitation of the "other." Actually it was never totally absent from the colonial debate, especially in the Maghreb, where Islam transcended the dispute.

Let us recall the figure presented earlier. A movement proceeding from an insulated inner core, influenced by the outside only slightly, if at all, is perhaps of greater significance than the peripheral response of the group affected by external stimuli. In fact it has taken north Africa only a few years— months in the case of Algeria—to shift the emphasis from the debate against the colonial partner to the internal debate. This shift has occasioned no loss of vehemence, but exactly the contrary. For this vehemence has a structural basis in the renewal of direct exchanges between the group and its territory. The dynamics of the *thawra,* most often translated "revolution," go beyond the English or French meaning of the term and include the quality of "liberation" which pervades life during the transformation. The first task of independence is to harness these liberated energies to the process of social reorganization. Failure to do this constitutes a grave danger. The collectivity arms itself against the eventuality of failure through a great release of passion and a simple predetermination of good and evil. Enthusiasm for the future, yearning for the fundamental, schooling of the will, the cult of cathartic violence, and a constant watchfulness—these are the values through which Maghrebi society, along with other Islamo-Mediterranean societies, fights to salvage its identity.

It is certainly natural that as calm returns and the requirements of order and work begin to win out, a reconstruction will take place. The social ethic will be severe with everything that sidetracks, opposes, or slackens the historic forward movement. The collective effort, through partisan trials, seeks a middle road between the excessive and the tepid. The rearrangement is in relation to this axis, which is itself uncertain because the Maghreb is looking for its place in a world setting to which it is peripheral.

Activation and inertia.   It is against the background of violence and watchfulness that one should evaluate a situation in which the call for "true socialism" is contrasted with tenacious manifestations of "neocolonialism" and historical movement is contrasted with inertia. But this inertia is not only the result of internal or external resistance

to change, of checks ascribable to mistakes or excesses, and still less of conspiracies between the "feudalists" or "bourgeois" and an ever-lurking "imperialism."

The inertia also proceeds from the limitations of the historical process itself, or at least from the persistence of geographical, social, and ideological preserves that are in large measure indifferent to the historical spirit. It is true that measures such as planning, industrialization, and agrarian reform stimulate intense activity, create new groupings and alliances, and out of the friction between the social group and the individual orient group-directed events. But they also create divergences of which the ideologies are often only a distorted reflection. Radicalism may well at times be inspired by foreign experiences; in contrast, a certain liberalism may be suggested by religious ideals; but these are only incomplete and perhaps fallacious formulations. Certainly we have noted a direct relationship between the concrete achievements of independence and value conflicts. But this relationship becomes less direct, even nonexistent, for those segments of the culture that the historical process touches only lightly.

Our figure encompasses many of these areas in the internal sphere, where they are linked with certain social and psychological "preserves" as well as with certain land areas of north Africa. I have spoken of the decay and disavowal that presently invest these areas with a negative quality. Thus it is, for example, with bedouinism throughout Mediterranean Islam. But although bedouinism is excluded from the visions of Arab modernization and is a pejorative term for a consciously repudiated social grouping, it nevertheless still exists; it does so both because of its statistical weight and because it corresponds with the extensive exploitative system, which remains appropriate to a whole section of the Maghreb (Poncet 1962). The persisting values and real importance of bedouinism make suspect any application of the idea of "underdevelopment." Nevertheless, under the influence of foreign examples, this idea is becoming daily more widespread. The concept of underdevelopment is used to explain the archaic survivals, which are in fact functionally related to the physical and cultural requirements of the extensive system, and the more recent decline, which is related to impoverishment and disintegration.

One of the first measures taken by the government of Ben Bella was for the re-education of the *yaouled's* of Algiers. But if some of these *olvidados,* shoeshine boys, and newspaper vendors have thus been enabled to leave the ranks of juvenile delinquency and enter vocational schools, other disturbing silhouettes have not disappeared from the sidewalks of the big cities. The adult "hoodlum" bothers passing couples. Bands of unemployed block the public thoroughfares and fill the *cafés maures*. A flood of human life dissipates itself at card games and *jacquet*. Despite the strictness encouraged by revolutionary morality, alcoholism is growing in the countryside, as if the throwing off of colonial restraints entailed casting aside all restrictions. Although it is not the scourge it has become in Egypt, the use of hashish is beginning to plague the country. The administrators of public assistance and employment projects start from a premise of pessimism concerning their ability to absorb unemployment, which in the last analysis they ascribe to the growth of population. Thus, in Tunisia birth control counseling has become a public policy, even though it is completely contrary to the family ethics of the rural population.

There is a contradiction between Maghrebi lifeways and technical advancement. According to economists, the "underemployed" include not only the partially or wholly urban and rural unemployed and the day or seasonal workers but also the farmers of tiny plots, the nomads, and the transhumants. Step by step the whole essence of bedouinism, labeled as "traditional sector" or "underdeveloped," is being swallowed up in the technicians' Hades. The colonial period had disowned the national culture. Are the independent states now going to do the same? If so, they will perpetrate an even more serious denial, for there is no power of appeal. Through hasty application of external lessons, there is a risk that the ancestral will be classified with that which is shorn of status and downgraded. It is hoped that the people of the Maghreb will make a deeper analysis of themselves and thus dissipate this too easily accepted contradiction.

Islam and secularism. Other values, which are part of the century but which relate to the transcendental, are involved in the Maghreb. Sometimes these converge with, sometimes conflict with, and sometimes remain untouched by, the values of changing historical processes.

One of the areas of involvement is the relationship between the theological and civil societies. In Tunisia the fast of Ramadan was abolished and became the object of a governmental campaign because of its negative economic effects. The popular reaction, especially at Kairouan, has subsequently brought about a more subtle policy, but one which still reflects the growing secularism. In addition, at Tunis and at Fez, the cathedral mosques of az-Zitouna and al-Qarawiyin have ceased to be

seats of learning as this function has become more and more the province of the national universities. The Koran schools, which were once very specialized, also tend to be gradually absorbed into the national school system. This integration, which the colonial regime did not want and could not have accomplished, appears today as a normal and irreversible development. The sermons from the pulpit, *wal'z*, *khutba*, and *irshād*, are subject to the same tendency. The sermon on the 27th night of the 1964 fast of Ramadan was, most significantly, preached by the mufti of Tunisia in the auditorium of the Grand Théâtre and not in the mosque; the Islam expressed under such circumstances is a modernist Islam. Also in Tunisia, the canonical magistracy of the *qādi* has been absorbed by the common-law judiciary. The wealth accumulated by the foundations, or *hubu*'s, has been returned either to their beneficiaries or to the public domain. It is true that in Morocco the Ministry for Islamic Affairs has demonstrated the opposite tendency, related to the school of the Salafiya. In contrast with the secularism of Bourguiba in Tunisia, the canonical reform of former Islamic Affairs Minister Allal el-Fasi has materialized in political and scientific action, extending even to juridical condemnation of apostasy, as demonstrated in the 1963 affair of the Bahais; nevertheless, it does not seem to have captured the masses as a counterbalance to the strong opposition it has met from the avantgarde.

The situation in Algeria is more complex. The young republic wrote Islam into its constitution. The role of the faith during the resistance was conspicuous, and after independence, the prominent place of Islam led to demands that it have cultural and moral leadership, demands that were naturally contested by the lay state. What one might call a clerical position, supported by the Algerian cultural association al-Qiyām, was thus significantly brought up against a secular and socialist orientation. But compromises could be found. No matter how much the revolutionary enthusiasm may draw for inspiration upon international models, it cannot ignore the mores that are rooted in faith and ritual. This is why the republic was able to accept Tawfiq al-Madani and his religious tendencies within the Ministry of Habous. Semiofficial campaigns to collect the canonical tax, *zakāt*, have been launched and have met with some success. Mosques have been dedicated with promising names such as Liberty and, at Mostaganem, Revolution. But modernization, which is in fact the secularization of life, is accelerating. As it does, it leads even the faithful to question customs surviving from the past, such as those attending the status of women. Practices such as polygamy and unilateral repudiation are already disavowed by the popular morality; at times they have been officially discouraged and even abolished, as in Tunisia in 1956. More and more these customs appear as archaic characteristics and are rejected as readily by the believer as by the progressive.

One after another the social implications of the creed are losing importance as the colonial situation that utilized them to set people apart disappears. Although individuals still fear starting debates on such questions, they tend to merge them with problems which go far beyond the Maghreb and Islam. The division between the temporal and the spiritual in behavior no longer invariably entails fixed formulations. The new ideology of the intelligentsia tends to avoid dogmatic disputation. Socialism does not always appear as a rival of Islam in thought, and even less in behavior.

In search of the self

By the very fact of challenging the established order, even the one it has itself created after destroying the colonial order, Maghreb society is seeking a part of its identity in the uncultivated or little understood zones of its nature and culture. Often these are zones which in the past were feared by all officialdom. Like the *maharam*, "lands it is forbidden to cultivate," which surround the tilled acres of the Moroccan encampment, they envelop the established, the recognized "self." But the forces of emancipation and the promise of the future are to be found in part in these preserves. These societies in their efforts at self-realization have been led astray by their failure to incorporate the ambiguous power, diffuse vehemence, and spontaneity of the "uncultivated" zones of culture. It is almost always the regularities and the constants that the new states worry about and with which they busy themselves. Of necessity drawn by schematized formulas of development, they allow many a discordance between the tide from which they flow and the projects they enter into to persist and even to become aggravated.

But this lack of completeness leads to new problems. Attempting to solve them is the most valuable contribution of independence: all is research in the new Maghreb. From the new-born self-consciousness of groups to the reports swarming around the social planner, from the gropings of collective behavior to the questioning reflected in the arts, the search continues.

The search is first of all a look. But this look is obviously not limited to the pseudo objectivity of the mirror or recording machine; rather, it strives toward a dialogue with the model. It is not by chance that a school of painting, a theater, and a romantic literature have exploded simultaneously into the art life of present-day north Africa. The coming of independence to the three north African countries, spread as it was over ten years, is not a chronological point of departure, but a climate which one particular artist may have sensed before another. Still, independence provides the impetus for an event such as the exposition that took place at the Musée des Beaux-Arts in Algiers on November 1, 1963. "We shall have the courage of our own riches. . . . In this abundance we see once more the sun of our own consciousness." All of the painters —abstract, representational, naive, baroque—were trying through the immediacy of their vision to reflect the collective "me." The *homme de l'œil*, whose advent characterized the Western renaissance, makes his appearance here. His first look is naturally directed toward himself. The public is being attracted en masse to the theater in order to engage in a dialogue with its own image. Thus Ali ben Ayed of Tunis attempts to combine the popular playlet in dialect—in the *commèdia dell'arte* genre —with the nobler play in the classical vein. The surprisingly youthful dramatic patterns of Shakespeare and Molière are being made available to a public that little by little will endow them with a Maghrebi content.

In the novel, an art form most highly developed in Algeria, a Kateb Yacine and a Muhammad Dib, forsaking the naturalism that provided Algerian literature with its initial rise, are committing themselves to a new kind of realism. Herein the collective myth, transfigured history, and verbal alchemy have produced two powerful encounters, in *Nedjma* (1957) and *Qui se souvient de la mer* (1963). In the latter work one finds the grotto of Keblout, from whence the hope of the tribe will spring. In the former, one finds Algiers, or perhaps Tlemcen, with tall houses sent crumbling down by an earthquake. These are telluric links of a history in quest of consciousness.

The language dispute. Most of the current works, including the two significant ones mentioned above, make use of the French language, a fact that has not failed to arouse concern and controversy. If emancipation is the rediscovery of the authentic, to what level should the Arabic language be resurrected from beneath the alluvia of the French?

Even in music this search and this ambiguity are manifested. It is true that Morocco has its Andalusian melody and its Berber songs, and

Tunisia its *mālūf,* which is still the object of delectation and a degree of snobbishness. Algeria has its *shaʿbī,* which compete with the invasion of Egyptian records on the radio. But will a classicism come out of this? Classicism, says Bachir Hadj Ali, must be drawn from popular feeling rather than from artificial imitation (Hadj Ali 1963). But this effort to achieve uniqueness and involvement must not succeed at the expense of style. If the Maghreb's music confronts us with such a dispute between the inherited and the nameless, the spontaneous and the organized, what can be said of the spoken language and the formidable practical associations it involves? The dispute cannot help but become grave, considering that it involves the creation of an educational system, an efficient bureaucracy, and international relationships.

In many north African circles the French language has been more assumed than endured, and independence has increased rather than decreased its diffusion. Moreover, "this Arab land, in spite of all impregnated with French culture," as Ben Bella, the first Algerian chief of state, described it, inclines toward plurality. The depth of its attraction to French culture seems to have carried the country beyond the lexicon upon which the research of the Arab academies has been based for a generation. To avoid creating a form as a mere disguise for an alien content, some believe that the Arabicization of the language should follow rather than precede the rise or the resurrection of a civilization. Here again we encounter the need that recovering nations have for self-realization. In language, as in technology, there are many methodological conflicts because of the practical effectiveness of importations that are already part of the scene.

In this connection independence has in many respects already given the problem a healthier complexion. In effect, the larger place assumed by bilingualism in the modern educational systems—not endured, but governed according to the needs of the individual or collective personality—permits some optimism. In spite of the liveliness of the polemics on the subject, the maturity of the practical approach to these problems in such sectors as educational programing substantiates this hope. Western culture can only gain as the sense of a national personality replaces the disequilibriums of colonial education. In this regard it may be said that the use of French will diminish as the people of these countries become re-Arabicized.

Besides the role of art, we must also note the role of sociological research. Planned change in the Maghreb has required the preparation of studies which are important contributions to knowledge,

but more significantly, it has been necessary to devise a methodology, whose successes and failures are equally revealing. The broad exposés undertaken by the parties themselves, such as those by the Néo-Destour and the FLN at the time of their respective foundings, aimed also at the analysis of the societies. Research is beginning in the universities of Tunis, Rabat, and Algiers, and this has already provided some interesting material. It would be premature here to place too much emphasis on these accomplishments, although future studies should be devoted to them.

The future. Perhaps the language dispute in the Maghreb is indicative of other contradictions. Insoluble on a superficial basis, they are amenable to solution through reference to the depths of Maghrebi life. That is why it is important to emphasize the basic areas of confrontation of the spontaneous with the organized and of nature with culture, for it is there that one encounters the collectivity in search of itself. It is equally important to correctly evaluate and understand that core of the Maghrebi personality which historical vicissitudes, in spite of their violence, have succeeded only in transposing rather than destroying. To its native internal pattern of alternation, the Maghreb now adds the patterns of industrial civilization, a variation ambiguous in its origins and prospects but whose power daily increases. For henceforward this new variation is not only an external element but a hypothesis of the self. It can remake the Maghreb, integrating it with the world from which it had been separated. However, it is reacting upon the most ancient of bases to a point where it threatens to destroy them. Is this the price of modernization? Maghrebi man is looking into himself in order to maintain through modernization—and despite it—another kind of self.

Jacques Berque

[*Directly related are the entries* Colonialism; Islam; Modernization; Near Eastern society.]

BIBLIOGRAPHY

Amin, Samir 1966 *L'économie du Maghreb.* 2 vols. Paris: Éditions du Minuit.

Anthologie maghrébine. 1965 Paris: Hachette.

Ayache, Albert 1956 *Le Maroc: Bilan d'une colonisation.* Paris: Éditions Sociales.

Berque, A. 1937 *L'Algérie, terre d'art & d'histoire.* Algiers: Heintz.

Berque, Jacques 1955 *Structures sociales du Haut-Atlas.* Paris: Presses Universitaires de France.

Berque, Jacques 1958a Droit des terres et intégration sociale au Maghreb. *Cahiers internationaux de sociologie* 25:38–74.

Berque, Jacques 1958b Médinas, villeneuves et bidonvilles. *Cahiers de Tunisie* 21/22:1–42.

BERQUE, JACQUES   1962   *Le Maghreb entre deux guerres.* Paris: Seuil.

BIROT, PIERRE; and DRESCH, JEAN   1953–1956   *La Méditerranée et le Moyen Orient.* 2 vols. Paris: Presses Universitaires de France. → See especially Volume 1: *La Méditerranée occidentale: Péninsule Ibérique, Italie, Afrique du Nord.*

BOURDIEU, PIERRE   (1958) 1962   *The Algerians.* Translated by Alan C. M. Ross, with a preface by Raymond Aron. Boston: Beacon. → First published as *Sociologie de l'Algérie.*

CHARNAY, JEAN-PAUL   1965   *La vie musulmane en Algérie d'après la jurisprudence de la première moitié du XXᵉ siècle.* Paris: Presses Universitaires de France.

COLLOQUE SUR LES CONDITIONS D'UNE VÉRITABLE RÉFORME AGRAIRE AU MAROC, PARIS, *1962*   1963   *Réforme agraire au Maghreb.* Paris: Maspéro. → Seminar organized by the Union Nationale des Étudiants du Maroc.

CUISENIER, JEAN   1963   *L'Ansarine: Contribution à la sociologie du développement.* Tunis (City), Université, Faculté des Lettres, Publications, Series 3, Vol. 7. Paris: Presses Universitaires de France.

DESCLOITRES, ROBERT   1961   *L'Algérie des bidonvilles: Le tiers monde dans la cité.* Paris, École Pratique des Hautes Études, Section des Sciences, Économiques et Sociales, Le monde d'outre-mer, passé et présent, Series 2, Documents, No. 6. Paris: Mouton.

DESPOIS, JEAN   (1949) 1964   *L'Afrique blanche.* Volume 1: Afrique du Nord. 3d ed. Paris: Presses Universitaires de France.

DOUTTÉ, EDMOND   1908   *Magie & religion dans l'Afrique du Nord.* Algiers: Jourdan.

FANON, FRANTZ   (1961) 1965   *The Wretched of the Earth.* Preface by Jean-Paul Sartre. New York: Grove Press. → First published as *Les damnés de la terre.*

GAUTIER, ÉMILE F.   (1931) 1959   *Moeurs et coutumes des musulmans.* Preface by Jacques Berque. Paris: Club du Meilleur Livre.

GOLVIN, LUCIEN   1950   *Les arts populaires en Algérie.* Volume 1. Algiers: Gouvernement Général de l'Algérie. → First volume of a projected series.

GUEN, MONCEF   1961   *La Tunisie indépendante face à son économie: Enseignements d'une expérience de développement.* Paris: Presses Universitaires de France.

HADJ ALI, BACHIR   1963   Culture nationale et révolution algérienne. *Nouvelle critique* No. 147:33–56.

JULIEN, CHARLES A.   (1931) 1961   *Histoire de l'Afrique du Nord: Tunisie, Algérie, Maroc.* 2d ed. 2 vols. Paris: Payot.

LACOSTE, YVES; NOUSCHI, ANDRÉ; and PRENANT, ANDRÉ   1960   *L'Algérie, passé et présent: Le cadre et les étapes de la constitution de l'Algérie actuelle.* Paris: Éditions Sociales.

LAUNAY, MICHEL   1963   *Paysans algériens: La terre, la vigne et les hommes.* Paris: Seuil.

LE TOURNEAU, ROGER   1962   *Évolution politique de l'Afrique du Nord musulmane, 1920–1961.* Paris: Colin.

MARÇAIS, WILLIAM   1902   *Le dialecte arabe parlé à Tlemcen: Grammaire, textes et glossaire.* Paris: Leroux.

MAUNIER, RENÉ   1932   *Loi française et coutume indigène en Algérie.* Paris: Domat-Montchrestien.

Mélanges Charles André Julien.   1964   Paris: Presses Universitaires de France. → See especially "Le tapis maghrébin" by Jacques Berque.

MONTAGNE, ROBERT   1930   *Les Berbères et le Makhzen dans le Sud du Maroc: Essai sur la transformation politique des Berbères sédentaires (groupe Chleuh).* Paris: Alcan.

NOUSCHI, ANDRÉ   1961   *Enquête sur le niveau de vie des populations rurales constantinoises, de la conquête jusqu'en 1919: Essai d'histoire économique et sociale.* Tunis (City), Université, Faculté des Lettres, Publications, Series 4, Vol. 3. Paris: Presses Universitaires de France.

OUZEGANE, AMAR   1962   *Le meilleur combat.* Paris: Julliard.

PARIS, UNIVERSITÉ, INSTITUT D'ÉTUDES DU DÉVELOPPEMENT ÉCONOMIQUE ET SOCIAL   1962   *Le développement agricole en Algérie.* Paris: Presses Universitaires de France.

PLANHOL, XAVIER DE   1961   *Nouveaux villages algérois.* Paris: Presses Universitaires de France.

PONCET, JEAN   1962   *La colonisation et l'agriculture européennes en Tunisie depuis 1881: Étude de géographie historique et économique.* Paris: Mouton.

Problèmes de l'Algérie indépendante. Étude présentée par François Perroux.   1963   Paris: Presses Universitaires de France.

RODINSON, M.   1966   *Islam et socialisme.* Paris: Seuil.

SEBAG, PAUL   1951   *La Tunisie.* Paris: Éditions Sociales.

TIANO, ANDRÉ   1963   *La politique économique et financière du Maroc indépendant.* Paris: Presses Universitaires de France.

Travail et travailleurs en Algérie. By P. Bourdieu et al.   1963   Paris: Mouton.

UNITED NATIONS EDUCATIONAL, SCIENTIFIC AND CULTURAL ORGANIZATION   1963   *Nomades et nomadisme au Sahara.* Arid Zones Research, Vol. 19. Paris: UNESCO.

II

SUB-SAHARAN AFRICA

In traditional Africa, south of the Sahara, there were from eight hundred to one thousand societies; in modern Africa there are some forty or fifty. Society, in the present analysis, will refer only to that social unit which is *global* in that the activities of all its members are organized in such a way that the survival and the development of the whole unit is made possible. The global society encompasses the networks of social relations in which individuals interact with one another during the entire course of their lives; identified by a name, it is perceived as a unit by its members and by the outsiders who belong to neighboring global societies. Usually a global society has its political expression in a single, but not necessarily centralized, system. Relations between rulers and subjects are organized across the whole society according to the same patterns, and there is no permanent contention within the rulers' group.

Global societies in traditional Africa. "Traditional Africa" is a cultural period which began with the neolithic revolution (the development of agriculture and/or cattle herding) and ended with the industrial revolution. The traditional period did not begin all over sub-Saharan Africa at the same time. It is certain the agricultural techniques spread from

Egypt, where they had been introduced from adjacent southwest Asia in the fifth millennium B.C.; it is probable that they had been independently invented in the Upper Niger Valley and diffused from there at about the same time (Murdock 1959, pp. 64–68). From these centers, agriculture finally reached every part of the continent south of the Sahara, although the transition was still in progress in the nineteenth century. The beginning of the modern period can be more precisely determined. Although some nonagricultural societies persisted until modern times, most of the societies upon which the industrial revolution later impinged were agrarian and/or pastoral. Political colonization of the interior of Africa was at the same time a consequence of European industrialization and the starting point of the process of African industrialization. The Berlin treaty in 1885 set the diplomatic rules for the partition of Africa among European powers. It is thus convenient and justifiable to choose this date as symbolic of the beginning of the modern period in Africa.

From the point of view of societal analysis, the modern period must be divided into the colonial period and the period of independence. The first states to achieve political independence did so in the 1950s (the Sudan in 1956, Ghana in 1957) but the movement culminated in 1960, the year in which 17 independent states emerged. Thus we take 1960 as the end of the colonial period.

Global societies in colonial Africa. In traditional Africa the hundreds of global societies were kingdoms or tribes, "federations" of bands or "unions" of villages. During the 75 years of colonization, we do not find clear-cut units which may be called global societies. Kingdoms and tribes continued to constitute the framework in which the great majority of Africans lived most of their lives; the social organization of production and consumption, marriage and inheritance, religious and community relations were regulated by traditional institutions. However, the networks of social interaction transcended the boundaries of the tribes or kingdom and involved the entire colony (no distinction need be made between crown colonies, protectorates, mandate territories, trust territories, and overseas "provinces").

Systems of political, administrative, educational, commercial, and juridical relations were based on the colony as a social unit. The governor was at the apex of a single structure in which everybody was included; tribunals and courts were integrated into a single system. Everyone had to pay taxes calculated according to the same schedule; every child was, in theory, expected to take part in a colony-wide school system; the same imported goods were usually available throughout the colony and were paid for with the same kind of money. It should be noted, too, that as the decades progressed from 1885 to 1960 the proportion of the interactions circumscribed by the colony increased, whereas the tribe-framed or kingdom-framed interactions diminished. On the other hand, a psychological identification with the colony was never achieved. There were obvious reasons for this: the colonial society was a white man's creation, imposed by force; the African populations understood more or less clearly the social stratification of a colonial society—a privileged minority supported by an exploited majority—and were not inclined to feel a deep attachment to such a society. Except for the very last years of the colonial period, there was no African participation in government, no recognized political discussion, no political parties, no elections.

One could analyze this fluid, and somewhat confused, societal situation in terms of a polarized continuum: at the traditional end, the global society is the tribe or kingdom; at the modern end, the global society is the nation. On the continuum, the colony is a historical stage between traditional society and national society, nearer to the latter than to the former. During the colonial period there was a certain overlapping of global societies or, to avoid contradiction, let us say that each individual belonged to two societies, neither of which succeeded in being fully global. Each individual was an actor in several systems of interaction, some systems covering only the tribe and others the whole colony. Since the precolonial traditional societies were global, that is, had complete sets of relational networks, there were conflicts between the duties of individuals as actors in the traditional and modern systems of politics, education, commerce, and so on.

Global societies in independent Africa. With independence, the importance of the sector controlled by the larger society has grown. The reality of the colony as a social unit has been proved by its persistence through decolonization and independence. As has often been pointed out, boundaries of the colonial territories were drawn with little or no attention to the boundaries of traditional societies. For example, the traditional Kongo kingdom found itself divided among three large territories: Portuguese Angola, Belgian Congo, and French Equatorial Africa. In spite of these frequent discrepancies, however, the new states that succeeded the colonies have rarely attempted to modify the colonial frontiers. The new African states are built on these artificial colonial units, although the national qualification of these units has been questioned.

Several processes have acted, since independence, to accelerate identification with the larger societies at the expense of the traditional units. Each citizen of the new state is increasingly involved in nationwide systems of interaction: he participates in the election of representatives to the national assembly; he is submitted to the propaganda of one or several nationally based political parties; he is urged to make his contribution to the country's economic development; if he is a wage earner, he may seek employment outside the area of his traditional society.

Once these extended systems of interaction and, consequently, of a common interdependence have been established, what remains to develop is the awareness of these patterns. Identification with the societal unit larger than the traditional society was born with independence and develops slowly. Some of the obstacles to that recognition—the colonial conditions mentioned above—have disappeared or at least have considerably diminished with independence. Of course, other obstacles remain: the memory of past tribal conflicts; the use, by some politicians, of the former tribal identifications; and regional interests. Certainly, traditional societies are still functioning in some respects, but the global societies of modern Africa are the nations embodied by the new states. Statehood has preceded nationhood, whereas in Europe the opposite occurred.

Civilizations. The term "civilization" has been used with so many different meanings that one feels free to use it to designate a specific concept. A civilization in the present discussion is an integrated cultural totality that is not linked to a particular global society. Its content may be induced from several social heritages: it summarizes what we believe to be common and essential to several societal cultures (Maquet 1962, p. 18). What is formulated on the basis of induction is an abstract construct, which may be applied not only to the specific cultures where it has been observed but to others as well.

As integrated totalities expressing what is thought to be essential, all civilizations are elaborated on an identical structure. Indeed, it is with reference to a structure that what is essential will be distinguished from what is not, that the integration will appear, and that it will be possible to compare different civilizations.

The concept of civilization is a useful tool for the analysis of African societies. It enables us to reduce the great number of global social entities and permits analysis of broadly articulated systems. These systems are composed of three levels. The first level concerns acquisition and production of goods. These processes depend on a natural factor, environment, and on a cultural one, the techniques through which food and other goods are obtained. As culture is made by men who have material needs, material adjustment is basic to all other cultural achievements. The second level is made up of social institutions that regulate the different systems of interaction: the economic system, through which goods are channeled to consumers; the political system, which organizes the relations between rulers and subjects; the kinship system, according to which descendants of a common ancestor and affines pattern their behavior toward one another; associations, in which people congregate on a voluntary basis to reach, by their common action, certain targets. On the third level there are collective representations, or systems of ideas and symbols shared by all the members of a society. These include religious and magical beliefs, ethical conceptions and world views, philosophy and art, language and poetry.

The principal previous attempts to delineate African cultural units larger than societal cultures have given priority either to temporal dimensions (Baumann et al. 1940; Murdock 1959) or to spatial distributions (Herskovits 1930; 1962). Although history and geography are taken into account, this classification is based on cultural criteria. Fundamental are the techniques for the extraction of food and other goods from nature. When, as in traditional Africa, these techniques are not very efficient, the environment plays a very important role in production. Thus, in the present classification, culture "types" will be found to correlate with similar ecological conditions, in substantial agreement with Herskovits' division of Africa into culture areas.

The acquisitive or productive techniques characteristic of the six main types of civilizations are (1) hunting and gathering, (2) forest horticulture based upon root crops, (3) savanna agriculture based upon cereal, (4) cattle herding combined with agriculture, (5) exploitation of natural resources for handicrafts and external trade, (6) industrial techniques.

In the analysis of each civilization, we shall proceed according to the categories set forth above: in each case, we shall describe the pattern of acquisitive and productive techniques, the struc-

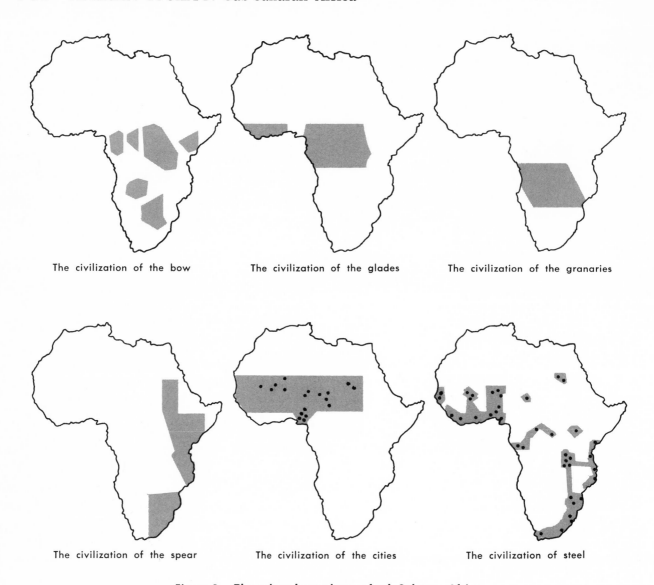

The civilization of the bow

The civilization of the glades

The civilization of the granaries

The civilization of the spear

The civilization of the cities

The civilization of steel

Figure 1 — The cultural complexes of sub-Saharan Africa

ture of institutions, and the pattern of collective representations (see Figure 1).

The civilization of the bow

Acquisitive techniques. The technology involved in hunting and gathering activities is not productive: the goods necessary for the life of the society are obtained from the environment without modifying it. Subsistence depends more upon collecting vegetable foods (roots, berries, mushrooms, leaves, fruits) and small animals (tortoises, snails, frogs, lizards, ants, locusts) than on hunting large game. The primary tools of the gatherers are digging sticks and stone knife-blades; the weapons of the hunters are bows and stone-tipped arrows, nets, traps, and snares.

Obviously the success achieved by these tech-

niques depends very much on the resources of the environment; these range from the rich equatorial forests to the humid savanna, in which large animals are abundant, to the dry semideserts, where every resource is scarce. Hunting and gathering are indeed the least efficient ways of exploiting the environment: the land area required to feed an individual is considerably larger than that required in cultivated areas.

Marginal peoples. It is difficult to estimate the numbers of hunters and gatherers in Africa at the end of the traditional period; one century later, around 1950, there were probably between 200,000 and 300,000. They were, and still are, found only in the refuge areas to which they have withdrawn: the equatorial forest, particularly in the eastern part; the mountains of east Africa, particularly in the region of the Congo–Nile divide; the deserts of southwest Africa; and, until the end of the nineteenth century, the highlands of southern Africa. Almost never are these peoples able to live a self-contained economic life, but they establish relations —frequently symbiotic—with groups of cultivators: through a permanent arrangement, a band of hunters and a village of cultivators living very near one another will carry on a constant exchange of goods and sometimes even enjoy common rituals.

Most African hunters are either pygmies or bushmen. Physical anthropologists consider the two groups to be very different genetically. The former are classed as Negrito (or pygmoid), and the latter are classed as Khoisan. All they have in common physically is their short stature. These racial characteristics have, of course, no relevance to our sociocultural analysis.

There has been a cultural continuity from the African preagricultural hunter to the marginal gatherer of the nineteenth century: the typical prehistoric art of rock painting was still practiced in 1869. Before the appropriation of most of the continent by agriculturalists, hunters and gatherers had occupied much more favorable environments; the description of the hard life of their descendants, limited to the marginal areas, should not be taken as applying to all preagricultural hunters and gatherers.

The band—the economic unit.   The low returns of their acquisitive techniques do not provide a basis for a broad choice of social systems for marginal hunting and gathering peoples.

The working unit of the economic system is composed of all the adults who hunt (the men) and gather (mainly the women) together. The number of adults who constitute the unit is limited by the subsistence factor. The elementary family (a hunter, his wife—or wives—and their unmarried children) is too small to constitute an economic unit of acquisition; if one of the adults of the group were unable, for whatever reason, to carry on his search for food, even for a few days, the survival of the unit would be threatened. Many hunting techniques—for example, beating the game toward traps or nets or killing a large animal—require a team. A too intensive exploitation of a certain area of forest or savanna would very rapidly exhaust it. Thus, there is an optimum size for the working unit which varies with the vegetal and animal resources of the environment; even in the best of situations, these units do not exceed one or two score of adults.

The unit of consumption is identical to the working unit with the addition of young children and old people. Distribution follows very strict rules which take into consideration the patterns of authority, of kinship, and the differential participation of the hunters in the successful operation.

The camp—the residential unit.   The residential arrangements for the band are dependent on the essential requirement of mobility. A camp cannot become a sedentary settlement: when the area that can easily be reached in less than a day's walk no longer supplies enough food, the camp must be moved.

The internal organization of the band is largely structured by relations established through descent and affinity. When the sons of a hunter marry and remain in their father's band the ties of filiation prevail. Also important are the ties of affinity, which determine the roles of persons linked through marriage. (Affines are understood here as including the kin of one's spouse and the spouses of one's kin.) Since all the members of one camp may not be related through kinship or affinity other systems of interaction are also present.

Nonpolitical decision making.   There is in the group a system of authority. As is well known, even in small, temporary groups leadership arises: one person gains influence over others and his opinions are usually influential. In the band such influence is wielded by an individual who exhibits competence in hunting, an ability to deal with tensions within the group, wisdom in difficult situations, or by one who has seniority, or numerous offspring, or magical powers. All decisions concerning the group will in fact be made by these influential persons: in a general discussion, their opinion will be accepted by the group, particularly in fields in which they are recognized as especially competent. In the small hunting and gathering group, this fluid pattern of authority is sufficient to ensure that the necessary decisions will be made.

In such societies the process of decision making does not require the existence of a political authority—that is, a ruler who has coercive means at his disposal. In this sense, there is no political system in African hunting bands.

In addition to making decisions, political authorities ensure conformity to the rules of social behavior. In a small society this may be achieved by other than political sanctions. Turnbull describes how the pressure of community feelings on the deviant is usually sufficient to oblige him to resume accepted behavior (1961, pp. 97–110). If he should resist, community disapproval may mean banishment. No physical coercion need be exerted; the refusal of others to cooperate with him is enough. In addition to community pressure, beliefs in magical powers provide other efficient sanctions: when someone does not behave properly the forest spirits may cause game to escape him when he hunts.

To be effective, nonpolitical sanctions require the unanimous support of the group. In African assemblies generally, the importance of unanimity, as opposed to simple majority decisions, has often been stressed: a decision is reached when, after long discussions, everybody finally agrees. Of course, some individuals carry greater weight; where societies are more differentiated politically, agreement becomes, to a greater extent, a passive acceptance of the opinions of people of prestige. Among hunters, where there is no political authority, unanimity is required in the execution as well as in the making of decisions, and this requires a deeper level of agreement in the community. If only a tiny minority does not apply the sanctions of social avoidance toward the deviant, this ruins the effectiveness of the process. Consequently, reactions to nonconformity to the rules are rarely extreme: moderation is imperative when every member of the group, including the relatives of the deviant, must apply the sanctions.

Global societies—the matrimonial criterion. Although the band encloses most of the systems of interpersonal action, the hunter's network of relations extends beyond the camp in some important respects. Among the southern hunters, several bands congregate at certain periods for common celebrations; everywhere, a hunter may leave his band to join another; if a group becomes too numerous it may split into two bands, between which ties will obviously remain. When bands of hunters have contacts with agricultural people, they become aware of their own cultural distinctiveness.

The most important links between bands, however, are matrimonial. Incest prohibitions within a camp composed largely of the descendants of a single ancestor compel members to look to other groups for spouses. Among the equatorial hunters, marriage is virilocal; the wife lives in her husband's camp, although she may return for long stays to the camp of her parents. Among some of the southern hunters, marriage is uxorilocal, although, again, relations between the young man and his father's band are not cut off.

Thus, the limits of the global society in the civilization of the bow are not clearly defined. It is larger than the band: it includes all the bands among which matrimonial exchanges take place.

Marriage by exchange is common among hunt-

ers. In its simplest form, a brother and a sister of group A marry a sister and a brother of group B. Thus, when a man wishes to marry, he must at the same time arrange a second marriage between a girl of his kinship group and a kinsman of the girl he wishes to marry. This form of marriage, which in many African societies seems to be older than marriage by bridewealth, is directly related to the technological arrangements for the acquisition of goods. A small group living in a difficult environment finds the problem of generational continuation a severe one; the child-bearing capacity of a girl concerns her whole group. To give away a girl to another group is to lose a potential mother. Marriage by exchange, in which the donor group receives a potential mother from the receiving group, is a very good adjustment to the demographic requirements of a band, obliged by ecological conditions to remain small and yet to maintain minimal membership.

Collective representations. The world views of African hunters have been the object of many studies and speculations. Catholic anthropologists of the Vienna school were eager to disprove evolutionary theories according to which men arrived at the conception of a high creator-god after having passed through animistic and polytheistic phases and to show that, on the contrary, mankind had "degenerated" from an original monotheistic faith. Since the hunters were thought to be most similar among contemporary peoples to our earliest ancestors, the Vienna anthropologists sought to find in their idea of divinity a kind of primitive monotheism.

Equatorial as well as southern hunters may be said to believe in a high divinity, but it is impersonal to the point of not being clearly distinct from the forest. It is benevolent but has "to be kept awake" so that nothing may go wrong. This idea seems to result from a projection of the everyday experience of men who are entirely dependent on what their environment offers them. They see the environment as good, but indifferent; they hope that the indifference is not deep and that, if kept "awake," nature will actively be good to them. It could be argued that many of the hunters' stories personalize the divinity and that the translation of its name as "god" is therefore justified. Most of the time, however, his adventures are quite undignified and "god" plays the role of a not-so-clever hero.

The ordering of relations between the hunters and their gods is straightforward. Rituals express through offerings and prayers the attitudes consistent with their world view: recognition of the weakness of man before the powerful gods, which are identified with natural forces, and the demand that they favor men by granting them abundance of game and fecundity of women.

In the system of values of the civilization of the bow, social harmony has, perhaps, the first place. The reason is obvious: hostility or tensions within a group threaten the group's survival. As soon as a possible cause of disagreement arises, it is removed at the cost of individual comfort or even equity. In a conflict between two members of the band, the aim of the influential men is the restoration of peace rather than exact assessment of rights and wrongs (Thomas 1959, pp. 22, 115–117).

This culture has a form of art that is unique in traditional Africa in both medium and style. The rock paintings and engravings, which have been found by the thousands, reflect in their subject matter the focal interests of the civilization of the bow: in representational style they portray games, the hunt, battles against pastoral and agricultural peoples, and punitive expeditions of white soldiers.

The dating of these pictures has been much debated. The balanced opinion of Clark (1959, p. 280) is that most of the rock paintings are not older than two thousand years, but that they belong to an artistic tradition which may go back as far as the middle Stone Age, that is, from twelve thousand to seven thousand years ago.

In the perspective of such antiquity and continuity, the way of life represented by the few scattered bands of hunters and gatherers remaining in the nineteenth century deserves to be counted among the great African civilizations.

The civilization of the glades

The traditional period, we have said, began with agriculture. It is very unlikely that agriculture began in the rain forest: the plants of the Nile and Niger valleys, from which the first agricultural complexes of sub-Saharan Africa were derived, were not suited to forest conditions. Agriculture probably spread to the forest areas in relatively recent times, perhaps with the migrations of the Bantu-speaking peoples in the first centuries of our era. That the forest agriculturalists are discussed after the hunters and before the savanna peasants is not meant to suggest an evolutionary sequence, for the production of goods by the techniques of forest cultivation does not provide people with a supply of food significantly more plentiful than that obtained from the environment by hunting and gathering. There are many similarities between the cultures built upon these two material bases, which provide approximately the same amount of food.

Forest agricultural techniques. The rain forest environment is homogeneous. It covers approximately the region extending from the fourth parallel north of the equator to the fourth parallel south and from the Rift Valley to the Atlantic Ocean. There, it stretches along the coast of the Gulf of Guinea up to Sierra Leone, with the exception of the Bight of Benin hinterland, a less densely forested area that has permitted the growth of another civilization, that of the cities. Vegetation is heavy; under very high trees, part of whose roots are above the soil, there is a dense undergrowth of shrubs, creepers, weeds, and grass. Swidden agriculture is practiced in the forest region.

The main tool is an iron ax (iron working is believed to have been introduced south of the Sahara from the kingdom of Meroë, in the Sudanic Nile Valley, during the last three centuries B.C.), used to cut the underbrush and to fell trees, which are left to dry for a few weeks and then burned.

The cleared spaces are cultivated with an iron hoe. Crops include plants with edible tubers (such as cassava, sweet potatoes, yams); bananas and plantains; and some cereals (corn, sorghum, millet, rice).

In spite of the abundance of natural vegetation, the soil of the rain forest is poor; deforested soil is of low fertility and is rapidly leached by the heavy rains. There are additional obstacles to cultivation in the forest: insalubrity breeds endemic diseases (malaria, sleeping sickness, various intestinal diseases), which diminish the working capacity of the agriculturalists; cattle breeding is impossible in many regions because of the tsetse fly, which transmits animal sleeping sickness. The technology is able to produce barely enough to ensure the subsistence of those who live in the glades of the equatorial forest.

The clearing team. Forest agriculture calls for a certain kind of social organization. Nearly every year some new part of the forest must be cleared. This is a communal activity, requiring the cooperation of a team of men; cultivation may then be carried on by the women of each elementary family. The residential unit—the village—comprises several elementary families. The lower limit to the population of a village is set by the labor requirements of slash-and-burn agriculture.

Because of the poor soil, large areas of land, either actually under cultivation or lying fallow, are required to feed a small group of people. Ecological factors limit the size of the village of forest cultivators, just as they do that of the hunters' camp.

There are two other social consequences of the low fertility of the soil. When the soil is depleted it is economical in time and effort to move the village. Agricultural nomadism does not imply, as does pastoral nomadism, the moving of the community over great distances. The village moves to the nearest unexhausted land and may return to its earlier location after several moves. A second consequence is the relative isolation of villages: villages in the forest are rather distant from their nearest neighbors.

Economic and residential patterns are thus closely interconnected. Members of the clearing team, with their dependents, constitute the residential unit, the village. The unit of production, which is also the unit of consumption, is the elementary family. It is a subsistence economy, since there is no significant surplus. There is very little exchange, the family producing what it consumes, except for iron tools and, in some cases, wood carvings and pottery made by specialists.

Kinship organization.   Relations between individuals are almost exclusively based on descent and marriage rules. Most of the societal cultures of the forest are patrilineal, and marriage is generally virilocal.

The main subgroups of the forest global societies are exogamous, corporate lineages and the non-localized combination of lineages—the clans.

There is more than one clan in a global society. When all the members of a society consider themselves descendants of the same ancestor, the society becomes a tribe, as in the case of the Mongo of the Congo Basin forest, who number more than one million.

Kinship roles and groups supply the framework for almost all social interaction among the people of the glades. As among hunters, decision making and conformity to the social rules do not require either the sanction of potential physical coercion or a specialized office of authority. The sanctions of community pressure and ancestral influence are sufficient to maintain order. In any case, the low productivity of forest agriculture does not offer the material basis necessary for the emergence of a system of political relations.

The residential unit, the village, usually does not, however, correspond to a single lineage—although this occasionally occurs. Village concerns are discussed, and disputes arbitrated, by the elders of the different lineages. The patriarch of the lineage that first settled in the village will be *primus inter pares,* but he will not have a direct authority over members of lineages other than his own.

A kinship philosophy.   The paramount importance of the kinship principle is reflected on the level of collective representations. The lineage unites the dead as well as the living offspring of the ancestor. The individual is never alone: a link in a series of generations, he transmits the life and the force of his prestigious ancestor and of all his ascendants to his children and to all his descendants. The idea of group destiny provides the central meaning of life; the idea of personal destiny is not congruent with the experience of everyday social relations, in which the individual is nothing outside the kinship groups of which he is a member. In this perspective, death is not seen as an absurdity or a tragedy: the lineage has continuity and the individual will survive with it. Among the Kissi of the Atlantic coastal forest, the first grandson of a man is given the name of his grandfather because the grandfather's shade, one of the three elements of the living being, which has left the body at death, is reincarnated in the grandson (Paulme 1954).

Such an idea of reincarnation is not universal in the civilization of the glades, but the belief in the influence of the dead on their descendants is to be found everywhere. The ancestors are not always benevolent: their after-death existence is a diminished one and they resent not being properly honored. The cult is thus prominent in religious ritual. Kinship regulates not only relations among the living but also those between the living and the "spirits" of the dead.

Kinship also pervades art. The rain-forest region is an area rich in sculpture. The statues, often called fetishes—an unfortunate term, since they are not worshiped—represent ancestors or even, one is sometimes inclined to say, the kinship principle. They are not portraits; they express a certain conceptual image, not a visual impression, of the men and women from whom the group traces its origins. They are figurative, but abstract: the natural proportions of the body have been purposely modified in order to convey a certain idea of the ancestors. The head, the seat of life, is enlarged up to a third of the total height; the sexual attributes, which evoke the fecundity of the lineage, are stressed. In spite of the relatively small dimensions of the carvings (they rarely reach one meter), they give an impression of strength, of great dignity, and of an austere vitality. The art of the civilization of the glades, discovered at the beginning of the twentieth century by the amazed and admiring painters and sculptors of the Western world, was the mirror of the main values of the small societies of the forest cultivators.

The civilization of the granaries

South of the equatorial forest and of the lower Zambezi Valley, there is a savanna zone which extends down to the southern end of the continent, with the exception of the Kalahari and Namib deserts and of the eastern highlands. The farther from the equator, the more and more marked become the seasons, which impose their rhythm upon the life of nature and of men.

The threshold of surplus.   The soil is not very rich. As in the forest, land must be left fallow for long periods; the topsoil is very thin and cannot be plowed. Agricultural returns, however, are higher in the savanna than in the glades.

Savanna agriculture rises above the subsistence level and yields a surplus. Output of savanna agriculture, however, should not be compared with the returns of such fertile lands as those of classical Egypt or the modern American Middle West. It should be added that the notion of surplus is to be related to the culturally determined level of consumption in a society and not to a physically desirable nutritional level. A producing unit may be undernourished, yet not consume all it produces.

The sorghum, millet, peas, and beans may be preserved and may be easily measured and transported. Kept in granaries, the surpluses constitute a reserve of wealth. The surplus may be exchanged for other foods (meat from pastoralists, game from hunters) or for tools and services. It may also be transferred to a beneficiary without any return in goods.

The emergence of political power.   The man who accumulates in his granary the surplus produced by the members of his community may become their chief: he may devote all his activity to government, since he himself is not obliged to take part in the productive processes. Still more important, he may support agents who will see that his orders are executed, using physical coercion if necessary. Such a society may exhibit the political relation: the coercive relation between actors who, through it, become rulers and subjects.

It is not implied that the concentration of the surplus, in totality or in part, in the chief's granaries constitutes a unilateral appropriation. As is often pointed out, the functions of the political rulers—decision making for the whole community, maintenance of peace and order within the society, defense against external dangers—may constitute real returns in exchange for the surplus; but they do not constitute economic returns.

Chiefdoms.   Political systems of interaction are thus possible in the civilization of the granaries. Full advantage has been taken of that possibility, and a variety of political organizations has developed in the southern savanna. The smallest is the chiefdom, limited to a few neighboring villages or even to a single village; the chief, assisted by his followers, governs his subjects directly. Even when

the subjects are few, the chief's power appears to be clearly of a different order from that of the lineage elders of the forest villages. In her analysis of the Bemba chiefdom, Richards (1939) indicates that the Bemba chief's power rested on four bases: (1) wealth in labor provided by villagers, war captives, and condemned delinquents and in such goods as elephants' tusks and meats provided by his hunter-subjects; (2) a staff of followers, some to arrest criminals, execute sentences, and collect taxes; (3) the adjudication of disputes; (4) the power of the guardian spirits and magical force inherited from his predecessor, whose name had been assigned to him. Even in a small Bemba chiefdom, we find not only political power (recognizable by the criterion of coercion) but also the main characteristic of a state structure: specialization and permanence of the ruler.

There is, apparently, a tendency for each chief to extend the network of political relations of which he is the beneficiary, that is, to increase the number of subjects who pay him tribute. When such attempts are successful, and when other villages recognize the power of the chief by sending him laborers and the produce of their fields, an organization more complex than the chiefdom becomes necessary. The two commonest forms are the kingdom and the hierarchical union of chiefdoms.

A king delegates his ruling power to representatives who govern parts of the state territory on his behalf. These province or district governors collect taxes, maintain order, and adjudicate in the name of the king. Nominated by the king, they are directly responsible to him and do not have an inherent right to their positions; they may be moved and replaced by other appointees. The succession of kings—dynasties—usually entails some form of historical recording of names and events. In the Lunda kingdom, for instance, there were people entrusted with keeping the oral traditions concerning the past.

Through such traditional history, sometimes confirmed by archeological discoveries, we know that several kingdoms flourished in the region now making up northeastern Angola, the southern Congo (Leopoldville), and northern Zambia. These developments were probably contemporary with the European Middle Ages. The first kingdom was Luba in population, but the rulers were Songe, who still reside in the Kasai region; after freeing themselves, the Luba founded what some historians call the second Luba kingdom, which extended its influence to the present-day Katanga province. In the seventeenth century the Lunda, their neighbors, dominated a very large area from Kwango to

Lake Mweru and, at certain times, subjugated the Bemba chiefdoms, the Rotse kingdom of Zambia, and the Ovimbundu chiefdom of Angola. In the nineteenth century, a new power, the Chokwe, arose in the region.

At the western end of the savanna, near the Atlantic Ocean, the kingdom of Kongo was already declining when the Portuguese reached the mouth of the Zaire River in 1482. From Mbanza Kongo, the capital, the king ruled over the six provinces of his state. The first Portuguese, traders and missionaries, seem to have been well received. The kings became Catholics and allied themselves to the kings of Portugal. Young noblemen were sent to study in Lisbon, a Kongo ambassador was appointed to the pontifical court in Rome, and the first Congolese bishop was consecrated in 1521. During the last decade of the fifteenth century, blacksmiths, carpenters, masons, farmers, and even two German printers were sent to Kongo by Portugal. The traditional Kongo state had sufficiently strong political institutions to play the part of Portugal's partner even if that partnership was in some respects more fictional than real.

In the Katanga region, the Yeke kingdom is an interesting example of the way in which political domination may be rapidly established. Because these events occurred in the nineteenth century, the process of state formation is well documented. Msiri, the son of an ivory trader of the Sumbwa chiefdom near Tabora, in Tanzania, came with a caravan to the chiefdom of Katanga around 1850. He wanted to obtain copper, which was mined by the subjects. The trading party was very similar to a band of warriors: Msiri's comrades had guns, obtained from the Arabs, and this gave them a significant superiority over the Katanga population. By intervening in local struggles, Msiri eventually established himself as king of a certain territory. Other Sumbwa men joined him and married local girls. With their aid, he organized a kingdom by extending his domination over neighboring chiefdoms. He gave a new name—Garenganze—to his kingdom, created a ritual complex, set up a capital at Bunkeya, and continued his trading activities. With the Arab merchants of Lake Tanganyika he exchanged ivory, copper, salt, and slaves for guns, powder, cloth, and pearls. When he died in 1891, killed by a Belgian officer of the Congo Free State Army, he left a large and prosperous kingdom built in less than forty years by a small group of warriors who had come from a place some eight hundred miles away.

Another form of large political unit is the union of chiefdoms, in which each component part retains its own ruler. All the rulers recognize the paramountcy of one of their number and pay him tribute. This was the situation among the Bemba chiefs, who admitted the pre-eminence of the Citimukulu, and among the Kuba chiefs, who obeyed the Nyimi.

Although political relations are important guidelines to behavior in the societies of the savanna, kinship and affinity continue to regulate large fields of social interaction. What has been said of kinship roles and groups in the societies of the glades remains applicable here, with the difference that in the savanna the mechanisms for decision and sanction are primarily political, whereas in the forest they are based on the influence of the elders and on community pressure.

Marriage by bridewealth. Marriage is considered to be more a lineage matter than an individual one. The initiative for arranging a marriage belongs to the relatives of the future spouses; if either the man or the girl rejects the choice, he or she may, with ingenuity and energy, escape their decision. The interest of the lineage in the marriage is also evident in the institution of the bridewealth. The bridewealth consists of a certain quantity of goods, and sometimes of services, given by the future husband's relatives to those of the future wife. In the author's view, marriage by bridewealth is a development of marriage by exchange. There are disadvantages in exchange marriage: when one marriage is contracted, it is not always easy to find counterparts available for the second marriage. This difficulty is avoided if the group providing the wife receives privileged goods which later on can be used to obtain a wife from any other lineage. Thus, the circulation of women is no longer restricted to two lineages but may link, through matrimonial ties, many lineages within a global society. Bridewealth is thus not a price but a claim: through it the donor lineage is given the means with which it may ensure another marriage and thus the offspring.

Luxury and prestige art. The art of the civilization of the granaries clearly expresses, on the level of ideas and images, its characteristic values: political power and wealth. Statues of the Kuba kings are not portraits; although they are personalized they primarily symbolize an important event of the reign. Among the Kongo, the Songe, and the Luba scepters, walking sticks, axes, and adzes are carved in a very refined manner: these are insignia indicating that the persons who possess them command much more power than ordinary men. Drinking cups, powder boxes, neck rests, seats, pipes, and other secular luxury objects made by professional craftsmen attest to the existence of an affluent group—a ruling minority who, disposing of the excess production of the global society, could afford to have specialists working for their pleasure.

Except for the hunters and a few pure pastoralists, agriculture is an experience common to all Africans. This is why the world view rooted in that experience extends beyond the borders of the civilization of the granaries. The cultivator observes, anticipates, and hopes for the recurrent growth of crops. He does his part, but after that he must depend upon the processes of growth, an experience very similar to that of human procreation, which means so much for the continuity of the descent group. For what matters most to him—crops and children—the African peasant feels dependent on a kind of energy present in all living beings but not limited to any of them. This precious energy, which is active in all processes of natural development, is conceived as something that may be communicated to the living. Those whose strength proves that they are recipients of an abundance of that energy—such as the great ancestors with many descendants, the kings who command many subjects, the tall isolated trees with opulent foliage—are respected. Some men, through their secret knowledge, control the flow of some sources of energy; by magical means they may communicate it to those who need it most—those who are ill or sterile.

This world view is rarely, if ever, openly expressed; it is an implied or covert philosophy, which an observer may grasp only through an inductive method. Fagg and Plass (1964, pp. 148–158), for example, have shown convincingly that a visual symbol of the growth principle—the exponential curve—is found in the sculpture of the Kuba and many other groups.

The civilization of the spear

Cattle herding as a technique of production opens possibilities on the levels of institutions and ideas which are very different from those based on agriculture. Few African societies, however, have purely pastoral economies. The economy of the nineteenth-century civilization that we shall call the "civilization of the spear" possessed a pastoral component, but in reality agriculture played the major role in subsistence activities.

Cattle herding has flourished in the eastern part of the continent: in the marshland of the White Nile, on the highlands east of the Great Lakes, and in the hilly grasslands south of the Limpopo River in southern Africa. There, the minimal environmental requirements for cattle are realized: grass and water are to be found even during the dry season; it is possible to move from one grazing ground to another; the tsetse flies, which transmit animal sleeping sickness, are absent.

A herd of cattle is a remarkable instrument for the production of goods. It requires little investment of labor: a few experts in cattle breeding and a few herdsmen who know the grazing grounds are sufficient to ensure good returns in milk, meat, blood, and leather. If properly kept, a herd will increase, even if an important part of its products is consumed. A herd can directly supply a group with all that is necessary to its subsistence.

For all these reasons, cattle raising is a very efficient technique of production for the group that possesses it. Of course, pastoralism without stall feeding requires very large land areas, but when advanced agricultural techniques, such as irrigation and fertilization, are not available and when the soil is poor, a small group of pastoralists enjoys a distinct advantage as compared with a similar group of peasants.

Cattle, a form of natural capital. The link between a group of people and their fields in traditional Africa has often been called collective ownership. In contrast to the Western concept of private property, the use of land was distributed among various individuals and groups; the right to allocate a plot for cultivation and, if not used, to take it back, belonged to the lineage elders or to the chief; the right to cultivate and to collect the harvest belonged, as long as it was effectively exercised, to an elementary family. Rights of usage were sometimes further divided into the right to grow certain crops, to plant trees, to build a dwelling. Alienation was seldom included among these rights. A plot was in fact freely granted to anyone who needed it.

The value of noncultivated land lay in the labor which had to be applied to it to make it produce crops. A herd of cattle, on the other hand, was never a free good: it was valuable in itself, since it was inherently productive. For this reason, it has been likened to a capital good. It was indeed a "natural" form of capital in the sense that the returns it gave were not founded on a complex economic system but were inherent in its nature.

Patterns of residence. Cattle herding as an economic activity had consequences for the systems of interaction of pastoral societies. Pastoral production in Africa did not support dense populations. Herds had to be scattered over large areas during the dry season and even during the rains, since the threat of overgrazing prevented heavy concentrations of cattle.

Nomadism was thus a necessity. Sometimes the pattern of movement was transhumant—a seasonal shifting of herds through a fixed series of grazing grounds; sometimes it was a true migration—a slow displacement of the whole range over a long distance. The latter was the case with the Luo: starting from the Rumbek region, in the south of the present-day Republic of Sudan, the Luo pastoralists migrated slowly—first to the north, then to the east, and finally southward; eventually in the late fifteenth century they reached the interlacustrine region, where they set up the Nyoro kingdom. The migration probably took a couple of centuries, and several Luo groups settled down along the way.

Kinship was one basis of communal life: the units controlling cattle were lineages; women and bridewealth, paid in cattle, were exchanged among lineages. But there was another basis: the fighting unit.

The bands of warriors. It was not by chance that pastoral societies were also warlike societies. Cattle, the most desirable form of capital, had to be defended against raiding; if it were stolen, one had to be able to retrieve it; if the opportunity arose to raid another group for its cattle or a village for its granaries, one had to be ready to take advantage of it. Pastoralists were able to devote time and effort to their training as warriors. The unit of people moving together with their herds was organized around a group of warriors numerous enough to constitute an efficient fighting unit. Within the group of warriors and their dependents, authority was based on status deriving from kinship position, warlike achievements, and pastoral wealth. In spite of the possibilities offered by the surplus production of large herds, it seems that there was no system of political relations within the warriors' bands, probably because of the restricted size of the bands and their constant mobility. Among homogeneously pastoral Nilotic societies of the present day, such as the Nuer, Dinka, and Shilluk, there is no distinct political structure.

The interlacustrine mixed societies. In the mixed societies composed of herdsmen and peasants there existed an extremely developed political system. Societies in the eastern part of Africa were not exclusively pastoral. Villages of hoe cultivators were scattered through the highlands, and bands of warriors passing through the region occasionally raided them. When herders decided to settle, however, as happened in the Great Lakes area, raiding was no longer a good policy. In some cases, we know the history of what happened.

The herders slowly occupied the noncultivated grassland between the villages. They had two advantages over the peasants: their warrior's training, tradition, and spirit, and that impressive form of natural capital, their cattle.

Two or three hundred years later, at the end of the nineteenth century, we find global societies organized as kingdoms that included the descendants of both herdsmen and peasants. The former had been able to establish and maintain a privileged position. In two interlacustrine kingdoms, Ankole and Rwanda, this was achieved by the clever manipulation of three systems of social interaction: the political, the stratificatory, and the feudal.

The political system established asymmetric relations between rulers and subjects, but the ruling function was in fact monopolized by the pastoral group. The king, the chiefs residing at the royal court, the province chiefs, and all their executive agents belonged to the pastoral minority. The instrument of physical coercion, the army, was manned exclusively by the young descendants of the nomad warriors. (The term "ruler" is not restricted here to the king or even to the important chiefs who had the right to make decisions; it includes all those who, as officers of governing agencies, had a certain share in the surplus collected by imposition of tribute.) Not all members of the pastoral group were rulers, but all of them benefited from the fact that the government was exclusively in the hands of members of their group.

Social stratification. The descendants of the pastoral invaders and the descendants of the conquered tillers constituted two ranked strata, horizontally cutting across the entire global society. They were called, respectively, *tutsi* and *hutu* in Rwanda and Burundi; *huma* and *iru* in Nyoro, Toro, and Ankole. In some cases the strata constituted "castes," since their memberships were entirely hereditary; in other cases, in which it was possible for an individual born in an inferior stratum to be admitted to a superior one on certain conditions, "class" is a more fitting term. Whether castes or classes, however, the strata in each society had different and unequal statuses.

In Ankole and Rwanda, where the system was particularly rigid and where the strata were castes, it may be said that each of them had a particular subculture within the societal culture of the global society. Huma and Tutsi, like their conquering ancestors, were cattle owners and warriors; Iru and Hutu tilled the soil, and even if they took care of the cattle, they could not own them. Marriages across the caste line were exceptional; dietary habits, leisure activities, religious beliefs, were all different. Huma and Tutsi had a genetic origin different from that of the Iru and Hutu, and in the nineteenth century a certain proportion of them continued to display distinct physical characteristics: a tall, thin build contrasted with the stockiness and medium stature of the peasants. Around these physical characteristics the superior stratum built caste stereotypes, assigning to themselves noble physical and psychological qualities and to the peasants the characteristics of, at best, good manual laborers. Thus, the differences between the strata were stressed because they justified the privileged position of the Huma or Tutsi.

The privileges of a member of the superior stratum were not automatic; he was not necessarily either a ruler or a rich man. But it was only to members of the superior stratum that the opportunity to become a ruler was open; members of the inferior group were excluded from governmental office. Men of the upper stratum, irrespective of personal abilities, were in a position to exert various kinds of pressure on inferiors to oblige them to provide services and agricultural goods. The stratified global society thus operated to maintain, over many generations, the superiority of the pastoral invaders over the peasants of the Great Lakes region.

Feudal institutions. In some of the interlacustrine societies—Ankole, Rwanda, Burundi, and Ha—feudal institutions developed in the stratified political and social systems, intensifying the social *status quo* so profitable to the upper caste. The feudal relation, based on voluntary agreement, established between a lord and his dependent a set of reciprocal obligations which offered protection to the dependent in return for services and products supplied to the lord. The economics of this exchange were not reciprocal. Such institutions channeled goods upward for the benefit of the Huma or Tutsi, just as political institutions channeled taxes from the subjects for the benefit of the rulers.

In 1871 an impressive complex of ruined stone buildings was discovered near the town of Victoria, in Rhodesia. When the Portuguese came to that region in the sixteenth century, the descendants of those who had built part of the constructions were no longer in Zimbabwe but in the kingdom of Monomotapa, a powerful monarch. The similarities in the political and dynastic institutions of the Zimbabwe–Monomotapa culture and of Ankole and Rwanda are such that some historians think that they have a common origin. If this is so, the architectural remains of Zimbabwe would be the ultimate stage of development for societies of the spear, very different from their pastoral and warlike austere beginnings.

War as an institution. In most of the societies of the spear, war was not a factor of social dis-

equilibrium, a tragic crisis, but rather an institutionalized phenomenon, integrated into the political and economic organization. Among the Masai and the Kikuyu, raiding expeditions—which caused few casualties—were organized for the purpose of gaining cattle, which would then be shared according to well-defined rules. The Zulu under Shaka, at the beginning of the nineteenth century, were a notable exception to this pattern—their object was to dominate vast territories. The conquered peoples did not continue as distinct social and cultural units: the young men were recruited into the army and the rest of the population was scattered or killed.

Collective representations. The human qualities admired in the societies of the spear were those of individual self-assertion, courage, self-confidence, self-control. Myths concerning the origin of mankind or of a particular global society (often the two were not distinguished) explained and justified the privileges of the superior stratum. Their founding ancestor, because he was more clever than his brothers, was given by their common father, sometimes deified as a creator, power and authority over his brothers and their descendants, the people of lower strata. Stratification was thus based on a belief in inherent capacity and confirmed by the decision of the most respected beings: the spirits of the ancestors.

The plastic arts were little developed in this region of Africa. Aesthetic values were expressed in ornamentation, music, and, above all, the verbal arts. Elongated and austere patterns on weapons and basketry seem to convey very well in aesthetic form the aristocratic outlook of warriors. The music was also restrained: songs and stringed instruments were as important as—in some places, more important than—the rhythm of drums. Poems extolling the great warriors of the past and their opulent herds of cattle were memorized. In the interlacustrine kingdoms, the accomplished "superior" men were expected to be able to compose poems, to speak eloquently and elegantly, and to enjoy as connoisseurs the sweet love tales sung in the evenings by their wives and sisters, the ladies of leisure of the civilization of the spear.

The civilization of the cities

The traditional cities with which we are concerned here were situated over a vast area extending from the southern fringe of the Sahara to the Atlantic and equatorial forest (and even to the Bight of Benin) and from the Atlantic Ocean to the Nile. The environment is very similar to the one found in the southern savanna: grassland with low bushes and trees, except in the coastal area of Yorubaland, which is covered with a not too dense forest.

Scarce materials and skilled craftsmen. The environment of this cultural complex is varied but is everywhere suitable for cereal agriculture and herding. The abundant wild game was hunted. Gold in dust and nuggets was found in relatively large quantity not far from the Niger's northern bend. High-quality timber exists in the region. Ivory and feathers, pelts and leather, were also available.

The originality of the civilization of the cities was not based on hunting, cultivating, and herding but on other techniques permitting new uses of the potentialities of the environment. The specialized utilization of raw materials through new techniques resulted in a system of production that provided the foundation for an original civilization.

The term "technique" is used here, as it has been consistently in this article, to mean a relationship to natural resources. Except in the case of gold, the new uses of raw materials did not require new tools. What then stimulated the people of the northern savanna to develop these new patterns of production? First, there developed a new internal demand for the craftsmen's products; second, and more important, the establishment of external trade produced an external demand for these goods, either as raw materials (gold, timber, ivory, kola nuts) or as finished objects (jewelry, "Morocco" leather goods).

The demand for Sudanic goods (goods from the whole sub-Saharan savanna belt—called the "country of the Negroes" by the Arabs) came first from the Maghreb and then, via the Maghreb, from the whole Mediterranean world. To the commodities already mentioned as objects of this trade may be added slaves. Like the other items, they were luxury goods, expensive and prestigious, since they were used not as laborers in a plantation system but as domestic servants in the households of rich Muslims and European aristocrats.

International trade. Men and commodities from the Sudan reached the Mediterranean fringe of Africa through the Sahara via several caravan routes, the three main ones being the western (Fez and Marrakesh to Timbuktu and Gao), the central (Kairwan to Kano), and the eastern (Tripoli to Abéché and the Lake Chad region). Horses and camels, introduced from the north, made possible the trans-Saharan crossings.

The traffic in commodities between the Sudan and the Maghreb was not one-way. From the north, caravans brought salt and copper, beads and cowries, figs and dates, cloth and fabrics, weapons and horses. Commercial profits on these transactions were high. In the south this trade was not carried on exclusively by private merchants. Sudanic rulers very closely controlled the exploitation of natural resources and trade. According to an Arab report written by al-Bakri in 1067, all the gold nuggets from the Ghana mines belonged to the king, whereas the gold dust was left to the gold washers. Duties were also levied on exported and imported goods.

Despotic kings. Political power in the civilization of the granaries was founded on the agricultural surplus produced by the peasant-subjects. In the civilization of the cities, the agricultural surplus is present, but it is supplemented by taxes on the exploitation of raw materials and on trading activities. The dual origin of the rulers' income gave to the societies they governed a very distinctive societal and cultural structure. Disposing of a very considerable amount of wealth, kings and chiefs commanded important means of coercion: soldiers, weapons, horses. Consequently, the royal power was in theory absolute and in practice despotic.

The king was very remote from his peasant-subjects. He did not rely exclusively upon their agricultural tribute and labor, as did his counterparts in the civilization of the granaries. On the contrary, his most significant wealth was entirely alien to the peasants; it consisted of objects imported or made for the ruler by highly specialized craftsmen. The social distance between the governors and the governed accounts, at least in part, for the cruel punishments and the huge human sacrifices reported by eighteenth- and nineteenth-century travelers and explorers. It may also help explain the sale of African men and women to the slave-ship owners who supplied the New World plantations from the sixteenth to the nineteenth centuries. European slave traders did not capture Africans; they bought them from the rulers of the coastal societies, who were accustomed to consider strangers and subjects as people so different from themselves that they could be treated as mere commodities.

International trade was the specific component in the kings' income that gave them such overwhelming political power. The commercial centers that developed at caravan terminals were also political capitals: merchants needed the support of kings and chiefs to obtain raw materials and manufactured goods; rulers wanted to be where they could exert profitable control over the transactions. Around the ruler's residence and the merchants' stores, other activities developed: craftsmen set up their workshops; peasants from the neighboring villages came to sell the food required by the city dwellers; in some places, such as sixteenth-century Timbuktu, Koranic scholars gathered and were respected and well paid for their teachings.

The urban phenomenon was so characteristic of the societies of the northern savanna that their civilization deserves to be called the civilization of the cities. These cities were quite different from the capitals of the kingdoms of the granaries and of the spear. Their prosperity resulted mainly from their situation in a network of international trade relations and only very secondarily from their dominance over the surrounding territory. Like the medieval seaports of western Europe and the Renaissance cities of northern Italy, the Sudanic centers were city-states. As a result of the primary orientation of the ruling groups of each city toward one another, many peasant communities in the intervening rural areas were left undisturbed. Thus, the civilization of the area we are considering may be thought of as a dual structure, combining quite distinct peasant and urban elements.

In the peasant villages were lineage heads, whose authority was based on ancestors, and local chiefs, who lived very close to their subjects and collected from them the surplus of their agricultural production and exercised authority and sanctions against deviant behavior. Another institution for social control that flourished in the savanna was the masked association. The masks of the Sudanic savanna—of the Bambara, Mossi, Dogon, Senufo—are as familiar to Westerners interested in African art as are the ancestral statues of the civilization of the glades. But the masks were not meant to be seen motionless in the daylight; it was rather at night that they came to life, their wearers dancing to the accompaniment of music and song. The men who carried them were not merely masked men: they lent their bodies to the spirits symbolized by the carved wood. The masked associations acted as agents of social control when other sanctions were not operative, either because the ruler was not strong enough to deal with some habitual offender or because the deviation involved belonged to a field outside the ruler's authority.

The ideology of urban culture reflected its distinct economic political institutions. As trade oriented them toward the distant cities of the Maghreb, the reigning dynasties of the savanna belt kingdoms, such as Ghana, Mali, and Songhai, adopted Islam. For this reason these kingdoms are often said to have been set up by "Arab invaders." This assertion is not supported by historical evidence. On the contrary, it seems that Ghana existed as a kingdom before the establishment of contact with the north. Except for short periods the rulers of these kingdoms have for centuries been African Negroes. The coastal cities of Yorubaland, Dahomey, and Benin were flourishing when the first European ships landed at the end of the fifteenth century and the beginning of the sixteenth century. They were not Islamized; they traded primarily with other non-Muslim peoples. Thus, these were not Arab conquest-states, although Islam contributed substantially to the culture of those states which were in closest commercial contact with the Maghreb.

Professional craftsmen and artists. The artistic traditions of the urban layer of the civilization of the cities are rich. The bronze heads of Ife are universally known. Made in the twelfth or thirteenth century, these heads are realistic in the sense that the features are represented according to their anatomic proportions, yet they are idealized. As in classical Greek sculptures of the fifth century B.C., they exhibit more harmony, more serenity, and more intensity than is found in reality, indicating that these beautiful heads are not portraits. Numerous copper plaques in high relief were made in Benin from the fourteenth to the nineteenth century. In the cities of Abomey and Kumasi bronze figurines were used to weigh gold dust.

These artistic creations tell much about the societies in which they originate. Metal casting was done by the lost wax process, which requires great professional skill, to produce masterpieces such as the perfect Ife heads. The Benin copper plates portray warriors, kings, and royal symbols and were obviously made to decorate public buildings. It is known, on the other hand, that the founders were not allowed to work for anyone but the king. From the number of gold weights to be found today in museums and private collections, we may safely infer that transactions in gold dust were very common.

Thus, over a period of several centuries, an urban civilization based on the exploitation of scarce and precious raw materials, on professional craftsmanship, and on international trade developed in many global societies of traditional Africa, some of which were contemporary with very similar European centers of the late Middle Ages.

The civilization of steel

Industrial centers are not numerous in contemporary sub-Saharan Africa. The largest are situated in south Africa, in the copper belt of Zambia and Katanga, and in west Africa. All are dominated by mining rather than by industrial production proper, although industrial workers and their dependents constitute a tiny minority among present-day Africans. Yet industry as a technique of production is the basis of a new civilization which coexists with the traditional ones, which transforms them, and which is in the process of superseding them.

Industrial techniques. As a technique, industry is a method of production which, using nonhuman sources of energy and advanced mechanical equipment, obtains a much higher output than does handicraft production. This technological revolution, first introduced in Britain in the eighteenth century, has continued to unfold its societal and cultural consequences throughout the Western world and beyond.

The first impact of the new techniques on sub-Saharan Africa was indirect: the industrialization of western Europe created in the nineteenth century a colonial expansion into Africa. Because consumer goods had been the first products of industrialization, the increased output required a broader market than Europe could offer; it also required cheap raw materials. Later, when industrial techniques were applied to the production of such capital goods as heavy machinery, engines, and railroads, these expensive commodities also had to be exported. To organize Africa as a producer of cheap raw materials and as a consumer of industrial products ranging from Manchester cotton to heavy equipment, it appeared necessary at the end of the nineteenth century to effectively occupy the interior of Africa to establish political dominion. The result was the establishment of administrative networks covering the territories granted to England, France, Germany, Belgium, and Portugal by the Berlin treaty of 1885.

The more direct impact of industrialization followed: mining concerns, processing plants, roads, ports, and railways were built, and for these projects African labor, both unskilled and skilled, was needed. Schools were provided, urban centers developed. Once begun, the colonial process, like many other historical currents, spread in many directions not intended by its initiators or even recognized: the missionary movement, the establishment of European agricultural settlers, the growth of scientific research institutes were all by-products of the colonial endeavor.

The new societies. Like other societies in the world into which industrial techniques have been introduced, the African societies have been deeply affected. New technique of production, whether organized by a capitalist or a collectivist economic system, opens for a society a broader range of potentialities on the levels of social institutions and collective representations. It also rules out certain possibilities which are incompatible with the requirements of industrial production. Slowly a new societal culture emerges that is the ever-changing result of the conflict between the forces of tradition, which tend to maintain institutions and representations corresponding to a partly discarded system of production, and the forces of the new system, which tend to create institutions and representations coherent with the new material basis of the society.

If the modern civilization of Africa is called "industrial," in spite of the fact that relatively few Africans are directly engaged in the process of industrial production, it is not only because the industrial revolution has been the cause of colonial expansion and the result of colonial occupation but also because the new states of independent Africa are shaped by the necessities of the industrial era.

Urban habitat. On the level of societal organization, the civilization of steel—the metal characteristic of the industrial technique—is expressed by urban patterns of residence. Except for the traditional cities previously discussed, urban aggregations were born in Africa during the colonial period and grew up around administrative, commercial, and mining centers. Since those who live there are more influenced by modern patterns of behavior and thought, urbanization may be considered a principal characteristic of the new civilization.

The new towns permit one to locate on a map the civilization of steel. But it is not, like other civilizations, closely linked to particular natural environments. Except for extractive activities, obviously situated near the underground natural resources upon which they are based, neither industrial techniques nor their consequence, the urban habitat, require a specific kind of environment. The distribution of urban centers south of the Sahara indicates that the civilization of steel is widely spread. The density of towns is higher in some regions than in others, but the phenomenon is obviously general. According to the estimates of demographers, some 22 million Africans—about 10 per cent of the total population of sub-Saharan Africa—were living in urban centers in 1961.

Many of these towns are not large: often their population does not number more than twenty thousand. But even in such small centers the individual leads a life very different from that of the peasant, the herdsman, the traditional craftsman, or the hunter. Often his dwelling is provided by his employer: he does not build it himself with the help of his lineage. If he attempts to do so on the outskirts of the town, the result will often be not a traditional dwelling in which the traditional good life can be led but, rather, a slum shanty. The urban African seldom grows crops. He receives wages and from these must buy all that is necessary for his subsistence, although by maintaining connections with his kinsmen in the countryside he may sometimes supplement his wages with agricultural produce. His dwelling and income permit him, at best, to care for his elementary family, his wife and children. They do not allow him to fulfill his duties to share with his lineage-mates. Polygyny, which in traditional Africa was wealth producing, since each wife cultivated her own fields for herself, her children, and her husband, is not easily practiced in urban conditions, where it is often an economic liability for the husband.

Traditional villages constituted very homogeneous communities where many kinsmen lived, where often one spent all one's life, from birth to death, where everyone knew everyone else personally. Elders were respected and obeyed, and their authority was a powerful deterrent to any deviant behavior. An urban population is heterogeneous and mobile and requires strict control by coercive agencies. The legitimacy of a village chief rested in large part on heredity: he was chief because his father had been chief of that village. This principle cannot be applied in towns with their heterogeneous populations; local authorities are either appointed by the central government or elected. The functions of the local authorities, too, are different in the two settings. Chiefs could administer the village directly because "public affairs" did not include such specialized activities as primary education, medical services, garbage disposal, water supply, and the like.

The global societies of the industrial civilization are larger than traditional global societies. Except for the Rwanda republic and the kingdom of Burundi, there are no independent states whose boundaries coincide with those of traditional global societies. This is due partly to the legacy of colonial organization—independence has been gained by colonial territories, not by traditional societies—but also to the necessities of industrial civilization: to be viable in the modern world, a state must be of a certain size in territory, population, and national income.

Outside influences and internal dynamism. On the level of collective representations, the industrial system of production has also brought many changes. On the one hand, the profound experience of being a citizen of a modern state living in a monetary economy generates new perceptions of the world; the industrial era has opened sub-Saharan Africa to world cultural currents, which until the end of the nineteenth century had not penetrated into the interior of the continent.

We have already mentioned two conflicting forces shaping the new societal cultures of Africa: tradition and the dynamism of the new productive techniques that tend to create institutions and representations coherent with techniques. Both forces operate within the framework of a societal unit and, for that reason, may be said to be internal to the unit. The third force we refer to here comes from outside, but it converges with the inner dynamism to bring about continuous change. It consists of systems of thought, such as socialism and liberalism, which have been developed in the West to explain and assimilate the industrial revolution; of political theories concerning the proper organization of the commonweal; of religions with universalistic ambitions.

Painting, music, and literature. This complex interplay of conservatism, inner dynamism, and outside influences may be observed in the field of art. Painting is very popular in the largest towns: Dakar, Abidjan, Brazzaville, Leopoldville, Kampala, Nairobi, Elisabethville. In traditional Africa, painting hardly existed and easel painting not at all. Some of the most gifted painters have been trained by European artists who refrained from a formalistic teaching, even avoiding art history. They have almost reinvented painting in an African setting. Traditional wood carving still subsists in some places where ancestors' statues are needed for rituals, but with the decline of the old cults, which during the colonial period have been persecuted by European administrators and missionaries, the necessary skills tend to die out. Other carvers, established in towns, produce poor substitutes of traditional masks and statues to be sold as art objects or curios.

Music obviously much more influenced by Latin American rhythms and by jazz than by the traditional music of the region is very much alive in the barrooms of African towns. This influence is not restricted to Africa, of course. The popular music of all the industrialized countries of the world presents the same characteristics. In the case of Africa, one should stress that the universal popular music adopted now had one of its original sources in Africa's own traditional music: brought to the New World by the slaves, traditional African music is one of the sources of the Latin American dances and of jazz.

In the realm of literary creation, we also find the three social forces at work: the form itself has been introduced from outside, while the themes are sometimes suggested by traditional tales, sometimes by new problems faced by African intellectuals in the situation in which they live.

In this article, societal phenomena—global societies and, within them, systems of interaction—have been approached from a cultural perspective. This has been done, first, because to consider societal phenomena apart from their cultural matrices would have been artificial. As has been shown, their interrelatedness with all aspects of societal culture is such that to abstract them would have prevented us from grasping their full significance. Second, the cultural approach permits us to discern, among the multiplicity of global societies in traditional and modern Africa, a limited number of basic cultural complexes, a number of themes upon which particular societal cultures may be seen as variations. Where, as in Africa, cultural and societal boundaries do not neatly coincide, this approach seems a useful one.

JACQUES MAQUET

BIBLIOGRAPHY

SUB-SAHARAN CULTURES

BAUMANN, HERMANN; THURNWALD, RICHARD; and WESTERMANN, DIEDRICH 1940 *Völkerkunde von Afrika: Mit besonderer Berücksichtigung der kolonialen Aufgabe.* Essen (Germany): Essener Verlagsanstalt.

BOHANNAN, PAUL 1964 *Africa and Africans.* Garden City, N.Y.: Natural History Press.

ELISOFON, ELIOT; and FAGG, WILLIAM B. 1958 *The Sculpture of Africa.* New York: Praeger.

FAGE, JOHN D. 1958 *An Atlas of African History.* London: Arnold.

FAGG, WILLIAM B.; and PLASS, MARGARET (compilers) 1964 *African Sculpture: An Anthology.* New York: Dutton.

FORTES, MEYER; and EVANS-PRITCHARD, E. E. (editors) 1940 *African Political Systems.* Published for the International Institute of African Languages and Cultures. Oxford Univ. Press.

HERSKOVITS, MELVILLE J. 1930 The Culture Areas of Africa. *Africa* 3:59–77.

HERSKOVITS, MELVILLE J. 1962 *The Human Factor in Changing Africa.* New York: Knopf.

INTERNATIONAL AFRICAN INSTITUTE 1954 *African Worlds: Studies in the Cosmological Ideas and Social Values of African Peoples.* Edited by Daryll Forde. Oxford Univ. Press.

INTERNATIONAL AFRICAN SEMINAR, THIRD, *1960*, SALISBURY 1965 *African Systems of Thought.* Preface by M. Fortes and G. Dieterlen. Published for the International African Institute. Oxford Univ. Press.

MAQUET, JACQUES J. 1962 *Afrique: Les civilisations noires.* Paris: Horizons de France.

MURDOCK, GEORGE P. 1959 *Africa: Its Peoples and Their Culture History.* New York: McGraw-Hill.

OLIVER, ROLAND A.; and FAGE, JOHN D. (1962) 1963 *A Short History of Africa.* New York Univ. Press.

OTTENBERG, SIMON; and OTTENBERG, PHOEBE (editors) (1960) 1961 *Cultures and Societies of Africa.* New York: Random House.

RADCLIFFE-BROWN, A. R.; and FORDE, DARYLL (editors) 1950 *African Systems of Kinship and Marriage.* Published for the International African Institute. Oxford Univ. Press.

SELIGMAN, CHARLES G. (1930) 1957 *Races of Africa.* 3d ed. Oxford Univ. Press.

THE CIVILIZATION OF THE BOW

CLARK, JOHN D. 1959 *The Prehistory of Southern Africa.* Harmondsworth (England): Penguin.

COLE, SONIA M. (1954) 1964 *The Prehistory of East Africa.* London: Weidenfeld & Nicolson.

SCHAPERA, ISAAC 1930 *The Khoisan Peoples of South Africa: Bushmen and Hottentots.* London: Routledge.

SCHEBESTA, PAUL (1932) 1933 *Among Congo Pigmies.* London: Hutchinson. → First published as *Bambuti, die Zwerge vom Kongo.*

THOMAS, ELISABETH M. 1959 *The Harmless People.* New York: Knopf.

TURNBULL, COLIN M. 1961 *The Forest People.* London: Chatto & Windus.

THE CIVILIZATION OF THE GLADES

DOUGLAS, MARY 1963 *The Lele of the Kasai.* Oxford Univ. Press.

LITTLE, KENNETH L. 1951 *The Mende of Sierra Leone: A West African People in Transition.* London: Routledge.

PAULME, DENISE 1954 *Les gens du riz: Kissi de Haute-Guinée française.* Paris: Plon.

WINTER, EDWARD H. 1956 *Bwamba: A Structural–Functional Analysis of a Patrilineal Society.* Cambridge: Heffer.

THE CIVILIZATION OF THE GRANARIES

BALANDIER, GEORGES 1965 *La vie quotidienne au Royaume de Kongo du XVIe au XVIIIe siècle.* Paris: Hachette.

COLSON, ELIZABETH; and GLUCKMAN, MAX (editors) 1951 *Seven Tribes of British Central Africa.* Oxford Univ. Press.

RICHARDS, AUDREY I. 1939 *Land, Labour and Diet in Northern Rhodesia: An Economic Study of the Bemba Tribe.* Oxford Univ. Press.

THE CIVILIZATION OF THE SPEAR

EVANS-PRITCHARD, E. E. (1940) 1963 *The Nuer: A Description of the Modes of Livelihood and Political Institutions of a Nilotic People.* Oxford: Clarendon.

FALLERS, LLOYD A. 1956 *Bantu Bureaucracy: A Study of Integration and Conflict in the Political Institutions of an East African People.* Cambridge: Heffer.

HERSKOVITS, MELVILLE J. 1926 The Cattle Complex in East Africa. *American Anthropologist* New Series 28: 230–272, 361–388, 494–528, 633–664.

KENYATTA, JOMO 1938 *Facing Mount Kenya: The Tribal Life of the Gikuyu.* London: Secker & Warburg.

MAQUET, JACQUES J. 1961 *The Premise of Inequality in Ruanda: A Study of Political Relations in a Central African Kingdom.* Published for the International African Institute. Oxford Univ. Press.

THE CIVILIZATION OF THE CITIES

DIETERLEN, GERMAINE 1951 *Essai sur la religion bambara.* Paris: Presses Universitaires de France.

FORMAN, WERNER; FORMAN, BEDRICH; and DARK, P. 1960 *Benin Art.* London: Hamlyn.

GRIAULE, MARCEL 1938 *Masques dogon.* Paris: Institut d'Ethnologie.

GRIAULE, MARCEL; and DIETERLEN, GERMAINE 1965 *Le renard pâle*. Paris: Institut d'Ethnologie.

MAUNY, RAYMOND 1961 *Tableau géographique de l'ouest africain au moyen âge, d'après les sources écrités, la tradition et l'archeologie*. Dakar (Senegal): IFAN.

PAULME, DENISE 1940 *Organisation sociale des Dogon (Soudan Français)*. Paris: Domat-Montchrestien.

SMITH, MICHAEL G. 1960 *Government in Zazzau: 1800–1950*. Published for the International African Institute. Oxford Univ. Press.

THE CIVILIZATION OF STEEL

BALANDIER, GEORGES 1955 *Sociologie actuelle de l'Afrique noire: Dynamique des changements sociaux en Afrique centrale*. Paris: Presses Universitaires de France.

BALANDIER, GEORGES 1957 *Afrique ambiguë*. Paris: Plon.

BASCOM, WILLIAM R.; and HERSKOVITS, MELVILLE J. (editors) 1959 *Continuity and Change in African Cultures*. Univ. of Chicago Press.

FALLERS, LLOYD A. (editor) 1964 *The King's Men: Leadership and Status in Buganda on the Eve of Independence*. Oxford Univ. Press.

AFRO–AMERICAN SOCIETY

See CARIBBEAN SOCIETY.

AFTALION, ALBERT

Albert Aftalion (1874–1956) was a French economist born in Bulgaria. He was a professor at the University of Lille and then at the University of Paris. His entire life was devoted to his work, and he left his mark on the entire generation of French academic economists who began their careers between the two world wars.

Aftalion's theoretical work was in the tradition of the first Viennese school. Like Eugen von Böhm-Bawerk, he attached great importance to the duration of the process of production, which for him provided an explanation of cycles. From Friedrich von Wieser he derived his theory of imputation, which he used as an argument against socialism (Aftalion 1923); his theory of the marginal utility of money; and the income theory (1927–1950, vol. 1), which marked a stage in his monetary thinking. Aftalion was also a statistician (1928) and fond of numerical data, which he interpreted practically in their raw state. He calculated correlation coefficients, standard deviations, and average lags but was suspicious of overly audacious techniques. He refused to take sides in the *Methodenstreit* and believed in using both theory and statistics to interpret contemporary events.

Aftalion is best known for his theory of crises (1913), which is in effect a theory of cycles. His explanation of cycles is a "real" one. Cycles occur because the process of production takes time. Production of capital goods responds to changes in the demand for consumption goods only after a certain delay. Just as a fire that is alternately stirred up and damped down takes time to become hotter and cooler—and thus also alternately makes a room too hot or too chill—so, because of the rigidity of manufacturing plant, do phases of upswing and depression succeed one another in the life of the economy (1921). The response of the producer goods sector to changes in the demand for consumption goods is not only late but is also magnified. "A small expansion of the consumption goods industries requires a much larger expansion in the fixed capital producing industries" (1913, vol. 2, p. 372). If Aftalion did not coin the phrase "acceleration principle," he clearly developed the concept.

In his theoretical criticism of socialism Aftalion asserted that the equal distribution of wealth would weaken the incentive to work and that the suppression of private property would dry up savings and kill capital formation.

His interpretation of the French inflation of 1919–1924 is noteworthy both for the method he used and the conclusions he drew. *Monnaie, prix et change* (1927–1948, vol. 1) is a typical instance of his characteristic intellectual procedure. Although eager to know, measure, and understand the facts, Aftalion was anything but an empiricist, a historicist, or a pure statistician. At the outset he made sure that he had a solid and precise theoretical point of reference: the quantity theory of money, in its Ricardian form, which states that general price changes are never more than reflections of changes in currency circulation. Aftalion compared this doctrine with the actual monetary experiences of his country and his era. Drawing a curve for the general price index and for the quantity of money in circulation in France after World War I, he found that (1) the variations in price were not proportional to the variations in banknote circulation but much broader; (2) the two phenomena often varied in opposite directions over considerable periods of time; and (3) the price movements preceded, and by several months, the changes in the quantity of money. Therefore, circulation was not the determining variable. Rather, it was the rate of exchange (itself controlled by psychological factors) that carried internal prices along with it, and it was only later that the rise in internal prices brought about the inflation of fiduciary issues. Aftalion inverted the "traditional order of the procession."

Thus, the classic theory was found to be deficient. Aftalion did not say that it was false; he showed that it was not a good explanation of all the cases of currency depreciation or of all the phases of that depreciation and that it needed to be refined. The Austrian value theory shows the way to this necessary reworking. From the point of view of the economic actor, the value of the monetary unit reflects the marginal utility of the currency. Now, marginal utility does not depend directly on the total amount of money, that is, on the sum total of currency, but on the income at the disposal of individuals. Aftalion therefore first substituted a Wieserian income theory for the quantity theory of money. But he went beyond that. The marginal utility of money does not depend only on the amount of money income; it reflects a subjective evaluation of the monetary unit, into which there enter memories (the past history of a currency has endowed it with more or less prestige) and forecasts (relating to the monetary and budget policy of the government). Aftalion stressed psychological factors: confidence as well as mistrust in the future value of money. This is by no means an abandonment of theory on his part. He still attributed importance to quantitative phenomena, even if he did not believe that they explain everything. Also, he asserted that social psychology has laws, being based on scientific knowledge. The psychological explanation that Aftalion superimposed on the classical theory was intended to be no less theoretical than the classical theory itself.

Aftalion studied international gold movements between the two wars (1932*b*; 1938) and constructed a precise and novel theory of the "stimulants" that produced a new equilibrium in the balance of accounts (1937). Here Aftalion used a terminology of his own. He called the sum total of everything that gives rise to settlements between the nation and countries abroad the balance of payments (*balance des paiements*). (This includes movements of gold and capital.) As thus defined, the balance of payments is always in equilibrium but a formal equilibrium. On the other hand, the balance of accounts (*balance des comptes*) —which is the balance of payments minus movements of gold and capital—is usually in imbalance. But Aftalion questioned whether it is true that its imbalances tend to be self-correcting, as is affirmed by Ricardo's classical theorem, according to which any imbalance in accounts brings about transfers of gold, which produce changes in relative prices that restore equilibrium. Aftalion analyzed current facts and observed that (1) by virtue of international credits, monetary instability, etc., migrations of gold depend today on many factors other than the balance of accounts; (2) the practices of sterilizing gold and credit inflation have made price movements largely independent of changes in national gold stocks; and (3) the

ratios of prices (and interest rates) current in different nations are no longer anything more than a secondary factor in international accounts. Hence, the automatic Ricardian mechanism no longer operates. This does not mean that there is no longer any natural tendency toward spontaneous restoration of equilibrium. The movements of incomes play an ever more effective corrective role than do price movements. Any deficit in the balance of accounts brings about, in the country showing the deficit, an excess of total monetary income over the monetary value of the national production; this (all other things being equal and even without any rise in internal prices) favors importation of merchandise and exportation of capital. While this represents a "stimulant" to restoration of equilibrium, there are countervailing "obstacles" of a political and psychological nature (commercial and monetary protectionism, general and budgetary economic policies, future diplomatic and military perspectives, etc.). Which, then, will prevail: these forces producing disequilibrium or the natural stimulant to the restoration of equilibrium? The answer will depend entirely on the circumstances, and Aftalion erected a theory of the various constellations of circumstances that can arise.

Aftalion's thought was always subtle, his approach scientifically rigorous and meticulous. His work exemplifies the revisions imposed by the events of the interwar period on several traditional aspects of classical economic theory: J. B. Say's law of markets, the quantity theory of money, and the Ricardian theory that describes how gold shipments ensure an automatic equilibrium in international accounts.

DANIEL VILLEY

[*For the historical context of Aftalion's work, see* ECONOMIC THOUGHT, *article on* THE AUSTRIAN SCHOOL; *and the biographies of* BÖHM-BAWERK; RICARDO; *and* WIESER. *For discussion of the subsequent development of Aftalion's ideas, see* BUSINESS CYCLES; INTERNATIONAL MONETARY ECONOMICS, *article on* BALANCE OF PAYMENTS; MONEY, *article on* QUANTITY THEORY.]

WORKS BY AFTALION

1899 *L'oeuvre économique de Simonde de Sismondi.* Paris: Pedone.

1904 *La crise de l'industrie linière et la concurrence victorieuse de l'industrie cotonnière.* Paris: Larose.

1911 *Les trois notions de la productivité et les revenus. Revue d'économie politique* 25:145–184, 345–369.

1913 *Les crises périodiques de surproduction.* 2 vols. Paris: Rivière. → Volume 1: *Les variations périodiques des prix et des revenus: Les théories dominantes.* Volume 2: *Les mouvements périodiques de la production: Essai d'une théorie.*

1921 Le rythme de la vie économique. *Revue de metaphysique et de morale* 28:247–278.

1923 *Les fondements du socialisme: Étude critique.* Paris: Rivière.

1925 Existe-t-il un niveau normal du change? *Revue économique internationale* [1925], no. 4:423–450.

1927–1948 *La valeur da la monnaie dans l'économie contemporaine.* 2 vols. Paris: Sirey. → Volume 1: *Monnaie, prix et change,* 1927. Volume 2: *Monnaie et économie dirigée,* 1948. A 3d edition of Volume 1 was published in 1950.

(1928) 1931 *Cours de statistique.* Compiled and edited by Jean Lhomme and Jean Priou. 3d ed. Paris: Presses Universitaires de France.

1929 *Monnaie et industrie: Les grands problèmes de l'heure présente.* Paris: Sirey.

1932a Die Einkommenstheorie des Geldes und ihre Bestätigung durch die gegenwärtigen Phänomene. Volume 2, pages 376–390 in *Die Wirtschaftstheorie der Gegenwart.* Edited by Hans Mayer. Vienna: Springer.

1932b *L'or et sa distribution mondiale.* Paris: Dalloz.

1937 *L'équilibre dans les relations économiques internationales.* Paris: Domat-Montchrestien.

1938 *L'or et la monnaie, leur valeur: Les mouvements de l'or.* Paris: Domat-Montchrestien.

WORKS ABOUT AFTALION

BOUNIATIAN, MAURICE 1966 *Mes théories économiques et Albert Aftalion.* Paris: Librairie Général de Droit et de Jurisprudence.

DIETERLEN, PIERRE 1960 Albert Aftalion et la pensée économique. *L'année sociologique* 3d series [1959]: 127–181.

HORNBOSTEL, HENRY 1957 À la recherche d'Albert Aftalion: 1874–1956. *Revue d'économie politique* 67: 789–802.

LECAILLON, JACQUES; and HOSMALIN, GUY 1957 Liste des travaux d'Albert Aftalion. *Revue économique* [1957]:363–366.

LHOMME, JEAN 1957 L'influence intellectuelle d'Albert Aftalion. *Revue économique* [1957]:353–362.

L'oeuvre scientifique d'Albert Aftalion. Preface by Gaetan Pirou. Articles by F. Perroux et al. 1945 Paris: Domat-Montchrestien.

ROBERTSON, D. H. 1914 *Les crises périodiques de surproduction,* by Albert Aftalion (Book review). *Economic Journal* 24:84–89.

AFTEREFFECTS

See PERCEPTION, *article on* ILLUSIONS AND AFTEREFFECTS, *and the biography of* JAENSCH.

AGE DIFFERENTIATION

Any analysis of social structure is concerned with the integration of social groups and the recognized network of status positions that are part of, or cut across, those groups. Expectations in terms of interpersonal behavior patterns are formulated by the role differentiation appropriate to status distinctions. In all societies only two reference points for the ascription of status seem to be universal: sex and age.

The institutionalization of age makes it clear that cultural rather than biological factors are of prime importance in determining the content of status. All human societies recognize a number of life stages, to which rather diffuse patterns of activities, attitudes, prohibitions, and obligations are ascribed. Age-categories may be few in number— e.g., youngsters, mature adults, and elderly people —or they may be numerous. For example, the Kikuyu of central Kenya have six age-categories for males and eight for females, emphasizing the continuous development of the individual as a social person. An age-category, as Eisenstadt has written, is a generalized role disposition into which specific roles may be built (1956, p. 22).

Age-grades. Ascribed roles relating to age may be specific, defining and limiting the nature of interconnected roles. The total range of age-defined roles may constitute a *graded* system, which emphasizes the progressive movement from role to role, i.e., from grade to grade, and prescribes the relationships between people in different grades. There is usually a specific time for moving from a younger grade to an older one, often ritually established (or at least marked) by *rites de passage.* In this case there is a periodic achievement of increasing seniority.

Persons of junior status may give respect and some degree of obedience to those of more senior status; conversely, the seniors expect deference but may also acknowledge obligations to assist, teach, test, or lead their juniors. One of the best-known cases of age-grades is that of the Masai of east Africa: for males, the grades are uninitiated youths (*ilaiyok*); young men or warriors (*ilmurran*), who are divided between junior and senior subgrades; elders (*ilmoruak*), who are divided into junior, senior, and retired subgrades; and ancient elders (*ildasati*). There are thus seven effective age-grades. For each there are well-established norms that prescribe the general lines of behavior, expectations, and obligations, both in public life (community, political, and ritual affairs) and in private life (family, kinship, and interpersonal affairs).

This system establishes the areas of competence, privilege, and obligation of males in Masai society. These basic role allocations are supported and emphasized by secondary ascriptions of dress and deportment, access to food and drink, sexual opportunities, etc. For example, junior *ilmurran* are learning warriors, able-bodied men available for protecting the community and its herds and for acting as messengers among the dispersed population. They are responsible for fence building and for the laborious watering of stock in the dry season. They may not marry. They may not eat meat in public. They have characteristic dress, hair style, and weapons. Senior elders are the "elder statesmen" and experienced diplomatists of the community, whereas the junior elders implement decisions and policies. The senior elders are characterized as sober, reliable men and heads of established families.

Age-class. Of course, the difference between age-categories and age-grades is largely one of degree rather than of kind, but the distinction is worth making if only to indicate the special significance of age-grades. There is often a considerable emphasis on one particular age-grade. Significantly, this is frequently the one relating to adolescents and young adults: for example, the teen-agers of modern Western societies, the bachelors in a number of Melanesian societies, or the militant warrior grades of many societies that engage in raiding or warfare. Elsewhere, as in some Australian tribes, it is the grade of elderly men which is specially stressed and defined. The general explanation for this kind of emphasis is that the particular stage of life is one that either presents a special problem to the society or is of such importance that it calls for marked attention.

In these cases the collection of people currently occupying the grade form an age-class, which is a noncorporate grouping. Entry into the grade and, where relevant, transfer out of it, are accomplished individually. This may happen by the attainment of a certain biological state (puberty) or a socially recognized status change that typically occurs at certain age periods (marriage, birth of a child, etc.). People in the same grade, that is, playing the same role, have much in common: they share their differentiation from younger and older statuses; they engage in similar activities and often cooperate with each other; and they share the same orientation and aspirations. There may even be subgrades through which a person is promoted. Among the Oraon of eastern India there are three three-year periods in the adolescents' grade. Among the south Irish peasants the lengthy age-grade between adolescence and the status of independent farm-owner and family head is divided between "boys" and "married boys." On any social occasion (a party, a wake, before and after Sunday mass) men cluster according to their subgrades, which are separate from the cluster of family heads (Arensberg 1937). Thus, the adolescents, who are neither children nor adults, and the peasant men, who remain subservient to their aged fathers, are set apart and seek the companionship of each other in extrafamilial situations.

A quite different form of noncorporate age-class occurs in some cases in which men who were initiated together or during the same period are considered to have a special egalitarian and friendly relationship. Such men acknowledge a common status within the total range of classes, and they acquire increasing seniority contemporaneously. Yet these classes do not emerge as integrated groups: the class never assembles or acts as a unit, nor does it pass through a series of grades. Instead, like the Irish peasants, these men are able to order their relations with one another in terms of their equality (same class), seniority, or juniority. Among the nomadic Turkana of Kenya, where local groups are highly unstable, kinship narrow in range, and political institutions weakly developed, the age-class system is most important. "Wherever a man goes in the course of nomadic pastoral movement or in traveling, he finds men who are his age-mates, comrades, and supporters. He finds also his seniors and juniors to whom he can fairly easily adjust his attitudes and behavior. He can never become socially isolated" (Gulliver 1958, p. 917). A temporary cluster of nomadic neighbors has a ready-made pattern of relative statuses and behavior norms that give it form and a degree of cohesion. Among the Nuer of the Sudan, where local communities are stable and kinship is both wide in range and powerful in practice, the class statuses of equality, seniority, and juniority usefully reinforce these other relations.

The allocation of roles by age-category or age-grade and membership of an age-class are not entirely coterminous with physiological age. For example, although the normal expectation is that initiation occurs at a given age, it can be subject to various other factors: the individual's position in the range of siblings and economic considerations, such as the need for labor in the family (where an initiate eschews labor) and the wealth of the father (where a payment is required). Co-initiates may thus be of ages ranging over a number of years. A man leaves the bachelor grade on marriage, but the time of first marriage is obviously dependent on many factors other than age. The young Irish peasant whose father dies early leaves the company of "boys" and becomes a family head more or less equal in status to his father's coevals. The ascription of role and status by age is thus subservient to other factors arising in family and community life.

There is a further point about which there has been confusion in the past. It should be remembered that the age-grade always implies the differentiation, or ranking of role, according to ascribed status. This differs essentially from stratification by achievement. The grade systems within the male clubs of some Melanesian villages (e.g., Banks Islands and New Hebrides) have sometimes been wrongly classified together with true age systems. But, as Lowie pointed out long ago, these Melanesian grades are principally ends in themselves, scales of prestige in the village club, with little concrete content. True age-grades, age-classes, and age-groups are principally means to other social ends, and they commonly have a considerable elaboration of roles and relationships (Lowie 1916, pp. 962 ff.). The various grades of so-called elders among the Kikuyu of Kenya are comparable to the Melanesian grades, although more complex. It is detrimental to sociological understanding either to confuse these grades with the true age-group system of the Kikuyu (largely applicable only to young men) or to emphasize that all elders together constitute a single age-category. The latter is, of course, roughly correct, although entry into the category occurs only after a man's first child is born. Since promotion through the grades is a matter of individual achievement (e.g., initiation of first child), ability to pay fees and provide feasts, and personal qualities, not all men reach the higher grades. Outstanding men may become acknowledged as leaders and are rapidly promoted. This may also be true for those with seniority in their patrilineages, for it is desired to have influential men in the higher grades where they may participate in political life.

Age-groups. In the literature of social anthropology there has been some confusion in the terminology of age and social structure. The terms "set," "class," "section," and, misleadingly, "grade" have been used interchangeably and have thus lost discrete meanings. The age-group, as defined here, deliberately emphasizes the corporate nature of this social group that is based on the criterion of co-evality. As a corporate group, it is a permanent collection of people who recognize a degree of unity, a unity that is acknowledged by nonmembers. Together, the members engage in particular activities, accept mutual obligations, and function as a group in relations with outsiders. Age-groups are usually named, may possess property (songs, shield designs, rituals, etc.), and are internally organized for decision making and leadership. Age-groups in historically known preindustrial cultures are largely confined to sub-Saharan Africa, certain Plains Indians of the United States, and some tribes of Brazil and India.

Transitory age-group system. Empirically, there are two kinds of age-group systems: those which initially concern younger men (and perhaps women) but become less important and disintegrate as the members grow older, and those which are comprehensive and affect people through the whole of their lives. The first type—the transitory age-group—is created specifically for the purpose of organizing the activities and potentialities of the younger men. It operates as an educational institution, providing a specialized means of bridging the gap between childhood and adulthood, and teaching young people the obligations and rights, manners, ritual behavior, sex knowledge, etc., of their society. In describing such groups among the Nupe of Nigeria, Nadel (1942) described this as "education for citizenship." There, each age-group passes through three age-grades, until the members have reached the age of 30 (when most have married); then the group's importance declines sharply, although older coevals retain a degree of comradeship.

The educational function of the transitory age-group may be less important than the organization of manpower. This was a feature of the centralized states of the Zulu, Swazi, Sotho, and Tswana in southern Africa. Among the Swazi, every five to seven years the paramount chief recruited a new age-group from the youths "about to mature and those who had recently matured" (Kuper 1952, p. 23). Each group had its own name, insignia, songs, barracks, and officials. Each operated, according to requirements, as a military regiment or as a labor battalion for chiefs and aristocrats. Age-groups had public responsibilities in national rituals and as "police." Each group was, to a considerable extent, responsible for the good behavior of its members, and age-mates acknowledged reciprocal assistance and loyalty.

In noncentralized societies, such as Nandi, Kipsigis, or Kikuyu of east Africa, the age-group system is similarly applicable principally to the young men. Among the Nandi a new group is recruited approximately every 15 years, and each one occupies the "warrior" grade for the same period of time and then abdicates to its chronological successors. The group in the warrior grade is a highly integrated, active unit, but afterward it degenerates to no more than an age-class. Among the Kikuyu a new age-group was founded almost every year when the uninitiated youths were circumcised.

Each group remained in the warrior grade for about 12 years, acting as a military regiment for its community; but after warriorhood a group lost virtually all significance.

Comprehensive age-group system. By contrast, in a comprehensive age system males form a new group when they are adolescents and remain in it for life, acting as a unit and engaging in intergroup relationships under their leaders. In many, but not all, cases an age-group passes successively through a series of age-grades so that the common roles of its members change from period to period; but transfer is specifically by group and not individually. The classic example is that of the Masai, whose age-grades have been described above. A new Masai age-group begins as junior learning warriors and is successively transferred to the grades of senior warriors, executive elders, senior elders and advisers, and retired old men. Transfer from one grade to the next is ideally accomplished through ritual. In fact, members of a group tend to shift gradually into an older grade before ritual prescription occurs, and indeed the imbalance between a real and ideal pattern is one of the forces impelling the ritual and maintaining the dynamics of the system. Nevertheless, age-groups, however well or poorly they follow the ideal, remain strong corporate groups. Alternate groups are linked through a father–son ideology, so that "fathers" are responsible for the transfer of their "sons" through the young men's grades. These two groups associate in politico-jural opposition to the complementary groups—i.e., groups 1 and 3 against groups 2 and 4. Although the two younger groups have pronounced military duties, the principal significance of Masai age-groups is in political affairs and in the wider field of social control. With somewhat unstable local communities, very shallow kin-groups, and no specialized political institutions, public life among the Masai is administered through the age-group system.

Other examples of age-groups passing through a series of age-grades can be found in a number of west African societies. Among the Ibo of eastern Nigeria young men's groups are allocated such tasks as clearing paths and market places, cutting forests, and guarding the settlement; older groups act as "police," and elders' groups act as arbitrators, conciliators, and repositories of law and custom. Each group provides mutual aid for and exercises collective discipline over its members.

A quite different system applied in a few Plains Indian tribes—Blackfoot, Mandan, Gros Ventre, Arapaho, and Hidatsa. A new group was made up of coeval youths who individually purchased the right of entry from a sponsor in the next older group. Groups aimed to gain possession over sets of rights and paraphernalia that were strictly graded and consisted chiefly of songs and dances. Achievement of a further grade was by collective purchase of the rights from their existing owners, and not by virtue of age; and a group that had sold its rights might exist outside the system until it later purchased rights in a new grade. Unfortunately, despite a considerable literature, the sociological aspects of these systems are far from clear; the nature of intragroup and intergroup relations, and their connection with social control and other activities, is vague (e.g., Lowie 1916). Useful comparison with the graded African systems is not, therefore, possible.

Not all African age-groups occupy specific grades. Among the Jie of Uganda, for example, initiation and group membership primarily give ritual efficacy to a man, and groups are principally significant in ritual contexts. In the frequent performances of public rituals a group's activities are given a general orientation in the range of assessed seniority between all extant groups: the juniormost groups act as servants and messengers and get the smallest shares of sacrificial meat; middle groups form the basic congregation and learn ritual procedures; the senior-most groups are conveners, ritual experts, and prayer leaders, and they get the best shares of meat. The actual allocation of tasks depends on the numbers of men in attendance on a particular occasion. Men invariably sit in their groups at rituals, and each group has its own senior men and leaders (Gulliver 1953).

Age-villages. The ungraded age-group system of the Nyakyusa of southern Tanganyika is probably unique. There, boys form their own distinct hamlets, separate from those of their fathers and older and younger brothers. Eventually, these become fully independent villages of adult coevals with their wives and children. Each has its own selected headman, and these villages form the basis of new chiefdoms in the territorial expansion of the tribe. In each generation, ideally, an old chiefdom divides into two; the old chief is replaced by his eldest sons, and the fathers' villages by those of their sons. Because of intervillage movement, the coeval basis of mature villages tends to diminish, although it persists strongly as the ideal for egalitarian cooperation among villagers. Wilson considers that this system is directly related to potential conflict between father and sons and the need to segregate the generations to avoid the fear of sexual shame and incest (Wilson 1949; 1951). The regularization of intergenerational conflict is also apparent in aspects of the Kikuyu and Jie systems, although, in contrast, father–son cooperation is integral to the Masai system.

Kinship and age-groups. Empirically, there is a marked difference between the societies in which comprehensive age-group systems occur and those in which age-group systems apply only to younger age-categories. Where social roles are defined in a centralized political system and/or a well-developed kinship system (especially one involving corporate kin-groups), age-groups have little or no importance among older men. As men mature, marry, and become family heads, right-holders in property, and responsible citizens, their obligations are to their families and kin-groups and to their political superiors. In these institutions men find their rights safeguarded and assistance rendered. Age-grouping cuts across and thus conflicts with both political and kinship ties. Furthermore, an essential feature of age-groups is the fraternal equality of co-members (age-mates) and the collective ascription of social roles by universalistic criteria. This conflicts with the possibilities of specialization and the achievement of privilege by individual effort or good fortune (e.g., birth) in a stratified structure. Among younger men this conflict matters less, for such people tend to be less differentiated. Since they usually have not yet begun to acquire obligations and rights of a kinship or political nature, it is highly convenient to use their physical power for military and labor services. Conversely, where a comprehensive age-group system operates, there are significant roles and social functions that are not determined by kinship and state. There may be no specialist political institutions and only a limited kinship system, as among the Masai and Plains Indians. Alternatively, the field of activities involving age-groups is strictly separate from the field involving kinship. Among the Jie, age-groups are devoted to the administration of rituals, a field in which kinship is not invoked; the Arusha of Tanganyika maintain a Masai-like age-group system in their autonomous local communities, and the field of kinship applies largely to nonlocal and extracommunity affairs. In brief, the establishment of social roles by kinship and by a specialist political system takes precedence over their establishment by age; kinship especially is dominant where conflict might arise through antipathetic roles.

Women's groups. Before marriage, girls' age-groups sometimes occur, but the rights and obligations individually acquired in marriage and motherhood effectively curtail relationships by age. Affairs purely for women are often organized by married women's groups, but the criterion of age is infre-quently utilized and the groups are weakly developed.

Political significance. It is sometimes assumed that age-group systems as such establish a distinct type of political system. Only for the Masai peoples is this true. Among others, to be sure, most age-groups systems have political aspects (such as among the Swazi, Nandi, and Ibo), but the political systems of these societies are very dissimilar. Jie age-groups serve ritual requirements and have only marginal and indirect political significance, and Plains Indians' groups seem not to have been politically important.

The literature. Despite considerable literature on age institutions, sociological analysis has been inadequate. Problems of historical reconstruction have loomed larger than functional interpretations. One of the critical problems has been the confusion of concepts resulting from the concern with ideal structure rather than careful observation of the personnel involved in age institutions, their respective roles, and the dynamics of these institutions in relation to the social structure.

The best general survey of the field is by Eisenstadt (1956). In addition, we need to have reliable information on modern change in age-grades and age-groups. Older systems have sometimes continued in changed form but with marked continuity of principle and function or simply persist in diluted importance and new systems seem to emerge. The reasons for this are not clear. Too often, age-oriented grades and classes in modern Westernized society have been considered as a social-psychological problem, or as an offshoot of political development; more sociological analysis of them is needed.

P. H. GULLIVER

[*Directly related are the entries* LIFE CYCLE; RITUAL; SOCIAL STRUCTURE. *Other relevant material may be found in* POLITICAL ANTHROPOLOGY.]

BIBLIOGRAPHY

ARENSBERG, CONRAD M. (1937) 1950 *The Irish Countryman.* Gloucester, Mass.: Smith.

DYSON-HUDSON, NEVILLE 1963 The Karimojong Age System. *Ethnology* 2:353–401.

EISENSTADT, SHMUEL N. 1954 African Age Groups. *Africa* 24:100–113.

EISENSTADT, SHMUEL N. 1956 *From Generation to Generation: Age Groups and Social Structure.* Glencoe, Ill.; Free Press; London: Routledge.

EVANS-PRITCHARD, E. E. (1940) 1963 *The Nuer: A Description of the Modes of Livelihood and Political Institutions of a Nilotic People.* Oxford: Clarendon Press.

FOSBROOKE, H. A. 1948 An Administrative Survey of the Masai Social System. *Tanganyika Notes and Records* 26:1–50.

GULLIVER, P. H. 1953 The Age-set Organization of the Jie Tribe. *Journal of the Royal Anthropological Institute of Great Britain and Ireland* 83:147–168.

GULLIVER, P. H. 1958 The Turkana Age Organization. *American Anthropologist* New Series 60:900–922.

GULLIVER, P. H. 1963 *Social Control in an African Society; A Study of the Arusha: Agricultural Masai of Northern Tanganyika.* Boston University African Research Studies, No. 3. Boston Univ. Press; London: Routledge.

HUNTINGFORD, GEORGE W. B. 1953 *The Nandi of Kenya: Tribal Control in a Pastoral Society.* London: Routledge.

JONES, G. I. 1962 Ibo Age Organization, With Special Reference to the Cross River and North-eastern Ibo. *Journal of the Royal Anthropological Institute of Great Britain and Ireland* 92:191–211.

KUPER, HILDA 1952 *The Swazi.* Ethnographic Survey of Africa, Southern Africa, Part 1. London: International African Institute. → A paperback edition was published by Holt in 1963 as *The Swazi: A South African Kingdom.*

LAMBERT, H. E. 1956 *Kikuyu Social and Political Institutions.* Published for the International African Institute. Oxford Univ. Press.

LINTON, RALPH 1936 *The Study of Man: An Introduction.* New York: Appleton.

LOWIE, ROBERT H. 1916 Plains Indian Age-societies: Historical and Comparative Summary. Volume 11, part 13 in American Museum of Natural History, *Anthropological Papers.* New York: The Museum.

MIDDLETON, JOHN; and KERSHAW, GREET 1965 *The Kikuyu and Kamba of Kenya.* Ethnographic Survey of Africa, East Central Africa, Part V. London: International African Institute.

NADEL, SIEGFRIED F. 1942 *A Black Byzantium: The Kingdom of Nupe in Nigeria.* Published for the International Institute of African Languages and Cultures. Oxford Univ. Press.

SPENCER, PAUL 1965 *The Samburu: A Study of Gerontocracy in a Nomadic Tribe.* London: Routledge.

WILSON, MONICA H. 1949 Nyakyusa Age-villages. *Journal of the Royal Anthropological Institute of Great Britain and Ireland* 79:21–25.

WILSON, MONICA H. 1951 *Good Company: A Study of Nyakyusa Age-villages.* Published for the International African Institute. Oxford Univ. Press.

AGGREGATION

Economic systems are composed of large numbers of individual economic units interacting to determine market prices and quantities of innumerable goods and services bought and sold by each unit. The inherent complexity of such systems has two important consequences for the methodology of economics, as compared with such experimental sciences as physics, chemistry, and even biology. First, one cannot hope to isolate individual economic units from their context, study them experimentally, and establish what could be called elementary laws of economic behavior. Second, even if one could rely on elementary laws of behavior deduced from logical arguments or adopted as plausible working assumptions, it may be extremely difficult, because of the innumerable complex interactions among the individual units, to determine what these laws imply concerning the behavior of the entire system.

Nevertheless, it is absolutely necessary to overcome these obstacles that stand in the way of determining economic relationships to be used within models intended to explain past economic developments or to forecast future developments. The subject matter of aggregation in economics is the study of the extent to which the difficulties presented by such large numbers of economic units and commodities can be surmounted by considering aggregates of subsets of decision-making units (firms, households, etc.) or of commodities or prices.

Scope of the aggregation problem. The aggregation problem arises in nearly all economic decisions and analyses. Every economic agent—the smallest *homo economicus*, the manager of a large firm, or the economic theorist—is confronted by numerous economic forces, although he may not be aware of them all. In making his economic decisions or in deducing the consequences of these forces, he must take account of them in the best possible way. Considered from this point of view, the aggregation problem would be confounded with that of economic science and would be devoid of specificity. Actually, a closer examination of the aggregation problem, initiated by Hurwicz (1952) and pursued by Malinvaud (1956a), narrows the role of aggregation in economic analysis.

The first object of economic theories is to reach general conclusions establishing either existence theorems for some classes of economies or the adequacy of particular economic means and structures for achieving particular economic goals. For example, economic theorists may initially be concerned with the existence and stability of a general equilibrium in an economy characterized by decentralized decision making; if a general equilibrium can be shown to exist for such an economy, they may then determine whether the equilibrium position is Pareto optimal in that no change can benefit anyone without injuring someone else. But too often these results are so general that they provide only loose guides for economic policy; even if they are formally correct, they do not provide answers to many fundamental questions encountered in formulating responsible economic policy. For instance, equivalence conditions between a

Paretian optimum and a value equilibrium do not afford any knowledge concerning the sociological aspects of the attainable states. On the other hand, an approximate idea of the values and determinants of global economic variables such as aggregate production or aggregate consumption can be much more useful in determining the need for, and appropriateness of, some economic policy.

The degree of complexity and precision needed in analyzing any economic question depends upon the nature of the actions to be undertaken on the basis of the analysis. Thus, it is advisable to make the best possible allocation of resources available for the analysis among (1) the gathering of data necessary to understand the situation, (2) the degree of precision needed in analyzing the situation, (3) the type and detail of decisions to be made, and (4) the choice and extent of the means by which these decisions are to be carried out. Keeping in mind these four general principles that are fundamental to the theory of decision making, it can be said that the specific concern of aggregation in economics is the study of the best way of making this allocation and of the choice of criteria to be considered.

Directions of research. Research on aggregation would be greatly facilitated if information on the development of an economy could be gained from a small number of variables that are functions of the actions taken by the numerous decision-making units. These variables should not be mere mental constructs but should lend themselves to actual numerical determination; hence, the functions describing them should be of a simple analytical form and readily determinable statistically. Beyond these general requirements, different writers have made various demands on the variables. May (1946) suggests that it should be possible to deduce *all* relevant economic variables from knowledge of this small number of variables, whereas Malinvaud (1956a) suggests that it need only be possible to determine a few simple, economically significant relationships among the small number of variables. In the following discussion of the approaches of May and Malinvaud, the terminology of aggregation theory will be defined and a historical sketch of developments of the subject matter and methodology of the theory will be given.

May considered a theoretical economic system S such that all its variables can be expressed as functions of p parameters only. The p parameters may vary freely or may be subject to constraints not expressed in S. This system is called the "microeconomic" system, and the same adjective will qualify the variables and functions in S. Although these microeconomic elements are conceptually defined, they may often be neither measurable nor explicit. The analytical form of S may present many difficulties in solving the system or in studying its qualitative properties. On the other hand, there might exist functions of several microeconomic variables in S, functions to be called "macroeconomic," that define macroeconomic variables or aggregates. For instance, suppose that after appropriate indexing, S is composed of I times K microeconomic relationships, f_{ik}, involving all conceivable microeconomic variables. Then it may be possible to find I functions, $F_i(f_{i1}, f_{i2}, \cdots, f_{iK})$, the F_i being the aggregates. The aggregates cannot be of an arbitrary nature but must have a simple and important economic meaning. A number $j > p$ of these aggregates being considered, there are, generally speaking, $j - p$ independent relationships that constitute a system, s, called the macroeconomic system. By combining microeconomic variables in S to obtain the j aggregates, one obtains s. Once the form and main features of s have been theoretically recognized, it is extremely desirable in practice that it be possible to determine s by statistical methods without relying directly on information contained in S. The great interest in the existence of a macroeconomic system, s, is now easily understood, for the existence of such a system enormously simplifies the study of economic systems and consequently the process of decision making at every level.

Before May, Klein (1946a) had presented the aggregation problem in a similar way except that he restricted himself to some part, say D, of S. Although his exposition did not portray the full generality of the aggregation problem, he nevertheless treated the problem as it is most often met in practice, where difficulties are encountered only for some economic variables or relationships. Aggregations in S restricted to D have a great advantage in that they can be used in some other system, say S', differing from S but involving the same part D. For instance, S and S' might present the same description of production, the part D, although they differ in their treatments of consumption, income distribution, etc. An aggregation procedure pertaining to D only could then be used in both S and S'. A general feature of research in aggregation is the twofold preoccupation of solving the aggregation problem in a specified economic framework and of finding partial solutions that may be utilized in many different frameworks.

Malinvaud noted that, as regards their consequences on actual economic actions and realizations, varied decisions might have the same practical implications or implications that can at least be considered equivalent. For example, aggregate fruit consumption may be largely unaltered by some variations in the composition of the fruit bundle; hence, a particular explanation of aggregate fruit consumption may be approximately valid for various decisions that determine the composition of fruit purchases. Consequently, every aggregation of a system S resulting not in exactly the same implications but in equivalent ones must be accepted. This approach usefully enlarges that of May, for it does not vitiate the conclusions derived from an exact system. Malinvaud calls this type of aggregation "intrinsic aggregation"; it includes the types of aggregations considered by Klein and May.

As will be seen below, intrinsic aggregations do not exist in general. Therefore, a solution is sought (1) by imposing restrictions on the range of variation of the microeconomic variables, the restrictions being based on certain economic considerations; or (2) by allowing the aggregates to be tolerably approximate, the permissible range of errors being determined by the uses to be made of the aggregates. The last approach is also the result of Malinvaud's study, and he calls it "representative aggregation."

The foregoing discussion suggests that the principal results obtained in the study of aggregation might be grouped under two headings, intrinsic aggregation and representative aggregation; and this dichotomy will be followed below. Systematic studies, consciously noting the difficulties due to aggregation in over-all economic problems, are rare when methodological studies are excepted. They are to be found especially in the literature dealing with the determination and empirical testing of economic laws. Because of their basic importance, they are grouped here in a special section (see section 3 below), although they could technically be placed under the heading of "representative aggregation."

1. Intrinsic aggregation

Intrinsic aggregation has been studied in the context of production relationships and in the context of consumption relationships.

Aggregation of production functions. Klein (1946a) examined the circumstances necessary for the existence of an aggregate production function that could be employed in the type of macroeconomic analysis developed by John Maynard Keynes in *The General Theory*. In doing so, he presented, probably for the first time, a precise

statement of an aggregation problem. The following problem was posed: Let there be n microeconomic production functions that may be written in their implicit forms as

$$R_i(\boldsymbol{a}_i, \boldsymbol{b}_i, \boldsymbol{c}_i) = 0 \qquad i = 1, 2, \cdots, n,$$

where $\boldsymbol{a}_i$ is the vector of outputs, $\boldsymbol{b}_i$ the vector of labor inputs, and $\boldsymbol{c}_i$ the vector of capital inputs for the ith firm. Can three functions,

$$A = A(\boldsymbol{a}_1, \cdots, \boldsymbol{a}_n)$$
$$B = B(\boldsymbol{b}_1, \cdots, \boldsymbol{b}_n)$$
$$C = C(\boldsymbol{c}_1, \cdots, \boldsymbol{c}_n),$$

be found such that a nonvanishing relation $R(A, B, C) = 0$ holds for all values of $\boldsymbol{a}_1, \cdots, \boldsymbol{a}_n$, $\boldsymbol{b}_1, \cdots, \boldsymbol{b}_n, \boldsymbol{c}_1, \cdots, \boldsymbol{c}_n$ satisfying the microeconomic production functions? Aggregate output, labor input, and capital input are denoted, by A, B, and C, respectively, and $R(A, B, C) = 0$ is the aggregate production function.

Nataf (1948) established that such aggregates could exist only under the condition that each R_i can be written as a sum of function A_i of the $\boldsymbol{a}_i$'s, B_i of the $\boldsymbol{b}_i$'s, and C_i of the $\boldsymbol{c}_i$'s, that is: only if $R_i = 0$ is equivalent to $A_i(\boldsymbol{a}_i) + B_i(\boldsymbol{b}_i) + C_i(\boldsymbol{c}_i) = 0$. Then the aggregates A, B, and C are, up to a transformation, equal to $\sum A_i$, $\sum B_i$, and $\sum C_i$ respectively, and $R = 0$ is equivalent to $A + B + C = 0$. These conditions are obviously unrealistic.

Aggregation in Leontief systems. Problems similar to that of Klein have been solved for aggregation of goods in a linear system of industrial relationships of the Leontief type. Ara (1959), Hatanaka (1952), McManus (1956), and Malinvaud (1956b) studied the conditions that must be met in order that the linear production relationships assumed by Leontief continue to hold for some aggregates of microeconomic goods. Aggregation within such systems is necessary in order to apply Leontief's theory to actual forecasting or planning. The conditions are always extremely strict for aggregation to be possible in the purely algebraic range of validity of these tableaux [*see* INPUT–OUTPUT ANALYSIS].

Disaggregation problems. In considering the utilization of interindustrial tableaux, Fei (1956) raised an interesting problem perfectly within the realm of intrinsic aggregation, although the problem presents itself in exactly the reverse form. In practice, examining whether any appreciable information can be gained by disaggregating aggregated variables or relationships may be of more immediate interest than examining whether information is lost in constructing aggregates. Of course, any gain in information realized by disaggregation must be weighed against the costs involved in doing so. Fei assumed there is a known aggregated Leontief matrix A, while the ideal unknown matrix is B. For computing production levels corresponding to a given final demand, we need the inverse of $(I - B)$. In fact, we can only use that of $(I - A)$. In order to judge the usefulness of determining B, of which only some structural properties are known in excess of its aggregation in A, Fei builds matrix operators that disaggregate A to A^*. The inverse of the transformation that disaggregates A to A^* will not only aggregate A^* to A but will also yield $(I - A)^{-1}$ when applied to $(I - A^*)^{-1}$. With knowledge of a particular A^* and structural information on B, and using the numerous mathematical studies on approximations and errors in matrix inversion, one can often express bounds on errors resulting from the substitution of A^* for B. Hence, since A^* and $(I - A^*)^{-1}$ give the same aggregated results as A and $(I - A)^{-1}$, one can determine whether the magnitude of the established errors warrants actual determination of B. Similar problems have been studied by Fisher (1958; 1962).

Aggregation in consumption problems. Gorman (1953) considered the problem of aggregating the indifference functions of all individuals in a population into a single function expressing the population's mean consumption in terms of the population's mean disposable income. He showed that this is possible only when Engel curves for each individual are straight lines and have the same direction for all individuals for a given set of prices, although the direction of the curves may be a variable function of prices (see also Nataf 1953, p. 20).

Nataf (1958), considering cases where all individuals have the same income or, more generally, where individuals have different incomes that depend on the same unique parameter, found the least number of representative consumers whose behavior is in accord with the theory of choice and whose mean consumption is that of the population. Curiously, this number is equal to the number of goods minus one, that is to say, considerably smaller than the number of individuals in the population. This result suggests that there is some hope of finding a few explanatory relations of consumption.

Very similar results appear as by-products in studies by Stone (1954), Fourgeaud and Nataf (1959), and others. Their results are more precise because more restricted families of demand functions are considered. In determining individu-als' demand curves, these authors find that the curves obtained imply that the total amount of every good consumed by the population may be expressed as a function of simple aggregates of individual incomes and of coefficients or parameters contained in the individual functions. These properties might facilitate explicit determination of the aggregate coefficients from global statistical data and permit testing of the goodness of fit of the type of individual functions involved.

Aggregation of sets of goods. Hicks (1939) and Leontief (1936) have studied a group of goods whose prices always change by the same proportion. Leontief showed that the total expenditure of an individual consumer on such a group of goods can be determined from an indirect utility function that depends only on his total income, prices of other goods, and the proportionality coefficient of variation of prices of goods in the group. However, it is not possible to determine the individual's consumption of each of the goods in the group.

Gorman (1959), following an initial study by Strotz (1957), defined aggregates $A, B, C, \cdots$ of goods and examined the conditions that must be satisfied by an individual's utility function in order that determination of the individual's consumption bundle be possible, either rigorously or approximately, in two stages. In the first stage, expenditures on each of the aggregates are determined given total money income and price indexes for each of the aggregates. In the second stage, expenditures on each good in aggregate A are determined given total expenditures on A and the prices of every good in A; and similarly for $B, C, \cdots$. Employing realistic approximations, Gorman concluded that the utility function required can be expressed as a summation of (1) arbitrary functions of each of the aggregates $A, B, C, \cdots, J$ and (2) a unique arbitrary function of the aggregates $K, L, \cdots$, each aggregate $K, L, \cdots$ being a homogeneous function of degree one of its component goods. This result is valid for the case where the distribution of expenditures on the aggregates applies locally for small deviations of prices and income from a known origin. Since this is the case generally met in practice, these approximations, as Gorman noted, are more interesting than the rigorous solution holding for any changes in prices and income.

2. Representative aggregation

Representative aggregation encompasses studies of the errors introduced into an economic theory or a practical decision when an aggregated model is substituted for a detailed model.

Macroeconomic validity of a microtheory. Morishima and Seton (1961) attempted to determine the extent to which aggregation phenomena might partly or wholly invalidate Marx's microeconomic results on the comparison of price and value systems. They not only found the types of aggregation that left Marx's results invariant to the level of aggregation (a matter relevant rather to intrinsic aggregation) but also searched for aggregation procedures that resulted in deviations of the same order of magnitude between aggregates as between microeconomic elements, allowing for random deviations within the microeconomic system. Their study could equally well be discussed in section 3, since it is an elaborated investigation of methods of verifying economic laws deduced from a given theory.

Aggregation of intertemporal relationships. Simon and Ando (1961) studied an intertemporal model with the following properties: (1) the current values of the variables in the model depend on their past values and are obtained through a linear stationary transient transformation of the past values, and (2) the variables for any period can be subdivided into groups in such a way that the values of the variables in a particular group depend only on the values of the variables in that group in the preceding period. Consequently, the transformation that gives the current values of all the variables in the model from their values in the preceding period is a matrix consisting of block submatrices on the principal diagonal, all other elements of the matrix being very small. Each submatrix corresponds to a particular group of variables. Due to the stationarity property of the transformation, the authors were able to define representative aggregates—one for each of the block submatrices—and to deduce the behavior of the aggregates from a simpler system than the original one.

Errors due to aggregation. Fisher, proceeding in the line of thought of Fei, considered not only the problem of aggregating sets of microeconomic variables but also the problem of going back from aggregates to a microeconomic set in such a way that the deviations from the true values of the microeconomic variables would be as small as possible from a certain point of view. He studied these problems for the classical cases of interindustrial exchanges (1958) and also for cases where stochastic features of the problems might be of relevance in selecting the aggregate model (1962).

Balderston and Whitin (1954) studied numerically the errors resulting from different aggregations associated with different treatments of imports in a Leontief system. They found the errors to be quite important, thus stressing the need to take careful account of aggregation phenomena.

3. Aggregation and the determination of economic laws

Economic laws generally emerge from an abstract microeconomic analysis, and their validity can seldom be tested by basic experiments and measurements. Rather, theories are tested by examining the extent to which their global implications are verified. Depending upon the type of problems studied and the aggregations made, various questions of aggregation theory will arise, belonging, technically speaking, to representative aggregation. Theil (1954) initiated the study of these questions. He assumed that microeconomic relationships are stochastic linear functions of microeconomic variables and that linear combinations of microeconomic variables are used as aggregates. He then examined whether there exist stochastic relationships among the aggregates of the same general form as the microeconomic relationships. The aggregates were shown to be tied by relationships involving functions of other unaggregated microeconomic variables of the system. This result points out the difficulties encountered in testing the validity of elementary laws (the microeconomic relationships) through aggregated relationships.

In other works, Theil (1957; 1959; 1960) and Mundlak (1961) have studied other examples where aggregation may generate errors or losses of information impeding the determination or testing of economic theories. For example, Theil (1959), using the two-stage least-squares estimation method, attempted to evaluate the loss of information in an estimate of a relationship directly based upon already aggregated variables, rather than the loss resulting from aggregation of the corresponding microeconomic relationships.

In a linear regression model for monthly data, Mundlak (1961) investigated the error in the regression coefficient when monthly data were grouped in yearly aggregates. Mandelbrot (1960; 1961) was able to demonstrate how some assumptions regarding stochastic variations of individual incomes over time result asymptotically in a general Pareto distribution of income.

Conclusions

Choice of a convenient aggregation is an absolutely fundamental problem in practical applications and even in the material interpretation of economic theories. It is generally impossible to build aggregated rigorous models of an economy valid through time and space, a fact that must be kept in mind (1) in interpreting real economic laws and (2) in conceiving the methodology of applied economic research. As for the first point, it seems that the results of aggregation have not yet been fully turned to account, and they might shed much light on such important problems as imperfect competition due to lack of complete information on the part of buyers and sellers, resulting in poor aggregate knowledge of their reciprocal reactions. This subject is probably a very fruitful one that has yet to be explored.

On the other hand, constructive ideas concerning the second point have appeared. Hurwicz' and Malinvaud's concepts provide a framework for rationally estimating the useful degree of precision in the elaboration and application of economic models. But before these ideas can be translated into practical methods, knowledge of representative aggregation must be enlarged for economic variables such as production, consumption, and investment. Some progress has been made in this matter; but much work, essentially in two directions, remains to be done. First, more studies of representative aggregation problems must be undertaken, a task related to obtaining much better knowledge of actual microeconomic laws regarding these phenomena. Second, these sectoral studies of production, consumption, etc., must be synthesized and incorporated in economic models to be tested as explanations of past economic developments or to be applied in economic planning at the sectoral, national, or even international level. Before progress can be made in these important areas, the results of theoretical analysis must be related to knowledge of the practical problems to be dealt with and solved. Theoreticians and practical economists should be aware of these problems and closely cooperate in resolving them.

ANDRÉ NATAF

BIBLIOGRAPHY

ARA, KENJIRO 1959 The Aggregation Problem in Input–Output Analysis. *Econometrica* 27:257–262.

BALDERSTON, J. B.; and WHITIN, T. M. 1954 Aggregation in the Input–Output Model. Pages 79–128 in Oskar Morgenstern (editor), *Economic Activity Analysis*. New York: Wiley.

FEI, JOHN C. H. 1956 A Fundamental Theorem for the Aggregation Problem of Input–Output Analysis. *Econometrica* 24:400–412.

FISHER, FRANKLIN M. 1965 Embodied Technical Change and the Existence of an Aggregate Capital Stock. *Review of Economic Studies* 32:263–288.

FISHER, WALTER D. 1958 Criteria for Aggregation in Input–Output Analysis. *Review of Economics and Statistics* 40:250–260.

FISHER, WALTER D. 1962 Optimal Aggregation in Multiequation Prediction Models. *Econometrica* 30:744–769.

FOURGEAUD, C.; and NATAF, ANDRÉ 1959 Consommation en prix et revenu réels et théorie des choix. *Econometrica* 27:329–354.

GORMAN, WILLIAM M. 1953 Community Preference Fields. *Econometrica* 21:63–80.

GORMAN, WILLIAM M. 1959 Separable Utility and Aggregation. *Econometrica* 27:469–481.

HATANAKA, MICHIO 1952 Note on Consolidation Within a Leontief System. *Econometrica* 20:301–303.

HICKS, JOHN R. (1939) 1946 *Value and Capital: An Inquiry Into Some Fundamental Principles of Economic Theory.* 2d ed. Oxford: Clarendon.

HURWICZ, LEONID 1952 Aggregation in Macroeconomic Models. *Econometrica* 20:489–490. → An abstract.

KLEIN, LAWRENCE R. 1946a Macroeconomics and the Theory of Rational Behavior. *Econometrica* 14:93–108.

KLEIN, LAWRENCE R. 1946b Remarks on the Theory of Aggregation. *Econometrica* 14:303–312.

LEONTIEF, WASSILY W. 1936 Composite Commodities and the Problem of Index Numbers. *Econometrica* 4:39–59.

MCMANUS, MAURICE 1956 On Hatanaka's "Note on Consolidation." *Econometrica* 24:482–487.

MALINVAUD, EDMOND 1956a L'agrégation dans les modèles économiques. France, Centre National de la Recherche Scientifique, Séminaire d'Économétrie, *Cahiers* 4:69–143.

MALINVAUD, EDMOND 1956b Aggregation Problems in Input–Output Models. Pages 187–202 in Pisa, Università di, Facoltà di Economia e Commercio, *The Structural Interdependence of the Economy: Proceedings.* Edited by T. Barna. New York: Wiley.

MANDELBROT, BENOÎT 1960 The Pareto–Lévy Law and the Distribution of Income. *International Economic Review* 1:79–106.

MANDELBROT, BENOÎT 1961 Stable Paretian Random Functions and the Multiplicative Variation of Income. *Econometrica* 29:517–543.

MAY, KENNETH O. 1946 The Aggregation Problem for a One-industry Model. *Econometrica* 14:285–298.

MAY, KENNETH O. 1947 Technological Change and Aggregation. *Econometrica* 15:51–63.

MORISHIMA, MICHIO; and SETON, FRANCIS 1961 Aggregation in Leontief Matrices and the Labour Theory of Value. *Econometrica* 29:203–220.

MUNDLAK, YAIR 1961 Aggregation Over Time in Distributed Lag Models. *International Economic Review* 2:154–163.

NATAF, ANDRÉ 1948 Sur la possibilité de construction de certains macromodèles. *Econometrica* 16:232–244.

NATAF, ANDRÉ 1953 Sur des questions d'agrégation en économétrie. Paris, Université de, Institut de Statistique, *Publications* 2, no. 4:1–61.

NATAF, ANDRÉ 1958 Forme réduite d'agrégats de consommation dans le cadre de la théorie des choix. Paris, Université de, Institut de Statistique, *Publications* 7:3–13.

PU, SHOU SHAN 1946 A Note on Macroeconomics. *Econometrica* 14:299–302.

SIMON, HERBERT; and ANDO, ALBERT 1961 Aggregation of Variables in Dynamic Systems. *Econometrica* 29:111–138.

STONE, RICHARD 1954 Linear Expenditure Systems and Demand Analysis: An Application to the Pattern of British Demand. *Economic Journal* 64:511–527.

STROTZ, ROBERT H. 1957 The Empirical Implications of a Utility Tree. *Econometrica* 25:269–280.

THEIL, HENRI 1954 *Linear Aggregation of Economic Relations.* Contributions to Economic Analysis, 7. Amsterdam: North-Holland Pub.

THEIL, HENRI 1957 Linear Aggregation in Input–Output Analysis. *Econometrica* 25:111–122.

THEIL, HENRI 1959 The Aggregation Implications of Identifiable Structural Macrorelations. *Econometrica* 27:14–29.

THEIL, HENRI 1960 Best Linear Index Number of Prices and Quantities. *Econometrica* 28:464–480.

AGGRESSION

I. PSYCHOLOGICAL ASPECTS   *Leonard Berkowitz*

II. INTERNATIONAL ASPECTS   *Frederick L. Schuman*

I
PSYCHOLOGICAL ASPECTS

The study of aggression—here regarded as any behavior whose goal is the injury of some person or thing (cf. Dollard et al. 1939)—has long been governed by philosophical preconceptions and clouded by hopes and fears. Writers have accounted for aggressive behavior in strikingly different ways: as the manifestation of an innate destructive drive, as an inborn reaction to frustrations, or as a learned way of responding to particular situations. Many of these interpretations have clearly been influenced more by metatheoretical beliefs regarding the nature of man or religiophilosophical hopes as to what human beings should be like than by carefully controlled and precise observations. Freud, as an example, at first had maintained that aggression was a "primordial reaction" to the blocking of pleasure-seeking or pain-avoiding strivings. However, partly because of his pessimism growing out of World War I, he revised his formulation and postulated the existence of an instinctive force of destruction and death (1920). Other psychologists have advanced entirely different conceptions. Some were predisposed to deny or minimize the role of innate factors in human behavior, while for others the notion of inherent aggressiveness was incompatible with their view of man as being basically good. Whatever the exact nature of their analysis, all too often their general theoretical or philosophical assumptions resulted in a relatively extreme stand in which some factors were given very heavy emphasis and others were played down or denied altogether.

Instinct conceptions

The Freudian "death instinct." In Freud's post-1920 discussion of aggressive behavior, the dominant tendency in all organic life was held to be the effort to reduce nervous excitation to the lowest possible level (1920). Just as all pleasure-seeking was supposedly oriented toward tension reduction, all organic life presumably sought death, for to die was to be free from stimulation. (Freud also proposed that death was often sought violently rather than quietly and peacefully.) But this initial striving for active self-annihilation did not find fulfillment, Freud maintained, because the death instinct, Thanatos, was opposed by the life instinct, Eros, which diverted the destructive drive from the self to others. Thus, in attacking other people the person found a release for pressures that otherwise would impel him to seek his own death.

Empirical evidence provides little support for Freud's analysis of aggressive behavior (cf. Berkowitz 1962). To cite just one difficulty, research clearly indicates that organisms do not seek the complete elimination of excitation. There are many situations in which human beings, as well as lower animals, work for an increase in stimulation (White 1959). Death is not necessarily the inherent aim of all organic life.

Other instinct doctrines. A number of biologists as well as orthodox psychoanalysts have accounted for aggression solely in terms of some inner force. The ethologist Konrad Lorenz (1952) has suggested, for example, that excitation is built up in each instinctive center within the central nervous system and is then dissipated when the instinctive act is performed. If an animal did not engage in aggressive behavior, "action-specific energy" would supposedly accumulate within the instinctive center controlling aggression. When enough energy is built up the action pattern presumably would go off by itself, that is, there would be "vacuum activity." In contrast to this notion of spontaneous aggression, others (for example, Scott 1958) have maintained that there is no evidence of a spontaneous stimulation for fighting arising within the body. Actual fighting, which usually involves males belonging to the same species, is relatively rare in nature; in most cases the opponents display threat ceremonies instead of coming to blows.

Exteroceptive cues. In contrast to the model based on notions of energy accumulation, many students prefer to analyze instincts as species-specific behavior patterns governed by exteroceptive stimuli, which activate and terminate the actions. External stimuli are thus considered to be important contributors to aggressive behavior. Fighting behavior in many species varies with the nature of the antagonist—whether the animal's opponent is from its own or some other species, and if the latter, whether it is a predator or some prey (Eibl-Eibesfeldt 1963). More than determining merely the form of the response, external cues often appear to be necessary for eliciting any kind of hostile actions. Tinbergen (1951) observed that the male stickleback fish attacked a dummy with a red spot on its belly but ignored a detailed replica of the stickleback that did not have this characteristic of the breeding male or that had the red spot on its back.

Fighting arising from competition for dominance, food, sexual partners, or territory clearly attests to the role of external stimulation in animal aggression. The aggressive activity in these cases is the product of some perceived obstacle to the attainment of a desirable goal state. Even apparently noncompetitive fighting may be explained in these terms; the combat may have been instigated in order to achieve such things as dominance or undisturbed possession of living space (cf. Berkowitz 1962, p. 17).

Internal conditions. The efficacy of external stimuli in evoking aggressive behavior, however, is probably contingent upon the presence of some suitable internal condition. In the case of the stickleback fish the necessary internal prerequisite seems to be the production of the hormones involved in reproduction. Given the required internal state, a particular stimulus evokes the aggressive response. As yet another illustration of this principle, von Holst and von Saint Paul (1962) have shown that electrical stimulation of a certain region of the fowl brain results in recognizable aggressive actions only in the presence of relevant cues, "an enemy real or artificial." Applying this formulation to competitive fighting, we can say that the rivalry produces an emotional state creating a readiness to engage in aggressive activity and that the competitor then provides the cue that releases (or evokes) the aggression.

The frustration–aggression hypothesis

The principle just advanced is a version of the "frustration–aggression hypothesis," which has long been used to account for aggressive behavior. Independently espoused by such writers as Freud (prior to World War I) and McDougall (1908), the hypothesis was spelled out most clearly by Dollard, Doob, Miller, Mowrer, and Sears in a now-classic monograph published in 1939. Briefly, these psychologists maintained that a frustration—"an interference with the occurrence of an instigated goal–response at its proper time in the behavior sequence"—arouses an instigation to aggression (Dollard et al. 1939, p. 7). Since this formulation has been criticized frequently, some additional points should be made clarifying and defending it. First, Dollard and his colleagues did not claim that frustration had no consequences other than

aggression. A thwarting will produce instigations to many different kinds of responses. Some of these other response tendencies may be stronger than the instigation to aggression, and the aggression is not revealed openly (Miller 1941). Moreover, although the hypothesis did say that all aggressive actions presuppose the existence of frustration, a person does not have to be frustrated in order to engage in aggressive actions (Bandura & Walters 1963). A contemporary revision of the frustration–aggression hypothesis must be less sweeping and all-explanatory than the original version.

This is not to say, however, that the hypothesis must be discarded altogether, as a number of writers have insisted (e.g., Buss 1961). While we cannot deal here with all of the criticisms (cf. Berkowitz 1962 for a more complete discussion), several of the arguments against the hypothesis can be answered.

Do only some frustrations produce aggression? To begin, several psychologists have contended that only certain kinds of frustrations give rise to aggressive responses. Threats or attacks upon the self produce aggressive tendencies, they say, but mere deprivations supposedly lead to other consequences. In a similar vein, other critics have suggested that arbitrary or unexpected thwartings lead to aggression, while less arbitrary or expected frustrations presumably do not.

Two comments can be offered in rebuttal. Dollard et al. (1939) proposed that the strength of the instigation to aggression resulting from a frustration is in direct proportion to the strength of the thwarted drive. Since the desire for self-enhancement is typically fairly strong in our society, we would expect attacks upon the self to lead to stronger aggressive reactions than, say, interference with the performance of some unimportant task. Attacks upon the self then may lead to overt aggression, while the hostile responses produced by the interruption of a task that is not relevant to the self may be too weak to be apparent. But the frustration need not even be a *direct* attack on the self in order to produce aggression. Buss (1963) has demonstrated that college students who were prevented by a peer from attaining a desirable goal (such as a money prize) tended to display more intense open aggression toward the peer than did a nonfrustrated control group. The thwarting was not an arbitrary one, and the allowable aggression was not instrumental to the attainment of other ends, but there was a definite aggressive reaction, if only a weak one.

The second comment deals with the matter of deprivations and arbitrary frustrations. According to the definition employed by Dollard and his colleagues, a frustration is the blocking of some *ongoing*, goal-directed activity. A person thoroughly engrossed in his work is not frustrated just because he has been without food for a number of hours. He may be deprived of food, but there are no ongoing eating response sequences, either in his thoughts or his overt activity, that are prevented from reaching completion. His failure to eat at his regular mealtime will therefore not produce an aggressive reaction. But what if this person had been prepared to eat at a certain time and had been thinking of the food he was soon going to enjoy? Suppose his employer unexpectedly gives him a sudden job that keeps him working late at night and causes him to miss his meal. We would now expect him to become angry. Whereas some psychologists would say he has now experienced an arbitrary or unexpected frustration, in contrast to an expected frustration, the present writer maintains that only now is he frustrated, whereas formerly, before he had anticipated eating, he was not. Only now is an ongoing response sequence prevented from reaching completion at its anticipated time (cf. Berkowitz 1962, pp. 36–42).

The innate nature of the aggressive reaction. American psychologists are characteristically reluctant to refer to instinctive or innate mechanisms in accounting for human behavior. Some of the objections to the frustration–aggression hypothesis seem to be dictated by this prejudice against the notion of innate reaction patterns.

Animals and humans can be trained to respond nonaggressively to situations that ordinarily produce hostile responses. For that matter, they can also learn to act aggressively in situations where formerly they had displayed little violence. In an experiment with school children, for example, Davitz (1952) rewarded one group of youngsters for acting aggressively and competitively, while another group was rewarded for cooperative and constructive behavior. After several training sessions all of the children were frustrated when a movie they were seeing stopped and, at the same time, their candy was taken away. Observations showed that the aggressively trained group exhibited more aggression in a free-play period immediately afterwards and that the constructively trained youngsters reacted more constructively to the thwarting. Scott (1958), after reviewing several of his animal experiments that had obtained essentially similar results, concluded that aggression was the product of previous learning. Taking much the same position, others (Bandura & Walters 1963) have argued that frustration produces a heightened motivational state that enhances the strength of whatever responses the individual has learned to make in the given situation; these may or may not be aggressive in nature.

Yet the experiments just mentioned do not really invalidate the frustration–aggression hypothesis. They demonstrate that previous experience can enhance or reduce the likelihood of aggressive behavior, *but they do not prove that aggression will not occur under suitable conditions in the absence of any aggression training.* Indeed, several experiments indicate that animals reared in isolation, and who had not previously learned to be aggressive, can react aggressively to arousing stimuli (Eibl-Eibesfeldt 1963, p. 11). In another demonstration that prior learning is not necessary for aggressive reactions, Seay and Harlow at the University of Wisconsin Primate Laboratory thwarted some infant monkeys by separating them from their mothers (1963). Six of the eight young animals subsequently displayed some aggression against a peer–playmate—but primarily when the previously frustrated infants were in their mothers' presence. Two aspects of this finding are noteworthy. First, and most important, monkeys of the species used (rhesus) rarely show any aggression at all during the first year of life, and these particular infants had never before been observed to act aggressively. It is very unlikely, then, that they had learned aggressive actions earlier. Second, and we shall return to this point later, the aggressive response to a frustration is clearly revealed only under certain conditions.

Inflicting injury as a goal response. Another criticism of the frustration–aggression hypothesis as advanced by Dollard and others stems from a particular philosophy of science embraced by some psychologists. In saying that aggression was a behavioral sequence whose goal was the injury of the person to whom the activity was directed, the authors of the 1939 monograph implied that this behavior was purposive or intentional. Some writers, taking the position of Watsonian behaviorists, object to the inclusion of intentionality in the definition of aggression. Intentionality usually has to be inferred, and these critics prefer to confine themselves to a strict operationism having little room for inferences. While we cannot here debate the merits and demerits of this approach, there is reason to believe that aggressive frustration reactions are frequently purposive in nature. Hokanson and his students have shown that provoked subjects who are permitted to aggress against their tormentor often display a drop in systolic blood pressure that brings their pressure level close to that exhibited by a nonaroused control group. Systolic pressure does not decline as much, however, when the angered people can carry out some activity, but do not believe they have inflicted injury on their frustrater (even though the activity is physically comparable to the aggressive response), or when the aggression is directed against someone other than the person who had provoked them (cf. Hokanson et al. 1963). If the decrease in systolic blood pressure is a sign of physiological relaxation brought about by the performance of a goal response, engaging in mere activity or aggressing against just anyone does not seem to be sufficient to produce this tension reduction; the frustrated person (who wants, and is prepared, to attack his frustrater) may be primarily concerned with injuring the person who had provoked him.

A revised frustration–aggression hypothesis

Elsewhere (Berkowitz 1962) I have suggested that the original version of the frustration–aggression hypothesis should be modified in three ways. First, I would contend that a frustration—preventing the occurrence of some goal response at its proper time in an ongoing response sequence—arouses, among other things, an emotional state, anger, that creates a *readiness* for aggressive acts. (The arousal state produced by a thwarting also increases the strength of the ongoing responses, whether these are aggressive or not.)

Second, it is important to make explicit what was only implicit in the formulation advanced by Dollard and his coworkers. Aggressive responses do not occur, even given this readiness, in the absence of suitable cues—stimuli associated with the present or previous anger instigators. These cues, in other words, evoke aggressive responses from a person who is "primed" to make them. The strength of the aggressive response resulting from a frustration presumably is a function of the intensity of the aroused anger and the degree of association between the available stimuli and past and present anger instigators.

By suggesting that cues are necessary to elicit aggressive actions, we can explain two propositions advanced by Dollard and his coworkers: In the absence of inhibitions, the strongest hostile responses supposedly are directed toward the perceived source of the frustration; and progressively weaker aggressive responses theoretically are evoked by objects having less and less similarity to the frustrater. In both cases, the more direct the association with the anger instigator the stronger is the aggressive reaction that is elicited.

A third necessary revision of the frustration–aggression hypothesis restricts the extent to which thwartings are employed as an explanation of aggression. Instead of maintaining that *all* aggression "presupposes the existence of frustration," we now recognize that (*a*) suitable cues may lead to aggressive behavior by arousing previously acquired aggressiveness habits and (*b*) such habits may be formed through learning—for example, by observing the behavior of some adult model—without involving a thwarting (Bandura & Walters 1963). To repeat, the revised hypothesis now would claim only that frustrations create a readiness for aggressive behavior.

Hostility displacement. The revised formula discussed above has some important implications for such phenomena as displacement and "scapegoating." In the scapegoat theory of prejudice the victim is said to be attacked primarily because he is a visible and safe target for pent-up hostility within the prejudiced individual. The aggressive "drive" supposedly "pushes" aggressive acts onto safe, available targets. Contrary to such a view, the present position contends that a target with appropriate stimulus qualities "pulls" (evokes) aggressive responses from a person who is ready to engage in such actions either because he is angry or because particular stimuli have acquired cue value for aggressive responses from him.

Several experiments by the writer and his students offer support for this analysis of hostility displacement. In one study (Berkowitz & Green 1962) it was shown that subjects who were deliberately provoked by the experimenter subsequently exhibited greater hostility toward a person who had angered them some time earlier than toward someone else who had not provoked them. By having angered the subjects previously, the former person had acquired the cue value that now enabled him to evoke hostile responses from them when they were later thwarted by the frustrater. The writer suggests that those minority groups that frequently are the victims of displaced hostility, such as Negroes and Jews, are capable of eliciting aggressive responses from thwarted people because these groups are strongly disliked, that is, they had previously aroused anger. The dislike could arise from learning that the groups have unpleasant qualities as well as from prior frustrating experiences with them.

According to this reasoning, most explanations of social prejudice are too one-sided. Typically they either explain why some people are ready to act aggressively, or they provide reasons why certain minority groups are disliked. The present formulation attempts to integrate the two sets of explanations: we have to know both (*a*) why some people are "primed" to act aggressively and (*b*) what stimulus qualities are possessed by certain groups which enable them to evoke hostile responses from the people having a readiness to behave aggressively.

Comprehensive analyses of scapegoating must deal with those people who characteristically display relatively strong hostility toward minority groups. Recent research (Berkowitz 1959) indicates that highly ethnocentric college students typically have a strong tendency to attack other people when frustrated by someone else. It is not altogether clear, however, whether this tendency is due to (*a*) previously acquired aggressiveness habits; (*b*) a proclivity to establish broad categories, especially when under stress, so that in essence the immediate frustrater is not sharply differentiated from the others; (*c*) intense emotional arousal; or (*d*) some combination of these factors.

Inhibiting aggressive reactions. When an angered person displaces hostility, he presumably does so *because* fear or anxiety inhibits direct aggression against the frustrater. The analysis presented here helps explain why the displaced aggression is frequently quite intense. Miller's (1948) translation of the psychoanalytic formulation maintains, as I indicated earlier, that stimulus objects increasingly removed from the frustrater on some appropriate generalization dimension would evoke weaker and weaker aggressive responses from the angered person. Attacks upon some bystander should thus be relatively weak and never stronger than the aggression that would be directed against the anger source. At least two studies, however, have obtained a substantial departure from this prediction. In one experiment (Pepitone & Reichling 1955), angered men whose inhibitions were presumably lowered by placing them in the company of others they liked exhibited the expected aggression gradient: much stronger attacks upon their tormentor than upon other associated stimuli. However, a more strongly inhibited group of men did not show this difference; the aggression they directed against the associated stimuli was practically as intense as the aggression against the anger instigator. Essentially similar findings have been obtained in other studies. Where members of a less inhibited group generally directed the strongest aggression against the source of their anger, most of the men in a more inhibited condition actually were more hostile toward the associated stimuli than toward the anger source (Berkowitz et al. 1963).

This last finding can be explained readily by noting that the inhibition of an aggressive response is a frustration. The emotional reaction produced by the thwarting should increase the strength of the individual's aggressive proclivities. Since there is a restraint against a direct attack on the frustrater, attacks evoked by other stimuli should be strengthened. (Dollard and his colleagues had made this prediction in their 1939 monograph.)

Expectations to aggress. Anger arousal does not in itself necessarily lead to an instigated aggressive response sequence. Stimuli associated with the anger instigator must also be present. These cues may be provided either by the external environment or the individual's thought processes. If a person is thinking of injuring his tormentor, the aggression goal (his frustrater) is symbolically represented in his thoughts. This symbolic representation serves as a cue setting an aggressive sequence into operation, if only internally. Preventing him from attacking his frustrater would then be an additional thwarting. Suppose, on the other hand, that the angered person does not see his tormentor, or any associated stimuli, and, for that matter, does not even think of "getting even." There would be no ongoing aggressive sequence, and an inability to attack the anger source would not be a frustration.

Berkowitz and Luehrig have obtained data consistent with this reasoning (Berkowitz 1964*a*), demonstrating that angered male college students who had expected to be able to attack their frustrater but were prevented from doing so subsequently exhibited a high level of aggression toward him at the end of the session. The aggression they displayed toward him was stronger than that shown by other provoked people who had been able to attack this person earlier with electric shock or who, although not having been given this earlier opportunity, had not previously expected to be able to attack him. It is not enough just to say that a "set" or expectation had been thwarted in the former group without explaining the meaning of "set." "Set" may consist of an implicit but nevertheless ongoing chain of responses. In the present case the implicit response sequence was activated by the anticipation of the aggressive opportunity, and the inability to satisfy this expectation was thus frustrating.

Hostility catharsis. Since the time of Aristotle, social science folklore has contended that an individual can be "purged" of his emotions by displaying his feelings. Aggressive behavior should therefore weaken the instigation to further aggression (unless he is frustrated again) and should somehow make the person feel better. But although such a proposition is almost universally accepted, empirical evidence regarding this catharsis hypothesis is far from unequivocal. We cannot be sure that catharsis takes place as readily and frequently as many people seem to assume.

There are manifold problems confronting research in this area. One difficulty is that observers have often regarded the intensity of the overt aggression following an initial attack as being a good indicator of the strength of the remaining "aggressive drive." They forget that inhibitions produced by guilt or anxiety arising from the initial aggression may weaken any subsequent expressions of hostility. But even in the absence of such inhibitions, diminutions in aggressive tendencies following an intervening experience are also not necessarily due to a cathartic drainage of aggressive "energy." An angered person who then watches a movie or a football game may calm down and become friendlier to his frustrater, not because he has discharged his anger vicariously but because he has been so distracted by the movie or game that he does not think of the thwarting he has experienced and ceases to stir himself up. Since he does not stimulate himself, his anger dissipates. To mention one other problem, the catharsis hypothesis is frequently tested by comparing an angered group that is permitted to aggress against someone with a similarly provoked group not given this aggressive opportunity. However, as we have already seen, if measurements obtained later should suggest there is a greater level of residual hostility in the latter (nonaggressing) condition, this difference may not be due to a catharsis in the group permitted to aggress; the angered people in the nonaggressing condition may have been frustrated —assuming they had wanted to, and had been prepared to, attack the anger source—and, so, they became more strongly aroused.

Clearly, given such difficulties, we cannot definitely say now that the free expression of aggression will automatically reduce the likelihood of subsequent aggression. Indeed, several studies of children in situations similar to play therapy suggest that the expression of aggression under such permissive conditions frequently serves to *increase* the probability of later violence (cf. Berkowitz 1962). The permissive situation may weaken inhibitions, and the performance of aggressive actions can strengthen aggressiveness habits. Nor does the observation of other people engaging in violence generally reduce aggressive tendencies. (1) The person who watches others acting aggressively often learns to behave aggressively through modeling himself after these others. (2) The wit-nessed hostility may provide cues activating previously acquired aggressiveness habits. (3) The witnessed hostility may affect the observer's judgment of the propriety of his own aggressive desires.

To demonstrate this last-mentioned possibility, in three separate experiments Berkowitz (1964*b*) and his students showed a filmed prize fight scene to deliberately angered college men. In some cases the aggression they watched was made to appear justified (in that a villain received his "comeuppance"), while for other men the witnessed aggression was made to appear less warranted. Since the justified fantasy aggression lowered inhibitions against aggression—as indicated by several measures—the catharsis hypothesis would predict that the angered men in this group would participate vicariously in the filmed violence and, thus, would purge themselves of their anger. But contrary to this expectation, the angered men in this justified fantasy-aggression condition later displayed stronger aggression against their frustrater than did the similarly provoked group shown the less justified aggression. If aggression was warranted on the screen, the former may have thought, it was all right to attack the villain in their own lives.

Performing an aggressive act may well be a goal response completing an ongoing aggressive response sequence, but satisfactory completion is apparently attained only to the extent that (*a*) the angered person himself (or perhaps someone the person associates with himself) does the attacking and (*b*) the frustrater (or perhaps someone associated with him) is injured. Further, we are not altogether certain as to what the effects of this completion would be. It may well produce a feeling of tension reduction, especially if the angered person had wanted to, and had been prepared to, aggress against the anger instigator but, for some reason, had not been able to do so right away. Whether the tension reduction signifies a decreased likelihood of subsequent aggression is not altogether clear, however. The aggressive act may lessen the thwarted person's anger at the moment, and thus may lower the probability of aggression at this time. But this frustrater has also acquired cue value for aggressive responses. Much like a red flag waved in front of a bull, under appropriate conditions (such as another thwarting experience) this individual may again evoke aggressive responses from the aroused person, whether or not he was the cause of the thwarting.

The reasoning just advanced obviously differs sharply from the "drainage" conception of aggressive behavior. Contrary to the notion of a free-floating aggressive energy that may be released through many different activities (for example, attempting to master others), or in attacking a wide variety of objects, available evidence suggests that the catharsis hypothesis must be restricted in scope. Moreover, if the view given here is correct, it is not necessary to provide substitute activities in order to "drain" a supposed reservoir of pent-up emotion. Unless the thwarted person is kept aroused or is rearoused, his anger probably will dissipate with time, and the probability of aggression will decline. But even if he is angry or has developed aggressiveness habits, aggressive behavior presumably will not occur unless appropriate cues are present.

LEONARD BERKOWITZ

[*Directly related are the entries* CONFLICT; WAR. *Other relevant material may be found in* INSTINCT; PSYCHOANALYSIS; STRESS.]

BIBLIOGRAPHY

BANDURA, ALBERT; and WALTERS, R. H. 1963 *Social Learning and Personality Development.* New York: Holt.

BERKOWITZ, LEONARD 1959 Anti-Semitism and the Displacement of Aggression. *Journal of Abnormal and Social Psychology* 59:182–187.

BERKOWITZ, LEONARD 1962 *Aggression: A Social Psychological Analysis.* New York: McGraw-Hill.

BERKOWITZ, LEONARD 1964a Aggressive Cues in Aggressive Behavior and Hostility Catharsis. *Psychological Review* 71:104–122.

BERKOWITZ, LEONARD 1964b The Effects of Observing Violence. *Scientific American* 210, February:35–41.

BERKOWITZ, LEONARD; CORWIN, R.; and HEIRONIMUS, M. 1963 Film Violence and Subsequent Aggressive Tendencies. *Public Opinion Quarterly* 27:217–229.

BERKOWITZ, LEONARD; and GREEN, J. A. 1962 The Stimulus Qualities of the Scapegoat. *Journal of Abnormal and Social Psychology* 64:293–301.

BUSS, ARNOLD H. 1961 *The Psychology of Aggression.* New York: Wiley.

BUSS, ARNOLD H. 1963 Physical Aggression in Relation to Different Frustrations. *Journal of Abnormal and Social Psychology* 67:1–7.

DAVITZ, JOEL R. 1952 The Effects of Previous Training on Postfrustration Behavior. *Journal of Abnormal and Social Psychology* 47:309–315.

DOLLARD, JOHN et al. 1939 *Frustration and Aggression.* Yale University Institute of Human Relations. New Haven: Yale Univ. Press.

EIBL-EIBESFELDT, IRENÄUS 1963 Aggressive Behavior and Ritualized Fighting in Animals. Pages 8–17 in Jules H. Masserman (editor), *Violence and War: With Clinical Studies.* Academy of Psychoanalysis, Science and Psychoanalysis, Vol. 6. New York: Grune & Stratton.

FREUD, SIGMUND (1920) 1950 *Beyond the Pleasure Principle.* Authorized translation from the 2d ed., by C. J. M. Hubback. International Psycho–analytic Library, No. 4. New York: Liveright. → First published under the title *Jenseits des Lustprinzips.* A paperback edition, translated by James Strachey, was published in 1959 by Bantam Books.

HOKANSON, J. E.; BURGESS, M.; and COHEN, M. F. 1963 Effects of Displaced Aggression on Systolic Blood Pressure. *Journal of Abnormal and Social Psychology* 67:214–218.

HOLST, ERICH VON; and SAINT PAUL, URSULA VON 1962 Electrically Controlled Behavior. *Scientific American* 206, March:50–59.

LORENZ, KONRAD 1952 *King Solomon's Ring: New Light on Animal Ways.* New York: Crowell; London: Methuen.

McDOUGALL, WILLIAM (1908) 1936 *An Introduction to Social Psychology.* 23d ed., enl. London: Methuen. → A paperback edition was published in 1960 by Barnes and Noble.

MILLER, NEAL E. 1941 The Frustration–Aggression Hypothesis. *Psychological Review* 48:337–342.

MILLER, NEAL E. 1948 Theory and Experiment Relating Psychoanalytic Displacement to Stimulus–Response Generalization. *Journal of Abnormal and Social Psychology* 43:155–178.

PEPITONE, ALBERT; and REICHLING, GEORGE 1955 Group Cohesiveness and the Expression of Hostility. *Human Relations* 8:327–337.

SCOTT, JOHN P. 1958 *Aggression.* Univ. of Chicago Press.

SEAY, B. M.; and HARLOW, HARRY F. 1963 Personal communication.

TINBERGEN, NIKOLAAS 1951 *The Study of Instinct.* Oxford: Clarendon.

WHITE, ROBERT W. 1959 Motivation Reconsidered: The Concept of Competence. *Psychological Review* 66:297–333.

II
INTERNATIONAL ASPECTS

Power holders and decision makers in the parochial sovereignties into which mankind has been habitually divided have repeatedly resorted to armed violence against neighboring communities in pursuit of political objectives. Every such resort to force has invariably been regarded as aggression (hence as unjustified, illegal, and immoral) by its victims and, also invariably, been deemed moral, legal, and justified by the alleged "aggressors" on the grounds of "self-defense," "preservation of the balance of power," "national honor," or some other plausible formula for rationalizing recourse to war.

Aggression as a concept or abstraction poses, therefore, a semantic and psychological problem rather than a problem admitting of solution by reference to traditional criteria of international law, diplomatic practice, military science, or international organization. In our time, aggression is a term of disapproval, usually limited to acts of military violence by "enemy" states whose purposes must be resisted. It is a prime article of faith, in the cult of nationalism, that aggression is always a crime committed by enemy governments and never a sin of one's own nation-state. The obvious falsity of this dichotomy has had little or no effect on the behavior of those committed to its fallacies.

The problem is not so simple, however, as these introductory comments suggest. Whether the propensity of human beings to resort to violence against other human beings is attributable to "instinct" or to "culture" has long been debated inconclusively. Some hold, with Sigmund Freud, that the human psyche is afflicted with a "death instinct," which avoids suicide only by a triumph of Eros over Thanatos, or, more commonly, by deflection of aggression against the self to aggression against others. Others, along with Bronislaw Malinowski, hold that aggression is not innate but is a product of the frustration of other human aspirations.

The issue in international law. In the realm of interstate relations many people, and policy makers, confronted with the recurring tragedies of worldwide violence in the twentieth century, have earnestly striven to outlaw war and to forbid aggression by international agreement. All such efforts have thus far failed.

The "outlawry of war" was anticipated in many late medieval and early modern treaties whereby sovereignties solemnly pledged themselves to perpetual peace. Since such pledges had no discernible effect on the subsequent decisions of statesmen, the formula was abandoned in the nineteenth century. It was revived in the twentieth by the shock of World War I. The League to Enforce Peace, 1915–1919, championed American membership in a league of nations in which "aggression" was to be met with such overwhelming economic and military force that it would not be attempted.

The League of Nations Covenant of 1919 forbade recourse to war, with qualifications. The Kellogg–Briand Pact of 1928, which pledged its signatories to renounce war as an instrument of national policy, save in "self-defense," was largely vitiated by the numerous national interpretations and reservations. Other bilateral and multilateral treaties of the 1930s reiterated the same goal. The Charter of the United Nations bound its members "to ensure, by the acceptance of principles and the institution of methods, that armed force shall not be used save in the common interest" and, further, "to maintain international peace and security, and to that end to take effective collective measures . . . for the suppression of acts of aggression or other breaches of the peace" (art. 1).

The assumption of the framers of the charter at San Francisco in the spring of 1945 was that a concert of powers, cooperating for common purposes, would guarantee peace and halt aggression by collective action, provided that the great powers with permanent seats on the Security Council would act unanimously on all measures of "enforce-ment" (cf. art. 27, the "veto" article of the UN Charter). The assumption proved false with the advent of the cold war in 1945/1946. Common action against aggression was henceforth impossible, with each contestant using real or alleged "aggression" by others as a weapon of propaganda, diplomacy, and strategy against the "enemy."

Within the context of the logic of international law, aggression consists in resort to war or to measures of armed coercion short of formal war, undertaken in violation of treaty obligations not to resort to war or to other acts of force. In the years that followed the signing of the Kellogg–Briand Pact, national policy makers, with the support of all patriots, paid no attention to the legal duties they or their predecessors had assumed whenever prevailing concepts of "national interest" dictated an opposite course. Law is an effective guide to conduct only in organized communities whose members accept its purposes as paramount. The Western state system is not such a community.

The totalitarian states have provided numerous examples of violations of treaty obligations forbidding aggression—for example, the fascist conquest of Ethiopia in 1935–1936; the Nazi seizure of Austria and Czechoslovakia in 1938–1939; Axis intervention in Spain in 1936–1939; Hitler's invasion of Poland in 1939; the Japanese assaults on China in 1931 and 1937 and on the United States in 1941; Stalin's partition of Poland with Hitler in 1939; the Soviet attack on Finland in 1939–1940 and conquest of the Baltic states in 1940. However, the democracies have no better record. Witness, among recent instances, the abortive Anglo–French–Israeli attack on Egypt in 1956; India's seizure by force of Hyderabad and Goa and attempted seizure by force in 1962 of territories in dispute between New Delhi and Peking; and the U.S. "spy flights" over the U.S.S.R. by U-2 planes (1955–1960), the Bay of Pigs invasion of Cuba in April 1961, and the "quarantine" of Cuba in October 1962. Other instances of resort to force come readily to mind, with each side accusing the other of "aggression": the U.S. war on North Vietnam, launched February 7, 1965; the U.S. intervention in the Dominican Republic, April 28, 1965; the India–Pakistan war over Kashmir, September 1965.

The problem of definition. It is evident that decision makers in sovereign states do not abide by treaty obligations when "security" or "defense" or ambition dictates contrary conduct. This circumstance has led diplomats and legalists to cultivate the illusion that obedience to law could somehow be assured if only a more precise definition of aggression could be formulated and generally accepted. Laborious efforts at Geneva in the 1920s in the name of the League of Nations were devoid of operational results. Similar efforts by the United Nations since 1946 have been equally in vain. The most notable, albeit futile, attempt to define aggression was made by Maxim Litvinov, foreign minister of the U.S.S.R., at the London Economic Conference of 1933. On July 4 of that year he signed a "Convention for the Definition of Aggression" with envoys of Rumania, Yugoslavia, and Turkey (a few other states subsequently adhered). The signatories to this convention agreed to define the aggressor in an international conflict as that state which is the first to commit any of the following actions: (1) declaration of war upon another state; (2) invasion by its armed forces, with or without a declaration of war, of the territory of another state; (3) attack by its land, naval, or air forces, with or without a declaration of war, on the territory, vessels, or aircraft of another state; (4) naval blockade of coasts or ports of another state; (5) provision of support to armed bands formed on its territory which have invaded the territory of another state, or refusal, notwithstanding the request of the invaded state, to take on its own territory all the measures in its power to deprive those bands of all assistance or protection (art. 2). Furthermore, it was stipulated that no political, military, economic, or other considerations could serve as an excuse or justification for such acts of aggression (art. 3).

No better definition of aggression has been formulated since 1933. The futility of the enterprise is shown by the fact that Soviet policy makers in their "winter war" against Finland in 1939–1940 violated all the obligations they had so recently assumed. Other instances of violations of pledged words are innumerable in the diplomatic and military history of the twentieth century.

The dilemma. The premise of all efforts to outlaw war and to define and forbid aggression by bilateral or multilateral accords among sovereignties is that national policy makers will be deterred from misbehavior by their promises and by threats of action against them from the entire community of nations. In practice, the promises are frequently ignored, for reasons pointed out by Machiavelli more than four centuries ago. As for the efficacy of threats against aggressors in the name of collective security, the verdict of experience thus far is negative. National policy makers, dedicated to the pursuit of the national interest, whether this is defined in terms of power, pride, profit, or prestige, can always be relied upon, whatever their rationalizations, to ignore their commitments to refrain

from aggression whenever they believe that resort to force will serve their purposes.

Aggression can probably never be prevented by legalistic formulae or by the artifacts of international organization and collective security, so long as the state system remains an arena of international anarchy among polities possessed of unlimited national sovereignty. Aggression will cease only when mankind reluctantly accepts the necessity of a drastic alteration of values and purposes in international relations and gives operational meaning to the ideal of world government. This goal is remote because of the universal disposition of *Homo sapiens* to cling to ancient ways in the face of new circumstances calling for new thought and threatening disaster if rethinking is resisted. In the absence of significant progress toward this objective, aggression in interstate relations will continue in the future, as in the past, with potentially catastrophic consequences—and all efforts to define, outlaw, and forbid recourse to force by one state against another must inevitably fail of their purpose.

FREDERICK L. SCHUMAN

[*See also* COLLECTIVE SECURITY; INTERNATIONAL LAW; WAR.]

BIBLIOGRAPHY

BOGGS, MARION WILLIAM 1941 *Attempts to Define and Limit Aggressive Armament in Diplomacy and Strategy.* Columbia: Univ. of Missouri Press.
LANGER, ROBERT; and SCHUMAN, FREDERICK L. 1947 *Seizure of Territory: The Stimson Doctrine and Related Principles in Legal Theory and Diplomatic Practice.* Princeton Univ. Press.
LITVINOV, MAXIM 1939 *Against Aggression.* New York: International Publishers. → Speeches, together with texts of treaties and of the Covenant of the League of Nations.
RESEARCH IN INTERNATIONAL LAW, HARVARD LAW SCHOOL 1939 *Draft of Conventions Prepared for the Codification of International Law.* Concord, N.H.: Rumford Press. → Also published as a supplement to Volume 33 of the *American Journal of International Law,* 1939.
STONE, JULIUS 1958 *Aggression and World Order: A Critique of United Nations Theories of Aggression.* Berkeley: Univ. of California Press.

AGING

I
PSYCHOLOGICAL ASPECTS

Description and explanation of adult behavior as it evolves over the life-span is the subject matter of the psychology of aging. This includes the study of capacities, perception, learning, problem solving, feelings, emotions, skills, and social behavior as they emerge and change.

Types of age and aging. There are three kinds of aging: biological, psychological, and social. Although the psychology of aging may be studied without regard to biological and social forces, it is best viewed as both a biological and a social science, reflecting the fact that the way in which individuals are transformed over time is a function of a complex field of biological and environmental forces.

Biological age. Biological age refers to the present position of an individual relative to his potential life-span. Research on the biology of aging is concerned with studying the processes that limit the life-spans of species and individuals, or with finding out why species and individual members of species have determinate lengths of life (Verzar 1963; Shock 1960). There is no consensus that the same factors limit the life-spans of different species. Although there is little doubt that the major factors must be genetic, their ultimate nature and the sequence of steps in their expression has yet to be described. The biological age of an individual is closely related to chronological age, but the two are not identical, since they are derived from different concepts as well as different sets of measurements.

Psychological age. Psychological age refers to the position of individuals relative to some population with regard to adaptive capacities as observed or inferred from measurements of behavior. Psychological age may also include subjective reactions to development. Although psychological age is related to both chronological age and biological age, it is not fully accounted for by the combination of these (Birren 1960).

Social age. Social age refers to the social habits and roles of the individual relative to his group or society. An individual's social age is related to his chronological, biological, and psychological ages, but it is not completely defined by them. Within societies there are often elaborate age-status systems that lead to expectations of how an individual should behave in relation to others. The age-grading of expected behaviors is a long-evolving process in society, and it is only partly determined by the biological and social characteristics of individuals at a given age (Tibbitts 1960).

In all three aspects of aging—biological, psychological, and social—the adult seems to develop or change in characteristically orderly ways. But as a result of many random events, these transitions are uniform but vary around the average trend for some defined population. The idea that individuals develop and age with variations around an average trend was a powerful conceptual innovation of the early nineteenth century.

Historical background. With the growth of science in the nineteenth century it became apparent that how long and how "well" man lived his life were matters for systematic observation. Although profound philosophical views had been set forth earlier, research on the psychology of aging began with the work of Lambert Adolphe Jacques Quetelet in 1835 and was further advanced by Francis Galton in the last quarter of the nineteenth century [*see* GALTON; QUETELET]. G. Stanley Hall brought attention to the subject by his book *Senescence* (1922), which is useful as a source of ideas and references. Hall (1922, p. 100) recognized the superficiality in regarding aging as the inverse of development and, despite his specialization in child psychology, struck an independent note, suggesting that older people, like adolescents, have unique psychological processes, which probably exhibit a higher degree of variability than do the functions of youth [*see* HALL].

Around this time, studies of the spontaneous activity of rats suggested that there was a reduction in drive with age (for references see Birren 1961). The topic aroused less interest in the 1930s, but more recently Anderson (1956) has reasserted the significance of studying age differences in activity level and has suggested the roles of both acquired motivational influences and biological effects.

Mental tests developed just before World War I, used for classifying recruits, showed age differences in test scores that had to be explained if one were going to take seriously what such tests purported to measure. These findings began a continuous line of research to the present day.

In Vienna during the 1930s the work of Charlotte Buhler and Else Frenkel-Brunswik was taking a philosophical turn, an approach that considered man more holistically than did contemporary experimental studies (Buhler 1961). Buhler and her students studied age changes in values and the progression of individuals toward their life goals as revealed by biographical studies. Since 1946 the process and problems of aging have received considerable attention from government and research agencies and from the behavioral sciences.

Approaches and problems. The psychology of aging can be approached as a basic field of knowledge and research; as a way of testing ideas or hypotheses from other areas of special interest, such as perception, learning, or personality; or as an application of psychological knowledge to the problems of older persons, since older persons are in an unfavored position in society and generally after mid-life there is an increase in social and medical problems.

One should distinguish in the older population those characteristics that do not necessarily affect the entire population and those that are so typical of the age range that they can be viewed as developmental, or aging, in nature.

Social problems. The social problems of older persons include income maintenance and employment, housing, medical services, social mobility, and opportunities for compatible interpersonal relations. Aged persons tend to have low incomes and little accumulated wealth and are therefore in a poor position to maintain their standards of food, clothing, housing, and social amenities. In addition, poor health and sensory defects frequently limit social mobility, resulting in a still further lowering of the standard of living.

There tends to be a high interaction on older populations of economic, health, and psychological factors. For example, the young adult who is cured of an illness may return to his original environment with the expectation that he will resume his pattern of living. The older person, discharged from a hospital, more commonly cannot return to his environment with the same expectation that he will resume his previous pattern of living. Many factors, including those of social isolation, transportation, and the need for supporting services (housekeeping and meals), form a complicated matrix of forces in which the older person is embedded and which limit his choices of behavior. Social and medical services are most commonly organized according to patterns that best serve the child or the young to middle-aged adults, although many countries and communities are beginning to organize services for older persons, taking into account the more highly interdependent social, psychological, and physical environment of the older person. The situation is in some respects like that of the young child, although the child's dependency is focused on the parents. There is often no similar major focus of responsibility for the older adult in relieving the effects of social deprivation and disease.

Health problems. Health statistics define important aspects of the psychological context of older persons. The number of older persons (over 65) classified as deaf or blind is 10 to 50 times greater than in the young adult group. The number of days of restricted activity because of medical problems rises markedly after age 65. One survey by the U.S. Public Health Service (1959) reported that about 13 per cent of those in the 45 to 54 age range have some limitation of activities compared to 55 per cent over the age of 75. More than half the persons over the age of 65 actually have two or more sources of limitation of activity.

Statistics from examinations of men called for military service in World War II show a relation between age and rejection for service. Nearly 18 million men were given examinations for military service by the U.S. forces between 1940 and 1945. If the number of totally disqualified men and men with limited or remediable defects are added together, the total percentage of rejected men 18 to 20 years old was 29.3 per cent, whereas for men aged 38 to 44 the rejection rate was 64.7 per cent (Goldstein 1951).

Not all of the age changes in health and fitness are a result of biological changes of aging. An analysis of selective service statistics suggests the importance of regional and social class differences. Some factors, such as the chronic disability resulting from accidents, vary with exposure, which in turn varies with occupation and social class. Other factors in the social context of the individual not only contribute to the occurrence, but also enlarge upon the consequences, of adverse events because of inability or failure to take remedial steps. The social context of the individual is both a cause of and a result of his biological characteristics and health. The capacity of the older individual to cope with disabilities common to older persons depends upon his educational level, lifelong styles of behavior, and the supportive level of his present environment. Membership in the lowest social classes of society is associated with a higher than average likelihood of joint adverse factors involving physical and mental health, educational opportunity, income, and marital and family relationships.

The number of days of disability for families with incomes under $2,000 was found to be 29.9, compared with only 13.0 days per year for those with incomes of $7,000 or more (U.S. National Center for Health Statistics 1963). Since most persons over 65 have reduced incomes, they must make compromises with their previous standards of living, including that of health maintenance.

Although age is related to vulnerability to adverse environmental circumstances, adverse circumstances may also increase as a function of age. For example, bereavement affects death rates. Death of a spouse apparently significantly hastens the death of the survivor.

The life cycle

Some of the problems facing individuals are characteristic of their age level and may thus be looked upon as "developmental tasks." The life-span is marked by familiar epochs, or phases, giving rise to the notion of a normal life cycle of events. As adults move forward in time, they successively make educational and occupational choices, marry, have children, advance in occupation, and retire. It is often difficult to avoid viewing such events as problems, although from a developmental point of view they are part of the normal content of human life. All developmental tasks challenge the individual somewhat. However, with adequate adaptation or resolution of the challenges and dominant concerns of an age level, the individual becomes an increasingly more differentiated and competent person. The principle to be emphasized is that the adult, like the child, is always evolving to become a more differentiated individual.

The analysis of biographical material has suggested to some psychologists that there is a tempo or rhythm to adult life. Buhler (1961) examined biographies for various kinds of information and was led to the opinion that there were clearly demarcated phases through which every adult passes. In general these phases correspond to concepts of construction, culmination, and reduction. The change from striving to withdrawing from life has also been described as a process of "disengagement" (Cumming & Henry 1961). Given a reduction in energy, the individual may become a willing accomplice in the process of separation from active roles in society. Thus, life satisfaction in the very aged may improve with some degree of disengagement. The extent to which all older individuals withdraw from activities and retrench emotionally or affectively is not certain. Probably there are those who would gain in morale from more involved affective and social relationships in late life, just as there are those who gain from moving toward a less involved status. Implied here is the fact that the aging individual is a biological and behavioral system that is interacting with stimulation from a particular social environment. It must be added that the psychological capacities of the individual will limit his effectiveness in adapting to the continually emergent features of his life.

Psychological capacities. Changes in the psychological capacities of individuals over the adult life-span have been well studied. Occasionally, contradictory results have been obtained, apparently because of differences in the educational level or health status of the groups studied. Disease, particularly cerebrovascular and primary brain disease of late life, can seriously impair mental functioning and limit effective behavior. Pres-ence of such afflicted persons in a sample distorts what may be regarded as the developmental, or normative, changes of aging. What constitutes adequate sampling in studies of aging is difficult to determine, since persons of different ages cannot be matched for many important background characteristics.

Sensory function. The changes in the central nervous system and in the peripheral sensory receptors and their specialized structures result in reduced sensory input with age. Thus, compared with young adults, the older person generally makes discriminations among stimuli of lower intensity. Another effect of the reduced sensory input may be the lowering of the total level of excitation imparted to the nervous system, thereby affecting the level of activity of the individual.

The different types of sensory receptors have in common their essential nature as neural structures or extensions of the nervous system. Thus the tendency toward generally reduced receptor efficiency may be based on the ability of cells of the nervous system to survive and function. In addition to sharing a common primary process of neural aging, receptors may exhibit deterioration in their specialized structures, such as the lens of the eye tending to become opaque (cataract) in many older individuals.

Speed and timing. One of the most distinguishing features of aging persons is their tendency to behave lethargically. Whereas young adults behave quickly or slowly in accord with the demands of the situation, older adults exhibit a generally slower rate of behavior. Slowness in the young adult can be thought of as a function of many factors, such as stimuli or signals that are weak or of low intensity, stimuli that are complex or ambiguous or unfamiliar, stimuli that are unexpected, and stimuli that tend to evoke conflicting responses. Responses that must be made in a sequential manner or responses in which the consequences may be inordinately great may be delayed until the individual feels the conditions are optimum. These factors affect the differential speed of response in older persons, too, but represent an impediment to behavioral speed in addition to a generalized tendency to slowness in the aged.

The generalized slowness of behavior in older persons is looked upon as being most probably an expression of a primary process of general neural aging. Explanations involve the loss of nerve cells, reduced neural excitability, physical–chemical changes at the synapse that limit transmission speed, and a lowered excitation resulting from changes in subcortical centers.

Although much has been learned about psychomotor speed and aging, not much is known about the modifying conditions that maintain an alert organism with a potential for precise and rapid response. Thus, whether continuous high-level stimulation in later life will retard or advance psychomotor slowing is not known.

Slowness can be looked upon as a change dependent upon the more elementary processes in the nervous system, or it can be examined with regard to its consequences for behavior. In the latter view, the slowness of advancing age comes as close as does any identifiable process to being an independent variable. That is, slowness defined as a minimum operations time in the nervous system can be used in turn to explain other psychological phenomena of aging. One consequence of the slowing-down process is that the individual is limited in the amount of activity or the number of behaviors he can emit per unit of time.

To some extent the psychomotor slowness of older persons may be affected by a depressive mood, although a heavy lethargic mood may be superimposed on a pre-existing slowness. Depression of affect is not an adequate explanation for the slowness of advancing age, although it can be a factor that amplifies its consequences.

The older person adapts to his slowness by avoiding situations with unusual time pressures. Slowness itself can be in part a manifestation of adaptation. As the individual becomes less sure of himself in walking, fearing the consequences of a fall, he may tend to slow his movements considerably. Also, with a reduction of activities in later life slowness may accompany adaptation to the level of stimulation of the environment. Long-term adaptation to a characteristic level of activity may result in the speed of response becoming fixed so that increased stimulation will not reinstate the previous limits of behavior. The view that the organism is reacting to a changing environment must be balanced with the view that the organism is also a self-activated system that may change over time and show a reduction in the number of behaviors emitted per unit time. Limiting the number of behaviors that can be emitted per unit time is a function of the central nervous system, a basic process that appears to change with age.

Psychomotor skills. Over the years of employment, individuals develop work methods and by so doing simplify their tasks. The inexperienced worker is apt to be working near the limits of his physiological capacities. With experience, compensations are developed by the individual so that limitations on performance are circumvented or minimized. There is thus no one-to-one or simple relation between complex occupational or athletic skills and specific physical or physiological capacities.

Older workers tend to drift from jobs requiring continuous activity under paced conditions. This confirms the evidence from experimental studies that slowness of perceptual and motor processes is a basic correlate of aging of the nervous system. Over the usual years of employment, there is generally a reduction in accidents resulting from failure of judgment and an increase in accidents involving rapid evasive movements or falls.

Much of the evidence from industrial studies indicates that little change in worker performance is found up to age 60–65. How definitive these facts are is uncertain, since older workers who have managed to survive are a highly selected subpopulation from a total initial population. Except for individuals with cumulative injuries or problems of health, worker performance up to age 60 should be little influenced by physiological changes in aging. Exceptions are instances where time pressures are great.

The individual's adaptation to his working conditions, as well as his own capacities, is significant for his total effectiveness. Few studies have attempted to measure long-term consequences of practice and experience on psychomotor skills. From laboratory studies and data on athletes, it is known that from about age 40 there is commonly found a reduction in such capacities as strength and sensory acuity and an increase in reaction time. The individual's limits are not often taxed in occupational performance, however, and tend to be well counterbalanced by experience and better work methods. Capacities change so gradually that adaptation is an almost unconscious process. When dramatic changes in skills occur they are likely to be the result of injury or disease with accompanying neurological damage. It is perhaps only after age 70 that the individual's skills show a quality of being "old," primarily because of the slowness of action and the tendency to work according to an internal tempo rather than to an external pace. Some researchers believe that individual differences in skills increase in persons over age 70, so that group averages or norms are less useful than they are for younger persons. Individual differences in rates of aging, specialization of experience and skills over the life-span, and consequences of diseases and injuries, including sensory defects, make the increased range of individual differences a likely and important fact, although there are not many data on the matter.

Learning.   The evidence that has been accumulating on both animal and human learning suggests that changes with age in the primary ability to learn are small under most circumstances. When differences do appear, they seem to be readily attributed to processes of perception, set, motivation, and the physiological state of the organism, including disease states, rather than to a change in the primary capacity to learn. There has been a general tendency since the work of Edward L. Thorndike in the 1920s to advance continually the age at which subjects in learning research are regarded as aged. At the present time there is little evidence to suggest that there is an intrinsic age difference in learning capacity over the employed years, i.e., up to age 60. This is not to say that learning of certain psychomotor skills may not show limitations in older persons because of problems of performance or speed limitations, or of lifelong habits that usually elude laboratory study. Clearly, further studies are needed to indicate the optimum conditions for adult learning over the life-span. These include studies on the optimum massing or distribution of practice; the focusing of attention and set; and the re-employment of learning strategies by the older subject, which may have fallen into disuse during the long years since schooling.

Because of the rapid changes in industry, particularly those brought about by automation, occupations change rapidly. Some jobs are eliminated and new jobs are created. Generally, the new jobs emphasize control over production rather than primary productive skills; hence automation brings with it an emphasis on abstract learning rather than on psychomotor skills. Training and retraining is becoming a commonplace characteristic of adult employment. It is expected that increasing information about adult learning and the conditions that best facilitate it will be provided by industrial studies of learning. Attitudes will change still more as training becomes an accepted feature of a work life in which individuals spend more time in training and less time in direct production. Through the work life, years-of-schooling is a more important variable than age in relation to learning.

Intelligence and problem solving.   Problem solving involves many component abilities, each with a limit that may change with age. The changes with age in component abilities are both incremental and decremental, and some show almost no change over the adult years. Generally, the amount of information possessed by an individual rises over the life-span. The extent, then, to which a problem contains familiar elements determines whether it will be solved more efficiently by the old adult in comparison with the young. If a problem emphasizes perceptual capacity or retention of instructions, the young adult will probably perform more effectively. It seems plausible that the adult enlarges his repertory of ready-made solutions over a lifetime and becomes more effective by virtue of them. The mode of addressing a problem thus tends with age to be one of searching within the existing repertory of responses rather than one of generating novel approaches. Age, therefore, brings with it not only differential changes in component mental abilities but involves the adaptions of the individual to problem-solving situations.

Rigidity is a descriptive term referring to a tendency to hold to a particular point of view and to resist change when the situation suggests that change is appropriate. In older adults most rigidity in problem solving seems to lie not in attitudes per se but in changes in abilities. Rigid behavior can result from disease and brain damage occurring with age. Thus, a population of individuals over the age of 65 years is a mixture of those who have limitations of mental abilities because of somatic disease affecting the brain and those who are relatively healthy. Up to about age 65 the number of years of education shows, in the relatively healthy, a greater relation to mental abilities than does chronological age. Furthermore, healthy individuals over the age of 65 will tend to perform better than young adults on certain mental tests, such as vocabulary, comprehension of verbal statements, and arithmetic operations, and they will perform more poorly than young adults on tests involving spatial perception and rapid decoding of information. Because of these differential changes with age no simple answer can be given to the question of whether problem solving and intellectual capacity rise or fall over the adult years.

Longitudinal studies of mental abilities indicate that some individuals decline rapidly in abilities over a short period of time, reflecting changes in health. If many such persons are included in a sample, the averages will show gradual decline, when in fact the results are a mixture of two populations: those who are stable in their abilities and those who decline abruptly and seriously. In statistical terms this means that changes in ability in later life are not randomly distributed, but that, with age, there is an increasingly skewed distribution of abilities.

Several studies show that the likelihood of survival is related to mental-test performance. The probability of survival is less in the persons showing drops in test performance. This seems reasonable, since the performance of psychological tests is a function of complex activity in the nervous system. Such activity may be particularly sensitive to disturbances in blood flow to the brain, arteriosclerosis, and loss of cells in senile brain disease. A new field of research is emerging, concerned with behavioral measurements that identify persons who have latent or active somatic disease and that show the relations of mental abilities to brain damage in later life.

Tests of mental ability have been criticized as being inappropriate for use with older adults because much of their content was developed for young adults and children. Intelligence tests for children are used mostly in school-like situations for the prediction of school success. No such simple criterion of adult intelligence can be agreed upon, and in general adult intelligence is difficult to define. The term has meaning in a particular context, such as occupational training, vocational guidance, or medical diagnosis and therapy. Measurements of behavior will increasingly have to indicate the extent to which particular areas of the nervous system and the body are involved in a disease process limiting social effectiveness.

As progress is made in research on the analysis of logical problem-solving behavior of persons over a wide age range, it will be possible to specify the individual differences in the sequence between some problem input and the resulting solution, or behavioral output. These sequences will no doubt be found to differ with age between the healthy person of high initial ability, with good education and supporting environment, and an individual of poor health, of low initial ability, with poor education and an unsupporting environment. At present there are only intimations about the nature of these efforts.

Personality. With advancing age there are reductions in drive level, including spontaneous physical activity and sexual behavior. Studies of many kinds of activities have shown a tendency toward declining social activities and interpersonal relationships. This has given rise to concepts of psychological and social disengagement. To some extent social role decline is initiated by the environment placing the individual in a less engaged position, e.g., retirement or the death of the spouse. In addition, there is an affective detachment from the environment, in which older persons have less ego involvement in their roles and activities. Students of personality and aging have described this as partially a consequence of a reduced "ego energy."

Generally, personality traits are more variable over the adult years than are mental abilities; how-

ever, some traits, like those of personal values and vocational interests, are relatively stable, whereas self-regarding attitudes change markedly. Studies of personality traits in relation to age and intelligence indicate that age is less important than intelligence in the personality adaptations over adult life. An important qualification must be made, however, in that nonverbal intelligence becomes highly correlated with psychomotor speed in older adults. Reflected in these three aspects of the individual—psychomotor speed, nonverbal intelligence, and personality adaptations—may be a factor of central nervous system change. What the student of personality observes at one level and calls "ego energy" may at another level be measured as psychomotor speed.

The possibility exists that there is physiological registration of the effects of psychological events of later life, just as there are physiological or somatic changes with behavioral consequences. This does not imply either a complete persistence or a complete fluidity of behavior. There are relative fixations of habit systems and physiological adaptations that make the older adult a more differentiated organism than the child. Changes with age in the environment and within the individual continually provoke further differentiation of behavior. There is always some environment that is optimum for the age and state of a particular organism.

Changes in interests and activities of adults reflect the changing position of the older adult in his environment as well as his motivations and long-established patterns of behavior. The habit systems that are built up in the individual over time impose controls over the behavior elicited in response to somatic changes in internal drives and external stimulation. One stable element in the choices of behavior is personal values, although these too may be modified or superseded if the cognitive load placed on the individual becomes excessive, or if the values are in dramatic conflict with the changes and drift in the content of the individual's life. The adaptive person modifies his behavior over time, thus "aging successfully." The internal habit systems that promote adaptation are not fully known. Apparently, successful adaptation may be brought about by quite different and almost opposite types of personality organization.

The attitudes of an aged person toward "old people" may be differentiated from his attitude toward himself in growing old. In general, the self-concepts of older subjects contain negative feelings of self-worth, although older persons living independently may regard themselves somewhat less negatively than do the institutionalized aged. This suggests that the personal circumstances of the individual over the age of 60 tend to be more important in determining his attitudes and his level of functioning than is his chronological age.

There are many issues to be explored more fully in relation to aging, such as what happens in late life to the early-life compulsive neurotic. It has been shown that schizophrenic patients may develop senile mental disorders; the superimposition of aging and senile brain changes upon early-life psychosis may reveal something about the basic processes of each. Similarly, it will be useful to know what happens to the homosexual in late life, as drives slacken, and to know what happens in late life to those men and women who have had excessively strong sexual drives, erotomania. Improvements in research methods can now lead to better distinctions between the transient emotional states and moods and persistent symptoms that appear in such regular form that they are found to constitute a syndrome. It seems likely that new syndromes will be identified in the older population as the normal psychology is better defined and understood and as more detailed attention is given to older deviant individuals. Knowledge in this area is far from static, and it is to be expected that finer discriminations will continually be made among the mental problems associated with advancing age.

Maladjustment. Many forms of deviant behavior and mental illness change in their frequency with age. The changes in the relative frequencies of forms of socially deviant behavior suggest that with age there are shifts in the motivation to act as well as in the controls over behavior. Rape tends to be a young man's crime; only 7 per cent of men arrested for rape are over 40. Arrests for exhibitionism, by contrast, are greater with age. In terms of arrests, younger men steal automobiles and older men deal in stolen property or engage in embezzlement and forgery. Property offenses tend to be related to unemployment, but unemployment affects younger and older men differently: crime in the 25 to 35 age group rises with unemployment and declines in those over 35 (U.S. Federal Bureau of Investigation 1963).

Suicide rates rise greatly and consistently with age in men; it is higher for whites than nonwhites. A sex difference is also seen, with women's suicide rates showing a slight rise in the middle years and then a decline after 60. Illness and physical infirmity seem to play a precipitating role in suicides. The large age, sex, and white–nonwhite differences in suicide rates indicate that the social environment as well as personal values is of major importance. The violent modes of suicide chosen by older men leave little doubt of their serious intent, in contrast to more ambivalent suicide attempts of younger persons.

Although patients with mental diseases associated with later life constitute the largest group of first admissions to mental hospitals, they do not constitute the largest group in the hospitals, for their death rates are high. Schizophrenic patients tend to remain in hospitals longer (average 10 years) than do senile patients (average 2.5 years), most of whom die in the hospital. Relative to the total population, few persons over 65 become mental hospital patients—only about 1 to 2 per cent (Confrey & Goldstein 1959). This figure, however, does not fully represent the frequency of mental disorder in the older population. Populations differ in their capacity to tolerate the older deviant person, although in general the community is more permissive with deviant behavior of older than of younger persons. The widowed, single, and divorced occupy many more beds in institutions than do married persons. Thus, social isolation is a factor in the likelihood of institutionalization.

Circulatory impairment and senile brain deterioration occur both separately and together in older patients. Studies indicate that advancing age is not necessarily related to a reduction in blood flow to the brain. Other studies show that the type of brain deterioration is related to the kind of symptoms shown by a patient, but that mixtures of organic and functional factors are frequently found. Diagnosis tends to be multiple in the older person, with interaction taking place between somatic and mental illness and the social environment throughout the course of the illness. Physical factors are being increasingly recognized as having functional consequences in older persons, not only in depressive affect, which may lead to suicide, but also as factors in precipitating mental disorder.

More emphasis is being given to mixed etiology in mental illness in older persons, and fewer persons have symptoms that are regarded categorically as either functional or organic in background. It is expected that additional disease patterns in the older population will be defined as research methods now available are applied to representative samples of the populations as well as to selected clinical groups. As more knowledge of the normal psychology of aging is acquired, the treatment of the older patient will become more specific and more rationally based.

Productivity. As the average life-span of modern man has increased, the amount of time spent outside the labor force has increased more than the amount of time spent in it. The length of time prior to entering employment has increased, but more dramatic has been the increase in the length of retirement, which has doubled. This creates a special problem; the individual must earn a sufficient income during the work life to provide for a longer retirement. Since retirement incomes are generally low, the standard of living drops, and the need for income to subsist and maintain previous activities is a primary concern for most older persons. It is not likely that there will be a reversal of the trend toward decreasing employment of older persons, for their employment would in many instances necessitate competition for jobs with young adults.

In periods of high technological change, older persons and those with less education tend to be dropped from employment. Industrial trends are such that education and continuing training through the employed life are becoming characteristic. The distinction between working and training is less clear than it once was. Previously, the worker trained before entering the labor market; now, there is continuing on-the-job training as industrial processes are modified. Older workers tend to have obsolete skills, and the basis for unemployment among older workers is technological change rather than the worker's lack of capacity. Because of the work orientation of society, the transition to free-time activities is not easy. Along with the expansion of leisure-time activities there exists a need for a reorientation in attitudes toward the uses of time; the meaningful use of free time in retirement can be a major problem of personal values.

Past generations of scientists and scholars tended to show peak productivity in the age range 30 to 40 years. Major contributions to mathematics, chemistry, and physics tend to come earlier in life than do those in medicine and philosophy. While sustained productivity in most learned fields occurs over the life-span, the most notable works appear to be produced by individuals in their thirties. Not much is known about scientific and artistic achievement by women, because few women entered these fields until recently and women often do not indicate their ages in their biographies.

Athletic achievement in sports declines by age 45 to a level not reached until age 70 in the sciences. There seems some basis for accepting the general view that physical capacities develop and decline earliest and that psychological capacities develop later and permit high-level achievements during most of the usual employed life-span. Social skills mature latest and in individuals in good health in a favorable environment are maintained at a high level throughout the life-span.

Total family income is at peak in the mid-fifties, suggesting that income trails somewhat the age of maximum productivity and the age of maximum need. What effects the current emphasis on education and research will have on productive careers and life achievement are not apparent. The effects of age and social climate probably differ, depending on whether the motives underlying employment are income, recognition, achievement, or desire for knowledge. A change in the social climate is giving increasing emphasis to maximum self-development, particularly through education, in contrast to the older ethic of work, which held that it was more moral to "work" hard than to study hard. Because of conflicts with earlier formed attitudes, older adults necessarily show some lag in responding to evolving attitudes toward education, work, and the uses of free time.

Last stages of life. At the end of life, early-life events may be evoked with surprising recall. Some time before the terminal stages of life an individual may become involved with a review of his life. Individuals react differently to the stimulus provided by the indications that life may be ending: some may deny it, some may react passively, and others may welcome it without reflection. Many people become involved in varying degrees in re-examining their lives in the face of an uncertain future. The life review is an active or purposeful examination of the events of one's life accompanying an impression of impending death. The intent of the life review is to reconcile one's values with the behaviors of one's life and to leave behind an acceptable image.

At present there is not much systematic research on reminiscing and the life review, so it is not possible to contrast individuals and experiences in a quantitative manner. This facet of the psychology of aging will, no doubt, become increasingly recognized. As more information becomes available, professional services for the aged will become more constructive.

Meeting and coping with frequent bereavement is one of the particular tasks of old age. Individuals learn to manage their grief by many devices—some by diverting their thoughts or avoiding provocative situations, others by developing abstractions of life principles.

The experience of loss is, of course, lifelong, and one of the elements of maturity is the management of the reactions to loss and the resumption of acceptable behavior.

The dying person has four tasks: (1) managing his reactions to the symptoms of his terminal state and altered physiology; (2) reacting to the impending separation from loved ones and friends; (3) reacting to a transition to an unknown state; and (4) adjusting his perception of his life.

Because of the frequency of deviant reactions in later life and the dramatic circumstances surrounding the end of life, the late years of life tend to be clouded in an aura of pathology, somatic and psychic. Terminal decline should be separated conceptually from the normal adaptations to living in the later years. Centenarians need not be debilitated but often have reasonably good health and mental lucidity. The normal psychology of later life is becoming understood, leading to expectations for successful adaptations for most persons. As further research is done on the relations of psychological, physiological, and social changes in later life, the characteristics which promote optimum adaptations should become better known.

The psychology of aging has as long a history as other areas of psychology, but the impetus to research and the organization of information did not come until recent years, with the increase in the percentage of older persons in Western societies. The subject is one of basic research and of application. Surveys indicate that older persons tend to be in a disadvantageous position in society with regard to income and services. Much of current research shows an awareness of the fact that aging is jointly a psychological, biological, and social problem. It seems very likely that most countries will increasingly organize social and medical services for older persons, taking into account the fact that biological, social, and psychological problems show greater interdependence in older than in younger adults.

The pattern or scope of research that is most relevant to aging is multidisciplinary, having an emphasis somewhat contrary to research in other areas of psychology, which tend to stress segmentation of problems within narrow conceptual systems. One deterrent to the study of the psychological aspects of aging has been the wide scope and complexity of variables that are relevant to how long and how well individuals live.

A recent development in the field is the reporting of longitudinal studies of adults; longitudinal data have even been collected on senescent one-egg twins. Although the major approaches and ideas in the psychology of aging have in the past come from other areas of research, there is evidence that theory and methods special to the psychology of aging are emerging.

The individual life with its contents and processes is the basic unit of reference for psychology as a science. In the past little recognition was given by investigators in other areas that age is one of the most pervasive of variables, and research was done on a hypothetical age-constant organism. Probably no psychological law can be properly stated without qualification in terms of the reference group in mind. One of the contributions of the psychology of aging to general psychology and the social sciences is that of providing a context within which to fit diverse research findings, i.e., a developmental psychology of the life-span.

JAMES E. BIRREN

[*Other relevant material may be found under* DEATH; DEVELOPMENTAL PSYCHOLOGY.]

BIBLIOGRAPHY

ANDERSON, JOHN E. (editor) 1956 *Psychological Aspects of Aging.* Washington: American Psychological Association.

BIRREN, JAMES E. (editor) 1960 *Handbook of Aging and the Individual: Psychological and Biological Aspects.* Univ. of Chicago Press.

BIRREN, JAMES E. 1961 A Brief History of the Psychology of Aging. *Gerontologist* 1:69–77, 127–134. → Contains a bibliography.

BIRREN, JAMES E. 1964 *The Psychology of Aging.* Englewood Cliffs, N.J.: Prentice-Hall.

BUHLER, CHARLOTTE 1961 Meaningful Living in the Mature Years. Pages 345–387 in Robert W. Kleemeier (editor), *Aging and Leisure.* New York: Oxford Univ. Press.

CONFREY, E. Q.; and GOLDSTEIN, M. S. 1959 The Health Status of Aging People. Pages 165–207 in C. Tibbitts (editor), *Handbook of Social Gerontology.* Univ. of Chicago Press.

CUMMING, ELAINE; and HENRY, W. E. 1961 *Growing Old.* New York: Basic Books.

FRANCE, CENTRE NATIONAL DE LA RECHERCHE SCIENTIFIQUE 1961 *Le vieillissement des fonctions psychologiques et psychophysiologiques.* Colloques internationaux, No. 96. Paris: Éditions du Centre. → Contains English translations of the papers, and summaries in both French and English.

GOLDSTEIN, M. S. 1951 Physical Status of Men Examined Through Selective Service in World War II. *Public Health Reports* 66:587–609.

HALL, G. STANLEY 1922 *Senescence: The Last Half of Life.* New York: Appleton. → Contains a discussion of early philosophical views about aging.

HAVIGHURST, ROBERT J.; and ALBRECHT, RUTH 1953 *Older People.* New York: Longmans.

Journal of Gerontology. → Published quarterly since 1946 by the Gerontological Society. Contains current psychological research on aging.

KUHLEN, RAYMOND G. (editor) 1963 *Psychological Backgrounds of Adult Education.* Papers presented at a Syracuse University conference, October 1962. Chicago: Center for the Study of Liberal Education for Adults.

KUTNER, BERNARD et al. 1956 *Five Hundred Over Sixty: A Community Survey on Aging.* New York: Russell Sage Foundation.

LEHMAN, HARVEY C. 1953 *Age and Achievement.* Princeton Univ. Press.

SHOCK, NATHAN W. (editor) 1960 *Aging: Some Social and Biological Aspects.* Symposia presented at the Chicago meeting of the American Association for the Advancement of Science, Dec. 29–30, 1959. Washington: The Association.

TIBBITTS, CLARK (editor) 1960 *Handbook of Social Gerontology: Societal Aspects of Aging.* Univ. of Chicago Press.

TIBBITTS, CLARK; and DONAHUE, WILMA T. (editors) 1962 *Social and Psychological Aspects of Aging.* New York: Columbia Univ. Press.

U.S. FEDERAL BUREAU OF INVESTIGATION 1963 *Uniform Crime Reports for the United States and Its Possessions, 1962.* Washington: Government Printing Office.

U.S. NATIONAL CENTER FOR HEALTH STATISTICS 1963 *Family Income in Relation to Selected Health Characteristics, United States.* Vital and Health Statistics, Series 10, No. 2. Prepared by Robert R. Fuchsberg. Washington: Government Printing Office.

U.S. PUBLIC HEALTH SERVICE, NATIONAL HEALTH SURVEY 1959 *Impairments by Type, Sex, and Age; United States, July 1957–June 1958.* Health Statistics, Series B, No. 9. Prepared by Louise E. Bollo. Washington: Government Printing Office.

VERZAR, FRIGYES 1963 *Lectures on Experimental Gerontology.* Springfield, Ill.: Thomas.

WELFORD, A. T. 1958 *Ageing and Human Skill.* Oxford Univ. Press.

WILLIAMS, RICHARD H.; TIBBITTS, CLARK; and DONAHUE, WILMA (editors) 1963 *Processes of Aging: Social and Psychological Perspectives.* 2 vols. New York: Atherton.

II

SOCIAL ASPECTS

Old age is the last phase of the life cycle. The timing of this phase, its impact on role relationships, and the meaning attached to it vary in different societies and in different subgroups within any given society. Differentiation in this sphere is effected by a complex combination of demographic, economic, social, and cultural factors. In industrial societies, falling death rates and decreasing birth rates have resulted in a considerable aging of the population. While the maximum span has changed very little, if at all, and the range of variation of the percentages of old people in various countries is still wide, there is a strong over-all upward trend in the average length of human life (Sauvy 1963).

Comparative analysis

Paradoxically, there is an inverse relationship between the demographic weight of aging people and their position in society. In most societies with a low proportion of old people, the aged are revered, whereas steady increases in the population of the aged impose an increasing burden on the younger age groups and engender a negative image of aging. However, the effect of demographic weight is not wholly negative; the growing proportion of old people in the population enhances their political importance.

Economic factors. There is a direct relationship between a society's level of productivity and the welfare of its aged. Societies that live at the edge of starvation find it difficult to maintain old people and often revert to the solution of abandoning them or putting them to death. At the other extreme, only highly productive systems can allow early retirement and provide adequate pensions. It should be noted, however, that when we shift the emphasis to the *usefulness* of their working capacity, the relationship between productivity and the position of the aged is reversed: low productivity tends to preserve the marginal utility of increments of labor, whereas high productivity and technological advance engender a labor surplus and older workers become increasingly redundant.

In economic systems where ownership rights are vested in the aged, the aged control to a considerable extent the life chances of the young and thereby command their assistance and deference. The time and the manner in which property rights are transferred from one generation to the other have far-reaching repercussions on the relations between old and young. Limitation of property rights, separation between ownership and control, and the proliferation of open opportunities for the young undermine the authority and autonomy of the old.

The extent of development of a market economy and the extent of bureaucratization also affect the position of the aged. Recruitment to work in a premarket economy is ascriptive, whereas the policy of recruitment in a market economy is based on tests of competence and competition that put the partly disabled older worker at a disadvantage. Nonbureaucratic institutions are flexible and can adapt their internal division of labor to suit the changes in capacities and needs of the available workers. Bureaucratic organizations have standardized and highly coordinated work routines and find it hard to vary their job requirements in order to adjust them to personal capacities and needs.

The impairment of skills by age does not proceed at the same rate for all occupations. Other things being equal, the capacity to perform tasks requiring a high degree of physical strength or coordination begins to decline much earlier in life than the capacity for decision making and administration; indeed, the seasoned executive is likely to be at his best around middle age. Yet the strain of executive life is bound to have a more or less corrosive effect. Far better suited to the capacities of aging people is the performance of such "integrative" societal roles as that of judge or religious functionary, since these involve concern with long-run considerations and guardianship of cultural traditions. It should be noted, however, that the developmental patterns of the different capacities are not determined solely by physiological processes and that health care and continuous training can maintain a high level of capacity and postpone gross disability considerably.

Finally, the function of the aged as bearers and transmitters of the techniques, knowledge, and skills of their society depends to a large extent on the rate of technological and social change in their society. Slow change puts a premium on accumulated knowledge and long experience; it makes possible an age-graded role allocation, which shifts older people to positions that are less arduous and exacting and yet are of central importance in their society. Conversely, rapid and pervasive change undermines their importance.

Group supports. The position of the aged is strongest, and they are best protected, in kin-centered societies. Corporate kin groups are based on lineal intergenerational continuity; within them, the old occupy positions of authority and serve as crucial intermediary links. Intergenerational living arrangements supply them with direct contact with the young. Yet another factor is the extent of community integration of the aged, which depends on the localization and connectedness of the network of social relations and on the continuity of contacts over the life cycle. Thus lifelong, overlapping, and mutually reinforcing ties with kin, neighbors, friends, and former colleagues integrate old people into the community as a whole. The accessibility of significant persons and service institutions is an important feature of such communities. Since old people become increasingly dependent on their immediate environment, they are usually at a disadvantage in urban communities, where the networks of informal relations are typically loose and where vital associations usually lie outside the local neighborhood.

Cultural factors. Closely related to the factors discussed so far, but partly independent of them, are certain basic orientations and value premises that affect the predominant view of the aged in any society (Parsons 1960). First, the extent to which old age is valued in any society depends partially on its dominant *time orientation*. In past-oriented societies, the aged are meaningful links to tradition and ensure historical continuity. Their role is particularly important in societies where continuity has a religious connotation; they serve as direct links to or even as incarnations of divine powers in societies based on ancestor worship. A present-orientation centers on short-range concerns and devalues old age. An even more radical devaluation of old age is inherent in a forward-looking orientation, which stresses innovation and progress.

Partly independent of the location of the domi-

nant time dimension is the extent of differentiation of the phases of the life cycle. Life may be viewed as an orderly succession of distinct phases, each posing its distinctive developmental dilemmas and tasks and each involving more or less clear, phase-specific normative injunctions and rewards. On the other hand, the view of life may be "fixated" on one of the life cycle phases, while the other phases are considered devoid of intrinsic interest or value of their own. A conception of life that is based exclusively on youth or middle age puts aging people at a serious disadvantage. Devaluation of old age coupled with lack of unequivocal normative standards undermines the ability of the elderly to adjust to the role transitions involved in aging.

Yet another important factor is an "otherworldly" versus a "this-worldly" orientation. An otherworldly orientation mitigates the onset of decline and the finality of death by projection to an afterlife or by an emphasis on a purely spiritual, nonterrestrial salvation; radical world rejection leads to glorification of death as the true goal of life. The awareness of time running short and the regret over physical deterioration are more acute when the prevalent culture emphasizes sensual enjoyment of material things and does not offer the consolation of life in the hereafter (Jeffers et al. 1962). Of crucial importance is the distinction between an emphasis on detachment or release versus an emphasis on active mastery. Adjustment to the role loss and contraction of activity entailed in aging is easiest when the dominant orientation encourages a passive and contemplative attitude toward the world and values highly detached meditation. Aging can be accepted with relative equanimity when the prevalent values legitimize release from duties, relaxation, and ego-gratification. On the other hand, adjustment to old age is most difficult and involves a serious reorientation when the value system puts the main stress on active striving and mastery of external reality; under these circumstances aging signifies being cut off from productivity and utility. Similarly, a cultural emphasis on achievement rather than ascription reduces the importance of seniority; social status becomes a function of ability, not of age. In an ascriptively oriented society, on the other hand, age progression is a major criterion of role allocation (Eisenstadt 1956).

Collectivism and individualism are also major orientations affecting treatment of the aged. The isolated individual is confined within the narrow limits of his life span and cannot see beyond it. The collectivistic orientation emphasizes the unity and continuity of the group as it evolves from generation to generation; thus the time perspective of the aging person is extended—the future of the group is also his future. The tendency toward individualism or collectivism affects the position of the aged in yet another way. The collectivistic orientation stresses the welfare of the group as a whole and emphasizes the interdependence of all its members. It fosters a binding sense of obligation toward those in need of support and encourages mutual aid and group action. Individualism stresses independence and fosters self-centeredness and self-sufficiency. It undermines the sense of moral duty toward the aged and hampers attempts to solve their problems by concerted action.

The position of the aged is thus dependent on a very complex combination of factors. One or another factor may be dominant in a given situation, but all of them have to be considered. Comparative research in this field has just begun; here it must suffice to say that the optimal balance between the forces that enhance the position of the aged and the factors that undermine it is in fact reached both in primitive societies that are well beyond the mere struggle for survival and in traditional agrarian societies (Fortes 1949). The most important mechanism operating in such societies is the transfer of the aged to the political and religious sphere; the young take over responsibility for work and welfare, but the old maintain over-all control. The injunctions to respect parents and old people in general are the pivot of the moral, jural, and religious systems. By contrast, processes of development in modern society have, on the whole, undermined the position of the aged. Aging leads to loss of status and control, and the prevailing negative image of old age is shared by both young and old (Tuckman & Lorge 1953; Barron 1953). However, there are many counteracting factors, and the balance is by no means wholly negative.

Aging and the modern kinship system

Demographic analysis of the family cycle reveals that the postparental stage has lengthened considerably and now lasts an average of 16 years (Glick 1957; Nimkoff 1962). The relationship between spouses is determined by the key events which punctuate the process of aging: termination of child-rearing tasks, retirement, and dissolution of the marital bond by death. In the first phase of aging the main burden of adjustment falls on the wife, who loses her cardinal role while her husband is at the peak of his career. During the second phase the main burden falls on the husband, who loses his major role as a member of the occupational system and has to redefine his relationship with his wife. The process of aging therefore brings

about a shift in the basis of solidarity between husband and wife, who move into a more equalitarian relationship with each other and with the world around them (Cumming & Henry 1961). The data suggest that couples react to this shift either by a *rapprochement* or by increasing estrangement. The departure of the children is sometimes followed by a period of renewal and intensification of attachment that is experienced as a second honeymoon. It should be noted, however, that the pattern of estrangement predominates. Examination of marital satisfaction over time in a large sample of families in Detroit (Blood & Wolfe 1960) indicates that marital satisfaction reaches a low point at the stage of unlaunched adult children, rises somewhat in the beginning of the postparental stage, but declines again after retirement.

As in earlier stages, segregation between aging husband and wife varies directly according to the connectedness of their social network and is most marked in couples with close-knit kin and community ties (Bott 1957). A study of a working-class suburb in London (Young & Willmott 1957) indicates sharp segregation and growing estrangement between aging spouses; the close relationship of the wife with her children and kin takes clear precedence over her relationship with her husband, and retirement of the husband engenders considerable tension. In an attenuated form, estrangement also appears among more mobile middle-class couples. Research on a primarily middle-class sample in Kansas City reveals that there is surprisingly little emphasis on the relationship with the spouse and that, especially for the wife, the parent–child and sibling bonds seem to override it (Cumming & Henry 1961). There is considerable evidence that in spite of the fact that widows face more serious economic problems than widowers and in spite of the greater centrality of the familial role for the wife, aging women overcome the shock of bereavement more easily than men (Townsend 1957; Marris 1958; Cumming & Henry 1961).

The parent–child relationship. Recent research indicates that in spite of the considerable intergenerational discontinuity brought about by processes of accelerated change, the parent–child bond is of crucial importance during the process of aging. Scrutiny of actual living arrangements suggests that, although the prevalent ideology emphasizes separation and independence, about a third of the people over 65 who have children live with one of them. The over-all trend, however, is one of decline in the number of such joint households; increases in some countries were caused by the postwar housing shortage (Schelsky 1953). The emergent pattern is that of living near children rather than living with or far away from them.

There is evidence that joint living engenders considerable strain and that it is easier to maintain amicable relations when the parents live in proximate but separate dwellings (Tartler 1961; Robins 1962). The highest proportion of joint households has been found among peasants, small craftsmen, and tradesmen. Living arrangements based on close proximity are typical of the nonmobile working class and of minority ethnic groups during the initial stages of their acculturation; such arrangements are less prevalent in families of people employed in professional and bureaucratic careers but do not disappear altogether. A typical pattern in such families is that of a two-phased movement—a period of dispersion is followed by a period of family coalescence. Adult children may go far afield in search of career openings, but the aging of the parents often brings about a reunion (Young & Geertz 1961).

During the later stages of aging, the parents, who have hitherto given more to their children than they have received from them, gradually become the main beneficiaries of the exchange. Although the importance of supporting parents in the economic sense is declining with the development of public and private pension schemes, there is considerable evidence that this trend has not undermined the filial sense of responsibility (Schorr 1960). Most assistance in such tasks as housekeeping, personal care, and nursing during periods of illness comes from children. In general, daughters are much more involved in the relationship than sons; the mother–daughter bond is particularly strong and persists throughout the process of aging, especially in working-class families.

Recent research also indicates that inherent strains are involved in the parent–child bond. Although there is a considerable congruence between the norms of aging parents and children in this sphere (Streib 1958), the relationship is basically asymmetrical (Reiss 1962): aged parents seem more attached to their children than vice versa. Most children have a more or less strong sense of duty toward their aging parents, but the intensity of such a commitment varies according to the nature of the affective bonds between them, compatibility of values and style of life, and the possibilities of reciprocal services. There is also some evidence that there is an inverse relationship between the urgency of the need of the parents and the children's readiness to help (Dinkel 1944).

Grandparents. Reaching grandparenthood is one of the key events in the onset of aging, and it occurs early in the process; there is a strong likelihood of becoming a grandparent well before one's fiftieth birthday (Glick 1957). There is evidence that grandparenthood is accepted with considerable ambivalence (Winch 1952). Grandchildren are tangible reminders of the passage from adulthood to old age, and they start to arrive at a time when such an awareness is still alien to the self-image. One of the most important factors affecting the position of grandparents in modern societies is the change in the patterns of familial authority. Comparative data on grandparents in primitive and traditional societies reveal that they perform either of two alternative roles (Apple 1956). In some societies they are typically strict and remote figures at the apex of the familial authority structure; in others they are permissive and easygoing and counteract the rigorous discipline imposed by parents. Grandparents are no longer authority figures in modern societies, and since parents have become much more permissive toward their children, there is also less need for grandparents to offer nurturance and tension release. Hence there has been a decline in the significance of grandparents in the life of their grandchildren, even though close contacts are often maintained through childhood and adolescence (Townsend 1957). The emergent pattern is based on intermittent contact, informality, and playfulness. The emphasis is on giving the grandchildren treats and having fun together rather than on transmission of values or nurturance (Neugarten & Weinstein 1964).

More distant kin. Aging people maintain contact and some interchange with a variety of more distant kin. Consanguinal kin tend to be more important than affinal ones and the wife's relatives more important than the husband's. Interaction among kin emphasizes ritual activities, friendliness, and sociability more than mutual aid (Cumming & Schneider 1961). There is a considerable amount of regular communication and visiting among kin, which provides aged people with their most important links with the outside world. Large family gatherings are less frequent than they used to be, but they have not disappeared; old people are often at the center of elaborate family rituals that draw relatives from far and wide (Albrecht 1962). Aging people serve as repositories of family lore and knowledge about kinsmen and are important connecting links in the kinship network (Young & Geertz 1961).

It should be noted that at times secondary and tertiary relatives replace and substitute for primary ones. When aging parents have sons but no daughters they see more of their daughters-in-law.

When they have no children, they have more contact with and get more assistance from nieces and nephews (Townsend 1957; Rosenmayr & Köckies 1963). Dormant ties are often reinvoked and reactivated. The obligations toward more distant kin are less binding than the obligations toward primary ones, but they are often strong enough to form a second line of defense around the aging person. In case of unavailability of closer relatives, they may step in and close the gap. Thus, kinship provides a field of actual and potential sources of support and aid.

Considerable interaction between aging people and their kin occurs in most sectors and strata of modern society. In certain subcategories of the population—in the nonmobile working class, among the self-employed in the lower middle class, in the upper class, and in certain ethnic groups—the kin bond is anchored in traditional obligations that persist and are reinforced by social and cultural intergenerational continuity. In other subcategories, pre-eminently among those employed in bureaucratic and professional careers, the kin network is loose, more elective, and more flexible but persists in spite of considerable geographical and occupational mobility. Although the majority of old people get considerable emotional support and aid from kin, this fact should not obscure the inherent limitations of the familial system of care. The emerging pattern of family relations in industrialized countries is not set by unequivocal norms, and much depends on personal relations and personal choice. A certain percentage of old people are neglected and isolated, either because they do not reach a modus vivendi with their kin or because they have few kin. Furthermore, families find it extremely difficult to cope with severely disabled old people. There is a sizable minority of old people who require a considerable amount of extrafamilial aid.

Aging and the occupational system

The proportion of old people in the labor force has declined considerably in all industrialized countries; except for the period of World War II, this trend has been steady and cumulative. In the United States about two-thirds of the men past 65 were working in 1900, as compared to one-third today (only 18 per cent of them full time). Almost half of those still working are self-employed, primarily in agriculture, small businesses, and the independent professions. Inasmuch as long-range trends of limitation of opportunities for self-employment continue, the labor force participation rates of older people will continue to decline. Increases in the average length of life, together with decreases in employment opportunities for the aged, result in great increases in the length of retirement (Kreps 1963; Michigan, Univ. of, 1963). It should be noted that there are considerable differences between men and women in this respect. While the participation of men past 65 in the labor force has declined, the participation of women in this age range has increased. Withdrawal from the occupational system is the major problem for aging men, whereas it is far less important for working women (Cumming & Henry 1961).

Patterns of retirement. Four major patterns of reaction emerge from research on aging in the sphere of work (Schneider 1962). The pattern of *full engagement* is based on the assumption that a man should not relinquish his work role or relax his efforts in this sphere until he dies; at the other extreme, *full disengagement* entails abrupt and total cessation of work. In between these extremes there are the patterns of *gradual disengagement* from the work role and of *disengagement and reengagement*. Many men "practice" for retirement by giving up work, starting again, and changing their status several times before finally retiring for good.

There is considerable variation with respect to the timing of retirement (Clark & Dunne 1956; Michigan, Univ. of, 1963; Wilensky 1960). Dropping out of the work force is already observable in the age span of 45–55. The most important reason for early retirement is ill health; another important factor is fluctuation in the economic situation. In most cases, retirement regulations set the limit at 60 for women and 65 for men. Although the majority of workers discontinue work either before or after the prevalent retirement age, there is a growing tendency to view it as the "normal" age of retirement.

The demand for mandatory retirement is rooted in both organizational and personal needs and thus is gaining the upper hand. The over-all trends are toward curtailment and standardization of the work span. Yet since the majority of aging workers are reluctant to retire and many are forced by adverse economic circumstances to seek work, there is considerable pressure to increase substitute employment opportunities. Attempts to solve this problem have developed in two major directions (Donahue 1955; Townsend 1957). First, there has been some exploration of marginal possibilities of employment in existing enterprises. For example, retired company directors and experts often act as consultants in their own or in other firms; in the lower echelons of the occupational ladder there are "old men jobs," such as watchman and janitor.

Second, sheltered and partly subsidized enterprises have been developed for those who can no longer earn a living any other way.

Effects of retirement. Retirement has far-reaching repercussions on most aspects of life. In the first place, it usually brings about a noticeable fall in the standard of living. However, the most important aspect of retirement is the loss of what is to most men their cardinal role (Blau 1956). The society's emphasis on productivity and achievement leads to a fixation on the occupational role, which becomes the core of personal identity. Cessation of work also disrupts basic life routines. No less problematic is the blurring of status position; past occupational history can fully articulate the family to the social structure only in cases in which the accomplishments of the retired men are cumulative or not easily forgotten. Yet another source of strain is the disruption of peer-group solidarity with colleagues, which is for the majority of men the main source of companionship outside the family. Thus the combined effects of retirement usually lead to serious disorientation. Many retired workers experience feelings of deprivation, boredom, and isolation, and in some cases retirement leads to sudden physical and mental degeneration.

However, such negative features are not universally associated with retirement. Lowered morale stems in many cases mainly from ill health and economic deprivation. The higher the retirement income, the more closely it approximates living costs, and the smaller the gap between preretirement and postretirement income, the more optimistic is the old person's evaluation of retirement and the easier his adjustment to it. Yet another key factor is the ideological premise that shapes the institutionalization of retirement (Donahue et al. 1960). The reaction to retirement is much more favorable where the old-age pension is defined as an inalienable right of every old person rather than as a degrading grant-in-aid for the needy. Work-centered values prevent the legitimation of retirement and engender serious problems, even when cessation of work is not accompanied by economic difficulties or ill health (Talmon 1961). The more positive view of retirement that is gradually emerging in affluent industrialized societies is an outcome of the transition from the emphasis on production to an emphasis on consumption and the concomitant legitimation of leisure and immediate gratification (Wilensky 1961a).

Participation in formal organizations

The peak of over-all organizational participation in voluntary associations occurs during middle age, followed by a slight decline that becomes definite around 65 (Wilensky 1961b). There is a certain variation of the participation cycle by sex (Havighurst 1957; Cumming & Henry 1961). Women react to the early loss of their child-rearing role by a temporary expansion of their organizational activity, whereas in the case of men the loss of their cardinal role is accompanied by cumulative withdrawal. Middle-class people are more active than members of the working class, both before and after the onset of aging. And, of course, individual organizational activity varies according to the opportunities and stimulus provided by the community of residence.

Attendance at church services and church-sponsored functions is the most prevalent form of organizational participation of the aging. Attendance rises during the age range of 50–65 and then decreases with age. There is some evidence that religious piety and especially belief in an afterlife have a similar developmental pattern, rising at the age when crises such as retirement and widowhood occur and then subsiding.

Examination of patterns of participation throughout the life cycle underlines the importance of pre-aging patterns. In general, people who were inactive before aging usually remain inactive; however, not all who were active remain active. Even those who continue their activity, and even enhance it, tend to relinquish it when they approach advanced old age. The key determinants seem to be the relationships between the interlocking cycles of family life, work, and organizational participation. The fact that the role loss of the woman occurs while her husband is still at the peak of his career engenders in her a quest for substitute roles outside the orbit of the nuclear family. Although the majority of women turn to cultivation of informal relations, a sizable minority enhance their organizational affiliation and participation. The withdrawal of both husband and wife after the retirement of the husband stems from the fact that much voluntary participation is career-connected.

Age-segregated organizations. In and by itself, similarity of age does not provide an adequate basis for the development of group consciousness and identification. Aging people are widely dispersed geographically, and the age category is subdivided by crosscutting kinship affiliations and by ethnic, religious, and class allegiances. The emergence of group consciousness and identification is also hindered by the stigma attached to aging; pride, denial, and apathy are often stronger than collective interests.

There are, however, a number of factors that

enhance age-group consciousness and, under certain conditions, lead to group organization and action (Rose 1962). Economic deprivation, ill health, and status insecurity engender resentment and a sense of common lot. The issues of pensions and medical care have led to the emergence of the aging as a voting bloc, sometimes with a leadership that acts as a political pressure group. Recent research into a pension movement that has organized about a quarter of all pensioners in California (Pinner et al. 1959) reveals certain characteristics that may be typical. This movement did not develop effective over-all leadership from within; the leader is middle-aged and is, in addition, marginal in the community. Communication runs directly from the leader to a loosely connected audience. While there is a considerable core of devoted, hardworking, and self-sacrificing members, the majority are passive, and their participation is fluctuating and very unstable. Yet another important characteristic of the movement is the narrowness and specificity of goals; members are in favor of radical measures with regard to provision for the aged but take a conservative position with regard to most other issues. The main motive for enrollment and participation was found to be status anxiety: most members are from the slightly privileged aged rather than from the most underprivileged. It seems that those who have some hold on the material and social foundations of respectability are more likely to resent their loss of status and are more amenable to political organization.

Yet another type of age-segregated organization is the old-age club or day center that is set up by various bodies, such as municipalities, trade unions, and religious organizations. Such clubs may put the main emphasis on organization of special interest groups and on providing facilities and instruction for the development of hobbies, or they may concentrate on providing a congenial atmosphere for sociability. Only a small proportion of those above 65 patronize the centers in metropolitan areas (Kutner et al. 1956; compare Townsend 1957). Participation in club activities is much greater among aged people living in retirement housing and retirement communities (Hoyt 1954). Most of these clubs are set up *for* rather than *by* old people and are managed by professionally trained directors.

Informal relations

During the period of aging, there is a gradual thinning out of the number of people surrounding the individual and a lessening of the amount and intensity of interaction; the majority of aged people do not wish to maintain extensive social contacts. There is considerable similarity in the developmental trends in formal and informal participation. However, since primary relations are less affected by the withdrawal from the major institutional roles than secondary relations, the level of interaction with the informal network remains higher than that of interaction within formal organizations.

Evidence on the developmental pattern of informal relations during the aging process—which is unsatisfactory and often contradictory (Townsend 1957; Cumming & Henry 1961)—gives the general impression that the dominant pattern for men is the continuation of preaging level of interaction and then decline, while the pattern typical of women is upsurge and decline. Since the main emphasis in the feminine role is expressive and inasmuch as the wife is the main mediator between the family and its network of informal relations, she finds it easy to enhance and revoke such relationships; an increasingly important source of companionship and diversion is the growing peer group of widows (Blau 1961). By contrast, since the man's role is mainly instrumental, he finds it difficult to shift from goal-oriented relationships to sociability for its own sake.

The durability of informal relations during the process of aging is affected by several factors. Bonds based on long association and common memories are more durable than short-range ones. Moreover, diffuse and comprehensive ties, such as those with kin and close friends, are more age-resistant than the more specific and limited ties that exist, for instance, between colleagues. Ascriptive bonds stand the test of deterioration and dependency better than more selective relations, and close kin are more important than close friends during the later stages of aging; the most persistent friends are those who through long service as substitute kin have become quasi relatives.

Another important factor operating in this process is accessibility. With the decline of physical mobility comes a gradual increase in the importance of neighbors. However, research clearly indicates that social interaction between the aged and their young and middle-aged neighbors is very limited and that the large majority of closer as well as the more superficial ties of old people are within their own age group (Aldridge 1959). The social distance between members of different age groups who are not tied by kinship bonds reflects the tendency to age-graded interaction that is dominant in modern societies (Neugarten & Peterson 1957).

Although old age usually entails a more or less marked contraction of the social world of the individual, research indicates that in the majority of cases it does not lead to extreme isolation or loneliness. It is significant that the extent of loneliness is *not* directly related to the extent of isolation (Kutner et al. 1956; Townsend 1957); it stems, rather, from a gap between desired and actual interaction. The intensity of loneliness experienced by the aged individual is a reaction to a discrepancy between his past and present patterns of association.

Leisure

The majority of aging people spend at least part of their day doing nothing whatsoever, and the amount of time spent in semisomnolent idleness increases with age (Beyer & Woods 1963). The problem is not so much the increase of the quantity of unobligated time as the shift in its function and significance. During adulthood leisure is delimited and patterned to a large extent by work; once the rhythm of work and leisure is upset, free time is often experienced as unstructured.

After retirement, activities that were fully absorbing and gratifying throughout adulthood often lose much of their meaning. Solitary hobbies, for instance, may provide a much needed respite from the hectic interaction during working hours, but the same hobbies do not necessarily facilitate adjustment to retirement and may even have a confining or isolating effect. Similarly, leisure-time activities that are part of a full-fledged family life may lose much of their attraction after the onset of aging, when the children have homes of their own. There is also the problem of the synchronization of leisure; the retired are free at times when most other members of the community are occupied, and this may increase aging people's feelings of alienation from the community.

Development of variegated leisure-time interests during adulthood facilitates the shift of dominant emphasis from work to free time (Havighurst 1954). Usually, however, these preaging patterns cannot be carried over into old age without a reassessment and at least some restructuring. During the early phases of aging there is an increase in recreational activities outside the home—activities such as visiting, traveling, fishing, and gardening. During the later phases recreation becomes increasingly centered on and confined to the home. Card games, handicrafts, reading, and above all television watching become the main preoccupations. A small but significant minority emphasize creativity and culture (Riesman 1954). But the majority of aging people cling to their preaging patterns (Dumazedier & Ribert 1963); there is some restructuring and change of pace, but little experimentation with new pursuits. It should be noted, however, that a certain proportion of aging people manage to develop new interests and to branch out into new spheres of activity (Riesman 1954). In such cases there is a redirection of involvement and a discovery of hitherto untapped personal abilities. A central characteristic of many of the activities that serve as focuses of re-engagement is that in one way or another they constitute a bridge between work and recreation. These pursuits are taken on voluntarily and felt to be genuine expressions of self, yet they require self-imposed obligations and self-discipline. Thus, re-engagement involves cumulative gains in understanding, knowledge, or proficiency which counterbalance the sense of over-all decline.

Major issues in the study of aging

The sociological study of aging centers on two major issues: the competition between the "engagement" and "disengagement" theories of aging and the controversy between the adherents of "community integration" and those of "age-group segregation."

Engagement–disengagement. The study of aging was dominated for a long time by a theory of engagement (see, for example, Cavan et al. 1949), which assumed that old age does not differ much from middle age. It asserted that most aging people resent the role loss imposed on them by society and resist the shrinkage of their social world. According to this view, the best way to avoid the adverse effects of aging is to continue to maintain the level of activities and the associates of middle age as long as possible and to find suitable substitutes when forced to relinquish preaging patterns. The keys to optimal aging are activity, outgoingness, and involvement.

The theory of disengagement, developed recently by Cumming and Henry (1961), discards the view of old age as an extension of middle age. Aging leads to a triple withdrawal from society: a loss of roles, a contraction of relationships, and a decline in commitment to norms and values. Thus the aging person becomes increasingly egotistical—relaxation, comfort, and self-gratification are his main preoccupations. Cumming and Henry argue that disengagement is an intrinsic developmental process inherent in aging as such and not just a result of external social pressures. Withdrawal is seen as functional for the individual as well as for society, in that it prepares the aging person for his approaching final withdrawal and minimizes the effect of his death on the social system.

These two theories of aging are based on competing ideologies, and the transition from one to the other reflects the value reorientation occurring in affluent industrial societies. The engagement theory expresses the high evaluation of active mastery of external reality, whereas the disengagement theory reflects the emergent emphasis on release and gratification. A critical examination of the data leads to the conclusion that both theories are inadequate and require modification (Rose 1964).

Our analysis of the process of aging indicates that there is a considerable difference between the first and the last stages of aging. The onset of aging is often accompanied by an upsurge of activity and involvement, whereas the downward trend dominates during the later stages. Also, as has been noted above, there are considerable differences in the reaction to aging in different spheres of participation. Aging is, in many cases, a restructuring of roles and relationships and a change in their relative significance, rather than mere decline.

Identification with values is partly independent of participation and may persist in spite of the decline in activity and interaction. There is some evidence that aged people are less pious, less conformist, and less concerned about moral issues and about matters of principle (Cumming & Henry 1961). However, there is considerable evidence that the aging identify with the central values of their society and do not differ much from other age groups as far as their conceptions of the good life are concerned (Rosow 1963). We find little to substantiate the contention that old people abandon the interests and causes that occupied the center of their life in order to become late-day hedonists. It seems that lifelong commitments can persist in spite of the weakening of institutional supports and controls, and there are some indications that the growing distance from everyday affairs may enhance rather than undermine the concern with ultimate values (Talmon 1963).

We turn now to the concept of *optimal aging*. Although not all old people fit the mold of "good adjustment" recommended by the engagement theory, it is true that the large majority of studies report a very strong correlation between engagement and morale. Furthermore, this correlation does not decline with age. Successful aging seems to depend to a large extent on a flexible combination of disengagement and engagement; adjustment is easiest when the aging person accepts the withdrawal from his central roles and reorients himself to other spheres.

The theories of engagement and disengagement have evolved out of research in industrialized countries, yet they purport to have universal application. The limitations of both theories become even more apparent if we try to apply them to primitive or traditional societies. The withdrawal and alienation of the aging in modern society are a reaction to the strains inherent in its structure and value orientations, and thus they cannot be assumed to be intrinsic to old age as such. The disengagement theory admits that the process of aging takes different forms in different societies and in different subgroups in any given society, but it has not spelled out the structural and ideological determinants that affect this process in a systematic way. There is great need for a wide-ranging and rigorous comparative analysis.

Integration–segregation. Classification of living arrangements of old people from the point of view of their opportunity for contact with members of other age groups and with each other yields a continuum ranging between maximal residential integration to maximal residential segregation. Scrutiny of the literature reveals that there is a fairly widespread rejection of the two extreme solutions: three-generation households are regarded as incompatible with the values and structure of the modern family, while there is growing opposition to closed and isolated homes for the aged.

However, we find controversy with regard to the intermediate patterns. Two seemingly opposed viewpoints have emerged in this sphere. Upholders of the age-heterogeneous pattern continue to put the main emphasis on intergenerational community integration (Mumford 1956; Townsend 1957). They hold that intergenerational relationships with kin are the main axis of the social integration of the aged. Living on their own in a "mixed" neighborhood in which they are long-term residents, with children or other close kin within easy reach, is considered to be the optimal solution.

Advocates of this view can cite a recent survey of old-age institutions in Britain (Townsend 1962), which has revealed that the majority of residents deplored their transfer to an old-age home and that it had an adverse effect on their morale. Furthermore, more than half of the residents were able to take care of themselves with either no assistance or very little; an additional fifth could live on their own if they were provided with considerable aid. The results of this survey have led to a demand to abolish all old-age institutions and to transfer the care of the aged to the community, where they can maintain partial independence with the help of community and domiciliary services.

Advocates of semi-segregated residential settings (Rosow 1961) hold that relationships with age peers are the major axis of social integration of the aged. They point out that the semi-integrated pattern works only in cases in which the aging person is a long-term resident in a relatively homogeneous and stable neighborhood and as long as his network of informal relations is localized and fairly intact. A partly segregated age-homogeneous setting maximizes opportunities for contacts with peers and protects the aged from invidious evaluation yet at the same time does not cut them off from outside contacts. Research on different types of semi-segregated settings reveals extensive social participation and intensive use of the variegated facilities provided by the management (Kleemeier 1954; Hoyt 1954).

Those recommending semi-segregated arrangements have also pointed to certain practical difficulties involved in the anti-institutional position. Given the shortage of personnel and equipment, institutionalization of a certain proportion of relatively isolated or severely disabled aged seems imperative (Fiske 1964). Furthermore, comparative analysis of different types of institutions for the aged indicates that homes that are not isolated from the community and allow their residents as much privacy and independence as possible neither cut them off from outside contacts nor produce the other adverse effects of isolated and highly bureaucratic institutions. It seems clear that aging people placed in different economic and social circumstances and at different stages of the aging process may require different solutions. There is also the need to take account of variations in temperament and value orientations. The intermediate patterns that combine contact and segregation, dependence and independence, are complementary rather than alternative solutions.

YONINA TALMON

[*See also* FAMILY; LABOR FORCE, *article on* PARTICIPATION; LEISURE; PENSION FUNDS; PLANNING, SOCIAL, *article on* WELFARE PLANNING.]

BIBLIOGRAPHY

ALBRECHT, RUTH 1962 The Role of Older People in Family Rituals. Pages 486–491 in Clark Tibbitts and Wilma Donahue (editors), *Social and Psychological Aspects of Aging.* New York: Columbia Univ. Press.

ALDRIDGE, GORDON 1959 Informal Social Relationships in a Retirement Community. *Marriage and Family Living* 21:70–72.

APPLE, DORRIAN 1956 The Social Structure of Grandparenthood. *American Anthropologist* New Series 58: 656–663.

BARRON, MILTON 1953 *The Aging American.* New York: Crowell.

BEYER, GLENN H.; and WOODS, M. E. 1963 *Living and Activity Patterns of the Aged.* Ithaca, N.Y.: Cornell Univ. Press.

BLAU, ZENA 1956 Changes in Status and Age Identification. *American Sociological Review* 21:198–203.

BLAU, ZENA 1961 Structural Constraints on Friendships in Old Age. *American Sociological Review* 26:429–439.

BLOOD, ROBERT O.; and WOLFE, DONALD M. 1960 *Husbands and Wives.* Glencoe, Ill.: Free Press.

BOTT, ELIZABETH 1957 *Family and Social Network: Roles, Norms and External Relationships in Ordinary Urban Families.* London: Tavistock.

BURGESS, ERNEST W. (editor) 1961 *Retirement Villages.* Ann Arbor: Univ. of Michigan, Division of Gerontology.

CAVAN, RUTH S. et al. 1949 *Personal Adjustment in Old Age.* Chicago: Science Research Associates.

CLARK, F. LE GROS; and DUNNE, AGNES C. 1956 *Aging in Industry: An Inquiry Based on Figures Derived From Census Reports Into the Problem of Aging Under the Conditions of Modern Industry.* New York: Philosophical Library.

CUMMING, ELAINE; and HENRY, WILLIAM 1961 *Growing Old: The Process of Disengagement.* New York: Basic Books.

CUMMING, ELAINE; and SCHNEIDER, D. M. 1961 Sibling Solidarity: A Property of American Kinship. *American Anthropologist* New Series 63:498–507.

DINKEL, ROBERT M. 1944 Attitudes of Children Toward Supporting Aged Parents. *American Sociological Review* 9:370–379.

DONAHUE, WILMA (editor) 1955 *Earning Opportunities for Older Workers.* Ann Arbor: Univ. of Michigan Press.

DONAHUE, WILMA; ORBACH, HAROLD; and POLLACK, OTTO 1960 Retirement: The Emerging Social Pattern. Pages 330–406 in Clark Tibbitts (editor), *Handbook of Social Gerontology.* Univ. of Chicago Press.

DUMAZEDIER, JOFFRE; and RIBERT, ALINE 1963 Retirement and Leisure. *International Social Science Journal* 15:438–447.

EISENSTADT, SHMUEL N. 1956 *From Generation to Generation: Age Groups and Social Structure.* Glencoe, Ill.: Free Press.

FISKE, MARJORIE 1964 *Lives in Distress: The Paths of the Elderly to the Psychiatric Ward.* New York: Basic Books.

FORTES, MEYER 1949 *The Web of Kinship Among the Tallensi: The Second Part of an Analysis of the Social Structure of a Trans-Volta Tribe.* Oxford Univ. Press.

GLICK, PAUL C. 1957 *American Families.* New York: Wiley.

HAVIGHURST, ROBERT J. 1954 Flexibility and the Social Roles of the Retired. *American Journal of Sociology* 59:309–311.

HAVIGHURST, ROBERT J. 1957 The Leisure Activities of the Middle Aged. *American Journal of Sociology* 63: 152–162.

HOYT, G. C. 1954 The Life of the Retired in a Trailer Park. *American Journal of Sociology* 59:361–370.

JEFFERS, FRANCES C.; NICHOLS, CLAUDE R.; and EISDORFER, CARL 1962 Attitudes of Older Persons Toward Death: A Preliminary Study. Pages 709–715 in Clark Tibbitts and Wilma Donahue (editors), *Social and Psychological Aspects of Aging.* New York: Columbia Univ. Press.

KLEEMEIER, ROBERT W. 1954 Moosehaven: Congregate Living in a Community of the Retired. *American Journal of Sociology* 59:347–351.

KREPS, JUANITA (editor) 1963 *Employment, Income and Retirement Problems of the Aged.* Durham, N.C.: Duke Univ. Press.

KUTNER, BERNARD et al. 1956 *Five Hundred Over Sixty.* New York: Russell Sage Foundation.

MARRIS, PETER 1958 *Widows and Their Families.* London: Routledge.

MICHIGAN, UNIVERSITY OF, CONFERENCE ON AGING, *1962* 1963 *Aging and the Economy.* Edited by Harold L. Orbach and Clark Tibbitts. Ann Arbor: Univ. of Michigan Press.

MUMFORD, LEWIS 1956 For Older People—Not Segregation, but Integration. *Architectural Record* 119:191–194.

NEUGARTEN, B. L.; and PETERSON, W. A. 1957 A Study of the American Age Grade System. Volume 3, pages 497–502 in International Association of Gerontology, Congress, Fourth, Merano, Italy, 1957, *Proceedings.* Florence (Italy): Mattioli.

NEUGARTEN, B. L.; and WEINSTEIN, K. K. 1964 The Changing American Grandparent. *Marriage and Family Living* 26:199–204.

NIMKOFF, M. F. 1962 Changing Family Relationships of Older People in the United States During the Last Fifty Years. Pages 405–414 in Clark Tibbitts and Wilma Donahue (editors), *Social and Psychological Aspects of Aging.* New York: Columbia Univ. Press.

PARSONS, TALCOTT 1960 Towards a Healthy Maturity. *Journal of Health and Human Behavior* 1:163–173.

PINNER, FRANK A.; JACOBS, PAUL; and SELZNICK, PHILIP 1959 *Old Age and Political Behavior.* Berkeley: Univ. of California Press.

REISS, PAUL J. 1962 The Extended Kinship System: Correlates of, and Attitudes on Frequency of Interaction. *Marriage and Family Living* 24:333–339.

RIESMAN, DAVID 1954 Some Clinical and Cultural Aspects of Aging. *American Journal of Sociology* 59:379–383.

ROBINS, ARTHUR J. 1962 Family Relations of the Aging in Three-generations Households. Pages 464–474 in Clark Tibbitts and Wilma Donahue (editors), *Social and Psychological Aspects of Aging.* New York: Columbia Univ. Press.

ROSE, ARNOLD M. 1962 The Subculture of the Aging. *Gerontologist* 2:123–127.

ROSE, ARNOLD M. 1964 A Current Theoretical Issue in Social Gerontology. *Gerontologist* 4:46–50.

ROSENMAYR, LEOPOLD; and KÖCKIES, EVA 1963 *Umwelt und Familie alter Menschen.* Berlin: Luchterhand.

ROSOW, IRVING 1961 Retirement Housing and Social Integration. *Gerontologist* 1:85–91.

ROSOW, IRVING 1963 Adjustments of the Normal Aged: Concept and Measurement. Volume 2, pages 195–223 in Richard Williams, Clark Tibbitts, and Wilma Donahue (editors), *Processes of Aging: Social and Psychological Perspectives.* New York: Atherton.

SAUVY, ALFRED 1963 Demographic Aging. *International Social Science Journal* 15:355–365.

SCHELSKY, HELMUT 1953 *Wandlungen der deutschen Familie in der Gegenwart.* Stuttgart (Germany): Enke.

SCHNEIDER, BETTY V. H. 1962 *The Older Worker.* Berkeley: Univ. of California, Institute of Industrial Relations.

SCHORR, ALVIN 1960 *Filial Responsibility in the Modern American Family.* Washington: U.S. Department of Health, Education and Welfare, Social Security Administration, Division of Program Research.

SHANAS, ETHEL 1961 *Family Relationships of Older People.* New York: Health Information Foundation.

SHANAS, ETHEL 1962 *The Health of Older People: A Social Survey.* Cambridge, Mass.: Harvard Univ. Press.

STREIB, GORDON F. 1958 Family Patterns in Retirement. *Journal of Social Issues* 14, no. 2:46–60.

SYMPOSIUM ON THE FAMILY, INTERGENERATIONAL RELATIONS AND SOCIAL STRUCTURE, DUKE UNIVERSITY, *1963* 1965 *Social Structure and the Family: Generational Relations.* Edited by Ethel Shanas and Gordon F. Streib. Englewood Cliffs, N.J.: Prentice-Hall.

TALMON, YONINA 1961 Aging in Israel, a Planned Society. *American Journal of Sociology* 67:284–295.

TALMON, YONINA 1963 Dimensions of Disengagement. Unpublished manuscript.

TARTLER, RUDOLF 1961 *Das Alter in der modernen Gesellschaft.* Stuttgart (Germany): Enke.

TOWNSEND, PETER 1957 *The Family Life of Old People.* London: Routledge; Glencoe, Ill.: Free Press.

TOWNSEND, PETER 1962 *The Last Refuge.* London: Routledge.

TUCKMAN, JACOB; and LORGE, IRVING 1953 Attitudes Toward Old People. *Journal of Social Psychology* 37:249–260.

WILENSKY, HAROLD L. 1960 Work, Careers, and Social Integration. *International Social Science Journal* 12:543–560.

WILENSKY, HAROLD L. 1961a The Uneven Distribution of Leisure: The Impact of Economic Growth on "Free Time." *Social Problems* 9:32–56.

WILENSKY, HAROLD L. 1961b Life Cycle, Work Situation, and Participation in Formal Associations. Pages 213–242 in Robert W. Kleemeier (editor), *Aging and Leisure.* New York: Oxford Univ. Press.

WINCH, ROBERT F. (1952) 1963 *The Modern Family.* Rev. ed. New York: Holt.

YOUNG, MICHAEL; and GEERTZ, HILDRED 1961 Old Age in London and San Francisco: Some Families Compared. *British Journal of Sociology* 12:124–141.

YOUNG, MICHAEL; and WILLMOTT, PETER 1957 *Family and Kinship in East London.* London: Routledge; Glencoe, Ill.: Free Press.

III

ECONOMIC ASPECTS

Since the end of World War II, mortality rates in Asia, Africa, and Latin America have begun to warrant the expectation of long life for the people of those areas, a hope realized by a growing number of Europeans and Americans for more than half a century. But the twentieth century has not yet contrived economic circumstances that will furnish the majority of those who reach old age the means to solve its accompanying problems. To be sure, money alone does not assure independence, self-esteem, and good health. It is a facilitating condition, however; and the overriding economic fact about the aged—those age 65 and over —is that most of them are still living on considerably less than an adequate income. According to United States census figures for 1960, aged persons living alone had a median yearly income of $1,055. For two-person families it was $2,530. Included in the 16.5 million aged were over thirty thousand persons who that year reported a taxable income of $50,000 or more, and over two million men and women who had no money income at all.

While these people, and those in like circumstances in other urbanized countries, are often counted as victims of industrialism, the adverse economic consequences of aging were suffered by individuals long before the age of industrialism, and the emergence of the aged poor as a pressing social problem is more accurately described as a function of modern urban life (Gordon 1960, pp. 208–209). Its prime ingredients are (1) an increased proportion of older people whose salable skills are being outstripped by changing technology and (2) conditions of urban life that undermine the family as a source of economic security. Its frequent result is poverty among the aged who, since the beginning of this century, constitute a growing portion of the population.

If current income figures identify poverty in old age as a persistent problem, a comparison with income figures of earlier decades reveals that, on the whole, the livelihood of the aged is improving and that it is increasingly dependent upon sources other than current earnings. In 1950, approximately twelve million older Americans shared a $15,000 million income, half of which came from their earnings. By 1961, the seventeen million aged received $35,000 million; but of this total, less than one-third came from earnings.

The fact that older Americans are better off despite declining earnings is accounted for by the growth of public and private payments on which the livelihood of the aged must increasingly depend. The decreasing importance of earnings reflects a decline in the percentage of older men in the labor force—an increasingly important aspect of the age–income cycle.

The age–income cycle.   The impact on earnings of those influences associated with age was first observed in English data near the turn of the century. Income tended, on the average, to rise in the early years, reach a peak in middle life, and then decline. Other studies, both in Europe and in the United States, using similar cross-sectional data, have confirmed the existence of this life cycle relationship between age and income.

It must be emphasized that these figures tell us only the relationship of income to age at a particular moment of time. They reflect the fact that older workers tend to have less education than younger workers; that there is downward occupational mobility and declining labor force participation; and that there is an increase in illness, in the amount of part-time work, and in the incidence of unemployment.

In his pioneering analysis of the age–income cycle, Woytinski (1943) cautioned against use of age–income data alone in predicting future family needs, since his analysis showed that over the long run the economic cycle in the life of an individual is overshadowed by secular variations in his earnings. Indeed, within its stable, approximately bell-shaped profile, the age–income curve shifts in response to changes in employment requirements, perquisites, and patterns. United States census data for the two decades after World War II show that the income peak for men, although still in the age 35–44 range, has moved to a slightly younger age. The long-run trend of income is up, but it is noteworthy that the margin of increase in the middle years is greater than at retirement. Increasing labor force participation by women is steadily transforming their age–income curve to a male variety.

Age–income data reveal, therefore, that, relative to income of persons in mid-working life, income of those at retirement age is low. With an income of $2,530, the average older couple in 1960 had less than one-half the average income of younger couples and about three-fourths the money that the Bureau of Labor Statistics estimates is required for an older couple's "modest but adequate" budget. Even so, the average couple is better off than older people who live alone. Their average yearly income was $1,055. Single women constitute the largest single class of aged economic units—about 43 per cent. There are almost as many aged widows as there are married men age 65 and over, but very few of these women are in the labor force. In 1961 their average yearly income was $960.

The aged represent about 10 per cent of the entire United States population and include people of widely varying economic circumstances. When these are all considered, however, it is not surprising that the U.S. President's Council on Aging, in its first annual report, concluded: "No matter what standards might be used to judge the adequacy of income of today's older people, one point is clear: their incomes are usually inadequate for even a modest level of living" (1963, p. 7).

The cost of providing for old age.   Some of the expenses of older people—such as the costs connected with working, educating children, and housing—are lower than those of younger people. But basic expenses continue, and some are increased, particularly medical expenses.

Older people in good health must spend more to retain it, and those in poor health face formidable, and steadily rising, expenses. Old age carries with it a high incidence of illness; in the United States the average medical expenses incurred by a person over 65 in 1961 were approximately 2.5 times greater than the medical expenses of a person under age 65. It is estimated that the ratio shortly will be 3 to 1.

Provision for old age is a difficult economic problem—and harder to solve than is generally realized. Consider a U.S. couple planning for retirement, who might prudently expect average monthly expenses to exceed retirement income by $125. Since to provide this $1,500 yearly sum from interest alone would require, at 3 per cent, a principal of $50,000 (at 4 per cent, it would require $37,500), most couples with investments will have to plan to spend both interest and principal.

In the United States, a man who retires at age 65 has a life expectancy of about 13 additional years. If his wife is the same age, mortality tables grant her 16 years. Assuming interest at 3 per cent, a joint-and-survivor annuity of $1,500 a year, payable as long as at least one spouse survives, would cost about $21,000. By reducing the annuity to $1,000 during the period only one spouse is alive, its cost is cut to approximately $18,000.

How realistic are these capital requirements? In 1961, the average aged U.S. couple had about $1,000 in liquid assets such as savings bonds or money in the bank; life insurance with a total face value of about $1,850; and those who owned a home had an equity of less than $10,000 (U.S. President's Council on Aging 1963, pp. 10–11). Those who lived alone had less. A 1957 survey of aged people drawing social security benefits revealed that of those who entered a general hospital that year, 40 per cent of the two-person families and 60 per cent of nonmarried people did not meet all their medical expenses from income, health insurance, and assets. The balance was paid by relatives, charity, or public assistance—until the depression the only methods, along with poorhouses, to help aged needy Americans.

Origin and evolution of social security. Although Germany had a fairly complete national insurance system by the close of the nineteenth century (compulsory old-age and invalidity insurance in 1889) and England introduced social insurance for the aged in 1925, the rise of these programs had little impact in the United States, where the efforts of energetic social reformers had made scant headway against the philosophy of individualism.

Soon after America became a nation, English, Elizabethan-type, poor laws were adopted, based on local responsibility, liability of relatives for support of indigent family members, and residence laws restricting eligibility for relief to residents of the locality. In the United States, before the twentieth century, government assistance to the aged consisted almost entirely of poorhouses. The power of

the states and their competition for business investments, the frontier and cheap land, and an enduring belief in individualism maintained this situation for a long period. Only seven states had passed old-age assistance laws prior to the depression, and two of these had been declared unconstitutional. And these old-age pension laws were merely liberalizations of the poor laws, with similar standards of eligibility.

In June 1934, when President Roosevelt appointed the Committee on Economic Security to study and recommend legislation that would promote economic security for the individual, the poverty and suffering of the depression were overwhelming relief programs for the poor. These conditions acquainted millions with the indignities of these programs and created a deep determination to eliminate this approach entirely. This committee, together with three other bodies established by the president's executive order, on January 15, 1935, completed an exhaustive study of foreign experience with, and the need for, social assurance and assistance. Two days later President Roosevelt transmitted the report of the Committee on Economic Security to the Congress, with a special plea for fast action.

Faced with the reality and implications of vast human suffering and enormous relief costs, the U.S. Congress, in seven months of heated hearings and debate, reconciled the philosophy of individualism with the facts of economic interdependence. President Roosevelt signed the Social Security Act on August 14, 1935, and the United States became the 21st nation to enact an old-age insurance program. Today the right to social security is a recognized aspiration throughout the world.

United States legislation. In its original form, the Social Security Act established a federally administered compulsory old-age insurance program and provided (1) federal financial participation in state old-age assistance programs and (2) a supplementary program designed primarily for those who would be ineligible for old-age insurance. In addition, the act provided for a state-operated system of unemployment insurance (actually, inducements to states to enact unemployment insurance legislation) and offered grants to states in six major fields to enable them to make more nearly adequate provision for needy dependent children, crippled children, maternal and child welfare, aid to the blind, public health activities, and vocational rehabilitation programs. The income security titles of the act authorized the federal government to participate financially in individually enacted state measures.

When President Roosevelt signed the act, he

called it the "cornerstone in a structure which is being built but is by no means complete." Since the original act was passed, major amendments affecting the aged have greatly broadened coverage and extended types of benefit protection, raised the dollar amount of benefits, and liberalized eligibility qualifications and the retirement test. By 1965 the program approached almost universal coverage. Virtually all types of employment were covered by social security (90 per cent of employed workers) or by some other public retirement program (including those for railroad workers, government employees, and veterans). About 83 per cent of aged Americans were drawing benefits or would be eligible for them on retirement. Since the act was passed, the types of protection have been expanded from the original limited old-age coverage (OAI) to include survivorship and disability protection (OASDI) and hospital and medical benefits (Medicare). Benefit increases since 1935 have kept pace with rising living costs, although not with the rising productivity of the economy and the consequent rising standard of living of the American worker. Also, the maximum wage and contribution base has not been raised sufficiently to keep abreast of the wage level, which has more than tripled since 1935.

World-wide programs. A study of the principal provisions of social security programs in all countries of the world (U.S. Social Security Administration 1964) reveals that 112 nations have at least one branch of social security and 78 nations have old-age, invalidity, and survivor programs. Included are all the European and North American countries. Of the 11 Middle Eastern countries, 8 have such programs, as do 15 of the 21 Central and South American countries; 10 of the 19 countries of Asia and Oceania; and 15 of the 36 African countries. In a number of countries, programs cover only small segments of the population and sometimes list benefits that are planned but not yet paid.

Canada, Denmark, Finland, Iceland, New Zealand, Norway, and Sweden now provide their aged with universal pensions, with payments available to every resident past a specified age without regard to qualifying conditions, past contributions, or employment. Australia, Saudi Arabia, South Africa, Trinidad, and Tobago potentially provide pensions to any aged resident but require a means test.

Principles of social insurance. Most of the programs providing protection to the aged are based on principles of social insurance as distinguished from the other two methods of providing "social security"—social assistance and direct public serv-

ices (poorhouses, etc.). Thanks in some part to the eloquent strictures of Lord Beveridge on "the nasty, dirty means test," more than three-fourths of the countries rely on social insurance concepts, whose unifying characteristics are (1) compulsory coverage, with qualifying conditions prescribed by statute; (2) benefits paid as a matter of right and linked to contributions or to coverage under the program; (3) benefit amounts often, but not always, related to prior earnings and rarely dependent upon means or needs of the recipient, as is the case with social assistance; and (4) financing entirely, or in large part, from social insurance contributions paid into a special fund by employers, employees, and sometimes by government.

Some of the countries with social insurance systems supplement them with assistance payments to the needy aged, invalids, or survivors. Such programs are found in Austria, Czechoslovakia, France, West Germany, Ireland, the Netherlands, the United Kingdom, and the United States.

Of the 65 countries whose statutory old-age benefit or pension systems cover significant segments of the population, all but 18 include statutory protection against medical care costs, either through general sickness insurance or through health service programs. Almost thirty years to the day after its inception, the social security system in the United States in 1965 finally joined these more advanced systems by adding Medicare benefits.

Social insurance has become the important approach to the economic problems of old age. Within the broad, general principles summarized above, its application depends upon statutory provisions, myriad regulations, and administrative rulings whose complexity defies the grasp of all but those who make it the subject of specialized study.

In broad outline, however, the issues and economic problems are similar in most countries, and these may be best illustrated by examining in somewhat more detail the principles underlying a single system, in this case that of the United States.

Four of the important principles underlying the OASDI program may be summarized as follows:

(1) *The right to benefits is based on presumptive need.* A key element in the theory of social insurance is that benefits are paid not as a matter of grace, but as a matter of right for social risks defined by law. Under the U.S. system, the need is economic adversity in old age, not old age itself. Thus, benefits are not automatically paid upon attainment of a specified age, but only upon actual retirement. By the same benefit theory, surviving widows are eligible for payments only as long as they do not remarry or are not substantially em-

ployed, and the eligible disabled receive payments because they are unable to do substantial, gainful work. (In the case of Medicare benefits, the need is ill health, and benefits are paid upon the attainment of the required age, whether individuals are retired or not.) A majority of social insurance systems have a similar approach to presumed need, but in a number of countries (among them, France, West Germany, and Switzerland) retirement is not a precedent condition for benefit payments. Within the age range 50–70, 60 and 65 are the most typical ages at which retirement benefits are first payable. Because life expectancy generally is shorter in tropical latitudes, age requirements tend to be lower in these areas.

(2) *Benefit amounts should establish a basic floor of protection.* Along with the definition of presumed need, the concept of a minimum floor of protection is designed to encourage saving and, when combined with private pensions and other assets, to provide a reasonably comfortable level of retirement. Approximately 40 per cent of the labor force is covered by both social security and supplementary retirement pensions; but since most private plans are not portable, it is difficult to predict how many persons will actually secure private pensions upon retirement, and of what magnitude.

Given the continuing and rapid growth of private retirement plans and life insurance, this benefit theory, which requires savings and private supplements for adequate retirement income, may become reality in the future for almost all beneficiaries. Its failure to do so at present means that 12.5 per cent of aged persons must still rely on social assistance payments for their livelihood and brings continuing criticism that the benefit floor is too low.

This criticism applies with equal, or greater, force to most other countries. Provisions for automatic adjustments related to the trend of wages or the cost-of-living index have been adopted in a small number of nations, among them Belgium, Denmark, Israel, West Germany, and Sweden. These are satisfactory, however, only where the basic benefit is adequate.

(3) *Benefits are financed entirely by contributions from workers and employers.* Most nations finance social insurance protection for their aged under a tripartite system of contributions from insured persons, employers, and government. A few countries, including the United States, have no direct government contributions for social insurance benefits except for social assistance to the needy aged. When tripartite financing is proposed for the United States, it is resisted by critics on the ground that the system should be kept self-supporting and by others who fear that government participation might slow down the rate of benefit increases. Experience under the German system, however, contradicts this latter contention.

A much larger and changed role for government is proposed by those critics who contend that the present financing system is unsound and that the entire system should be financed on a current basis by annual government appropriation or made subject to the financial requirements of private insurance. Although the former proposal, which has several times been urged on the Congress, has made no headway, its major premise—that the present system of financing is unsound—continues to be a subject of popular writing and discussion. The issue arises because the goals of social adequacy and individual equity conflict. The former requires reasonable benefit levels; the latter requires benefits that are actuarially equivalent to contributions. Since the social security system requires contributions from potential beneficiaries who may not collect benefits and seeks to afford reasonable benefit levels on a current basis to many who have been covered only a few years, it must compromise between these two goals. It is estimated that in the early 1960s the proportion of current benefits "bought" by the contributions of the workers involved was about 5 per cent (Myers 1961, p. 3). Benefits and administrative expenses are paid from current contributions plus interest earned by the fund representing past contributions that exceed payments. This is as planned, for financing by private insurance principles would defeat the goal of social adequacy, and in any case is not necessary for public programs with nearly universal coverage and implicit federal backing—should such backing be required. The system is not intended to have a fully funded reserve, but it is nonetheless fully self-supporting and fiscally forthright.

(4) *Benefits are related to prior earnings.* A basic decision faced by any country establishing a social insurance system is whether the benefits paid should be related to prior earnings or whether all beneficiaries should receive an identical benefit.

The social security system in the United States adopted the earnings-related benefit from the beginning, despite the administrative difficulties and costs it involves, on the assumption that a relationship between contributions and benefits would be more acceptable to Americans. Although a flat-rate benefit would no doubt improve the relative position of low-income groups, the benefit formula adopted by the Social Security Act was not a simple earnings–benefit ratio but was weighted to result in a relatively larger benefit for those with low earnings than for those with high earnings. Thus, although the benefit increases as the average monthly wage increases, the *ratio* of benefits to average monthly wage decreases as the wage increases, so that the lower paid workers get more out of the system in relation to what they paid in than do the higher paid workers.

Until 1959, the British system relied entirely upon a flat-rate benefit, paid to all adult claimants (except widowed mothers). This system was criticized as being outdated and resulting in "fair shares in poverty." In 1959, a limited wage-related benefit system was inaugurated, but there is still serious concern over its adequacy (Burns 1963, pp. 20–23).

Adequacy, the immediate issue.   In its first annual report, the U.S. Social Security Board acknowledged that: "An attempt to find security for a people is among the oldest of political obligations and the greatest task of the state." The legitimacy of this search is no longer seriously challenged; the immediate problem is how to attain adequate security, how to ensure that the steadily increasing number of old people are not left behind but will share the social and economic progress of the community. At the end of World War II, an expansion in employment opportunities was often proposed as a partial solution to the economic problems of the aged. Ideally, an older worker would have the choice between employment and adequate retirement benefits. But by the 1960s, the aged found it increasingly difficult to compete for jobs; and as their range of choice became more and more limited, their demand for more adequate income maintenance programs was intensified.

If adequacy depended solely upon the economic capacity of society to provide greater economic support for the aged, social insurance systems of most nations could protect them from want. But how much a nation is willing to spend is a political as well as an economic matter; and the compromise is often struck below what is economically possible.

Private pension plans.   In some countries the tendency to enlarge social security benefits and contributions seems to be reducing the influence of private pension plans. In the United States, however, dissatisfaction with the benefit floor has spurred a strong labor movement to bargain for private pension plans, which are growing rapidly and promise to provide for a large segment of the population a comfortable "second story" to the "floor" of protection offered by social security. But those not employed by large corporations or protected by collective bargaining are in danger of being relegated to a second-class category, justified neither by logic nor equity.

Moreover, the pension funds behind these private programs, like the funds some nations have amassed under social insurance, are becoming a major source of new capital, whose economic implications and potential power are, as yet, only dimly perceived.

The future course.   In the near future, social security programs throughout the world may be expected to follow a predictable course providing income and services to ease the encumbering costs of old age. Evidence of a significant shift away from this cash indemnity approach can be found in some social security programs that are slowly adopting the view that cash benefits are part of a broad national program of investment in human resources (Gordon 1963*a*, p. 35). With training, retraining, and rehabilitation at its core, this approach does more than pay benefits to help prop up the failing economic status of the aged; it seeks to restore individuals to a fuller economic and social life. This development, together with the growing interest in preventive approaches to the economic problems of aging—health education, medical care, training, and planned retirement— hold for the aged the promise, not of a new life, but of continued enjoyment of the old.

EARL F. CHEIT

[*See also* LABOR FORCE, *article on* PARTICIPATION; MEDICAL CARE; PENSION FUNDS.]

BIBLIOGRAPHY

BURNS, EVELINE M. 1956   *Social Security and Public Policy.* New York: McGraw-Hill.

BURNS, EVELINE M. 1963   Social Security in Britain: Twenty Years After Beveridge. *Industrial Relations* 2, no. 2:15–32.

GORDON, MARGARET S. 1960   Aging and Income Security. Pages 208–260 in Clark Tibbitts (editor), *Handbook of Social Gerontology: Societal Aspects of Aging.* Univ. of Chicago Press. → A lucid economic analysis, well documented. An excellent reference source for basic data in the field.

GORDON, MARGARET S. 1963*a*   *The Economics of Welfare Policies.* New York: Columbia Univ. Press.

GORDON, MARGARET S. 1963*b*   U.S. Welfare Policies in Perspective. *Industrial Relations* 2, no. 2:33–61.

GREAT BRITAIN, INTER-DEPARTMENTAL COMMITTEE ON SOCIAL INSURANCE AND ALLIED SERVICES 1942   *Social Insurance and Allied Services.* Papers by Command, Cmd. 6404. London: H.M. Stationery Office; New York: Macmillan. → Known as the Beveridge Report.

HABER, WILLIAM; and COHEN, WILBUR J. (editors) 1960   *Social Security: Programs, Problems and Policies; Selected Readings.* Homewood, Ill.: Irwin.

MICHIGAN, UNIVERSITY OF, CONFERENCE ON AGING, *1962*

1963 *Aging and the Economy.* Ann Arbor: Univ. of Michigan Press.

MYERS, ROBERT J. 1961 Social Security: The Years Ahead. Pages 1–9 in California, University of, Chancellor's Committee on the 25th Anniversary of the Social Security Act, *Social Security in the United States: Four Lectures.* Berkeley: Univ. of California, Institute of Industrial Relations. → An easy-to-read analysis, by the actuary of the U.S. system, of the basic financing principles of the social security program.

SCHOTTLAND, CHARLES I. 1963 *The Social Security Program in the United States.* New York: Appleton. → A readable account of the U.S. social security program.

Social Security Bulletin. → This monthly publication of the U.S. Social Security Administration presents current research, operating statistics, and a current listing of recent publications in the field. Published since 1938.

STEINER, PETER O.; and DORFMAN, ROBERT 1957 *The Economic Status of the Aged.* A publication of the Institute of Industrial Relations. Berkeley: Univ. of California Press.

TURNBULL, JOHN G.; WILLIAMS, C. ARTHUR, JR.; and CHEIT, EARL F. (1957) 1962 *Economic and Social Security.* 2d ed. New York: Ronald.

U.S. PRESIDENT'S COUNCIL ON AGING 1963 *Report [First].* Washington: Government Printing Office. → A good popular summary of the current programs and research findings about the status of older Americans.

U.S. SOCIAL SECURITY ADMINISTRATION 1960 *Basic Readings in Social Security: 25th Anniversary of the Social Security Act; 1935–1960.* Washington: Government Printing Office.

U.S. SOCIAL SECURITY ADMINISTRATION 1964 *Social Security Programs Throughout the World.* Washington: Government Printing Office.

WOYTINSKI, WLADIMIR S. 1943 *Earnings and Social Security in the United States.* Washington: Social Science Research Council, Committee on Social Security. → See especially "Wages by Age of Workers," pages 124–133.

AGRARIAN MOVEMENTS

See AGRICULTURE; CHINESE SOCIETY; LAND; MIDDLE AMERICAN SOCIETY; PEASANTRY; SOCIAL MOVEMENTS.

AGRICULTURE

In addition to the articles listed below, agriculture is discussed in a number of other articles. DOMESTICATION *describes the early history. Other aspects of the social structure of agriculturalists are discussed in* COMMUNITY, *article on* COMMUNITY DEVELOPMENT; MANORIAL ECONOMY; RURAL SOCIETY; *and* VILLAGE. *Other aspects of the economy of agriculture are discussed under* COMMUNISM, ECONOMIC ORGANIZATION OF; CREDIT; FAMINE; FOOD; LAND; LAND TENURE; *and* PLANTATIONS.

I
COMPARATIVE TECHNOLOGY

There are several ways of comparing the agricultural economy of one region with that of another. It can be done in terms of crop distributions, or relative productivity, or the effect on the rural landscape. The method used here will be a classification of agricultural practice in terms of the basic method or technology by which the farmer tackles the job of wresting crops from the earth.

Agricultural technology, as it functions in various natural settings, not only influences crop patterns, productivity, and the landscape, but also affects population density, possibilities for trade and urbanization, and social structure.

If we look around the world and attempt to plot on a map the varying techniques with which different societies face the fundamental tasks of cultivation, we are bound to be struck by the existence, over wide areas containing many millions of people, of relatively unsophisticated techniques that seem to be survivals from an age which the more sophisticated societies have left far behind. There are today but few regions where these unsophisticated techniques are entirely unaffected by new ideas that have spread with modern trade and commerce from those countries with early experience of agrarian revolution (as defined below). The degree of penetration by these new ideas varies widely, however, from place to place.

The agricultural systems of the world may be considered in terms of the following very broad categories, which may, as will be seen, be further subdivided (in some cases using criteria other than technology): (1) shifting cultivation; (2) simple sedentary cultivation with hand tools; (3) simple plow cultivation; (4) cultivation dominated by the effects of the agrarian revolution.

Shifting cultivation

Shifting cultivation is a system under which temporary clearings are made, usually but not invariably in forest country, and cultivated for a short period of years before being allowed to revert to natural vegetation while the cultivator moves on to a succession of new clearings. Typically, the period for which any one patch is in cultivation is a good deal shorter than the period for which it is allowed to lie fallow under naturally regenerating vegetation.

Shifting cultivation as just defined is the dominant agricultural system over wide areas of the earth's surface. Most of these areas are within the tropics, notably in the Amazon Basin and adjacent areas of South America, in most regions of intertropical Africa, in a number of remote jungle areas in India, in most of the less populated parts of both peninsular and insular southeast Asia, in the highland areas of Manchuria and Korea, and in aboriginal southwest China. This system of agriculture was formerly widespread in many parts of Europe, notably in northwest Spain and in the Black Forest and other forested highland regions of central Europe; survivals may still be encountered. Possibly something like 200 million people, occupying 14 million square miles, are engaged in shifting cultivation.

In addition to the impermanence of cultivation and to the system of "bush-fallow" already mentioned, many but not all systems of shifting cultivation also involve other characteristic traits, notably clearing by slashing and burning the forest or other vegetation (leaving stumps and often bigger trees), and cultivation by hoe, dibble, or digging stick but not by plow.

Perhaps because in western and central Europe shifting cultivation has receded in the face of more advanced techniques of cultivation, there has been a tendency to see it as a primitive method of land use that ought to be replaced or even forbidden. Foresters tend to be particularly hostile to it, because of its undeniably destructive effect on vegetation—shifting cultivators usually (although not always) prefer high forest to low jungle or scrub because under high forest conditions there tends to be a higher humus content and higher fertility. It should be noted, however, that foresters in a number of tropical countries have exploited a system first developed in Burma, the so-called *taungya* system, under which shifting cultivators are allowed to cultivate clearings on condition that when they abandon them they replant the forest in the form of teak. Hostility to shifting cultivation also springs from those who see it as a cause of soil erosion, particularly when it is practiced on steep slopes—as it is, for example, in Orissa (India) and in the hill tracts behind Chittagong (Pakistan). There can be no doubt that erosion *is* accelerated in such circumstances. It is worth noting, however, that some shifting cultivators deliberately choose slopes rather than flatter land because it

is the former that, under tropical conditions, tend to have the less mature (and therefore less leached and more fertile) soil. There can also be no doubt that shifting cultivation, notably in parts of Africa and Indonesia, has degraded the natural vegetation from forest to grassland.

In a broader sense, too, shifting cultivation may often be seen as an adaptation to tropical soil conditions under which continuous cultivation may be highly dangerous in the absence of advanced techniques for conserving soil and maintaining soil fertility; under such circumstances it may be preferable to cultivate for a year or two and to abandon the plot before too much damage is done to the soil (although in point of fact it is often the impossibility of controlling weeds with hand tools alone, rather than diminished fertility, that drives the cultivator off his plot). It is significant, in this connection, that European settlers in Brazil have, in some areas, taken to a form of shifting cultivation.

It is impossible in the present state of our knowledge to say of all systems of shifting cultivation whether they are in equilibrium with their environment or destructive of it; in many cases more research is needed. A clearer definition of the problem is required because of the wide range of practices, all subsumed in the term "shifting cultivation." Conklin (1961), for example, shows that "swiddens" (clearings made by shifting cultivators) may or may not be worked with hoes, may or may not be fenced, may be worked from temporary huts or permanent villages, and vary enormously in such features as methods of clearing and duration of fallow. (In this last connection it is important to emphasize that in many regions, notably in west Africa and parts of India and Ceylon, the pressure of population and the demands of cash cropping are such that the period of regeneration between successive periods of cultivation grows shorter and shorter, sometimes until it even disappears altogether. In the absence of techniques of manuring and soil conservation the result is usually the degradation of the soil.) Conklin goes on to point out the merits of "a combined ethnographical and ecological approach" to the study of shifting cultivation and the rarity with which this approach has hitherto been followed.

G. J. A. Terra (1958), writing on southeast Asia with special reference to Indonesia, demonstrates a wide variety of practice among shifting cultivators (who, however, have tended to become sedentary, especially in Java). Thus in Bangka, Billiton, and Minahassa, as well as Halmahera and many other islands of the Moluccas, shifting cultivators have no cattle and depend almost entirely on plots planted with the dibble; but a system of even wider distribution (e.g., in many parts of Sumatra, in southern Celebes, and in the Lesser Sundas) involves shifting cultivation by people who also own cattle and among whom cattle ownership, as in eastern and southern Africa, confers status.

R. F. Watters (1960) also records the wide variety of practice covered by the term "shifting cultivation" and distinguishes a number of major types. He brings out an important point that is often overlooked: shifting cultivation is in a number of areas practiced by people who are perfectly well aware of methods of sedentary cultivation, but use shifting cultivation for a particular category of land. For example, shifting cultivation is practiced in the unirrigable "highlands" in the dry zone of Ceylon, a country where irrigated rice and coconuts are grown respectively in permanent fields on irrigable land and on land with a permanently high water table. In northern Burma, again, culturally identical peoples practice, on the one hand, terraced rice cultivation of hill slopes in areas of high population density, and, on the other, shifting cultivation of similar slopes where population density is low (Leach 1959).

There is, in fact, a close connection between shifting cultivation and low population density: beyond a critical density (which varies with local conditions) the period of regeneration allowed to the natural vegetation becomes too short, and deterioration tends to set in unless the cultivators adopt some of the techniques by which sedentary cultivators manage to cultivate the same field year in and year out. This is one way by which the transition from shifting to sedentary cultivation may be effected; another is the planting of commercial crops, especially permanent tree crops, in abandoned clearings by shifting cultivators (the rubber grown in Sumatra is a good example).

Simple sedentary cultivation with hand tools

It does not follow, however, that all simple sedentary cultivation (that is, for present purposes, sedentary cultivation without recourse to the plow) represents the fixation of shifting cultivation. In southeast Asia, for example, it may well be that the most ancient surviving form of cultivation is the use of permanent gardens to grow bananas, various tubers such as *Dioscorea* yams and taro (*Colocasia esculenta*), and tree crops such as the coconut and, less frequently, the sago palm. Carl O. Sauer (1952) believes that this was the earliest of all forms of cultivation. It survives as the sole form of land use in remote Indonesian islands like

the Mentawai Islands; and something very like it provides the basic system in Polynesia, where it survives (e.g., in Fiji) in the form of specially prepared and irrigated taro beds. In all these cases, except where modern influences have prevailed, cultivation is by digging stick or, less commonly, by hoe. Fertility in tuber gardens is maintained by a rest period. Tree crops can, of course, be permanent, for trees bring nutriment up from lower horizons of the soil and protect the earth from erosion; they are therefore relatively easy to maintain in equilibrium with the environment—provided the climate is suitable—though yields are often very low indeed in the absence of pest control and fertilizers.

The mixed garden (containing both tree crops and a wide variety of vegetables) that is so characteristic of much of the rice-growing regions of southeast Asia and the Indian subcontinent may be regarded as a special development from the system just described.

In many parts of Africa south of the Sahara "women's gardens" are to be found immediately around the village. In them vegetables, bananas, and other crops are grown by hand tillage on a more or less permanent basis. The gardens are kept fertile by means of manure from goats, chickens, and the villagers themselves, together with household refuse and ashes.

The agricultural systems of the Inca in pre-Columbian America and of their latter-day successors represent a fine example of sedentary but plowless agriculture in part dependent on irrigation and the terracing of steep slopes.

It must be recognized, however, that it would be extremely difficult to draw a map of the world and to plot on it all examples of the land-use technique currently under discussion and, in particular, to identify all existing cases of the fixation of cultivation in areas traditionally devoted to shifting cultivation. Much more work on this problem is needed.

Simple plow cultivation

It will be appreciated that two of the basic problems that confront the sedentary cultivator are the maintenance of soil fertility and the control of weeds. If fertility cannot be maintained fields must be periodically abandoned, and the cultivation is no longer truly sedentary; if weeds proliferate too extensively (as in the *chena*, the patch of the Ceylonese shifting cultivator), the same applies. The use of even the simple wooden plow goes a long way toward the solution of both problems. The ability of the plowman to cover at least some of his weeds, and thus to kill them, also adds to the humus in the soil. The deeper and more systematic cultivation made possible by the plow tends to bring to the surface plant-nutrients taken down by percolating rainfall and to improve soil structure; the presence of draft animals to pull the plow at least gives the possibility of stall-feeding and hence systematic manuring—a possibility that is unfortunately not always realized in practice.

Over a vast area stretching from the Mediterranean and the Balkans to the Japanese archipelago, and from central Asia to Ceylon, agricultural technology is still dominated by a simple, traditional plow culture, only marginally affected by the agrarian revolution and those other developments that have transformed the agriculture of such regions as western Europe, North America, and Australia. The vast populations of India, China, and the Middle East depend for their food supply on traditional methods of sedentary tillage using the types of wooden plow handed down from remote generations.

Within this great cultural region there may be recognized a number of subcultures, separated on grounds of technology and associated crop pattern.

In the Middle East, from Afghanistan and Iran to Egypt, one can recognize a belt of plow cultures, perhaps the most ancient of all, where animal-drawn plows appeared much before 3000 B.C. It is characterized, among other things, by a reliance on irrigation of a wide variety of types, from the ancient and modern systems dependent on the Nile to the ingenious tunnels (*karez*) of Iran and the multitudinous devices used by the oasis dweller. In this area, too, the terracing of hill slopes is in many places a highly developed traditional technique.

The lands around the Mediterranean, with their highly distinctive climate and cultural history, also form a subregion within the belt of plow cultures. The most characteristic and traditional technology hinges on a twofold system of land use: the fields, traditionally growing the staple cereal crops, wheat and barley, and in some places irrigated; and the hillside plantations of vines and olives, figs, and other tree crops. Everywhere (especially in the south of France, in Italy, and in Israel) traditional methods are, however, being rapidly replaced by more specialized cultivation under the impact of commerce and of the agrarian revolution.

In the Balkan peninsula and in certain geographical pockets in western, central, and northern Europe one reaches what may, for convenience and brevity, be regarded as the cool temperate variant of traditional plow culture—the cultiva-

tion, using oxen or horses as draft animals, of wheat and barley in favorable places, and of oats and rye in wetter and cooler places, with a fair range of ancillary crops. Here are European peasant societies still relatively unaffected by the agrarian revolution: but the word "relatively" is used advisedly, for almost everywhere today, under the impact of modern communications or commerce, and of institutional changes in communist countries, the old order is vanishing and the transition to a more modern agricultural technology and economy is being effected, here slowly, there more rapidly. Some of the largest agglomerations of population depend on an association of the plow and of other simple animal-drawn tools (harrows, leveling boards, and the like) with irrigated (or, at any rate, flooded-field) rice cultivation. This subculture covers much of Ceylon, southern India, Bengal, and Assam, the deltas of mainland southeast Asia, Java, Sumatra, the Philippines, and southern China and Japan. The total area under "wet" rice (as distinct from "dry" rice grown by shifting or rudimentary sedentary cultivation) exceeds 200 million acres, and rice forms the staple food of well over half the world's people. Rice is a remarkable crop in other ways too. Because it exists in so many varieties it can be grown under widely varying conditions, from brackish or even saline soils to deeply flooded deltas like those of Thailand and South Vietnam. In many places, given enough water, it can supply two crops on the same land each year. And—a very important point —it can give worthwhile yields on the same land year after year for generations without manuring, although, of course, yields may be greatly increased by the judicious use of manure; dry crops under similar conditions tend, in the tropics at any rate, to give declining yields that may well stabilize at an uneconomic level. The reasons for this valuable property of wet rice are probably to be sought in such factors as the nutrients and clay minerals brought in by irrigation water and the lower temperatures preserved by flooding, which, with anaerobic conditions for much of the year, lower the rate of oxidation and loss of nutrients of vegetable matter. Just as irrigated wheat cultivation historically became identified with the rise of many sociocultural institutions of Western civilization, so with rice cultivation goes a whole way of life, a whole type of civilization, together with the possibility of supporting dense populations for centuries, if not for millennia.

Among the populations supported by plow cultivation of rice there are, not surprisingly, many variations in agricultural economy and technology.

Some rice cultivators have highly developed techniques of terracing hillsides and of controlling water in the terraces (e.g., in the hills of Ceylon, in Java, and in the interior of Luzon); others tackle land that is almost flat (e.g., in southern Thailand and in the Malay Peninsula). Again, some rice cultivators, as in China, employ almost incredible ingenuity in seeing that every scrap of waste organic matter finds its way back to the soil —indeed, their technology tends to be intensive gardening rather than plow culture—whereas others, in regions that until recently felt but little pressure of population, use no manure at all except under the modern pressure exerted by a cash economy and by government agencies (e.g., in lowland Ceylon).

North and west of the great rice-growing areas of India and China, in the dry plateaus of the Deccan and the great Indo-Gangetic plains, and the loesslands and delta of the mighty but dangerous Hwang Ho, are other large populations of farmers, densely settled in fertile plains, less densely (but still thickly by American standards) in rockier plateaus with thinner soils. These form two more subcultures, as it were, of the great Old World belt of plow cultures, devoted to millets, wheat, oilseeds, sugar cane, and cotton rather than to rice and its ancillaries. The north Indian peasant tends to have less intensive techniques and lower yields than his north Chinese counterpart, although in India the situation is changing (albeit rather patchily) and China, of course, feels the impact of the communist agrarian measures.

The agrarian revolution

In Europe, agricultural developments of the last three hundred years have wrought such changes in technology and economy that they demand separate, though necessarily summary, treatment. The source of the changes concerned lies, of course, in the agrarian revolution in the widest sense of that term, including not only technical changes but changes in conditions of land holding. A whole complex of developments is thus involved, including the replacement of fallowing with constant tillage; the introduction of new crops and of new breeds of animals; the effects of evolving communications on the specialization of agricultural production; structural change in the agrarian system (evolutionary in the West, revolutionary in Russia); and, more recently, the impact of modern science and engineering as seen in mechanization, pest and disease control, artificial fertilizers, and the evolution of strains of crop suited to particular conditions and resistant to specific diseases. One has only to compare a modern farm in, say, East Anglia (England) or the United States with a peasant holding in India or Egypt to see the contrast. Yet an increasing number of peasant holdings in India and in Egypt are feeling some of the effects of the revolution in question. In both countries, for instance, the peasant may have a very small holding and be cultivating it with a wooden plow and draft animals that have changed little since the time of Ashoka or of the pharaohs; but in both countries he may well be growing, for a distant market, an American variety of cotton developed by scientific genetic research.

It would be difficult to attempt a description of all the types of agricultural technology or of cropping patterns that have emerged and are constantly evolving from the revolutionary changes just mentioned, even if the requisite data were everywhere available. One or two salient characteristics may, however, be highlighted and one or two technological subtypes enumerated. One of the outstanding characteristics of modern agriculture—whether in land of comparatively new settlement such as North America, Argentina, or Australia, or in older agricultural areas such as western Europe—is the high and mounting degree of mechanization, characterized first by new plows, harvesters, and other implements drawn by horses, and then by tractor-drawn implements and self-propelled machines like the combine harvester or the rotary tiller. Originally a response mainly to the need for constant tillage, weed control, and other desiderata of the earlier agrarian reformers, the movement toward mechanization has been vastly stimulated by the existence in lands of new settlement of enormous areas of virgin soil combined with a great dearth of labor. The relationship between mechanization and the relative abundance of land and of labor seems to be forgotten by those who advocate wholesale mechanization in underdeveloped and overpopulated countries. Wholesale mechanization of Indian agriculture would, for example, merely swell to uncontrollable numbers the already large army of rural unemployed or grossly underemployed, at the same time *reducing* yields per acre where at present, as in parts of Madras State, the intensive application of hand methods gives phenomenal yields, in this case of rice. The answer would appear to be *selective* mechanization of processes such as plowing hard-caked soil, impossible under present methods, or of processes handicapped, despite the over-all surplus of labor, by seasonal shortage—for example, weeding the standing paddy crop. In western Europe and elsewhere, mechanization has been associated with a drift of labor from the land into other occupations and often into towns, and with a decline in the proportion of the national labor force engaged in cultivation to a figure that sounds unbelievable to, say, Indian ears.

Another outstanding characteristic of modern agricultural technology is the breeding of new varieties of crops. These new varieties have in some cases revolutionized agricultural geography; for example, it seems probable that none of the lands in the United States west of the Mississippi would be growing wheat today if the only available varieties were those brought by the Pilgrim Fathers. The poleward and desertward march of agriculture is a feature of our times, but it carries with it its own dangers—notably of soil erosion in the case of the extension of cultivation toward and into arid regions.

Monoculture. An outstanding characteristic of modern agriculture is its high degree of specialization. Most African farmers would find it very hard to understand the agricultural methods of, say, a Wiltshire (England) dairy farmer, who produces nothing but liquid milk, of which he consumes only a few pints a day, and who must buy everything else he needs, including even milk products like butter and cheese. It is, of course, the rise of urban and industrial markets, the spread of modern communications, and the development of an exchange economy that have, with changes in methods of production, brought about the world of specialized agricultural production in which we live. Wheat farming in the Canadian prairies, cocoa farming in Ghana, citrus planting in Israel, truck farming in Florida, and cotton production in Russian central Asia are a few examples out of thousands that might be cited. The modern farmer chooses his crop not by applying a traditional technology and a limited range of crop choices to local natural conditions but by watching the market (often distorted, or at any rate affected, by state action). But the farmer still flouts natural conditions at his peril, as those in the dust bowls of the 1930s found to their cost. Monoculture in particular carries grave perils—not only of declining fertility, but of diseases that spread like wildfire when they find ready victims of the same species, or even variety, for mile after mile across country.

One of the most familiar examples of monocultural techniques is the tropical plantation—of tea in Ceylon, of rubber on the Malay Peninsula, of sisal in Tanganyika, and so on. Originally these large units of production, opened up by means of imported capital, often operated by imported labor, and working for distant markets, stood in stark contrast to minuscule local peasant holdings: hence (in part) the theory of the "dual economy,"

two contrasting economies side by side in the same area. But in many countries today—notably in Ceylon—local capital and enterprise is active in the plantations, and small holders and peasants are planting the crops once almost entirely confined to the large alien holdings. In other countries, for example Indonesia, the plantation is seen as an alien, colonialist intrusion, and is on the way out.

Conclusions

It cannot be denied that, taking the world picture as a whole, the shifting cultivator, the plowless sedentary cultivator, and the traditional plow cultivator are retreating before the advance of modern commercial agriculture; to be more precise, elements of the modern agricultural technology and of modern agricultural organization are penetrating the formerly almost static world of traditional agriculture. It may be in the form of a new crop (for example, the spectacular spread of manioc—*Manihot utilissima*—from the New World tropics to almost all parts of the Old World tropics); or the use of artificial fertilizer; or a new system of green manuring. It may be the addition of a steel tip and mold board to a traditional wooden plow, or the development of truck farming, or heavy emphasis on a commercial crop such as cocoa in Ghana or rubber in Malaya.

But this is not to say that all the features of the more ancient agricultural economies are about to disappear, still less that they ought to disappear. There is great danger in the wholesale transplantation of an agricultural technology from one environment to another—witness the spectacular failure of the scheme for mechanized production of groundnuts in Tanganyika. And the dangers are not only physical dangers, dangers to soil and plant cover. There are also grave social dangers. The effects of wholesale and indiscriminate mechanization on an overpopulated society have already been discussed. It is always useful, and often essential, to start from the assumption that a long-standing system of agricultural technology represents an adaptation to local physical and social conditions, albeit at a lower technical level and sometimes in terms of past social conditions, especially where the population/land ratio is concerned.

There is much research to be done everywhere on the relationships involved. Only when there is an understanding of the existing system can changes safely be introduced or adapted.

B. H. FARMER

[*See also* LAND TENURE. *Other relevant material may be found in* ASIAN SOCIETY, *article on* SOUTHEAST ASIA.]

BIBLIOGRAPHY

CONKLIN, HAROLD C. 1961 The Study of Shifting Cultivation. *Current Anthropology* 2:27–61. → A bibliography appears on pages 35–59.

CURWEN, ELIOT C.; and HATT, GUDMUND (1946–1953) 1953 *Plough and Pasture: The Early History of Farming.* New York: Schuman. → Part 1: *Prehistoric Farming of Europe and the Near East,* by Eliot C. Curwen. Part 2: *Farming of Non-European Peoples,* by Gudmund Hatt. Part 1 was published in 1946 as *Plough and Pasture.*

DUMONT, RENÉ (1954) 1957 *Types of Rural Economy: Studies in World Agriculture.* New York: Praeger. → First published as *Économie agricole dans le monde.*

FAUCHER, DANIEL 1949 *Géographie agraire: Types de cultures.* Paris: Librairie de Médicis.

FORDE, C. DARYLL (1934) 1963 *Habitat, Economy and Society: A Geographic Introduction to Ethnology.* London: Methuen.

GEORGE, PIERRE 1956 *La campagne: Le fait rural à travers le monde.* Paris: Presses Universitaires de France.

GOUROU, PIERRE (1947) 1964 *The Tropical World: Its Social and Economic Conditions and Its Future Status.* 3d ed. New York: Wiley. → First published as *Les pays tropicaux: Principes d'une géographie humaine et économique.*

GRIST, DONALD H. (1953) 1959 *Rice.* 3d ed. London: Longmans.

KING, FRANKLIN H. (1911) 1927 *Farmers of Forty Centuries: Or, Permanent Agriculture in China, Korea and Japan.* New York: Harcourt.

LEACH, EDMUND R. 1959 Some Economic Advantages of Shifting Cultivation. Volume 7, pages 64–66 in Pacific Science Congress, Ninth, Bangkok, 1957, *Proceedings.* Bangkok: Secretariat, Ninth Pacific Science Congress.

SAUER, CARL O. 1952 *Agricultural Origins and Dispersals.* New York: American Geographical Society.

SIEGFRIED, ANDRÉ (1943) 1947 *The Mediterranean.* New York: Duell, Sloan & Pearce. → First published as *Vue générale de la Méditerranée.*

TERRA, G. J. A. 1958 Farm Systems in South-East Asia. *Netherlands Journal of Agricultural Science* 6:157–182.

WARRINER, DOREEN (1939) 1965 *The Economics of Peasant Farming.* 2d ed. New York: Barnes & Noble.

WATTERS, R. F. 1960 The Nature of Shifting Cultivation: A Review of Recent Research. *Pacific Viewpoint* 1:59–99.

WEULERSSE, JACQUES 1946 *Paysans de Syrie et du Proche-Orient.* Paris: Gallimard.

WHITTLESEY, DERWENT S. 1936 Major Agricultural Regions of the Earth. Association of American Geographers, *Annals* 26:199–240.

WITTFOGEL, KARL A. 1957 *Oriental Despotism: A Comparative Study of Total Power.* New Haven, Conn.: Yale Univ. Press. → A paperback edition was published in 1963 by Yale University Press.

II

SOCIAL ORGANIZATION

Agriculture-related social action is typically organized through such groupings as the following: the *family,* which is both a producing and consuming unit, as is also the *large estate,* such as the manor, the hacienda, the cooperative farm, or the collective; *work teams* of various composition; *associations* organized for such purposes as irrigation, drainage, marketing, and purchasing; and *related systems* from which issue such services as education and religion. The student of agricultural organization is interested in the relationships that compose these units, the relations of these units to one another, and their relationships or linkages to larger pluralities, such as the society and nation and their various subsystems.

The pursuit of such knowledge is impeded by the following factors. First, there is a lack of adequate historical records. A second problem is the vagueness of the term "agricultural organization" and the lack of specificity in its use. If all activities related to agriculture are included, as in the case of "agribusiness," a sizable proportion of the population may be involved, even in an industrialized nation (for example, 30–40 per cent of the United States labor force); if only those engaged in farming are included, the proportions, especially in industrialized nations, will be much smaller (for example, 12 per cent of the United States labor force). The incomparability of unlikes is also a problem: a farm run by a nuclear family cannot be effectively compared with a hacienda run by hundreds of people. Outwardly similar units may be rendered incomparable by fundamentally different forms of tenure, distribution of power, and extent of status-role differentiation. Finally, ideological differences complicate the study of agricultural organization. For example, the idealization of the peasant family form of agriculture under the German Nazis and similar groups leads to a different viewpoint than that arrived at by the communists, whose view of agriculture is essentially pragmatic. Studies of agriculture undertaken by the Nazi government revealed that family-sized farms, as compared to large estates, yielded as much or more of all crops to the market (per unit of land), as well as more human beings; more "cannon fodder" was often the interpretation of this phenomenon by those of different ideological persuasion. Also, the persistent belief that social stability and military strength, viewed as national needs, can be maintained only by a large and prosperous rural population, is an a priori point of view that is not conducive to objectivity.

The typological approach

Almost from the beginning of sociology, concepts that have facilitated the ordering of social action on and between ideal or constructed poles (often called "types") have been employed in the analysis of many forms of organization, particularly in the case of agricultural organization. Probably the most generally used of these types are Ferdinand Tönnies' concepts of *Gemeinschaft* and *Gesellschaft* (1887), which arose from their author's familiarity with both agricultural and nonagricultural organizations. The essence of the *Gesellschaft*-like organization (such as a factory or army) is the all-important, functionally specific goal (such as profits for the factory or winning a battle for the army) shared by the actors; in the pursuit of that goal, facilities and means, including human relationships, are used in a manner that is instrumental, efficient, and economical. The opposite of the *Gesellschaft*-like organization is "farming as a way of life" carried on for its own sake. The greater the tendency for agricultural organization to be a "way of life," the less functionally specific are both goals and norms and the more *Gemeinschaft*-like the organization will be. The essence of *Gemeinschaft*-like organization and the social relations that compose it is the goal of furthering and maintaining the social relations themselves, which are never subordinated to functionally specific goals. *Gemeinschaft*-like organizations typically give high priority to the communication of sentiment for effective goal attainment. Status roles, rank, and power tend to be allocated by such ascriptive factors as sex and age in *Gemeinschaft*-like organizations, whereas these are typically allocated by achievement—demonstrated or potential—in the *Gesellschaft*-like organizations.

Such polar types (which are not to be confused with classificatory concepts, with variables, or with models) represent dimensions that do not exist in the real world—a fact that does not reduce their analytical utility. There probably is no organization, for example, all of whose members always place goal achievement above any consideration for social relationships, as is typified in the pure *Gesellschaft*. Similarly, there probably is no organization all of whose members always subordinate instrumental goals to make only the relationship, such as love, revenge, or friendship, an end in itself, as is typified in the pure *Gemeinschaft*. Determinative system theory, such as is employed in physics, often cannot utilize ideal types, which are of greatest use in the preliminary exploration of the general nature of phenomena. Among the most useful types are local versus cosmopolitan, traditional versus modern, folk versus urban, primary versus nonprimary, and the trilogy—familistic, contractual, and compulsory [see COMMUNITY–SOCIETY CONTINUA; see also Tönnies 1887].

The processual–structural approach

Certain general processual patterns may be noted as one traces the development of man's effort to produce more and better food and fiber with minimum effort. Different as is primitive agriculture from the sequential stages of technological advance now culminated in the agriculture of urbanized Western society, certain common elements and processes are apparent at all stages. One way of approaching the analysis of these general patterns is by specification of the elements and processes observed to be common to all social systems (Loomis 1960, pp. 1–47, especially fig. 1, p. 8). The following discussion of agricultural organization will be guided by this approach and reinforced by use of concepts from the *Gemeinschaft–Gesellschaft* typology.

Up to the time of the industrial revolution, relationships in agricultural organization were almost universally *Gemeinschaft*-like, and kinship ties were of utmost importance. Child–parent relations in the family or extensions of such patterns to the feudal manor controlled by a surrogate father or lord (patron) were evaluated most highly—so highly that they were ends in and of themselves and diffused with intense sentiment. In *Gemeinschaft*-like agricultural organizations, processes such as that of allocation of status roles, rank, and power conformed to age-old patterns, and the actors observed norms that specified action for every possible exigency (Loomis 1960, pp. 57–118, especially fig. 2, p. 61). The principle of ascription, or *who* the actor was, was followed, rather than that of achievement, or *what* the actor could do. These considerations restricted the rational, efficient, and economic use of nonhuman facilities and human services.

Barriers to rational action. Nonhuman facilities, such as real estate and instruments of production, are alienable and subject to successive allocations in the *Gesellschaft*-like organization, such as the farm that is run for profit. The more *Gesellschaft*-like the organization is, the freer its members are to enter or be placed in new social relations, discontinue old ones, move in space, and be subject to change in status roles, power, and rank. Inalienable instruments of production, unchanging social relations, and inviolable allocations of status roles, power, and rank constitute inhibitions to the rational use both of human and nonhuman resources. Agricultural organizations of the past and so-called underdeveloped agricultural societies of the present tend to harbor such inhibitions.

It has frequently been hypothesized by sociologists that the higher the value of an object (especially if its use is fused with sentiment), the greater are the inhibitions to its rational use. In the case of ends, value may be measured in terms of willingness of actors to make sacrifices to obtain or to retain an object. In the case of a norm, value may be measured by the intensity of indignation when the norm is violated and by the degree of harshness of the negative sanction imposed upon the violator. Societies in which malnutrition is commonplace and famines are frequent would, according to the hypothesis, tend to value land very highly and to accord it a quality of sacredness; other facilities requisite to a basic food supply would become fused with affectivity and hedged about with restrictions. The hypothesis would explain the widespread restrictions on free sale, purchase, or exchange of land, which in turn is often the most important basis for allocation of status roles, rank, and power, since these latter are often ascribed by the relationship of a given actor to the land; the manor's lord, cotters, and villeins are well-known examples (Loomis & Beegle 1950). It has been observed that food crops in the field and immediately after harvest are often considered sacred; their movement and use during this period must be accompanied by proper ritual. Once the crops are sold, they lose their sacred nature. Similarly, the hypothesis may be applied to explain various types of restrictions on the mobility and alienability of human services in feudal and other traditional organizations.

The limits of rationality in agriculture. Contrary to the cyclical theories of development, agricultural organization has, at least since the industrial revolution, become increasingly efficient and economical in respect to human effort and facilities. Exceptions may be cited in various cases of extreme anomie, as disorder becomes so common and painful that reaction in the form of ultraconservative movements occurs, such as in the German Nazi and Italian fascist movements. The over-all trend, however, has been a shift from *Gemeinschaft*-like restrictions on utilization of nonhuman facilities and human services in goal attaining activities toward *Gesellschaft*-like relations in which these restrictions are at least partially eliminated.

Is it likely that the degree of rationality that attends industrial and market organization in its most *Gesellschaft*-like form can be made to attend agricultural organization? To explore this possibility, let a given agricultural facility, for instance a unit of land, be likened to a unit of money, say a hundred dollar bill. When the possession, exchange, and transfer of a unit of land can be effected with the same sentimental detachment that would mark the possession, exchange, and transfer of a hundred dollar bill, then a parallel degree of rationality will be evinced by the two

types of organization. Most students of rural life and agricultural organization cannot foresee as a likely occurrence early rationalization of agriculture, when land, livestock, machinery, and plant would be as removed from the sacred and as imbued with the secular as are parallel operations in nonagricultural production.

Feudal tenures and relationships. Under medieval European tenure, the feudal manor operated with some slaves who could be sold, but most agricultural workers were, in effect, bound to the soil as serfs and were transferred with the estate, although there were degrees of serfdom and some serfs eventually became free peasants. In rank the bondsmen were below the lesser gentry, the nobility, and the royalty. The basic unit was the tribal group or peasant family, which was characteristic of the less fully developed form of German feudalism that spread to the Low Countries and to the north of Italy, as well as of the fully developed French feudalism that came to prevail in England, northern Spain, the two Sicilies, and the Levant (Boissonnade 1921, p. 120 in 1929 edition). How each man was related to the land determined whether he could marry and under what conditions, what services and payments he would have to render, and under what conditions he could leave the estate. His tenure status prescribed his status role, his rank, and his power. The concept *Gemeinschaft* from Tönnies and the similar concept "status" from Maine (1861) arose out of the great differences that they noted between the feudal tenures of the Middle Ages and (*a*) the *Gesellschaft*-like and contractual relations of the present day and (*b*) the latifundia (arising out of the enclosure movement in England from 1450 to 1600) and other developments elsewhere, as the customary rights of the various tenure groups of lower rank were disregarded and latifundia came into being.

Out of the feudal system grew a stratification pattern based upon the estates, or *stände* as they are called in Germany. These specified the status roles, rank, power, and life-style of members and institutionalized the means of entry or expulsion by ritual forms. Most of the bases for allocation of placement as exercised under this form of stratification are ascriptive; they have long been associated with rural societies and are still found today in many parts of the world. Since modern business, commerce, and industry require a *specified* performance, they tend to dissolve the estate form of stratification and replace the ascriptive allocation of its members with allocation by achievement. In the ideal typological form of complete *Gesellschaft*, there emerges an open-class system in which all persons find their places according to their skills, technical competency, and contributions, with no importance attached to the class position of one's antecedents or to one's age or sex. Opposite to this is the caste system of stratification that is found most commonly in agricultural and rural societies, the most extreme example of which exists in India.

Importance of the feudal system. There has been considerable transmission of feudal ideology and of feudal norms, especially those related to rank and power, to the present industrial organization in areas of feudal background, such as England and Germany. Other legacies, however, from the feudal era are probably of greater importance. One such is the influence it had upon the thinking of Marx and Engels, who furnished the basic ideology for communism in Russia and China. The once feudal nations are often contrasted with those having no feudal history in respect to class structure and attitudes toward authority. Marxian doctrine places capitalism in an important intermediary stage between feudalism (or something comparable) and communism. Marx had an unusual interest in the United States, perhaps because of its lack of feudal background. Lenin on the other hand studied the exploitation of Negroes in the rural South and leaped to the conclusion that the United States would follow the European pattern. Marxist and Leninist doctrine aside, recent history shows that industrializing societies without feudal backgrounds more easily adopt equalitarian achievement motivation than do others.

Successors to the feudal pattern. Most of the agriculture of the noncommunist world may be classified according to whether the central producing and consuming unit is the farm family, the large estate, such as the hacienda or the latifundium, or a mixture of these two types of units. The haciendas, latifundia, and similar forms frequently arose out of feudalism. In England, the enclosure movements and other pressures resulted in virtual dispossession of those villagers and farmers that possessed communal property. Much the same development occurred along the Baltic coast in Mecklenburg and Holstein, and in Swedish Pomerania, where the peasants, who were long accustomed to communal tenure of grazing and grass lands, had no protection against property appropriation. The rapidity of change from *Gemeinschaft*-like relations, with protection based upon custom, to *Gesellschaft*-like norms of contact left rural dwellers in many areas in a state of semishock, without the necessary knowledge and linkages for secure existence in the new order. The right to ownership and transfer of property in fee simple was not achieved for the peasants in the French Revolution. Owing in part to this failure almost half of the land of France, Italy, and Spain came to be worked by tenants and sharecroppers (Dietze 1933, p. 49). Outright ownership by peasants occurred in much larger proportions in Germany and in the Scandinavian kingdoms.

The farm family. Even during the feudal period, when most rural dwellers were subjected to the feudal system, there were yeomen who, as small independent landholders, continued a free existence in limited areas of Europe, such as Upper Bavaria, Swabia, Thuringia, Saxony, Frisia, and Holstein. An ideology of the yeoman—a farm owner and operator without indebtedness—can be traced to areas where substantial numbers of farm families remained free from bondage to the land. A number of leaders, such as Thomas Jefferson, believed that democracy could best survive when many such farmers, who were ready to fight any attempts to subordinate them, peopled the countryside. For Jefferson, who believed that an occasional revolution was good for the political health of nations, it would be these "free yeomen" who would begin such revolutions.

The so-called family farm is a productive unit in which the family is the central entrepreneurial work unit. The designation covers enterprises of widely different character. A family farm in New Jersey may consist of three acres and one thousand laying hens; in Oregon it may comprise 3,200 acres of wheat and grazing land. In the Western Hemisphere the family farm is a vital force in the agriculture of widely dispersed societies, such as Costa Rica, Chile, southern Brazil, Colombia, the United States, and Canada. Turkey, India, Pakistan, Japan, and Korea are examples of areas in the Eastern Hemisphere where the family farm organization is extensive and important. In some respects it constitutes an American ideal. It became the model used by the Allies in reorganizing conquered areas under their control at the end of World War II. Like other American businesses, farms and ranches tend to become larger and larger for many purposes of production. Nevertheless, the "sacredness" of the family farm is frequently demonstrated in American political action at home, as well as in policy for improving agricultural practices abroad.

In most of the industrialized countries where the family farm has predominated, family control is decreasing as the farming operations become larger. An example may be taken from the Heide areas of Germany, which have long been famous for a free peasantry. There the once independent peasants are increasingly beholden to authorities and creditors, many of whom are from the cities, as competitive agriculture fosters the use of costly overhead irrigation systems, which at once irrigate and fertilize the soil and crops. Other developments that may decrease control by the farm family are the following: increased specialization, greater capitalization, greater dependence on both domestic and foreign markets, and increasing employment of farm family members in industry, resulting in part-time farming and dependence upon the urban wage economy. In addition, *vertical integration* increasingly links the farm family to various other systems, thereby depriving it of autonomy. An example is provided in the widespread practice of contract farming in the poultry industry, organized by hatcherymen or feed dealers who agree to supply chicks, feed, medicine, capital, electricity, heat, and supervision. Although the prices for poultry are guaranteed to the farmer, the system tends to deprive previously independent farm families of the "yeoman freedom," making them semi-share-croppers under control of urban contractors and capital suppliers.

Changes in agricultural organization

Rapid change in agricultural practices and organization usually comes from societal units outside the immediate agricultural system. Perhaps the chief exception to this generalization in the literature on agriculture is the manner in which there developed a relatively highly advanced form of agriculture among the various Protestant sects, such as the Mennonites and the Amish, especially in the German Palatinate. They were known as "clover" farmers and, because of their great ability as agriculturists, were sought by princes of the time to operate farms of the nobility. Farmers from this same strain also became outstanding agriculturists in Pennsylvania and elsewhere in the New World without outside assistance. I conjecture that this exceptional development may have issued from the knowledge of scholarly Roman Catholic priests who had access in the universities and the monasteries of the time to advanced knowledge about agriculture and who defected in sizable numbers during this epoch, often to found or to join such nonconformist religious groups as those later known as the Mennonites and the Amish. If this interpretation is correct, it is a most interesting form of systemic linkage, by which the defecting priests brought knowledge beyond that of the traditional base to the peasant groups of which they became a part.

Systemic linkage. The traditional base of knowledge gathered from generations of actual farming experience is generally insufficient to spark rapid change. *Gemeinschaft*-like societies, which typically live by tradition, distrust innovations. Only as agricultural organizations are linked to various knowledge producing and distributing centers does rapid change in agriculture take place. Typical linkages promoting changes are those with credit facilities, organized experimental animal and plant stock breeding, and market economies. Wherever very rapid change in agriculture has taken place, these facilities have been available. No country with advanced agriculture is today without agricultural experiment stations or other forms of scientific activity, operating to improve planting and animal stocks as well as agricultural practices, organization, and technology generally.

Systemic linkage between these agencies and the agricultural production units may take many forms and should receive more careful study than it has been given. The folk schools, universities, and agricultural services have been important in Denmark. Extension services in the United States, rural academies in Pakistan, national ministries of agriculture in Latin America, and agencies of community development and cooperation in India are other examples of the institutionalized linkages between agricultural research and practice. Everywhere that rapid progress has been made, agricultural credit has been made available on a rational basis at interest rates comparable to or lower than those prevailing in other productive enterprises. The credit system of usury, common in the underdeveloped areas of the Far East (which often require that the borrower pay 100 to 300 per cent per annum to a local moneylender bearing a semi-*Gemeinschaft*-like, personal, or *patron* relation to the debtor), usually must be abolished or radically modified before rapid progress in agricultural production can take place.

Of utmost importance is the form of the linkage between the agricultural production organizations —whatever type of farm that might be—and the centers of knowledge about such facilities as credit, markets, and the results of basic and applied research. Especially in underdeveloped areas, the chief lack is not in knowledge itself but rather in the transmission of that knowledge. Such scientific establishments as experiment stations, research laboratories in government bureaus, and universities do the "cognitive mapping" necessary to improve the practices, stocks, and technology (Loomis 1960, pp. 12–13, 68–69). The incumbents of certain status roles, such as teachers and extension workers, link the systems in which the concern is cognitive mapping with the systems in which the concern is efficient production. To be effective in their status roles, such professionals not only must have mastered their own specialties in the agricultural sciences but must also be adept at appraising those systems most amenable to linkage. The rate of adoption of new agricultural practices will vary as these factors vary in effectiveness.

Diffusion of innovations. An important aspect of social change in agricultural organization is the relative willingness to adopt improved stocks, facilities, and practices. A series of types or semi-status roles has identified agriculturists relative to their time and manner of adopting new practices once these are made available. In the industrialized West only 3 per cent are "innovators" who are frequently linked directly to agricultural scientists whom they know personally. They evaluate science highly, do much of their own cognitive mapping in accordance with the canons of science, consider profits in agriculture as a most important goal, and take risks to attain this goal by borrowing money. Innovators make decisions and act upon them more quickly than others. In terms of systemic linkage, innovators are not linked to their neighborhoods as closely as others, are more cosmopolitan in orientation, and, although relatively well off financially, usually do not rank as high in local neighborhood affairs as do the next group to adopt practices, namely the "early adopters." These latter may constitute something like 14 per cent of the agricultural producers. Early adopters and the next group—"early majority adopters"—may constitute together more than 35 per cent of the agricultural producers. They are linked both to the local neighborhood and community groups and to the knowledge centers, such as universities and experiment stations. The last groups to adopt improved stocks and practices have been called the "laggards" and "late adopters"; they evaluate science less highly than do earlier adopters (see Rogers 1962).

The case of an effective and generally adopted weed killer may serve as an example of differential adoption rates; it was adopted almost as soon as it was available by the innovators, whereas it was adopted after a ten-year delay by the laggards (North Central . . . 1961, p. 6). Laggards confine their interaction almost completely to their neighborhoods and localities, have a minimum of systemic linkage with knowledge centers, have relatively low rank, and are usually older and less well educated than innovators and early adopters. Laggards and late adopters engage frequently in a type of cognitive mapping akin to magic, such as the effect of the moon on seed germination. They tend to seek evaluations and reinforce their own judgments by asking the opinion of friends and neighbors. The end for which farming is conducted for the laggards is often "farming as a way of life," in contrast to the profit motive, which is a highly valued end for the innovator. Usually the norms for agriculture and for life are highly traditional. Various studies in underdeveloped agricultural societies indicate that, in the above respects, the majority of peasants and laborers resemble the laggards and late adopters. One of the prime problems in the effort to increase the productivity of areas of traditional agriculture is to increase the proportion of innovators and early adopters [see DIFFUSION, *article on* THE DIFFUSION OF INNOVATIONS].

Agriculture and society

As agricultural production becomes more efficient and markets and credit facilities more accessible, cities become larger, with the urban increase accruing largely from rural populations, which almost always have higher replacement rates. It has been suggested that high mobility is the chief differentiating feature of urbanized and developing societies. However, the movement of people is not always from the farms to the cities. During the depression of the 1930s a great "back to the land movement" began throughout the urbanized world, and in both Europe and America various forms of settlement designed to combine a home garden or subsistence with city wage work were established. This phenomenon throws in relief some of the fundamental patterns involved in the development of modern differentiated and industrialized societies.

Throughout history man has dreamed of establishing communities that are organized and designed to eliminate human conflict, poverty, and ignorance. Although such blights are often found in agricultural societies, the differentiated, industrialized urban societies generally manifest higher suicide rates, more anomie, and more alienation of man from man than do rural societies. Although it is the belief of many, including the author, that man's flexible and rational nature, coupled with his ability to transmit knowledge, makes it possible for him to develop organizational techniques suited to conditions in which the division of labor and institutional differentiation dominate, many thinkers disagree. They believe an urban existence is unnatural and dysfunctional for mental and physical well-being. Such thinking is sometimes based upon the following facts and logic. Rural societies, particularly those not linked to modern industrialized cities, are less differentiated and more integrated, in the sense that their members fill fewer conflicting status roles (for example, the policeman who is a neighbor of a habitual delinquent) and manifest greater consensus on the goals and norms that guide life. Moreover, fewer members find existing institutions so meaningless that identity is sought with deviant groups, especially those that take pride in and flaunt their deviancy, as is fairly common in Western industrial society.

To understand the variation among agricultural organizations and rural societies, it may be helpful to visualize the "perfectly integrated society": the quintessence of societal integration that has no empirical existence but may be projected as an ideal type (see Williams [1951] 1960, pp. 374, 378). It would be small in size, stable in demographic composition and in physical milieu, with relatively few linkages with other societies. It would have few "center activities," whereby man refines and converts for his final use the products of "field activities," such as agriculture, mining, lumbering, and herding. In a perfectly integrated society, there is complete consensus on goals and unwavering dedication to the norms of goal fulfillment. People find it a pleasure to do their duty, and spontaneous approval is given to all who do so. In such a society, there would, of course, be no need for social control and no police force or other sanctioning agency.

The impact of urbanization. Factors of differentiation, however, have emerged very early, as recorded history demonstrates. Simple agricultural societies, which are subject to the vicissitudes of flood, drought, and other natural calamities, employ religious rituals, especially at planting and harvest time. The keepers of such rituals—the holy men and the medicine men—not only supply through their activities much needed integration but also frequently specify planting stocks and times and probably become the first agricultural as well as religious experts. Thus, integration becomes increasingly difficult to achieve as status roles become differentiated not only in agriculture and religion but also in many other spheres, such as health, education, and government. "Center activities" become more numerous and important. As societies have become industrialized and urbanized, many variations have been observed, but some similarities and patterns may be mentioned.

First, power or control, even during periods when an agriculturally based nobility rules, comes to be highly concentrated in the urban centers. Moreover, societal integration and boundary maintenance are limited when these centers are few and weak. This is the chief reason why in modern times the spread of communism, contrary to Marx's prediction that it would be introduced by the city proletarian masses, has been most prominent in peasant societies with weak central activities and government. The rank of various incumbents of status roles in the systems located in the field de-

creases as urbanization places greater emphasis upon center activities. These differences in rank are determined not so much by the difficulty of learning the skills demanded by the new status roles (it is probably more difficult to learn to train and use oxen and horses as draft animals than it is to operate an elevator in a hotel, for instance) as they are by the fact that the higher replacement rates of families that teach these skills to their children, as well as the lower demand for rural skills, generally disparages field activities. Because of available financial support, most able professionals tend to gravitate to the larger centers, whereas fewer elect to practice in rural areas; thus, there are fewer highly trained specialists (per ten thousand people), such as doctors and dentists, in rural than in urban areas.

Those engaged in center activities over several generations less frequently participate in conservative and reactionary movements and more frequently participate in liberal and radical movements than those engaged in field activities. It is often found that in urban areas the ultraconservatives and reactionaries frequently have recently come from the areas where field activities predominate. This in part explains the emphasis in such ultraconservative or reactionary movements as those of the German Nazis on returning agriculture to its earlier forms.

Those engaged in field activities have higher demographic replacement rates than those engaged in center activities. As centers emerge, the migration results in larger proportions of females and persons of employable age in the areas where center activities predominate. On the other hand, areas in which field activities predominate have larger proportions of males and persons in the younger and older less productive ages. Finally, urbanization—especially rapid urbanization—produces strains that are reflected in increasing rates of suicide and certain forms of criminality, such as homicide. However, when urbanization is in advanced stages and urban traits are being rapidly diffused to the countryside suicide rates of rural areas may sometimes, if only rarely, exceed urban rates.

CHARLES P. LOOMIS

[*Directly related are the entries* COMMUNITY–SOCIETY CONTINUA; RURAL SOCIETY. *Other relevant material may be found in* FOOD, *article on* WORLD PROBLEMS; PEASANTRY; TECHNICAL ASSISTANCE; *and in the biographies of* MAINE; TÖNNIES.]

BIBLIOGRAPHY

BOISSONADE, PROSPER (1921) 1964 *Life and Work in Medieval Europe: The Evolution of Medieval Economy*

From the Fifth to the Fifteenth Century. New York: Harper. → First published as *Le travail dans l'Europe chrétienne au moyen âge.*

DIETZE, C. VON 1933 Peasantry. Volume 12, pages 48–53 in *Encyclopaedia of the Social Sciences.* New York: Macmillan.

FUSTEL DE COULANGES, NUMA DENIS (1864) 1956 *The Ancient City: A Study on the Religion, Laws, and Institutions of Greece and Rome.* Garden City, N.Y.: Doubleday. → First published in French.

LOOMIS, CHARLES P. 1960 *Social Systems: Essays on Their Persistence and Change.* Princeton, N.J.: Van Nostrand.

LOOMIS, CHARLES P.; and BEEGLE, J. ALLAN (1950) 1955 *Rural Social Systems: A Textbook in Rural Sociology and Anthropology.* London: Bailey & Swinfen. → See sections on land tenure for a comprehensive bibliography.

MAINE, HENRY J. S. (1861) 1960 *Ancient Law: Its Connection With the Early History of Society, and Its Relations to Modern Ideas.* Rev. ed. New York: Dutton; London and Toronto: Dent. → A paperback edition was published in 1963 by Beacon.

NORTH CENTRAL RURAL SOCIOLOGY SUBCOMMITTEE FOR THE STUDY OF DIFFUSION OF FARM PRACTICES 1961 Adopters of New Farm Ideas: Characteristics and Communication Behavior. Unpublished manuscript, Michigan Agricultural Extension Service, East Lansing.

ROGERS, EVERETT M. 1962 *Diffusion of Innovations.* New York: Free Press.

TÖNNIES, FERDINAND (1887) 1957 *Community and Society (Gemeinschaft und Gesellschaft).* Translated and edited by Charles P. Loomis. East Lansing: Michigan State Univ. Press. → First published in German. A paperback edition was published in 1963 by Harper.

VINOGRADOFF, PAUL (1905) 1920 *The Growth of the Manor.* 3d ed. New York: Macmillan.

WILLIAMS, ROBIN M. JR. (1951) 1960 *American Society: A Sociological Interpretation.* 2d ed., rev. New York: Knopf.

III

HISTORY

We now know that the historian's desire to set in order and tighten the history of agriculture must not go so far as to dissolve the diversity of events into a single trend of evolution or even into a "law," as did the writers of antiquity with their rigorous sequence of nomadism developing from hunting and fishing and agriculture from nomadism or as did the historians of the nineteenth century, who held that communal ownership was a necessary phase in the evolution of society (de Laveleye 1874; von Below 1920).

Much archeological evidence, including that from recently developed techniques of aerial photography and research on organic remains, indicates that hunting, fishing, and food gathering persisted side by side with simple cultivation during long periods of prehistory. Similar evidence, particularly from implements and aerial photography, discloses early field arrangements throughout Europe that give no appearance of having been farmed in common. [For *fuller treatment of the origins and early history of agriculture, see* DOMESTICATION; URBAN REVOLUTION.]

With the development of advanced civilizations in the Near East there came new plants, new implements, new techniques (irrigation, fertilizer, regular succession of crops), and new forms of organization of agriculture (*latifundia,* slave plantations). These innovations reached the countries north of the Alps via Greece and Rome, although many of them vanished again with the Romans.

Europe's population, however, had reached a low point at about the middle of the first millennium A.D. It is estimated that no more than four million people (about four per square kilometer) then lived in the area today occupied by England, France, and the Federal Republic of Germany. This in turn meant wide-open stretches for man and animal, little agriculture, emphasis on animal husbandry, and widely scattered settlements.

The medieval expansion. The middle of the first millennium may be regarded as the turning point at which a new expansion set in, an expansion that has continued with reverses and interruptions to the present day. Starting in the sixth and seventh centuries and expanding after the year 1000, forests were cleared, marshes drained, and land along the coasts reclaimed from the sea. The higher elevations were opened up in the lower mountain ranges; the upper limit of permanent settlement in the Alps was higher about the year 1300 than ever before or since. By the time this wave of land expansion subsided (at the beginning of the fourteenth century) the arable land of the old Europe had been increased many times over.

Most of the villages still in existence in central Europe existed at the end of the medieval expansion of cultivated land. Only few inhabited places have been added since, while many have disappeared since the high Middle Ages. For example, it is estimated that about the year 1300 there were some 170,000 independent—that is, territorially separate—settlements in Germany (within the confines of the Germany of 1933). Since there were no more than about 140,000 localities there in 1933, and since several thousand of these were founded in modern times, we may assume that every fifth inhabited place disappeared during the late Middle Ages—i.e., in the fourteenth and fifteenth centuries—and was never re-established.

As large numbers of such *deserted villages* likewise appeared in the Scandinavian countries and in England, France, and Poland in the late Middle Ages (although in those countries they were re-established more often than was the case in Germany), we must look for explanations that enable us to comprehend the accumulation of deserted

PRICE AND WAGE MOVEMENTS IN EUROPE, 1351–1525

50-year average, based on the silver content of coins, 1351–1375 = 100

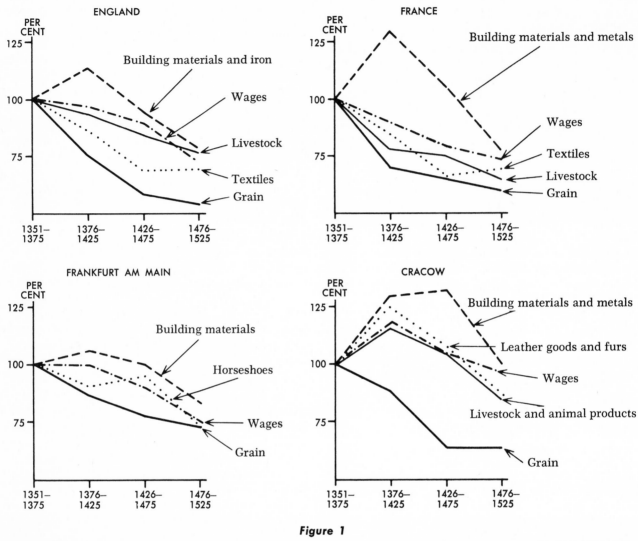

Figure 1

Source: Abel (1935) 1966.

villages in the late Middle Ages as a universal European phenomenon. The falling population in Europe of the late Middle Ages affords one explanation. The population of central Europe dropped perhaps as early as the great famine of 1307–1317, but certainly during the bubonic plague (the Black Death) of 1348–1350, which came out of the Orient and swept over Europe; and it remained low, for the first wave of the plague was followed by others. The depopulation was followed by migrations. The peasants abandoned the settlements in inaccessible and elevated localities (Norway, the Alps), on infertile soil, or in perilous social circumstances. They migrated into the valleys—to a more productive agriculture or a smaller burden—or else into the towns. The naturalization lists of many towns in the late Middle Ages, and sometimes the very names of those naturalized (which reveal their origins), are evidence of this flight from the land in the late Middle Ages.

Economic conditions must also be acknowledged as a causative factor in the movement from the countryside to the city. During the late Middle Ages the prices of agricultural products fell; the prices of craft products and wages were much steadier (Figure 1). Unskilled laborers often received the counterpart of 20 to 30 kilograms of grain as their day's wages. This, too, was a consequence of the decreased population, and although the peasants did not comprehend these relationships, they saw that work was easier, life was safer, and burdens were lighter in the towns than on the land. Therefore they migrated to the city, and when they were no longer able to do so, they sent their sons to the townsfolk—as reported in a Prussian source, "to serve or to learn a trade."

Field arrangements. When the period of deserting the villages came to an end, clearing and settling were resumed, and the manorial system that had come down from the Middle Ages was extended still further. Over large areas of central Europe this was the three-field or multifield economy, with common pasturage and the open-field system.

For a long time it was thought that these field arrangements were linked to the taking over of land during the barbarian invasions. It was believed that the initial settlers had occupied the land in common and divided it into farmstead land, arable land, and meadows, with the arable land divided into larger plots and these plots subdivided into strips, each family then being allocated several strips. This implied that the strip farming of the fields and the broad parceling out of the strips with regular crop rotation had existed "from the very outset," a notion that had to be abandoned. The village with "open fields" (*Gewanndorf*) had precursors from which its subsequent form, which has come down to us, evolved through expansion, alteration, and reconstruction.

Expansion signifies the gradual growth of arable land by the extension of clearing. In many cases the later fields can be distinguished from the earlier ones by their names, their location with respect to the village, and their shape; and even today we can perceive the original fields, to which usually only a few farmsteads were attached. As the number of peasant families increased the area of arable land had to be expended. If enough waste land and woodland were available, the arable land could be extended by clearing from the village as a center. Since this work of clearing, especially in the bush and forest, could rarely be handled by a single peasant family, it is easy to understand the parceling out of the newly cleared land. It reflected the individual's share in the work done in common. The expansion theory explains the gradual growth of arable land, although it does not explain the combining of parcels and strips into large fields, which were cultivated according to strict rules in the old villages.

The *alteration theory* proposes to explain the origin of this utilization of the arable land in common. It depicts conditions that might well have necessitated a transition from a more individual to a more cooperative economy, perhaps in the following manner. As the populations increased, real properties began to be subdivided; fields were cut up into irregular shapes and locations. This gave rise to the "medley" of pieces of land, which compelled cooperation. Crossings had to be regulated, water rights settled, and cultivation plans attuned to one another. The sown fields also had to be fenced in to protect them from grazing cattle, shepherds had to be appointed, and other arrangements made that could be effected only in agreement with neighbors. This promoted a constant association of the joint proprietors of a field, as well as the arising of a collective consciousness that facilitated renunciation of individual rights, no longer so useful.

We cannot say with certainty when this took place. The origins of these utilizations in common of arable land probably go far back in time. Tacitus describes conditions that might be interpreted as such commons, but these are probably attributable to special circumstances, such as migrations or states of war. It is unlikely that most of the common utilizations of land originated much earlier than the expansion period of the high Middle Ages, and many new villages in the formerly Slavic East were founded in the same period (eleventh to thirteenth centuries). The system of strip farming, which had proved its worth, was transferred to these commons. Field areas were demarcated according to soil quality and distance from the village. On the resulting scattered holdings all the peasants were treated as equitably as possible and moreover were equally affected by wet weather, rain, or hail, a situation that diminished individual risk.

Recent research has shown, however, that a large-field economy had by no means gained as much ground in the high Middle Ages as had previously been assumed, even where it subsequently became the rule. Here we are aided by the *reconstruction theory*. This theory makes allowance for the period of deserted villages. Once the villages had decayed, the fields had gone to weeds, and property rights had been obscured, planning, distribution, and rearrangement could be effected as in virgin territory. Parcels could be laid out and strips staked out and assembled into large fields without disturbing older rights. Here and there the old field boundaries remained, but as a rule they disappeared on cultivated land. Then, and in many instances only at the beginning of modern times, did the dominant picture become that of the large-field economy of a group of peasants joined in a working association.

Yet a countermovement developed at an early date, leading from the (relative) collective to greater individuation of property and usufruct rights. In England, enclosures, the fencing of sections of fields and forests for individual use, began as early as the fourteenth and fifteenth centuries. In the sixteenth century the peasants of the bishopric of Kempten in Allgäu began to dissolve their villages and common lands and to shift their farmsteads to the former common lands. The north European nobility began to withdraw their fields from the village common lands in the seventeenth and eighteenth centuries, and this trend became stronger in the nineteenth century. Yet the elimination of farming strips, which began thus—with or without the initial disintegration of the villages —remains even today one of the major tasks of agrarian policy in many European countries.

Social arrangements. The little settlements and balk-enclosed fields uncovered by the spade and revealed by genetic research on arable land are evidence of a peasantry that was organized in tiny groups around house and family. Their arable land was sufficient to be cultivated by and to support the inhabitants of the house. Over and above all regional peculiarities, the shape of the Carolingian *mansus*, the Danish *bool*, the English *hide*, the Breton *ran,* and the German *Hufe* all bore the stamp of the *terra familiae* thus delimited and established.

This does not exclude social differentiation. Greater economic power and prominent social status were not lacking even in earliest times, although it was only with the increasing density of population and with the increasing shortage of land that the phase of social differentiation and integration that produced the social pattern of the Middle Ages began.

The central factor was *territorial dominion.* It set up a relationship to the soil. As long as land was available in abundance, man was the more valuable property and villenage the adequate form of dominion. As land became scarce, rights and obligations could be linked to its transfer. This is what happened in many countries; a rather uniform form of territorial dominion resulted, notwithstanding many differences in detail. The core of such dominion was the manor. This was the seat of the manorial administrators (steward, *villicus*) who collected dues from the peasants and were overseers of the services the peasants had to perform on the land belonging to the lord of the manor (the *terra salica*). Most of the land was parceled out to the peasants, who constituted an association subject to manorial law. Manorial law governed their rights and obligations and also sub-

jected the lord's claims to the verdict of a manorial court, on which the peasants also sat and had a vote as long as the ancient peasant freedoms lingered.

About A.D. 1000 the large landed estates of the kings, the church, and the counts that had characterized the era of the Franks were succeeded by small landed estates. The *villicus*, who had been a farmer, was succeeded by the manorial feudal knight, who followed the profession of arms and hunting, and pleasures of chivalry, losing interest in his private property. Many of the manors were dissolved or transformed. Rents became important. In some parts of Europe this process went so far that hardly anything more of the old manorial associations than a sheaf of rent rights and rent obligations survived. Elsewhere leaseholdlike conditions evolved, leading in some places to exclusive ownership by the lord of the manor (England) and in others to the peasants' sole ownership (northwest Germany, Denmark, and Scandinavia). We cannot trace these details in this article, but we do have to point out a special formation that arose in east Germany and the adjacent Slavic lands. In these areas a new structure, the so-called *Gutsherrschaft* (manorial domain), grew out of the *Grundherrschaft* (landed estate).

During the period of settlement peasants and knights, still only little differentiated socially and economically, cultivated side by side the land in east Germany. When many peasant farms were deserted in eastern Europe during the late fourteenth and the fifteenth centuries, the knights annexed to their own estates the land thus left vacant. This involved little change in the economy at first, since no markets were available. Only in the sixteenth century, as the population began to increase again, did markets improve. Prices of agricultural products rose, and the markets in the West were opened up to the products of east European agriculture. By the end of the sixteenth century Danzig alone exported as much as 130,000 metric tons of grain annually.

The rising real prices of agricultural products formed the economic background for the expansion of large grain farms in the East (Figure 2). And there were other factors. The rise of mercenary armies relieved the knights of the obligation of military service. Once their military function vanished they were freed for the tasks of agriculture. The weakness of the central power (the state) was another important factor. It resulted in the transfer of major sovereign rights, such as the rights of judicature, taxation, and *corvée* labor for

PRICE AND WAGE MOVEMENTS IN EUROPE IN THE SIXTEENTH CENTURY

25-year average, based on the silver content of coins, 1501–1525 = 100

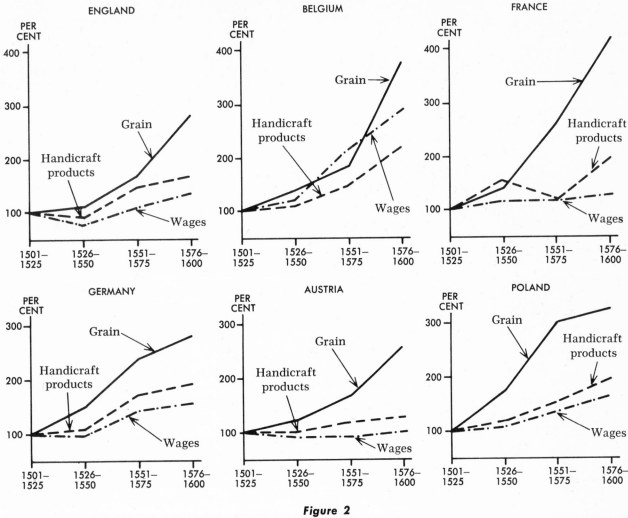

Figure 2

Source: Abel (1935) 1966.

public works, to the knights and landowners. This made possible the confiscation of much peasant ownership (*Bauernlegen*), which contributed in no small degree to the expansion of estate size during the periods of agricultural boom, particularly around 1600 and again around 1800.

At the same time the peasants' property rights were impaired. Hereditary, little encumbered property became the exception, nonhereditary property the rule. The peasants, with wife and children, were forced to do *corvée* labor, manual haulage with teams of draft animals; as servants they were bound to the soil and became subjects of their lord.

The emancipation of the peasants (*Bauernbefreiungen*) eliminated landed estates and manorial domains, thus releasing forces that, together with the industrial and technical advances of the nineteenth century, initiated a new phase in agriculture. [*For further discussion of these aspects of medieval agriculture, see* MANORIAL ECONOMY.]

Agriculture and the economy. An endeavor to place agriculture within the framework of general economic development may begin with the theories advanced by the classical economists around the turn of the eighteenth century. Malthus proclaimed that population always tends to increase faster than the foodstuffs available. Ricardo added that the condition of the workers grows steadily worse over-all, while that of the landlords constantly improves.

When we compare prices and wages in the fifteenth century with those at the beginning of the nineteenth century, the historical data appear fully

Table 1 — Price and wage movements in the agrarian period: Indices at 1801–1850 based on 1401–1450 = 100

England		Germany	
Wheat	563	Rye	378
Wages	310	Iron	173
Iron	104	Wages	149

Source: Abel (1935) 1966.

to confirm the theorists' assertions (see Table 1). In addition, grain prices rose absolutely as well as relatively to the prices of handicraft products. Land rents, measured, say, in rentals for unencumbered plots of land, rose even more. Wages lagged behind. Around 1800 a Berlin mason, for example, earned hardly more than the equivalent of 7 kg. of rye per day. How he fed, clothed, and housed himself and his family on such an income remains a mystery.

The theorists had less success with their predictions of the future. Population continued to grow in the nineteenth and twentieth centuries, but the living standard of the masses improved. Wages rose much faster than the prices of grain or iron (see Table 2). We find a break in price, wage, and rent trends at the threshold of the industrial era.

Table 2 — Price and wage movements in the industrial period: Indices at 1951–1960 based on 1801–1850 = 100

England		Germany	
Wages	995	Wages	1,216
Iron	201	Rye	286
Wheat	111	Iron	200

Source: Abel (1935) 1966.

There is analogous evidence in the narrower field of agriculture. During the initial period farming took precedence over livestock raising, for, as Adam Smith pointed out, a corn field of moderate fertility produces much more food for man than the best pasture of the same size. During the following period field crops were also placed in the service of livestock raising. Meat consumption fluctuated similarly, sinking from far above 100 kg. per capita per annum in the fifteenth century in Germany to about 14 kg. per capita per annum around 1800, after which it began to rise again. Thus, there have been two clearly distinct phases or periods in the history of European agriculture and food supply since the high Middle Ages.

Still, this break indicates only part of what actually happened. The watershed dates can be derived from the statistical data only by omitting the intervening data (as in Tables 1 and 2). The

predominating, or at least the more obvious, trend in the statistical series of agricultural production, prices, income, and foodstuff consumption was not a continuous rise or fall, but rather a repetitive (pulsating) oscillation, in turn made up of several superimposed cycles.

Secular cycles. When we employ appropriate statistical methods to eliminate the short-term and medium-term grain-price fluctuations, we find secular cycles, which can be traced back into the Middle Ages in northern Italy, France, England, Germany, and Austria (Figure 3). Ever since Jean Bodin, in 1568, termed the surplus of precious metals the most important and almost sole cause of the rise of prices, we have tended to look to money for the causes of such long-term price changes. Yet prices varied with respect to one another and to wages, both during the upward and the downward general price trends, and these relative changes cannot be explained by the simple quantity theory of money. They point back to the change in population, which paralleled the change in grain prices in central Europe and has been inversely proportional to the change in real wages ever since the late Middle Ages. This is true not only of the Middle Ages but also of modern times. Population rose sharply in all the countries of central Europe during the sixteenth century and through the beginning of the seventeenth century, after which this increase came to a halt. Population began to rise once more only after about the middle of the eighteenth century, a trend that is even more pronounced today.

The effects of population trends cannot be separated from the effects of the price–wage ratio, since both exhibit the same trend as far as agriculture is concerned. All we can say is that agricultural output and agricultural income paralleled population *and* price changes.

This is true, first of all, of *agricultural acreage*. The period of clearing in the twelfth and thirteenth centuries was followed by the period of deserted villages in the late Middle Ages. The price rise of the sixteenth century was accompanied by a second wave of farmland expansion. A third wave set in during the eighteenth century (even earlier in Germany, where it occurred soon after the end of the Thirty Years' War), again resulting in a substantial increase in farm acreage.

Second, the secular cycles of grain price changes were accompanied by changes in the *intensity of agriculture*. No matter where we look, at the development of operating technology, yields, expenditures, or the systems of farm management, the decisive advances took place during the periods of

GRAIN PRICES IN EUROPE FROM THE THIRTEENTH TO THE TWENTIETH CENTURIES *
Three-term moving average of ten-year averages, in grams of silver per 100 kg.

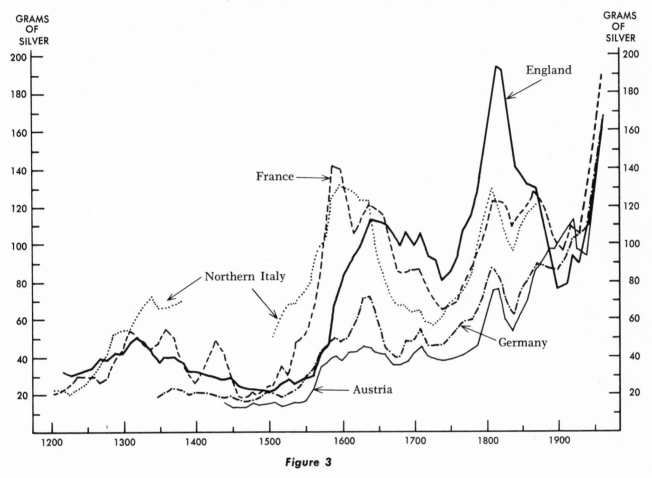

Figure 3

* Wheat prices used for France, England, and northern Italy; rye prices used for Germany and Austria.

Source: Abel (1935) 1966.

long-term price rises. The periods of falling agricultural prices, i.e., the close of the Middle Ages and the decades after the Thirty Years' War, were associated with extensive farming (e.g., the increase in sheepraising in England during the late Middle Ages at the expense of grain farming) or stagnation in the evolution of agriculture.

Third, the secular price fluctuations were associated with changes in *agricultural income*. This applies above all (in fact, by definition) to those shares of agricultural income that are to be allocated to the soil as a unique factor of production, that is, to the rent of Ricardo's theory. It also applies, however, even if in a somewhat qualified way, to the stipulated dues and services of an economic order that conceded influence upon income distribution to authority as well as to the market, i.e., to the "feudal rent charges" of the incipient trading economy. Last, it also applies to peasant income, which usually consisted of wages and rent, but which actually tended to follow rent

even on farms of moderate size as soon as wages and rent began to diverge.

Short-term fluctuations. Shorter-term fluctuations were embedded in the secular cycles. They were caused by crop fluctuations, wars, stagnation of trade, and other events, but it should be borne in mind that the effects of even these short-term fluctuations were substantially affected by the long-term changes in prices and income and by the underlying man–land ratio. (For instance, the devastating consequences of the great famine of 1307–1317 can be explained only in association with the long-term shortage of land during the high Middle Ages.) Thus abundant harvests during periods of secular depression in agriculture often brought about what may be termed *agrarian crises* comparable to recent phenomena of a similar nature. Yet, in addition to the factors in common (often underestimated in the past), the differences between the early and later marketing crises of agriculture are also significant. To begin with, the

WHEAT PRICES IN ENGLAND, FRANCE, AND GERMANY, 1790–1960
Seven-term moving averages of annual prices, in marks per 100 kg.

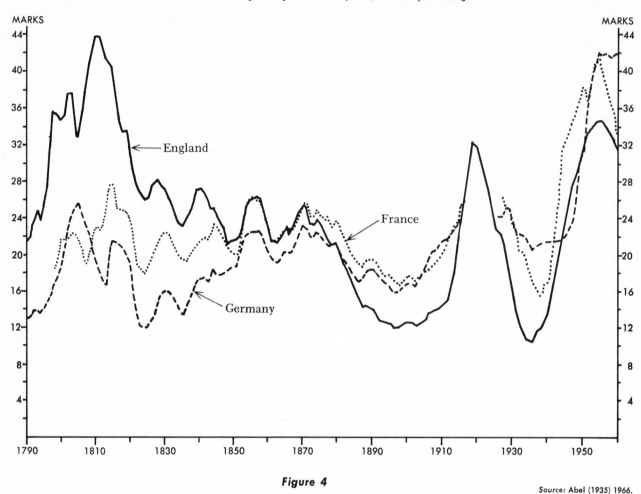

Figure 4

Source: Abel (1935) 1966.

interdependence of market and agriculture increased and with it the territorial and functional scope of the crises; second, the secular cycles of grain prices broke down during the nineteenth century into cycles that were still "long" but which were much shorter than before (Figure 4); and third, the causes of these secular fluctuations and hence the causes of more recent agrarian crises (around 1820, 1890, 1930) were quite different from those of previous depressions. The earlier crises occurred in an era of halting population growth or even of decreasing population, while the agrarian crises of the nineteenth century and even of the twentieth century coincided with a marked population increase.

Insofar as ultimate causes can be cited, they must be sought in the participation of agriculture in the powerful expansionist drive that has been manifested ever since the technical and social revolutions of the end of the eighteenth century. Theodore W. Schultz came to the same conclusion

(1945, p. 45). Schultz thought that "three sets of circumstances are possible in the rate of growth in the demand and the supply of farm products: (a) an equal increase in both demand and supply; (b) an unequal expansion, in which demand pushes hard against supply; (c) an unequal expansion, in which supply outdistances demand." He did not discuss the first situation, because it is of no theoretical or historical interest. The second, "with demand for farm products pushing hard against the supply (the state of affairs now present in China and India) . . . worried Malthus, Ricardo, and their contemporaries. The third condition, where the supply of farm products increases so fast that it presses hard against the demand, is the one that has in fact (since Malthus and Ricardo) occurred." This is a simple, but quite accurate, formula for making a distinction between the two periods we find in the history of Western agriculture since the high Middle Ages.

WILHELM ABEL

BIBLIOGRAPHY

BOOKS

ABEL, WILHELM (1935) 1966 *Agrarkrisen und Agrarkonjunktur: Eine Geschichte der Land- und Ernährungswirtschaft Mitteleuropas seit dem hohen Mittelalter.* 2d ed., enl. Hamburg (Germany): Parey.

ABEL, WILHELM (1943) 1955 *Die Wüstungen des ausgehenden Mittelalters.* 2d ed. Quellen und Forschungen zur Agrargeschichte, 1. Stuttgart (Germany): Fischer.

L'agriculture à travers les âges, histoire des faits, des institutions, de la pensée et des doctrines économiques et sociales. 5 vols. 1935–1965 Paris: De Boccard. → See especially Volume 2: *Première période de Hammourabi à la fin de l'empire romain,* by E. Savoy, 1935. Volume 3: *L'agriculture au moyen âge de la fin de l'empire romain au XVIe siècle,* by R. Grand and R. Delatouche, 1950. Volume 4: *L'agriculture du XVIIe siècle à la fin du XVIIIe,* by E. Soreau, 1952.

BELOW, GEORG VON (1920) 1926 *Probleme der Wirtschaftsgeschichte: Eine Einführung in das Studium der Wirtschaftsgeschichte.* 2d ed. Tübingen (Germany): Mohr.

Cambridge Economic History of Europe. Volume 1: The Agrarian Life of the Middle Ages. Edited by T. H. Clapham and Eileen Power. 1941 Cambridge Univ. Press.

DUBY, GEORGES 1962 *L'économie rurale et la vie des campagnes dans l'occident médiéval France, Angleterre, Empire, IXe–XVe siècles: Essai de synthèse et perspectives de recherches.* 2 vols. Paris: Aubier.

LAVELEYE, ÉMILE DE (1874) 1901 *De la propriété et de ses formes primitives.* 5th ed. Paris: Alcan.

MEITZEN, AUGUST 1895 *Siedlung und Agrarwesen der Westgermanen und Ostgermanen, der Kelten, Römer, Finen und Slawen.* 3 vols. and Atlas. Berlin: Hertz.

SCHULTZ, THEODORE W. 1945 *Agriculture in an Unstable Economy.* New York: McGraw-Hill.

SLICHER VAN BATH, BERNHARD H. (1960) 1963 *The Agrarian History of Western Europe, A.D. 500–1850.* London: Arnold. → First published as *De agrarische Geschiedenis van West-Europa, 500–1850.*

PERIODICALS

Agricultural History. → Published since 1927 by the Agricultural History Society.

Agricultural History Review. → Published since 1953 by the British Agricultural History Society.

Annales: Économies, sociétés, civilisations. → Published since 1946. Supersedes *Annales d'histoire sociale,* Vols. 1–3 (1939–1941), which superseded *Annales d'histoire économique et sociale,* Vols. 1–10 published between 1929 and 1938.

Rivista di storia dell' agricoltura. → Published since 1961 by the Istituto di Tecnica e Propaganda Agraria.

Zeitschrift für Agrargeschichte und Agrarsoziologie. → Published since 1953.

IV

PRODUCTION

Until some yet unanticipated chemical revolution occurs, the production of food, fiber, and related products will remain an economic activity essential to the continued survival of man on this planet. Anthropologists have found civilizations or groups that did not travel, exchange goods, or manufacture. They have not, however, reported groups that did not eat, and the civilizations that have not used some method of protecting the human body from the elements have been few. Thus, the economic activity embraced in agricultural production has as its primary purpose the meeting of the physiological needs of man, although in most economies agricultural production involves products that go beyond meeting these needs.

Until a society has met its basic needs for food and fiber its economic activity is directed to little else. In a wealthy or advanced economy the production of food and fiber constitutes a small fraction of its total economic output and often an even smaller fraction of its total consumption. Even so, the importance of agricultural production should not be underestimated and an understanding of the nature of the economic activity involved should not be neglected.

Definition and measurement. The problem of defining agricultural production involves defining both "agricultural" and "production." Agricultural production as used in this discussion will include the growing and/or harvesting of food and fiber products grown for legal human consumption. Thus, economic activities that may take place within the unit producing an agricultural product, but that occur after harvest, such as processing, curing, or marketing, generally are not considered production. It should be noted that products not classified as either food or fiber—such as flowers, tobacco, and industrial oilseeds—are also usually included as agricultural production. Such products as natural rubber and forest products are often classified as agricultural production.

Agricultural production usually means the production of a product via a biological process: the idea of growing is involved. Even if growth takes place entirely removed from natural processes or the earth, as in modern-day broiler and egg production, it is still classified as agricultural production.

Defining agricultural production is a relatively simple problem; measuring agricultural production is not so simple, and the results are somewhat inexact, even in advanced economies. One problem is the avoidance of double counting in determining agricultural production; another is not counting very large parts of the production that actually occurs.

The problem of double counting occurs because many agricultural products are not consumed directly by humans but are used as intermediate products in other agricultural production. In some countries much of the crop acreage is devoted to the production of forage and feed grains that in turn are fed to livestock: the livestock is eventually used for human consumption. In many parts of the world the farm power is supplied by animals, and much of the crop production is to provide food for these animals which in turn are used to produce food for human consumption. If we are to avoid double counting we cannot count total crop production and total livestock production as net product. It is necessary to deduct that portion of crop and livestock production used for farm power and that portion of crop production used to produce livestock output. If this deduction can be accurately made, the resulting measurement consists of net farm output destined for human consumption. It should be recognized, however, that even in wealthy countries with good statistical measures of gross crop and livestock output the deductions are only approximations. In countries with poor statistical estimating methods, the estimates are only gross approximations—if they are made at all.

The second problem in measuring agricultural production is that of accounting for much of the production in subsistence agriculture. In parts of the world up to 80 per cent or more of the population live by primitive agricultural production that is primarily for personal or family consumption. Little, if any, of the product that is produced is sold outside the family or the village, unless there is a surplus above family or local wants. In such areas of the world the population estimates carry wide margins of error, and estimates of production and consumption in such areas have an even wider margin of error. One of the reasons that some areas have shown notable increases in agricultural production in the early stages of economic development may be that for the first time production that was previously unmeasured is caught in the newly developing market economy or by improved statistical measurements.

Thus, in using statistics relating to agricultural production one should view them with more caution than is sometimes exhibited. In the wealthy noncommunist countries the statistics generally are reasonably accurate and complete. In the underdeveloped countries wide margins of error are frequent in statistics relating to agricultural production. In some countries the usual margins of error are compounded by national policy deliberately designed to mislead observers regarding actual production, so that such statistics on agricultural production may be of little value.

Types of organization. Agricultural production has been organized in several different ways in different parts of the world and at different periods of time. These various forms of organization have had significant effects upon the rates of change and growth in productivity in agriculture and, in some cases, upon the entire society in which they existed.

It should be recognized that in most respects the different types of organization of agricultural production are not distinct and clear-cut. Classifications of types of organization are in part a function of the economic system in which they are found. Units that would be classified as low-production or subsistence farms in the United States might be classified as medium or large-scale farms in other agricultural economies.

For purposes of classification it is useful to consider four elements: (1) the quantity of resources involved in the production unit; (2) the proportions of those resources (land, labor, and capital) involved in a typical production unit; (3) who has the power to decide how the resources of the production unit are used; and (4) the extent to which such economic factors as product and resource prices determine the way in which the resources of the production unit are used.

Subsistence. Probably the largest in numbers of persons involved, if not in production, is the subsistence agricultural production typical of many of the underdeveloped areas of the world. Subsistence agriculture is often organized around tribal or village groups, with members of the village engaging in agricultural production in the areas adjacent to the village. This organization is marked by a low ratio of land per worker and the almost complete absence of capital goods. Production processes are heavily influenced by custom, superstition, and long-standing experience. Not only is the individual producer capital scarce but community capital in the form of roads, irrigation, communication, and transportation is often absent. In such areas neither the market for products nor the market for productive factors is well developed, so that the usual economic forces of prices and incomes may produce less response than is typically expected in a production process. Thus, much of the subsistence agricultural production in the world is primarily for consumption by the members of the family producing it, although some of its products do move into market systems, both local and international.

Plantation. In those economies where subsistence agriculture is found there is often another form of economic organization of agricultural production—plantation agriculture. Its economic organization contrasts sharply with that of subsistence agriculture: typically, it is entirely market oriented, selling its products in national and international markets. In fact, agricultural production from such organizations often is the major source of foreign exchange for underdeveloped countries. The economic organization of plantation agriculture frequently involves large capital investment, often from foreign sources. The ratio of land and capital to labor in production is higher than in subsistence agriculture. The labor supply for plantation agriculture usually is local, with payment in wages or goods rather than by sharing in the returns. The technical production processes are centrally determined by the managers. Quite often the auxiliary services necessary to the specific production and marketing of the particular commodity involved are highly developed, in striking contrast to similar developments for the rest of the agricultural economy concerned. [See PLANTATIONS.]

Hacienda. Another form of economic organization of agriculture is that of the hacienda, found in Latin America. These organizations are privately owned, with the owners generally living elsewhere. Unlike plantations, haciendas usually do not involve high capital investments and modern technical methods. In fact, much of the problem of inadequate agricultural production in many Latin American countries can be attributed to the lack of intensive use of some of the most productive land—which is generally on haciendas. Haciendas are typically used for livestock grazing and cereal crop production, involving low capital and labor inputs per unit of land. The labor used in such production receives little pay and has little or no incentive to adopt new technologies. Almost all observers agree that this system of agriculture is relatively inefficient at both the individual firm and national levels, but since land ownership and political power are closely related there is little incentive to change unless change is forced by outside events.

Large-scale production with collective ownership. Another form of organization of agricultural production is found in the large-scale farms that dominate agriculture in the Soviet Union and some other eastern European countries. These are state or collective farms. In some other areas, notably Israel, agricultural production is organized along similar lines, but the farms are cooperative in structure. The capital for this type of large-scale agricultural production is public capital, not owned or controlled by those who actually produce the farm products. In general, large quantities of capital are involved, in the form of both land and machinery. Such farms are primarily for the purpose of producing for nonfarm consumption and are usually heavily dependent upon nonfarm-produced

goods for productive inputs. Even in the communist countries a price system is used as one of the methods of allocating productive resources to and within the agricultural sector. Moreover, some type of incentive system frequently is used in order to induce workers on the large-scale farms to increase output. Since these large-scale farms often are specialized in the production of field crops, workers on such farms often are allowed to maintain their own small plots or farms for the production of fruits, vegetables, and livestock products. Even in communist countries the agricultural workers usually are allowed to market some of the products from these private plots [see COMMUNISM, ECONOMIC ORGANIZATION OF, *article on* AGRICULTURE].

Large-scale production with private ownership. In the United States and other countries there are some large-scale agricultural production units which are privately owned; sometimes they are corporate in structure. They involve large capital inputs, use the most advanced technology, and often are highly efficient units of production. Such farms are almost totally dependent upon hired labor; the capital-to-man and land-to-man ratios are usually very high; and the management decisions are usually centralized, with the production specialized in one or a few products.

Large-scale organization of agriculture has proved to be less effective in the production of some livestock products than it is in the production of crops. One exception is the production of range livestock, for which large acreages of land can be used extensively without significant labor inputs. The difficulties of organizing large-scale units to produce livestock products appear to be the result of diseconomies in the areas of disease control and production management decisions that arise in livestock production. Large-scale agricultural production involves centralized decisions on technology and management, whereas almost constant contact between manager and product appears to be a prerequisite to most successful livestock production. However, technical breakthroughs in disease control have made large-scale agricultural production feasible for poultry products, and similar technical developments may make large-scale production units feasible for other livestock as well.

Small-scale production. Somewhat above the primitive subsistence agricultural production units described earlier are the small farms that are common in western Europe, Japan, parts of Latin America, and in the United States. Such farms may involve from one to ten or more acres, so that the ratio of land to labor is low. The capital input usually is low also, and the total output of the unit may not be high. Such farms produce in excess of family consumption needs; in fact, their production often is primarily for sale. However, the resources available are usually too few to employ profitably all of the available labor, so that the level of living of these farmers is low for the society in which they are found.

Medium-scale production. There are, finally, farms that are larger scale than those just discussed but that fall short of the large-scale farms in some continuum of size. This type of agricultural production typifies the agriculture of the United States and western Europe. It is marked by private ownership of the productive resources, with the ownership, management, and labor function carried out by a single family. This type of organization has come to be called the "family farm" in the United States, and its strengthening vis-à-vis other forms of economic organization of agricultural production has always been a major goal of U.S. farm policy.

Despite the rather modest size of these farms relative to the large-scale farms previously discussed, their capital-to-man ratio often tends to be high. This is because the response to technical and economic change in agricultural production in the United States and western Europe has been primarily to increase the capital used in conjunction with the labor of the farm operator and his family, thus enabling them to increase agricultural production substantially. Technical advances in agricultural production in the United States have not led to a shift from small-scale to large-scale units but rather to a reduction in the number of subsistence farms. In the United States these small-scale and medium-scale farms accounted for 70 per cent of total agricultural production in 1959, and their contribution to output actually has risen relative to that of large-scale farms over the past two decades.

These medium-scale and small-scale farms are organized to produce almost entirely for market consumption. They are increasingly dependent upon nonfarm-produced capital items and productive resources beyond the land and family labor. A market price system is the primary determinant of resource allocation to and within these producing units. Decision making about all phases of production is almost completely decentralized to the level of individual producers. Of course, such a system of economic organization requires an extensive public investment in education of the operator and family members, roads, market information, and other overhead services if it is to function effectively.

From historical performance, it appears that, based upon economic criteria, the decentralized medium-scale and small-scale production units in agriculture have excelled in their ability to produce farm products. Rates of growth in output and productivity on such farms have far exceeded those achieved by other types of economic organization of agricultural production. It is probably a mistake to say this superior performance is due to a "free" price system rather than to recognize that it is the result of a complex decentralized production system, heavily dependent on its outside auxiliary services, both private and public, to provide a constant flow of new methods of production and on managers able to absorb and apply these changes in a market economy.

The distribution of world production. Neither population nor agricultural production is distributed equally around the world, and foreign trade does not serve to cause consumption patterns to vary significantly from the population–production distribution. Table 1 shows the distribution of population, arable land, and agricultural production, as estimated by the United States Department of Agriculture in 1958.

Table 1 — Distribution of world population, arable land, and agricultural production, by regions, 1958

	Population	Arable land	Agricultural production
	(Per cent of world total)		
United States	6.1	13.5	15.8
Canada	0.6	2.9	1.5
Australia and New Zealand	0.4	2.0	2.2
Western Europe	10.6	6.9	15.7
Eastern Europe	11.2	19.9	14.2
Mainland China[a]	23.5	8.0	16.0
Japan[b]	3.2	0.4	2.1
South, southeast Asia and other Far East	26.7	18.3	14.2
Latin America	6.7	7.3	9.1
Africa and Near East	11.0	20.8	9.2
World	100.0	100.0	100.0

a. Also North Korea, North Vietnam, and Mongolia.
b. Includes Pacific Islands.

Source: Adapted from U.S. Department of Agriculture [1961] 1962, p. 9, table 1.

The United States, Canada, Australia, New Zealand, and western Europe had 17.7 per cent of the world's population, contained 25.3 per cent of its arable land area, and, because of the advanced agricultural production techniques used, accounted for 35.2 per cent of the world's agricultural production. At the other end of the scale the Far East

Table 2 — Distribution of world population and food supplies, by regions, 1957–1959

	PERCENTAGE OF POPULATION	PERCENTAGE OF FOOD SUPPLIES		
		Total	Animal	Crops
Europe	21.6	34.2	38.4	26.2
North America	6.6	21.8	29.2	10.4
Oceania	0.5	1.3	1.6	0.9
Far East, including mainland China	52.9	27.8	18.5	44.2
Near East	4.4	4.2	2.8	5.5
Africa	7.1	4.3	2.8	6.3
Latin America	6.9	6.4	6.7	6.5
World	100.0	100.0	100.0	100.0

Source: Food and Agriculture Organization of the United Nations 1963, p. 20, table 9.

(omitting Japan) had one-half of the world's population, 26 per cent of its arable land, and accounted for only 30 per cent of its agricultural production.

Total world agricultural production is highly skewed in favor of the developed countries, and trade does little to correct this imbalance. This is especially true for the more preferred products, the animal products, which are even less equally distributed in relation to population than is total agricultural production (Table 2). Europe and North America, with 28.2 per cent of the world's population, consume 67.6 per cent of the food supplies coming from animal sources. Peasant or subsistence agriculture tends to be crop agriculture, for only after a relatively high income level is reached is it feasible to pay the cost, in terms of energy loss, that is involved in the conversion of crops to livestock products prior to their use for human consumption.

Thus, agricultural production relative to population is greatest in those areas where medium-scale and small-scale market-oriented agriculture, with

decentralized decision-making units of production, predominates. In the Soviet Union and other communist countries, where large-scale agriculture is most common, private small-scale farms still are a major source of production of livestock and fruit and vegetable products. The inability of subsistence agriculture to provide an adequate base for economic growth has long been recognized and underlies the various attempts at the reorganization of agricultural production underway in almost every underdeveloped country.

Trends in agricultural production. Total agricultural production in the world has risen markedly in the two decades from pre-World War II to 1960 (Table 3). Despite many impressions to the contrary, agricultural production has risen at a more rapid rate than has population over the past two decades. World agricultural production per capita is reported to have risen about 12 per cent and the per capita production of food products about 14 per cent.

However, despite this encouraging trend in agricultural production, the trends in production and population growth have been adverse to the underdeveloped areas of the world (Table 4). North America, Europe, and Oceania have experienced huge increases in agricultural production, starting from a level that was already favorable relative to their population. As a result, the major agricultural problem in these areas has been the maintenance of income levels of agricultural producers in the face of increases of output of products with an inelastic demand. The less developed areas of the world have experienced almost the same percentage increases in production as the developed areas; but in most cases population growth has exceeded that of agricultural production, so that production per capita actually has declined from prewar levels. Thus, little or no gain has been

Table 3 — Indices of world agricultural production in relation to population, 1952/1953–1956/1957 average = 100*

	Prewar (average)	1948/1949– 1952/1953 (average)	1953/1954– 1957/1958 (average)	1958/1959	1959/1960	1960/1961	1961/1962 (preliminary)
Total production							
All agricultural products	77	88	102	113	116	119	119
Food products only	76	88	103	114	116	119	119
Population	81	94	102	107	109	112	114
Per capita production							
All agricultural products	95	95	101	106	106	106	105
Food products only	94	94	101	106	106	107	105

* The indices have been calculated by applying regional weights, based on 1952/1953–1956/1957 farm-price relationships, to the production figures, which are adjusted to allow for quantities used for feed and seed. The indices for food products exclude coffee, tea, tobacco, inedible oilseeds, animal and vegetable fibers, and rubber. Mainland China is excluded because of incomplete data.

Source: Food and Agriculture Organization of the United Nations 1962, p. 13, table 11-1.

Table 4 — Changes in food production and population, 1959/1960–1961/1962 average in relation to prewar period

	Population	Total food production	Per capita food production
		(Percentage increase[a])	
North America	43	65	16
Western Europe[b]	19	43	20
Eastern Europe	12	62	46
Oceania	52	44	−5
Four above regions	21	56	29
Latin America	71	69	−1
Far East[c]	46	45	−1
Near East[d]	50	66	11
Africa	53	52	−1
Four above regions	51	54	2
All above regions	38	56	13

a. Minus sign indicates decrease.
b. Includes Yugoslavia.
c. Excludes mainland China.
d. Extends from Cyprus and Turkey to Afghanistan and includes Libya, Sudan, and the United Arab Republic.

Source: Food and Agriculture Organization of the United Nations 1962, p. 16, table 11-3.

achieved from the low levels of output per person that marked these areas of subsistence agriculture more than two decades ago.

The comparative ability of certain types of agricultural organization to expand output is further illustrated by Table 5. Here we see that the underdeveloped, peasant agricultural economies have barely regained their prewar levels of crop output per capita and that most of the postwar increase in agricultural production has been in the form of livestock products and has taken place in the developed countries. Thus, the period since 1950 has been marked by attempts by underdeveloped countries to rapidly expand agricultural production to keep pace with population growth, whereas that of developed countries has been to retard rates of increase in farm output to forestall sharp declines in the price of farm products and the income of agricultural producers.

Sources of increased production. Early economists postulated that agricultural production would place a limit upon economic growth and, finally, population growth in an economy. They predicted that expansion of output would require recourse to increasingly inferior land, to the point where food production would limit the amount of other goods that could be produced and even the population. For much of the world this model still threatens to become reality, yet in some economies agricultural products are produced in great quantity and with a declining proportion of the nation's resources. It is this latter model of agricultural production that has attracted world attention and offers hope that the world can feed and clothe an expanding population and still produce increasing quantities of other goods and services.

This marked increase in agricultural production in the developed countries has been accomplished without expanding the land under cultivation and despite a major decline in labor used. It has been the result mainly of the addition of major capital equipment, in the form of machines, and the application of science to agricultural production. Science has made possible the development of new breeds of animals that produce more product per pound of feed; science has developed crops that produce more usable product from an acre of land; and science has produced new machines that make new capital investment more productive than that which previously existed. Research workers and individual managers have devised improved forms of economic organization that benefit from specialization and the economies of scale.

Thus, most of the increase in agricultural production in the advanced economies has been the

Table 5 — Per capita food supplies available for human consumption, by regions, prewar world average = 100

	PREWAR YEARS		POSTWAR YEARS		CURRENT PERIOD	
	Crops[a]	Livestock and fish[b]	Crops[a]	Livestock and fish[b]	Crops[a]	Livestock and fish[b]
North America	178	394	172	460	157	495
Europe	120	154	120	147	120	199
Oceania	181	355	194	346	179	354
Far East, including mainland China	84	38	75	30	83	38
Near East	112	72	108	71	125	72
Latin America	77	123	86	97	93	110
Africa	c	c	c	c	87	44
World	100	100	94	95	99	112

a. Vegetable oils and fats are not included.
b. Animals fats and oils are not included.
c. Not available.

Source: Food and Agriculture Organization of the United Nations 1963, p. 18, table 8.

result of growth in productivity concurrent with sharp changes in factor proportions in the agricultural economy. One of the major problems of the advanced agricultural economies is to continue to adjust to the sharp changes in factor proportions that are necessary as a result of sharply differing rates of growth in factor productivity.

One of the characteristics of advanced agriculture is its heavy dependence upon reproducible factors of production, in contrast to the traditional dependence of agricultural production upon land. Since these reproducible items used in agricultural production generally constitute only a fraction of the total demand of an economy for steel, chemicals, and petroleum products, the supply of these productive factors is relatively elastic to the agricultural industry. Thus, if the price level for farm products is favorable to the increased use of reproducible factors of production, it is possible to expand agricultural production substantially in a short period of time. This is in sharp contrast to the traditional or peasant agricultural economies, where production is still dependent primarily upon the natural resources of land and water, family effort, and little, if any, reproducible capital. Since the supply of these traditional factors of production is not readily expandable, the output of farm products is not very responsive to favorable prices.

Although the expansion of advanced agriculture is relatively responsive to changes in output or input prices, contraction of aggregate output is much less so. Much of the reproducible capital used in modern agriculture has a useful life extending over several years or production periods, and once put into use in agriculture the capital is likely to continue in production until its productive value is exhausted. Even so, the dependence of advanced agricultural production upon a steady use of expendable flow inputs (fertilizer, insecticides, fuel) means that the prices of these productive factors relative to output prices can and do influence aggregate production.

If total agricultural production in the world is to expand sufficiently to provide for the growing world population, much of world agricultural production must be shifted from peasant or subsistence agriculture to some kind of market-oriented production units making use of advanced technology and large quantities of reproducible capital and having an economic organization capable of dealing with and responsive to economic change. Thus far only a small fraction of the world's agricultural production is so organized, and improved organization of agricultural production stands as a major task in the underdeveloped economies. In the developed economies, where such advances in the organization of agricultural production have occurred, too little still is known about the basic economics in agriculture of capital flows and technological advance. Thus, the economics of agricultural production remains important throughout the world.

DALE E. HATHAWAY

[See also FOOD and LAND.]

BIBLIOGRAPHY

BROWN, LESTER R. 1963 Man, Land, and Food: Looking Ahead at World Food Needs. U.S. Department of Agriculture, Foreign Agricultural Economic Report, No. 11. Washington: Government Printing Office.

EICHER, CARL; and WITT, LAWRENCE (editors) 1964 Agriculture in Economic Development. New York: McGraw-Hill.

FOOD AND AGRICULTURE ORGANIZATION OF THE UNITED NATIONS 1962 The State of Food and Agriculture, 1962. Rome: The Organization.

FOOD AND AGRICULTURE ORGANIZATION OF THE UNITED NATIONS 1963 Third World Food Survey. Freedom From Hunger Campaign, Basic Study No. 11. Rome: The Organization.

Freedom From Hunger Campaign, Basic Study, Nos. 1–11. 1962–1963 Rome: FAO.

SCHULTZ, THEODORE W. 1964 Transforming Traditional Agriculture. New Haven: Yale Univ. Press.

U.S. DEPARTMENT OF AGRICULTURE, ECONOMIC RESEARCH SERVICE (1961) 1962 The World Food Budget, 1962 and 1966. Rev. ed. Foreign Agricultural Economic Report, No. 4. Washington: Government Printing Office.

V

CAPITAL

Viewed broadly, agricultural capital (or, for that matter, capital in general) includes investments in the production of technological change (Schultz 1964, chapter 10) and in the training of people (Schultz 1964, chapter 12) as well as in physical properties such as barns, tractors, irrigation ditches, hoes, draft stock, cattle, hogs, and growing plants (Tostlebe 1957). So viewed, capital investment in agriculture varies widely from undeveloped to developed countries, from competitively organized to highly controlled economies, and from indigenous systems to plantation systems of farming in tropical regions. The movement of capital into and out of agriculture also varies widely among different kinds of agricultural economies, thereby having profound impacts on the development of the nonfarm sector as well as on the farm sector.

Agricultural capital is thus a most interesting subject of study. The formation, use, and movement of agricultural capital help explain differences in the productivity of diverse agricultural economies and in the welfare of farmers and nonfarmers the world over. By studying capital we can understand some of the differences in productivity between (1) private and publicly managed agricultural systems, (2) Nigerian and Thai rice producers, and between (3) western European and Soviet or mainland Chinese agriculture.

When one considers the formation and use of agricultural capital from a world-wide historical perspective, it is helpful first to examine what goes on in primarily agricultural societies. As such societies develop capacity to produce more than subsistence, it becomes possible for them to save and invest. The diversion of what might have been consumption into investment takes place first privately and later as a matter of public policy.

Once a farmer has acquired the ability to produce enough to feed himself and his family, he can divert part of his energy and resources to producing more tools, buildings, paddocks, and livestock for use in further production. These articles are capital equipment which he invests in production. The resulting increase in production in turn becomes available either for sale or reinvestment in production. If the extra product is sold, the income produced is available to purchase either capital or consumer goods. Often both capital and consumer goods are acquired, and output increases still further. Per capita farm incomes increase if the value of the increased output remains with the producers and if their population increase is less than the increase in output.

At various times in all societies, and typically in some, the process of diverting agricultural output away from consumption into investment has failed to develop, has broken down, or has proceeded slowly. The reasons for this are numerous, including, among others: (1) high birth rates and, hence, high demands for the means of subsistence; (2) meager natural resources and harsh climatic conditions; (3) military action, by either invaders or indigenous governments, which reduces agricultural output or curtails capital investment in agriculture; (4) demands for agricultural output and capital to develop the nonfarm economy; and (5) exploitation of agriculture by public measures. As a result of these and other conditions, governments, organizations of farmers, and other groups have often taken public steps to promote capital formation and investment in agriculture.

Public promotional policies and programs. Public steps to promote capital formation and investment in agriculture include the organization of public agricultural credit systems. Some are highly subsidized, such as the U.S. Farm Security Administration, and others relatively self-sufficient once brought into existence, like the Production Credit Association. Both of these arose as part of a public effort to expand and maintain the use of capital in U.S. agriculture in the depression years of the 1930s.

Also involved have been direct grants of capital to individual farmers. Recipients of such grants include Norwegians whose farms were damaged by the Germans retreating to the sea from northern Finland in World War II; low-income farmers in the mid-1930s, covered by the U.S. Resettlement Administration; and Nigerian farmers under the Eastern Nigerian government's tree-crop rehabilitation scheme.

Capital is also moved into agriculture as *indirect* public investment not going to individual farmers. It may be in the form of irrigation systems, roads, public market facilities, electrical facilities, drainage ditches, and flood control, to mention but a few. These investments may take place through direct grants, subsidized loans, or credit facilities which become self-supporting once established.

Though infrequent in the United States and western Europe, large-scale investment of public funds *directly* in farm production often occurs in countries with state-operated farms and plantations. In some instances these funds come from taxes levied on the nonfarm economy. In other instances, and perhaps more frequently, they come from levies of various forms on cash export crops such as rice, rubber, and oil-palm produce. The 1962–1968 development plan of the Eastern Nigerian government, for instance, provides for large direct investments in state-operated plantation and settlement schemes. A major source of this money is a "tax" levied on oil-palm producers by a marketing board which pays farmers less than the world price for the palm oil exported through it.

There are also important public capital investments in agriculture which are *still more indirect* than public investment in roads, irrigation projects, electrical facilities, and the like. These involve public-supported research and education, two of the hallmarks of the truly advanced agricultural economies of the world (Schultz 1963; 1964). The research and educational programs of the U.S. land-grant colleges and the Department of Agriculture are outstanding examples of public investment in human and technological capital. Heavy public investment in agricultural research and training is especially characteristic of the other advanced agricultural economies of the world such as Denmark, England, the Netherlands, Canada, and Australia.

In many economies public investment in agriculture is carried out with money obtained from the farm economy through direct taxes, export assessments, profits from state-owned or operated marketing agencies, or state income from appropriated farm properties. In Thailand, for instance, heavy export charges on rice support extensive public investment in irrigation facilities and in agricultural extension and research. In Nigeria, marketing board profits (taxes) provide capital to promote the agricultural projects of the 1962–1968 development plan.

In some instances, privately organized groups of farmers sell bonds and make credit contracts for the installation of drainage ditches, pumps, and irrigation equipment. In some such cases the savings come from the farm economy; in others, from the nonfarm economy.

Public policy is an important determinant of the rate of capital formation in agriculture. Some policies and programs exploit farmers heavily, leaving little surplus to accumulate in agriculture. If such taxes are levied on commodities in whose production the country has a comparative advantage, the over-all rate of capital accumulation in the country's agriculture may be reduced substantially even though the tax moneys are reinvested in agriculture. This is especially true if corruption and inefficiency are associated with the expenditure of the funds and if the investments are in the production of crops and commodities in which the country has a low comparative advantage. If the funds are invested outside of agriculture, capital formation in agriculture may be reduced to zero. If taxes from parts of the agricultural economy with a comparative advantage are invested corruptly and inefficiently in the production of nonfarm products which have a comparative disadvantage, the country's over-all capital formation and economic growth may be greatly curtailed or may even cease entirely.

Various countries have used different combinations of policies and programs both to promote agricultural production and to obtain capital to develop their nonfarm economies. The results have varied from starved people and unsupported industry at one extreme, to farm surpluses, rapid farm capital formation, low food prices, and substantial transfer of people and income out of agriculture for industrial development at the other extreme. Among the countries successful in finding a fairly effective combination of policies and programs is the United States.

U.S. experience. The role which expanded use of capital has played in increasing the output of the U.S. agricultural economy is of special interest to nations faced with the problem of expanding their agricultural output. It commands the interest of administrators and students of economic development the world over.

Strauss and Bean estimated that U.S. farm production *doubled* from 1870 to 1895 (1940). This expansion involved the use of more land, labor, and capital and better technology. The new technology was largely that developed by "free-lance" inventors and an aggressive group of agricultural entrepreneurs. It brought new equipment, improved breeds of animals, improved plant varieties and species, and advancing methods of organizing individual farms.

From 1895 to about 1925 the nation's total agricultural output rose about as much as it had from 1870 to 1895 (Barger & Lansberg 1942). This increase was based on the use of more land, additional capital, and improved technology. The amount of labor used stayed essentially the same, but its quality improved with the expanding base for education (Johnson 1955). The capital used in this expansion was different from that of the preceding period. It involved mechanical power and improved varieties of plants and animals. This expansion also involved changes in tillage practices, crop rotations, and control of pests and diseases. At least as important as the new technology was the improvement in the human agent resulting from capital investments in both general and vocational training of farm people.

The next 17 years, from 1925 to 1942, resulted in another increase in production equal to the total output of 1870. When the prices of farm products fell relative to costs, special price-support programs maintained incentives to individual farmers, and special credit programs were developed to bring capital into agriculture. After the early 1940s agricultural production continued to expand at a rate which brought about, by the early 1960s, another increase equal to 1870's output. By then agricultural production in the United States was approximately four times as high as in 1870. The expansions from 1925 to the early 1960s followed the general pattern of 1895 to 1925. Land use did not expand greatly but labor use contracted sharply, while capital use increased. The expansion of capital use went to improve technology and to educate farmers as well as to provide physical items of production such as tractors, breeding animals, buildings, fences, wells, orchards, and tools.

In the 1870–1960 period there were also important reallocations of agricultural production from farm to farm within regions, from region to region, and between the farm and nonfarm economy. These reallocations greatly increased the productivity of American agriculture relative to small-unit agricultural economies such as those found in Europe in the same period. Capital-embodying technological advance was instrumental, along with institutional changes, in making possible and in bringing about these reallocations of production. Increases in production exceeded, both proportionately and absolutely, the increased use of resources in agriculture. Examples of farm-to-farm reallocations of production are found in the emergence of specialized dairy, stock-fattening, and cash-crop farms in areas formerly characterized by generalized farming. At the regional level fruit, vegetable, and livestock production has been specialized in areas of high comparative advantage. Similarly, the farm economy has come to specialize in crop and livestock production while transferring to the nonfarm economy the production of marketing and processing services, such as power units (tractors instead of horses) and fuel (petroleum products instead of horse feed). Specialization became the outstanding characteristic of the modern American farm.

In addition to the higher output which has resulted from increased use of capital, improved technology, and greater specialization in U.S. agriculture, there is the vast amount of income transferred for investment as capital in the nonfarm economy. This income flow has been largely voluntary in the form of inheritances to off-farm migrants, a process free of the social and political problems involved in taxing and conscripting farm capital for the development of nonfarm economies.

At times this outflow, the pattern of capital accumulation, and the impact of business booms and depressions were such as to reduce the capital available to U.S. agriculture below its needs. This situation has been remedied, intentionally and sometimes unintentionally, with partially subsidized credit programs for farmers and with price-support programs which have increased the income available to farmers for use in capital formation.

While major public investments have been made in U.S. agriculture in education, roads, research, irrigation schemes, etc., no extensive public investment has been made directly in agricultural production; instead, an environment conducive to such private investment has been maintained. This is in sharp contrast to many developing countries. They have taken drastic steps, including taxation, appropriation, and export or other levies on exportable farm products, to transfer income out of agriculture to develop the nonfarm economy. When the depressing effects of these actions on farm

production and farm capital formation become apparent, attempts are often made to stimulate agricultural production with direct governmental investment. Results of such policies to date, both in communist and in noncommunist countries, have been far from encouraging—the Soviet Union, China, Thailand, Argentina, and Nigeria being cases in point [see COMMUNISM, ECONOMIC ORGANIZATION OF, *article on* AGRICULTURE].

An alternative policy, followed in the United States from 1870 to 1960, has also been characteristic of Denmark, Australia, New Zealand, and England. It is the basis for the current expansion in agricultural output in western Europe. There, new institutional arrangements facilitate more specialization, better prices to farmers, and/or wider markets for those products which can be produced at a comparative advantage. Also, greatly expanded capital investments are being made in both the education of farmers and in the development of agricultural technology, while capital investment in direct farm production is left in the hands of farmers rather than carried out by governments. [See AGRICULTURE, *article on* DEVELOPING COUNTRIES.]

Experience of other countries. A brief survey of the creation and use of agricultural capital in different countries suggests certain generalizations about the types of institutions and policies which lead to rapid formation of capital in agriculture and to the transfer of income out of farming to promote nonfarm capital formation.

Broadly speaking it is possible to group the experience of various countries, at different times, into four categories:

(1) *Success* in increasing the stock of capital in agriculture, so as to obtain both high-level farm output and the transfer of substantial income out of agriculture for nonfarm development, *in the presence of* substantial natural resources relative to population.

(2) *Success* in obtaining sufficient growth of capital in agriculture to obtain both a high-level agricultural output and a transfer of substantial income out of agriculture for nonfarm development *despite meager* natural resources relative to population.

(3) *Inability* to obtain adequate capital growth in agriculture for high-level farm output and a significant transfer of income out of agriculture for nonfarm development *despite substantial* natural agricultural resources relative to population.

(4) *Inability* to obtain adequate capital growth in agriculture for high-level farm output and signif-

icant transfer of income out of agriculture for nonfarm development *in the absence of* substantial natural resources relative to population.

These categories suggest that agricultural capital formation and use of farm income are not determined solely by initial man–land ratios. Whether this independence is apparent or real is not too important. Obviously, if it is real other factors explain success and failure; if it is only apparent other factors obscure the true relationship. In any event, the other factors are of crucial importance as variables to be controlled by the policies and programs of a country.

The first step in isolating the other factors at work is to examine the countries which fall into the four categories: (1) success with substantial resources, (2) success despite meager resources, (3) inability despite substantial resources, and (4) inability in the presence of meager resources. In the first category are the United States (already discussed) and New Zealand; in the second, Japan (since early in this century) and Switzerland. In the third, we find the Soviet Union and Argentina (since the 1930s); in the fourth, Albania, Haiti and, perhaps, India. Further examination would extend the number of countries, but this list is sufficient to reveal common characteristics of the successful ones. Following are some major differences between the successful and unsuccessful countries.

(1) In successful economies favorable rates of return have been maintained as incentives for private farmers to adopt new technology and acquire new skills. In the unsuccessful economies, farm incomes have often been taxed or otherwise reduced and seldom if ever supported; rewards have not been tied specifically to adoption of new technology and acquisition of new skills.

(2) Whereas in successful countries land rents have been permitted to allocate use of land, in unsuccessful countries land rents have been eliminated or prevented by policy or custom from playing an allocative role.

(3) In the successful countries there has been extensive public investment to provide a broad educational base for farmers. In those not successful general education of farmers has been restricted; little public investment has been made in such education.

(4) Generally in successful countries there has been heavy investment in the agricultural sciences and disciplines devoted to technological advances in farming. In unsuccessful countries there has been little investment of this type.

(5) In the successful countries there has been large-scale public investment in extension programs aimed at helping private farm entrepreneurs adopt new technology, whereas in unsuccessful ones there have not been extensive investments in such extension programs.

(6) In successful countries public programs have not forced capital out of agriculture; at times movements of capital into agriculture have been encouraged. In some unsuccessful countries capital has been forced out of agriculture into the nonfarm economy, and in some instances political considerations have led to the actual destruction of agricultural capital.

(7) Whereas all successful countries have experienced large transfers of income from the farm to create capital in the nonfarm economy, in unsuccessful countries such transfers have been small or, when forced, moderate.

(8) All the successful countries, but only some of the unsuccessful, have made substantial public investments in roads, communications, irrigation, drainage, market facilities, etc., in indirect support of farm production.

(9) None of the successful, but several of the unsuccessful, are characterized by fairly permanent public investment in direct agricultural production.

(10) All of the successful show a tendency to overinvest in direct production to the extent of expanding production so as to put adverse pressure on farm product prices and returns on investment. The unsuccessful do not show this tendency; consequently food prices are high, but there is little evidence of high returns on investment.

(11) In successful countries, when investment in direct farm production has proven inadequate, individual farmers have been helped. In the unsuccessful, on the other hand, little help has been given individual farmers in similar circumstances.

(12) Among both the successful and unsuccessful there are countries that have benefited from substantial foreign markets and countries that have not.

(13) Among both successful and unsuccessful countries, some have received foreign aid and some have not.

Role of management. Our analysis of the performance of different economies in creating and using agricultural capital suggests that management—private and public—is a crucial variable. Publicly managed farm economies tend to underinvest in direct agricultural production while capital formation tends to lag. On the other hand, privately managed farm economies tend to over-invest. While many privately managed agricultural economies have substantial programs for public investment in the education of farmers and in the development of technology, it appears that both kinds of economies tend to underinvest in public facilities, the privately managed less so, however, than the publicly managed. The economies placing high reliance on private managers for direct-investment decisions are of two kinds: those characterized by rapid technological, economic, and institutional change; and those characterized by low-level technology, with few advances in technology, education, and institutions. The latter have tended to reach equilibriums not characterized by substantial capital accumulation.

The above observations raise the question: What is the role of management in the development of these tendencies in the use of capital?

Managers, private or public, make decisions. Decisions are made in order to obtain objectives that are private as well as public—even in the case of public managers, because *private success,* as a public servant, is also an objective for a public decision maker. Private interests of public decision makers do not coincide entirely with high output and rapid capital formation. There is little incentive, for example, for the public servant managing an agricultural unit to pay attention to biological and agronomic problems: the small details of insect, pest, and disease infestations, and the variations of land with respect to fertility, drainage, soil structure, etc. Instead, the public servant often finds it advantageous to concern himself with the politics of his governmental unit. Skill applied in "managing" bureaucratic details is often likely to increase the public manager's remuneration more than skill applied to the details of biological production problems.

The private agricultural manager, on the other hand, maximizes his personal gain by close attention to biological and agronomic detail *if* the market pays enough to provide the motivation. The requirement of "pay to motivate" explains why direct attempts to transfer capital from agriculture to industry by taxation and confiscatory methods often retard both production and capital formation in agriculture.

There is a tendency for private managers to exhaust possibilities for gain. This explains why traditional farm societies not subject to technical, social, political, and economic change are so organized that it is difficult to improve income by better economic adjustment of their operation under the existing technology and the existing socioeconomic and political system. When, however, rapid changes take place in technology, human skills, and tastes as a result of public investment in research, agricultural extension, and general education, many opportunities develop for advantageous changes provided the gains are not taxed away or confiscated.

In the case of heavy taxation or confiscation, expansion in farm output and farm capital formation is retarded. Examples here include rice production in Thailand and oil-palm production in Nigeria. In these instances, public investment in research and education results in little expansion of production and little capital formation, given restrictive assessments which absorb 40 to 50 per cent of world prices for rice and oil-palm produce. On the other hand, just the opposite situation exists with respect to untaxed commodities in the same two countries. From 1944 to 1962, for example, in the absence of assessments and with publicly supported research and extension programs, swamp rice acreage in Nigeria expanded from virtually none to 85,000 acres. In Thailand, corn production expanded rapidly in the absence of restrictions and in the presence of publicly supported research and extension. In both countries, with expansion in production has come substantial formation of capital both in agriculture and in related supporting activities.

The tendency of private managers to overinvest in direct production remains to be discussed. As agricultural production requires space, transportation costs introduce large differences between the acquisition costs and salvage values of durable items of capital. This difference between acquisition costs and salvage values makes it difficult to correct mistakes of overinvestment and contributes to the high level of fixed costs in agricultural production. Private managers find it difficult to foresee the increase in total production and fall in prices which take place when many farmers respond to favorable changes in technology, human skill, or economic conditions. It is difficult to correct the overinvestment because of the transportation and other costs of disinvestment. If, on the other hand, mistakes of underinvestment are made, they are easy to correct as it will still be advantageous and easy to expand production. The result is a tendency toward overinvestment in those privately managed agricultural economies which are characterized by rapid technological change, improvements in the human agent, and unrestricted prices (Johnson 1958; Johnson et al. 1961).

The tendency toward overinvestment in privately

managed farm economies results in some waste of capital relative to a possible optimum. But capital formation, farm output, and lower food prices (benefiting consumers) appear to be almost uniformly superior in privately managed, unrestricted farm economies to those achieved in either publicly managed or severely taxed, privately managed farm economies.

The tendency of both privately and publicly managed farm economies to underinvest in research, education, farm services, roads, and the like now needs to be considered. There seems to be fair evidence that this tendency to underinvestment is less pronounced in privately managed than in publicly managed farm economies attempting development. The tendency of public managers to pursue private ends has been used to explain underinvestment in farm production when such managers operate farms directly. The same argument applies to public managers of investments in public facilities, whether those facilities serve publicly or privately managed farms. The somewhat lesser tendency to underinvest in public facilities serving adequately motivated privately (as contrasted to publicly) managed farm economies can be explained by (1) the pressure that rather well-to-do farmers can put on public managers and (2) the higher rate of capital formation in such economies.

In summary we may make the following observations suggested by empirical findings:

(1) Farm capital formation takes place rapidly when farmers are in a position to gain from reinvesting part of their income and when they have major responsibility for investment in direct farm production. Public investment in direct farm production has rarely proven as effective as private investment.

(2) Rapid capital formation occurs when the public makes substantial investments in both the general and technical education of farmers, in improved technology for farming, and in its extension to farmers. Investments of this kind, however, have not been effective unless substantial incentives are given to private farm managers.

(3) Formation of farm capital is accelerated when the transfer of capital from the farm to the nonfarm sector is left to voluntary processes, including transfers in the form of inherited monetary capital as well as training received by farm children who migrate to nonfarm occupations. On the other hand, programs designed to force income out of agriculture make private agricultural investment unattractive; this leads to low capital formation, retarded farm production, high real farm-product prices, and a lack of income to transfer to the nonfarm economy.

(4) Lagging farm capital formation can be stimulated with favorable price programs and credit assistance to individual farmers.

(5) However, privately managed farm economies subject to price incentives tend to overinvest in direct farm production in the presence of favorable changes in technology, human skills, human tastes, and the economic environment. Publicly managed farm economies underinvest in direct farm production, even given similar changes in technology, human skills, and tastes.

(6) Privately managed farm economies move into a stagnant equilibrium in the absence of changes introduced by publicly supported research, technical extension, and general education.

(7) Both publicly and privately managed systems of direct agricultural production tend to be characterized by underinvestment in public facilities for agricultural research and extension and in general education, roads, and other public facilities.

GLENN L. JOHNSON

[See also AGRICULTURE, article on DEVELOPING COUNTRIES; CREDIT, article on AGRICULTURAL CREDIT.]

BIBLIOGRAPHY

BARGER, HAROLD; and LANSBERG, HANS H. 1942 *American Agriculture, 1899–1939: A Study of Output, Employment and Productivity.* New York: National Bureau of Economic Research.

JOHNSON, GLENN L. 1955 Agriculture's Technological Revolution. Pages 27–44 in The American Assembly, *United States Agriculture: Perspectives and Prospects.* New York: The Assembly.

JOHNSON, GLENN L. 1958 Supply Function: Some Facts and Notions. Pages 74–93 in *Agricultural Adjustment Problems in a Growing Economy.* Edited by Earl D. Heady et al. Ames: Iowa State College Press.

JOHNSON, GLENN L. 1964 A Note on Nonconventional Inputs and Conventional Production Functions. Pages 120–124 in Carl Eicher and Lawrence Witt (editors), *Agriculture in Economic Development.* New York: McGraw-Hill.

JOHNSON, GLENN L. et al. 1961 Implication of the IMS for Study of Responses to Price. Pages 150–169 in *A Study of Managerial Processes of Mid-western Farmers.* Edited by G. L. Johnson et al. Ames: Iowa State Univ. Press.

SCHULTZ, THEODORE W. 1963 *The Economic Value of Education.* New York: Columbia Univ. Press.

SCHULTZ, THEODORE W. 1964 *Transforming Traditional Agriculture.* New Haven: Yale Univ. Press.

STRAUSS, FREDERICK; and BEAN, LOUIS H. 1940 *Gross Farm Income and Indices of Farm Production and Prices in the United States: 1869–1937.* U.S. Department of Agriculture, Technical Bulletin No. 703. Washington: Government Printing Office.

TOSTLEBE, ALVIN S. 1957 *Capital in Agriculture: Its Formation and Financing Since 1870.* Princeton Univ. Press.

U.S. Department of Agriculture, Agriculture History Branch 1963 *Century of Service: The First Hundred Years of the United States Department of Agriculture,* by Gladys Baker et al. Washington: Government Printing Office.

VI

LABOR

This article is concerned with farm labor, both self-employed operator families and hired workers, in the more highly industrialized countries. It centers principally on the United States, with comparative references to other industrial economies, mainly European. In all industrial countries, agriculture is becoming predominantly commercial, not only in the sale of output but in the purchase of production materials and services. Subsistence production (autoconsumption) is rapidly disappearing. Within each national system of agriculture one finds a complex of government actions and interventions mixed with components of competitive market forces. In their diverse effects these complexes of economic and political forces tend simultaneously to promote the absorption of agriculture into the industrial sphere and to perpetuate its insulation. These forces profoundly affect farm occupations and at the same time determine the efficiency with which the productive resources associated with farming are utilized in the various national economies.

This essay seeks to develop two perspectives: (*a*) an examination of the characteristics and composition of the farm labor forces and their employment from the standpoint of manpower utilization; and (*b*) an examination of the occupational categories of agriculture in terms of their opportunities, requirements, and rewards. For both perspectives, the essence is change and transition. Consequently, one can scarcely avoid being challenged to try to understand the forces that appear to be shaping the future. At the risk of neglecting an adequate survey of the contemporary situation in farm labor, the motivation underlying this essay is concern with future trends and prospects.

Off-farm migration and national policy. With varying degrees of awareness, with mixed feelings of satisfaction and regret, and with ambivalences of political posture and policy, the industrial nations have been witnessing the rapid decline of their farm populations. Those who view this with regret are mainly agrarian fundamentalists who see in migration off farms an erosion of cherished values; those who view it with satisfaction include industrial employers interested in filling job vacancies and the many persons who believe that farm incomes would improve if fewer people were engaged in agriculture.

In most of the industrial nations, postwar rates of off-farm migration have been so high that, if sustained for another two decades, they will virtually eliminate the farm population. National governments have not usually (with the principal exceptions of Austria and Switzerland) tried to restrain off-farm migration nor have many governments (excepting Italy and Sweden) taken direct action to accelerate it. Indirectly, through other interventions, governments typically have followed a complex of practices that have had the effect of simultaneously aiding and retarding occupational adjustments out of agriculture. The clash has come mainly between policies designed for the protection of agriculture in general and those aimed at structural renovation. Most countries have officially acknowledged the comparatively poor income position of farm people and have invoked protective measures, such as import restrictions, price supports, and various subsidies. Governments have also acknowledged that one of the main reasons for low farm income is low agricultural efficiency. With exceptions, they have also recognized that larger and (in Europe) less fragmented farms are an essential step in achieving the efficiency that would lead to more satisfactory incomes. Most countries have both protective and "structural" policies. Although the protective measures have long traditions, they are now usually viewed as transitional to achieving structural renovation. This relationship is explicit in Swedish law, and it is at least implicit in German law. Similarly, "agricultural adjustment," as well as income improvement, was implied in the United States Agricultural Adjustment Act of 1933 and its numerous subsequent amendments.

The dilemma is that policies of transitional protection and policies of renovation and adjustment have not demonstrated compatibility. Protective measures, including subsidies, have a here-and-now quality that gives them considerably more political appeal than do the uncertain future prospects of structural transformation. Accordingly, national governments in their current budgetary and administrative actions are prone to give greater emphasis to protection and thereby to impede adjustments that would raise the efficiency of farm labor.

Yet in environments favorable to off-farm employment, as in the industrial countries in the postwar years, the magnitudes of occupational movement out of agriculture have been unparalleled in modern history.

For comparison of the differential effects of national policy and off-farm employment opportunity, we may look at what has happened in West Germany, Sweden, and the United States. West Germany has had overfull employment; labor has been imported in substantial volume for industry and construction; no significant effort has been made to facilitate the transfer of farm people into nonfarm employment; German agricultural policy is one of the world's most highly protective. Sweden has had more than full employment; its agricultural policy is protective and yet designed to achieve structural rationalization; it has an affirmative manpower policy, which includes state support for relocation of the farm labor force. The United States had a favorable level of employment until 1958 but thereafter a high unemployment level ranging from 5 to 7 per cent; its agricultural policy is protective but less so than that of Germany, and it lacks structural objectives; until 1962 it had no cohesive national manpower policy; farm people seeking an occupational adjustment have had to depend upon their own resourcefulness.

The effects of these differing combinations of state policy and prosperity are reflected in the average annual rates of decrease in the farm labor force during the decade 1950–1960: Germany, 2.25 per cent; Sweden, 3.5 per cent; United States, 2.5 per cent.

These results suggest two generalizations of considerable significance: (a) policies of agricultural protectionism may have retarded the migration out of agriculture but have not effectively obstructed it; (b) farm people aspire to more satisfactory levels of income and, given a reasonable opportunity to achieve an improvement, are quite ready to give up whatever they may hold to be the cherished values of farm life.

Structural adjustments have accompanied outmigration. The number of farms has declined, though not as rapidly as the active farm population. The reduction in farm numbers has been achieved mainly by the amalgamation of small farms. Only in Sweden has the discontinuance of farms been significant, which is a reflection of a rationalization policy that includes eliminating farms in areas not well suited to agriculture. Amalgamation has typically not involved the very tiny farm to the same extent as the larger-sized small farm. In Germany and Sweden the decline was principally in the 2–2.5 hectare category, while the principal gain was in the 10–20 hectare size. The persistence of the very small farm is explained by the growing practice of part-time farming and off-farm employment.

Partial and provisional out-movements. Part-time farming appears to be on the increase in all industrial countries. This may be interpreted as a form of partial and provisional movement out of agriculture. A related practice is for farmers to discontinue operation while retaining ownership of their farms and leasing them to farmers who have other land. These partial occupational adjustments may imply a feeling of uncertainty about off-farm employment prospects and the desire to maintain some provision against this uncertainty. Since land values and rents are rising sharply in all industrial countries, there may also be the motivation to retain landownership as a source of income and of capital gain; for many it also provides a place to live.

Even if the opportunities for the provisional and partial forms of occupational adjustment should decline, agriculture will apparently continue in its traditional role as a reservoir of industrial manpower, but on a diminishing scale. For the immediate future, this potential is reduced somewhat by the tendency of off-farm migration to leave behind persons in older age categories. Even if farm policies continue to have a restraining effect on mobility, which appears likely, off-farm movement will probably continue to draw off significant numbers of people. In the European economies off-farm migration will apparently rest heavily on the "pull" factor, that is, on whether full and overfull employment can be maintained. In the United States, where a high rate of off-farm migration has continued despite substantial unemployment, it appears that a combination of "push" forces will sustain off-farm migration even without a climate of favorable opportunity. This expectation is supported by the fact that agricultural transformation in the United States is financial and managerial as well as technological. For example, efficient farmers are motivated to enlarge their operations and consequently to offer other farmers a price or a rent for their land that is persuasively attractive. The demand for land for enlargement is brisk, and so long as there are attractive opportunities to sell or rent, off-farm employment need not always offer a full replacement of the income to be realized from continuing to operate the farm.

The most likely future for the industrial countries is that the farm proportion of all gainfully occupied will decline to as little as one-half or perhaps even one-fourth of its present size. National governments almost universally are committed to the maintenance of high levels of economic growth. These policies should continue to provide off-farm opportunities. Even if political devotion to agricultural fundamentalism continues to nurture highly protective programs for farmers, such programs are not more likely in the future than in the past to generate satisfactory levels of income for all farmers. Consequently, it may be expected that individuals on their own initiative will continue to seek more favorable situations. Whether or not national policies to sustain growth and full employment are fully successful will make little difference to the older-age farm people, for their prospect is retirement. The critical question is whether the level of off-farm employment, together with manpower policies, including those for basic education and occupational training, will provide a favorable climate for the release of farm youth.

Although the farm labor force component in industrial economies will probably drop to 4 or 5 per cent, or even lower, one can be quite certain that the base of agriculture as a political interest will remain substantially larger. Farm landowners have as keen an interest in agricultural prosperity as do their tenants. Moreover, the decline in the number of farmers has been considerably offset by the rising participation of off-farm industries and service agencies—those that supply machinery and production materials, those that process farm products, the banks, and other investors. All have a stake in farm affairs and will add significantly to the political base from which farm and manpower policies are fashioned.

Changes in and among farm occupations. Notwithstanding the great changes of recent years, the dominant form of engagement in agriculture is still that of self-employed owner-operator, whose labor is customarily supplemented by family members and frequently also by temporarily employed wageworkers. Deviations from the dominant form occur principally when: (a) the farm is rented, entirely or in part; (b) the farm is so large that hired workers do most or all of the work; (c) the land is in a large ownership, and its use is divided into controlled rental or sharecropper units; (d) the owner is an absentee investor who employs a manager who in turn hires a work force.

In some places one or another of these deviations becomes the dominant form. The United Kingdom has mainly tenant farming, and its work force is composed principally of hired men. California is notable for large-scale employment of seasonal and migratory workers. Sharecropping continues to be a prominent form in Italy.

The occupational category of hired farm worker is also heterogeneous, but its range of diversity is perhaps less. Both operators and hired workers are to be found at the minimum level of skill and capacity, and at this minimum level both are likely to live in a state of poverty. But at the upper ranges of skill, capacity, and standard of living there are only operators; the hired worker who seeks occupational advancement in agriculture must become a farm operator to do so. Hired workers fall into two broad categories: (a) permanent, or year-round; and (b) temporary, or seasonal. Migratory workers, a widely and dramatically known group, are one portion of the large total of temporarily hired workers, all of whom are confronted with irregularity, insufficiency, and uncertainty of employment.

Growing importance of management function. In traditional farming systems the farmer had few entrepreneurial decisions to make; his primary activity was as self-employed laborer. Farming was indeed an uncertain business in terms of the hazards of weather, disease, and crop failure, but it was mainly the input of self-employed labor that was being risked. Now, as the ratio of capital to labor has risen multifold and production requires large money outlays for commercial inputs, the capital-managing and decision-making functions of the farm operator have become far more prominent. It is not unusual now for the American family farm operator to have a highly mechanized farm representing a total investment of $100,000 to $250,000. Production outlays may run to $50,000 per year. Yet the total labor requirement for such an operation (if it is in livestock or general crops, as opposed to vegetables or fruit) is not likely to involve more than 100 to 200 man-days of hired labor per year. It is easily seen that the management capabilities of such a farmer are more critical to success than the willingness to work diligently.

The average (or typical) size of farm, measured either in acreage, investment, or value of output, has risen significantly in all industrial countries. The increase in scale has tended to be in proportion to the labor substitution effect of mechanization; had this not been true, hired labor employment per farm would have risen in proportion to the increase in farm size, which it has not. As it has developed, the farm operator and family members typically supply most of the labor needs of the highly mechanized and capital-intensive farms. Thus, while the farmer has had to become ever more a capitalist, risk taker, and decision maker, he nevertheless has continued the tradition of being also a *workingman*, with the supplemental participation of other members of the family.

Given an environment favorable to the development of entrepreneurial talent, offering at the minimum good basic education and a public advisory service, it seems reasonable to expect the occupational combination working-farmer–manager–decision-maker to continue even in the face of further advances in mechanization and technology. But will the minimum conditions for widespread development of entrepreneurial ability be met? And—an equally urgent question—in view of steeply mounting capital requirements, can the self-capitalizing role of the farmer be sustained? The answers to these questions are somewhat interrelated, as we shall see.

Traditionally, farm capital is operator owned and borrowed—it originates from individual savings and debt obligations. Equity share participation, the foundation of industrial capitalism, is rare in agriculture. Consequently, entry into farming is largely determined by inheritance or marriage. Otherwise, the capital requirements exceed the ability of individuals to accumulate sufficient savings even if they are willing to assume large debt obligations. In former times Americans spoke of the "agricultural ladder," a concept implying that a person could commence as a hired hand and, with hard work and parsimony, advance to tenant and ultimately to owner-operator. It was a romantic idea which long ago—when land on the frontier was abundant and cheap—had prospect of realization.

The requirements of self-capitalization may operate as an obstruction to the entry of entrepreneurial talent. In the nonfarm population there undoubtedly are capable individuals interested in farming who are not able to enter agriculture through inheritance; if they do not possess considerable wealth or the willingness to commit themselves to a large debt obligation, they will find opportunities for entry severely restricted. The traditional system imposes an obligation to "live poor and die rich," that is, to commit a substantial proportion of current income to an obligatory savings program through debt amortization—from which only inheritors may realize any substantial benefit. Agriculture long remained the major sector of the economy in which enterprises were small enough to permit self-employment, self-management, and self-capitalization. But that day appears to be approaching its end, with the pressure for division coming principally through the capital function.

The implications of this analysis are that a separation of farm occupational functions is likely to become a necessity and, moreover, that it may be desirable. There are indications that such a separation is already beginning to occur. It is appearing mainly in three forms: (a) increasing rental of land (ownership thereby becoming separated from operation); (b) contractual arrangements, usually called "vertical integration," through which capital or supervision, or both, are supplied by an outside agency, usually a marketing or processing firm; (c) incorporation, with the ownership of shares distributed among several investors.

Ownership of farmland by nonfarm investors is occurring in two ways: direct investment in farms by outside individuals; and retention of ownership of land by discontinuing farmers. But this process is not reflected in increased numbers of tenant farmers; rather, the rental land is being taken up by owner-farmers who wish to expand. In United States statistics, this shows up in some rather dramatic, but little noticed, data on "part owner" farms. These combined ownership and rental units have been increasing and now incorporate far more acreage under lease than that held by tenant operators. With the present trend, more than half of United States farmland will very soon be operated by part owners. As this is a means of consolidating and enlarging operating units without entering into the land-purchase obligation, the practice can be expected to continue.

The vertical integration (contractual) arrangement has both a capital and a management rationale. In addition to advancing credit, the processing or marketing company provides guidance and supervision as well as the assurance of a marketing outlet. Some observers are apprehensive of this arrangement because of the constraints it imposes on the farmer's freedom. However, it does serve a purpose, and unless the obstructions to capitalization and the entry of entrepreneurial ability are otherwise overcome, further such expansions may be expected.

Incorporation of farms with distributed ownership of shares also continues to occur. There is little knowledge of its extent or rate of development. It is a form of organization that facilitates consolidation of valuable landholdings and offers the usual tax, inheritance, and other advantages long enjoyed by large industrial corporations.

Farms do not need to become the counterparts of the large industrial corporations to achieve production efficiency. Nevertheless, there is ample evidence that the basic efficiencies required to produce an acceptable level of income require a great deal more enlargement than has yet occurred in most areas. One may roughly estimate the minimum capital required for an efficient commercial farm at around $100,000. Whereas the mechanisms for assembling multimillion dollar participating capitalizations are well perfected, those for assembling farm capital in the range of $100,000 to $250,000 are not. One may speculate, accordingly, that unless there emerge mechanisms and procedures for shared financial participation in the larger commercial family farms, the tendency for them to be absorbed into multimillion-dollar corporate ownership is likely to accelerate.

Declining position of hired labor. Only exceptionally has farm work represented more than the residual chance for those unable to obtain more desirable employment. Recent years of economic growth have brought advances in welfare to many, but few to the farm worker. These generalizations have their greatest validity in the United States; perhaps Holland stands out as nearest to being exceptional. Whereas the Dutch farm worker is regarded as an integral part of the national occupational structure and is included in all social legislation, the American farm worker is regarded as, in effect, outside the national occupational structure and generally is excluded from such social measures as minimum wage requirements, unemployment insurance, and protection of the right to unionize.

In the United States the number of persons who do some farm work for wages has remained substantially constant throughout the postwar years, whereas the self-employed have declined sharply. But while the number of hired workers has been maintained, the proportion having only short-term, seasonal employment has risen. This development reflects the persistently slack nonfarm demand for the occupationally ill-prepared, whether the general level of unemployment is low or high. It also reflects a change in farm labor demand.

This trend toward less regular and more casual employment for farm workers is also observed in most European countries. In West Germany, for example, the prewar ratio of regular to temporary hired workers was 2:1; by 1962–1963 the proportions were approximately equal. Underlying the shift away from regular employment of hired workers is the change in labor requirements associated with technological change. Tractors eliminate the need to care for work stock and to raise their feed and mend their harnesses. Commercial fertilizers eliminate the necessity of handling barnyard manure; milking machines replace hand milkers. Processing and hauling of products to market have been taken over by off-farm agencies. But many farmers who can handle their basic activities of land preparation and planting still are likely to need outside help at harvesttime, particularly if they produce fruits and vegetables or similar crops that are not yet harvested by machine.

Concurrently with mechanization and other forms of technological change there has occurred a tendency to reduce the diversification of production on individual farms. The resulting specialization means less spreading of labor requirements through the year. The combined effect of technological change and farm specialization has tended to convert the hired labor demands of agriculture into an aggregation of temporary seasonal needs, thereby rapidly reducing the few remaining op-

portunities for farm wagework to be an occupation or a career. Regularly employed workers are now found mainly in poultry or livestock raising and in specialist and supervisory categories on the largest farms.

Attempts have been made to improve the economic situation of hired farm workers through collective bargaining and legislation. These efforts have been successful in Holland and the Scandinavian countries; they have had limited success elsewhere in Europe and Great Britain; they have almost completely failed in the United States. The failure in the United States is basically attributable to the fact that farm work is regarded as transitional—a job to be gotten out of as soon as possible, rather than one to be protected and improved. This attitude, shared by the workers as well as the community at large, has obstructed the development of group consciousness and cohesiveness, as has the fact that the bulk of employment is geographically spread, fragmented into small units, and temporary. The many sporadic efforts to unionize, almost none of which have been initiated from within the farm-worker population, have been failures. With farm workers having no organizations to protect their own interests, other interest groups sympathetic to their needs have attempted to have them included in legislation on minimum wages, unemployment insurance, and protection of the right to organize. Against the opposition of well-organized farmers, these efforts have enjoyed only a pittance of success.

Farming occupations in the future.   It is scarcely conceivable that commercial farming will not become ever more technologically intricate and capital intensive. Increases in farm size are necessarily associated with effective use of technology and capital. Nevertheless, technical efficiencies of scale can still apparently be realized, for most types of farming, on units that are not too large for the operator and his family to work. But such a farm is becoming increasingly difficult to finance, except by inheritance. Financial organization may therefore become a more influential determinant of farm size than the technical requirements of efficient production. Techniques and procedures of financial organization may become the deciding factor in whether commercial farms remain essentially family enterprises or become large-scale corporations. Outside financial participation is essential under either alternative. If farms can be efficiently financed within the range of family enterprise, the farmer will be able to retain the major part of his traditional role, that of the self-employed entrepreneur. If the capital solution favors large aggregations, the complex of activities that have traditionally been those of the farmer will likely be split in such a way as to leave the hired manager as his counterpart. In any realistic view of the future, the farmer is not likely to remain a self-capitalist to the same extent as in the past.

The economic future of the farm worker is quite uncertain. Some atractive full-time jobs will remain in family-scale farm enterprise, particularly where livestock are involved. However, in family units that need an additional man or two on a steady basis, partnerships are likely to be more frequently used. There is no promising future in agriculture for workers who are employed seasonally and casually, at least not for those who depend upon it as a full-time occupation. Mechanization of hand labor tasks will be developed and extended; seasonal activities will continue to become shorter in duration. Whether agriculture can offer a substantial and attractive occupational base for hired laborers depends mainly upon the evolving pattern of farm size, for only on the large farm does the labor of the hired worker become more than merely supplementary to that of self-employed members of the farm family.

VARDEN FULLER

BIBLIOGRAPHY

Disparities in Pace and Form of Rural Development.   1964   *International Journal of Agrarian Affairs* 40, no. 3.

DOVRING, FOLKE (1956) 1960   *Land and Labor in Europe, 1900–1950: A Comparative Survey of Recent Agrarian History.* 2d ed. The Hague: Nijhoff.

HOFSTEE, E. W.   1957   *Rural Life and Rural Welfare in the Netherlands.* The Hague: Government Printing and Publishing Office.

MÜLLER, PETER   1964   Recent Developments in Land Tenure and Land Policies in Germany. *Land Economics* 40:267–275.

U.S. DEPARTMENT OF AGRICULTURE   1963   *Yearbook of Agriculture: A Place to Live.* Washington: Government Printing Office.

WRIGHT, GORDON   1964   *Rural Revolution in France: The Peasantry in the Twentieth Century.* Stanford (Calif.) Univ. Press.

VII

PRODUCTIVITY AND TECHNOLOGY

Increase in productivity. Agricultural productivity in most economically advanced countries is now apparently growing at a much higher rate than was true in previous periods in history and, at least since World War II, at a much higher rate than productivity in other sectors of these economies (Fabricant 1959). In the northwest European countries "total factor productivity" in agriculture grew between 1950 and 1959 at the rate of 2.0 per cent per year, a rate that was slightly above

the one achieved by U.S. agriculture during this same period (FAO 1962). Similarly high rates of growth are reported for the Soviet Union, although the margin of error in Soviet statistics is quite large (Johnson 1963). But neither northwest Europe nor the Soviet Union has had declines in labor used in agriculture comparable to those in the United States, although in both areas the agricultural labor force has begun to decline. In this respect, the recent United States and Canadian experience is almost unique.

As Table 1 shows, agricultural output in the United States grew at the approximate rate of 1.8 per cent per year during the 1949–1963 period. At the same time, man-hours used in agriculture were declining at the rate of 4.5 per cent per year. As the result of these trends, output per man-hour in agriculture rose at the astonishing rate of 6.3 per cent per year. While the use of purchased inputs such as fertilizer and machinery also increased at a relatively rapid rate, conventional measures of total input use in agriculture (which combine all the standard categories into one over-all input index) changed very little, leaving almost all of the observed growth in output to be explained by growth in total factor productivity or technical change (USARS 1963).

Historically, the recently observed rate of growth in U.S. agricultural output is not particularly high. During the 30-year period from 1880 to 1910, U.S. farm output grew at an average rate of 1.6 per cent per year. During that same period, however, most of the growth in output could be accounted for by comparable growth in inputs used, mainly land, labor, and machinery, leaving only a small fraction of the total growth (0.2 per cent per year) to be explained by growth in "total factor productivity" (Loomis & Barton 1961). What is unique about the recent experience of U.S. (and Canadian) agriculture is the almost complete stability in the conventional total inputs index.

This growth in output, which cannot be explained by comparable growth in inputs as conventionally measured (and that is what an increase in "total factor productivity" actually means), raises several interesting questions: (1) What were the actual sources of this growth? (2) What were the economic factors that determined the date and rate at which these various sources became operative? (3) Is it possible to improve the methodological framework for asking such questions so that at the end one does not remain with "productivity" accounting for most of the observed growth without productivity itself being accounted for in turn by other known factors?

Table 1 — Average annual rates of growth of agricultural output and productivity, selected countries and periods

		Output	Labor productivity	Total factor productivity	Approximate per cent of output growth accounted for by growth in conventional inputs
			(Per cent per year)		
United States:	1880–1910	1.6	0.6	0.2	88
	1910–1929	1.0	0.8	0.1	90
	1949–1963	1.8	6.3	1.8	0
Canada:	1926–1947	1.3	1.6	0.0	100
	1947–1957	1.1	5.4	3.0	0
Northwest Europe:	1950–1959	2.7	4.6	2.0	26
Israel:	1952–1961	13.2	9.4	5.3	60
Soviet Union:	1950–1959	4.9	5.7	3.3	28

Sources: U.S. Agricultural Research Service 1963; Loomis & Barton 1961; Food and Agriculture Organization of the United Nations 1962; Johnson 1963; Lok 1961; Mundlak 1964.

Sources of the increase. Since the acreage of land used in agriculture in the United States has changed very little during the last twenty years, one can view the growth in output per man-hour in agriculture as the approximate sum of two components: the increase in yield per acre and the decline in labor used in agriculture. Because of the particular technological conditions of production in agriculture these two components of growth are somewhat independent, at least over a certain range, and can be discussed separately. The major sources of increases in yield per acre have been biological improvements in varieties (mainly hybrid corn and sorghums), increased applications of plant nutrients (fertilizers) and water (irrigation), improved cultural practices such as chemical weed control and denser plantings, shifts of crops to areas of higher comparative advantage (the localization of corn in the corn belt and the move of cotton into the western and southwestern states), and the introduction of crops that are higher yielding and more valuable, such as soybeans. Much of the growth in yields during the 1938–1949 period was due to hybrid corn and other similar biological developments. In the postwar period, the single most important influence on yields has been the rapid growth in the application of fertilizers, particularly of nitrogen materials, which more than tripled between 1949 and 1962. Varietal improvements were still important (as, for example, in hybrid sorghum) but affected a much smaller portion of the aggregate (Durost & Barton 1960; Johnson & Gustafson 1962).

The decline in labor in agriculture was made possible by the substitution of mechanical power and by a rise in the rate of utilization and in the quality of the remaining labor force. While the mechanization of U.S. agriculture was proceeding at a rapid pace in the 1920s, and even earlier, the substitution that was occurring at that time was mainly one of machines for horses and mules and not one of machines for human power. This substitution of mechanical for animal power actually had an important output-raising effect of its own. It released for human consumption a substantial amount of grain previously used by horses and mules. Labor use in agriculture did not begin to decline at a rapid rate until the early 1940s, when the increase in the demand for labor in the rest of the economy began to pull substantial amounts of labor out of agriculture. At the same time, farm machinery began to change from a substitute for animal power into a substitute for manpower. This process was aided by the increase in the effective size of farm machinery and by the rapid growth in the availability of various "attachments," increasing the versatility of farm machinery and allowing one man to do a much wider variety of tasks with the same machine.

The impact of an approximate halving of the farm labor force between 1940 and 1962 was mitigated by the increased efficiency with which family labor was being used, mainly as the result of the very rapid increase in the average size of commercial farms and by the improved quality of the remaining labor force. Measured by an index of formal schooling per man, the average quality of the agricultural labor force increased by 15 to 20 per cent between 1940 and 1960.

Adoption of new techniques. There were many different economic forces behind these changes. Much of the original inventive effort occurred outside of agriculture. Agriculture benefited from general developments in genetics and chemical technology and from the decline in the real price, per horsepower-hour, of mechanical power. Economic incentives played a crucial role in determining the responsiveness of the farm sector to these developments. When the superiority of a particular new technique was clear and substantial, as was the case for hybrid corn in the corn belt, it was adopted relatively rapidly. It took only about four years for Iowa farmers to switch from mainly open-pollinated varieties of corn to almost entirely (90 per cent) hybrid varieties. In the southern United States the spread of hybrid corn lagged initially because no varieties adaptable to southern conditions were available until much later in the period. This lag in "availability" was largely due to the reluctance of private (and public) seed companies to enter into a substantially smaller and poorer market for their product. Furthermore, once they did enter the South, their product was accepted at a slower rate because the absolute profitability of the shift to hybrids was much smaller in the South, generally owing to the originally lower yield levels (Griliches 1960).

The rate of acceptance by farmers of new, superior techniques is largely determined by the absolute profitability of the shift to these techniques. On the other hand, the rate of adoption of more established techniques, such as fertilization, depends more on the rate at which their price (cost) declines relative to product and other factor prices. In either case, the crucial factor is the existence and magnitude of the economic incentive for the move. The use of fertilizers in U.S. agriculture, which has more than quadrupled since 1940, was greatly stimulated by the approximate halving of fertilizer prices (from their pre-World War II levels) relative to both farm product and other input prices. This fall was due to a series of developments in the nonfarm sector: the decline in the real price of energy, a main input in the production of synthetic nitrogen; the breakup of the nitrogen cartel as the result of government construction of new nitrogen plants during the war and their subsequent resale to new entrants into the industry; and the savings in transportation and handling costs, both at the manufacturing and retail levels, as the result of a continuous shift toward stronger mixtures. Similarly, the substitution of mechanical power for human labor was induced by the rising price of labor, which was due to the higher wages in the rest of the economy, and the resulting out-migration of farmers, and the decline in the real price of machinery, which was mainly the result of

the decline in the real price of horsepower with the development of higher-compression engines.

Problems of measuring productivity. Given all the specific sources of output growth, why are they not reflected in the conventional productivity measures? The answer to this question lies in the way inputs are usually measured and combined to give "total factor productivity." Most input measures make no, or only inadequate, allowances for quality change. In some cases the inputs are just counted, as if a ditchdigger's and an agronomer's man-year were equivalent. Many input series are constructed by "deflating" value series by some corresponding price index. This just pushes the problem of quality change back one step, to the question of how much price has really risen per constant-quality unit. Most price indexes are not very good at keeping the quality of the commodity price constant, but input price indexes are especially suspect. This is partly a reflection of the amount of resources spent (usually very small) on collecting input data compared to the resources spent on the collection of product data. The Consumer Price Index and its components are of more general interest, and much more money is spent on collecting data for them and on investigating their validity. While not perfect, they are thus much less subject to a secular upward drift caused by unmeasured improvements in the quality of the goods they price. By comparison, input price indexes are orphans in the world of social statistics and hence, because of poor measurement procedures and inadequate adjustments for quality change, have a much more pronounced tendency to drift upward. [See INDEX NUMBERS, *article on* PRACTICAL APPLICATIONS.]

In some cases, no direct price information is used at all. For example, the indexes used to deflate construction expenditures use input prices instead of product prices. The price of a well-specified house or structure is not collected; instead, the wages of construction labor, the price of lumber, etc., are averaged to arrive at an index of construction *cost* rather than an index of the *price* of construction. The difference between these two concepts is exactly equal to productivity growth in the construction industry. Using cost indexes instead of price indexes to deflate construction expenditures assumes that there were no improvements in productivity in the construction industry. This assumption leads to a very large downward bias in the resulting input series (the services of structures) and to the shifting of all the productivity growth in the construction sector to the productivity measures for sectors using its output.

In other cases, the commodity that is being

priced may be quite complex, and it may be very hard to keep up with all the changes that are occurring in it. Some progress has been recently made in tackling this difficult problem through the use of statistical techniques. If one has an array of different models of a particular machine, differing widely in some important dimensions and consequently differing in price, it is possible to derive the implicit price per unit of a particular dimension (such as horsepower) and use this price to adjust for the change that has occurred in this dimension over time (Griliches 1964*a*). In principle, if we could measure inputs better, allowing for all the quality changes that have occurred, we should be able to account for a substantial fraction of what currently is attributed to "productivity."

The usual total input indexes combine the various input series in proportion to the market price of these inputs in some base period or, what is almost the same thing, in proportion to the share of these inputs in total costs. This procedure assumes that market prices measure adequately the contribution of the individual inputs to the growth in output. For this to be true the relevant markets have to be in competitive equilibrium and there must be no economies of scale. But disequilibrium is the essence of change. It is quite likely that the contribution of those inputs whose use is growing is larger than would be measured by their market price. If this view is correct, then the standard measures may underestimate input growth in agriculture by overweighting declining inputs, such as labor, and underweighting growing inputs, such as fertilizer and machinery. The results of several statistical production function studies, which attempt to estimate directly the contribution of specific inputs in agriculture, seem to support this conjecture.

Similarly, the standard measures assume that no gain in efficiency can be had from increasing the scale of operations of a firm or farm. There is, however, a large body of evidence that points in the direction of substantial economies of scale in agriculture, at least in the size range where most farms are currently concentrated. The exact source of these economies is not very clear. One important source is the availability of larger and faster machines at lower prices per relevant work unit (horsepower-hour or acres plowed per hour). Another source is the possibility of more complete utilization of the available machine power and manpower on larger farms. The very substantial increase in the size of the average farm in the United States in recent years (over 50 per cent

since 1950) seems to support the reality of these economies.

A recent study estimated the contribution of individual input categories by fitting a production function to data on agricultural output and input in 68 regions of the United States in 1949 (Griliches 1963). It found that the implied weights differed somewhat from the official ones in the conjectured direction (less weight given to labor and more to machinery), that differences in education per man did affect productivity, and that there was strong evidence of substantial economies of scale. In addition, on the basis of other studies and data, it concluded that the conventional measures of input change over time seriously underestimate the actual growth in inputs used in agriculture, in particular when the concept is broadened to include not only the growth in the quantity of inputs used but also the growth in their quality. Making a series of adjustments to correct for some of the biases in these conventional measures and combining the resulting adjusted input series by using the new weights, this study succeeded in explaining most of the growth in U.S. agricultural output between 1940 and 1960, leaving almost nothing to the residual "total factor productivity growth" category. The results of this study imply that (very) roughly about a third of the measured productivity increases are due to improvements in the quality of the inputs used (among which the rise in education per worker plays an important role), about a quarter to a half are due to a move toward the elimination of relative disequilibria, which were reflected in the overpricing of labor and the underpricing of capital services by conventional market measures, and that the rest are due to the expansion that occurred in the scale of the average farm enterprise.

A subsequent study reached similar conclusions (Griliches 1964*b*). That study, however, focused primarily on estimating the previously unmeasured contribution of public investments in agricultural research and extension services to the growth in aggregate output. It fitted an aggregate production function to state output and input data for 1949, 1954, and 1959, including an estimate of public expenditures on research and extension for each state (per farm, lagged) as an additional output-determining variable. The coefficients of this variable, which were relatively large and statistically significant, provided an estimate of the contribution of these expenditures to the observed increases in output and imply that about 30 per cent of the increase in the aggregate output of U.S. agriculture between 1949 and 1959 is attributed to the rise in public research and extension expenditures per farm. The rest of the accounting was similar to that arrived at in the previously quoted study (Griliches 1963), except that the later study attributed a somewhat smaller role in the total to economies of scale.

Such "complete" accounting for the observed productivity increases does not mean that there were no meaningful increases in agricultural productivity during these periods or that no important changes occurred in the techniques of production used in agriculture. It does, however, indicate a way of providing an explanation for what were previously unexplained increases in farm output.

ZVI GRILICHES

[*See also* PRODUCTIVITY.]

BIBLIOGRAPHY

DUROST, DONALD D.; and BARTON, GLEN T.   1960   *Changing Sources of Farm Output.* U.S. Department of Agriculture, Production Research Report, No. 36. Washington: Government Printing Office.

FABRICANT, SOLOMON   1959   *Basic Facts on Productivity Change.* New York: National Bureau of Economic Research.

FOOD AND AGRICULTURE ORGANIZATION OF THE UNITED NATIONS   1962   *Agricultural Commodities: Projections for 1970.* FAO Commodity Review, Special Supplement. Rome: United Nations.

GRILICHES, ZVI   1960   Hybrid Corn and the Economics of Innovation. *Science* New Series 132:275–280.

GRILICHES, ZVI   1963   The Sources of Measured Productivity Growth: United States Agriculture, 1940–1960. *Journal of Political Economy* 71:331–346.

GRILICHES, ZVI   1964a   Notes on the Measurement of Price and Quality Changes. Pages 381–404 in Conference on Models of Income Determination, Chapel Hill, N.C., 1962, *Models of Income Determination.* Conference on Research in Income and Wealth, Studies in Income and Wealth, Vol. 28. Princeton (N.J.) Univ. Press.

GRILICHES, ZVI   1964b   Research Expenditures, Education, and the Aggregate Agricultural Production Function. *American Economic Review* 54:961–974.

JOHNSON, D. GALE   1963   Agricultural Production. Pages 203–234 in Abram Bergson and Simon Kuznets (editors), *Economic Trends in the Soviet Union.* Cambridge, Mass.: Harvard Univ. Press.

JOHNSON, D. GALE; and GUSTAFSON, ROBERT L.   1962   *Grain Yields and the American Food Supply: An Analysis of Yield Changes and Possibilities.* Univ. of Chicago Press.

LOK, SIEPKO H.   1961   An Enquiry Into the Relationships Between Changes in Over-all Productivity and Real Net Return Per Farm and Between Changes in Total Output and Real Gross Return: Canadian Agriculture, 1926–1957. Ottawa (Canada): Department of Agriculture, Economic Division.

LOOMIS, RALPH A.; and BARTON, GLEN T.   1961   *Productivity of Agriculture: United States, 1870–1958.* Technical Bulletin, No. 1238. Washington: U.S. Department of Agriculture.

MUNDLAK, YAIR   1964   *Long-term Projections of Supply and Demand for Agricultural Products in Israel.* Volume 1: General View and Summary. With projections of population and income by Nadav Halevi. Jerusalem (Israel): Hebrew Univ., Faculty of Agriculture.

U.S. AGRICULTURAL RESEARCH SERVICE, FARM ECONOMICS RESEARCH DIVISION   1963   *Changes in Farm Production and Efficiency: Summary Report, 1963.* Statistical Bulletin, No. 233. Washington: U.S. Department of Agriculture.

VIII

MARKETING

Marketing, in the usage of agricultural economists, encompasses virtually all activities relating to agricultural commodities from sale by original producers to purchase by final users. It includes the physical operations of transportation, storage, processing, and related sorting, packaging, and other handling. It includes buying and selling and pricing, trading practices and organizational arrangements, and the competitive structure of markets. It includes such related activities as grading and standardization of products; provision of market information; financing of trade; the bearing and shifting of risks; merchandising, advertising, and promotion; and the development and market testing of product innovations. It also includes related governmental activities, such as those aimed at regulating and facilitating trade or intervening in pricing.

This usage is more comprehensive than that of general economists, who restrict marketing primarily to pricing and the activities involved in transfer of ownership. It differs also from the usage of business economists, whose focus is primarily upon policies of firms in planning their operations for most effective distribution of their products.

Marketing is, of course, the concomitant of specialization in production. In a truly subsistence economy there would be no marketing. In an economy in which trade occurred only between original producers and final users there would be no "marketing margin" between producer prices and consumer prices. Marketing costs would be borne directly by producers and users, and farmers would receive all of the "consumer's dollar."

Marketing becomes of distinct concern where there are intermediaries—"middlemen"—involved in the transfer of goods from specialized producers to final users, whose return comes from a margin between the price paid producers and that charged consumers. The "costs" of marketing then become evident as an offset to the benefits of specialization in production. These costs typically increase as the economy develops. It is not fortuitous that explicit concern with agricultural marketing developed in the United States at a time when agricultural production was becoming predominantly specialized and when the growth of cities was coming to require an elaborate and far-flung system of supply, the costliness of which was reflected in a substantial and widening margin between farm and retail prices.

Inherent complexities. Part of the costliness of marketing agricultural products arises from the dispersion of production and consumption. Farm production over most of the world is carried on by many small producers. Even where it is conducted on large, centrally managed plantations or collectives, it is necessarily spread out—it cannot be concentrated in factories, as can production in many other industries. Similarly at the consuming end, marketing must make products available in small quantities to meet the daily needs of individual families. Hence a widespread marketing system has a gross task of first assembling products and then redistributing them.

The biological production process in agriculture creates further problems in the marketing of its products. Production is seasonal; the whole year's output of some crops is harvested in a few weeks. The production period is long; several months elapse from preparation for planting to time of harvest for most crops, and for tree crops and animals of long gestation the period is longer still. The products are perishable, many of them highly so. Output is uncertain; weather conditions, diseases, insect infestations, and the like affect both the quantity and the quality of product. And quality varies from unit to unit within a crop; the agricultural production process does not yield a standardized product.

These conditions of production have several consequences for marketing. The volume coming to market varies seasonally; for some commodities the seasonal peaks are very sharp. To avoid spoilage losses, perishables must be utilized quickly—either consumed or processed into storable form. Special handling is required for their protection. Processed products and the less perishable staple commodities must be stored to meet year-round consumption needs. Year-to-year variations in supply add to the uncertainties in marketing. Variability in product quality makes market valuation difficult and complicates processing.

Both the variability of supply of farm products and their perishability make marketing costly. They also make it risky, not only because of the danger of spoilage losses but also because of price uncertainty. Since food serves a satiable want, the demand for food commodities is typically inelastic at high levels of supply. Prices thus tend to be unstable. For perishables that must be disposed of before they spoil, a small oversupply can cause a drastic drop in price. And while sudden price decreases are less likely in storables, over the long period of storage they can suffice to cause substantial losses, especially in view of the large investment where the year's supply must be held from harvest to harvest.

The long production period of agricultural products is a further unstabilizing factor in marketing, since it delays the response of supply to price. Once the planting season of a crop is past, little can be done to increase the current season's supply, and it can be decreased only by abandoning the investment already sunk in it, which will not be done so long as the prospective price gives hope of covering the remaining costs of carrying it through to market.

The organization of markets. The widening of markets, in addition to permitting specialization in production, also mitigates some of the problems just described, by diluting their effects. It is of interest, therefore, to review some prerequisites of a widely organized marketing system.

Even in relatively primitive economies, presumed to have only a "subsistence" agriculture, there is, typically, considerable marketing. Each community has its market where produce is exchanged on certain days. Even though trade is predominantly local, there are usually some persons who specialize in buying and selling and in such supporting activities as carrying. In such widely separate societies as Java, west Africa, and the Indian communities of Guatemala, women traditionally do much of the local marketing.

The local markets are often structured throughout an area, each operating on a different day of the week so that professional traders can carry wares from one to another. This encourages local specialization in production by providing an expanded market for local surpluses. Typically, a group of small markets is tributary to a central market where trade, on a larger scale, includes wholesale transactions with central markets of other areas. Thus a network of markets is built up throughout a region, which may tie in with other regional or international systems of trade.

This larger, longer-distance trade is more often carried on by men, and in many societies it is dominated by aliens—the Chinese in southeast Asia and Indonesia, the Indians in east Africa, and people of Levantine origin in west Africa. This has been explained by the freedom of such immigrants from the disapprobation that some indigenous groups attach to trade; also by the cohesiveness of alien minorities, which enables them to enforce codes of ethical trade conduct among their members over large areas.

The breadth of markets—and the kinds and degree of regional specialization in production that are possible—depend first of all upon the density of population and the means of transport available. Where transport is upon the backs of men or the heads of women or, at best, by oxcart, the area that a market can serve is limited and the individual lots traded are small. Marketing of perishables is restricted to the local area; for bulky staples, the cost in human time and effort is a barrier to intensive specialization in production for distant markets.

The technological basis for a widespread agricultural marketing system thus rests first of all upon rapid, low-cost transportation. It depends equally upon rapid, low-cost communication. Also important are efficient methods of storage, of processing, and of protecting products from spoilage and damage.

But the widening of markets also depends upon devising effective organizational arrangements for managing the movement of products and the flow of payments for them. There must be an "intelligence" system, providing the information needed for correct decision making. There must be arrangements for transfer of payments and for mobilization of capital funds to finance commodities in marketing channels, including the spreading of risks involved in interseasonal holding of commodities. Needed in support of all of these are standard measures of quantity and accepted methods for identification of quality of commodities in trade channels, as a basis for proper evaluation. Most important of all is the need for a framework of legal and ethical arrangements within which large-volume, long-distance transactions can be entered into rapidly with mutual confidence among the parties concerned.

In a marketing system coordinated through open, competitive markets, pricing is the heart of the coordinating system. Price theory and agricultural prices are discussed under other headings [see COMPETITION and DEMAND AND SUPPLY]. It suffices here to point out that effective coordination of agricultural markets requires rapid collection and dissemination of information on current and prospective supplies and movements of commodities and on prices throughout the market. In many countries the private communication between buyers and sellers and the brokers and other agents who represent them is supplemented by an extensive trade press and radio service that reports current market information and by publicly maintained crop-forecasting and market-reporting services. There is also public establishment of standard weights and measures, and of standards of quality for major commodities, and frequently public maintenance of an impartial inspection service for certifying the quality and condition of lots of commodities in trade channels. Flow of funds is provided by a widespread commercial banking system —both for facilitating payment in long-distance transactions and for making credit available for financing market operations.

Longer-term problems. The longer-range coordination of production and consumption of agricultural commodities presents more difficult problems because of characteristics previously pointed out: the long production cycle and consequent slowness of response of supply to price; and the uncontrollable variations in production, especially in the face of inelastic demands. Farmers cannot know at planting time what the prices of alternative crops will be at harvest time; they cannot even know what their own yields will be. Processors and distributors face corresponding uncertainties.

One response to this difficulty is the pressure for government intervention in markets to stabilize prices and manage supplies. Measures sometimes undertaken for this purpose include: year-to-year storage of staple crops, purchase and extracommercial distribution of price-depressing surpluses, the setting of quotas limiting the acreages that farmers may plant to certain crops, price fixing, subsidies to producers and low-income consumers, collective-bargaining schemes, the sponsoring of marketing boards or marketing agreements or quasi-public corporations with varying degrees of monopoly powers in the management of supplies, discriminative pricing schemes for diverting surpluses to secondary uses, and the many devices used for controlling or managing foreign trade in agricultural commodities. Various such measures are discussed under other headings [see particularly AGRICULTURE, article on PRICE AND INCOME POLICIES].

Forward contracting. A variety of private devices are also used to improve longer-term coordination. One is vertical integration, in which several of the stages between farm production and retail distribution are brought under single ownership and management. Similar results are achieved in part by forward contracting. A feeder may contract with a cattle raiser for future delivery of feeder stock. A distributor may contract with a processor in advance of the packing season. In turn, the processor may contract with growers for specified acreages of canning crops. Such contracts give buyers assurance of future supplies and give growers assurance of an outlet for their produce. Futures trading [see SPECULATION, HEDGING, AND ARBITRAGE] is, of course, a highly organized form of forward contracting in which the contracts themselves are negotiable in trade.

Forward contracting has been encouraged by the increasingly close technological relation between farm production and processing. For example, processors contract with raisers of broiler chickens in order to be able to schedule the flow of raw materials to the processing plants. Contracts likewise facilitate quality control, as when a contract for a canning crop specifies the variety of seed to be sown and gives the canner supervision over spraying and other cultural practices and over the maturity of crop at harvest.

Such vertical "contract integration" reduces market uncertainties for the parties engaging in it. Because it bypasses the open market, however, it reduces the coordinating role of the price mechanism of that market.

The lengthening of marketing channels in a highly developed economy, and especially the increased processing to which modern technology has given rise, creates a further problem of vertical coordination. The wide separation of consumers from original producers attenuates the effectiveness of consumer demand as a guide to production. This is reflected in the increasing emphasis upon research into consumer preferences and buying behavior and the increasing use of advertising promotions and other merchandising schemes to manipulate final demand.

A further consequence of modern technology (including in this term techniques of management organization), coupled with the growth in scope of markets, is that economies of scale lead to the growth of very large enterprises. In the United States, some food processors are among the largest corporations, as are some chain-store food distributors. This need not indicate monopolistic concentration, for monopoly must be defined in terms of the size of the market: a small firm may enjoy a monopoly position in an isolated local market, and giant corporations may compete intensively in a market of nationwide scope. Growth in size of enterprises in the food industries nevertheless constitutes a change in market structure whose consequences have been inadequately analyzed. An enduring policy problem is how to retain the efficiencies of large-scale operations, yet prevent abuses of the market power that may be associated with them.

Farmers have attempted to secure advantages of size through cooperative marketing associations, a number of which in the United States are significant in the national market. Encouragement of farmer cooperatives is public policy in many countries. Their management presents unique problems if the farmer members are to retain effective control, yet permit flexible and progressive operation. They can, however, strengthen the market position of farmers vis-à-vis proprietary firms. Typically, their major advantage has been found to arise not simply from their activity as bargaining organizations but from efficient performance of processing or other marketing functions on a scale beyond the resources of individual members.

Government interest.   Because agricultural marketing plays so important a role in supplying foods and other essentials to consumers as well as in determining the incomes of the farm population, it has traditionally been a subject of public concern. In economies that have developed under a predominantly laissez-faire philosophy, this concern has expressed itself chiefly in regulation to restrain abuses, in public provision of services that private trade cannot readily provide, and in intervention where free markets give unsatisfactory results.

In the United States agricultural marketing was recognized as a distinct area of study in the U.S. Department of Agriculture by 1913. The early concern was with the apparently disadvantageous market position of farmers; with things farmers might do to improve their position, either individually, as by better sorting and packing of products and better selection of market outlets, or jointly through cooperative marketing associations; and with the need for public action to curb abuses in marketing and to provide such services as market reporting, promulgation of grade standards, and product inspection.

The collapse of farm prices following World War I and the extreme deterioration of markets during the depression of the 1930s brought great interest in schemes for stabilizing and supporting farm prices, controlling market supplies, and subsidizing both domestic consumption and exports. During World War II price guaranties were used to encourage increased production of farm products; and price controls, allocation orders, and consumer rationing were part of a wide-reaching program for wartime management of supplies of foods and other essential commodities.

At the close of the war, concern lest markets

might again collapse led to substantial expansion of agricultural marketing research. Special emphasis was placed upon increasing the efficiency of physical handling of products at all stages of marketing in order to reduce marketing costs, and upon expansion of markets through study of consumer wants, preferences, and buying behavior, improvement of products and services, and more effective merchandising and promotion.

The chronic depression of prices for farm products during the 1950s and continuing into the 1960s, accompanied by the accumulation of large surpluses in government hands, led to renewed interest in pricing and the competitive structure of markets, and in schemes for using surplus commodities as a form of aid to developing countries.

At the same time, the extension of technical aid to these countries opened the eyes of agricultural economists to the importance of marketing in facilitating or hampering the transition to commercial agriculture. In agricultural development in such countries, primary emphasis is usually placed upon increasing production. But there is need for simultaneous planning of market development, not only to assure the most effective use of increased commercial supplies but to provide adequate incentives to farmers to produce for the market in the first place.

At the same time, the intricacy of activities involved in a widespread, flexibly operating, efficient marketing system strongly recommends much decentralization of decision making. The need is for the kind of entrepreneurship by which many individuals will make decisions on their own initiative and use ingenuity in devising improved methods and meeting emergent needs. In this way, market development can proceed autonomously, with minimum burden upon the scarce resources of central government management. How to encourage this within a planned economy presents a most interesting problem.

Agricultural marketing, in short, encompasses the system of managing a country's supplies of food and other essential commodities. Upon the efficiency of this system depends the possibility of maintaining an urban industrial population. The system thus plays a vital role in economic progress.

HERMAN M. SOUTHWORTH

BIBLIOGRAPHY

Much marketing research is reported in the U.S. Department of Agriculture's Marketing Research Reports *and in bulletins of state agricultural experiment stations.*

ABBOTT, JOHN C. 1962 The Role of Marketing in the Development of Backward Agricultural Economies. *Journal of Farm Economics* 44:349–362.

ABBOTT, JOHN C. et al. 1962 *Marketing: Its Role in Increasing Productivity.* Freedom from Hunger Campaign, Basic Study No. 4. Rome: FAO.

BAUER, PÉTER T. (1954) 1963 *West African Trade: A Study of Competition, Oligopoly and Monopoly in a Changing Economy.* London: Routledge.

BOHANNAN, PAUL; and DALTON, GEORGE (editors) 1962 *Markets in Africa.* Northwestern University Africa Studies, No. 9. Evanston, Ill.: Northwestern Univ. Press.

BOWRING, JAMES R.; SOUTHWORTH, HERMAN M.; and WAUGH, FREDERICK V. 1960 *Marketing Policies for Agriculture.* Englewood Cliffs, N.J.: Prentice-Hall.

CLODIUS, ROBERT L.; and MUELLER, WILLARD F. 1961 Market Structure Analysis as an Orientation for Research in Agricultural Economics. *Journal of Farm Economics* 43:515–553.

COLLINS, NORMAN R.; and HOLTON, R. H. 1963 Programming Changes in Marketing in Planned Economic Development. *Kyklos* 16:123–136.

DEWEY, ALICE G. 1962 *Peasant Marketing in Java.* New York: Free Press.

HOFFMAN, AUSTIN C. 1940 *Large-scale Organization in the Food Industries.* U.S. Temporary National Economic Committee, Monograph No. 35. Washington: Government Printing Office.

IRWIN, HAROLD S. 1954 *Evolution of Futures Trading.* Madison, Wisc.: Mimir Publishers.

IRWIN, HAROLD S. 1962 The Intangible Side of Agricultural Marketing: A Neglected Area of Research. *Journal of Farm Economics* 44:808–819.

KOHLS, RICHARD L. (1955) 1961 *Marketing of Agricultural Products.* 2d ed. New York: Macmillan.

Marketing Evolution and Innovation. 1963 *Journal of Farm Economics* 45:1243–1271. → A symposium.

Market Organization and Economic Development. 1959 *Journal of Farm Economics* 41:1307–1331. → A symposium.

MIGHELL, RONALD L.; and JONES, LAWRENCE A. 1963 *Vertical Coordination in Agriculture.* Agricultural Economic Report No. 19. Washington: U.S. Department of Agriculture, Economic Research Service.

NICHOLLS, WILLIAM H. 1941 *A Theoretical Analysis of Imperfect Competition With Special Application to Agricultural Industries.* Ames: Iowa State College Press.

SHEPHERD, GEOFFREY S. (1946) 1962 *Marketing Farm Products: Economic Analysis.* 4th ed. Ames: Iowa State Univ. Press.

SKINNER, GEORGE 1964–1965 Marketing and Social Structure in Rural China. *Journal of Asian Studies* 24:3–43, 195–228, 363–399.

TAX, SOL (1953) 1963 *Penny Capitalism: A Guatemalan Indian Economy.* Univ. of Chicago Press.

U.S. DEPARTMENT OF AGRICULTURE 1954 *Yearbook of Agriculture: Marketing.* Washington: Government Printing Office.

U.S. FARMER COOPERATIVE SERVICE (1948) 1965 *Farmer Cooperatives in the United States.* Rev. ed. FCS Bulletin No. 1. Washington: U.S. Farmer Cooperative Service.

WAUGH, FREDERICK V. (editor) 1954 *Readings on Agricultural Marketing.* Ames: Iowa State Univ. Press.

IX
PRICE AND INCOME POLICIES

Agricultural price and income policies involve the use of governmental authority to increase and/or stabilize agricultural prices and incomes. The measures used to stabilize prices include stock acquisitions, control of domestic and foreign supplies, price supports, and direct subsidies. Programs to increase prices have used similar methods; in fact, most programs to stabilize prices have involved efforts to achieve a long-run average level of prices in excess of what would have otherwise prevailed. The measures to increase the income of farmers have included research to improve farm production methods, farm management advisory services, low-cost credit, aids to farm consolidation and off-farm migration, direct subsidies, control of output or marketings, and price supports.

Historical development. Governmental interference with, or regulation of, the prices of farm products can be found throughout recorded history. An example, more than three millenniums ago, was Joseph's granaries in Egypt. During the mercantilist period, most of the advanced nations of the world regulated the trade in certain agricultural products. The most famous of the regulations in modern history were the British corn laws, whose beginnings can be traced to 1463. The British corn laws were in existence for approximately four centuries and included many of the devices for influencing price and trade that are now used. These included prohibitions on exports (unless the domestic price was below some given level), export taxes, export bounties or subsidies, and import duties that varied with the domestic price. From 1796 through 1810, bounties were paid in most years to encourage the importation of grain; during some of the same years, export bounties were also paid. Furthermore, in 1623 a proclamation was issued authorizing the construction of public granaries for keeping the surplus of one year to offset the poor crops of another year; apparently none were built.

It can be said that the corn laws had two basic purposes: (1) to maintain the price of grains at a level that would encourage domestic production and (2) to moderate the variability in the price of grain. Until 1814, when export bounties were abandoned, these two objectives were to be achieved by a sliding scale of import duties, which were prohibitive at low grain prices and nominal when grain prices were high, and a bounty on exports when the grain price fell below a specified level. It is reasonably clear that the corn laws were ineffective in stabilizing grain prices; a moderately

short crop tended to force the price of grain to the maximum at which almost free importation was permitted, and an above average crop forced prices down to the point at which exportation was permitted and, if the prices were still lower, subsidized.

The effect of the corn laws upon the price of grain has never been adequately determined and probably cannot be from the available data. From 1697 through 1792, exports were substantially larger than imports; during this period, the export bounty was perhaps 5 per cent to 10 per cent of the domestic price. After 1792, England was generally a net importer of grain and the export bounty was of little significance. Under the schedule of import duties that became effective in 1828 and which remained unchanged until 1842, the duty was nominal when the British grain price was 73 shillings per quarter but increased to about 50 per cent of the c.i.f. price when the domestic wheat price was 65 shillings. Most wheat imports were made when the tariff duty was low and the domestic price quite high. However, from 1828 through 1840, almost a tenth of all wheat imported paid a duty of £1 or more, which was equal to a duty rate of 30 per cent or greater. Thus it is fairly clear that the corn laws had the effect of increasing grain prices during this period, but it is not possible to estimate the magnitude of the increase. The very substantial increase in imports following the reduction of the duties in 1842 and their elimination in 1846 also supports the contention that grain prices were increased significantly by the corn laws.

If we exclude the many governmental monopolies that have been established for centuries for various agricultural products, such as tobacco, opium, and alcohol, the first use of the modern technique of price support was probably the Brazilian coffee valorization scheme, which had its beginnings in 1902. The coffee scheme involved government loans to coffee producers, enabling them to hold stocks and thus reduce the quantity marketed, and prohibitions on further planting of coffee trees. Other early examples of price supports include a loan and storage program for currants, established in Greece in 1905; a program for controlling the types, acreages cultivated, and purchase prices of tobacco, established in Japan in 1905; and, in Great Britain during World War I, minimum or guaranteed prices for grains.

General adoption of price and income measures is largely a phenomenon of the past three decades. In the United States, the Federal Farm Board was established in 1929 to provide loans to hold farm commodities off the market in the face of the rapid decline of farm prices during the early years of the great depression. Within a period of little more than two years, the financial resources available to the Federal Farm Board were largely exhausted and the decline in farm prices had been little affected by its actions. It was argued that a primary reason for the failure of the Federal Farm Board was that it did not have authority to limit production to the amount that could be sold at reasonable prices. The Agricultural Adjustment Act of 1933 provided for a wide variety of measures to improve farm prices and incomes—acreage or output limitations, price supports, processing taxes, and subsidies. Significant parts of this act were declared unconstitutional in 1936; however, except for the processing taxes (which had an adverse effect on farm prices in any case), all of the major features of the act, plus other extensions of authority, were re-enacted by Congress between 1936 and 1938. Except for some changes in emphasis, the farm legislation of the period from 1933 through 1938 is still the basis of current farm income and price programs in the United States.

The farm price and income problem. Government action in agriculture has been based on one or both of two assumptions: (1) farm prices and incomes are too variable over time, and (2) the returns to farm resources are too low. The rather substantial variability of farm prices and incomes from crops and from a number of livestock products has been substantiated. The extensive work done by T. W. Schultz (1945) may be noted. In the absence of government programs, farm prices have varied over time as a result of changes in the level of business activity, variations in the output of individual crops, and substantial annual variations in the output produced on individual farms. For many farm products the intrayear variations in prices have also been very large.

The basic sources of the instability of farm prices and incomes can be briefly noted. First, the price elasticity of demand for farm products is low. Thus, for any given demand situation, a small variation in the quantity supplied can result in a much larger and opposite variation in price. Second, in the short run, the elasticity of supply of farm products is very low. In any given country, crops are produced in a given season and the output available for sale for the entire year is determined in a relatively short period of time. Consequently, most of the effect of a change in demand will be felt in price changes, rather than in changes in the quantity offered for sale. Third, production decisions often must be made several months or a year before the product is available for sale. If the price expectations underlying the production decisions turn out to be inaccurate, large changes in prices and income may result. Finally, many farmers live in areas where there are substantial year-to-year climatic variations—the Great Plains of North America, for example. The yield of a given crop on a farm may vary from nothing to two or three times the long-run average yield. At least for the major industrial countries, it appears that instability of demand has been much less important as a source of price instability since World War II than in the years before.

In an economy with rising per capita incomes, it is almost certain that the return to farm labor will be less than the return to comparable labor elsewhere in the economy. In such an economy, a transfer of labor resources from agricultural to nonagricultural occupations is almost certain to occur. The transfer will occur if two phenomena exist: (1) if the income elasticity of demand for farm products is less than unity, and (2) if technological change or other forces result in rising output per unit of labor and land engaged in agriculture.

The existence of the required transfer and its magnitude depend upon the income elasticity of demand for farm products and the relative rate of change in productivity in agriculture compared to the rest of the economy. After an economy has reached a level of per capita income approximating $100 (United States), the income elasticity of demand for farm products is significantly less than unity. Thus the demand for farm products will increase less rapidly than the demand for nonfarm products, since the income elasticity of demand for all output is unity. If it were not possible to increase resource productivity in agriculture, resource transfers out of agriculture would not be necessary, since, with a positive income elasticity of demand, the absolute demand for farm products would grow with rising per capita income. However, the history of the industrial nations indicates that technological and other changes that increase productivity are of roughly the same significance in agriculture as in the rest of the economy.

No nation that has had significant increases in real per capita income has been able to avoid a decline in the share of its total labor force engaged in agriculture. In the past century, the percentage of all workers engaged in agriculture in the United States has declined from about 60 per cent to about 8 per cent; since 1940, farm employment has decreased from 9.4 million to 5.0 million. Since the end of World War II, farm employment has declined by approximately 30 per cent in western Europe.

A decline in the percentage of the labor force engaged in agriculture is one of the adjustments required as a result of increasing real incomes. It is a reflection of the fact that as people become richer they desire to spend a smaller fraction of their income for food and other farm products. It is also an indication that the forces that make it possible for the economy as a whole to enjoy higher incomes—increased capital, new knowledge, and a better educated labor force—are also operative in agriculture.

But, as noted above, one of the consequences of the forces that caused the decline in the relative and absolute employment in agriculture is that the return to farm labor is less than the return to comparable labor elsewhere in the economy. Thus, there is an incentive for young people born on farms to choose another occupation; for most farm youth, this implies leaving the home community and migrating to an urban community.

The size of the differential in income associated with the transfer of labor from agriculture to the rest of the economy appears to vary a great deal from country to country. It appears to be quite large in the United States and Canada—perhaps as much as a quarter or a third—and substantially smaller in France and England.

Remedial techniques. Price and income policies generally have one of two objectives, although sometimes both objectives are pursued simultaneously. One objective is the stabilization of the level of farm prices or incomes; the other objective is the increasing of the level of farm prices or incomes. The latter objective may also seek to increase output, or the end may be primarily the improvement of the income position of farm families, with any output effects being unintended. The price and income policies followed in Great Britain since the end of World War II have had the increasing of output as one of their major objectives. Over the same period of time, the policies in the United States have attempted to use price and income measures as a means of increasing farm incomes, and programs were devised to offset the output effects of the higher prices and incomes.

The techniques that have been used to increase or stabilize farm prices fall into a number of categories; frequently several techniques may be used in combination. The principal techniques include output control, storage financed by loans or government purchase, deficiency payments, import controls, and export subsidies. The main features of the wheat program of the United States in 1963

were approximately the same as the programs followed for several major crops during the previous decade and may be used as an example. The total area sown to wheat was limited to fifty million acres; each farmer who grew wheat was allocated a specific acreage based upon previous area seeded. When the wheat was harvested the farmer had the choice of selling his wheat on the market or of obtaining a nonrecourse loan from the Commodity Credit Corporation. The meaning of the term "nonrecourse loan" is that the farmer could deliver his wheat in full payment of the loan even if the market price of the wheat were below the amount loaned to him. The general idea of this loan program was that enough farmers would place their wheat in storage to increase the market price to approximately the loan rate, which was $2.00 per bushel in 1963.

The production of wheat in the United States in recent years has been approximately double the domestic use for food, feed, and seed. As the domestic price averaged about $0.65 per bushel more than the price received by exporters abroad, any sales of wheat in foreign markets required an export subsidy of about that amount. However, even with an export subsidy, sales in regular commercial export markets were equal to about half the excess of production over domestic use. The remainder of the wheat, plus some additional amount to reduce the relatively large stocks held by the Commodity Credit Corporation, was disposed of as a part of the United States foreign economic assistance program. The wheat was sold for local currencies, with no anticipation that payment would be made later in dollars. Most of the local currencies have been, or will be, returned to the nations receiving the wheat, although some have been used to cover United States expenditures in the recipient nations.

One consequence of the price support programs that resulted in domestic prices in excess of world market prices has been the necessity to control the importation of the farm products involved. Again using wheat as an example, for almost three decades there has been an import quota that prohibits the importation of more than a few thousand bushels of wheat or its equivalent in flour.

In the United Kingdom, which is an important importer of wheat, price supports for wheat have been maintained by deficiency payments. The deficiency payment to the farmer represents the difference between the guaranteed price and the average market price for the year. In this system, imports are allowed to enter the country freely; and because there is no tariff on wheat, the price paid by consumers represents the lowest price at which wheat is available from anywhere in the world.

In West Germany, which also imports wheat, the government establishes a target price for wheat. The target price is a threshold price at the major ports (the target price minus transport costs to the major interior markets). On any wheat that is imported from outside the European Economic Community, a variable levy is imposed, equal to the difference between the threshold price and the average price of wheat offered for sale by exporters. Thus, the price at which imported wheat is available to German millers does not vary; a decline in the exporter's offering price is offset by an equal increase in the variable levy. The variable levy, which is a major instrument of the common agricultural policy of the European Economic Community, is a modern version of the English corn laws of the early nineteenth century.

The price and income programs of most nations have included measures other than increasing the prices received by farmers. In the United States, various payments are made directly to farmers for carrying out certain farm practices, such as terracing, tiling, liming, and the planting of cover crops. Substantial payments have also been made for diverting land from productive use. In the United Kingdom, subsidies have been paid for the use of fertilizers and limes, for drainage, for the ploughing up of land, and for the production of cattle in hill regions. In West Germany, payments have been made for reduction of fertilizer prices, for improvement of farm buildings, and for land consolidation and enlargement of farms.

Determination of price support levels. The determination of the price support level varies from country to country. In the United States, an attempt was made in the Agricultural Adjustment Act of 1933 to specify an objective criterion. This criterion was called the parity price, which was the price of an agricultural commodity that would give the same purchasing power, in terms of the goods and services purchased by the farmer for production and living, that the commodity had in 1910–1914. Thus the price received per bushel of wheat during 1910–1914 was 88 cents; if prices paid by farmers doubled, the parity price would be $1.76 per bushel. Price supports, however, were never established at 100 per cent of parity. During the 1930s, support prices were established in the general range of 50 per cent to 70 per cent of parity; it was not until World War II that price supports were established at 90 per cent of parity.

The specific definition of parity was changed on

several occasions; for example, property taxes and wage rates for hired workers were added to the prices-paid index. One serious objection to the concept was that demand and supply conditions change over time and that the relative prices of agricultural products that prevailed in 1910–1914 did not fit the circumstances four decades later. An important modification was introduced in 1948, when the relative parity prices were determined by the average prices received by farmers during the previous ten years. However, since the revision in the formula resulted in the reduction of parity prices for "politically important crops," primarily wheat and corn, the revised formula did not become fully effective for certain crops for almost a decade.

Other nations have not adopted such specific and rigid concepts as parity prices to define their farm price objectives. In the United Kingdom, the price objective was defined in the Agriculture Act of 1947 as "promoting and maintaining a stable and efficient agricultural industry capable of producing such part of the nation's food and other agricultural produce as in the national interest it is desirable to produce in the United Kingdom, and of producing it at minimum prices consistent with proper remuneration and living conditions for farmers and workers in agriculture and an adequate return on capital invested in the industry." In West Germany, the Agricultural Act of 1955 had the objective of providing the same return to agricultural labor on properly managed holdings of average production conditions as to wage earners in comparable nonagricultural occupations in rural areas; additional criteria included adequate reward to managerial activity and capital in agriculture.

Effects of price and income policies. The agricultural price and income measures of the industrial countries have a number of consequences, some intended and some unintended, that merit examination. The major intended effect is to increase the level of return to resources engaged in agriculture. Other important areas of effect are output consequences, cost to consumers, cost to taxpayers, and international trade.

Resource and output effects. Of the various effects, the one that is subject to the most dispute is the return to resources engaged in agriculture. The intent of the governments that enact and administer agricultural price and income measures is to increase the return to farm labor, land, and capital. There is considerable dispute among economists about the effects of higher prices and other income measures upon the return to farm labor.

One school of thought argues that the increase in net income resulting from an increase in farm product prices is of almost the same absolute size as the increase in gross farm income. Another school of thought argues that the effect of a given increase in product prices upon the average return to farm resources depends on the characteristics of the production function and the elasticity of supply of the various farm resources.

The basic assumption of the first school is that farmers do not adjust the level of output in response to changes in the average level of all product prices. Following an increase in product prices, production expenditures, except for purchases from other farms, remain essentially the same. Since production expenses in modern agriculture constitute half or more of gross income, a change in gross income of 10 per cent would result in a change of net farm income of more than 20 per cent, if the stated assumption were correct.

The above approach to the effects of changes in product prices upon the returns to farm resources is inconsistent with the expected result derived from the application of modern price and production theory, unless the elasticity of supply of agricultural output is, in fact, zero.

In brief summary, price and production theory implies the following consequences from an increase in farm product prices: (1) farm output would increase; (2) more inputs or resources would be used; (3) total payments to nonfarm resources—fertilizer, gasoline, feed supplements, machinery—would increase; and (4) the relative increase in factor prices will vary inversely with their elasticities of supply. Whether the increase in the return to farmer-owned resources—the labor of the operator and his family and his owned capital and land—will increase more than, the same as, or less than the increase in product prices depends upon the conditions of production and the elasticities of factor supply.

Some of the above implications are directly derivable from the formula $[1/(s+1)][1+e]$, in which s is the elasticity of supply for a factor and e is the elasticity of supply of output. The above formula is based upon the assumption that the elasticity of substitution among inputs is unity; if the elasticity of substitution varies between 0.5 and 2.0, the results are affected only slightly.

The implications of the formula can be illustrated by assuming that government action results in an increase of product price by 10 per cent. Let us assume that the elasticity of supply of output is 0.1. If the elasticity of factor supply is zero, which, in the short run, may be approximately true

of land, the return to land (rent) will increase by 11 per cent. If the elasticity of supply for an input is 10, which might be the case for fertilizer, the increase in price would be about 1 per cent. If the elasticity of factor supply is 0.25, which might represent all labor used in agriculture, the increase in the return to labor would be 9 per cent. If the elasticity of factor supply is unity, the increase in factor price would be between 5 per cent and 6 per cent. If the elasticity of factor supply is equal, or greater than, the output elasticity, the increase in factor price will be less than the increase in product price.

It is almost certain that land will be the input that will gain most from an increase in product price due to government action. It is also most unlikely that the increase in the return to labor will be greater than the increase in product price.

The above results can be put differently. A significant fraction of the cost of the higher prices will be required to pay for additional inputs; of the increase in net returns to farm resources, the largest percentage increase will go to the owners of land.

The effects of changes in product prices upon the return to resources are affected only slightly if output is controlled by reducing the quantity of one of the inputs, such as land. The major effect of limiting the quantity of one of the inputs that may be used is to reduce the level of output somewhat and thus perhaps to reduce the governmental costs of the effort to increase product prices.

In the short run, the formula given above may not apply. This is true because the change in prices may not be fully anticipated or, if anticipated, complete adjustment is not possible. For example, in the United States between 1948 and 1949, farm prices received decreased by 12.5 per cent, and net farm income per capita declined 22.5 per cent; between 1950 and 1951, prices increased by 6 per cent, and net farm income per capita increased 11 per cent. However, if periods of somewhat greater length are compared, the formula appears to be supported by changes that can be observed in prices and incomes. Between 1945–1948 and 1949–1953, farm prices decreased by 11 per cent and farm income per capita by 10.5 per cent; between 1949–1953 and 1954–1958, farm prices decreased by 13 per cent and farm income per capita by 5 per cent.

The United States has been the only major industrial country that has followed a conscious policy of attempting to restrict farm production. However, the effectiveness of the programs followed—restriction of land cultivated for certain crops—is subject to debate. First, it is possible to substitute other inputs for land—more fertilizer, labor, machinery, herbicides, and insecticides. The higher prices that have been associated with the reduction in land cultivated have encouraged such substitutions. Second, the relative importance of land, as a factor of production, is relatively small in modern agriculture. In the United States, at present, land, including buildings used for production, accounts for about 15 per cent of all farm resources. If the elasticity of substitution between land and all other inputs is unity, a 20 per cent reduction in land use (which has never been achieved in the United States) would cause farm output to decline no more than 4 per cent or 5 per cent. Third, while the United States has attempted to reduce farm output by reducing cultivated land, it has simultaneously had subsidized farm credit. In addition, there has been an effective research and education program to improve farm efficiency and, thus, production. On balance, it appears most unlikely that the United States has reduced farm production by government programs, and it is probable that the higher prices have resulted in an increase in the level of production.

Costs of programs. The total costs of efforts to increase farm prices as a means of increasing farm incomes have proven to be very substantial in the major industrial nations. These costs take several forms, depending upon the particular methods adopted for increasing returns to farmers. In the United Kingdom, where the policy has been to allow prices in consumer markets to clear the markets, the major costs have represented subsidies paid to farmers. These subsidies have taken two forms: (1) a payment to farmers equal to the difference between the guaranteed price and the market price, and (2) production subsidies for such items as fertilizer and lime or for improvements of buildings and other structures. In West Germany, the costs have included relatively high prices for consumers, payments for improving the quality and marketing of milk, payments for enlargement of farms and improvement of farm buildings, and subsidies to reduce the cost of certain farm inputs (principally fertilizer and petroleum products).

In the United States, the cost of the farm price programs have included payments to induce farmers to withdraw part of their land from cultivation, payments for land improvements, export subsidies to compensate for the difference in domestic and foreign prices, and storage costs—as well as higher prices to domestic consumers. In the United States, storage costs of commodities acquired by the government in its efforts to maintain market prices near some specified level have been a significant element in the total costs of the farm price support program. In recent years, for example, if the cost of storage for wheat owned by the government is calculated on a first-in–first-out basis, the cost of accumulated storage is greater than the amount received by the farmer for the wheat.

International trade effects. The efforts on the part of governments to increase farm prices and incomes have major implications for international trade in farm products. The nations that increase prices to consumers restrict consumption of farm products. If the nations are importers of farm products, the volume and value of imports are reduced. If the nations are exporters, the quantity of products available for export is increased, and export subsidies are often used to increase the quantity of farm products exported. Equally important, the methods used to increase farm incomes—higher prices and production subsidies—also increase farm production in the industrial countries. In a nation that normally imports part of its food supply, the net effect is to reduce the demand for imports. An exporting country is faced with the necessity of increasing exports.

One of the important, but often ignored, consequences of the farm income programs of the industrial nations is the effects upon the export possibilities of underdeveloped areas. By reducing consumption through higher prices to consumers and by increasing farm output by higher prices and various subsidies, the industrial nations have reduced the export potentials of underdeveloped areas. While it is true that many of the tropical farm products produced by underdeveloped areas are not produced in the industrial countries, there is competition at both the production and consumption level. In production, the industrial countries compete in rice, fats and oils, and sugar. In addition, subsidized exports, often under the guise of foreign aid, reduce the market for domestically produced food products, especially the grains, in the recipient countries.

Alternatives. The price and income policies described above have numerous and serious disadvantages, higher prices to consumers, large treasury costs, increased farm output, and restraint on the potential gains from international specialization; but perhaps the most serious limitation is that there is no evidence that the income gaps that exist between farm and nonfarm families have narrowed as a result of these programs. At best, it can be argued that the income differentials are generally narrower than would have been the case if the various nations had not pursued these policies. But this proposition has not been demonstrated in any systematic way, despite the billions of dollars spent each year on these programs by the industrial nations.

One of the consequences of economic growth is a decline in farm employment, first relatively and later absolutely. A major factor, although not the only one, in the observed differences in the incomes of farm and nonfarm workers is that many farm people must continually shift to nonfarm jobs. No developing country has been able to avoid this transfer. Yet there are very few instances where the necessity for the labor transfer has been recognized as an element that needed to be considered in developing agricultural income programs.

While it is probably true that the policies followed by the industrial nations have not held a significant amount of labor in agriculture—in most countries significant income differentials have persisted—the programs can be criticized on two grounds. First, most countries have had programs that have encouraged farmers to make additional investments in land improvements, buildings, fertilizer, and machinery. These increased investments, where not justified by their returns, have reduced the demand for farm labor and depressed the returns to farm labor. Second, the programs have failed to aid farm people in making the adjustment that economic growth required, namely the transfer from farm to nonfarm occupations. If the funds invested in farm price supports and production and investment subsidies had been used for rural education, training of adult farm workers for nonfarm jobs, improving employment information, and subsidies for labor transfers, the returns to farm resources would be no lower than they now are. Furthermore, the adjustments that the agricultures of all industrial nations face would by now be much smaller in magnitude.

The transfer of workers from agriculture to the rest of the economy is influenced, of course, by the state of employment in the economy as a whole. If there is an active labor market, the transfer can occur more rapidly and more easily than if there is serious unemployment. With some exception for Canada and the United States, most of the major industrial countries have not had high unemployment rates for the past two decades. In the United States, during the years 1960–1962, when unemployment rates averaged almost 6 per cent, the annual migration from the farms averaged 5 per cent of the farm population. And this was in a setting in which little was done by government to aid the transfer and employment opportunities were relatively limited.

I should note that there is not general agreement among agricultural economists that it is possible to remove the disequilibria in agriculture by assisting the transfer of labor out of agriculture. Heady (1962) has argued that while it is desirable to do all that can be done to make the elasticity of supply of farm labor as large as possible, technological change and the substitution of other inputs for labor will make it difficult, if not impossible, to increase the returns to farm labor to a satisfactory level, unless the amount of land used in agriculture is also reduced. Heady's conclusion implies that the long-run elasticity of substitution between labor and other inputs, given the existing supply of land, is very high, and large changes in the quantity of labor will not have much influence upon the marginal returns to labor. However, if the elasticity of substitution between land and purchased inputs is also very great, reducing the amount of land used in agriculture would also have little effect upon output, product prices, or the marginal return to labor.

The questions posed by the previous paragraph are questions of fact. Unfortunately, we do not yet have the research that could clearly substantiate one view or the other.

D. GALE JOHNSON

BIBLIOGRAPHY

BENEDICT, MURRAY R. 1953 *Farm Policies of the United States, 1790–1950: A Study of Their Origins and Development.* New York: Twentieth Century Fund.

BENEDICT, MURRAY R.; and STINE, OSCAR C. 1956 *The Agricultural Commodity Programs: Two Decades of Experience.* New York: Twentieth Century Fund.

COCHRANE, WILLARD W. 1965 *The City Man's Guide to the Farm Problem.* Minneapolis: Univ. of Minnesota Press.

HATHAWAY, DALE E. 1963 *Government and Agriculture: Public Policy in a Democratic Society.* New York: Macmillan.

HEADY, EARL O. 1962 *Agricultural Policy Under Economic Development.* Ames: Iowa State Univ. Press.

JOHNSON, D. GALE 1947 *Forward Prices for Agriculture.* Univ. of Chicago Press.

MCCRONE, GAVIN 1962 *The Economics of Subsidizing Agriculture: A Study of British Policy.* London: Allen & Unwin.

NICHOLSON, JOSEPH S. 1904 *The History of the English Corn Laws.* New York: Scribner.

ORGANIZATION FOR EUROPEAN ECONOMIC COOPERATION 1961 *Trends in Agricultural Policies Since 1955.* Fifth Report on Agricultural Policies in Europe and North America. Paris: The Organization.

SCHULTZ, THEODORE W. 1945 *Agriculture in an Unstable Economy.* New York: McGraw-Hill.

TONTZ, ROBERT L. (editor) 1966 *Foreign Agricultural Trade: Selected Readings.* Ames: Iowa State Univ. Press.

TRACY, MICHAEL 1964 *Agriculture in Western Europe.* London: Cape; New York: Praeger.

X

DEVELOPING COUNTRIES

Most typically, agricultural activity in developing countries is carried on by persons who combine in a single household the functions of managing and providing labor for a settled farm. This type of agriculture may be called peasant farming. The definition includes a vast number of farmers who have very similar economic problems and who produce much of the world's food and fiber. The definition excludes both the farm laborer who has virtually no decision-making power and the specialized farm manager who does little or no manual labor. It also excludes large corporate, state, and collectivized farms, as well as plantations. (The latter, in particular, are important in a number of developing nations.) On such farms the functional division into manager and laborer is usually accompanied by sharp social distinctions as well. The practitioner of shifting cultivation is also excluded from this definition of peasantry. Shifting cultivation occupies a large area in many developing countries, but because of its extensive nature, it accounts for only a small proportion of agricultural production. [See AGRICULTURE, *article on* PRODUCTION; COMMUNISM, ECONOMIC ORGANIZATION OF, *article on* AGRICULTURE; PLANTATIONS. *For discussion of shifting agriculture, see* AGRICULTURE, *article on* COMPARATIVE TECHNOLOGY; *and* ASIAN SOCIETY, *article on* SOUTHEAST ASIA.]

The peasant farmer occupies an intermediate position on the continuum between agricultural laborer and specialized manager. Thus, the definition of a peasant farmer is necessarily arbitrary at its edges. On the one hand, farm laborers may own small pieces of land which they till and about which they make management decisions. On the other hand, some peasants operate such large farms that they in fact participate little in laboring and serve largely as specialized managers. Nevertheless, there is sufficient homogeneity of economic problems and decision-making responsibility included in this definition to make it operationally useful.

Peasant farming includes a wide range of economic conditions, since both the largely subsistence farmer characteristic of much of Asia and the highly commercialized family farmer of North America combine the farm-labor and farm-management functions in the same household. The peasant or family farm in the dynamic high-income economies is discussed in other articles in this group. The emphasis of this article will be on the peasant farmer in the context of a relatively traditional economy.

The complexity of executive management required and the necessity of day-to-day decisions under highly varied conditions give considerable advantage to the family-size farm and explain the dominance of the peasant farm in the world's agriculture. Farms with large labor forces and a sharp division between management and labor are largely limited to special situations: where integrated operations offer special marketing advantages; where other services having major economies of scale, such as research, must be rendered on each individual farm; or where special problems of handling unskilled labor arise. Most of the farming in the United States is still basically family farming, even though the American farmer is competent in a highly advanced technology, is highly commercialized, and uses large amounts of capital and land.

As broadly defined, peasant agriculture dominates the low-income economies of much of Asia and to a large extent those of Africa and Latin America as well. In these areas peasant agriculture often produces over half of the national income and absorbs well over half of the nation's population. The future course of food production for growing populations and, in early stages of development, the future rate of increase in per-capita national income itself depend in important part upon production trends in the dominant peasant-farming sector (Johnston & Mellor 1961). With recognition of the critical role of peasant agriculture in economic development, substantial research and policy attention is directed to analysis of the means of development of this sector of the economy.

Means of increasing production. Peasant agriculture has two characteristics that distinguish it sharply from other sectors of the economy in the development process.

First, early in development, peasant agriculture already commands the economy's basic stock of land, labor, and capital, which it uses at low levels of productivity. Thus, for this sector the problem of development is not so much one of raising a large stock of new resources, as is the case for much new industry, but one of how to make the existing stock of resources more productive. Peasant agriculture thus offers substantial opportunity for rapid increase in production through increasing the productivity of existing resources, but concurrently it presents major problems of inertia in changing an existing system.

The second distinguishing characteristic of the peasant-farming sector is that it consists of a large number of heterogeneous small-scale units of production. This creates problems of communication and of rendering production-related services. Although the farming operation itself offers few economies of scale beyond a family-size operation, many of the services, such as research, education, transport, and so on, which are associated with high-productivity agriculture, do offer major economies of scale. If peasant agriculture is to develop, devices must be found for providing such services to literally millions of small-scale farming units. The problems to be met and the inertia in the existing system seriously retard the development process.

Four quite different approaches are currently proposed as means of increasing production in a peasant agriculture. They differ in the extent to which they require increased allocation of scarce resources from other sectors of the economy and in the implicit level of returns such resources are expected to receive from their use in agriculture.

First, it is argued that peasant farmers in traditional economies use the resources currently at their disposal inefficiently. It then follows that systematic study of resource utilization will provide the basis for reorganizing agriculture with a consequent increase in production. However, increasingly it is recognized that, given their environment, peasant farmers in fact operate rather efficiently and that major increases in production cannot be expected from this source (Schultz 1964).

Second, it is argued that traditional peasant agriculture contains a large stock of idle labor and even land resources that may be brought into production. However, it is now being recognized that although such idle stocks of resources do occur, their productivity, with current technology, is too low to make them meaningful to either individual peasants or to society as a whole (Mellor 1963).

Third, it is argued that increased production in peasant agriculture requires heavy input of capital and other resources of a largely traditional type in the form of land-reclamation schemes, major irrigation projects, and large-scale machinery. However, experience to date indicates that returns on this kind of investment in peasant agriculture are generally low unless major changes in technology occur simultaneously.

Fourth, it is argued that increased production may be achieved largely on the basis of the existing set of traditional resources through introducing technological change, which raises the productivity of existing resources and concurrently attracts idle resources into production. Such technological change, of course, has a cost and involves a number of planning problems. The approach has been successful in many high-income countries, including most notably Japan.

The relative merits of these several positions will become clearer in the succeeding discussion of the economics of traditional peasant agriculture and its modernization.

The resource base. The family labor force is the basic labor unit of peasant agriculture. Farms in the United States normally have a labor force equivalent to two full-time persons, and that typical size has not changed significantly for decades. The typical farm in India and Indonesia also has roughly a two-man labor force. Of course, the extent to which other resources are combined with labor, the extent to which the labor force is fully occupied, and the size of income accruing to that labor force differs greatly from one peasant agriculture to another.

Typically, in traditional economies there are large stocks of idle labor during much of the year, and in some peasant agricultures there is a stock of idle labor even at seasonal peaks of labor requirements. The productivity of labor in traditional peasant agricultures is low. Typically an increment of a man-day of labor in India provides the basis for only an additional 20 to 40 cents increment to production. Such a return provides little incentive for either full or efficient utilization of labor.

The size of the land resource per peasant family differs greatly from one situation to another. In a high-income country the family farmer may command hundreds of acres of land. In India peasant farmers typically command only five or ten acres. In Japan peasant farms are even smaller, averaging only about two acres per farm.

As in the case of labor, there is great variability in the production that is drawn from an acre of land. Japanese farmers gain several times as much production per acre as do Indian farmers. And the differences are more matters of technological stage than inherent productivity of the land. Typically in peasant agricultures of low-income countries yields per acre are very low compared to what is expected from similar land in a high-income nation.

The capital resource per peasant family also ranges widely—from the tens of thousands of dollars of nonland capital of a family farm in the United States to the mere tens of dollars of capital of a peasant farm in a low-income country. In

India nonland capital typically consists of a team of bullocks worth $100–$200 and perhaps only $50 worth of tools. In many low-income countries working livestock is not common, and nonland capital, therefore, includes only a few dollars' worth of hand tools. In such agricultures the major opportunity for capital formation within agriculture is in the form of improvements to land, such as wells, land leveling, fencing, and so on. Since these forms of investment are largely a direct embodiment of labor, the returns on them tend also to be driven to low levels.

Technology in the form of improved plant and livestock varieties and advanced production practices is one of the most important resources of high-income peasant agricultures. The peasant agricultures of low-income parts of the world lack such technology, and its provision represents a key aspect of the process of modernization.

The economic efficiency of resource use. Resource *productivity* in the peasant agriculture of traditional economies tends to be low, in the sense that output per unit of input of resources is low. However, the economic *efficiency* with which resources are used in peasant agricultures is generally quite high, in the sense that with the given objectives of peasant farmers a simple reorganization of resources within the present environment will not provide a substantial increase in production. This distinction is important because if economic efficiency is already high, then an increase in productivity requires a change in the environment within which decisions are made, rather than just a process of education.

Carefully drawn empirical studies of resource efficiency, which recognize the objectives of peasant farming, generally show peasant farmers to be combining inputs and production objectives in close to an optimal pattern (Schultz 1964; Tax 1953; Jones 1960). The objectives of a family enterprise such as a peasant farm may be complex and may certainly include, in addition to money income, consideration of the value of family time for leisure and other nonmonetary uses. Peasant farmers are not alone in introducing broad objectives into their economizing decisions.

Peasant farmers face two basic types of management decisions: those concerned with factor combinations (the intensity with which factors of production are used) and those concerned with the combination of enterprises (the output mix).

No farmer faces a completely static environment, although in a traditional peasant agriculture the decision-making environment changes relatively slowly. Even in a traditional peasant agricul-ture, population growth increases the availability of labor and pressures on income, calling for adjustment of labor input and product output. Occasional changes in technology, such as cultivation practices, or in water availability provide opportunity for new combinations of input and output. Occasionally the physical environment itself changes, with new insect and disease problems changing factor costs and returns. And even if agriculture itself is not dynamic, changes in incomes and tastes in other sectors may bring about price changes, which in turn change the relative profitability of alternative cropping patterns. Particularly if incomes are already low, peasant farmers must adjust effectively to many of these changes.

As economic development and the modernization of agriculture occur, changes in the decision-making environment become more rapid, and the pressure on the decision-making ability of peasant farmers increases substantially. In a traditional agriculture peasants may maintain efficiency by slow evolution of a trial-and-error nature. With modernization, decision making must become much more systematic and rapid. Thus, the relatively high level of economic efficiency in traditional peasant economies probably shows more about the simplicity and static nature of their environment than about the excellence of their decision-making ability.

Three special features of peasant farming in low-income countries may give the appearance of economic inefficiency. They are discussed below:

Variability in economic efficiency. Studies that demonstrate peasant farmers to be, on the average, in good economic adjustment with their environment normally include considerable variability around that average. It is usually not clear to what extent such variability arises because many peasant farmers are not in optimal economic adjustment and to what extent the environment itself differs significantly from one farmer to another. Certainly the latter is true in part. Soils and other physical features differ widely even within small areas, so that the optimal organization and combination of factors will vary from one farm to another. A gross study is not likely to make the necessary adjustments in all the data. Perhaps even more important, costs of labor and capital differ substantially from one farm to another. Farms with relatively more land per family member may feel less pressure to squeeze the last bit of gross income out of the farm through more use of labor, and thus they in effect act as though labor were more expensive to them than to other farmers (Mellor 1963). Likewise, such farmers, because of their higher incomes, have effectively lower costs of capital. Such variation in labor and capital costs may be greater than in the high-income nation where resources may be more freely mobile. As a result, greater variability in farm organization and operation may occur in traditional, as compared to modern, peasant-type agricultures.

Peasant conservatism. Farmers in low-income countries tend to be conservative. That is, they weigh risks and uncertainty heavily in making decisions. In addition, certain types of risks may in fact be greater in a traditional agriculture. Judged by standards that presume no risk, farmers in such a situation may appear out of adjustment. Risks of importance occur in regard to weather, prices, and technology.

Because peasant farmers in low-income countries have low incomes and relatively fixed consumption patterns, they tend to attach a very high value to achieving the normal pattern of income and relatively less value to comparable increments in excess of the normal pattern. Thus, peasant farmers in a traditional agriculture often choose a cropping pattern that provides little variability in production over a wide range of weather conditions, even though it may provide somewhat less on the average or in total over a period of years. Such organization may appear inefficient if the peasant's weighing of risk and uncertainty is not recognized. Peasants may react to new price relationships in the same manner. Even more important, peasant farmers may be slow to accept technological change because of the risks involved.

It should be clearly noted that in a traditional peasant agriculture, which does not have institutions for developing and testing innovation, long experience has shown that innovation generally does not pay. Conservatism in such a situation has important survival value, particularly if peasant farmers are living close to the subsistence margin. In such circumstances a society may institutionalize conservatism by placing decision-making power in the hands of the older members of the family and community who have learned from observation to move very cautiously into anything new. Such institutionalization of conservatism is valuable in a traditional economy. However, it slows progress toward a modern agriculture in which there are institutional means for developing and testing innovation so as to reduce its risk and increase its profitability. In any case, conservatism will in the short run cause farmers to be out of adjustment with a dynamic environment.

Subsistence-mindedness. Peasant farmers may be in significant part subsistence-minded—attaching special value to crops and livestock produced for home use relative to production for sale. Individual peasants may thus appear out of economic adjustment and unresponsive to price changes. In general, however, peasant farmers are not completely rigid in following production patterns that favor subsistence commodities. The apparent inflexibility arises from two sources, the first a matter of price relationships and the second a matter of risk and uncertainty.

In deciding upon relative emphasis on subsistence crops, farmers compare the farm price of crops they will sell and the retail price for crops they are to buy. Since marketing costs may provide a significant difference between these prices, there will be a range of prices within which individual farmers will not respond to changes in price. The effect of this will be to reduce the average extent of response of supply to changes in price relationships at retail.

This tendency will be increased by farmer reaction to risk and uncertainty. It is of great importance to peasant farmers that they be able to supply their subsistence needs. It happens that in most low-income countries there are great seasonal and year-to-year fluctuations in market prices and in market availability of food crops. As a result, farmers fear that if they produce certain crops for sale and then later buy subsistence crops on the market, they will be caught purchasing at a time of seasonally or cyclically high prices or low supply. This simply means that farmers would structure production to given price relationships if those prices were certain, but with price uncertainty they will give added favor to production for subsistence needs. Such behavior is inefficient only by the use of inappropriate measures.

Price responsiveness of peasant farmers. Given similar physical conditions, peasant farmers in a traditional agriculture tend to be as responsive to change in the relationship among farm prices as farmers in more modern agricultures, or even more so. This is documented by a number of careful studies of price behavior in peasant agricultures of Asia (Krishna 1963; Falcon 1964). This is not surprising, since peasant farmers in a traditional agriculture use forms of labor and capital which are quite flexible in production—in contrast with peasant farms in high-income agricultures, where capital tends to be highly specific in, say, cotton-picking machines, which will not harvest wheat, and in technical know-how regarding, say, onions, which is not transferable to beets. It is this flexibility of resource use in traditional agricultures that permits a substantial response to changes in price relationships.

On the other hand, peasant farmers in low-income economies tend to alter the aggregate level of agricultural production relatively little in response to price changes. This is because they operate in an agriculture using largely fixed resources, such as land and family labor, and use little of such purchased variable inputs as fertilizer. In addition, labor is relatively immobile, with little opportunity to move in and out of agriculture. Thus, there is little opportunity to vary the quantity of resources in production in response to change in the over-all level of prices for agricultural commodities. Occasionally, higher prices may pull additional labor into production from idle stocks. However, in a traditional agriculture the tendency for that to happen on some farms may be counterbalanced by the tendency on some other farms for income incentives to be satisfied with less work at higher prices, causing a perverse response of labor input to price.

Peasant response to new technology. There are many examples of peasant farmers in traditional agriculture who quickly adopt an innovation that is profitable under their conditions. Earlier exposition suggests that they may be cautious in decisions regarding change; but this is not because they are not economically motivated, but because they know from experience of the risks involved. However, even on this count the stereotype of peasant conservatism tends to be overstated. It must be remembered that there is normally considerable variability in size of farm and income among peasant farmers in a given community. The operators of the larger farms are well able to experiment and to accept some risk—and to a surprising extent experimentation does occur. All too often what is interpreted as a reluctance toward change is in fact no more than good sense on the part of peasants in rejecting innovation that under their conditions is unprofitable (Herdt & Mellor 1964).

The requisites for modernization. Modernization of peasant agriculture does not require change in its basic structure. Peasant agriculture is well suited to modernization, and peasant farmers are already reacting in an economically rational way to their environment. What is needed to bring about decisions that will increase production and incomes is to change the environment within which peasant farmers make decisions. That is largely a matter of institutional change. And although it is true that major increases in production require a complex

reformation of institutions, it is often the case that only one or two sets of institutions are limiting at a specific time. The following sets of institutional changes are set forth in the order in which they are most likely to be limiting (Mellor 1963).

In some peasant agricultures *land tenure* and other arrangements may be repressive and hence discouraging to income-increasing innovation, because the landlords or others appropriate an undue proportion of gains, while letting the risk and uncertainty and the cost of added inputs fall on the peasant farmer. Land reform and related institutional changes may be needed [*see* LAND TENURE].

If efficiency is to increase, a prime requisite is *new technology*. This is rarely transferable directly from one region to another, hence peasant agriculture must be supported by a program of research. Research institutions need to be centrally provided. This is often the source of unfavorable contrast between peasant agriculture and plantations or other large-scale methods of farming. The latter tend to have their own experiment stations. Peasants in traditional agriculture do not. In high-income agricultures of Europe, North America, and Japan the state has provided such facilities to family farmers, with a salutary effect on production and incomes.

Much technological change is based on *new forms of inputs*, particularly improved seeds and fertilizers. These require new lines of production and distribution. Traditional peasant agriculture can improve very little until these lines are opened and developed.

As innovation becomes more complex, *educational institutions* are required to teach farmers to use complex innovation and to handle increasingly complex decisions more rapidly.

Eventually, improved *credit facilities* are needed. Initially this may be less important than is sometimes thought. Innovations in early stages of development normally have cash costs sufficiently low for current income to provide the basis for adequate capital formation, at least on the larger farms. As innovation requires more and more purchased inputs, credit problems may increase [*see* CREDIT, *article on* AGRICULTURAL CREDIT].

Likewise, increased *marketing efficiency* may be important in modernization, particularly when output combinations change or bulky perishable products are produced in much larger quantity.

The key to modernization of traditional peasant agricultures is to provide institutions for facilitating the development and application of technological advance, thereby increasing the productivity of the existing stock of resources. The economic returns to such an effort tend to be high.

JOHN W. MELLOR

[*See also* AGRICULTURE, *articles on* CAPITAL, LABOR, *and* MARKETING.]

BIBLIOGRAPHY

CLARK, COLIN; and HASWELL, M. R. 1964 *The Economics of Subsistence Agriculture.* London: Macmillan; New York: St. Martins.

DEWEY, ALICE G. 1962 *Peasant Marketing in Java.* New York: Free Press.

EDWARDS, DAVID 1961 *Report on an Economic Study of Small Farming in Jamaica.* Kingston: Univ. College of the West Indies, Institute of Social and Economic Research.

FALCON, WALTER P. 1964 Farmer Response to Price in a Subsistence Economy: The Case of West Pakistan. *American Economic Review* 54:580–591.

FIRTH, RAYMOND; and YAMEY, B. S. (editors) 1964 *Capital, Savings, and Credit in Peasant Societies: Studies From Asia, Oceania, the Caribbean and Middle America.* London: Allen & Unwin.

HERDT, ROBERT W.; and MELLOR, JOHN W. 1964 The Contrasting Response of Rice to Nitrogen: India and the United States. *Journal of Farm Economics* 46: 150–160.

JOHNSTON, BRUCE F.; and MELLOR, JOHN W. 1961 The Role of Agriculture in Economic Development. *American Economic Review* 51:566–593.

JONES, WILLIAM O. 1960 Economic Man in Africa. *Food Research Institute Studies* 1:107–134.

KRISHNA, RAJ 1963 Farm Supply Response in India–Pakistan: A Case Study of the Punjab Region. *Economic Journal* 73:477–487.

MELLOR, JOHN W. 1962 The Process of Agricultural Development in Low-income Countries. *Journal of Farm Economics* 44:700–716.

MELLOR, JOHN W. 1963 The Use and Productivity of Farm Family Labor in Early Stages of Agricultural Development. *Journal of Farm Economics* 45:517–534.

MELLOR, JOHN W. 1966 *The Economics of Agricultural Development.* Ithaca, N.Y.: Cornell Univ. Press.

NAIR, KUSUM (1961) 1962 *Blossoms in the Dust: The Human Factor in Indian Development.* New York: Praeger.

SCHULTZ, THEODORE W. 1964 *Transforming Traditional Agriculture.* New Haven: Yale Univ. Press.

TAX, SOL (1953) 1963 *Penny Capitalism: A Guatemalan Indian Economy.* Univ. of Chicago Press.

WARRINER, DOREEN (1939) 1965 *The Economics of Peasant Farming.* 2d ed. New York: Barnes & Noble.

WISER, WILLIAM H.; and WISER, CHARLOTTE (1930) 1963 *Behind Mud Walls: 1930–1960.* Berkeley: Univ. of California Press.

ALCOHOLISM

See DRINKING AND ALCOHOLISM.

ALEXANDER, FRANZ

Franz Gabriel Alexander (1891–1964), physician and psychoanalyst, was born in Budapest, the son of a professor of history and philosophy at the University of Budapest. In the scholarly environment of the university Alexander's interests early focused on the world of ideas: the humanities, languages, and aesthetics. His uncle, a successful chemical engineer, introduced him to the precision of scientific discipline.

As early as high school Alexander's scientific interests became predominant, although he never entirely abandoned humanistic philosophy. He went to the University of Göttingen to study medicine and was attracted to the new mathematical formulations of David Hilbert and Hermann Minkowski, the innovations in theoretical physics of Theodor von Karman, and the philosophical dissertations of Edmund Husserl. Husserl and Alexander clashed over the latter's refusal to abandon the position that knowledge of a thing is a function of both the nature of the object and the perceiving mind. In a sense, Alexander's position foreshadowed his later commitment to psychoanalysis and psychosomatic medicine.

After Göttingen, Alexander returned to Budapest to complete his medical training and do further research in biochemistry and physiology. In World War I he served as a military physician on various battlefronts, and at the end of the war he returned to Budapest to work in brain physiology at the Neuropsychiatric Clinic of the university.

Although he had read Freud's *The Interpretation of Dreams* as a medical student, its relevance and applicability to clinical matters became clear to him only during this period in the psychiatric department. Not entirely convinced—but increasingly becoming so—that the various examinations and tests then employed in psychiatric diagnosis and study were meaningless in comparison to the approach of psychoanalysis, Alexander went to Berlin in 1919, where he became the first student in the recently founded Berlin Psychoanalytic Institute. He underwent analysis with Hanns Sachs and became an assistant in the institute. In 1921 he won a prize awarded by Freud for research in the field of psychoanalysis for his study "The Castration Complex in the Formation of Character" (1923).

In 1924 and 1925 Alexander gave a series of lectures at the Berlin Institute that formed the basis of his first book, *The Psychoanalysis of the Total Personality* (1927), an elaboration of the theory of the superego. This work excited the psychoanalytic community generally and moved Freud to write, "The young man is extraordinarily good," and to express his confidence that Alexander would become one of the pillars of the psychoanalytic movement.

Developing the ideas on the superego that he had presented in his book, Alexander began to work with Hugo Staub, a lawyer, on the application of psychoanalytic principles to the field of criminology. Together they published *The Criminal, the Judge, and the Public* (1929), dealing with the understanding and diagnosis of criminal personalities. The direct result of this contribution to criminology was that Alexander was invited to attend the 1930 International Congress for Mental Hygiene, in Washington. Indirectly, it led to the beginning of a new phase of his career in the United States.

While in Washington, Alexander was offered a one-year visiting professorship in psychiatry at the University of Chicago Medical School by Robert Hutchins, the newly installed president of the university. Hutchins hoped in this way to introduce psychiatry into the medical school curriculum. Alexander suggested instead that he be visiting professor of psychoanalysis and proposed that he teach only psychoanalysis and psychoanalytic psychiatry. After careful consideration Hutchins, as well as the director of the university clinics, Franklin McLean, agreed, and the world's first university chair in psychoanalysis was created. However, Alexander's hope that the psychological approach to the study and treatment of disease would become an integral part of medical education was not immediately realized. (Indeed, Freud had predicted that Alexander's insistence on being called professor of psychoanalysis would aggravate the problem of acceptance.) It was the social scientists, philosophers, and lawyers who showed interest in the new field, rather than the physicians—with the exception of a few who became involved in work on the psychological aspects of medicine.

Following his year in Chicago, Alexander spent a year in Boston collaborating with William Healy, director of the Judge Baker Foundation, on problems of delinquency. Their insights derived from the psychoanalyses of a number of offenders are presented in *Roots of Crime* (1935). Then, in 1932, Alexander returned to Chicago to organize the Chicago Institute of Psychoanalysis (a separate entity from the Chicago Psychoanalytic Society).

To staff the new institute Alexander invited analysts already in Chicago and also recruited people from elsewhere to collaborate in training and research activities. He made considerable efforts to integrate the institute with Chicago's medical community, in part by familiarizing medical leaders with psychoanalytic principles. This not only furthered the acceptance of the institute by the medical community but also set the stage for the psychosomatic research that became Alexander's hallmark and that of the Chicago institute.

Alexander held many important professional positions. He was president of the American Psychoanalytic Association in 1938 and 1939, president of the American Society for Research in Psychosomatic Medicine in 1947–1948, and president of the Academy of Psychoanalysis in 1963–1964. He was also one of the founding editors of *Psychosomatic Medicine*, which first appeared in 1939 under the sponsorship of the National Research Council, and served on the editorial boards of many other professional journals.

Alexander was on the faculty of the University of Illinois department of psychiatry from 1938 until his retirement in 1956. That year he also retired as director of the Chicago institute after nearly 25 years, only to start new ventures in psychosomatic research and psychotherapy on the west coast. While he was affiliated with Mount Sinai Hospital in Los Angeles, with the University of Southern California, and with the Southern California Psychoanalytic Institute, he began a research project on the principles and factors involved in psychoanalytic and psychodynamic treatment, especially the role of the personality of the therapist in the therapeutic process.

At the time of his death, in 1964, Alexander had several major addresses scheduled and some papers ready for publication and was in the process of completing three books in collaboration with different teams in Chicago and Los Angeles. These writings reflect his constant attempt to fuse science and humanism, for they deal with the history of psychiatry, the psychoanalytic pioneers, and psychosomatic medicine.

GEORGE H. POLLOCK

[*For the historical context of Alexander's work, see* PSYCHOANALYSIS, *article on* CLASSICAL THEORY *and the biography of* FREUD. *For discussion of the subsequent development of his ideas, see* PSYCHOSOMATIC ILLNESS.]

WORKS BY ALEXANDER

1922   Kastrationskomplex und Charakter: Eine Untersuchung über Passagere Symptome. *Internationale Zeitschrift für Psychoanalyse* 8:121–152.
1923   The Castration Complex in the Formation of Character. *International Journal of Psycho-analysis* 4:11–42.
(1927) 1930   *The Psychoanalysis of the Total Personality: The Application of Freud's Theory of the Ego to the Neuroses.* Nervous and Mental Disease Monograph Series, No. 52. New York: Nervous & Mental Disease Pub. → First published in German.
(1929) 1956   ALEXANDER, FRANZ; and STAUB, HUGO *The Criminal, the Judge, and the Public.* Glencoe,

Ill.: Free Press. → First published as *Der Verbrecher und seine Richter.*

1935 ALEXANDER, FRANZ; and HEALY, WILLIAM *Roots of Crime: Psychoanalytic Studies.* New York: Knopf.

1950 *Psychosomatic Medicine: Its Principles and Applications.* New York: Norton.

1952 ALEXANDER, FRANZ (editor) *Dynamic Psychiatry.* Univ. of Chicago Press.

1960 *The Western Mind in Transition: An Eyewitness Story.* New York: Random House.

1962 *The Scope of Psychoanalysis: 1921–1961.* New York: Basic Books.

SUPPLEMENTARY BIBLIOGRAPHY

GLOVER, EDWARD 1964 Freudian or Neofreudian? *Psychoanalytic Quarterly* 33:97–109.

ALIENATION

Alienation, or estrangement, is a concept of considerable antiquity, whose metaphysical origins have been veiled in the course of time by the progressive secularization of Western thought. Historians of philosophy trace the concept back to the writings of Plotinus, whose doctrine of emanation assumed a procession from an ultimate undefinable source or principle to a multiplicity of finite beings: the undivided One unfolds into its various manifestations by a downward process linking the supersensible Being with a hierarchy of lower spheres and ultimately with the world of nature and material existence, matter being the lowest stage of the universe and the antithesis to the One. These Neoplatonic speculations had their counterpart in certain themes of early Christian theology, the gradual fusion of Christianity and Neoplatonism forming an important aspect of the Hellenistic era. For example, the Plotinian identification of matter with the principle of evil may be said to represent a link between Gnostic speculation and the theology of Augustine, whose writings in turn were to become an important source for the Lutheran interpretation of Christianity and therewith for the German Protestant tradition, which in the nineteenth century was secularized in the philosophical writings of Hegel and Feuerbach.

By a different route the Pauline view of the Incarnation furnished a theme for Luther, whose translation of the Greek term *ekenosen* (in the Latin Vulgate: *exinanivit*) as *hat sich selbst geäussert* led directly to Hegel's use of the term *Entäusserung.* This may be freely translated as "self-alienation" if it is borne in mind that Hegel employed the concept in the Christological sense, since he inherited a theology that enabled him to conceive world history in terms leading back to the Lutheran tradition. Later usage, however, treated "alienation" as signifying "loss of being" or "estrangement." In Feuerbach and Marx, *Entäusserung* became a synonym for *Entfremdung* (estrangement).

In his youthful theological writings (which were unpublished until the early twentieth century), Hegel, unknown to his contemporaries, had outlined a critique of historical Christianity which on some points anticipated Feuerbach's treatment of the subject; but the notion that religion as such constitutes the alienation of man from his true being belongs to Feuerbach. Feuerbach's transformation of theology into anthropology (a radicalization of certain elements of Hegel's early thought) in turn served Marx as the starting point for his own reflections on the subject. Yet Hegel's *Phenomenology of Mind* (1807), with its celebrated analysis of "the alienated spirit," constitutes an important link with the postreligious view. It anticipated the secularization of an originally metaphysical concept. This process reached its critical point in the writings of the Young Hegelians, and notably in Marx's *Economic and Philosophic Manuscripts of 1844* (also known as the "Paris Manuscripts").

In these writings of the young Marx, which remained unpublished until 1932 and which became genuinely influential only after 1945, the concept of "alienation" shed the metaphysical aura that it had still retained in Feuerbach and assumed a historical character. Alienation was no longer held to be inherent in man's "being in the world," but rather in his being in a particular historical world, that of "alienated labor." Thus, *Entfremdung* was no longer seen as a particular moment in the *Entäusserung* of the pre-existing *logos,* although the notion of a "fall" from a state of perfection was retained in the concept of an anterior stage when men were not yet subject to that "alienation" which the division of labor, under capitalist exploitation, later imposed upon them.

It has been suggested that in thus emptying the Hegelian terminology of its theological content, Marx lost his hold on the philosophical dimension which sustained the thought of his contemporaries. Yet Feuerbach had already preceded him in inverting the traditional hierarchy of values that Hegel inherited from the Augustinian–Plotinian sources of Christianity. Feuerbach's naturalism implied a rejection of the belief that matter was somehow inferior to spirit and thus signaled a reversion to the "materialist" naturalism of antiquity. The process was carried further in Marx, whose fragmentary anthropology—as outlined in the "Paris Manuscripts"—had cut its connection with religion altogether. Feuerbach's deification of man, like

Goethe's "Promethean" poetry, was an important precondition of the Marxian viewpoint, but Marx was more down-to-earth, in a manner analogous to contemporary positivism. Where Feuerbach had sought to overcome man's alienation by reintegrating his "split personality" through a religion of humanity, Marx emphasized the need for a radical transformation of society that would permit men to lead a "truly human" existence. The "true socialism" of Moses Hess, which by 1847 had begun to furnish Marx and Engels with a topic for their irony, may be described as the consistent application of Feuerbach's anthropology to politics. By contrast, Marx from about 1846 onward no longer emphasized the theme of human self-estrangement, although in an important sense it remained a part of his mature thinking and even influenced his analysis of the economic process in *Capital*, e.g., in the well-known passage on the "fetishism of commodities." The interest which the subject has retained for contemporary socialists is thus in the main bound up with a particular phase in Marx's intellectual development.

The concern with human life under conditions of growing mechanization, specialization, and dependence on an "objectified," or "reified," external world, is a theme common to Marx and the post-Marxists. Its roots may be traced back to eighteenth-century writers such as Herder and Schiller, whose reflections on history lent powerful support to the fashionable idealization of classical antiquity as a golden age in which man's faculties developed to a totality whose conflicting elements were, for a brief moment, held in harmonious balance. The notion of "self-alienation" here acquired a meaning more in tune with the usual sense of "estrangement." Even the Marxian critique of dehumanized proletarian existence under industrial capitalism was foreshadowed in Schiller's remarks (in his *Briefe über die aesthetische Erziehung des Menschen* 1795) on the deadening and soul-destroying effect of specialization. There is a straight road from Schiller's *Aesthetic Letters* of 1795 to the "Paris Manuscripts of 1844," though Schiller's solution—which envisaged a recovery of the lost harmony in the spheres of art and education—seemed to Marx a characteristic example of the idealist tendency to seek refuge in a realm beyond that of ordinary material existence.

Objectification and estrangement

From the viewpoint of contemporary sociology, Marx—specifically the Marx of 1845–1847, who was no longer a philosopher and not yet an economist—appears as the crucial figure in the process

whereby "alienation" was transformed from an ontological into a sociological concept. As an element in the idealist ontology of the early nineteenth century, alienation had once signified an ultimate datum of human existence, a theme developed at length by Hegel in his *Science of Logic* (1812–1816), where he makes play with the self-alienation inherent in the subject–object relationship, which is the precondition of knowing the world. What Hegel called *Selbstentäusserung* (self-externalization) is Spirit's characteristic mode of presenting the world of nature and history to the individual consciousness. This consciousness is "alienated" insofar as it does not apprehend the external world as objectified Mind, and its self-alienation (*Selbstentfremdung*) is overcome to the extent that this gap is closed by self-awareness. The stages whereby this metaphysical doctrine was transformed into the Marxian "materialism" can be followed in the writings of the Young Hegelians, culminating in the work of the youthful Marx. The crucial importance of Feuerbach's atheism in this context lies in the fact that his self-alienated man has only an earthly habitation and thus requires a humanized world, a world made manlike, in order for him to feel at home. Feuerbach's contemporary Søren Kierkegaard, who retained his hold on the Lutheran faith which the Young Hegelians had abandoned, arrived at a different conclusion and thus became the founder of religious existentialism. The point here is that Marx, by traveling in the opposite direction, was necessarily driven to the "materialist" conclusion that the solution to the *theoretical* problem of "alienation" lay in the *practical* activity of transforming a world in which men do not feel at home. This was the gist of the 1845 "Theses on Feuerbach," which set out the credo of revolutionary humanism.

But in the process of reaching this position Marx had made use of the Hegelian categories of "externalization" and "estrangement," notably in the 1844 "Paris Manuscripts," where he transformed Hegel's rudimentary analysis of the labor process (in the "Lordship and Bondage" chapter of the *Phenomenology*) into something new and revolutionary. Man, that is to say, generic man as a "species being" (*Gattungswesen*), is seen to have his *essential being* in labor, but this essence is at the same time taken away from him, i.e., "alienated," by a world which is a *verkehrte Welt* (one standing on its head), a world in which "the worker becomes all the poorer the more wealth he produces."

With the *increasing value* of the world of things proceeds in direct proportion the *devaluation* of the world of men. . . .

This fact expresses merely [the circumstance] that the object which labor produces . . . confronts it as *something alien*. . . . The product of labor is labor which has been embodied in an object, which has become material: it is the *objectification* of labor [*die Vergegenständlichung*]. Labor's realization is its objectification. . . . [This] realization of labor appears as . . . *loss of the object* and *bondage* to it; appropriation as *estrangement*, as *alienation*.

So much does labor's realization appear as loss of realization that the worker loses realization to the point of starving to death. So much does objectification appear as loss of the object that the worker is robbed of the objects most necessary not only for his life but for his work. (Marx [1844] 1964, pp. 107–108)

It is this state of affairs which defines the worker as a proletarian. "All these consequences result from the fact that the worker is related to the *product of his labor* as to an *alien* object" (*ibid.*, p. 108). Alienated labor creates a world in which the real producer cannot recognize himself. Work, man's existential activity, estranges him both from nature and from himself. This alienation (which the romantics had attributed to the increasing rationalization and specialization of the life process), Marx attributed to society, and specifically to the exploitation of the worker by the nonworker, i.e., the capitalist. This diagnosis underlay all Marx's theorizing, although in his later writings it was no longer explicit. It had an obvious counterpart in the socialism of his contemporary Proudhon, in whom however the Rousseauist element was stronger. When Proudhon said, "Ce que l'Humanité cherche dans la Religion et qu'elle appelle DIEU, c'est elle-même" ([1849] 1929, p. 62), he was echoing both Rousseau and Feuerbach. The political application appears in the statement immediately following: "Pour tout le reste, nous n'admettons pas plus le gouvernement de l'homme par l'homme, que l'exploitation de l'homme par l'homme . . ." (*ibid.* p. 62). The difference in tone points to the subsequent disputes between socialists and anarchists, whose "libertarian" credo was adequately formulated by Proudhon in the passage cited above.

The Marxian tradition, then, sees human self-estrangement as rooted in the form given to the labor process by modern society, i.e., industrial society. But unlike the romantics and their predecessors of the eighteenth-century Enlightenment, Marx attributed this dehumanization not to the division of labor as such but to the historic form it had taken under capitalism. That specialization was at the root of the trouble Marx did not doubt; but as late as 1875 he believed that "in a higher phase of the communist society" not only would

"the enslaving subordination of the individual to the division of labor" disappear but even the "antithesis between mental and physical labor" would vanish. To say that this belief could only be grounded on irrational faith is perhaps to underrate the strength of Marx's commitment to the optimistic world view of the Enlightenment with its hope of a better future in which man would at last be master over his circumstances. From this vantage point, which Marx shared with both the French materialists and the German idealists, the impetus given to the division of labor by modern technology appeared as a means for raising mankind to a higher level where these crutches might be discarded. The manner in which Marxism, and socialism generally, have developed this theme, however, is tied to the critique of one particular form of social organization. It therefore runs up against the argument that the division of labor itself, and the resulting fragmentation of the human personality, are rooted in technological conditions which are likely to survive any conceivable rearrangement of society.

Rationalization and disenchantment

In the generation following Marx the tacit abandonment of the earlier utopian perspective was clearly an element in the emancipation of sociology from philosophy. The notion of a descriptive "science of society," as developed in particular by Max Weber and his school, emerged *pari passu* with the positivist demotion of philosophy to a purely synoptic function, as the general link between the sciences or, alternatively, as the study of concepts common to all scientific investigators. With this view prevailing, a social science not grounded in traditional philosophy or metaphysics could easily dispense with general notions supposedly derived from the study of human nature or the human essence. The role of Marxism in this process was ambiguous, the later writings of Engels forming a link with the general trend of positivism. The dominant schools associated with Weber and Durkheim cut their connection with all branches of philosophy except for the theory of knowledge. The same process occurred in traditional psychology and in the new forms developed after about 1900 by Freud and his followers, although the Jungian school attempted to conserve the romantic universalism of the "philosophy of nature," which had once formed a bond between Goethe, Hegel, and Schelling.

The importance of this break with philosophy is exemplified by the key role played in modern sociology by the ideal of a "value-free" science, which no longer sets itself up as a judge of social institutions, let alone as an instrument for helping men to attain either freedom or felicity. This deliberate refusal to transcend the limitations imposed by empirical description is an aspect of the progressive rationalization of life, which exacts its tribute from the scholar no less than from the worker, technician, or administrator. The disillusionment inherent in the acceptance of the situation as unalterable is experienced not sadly as "estrangement" from a better world but stoically as the endurance of reality. Positivist sociology asserts the need for scientific neutrality in the face of structures whose permanent features are indifferent to individual desires and hopes, whether religious or secular. It draws its ethos from the refusal to indulge in a modernized version of the pathetic fallacy.

The classic statement of this position is to be found in the writings of Weber, where the disjunction of fact finding and valuation is accepted as the necessary fate of science in a disenchanted universe. "Disenchantment" (*Entzauberung*) is a key concept for Weber, just as *Entäusserung* is for Hegel or *Entfremdung* for the young Marx and the contemporary neo-Marxians. It relates to the discovery that the world is, in the literal meaning of the term, senseless, i.e., not the seat of a divinity or some other agency responsive to human desires. Tacit acceptance of this state of affairs forms part of that process of "rationalization" which Weber saw as the underlying element in the historical process. As mankind gradually sheds its illusions, it discovers itself in a world which, owing to the progressive application of science, becomes steadily more complex and at the same time less satisfying to the romantic craving for harmony. Technology imposes fresh burdens upon men at the very moment when—owing to a parallel process of rationalization—the old metaphysical hopes and certainties have crumbled. A broadly similar analysis, likewise remarkable for its stoical pessimism, is to be found in the later writings of Freud, where the stress falls on the abandonment of religious hopes and consolations (cf. his *Future of an Illusion* 1927 and *Civilization and Its Discontents* 1930).

The transformation of socialism into sociology, under the impact of political shocks and disappointments (notably since World War II), runs parallel to this development. Its most recent manifestation, the acceptance of a totally rationalized environment as unalterable and common to all major industrial societies, relates back to a theme already present in Saint-Simon, Comte, and Marx: the belief that the study of society discloses a mechanism of causation which asserts itself with the relentless force of natural law. In nineteenth-century socialism this conviction was balanced by faith in the ability of men—when delivered from their previous ignorance—to plan their lives in accordance with innate human needs and strivings, notably the desire for freedom, understood as the unfolding of personality in every individual. This faith, which binds the socialist movement to its ancestral liberal–humanist origins, still persists in an attenuated form wherever technology has transformed the preindustrial environment, but with the significant difference that the "humanization" of work is now envisaged as no more than a palliative. In the newer centers of industrial civilization a similar degree of skepticism will presumably have to await the dissipation of the inevitable first flush of technological enthusiasm. The alienation of labor as the self-alienation of man from his essence is a concept that presents considerable intellectual difficulties, and in any case it fails to satisfy the emotional needs of societies newly launched upon the adventure of modernization.

Since intellectual life generally reflects the prevailing social situation, the prominence in modern literature and art of concern over the role of the alienated individual in a "reified" world need occasion no surprise. This phenomenon dates back to the early years of the present century, when individualism first began to look problematical in western and central Europe, even though the societal organization of existence, by and large, still followed liberal–individualist lines. The impact of totalitarianism in the 1930s and 1940s upset the traditional equilibrium between the individual and society, even in countries where the totalitarian experiment failed or was not permitted to occur. Both the official culture and the unofficial criticism of this culture show the marks of this experience, whose extreme point was the massive "liquidation" of individuals and groups in the interest of a "new order" imposed upon society by the state. This experience could not be accommodated within the traditional liberal–democratic conceptions. Hence it gave rise to critical reflections upon the probable character of a planned and centralized society in which human beings might be "alienated" en masse, not merely from their metaphysical essence but from their earthly existence, at the command of rulers raised by technology above the customary safeguards of popular control.

At a more trivial level, the situation reflects itself in the concern shown by intellectuals over the control of mass communications and the alarming possibility of an artificially contrived and predigested "pseudo culture" taking the place of creative spontaneity. Closely related are the controversies over the role of a therapeutic psychology whose conformism increasingly condemns it to the provision of spiritual tranquilizers (a function hitherto monopolized by religion).

These concerns appear to represent the contemporary form of a debate whose philosophic origins are attested by the very terms in which it is conducted. As has been shown in the preceding discussion, positivist sociology in the later nineteenth century fell heir to the unsolved problems of traditional metaphysics. These problems are related, in an obscure and mystifying fashion, to permanent human concerns which assert themselves with special force whenever a particular social and cultural integration fails to satisfy the elites of a given society. What appears at one level as the disintegration of traditional ways of life is reflected at a different level in the dichotomy of "facts" and "values." Since the intellectuals as a group form a stratum of society in which material tension is immediately experienced in theoretical terms, their role in developing concepts which reflect their own peculiar situation is obviously crucial. Provisionally it may be suggested that the intelligentsia's rejection of the modern world is central to the contemporary situation in philosophy. Yet this world is itself the creation of a rational science in which intellectuals have traditionally placed their faith. The paradox suggests that we may have come to the end of an important chapter in modern cultural history.

GEORGE LICHTHEIM

[See also LITERATURE, article on POLITICAL FICTION; MARXISM; PERSONALITY, POLITICAL; and the biographies of ENGELS; FREUD; HEGEL; MARX; PROUDHON; WEBER, MAX.]

BIBLIOGRAPHY

ADORNO, THEODORE W. 1962 Einleitung in die Musiksoziologie. Frankfurt am Main (Germany): Suhrkamp.

AXELOS, KOSTAS (1961) 1963 Marx: Penseur de la technique. Paris: Minuit.

BELL, DANIEL 1959 The End of Ideology. Glencoe, Ill.: Free Press. → A paperback edition was published in 1961 by Collier.

CALVEZ, JEAN-YVES 1956 La pensée de Karl Marx. Paris: Seuil.

COTTIER, GEORGES M.-M. 1959 L'athéisme du jeune Marx: Ses origines hégéliennes. Paris: Vrin.

FEUERBACH, LUDWIG A. (1840) 1957 The Essence of Christianity. New York: Harper. → First published in German.

FREUD, SIGMUND (1927) 1960 The Future of an Illusion. Garden City, N.Y.: Doubleday. → First published in German.

FREUD, SIGMUND (1930) 1958 Civilization and Its Discontents. Garden City, N.Y.: Doubleday. → First published as Das Unbehagen in der Kultur.

GURVITCH, GEORGES 1962 Dialectique et sociologie. Paris: Flammarion.

HEGEL, GEORG WILHELM FRIEDRICH (1795–1809) 1961 On Christianity: Early Theological Writings. Gloucester, Mass.: Smith. → Written during the years 1795–1809. First published in 1907 as Hegels theologische Jugendschriften.

HEGEL, GEORG WILHELM FRIEDRICH (1807) 1961 The Phenomenology of Mind. 2d ed., rev. London: Allen & Unwin; New York: Macmillan. → First published in German.

HEGEL, GEORG WILHELM FRIEDRICH (1812–1816) 1951 Hegel's Science of Logic. 2 vols. London: Allen & Unwin; New York: Macmillan. → First published in German.

HYPPOLITE, JEAN 1955 Études sur Marx et Hegel. Paris: Rivière.

KAMENKA, EUGENE 1962 The Ethical Foundations of Marxism. London: Routledge; New York: Praeger.

LICHTHEIM, GEORGE (1961) 1965 Marxism: An Historical and Critical Study. 2d ed., rev. London: Routledge; New York: Praeger. → A paperback edition was published by Praeger in 1965.

MARCUSE, HERBERT (1941) 1955 Reason and Revolution: Hegel and the Rise of Social Theory. 2d ed. London: Routledge. → A paperback edition was published in 1960 by Beacon.

MARX, KARL (1844) 1964 Economic and Philosophic Manuscripts of 1844. New York: International Publishers; London: Lawrence & Wishart. → First published in German in 1932. Sometimes referred to as the "Paris Manuscripts of 1844."

MARX, KARL (1845) 1935 Theses on Feuerbach. Pages 73–75 in Friedrich Engels, Ludwig Feuerbach and the Outcome of Classical German Philosophy. New York: International.

MARX, KARL. Selected Writings in Sociology and Social Philosophy. Edited by T. B. Bottomore and M. Rubel. New York: McGraw-Hill, 1964.

POPITZ, HEINRICH 1953 Der entfremdete Mensch: Zeitkritik und Geschichtsphilosophie des jungen Marx. Basel: Verlag für Recht und Gesellschaft.

PROUDHON, PIERRE JOSEPH (1849) 1929 Oeuvres complètes. Volume 8: Les confessions d'un révolutionnaire. Paris: Rivière.

RUNCIMAN, WALTER G. 1963 Social Science and Political Theory. Cambridge Univ. Press.

SCHILLER, JOHANN C. FRIEDRICH (1795) 1845 The Aesthetic Letters, Essays and the Philosophical Letters of Schiller. Boston: Little. → First published as Briefe über die aesthetische Erziehung des Menschen.

SCHILLER, JOHANN C. FRIEDRICH. Philosophische Schriften und Gedichte. Edited by Eugen Kühnemann. Leipzig: Meiner, 1922.

TUCKER, ROBERT C. 1961 Philosophy and Myth in Karl Marx. Cambridge Univ. Press.

ALLIANCES

In the technical language of statesmen and scholars the term "alliance" signifies a promise of mutual military assistance between two or more sovereign states. Although some propagandistic advantages may be gained by applying the term to loose agreements for cooperation, such as the United States program for Latin America known as the Alliance for Progress, this use obscures the peculiarly far-reaching commitment contained in military pacts by which a nation formally promises to join another in fighting a common enemy.

Alliances are instruments of national security. They are sought in order to supplement national armed forces. The military support that is promised will usually, but not always, comprise the dispatch of military forces in time of need. It is not necessarily limited to such assistance. One country may also give the other permission to deploy forces on its territory or the right to move forces across its territory. Alliances may extend to forms of cooperation other than military ones, but they are unlikely to survive if the military reason disappears. When a country promises military assistance without receiving a similar promise in return, it is customary to speak of a guarantee pact. The guarantor may enter into such a pact when an enemy take-over of another, usually weak country would strike a blow at the guarantor's security.

To be an effective instrument of security, the treaty must define as clearly as possible the circumstances known as *casus foederis,* under which the promise of mutual assistance is to become effective. Prior to World War I, alliance treaties usually contained a nonprovocation clause by which an ally was relieved of its obligations if its partner became guilty of provoking the war in which assistance was expected. The clause came into disrepute because it made it easier for a country to evade its obligation on the ground that its ally had caused the war. Remembering the lack of a firm British commitment prior to the war of 1914, the French have insistently claimed that military pacts lack deterrent value if the promised assistance is not virtually automatic.

No alliance is likely to be an unqualified blessing: in some cases it may prove more of a drain on a country's strength than a supplement, and uncertainty is inherent in any promise of future assistance. The outstanding asset of an alliance is the military assistance expected in case of need and its deterrent effect on the enemy, even preceding any armed conflict. Moreover, a country may gain prestige from having powerful allies or from denying them to its opponent. The chief liability of an alliance is the obligation to come to the assistance of an ally possibly under conditions that, from a strictly national point of view, might suggest abstention from the conflict. A country fearing that the cost of involvement or "entanglement" in the quarrels of others will not be compensated by gains from the alliance may decide to "go it alone." The weak country often fears that it may become dependent on an ally who can involve it in wars it can do nothing to prevent; the strong one fears that it will lose its freedom of action by tying itself to another.

Development.   Despite these inhibitions, wherever in recorded history a system of multiple sovereignty has existed, some of the sovereign units when involved in conflicts with others have entered into alliances. Changing alliance patterns characterized interstate relations in ancient China from the eighth century B.C. to the middle of the third century A.D.; alliances were an accepted technique of foreign policy in ancient India, as shown by Kautilya in his *Arthaśāstra* (c. 300 B.C.). The polarization of the world of Greek city-states has been described by Thucydides in the *Peloponnesian War,* and the pitfalls of alignment and neutrality in the days of the Italian city-states have been examined by Machiavelli. Only within a system dominated by a single country, such as the Roman Empire, has there been little room for alliances.

Alliance policy became a specially prominent feature of the Western state system with the rise of nation-states in the fifteenth century. Coalitions of allied states were repeatedly formed against countries assumed to be seeking hegemony, and they, in turn, led to the formation of rival coalitions, as in the case of the Triple Alliance and the Triple Entente that preceded World War I. The establishment of the League of Nations did not dissuade France—a long-time advocate of alliance policy—from seeking security through a network of alliances during the interwar period. These alliances proved too weak, however, to deter Nazi Germany. Following World War II, the renewal of alliance policy came to center in Washington. Under the threat of Soviet expansion the United States broke with its traditional policy of nonalignment or isolation and built up a global system of alliances embracing more than forty noncommunist nations in Europe, Asia, and Latin America. In the meantime, the Soviet Union, and subsequently Communist China, supplemented its military power with that of other communist countries, allies in name but satellites in fact in that they took their orders from Moscow or Peking.

As a result of these developments, the nonaligned countries, many of them new states in Asia and Africa, came to see the rest of the world in the image of two opposing military blocs. Competition between the blocs for the support of the neutrals became a striking feature of the power struggle between the two opposing camps. Each side insisted that its alliances, no less than its armaments, were purely defensive, as has been customary throughout the ages. The claim cannot be refuted by reference to particular features of the alliances and armaments; both are instruments of policy that can serve defensive as well as offensive purposes. The claim may be belied, however, by the open and persistent assertion of foreign-policy objectives that cannot be attained except by the threat or use of military force.

Religious or ideological homogeneity has not been a traditional prerequisite of alignment among states, as demonstrated by French alliances with non-Christian Turkey in 1535, with Protestant Sweden during the Thirty Years' War, and with the Soviet Union in 1935, as well as by alliances formed after World War II between the United States and such authoritarian regimes as Portugal, Nationalist China, and South Korea. Although domestic dissatisfaction and a loss of propagandistic advantages may arise from such heterogeneous alignments, these disadvantages are considered outweighed by strategic gains. However, the more the international conflict takes on the character of a war between transnational ideological camps, the stronger public resistance tends to become to alliances with governments of the opposing ideology. Under conditions of ideological conflict alliances may also be used to bolster regimes that share the ideology of the ally; they thereby become instruments of subtle intervention in the domestic affairs of other countries and may provoke displeasure there among political groups whose cause is harmed by such intervention.

Evaluation. Alliances have been variously praised and condemned for their effects on the community of nations and on world peace. They have been declared responsible for the power struggles among nations, although, as a rule, they are a symptom rather than a cause of such struggles. However, when a crystallization into two antagonistic blocs takes place, the race for allies coupled with the arms race may cause an intensification of the conflict and its expansion beyond the area in which it arose. In view of this danger, nations that remain unaligned and neutral may play a pacifying role as buffers or mediators and help to localize wars. In support of alliances, it can be said that they play a decisive role in the balancing-of-power process by which adequate counterpower is mustered to deter aggression. It is sometimes claimed that they also serve as stepping stones to more intimate and lasting bonds culminating in con-

federate or federal unity among the one-time sovereign parties. There have been cases—Germany and Switzerland offer illustrations—in which unification was preceded by wartime alliances that served to create or strengthen a sense of affinity and solidarity among the allies. Usually, however, alliances break up when the original common danger lessens or disappears; often, they break up earlier, especially if one ally sees no other way of saving itself than by capitulating to the enemy.

With the establishment of the League of Nations in 1919 and subsequently of the United Nations, the member countries seemed to have found in what has been called collective security an alternative to the traditional alliance [see COLLECTIVE SECURITY]. In practice, the hope that these universal international organizations could serve as a substitute for pacts of mutual assistance has proved to be an illusion. Nations have not been ready to fight any aggressor irrespective of their national interests.

No matter what is done to formulate an alliance treaty with care and with an eye to the interests of all the parties concerned, considerable strains within the alliance must be expected, particularly if the alliance is of long duration and goes into effect in time of peace. The interests of the allies may come to diverge even with respect to the identification of their chief enemy; conflicts among the allies may undermine their solidarity and with it their confidence in the reliability of the promises made to them by their allies. In the case of the American alliance system established after World War II special kinds of strains have materialized, particularly within the relatively tight-knit multilateral North Atlantic Treaty Organization. These strains have arisen partly because the United States alone has possessed substantial strategic nuclear forces, which have constituted the main instrument of NATO deterrence, and partly because America's global interests could not be fully harmonized with the purely local or regional interests and perspectives of her partners.

Alliances that include major nuclear powers may run into increasing difficulties in the future. Any power committed to assist an allied victim of attack through nuclear intervention risks national suicide; its threat to accept such a risk may not be credible to the opponent and thus fail to deter him. Moreover, the nonnuclear allies lose control over their national security if it comes to rest on the independent decision of their nuclear protector. As a result, a tendency toward nuclear proliferation develops which, in turn, may have a divisive effect on existing alliances. Whether collective control of a nuclear deterrent by a group of allies is practical only the future can tell.

Although the literature on alliances considered in the abstract is not abundant, theorists in the future may expect to gain new insights into the military, psychological, and political aspects of interallied relations from two sources: first, from a wealth of specialized studies of NATO, many focused on allied nuclear policies; second, from analyses of interstate alignments employing the methodology of game theory, systems analysis, or simulation theory. See, for example, William Riker (1962) or Morton Kaplan (1957).

Most of the recent work on international integration, community building, and regionalism touches on alliances only incidentally, to suggest either that they gain in stability by incorporating a more than military identification of interest among their members or that they may serve as stepping stones toward political integration. In this connection, see Karl Deutsch et al. (1957), Amitai Etzioni (1961), and Ernst Haas (1958).

ARNOLD WOLFERS

[See also COALITIONS; COLLECTIVE SECURITY; CONTAINMENT. *Other relevant material may be found under* INTERNATIONAL POLITICS; INTERNATIONAL RELATIONS; ISOLATIONISM; NEUTRALISM AND NONALIGNMENT.]

BIBLIOGRAPHY

ARON, RAYMOND 1962 *Paix et guerre entre les nations.* Paris: Calmann-Lévy.

BRZEZINSKI, ZBIGNIEW K. (1960) 1961 *The Soviet Bloc: Unity and Conflict.* Rev. ed. New York: Praeger.

CARR, EDWARD H. 1951 *German–Soviet Relations Between the Two World Wars, 1919–1939.* Baltimore: Johns Hopkins Press.

DEUTSCH, KARL W. et al. 1957 *Political Community and the North Atlantic Area: International Organization in the Light of Historical Experience.* Princeton Univ. Press.

ETZIONI, AMITAI 1961 *A Comparative Analysis of Complex Organizations: On Power, Involvement, and Their Correlates.* New York: Free Press.

FAY, SIDNEY B. (1928) 1938 *The Origins of the World War.* 2d ed., rev. New York: Macmillan.

GANSHOF, FRANÇOIS LOUIS (1953) 1958 *Le moyen âge.* 2d ed., rev. Paris: Hachette. → Published as Volume 1 of *Histoire des relations internationals,* edited by Pierre Renouvin.

HAAS, ERNST 1958 *The Uniting of Europe: Political, Social, and Economic Forces, 1950–1957.* Stanford (Calif.) Univ. Press.

KAPLAN, MORTON A. 1957 *System and Process in International Politics.* New York: Wiley.

LANGER, WILLIAM L. (1931) 1950 *European Alliances and Alignments, 1871–1890.* 2d ed. New York: Knopf.

LISKA, GEORGE 1962 *Nations in Alliance: The Limits of Interdependence.* Baltimore: Johns Hopkins Press.

OSGOOD, ROBERT E. 1962 *NATO: The Entangling Alliance.* Univ. of Chicago Press.

PHILLIPS, WALTER A. (1914) 1920 *The Confederation of Europe: A Study of the European Alliance, 1813–1823, as an Experiment in the International Organization of Peace.* 2d ed. London: Longmans.

RENOUVIN, PIERRE (editor) 1953–1958 *Histoire des relations internationales.* 8 vols. Paris: Hachette.

RIKER, WILLIAM H. 1962 *The Theory of Political Coalitions.* New Haven: Yale Univ. Press.

SCOTT, WILLIAM E. 1962 *Alliance Against Hitler: The Origins of the Franco-Soviet Pact.* Durham, N.C.: Duke Univ. Press.

TAYLOR, ALAN J. P. 1954 *The Struggle for Mastery in Europe 1848–1918.* New York and London: Oxford Univ. Press.

WOLFERS, ARNOLD 1940 *Britain and France Between Two Wars: Conflicting Strategies of Peace Since Versailles.* New York: Harcourt.

WOLFERS, ARNOLD (editor) 1959 *Alliance Policy in the Cold War.* Baltimore: Johns Hopkins Press.

ALLPORT, FLOYD H.

Floyd H. Allport is rightly regarded as the founder of social psychology as a scientific discipline. The early theoretical works of McDougall (1908) and Ross (1908) had indicated the need for this special field of study, but not until the appearance of Allport's *Social Psychology,* in 1924, was there a systematic treatise based upon experimentation and operational concepts for studying man's relations with man. Not only did Allport's book help to create the field, but his continuing contributions in the form of theory and research marked the major avenues along which social psychology was to travel through its youth and early maturity. His pioneer efforts in methodology were so deep and broad that most of the methods in use today are refinements of his early work in group experimentation, field studies, attitude measurement, and behavioral observation. Nevertheless, his greatest gift has been in the origination of theory and its outcomes in research. His early formulation of a sophisticated behaviorism and his later event-system theory anticipated developments in the field and in some respects are still in advance of it.

The major intellectual influences affecting Floyd Allport came in his graduate days at Harvard from two of psychology's great figures, Edwin Bissell Holt and Hugo Münsterberg. From Holt he derived his epistemological wisdom, his understanding of science, and his social behaviorism. From Münsterberg he learned the skills of the true experimentalist in operationalizing concepts for research testing and received the heritage of the German work on group influence. Mention should be made also of McDougall, against whose doctrines Allport rebelled, but in rebelling moved toward a constructive reformulation of the insights of that British evolutionist.

Allport was born in Milwaukee in 1890. He received his PH.D. from Harvard in 1919 and remained there as instructor until 1922, when he left to accept an associate professorship at the University of North Carolina. In 1924 he was called to a chair at Syracuse University's new school for the social sciences. As professor of social and political psychology in the Maxwell Graduate School of Citizenship and Public Affairs, he directed the first doctoral program in social psychology in the United States. He remained at Syracuse until his retirement, in 1956.

Although Allport's experimental work first appeared in 1920, his major impact came with the appearance of his *Social Psychology*, in 1924. This book was an excellent integration of the relevant psychological knowledge of the time—of group experimentation, personality research, and related areas in general psychology, child development, and applied psychology. It was much stronger on the psychological than on the sociological side, and its behavioristic translation of Freudian concepts of conflict and its use of Freudian mechanisms in relation to social problems set the stage for later attempts at linking the two approaches. Among other topics, this volume presented Allport's own classic experiments on group influence—research that made group experimentation one of the central streams of social psychology for most of the years of its history. In fact, the well-known experiments of Sherif on the formation of group norms (1935) and of Asch on the power of the group (1952) were but extensions of Allport's findings. And Dashiell's work on experimental juries in the evaluation of testimony (1935) followed directly from Allport's work.

Finally, Allport's *Social Psychology* provided a set of useful concepts for research—specifically, his notions of social facilitation, social increment and decrement, prepotent reflexes and habits, afferent and efferent conditioning, circular and linear social behavior, coacting and interacting groups, the impression of universality, attitudes of conformity, and self-expressive social attitudes.

Allport's contributions did not cease, of course, with the appearance of his famous text. Two of his interests in the late 1920s and early 1930s were the investigation of social attitudes and the study of institutional behavior. There had been scattered

attacks upon attitudes as intervening variables mediating between personality and social situation, but Allport and his students attempted the first systematic exploration of this area. In a research paper with D. H. Hartman, Allport demonstrated the similarity between extremists of the left and extremists of the right with respect to basic personality characteristics, thus foreshadowing the present work on the authoritarianism of the left (Allport & Hartman 1925). In another investigation Allport and Katz utilized attitude measurement to describe the student culture of a large university and of its subsystems (Katz & Allport 1931). George B. Vetter, another of Allport's students, assembled the first conclusive evidence of the generality of attitude patterns over a wide range of specific issues (1930). Allport turned to L. L. Thurstone for help on technical problems of attitude measurement; Thurstone's attitude scales and his development of psychophysical methods for social objects were the result (Thurstone & Chave 1929; Thurstone 1928).

In the late 1920s and early 1930s Allport waged a continuing battle against the use in the social sciences of group fictions and reified concepts. He demonstrated the persistence of the old tautology of the group mind in current concepts of social institutions (Allport 1927).

He argued vigorously against the confusion of concepts and percepts and anticipated the later developments in operationalism by insisting upon such criteria as explicit denotation for making concepts scientifically usable (Allport & Hartman 1931). This led to his work *Institutional Behavior*, in which he analyzed such institutions as the nation, the church, the law, and the industrial complex in terms of the motivations, attitudes, and habits of people (Allport 1933). Although his attack on group fictions was extreme, he played a major role in getting social scientists to rethink their conceptualizations and to move from their armchairs to empirical research to test their theories. In a sense he was one of the first political behaviorists. He conceptualized the public opinion process in individual but dynamic terms with reference to crystallized beliefs concerning some proposed social action, thus distinguishing it from a mere collection of individual opinions (Allport 1937).

Institutional Behavior was based partly upon Allport's theoretical study of accepted doctrines about social institutions and partly upon the research of his students on legal compliance, conformity in industrial settings, ceremonial religious observance, and the factors determining normative behavior in a small community. In this program of research Allport developed the concepts of pluralistic ignorance, partial inclusion, and public and private attitudes and the J-curve theory of conforming behavior (Allport et al. 1932; Allport 1934; Schanck 1932).

As F. H. Allport became involved in studies of social behavior outside the laboratory, he became increasingly dissatisfied with his earlier behavioristic theory, which neglected the problem of relationships and the problem of social structure. He was still unhappy with the traditional social science approach of meeting the difficulty with what he regarded as word-magic. Nor was he satisfied with the field theorist who recognized the problem of relationships but solved it in phenomenological fashion. Hence he became absorbed in the development of a new theory of behavior that would take account of the structure of social action in an objective and scientific manner.

To introduce his highly abstract event-system theory to the world of academic psychology, with its many specialized interests, Allport attempted a review of theories of perception as a focus of concern for many psychologists in his well-known *Theories of Perception* (1955). This volume has been widely regarded as the most scholarly and the most incisive analysis of theories of perception thus far available. It also presents some of Allport's own theory of individual and social behavior.

His theory, which he terms an event-system theory, is still in the process of refinement. It is something of an open-system approach that sees social structure as being made up of cycles of events that return upon themselves to complete each cycle (Allport 1954). Social structure has no anatomical or physical basis apart from the events themselves, so that social systems are made up of the interstructuring of specific acts: "Causation, in the structural view, is not historical nor linear, but continuous, time independent, and reciprocally cyclical. One looks for it neither in society *nor* in the individual, as traditionally seen as separate levels or agencies, but in the compounded patterns of structuring which are the essential reality underlying both" (Allport 1962, p. 19). Individuals relate to one another to maintain the intrinsic rewards from their patterned behavior as well as the more indirect rewards, including the assurances that the structure will be maintained. For Allport a group norm does not so much determine the behavior of individuals as provide a stipulation that will conduce to the creation or preservation of a structure (patterned activity) in which individuals have some degree of involvement. From

this theory Allport has proceeded to measure degree of structurance—i.e., potency of involvement—through a negative-causation technique. The relevance of behavior to the structure in question is measured by an index of interstructure to get at the reinforcing or inhibiting effects received from related structures.

The individual is thus seen as a matrix of involvements in many collective structures, with his own personality system a tangential structure. In one study, for example, Morse and Allport showed that hostility toward minority groups was a function of involvement in the national structure, whereas feelings of aversion toward minority group members were more clearly related to the personality syndromes of the prejudiced people (Morse & Allport 1952).

Allport's contributions have had two major consequences: (1) He shaped the field of social psychology as an area concerned with the basic problems of social influence in which measurement of individuals is the primary focus. Such measurement should be guided by theories of social process, but the data to be gathered are always at the individual level. (2) He furnished the rationale and the example for the behavioral trend in the social sciences. Allport's insistence upon translating institutional concepts into the measurable behavior of people, his refusal to permit social scientists to fall back upon an undefined higher level of constructs, and his research, as well as that of his students, have not been without effect. The concept of the behavioral sciences is the logical outcome of Allport's teachings. The voice crying in the wilderness forty years ago proved to be the voice both of the leader and of the prophet.

DANIEL KATZ

[*For the historical context of Allport's work, see the biographies* HOLT; MCDOUGALL; MÜNSTERBERG. *For discussion of the subsequent development of his ideas, see* ATTITUDES; GROUPS; SOCIAL PSYCHOLOGY.]

WORKS BY ALLPORT

1920   The Influence of the Group Upon Association and Thought. *Journal of Experimental Psychology* 3:159–182.

1924   *Social Psychology.* Boston: Houghton Mifflin.

1925   ALLPORT, FLOYD H.; and HARTMAN, D. A. The Measurement and Motivation of Atypical Opinion in a Certain Group. *American Political Science Review* 19:735–760.

1927   "Group" and "Institution" as Concepts in a Natural Science of Social Phenomena. *American Sociological Society Publications* 22:83–99.

1931   ALLPORT, FLOYD H.; and HARTMAN, D. A. The Prediction of Cultural Change. Pages 307–350 in S. A. Rice (editor), *Methods in Social Science.* Univ. of Chicago Press.

1931 KATZ, DANIEL; and ALLPORT, FLOYD H. *Students' Attitudes: A Report of the Syracuse University Reaction Study.* Syracuse, N.Y.: Craftsman Press.

1932 ALLPORT, FLOYD H.; DICKENS, MILTON C.; and SCHANCK, RICHARD L. Psychology in Relation to Social and Political Problems. Pages 199–252 in Paul S. Achilles (editor), *Psychology at Work.* New York and London: McGraw-Hill.

1933 *Institutional Behavior.* Chapel Hill: Univ. of North Carolina Press.

1934 The J-curve Hypothesis of Conforming Behavior. *Journal of Social Psychology* 5:141–183. → The article includes summaries in French and German.

1937 Toward a Science of Public Opinion. *Public Opinion Quarterly* 1:7–23.

1952 MORSE, NANCY C.; and ALLPORT, FLOYD H. The Causation of Anti-Semitism: An Investigation of Seven Hypotheses. *Journal of Psychology* 34:197–233.

1954 The Structuring of Events: Outline of a General Theory With Applications to Psychology. *Psychological Review* 61:281–303.

1955 *Theories of Perception and the Concept of Structure.* New York: Wiley.

1962 A Structuronomic Conception of Behavior; Individual and Collective: 1. Structural Theory and the Master Problem of Social Psychology. *Journal of Abnormal and Social Psychology* 64:3–30.

SUPPLEMENTARY BIBLIOGRAPHY

ASCH, SOLOMON E. (1952) 1959 *Social Psychology.* Englewood Cliffs, N.J.: Prentice-Hall.

DASHIELL, J. F. 1935 Experimental Studies of the Influence of Social Situations on the Behavior of Individual Human Adults. Pages 1097–1158 in Carl Murchison (editor), *A Handbook of Social Psychology.* Worcester, Mass.: Clark Univ. Press.

McDOUGALL, WILLIAM (1908) 1936 *An Introduction to Social Psychology.* 23d ed., enl. London: Methuen. → A paperback edition was published in 1960 by Barnes and Noble.

ROSS, EDWARD A. 1908 *Social Psychology.* New York: Macmillan.

SCHANCK, RICHARD L. 1932 A Study of a Community and Its Groups and Institutions Conceived of as Behaviors of Individuals. *Psychological Monographs* 43, no. 2:1–133.

SHERIF, MUZAFER 1935 A Study of Some Social Factors in Perception. *Archives of Psychology* 27, no. 187:1–60.

THURSTONE, LEON L. 1928 The Measurement of Opinion. *Journal of Abnormal and Social Psychology* 22: 415–430.

THURSTONE, LEON L.; and CHAVE, E. J. 1929 *The Measurement of Attitude.* Univ. of Chicago Press.

VETTER, GEORGE B. 1930 The Measurement of Social and Political Attitudes and the Related Personality Factors. *Journal of Abnormal and Social Psychology* 25:149–189.

AMBITION

See ACHIEVEMENT MOTIVATION.

ANALYSIS

See PSYCHOANALYSIS; STATISTICS, *article on* THE FIELD; SURVEY ANALYSIS.

ANALYSIS OF VARIANCE

See under LINEAR HYPOTHESES.

ANALYTICAL PSYCHOLOGY

Analytical psychology, also called complex psychology, is identified with the work of Carl Gustav Jung, who founded it. It is an attempt to expand Freudian psychology, from which it developed. Jung's doctoral dissertation, written in 1900 and published in 1902, reflects his acquaintance with one of the earliest of Freud's writings, *The Interpretation of Dreams,* although he drew equally on the books of Pierre Janet and F. W. H. Myers. Jung had read widely, not only in medicine and psychiatry but also in philosophy. Long before he found his way into the new movement of psychoanalysis, he wrote to Freud: "If there is a psychoanalysis there must also be a psychosynthesis" (Jacobi [1957] 1959, pp. 24–25). It was this search for a synthesis that was Jung's aim throughout his life and that first led him into closer association with Freud and later forced him to break away again.

From the very beginning of his career, Jung was interested in phenomena of the *unconscious,* a concept known to him not only from Freud's writings but also from his acquaintance with a long line of German philosophers and physicians (Schopenhauer, von Hartmann, Carus, etc.). Indeed, even in his student years at the University of Basel, 1895–1900, he became interested in occult phenomena and the psychological significance of dreams, largely as the result of personal experiences. This led him to specialize in psychiatry; his doctoral dissertation dealt with the psychology and pathology of so-called occult phenomena and bears witness to this early interest. In 1900 he become assistant to Eugen Bleuler, director of the Burghölzli, the psychiatric clinic of the University of Zurich. In 1905 he was made lecturer and psychiatrist-in-chief at this clinic, where he established a laboratory for experimental psychopathology. There he developed his word association experiments (later published as *Studies in Word-association,* 1904–1909), which were the first scientific studies to confirm some of Freud's findings, notably those relating to the concepts of repression and inhibition. In this experiment, a number of words were read to the patient, who had to reply to each with the word that came first to his mind. Jung found that often a response was unduly delayed, or the stimulus word was misinterpreted or answered by an apparently irrelevant association; and in some cases there was no answer at all. Whenever such response peculiarities occurred, the stimulus word seemed to have touched on some emotional memories, an affective "complex" that apparently was unconscious. This word association test is still a standard diagnostic procedure and was later developed into the so-called lie detector test.

Although at this time Jung seems to have had no difficulties interpreting these complexes in terms of sexuality, he was wary of accepting Freud's notion of the exclusive role of sexuality in psychic life. However, his first personal meeting with Freud, in 1906, seems to have convinced him, at least temporarily, of its primacy. In 1909 he was asked, together with Freud, to lecture at Clark University in Worcester, Massachusetts. Soon after his return, he resigned from his post at the Burghölzli, apparently because of increasing tension between him and Dr. Bleuler, who had at first been interested enough in the new science to join the International Psychoanalytical Society but who later withdrew because he came to disagree more and more with Freudian theory.

Jung, one of the few non-Jewish members of the circle around Freud, was favored by the master, often to the chagrin of his Viennese supporters. Freud felt, not unreasonably, that the always present anti-Semitism in German-speaking countries might seriously retard the spread of psychoanalysis if it were thought of as a Jewish enterprise. In 1910, largely for this reason, Freud made Jung the first president of the International Psychoanalytic Society.

In the next few years, Jung seems to have been continually torn between his interest in establishing the broader nature of the unconscious and his loyalty to the Freudian approach. Not unexpectedly, his essay "Theory of Psychoanalysis" (1913a) suggested a number of modifications in psychoanalytic theory; and after another two years of uncertain allegiance and nagging doubt, Jung finally resigned the presidency of the society in 1914. *The Psychology of the Unconscious* (1913b) made this step inevitable. The transformations of the libido, as he described them, are far removed from psychosexual development as Freud understood it.

Divergences from Freud. Jung uses the Freudian term "libido"; but while Freud conceives of libido as a set of component instincts (oral, anal, genital) combined into the adult sexual drive, Jung sees it as the product of the tension between conscious and unconscious. For Jung, energy flows ceaselessly between these two poles and manifests itself in every activity, including sexual activity. It is not composed of part instincts but is unitary, neutral, ever the same. For Freud, energy is essentially sexual because its aim, sexual pleasure, is considered the prototype of all pleasure. For Jung, however, pleasure can result from any activity.

Sucking and eating are pleasurable, but these pleasures have no necessary connection with sexual pleasure. The Oedipus complex, that bulwark of Freudian theory, in Jung's thinking becomes a name for the child's desire for food and protection, which orients him toward the mother. The prohibition of incest, far from being the sign of a repressed universal urge, is for Jung only the expression of the fact that daily companionship from childhood on does not make for powerful sexual attraction. Infantile repression can be merely a sign of the child's biological immaturity and not necessarily a sign that instinctive forces are threatening from the unconscious. Indeed, even in his early writings he asserts that the cause of neurosis is not to be found in such repression. Neurosis may be the result of man's inability to face his life task here and now; and out of inertia he turns his life force (libido) back to the past (regression) instead of using it to cope with the difficulties of the present. As for the unconscious, Jung stresses its complementary function. For Freud, the "primary process" provides in fantasy the desired fulfillment of a wish; for Jung, fantasy serves to draw attention to significant inner realities.

Development of Jung's own system. As Jung moved farther and farther away from Freud, his interest in unconscious symbolism increased. He devoted a large part of his time to the study of alchemistic texts and discovered in them parallels to the images and symbols that recurred in the analyses of his patients. He came to believe that Western man has lost the intuitive comprehension of symbolism that is universal in the East, and therefore is at a grave disadvantage in his search for maturity. After several works in which he used mainly early Christian and medieval symbolism in his interpretations, he published, with Richard Wilhelm, a translation of an old Chinese text, *The Secret of the Golden Flower* (1929), in which he interpreted Chinese symbols on the basis of his system. Later, he collaborated with the Hungarian philologist and mythologist Karl Kerényi (*Essays on a Science of Mythology*, 1941) and edited Heinrich Zimmer's *Der Weg zum Selbst* (1944). In 1948 he founded the Jung Institute in Zurich for training students in his methods of treatment and interpretation. The institute has been carrying on his work since his death in 1961.

Structure of personality

Jung seems to conceive of human personality as wider in scope than is usually assumed.

Conscious and unconscious. Of the conscious mental contents that man acquires in the course of his life, some are later forgotten, others are actively repressed; all fall back into the *personal unconscious*. This personal unconscious is continuous with the *collective unconscious*, also called the *objective psyche*. The collective unconscious represents the inherited basis on which the individual conscious and unconscious life is built. The larger personality, the total self, comprises both conscious and unconscious (individual and collective); but consciousness is the spearhead of activity, and the unconscious is the ground out of which action is born. Normally this is not one-way traffic. The conscious is continually replenished and nourished by the unconscious; and an increase in energy flow to the conscious always implies a compensatory flow to the unconscious.

Extraversion/introversion. Personality is developed through a movement out into the world and a temporary withdrawal, in a succession of cycles of progression and regression. This goes on from childhood, through the turbulence of adolescence, to maturity and old age; there is no standing still. Even in neurosis and psychosis, only the direction of energy is changed, flowing more strongly toward the unconscious than the conscious.

Jung distinguishes two main directions of activity. It may be turned toward outer objects, the world in all its forms; this he calls *extraversion*. Or it may be turned toward the inner world, the world of thought and imagination; this he calls *introversion*. These are both normal directions of activity and interest, but each is preferred by different types of people. The extravert is interested in the outer aspects of things, the world of sights, shapes, sounds, odors. As a scientist, the extravert is interested in facts, not theories; as an artist, in the forms or sounds or colors he uses, not in the meaning he wants to express. The introvert, on the other hand, is interested in what can be made out of the things he encounters. He is interested in the products of his own activity, in the shapes he gives the world according to his own inner dictates. The introvert scientist is interested in theories, not in facts. The introvert artist is passionately intent on giving shape to his convictions. He does not experiment with form or color for their own sake; he uses them solely as vehicles for his thoughts.

Normally, man spends his childhood years in exuberant extraversion until this is compensated by the period of adolescent introversion. In maturity, he has settled on one of these modes of reaction, although ideally the other should be available to him as circumstances require.

Four functions. Within his preferred mode of conscious activity, each person also has preferred functions. Jung distinguishes four main functions: thought, feeling, sensation, and intuition. Thought evaluates whether things are true or false; feeling, whether they are agreeable or disagreeable. Because this pair of opposite functions imposes our concepts of true/false, good/bad on reality, Jung calls them rational functions. Sensation and intuition, on the other hand, simply acquaint us with things. Whether we find that "this is red" or "1 and 1 is 2," we simply apprehend what is there. Jung calls intuition "a perception based on self-evidence," which illustrates his notion that both sensation and intuition help us apprehend reality. Since, in his view, outer reality is thus received without the imposing of reason upon it, he calls this pair of functions irrational.

As the child uses his functions, he will find one to be more adequate than the others. This becomes his "superior function." The function that is next most adequate becomes his "auxiliary function." In Jung's system, all energy (and thus all activity) is the product of the tension between two opposites, the one conscious, the other unconscious. This holds for the two pairs of functions also. Thought is the opposite of feeling; when thought is the superior function, the inferior (and unconscious) function will be feeling, and vice versa. With thought as the superior function, either sensation or intuition may become the auxiliary function, consciously employed in encountering the world. The remaining function will be partly conscious, partly unconscious. Ideally, with increasing maturity the inferior function also should become available, with the result that a man should finally be able to use all four functions with almost equal ease—an improbable event. For instance, the introvert for whom thought is a superior function should be able to comprehend something quickly, intuitively grasp its potentialities, sense its various aspects, and correctly evaluate it.

When a man uses his superior function exclusively and refuses to acknowledge other modes of action, the repressed inferior function will influence his actions indirectly and often disastrously. Therefore, an introvert thinking type might find himself fatally attracted to a girl with whom he has nothing in common and who is not even particularly attractive: his repressed feeling function has remained primitive and now exacts its revenge for long neglect.

The ego. That part of personality that represents the individual as he experiences himself and adapts to external reality is called the conscious *ego*. Each human being begins his life as a member of a family, a nation, and the human race and he draws on a heritage of experience and conduct that comes to him from the past. He lives on the conscious level as an ego, but is also an embodiment of the collective psyche and draws on the energy created by the tension between conscious and unconscious.

Persona. During the years prior to maturity, each man overemphasizes the conscious. Since he is master of his fate only on the conscious level, he will tend to neglect and even to deny everything that cannot be handled by means of his superior function. He lives his life on the surface: he takes a job, gets married, becomes a family man and taxpayer, and establishes himself in his world. He acquires what is called the *persona*—the face he turns toward the world. The persona is a real, even necessary, attribute, for without it a man would never achieve frictionless adjustment. The persona is not the total self. When a man consciously identifies himself with the persona, when he denies the unconscious aspect of his personality, the unconscious will have its revenge by breaking through into conscious life, either in the form of disquieting dreams or in the form of neurosis and even psychosis. Since energy flows between the conscious and the unconscious, there will be a backlash into the unconscious whenever the conscious is overcharged by identification with the persona.

Individuation. For the sake of his mental health as well as his maturity, a man must transcend his conscious ego, must relinquish his unthinking identification with the persona and try to reach his true self, the "midpoint of his personality," which makes both poles of his personality, conscious and unconscious, accessible to him. Such *individuation* is a natural, even instinctive, process. But if it is made conscious, the individual gains insight and enlarges his consciousness. If he does not take part in this process consciously, individuation will still occur; but it will victimize him ([1952] 1958, p. 460).

The process of individuation can be observed in therapy, where the personal unconscious is analyzed. But as soon as the patient begins to become aware of his unconscious inclinations, says Jung, there will arise images that clearly point beyond the personal to the collective unconscious. In the analysis of the personal unconscious, Jung, like Freud, used dreams and fantasies. But unlike Freud, Jung found himself unable to reduce dreams to the fantasied fulfillment of a libidinal wish. Indeed, actual sexual dreams often seemed to point to a meaning deeper than sexual desires.

The archetypes. Thus, Jung was led toward one of his more difficult conceptions, the *archetype*.

Over and over, in the dreams of his patients he found images that have held meaning for men throughout the ages. The individual dreamer may not understand the significance of these images and so could not have acquired them either through personal experience or through reading. Myths and fairy tales employ such archetypal images with the same meaning that they have in dreams, e.g., the fish, water, and particularly the mandala, a symbol of unity in Quaternity. Better known archetypal images are those of the hero, the savior, the magician, and the king. These images are not archetypes themselves; they are the experienced expression of the archetype. The archetype itself is "an inherited mode of psychic functioning" analogous to inherited behavior patterns. But, Jung adds, this is merely the biological aspect of the archetype. When experienced by an individual, the archetype appears fundamentally important. Whether or not it is expressed in symbols, the archetype "possesses" the individual (Jacobi [1957] 1959, pp. 43–44). Here it becomes clear that the archetype is an unconscious force expressed in images through which the collective unconscious influences the individual.

For Jung, the comprehension of reality is not confined to sense perception and logical understanding. The symbolic, imaginative apprehension of the world is another avenue of knowledge, just as natural, just as spontaneous. Indeed, the child seems more at home in this world of imaginative perception than he is in the world of logical understanding. According to Jung, the psyche meets the world with a symbolic archetypal image which apprehends the inner meaning, just as the biological organism uses the eye to see and the eye catches the light. "And in the same way as the eye bears witness to the peculiar and independent creative activity of living matter, the primordial image expresses the unique and unconditioned creative power of the mind" (Jung [1921] 1959, p. 557).

Since these are two equivalent ways of apprehending the world—one giving us physical reality, the other psychic reality—it is possible to *project*, that is, to ascribe our own unconscious tendencies to the outside world. Consequently, a man must learn to distinguish reality from projection. He must become conscious of the archetypal world by integrating and assimilating the archetypal images that he experiences.

The shadow. The first step in this process of integrating and assimilating is to transcend the conscious persona and face the *shadow* in the personal unconscious, if the person wants to tap the energy of the unconscious. The shadow represents the psychic aspects that are denied in conscious living. As long as his shadow side remains unacknowledged, man suffers a ceaseless conflict between conscious intentions and unconscious inclinations, between the persona and the shadow. The presence of such a conflict is betrayed by the *complex*, a set of emotionally charged ideas. And the complex can be discovered by the word association experiment, as we have seen above. Jung claims that every complex consists of a "nuclear element" that is unconscious and archetypal and a set of associations around this nucleus. If we consider, for instance, the archetypal image of the father as such a nucleus, we may find that a son's years of actual experience with his father have clothed this nucleus with a complex of highly emotional memories made virulent by the opposition between the hostile or resentful impulses created by these situations and the genuine love and gratitude he feels for his father.

Such a complex may remain unconscious, in which case it will grow unhindered. Sometimes it is intellectually known: the son may know that he has a "father complex." But it can be resolved only when he realizes that some of his negative feelings are his own projections. The father has not really earned all the resentment and hostility the son may feel. This projection of the shadow is unconscious; when it is withdrawn through the conscious realization that it *is* a projection, the complex is resolved and a realistic relationship to the father can be established.

In its envelope of acquired attitudes, the shadow represents the negative side of a man's persona and the effects of its projection can be resolved in therapy without too much difficulty. It is even possible to do this without therapy, provided the individual has a modicum of insight and can exercise some self-criticism. But it is next to impossible to realize and acknowledge the archetypal nucleus of the shadow. "It is quite within the bounds of possibility for a man to recognize the relative evil of his nature," says Jung, "but it is a rare and shattering experience for him to gaze into the face of absolute evil" ([1951] 1959, p. 10).

Anima, animus. When the projection of the shadow is resolved, what is next encountered in analysis is a personification of the collective unconscious in the figures of the anima (in men) and the animus (in women). According to Jung, both anima and animus consist of three elements: "the femininity pertaining to the man and the masculinity pertaining to the woman; the experience which man has of woman and vice versa; and, finally, the

masculine and feminine archetypal image" ([1951] 1959, p. 21). Although the contribution of a man's or a woman's personal experience can be integrated in the process of analysis, the archetypal nucleus of anima and animus remains autonomous. Thus, they have often been projected as gods (Hermes, Aphrodite, Persephone). These archetypes are again encountered in our Western culture as the symbols of Christ and the church.

According to Jung, the less a person is aware of these forces, the more powerful they become, and the more their influence will be negative. A man's anima will give rise to irrational moods while the animus of women produces irrational opinions, the feminine substitute for masculine logic. A man who denies his own femininity and so devalues women becomes the prey of his anima, suffers from her destructive aspect, and is the plaything of unreasonable likes and dislikes. But if he becomes aware of the anima, he will discover her positive aspect and be inspired by the eternal feminine. If a woman overemphasizes her femininity, plays up to men, depends on her seductiveness to get what she wants, her animus will show its negative side: she will become a shrew in her aggressive argumentativeness. (Jung, like so many great men of past generations, seems to assume that logic and rationality are altogether masculine, while emotionality and deviousness are a feminine heritage.)

According to Jung, the father acts as protection against the dangers of the outside world and so becomes a model persona for his son, while the mother protects him against the dangers that threaten from his unconscious and so becomes the model for his anima image. Primitive religions, as well as Christian rites (particularly in the Roman Catholic church), used to provide effective anima symbols (Virgin Mary, Mother Church) for the difficult transition from adolescence to maturity. But modern man has lost access to the meaning of such symbols and flounders in his attempt to become aware of his anima and thereby reach maturity.

The magician and the great mother. When the anima is encountered and acknowledged, there is a new danger: the newly available anima energy may give rise to a spurious feeling of power. A man who has faced his anima now feels himself divinely chosen, a hero, a prophet. But his seeming abundance of power is merely the sign of another invasion from the unconscious, represented by the archetype of the hero—saint, superman, magician —which must be made conscious in turn. For women, the corresponding archetype is the great mother. Identification with the magician or great mother invariably ceases, according to Jung, when man has differentiated himself from his unconscious and is able to use its energy without inflation.

The God image.   The last and most powerful archetypal image to be encountered in the process of individuation is that of the Divine. For Jung, "the idea of God is an absolutely necessary psychological function of an irrational nature, which has nothing whatever to do with the question of God's existence" ([1913*b*] 1953, p. 70). God must be acknowledged as a psychic reality, whether we are theists or not. The God image represents the archetype that is most powerful. If it is not an image of God, it will be that of some substitute, just as powerful but possibly malignant. Hence "the gods cannot and must not die" ([1913*b*] 1953, p. 70). As long as the human being either worships these archetypal symbols or denies them, he has not yet recognized them as being what they are—symbols of unconscious forces. As soon as the God image is experienced in dreams or fantasies, says Jung, the awakening of the larger self is at hand, the individuation process has reached its final stage. For this reason, he considers the God image the symbol of the total self in action, the self that includes the conscious and the personal unconscious and reaches into the collective psyche.

Religion

According to Jung, the religions of mankind, from the most primitive to the most highly developed, have a deep significance. In symbolic form they map out the path of salvation and so make it possible for the believer to embark consciously on the process of individuation. Among primitive peoples, the God image is still entirely a projection from the unconscious. As gods and demons, these projections protect the primitive from the inroads of the unconscious. Since the primitive is all persona, he is helpless against the sudden uprush of emotion from the unconscious. As an example, Jung mentions the case of a primitive who came home from an unsuccessful hunt and, full of rage, strangled his small son, only to mourn him bitterly the moment after. To think that his rage meant that he was possessed by an evil spirit made it possible for him to devise means of propitiating the spirits and so gain control over his emotions.

In the West Christianity had fulfilled a similar function. Through dogma and ritual, the church provided a blueprint for man's growth toward maturity. At baptism, the child was received into the church, thus releasing him from exclusive dependence on his parents and protecting him from the unknown by giving him a heavenly father. At confirmation, he was not only formally initiated into the world of men but was also confirmed in his membership in a spiritual family (church and pope as mother and father). Although the church was, and is, a positive factor, Jung feels that it has kept the individual confined in a collective world that should be abandoned as soon as self-confidence permits. With the Reformation, which exalted individualism, the unity of doctrine and symbolism gradually disappeared; and meaning has been bleached out of the sacred symbols until modern Protestantism is left with little more than the historical figure of Christ and an ambiguous and problematical idea of God.

This rootlessness of modern man has sometimes tempted him to look to Eastern religions for meanings as yet undiluted by usage, for newly minted symbols that might bring back an experience long forgotten, if ever known. This attempt will not succeed, says Jung, for religion must be firmly rooted in experience; it cannot be transplanted. For modern man, Jung sees only one remedy: to become aware that God is an archetype that is rooted deep in our collective unconscious and that conveys an experience of the numinous (in Rudolf Otto's term), of something that arouses awe and inspires deeds far surpassing everyday aims.

Jung and Christianity.   Jung has so often been accused of reducing religion to psychology and has so often protested that he is not guilty of such naive psychologism that it will be well to discuss this facet of his system.

Our Western Judaeo-Christian tradition assumes a dualism of matter and spirit. God, the creator of all that is, sustains what he has created and so is "in" his creation; but as pure spirit he immeasurably transcends his creation. Man, partly material, partly spiritual, can come to know him after a fashion, can love, worship, and serve him, but can also turn away from God and choose his own willful destiny. In contrast, Jung sees a duality of matter and psyche or mind. Indeed, the "objective psyche" is, if anything, more real than the physical world. Since he believes that even animals share archetypes ([1913*b*] 1953, p. 67), the archetypal organizing forces seem to regulate the activity of all living things. The objective psyche seems to penetrate everything ([1937–1944] 1955, p. 132). If living organisms are thus so grounded in the objective psyche, then it is really the spaceless, timeless realm out of which the material universe was somehow precipitated. Jung actually draws an analogy, admittedly speculative, between the nature of the atom and the nature of the archetype and defends this analogy insistently (Jung 1951).

In Jung's universe, the objective psyche is the ultimate reality. For this reason, he cannot understand the objections of theologians who accuse him of equating God with psychic reality—for is not psychic reality all there is? For Jung, the personified archetypal forces are the only real forces, and the God image is their most powerful expression. Why, then, should anyone accuse him of psychologism? Jung's is not a Christian world view; it is far closer to that of Carus and von Hartmann, for whom the supraindividual unconscious psyche, absolute and eternal, is the source of consciousness, "the Divine within us." Jung's process of individuation is really the reclamation of matter by the divine unconscious, and man has only the choice of going along or being dragged along.

The problem of evil.   This divergence of Jung's world view from the Christian tradition is at the root of the heated debates, engaged in by Jung and some of his theologian disciples, on the problem of evil.

For Jung, evil had to be substantial, a real archetypal force. Lucifer, Satan, the shadow, are archetypal images for him, the expression of psychic realities. In his system, they must be equally potent, equally real, opposites of the good—of God. Without opposites, he cannot conceive of energy, power, or any movement, even the movement toward individuation. For the Christian, on the other hand, everything has been created by God and so is good. Some creatures, having been given free will, broke away from God and set their will against his. They have become evil. But their substance, being God's creation, is good; only their will is evil and so works evil. The devils' sin is in having perverted God's good creation and having turned it against him. They are rebels, not evil gods. Consequently, the Christian can believe in the final victory of the good, while Jung is caught in his universe of absolute good and absolute evil, in which the increase of one always requires the increase of the other.

Trinity versus Quaternity.   Jung's view that the archetypal forces are the only reality also seems responsible for his often expressed conviction that the Trinity, as conceived by Christians, is incomplete without a fourth member. This is sometimes the feminine principle to complement God the Father, sometimes the principle of evil to complement God as the principle of good. He actually claimed that the dogma of the Assumption of the Virgin Mary adds the needed fourth to make a Quaternity ([1902–1959] 1958, vol. 11, p. 171).

In this interpretation, Jung has found a way to impose his own mold of thinking on Christian beliefs. For him, the Quaternity is the symbol of individuation, as he has found it in his analysis of patients. Here he has seen the emergence of the foursquare man who has faced shadow and anima, God and the devil; conceiving these images as expressions of the personified powers of the unconscious, the only realities, it was easy for him to believe that these must be the realities behind Christian dogma. So he interprets the Mass as "the rite of the individuation process" which "transforms the soul of the empirical man, who is only a part of himself, into his totality, symbolically expressed by Christ" ([1942] 1958, p. 273).

Possible objections.   Once the collective psyche is given the status of absolute reality, Jung cannot be charged with psychologism. But perhaps the logic of his own system would require a realization that the identification of the God image with the total self is also a projection. Just as other archetypal images do not merely symbolize unconscious forces but are ways of apprehending reality in the persons of real men and women, so the God image might be a way of apprehending extraindividual and extrapsychic reality. In Jung's system, a dangerous inflation follows if the archetypal energy is appropriated by the ego, as we have seen above. Might there not be a similar, even more dangerous, inflation if the God image is appropriated by the total self? After the unconscious projections of the shadow, the anima, and the magician are recognized and withdrawn, would not the logical last step be a resolution of the God complex through a withdrawal of the unconscious projection on the total self? Jung's philosophy does not allow him to take this last step toward individuation, and so he is left with a completely autonomous self, a veritable half-god.

The growing God.   This inflation is perhaps most noticeable in Jung's *Answer to Job* (1952), one of his most recent books. Here he explores the character of Yahweh in his treatment of Job. Yahweh is a combination of opposites: he is omniscient and omnipotent, yet he demands praise, worship, and sacrifice. He is total justice—but also total injustice, as demonstrated in the way he treats Job. Such an aggregate of opposites implies lack of insight, lack of self-reflection, total unconsciousness. Man, dependent and defenseless, had to compensate by a "somewhat keener consciousness." Thus, the creature has surpassed the creator in morality and wisdom, and God must become man to regenerate himself and become conscious ([1952] 1958, pp. 405–406).

With this notion of man as superior to God,

Jung's thinking has completed a full circle: the conscious ego is but a tiny part of the total self, and its energy depends on the tension of conscious and unconscious; God is an archetype in the unconscious, symbolizing the total self; this total self has to be achieved by a process of individuation in which one archetypal projection after another must be faced and transcended; but the archetypal force (God), symbolizing the total self, is inferior to the conscious ego. Apparently, this "most powerful" archetype is in need of constant regeneration through constant incarnation, first through Christ in one man, then through the Holy Ghost in many. Jung admits that "such a transformation [into complete God-men] would lead to insufferable collisions between them, to say nothing of the unavoidable inflation to which the ordinary mortal . . . would instantly succumb." His solution? ". . . even the enlightened person remains what he is, and is never more than his own limited ego before the One who dwells within him, whose form has no knowable boundaries, who encompasses him on all sides, fathomless as the abysms of the earth and vast as the sky" ([1952] 1958, p. 470). In other words, man affords regeneration to the unconscious God, is even superior to him, but still is not God. Is this perhaps a belated recognition that the identification of the total self with the God image is a projection?

Synchronicity.   In his later works, Jung suggested that the principle of causality should be complemented by the principle of *synchronicity*. This is the notion that events that occur apparently by chance may actually be the result of a common inner meaning. In Jung's own experience, on a day devoted to exploring the fish symbolism, he had fish for lunch, found an inscription that referred to fish, was shown pictures of fish and told a dream about fish ([1937–1944] 1955, p. 14). This principle is easy to explain in terms of Jung's system, in which the objective psyche interpenetrates the physical universe and pursues its own aims through the individuals it produces and nourishes.

Jung's method of treatment

Jung diverged as far from Freud's technique as he did from Freud's theory. He used dreams to discover the root of the patient's problem, as did Freud. But unlike Freud, he depended on dream sequences rather than on single dreams and used amplification rather than free association to arrive at the meaning of the dream. The difference is fundamental. Freud used the patient's associations to uncover buried memories; Jung asked for the meaning of the dream figures to arrive at the mean-

ing of the dream story. He quotes the dream of a woman patient to illustrate his method: "*She is about to cross a wide river. There is no bridge, but she finds a ford where she can cross. She is on the point of doing so, when a large crab that lay hidden in the water seizes her by the foot and will not let her go*" ([1913b] 1953, p. 80). The meanings are as follows: *River*—a boundary difficult to cross; she must reach the other side. *Ford*—a possible crossing; treatment is a way to health. *Crab* (German *Krebs* means crab and cancer)—an incurable disease; something is stopping her (a row with a woman friend). Interpreted on the objective level, the dream says that her friend is the obstacle that prevents her from getting well. But Jung also interprets dreams on the subjective level, treating dream contents as symbols of inner tendencies. On the subjective level, "the dream shows the patient that she has something in herself which prevents her from crossing the boundary, i.e., from getting out of one situation or attitude into another" ([1913b] 1953, p. 84). The relationship with her friend is sentimental and demanding, used as a defense against heterosexual entanglements. Objectively, this relationship is the "cancer"; subjectively, it is her unconscious need of such a defense that prevents her progress. The dream also suggests a remedy: to free herself from the cancer if she is to progress.

It is Jung's conviction that the therapist can bring the patient only up to the point in the process of individuation reached by the therapist himself. The therapist is a helper, a coexplorer in the discovery of the unconscious. In helping the patient, the doctor gains insights about his own personality and is transformed, together with the patient.

Evaluation

Jung's books are difficult to read because they are weighed down by references to mythology, alchemy, and Christian and Eastern symbolism, with which the reader has little firsthand acquaintance. Thus, it is next to impossible to assess the validity of Jung's inferences from these sources. Moreover, Jung's system has grown over many years and is not stated in full in any of his books. Consequently, it is necessary to read the better part of his writings before one can form a good notion of the scope of his theories.

Jung's empirical results represent a broadening of psychotherapy and personality research, which will continue to bear fruit now that the strictly mechanical view of man is beginning to be superseded by a more humanistic approach. Jung's conception of human personality is incomparably richer than that of Freud or his successors. Like Freud, he began by exploring memory (free associations) but soon realized that fantasy and imagination are the "royal road to the unconscious." Jung's findings demonstrate that man has aspirations as well as lusts and that his imagination is not restricted to fashioning disguises for libidinal wishes.

His clinical explorations seem to make it clear that the dreams and fantasies of his patients refer to something beyond the immediate situation, to a human desire for perfection or self-realization. However, the inference of a collective unconscious projecting its archetypal images in dreams and fantasies is not required by Jung's evidence. Strictly speaking, all our functions are unconscious. We do not know how we produce fantasy images, but neither do we know how we draw logical inferences. To explain fantasy images that express the same meanings, whether they occur in dreams of modern man or in myths and fairy tales, we need no more than the assumption that like human structure will mediate like human experiences pictured in similar images. Imagination is normally used for planning action. When released from such use, in dreams and fantasies, it still functions to picture a man's life situation, and his attitudes, as expressed in his actions, and their possible consequences. Imagination, then, is an adjunct to deliberate planning and conduct, well suited to draw attention to aspirations not acknowledged in conscious life. To go beyond this function of imagination and suggest a direct connection with an extra-individual "objective psyche" seems to have been dictated by Jung's personal philosophy rather than by his scientific training or clinical experience.

MAGDA B. ARNOLD

[Other relevant material may be found in DREAMS; LITERATURE, article on THE PSYCHOLOGY OF LITERATURE; PSYCHOANALYSIS; RELIGION; and in the biographies of BLEULER; FREUD; JUNG.]

BIBLIOGRAPHY

GOLDBRUNNER, JOSEF (1949) 1956 Individuation: A Study of the Depth Psychology of Carl Gustav Jung. London: Hollis & Carter; New York: Pantheon. → First published in German.

The Interpretation of Nature and the Psyche. 1955 New York: Pantheon. → Contains two essays: "Synchronicity: An Acausal Connecting Principle" by C. G. Jung and "The Influence of Archetypal Ideas on the Scientific Theories of Kepler" by W. Pauli.

JACOBI, JOLANDE (1957) 1959 Complex, Archetype, Symbol in the Psychology of C. G. Jung. New York: Pantheon. → First published in German.

JUNG, CARL GUSTAV (1902) 1957 On the Psychology and Pathology of So-called Occult Phenomena. Pages 3–88 in Carl Gustav Jung, Collected Works. Volume 1:

Psychiatric Studies. New York: Pantheon. → First published as "Zur Psychologie und Pathologie sogenannter occulter Phänomene."

JUNG, CARL GUSTAV (1902–1959) 1953– Collected Works. Edited by Herbert Read et al. New York: Pantheon. → Volume 1: Psychiatric Studies, 1957. Volume 3: The Psychogenesis of Mental Disease, 1960. Volume 4: Freud and Psychoanalysis, 1961. Volume 5: Symbols of Transformation, 1956. Volume 7: Two Essays on Analytical Psychology, 1953. Volume 8: The Structure and Dynamics of the Psyche, 1953. Volume 9, Part 1: The Archetypes and the Collective Unconscious, 1959. Part 2: Aion: Researches Into the Phenomenology of the Self, 1959. Volume 10: Civilization in Transition, 1963. Volume 11: Psychology and Religion: West and East, 1958. Volume 12: Psychology and Alchemy, 1953. Volume 14: Mysterium coniunctionis, 1963. Volume 16: The Practice of Psychotherapy, 1954. Volume 17: The Development of Personality, 1954. Forthcoming volumes include Volume 2: Experimental Researches; Volume 6: Psychological Types; Volume 13: Alchemical Studies; Volume 15: The Spirit in Man, Art, and Literature; and final volumes on his miscellaneous works, bibliography, and index.

JUNG, CARL GUSTAV (1904–1909) 1918 Studies in Word-association: Experiments in the Diagnosis of Psychopathological Conditions Carried Out at the Psychiatric Clinic of the University of Zürich, Under the Direction of C. G. Jung. London: Heinemann. → First published in German.

JUNG, CARL GUSTAV (1913a) 1961 Theory of Psychoanalysis. Pages 83–226 in Carl Gustav Jung, Collected Works. Volume 4: Freud and Psychoanalysis. New York: Pantheon. → First published as Versuch einer Darstellung der psychoanalytischen Theorie.

JUNG, CARL GUSTAV (1913b) 1953 The Psychology of the Unconscious. Pages 1–117 in Carl Gustav Jung, Collected Works. Volume 7: Two Essays on Analytical Psychology. New York: Pantheon. → First published as "Neue Bahnen der Psychologie." In 1917 revised and expanded into Die Psychologie der unbewussten Prozesse.

JUNG, CARL GUSTAV (1921) 1959 Psychological Types: Or the Psychology of Individuation. London: Routledge. → First published in German.

JUNG, CARL GUSTAV (1922–1931) 1959 Modern Man in Search of a Soul. London: Routledge. → First published as Seelenprobleme der Gegenwart.

JUNG, CARL GUSTAV (1929) 1962 Commentary. Pages 77–137 in T'ai i chin hua tsung chih, The Secret of the Golden Flower: A Chinese Book of Life. New York: Harcourt. → "Commentary" first published in German.

JUNG, CARL GUSTAV (1932–1936) 1939 The Integration of the Personality. New York: Farrar. → Originally published in German in the 1932–1936 volumes of Eranos Jahrbuch.

JUNG, CARL GUSTAV (1937–1944) 1955 Psychology and Alchemy. London: Routledge. → First published in German. Also appeared as Volume 12 of Jung's Collected Works.

JUNG, CARL GUSTAV (1942) 1958 Transformation Symbolism in the Mass. Pages 201–296 in Carl Gustav Jung, Collected Works. Volume 11: Psychology and Religion: West and East. New York: Pantheon.

JUNG, CARL GUSTAV (1951) 1959 Aion. Volume 9, part 2 in Carl Gustav Jung, Collected Works. New York: Pantheon.

JUNG, CARL GUSTAV (1952) 1958 Answer to Job. Pages

355–470 in Carl Gustav Jung, *Collected Works*. Volume 11: Psychology and Religion: West and East. New York: Pantheon. → First published as "Antwort auf Hiob."

JUNG, CARL GUSTAV; and KERÉNYI, KARL (1941) 1949 *Essays on a Science of Mythology: The Myth of the Divine Child and the Mysteries of Eleusis*. New York: Pantheon. → First published in German.

ZIMMER, HEINRICH 1944 *Der Weg zum Selbst: Lehre und Leben des indischen Heiligen Shri Ramana aus Tiruvannamalai*. Edited by Carl G. Jung. Zürich: Rascher.

ANARCHISM

Anarchism, like liberalism and democracy, carries more than a single connotation. This is because it has produced both a body of theoretical literature and a series of activist parties, the two only remotely related. The anarchism of Godwin, Proudhon, and Kropotkin, known to the scholarly community, stands at a far remove from the images of the Haymarket rioters, Sacco and Vanzetti, and the Spanish Civil War, familiar to the popular mind. Yet if relationships must be established, it may be said that both the literary and the activist traditions share a common view of man, society, and the state.

Any definition of anarchism must be derived more from its literature than from its record of political action. Leon Czolgosz, who assassinated President McKinley, and the Andalusian peasants who fought against Franco were probably stirred by the same impulses as were Godwin and Kropotkin. But the latter figures articulated their beliefs, and it is on the written work that we must rely. The major tenets of anarchist doctrine may be summarized under five major heads. Emphases may differ with different proponents, but most of the elements are at least implicit in all serious anarchist writings.

(1) Man is essentially a benign creature. He was born good, or with a potentiality for goodness, but has been corrupted by the habits and institutions of authority. Religion, education, politics, and economic life have all served to warp the natural goodness that inheres in mankind.

(2) Man is a social animal, and men reach their fulfillment when voluntarily and spontaneously cooperating with one another. Society is natural, the state is not; and the quest for the communal life is instinctive to all men.

(3) Prevailing institutions of society—particularly private property and the state—are artificial agencies through which men exploit and corrupt each other. Authority in any form, even democratic government or a socialist economy, stultifies the individual.

(4) Social change must be spontaneous, direct, and mass-based. Political parties, trade unions—indeed, all organized movements—are themselves creatures of authority. While pursuing reform or even revolution, they are so constituted as ultimately to replace one evil with another of a similar sort. Significant change, then, must express the natural sentiments of a mass of autonomous individuals acting without outside direction.

(5) Industrial civilization, no matter what the form of ownership of the means of production, warps the human spirit. Machines master men, narrowing their personalities and blocking creativity. Any society built on an industrial structure is bound to debase the motives and impulses of those who live in it.

The literature of anarchism. While elements of anarchist doctrine can be found as far back as the Stoics, the first meaningful exposition could not come until the advent of the industrial revolution. William Godwin's *Political Justice* (1793), appearing in the first and grimmest generation of that revolution, attacked the exploitation of man by man resulting from tyrannical government and unequal ownership of property. It is interesting to note that Godwin did not exhort men to revolutionary action, but hoped rather that people would educate themselves to a realization that justice would be secured only if they replaced the state with a network of voluntary arrangements.

Far more widely read was Pierre Joseph Proudhon, whose *What Is Property?* (1840) gave the notorious reply that "property is theft." Proudhon emphasized that society is a natural organism and the individual is a social creature. He, too, did not advocate revolutionary violence, but his call for the abolition of the state and the prevailing economic system implied that a forceful overturn was bound to come. Throughout his writings he elaborated many plans for setting up independent associations, decentralizing authority, and circumscribing the power of the state. The theoretical clash between anarchist and communist doctrine can be seen most vividly in Marx's attack on Proudhon, one of those rare cases where Marx displayed respect for the arguments of an antagonist.

Perhaps the most attractive of anarchist authors was P'etr Kropotkin, whose *Mutual Aid* (1890–1896) sought to rebut social Darwinism. Nature does not live under laws that permit only the fittest to survive, Kropotkin argued; not only in primitive societies, but also in the animal world, the basis of organization is mutual cooperation and help. With this "scientific" underpinning he proceeded to call for a thoroughgoing communist society, based on communes and devoid of either a division of labor or a money economy. He was explicit in advocating removal of the state by revolutionary means, but he was a "pure" anarchist in that he rejected any organized movement or party as the vehicle of change.

Of the major anarchist writers, Georges Sorel seemed least concerned with the goodness of man or the question of individual freedom. His *Reflections on Violence* (1908) is closest to the popular image of an anarchist handbook, detailing the various methods by which the working class can undermine and overthrow the capitalist state. The chief weapon is the "general strike," a rising of the proletariat that brings the wheels of the old order to a precipitous halt. Sorel was prepared to use existing trade unions as the vehicle for revolution, giving rise to the term "anarchosyndicalism." In making such a concession, he was, unlike Kropotkin, willing to use at least one institutional mechanism of the old regime to bridge the gap to the new society.

Anarchism as utopianism. It is easy enough to see how anarchism has remained a sectarian doctrine. Its tenets, taken singly, have much in common with those of other ideologies. Anarchism shares with liberalism an exaltation of the individual, a rejection of authority, and assumes a natural harmony of interests in society. Like both socialism and communism, it abjures private property and a state that supports the capitalist system; its stress on the need for revolutionary change clearly parallels the communist prescription. Anarchism has a democratic strand in its emphasis on human equality, and it is also in the classical conservative tradition in its suspicion of industrial society. Yet anarchism is the sum of its several parts, and the whole recipe is too rich a mixture for most. Those who rebel against authority may be attracted by parts of the anarchist creed; however, all but a handful balk when they learn that the entire doctrine must be regarded as an interlocking edifice.

Quite plainly, anarchists wish to have it all ways at once. If foremost priority is apparently accorded to the free and uncoerced individual, equal value is assigned to the harmonious social organism. Revolutionary violence is advocated, or at least implied, but unlike the communist variety it is to come to pass without benefit of a hierarchical party or leaders who impose their will on an organized movement. And the society of the postrevolutionary epoch, unlike any the modern world has ever known, will exist without law, state, or authority and will witness the flowering of hitherto unknown human potentialities.

Anarchism must be understood as a variety of utopianism—although differing from other utopian thought in that it considers not only ends but also means to the achievement of those ends. Like all utopianism, it is at least partly an attitude of mind rather than a rigorous theory. There is no difficulty in finding instances of ingenuousness in anarchist doctrine. It is easy enough to point out that coercion, real or threatened, is a necessary element in human relations; that revolutionary action can lead to dictatorial tyranny no less than to the promised land; that man has a propensity for evil as well as for good; that the anarchist utopia will be a monotonous plateau. But none of these objections, all based on common sense, attack the basic impulse that gives rise to the anarchist protest.

Anarchism, like any utopian doctrine, is first a critique of existing social arrangements, and second a blueprint for a problemless future. The principle that man is naturally good, for example, cannot be undermined by allusion to the evil behavior that has recurred throughout human history. For the reply is simply that man has never been given the chance to realize his potential, that his benign nature has heretofore been corrupted by institutional authority. Nor, by the same token, can the drabness of an equalitarian and conflictless society be used as a stick with which to beat utopian projections. To say that we, the corrupted products of an immoral era, would be bored is a myopic judgment on the conditions of society best conducive to the highest development of the human spirit. If anarchism is utopian, if its analysis and prescriptions seem unsophisticated, it nevertheless represents one of the fundamental expressions of dissatisfaction with the way men have chosen to order their lives up to the present.

Anarchism in the modern world. It is tempting to say that there is a little of the anarchist in everyone. Most individuals are sufficiently unquestioning to accept authority, at least as a necessary evil. But there is hardly a person who has not, perhaps in one moment of his life, stopped to wonder what he might have made of himself if agencies of coercion had not restricted his behavior at every turn. The businessman objecting to government intervention in his affairs, the factory worker resentful of the discipline imposed by management, the citizen who feels powerless in the face of party machines, even the adolescent chafing under regulations laid down by school authorities—all yearn for the freedom to be and to become themselves. To be sure, much of what sometimes passes as the spirit of anarchism is simply rationalization for a style of life an individual or group wishes to attain or preserve.

A good deal of the renewed interest in "alienation," "anomie," and personal "identity" stems from the assumption that men seek to be free of restrictions and are thwarted in their quest by the impersonal rules and personal relationships arising in the modern world. Critiques of corporations, trade unions, political parties, and even suburban life seem at first glance to reflect the anarchist temper. But in the final analysis it would be a grave error to confuse this social criticism with the anarchist tradition. For above all else the anarchist stands *outside* his society. He has no vested interests in it, and he is prepared to witness its destruction. The businessman, the politician, the intellectual, all of these may want the world shaped somewhat differently, but they still wish to preserve what are for them critical elements of that world. Few are so dedicated to freedom that they reject out of hand all organized forms of action and wait instead for the day when spontaneous and leaderless uprisings overthrow the social structure.

There may be concern with the kinds of problems that constitute anarchist doctrine, but there is a shortage of actual anarchists. This has been the case throughout history. Dedicated believers arise from time to time to assassinate princes and presidents, to encourage labor unrest, and to man a barricade in a civil war. But if states and economies have been overturned by revolutionary means, it has been by other movements acting under other inspirations.

ANDREW HACKER

[*See also* SOCIALISM; SYNDICALISM; UTOPIANISM. *Other relevant material may be found in the biographies* KROPOTKIN; PROUDHON; SOREL.]

BIBLIOGRAPHY

FLEISHER, DAVID 1951 *William Godwin: A Study in Liberalism.* London: Allen & Unwin.

GODWIN, WILLIAM (1793) 1946 *Enquiry Concerning Political Justice and Its Influence on Morals and Happiness.* 3 vols., 3d rev. ed. Univ. of Toronto Press.

HOROWITZ, IRVING L. 1961 *Radicalism and the Revolt Against Reason: The Social Theories of Georges Sorel.* London: Routledge; New York: Humanities.

KROPOTKIN, P'ETR (1890–1896) 1955 *Mutual Aid: A Factor of Evolution.* Boston: Extending Horizons. → Thomas Huxley's "The Struggle for Existence" is included in this book.

LUBAC, HENRI DE (1945) 1948 *The Un-Marxian Socialist: A Study of Proudhon.* New York: Sheed & Ward. → First published in French.

PROUDHON, PIERRE JOSEPH (1840) 1876 *What Is Property? An Inquiry Into the Principle of Right and of Government.* Princeton, Mass.: Tucker. → First published in French.

SOREL, GEORGES (1908) 1950 *Reflections on Violence.* Glencoe, Ill.: Free Press. → First published in French as *Réflexions sur la violence.* A paperback edition was published in 1961 by Collier.

WOODCOCK, GEORGE 1962 *Anarchism: A History of Libertarian Ideas and Movements.* New York: Meridian.

WOODCOCK, GEORGE; and AVAKUMOVIC, IVAN 1950 *The Anarchist Prince: A Biographical Study of Peter Kropotkin.* New York: Boardman.

ANDERSON, OSKAR N.

Oskar Nikolayevich Anderson (1887–1960), a pioneer of applied sampling-survey techniques, and remembered also for his contributions to the variate-difference method, has been described as "perhaps the most widely known statistician in Central Europe. . . . He provided a link between the Russian school of statistics . . . ([A.A.] Markoff [Sr.], Tschuprow) and the Anglo-American school. . . . Through his origin in the flourishing Russian school of 'probabilistes,' . . . Anderson belongs to the so-called 'continental' school of statistics, and worked in the tradition of the well known German statisticians [W.] Lexis and [L.] von Bortkiewicz. He might be the last representative of this approach . . ." (Tintner 1961, p. 273).

Anderson was born in Minsk, Byelorussia. His father was a professor of Finno–Ugric languages at the University of Kazan. Although the Andersons were Russian subjects, they were ethnically German. In 1906 Anderson was graduated from the gymnasium in Kazan with a gold medal. After studying mathematics at the University of Kazan for a year, he entered the economics department of the Polytechnical Institute in St. Petersburg. There he became an outstanding pupil of Aleksandr A. Chuprov (or Tschuprow), whose strong permanent influence on Anderson is evident, even in such detailed matters as taxonomic conventions. As B. I. Karpenko wrote: "The ideas of A. A. Chuprov penetrate into foreign science not only directly but also through the writings of his students . . . e.g., O. N. Anderson, who wrote a series of valuable works, in particular a serious book on the theory of statistics, which (in German) expounds A. A. Chuprov's ideas . . ." (Karpenko 1957, p. 317).

From 1912 to 1917 Anderson taught in a commercial gymnasium in St. Petersburg. While there he also obtained a law degree. In 1915 he took part in an expedition to Turkestan to make a survey of agricultural production under irrigation in the Syr Darya River area. There, as chief scientific consultant, Anderson made one of the earliest applications of sampling methods. It apparently had only one Russian precedent: on January 6, 1910, Chuprov had presented a paper on the application of sampling techniques to data from the 1898–1900 rural census, but this application had had an "experimental, rather than a practical, character" (Volkov 1961, p. 159).

In 1917 Anderson served as research economist for a large cooperative society in southern Russia and also underwent further training in statistics at the Commercial Institute in Kiev, where he became a docent in 1918. Concurrently, he held an executive position in the demographic institute of the Academy of Sciences in Kiev. While in Kiev, he came to know and was perhaps influenced by Eugen Slutsky.

Like many Russian students of his time, Anderson had leftist sympathies. In 1920, however, he and his family left Russia as a result of the political upheavals. The following year he became a high school principal in Budapest; from 1924 to 1933 he was a professor at the Commercial Institute in Varna, Bulgaria; and from 1935 to 1942 he held a similar position at the University of Sofia. From the mid-1920s on, he was a member of the Supreme Statistical Council of the Bulgarian government. He successfully advocated the use of sampling techniques—in addition to a complete enumeration—in the 1926 census of population and manufacture. Another large-scale sample survey instigated by Anderson covered Bulgarian agricultural production and producers in 1931–1932. In 1936 he began a complete redesigning of the acreage and crop statistics, basing them on purposive sampling.

In 1933 Anderson went to England and Germany on a Rockefeller stipend and, as a result of this trip, he published his first textbook (1935). He was a charter member of the Econometric Society. He contributed the article "Statistical Method" to the *Encyclopaedia of the Social Sciences* (1934). From the middle 1930s on, he served as an adviser for the League of Nations. In 1940 the Bulgarian government sent him to Germany, then at war, to study rationing. In 1942 Anderson accepted an appointment at the University of Kiel, Germany, and from 1947 to his death he was a professor of statistics in the economics department of the University of Munich. He was coeditor of the *Mitteilungsblatt für mathematische Statistik* (later *Metrika*) from its inception until he died. At the time of his death, his authority in German statistical circles was unrivaled. It was mainly through his efforts that the statistical training for economists at German universities was improved or was maintained at a reasonable level, despite various adverse influences.

Major contributions. One author has summed up Anderson's lifework in the following manner:

The course of outer events in Oskar Anderson's life reflects the turbulence and agonies of a Europe torn by wars and revolutions. His scientific work, always marked by personal involvement, is of sufficient stature to be of lasting interest. . . . Some of Anderson's endeavours were ahead of his time, along lines that have not yet received adequate attention. Thus his emphasis on causal analysis of nonexperimental data is a reminder that this important sector of applied statistics is far less developed than descriptive statistics and experimental analysis. . . . The main strength of Anderson's scientific *œuvre* lies, I think, in the systematic coordination of theory and application. Only to a relatively small extent does his importance derive from specific contributions. . . . (Wold 1961, pp. 651–653)

Despite the cogent appraisal by Wold, it seems desirable to take up some of Anderson's particular contributions.

Sample surveys. The Turkestan sample survey of 1915 and a demographic sampling study of 1916–1917 are contained in manuscripts that were lost; it seems safe to assume that the lost papers were valuable ones. We do have access to the first Bulgarian sample survey, which Anderson designed and whose implementation he supervised (1929*a*).

Variate-difference method in time series. Utilizing, in essence, the theorem that the nth difference of a polynomial of degree n is a constant and the $(n + 1)$st zero, the variate-difference method attempts to analyze time series on the basis of few assumptions, but including the sensitive one that random errors are not autocorrelated. Anderson developed the method concurrently with William S. Gosset (for details, see Tintner 1940, pp. 10–15). The method has not met with general favor, although it is still taken as a point of departure for various theoretical studies. Anderson himself was aware of its limitations (1954, pp. 178–180 in 1957 edition). In a different context, his incisive critique of the Harvard method of time-series analysis (1929*b*) is recognized as having definitively discredited mechanical procedures of that kind.

Quantitative economics. Anderson's study of the "verifiability" of the quantity theory of money (1931) is an econometric classic because Anderson took advantage of the then new awareness of the importance of random residuals. Several of his papers analyze the causes of divergent movements of agricultural and industrial prices. A critique of N. D. Kondratieff's work on long waves (in business cycles) is among Anderson's lost papers. His contributions to index-number theory were both constructive and critical. For reasons of error accumulation, he was specifically against chain indexing (1952).

Probability theory and nonparametric methods. Anderson's was essentially an eclectic, and somewhat modified, frequency point of view (e.g. 1954, pp. 98–100 in 1957 edition). In particular, he felt that finite, rather than infinite, urn models were more appropriate in most social contexts; correspondingly, he was against too facile an invocation of the central-limit theorem. In his papers on nonparametric methods (1955a; 1955b), he intended to make correlation and regression models applicable to a wider range of socioeconomic phenomena.

Textbooks. In his first textbook (1935), Anderson tried to expound twentieth-century statistical methods using preuniversity-level mathematics. Because of the time of publication and the then predominant doctrines, its influence seems to have been stronger outside of Germany than within. His second textbook (1954), however, went through three editions in three years; it was unusual for its highly personal anecdotal style and its abundance of historical, biographical, institutional, and mathematical asides.

Students. Anderson's best-known students, all professors in Germany, are Hans Kellerer, at Munich; Heinrich Strecker, at Tübingen; and Anderson's son Oskar, at Mannheim. What clearly characterizes them as Andersonians, especially the former two, is a strong interest and activity in sampling-survey design, a concern for the implemental side of statistics, and avowed reservations against abstractions unrelated to practice. Strecker has also worked on variants of the variate-difference method.

EBERHARD M. FELS

[*For discussion of the history and subsequent development of the fields in which Anderson worked, see* NONPARAMETRIC STATISTICS; PROBABILITY; SAMPLE SURVEYS; TIME SERIES.]

WORKS BY ANDERSON

(1929a) 1949 *Über die repräsentative Methode und deren Anwendung auf die Aufarbeitung der Ergebnisse der bulgarischen landwirtschaftlichen Betriebszählung vom 31. XII. 1926.* Munich: Bayerisches Statistisches Landesamt. → First published in Bulgarian.
1929b *Zur Problematik der empirisch-statistischen Konjunkturforschung: Kritische Betrachtung der Harvard-Methoden.* Bonn: Schroeder.
1931 Ist die Quantitätstheorie statistisch nachweisbar? *Zeitschrift für Nationalökonomie* 2:523–578.
(1934) 1959 Statistical Method. Volume 14, pages 366–371 in *Encyclopaedia of the Social Sciences.* New York: Macmillan.
1935 *Einführung in die mathematische Statistik.* Vienna: Springer.
1952 Wieder eine Indexverkettung? *Mitteilungsblatt für mathematische Statistik* 4:32–47.
(1954) 1962 *Probleme der statistischen Methodenlehre in den Sozialwissenschaften.* 4th ed. Würzburg (Germany): Physica–Verlag. → Pages cited in text refer to the 1957 edition.
1955a Eine "nicht-parametrische" (verteilungsfreie) Ableitung der Streuung (Variance) des multiplen ($R_{z.xy}$) und partiellen ($R_{xy.z}$) Korrelationskoeffizienten im Falle der sogenannten Null-hypothese, sowie der dieser Hypothese entsprechenden mittleren quadratischen Abweichungen (Standard Deviations) der Regressionskoeffizienten. *Mitteilungsblatt für mathematische Statistik* 7:85–112.
1955b Wann ist der Korrelationsindex von Fechner "Gesichert" (Significant)? *Mitteilungsblatt für mathematische Statistik* 7:166–167.
1963 *Ausgewählte Schriften.* 2 vols. Edited by H. Kellerer et al. Tübingen (Germany): Mohr. → Contains most of Anderson's extant papers—translated into German if originals are in other languages—and a biography.

SUPPLEMENTARY BIBLIOGRAPHY

KARPENKO, B. I. 1957 Zhizn' i deiatel'nost' A. A. Chuprova (The Life and Activity of A. A. Chuprov). Akademiia nauk SSSR, Otdelenie ekonomicheskikh, filosofskikh i pravovykh nauk, *Uchenye zapiski po statistike* 3:282–317.
TINTNER, GERHARD 1940 *The Variate Difference Method.* Bloomington, Ind.: Principia Press.
TINTNER, GERHARD 1961 The Statistical Work of Oskar Anderson. *Journal of the American Statistical Association* 56:273–280. → Contains a bibliography.
VOLKOV, A. G. 1961 Vyborochnoe nabliudenie naseleniia (The Sample Survey of Population). Akademiia nauk SSSR, Otdelenie ekonomicheskikh, filosofskikh i pravovykh nauk, *Uchenye zapiski po statistike* 6:157–184.
WOLD, HERMAN 1961 Oskar Anderson: 1887–1960. *Annals of Mathematical Statistics* 32:651–660. → Contains a bibliography.

ANGELL, JAMES ROWLAND

James Rowland Angell (1869–1949), psychologist, educational administrator, and public-service counselor, came from New England stock. His father, James Burrill Angell, a direct descendant of Thomas Angell, who went to Rhode Island in 1636 with Roger Williams, was at various times professor of modern languages at Brown University, editor of the *Providence Journal*, president of the University of Vermont, president of the University of Michigan for 38 years, and U.S. minister to China, 1880–1881, and to Turkey, 1888–1889.

His mother, Sarah Swope Caswell, was a descendant of Peregrine White, the first white child to be born to the *Mayflower* Pilgrims. She was the daughter of Alexis Caswell, an eminent mathematician, astronomer, president of Brown University, and charter member of the American Academy of Science.

The first two decades of James Angell's life were spent at the University of Michigan, where his father had become president when James was three years old. His home environment was distinctly academic. The Angell home was visited frequently not only by local faculty members but also by such widely eminent persons as Andrew White, Matthew Arnold, and Grover Cleveland.

In high school Angell took a conventional classical course; in college his major interests were logic, philosophy, and psychology. "But the psychology," he wrote in his autobiography, "instantly opened up a new world, which it seemed to me I had been waiting for, and for the first time I felt a deep and pervasive sense of the intellectual importance of the material I was facing. . . . With that experience began my real intellectual life, which ultimately led me on into my profession" ([1932] 1961, p. 5).

Psychology.   After graduating from the University of Michigan in 1890, he spent three years in graduate study of psychology and philosophy—one at Michigan, under John Dewey and James Tufts; one at Harvard, under William James and Josiah Royce; and one in Germany, mainly under Friedrich Paulsen at Berlin and Benno Erdmann at Halle. It was during these years that psychology was gradually becoming differentiated from philosophy and developing into an experimental science. About a dozen psychological laboratories had been started in the United States, mostly in the eastern states, but the expanding western universities were eager for well-trained experimental psychologists.

In 1893, before he had finished his work for a doctorate at the University of Berlin, Angell received an invitation from the University of Minnesota to become an instructor in psychology. His duties included teaching experimental methods and founding a psychology laboratory.

The following year Dewey, who had become chairman of the department of philosophy at the University of Chicago, brought Angell there as assistant professor of philosophy in charge of the psychology courses and a psychological laboratory. He was instantly in close contact with many of the distinguished scientists and scholars whom President William Rainey Harper had assembled. Being associated with such men as A. A. Michelson and R. A. Millikan in physics, Jacques Loeb in physiology, and H. H. Donaldson in neurology reinforced Angell's determination to bring the newly emerging science of psychology up to the highest experimental standards and to draw maximum support from cognate sciences; his background in philosophy and his contacts with philosophers like Dewey, J. H. Tufts, and G. H. Mead strengthened

his belief that the science of psychology should be grounded on a broad conceptual foundation.

Psychology based on such a foundation became known as "functional psychology," and Angell became its chief formulator and exponent. This formulation is most clearly expressed in his presidential address before the American Psychology Association in 1906 (Angell 1907). All mental processes and phenomena, such as perception, attention, memory, imagination, and thought, are viewed as products of organic evolution and, like all other similar products, perform certain functions for the survival and well-being of the organism. They are best understood by observing what they accomplish and the environmental conditions under which their various functions are performed. Thus, psychology is inevitably and intimately linked with the biological and social sciences and should have as its object the study of how humans and other animals adjust to, cope with, and modify the environments in which and by which they live.

All scientific activity has as one of its goals the harnessing of scientific knowledge to the solution of man's problems of survival and welfare. There is, therefore, no sharp dividing line between "pure" and "applied" science. The task of pure science is to provide basic understanding of the nature of man and his environment, and that of applied science is to direct this understanding to the control of the environment.

Angell's place in the history of psychology is well established (Boring 1929). He was one of the pioneers in organizing laboratory courses, in standardizing experimental procedures, in developing appropriate apparatus, and in systematizing the objectives and content of a growing young science. Although the term "functional" has largely disappeared, its point of view and basic principles are commonly accepted and taken for granted. Angell and his many distinguished students did not set out to establish a school of thought or a logically tight system, but rather to develop principles, methods, and objectives that have since permeated the whole of psychology.

Educational administration.   Angell's career as an educational administrator began in 1911, when he succeeded George E. Vincent as dean of the faculties of the University of Chicago, a position then next in rank to the president. This position brought him into first-hand contact with all of the administrative problems of a large university. During the year 1918/1919 he served as acting president of the university.

His next position of importance was that of

chairman of the National Research Council in 1919–1920, which brought him into close relation not only with the most distinguished scientists in all fields but also with many outstanding industrialists. It was during this year that he delivered a famous paper entitled "The Organization of Research" to the twenty-first annual conference of the Association of American Universities (Angell 1920). This paper contains his view on the "reproductive processes of science," that science, like the human mind, is a product of evolution and grows by a process of proliferation and selection. This conception of science guided his efforts to promote research when, a year later, he became president of the Carnegie Corporation and when, two years later, he was appointed the fourteenth president of Yale University.

His administration at Yale, from 1921 to 1937, was characterized by the phenomenal financial and physical growth of the university. Angell also took an active part in the shaping of educational policies. Many distinguished scholars and scientists were added to the faculty; residential colleges for undergraduates were adopted; a new undergraduate school of engineering was created, as well as new departments of anthropology, linguistics, government and international relations, and drama; and the Institute of Human Relations, an interdisciplinary research center, was established. According to Angell, one of the university's major objectives was to study human behavior in all its aspects.

Public service.   Angell reached Yale's compulsory retirement age of 68 in 1937. But being in good health, he decided to accept a position as educational and public service counselor to the National Broadcasting Company. He began by making a comprehensive study of the educational and cultural possibilities and public responsibilities of broadcasting in both Europe and the United States. He then drew up a plan for what he called "public-service programming," which would include not only educational programs but programs in the fields of social and economic problems, current events, music, drama, and religion.

Angell has been characterized as a man of profound wisdom and breadth of vision. He never embraced the extreme views of progressive education of his mentor, John Dewey, or the excessive behaviorism of one of his most distinguished students, John B. Watson. Angell's contributions to the social sciences are recorded not only in his books and articles on psychology and his many addresses and papers (1937) written while he was in educational administration, but also in the many deeds by which he advanced both the science of psychology and the art of education.

MARK A. MAY

[*For the historical context of Angell's work, see the biographies* DEWEY; JAMES; MEAD.]

WORKS BY ANGELL

(1904) 1908   *Psychology: An Introductory Study of the Structure and Function of Human Consciousness.* 4th ed., rev. New York: Holt.

1907   The Province of Functional Psychology. *Psychological Review* 14:61–91.

1920   The Organization of Research. Pages 27–41 in the Association of American Universities, *Journal of Proceedings and Addresses of the Twenty-first Annual Conference.* Chicago: The Association.

(1932) 1961   James Rowland Angell. Volume 3, pages 1–38 in Carl Murchison (editor), *A History of Psychology in Autobiography.* New York: Russell.

1937   *American Education: Addresses and Articles.* New Haven: Yale Univ. Press.

SUPPLEMENTARY BIBLIOGRAPHY

BORING, EDWIN G.   (1929) 1950   *A History of Experimental Psychology.* 2d ed. New York: Appleton. → See pages 554–558 on Angell in the 1950 edition.

HEIDBREDER, EDNA   1933   *Seven Psychologies.* New York and London: Century.

ANGLO–AMERICAN SOCIETY

The four largest English-speaking democracies —Australia, Canada, Great Britain, and the United States—are generally regarded as highly similar societies, which for the purposes of comparative social science may be treated as different examples of the same type. They vary greatly, of course, in area, size of population, and degree of ethnic, racial, and linguistic homogeneity. They differ, too, with respect to formal political institutions—monarchy as compared to republic, federalism contrasted with unitary national power, separation of powers contrasted with parliamentary–cabinet control. These differences, however, are often treated as minimal, given the common derivation of many cultural similarities, a common language which facilitates cultural interaction among the nations, extremely high standards of living and economic productivity, and stable democratic political institutions, such as a common-law tradition and a two-party political system in which each party consists of a broad coalition of interests and in which ideological differences are minimized. From the comparative perspective of world-wide cultural variations, there can be little doubt that these four nations represent different regional versions of one culture.

Any comparison of societies that are so greatly similar economically and politically (that is, as wealthy, stable democracies) must seek some conceptual distinctions to illuminate the peculiarities of institutions in highly comparable systems. In the tradition of Max Weber's methodology of social science, this discussion emphasizes those distinctions among key social values that are related to variations in certain of the social institutions found in Anglo–American societies.

One particularly effective method for systematically classifying the central values of social systems is a modification of the pattern-variable approach originally developed by Talcott Parsons (1951; 1960). Pattern variables are dichotomous categories of modes of interaction, such as achievement–ascription, universalism–particularism, specificity–diffuseness, self-orientation–collectivity orientation, and equalitarianism–elitism. (The last is not one of Parsons' distinctions, but one added here.) A society's value system may thus orient an individual's behavior so that he (1) treats others in terms of their abilities and performances or in terms of inherited qualities (achievement–ascription); (2) applies a general standard or responds to some personal relationship (universalism–particularism); (3) relates to a selective aspect of another's behavior or to many aspects (specificity–diffuseness); (4) gives primacy to the private needs of others or subordinates others' needs to the defined interests of the larger group (self-orientation–collectivity orientation); or (5) stresses that all persons must be respected because they are human beings or emphasizes the general superiority of those who hold elite positions (equalitarianism–elitism) (Parsons 1951, pp. 58–67; 1960).

Although the value patterns are dichotomous, for purposes of comparative analysis it is preferable to conceive of them as scales, along which nations can be ranked in terms of their relative position on each of the pattern variables. The terms themselves represent the polar values for each scale, and nations may be ranked in terms of their relative approximation to the "pure" expression of each of the polar values. While there is no absolute basis on which to make judgments in terms of the pattern variables, the nations can be fairly reliably ranked with respect to one another. For example, Britain is more ascriptive than the United States but much more achievement oriented than India.

The tentative rankings assigned the four major Anglo–American societies on these five dimensions are presented in Table 1, based primarily on im-

pressionistic rather than systematically collected empirical evidence.

Table 1 — Tentative estimates of relative rankings of the four English-speaking democracies according to strength of certain pattern variables (ranked according to the first term in the polarity)

	Great Britain	Australia	Canada	United States
Ascription–Achievement	1	2.5	2.5	4
Particularism–Universalism	1	2	3	4
Diffuseness–Specificity	1	2.5	2.5	4
Collectivity orientation–Self-orientation	1	2	3	4
Elitism–Equalitarianism	1	4	2	3

According to these estimates, Australia is slightly more egalitarian, but less achievement oriented, universalistic, specific, and self-oriented than the United States. It is less universalistic but more egalitarian than Canada. Canada systematically differs from the United States on all five dimensions, being less egalitarian, achievement oriented, universalistic, specific, and self-oriented; and Britain, in turn, differs consistently from Canada in the same way the latter differs from the United States. These ranks, of course, are based on abstracting ideal-typical aspects of the four societies.

To highlight the analytic utility of these distinctions, it would seem worthwhile to discuss the causes and consequences of national value differentiation. This may be done by indicating those variations in the social development of each country that presumably created and sustained structures embracing these values; differences in the institutional arrangements that relate to the separate value patterns may then be derived.

Sources of value differences

Although there are obviously many events and factors in the history of these nations that have determined the current variations among them, three particularly significant ones may be singled out: (a) the varying origins of their political systems and national identities; (b) different religious traditions; and (c) the presence or absence of specific types of frontier experiences.

The variations in the political systems of these four societies stem from revolution in the United States, counterrevolution in Canada, the transference of nineteenth-century British working-class culture to Australia, and a deference pattern in Britain sustained by a monarchy and aristocracy. The variations in religious traditions are reflected in the Puritan and subsequent Arminian doctrines of the United States, which have sustained a nonconformist Protestantism and the separation of church and state, and in a dominant Anglican tradition in England, which still provides that the large majority of persons are born into the established national church. And the diverse impact of the frontier experience helped sustain collectivity orientations in Australia and Canada but fostered self-orientations in the United States. Britain moved into the modern industrial and democratic period while retaining much of the formal structure that sustained the dominant classes and institutions of the previous period; thus, many of the preindustrial and predemocratic value orientations that emphasized ascription and elitism remained viable. In contrast, the growth of Canada, Australia, and the United States involved the settlement of relatively vacant frontiers. The differing development of the frontier and the varying approaches to the land question effected divergencies in the social structure and political ideologies of these three originally colonial societies.

The United States.   The American frontier development, the success of the small farmer tilling his own soil, supported the revolutionary emphases on egalitarianism and achievement. Postrevolutionary America provided individual economic opportunities, which inhibited the development of class antagonisms. At the beginning of the nineteenth century as many as four-fifths of the free people who worked were owners of their own means of livelihood (Corey 1935, pp. 113–114; Mills 1951, p. 7). Social status depended largely upon the amount of property owned. This development of a majority of propertied individuals gave American society the predominately middle-class structure on which its democratic political institutions have been based. From its beginnings, the United States lacked a social hierarchy linked to the presence of an aristocracy or peasantry.

The self-orientation so prevalent in the United States has many of its roots and impetus in the Arminian religious system which, contrary to Roman Catholic and Anglican tradition, asserts that everyone is judged individually and by his own achievements. As Max Weber pointed out, denominationalism and sectarianism helped create an ascetic work ethic that facilitated the emergence of modern capitalism and individual achievement. Thus, achievement, universalism, and self-orientation have been strengthened in the United States by a dominant religious tradition that emphasizes a nonconformist Protestantism, stressing individual

responsibility, self-pride, and individual ambition. As Tocqueville observed, in the United States even Roman Catholicism initially assumed something of an independent, sectarian character, at odds with the prospective elites, and thus contributed to liberalizing and populist tendencies ([1835] 1945, vol. 2, p. 312).

Canada.   The Canadian nation resulted from the defeat of the American Revolution in the northern British colonies. Its *raison d'être* is the victory of the "counterrevolution" which affirmed many of the values rejected by the United States. The Loyalist spirit was reflected in the plans of imperial authorities to establish a hereditary, colonial aristocracy in Canada:

> Efforts to strengthen the political ties of Empire or of nation led to deliberate attempts, through land grants and political preferments, to create and strengthen an aristocracy in the colonies . . . and, later, in a less obvious fashion, in the Canadian nation. The democratic movement, it was felt, was liable to draw Canadian people closer to their neighbours to the south; and a privileged upper class was a bulwark of loyalty and conservatism.   (Clark 1962, p. 194)

With a sort of Burkean pride, the pioneers of English Canada held an open disdain for the doctrine of the rights of man. The extent of this antirevolutionary feeling among English Canadians has been noted by a Canadian historian in these terms:

> The mental climate of English Canada in its early formative years was determined by men who were fleeing from the practical application of the doctrines that all men are born equal and are endowed by their Creator with certain inalienable rights amongst which are life, liberty and the pursuit of happiness. . . . In Canada we have no revolutionary tradition; and our historians, political scientists, and philosophers have assiduously tried to educate us to be proud of this fact. (Underhill 1960, p. 12)

Large numbers of the original post-1783 Canadian population rejected the American values of equalitarianism and universalism. In what was to become English Canada, the Tory émigrés who settled in the Maritimes and Ontario constituted the first United Empire Loyalists, loyal to the crown and British social and political institutions. In French Canada the dominant conservative clergy feared and inhibited the liberal doctrines of the American and French revolutions.

Democratic movements arose in Canada, which, like those to the south, drew support from the agrarian frontier of small, independent farmers striving to become economically prosperous. These settlers' "main concerns as a class were free land, abundant and accessible markets, monetary and and protection against the menacing interests of the urban centers" (Brady [1947] 1960, p. 463). financial policies advantageous to their economy, However, the self-orientations that seem endemic to the values of frontier communities were curbed in Canada by fear of the expansionist tendencies of the United States. Autonomous liberal frontier areas were prospective centers of sedition, of commitment to American values. The establishment of the centrally controlled Northwest Mounted Police to keep law and order on the frontier was designed to protect Canadian rule. The Canadian frontier was never permitted to extend beyond the direct control of the central government. Such centralization was necessary because local autonomy might result in support for efforts to join the United States. These conditions contributed to a greater sense of respect for law and authority (elitism) north of the border than was prevalent south of the border. "In the United States the frontier bred a spirit of liberty which often opposed efforts to maintain order. In Canada, order was maintained at the price of weakening that spirit" (Clark 1962, p. 192). Canada never glorified the frontiersman and his tendencies toward rebellion and independence; the bard of egalitarian populism, Walt Whitman, who was popular in America (and Australia), was not popular in Canada (Bissell 1956, pp. 133–134).

Significant differences in the religious development of Canada and the United States are also evident. Both societies have had their innovating sectarian movements, but in Canada the sects have been more prone to align themselves with traditional institutions and more ready to emulate the style of the established churches (Clark 1962, pp. 167–182). New religious movements in Canada have generally failed to increase achievement orientation significantly. In the United States the ascetic Protestant sects dominated the nation by the end of the first quarter of the nineteenth century and successfully institutionalized their values, which fostered hard work, savings, and investment. Thus, while Canadian frontier conditions were often just as destructive of traditional social relations as were those of the American frontier, the predominance of Anglican and French Catholic religious values, which sustained elitism and particularism, helped prevent the excessive individualism (self-orientation) and egalitarianism inherent in frontier communities.

Australia. From its beginnings as a British prison colony, founded in Sydney in 1788, Australia's social structure has reflected the influences of immigration (convict and nonconvict) and geography. Although the British hoped to develop Australia as a society of small, independent farmers, farming proved difficult in the poor soil and arid climate. Australia's wealth lay in sheep, not crops. Holdings of large pasture lands by individual owners operating with hired hands made Australia a business world where exploration of land by subsistence farmers was unknown. "The typical Australian frontiersman in the last century was a wage-worker who did not usually expect to become anything else" (Ward 1959, p. 226).

Australia's rural frontier resulted in a pastoral upper class and a large propertyless laboring class. The major port cities of the six Australian colonies became heavily populated, and the urban workers formed the front of the democratic movement. They pitted themselves against the oligarchy of the graziers and soon developed a class solidarity that was to influence Australia's subsequent economic and political development.

"Australia is one of the very few countries whose whole development has taken place since the beginnings of the Industrial Revolution" (Ward 1959, p. 18), and consequently it developed its national ethos and class structure in a period in which traditional and aristocratic values were under sharp attack (Rosecrance 1964, pp. 275–318). Structurally, Australian society has the lower strata of the British Isles without the upper strata. It has always reflected working-class values—egalitarianism, antielitism, and particularism (group consciousness).

The working-class solidarity and the corresponding set of value orientations imported from Britain were reinforced by the social structure of the Australian frontier. Australian bushmen turned to collective action and to the principle of "mateship," or the "uncritical acceptance of reciprocal obligations to provide companionship and material or ego support as required" (Taft & Walker 1958, p. 147). This mateship philosophy supports egalitarian values in Australia and, according to some, is responsible for thwarting the development of strong achievement orientations (Goodrich 1928, pp. 206–207).

A number of commentators have recently called attention to what they describe as the Americanization of Australia, by which they mean "the growth of competitiveness and the success ethic" (Jeanne MacKenzie [1961] 1962, p. 8). The rapid growth of higher education in Australia suggests that the Australians may be losing their disdain for achievement, but the value system apparently still emphasizes a commitment to egalitarian social relations beyond that found in other complex societies. For example, it is "the only western country which long resisted the noxious habit of tipping" (Jeanne MacKenzie [1961] 1962, p. 102). An Australian political scientist has commented that "in Australia there is little respect for wealth as such. . . . It is harder for an industrial magnate to enter politics than for a camel to pass through the eye of a needle" (Eggleston 1953, p. 11).

Little has been written relating Australia's religious institutions and traditions to other aspects of its development. The two major denominations are Anglican (34.8 per cent) and Roman Catholic (24.6 per cent). Denominations of Arminian and Calvinist origin are relatively small. The available data indicate, however, that the adherents of the latter groups tend to have been more successful achievers than those of the former. Thus, among Australian Christian denominations, the four whose followers have highest occupational status are Presbyterian, Congregationalist, Methodist, and Baptist, in that order (Taft & Walker 1958, p. 175). A question remains as to how much the weakness of the historic sects retarded the development of a hard-work-oriented ascetic Protestant ethic. Most commentators who seek to explain why Australians seem less work oriented and more concerned with leisure than citizens of some other nations attribute the origin of this ethos to the transplantation of the "restriction of output" norms of the nineteenth-century English workers rather than to religion (Rosecrance 1964).

If many of the differences between the United States and Canada may be related to the fact that one is the outgrowth of a successful democratic revolution and the other of its defeat, some of the differences between the two British Commonwealth nations, Canada and Australia, may also be tied to different political origins. Unlike Canada, Australia did not emerge from a vanquished democratic revolution and has no history of defeated nineteenth-century reformist movements. If anything, the reverse is true: the "left" played the major role in defining political and social institutions during the period in which national identity was established. Canadian unification in 1867 is associated with the Conservative party, whereas the federation of Australia around the turn of the century was pressed in most states by the Labor party. It is noteworthy that in Australia, as in the United States, it has been the "conservative" party that has changed its name to avoid association with traditional and privileged elements. "Not by accident but by design the term conservative early in the twentieth century disappeared from the

nomenclature of parties in Australia and New Zealand. . . . It could not obviously win enough varied backing among the surviving elements of conservative opinion. In Canada a conservative outlook in many respects found great favour" (Brady [1947] 1960, p. 528).

In a certain sense some of the persisting differences in outlook between Canada and Australia may be seen as reflecting the need of each country to dissociate itself from the major power that has had the most direct cultural and economic influence on it. Canadians are the world's oldest and continuing "anti-Americans." The Canadian has always felt his sense of nationality threatened by the United States, physically in earlier days, culturally and economically in more recent years. Not only have Canadians found it necessary to protect themselves against American expansion, they have also found it necessary to emphasize why they are not and should not become Americans; they have done so by disparaging various elements in American life, mainly those that are seemingly an outgrowth of mass democracy and an excessive emphasis on equalitarianism. Australian nationalism, in contrast, inspired efforts to dissociate Australia from Britain, first politically and later in terms of social values. Britain was perceived antagonistically as the stronghold of rigid inequality. Thus, where Canada justified a more elitist attitude in reaction to American equalitarianism, Australia emulated various American equalitarian patterns in reaction to British elitism.

Britain. The oldest of the Anglo–American societies, Britain clearly differs from the other three countries in having a visible resident monarchy which even today retains considerable social influence over the populace. Even socialist leaders, such as Clement Attlee and Herbert Morrison, accept aristocratic titles as great honors, a phenomenon that occurs in no other country in the world. In England a public-opinion study reported that "in 1957, three people in five *throughout the country were still keeping souvenirs from the 1953 Coronation*; and three in ten claimed to have a picture of a royal person in their house" (Harrisson et al. 1961, p. 232).

The characterization of British society as elitist and ascriptive with diffuseness and collectivity orientations is supported by institutionalized religion, which still performs a role of social integration. England, unlike the other three Anglo–American societies, does not sanction the split between church and state. The Church of England remains an Established church. In England the prime minister appoints the bishops; other ecclesiastics are also appointed by secular officials. In fact, the archbishops and 26 senior bishops sit in the House of Lords. The Prayer Book, which is the approved liturgical form of worship, is subject to the approval of Parliament, and an attempt to revise the Prayer Book in 1928 was rejected by the House of Commons (Richmond 1958, p. 108).

The traditional upper classes and their institutions—the public schools, the ancient universities, and the titled aristocracy—remain at the summit of the social structure (Crosland [1956] 1957, pp. 232–237; Williams 1961, pp. 318–321; Sampson 1962, pp. 160–217). George Orwell suggested that deferential sentiments are so strong among British workers that "even in socialist literature it is common to find contemptuous references to slum dwellers. . . . There is probably more disposition to accept class distinctions as permanent, and even to accept the upper classes as natural leaders, than survives in most countries. . . . The word 'Sir' is much used in England, and the man of obviously upper class appearance can usually get more than his fair share of deference . . ." (1947, p. 29).

Although elitist, ascriptive, particularistic, and collectivity-oriented values do persist in British society, Britain has been moving much closer to the opposite set of orientations. Industrialization, urbanization, and political democratization have all spurred the growth of universalistic and achievement-oriented values. But *relative* to the other English-speaking countries Britain still retains many of its preindustrial value orientations, which are sustained through their identification with the top of the social hierarchy. Thus, in the nineteenth century the British business classes rejected the *noblesse oblige* collectivity-orientation characteristic of the aristocracy: they denied responsibility for the poor and, instead, justified their claim to authority over the poor on the basis of their ownership of productive machinery (Bendix 1954, p. 271). However, within a relatively short period of time, the spokesmen for the new entrepreneurial classes imitated the old aristocracy by formulating an ideology that affirmed their responsibility for the workers and the lower classes generally and claimed that the duty was being performed (Bendix 1956, pp. 100–116). The British upper classes, unlike most Continental aristocracies, sustained their social prestige and influence by strong resistance to the claims of the new business classes, and later of the workers, to participate in politics. As Tocqueville pointed out, the British upper classes have maintained an "open aristocracy" that can be entered by achievement, conferring upon the entrants many of the diffuse privileges of inherited rank (Tocqueville 1833–1835).

Social structure and value emphases

It is extremely difficult to verify the assumptions concerning the rank-order differences in value emphases that have been posited here or to show the ways in which these differences affect patterns of behavior. Some of the economic indicators concerning distribution of income and wealth, size of national income, and per capita growth rates do, however, tend to support these assumptions.

Economic structure. The seemingly greater emphasis on equalitarianism in Australia than in the United States and Canada may account for the fact that Australia shows a lower income differential than do the United States and Canada. "The differential between the lowest and highest incomes is low in Australia. Within any commercial or industrial organization the salary of the second-highest-level executives is usually not more than three times that of the lowest paid adult male employee (before income tax, which levels the incomes considerably more)" (Taft & Walker 1958, p. 141). When the distribution of incomes in Australia and the United States is compared, it is clear that the majority of Australian incomes are distributed within a narrower range and with a lower midpoint than are the majority of United States incomes. Income data for 1957–1959 indicate that the difference between the income levels below which 25 per cent and 75 per cent of the population (taxpayers) fall is $1,300 in Australia, close to the 25 per cent income level (about $1,250). In the United States the corresponding difference between the 25 per cent and 75 per cent income levels (for families and unrelated individuals) is approximately $5,000, a figure more than double the 25 per cent income level (about $2,200). This comparison implies that there are proportionately fewer paupers and millionaires in Australia than in the United States (Mayer 1964). And reports of British income data indicate that there is a much greater concentration of low incomes in the hands of the many and of high incomes in the hands of a few than in the United States or Canada (Lydall & Lansing 1959, pp. 59–64; Bryden 1964, p. 30; Great Britain, Central Statistical Office, 1960, pp. 254–257; Australia, Department of the Treasury, Taxation Office, 1960–1961, p. 42). There is also abundant evidence that in spite of six years of a Labour government following the war, and an extensive commitment to a welfare state, the distribution of wealth in Great Britain is far *less* equal than in the United States (Lampman 1962, pp. 211, 215; Lydall & Lansing 1959, p. 64). A recent study of income distribution in Great Britain concludes that "the ownership of wealth, which is far more highly concentrated in the United Kingdom than in the United States, has probably become still more unequal and, in terms of family ownership, possibly strikingly more unequal, in recent years" (Titmuss 1962, p. 198).

Australia currently stands at the egalitarian end of the income-distribution scale among the four nations, while Great Britain remains the most inegalitarian. In recent years, however, various commentators on the Australian scene have suggested that achievement values are gaining, indicated by increasing support for greater income differentiation among jobs on the basis of the level of skill and education required, and that the sentiment for preserving a small wage spread is declining. Professional associations and skilled workers' unions have been demanding substantial increases in the salary margins between themselves and those with less skilled occupations. The Arbitration Commission has begun to acknowledge such claims (Encel 1964, pp. 61–66). In deciding on the demands of the engineers' association, which argued against past egalitarian wage policies on the grounds that "the prestige and social importance should be reflected in its remuneration . . . [a recent judgment by the Arbitration Commission] acknowledges that 'this is a technological age in which the needs of mankind continue to become more comprehensive and complex,' that the satisfaction of these needs depends greatly on the skill of the engineer, and that low salaries prevent the professional engineer from occupying 'the honoured place in the community which was his right and entitlement'" (Davies & Encel 1965, pp. 30–31). The United States has traditionally emphasized that achievement (equality of opportunity) and social equalitarianism (equality of manners) do not imply "equality of income," whereas Australia has assumed that "mateship" and "equality of status" require the maintenance of low income differentials among high-status and low-status occupations. On the whole, manual workers' unions in Australia are still more likely than those in North America to bargain for "across-the-board" increases rather than for differentiation among various skill groupings and are also more likely to prefer shorter hours to increased pay, policies which may reflect the lower level of achievement motivation there.

Educational system.   Perhaps no other institution is as intimately connected with the values of achievement and equalitarianism as the educational system. Here also it seems possible to relate many of the available facts concerning institutional variations among these four countries to assumptions concerning value differences. Perhaps the most striking evidence of the difference in values between the United States and the other societies is the variation in opportunities for higher education. The other three countries have a considerably lower proportion of college-age youth enrolled in higher education than does the United States, although Australia is somewhat closer to the United States than is Canada, which in turn has a larger cohort in higher education than does Great Britain (see Table 2).

Table 2 — Students enrolled in educational institutions as per cent of age group 20–24, about 1960

United States	30.2
Australia	13.1
Canada	9.2
England and Wales	7.3

Sources: *Compendium of Social Statistics,* 1963, pp. 329, 331, 324–325; *Demographic Yearbook,* 1960, pp. 182, 191–192, 245–246.

The strong and successful efforts in the United States to extend opportunities for higher education reflect both the pressures exerted by those in lower-status positions to secure the means to success and the recognition by the privileged that American values of equality and achievement require that those who are qualified be allowed the means to take part in the "race for success."

There are varying estimates of the numbers entering and attending institutions of higher education in different countries, owing in large part to the differing definitions of higher education in each nation. But even when the rather narrow British definitions and assumptions are applied, it seems clear that the proportion of college-age Americans enrolled in higher education is at least four and possibly seven times the proportion of Britons and that the American ratio is two to three times that of Canada and Australia (Great Britain, Committee on Higher Education, 1964).

Some evidence that these differences reflect variations in values, and not simply differences in wealth or occupational structures, may be deduced from the fact that the two major former American colonies, the Philippines and Puerto Rico, though low in per capita income, have a much larger proportion of the college-age cohort enrolled in colleges and universities than any country in Europe or the Commonwealth, a phenomenon that appears to reflect the successful effort of Americans to export their belief that "everyone" should be given a chance at college education. Similarly, the Scots, whose society is both more equalitarian and achievement oriented than the English, though much poorer economically, have proportionately many more students enrolled in universities. The rapid growth in the proportion of Australians still at school in the 20–24 age group, placing Australia considerably ahead of Canada, indicates that observers of the Australian scene may be correct in reporting that achievement values are gaining there. It also points to the close relationship between achievement and equalitarianism. One Australian educational expert accounts for the growth in education as inherent in "the objective of equality of educational opportunity which stems from the social philosophy of the country" (Bassett 1963).

The content of educational curricula also appears to reflect national value differences. In the United States and Australia, where status differences are seemingly less emphasized than in Canada, not to speak of the much more status-bound British society, curricula include more vocational, technical, and professional courses in schools and universities. These courses reflect the view that education should be concerned with imparting not only intellectual and purely academic skills but also practical knowledge directly applicable to a specific occupational situation (Conant 1961). As in the United States, Australian universities "are increasingly becoming high-level training institutions. Courses in pharmacy, forestry, surveying, physiotherapy, social work, town planning, agricultural economics, radiography, and many other new subjects have appeared on the scene to swell the number of university students and create new professions where only occupations existed before" (Bassett 1963, p. 293).

In Britain, and to a lesser degree in Canada, technical training has been viewed as corrupting the "aristocracy of intellect," or those being trained for political and social leadership. The British have largely kept vocational higher education outside the universities, with separate nonuniversity-affiliated colleges or schools for those subjects. Canadians, though less successful in resisting the introduction of these subjects than the British, still differ from Americans in being more eager to maintain the humanist emphasis in the curricula, a point of view that seems to accompany ascriptive and elitist values in other societies as well (Woodside 1958, p. 20). It has been noted that in Aus-

tralia "a utilitarian approach to education is widespread. Schooling is seen as vocational training and social adjustment rather than as the extension of general education and knowledge" (Barcan 1961, p. 43).

The British educational system traditionally has been concerned with giving a separate and special education to those selected for the elite—whether on the basis of inheritance or demonstrated ability—by removing them from contact with the prospective nonelite in either public or grammar schools, in which there is great emphasis on inculcating the elite's aesthetic culture, manners, and sense of paternalism toward the nonelite (Young [1958] 1959, p. 40; Vaizey 1959, pp. 28–29; Middleton 1957, pp. 230–231). The American system, on the other hand, as James Conant once put it, demands as its ideal "a common core of general education which will unite in one cultural pattern the future carpenter, factory worker, bishop, lawyer, doctor, sales-manager, professor and garage mechanic (see Young [1958] 1959, p. 40). Some Canadian writers have pointed out that until very recently education in their country was designed to train an ecclesiastical and political elite, much in the British tradition (Woodside 1958, pp. 21–22; Wrong 1955, p. 20). Canada is caught in the painful dilemma between what might be termed the European orientation and the American orientation (Nash 1961).

Political structure. The same assumptions about the interrelated consequences of national value emphases apply to variations in political and class conflicts. Thus, differences in the backgrounds of the supporters of political parties are much more closely correlated with class lines in Australia and Britain than in the United States and Canada (Alford 1963, pp. 101–107). The two most class-polarized nations, Australia and Britain, are those in which working-class particularism (group consciousness) sustains a sense of political class consciousness. Conversely, the two North American polities have been characterized by a stronger emphasis on universalism and achievement orientation. Where these values are emphasized, the lower-status person is more likely to feel impelled to get ahead by his own efforts and consequently is less prone to accept political doctrines that stress collective responsibility for success or failure (Merton [1949] 1957, pp. 167–169). These varying emphases and pressures may also be reflected by differences in trade-union membership. In Australia, two-thirds of all workers belong to unions (Walker 1956, p. 325), whereas in the United Kingdom somewhat over 40 per cent of the employed population is unionized, and in the United States and Canada about 30 per cent of those in nonagricultural employment belong to unions (International Labor Office 1961, pp. 18–19; Cyriax & Oakeshott [1960] 1961, p. 14; U.S. Bureau of the Census 1964, p. 247; Canada, Bureau of Statistics, 1962, pp. 246–249).

Although more stress is placed on the relationship of class to party in Australia and Great Britain than in the two North American nations, the Labor party has been able to win much more acceptance among the electorate in Australia than in Britain. Australia had a minority Labor government as early as 1904, and the first majority Labor government in the world in 1910. Although the (conservative) Liberal–Country parties have dominated most federal governments during much of the postwar period, this has been in part a result of the presence of two rival Labor parties on the ballot. In Britain, on the other hand, the Conservatives have been the dominant party throughout most of the twentieth century. The Labour party, in fact, has never received a majority vote from the electorate. It may be suggested that these national differences reflect the prevalence in Australia of political values derivative from the particularistic mateship sentiments developed among a working class transplanted from the more ascriptive and particularistic society of the British Isles. In Australia the descendants of the British working class have not been subject to the countervailing influence of a traditional elite supported by deferential norms, such as continued in the United Kingdom. Thus, particularistic class values (mateship) have fostered strong class political and economic organization in Australia and Britain, but the absence of ascriptive (aristocratic) and elitist values in the former undercut the support for conservative institutions and parties.

The politics of the United States and Canada differ in that identification with the elite constitutes an electoral handicap in the United States. The Democratic party has had the historic advantage (apart from the aftereffects of the Civil War) of being perceived as the party of the common man, of the people, in opposition to the elite. Canada, on the other hand, has no such legitimate antielitist populist tradition. In contrast to the United States, it has emphasized the disadvantages of populism, an outlook that may have played a major role in preventing the emergence of a clear-cut left–right class-based party conflict in the country. In Canada also, class-differentiated politics have probably been hampered by the fact that particularism (group consciousness) has always been expressed much

more in religious and ethnic (linguistic) terms than according to class lines (Alford 1963, pp. 262–277; Regenstreif 1963, p. 63).

American and Australian equalitarianism and lack of status deference not only results in greater legitimacy for the "left" party but also contributes to the relatively greater strength in these nations of populist antielitist movements through which popular discontent is expressed. The seemingly lesser respect for the "rules of the political game" in the United States, and to some extent in Australia as well, may be viewed as endemic to a system in which equalitarianism is strongly valued and diffuse elitism is absent. Generalized deference is not accorded those at the top; therefore, in the two more equalitarian nations, there are repeated attempts to redefine the rules or to ignore them. In effect, the legitimacy and decisions of leaders are constantly being questioned. A comment made by an Australian political scientist concerning attitudes toward political leaders in his country could be applied to the United States: "The suspicion of established authority that permeates Australian society finds a particular outlet in a widespread distrust of politicians, who are regarded as corrupt, self-seeking, uneducated, of mediocre ability, and not fit to be trusted with power" (Encel 1962, p. 209).

Many have argued that the more widespread deferential respect for elites in Britain, and to a degree in Canada, as compared to the antielitism of the two other nations, underlies the freedom of political dissent and guaranteed civil liberties so characteristic of Britain and English-speaking Canada. The emphases on elitism and diffuseness are reflected in the ability of the more unified and influential elites to control the system so as to inhibit the emergence of populist movements that express political intolerance. The Canadian sociologist S. D. Clark notes that: "In Canada, it would be hard to conceive of a state of political freedom great enough to permit the kind of attacks upon responsible leaders of the government which have been carried out in the United States" (1954, p. 72). In seeking to explain why Britain has not witnessed attacks on the integrity of its governing elite, Edward Shils comments that "the acceptance of hierarchy in British society permits the Government to retain its secrets, with little challenge or resentment" (1956, p. 49 ff.; Hyman [1963] 1964, p. 294).

Diffuse elitism tends to place a buffer between the elites and the rest of the population. The ability of Britain to operate without a written constitution, or Canada without a bill of rights, which would place restrictions on parliamentary violations of civil liberties, is to some degree made possible by the emphases on diffuseness and elitism in the two systems. In these societies the elites, whether those of intellect, of business, of politics, or of mass organizations, are both protected and controlled by their membership in the "club," which prescribes norms governing conflict among the members.

The greater violation of minority-group civil liberties in the more equalitarian democracies may be viewed as a consequence of a social system in which elite status is more specific. Accordingly, contending elites do not receive diffuse respect and feel less acutely the need to conform to a commonly held set of rules when engaged in struggle. They do not see each other as part of the same club, as members of an "establishment." Hence, conflicts about *the rules*, as well as over policies, are put to the broader public for solution. And this entails appealing in some degree to a mass electorate to adjudicate on rules whose significance and applicability they cannot be expected fully to understand. Appreciation of the necessity for such rules often involves a long-term socialization to the nature of the political process.

Some of the differences in political reactions among the four nations may also be due to the varying emphases in self-orientation as distinct from collectivity-orientation values. An emphasis on particularism tends to be linked to collectivity orientations. Moreover, the *noblesse oblige* morality inherent in aristocracy is an aspect of collectivity orientation. Historically, Britain, Australia, and Canada have stressed collectivity orientations much more than has the United States. In the first two countries, even the nonsocialist parties have long accepted the logic of government intervention in the economy and of the welfare state. Canada has never had a major socialist party, but a large number of industries are government owned, and both major parties have sponsored significant welfare-state measures. That the collectivity orientation in Canada is stronger than in the United States seemingly reflects the greater stress in the former of the values of elitism and particularism.

Although modern industrial society appears to be moving generally toward a greater acceptance of collectivity orientations, in the United States the emphasis on self-orientation results in strong resistance to community-welfare concepts. The rise of right-wing extremist resistance to such changes may reflect the fact that the self-orientation values are stronger among large segments of the American population than they are within societies with an aristocratic and elitist background. Thus, the values of elitism and ascription may operate against the excesses of populism and facilitate acceptance of a welfare state by the privileged strata, whereas emphases on self-orientation and antielitism may be conducive to right-wing populism.

The greater similarity between Australia and the United States, and their difference from Canada and especially Britain, in the occurrence of populist threats to the principle of due process is reflected to some degree in the extent to which the former two tolerate lawlessness. The comparative lack of traditional, hierarchically rooted social control mechanisms results in only weak social pressure to obey the rules without coercion. As the Australian historian Russell Ward has well put it, the deferential "respect for the squire," which underlies the acceptance of authority and informal social controls in Britain, is "based on traditional obligations which were, or had been, to some extent mutual" (1959, p. 27). Status deference was not easily transferred to new equalitarian societies that emphasized the universalistic cash nexus as a basis of social relations. The complaints often heard in the United States about corruption as a means of achieving success have also been expressed by Australians (Bryce 1921, pp. 276–277; Jeanne MacKenzie [1961] 1962, pp. 154, 220–222). "They will put up with boss-rule and corruption in trade-unions; they are not greatly concerned about gerrymandering at elections" (Norman MacKenzie [1962] 1963, p. 154; Lipset 1963, pp. 199–202). Neither union corruption nor gerrymandering are as prevalent in Britain and Canada.

One indicator of the relative strength of the informal normative mechanisms of social control as compared with the emphases of legal sanctions may be the relative size of the legal profession. The rank order of the four nations with respect to ratio of lawyers to population suggests that the United States depends most heavily on formal legal rules (one lawyer per 868 people), Australia second (one per 1,210), Canada third (one per 1,630), and Britain last and least (one per 2,222 people) (Lipset 1963, p. 264).

The United States has the highest crime rate among the four and Australia has the second. Contempt for law in Australia is expressed by lack of respect for the police and for law enforcement in general. These attitudes, linked not only to equalitarian attitudes toward authority but also perhaps to the country's penal-colony origins, are evident in the comment that "it is not uncommon to hear of a crowd watching a fight between a policeman and some minor criminal and intervening only to obstruct the police and allow the criminal to escape" (MacDougall 1963, p. 273). A study of Australian national character states unequivocally that "dislike and distrust of policemen . . . has sunk deeply into the national consciousness" (Jeanne MacKenzie [1961] 1962, p. 149). Similarly, studies of American police report that the policeman typically perceives the citizenry to be hostile to him (Skolnick 1966, p. 50). British police are somewhat less likely to experience the community as hostile (Banton 1964, pp. 125–126). The difference between American and British respect for the police is evidenced in a content analysis of movie plots in the two countries: "In American films the police are often mistaken, and the private investigator must solve the mystery. In British films, the police are almost always right" (Wolfenstein [1953] 1955, p. 312). And the implications of these findings are strengthened by the results of a detailed study of the English public that reports "enthusiastic appreciation of the police," the author commenting that he does "not think the English police have ever been felt to be the enemy of sizable non-criminal sections of the population . . ." (Gorer 1955, p. 295). Similarly, there seems general agreement among Canadians that the respect given their national police force, the Royal Canadian Mounted Police, far exceeds that ever accorded police in the United States (Wrong 1955, p. 38; Lipset 1965, pp. 28–30, 50–51).

Other illustrations. The consistent pattern of differences among the four major English-speaking nations may be pursued along many lines. Studies of comparative literature suggest that since Britain is elitist and the United States egalitarian the former has had greater influence on Canadian literature and American writers have had a more significant impact upon Australians:

Canadian writers have been less responsive than the Australian to American influences. As between English and American models, they have preferred the English. . . . Canadian writers found it more difficult than the Australian to absorb the exuberant realism that went with the expansion of American democracy. Whitman excited only the feeblest discipleship in Canada, but he was a political bible and a literary inspiration to Bernard O'Dowd, perhaps the best of the pre-modern Australian poets. American Utopian and protest literature found eager readers in Australia, comparatively few in Canada.   (Bissell 1956, pp. 133–134)

Canadian intellectuals have attempted to demonstrate that they are superior to the crude vulgarities of populist American culture and almost as good as English intellectuals. Australian intellectuals have rejected the English cultural model as linked to a decadent elitist society and often hold up American equalitarian writings as a superior model. Thus, whereas Canadian critics praised the poet Charles Sangster because "he may be regarded as the Canadian Wordsworth," Australian critics praised the poet Charles Harpur for the fact that he "was *not* the Australian Wordsworth" (Matthews 1962, pp. 58–59).

The differences among the nations, particularly with respect to egalitarianism, are highlighted by their legends and folk heroes. In Australia the heroes are frequently men who challenge authority and remain loyal to their companions. A list of Australian folk heroes would include Ned Kelly, outlawed bushranger, and Peter Lalor, the rebel leader of the Eureka Stockade (Taft 1962, p. 193). Comparative analyses of Canadian and American culture stress that many American heroes are also rebels against authority: cowboys, miners, vigilantes, frontiersmen, who keep fleeing the coming of authority, "while in Canada the 'mountie,' a policeman who clearly stands for law and order and traditional institutional authority, is the corresponding symbol of Canadian westward expansion" (Wrong 1955, p. 38). Or, as S. D. Clark has reported, "we have tended to dismiss our rebels of the past as misguided individuals out of accord with their fellow citizens" (1959, p. 3). But English history and mythology, Robin Hood apart, glorifies the deeds of monarchs, aristocrats, and those who have defended the legitimacy of national hierarchical institutions.

Impressionistic reports concerning the different ways in which civilian conscripts of the four countries responded to the hierarchical organization of military life during two world wars coincides with estimates of the differences in national values. The British, and to a lesser degree the Canadians, are reported to have been more accepting of authoritarian structures, whereas Americans and Australians exhibited strong resentment at having to exhibit deference to military superiors. A study of the Australian Army reports that English "troops accepted the principle that the general business of the great world was the affair of their superiors alone rather than of themselves; if action outside routine was called for, they looked to their officers to tell them what to do and how to do it. In Australia the distinction into social classes was so resented that it was difficult to get born Australians to serve as officers' batmen and grooms . . ." (Crawford 1952, p. 155). And various observers have reported that in London bars during both world wars, Americans and Australians tended to associate together, while Canadians were more likely than

Australians to prefer British companions. More recently, an English observer commented that it "is very noticeable that Canadians are intimately at home when they go to England . . ." (Pritchett 1964, p. 189).

Unfortunately, there are few systematic studies of institutional differences in all four countries, and not many more that deal with any two of them. But those that do exist, whether they contrast education, family organization, religion, politics, the police, or the operation of the judicial system, tend to reinforce the general interpretation advanced here of the consequences of systematic variations in major societal values.

Congruence of values. Although important differences continue to exist among the four major Anglo–American nations, a reading of the historical record would suggest that the differences have diminished over the generations. Achievement orientations have increased outside the United States; class particularism seems less strong in Australia than in the past; the United States' self-image as a radical egalitarian democratic nation opposed to the reactionary monarchical, aristocratic, and imperialist regimes of Europe has been challenged by its recent world-wide role of supporting existing regimes against communist and sometimes noncommunist revolutionary movements; Canada's self-justification against the United States as counterrevolutionary and against mass democracy has undergone important changes as well. Many Canadians now seek to defend the integrity of Canada against the United States by defining their own country as the more humane, more equalitarian, more democratic, and more anti-imperialist of the two. And since World War II in Britain, the Labour party has been in a position to contest regularly for control of the government, has gained control on occasion, and can expect to hold power frequently in succeeding decades. The Labour party seeks to foster the values of achievement, of universalism, and of equalitarianism. In the United States collectivity-orientation values are winning increasing respectability; the concept of the welfare state, although still less universally accepted than in the other three nations, is favored by growing numbers of Americans. It is obviously impossible to predict how similar the values and cultures of these four societies will be in the future, but the general trends are clear—structural change and political events are pressing them toward a congruence of values.

SEYMOUR M. LIPSET

[See also the biography of TOCQUEVILLE.]

BIBLIOGRAPHY

A comprehensive bibliography appears in Lipset 1963.

ALFORD, ROBERT R. 1963 *Party and Society: The Anglo–American Democracies.* Chicago: Rand McNally.

AUSTRALIA, DEPARTMENT OF THE TREASURY, TAXATION OFFICE 1960–1961 *Report of the Commissioner of Taxation.* No. 40. Canberra: Commonwealth Government Printer.

BANTON, MICHAEL P. 1964 *The Policeman in the Community.* London: Tavistock.

BARCAN, A. 1961 The Government of Australian Education. Pages 31–50 in R. G. Menzies et al. (editors), *The Challenge to Australian Education.* Melbourne: Cheshire.

BASSETT, G. W. 1963 Education. Pages 276–312 in Alan L. McLeod (editor), *The Pattern of Australian Culture.* Ithaca, N.Y.: Cornell Univ. Press.

BENDIX, REINHARD 1954 The Self-legitimation of an Entrepreneurial Class: The Case of England. Volume 2, pages 259–282 in World Congress of Sociology, Second, *Transactions.* London: International Sociological Association.

BENDIX, REINHARD 1956 *Work and Authority in Industry: Ideologies of Management in the Course of Industrialization.* New York: Wiley.

BISSELL, CLAUDE T. 1956 A Common Ancestry: Literature in Australia and Canada. *University of Toronto Quarterly* 25:131–142.

BRADY, ALEXANDER (1947) 1960 *Democracy in the Dominions: A Comparative Study in Institutions.* 3d ed. Univ. of Toronto Press.

BRYCE, JAMES 1921 *Modern Democracies.* Volume 1. London: Macmillan.

BRYDEN, MARION D. 1964 Statistical Comparisons: Personal Income Taxes. *Canadian Tax Journal* 12, no. 1 (Supplement): 19–32.

CANADA, BUREAU OF STATISTICS 1962 *Canada Year Book.* Ottawa: Queen's Printer.

CLARK, SAMUEL D. 1954 The Frontier and Democratic Theory. Royal Society of Canada, *Transactions* Third Series 48, section 2:65–75.

CLARK, SAMUEL D. 1959 *Movements of Political Protest in Canada: 1640–1840.* Univ. of Toronto Press.

CLARK, SAMUEL D. 1962 *The Developing Canadian Community.* Univ. of Toronto Press.

Compendium of Social Statistics: 1963. United Nations Statistical Office, Statistical Papers, Series K, No. 2. 1963. New York: United Nations.

CONANT, JAMES B. 1961 *Slums and Suburbs: A Commentary on Schools in Metropolitan Areas.* New York: McGraw-Hill. → A paperback edition was published in 1964 by New American Library.

COREY, LEWIS 1935 *The Crisis of the Middle Class.* New York: Covici, Friede.

CRAWFORD, RAYMOND M. 1952 *Australia.* London: Hutchinson's University Library.

CROSLAND, CHARLES A. R. (1956) 1957 *The Future of Socialism.* New York: Macmillan.

CYRIAX, GEORGE; and OAKESHOTT, ROBERT (1960) 1961 *The Bargainers: A Survey of Modern British Trade Unionism.* London: Praeger.

DAVIES, ALAN F.; and ENCEL, S. 1965 Class and Status. Pages 18–42 in Alan F. Davies and S. Encel (editors), *Australian Society: A Sociological Introduction.* New York: Atherton.

Demographic Yearbook. → Issued by the United Nations since 1948.

EGGLESTON, FREDERIC W. 1953 The Australian Nation. Pages 1–22 in George Caiger (editor), *The Australian Way of Life.* New York: Columbia Univ. Press.

ENCEL, S. 1962 Power. Pages 207–224 in Peter Coleman (editor), *Australian Civilization: A Symposium.* London: Angus & Robertson.

ENCEL, S. 1964 Social Implications of the Engineers' Cases. *Journal of Industrial Relations* 6:61–66.

GOODRICH, CARTER 1928 The Australian and American Labour Movements. *Economic Record* 4:193–208.

GORER, GEOFFREY 1955 *Exploring English Character.* New York: Criterion.

GREAT BRITAIN, CENTRAL STATISTICAL OFFICE 1960 *Annual Abstract of Statistics.* No. 97. London: H.M. Stationery Office.

GREAT BRITAIN, COMMITTEE ON HIGHER EDUCATION 1964 *Higher Education.* Appendix 5. London: H.M. Stationery Office.

HARRISSON, THOMAS M. et al. 1961 *Britain Revisited.* London: Gollancz.

HYMAN, HERBERT H. (1963) 1964 England and America: Climates of Tolerance and Intolerance—1962. Pages 227–257 in Daniel Bell (editor), *The Radical Right: The New American Right Expanded and Updated.* Garden City, N.Y.: Doubleday.

INTERNATIONAL LABOR OFFICE 1961 *The Trade Union Situation in the United Kingdom: Report of a Mission From the International Labour Office.* Geneva: The Office.

LAMPMAN, ROBERT J. 1962 *The Share of Top Wealth-holders in National Wealth: 1922–1956.* National Bureau of Economic Research, General Series No. 74. Princeton Univ. Press.

LIPSET, SEYMOUR M. 1963 *The First New Nation: The United States in Historical and Comparative Perspective.* New York: Basic Books.

LIPSET, SEYMOUR M. 1965 Revolution and Counter-revolution: The United States and Canada. Pages 21–64 in Thomas R. Ford (editor), *The Revolutionary Theme in Contemporary America.* Lexington: Univ. of Kentucky Press.

LYDALL, HAROLD F.; and LANSING, JOHN B. 1959 Comparison of the Distribution of Personal Income and Wealth in the United States and Great Britain. *American Economic Review* 49:43–67.

MACDOUGALL, D. J. 1963 Law. Pages 252–275 in Alan L. McLeod (editor), *The Pattern of Australian Culture.* Ithaca, N.Y.: Cornell Univ. Press.

MACKENZIE, JEANNE (1961) 1962 *Australian Paradox.* London: Macgibbon & Kee.

MACKENZIE, NORMAN (1962) 1963 *Women in Australia: A Report to the Social Science Research Council of Australia.* London: Angus & Robertson.

MATTHEWS, JOHN P. 1962 *Tradition in Exile: A Comparative Study of Social Influences on the Development of Australian and Canadian Poetry in the Nineteenth Century.* Univ. of Toronto Press.

MAYER, KURT B. 1964 Social Stratification in Two Equalitarian Societies: Australia and the United States. *Social Research* 31:435–465.

MERTON, ROBERT K. (1949) 1957 *Social Theory and Social Structure.* Rev. & enl. ed. Glencoe, Ill.: Free Press.

MIDDLETON, DREW 1957 *The British.* London: Secker & Warburg. → American edition published by Knopf as *These Are the British.*

MILLS, C. WRIGHT 1951 *White Collar: The American Middle Classes.* New York: Oxford Univ. Press.

NASH, P. 1961 Quality and Equality in Canadian Education. *Comparative Education Review* 5:118–129.

ORWELL, GEORGE 1947 *The English People.* London: Collins.

PARSONS, TALCOTT 1951 *The Social System.* Glencoe, Ill.: Free Press.

PARSONS, TALCOTT 1960 Pattern Variables Revisited: A Response to Robert Dubin. *American Sociological Review* 25:467–483.

PRITCHETT, VICTOR S. 1964 Across the Vast Land. *Holiday* 35, April: 52–69; 184–189.

REGENSTREIF, S. PETER 1963 Some Aspects of National Party Support in Canada. *Canadian Journal of Economics and Political Science* 29:59–74.

RICHMOND, ANTHONY H. 1958 The United Kingdom. Pages 43–130 in Arnold M. Rose (editor), *The Institutions of Advanced Societies.* Minneapolis: Univ. of Minnesota Press.

ROSECRANCE, RICHARD N. 1964 The Radical Culture of Australia. Pages 275–318 in Louis Hartz, *The Founding of New Societies: Studies in the History of the United States, Latin America, South Africa, Canada, and Australia.* New York: Harcourt.

SAMPSON, ANTHONY 1962 *Anatomy of Britain.* New York: Harper.

SHILS, EDWARD A. 1956 *The Torment of Secrecy: The Background and Consequences of American Security Policies.* Glencoe, Ill.: Free Press.

SKOLNICK, JEROME 1966 *Justice Without Trial.* New York: Wiley.

TAFT, RONALD 1962 The Myth and the Migrants. Pages 191–206 in Peter Coleman (editor), *Australian Civilization: A Symposium.* London: Angus & Robertson.

TAFT, RONALD; and WALKER, KENNETH F. 1958 Australia. Pages 131–192 in Arnold M. Rose (editor), *The Institutions of Advanced Societies.* Minneapolis: Univ. of Minnesota Press.

TITMUSS, RICHARD M. 1962 *Income Distribution and Social Change: A Study in Criticism.* London: Allen & Unwin.

TOCQUEVILLE, ALEXIS DE (1833–1835) 1958 *Journeys to England and Ireland.* New Haven: Yale Univ. Press. → Written in the years 1833–1835. First published posthumously in French.

TOCQUEVILLE, ALEXIS DE (1835) 1945 *Democracy in America.* 2 vols. New York: Knopf. → First published in French. Paperback editions were published in 1961 by Vintage and by Shocken.

UNDERHILL, FRANK H. 1960 *In Search of Canadian Liberalism.* Toronto: Macmillan.

U.S. BUREAU OF THE CENSUS 1964 *Statistical Abstract of the United States.* Washington: Government Printing Office.

VAIZEY, JOHN 1959 The Public Schools. Pages 21–46 in Hugh Thomas (editor), *The Establishment: A Symposium.* London: Blond.

WALKER, KENNETH F. 1956 *Industrial Relations in Australia.* Cambridge, Mass.: Harvard Univ. Press.

WARD, RUSSELL B. 1959 *The Australian Legend.* New York: Oxford Univ. Press.

WILLIAMS, RAYMOND 1961 *The Long Revolution.* New York: Columbia Univ. Press.

WOLFENSTEIN, MARTHA (1953) 1955 Movie Analyses in the Study of Culture. Pages 308–322 in David C. McClelland (editor), *Studies in Motivation.* New York: Appleton.

WOODSIDE, WILLSON 1958 *The University Question: Who Should Go? Who Should Pay?* Toronto: Ryerson.

WRONG, DENNIS H. 1955 *American and Canadian Viewpoints.* Washington: American Council on Education.

YOUNG, MICHAEL D. (1958) 1959 *The Rise of the Meritocracy, 1870–2033: The New Elite of Our Social Revolution.* New York: Random House. → A paperback edition was published in 1961 by Penguin.

ANGYAL, ANDRAS

Andras Angyal (1902–1960) is one of the major representatives of the holistic point of view in psychology and psychiatry. Born in Hungary, he spent his childhood in a rural Transylvanian community. He received a PH.D. in psychology from the University of Vienna in 1927 and an M.D. from the University of Turin in 1932. No one of Angyal's teachers seems to have had a decisive influence on his intellectual development, which was determined largely by his own interests and experiences.

His early research in perception, in which he combined painstaking observation with ingenious theorizing, was centered on the role of spatial schemata, or systems of spatial coordinates, in orientation and perception (1930). In 1932 Angyal came to the United States as a Rockefeller fellow and participated in the cross-disciplinary seminar on the impact of culture on personality held at Yale University under the direction of Edward Sapir, with whom Angyal formed a lasting friendship. For the next 12 years he worked at the state hospital in Worcester, Massachusetts, where research on schizophrenia was being conducted. He held successive positions there as psychiatrist of the research service and as resident director of research. Angyal carried out a number of studies of schizophrenia, both psychological and physiological, including intensive investigation of a number of individual patients. He discovered a particular syndrome marked by bizarre "somatic delusions" and demonstrated that these and other symptoms, although seemingly disparate, had a common root in the loss of ego-reference of the patient's conscious experiences; the bizarre complaints were exact descriptions of perceptual alterations caused by mistaken attribution of tactile and kinesthetic sensations to purely environmental sources, instead of to the interaction of bodily and external events (1936, pp. 1029–1053).

Angyal's theoretical book, *Foundations for a Science of Personality*, appeared in 1941. In presenting this comprehensive view of total human functioning, he did not merely pay lip service to the concept of "the organism as a whole" but developed conceptual means for approaching each problem from a consistently organismic standpoint. The book was very favorably received by the dynamically and holistically oriented psychologists and psychiatrists, who praised it for its breadth of vision, its conceptual originality and clarity, and the wide range of the material integrated.

Angyal's growing interest in the dynamics of mental illness and its cure, furthered also by an intensive study of psychoanalysis, eventually led to a major change of activity. From 1945 until his death in 1960, Angyal was engaged in private psychiatric practice in Boston. Although he was also active as lecturer, consultant, and training psychiatrist in various guidance centers and schools, including Harvard and Brandeis universities, most of his time was devoted to therapeutic work with neurotics. A talented and devoted therapist, Angyal remained an eager explorer, bent on acquiring a better understanding of human phenomena. He developed a comprehensive theory of neurosis and treatment, which he considered a complement of his theoretical book and indeed his main contribution to knowledge. *Neurosis and Treatment: A Holistic Theory* appeared posthumously in 1965.

Personality theory. Like William Stern, Angyal advocated the use of "psychophysically neutral" concepts (such as system, set, shift of set), equally applicable to all aspects and levels of personality functioning. He viewed mental states as symbolic elaborations that reflect, sometimes in a distorted manner, only parts of the total life process, so that the realm of the "unsymbolized" is much larger than that of the repressed, and the self contains more than does the conscious self; the symbolic elaborations, in turn, potentiate and influence the organismic processes they reflect. Neither the mind–body division nor the subject–object dichotomy should be absolutized or reified: life is a continuous interplay of organismic trends and the "foreign" influences of the environment.

The basic human trends can be inferred from the most general patterns of these person–world interactions. Two such patterns, or trends, are observable. Angyal called them the "trend toward increased *autonomy*" and the "trend toward *homonomy*"; he also referred to them as "mastery" and "love." In the one attitude, the human being strives to impose his control on the environment; in the other, he seeks harmonious participation in something larger than himself—a relationship, a social group, a cause, an ordered universe. The specific diversified ramifications of this double dynamic pattern form the blueprint of the personality structure. The double pattern of life operates also on the physiological level, where processes serving the continuation of the species can be distinguished from those serving the individual. In accord with the holistic approach, Angyal saw no reason to ascribe greater reality to the physiological than to any other abstracted aspect of the organism; in this he differed with psychoanalysis, even though he respected its clinical findings and incorporated them into his scheme.

Both autonomy and homonomy are present in most behavior, but one usually predominates. A person can strive, for example, to influence nature to serve his needs, or he can "resonate" to it in an aesthetic experience. Social and cultural realities function in part as forces foreign to the person, but also as uniquely human opportunities for homonomous integration. Values and norms of behavior, despite their cultural relativity, are adopted by the individual not only for fear of ostracism; they may also function as genuine expressions of his homonomous trend. Real guilt, as distinct from neurotic guilt, is felt by the person when he has acted against, or betrayed, somebody or something with which he is genuinely identified; it is an expression of homonomy. The two basic trends, although seeming opposites, presuppose each other and are but two directions of one organizing process: while the individual fits environmental items into his own life as its parts, he also extends his life by becoming a part of a larger meaningful whole.

To provide conceptual tools for dealing with wholes whose functioning does not derive from that of their parts, Angyal outlined the logical properties of systems, as distinct from relationships. He defined "systems" as distributions of members in a dimensional domain governed by a single principle: the system principle of the circle is that all points are equidistant from the center; the system principle of human life, the double pattern described above. Members or parts of a system function as such only through those qualities that are relevant to the system principle and are connected only through their common participation in the system. According to Angyal, causal thinking, which looks for direct connections between antecedent and subsequent events, has only a limited value in exploring personality. In system thinking one connects two parts, or two events, by finding the superordinate system to which both belong. System dynamics, as distinct from atomistic causality, are governed by the trend toward a more complete realization of the system principle, of which trend the gestalt laws of "tendency to closure" and "tendency to *Praegnanz*" are partial expressions. In the temporal gestalt of an individual life, not only does the past determine the present, but the reverse is also true. Past events are immutable only when viewed in isolation from the system; a change in the system principle of the individual life will cause these past events to gain a different meaning, a different position within the new system. Since both health and neurosis are organized systems, a shift from one to the other changes the past.

Neurosis. Neurosis is not a focal disturbance, a "bad" part in a healthy organism: it is a complete way of life, an organization perpetuated by system dynamics. This complex structure is built to cope with the person's persisting *isolation* from the world, which is reflected in awareness as anxiety. Isolation is experienced by every child in the process of individuation, of growth and change, but normally the child overcomes it by relating himself to his environment through mastery and through affection. If opportunities for this are inadequate during the crucial early period, the world remains alien and threatening; the child starts diverting much of his energy into self-protection and thus perpetuates his isolation. Although the neurotic continues to pursue the basic human goals, his half-hearted, tortuous efforts result in a life both strenuous and impoverished.

Central to Angyal's theory of neurosis is the thesis of the dual organization of personality, or *universal ambiguity*. Every childhood contains both healthy and traumatic features; the child's early attempts to relate himself to the world succeed in part and in part fail. As a result, personality develops around two nuclei and forms two patterns, one of which may be underdeveloped but never absent. Confidence and diffidence, conviction and doubt that life is livable, mark the "great divide," the point at which the human life course acquires its dual organization and its basic existential conflict. Health and neurosis are two dynamic gestalten organizing the same material, each according to its own system principle, and competing for dominance. The person's state depends on which system is dominant: he is healthy when he lives in an atmosphere of realistic confidence and hope; he is neurotic when his thoughts and actions are organized by diffidence and anxiety. Potentially, each personality process has a position within these two patterns and, like a part of an ambiguous visual gestalt, changes its character when a shift occurs in which figure and background change places. Every personal event has a double meaning depending on whether it occurs within the framework of health or of neurosis; hence universal ambiguity.

The conception of personality as a dualistic organization led Angyal to review and reformulate many major principles of dynamics and therapy. Defense mechanisms, for example, he viewed as organizational devices serving either health or neurosis; each system uses them to complete and maintain itself and thereby prevents the alter system from gaining dominance. Thus, both the neurotic and the healthy trends can be repressed by the opposite organization. Therapy aims at reinstating to dominance the latent system of health, thus reversing an earlier shift from health to neurosis, but the self-perpetuating neurotic pattern is not easily overcome. Angyal advocated the use of holistic interpretations that uncover the patient's persisting broad attitudes, but he emphatically stated that neurosis is not overcome by mere insight. If the patient is to take a chance on a new unfamiliar way of life, he must have experienced in a vital way, even to the point of despair, the destructive effects of his neurotic attitudes; he must also have obtained at least a glimpse of his "real self," i.e., his individual pattern of health. Successful therapy requires a careful unearthing and fostering of this repressed healthy pattern; this reconstructive aspect of therapy is too often neglected.

Angyal supplemented his general theory of neurosis with an elaboration of its main dimensions, or patterns. Of particular interest to social scientists is his conception of the hysterical pattern as based on a near-suicidal obliteration of the person's genuine self and the substitution of an artificial personality fashioned largely from the reactions of others. This method of "vicarious living" results in emptiness and, at its extreme, in feelings of nonexistence; some patients struggle against this state by fighting the agents of external suppression. Angyal believed this condition to be the "neurosis of our time"; he felt that the hysterical pattern, in both its conformist and its rebellious variants, was much better understood and more effectively treated than the obsessive–compulsive type of character neurosis. The latter he viewed as originating in inconsistent treatment of the child; this results in lasting confusion and in ambivalence toward the "good–bad" world. A careful analysis of the paradoxical inner maneuvers of persons who develop the life-style of "noncommitment" shows that these behavior patterns and symptoms express both the patient's abiding confusion and his persistent, if ineffective, search for clarity and for an unambiguous emotional orientation.

As a European, Angyal shared in the phenomenological tradition, and some of his thinking on the nature of man, on illness and health, resembles the views of existential writers. He was also keenly interested in the perspectives on human existence revealed by various religions. Yet his concepts and his methods were firmly anchored in the empirical scientific tradition.

EUGENIA HANFMANN

[*For the context of Angyal's work, see* GESTALT THEORY; PHENOMENOLOGY; PSYCHOLOGY, *article on* EXISTENTIAL PSYCHOLOGY; *and the biographies of* KOFFKA; KÖHLER; STERN; WERTHEIMER.]

WORKS BY ANGYAL

1930   Über die Raumlage vorgestellter Örter. *Archiv für die gesamte Psychologie* 78:47–94.

1936   The Experience of the Body-self in Schizophrenia. *Archives of Neurology and Psychiatry* 35:1029–2053.

1941   *Foundations for a Science of Personality.* New York: The Commonwealth Fund.

1965   *Neurosis and Treatment: A Holistic Theory.* New York: Wiley. → Published posthumously.

ANIMAL BEHAVIOR

See COMMUNICATION, ANIMAL; ETHOLOGY; IMPRINTING; LEARNING; PSYCHOLOGY, *article on* COMPARATIVE PSYCHOLOGY; SEXUAL BEHAVIOR, *article on* ANIMAL SEXUAL BEHAVIOR; SOCIAL BEHAVIOR, ANIMAL.

ANOMIE

See CONFLICT; DEVIANT BEHAVIOR; IDEOLOGY; INTEGRATION; NORMS. *See also* DURKHEIM.

ANTHROPOLOGY

The six articles under this heading describe the fields of cultural, social, and applied anthropology. Other subdisciplines can be found under ARCHEOLOGY; LINGUISTICS; *and* PHYSICAL ANTHROPOLOGY. *Related entries are* ECONOMIC ANTHROPOLOGY; ETHNOGRAPHY; ETHNOLOGY; FOLKLORE; LINGUISTICS; *and* POLITICAL ANTHROPOLOGY. *The history of the major concepts of anthropology may be found under* CULTURE; ECOLOGY; EVOLUTION; KINSHIP; RACE; *and* SOCIAL STRUCTURE.

I
THE FIELD

Anthropology, in consonance with the etymology of its name, "study of man," is the most comprehensive of the academic disciplines dealing with mankind. This comprehensiveness is displayed in its concern with the full geographical and chronological sweep of human societies, the breadth of its topical interest, which embraces such diverse areas as language, social structure, aesthetic expression, and belief systems, and in the fact that it alone among the sciences of man treats him both in his physical and sociocultural aspects. In addition to these fundamental biological and social scientific components, anthropology has a significant humanistic aspect, as shown, for example, in its empathetic search for the bases of aesthetic valuation in the arts of alien people.

Although anthropology is thus in principle all-inclusive, it is in fact but one of a number of disciplines that study man. Indeed, the very richness and variety of its interests lead inevitably to fragmentation into a number of semiautonomous subdisciplines, practically all of which, moreover, must share their subject matter with some other well-established and independent field of study. Thus anthropology may easily appear to be a study whose definitional and programmatic claims of vast scope mask a factually disjunctive accumulation of relicts.

This apparent contradiction can be at least partially resolved; in terms of problems and methodology there are certain basic themes that provide a focus of distinctive interests and mark off anthropology from other disciplines. Even where it overlaps some other field of study in subject matter, it tends to approach the specific data somewhat differently and in terms of problems posed within the general frame of anthropological theory. One particular set of interconnected problems may be singled out as historically the core of anthropological interest—namely, the description and explanation of similarities and differences among human ethnic groups. This has been a central problem only in anthropology and thus serves to distinguish it from the other social sciences. Moreover, in the history of the subject it has not so much been superseded by other problems as subject to successive restatement in ever broader terms.

Since ethnic groups differ both in physical type and in sociocultural characteristics, anthropology has been concerned with both in its physical and sociocultural branches respectively. To explore the full range of human diversity it becomes of great importance to take into consideration precisely those societies whose isolation from the well-documented historical traditions guarantees the maximum divergence from those institutions with which we are most familiar. Further, their pre-

sumed isolation from each other ensures that these societies provide the maximum number of historically independent examples of the many types of human societal organization. Although in principle anthropology has always had an equal interest in societies of all types, in practice it has involved a concentration on primitive, or preliterate, peoples, most frequently defined as those that did not have writing at the time of first contact with the West. Many of the characteristics of cultural anthropological methodology and theory have resulted from this preoccupation. The basic descriptive technique is field study by observation and participation and verbal interview of relatively small groups typically organized on a tribal basis. The emphasis tends to become qualitative rather than quantitative. The ethnographer seeks to construct a coherent over-all picture of the institutions of the people being studied by a complex and not explicitly verbalized procedure of inference from the raw data of observation.

In analogous fashion, in order to recover the basic facts concerning past societies in regions and for periods in which the written records that constitute the basic materials of conventional historians are lacking, the skills of archeology are combined with other inferential methods, such as the use of oral traditions, ethnological trait distributions, and comparative linguistics.

The distinction between physical anthropology and allied biological sciences can also be understood in terms of this interest in human ethnic diversity. What is common physically to all human beings has been the concern of human biology as a specialized branch of general biology, while the traditional task of physical anthropology has been the description and explanation of human physical variation. In its historical dimension this connotes an interest in the reconstruction of past human forms from fossil evidence (human paleontology), just as archeology seeks to discover the facts regarding the cultures of the past.

Not only subject matter and methodology but the broader characteristics of anthropological theorizing can be largely understood in terms of this central problem. Thus the basic method of anthropology has been the comparative method, and such basic approaches as cultural evolutionism and environmentalism were attempts to account for cultural similarities and differences by some single variable.

An important shift in anthropological interests may be detected in the more recent period, the beginnings of which may be roughly dated to the third decade of the twentieth century. Attention turned to the internal organization of each culture, and while this interest was to a great extent a particularistic attempt to discover the peculiar "genius" of each culture, the comparative framework was not completely abandoned. It eventually became integrated in a broader framework, which tended to be taken for granted by anthropologists: features common to all cultures were investigated in order to throw into relief the basic over-all characteristics that may be presumed to make up common human nature. Problems of this order can be exemplified by a theoretical assumption that in all societies individuals become socialized in conformity with prevailing norms and that public order is maintained. The investigation of such assumptions regarding the internal functioning of societies was instrumental in the development of an interest in the relation between personality and culture, a field which previously was virtually unexplored.

To the extent that such questions had long been a focus of theoretical interest in sociology and psychology, this broadening of traditional anthropological interests involved the utilization of theoretical concepts developed in these other disciplines and interdisciplinary collaboration on a far wider scale than heretofore.

Even more recently, a contributing factor to this interdisciplinary emphasis has been the extension of anthropological interests, largely in connection with applied problems, to urban situations and literate societies. As a result, anthropology both in certain areas of object matter (e.g., community studies) and theory (e.g., functional theory) has become virtually indistinguishable from sociology. The persistence, however, of such traditional interests as prehistoric archeology, the study of unwritten languages, and the ethnographic description of tribal societies has ensured the continued existence and uniqueness of anthropology.

Subdivisions and interrelation of disciplines

In traditional American practice anthropology is often divided into four basic subdivisions—physical anthropology, cultural anthropology, archeology, and linguistics. Social anthropology is commonly added to these as a distinct branch under the influence of the social functionalism of Radcliffe-Brown and his followers, who draw a sharp line between a science of social structure and function (social anthropology) and a descriptive, historically oriented study of culture (ethnology, or cultural anthropology). In either form this division has, in certain respects, more of a practical than a theoretical basis and is oriented toward the

problems of training students in graduate doctoral programs. Thus, language is part of the culture of a people, and therefore its study is logically a subdivision of cultural anthropology. Archeology seeks to recreate as far as possible the culture of former peoples from the evidence of their material remains and to reconstruct the historical interrelationship of such cultures, so that it also may be considered an aspect of cultural anthropology. However, both linguistics and archeology require considerable training in highly specialized techniques; this is the fundamental reason in practice for their separation from other aspects of cultural and social anthropology. The separation of cultural and social anthropology is rather that of two different approaches to what is basically the same objective phenomenon of group behavior. Indeed, the distinction falls away for those who would not accept as theoretical doctrine the separation of social structure and culture as distinct fields of study.

From these considerations it follows that the truly fundamental division within anthropology as practiced in the United States is between the physical study of man (physical anthropology) and the sociocultural study of man (the remaining branches). The basic nature of this division is reflected in the fact that outside of the United States the term "anthropology" or its translational equivalents (e.g., German *Anthropologie*) corresponds to American "physical anthropology," while "ethnology" designates the sociocultural study of mankind. The significance of this division, along with a recognition of a special relationship between the two is reflected in the organization of the periodic international congress called the International Congress of Anthropological and Ethnological Sciences.

The fact that man is the only species that has developed culture introduces new factors of great significance from the purely biological point of view. In most general terms, the key adaptive mechanism of man as a species is culture itself. This has many practical consequences for the physical anthropologist. For example, mating in a human population takes place within a socially determined matrix. Such considerations render fruitful the integral association of the physical and sociocultural branches of anthropology.

More circumscribed bases of specialization either crosscut or subdivide the fundamental divisions just enumerated and bring into relief the complexity of the relationships between anthropology and a variety of other disciplines or fields of specialization. These are of two main types, areal and topical.

For example, the average anthropologist, while almost always a specialist in one of the major branches, tends to be restricted in his actual work to a specific world area. Thus an archeologist will normally have a predominant interest in some particular major geographical area, e.g., North America, and often within this area will have a regional specialty, such as the American southwest. Such specialization segments anthropology in the geographical dimension but tends to bring together the basic fields in terms of a common areal interest. Thus our hypothetical southwestern archeologist will feel the need to have at least an elementary control of the basic facts regarding the ethnographic and linguistic distributions of his area in order to interpret his own results. In certain cases this will lead to consultative discussion with his colleagues in these other branches or even to full-fledged collaborative research.

Anthropology is in principle concerned with all world areas, just as it is concerned with all types of society—primitive, literate, or industrialized. But here again in practice anthropology in all its branches has tended to concentrate its interest in areas such as Oceania or aboriginal America, where the societies have been exclusively or at least predominantly preliterate. However, anthropologists have come to realize more and more that societies of all types must be considered within the scope of the discipline's possible generalizations and that it is as dangerous to omit industrialized societies and the literate civilizations of the Near or Far East as it is to disregard preliterates. In extending its interest to geographical areas that include literate civilizations with extensively documented histories, anthropology necessarily treads on ground already occupied by traditional area-oriented specializations, e.g., Indology, Sinology, and Near Eastern studies. The approach of the expert in these latter fields is likely to differ from that of the anthropologist by its philological, humanistic, historical, and particularizing emphases. The cultural or social anthropologist is typically synchronic in his interest, thinks in terms of general social–theoretical problems, and is likely to study communities at the local level, since such objects of study as villages are the most closely adapted to the methods developed in the study of tribal society. There is thus room for both types of specialists. Moreover, increasingly each has incorporated interests and techniques from the other so that the differences have tended to become minimized.

The same basic criterion of writing forms the main line of demarcation between the anthropological archeologist, who concentrates on prehistory, and the classical and Near Eastern archeologist, who is concerned with literate cultures. Likewise, the anthropological linguist specializes in the study of hitherto unwritten languages. This carries with it an interest in linguistic field method and synchronic description and a lack of involvement with traditional philological techniques of textual analysis.

The other major basis for specialization within social and cultural anthropology is topical. Most anthropologists tend to confine their interests very largely to such specific aspects of culture as economic life, politics, religion, or music. Here once again anthropology encounters well-established disciplines, such as economics, political science, and musicology. All of these in practice, however, pay most attention to their object of study in the Western tradition and treat the relatively neglected branches of their subject which have to do with non-Western cultures under such rubrics as comparative politics or comparative economics. Anthropology, in turn, in spite of claims to universal interests, tends to focus its attention on non-Western, particularly preliterate, societies.

Anthropology also differs from the standard disciplines in another respect. It studies not only the comparable phenomenon in non-Western cultural settings but also the corresponding cognitive and valuational aspects of the culture with regard to the subject matter. This latter class of studies may well involve topics outside of the social sciences. For example, the anthropological specialty known as ethnobotany investigates the botanical knowledge of indigenous peoples. Applied interests supply a strong point of articulation for these two aspects. Thus, the medical anthropologist involved in medical action programs considers the varying incidence of diseases in specific ethnic groups as the result of biological and social factors but also studies native theories of diagnosis and treatment, since they constitute the cultural setting into which the new methods are to be introduced.

Another type of division particularly prominent in social and cultural anthropology is that between ethnography, the gathering and organization of observational data from the field, and ethnology, the theoretical subdiscipline that utilizes such information as its basic data. Analogous divisions exist in the other major branches of the subject, e.g., descriptive as against theoretical linguistics. Such divisions are not comparable to those described earlier, since virtually every individual scientist has both descriptive and theoretical interests that interact. However, there are individual predilections for one or the other aspect.

Finally, anthropology may be divided into theoretical and applied branches. Anthropologists have always maintained that a basic motive for the scientific study of man is the greater understanding and control it gives us of ourselves and of our society. On the other hand, unlike its sister science sociology, it has not been involved on the theoretical level in problems of societal reform. Yet an interest in the welfare of the people it studies has also been a part of the anthropological tradition. Further, in Western nations with colonial possessions, a form of applied anthropology was developed but was practiced for the most part by administrators with anthropological training rather than by professional anthropologists as such.

After World War II there developed a far deeper involvement in the form of schemes of local and national development, particularly in newly independent countries and often involving the collaboration of Western powers or international agencies. Such activities to a certain extent modified the exclusively observational method of anthropology in the direction of experimental methodology, though under the necessarily limiting conditions of policies not usually formulated by anthropologists.

History

Anthropology in its modern form is a product of the nineteenth century. Such organizational landmarks as the founding of the first anthropological society and the first academic chair in the subject date from this period, but its historical roots are, of course, much deeper. In its specifically nineteenth-century form it is dominated by the idea of the regular and progressive development of human society from a precultural state in which man did not differ essentially from other animals. This doctrine of cultural evolution received a great impetus from the scientific success of Darwinism, dating from the appearance of the *Origin of Species,* but it is clear that the basic components of nineteenth-century anthropology developed at a substantially earlier date and in essential independence of biological theory. Among these fundamental ideas are the notion of the possibility of applying the scientific method to the study of man; the abstract conception of culture—or the totality of socially acquired habits distinct from physical inheritance—as itself a possible object of scientific inquiry; and the notion of culture as undergoing cumulative and progressive change over a long time span.

As in other fields of endeavor, the first substantial contributions were made by the Greeks, but the classical heritage in anthropology is not to be compared to that in such fields as history and political science. The ancients developed a model of ethnographic description as the local setting for historical narrative. Geographical works also included facts and observations concerning physical anthropology and local customs. These figured in a general but rather vaguely developed theory concerning the influence of climate on culture and biological types, which foreshadowed the geographical determinism of the modern period. The ethnographic observation of cultural differences raised the question of the naturalness versus the conventionality of human custom and the existence of universally valid legal and moral regulations, a peculiarly anthropological philosophical problem. Finally, various theories regarding the over-all development of human culture were discussed, such as the traditional religious doctrine of a former golden age, the cyclical theories of the Stoics, and the progressive development of man's heritage by his own efforts as a corollary to the Democritean atomic theory, particularly as set forth in the famous poem of Lucretius, *On the Nature of Things.* This latter doctrine may be considered a distant precursor of cultural evolution, and it is of interest to discern here the same fundamental opposition between a theological theory of degeneration and a scientifically oriented belief in progressive development, which reasserted itself in the nineteenth century.

The next significant developments date from the period of Renaissance humanism and the geographical explorations of the fifteenth and sixteenth centuries. These contributed in new and important ways to the intellectual climate in which modern anthropology was ultimately to develop. The Renaissance struck a modern note of secularism with the notion that man's earthly career was of interest for its own sake and not merely as a preparation for an eternal hereafter. The attempt of humanists to recreate the world of Greece and Rome through the study of original documents rather than through inherited medieval spectacles gave them a kind of anthropological overview of cultural differences. The voyages of exploration broadened spatial perspectives even as humanism widened the chronological one. Whole continents of peoples unknown to the ancient world were revealed. This not only produced an accumulation of facts on a new scale but also raised theoretical questions of great import. Were the novel populations revealed by exploration of the same species as Western man and therefore the possessors of souls worth saving? That they were was the orthodox answer but one difficult to justify from the genealogical tables of Genesis. The theory explaining the existence of the American Indians as remnants of the ten lost tribes provided a welcome refuge, but other bolder spirits speculated on the possibility of other populations not descended from Adam (the pre-Adamites). So arose the rival theories of monogenetic and polygenetic human origins, theories in continued conflict for several centuries thereafter. Further, were the non-Western peoples who were at a simple stage of technological development representative of the state of nature posited by various theorists as prior to the contractual origin of political and legal institutions? Did they represent, perhaps, something like what our own ancestors were like before the rise of literate civilization? This latter view was eventually to gain considerable currency and provide an essential component in a theory of progressive development.

But before the idea of progressive development could gain ground the prevailing notion of the superiority of the classical world over the modern had to be overcome. This was accomplished in the course of the seventeenth century. In the great achievements of the physical sciences, which culminated in the Newtonian synthesis, the modern world clearly exhibited, at least in one respect, a superiority over the ancients. Under the apparent triviality of the "battle of the ancients and the moderns," satirized by Swift in his *Battle of the Books*, lies a serious point. Bernard Fontenelle, in his *Digression sur les anciens et les modernes*, distinguishes between noncumulative aspects of culture, such as literature, and cumulative aspects, such as science. In the latter, modern man is superior. Indeed mankind, in a favorite figure, is compared to an individual developing through the ages and now in his prime. But, according to Fontenelle, this man will have no old age, and infinite perfectibility is possible.

Newtonianism makes yet another contribution. In a universe ruled by law in its physical aspect, man cannot be an exception. It remains then to follow the path blazed by Newton; and indeed, literal application of such concepts as gravitational attraction were not lacking in the eighteenth century and after.

To depict a complete course of progressive development, all that was needful was to consider contemporary savages as representative of a stage preceding that of the ancient East and the classical world. This step was taken by Turgot in his "Plan de deux discours sur l'histoire universelle" (1844), a work that states for the first time the concept of three successive economic stages—hunting, pastoral, and agricultural—as well as the basic form of Comte's later law of the three stages of conceptual development—the theological, the metaphysical, and the scientific.

Another noteworthy work of the eighteenth century is Christoph Meiners' *Grundriss der Geschichte der Menschheit*, in which, quite in the spirit of modern cultural anthropology, he proposes a new science, which will take as its subject matter the customs of all peoples and will pay particular attention to the study of nonliterate peoples.

But certain methodological and intellectual advances that occurred only in the late eighteenth and the early nineteenth centuries were indispensable for the founding of a science embodying the already developed philosophical views and general programs. From this period date the first systematic racial classifications, those of Linnaeus and Johann Blumenbach, and the initiation of techniques of anthropometric measurements by Pieter Camper. It was also during this period that modern linguistics came into existence. The basic notion that dominated linguistics in the nineteenth century was that languages could be classified into families and that languages in the same family were divergent developments over time from an earlier single language. This idea had already been expressed quite clearly by a number of writers in the late eighteenth century, but by the efforts of Franz Bopp, Rasmus C. Rask, Jakob Grimm, and others in the first half of the nineteenth century it developed systematic methods of comparison to reconstruct the ancestral language. The important recognition of the regularity of sound correspondences in related languages was first pointed out by Rask; it was popularized by Grimm in 1822 and helped to establish the general idea of regularities in human cultural change.

During this period there were also notable discoveries that radically extended the time perspective regarding human development and thus added an essential note of plausibility to the concept of gradual cultural advance. The decipherment of Egyptian writing by Jean-François Champollion in 1821 and, even more dramatically, the description of the basic archeological ages of stone and metal (e.g., by V. Thomsen in 1819) drastically altered traditional ideas regarding the age of man. But it was not until 1859 that the eminent geologist Charles Lyell recognized the validity of Boucher de Perthes' discovery of human implements of the Old Stone Age contemporaneous with extinct mammals. Thus archeology and Darwinism combined to present a picture of man firmly anchored among other animal species of the past, developing from a cultureless anthropoid over more than a million years of the Pleistocene.

It was during the first half of the nineteenth century that anthropology began to emerge as a distinct discipline. In England, France, and Germany anthropological or ethnological societies were founded. In Germany *Kultur* became a technical term with practically its modern connotation, and it was taken over into English by E. B. Tylor in his classic work *Primitive Culture,* published in 1871. In its detailed overview of human cultural evolution in one major aspect (religion) and its clear statement of the theoretical perspectives of a science of culture, Tylor's book is a true landmark. [*See* TYLOR.]

Tylor's work is representative of the anthropological approach that was dominant in the English-speaking world in the latter part of the nineteenth century, that of cultural evolutionism. The basic procedure, nowhere explicitly described, was known as the comparative method. Cultural evolution took place, in any domain, in a series of stages, the earlier ones being documented through ethnographic data, the later through historical data leading up to European institutions of the nineteenth century. The earliest stage was often hypothetically deduced, as in the case of those who proposed that primitive promiscuity was the earliest form of marital institution. A prominent role was played by the methodological device of *survivals,* that is, the persistence of institutions in a later stage which gave some evidence of their origin at an earlier stage. Thus L. H. Morgan deduced that because in Hawaii the kinship term glossed as "father" was used for father's brother and mother's brother as well as for father, at a former stage all of these men were potential fathers of an individual [*see* MORGAN, LEWIS HENRY]. Another basic assumption was that of the psychic unity of mankind. The basic similarity of human nature explained the fact that even peoples geographically distant might agree in details of custom that were symptomatic of a particular stage of development. The tendency, therefore, particularly in later members of the school, was to interpret cultural similarities in terms of independent parallel development rather than through the historical process of diffusion.

In Germany during this period the leading anthropological figure was Adolf Bastian. In his doctrine there was little notice of "stages" as actual chronological periods and no systematic employment of the comparative method. The key concept of *Elementargedanke* played a role similar to that of psychic unity. The work of Bastian's lead-ing disciple, Richard Andree, consisted in the documenting of such cultural parallels. [*See* BASTIAN.]

Beginning in the 1880s powerful reactions against these ruling tendencies began to appear, and by 1910 they were largely dominant. Both in the German and English-speaking worlds the comparative method was called into question as deductive, question-begging, and leading to conflicting results. In place of the schematism of stages illustrated by customs from diverse parts of the world, the emphasis was on the reconstruction of a presumably more realistic culture history in which different areas had undergone different developments and in which the historical processes of diffusion and migration were called upon to explain cultural similarities. In Germany and Austria a systematic methodology was developed, that of the culture-historical school (*Kulturkreislehre*) under the leadership of Fritz Graebner and later of Wilhelm Schmidt [*see* GRAEBNER; SCHMIDT]. By application of criteria of similarity in culture traits it was believed that there could be constructed a number of distinct original cultures that succeeded one another in time of origin and that spread by migration all over the world. During this period of the first two or three decades of the twentieth century even more extreme theories of single cultural origins arose and had a certain vogue, as for example, pan-Egyptianism and pan-Babylonianism.

In the United States as well, under the influence of Franz Boas, the virtual founder of American academic anthropology, a critical reaction to cultural evolutionism was the dominant theme [*see* BOAS]. The emphasis was also on the reconstruction of cultural history but on a much more limited scale. Originally intended as a means of classifying cultures for descriptive purposes, the culture area was soon used as a device for historical reconstruction. Cultural similarities involving restricted and continuous distribution were interpreted in terms of diffusion. In this way histories of certain specific cultural complexes in circumscribed areas were reconstructed, often tending to show that, contrary to evolutionary doctrine, institutions had developed in different chronological orders in different areas. Methodologically, Boas' own approach was still more drastic, in that he raised fundamental questions regarding the validity of assumptions concerning the equatability of traits in different cultures. Thus under his stimulus, Alexander Goldenweiser sought to show that the label "totemism" had been applied to diverse phenomena, among which it was unlikely that there was either a real psychological or historical connection [*see* GOLDENWEISER].

Such investigations as Goldenweiser's involved an analysis of the particular phenomena in each culture and as a part of that culture. In diffusion studies the questions that began to be asked were not so much where and when a particular culture trait had spread, but why it was accepted by one people and rejected by another and how it was reinterpreted and integrated into the borrowing culture. Such studies inevitably raised questions of the internal organizing principles of each culture. One type of answer receives its classic exposition in Ruth Benedict's *Patterns of Culture*, in which the integrative factor is described in psychological terminology [*see* BENEDICT]. This line of interest led to the development of the interrelation between personality and culture as a field of study.

These general tendencies were reinforced during this same period of the 1920s and 1930s by the rise of functionalism. The leading exponents of this point of view, Malinowski and Radcliffe-Brown, agreed in emphasizing the importance of functional interrelationship among cultural traits and in disparaging the historical types of explanation of cultural phenomena that had characterized all previous schools. The functionalism of Malinowski views culture as consisting of organized institutions related functionally to the biological and derived needs of human beings. That of Radcliffe-Brown and his followers, which derives ultimately from the writings of the great French sociologist Émile Durkheim, has been called structural functionalism. It interprets function as contributing to the survival of the existing social structure and eschews psychological explanation of social facts. Also in contrast to Malinowskian functionalism, it has an important place for the application of the comparative method, because it contends that laws can be discovered by comparisons of structure. [*See* DURKHEIM; MALINOWSKI; RADCLIFFE-BROWN.]

Current trends

The years following World War II have witnessed, along with an almost explosive material expansion of anthropology, a diversity of new interests, though for the most part these no longer express themselves in over-all systems of the kind that characterized the "schools" of the past. In fact, most anthropologists are eclectic in terms of the traditional doctrines. Moreover, partly through the influence of sociology, there is a much more sophisticated interest in the philosophy of science. This is evident in an emphasis on the methodology of theory construction that has replaced the earlier characteristically informal and semi-intuitive approach of anthropologists.

A number of developments may be noted in the period following World War II. Most basic has been the extension of anthropological interests into areas with nontribal societies and to newly urban or otherwise Western-acculturated groups in non-Western societies. One characteristic form this has taken is in the expansion of community studies. This extension has been strongly interdisciplinary and in close connection with applied interests. In moving outside the confines of tribal societies, anthropologists have not avoided consideration of larger units such as national states. Thus the notion of *basic personality,* which was a central concept in earlier culture and personality studies, was taken over in the form of national character in the studies of Margaret Mead and her associates. [*See* CULTURE AND PERSONALITY; NATIONAL CHARACTER.]

Another trend has been the revival of interest in cultural evolution, chiefly under the stimulus of Leslie White. Emphasis was placed on those aspects of culture that were in fact cumulative, e.g., technological control of environment, and on the compatibility of historically known facts of the diffusion of custom with such over-all technological advance. [*See* EVOLUTION, *article on* CULTURAL EVOLUTION.]

Another interest has been social or cultural ecology. Older oversimplified forms of environmental determinism had generally been superseded by more realistic doctrines of possibilism. The aim was now, following the lead of the plant and animal ecologists, to examine in detail the interrelations of man and his physical environment and the mutual adjustments of sociocultural institutions within an over-all environmental situation. [*See* ECOLOGY, *article on* CULTURAL ECOLOGY.]

In the work of Julian Steward cultural ecological analysis leads to a typology of societies in terms of levels of sociocultural integration, ultimately based on levels of ecological adjustment to environment. This involves an interest in parallel, or so-called multilinear, evolution in the form of historically independent cases of like sequences of development from lower to higher levels of integration.

The method of making cross-cultural comparisons in order to discover lawlike associations of cultural phenomena, frequently of a statistical sort, was initiated by Tylor in his classic paper of 1889, "On a Method of Investigating the Development of Institutions, Applied to Laws of Marriage and Descent." This method has been greatly extended and systematized in the postwar period through the Human Relations Area Files at Yale University.

G. P. Murdock uses such data in his *Social Structure* (1949) to enunciate a series of statistical generalizations among variables in kinship and other aspects of social organization. Murdock's approach also involves a dynamic aspect, in that only certain transitions among types of kinship systems are postulated as being at all frequent and causal mechanisms are posited for such changes. Hypotheses of this order are employed in reconstructing the history of social institutions. Another example of a significant application of this methodology is the study by J. W. M. Whiting and I. L. Child, *Child Training and Personality: A Cross-cultural Study* (Whiting & Child 1953), in which various hypotheses in the field of culture and personality studies are tested cross-culturally. Among these hypotheses are some concerning connections between child-rearing practices, personality, and certain cultural institutions, derived from the Freudian-oriented theories of Ralph Linton and Abram Kardiner. [*See* ANTHROPOLOGY; *article on* THE COMPARATIVE METHOD IN ANTHROPOLOGY; ETHNOLOGY; SOCIALIZATION.]

These cross-cultural and other systematic comparative approaches highlight an interest in universal aspects of culture rather than cultural diversity. Given the complexity of human institutions, it is not surprising that little of a specific nature can be stated as true for all cultures. More typically, then, statements of a generalizing sort about human societies involve absolute or statistically based invariance among certain variables. An interest in such relationships in linguistics was pioneered by R. Jakobson. The volume of papers edited by J. H. Greenberg, *Universals of Language* (Conference on Language Universals 1963), gives evidence of the growing interest in the investigation of such cross-linguistic constancies.

Along with the continued flourishing of variant forms of functionalism, there is a strong trend toward structuralism proper, largely owing to the growing influence of Claude Lévi-Strauss. At least partly inspired by structural linguistics, the basic notion is to analyze social institutions in terms of highly abstract structural relationships. This is analogous to structural analysis of sound systems, which are accounted for in terms of opposition and contrast. Also of linguistic inspiration are the semantic analysis of kinship systems initiated in its modern form by Floyd Lounsbury and Ward Goodenough and the analysis of the semantics of folk taxonomy by Harold C. Conklin, Charles Frake, and others. These approaches presumably bring to light underlying factors that figure in the semantic structure and give deeper structural insights into

the systems being investigated. [*See* COMPONENTIAL ANALYSIS.]

In linguistics itself it is evident that a new development of revolutionary proportions occurred in the form of transformational theory, initiated by Chomsky in his book *Syntactic Structures* (1957). The basic idea is the generation of the grammatical sentences of a language by the successive applications of a set of underlying rules. The test of a grammar is not merely the conformity of the sentences generated with the intuition of the native speaker regarding the grammatically acceptable set of sentences but also, through the subset of transformational rules, the explicit relations between whole sets of sentences whose relations are intuitively recognized by native users of the language (e.g., active with corresponding passive). Previous descriptive linguistics is criticized as "taxonomic," in that it operates with an empirically given body (corpus) of linguistic behavior, which it seeks to describe (it is claimed, unsuccessfully) in terms of only operationally defined procedures. The influence of transformational linguistics is already evident in psychology and is likely to have a considerable impact on anthropology also. [*See* COGNITIVE THEORY.]

Trends in archeology and even more in physical anthropology also involve shifts in interest and methodology of very considerable proportions. Although archeology is, and by its very nature must remain, historical, it has not escaped the newer functional and ecological influences. Definition of the chronological succession of cultures characterized only by implement types is radically altered as archeological materials are being used as a source of inference regarding demographic patterns, for the relation of culture to environment, and for the reconstruction of the nonmaterial aspects of culture, as far as this is possible. An attempt is being made to arrive at broader interpretive historical syntheses and even at lawlike regularities of historical process [*see, for example,* URBAN REVOLUTION].

In physical anthropology, the older anthropology sought chiefly to unravel the racial history of mankind in terms of migration and mixture of relatively static types defined by anthropometric traits, ideally supposed to be fixed, nonadaptive, and not subject to major environmental modification, even though the genetic basis of such metrical traits was admittedly unknown. The reconstruction of racial history has become less important than the study of the dynamic processes of change in the genetic composition of populations. Human physical evolution has likewise been reinterpreted through the same mechanisms of genetic change and through a study of anatomical form in relation to physiological functioning in the context of developing human cultural and social organization. A significant broadening of the basis for such investigations is being provided by the burgeoning interest in comparative primatology, with specific attention to the nonhuman analogues of human social organization and communication. [See ETHOLOGY; EVOLUTION; GENETICS; SOCIAL BEHAVIOR, ANIMAL.]

Thus the initial period of system building in anthropology in the nineteenth century was succeeded by a critical epoch in which emphasis lay in the natural history type of observation and in the uniqueness of individual cultures and local historical sequences. The present period, by contrast, is characterized by a richness and diversity of constructive theoretical endeavors and is distinguished by a revival of interest in generalization, both on a synchronic foundation and in reference to diachronic processes of change. The time would seem to be approaching in which some new synthetic type of theory will be required to integrate and unify these diverse theoretical strands.

JOSEPH H. GREENBERG

BIBLIOGRAPHY

BOAS, FRANZ (1887–1936) 1955 *Race, Language and Culture.* New York: Macmillan.

CHOMSKY, NOAM 1957 *Syntactic Structures.* The Hague: Mouton.

CONFERENCE ON LANGUAGE UNIVERSALS, DOBBS FERRY, NEW YORK, *1961* 1963 *Universals of Language: Report of a Conference.* Edited by Joseph H. Greenberg. Cambridge: M.I.T. Press.

INTERNATIONAL SYMPOSIUM ON ANTHROPOLOGY, NEW YORK, *1952* 1953 *Anthropology Today: An Encyclopedic Inventory.* Prepared under the chairmanship of A. L. Kroeber. Univ. of Chicago Press.

KEESING, FELIX M. 1958 *Cultural Anthropology: The Science of Custom.* New York: Holt.

LOWIE, ROBERT H. 1937 *The History of Ethnological Theory.* New York: Farrar & Rinehart.

MURDOCK, GEORGE P. 1949 *Social Structure.* New York: Macmillan. → A paperback edition was published in 1965 by Free Press.

SPENCER, ROBERT F. (editor) 1954 *Method and Perspective in Anthropology.* Minneapolis: Univ. of Minnesota Press.

TURGOT, ANNE ROBERT JACQUES 1844 Plan de deux discours sur l'histoire universelle. Volume 2, pages 626–671 in Anne Robert Jacques Turgot, *Oeuvres de Turgot.* Paris: Guillaumin.

WHITING, JOHN W. M.; and CHILD, IRVIN L. 1953 *Child Training and Personality: A Cross-cultural Study.* New Haven: Yale Univ. Press. → A paperback edition was published in 1962.

YEARBOOK OF ANTHROPOLOGY (1955) 1956 *Current Anthropology: A Supplement to* Anthropology Today. Edited by William L. Thomas, Jr. Univ. of Chicago Press.

II
CULTURAL ANTHROPOLOGY

Cultural anthropology is that main part of anthropology in which human culture is studied. It thus takes in all branches of anthropology except those that are more directly concerned with human biology and with the interplay of biological and cultural factors. Its key concept is that of culture, and in the definition of culture are implied the scope and the principal methods of cultural anthropology.

Culture is all that a man learns to do as a member of his society. It includes all the knowledge, common understandings, and expectations that the people of a group share and that their children learn.

Seen in broadest perspective, culture refers to the main behavioral characteristics of the human species. Culture distinguishes mankind from the rest of the animal world. Only man has language, uses a variety of other symbols, and makes consistent use of tools. Thus, man alone can transmit to his fellows vast quantities of information and accumulated experience. Moreover, all men, of whatever kind and circumstances, have the capacity for using and developing culture. The continuities in biological evolution between mankind and other species have long been recognized, and more recently anthropologists have come to see that culture has been a factor in human biological evolution. There is no doubt that only mankind uses and transmits the capacities we summarize under the concept of culture.

Human culture is actually manifested in a great variety of particular cultures; that is, in the special ways of life of main groups of people. A culture, as contrasted with culture in general, comprises the selective modes of acting, thinking, feeling, and communicating which are used by people of one group and which distinguish their behavior from that of other groups. The participants in each culture not only use characteristic tools, values, ideas, words, but also maintain a distinctive arrangement of the component parts of their culture.

The central task of cultural anthropology, then, is to study the similarities and differences in behavior among human groups, to depict the character of the various cultures and the processes of stability, change, and development that are characteristic to them. Each main group of people has produced a different set of answers to the same questions which all groups must face; these questions are raised not only by the biological structure of men but also by the requirements of being the bearers and users of culture.

Scope and methods

The scope and the methods of cultural anthropology are implied in the definition of generic culture and distinctive cultures. It takes in all of human social behavior from the beginnings of man's career to the great movements of the present time. Cultural anthropologists study all cultures, whether carried on in tribal societies or in complex civilized nations. Every type of behavior is examined, whether rational, nonrational, or irrational. All aspects of a culture are considered, including the technical and economic means of dealing with the natural environment, the ways of relating to other people, the special experiences of religion and art. Not only are the activities within the several aspects studied but the interplay among them is of special interest, as the relation between family structure and economic forces or between religious practices and social groupings. Daily life no less than high achievement, the ordinary villager as well as the elite leaders, are taken within the cultural anthropologist's purview.

Given this scope, the basic methods of cultural anthropology follow. These entail a holistic view, field study, comparative analysis, and a particular kind of molecular–molar theorizing.

The holistic view. This view assumes that one is free to study any kind of human behavior relevant to the problem being examined. Thus, an anthropologist studying economic development in an African locale may find that he must look into the ceremonial cycle and into family relations if he is to depict fully the processes of economic change there. Or, in tracing the development of ancient civilizations, pottery styles as well as settlement patterns, trade routes, and subsistence techniques have to be taken into account. Any one book cannot show all of the culture of even a small and simple society, but through the combined efforts of cultural anthropologists, many cultures have been explored, many parts of particular cultures have been closely examined, and the characteristics of human culture have been outlined.

Field work. Cultural anthropologists typically gather their scientific evidence at first hand by direct observation. If it is evidence on an ancient culture, the data come mainly from excavations carried on by those anthropologists who specialize in the archeological side of the subject. The cultural anthropologists who study the ways of living peoples go to stay among them and learn about their society and culture by participating, interviewing, observing. It is in the first instance an observational rather than experimental method; the data are taken from the context of reality rather than from the more controllable confines of a laboratory. One consequence of such field work is that the cultural anthropologist becomes aware of the inside view of a culture, of how it looks to those who use it, what rewards and problems they see, as well as how that way of life appears to an outside observer. His analysis thus is able to take into account the inner forces as well as external forces and influences. Another consequence of intensive field work is that the anthropologist focuses on patterns of behavior that are meaningful in the culture, rather than on bits of behavior that may be convenient units for measurement. He looks for regular sequences of action and notes how they are changed in various contexts. He observes how patterns are distinguished from one another by the participants as well as in the eyes of the observer. Although a cultural anthropologist may use questionnaires and other techniques to elicit statistical data, his primary interest usually is to ascertain the regularities of behavior and the principal discontinuities among them. After he grasps these configurations he is better able to judge which numerical measurements are likely to be significant and how best to get them.

Comparative method. The comparative perspective is brought into play at every level of analysis. When, for example, a cultural anthropologist studies social organization in a village in India, he finds out how the villagers organize themselves and then compares the various groups of the village in order to ascertain the similarities and differences among them. Since the villagers rank themselves in a hierarchy of caste groups, one comparative task is to see which patterns of conduct are similar in all caste ranks and which differ among them. Armed with an understanding of the similarities as well as of the differences, the fieldworker can compare the organization of the village as a whole with that of other villages of the vicinity. Such comparison again enables him to delineate similarities and differences among villages or types of villages and so to explain some of the past behavior of the villagers and to say something about their probable responses to some future circumstances. Further, a comparison of village organization in the various regions in India may lead to some formulation of general features shared widely in Indian civilization. This, in turn, may permit a cross-cultural comparison of caste stratification in village India with types of social stratification in, say, parts of Japan or the United States. At the widest horizon of analysis these comparisons raise the question of social stratification as a general attribute of human culture and society.

This comparative approach is utilized at all levels of analysis. Thus, if the problem being considered is whether the earliest civilizations rose out of similar conditions of ecology and technology, the several early civilizations are compared to see if any similar conditions prevailed. If so, we may add to our understanding of the grand processes of human development. If no similarities appear, the process of comparison may still suggest useful ideas to be tested in the same comparative manner. To take another example, to understand the transition from more isolated or dependent economies to a modern, industrialized nation-state, we examine the record of national development—including societal and religious as well as economic changes —in a number of developing countries.

Development of concepts. There is, finally, a way of developing generalizations that is characteristic of the work of cultural anthropologists. They tend to begin theorizing from the empirical evidence, to build their concepts from what they see people doing or hear them saying or from the material remains of past cultures which they uncover from the earth. In selecting certain parts of reality for observation, in asking certain kinds of questions of the people and the data, cultural anthropologists, like other scientists, are informed and guided by accumulated theory. But the cultural anthropologist is less likely than are other social scientists to begin with a model or a set of abstract propositions and direct his field work to the testing of the model or the propositions. He is apt to shape his concepts more from the ground up than from the abstract formula down.

Similarly, the theoretical problems selected for analysis are likely to be suggested by the circumstances and problems of the people being studied. The cultural anthropologist does not typically observe people in order to shed light on a concept, but rather he marshals whatever concepts he can in order to understand a people—and people. Hence, when he finds previous concepts inadequate to explain important processes of behavior which he has observed, he tries to generate and test a new concept. In so doing he has the advantage of sharing common human qualities with the subjects of his study. Robert Redfield once wrote, "To be able to find out what it is that a Zuñi Indian is ashamed of, one must first know what it is to be ashamed" (1962–1963, vol. 1, p. 54).

There is a fundamentally humanistic component in much of cultural anthropology. It is not only that the arts of a people are studied, and these at the humblest levels as well as at the pinnacles of aesthetic achievement. It is also, as we have noted, that an anthropologist tries to see a culture from the inside as well as from the outside. As a participant observer, he experiences some part of the life he observes, and his personal experience finds expression in his studies, so that they entail humanistic insight as well as scientific objectivity. Having lived among the people whose culture he analyzes, the anthropologist is likely to depict the strains and conflicts they feel and to discuss the rewards and pleasures for which they strive. In working with his informants, he should ideally have a balanced attitude of both compassion and reserve, of attachment and detachment, of involvement and objectivity. Too great involvement will bias his account; too rigid objectivity may blind him to the realities of the society. Moreover, attachment and insight into other cultures does not mean that the anthropologist totally sheds the values of his own culture. He generally is able to view them in larger and wider perspective and so may be emancipated from the more parochial and intolerant pressures of the moment, but he does not necessarily reject wholesale the values of his own group or even remain indifferent to them. Anthropologists, for example, are as passionately attached to the values of science as they understand them as are any other toilers in the vineyard of science.

In appreciating the inside view of a culture, an anthropologist comes to appreciate the importance of the position of the observer in the analysis of culture and society. He gets different views from persons of different status, and their appraisal of his status may influence their responses; he finds that the same person may alter his view in the passage of time and through change of circumstance. This holds true in some measure for the observers as well as the observed. Yet there is also the constant of objective reality to be discerned within the shifting perspectives. Hence, he grasps that he must be able to change the angle of his vision—now seeing the village as the main unit, now as only one part of a larger social entity. He must describe village life as a stable ongoing system at this moment of time and then analyze the same behavior as continually in process of change, as part of the stream of history. Most important, he must try to reconcile the differing perspectives, so that he may draw from the study of continuous change in time some generalizations that may hold true across time, so that in his analysis of a larger system he may illumine the meaning of its component groups as smaller systems.

Such tasks require generalization at different

levels of analysis. At the more immediate level, an anthropologist studying a particular society abstracts the general form and functions of its activities, for example, in marriage ceremonies, using his observations and participants' accounts. He is aided by the fact that the subjects of his inquiry also generalize—though not necessarily with reliable accuracy—and can give him an already abstracted account by which they guide their behavior. At another level of analysis, he compares the patterns of marriage rites within a civilization to see whether the various versions together reflect some leading ideas and behavior patterns shared widely by the people of that civilization. At still more abstract levels he formulates concepts about the place of such rituals in society and tests these concepts against the widest available range of comparative evidence.

Problems of method. There are disadvantages as well as benefits in following the principles of method. The free-ranging holistic approach avoids arbitrary barriers to inquiry, but it also requires continual resetting of the framework of inquiry. Being unfettered brings on its own trammels. The emphasis on pattern, on the contours of thought and behavior, has made for less precision in measurement and in detailed specification than is now needed to advance anthropological concepts. As Clyde Kluckhohn pointed out, cultural anthropologists have frequently been cavalier about numbers (1959, pp. 259–261). They have not regularly given adequate information about the number and kinds of observations on which their generalizations are based. They have tended to assume more homogeneity in nonliterate cultures than may exist, emphasizing the dominant modalities of behavior and glossing over the variant as well as the deviant expressions.

The gains from field work have entailed certain losses as well. The natural history procedure, in which the observer maps what is there and follows the flow of events as he finds them, may lead more to description than to analysis, more to imparting disparate blocks of information than to constructing coherent and comparable accounts. In using this procedure, one may overlook significant underlying forces because they do not appear as such in a descriptive mapping of the culture. The very attempt to cover many facets of a culture during a stay of a year or so among a people necessarily makes an anthropologist's account of their farming or their music less detailed and perhaps less penetrating than a year's study by an agricultural specialist or a musicologist would yield. Some improvement in this has been brought about by re-peated field trips to the same people by the same anthropologist, through restudies by other observers, and through team research; yet a cultural anthropologist remains more of a jack-of-all-trades and less of a specialist-master of one field of research than are most other social scientists.

In the making of cultural comparisons, there are similar defects that are inherent in the methodological virtues. When the frame of inquiry and of reference differs somewhat from study to study, when profile rather than precise measurement defines pattern, it is not always easy to judge whether two accounts of presumably comparable behavior are really comparable. The inclination to build theoretical concepts from the observed data through successive levels of abstraction entails other difficulties. There is a temptation to leap too quickly from the immediate to the highest level of abstraction. It has been said that anthropologists are the astronomers of the social sciences. This role is complicated by the fact that insofar as they themselves go to far-off places to collect data on the universe of man, they take it upon themselves to be the astronauts as well.

Aware of these difficulties, anthropologists have worked steadily at improving their methods, yet are mindful that any method has cost as well as yield. Thus, the loss of rigor which comes from studying behavior in the context of real experience rather than in the controlled situation of the laboratory is more than made up for, they believe, by the relevance of field observation toward the explanation of significant problems. The results of laboratory research are essential for an understanding of some aspects of human behavior, but laboratory methods, too, have their limitations. Similarly, statistical data are imperative for some types of analysis but are not directly relevant for others. A sample poll of buying preferences can be used to forecast certain limited economic trends with considerable accuracy, but a poll of the same sample on theological matters would hardly be very enlightening about the structure of religious belief and practice in the culture. On such questions it is the pattern of religious allegiance and behavior that is significant; it is the relation of a part of religious practice to other parts and to other institutions that requires examination before one attempts precise measurement of a particular point of belief.

Just as each discipline of the social sciences is both the master and the captive of its prevailing methodology, so the work of cultural anthropologists is in some ways limited as well as advanced by their chief methods. The use of these methods does contribute fruitful results not characteristically provided by the other behavioral sciences, and in that contribution to the common enterprise of understanding human behavior the cultural anthropologist finds the basic justification for his methods.

Results of cultural anthropology

From the several fields of cultural anthropology have come a number of significant results. One simple outcome is that the outlines of most of the principal cultures of the world have been charted. For many of these, it is only a preliminary kind of mapping; there are large societies for which we have only quite meager data and little of that is from the observations of social scientists. Yet the main dimensions of human culture can be discerned. Universal components as different from one another as incest prohibitions and art forms have been noted and the range of variation within each general component has been recognized. Thus, incest taboos in one culture may be applied to only a few relationships, in another they may involve scores of social positions. Art forms may be expressed in a huge variety of media, but what is selected by the people of one culture as a proper vehicle for aesthetic enjoyment, say elaborate skin tattooing, is disdained by or unknown to others.

Even such preliminary mapping of culture, in itself, can have an impact on students. Once it is recognized that each culture is worthy of serious study and that there are many potential variations, then differences from one's own patterns need not be seen, as they often naively are, as threatening one's own values. Even this first step in the use of the concept of culture can convey important meanings. These, in turn, foster further explorations, which then carry a student into realms of knowledge and research opened up by the broad concept of culture and for which the broad concept must be developed in much more specific ways.

That development of anthropological ideas has yielded two main kinds of results: those dealing with cultures seen as systems, that is, as organized, interrelated patterns of activities and of people; and those dealing with the growth of cultures, the regular ways by which culture systems are changed, are adapted, and evolve. Social anthropologists whose main efforts are in the systemic, synchronic mode of analysis have produced studies of such matters as the processes of kinship and marriage, the relation of conflict to solidarity, the interchange between religious and societal activities. Much of this kind of analysis has been based on observations of small-scale, tribal societies of Africa,

Oceania, the Americas. The testing of these findings in complex cultures carried on by millions of people and the consequent refinement of the concepts are promising but difficult challenges for synchronic studies.

One approach to the broadening of analysis is that of cultural ecology, in which the system of a particular culture and society is seen as being in constant interchange with larger systems, both of man and of nature (Steward 1955; Sahlins & Service 1960). Another approach follows the model of linguistic analysis to study the categories of thought used within a culture as expressed, for example, in kin terms, myth, rituals. Comparative studies of a selected aspect in different cultures, as in cross-cultural studies of religion or technology, have long been undertaken to ascertain the constant core of behavior and the potential variations; added to these research pursuits more recently has been the comparative study of values, that is, the effort to state the basic outlook and choices taken by the people of a culture and to compare the syndromes of values among cultures (Kluckhohn 1959).

Studies in psychological anthropology (also called culture–personality studies) are relevant to the analysis of a culture both as a maintained system and as a changing, evolving life-tool. Culture institutions are maintained by people; that maintenance is shaped by the cognitive perceptions and the personality dimensions common to those people. Hence, two societies may maintain the same cultural form, say, of parliamentary democracy yet carry it on with quite different results if each group has differing attitudes toward authority or differing values about egalitarianism. The institutions, in turn, notably those of education, mold the developing personalities of the children. Both kinds of influences operate; both should be taken into account in a full analysis of a culture. Further, culture change comes about through changes in the day-to-day behavior of individuals and groups of individuals. The reasons why people select certain changes and not others are not unconnected with their personality characteristics. And when a major change in one part of a culture is made, as when a people shift to a new level of technology, the reverberations of that change not only touch other aspects of the culture, often giving a new context to kinship or a new emphasis in religion, but are also likely to affect the manner in which personalities typically take shape in that society.

To turn to studies of culture growth, all time spans in the human range are included, from small, limited shifts to a view of all of the human career considered as one course of biological and cultural evolution. When cultural anthropologists began to examine how a particular culture came to be, they were impressed by how little of it had originated within the one society. There has been a constant borrowing of culture elements by one group from another, even among peoples who were bitter enemies and across formidable geographical barriers. This process, called "diffusion," occurred in the earliest eras of culture history and has vastly accelerated in recent times. Yet there are limits and resistances to diffusion. The analysis of the conditions that favor culture transfer and those that impede it is a central problem in the study of culture change. Coupled with this study are questions about the conditions for innovation and creativity within a culture, how inventions arise and how they become accepted.

The rates of culture change are another facet of this inquiry. The findings of archeological anthropology demonstrate that there has been an accelerating pace of change, at least in certain phases of culture. Although the accelerating development of human command of energy can be demonstrated, not all parts of a culture change at the same rate, nor is there clear evidence for cumulative development in such matters as forms of marriage, kinship, or ritual.

In the perspective of human evolution, culture growth began while biological evolution was still going on, before the human organism had evolved to its present state. When the biological precursors of man began to acquire the rudiments of culture, according to recent findings, this capacity advanced their physical evolution in the human direction. Hence, man is the product of culture as well as the producer of it. Culture patterns are best seen not as constraints imposed for the common good but as integral elements of human life and as the means of developing and realizing man's potential.

In certain respects, man's potential has risen successively as new thresholds of culture have been reached, as with the development of the Neolithic inventions, of civilization, of science. Once a society attains such a threshold, many new cultural opportunities become open to its people. Not all societies necessarily cross that threshold at the same period, nor do all exploit the potentialities in the same way, but the attainment of a cultural divide by one people makes it possible for all mankind eventually to share in its consequences. Thus the current press for economic development in new nations can be seen as an episode of contemporary cultural evolution.

The idea of cultural evolution was salient in the nineteenth-century beginnings of cultural anthropology, but it was chiefly propounded as a series of a few stages through which each people had to pass. The validity of these stages was challenged, especially by those who became aware of the importance of diffusion. They demonstrated that not every society had to go through the same developmental stages and, moreover, that the critical features postulated for the respective stages did not hold true when tested against the ethnological evidence. The diffusionists took as their main task the reconstruction of particular culture histories, especially of primitive peoples. Their efforts, in turn, were criticized by those who saw the primary task for anthropology not as that of formulating conjectural history but as depicting the functional interrelations and social rationale within a culture. The pioneering functionalists, in their turn, are now criticized as overdogmatic in their restriction of the focus of inquiry and in their assumption of a close, organic interrelation among all parts of a culture. Each of these trends of thought has made positive contributions, although the proponents of each, in their critiques of their predecessors, now appear to have provided oversimplified refutations of too simple concepts.

Trends

Since World War II there has been a great spurt of activity in almost every part of cultural anthropology. Peoples not much noted by anthropologists before, especially those of complex societies, have been described in intensive studies of particular villages and neighborhoods. Topics little examined anthropologically, such as law or leadership, have been better explored, and our knowledge of such standard anthropological topics as kinship has been deepened.

There has also been development of the basic precepts underlying all parts of cultural anthropology. Eric Wolf (1964) has noted that there is a greater emphasis on constructing systems of general propositions and that there has been a lessening of the fluidity and ambiguity of the more romantic approach. There is also growing interest in the peoples of civilization and the characteristic features of civilization, an interest that was never absent from cultural anthropology but one that had been second to the concentration on small, primitive (i.e., nonliterate) societies. There is a re-emphasis on the constant features of human psyche and society, on the limitations to change at any one time, and on the inevitable requirements of social life. Human potentiality is seen as flexible but not quite as open and unbounded as some cultural anthropologists used to hold. Cultural relativism remains a necessary condition for gathering data; one cannot observe objectively if one's own ethical judgments about the way of life being observed intrude into and color the observations. But the suspension of value judgment is not indefinite; complete moral relativism is not defended. Each person and society has to take some moral stand in order to function.

There is also a freshening challenge to cultural anthropology as a valid, unified field of study. It is a challenge raised previously by the founders of the functionalist approach and not abandoned by some of the social anthropologists who have ably carried forward this approach. The challenge is simply that no one discipline can usefully cover so vast a scope as cultural anthropology claims, that so ambitious a reach inevitably impairs one's grasp of any worthy topic and defeats the kind of intensive investigation essential for scientifically useful results. These challengers do not question the scientific validity of linguistic or archeological or evolutionary studies, but they find no special advantage and considerable disadvantage in trying to maintain closer nexus with these fields than with others in the social sciences. Those who express this doubt find the study of contemporary, small-scale societies, with concentration on social relations, to be ample enough field for research efforts.

Yet, although it is true that the immense scope of cultural anthropology does sometimes impede more intensive studies, cultural anthropologists do not feel at all precluded from doing intensive studies or from utilizing the results of social anthropological work. They believe that there are times and occasions when the narrower range is needed and others when the broad strategy is suitable. They do not want to abandon the broad policy which enables them to shift from one level of analysis to another and from one field of investigation to another. This may prejudice their mastery of a particular subject, but it keeps open their intellectual mobility. It is this mobility—feeling free to ask such questions as whether a cultural process discerned in one era or civilization holds true in another, how the findings from the microscopic examination of a culture fit into macroscopic understanding of culture—that has yielded useful results for cultural anthropology.

DAVID G. MANDELBAUM

[*Directly related are the entries* ARCHEOLOGY; ETHNOGRAPHY; ETHNOLOGY; LINGUISTICS. *Other relevant material may be found in* CULTURE, *article on* CULTUROLOGY; DIFFUSION, *article on* CULTURAL DIFFUSION; ECOLOGY; EVOLUTION, *article on* CULTURAL EVOLUTION; FIELD WORK; OBSERVATION.]

BIBLIOGRAPHY

CLARK, JOHN G. D. (1939) 1957 *Archaeology and Society: Reconstructing the Prehistoric Past.* 3d ed., rev. London: Methuen.

GEERTZ, CLIFFORD 1962 The Growth of Culture and the Evolution of Mind. Pages 713–740 in Jordan M. Scher (editor), *Theories of the Mind.* New York: Free Press.

HEIZER, ROBERT F. 1959 *The Archeologist at Work: A Source Book in Archeological Method and Interpretation.* New York: Harper.

HERSKOVITS, MELVILLE J. 1955 *Cultural Anthropology.* New York: Knopf. → An abridged revision of *Man and His Works,* 1948.

HYMES, DELL H. (editor) 1964 *Language in Culture and Society: A Reader in Linguistics and Anthropology.* New York: Harper.

KLUCKHOHN, CLYDE 1958 The Scientific Study of Value, and Contemporary Civilization. American Philosophical Society, *Proceedings* 102, no. 5:469–476.

KLUCKHOHN, CLYDE 1959 Common Humanity and Diverse Cultures. Pages 245–284 in Daniel Lerner (editor), *The Human Meaning of the Social Sciences.* New York: Meridian.

KROEBER, A. L. (1923) 1948 *Anthropology: Race, Language, Culture, Psychology, Prehistory.* New rev. ed. New York: Harcourt.

KROEBER, A. L. 1952 *The Nature of Culture.* Univ. of Chicago Press.

LEWIS, OSCAR 1961 *The Children of Sanchez: Autobiography of a Mexican Family.* New York: Random House.

LOWIE, ROBERT H. 1937 *The History of Ethnological Theory.* New York: Farrar & Rinehart.

MEAD, MARGARET 1964a *Anthropology: A Human Science; Selected Papers 1939–1960.* Princeton, N.J.: Van Nostrand.

MEAD, MARGARET 1964b *Continuities in Cultural Evolution.* New Haven: Yale Univ. Press.

MURDOCK, GEORGE P. 1949 *Social Structure.* New York: Macmillan.

REDFIELD, ROBERT 1955 *The Little Community: Viewpoints for the Study of a Human Whole.* Univ. of Chicago Press. → A paperback edition, bound together with *Peasant Society and Culture,* was published in 1961 by Cambridge Univ. Press.

REDFIELD, ROBERT 1956 *Peasant Society and Culture: An Anthropological Approach to Civilization.* Univ. of Chicago Press. → A paperback edition, bound together with *The Little Community,* was published in 1961 by Cambridge Univ. Press.

REDFIELD, ROBERT 1962–1963 *Papers.* Edited by Margaret P. Redfield. 2 vols. Univ. of Chicago Press. → Volume 1: *Human Nature and the Study of Society.* Volume 2: *The Social Uses of Social Science.*

SAHLINS, MARSHALL D.; and SERVICE, ELMAN R. (editors) 1960 *Evolution and Culture.* Ann Arbor: Univ. of Michigan Press.

STEWARD, JULIAN H. 1955 *Theory of Culture Change: The Methodology of Multilinear Evolution.* Urbana: Univ. of Illinois Press.

WHITE, LESLIE A. 1959 *The Evolution of Culture: The Development of Civilization to the Fall of Rome.* New York: McGraw-Hill.

WOLF, ERIC R. 1964 *Anthropology.* Englewood Cliffs, N.J.: Prentice-Hall.

III
SOCIAL ANTHROPOLOGY

Social anthropology aims at understanding and explaining the diversity of human behavior by a comparative study of social relationships and processes over as wide a range of societies as possible. The social relationships studied are primarily those that are standardized or institutionalized, that is, in which people are regularly concerned as members of particular social groups or categories. Typically, these institutions are the family, marriage, and kinship; complexes of economic and political organization; social control (including law); morality, ritual, and religion. No "explanation" of social relationships can be final in any social discipline; the findings of social anthropology must be supplemented by other data, for example, demographic and psychological data. But a social anthropologist provides understanding of social relationships in his field by precisely defining and describing behavioral connections. An exotic custom such as a "joking relationship," whereby certain named categories of kin not only may engage in horseplay and other privileged familiarities but also are expected so to behave, is "explained" to a degree, i.e., made more intelligible, when contrasted with customs of "avoidance" that show other categories of kin treated with the greatest respect, even to the point of shunning all contact. These parallel but opposite ways of behaving "make sense" (especially when compared over a range of societies) as methods of symbolic treatment of categories of kin who may stand in different but equally important structural and operational relationships. Polarization of behavior patterns gives a strong delineation to the kinship structure and provides a relatively simple framework for canalization of conflicting interests, thus allowing for more effective performance of social tasks.

The general conceptual apparatus of the social anthropologist and his theoretical approach are broadly similar to those used by his colleagues in other social sciences, especially sociology. (Conventionally, the anthropologist has been concerned with the "primitive," or non-Western, societies.) His method is differentiated to some extent, however, by a more holistic approach. Social anthropology explicitly recognizes that behavior is intrinsic to a relatively systematized pattern of interrelated institutions. This notion of functional interrelatedness, while shared by other social sciences, has been more forcibly presented to the working social anthropologist by his field experience in relatively small-scale societies—in some

of which every member has been personally known to the observer.

History. The comparative study of institutionalized social relations can be traced far back in the history of intellectual exploration. The theoretical content of Herodotus may be overestimated, but Montesquieu, Jens Kraft, Izaak Iselin, and Adam Ferguson are examples of early forceful thinkers about society to whom social anthropologists still turn. An early descriptive ethnographic tradition—exemplified in the work of J. F. Lafitau (1724) on the Huron, Garcilaso de la Vega (b.1539–d.1616) on the Inca, and James Cook (1768–1775) on the peoples of the central and western Pacific—has also contributed to the making of social anthropology. Many of the ideas of social anthropology derived from the theoretical work of H. Maine, J. J. Bachofen, and especially L. H. Morgan. Later, the work of J. F. McLennan and C. N. Starcke on family and kinship, and of E. B. Tylor, W. Robertson Smith, and J. G. Frazer on religion, conceptually and analytically influenced the emerging discipline, and a fundamental contribution came from E. Durkheim and his "school" of followers who write for the journal *L'année sociologique*. Much of the interest lay in the search for evolutionary and historical sequences in human custom, but the converging ethnographic and theoretical influences gave rise to more realistic studies. F. Boas in the United States and A. C. Haddon in Britain initiated systematically planned field expeditions. In the early twentieth century ethnographic studies contributed to our understanding of age-grades and men's associations, kinship and marriage, and primitive law. Missionaries and government officials also added materially to the ethnographic record and drew upon and stimulated the comparative theorists. The book that for the first time drew together much of the material on social anthropology in a systematic, theoretical way was R. H. Lowie's *Primitive Society* (1920). Meanwhile, A. R. Radcliffe-Brown (1922) and B. Malinowski (1922), who had combined extensive field work with a high degree of theoretical training and insight, were beginning to set the conceptual framework for the intensive study of contemporary institutions which, largely under their influence, has come to be known as social anthropology.

Modern social anthropology has passed through several phases, beginning with a major emphasis on functionalism. A noticeable contrast here was between Malinowski's insistence upon the ultimate biological basis of human behavior, radically transmuted though it is by culture, and Radcliffe-

Brown's emphasis upon the comprehension of function as it related to the requirements of society rather than to those of individual members (Radcliffe-Brown 1952). Linked with his emphasis upon social structure was his stress on the concepts of social integration and social equilibrium. The latter assumption has been criticized inasmuch as it tends to negate the social potential for change (Leach 1961). Moreover, Radcliffe-Brown's insistence upon the primacy of institutional factors in controlling individual behavior has seemed like a too rigid structural determinism. Even apart from frontal attacks launched upon such functional and structural assumptions, recent studies in social anthropology have shown more awareness of the methodological problems involved.

Modern interest in models. Modern interest in structure has taken the form of the explicit construction of models. Interest in this development was probably influenced by mathematical practice, for example, in mechanics, and perhaps by contemporary usage among economists. It was demonstrated for kinship studies by E. R. Leach (1954) in a study of Jinghpaw kinship terminology, in which he constructed a hypothetical society organized in accordance with seven structural principles, and then demonstrated that the highly complex Jinghpaw empirical system could be seen as a modification of the formal simplicity of this theoretical scheme. He called this essay an experiment in ethnographic algebra, possibly with the memory of a gibe that Malinowski leveled at Radcliffe-Brown's Australian kinship diagrams. Social anthropologists were especially stimulated, however, by the massive analysis of C. Lévi-Strauss (1949), in particular by his models of restricted and generalized exchange applied to the field of kinship and marriage. Model-building in the developed manner involves a high degree of abstraction and the articulation of a set of abstract propositions for heuristic purposes. The logical inferences proceeding from such a method have been very illuminating, especially in the field of kinship, which lends itself particularly to such treatment. A variation of model treatment, the "theory of games," has been applied with more limited effect by F. Barth (1959) to the political organization of Pathan society. Barth points out that the crucial step in a transformation from real life to a theory-of-games model depends upon the formulation of the rules by which the members of the society govern their actions. This involves highly significant levels of abstraction. In the selection and formulation of elements for manipulation in the model, the specific choices made by the analyst himself are of prime importance for the final interpretation. This method was invented in terms of economic problems that depend upon the operations of only a few "players." When one applies it to social problems, extreme reductionism is required.

Use of the model concept by social anthropologists has covered a wide range (Association of Social Anthropologists 1965a); it has even been applied, with rather dubious accuracy and significance, to the recognition of personal bias in the analyst's choice of material for examination. A feature of modern social anthropology is its self-consciousness. Obviously, personal elements in the situation of the observer are recognized as affecting the collection of his data, including the possibility that he may influence to some degree the behavior of the people whom he is studying. The idiosyncratic role of the analyst in handling this material and his personal involvement with the people may condition the form that he attributes to the society he studies.

Analyses of social process. Side by side with the more precise conceptualization of structural studies there has developed a more definite interest in the analysis of social process. Argument still proceeds as to the degree to which the behavior of members of a society is to be understood in terms of the jural rules of the society or in terms of their individual choice and decision. There is also difference of view as to whether the concept of social structure should be applied primarily to a summation of rules or to a summation of behavior, whether it should refer to ideal or statistical norms. But whichever is the emphasis in definition, in practice both are studied. Studies of social process in kinship and marriage have focused on such problems as the developmental cycle in domestic groups, the operation of prescriptive marriage rules, the stability of marriage, the relations between residence and descent. Variant and changing relations between kin in matrilineal systems have been given much comparative study (Eggan 1950; Schneider & Gough 1961), and the structure of unilineal descent groups has been elaborately examined (Fortes 1953). There has been much concern with the definition of descent groups that recognize membership by optative rather than by definitive criteria (Firth 1957). Whether such units are patrilineal descent groups admitting of many exceptions to the unilineal membership rule or whether they are nonunilineal groups with a patrilineal descent emphasis is still a matter of argument. But until the concept of descent itself is further clarified this issue is unlikely to be solved by field research.

In the field of political organization, many analyses have demonstrated the dynamic social, economic, and ritual relationships involved in the struggle for power and its exercise. There has been an interest in the theory of conflict, which questions the degree to which conflict of a sectional order strengthens the over-all structure (Gluckman 1956). Such conflict theory may owe something to Marxist emphases and perhaps also to psychological views about the cathartic effects of aggression. In sociojuridical analysis, issues of a legal character—including problems connected with suicide and homicide—have been refined, while clarity has emerged from the study of such economic institutions as market processes and allied operations. Other functional analyses of this order have been done in the field of ritual and myth. Interest in relating millenarian movements to economic and political conditions has been helped and stimulated by historians and social scientists in other disciplines.

Undoubtedly, much of the orientation in recent studies of social process has been due to the large-scale, irreversible changes that have occurred in the African, Asian, Oceanic, and American societies, which have been the concern of social anthropologists. But whereas earlier "social change" tended to be isolated as a separate field of study, it is now realized that changing conditions are an integral part of the data field of the anthropologist. There has been a renewal, in more sophisticated form, of claims for the study of history as a legitimate and indeed necessary aspect of the work of the social anthropologist.

The philosophical problems involved in explanations of causality have not been ignored (Nadel 1951). Some social anthropologists, especially in the United States, have not been content with the indication of correlates or concomitant variations in institutional patterns. The search for antecedent conditions to existing phenomena and the posing of questions in the form of *why* as well as *how* institutions exist and work have resulted in increasingly precise formulations. Apart from the indication of historical antecedents from documentary materials and oral tradition, attempts have been made to indicate the significance of ecological factors as conditions for institutional development. Generalizations have usually been cautious, for instance, of the order of suggesting broad correlation between the political system and mode of subsistence (Schapera 1956, p. 219). However, in terms of cultural evolution more dynamic relationships have also been suggested. An example of this is the proposition that the patrilineage of Nuer type is a unit of predatory expansion (Sahlins 1961). Problems of how to handle the historical dimension in the absence of written records have still, however, to be adequately solved, and various assumptions about plausibility of tribal traditions must be tested more fully before being completely acceptable in interpretation.

Studies of symbolic forms. A very important part of the work of social anthropologists in recent years has been in the study of symbolic forms. Particular attention to the need for the study of symbolic behavior was drawn by S. F. Nadel (1951, pp. 261–264). Description and analysis have proceeded particularly within the area of several related major topics. For example, analyses of witchcraft accusations have indicated symbolic correspondences with structural tensions in a given society. This is clearly seen when it appears among affinal kin. Studies of totemism have indicated some of the formal qualities of thought beneath apparently bizarre and inconsequent selection of objects as emblems. The symbolism of myth has been explored, especially by Lévi-Strauss, who by a comparative analysis of the constituent elements in all available versions of a myth, and of their interrelatedness, has gone far to demonstrate significant modes of human thinking (1955). E. R. Leach (1954) has argued that ritual is a form of symbolic, nonverbal behavior equivalent to verbal statements about the structure and values of the society concerned. A. I. Richards (1956) has demonstrated the complexity of the symbolism that may be expressed in girls' initiation rites.

Anthropological studies of "primitive" religious systems are now numerous, and analyses of such actions as sacrifice and of such concepts as god and spirit have contributed much to our understanding of their complexity and sophistication (for example, Evans-Pritchard 1956). The study of religious systems has revealed more clearly than in most other fields the differences of basic philosophical assumptions in the work of social anthropologists. Some have adopted a rationalist or humanist standpoint, regarding the religious concepts and behavior of the people studied as being essentially human constructs, responsive to both general and specific issues of their social and economic existence (Firth 1951). Other anthropologists have proceeded from the standpoint of believers in the separate, absolute character of religious phenomena and have regarded the institutions of the people they have studied as special instances of general truth (Evans-Pritchard 1956).

Method of social anthropology. The hallmark

of a social anthropologist tends to be the pursuit of field investigations of an intensive character. Commonly using the vernacular of the people studied, he combines some participation in affairs of members of the society with the collection of data by inquiry and observation. By none of these criteria can a social anthropologist be separated absolutely from his colleagues in other social sciences, but the combination of them has given him a characteristic "grass roots" approach and a closely personal experience of societies different from his own.

The intensive field methods of the social anthropologist carry with them certain difficulties. The relative shortness of the period of observation has sometimes resulted in a lack of historical sensitivity. Institutions have been described as permanent when they may have been only contingent upon the operation of demographic or ecological factors of relatively brief duration. Perception of trends of change in social forms has been difficult and subject to considerable error. Partly to meet such problems and partly from a wish to repeat experiences of considerable scientific and aesthetic interest, some social anthropologists have returned after a considerable period of years to the societies they formerly studied. A variant procedure has been for a different social anthropologist to make a restudy of a community investigated earlier. This "replication analysis" presents such theoretical issues as the length of time that should be allowed to elapse before the restudy, the criteria that should be used to establish identity and difference over the period, and the relation of these "dual synchronic" studies to a full diachronic analysis. Replication studies have yielded valuable data on the pace of social change and the most sensitive areas of influence.

The necessity of securing rapport has meant an emphasis on personal, intimate contact with members of the society under study. This has made it difficult to ensure the representativeness of the sample of people selected for close inquiry. In societies of tiny population such lack of adequate sampling has probably resulted in minimal distortion. But in societies with a membership of several hundred thousand, such as some African tribes, anthropological study has had to assume homogeneity rather than to prove representativeness, although some efforts at crude sampling have been made. Available evidence does not suggest any great bias, nor would simple methods of random sampling necessarily have yielded more accurate data, given the intricate and sensitive character of much of the material required. Linked with this

problem is that of the use of quantitative data. Ever since W. H. R. Rivers (1910), social anthropologists have freely used a genealogical method of inquiry to obtain data about kinship structure and terminology, marriage patterns, and so on. This has yielded much numerical information. Until recently, social anthropologists were content to express roles and behavior patterns of members of the society in general terms, on the basis of very few instances or indeed without specifying the range of instances at all. Now, in such fields as patterns of household composition and residence, exchange, landholding, and political allegiance, generalizations are commonly supported by figures of distribution. One widely used technique for such a purpose is a sociological census.

Areas of needed research.   To specify areas of most needed research in social anthropology is difficult because of the relative novelty of the study among the social sciences and the need for development in every field. But certain areas seem to need special attention. The rapid cultural—in some cases physical—disappearance of "primitive" peoples demands that energetic efforts be applied to map the social systems of those as yet relatively unexamined. (The UNESCO Committee for Urgent Anthropological Research has been engaged in drawing up regional programs for such study.)

Sophisticated comparative analyses of kinship institutions, patterns of domestic grouping, residence, and landholding are still needed. This field is pre-eminently that of the social anthropologist; no other social scientist has his skills in the study of comparative kinship. In religion a vast body of ethnographic data still awaits more rigorous theoretical analysis. Not only is more intensive study of the religious systems of particular primitive societies required, but also closer contact with philosophers, psychologists, and modern theologians, so that the very difficult and delicate problems of interpretation that arise may be handled more effectively.

In political anthropology, with which is linked the anthropological study of law and social control, solid advance has taken place over the last decades (Association of Social Anthropologists 1965b), especially in studies of the less highly centralized systems. More extensive studies must be made of political and administrative processes as distinct from governmental structures. Collaboration with political scientists is advisable, particularly in the study of the structure and activities of political parties and of relations between central and local government. The rapidity with which traditional political systems are being superseded in favor of or combined with those of more complex societies makes this all the more urgent.

Collaboration is also necessary in economic anthropology. Here the body of general theory, derived largely from the parent discipline of economics, must be applied and interpreted by people trained in empirical field work as well as in the theoretical discipline of social anthropology. The significance of the study of incentives to production, of exchange as a social as well as an economic process, and of the uses of capital and credit in peasant conditions is beginning to be appreciated in the work of economic anthropologists. The results have a practical as well as theoretical relevance in connection with the demands of economists for provision of acceptable generalizations about economic growth.

The modern social sciences, although not necessarily called upon to justify themselves simply by their practical application, have increasingly shown their utility in such directions. Cooperation of anthropologists with public health administrators is particularly promising. Social anthropology has contributed to a broader understanding of many types of social relationships, the nature of family structure and roles, and the significance of kinship in industrial as well as in nonindustrial societies. Its general diagnostic and productive value may be fairly limited, but when applied to the analysis of small communities in any type of society, it has been able to demonstrate and illustrate the need for a more sensitive, more holistic approach to the study of social relations. This does raise a basic problem as to how the microanalysis of the social anthropologist can be translated into macroanalytical terms. In this respect a movement of social anthropology in the direction of the adoption of more adequate statistical procedures as now used by sociologists may be necessary.

RAYMOND FIRTH

BIBLIOGRAPHY

ASSOCIATION OF SOCIAL ANTHROPOLOGISTS 1965a *The Use of Models in Social Anthropology.* Monograph No. 1. London: Tavistock.

ASSOCIATION OF SOCIAL ANTHROPOLOGISTS 1965b *Political Systems and the Distribution of Power.* Monograph No. 2. London: Tavistock.

BARTH, FREDRIK 1959 Segmentary Opposition and the Theory of Games: A Study of Pathan Organization. *Journal of the Royal Anthropological Institute of Great Britain and Ireland* 89:5–21.

COOK, JAMES (1768–1775) 1955–1961 *The Journals of Captain James Cook on His Voyages of Discovery.* 2 vols. Edited by J. C. Beaglehole from the original manuscripts. Hakluyt Society Extra Series, nos. 34 and 35. Cambridge Univ. Press. → Volume 1: *The Voyage of the Endeavor, 1768–1771,* 1955. Volume 2: *The Voyage of the Resolution and Adventure, 1772–1775,* 1961.

EGGAN, FREDERICK R. 1950 *Social Organization of the Western Pueblos.* Univ. of Chicago Press.

EVANS-PRITCHARD, E. E. 1951 *Social Anthropology.* London: Cohen & West; Glencoe, Ill.: Free Press.

EVANS-PRITCHARD, E. E. 1956 *Nuer Religion.* Oxford: Clarendon.

FIRTH, RAYMOND W. 1951 *Elements of Social Organization.* London: Watts. → A paperback edition was published in 1963 by Beacon.

FIRTH, RAYMOND W. 1957 A Note on Descent Groups in Polynesia. *Man* 57:4–8.

FORTES, MEYER 1953 The Structure of Unilineal Descent Groups. *American Anthropologist* New Series 55:17–41.

GLUCKMAN, MAX 1956 *Custom and Conflict in Africa.* Oxford: Blackwell; Glencoe, Ill.: Free Press.

LAFITAU, JOSEPH FRANÇOIS 1724 *Mœurs des sauvages amériquains, comparées aux mœurs des premiers temps.* 2 vols. Paris: Saugrain l'aîné.

LEACH, EDMUND R. 1954 *Political Systems of Highland Burma: A Study of Kachin Social Structure.* A publication of the London School of Economics and Political Science. London: Bell; Cambridge, Mass.: Harvard Univ. Press.

LEACH, EDMUND R. 1961 *Rethinking Anthropology.* London School of Economics and Political Science Monographs on Social Anthropology, No. 22. London: Athlone.

LÉVI-STRAUSS, CLAUDE 1949 *Les structures élémentaires de la parenté.* Paris: Presses Universitaires de France.

LÉVI-STRAUSS, CLAUDE 1955 The Structural Study of Myth. *Journal of American Folklore* 68:428–444. → Also published in French in 1958, with modification and addition, in Claude Lévi-Strauss' *Anthropologie structurale.*

LOWIE, ROBERT H. (1920) 1947 *Primitive Society.* Rev. ed. New York: Liveright. → Also published in a paperback edition.

MALINOWSKI, BRONISLAW (1922) 1960 *Argonauts of the Western Pacific: An Account of Native Enterprise and Adventure in the Archipelagoes of Melanesian New Guinea.* London School Studies in Economics and Political Science, No. 65. London: Routledge; New York: Dutton.

MURDOCK, GEORGE P. 1949 *Social Structure.* New York: Macmillan.

NADEL, SIEGFRIED F. 1951 *The Foundations of Social Anthropology.* London: Cohen & West; Glencoe, Ill.: Free Press.

RADCLIFFE-BROWN, A. R. (1922) 1948 *The Andaman Islanders.* Glencoe, Ill.: Free Press.

RADCLIFFE-BROWN, A. R. 1952 *Structure and Function in Primitive Society.* London: Cohen & West; Glencoe, Ill.: Free Press.

RICHARDS, AUDREY I. 1956 *Chisungu: A Girls' Initiation Ceremony Among the Bemba of Northern Rhodesia.* London: Faber.

RIVERS, W. H. R. 1910 The Genealogical Method of Anthropological Inquiry. *Sociological Review* 3:1–12.

SAHLINS, MARSHALL D. 1961 The Segmentary Lineage: An Organization of Predatory Expansion. *American Anthropologist* New Series 63:322–345.

SCHAPERA, ISAAC 1956 *Government and Politics in Tribal Societies.* London: Watts.

SCHNEIDER, DAVID M.; and GOUGH, E. KATHLEEN (editors) 1961 *Matrilineal Kinship.* Berkeley: Univ. of California Press.

IV
APPLIED ANTHROPOLOGY

The studies that are given the name of applied sciences are concerned with techniques based on the recognition of scientific principles. The best-known examples are engineering, which applies the principles of physics, and medicine, which applies the principles of physiology. The student of engineering learns to apply scientific principles so as to construct works that will stand up against the strains to which they are likely to be exposed; the student of medicine learns to apply scientific principles to the relief of disease in the human body. Each is concerned with the attainment of limited, agreed objectives; and each has his objective chosen for him. The engineer is employed to build a dam or a bridge that somebody else has decided is needed in a particular place; he does not have to ask whether it is desirable, on some scale of values, to create an artificial lake or to link the two sides of a river. The doctor is consulted by a patient who thinks he is ill. The doctor does not—indeed, must not—debate whether it is right or wrong to cure the patient; he must just consider what is the best way.

Social anthropology is concerned with the whole field of social relationships. The analogy between it and engineering would suggest that it should prescribe techniques for constructing societies that would be in some sense desirable; the analogy between it and medicine would suggest that it should provide prescriptions for the cure of pathological states of society. But there is no such consensus in social anthropology as there is in engineering and medicine about what is to be considered desirable or pathological.

Definitions of the field.   Some social anthropologists have sought to establish indexes of community health. It has been suggested that a scientifically relevant concept of the healthy community may be stated in terms of an optimum balance of interrelated factors. In this context whole evolving human beings will be considered as they relate to one another and to an organized community. The community may be viewed as an entity that responds to an effective changing environmental setting (Thompson 1960, p. 773). This is a formula for asking questions, not for answering them.

Moreover, a different point of view, which has as much support, considers any study of change in social institutions as a study in applied anthropology. According to Eliot D. Chapple, "Applied anthropology is regarded as that aspect of anthropology which deals with the description of changes in human relations and in the isolation of the principles that control them" and includes "an examination of those factors which restrict the possibility of change in human organization" (Chapple 1953, p. 819).

The field of applied anthropology has, in practice, been taken to be any context in which it may be useful for people taking community decisions to know something about the population for which they are responsible. In this sense it has been applied to any kind of inquiry into the customs of non-European peoples subject to the rule of Europeans.

The first attempt of British anthropologists to turn their knowledge to practical use came at the close of the South African War of 1899–1902. The Royal Anthropological Institute addressed to the secretary of state for the colonies a proposal that the laws and institutions of the different south African tribes be recorded in order to provide the basis for an enlightened policy of administration. It was believed that this might mitigate the disintegration commonly caused by primitive institutions coming into contact with more advanced civilizations. (Mr. Joseph Chamberlain replied that the officials of the new south African colonies were too busy with "numerous questions of pressing practical importance.")

Anthropology in colonial administration.   During the period between the two world wars the appropriate field for the application of anthropology was thought to be the administration of colonial peoples. Although the different colonial governments held different views about the speed with which the subject populations could be westernized and the degree of westernization that was desirable, they all found it necessary to have some regard for traditional customs regulating social status and interpersonal relations.

After 1926 some study of anthropology was included in the training of administrative officials for the British colonies in tropical Africa. Nigeria and the Gold Coast seconded officials from this service to posts as government anthropologists. Similar posts were created in Papua, the Australian territory in southeastern New Guinea, and in the Anglo-Egyptian Sudan. In Tanganyika a deliberate experiment in applied anthropology was made in which an anthropologist directed his inquiries to answering specific questions formulated by an administrative official; the results were published in *Anthropology in Action* (Brown & Hutt 1935).

Research interests.   In the Northern Territories of the Gold Coast, Meyer Fortes, at the request of the government, produced an account of Tallensi marriage law (1937). We owe to R. S. Rattray, the government anthropologist of the Gold Coast, some valuable volumes on the ethnography of Ashanti and the territories to the north of it (1923; 1932) and to C. K. Meek, who held the corresponding post in Nigeria, studies of the Jukun (1931*a*), the Ibo, and some of the smaller tribes of northern Nigeria (1925; 1931*b*). F. E. Williams published some studies of Papuan peoples, including an account of a "nativistic" movement (1928; 1940). This study did not simply describe native institutions but also sought to explain a disturbance that had caused concern to the authorities and to suggest remedial measures. In this manner it came near to the concept of applied anthropology held today.

With the above exception, the work of these men was confined to describing indigenous institutions, particularly political institutions. It can be called applied anthropology because the researchers were employed by governments whose policy was to preserve native institutions as far as possible. The British governments of Nigeria and the Gold Coast at that time believed that persons holding authority by virtue of their traditional status were the best local agents of government policy and were anxious to know who would be the right person, or persons, to recognize as "native authority."

A Belgian writer on applied anthropology has described the policy of relying on traditional authorities as being inspired by motives "predominantly of a sociological order." He wrote that indirect rule attempts to avoid the disintegration of native society by influencing it through the medium of its own institutions and its own leaders (Nicaise 1960, p. 112).

In the training given to entrants into the colonial services of Belgium and Holland more time was devoted to the study of ethnography and customary law than in Britain. On the whole, however, it was concerned more with traditional institutions than with contemporary processes of change.

The International Institute of African Languages and Cultures (now the International African Institute) was founded in 1926 in order to promote anthropological and linguistic research. Its founders were impressed by the rapidity of social change in Africa and considered that this should be made the subject of scientific study by trained observers.

When the institute received a grant from the Rockefeller Foundation in 1932 for the expansion of its research program, the object of this program was defined as "bringing about a better understanding of the factors of social cohesion in original African society, the ways in which these are being affected by the new influences, tendencies towards new groupings and the formation of new social bonds, and forms of co-operation between African societies and western civilization" (International . . . 1932, p. 1).

"These questions," the institute stated, "are of the first importance to the African peoples themselves, to the administrator, to the educator, to the missionary, and to the settler and trader" (1932, p. 1). The understanding gained would enable the administrator "to foster the growth of a healthy, progressive, organic society" (1932, p. 2), and all the other persons mentioned would find in such a society the environment most favorable to the pursuit of their aims. At this time, then, applied anthropology did mean the use of anthropological knowledge to produce a healthy condition of society. The institute offered to put at the disposal of all persons with specific aims in Africa, including "the native leaders of African society," knowledge that would "assist them in determining the right relations between the institutions of African society and alien systems of government, education, and religion, in preserving what is vital in the former and in eliminating unnecessary conflict between the latter and African tradition, custom, and mentality" (1932, p. 3). In other words, it hoped to offer recipes for what Malinowski a few years later was to call "successful cultural change" (1945, p. 56). Topics to be studied would include the social consequences of the demand for wage labor, the effect on political institutions of subjection to a foreign overlord, and the relation of school education to traditional values.

Although the International African Institute as a body did not advocate specific policies, the general line taken in its publications was that the understanding of traditional institutions should make it possible to introduce necessary changes without causing unnecessary disintegration.

One of the recommendations with which Lord Hailey concluded his monumental survey of Africa was that the British government provide funds for research into all the sciences, natural and social, that were relevant to African problems. Shortly after the publication of his *African Survey* (1938), the report of the West India Royal Commission (Great Britain . . . 1940) urged that funds be made available from the United Kingdom Treasury for the stimulation of economic development and the provision of social services that were beyond the resources of the colonial territories. The Colonial Development and Welfare Acts, of 1940 and later years, earmarked funds for the two purposes just mentioned. Committees of experts, including social scientists, were set up to advise on the allocation of grants from the research fund. Applicants for grants were expected to be able to argue that their research would be of value to the government of the territory where they proposed to work; some, however, argued successfully that any addition to knowledge of the social structure of the people subject to its authority is of value to a government.

At the same time surveys were made of the major geographical areas with the aim of evaluating the existing state of knowledge and the areas in which further information was most urgently needed. These surveys encouraged a certain concentration of research in directions that could be expected to throw light on administrative problems.

Government sociologists. At this period some appointments of anthropologists to government service were made in Kenya and Tanganyika. These men were frequently given the title "government sociologist," which did not imply that their training or theoretical interests differed from those of social anthropologists but simply recognized the unpopularity in African circles of the word "anthropology," a term thought of as meaning the study of "primitive peoples." This generation of government anthropologists was expected to be able to turn its attention to limited questions on which answers were thought to be urgently needed. Thus Philip Mayer in Kenya made an exhaustive study of Gusii marriage law and a shorter examination of the difficulty of limiting the amount of bridewealth payment and discussed the neighborhood cooperative farming groups from the point of view of their suitability to undertake new economic activities (1950; 1951). Philip Gulliver examined the effects of migratory labor and other social changes among a people (the Nyakyusa) who had been largely unaffected by commercial influences up to the period of World War II (1955; 1958). In Australia Ian Hogbin was commissioned to estimate the damage suffered by the New Guinea peoples during the Japanese occupation and Camilla Wedgwood to estimate their educational needs.

Research institutes. Research with a practical bearing was also undertaken by the research institutes sponsored or assisted by the Colonial Office. Such institutes exist in east, west, and central Africa, in the West Indies, and in Malaya. The East African Institute studied the social consequences of the immigration of labor, the reasons for the ineffectiveness of African village headmen as agents of government policy, and the changing position of African chiefs. Later it embarked on a large-scale five-year study of urbanization. The Rhodes–Livingstone Institute has carried out intensive studies of urbanization in the copper belt of central Africa. The West African Institute sponsored a study of the mixed population employed on the agricultural estates of the Cameroons Development Corporation and the relations between immigrants and people of local origin. Studies of family structure have been conspicuous in the work of the West Indian Institute.

Belgian Congo. Increased attention was paid to anthropological research by Belgium in the period between World War II and the independence of the Congo. A center for the study of social problems (CEPSI), founded at Elisabethville in 1948, has concentrated on problems associated with urbanization. The Solvay Sociological Institute in Brussels created a Congo section, which paid special attention to social problems of the labor force—absenteeism, instability in employment, and unemployment. Studies were made of crime and juvenile delinquency, of new leadership in urban areas, and of the new elective institutions that had been created in preparation for independence. The Institute of Research in Economics and Sociology of the Lovanium University in Leopoldville, founded in 1956, has an ethnosociological division. It has organized a detailed analysis of the population of Leopoldville, taking different sections—primary school teachers, laborers, unemployed—and examining in each the characteristics of marriage and family life, religion, and recreational activities.

Applied anthropology in America. In the United States the employment of government anthropologists may be said to date from 1934, when at the request of John Collier, commissioner of the Bureau of Indian Affairs, the Unit of Applied Anthropology was created. The anthropologists' first task closely resembled that of the government anthropologist who had been appointed a few years earlier in Nigeria: to investigate Indian political institutions with a view toward utilizing them as agencies of local government. Other anthropologists were attached as advisers to a technical cooperative unit in which the Department of Agriculture cooperated with the Bureau of Indian Affairs on schemes for the improvement of land-use methods.

Private enterprise also employed anthropologists

as consultants. The first such venture was the study carried out at the Western Electric Company's Hawthorne Works in Chicago from 1927 to 1932 (Roethlisberger & Dickson 1939). Anthropologists recognized that a pattern of social relationships develops among any body of people who regularly work together and that unexpected resistance to disturbances of this structure may affect attempts to increase their efficiency or welfare. In Britain, after 1960, similar studies were sponsored by the Department of Scientific and Industrial Research.

The Society for Applied Anthropology was founded in the United States in 1941; it published a journal, *Applied Anthropology,* the name of which was changed in 1949 to *Human Organization.* The society described as its primary object "the promotion of scientific investigation of the principles controlling the relations of human beings to one another, and the encouragement of the wide application of these principles to practical problems." It had three main fields of interest: mental health, the study of industrial organizations, and the relation of economic development to cultural change. *Economic Development and Cultural Change,* a specialist journal for the last-named subject, was founded in 1951.

During World War II a number of anthropologists were employed in America by the United States government in connection with the relocation of Japanese populations. They also attempted to explain the culture of occupied areas to those members of the armed forces who required that natives cooperate as laborers, messengers, etc. In America, as in Australia (but not Britain), training courses for officers to be engaged in military government in occupied territories included instruction in anthropology. In its administration of the Trust Territory of the Pacific Islands, the United States from 1951 employed seven anthropologists, one at headquarters and one in each administrative district. They were to advise on the means of implementing government projects, interpret them to the native populations and evaluate their progress. These projects included health improvement, labor policies, education, legislative measures, and judicial procedures. The anthropologists were also expected to carry on the fundamental research on which their advice must ultimately be based.

Applied anthropology since World War II. Since the end of World War II the new political balance of power that has resulted in the almost complete liquidation of colonial rule has brought about a change in the emphasis of applied anthropology in the economically underdeveloped countries. The colonial powers, and many anthropologists who were not their nationals, were concerned primarily with stability, with gradual change, and therefore with the preservation of indigenous institutions. Their successors are determined on rapid change and have the support of world powers who, whatever may be their ideologies, value technical progress more than social stability. Politically uncommitted anthropologists have been forced to recognize the pressing problems that are created by increasing populations in territories where resources are limited and productivity is low. Technical specialists of all kinds are seeking to devise ways of improving standards of living. When the collaboration of anthropologists is invited, it is for them to show where traditional values and institutions are hindering the adoption of improvements.

Anthropologists have been employed as consultants in a number of technical-assistance projects undertaken by the United States and also by the specialized agencies of the United Nations, notably the World Health Organization. They have most to offer to public health projects, agricultural extension, and community development.

In the United States and the United Kingdom, since World War II, there has been increasing cooperation between anthropologists and medical specialists. For example in the United States, the Harvard School of Public Health has carried out a study of social reactions to proposals for the fluoridation of water supplies. In Britain an anthropologist has been included in a team studying the epidemiology of mental disease in South Wales.

Goals of applied anthropology. The change in the directions in which the application of anthropology is sought has had some influence on the anthropologists' interpretation of their role. Those who hesitated to make themselves responsible for deciding what an ideal society would be like have less hesitation in suggesting what approach would give the best chances of success for public health programs. Those who held that any help they might give to a colonial government must be a kind of treachery to its subjects need have no such inhibitions about independent territories.

Nevertheless, there has been much discussion of the question whether anthropologists should join in development projects or should simply present their facts and let administrative authorities do with them as they wish. This extreme view would stultify all attempts at applying anthropological knowledge, since the theoretical work of anthropologists is not focused on administrative problems, and its implications for action would be recognized only by other professionals. The opposite viewpoint is that anthropologists must themselves make policy recommendations. This is expressed in the code of ethics of the American Society for Applied Anthropology, which says, *inter alia*:

To his fellow men he [the anthropologist] owes respect for his dignity and general well-being. He may not recommend any course of action on behalf of his client's interests, when the lives, well-being, dignity, and self-respect of others are likely to be adversely affected, without adequate provisions being made to insure that there will be a minimum of such effect and that the net effect will in the long run be more beneficial than if no action were taken at all. He must take the greatest care to protect his informants, especially in the aspects of confidence which his informants may not be able to stipulate for themselves.

To his clients he must make no promises nor may he encourage any expectations that he cannot reasonably hope to fulfill. He must give them the best of his scientific knowledge and skill. He must consider their specific goals in the light of their general interests and welfare. He must establish a clear understanding with each client as to the nature of his responsibilities to his client, to science, and to his fellow men. (Statement on Ethics . . . 1963–1964, p. 237)

Nadel (1953) urged that if anthropologists did not claim the right to contribute directly to the framing of policy, the data provided by them could be used, in ways that he did not specify, to damage the societies that they described. The same attitude is implied in Barnett's statement that anthropology "exposes people who are powerless to state their own case" (1956, p. 80). Beals has urged that applied anthropology be concerned with finding out what inarticulate people want and then helping them to get it (1953, p. 188), an argument also put forward by Tax (1958, pp. 17–19).

All these interpretations of the anthropologist's role reject the idea that his advice is technically oriented and thus value-free. Of course, there is a sense in which no application of theoretical knowledge is value-free; if people seek to use knowledge, it is to attain ends that they value. But the question of values in applied anthropology had a special significance during the colonial era because of the type of situation in which the advice of anthropologists was sometimes sought and sometimes offered. Colonial governments interpreted their "civilizing mission" to mean, among other things, a process of moral improvement; anthropologists did not always see as moral improvement the kind of change that governments sought to bring about. On their side anthropologists were

concerned that the processes of social change to which the governments were committed be beneficial rather than harmful to the subject societies, an aim that entailed the introduction of value judgments at every turn. Those who believed that the changes being imposed on the simpler societies would of necessity be harmful could not expect the governments to share their view but nevertheless claimed a hearing. Obviously the difference between their values and those of the governments made it very difficult for them to offer advice of a kind that would facilitate the execution of government policies.

It is no accident that the focus of interest of applied anthropology has shifted with the withdrawal of colonial rule. The new independent governments see their functions as the older independent nations do: not to make over alien societies but to raise standards of living and to spread welfare. They are quite certain about the kind of society they want to create, and they are not asking anybody's advice about this. When they do seek advice, it is in fields where there is a consensus on values; all are agreed that health is good and that the pursuit of physical comfort and material wealth is at any rate permissible for those people who like it. Anthropologists are still not invited to pass judgment on the merits of the projects in which their cooperation is sought, but these are in practice congenial to most of them in a way that moral-improvement policies often were not. They are not asked, nor do they now seek, to advise on the total process of social change; their role is now to indicate where existing social structures and idea systems may present obstacles to specific projects.

LUCY MAIR

[*Directly related are the entries* ACCULTURATION; FIELD WORK; OBSERVATION.]

BIBLIOGRAPHY

ARDENER, EDWIN et al. 1960 *Plantation and Village in the Cameroons.* Published for the Nigerian Institute of Social and Economic Research. Oxford Univ. Press.
BARNETT, HOMER G. 1956 *Anthropology in Administration.* Evanston, Ill.: Row, Peterson.
BEALS, RALPH L. 1953 Problems of Application: Results. Pages 178–190 in International Symposium on Anthropology, New York, 1952, *An Appraisal of Anthropology Today.* Edited by Sol Tax et al. Univ. of Chicago Press.
BROWN, G. GORDON; and HUTT, A. McD. BRUCE 1935 *Anthropology in Action: An Experiment in the Iringa District of the Iringa Province, Tanganyika Territory.* Published for the International Institute of African Languages and Cultures. Oxford Univ. Press.
CHAPPLE, ELIOT D. 1953 Applied Anthropology in Industry. Pages 819–831 in A. L. Kroeber (editor), *Anthropology Today: An Encyclopedic Inventory.* Interna-

tional Symposium on Anthropology. Univ. of Chicago Press.

FORTES, MEYER 1937 *Marriage Law Among the Tallensi.* Accra (Ghana): Government Printing Department.

FOSTER, GEORGE M. 1962 *Traditional Cultures, and the Impact of Technological Change.* New York: Harper.

FREEDMAN, M. 1956 Health Education: How It Strikes an Anthropologist. *Health Education Journal* 14: 18–24.

GREAT BRITAIN, WEST INDIA ROYAL COMMISSION 1940 *Recommendations, 1938–1939.* Papers by Command, Cmd. 6174. London: H.M. Stationery Office.

GULLIVER, PHILIP H. 1955 *Labour Migration in a Rural Economy: A Study of the Ngoni and Ndendeuli of Southern Tanganyika.* East African Studies, No. 6. Kampala (Uganda): East African Institute of Social Research.

GULLIVER, PHILIP H. 1958 *Land Tenure and Social Change Among the Nyakyusa.* East African Studies, No. 11. Kampala (Uganda): East African Institute of Social Research.

HAILEY, MALCOLM (1938) 1957 *African Survey, Revised 1956: A Study of Problems Arising in Africa, South of the Sahara.* Issued under the auspices of·the Royal Institute of International Affairs. New York and London: Oxford Univ. Press.

INTERNATIONAL INSTITUTE OF AFRICAN LANGUAGES AND CULTURES 1932 A Five-year Plan of Research. *Africa* 5:1–13.

MALINOWSKI, BRONISLAW 1929 Practical Anthropology. *Africa* 2:22–38.

MALINOWSKI, BRONISLAW 1945 *The Dynamics of Culture Change: An Inquiry Into Race Relations in Africa.* New Haven: Yale Univ. Press.

MAYER, PHILIP 1950 *Gusii Bridewealth Law and Custom.* Rhodes–Livingstone Papers, No. 18. Oxford Univ. Press.

MAYER, PHILIP 1951 *Two Studies in Applied Anthropology in Kenya.* Colonial Research Studies, No. 3. London: H.M. Stationery Office.

MEEK, CHARLES K. 1925 *The Northern Tribes of Nigeria.* 2 vols. Oxford Univ. Press.

MEEK, CHARLES K. (1931a) 1950 *A Sudanese Kingdom: An Ethnographical Study of the Jukun-speaking Peoples of Nigeria.* New York: Humanities.

MEEK, CHARLES K. (1931b) 1950 *Tribal Studies in Northern Nigeria.* 2 vols. New York: Humanities.

MEEK, CHARLES K. (1937) 1950 *Law and Authority in a Nigerian Tribe: A Study in Indirect Rule.* New York and London: Oxford Univ. Press.

NADEL, SIEGFRIED F. 1953 *Anthropology and Modern Life.* Canberra: Australian National Univ.

NICAISE, JOSEPH 1960 Applied Anthropology in the Congo and Ruanda–Urundi. *Human Organization* 19: 112–117.

PAUL, BENJAMIN D.; and MILLER, W. B. (editors) 1955 *Health, Culture and Community: Case Studies of Public Reaction to Health Programs.* New York: Russell Sage Foundation.

RATTRAY, ROBERT S. (1923) 1956 *Ashanti.* Oxford Univ. Press.

RATTRAY, ROBERT S. (1929) 1956 *Ashanti Law and Constitution.* Oxford Univ. Press.

RATTRAY, ROBERT S. 1932 *The Tribes of the Ashanti Hinterland.* 2 vols. Oxford: Clarendon.

ROETHLISBERGER, F. J.; and DICKSON, W. J. 1939 *Management and the Worker: An Account of a Research Program Conducted by the Western Electric Company, Hawthorne Works, Chicago.* Cambridge, Mass.: Harvard Univ. Press.

SPICER, EDWARD H. (editor) 1952 *Human Problems in Technological Change.* New York: Russell Sage Foundation.

Statement on Ethics of the Society for Applied Anthropology. 1963–1964 *Human Organization* 22:237 only.

TAX, SOL 1958 The Fox Project. *Human Organization* 17:17–19.

THOMPSON, LAURA 1960 Applied Anthropology, Community Welfare, and Human Conservation. Pages 769–774 in International Congress of Anthropological and Ethnological Sciences, Fifth, 1956, *Men and Cultures: Selected Papers.* Edited under the chairmanship of Anthony F. C. Wallace. Philadelphia: Univ. of Pennsylvania Press.

WILLIAMS, FRANCIS EDGAR 1928 *Orokaiva Magic.* Oxford Univ. Press.

WILLIAMS, FRANCIS EDGAR 1940 *Drama of Orokolo: The Social and Ceremonial Life of the Elema.* Oxford: Clarendon.

V

**THE ANTHROPOLOGICAL STUDY OF
MODERN SOCIETY**

The anthropological study of modern society has two forms: one, the utilization of anthropological techniques in the study of the current scene; the other, the application of anthropological understandings to the behavioral sciences in general. Although these two are inevitably intertwined, it is useful to treat them separately.

Historical background. Research in anthropology had been so overwhelmingly concerned with primitive and preliterate societies that it was viewed as a radical departure when in the 1930s students began to make ethnological investigations of modern European and American communities. Yet, early anthropological discussion did not confine itself to primitive peoples but regularly used relevant data from classical antiquity, Asiatic civilizations, European peasant communities, and even urban social phenomena. E. B. Tylor, for example, cited animistic concepts of his contemporary world ([1871] 1958, especially vol. 2, chapter 11), chided Blackstone for misconstruing in his *Commentaries* the nature of kinship regulations and thereby reformulating them in legal practice. In his discussion of survivals he used children's games and idioms as data (*ibid.*, vol. 1). Similarly, Sir Henry Maine, whose interest was comparative law, very naturally demonstrated his theses with current local usages as well as data on those more exotic peoples who are the usual subjects of anthropological discourse. In that era, although those concerned with anthropology rarely had personal contact with the native peoples that were the chief subject of their theoretical treatises, Frédéric Le Play (1855) initiated field studies of the economic and social life of European peasants, craftsmen, and laborers; this work is an unusual example of an early effort to illuminate current social life at least partially within the anthropological frame of reference.

It is also worthwhile to note that anthropological generalizations were applied to current problems. Tylor, in a Victorian idiom and outmoded theoretical framework, concludes his *Primitive Culture* thus:

To the promoters of what is sound and reformers of what is faulty in modern culture, ethnography has double help to give. To impress men's minds with a doctrine of development, will lead them in all honour to their ancestors to continue the progressive work of past ages, to continue it the more vigorously because light has increased in the world, and where barbaric hordes groped blindly, cultured men can often move onward with clear view. It is a harsher, and at times even painful, office of ethnography to expose the remains of crude old culture which have passed into harmful superstition, and to mark these out for destruction. Yet this work, if less genial, is not less urgently needful for the good of mankind. Thus, active at once in aiding progress and in removing hindrance, the science of culture is essentially a reformer's science. ([1871] 1958, vol. 2, p. 539)

Tylor was justified in calling anthropology a "reformer's science," for anthropologists have repeatedly concerned themselves with the moral and practical implications of their special knowledge. Franz Boas, the empiricist who was so insistent on work among preliterate peoples, wrote as early as 1911 of the implications of anthropological study for an understanding of our own cultural milieu; in this latter summary he refuted the assumptions of moral progress implicit in nineteenth-century evolutionism. Robert H. Lowie (1929) endeavored not so much to show that primitive man had the same virtues and capacities as modern man as to demonstrate that modern man engages in follies and vices similar to those found among primitive peoples. Lowie later tried to construct an ethnography of the Germans (1945), based upon his personal experience and his wide reading in German literature. Anthropologists in England and on the Continent have not, in recent years, shown as much interest in modern culture, although a major exception prior to World War II is represented by the program called Mass Observation, which endeavored to elicit popular attitudes and behavior patterns in England by means of informal interviews and observation of large-scale but nonrandom population samples. Some interest in modern peasantry has recently developed, and the anthropological study of modern society in England is reported in Klein (1965).

By the early 1940s a professional association (the Society for Applied Anthropology), with its own journal (*Human Organization*, originally called *Applied Anthropology*), was created in response to growing interest in such subjects as factory organization, community life, and problems of native peoples in the modern world. In 1954 the American Anthropological Association held a symposium on the United States, which was subsequently published as a special issue of the *American Anthropologist* (Lantis 1955).

The empirical study of modern society

Although in the study of primitive customs and tribal life anthropologists had until recently a virtually *de facto* monopoly, in the study of modern society they came into competition (and frequent collaboration) with representatives of other fields and were constrained to justify their methods and approaches in the face of those already being employed. Anthropological studies of modern society have taken many forms but may be grouped into the following classes: (1) the study of the modern American community, (2) the study of peasant communities throughout the world, (3) the study of specific institutions of modern society, (4) the study of "national character," and (5) the study of modern adaptations of tribal cultures.

Studies of American communities. The study of American community life was initiated under Franklin H. Giddings as an investigation into the evolution of rural communities (for example, Williams 1906). Such studies came to be the special province of rural sociology; they were generally unsophisticated surveys but some, for example, Nelson's study of Mormon communities (1952), do have anthropological insights. Urban studies developed by the Chicago school, such as Zorbaugh's *Gold Coast and Slum* (1929), are also forerunners of an anthropology of modern life. It is, however, the Lynds' investigation of "Middletown" (Lynd & Lynd 1929; 1937)—the very name conjures up the notion of the normative for American culture—that has an explicit anthropological approach, and, significantly, the Foreword to *Middletown* was written by Clark Wissler, an anthropologist. This investigation of Muncie, Indiana, had a wide impact (both public and academic), in part because it revitalized the muckraker tradition but more because it succeeded in presenting a cultural view of ordinary modern life—a picture of middle-class tribalism in America. It proved to be the first and most successful of a long line of anthropological studies of the American community.

The most elaborate and extended of these were initiated by W. Lloyd Warner, who turned from field work among the Australian aborigines to field work in Newburyport, Massachusetts, and, subsequently, with the aid of numerous students, to other towns throughout the United States. The Newburyport study involved not only detailed interviews with a sample of the city's population but also analyses of its institutions. Several volumes have been published under the general title "The Yankee City Series." The first (Warner & Lunt 1941) presented the general social framework, namely, a sixfold class structure based upon identification, social interaction, and social attributes. Other volumes concerned themselves with particular aspects of social life, for example, the factory (Warner & Low 1947) and ethnic relations (Warner & Srole 1945). Among works on American community life for which Warner was directly responsible are the analysis of a southern city (Davis et al. 1941), of an urban Negro community (Drake & Cayton 1945), and of a midwestern town (Warner et al. 1949). Warner has summarized and generalized his class approach in *Social Class in America* (Warner, Meeker, and Eells 1949), in which he defines social classes and the measures he has developed for their determination. To Warner, social class is not economic class but refers, rather, to recognizable levels in a social hierarchy, based upon self-identification, divergent life-styles, and, particularly, differential prestige. Warner (1952) has also examined the status system and institutional behavior in terms of the symbol system and ritual (collective representations) of American life. Whatever the epistemological reality of the Warnerian social classes may be, the schema has offered a context for interpreting observed differences in child-rearing practices (Davis & Dollard 1940; Ericson 1947), in sexual attitudes and behavior (Kinsey et al. 1948), and in the classroom performances of children (Warner et al. 1944; Hollingshead 1949).

Meanwhile, many other anthropologists turned to an examination of the American community: Carl Withers (1945) focused on the life-cycle patterns as they varied according to social status groups in an Ozark rural community he called Plainville, U.S.A.; Hortense Powdermaker (1939) directed her attention chiefly to the mode of life of different status groups in a southern Negro community and the distinction between the reality of that society and the image the white people had of it; Walter Goldschmidt (1946; 1947) demonstrated the social cleavage between farm labor and the "nuclear group" in a California town and analyzed the effect of industrialized agriculture on community life. Studies investigating rural life were initiated at the University of North Carolina, and from this program emerged an analysis of plantation life by Morton Rubin (1951) and of Negro society by Hylan Lewis (1955). Arthur J. Vidich and Joseph Bensman (1958) analyzed the values and attitudes of persons in an upper New York State town and the discontinuity between the public image and reality in community life; William F. Whyte (1943) studied a community of slum youths. Governmental studies of rural community life were made by the Bureau of Agricultural Economics (*Culture of a Contemporary Community* series), and the Japanese Relocation Authority studied World War II internment camps.

Although anthropologists have regularly found a "class system" in the American community, characterized by differentials in economic roles, financial status, life-style, material conditions, power, and prestige, the specific class systems are not comparable. Thus, while Warner found six social classes in Newburyport, other students found diverse numbers ranging from two to seven, and Withers (1945) showed that persons of different standing see the "class structure" of Plainville quite differently. One might conclude that each community defines its own class system; however, Goldschmidt (1955) has pointed out that although there are great differentials in social status related to income, occupation, and life-style and that persons at different levels in the social hierarchy have different attitudes, values, and orientations to society, the important dynamic in American society is status mobility and anxiety, rather than fixity and class identification.

The description of social class (or the dynamics of status) is common to American community studies, but the more significant contribution of these studies has been to provide a rich ethnography of modern social life not only in its formal aspects but in an informal, intensely personal, intimate manner. They err in reflecting both the mood of the time and the predilections of the ethnographers, yet they are a remarkable reportage on the customs of modern America. They err, too, in their frequent tacit assumptions that the community represents the nation in microcosm, for modern America is a network of social communication in which the towns are merely at the termini. But they give the necessary matrix in which American life—as analyzed by other social scientists—can be understood [see FIELD WORK; OBSERVATION].

Study of peasant communities. Anthropologists more or less concurrently began to study modern peasant communities in diverse parts of the world. Few had examined village life among farmers of literate, politically oriented societies until Redfield studied Tepoztlán, Mexico, in 1928 (Redfield 1930). Redfield's close association with the Chicago sociologists and the then important dichotomy between rural and urban in sociological theory must have influenced this choice. However, Redfield never abandoned his essentially anthropological perspective and until quite late in his career continued to discuss peasant and primitive societies under the single term "folk." Village studies claimed increasing attention of anthropologists (and sociologists)—for example, Ireland (Arensberg 1937; Arensberg & Kimball 1940), Japan (Embree 1939), China (Fei 1939; Yang 1945), and, under the sponsorship of the Smithsonian Institution's Institute of Social Anthropology, many Latin American communities (Beals 1946; Brand 1951; Foster 1948; Gillin 1947; Pierson 1948; Tax 1953)—so that representative studies are now available for most countries where peasant farming is found. These studies usually concentrate on single local communities, carrying into the study of peasant life the methods and assumptions of tribal ethnography: reliance on informants rather than questionnaires or other instruments, the implicit assumption of cultural homogeneity, the focus on customary usages rather than on behavioral diversity. They also tend to treat communities as isolates, focusing upon the internal structure of community life rather than interrelationships with the broader society and assuming that the village is a microcosm of the whole. Redfield (1956, especially chapter 3) conceptualized the distinction between the little (peasant or local community) tradition and the great (national or intellectualized) tradition and discussed the interdependence between them. There have been no consistent efforts either to define the general characteristics of peasantry or to show the essential uniformities and diversities of peasant communities as they exist within a single country or culture area.

Like the study of the American community, the ethnography of peasant life has given us an understanding of the everyday life of the peoples it describes. We are much better able now to understand behavior of the people of India, for instance, than when we had merely the formal accounts and histories of the caste system and the teachings of Indian scholars. Furthermore, the inclusion of these different examples of customary social systems has enriched the literature of anthropology for purposes of comparative studies [see REDFIELD; PEASANTRY; VILLAGE].

Institutional studies. A third line of inquiry in the study of modern society may be called the ethnography of modern institutions. The classic studies made at the Hawthorne plant of Western Electric under the aegis of Elton Mayo (Roethlisberger & Dickson 1939) are an early example. The essence of this work was to demonstrate that the status system and the structuring of social relationships were essential ingredients in work satisfactions and factory output. There has flowed from this initial source a body of literature analyzing various work situations—increasingly for the practical aims of employers in the maintenance of orderly production—and institutions, for instance, the motion picture industry (Powdermaker 1950) and the restaurant industry (Whyte 1948). Harding (1955) has summarized the anthropological study of industrial enterprises, pointing out that the factory—or an entire industry—is a social system, that it operates on the assumption of communication among its component elements, that this involves not only the formal system but also the informal, and that the latter is a major consideration in the daily operations of the work routine.

Another example of institutional ethnology is Caudill's study (1958) of a psychiatric hospital, in which he analyzes the day-to-day personal relations of doctors, ward personnel, and patients, treating the hospital as a small society whose functions affect the behavior of its personnel in many subtle ways outside the awareness of the participants themselves. Among the elements that Caudill discovered were (1) that there is a hierarchical structure in the hospital, (2) that direct communication between levels is faulty, (3) that actions by persons are symbolic (communicative) expressions, (4) that these actions or events are disregarded or misunderstood, and (5) that an anthropological investigation can interpret these events and lead to a restructuring of action beneficial to the institution and hence to the patients. Although the hospital may be viewed as a community, it is not sealed off from the society around it; events in the homes of patients affect those in the hospital and vice versa; furthermore, the patterning of events in the hospital setting reflects generic American culture patterns, as a comparison with behavior in Japanese hospitals confirms.

American schools have been subjected to anthropological investigation. Early studies emphasized the role of social class, pointing out that the teachers have largely been of upwardly mobile lower-middle-class origin, strongly attached to the values of thrift, industry, cleanliness, competitiveness, and the virtues of success. This setting gives advantage to middle-class children and reinforces these values in the society at large. They not only appear in the formal structuring of class work and grades but also in the informal extracurricular activities and the interpersonal relations among the pupils. Jules Henry (1963) has shown the transmission of values and attitudes in the latent content of classroom discourse and their relationship to the domestic problems of the children: the reinforcement of materialistic over intellectual and moralistic values, the inculcation of attitudes of hostility and competitiveness in classroom recitation, and the continuity between the classroom events and problems in out-of-school relationships.

National character studies. Historians and men of letters have often depicted the character of a people or an epoch—a culture—as, for example, Burckhardt on the Italian Renaissance, Hamilton on classical Greece, and Tocqueville on America. Anthropology has contributed substantively to this literature and has endeavored to formulate both method and rationale for this enterprise. The anthropological investigation of national cultures was initiated during World War II to contribute to military decisions through better understanding of enemy cultures and has continued into the cold war period.

The study of national character is concerned with generalizations regarding the psychological attitudes and orientation of a population sharing a culture: a nation, a region, an ethnic group, such as east European Jews. It is therefore concerned with psychodynamics and has been much influenced by neo-Freudian thought. National character studies have attempted to substitute cultural explanations of manifest differences in personality attributes for racial or environmental explanations. The idea of national character is that these psychological attributes are formed early in an infant's life by the experiences it undergoes as a result of culturally established child-training practices. The theoretical basis has been set forth by Gorer (in Mead & Métraux 1953) and by Mead (1953).

National character studies attempt to trace the way in which the identified cultural behavior is represented in the intra-psychic structure of the individual members of the culture, combining cultural theory and psychological theory (principally learning theory, Gestalt psychology, Freudian psychology, and child development studies) into a new psychocultural theory to explain how human beings embody the culture, learn it, and live it. (Mead 1953, p. 651)

The first full-length anthropological national character study was Mead's book (1942) on the United States; the most widely referenced, Benedict's on Japan (1946). Others include Gorer on America (1948), Gorer and Rickman on Russia (1949), and Métraux and Mead on France (1954). The Columbia University research project in contemporary cultures gathered scholars from different disciplines to "study culture at a distance," that is, to investigate societies to which scholars did not have direct access. This involved not only the interviewing of immigrants, refugees, and prisoners of war but also the detailed analysis of current literature, humor, motion pictures, and other expressions of the current popular culture (Mead & Métraux 1953).

These studies have been much criticized for their lack of methodological rigor and for their involvement with psychodynamic theory. The study of national character cannot explain the origin of diverse forms of behavior, but it can describe them in an ethnographic sense and discuss the internal dynamics of how generic cultural practices engender in infants those attributes of character which, although not within the awareness of the people, are nevertheless an essential part of their culture. The culturally established common modes of handling children, the nature of cultural rewards and punishments, and the affect patterns between parents and children are seen as the mediating—not the causative—forces in transmitting and preserving the national character. Mead (1953, p. 652) is quite clear on this point, although such clarity is not displayed by all other students of national character [see NATIONAL CHARACTER].

Acculturation of tribal cultures. The unlettered peoples and tribal societies have in ever-increasing degree felt the impact of the modern world and the universalization of technology. Indeed, the opportunity to examine primitive society in its pristine state rapidly waned during the first half of the twentieth century, and even the pockets of tribal cultures still to be found are not entirely innocent of elements from more advanced economic systems. Furthermore, research has disclosed that many of the tribal cultures appearing in the ethnographic literature had been in varying degrees influenced by Europeanization, either through direct acquisitions, such as the horse on the American plains, or indirectly, such as by opportunities to engage in the fur trade or involvements with the slave trade. Malinowski (1945) despaired of finding a pristine condition—a point of departure —for the study of the acculturative process. But as native peoples became increasingly involved in modern society, and particularly as their adjustment to new conditions presented both theoretical and practical problems, anthropologists came to study the processes and products of acculturation. Acculturation studies constitute a large corpus of literature, but little systematic generalization on these data has been made; the fact is that very little generalization can be sustained. The most important of the recognized regularities in acculturation situations are the quick assimilation of certain kinds of material goods, the undermining of native systems of authority and social values, the recurrent tendency to develop millenarian or nativistic religious cults, and the greater resistance to change of religious beliefs and psychological sets or attitudes. But the most apparent conclusion regarding the entry of tribal peoples into modern society is that no generalization is universally applicable. Some peoples, notably the Masai in Africa and most Pueblos in the American southwest, show a high retention of native culture despite long and continuous contact with the West, whereas other peoples, for example, the Maori of New Zealand, readily adopt Western patterns of behavior [see ACCULTURATION; CULTURE, article on CULTURE CHANGE].

General theory and practice

Until recently, ethnographic fieldwork meant that an investigator, armed with such minimal tools as notebook and camera, went alone (later with his spouse) to study an as yet professionally unstudied tribe and to describe to the degree he saw fit all those departments of tribal life—economy, daily round, domestic life, social organization, theology, language—he found of interest and relevance. His studies were at first more concerned with rules and expectancies than with frequencies and contradictions, and for this purpose he sought out elderly informants who could verbalize these matters, while observing as much of the traditional events as were retained in the community. By internal checks and ever-increasing detail he established what was "true" for the culture under scrutiny. He neither bothered about nor expected statistical validation or replication and rarely had any documents to worry about. But as each fieldworker returned with new insights resulting from deeper investigation of particular aspects of culture, anthropology became increasingly aware of the intricacies, the subtleties, and the underlying unities of cultural behavior, so that his successors were able to penetrate still more deeply into tribal life.

Such practices do not make for sophistication

in research design, statistical manipulation, validity control, or replication. In the present era of increased identification of research methods with the statistical handling of data, the anthropological study of modern society is often disparaged. However, it emphasizes features increasingly neglected by other social disciplines. First, the holistic approach, which examines each phenomenon in the context of the totality, avoids (or at least minimizes) the error of treating each cultural department, for example, economics, politics, religion, as if it had a separate and at best only internally consistent meaning. Closely related is the capacity for finding patterns or integrative elements in cultural systems. Third, recognition that cultural features have deep psychological involvements for the individual participants makes it possible to see the interplay between individual sentiments and cultural institutions. Fourth, the anthropologist's very naïveté makes him willing to examine aspects of life not amenable to counting and statistical manipulation and thus to utilize evidence other scholars avoid as "methodologically unsound." On the whole, what the anthropological approach brings to the study of modern society is the use of insight, introspection, close attention to detail, validation through internal consistency, and the capacity to deal at the same time with all levels of behavior—from material artifacts to psychic life. If the results sometimes seem impressionistic, if there is a novelistic quality, nevertheless there is a closer sense of human reality than is generally provided by those social sciences traditionally concerned with modern society. Writing with particular reference to the community study, but more generally applicable to the anthropological approach, Vidich, Bensman, and Stein say:

The survival of the community study perhaps can be explained precisely because it has not absorbed too completely the major techniques of the more "advanced" social sciences. . . . [Community studies] have always shown, no matter how imperfectly, the interrelationship between the various segments of community life. As a result the "totality" has neither been neglected nor shattered into unrelated segments. . . . As a consequence of the unwillingness of most community researchers to forsake direct observation and direct reporting of the community life, we still have coherent images of the community and social life which are unattainable by other methodologies. . . .

In spite of the grandiose elaboration of research methodologies and abstract theories, it appears that the ear and the eye are still important instruments for gathering data, and that the brain is not always an inefficient mechanism for analyzing them. Because these ancient instruments are still effective, sociologists of all methodological persuasions as well as laymen have come to rely on the community study as a source for their over-all images of society. They use these studies for building their substantive theories of society, and they use them as reference points in doing other research and for their commentaries on the society at large. (1964, p. xi)

Culture theory and the other social sciences

Anthropology has made a contribution to the study of modern society that goes deeper than the mere building up of a corpus of empirically derived information. The concept of culture has had a pervasive influence on the other disciplines devoted to human behavior. So long as students of society are limited in their considerations to a single culture or closely related cultures, they are not able to see the force of culture at all, and their analysis is deprived of the major dynamic in the events their discipline is designed to illuminate. It is true that history provides some of the cultural diversity with which theoretical models of behavior may be tested, but history lacks the detailed data, especially of intimate and informal events, that is not recorded in historic documents. Furthermore, historical societies tend to be rather similar in their general character and hence provide only a narrow cross-cultural perspective; and, above all, the historians did not develop theories of culture which could serve as a basis for understanding the phenomena in question. A few scholars, notably the sociologist Max Weber, transcended these limitations, but the cultural point of view is fundamentally the contribution of anthropology.

The clearest illustration of the role of anthropology is provided by linguistics. Prior to the twentieth century, linguists had formulated taxonomic and philological relationships among the diverse tongues of the globe, but their grammatical analyses were based upon the model of Indo-European forms, especially Latin. It was the anthropologically oriented linguists, such as Boas, Bloomfield, and Sapir, who forced the linguists to examine each language in terms of its own grammatical structure and to discover that grammar, syntax, and semantic categories varied from one language to another. This enabled them to develop those general concepts by which to understand the phenomenon of speech and, through a "cultural" understanding, to arrive at a true comparison of linguistic phenomena and thereby at valid generalizations about verbal communication as a process. Significantly, these understandings returned to the linguist a better comprehension of the processes inherent in his own language, not only for purposes of understanding the nature of communication in his own society but even for such practical purposes as the teaching of language.

The influence of anthropology on psychoanalytic thought has also been dramatic. Until after World War I the psychology of human behavior was dominated by a fundamentally biological metaphysics—whether Watsonian behaviorism or Freudian psychodynamics. Anthropological study cast serious doubts on the simple biological models that such theories engendered and gave increasing emphasis to the essential element of culture as a formative force in determining the character of human responses. Thus, when Malinowski pointed out that in the Trobriand Islands the conflicts characteristic of the Oedipal relationship in Western society attach not to the father but to the mother's brother, though he has no sexual liaison with the mother and indeed stands in strict avoidance relation to her, some of the "instinctual" assumptions of Freudian dynamics were undermined. Again, when Mead reported the absence in Samoa of those puberty crises characteristic of middle-class Western girls, or the failure of the sexes in some New Guinea tribes to display the personality characteristics that we associate with sex roles, the physiological basis for such behavioral elements had to be seriously questioned. If men behave differently in different societies, then some situational aspect must be sought as explanatory hypothesis. This all the more so since other sources of data showed that genetic differences between peoples could not account for the manifest differences in their behavior, character, or ability.

The investigation of child training and growth in different cultural environments demonstrated that the psychology of everyday life varies in terms of culture context, with the result that psychoanalytic thought has divested itself of its uniform biological model and has reformulated its understandings in terms of cultural context—the human and symbolic environment in which the child grows up. This is found particularly in the works of Sullivan, Horney, Fromm, and especially Erikson (who has had intensive ethnographic experience with primitive peoples). Although the manner of transmission of attitudes and sentiments from generation to generation is not yet fully comprehended, there is no doubt that the cultural patterning of infantile experience is a crucial element in the formation of adult character. The social psychologists have also come to recognize the cultural dimension and to seek cross-cultural controls within which to test their hypotheses [see CULTURE AND PERSONALITY; LIFE CYCLE; see also Doob 1960].

Most of the social sciences have in varying degrees been influenced by anthropological understanding. Political scientists working with Western society may remain unconcerned with cultural forces, but political analysis in emerging nations of Africa and Asia requires recognition of the local cultural forces. An example of cultural continuities is documented for the ancient Buganda kingdom and modern Uganda (Apter 1961; Fallers 1964). Least influenced has been economics, which, largely holding to a dichotomy between market and nonmarket societies, finds no need to expand its explanatory system to the world of primitive man and hence remains relatively uninfluenced by the data of anthropology and the role of culture in the operations of the market place.

Policy implications

The infusion of anthropological thought into the scholarly understanding of modern society has had wide-ranging practical applications. The influence upon linguistics was noted in passing, and a comparable influence may be seen in changing attitudes toward child care. In the realm of business, anthropological consultants help management understand the practical problems of coping with informal social relations and culturally induced desires of its personnel. In government the earliest use of anthropological talent was, as might be expected, in the administration of Indian affairs, where John Collier, commissioner of Indian affairs under President Franklin D. Roosevelt, used anthropological understanding of native values and attitudes to help reconstitute internal tribal governments and reformulate school programs. Anthropological knowledge has long (but inconsistently) been applied in colonial administration. Recognition of the cultural dimensions in international relationships is widespread but not universal, and textbooks are available on the practical uses of anthropology for cultural relationships (for example, Foster 1962; Spicer 1952; Erasmus 1961). Many governmental agencies are now seeking anthropologists' advice in dealing with foreign countries. The awareness that cultural factors are responsible for the differential behavior of ethnic and racial groups has influenced policy in the United States. Not only do we recognize that members of various ethnic groups and social classes are raised in environments which foster different social outlooks and cultural values but we have also endeavored to ameliorate racial and ethnic relations through altering the cultural environment.

Anthropology has forced upon both scholars concerned with modern society and men of practical affairs a new metaphysics concerning the nature of man. This cultural viewpoint has the following features: (1) those behavior patterns which differentiate one community from another are not responses to differing genetically transmitted characteristics; (2) they are, instead, a product of cultural tradition; (3) this cultural tradition is transmitted in part unwittingly through the human and symbolic environment in which a community nurtures its children; and (4) modern society is not, in such matters, different from primitive societies, even though it has its peculiar complexities. By and large, the intellectual community and the policy-formulating elite in most technologically advanced societies accept and act on these basic anthropological tenets. Tylor's assertion that anthropology is a policy science and should be used for the improvement of the human condition is thus sustained, although the nature of the changes wrought by the anthropological understanding of modern society is not what Tylor anticipated.

WALTER GOLDSCHMIDT

BIBLIOGRAPHY

APTER, DAVID A. 1961 *The Political Kingdom in Uganda: A Study in Bureaucratic Nationalism.* Princeton Univ. Press.

ARENSBERG, CONRAD M. (1937) 1950 *The Irish Countryman.* Gloucester, Mass.: Smith.

ARENSBERG, CONRAD M.; and KIMBALL, SOLON T. (1940) 1961 *Family and Community in Ireland.* Gloucester, Mass.: Smith.

BEALS, RALPH L. 1946 *Cherán: A Sierra Tarascan Village.* Smithsonian Institution, Institute of Social Anthropology, Publication No. 2. Washington: Government Printing Office.

BENEDICT, RUTH 1946 *The Chrysanthemum and the Sword: Patterns of Japanese Culture.* Boston: Houghton Mifflin.

BOAS, FRANZ (1911) 1963 *The Mind of Primitive Man.* Rev. ed. New York: Collier. → A paperback edition was published in 1965 by the Free Press.

BOAS, FRANZ (1928) 1962 *Anthropology and Modern Life.* New York: Norton.

BRAND, DONALD D. 1951 *Quiroga: A Mexican Municipio.* Smithsonian Institution, Institute of Social Anthropology, Publication No. 11. Washington: Government Printing Office.

CAUDILL, WILLIAM 1958 *The Psychiatric Hospital as a Small Society.* Cambridge, Mass.: Harvard Univ. Press.

DAVIS, ALLISON; and DOLLARD, JOHN (1940) 1953 *Children of Bondage: The Personality Development of Negro Youth in the Urban South.* Prepared for the American Youth Commission. Washington: American Council on Education.

DAVIS, ALLISON; GARDNER, BURLEIGH B.; and GARDNER, MARY R. 1941 *Deep South: A Social Anthropological Study of Caste and Class.* Univ. of Chicago Press.

DOOB, LEONARD W. 1960 *Becoming More Civilized: A Psychological Exploration.* New Haven: Yale Univ. Press.

DRAKE, ST. CLAIR; and CAYTON, HORACE R. (1945) 1962 *Black Metropolis: A Study of Negro Life in a Northern City.* 2 vols., rev. & enl. New York: Harcourt.

EMBREE, JOHN F. (1939) 1950 *Suye Mura: A Japanese Village.* Univ. of Chicago Press.

ERASMUS, CHARLES J. 1961 *Man Takes Control: Cultural Development and American Aid.* Minneapolis: Univ. of Minnesota Press.

ERICSON, MARTHA C. (1947) 1951 Social Status and Child-rearing Practices. Pages 494–501 in Society for the Psychological Study of Social Issues, *Readings in Social Psychology*. Edited by Theodore M. Newcomb and Eugene L. Hartley. New York: Holt.

FALLERS, LLOYD A. (editor) 1964 *The King's Men: Leadership and Status in Buganda on the Eve of Independence*. London: Oxford Univ. Press.

FEI, HSIAO-T'UNG (1939) 1962 *Peasant Life in China: A Field Study of Country Life in the Yangtze Valley*. London: Routledge.

FOSTER, GEORGE M. 1948 *Empire's Children: The People of Tzintzuntzan*. Institute of Social Anthropology, Publication No. 6. Washington: Smithsonian Institution.

FOSTER, GEORGE M. 1962 *Traditional Cultures, and the Impact of Technological Change*. New York: Harper.

GILLIN, JOHN P. 1947 *Moche: A Peruvian Coastal Community*. Smithsonian Institution, Institute of Social Anthropology, Publication No. 3. Washington: Government Printing Office.

GOLDSCHMIDT, WALTER 1946 *Small Business and the Community: A Study in Central Valley of California on Effects of Scale of Farm Operations*. Washington: Government Printing Office.

GOLDSCHMIDT, WALTER 1947 *As You Sow*. New York: Harcourt.

GOLDSCHMIDT, WALTER 1955 Social Class and the Dynamics of Status in America. *American Anthropologist* New Series 57:1209–1217.

GORER, GEOFFREY (1948) 1964 *The American People: A Study in National Character*. Rev. ed. New York: Norton.

GORER, GEOFFREY; and RICKMAN, JOHN (1949) 1950 *The People of Great Russia: A Psychological Study*. London: Cresset. → A paperback edition was published in 1962 by Norton.

HARDING, CHARLES F. 1955 The Social Anthropology of American Industry. *American Anthropologist* New Series 57:1218–1231.

HENRY, JULES 1963 *Culture Against Man*. New York: Random House.

HOLLINGSHEAD, AUGUST DE B. (1949) 1959 *Elmtown's Youth: The Impact of Social Classes on Adolescents*. New York: Wiley.

KINSEY, ALFRED C. et al. 1948 *Sexual Behavior in the Human Male*. Philadelphia: Saunders.

KLEIN, JOSEPHINE 1965 *Samples From English Cultures*. 2 vols. London: Routledge.

LANTIS, MARGARET (special editor) 1955 The U.S.A. as Anthropologists See It. *American Anthropologist* New Series 57, no. 6, part 1. → An "Introduction" by Margaret Lantis appears on pages 1113–1121.

LE PLAY, FRÉDÉRIC (1855) 1877–1879 *Les ouvriers européens*. 2d ed. 6 vols. Tours (France): Mame.

LEWIS, HYLAN 1955 *Blackways of Kent*. Chapel Hill: Univ. of North Carolina Press.

LOWIE, ROBERT H. 1929 *Are We Civilized? Human Culture in Perspective*. New York: Harcourt.

LOWIE, ROBERT H. 1945 *The German People: A Social Portrait to 1914*. New York and Toronto: Farrar.

LYND, ROBERT S.; and LYND, HELEN M. (1929) 1930 *Middletown: A Study in Contemporary American Culture*. New York: Harcourt. → A paperback edition was published in 1959.

LYND, ROBERT S.; and LYND, HELEN M. 1937 *Middletown in Transition: A Study in Cultural Conflicts*. New York: Harcourt. → A paperback edition was published in 1963.

MALINOWSKI, BRONISLAW (1945) 1961 *The Dynamics of Culture Change: An Inquiry Into Race Relations in Africa*. New Haven: Yale Univ. Press.

MEAD, MARGARET (1942) 1965 *And Keep Your Powder Dry: An Anthropologist Looks at America*. New ed. New York: Morrow.

MEAD, MARGARET 1953 National Character. Pages 642–667 in International Symposium on Anthropology, New York, 1952, *Anthropology Today: An Encyclopedic Inventory*. Edited by Alfred L. Kroeber. Univ. of Chicago Press.

MEAD, MARGARET; and MÉTRAUX, RHODA (editors) 1953 *The Study of Culture at a Distance*. Univ. of Chicago Press.

MÉTRAUX, RHODA; and MEAD, MARGARET 1954 *Themes in French Culture: Preface to a Study of French Community*. Stanford (Calif.) Univ. Press.

NELSON, LOWRY 1952 *The Mormon Village: A Pattern and Technique of Land Settlement*. Salt Lake City: Univ. of Utah Press.

PIERSON, DONALD 1948 *Cruz das Almas: A Brazilian Village*. Smithsonian Institution, Institute of Social Anthropology, Publication No. 12. Washington: Government Printing Office.

POWDERMAKER, HORTENSE 1939 *After Freedom: A Culture Study in the Deep South*. New York: Viking.

POWDERMAKER, HORTENSE 1950 *Hollywood, the Dream Factory: An Anthropologist Looks at the Movie-makers*. Boston: Little.

REDFIELD, ROBERT 1930 *Tepoztlán, a Mexican Village: A Study of Folk Life*. Univ. of Chicago Press.

REDFIELD, ROBERT 1956 *Peasant Society and Culture: An Anthropological Approach to Civilization*. Univ. of Chicago Press. → A paperback edition, bound together with *The Little Community*, was published in 1961 by Cambridge University Press.

ROETHLISBERGER, FRITZ J.; and DICKSON, WILLIAM J. (1939) 1961 *Management and the Worker: An Account of a Research Program Conducted by the Western Electric Company, Hawthorne Works, Chicago*. Cambridge, Mass.: Harvard Univ. Press. → A paperback edition was published in 1964 by Wiley.

RUBIN, MORTON 1951 *Plantation Country*. Chapel Hill: Univ. of North Carolina Press.

SPICER, EDWARD H. (editor) 1952 *Human Problems in Technological Change*. New York: Russell Sage Foundation.

TAX, SOL (1953) 1963 *Penny Capitalism: A Guatemalan Indian Economy*. Univ. of Chicago Press.

TYLOR, EDWARD B. (1871) 1958 *Primitive Culture: Researches Into the Development of Mythology, Philosophy, Religion, Art and Custom*. 2 vols. Gloucester, Mass.: Smith. → Volume 1: *Origins of Culture*. Volume 2: *Religion in Primitive Culture*.

VIDICH, ARTHUR J.; and BENSMAN, JOSEPH (1958) 1960 *Small Town in Mass Society: Class, Power and Religion in a Rural Community*. Garden City, N.Y.: Doubleday.

VIDICH, ARTHUR J.; BENSMAN, JOSEPH; and STEIN, MAURICE R. (editors) 1964 *Reflections on Community Studies*. New York: Wiley.

WARNER, W. LLOYD (1952) 1962 *American Life: Dream and Reality*. Rev. ed. Univ. of Chicago Press. → First published as *The Structure of American Life*.

WARNER, W. LLOYD; HAVIGHURST, ROBERT J.; and LOEB, MARTIN B. 1944 *Who Shall Be Educated? The Challenge of Unequal Opportunities*. New York: Harper.

WARNER, W. LLOYD; and LOW, J. O. 1947 *The Social System of the Modern Factory.* New Haven: Yale Univ. Press; Oxford Univ. Press.

WARNER, W. LLOYD; and LUNT, PAUL S. 1941 *The Social Life of a Modern Community.* New Haven: Yale Univ. Press.

WARNER, W. LLOYD; MEEKER, MARCHIA; and EELLS, KENNETH (1949) 1960 *Social Class in America: A Manual of Procedure for the Measurement of Social Status.* New York: Harper.

WARNER, W. LLOYD; and SROLE, LEO 1945 *The Social Systems of American Ethnic Groups.* New Haven: Yale Univ. Press.

WARNER, W. LLOYD et al. 1949 *Democracy in Jonesville: A Study in Quality and Inequality.* New York: Harper.

WHYTE, WILLIAM F. (1943) 1961 *Street Corner Society: The Social Structure of an Italian Slum.* 2d ed., enl. Univ. of Chicago Press.

WHYTE, WILLIAM F. 1948 *Human Relations in the Restaurant Industry.* New York: McGraw-Hill.

WILLIAMS, JAMES M. 1906 *An American Town: A Sociological Study.* New York: Kempster.

[WITHERS, CARL] (1945) 1961 *Plainville, U.S.A.,* by James West [pseud.]. New York: Columbia Univ. Press.

YANG, MOU-CH'UN (1945) 1965 *A Chinese Village: Taitou, Shantung Province.* New York: Columbia Univ. Press.

ZORBAUGH, HARVEY W. 1929 *Gold Coast and Slum: A Sociological Study of Chicago's Near North Side.* Univ. of Chicago Press.

VI

THE COMPARATIVE METHOD IN ANTHROPOLOGY

Social and cultural anthropologists concern themselves with three main types of problems: (1) the description of ethnographic facts, (2) inductive reconstruction of long-term cultural history, and (3) the development of general propositions about culturally regulated human behavior. Cross-cultural comparison is an essential element in any form of either the second or third problem. Since anthropological theory building begins with inductive inferences from loosely associated ethnographic facts, the argument can always be *illustrated* by cross-cultural comparison. Some believe that, properly manipulated, this combination of induction plus exemplification can lead to the discovery of true sociological "laws," analogous to the "law" of gravitation or the "principle" of the conservation of energy. They claim that these regularities can be demonstrated, either as universal truths or as statistical probabilities. In this article some of the common variations of this doctrine will be examined.

Scientific explanation

The natural science analogy. In the natural sciences it is taken for granted that the behavior of all materials under observation is governed by laws of nature. Every experiment is repeatable, and inconsistencies in results imply either faulty technique or faulty understanding. Inconsistency can never lie in the behavior of the subject matter because the material of the experiment does not have a will of its own.

With this basic assumption underlying all theoretical formulations, exact descriptions and rigidly controlled experiment will always lead to an understanding of the mechanisms of natural process. This understanding should enable the scientist to predict with confidence the statistical probability of future events. An essential part of this scientific procedure is the development of precisely defined concepts (such as species, elements, molecules, atoms, elementary particles, mass, energy, pressure, spatial dimension, temperature), which together provide an internationally agreed upon frame of reference in terms of which the particular phenomena observed by different investigators may be described. Scientific progress is possible only because all the specialists in a given discipline use units of description that are commonly understood and have precisely defined meaning. The philosophy underlying all such science is atomistic, and the "model of reality" is that of a system of relationships between unit entities which are deemed, for the arbitrary purposes of the discussion, to be isolate and impermeable.

These characteristics of natural science have been consciously imitated by leading theorists of the social sciences, but they have been reluctant to admit that the two fields are analogous rather than homologous. Unfortunately there are several characteristics inherent in the data of social science that cast serious doubts as to how far a natural science methodology is really justifiable.

Human subject matter cannot be presumed to have a neutral attitude. At certain levels of organization human material does have a will of its own, and consequently all prediction based on the analysis of past experience must be subject to qualification. The question whether social phenomena consist of events which are governed by individual wills or of processes unaffected by individual intentions is the basic issue which distinguishes the method of history from the method of sociology. The sociologist searches for social facts which correspond to natural phenomena, in that they are predictable and resistant to manipulation by individual human wills. Durkheim believed that there were three main classes of social fact, namely: (1) language and other codes of communication by which the members of a society communicate with one another; (2) statistical facts of a demographic or economic kind, which are measures of the condition of society rather than of the will of individuals—e.g., the suicide rate or the unemployment rate, which have respectively been used as measures of the psychological health and the economic health of society as a whole; (3) "customs" and "jural rules." It is with this last category that there are the greatest difficulties. How far does it really refer to phenomena which are external to the individual? What is a custom? Is it a description of how people behave or of how they are supposed to behave? Consider the following examples. We can learn from the pages of a standard work of ethnography that it is *customary* among the Kurds for a man to marry his father's brother's daughter. We can also learn that in one particular Kurdish community in 1951, 45 per cent of all marriages conformed to this customary pattern (Barth 1954). On the other hand, whereas the standard ethnographic account of the Trobriand Islands says that it is *customary* for a man to marry his father's sister's daughter, a very detailed demographic survey carried out in 1951 recorded only one such marriage among several hundred (Powell 1957). What are we to make of such discrepancies? If customs are to be compared cross-culturally, what is it that we should compare? In the natural sciences this kind of difficulty does not arise. The sequence of research procedure is quite standardized: in any one experiment the individual observations are interpreted as exemplifying a regularity of nature, a *normal* event. From a series of such inferred normalities the observer deduces a principle of regularity or "law." But in anthropology, customs and jural rules are *normative,* not *normal*; although their natures can often be discovered directly by question and answer they cannot be discovered at all by averaging out the details of actual behavior. The raw material of ethnography can be assembled either as a set of individually observed events or as a set of normal events (average actual occurrences), or as a set of normative ideal patterns (verbalized customs). But the last class is not a derivative of the other two. It is not at all obvious why customs—i.e., normative ideal patterns of behavior—should have any characteristics comparable to those regularities we encounter in natural law. Natural law regularities are summaries of events which actually occur; customs are mere mental configurations.

Most social scientists, but especially anthropologists, feel that their concern is with people living in "ordinary" rather than "artificial" social conditions. Social anthropologists are precluded from laboratory experiment. However, it has sometimes been suggested that if an anthropologist compares "ordinary" phenomena in two or more different cultural contexts the procedure is equivalent to that of making repeated observations in a controlled laboratory experiment (see, for example, Ackerknecht 1954, p. 125). This is held to justify the statistical comparison of data derived from quite distinct cultural situations. For example, in many societies a rule of matrilineal descent is found to be associated with a kinship terminology in which the father's sister and the father's sister's daughter are placed in a single category. Some writers treat this association as a kind of natural law such that if the correlation were checked for all known matrilineal systems the statistical probability of it occurring in any newly discovered case could be specified. Thus, when in a sample of fifty societies with "exclusive matrilineal descent with exogamy" only 42 per cent conformed to the expected pattern, Murdock nevertheless claims that this correlation "tends to occur" and the theorem is thereby "conclusively validated" (Murdock 1949, pp. 166–167). A statistic of this kind seems to be devoid of any meaning. It does not tell us whether the correlation will or will not hold for any particular future case. Moreover, the resemblance between such a finding and a genuine scientific discovery is quite specious. The link between matrilineal descent and this particular kin-term usage is a matter of logic. The correlation can be directly inferred from the operations necessary to produce a satisfactory definition of the expression "matrilineal descent group." What is surprising is not the empirical association of facts but the lack of it. The circumstance that Murdock's statistic does not work out at 100 per cent provides us with the useful but scientifically disconcerting information that cultural data are not always consistent, and this in itself invalidates the whole methodology. Similar destructive criticism can be leveled against all attempts to show that correlations of custom conform cross-culturally to statistical probabilities (Köbben 1952).

Cultural facts are not readily discriminated into ultimate units which can be given precise taxonomic description. A generation ago it was quite common for anthropologists to write as if "a culture" was a simple assemblage of elementary particles or traits, the nature of which could be exactly specified. Social reality could then be described as a system of relationships between unit traits which recur in different cultural contexts, just as unit atoms of particular elements recur in different chemical contexts. This orientation to cultural data is untenable. The units of ordinary anthropological description—expressions like "patrilineal descent," "uxorilocal residence," "matrilateral cross-cousin marriage," "ancestor worship," "bride price," "shifting cultivation," etc.—which are still used as the discriminating traits in even the most sophisticated forms of cross-cultural analysis—are not in any way comparable to the precisely defined diagnostic elements which form the units of discourse in natural science. This is the heart of the whole matter. Those who claim to formulate "scientific" generalizations on the basis of cross-cultural comparison are asserting that they can recognize by inspection that a characteristic x found in culture A belongs or does not belong to the same subclass of social facts as a characteristic y found in culture B. The following is a case in point. The inhabitants of the tiny Polynesian island of Tikopia recognize that their social system is composed of social groups called *paito*; the Nuer of the Sudan recognize groups called *thok dwiel*; the Kachin of northern Burma recognize groups called *amyu*; the Chinese recognize groups called *tsung-tsu*; and so on. In the jargon of contemporary social anthropology all these entities are to be classed as patrilineal descent groups; they are examples of "the same thing." Such propositions clearly leave plenty of room for skepticism. To assert of even one particular that the Tikopia and the Chinese have "the same kind of social structure" must invite caution. What could such a proposition really mean? It is rather like pointing to the undoubted resemblance between a clock face and the stars of the zodiac. It is obvious yet utterly irrelevant. However, such comparisons are orthodox in anthropology.

The communication system analogy. Malinowski sought to evade the difficulties raised by simple trait comparisons by blandly affirming that every social event is uniquely defined by its total social context (Malinowski 1944; see also Goldschmidt 1966). If this were the case, all cross-cultural comparison would be futile. The thesis advanced by Malinowski has yielded little fruit. One trouble is the anthropologists' insistence that their generalizations are *scientific*. But if we frame our objectives with greater modesty, if we simply try to understand how human beings behave, the outlook need not be so depressing. In practice, despite the theoretical difficulties, all anthropologists, Malinowski included, have resorted to cross-cultural comparison to generate ideas. Such comparison may not prove anything, but it gives insight. We may need to get away from the natural science analogy and place stress on the fact that all customs and rules of behavior are human inventions. It is true that we do not ordinarily observe an individual inventing a custom, but customs can be described by individuals, and in this form they represent mental configurations of which all human minds are capable. Human beings do not all think alike, but they need not all think differently. Patterns of social behavior can and do recur in widely different contexts. That being so, our problem can be turned inside out. The issue should not be: How can we discover the social laws which govern cultural behavior? For in fact we have no valid ground for supposing that there are any such social laws. Instead, we can start with the observable fact that at different levels of abstraction similar configurations of cultural phenomena recur in different contexts. What significance should be attached to such recurrence?

This line of argument leads back to a position close to that adopted by the social evolutionists of the late nineteenth century. At that time it was assumed that cultural traits from different primitive contexts were comparable because they were products of human minds "at the same stage of development." Today the comparative structuralism of Lévi-Strauss implies a rather similar attitude. Cultures are not to be thought of as assemblages of social facts which exist *sui generis* but rather as systems of communication. We can compare cultures just as we can compare spoken languages, but if we do so, the similarities which emerge result from the fact that all human brains operate in the same way. We are not discovering truths of nature which are independent of human actors but rather the possibilities of human action as such. Such an orientation leads to a shift in view about the purpose for which cross-cultural comparison may be conducted. Instead of demonstrating that a particular correlation of cultural traits $p, q, r, \ldots$ is repeated in different cultural contexts A, B, C, $\ldots$, which is the ultimate objective in all indexing procedures such as the Human Relations Area Files, we are led to other considerations. First, what is the structural–functional logic which brings features $p, q, r, \ldots$ into association in context A? Second, what variations of this concatenation $p, q, r, \ldots$ are conceptually possible? Third, which of these variations actually occur and in what circumstances? The outcome of such a procedure is a comparison of contrasts rather than a comparison of similarities, and the objective of the exercise is to discover what is humanly feasible rather than to demonstrate what is statistically probable. Cross-cultural comparison here becomes a means of understanding the humanity of human beings. It is not a question of demonstrating that culture is like nature, but of showing how culture differs from nature.

Cross-cultural analysis

The following are some of the more distinctive types of cross-cultural comparison which have been adopted by anthropologists.

The British social evolutionists. The phrase "the comparative method" in English-language anthropological writings usually refers to a specific style of demonstration employed by a wide variety of authors from about 1860 onward. Outstanding exponents of the method during the period before 1914 were H. Spencer, E. B. Tylor, J. G. Frazer, E. S. Hartland, E. Westermarck, E. Crawley, and L. T. Hobhouse. More recent scholars who have employed similar procedures include R. Briffault, M. Eliade, and E. O. James. The technique rests on the notion that the development of human society has been analogous to the development of a human individual: primitive societies correspond to human infants, sophisticated societies to human adults. Whether a particular society is to be rated primitive or sophisticated can be judged by inspection. Just as human adults retain in their psychological make-up features which derive from childish experience, so also sophisticated societies retain "survivals" of primitive features. It is assumed that the objective of anthropology is to reconstruct a convincing picture of the early state of human society. Evidence for this primeval condition of mankind can be drawn either directly, from the observation of existing primitive societies, or indirectly, from the study of survivals persisting in contemporary sophisticated society. Since the anthropologist himself is the judge of what is primitive or sophisticated and since no clear distinction is drawn between myth and legend, on the one hand, and customary practice, on the other, almost any kind of ethnographic evidence can serve as illustrative evidence of hypothetical past social conditions.

Certain features are characteristic of all exponents of the comparative method among the earlier evolutionists. The practitioners displayed a prodigious range of erudition in that they were familiar with an extraordinary variety of ethnographic facts. This knowledge was derived exclusively from books. Very few of the writers concerned had first-hand knowledge of any particular primitive society. (Edward Westermarck, who had detailed knowledge of Morocco, is here the exception.) Each item of illustrative evidence was detached from its context and treated as directly comparable to any other. All varieties of evidence were considered uncritically: a detail mentioned by a classical author of the third century B.C. was given the same credibility as an item attributed to a sixteenth-century traveler, an eighteenth-century missionary, or a late nineteenth-century ethnographer. Evidence from myth was treated as the equivalent of fact.

The comparative method took no cognizance of quantitative factors or variations of scale. As Hartland put it, the objective was to "illustrate a great body of traditional philosophy, confined not to one race or country but common to mankind." Also, the ethnographic evidence was always used to exemplify general propositions with the implication that such propositions are validated by an accumulation of positive evidence. Neutral or negative evidence was never considered. This procedure is logically fallacious. The exponents of the "comparative method" did not in fact prove anything by their comparisons, and if some of the works in question—such as Frazer's *Golden Bough*—retain a certain residual attractiveness it is because of the exotic quality of the data rather than because of any intrinsic merit in the argument.

Culture history

From about 1890 onward the doctrines of the social evolutionists were gradually superseded by various forms of diffusionism. Evolutionists supposed that all human societies follow the same course of development: the occurrence of similar cultural features in different contexts of time and space was evidence for the standardization of human minds and a uniform capacity for invention. Diffusionists were disinclined to recognize invention at all; the geographical distribution of cultural traits was evidence for historical contact and dispersal by borrowing from a single original source. Historical reconstructions were elaborated from skilled exploitation of the theory of "survivals," which had originated among the evolutionists. Work of this kind ranges from the grandiose world histories of the *Kulturkreislehre* (see e.g., Montandon 1934, p. 97) to the reconstructions of Californian Indian history developed by Kroeber and Driver (Culture . . . 1937–1950) on the basis of meticulous statistical analysis of trait distributions. The works of the *Kulturkreislehre* suffer from the same defects as those of the social evolutionists. A formidable apparatus of comparative ethnographic evidence was marshaled so as to illustrate a thesis developed a priori. Negative evidence was not usually considered, and there was little discrimination concerning the quality or context of evidential sources. As was to be expected, trait distribution studies have become increasingly sophisticated with the passage of time, and distinction now needs to be drawn between arguments about the diffusion of artifacts and those in which the traits under discussion are such ephemeral things as customs, rules, and items of belief. The relative plausibility of some of the diffusionist historical reconstructions advanced by prehistoric archeologists depends on the fact that since material objects are part of nature as well as part of culture we can reasonably expect them to conform to "natural" regularities. By contrast, if we treat the abstract aspects of culture as natural we shall merely deceive ourselves.

Statistical analysis of nonmaterial cultural data

Tylor (1889) was among the first to attempt a statistical correlation of social institutions based on cross-cultural data—in this case between mother-in-law avoidance and certain other social conventions. A much more ambitious enterprise was that of Hobhouse, Wheeler, and Ginsberg (1915), which endeavored to establish an empirical correlation between basic modes of subsistence and the forms of social organization. These scholars classified 552 societies into lower hunters, higher hunters, dependent hunters, agricultural or pastoral on the first level, agricultural or pastoral on the second level, and agricultural on level three. They then developed a cross-cultural index that recorded for each "people" the presence or absence of such characteristics as types of legal sanction, mode of descent, patterns of residence, sexual conventions, treatment of women, modes of warfare, degree of social stratification. The Yale cross-cultural survey initiated by Murdock in 1937, which later developed into the Human Relations Area Files (Yale University . . . 1938; Moore 1961) and the Ethnographic Atlas of *Ethnology*, has greatly refined the procedures adopted by Hobhouse, Wheeler, and Ginsberg, but it remains a work of essentially the same kind and suffers from the same intrinsic defects, some of which have been pointed out in earlier sections of this article. The basic units of comparison, which are variously described as tribes, peoples, cultures, or societies, are treated as if they were naturally bounded and self-discriminating. They are investigated as if they were zoological pseudo species. The purpose of the analysis is to establish a taxonomy of culture species on Linnaean principles. Just as the classification of plants and animals throws light upon the sequences of evolution, so also a classification of societies according to their morphological characteristics will demonstrate laws of social evolutionary change.

To accept this thesis it is necessary to believe not only that "societies" ("cultures" etc.) exist in nature just as "species," but that the distinctive features of anthropological description (e.g., the contrast between the presence or absence of unilineal descent groups) are comparable to the distinctive features of biological description (e.g., the contrast between vertebrates and invertebrates). Those who reject this homology are likely to view the development of the Ethnographic Atlas with some dismay. The information recorded in this index is being coded to a numerical taxonomy, which will eventually make the whole apparatus directly accessible to computer analysis. This may seem splendidly up to date, but if the information which is being stored is defective in the first place the later application of statistical analysis, computerized or otherwise, will compound the confusion (e.g., Coult & Habenstein 1965).

Structural comparison (Radcliffe-Brown)

The classical comparative method, the diffusionist reconstructions of the cultural historians, and the various styles in cross-cultural statistical analysis all rested on the proposition that "a culture" ("a society," etc.) is to be conceived of as an assemblage of traits which can be separately compared. Functionalist social anthropology rejects this view. Societies are systems which can be compared only as wholes. In Malinowski's version of functionalism this wholeness was so comprehensive that all cross-cultural comparison became meaningless, but Radcliffe-Brown sought to discover universal sociological laws and was prepared to recognize that, for comparative purposes, the notion of functional totality could be raised to a somewhat abstract level. In this he followed Durkheim. A society must be analyzed as a system, not as a set of component parts, but the analyst may reduce his problem to manageable proportions by considering only one frame of reference at a time. It then becomes legitimate to compare the political system of society A with the political system of society B, or the kinship system of society A with the kinship system of society B, and so on. From this there might emerge certain general principles which can be applied to the analysis of politics or kinship everywhere. Although early work of this genre showed exaggerated optimism, it has achieved some notable successes. The procedure has not yielded general sociological laws, but close attention to details and patient step-by-step testing of limited hypotheses have led to genuinely increased insight into some particular aspects of human behavior. This style of comparison is most fruitful when all the societies under consideration share a common geographical environment and are broadly similar in scale and general culture (e.g., Radcliffe-Brown 1931; Eggan 1950; Schapera 1953).

Despite Radcliffe-Brown's emphasis on the notion of system and occasions when he invoked comparison as a means to solving problems of philosophy and psychology (e.g., 1951), he remained firmly attached to the natural science analogy. He thought of social structure as part of the social system in much the same sense as the bony skeleton is part of the living mammal, and he supposed that anthropologists might compare whole societies just as zoologists can compare mammalian species. But a skeleton is a tangible reality; a social structure is not.

Structural comparison (Lévi-Strauss)

If we think of society as a communication system rather than as a natural phenomenon we are led to think of the products of culture as structured, just as the sentences of the language, if they are to be comprehensible, must conform to certain transformational rules but are not predetermined as to content. Two expressions which exemplify the same principles of grammar and syntax may not resemble each other at all in their overt form. If this analogy is exact, it should be possible and rewarding to compare the structure of cultural systems at a more abstract level. Lévi-Strauss insists that cultural systems are in fact used like languages; it is through culture that men are able to recognize the world of nature and the world of society as an ordered place with which they can come to terms. Kinship systems, political systems, and mythological systems are systems of classification invented by men. The structures they embody are logical structures which correspond to ordinary human faculties. The regularities which we may expect to find in them are not a part of nature outside man but a part of nature inside man. Linguistics and psychology rather than biology are the proper models for the inquiring anthropologist. Although an appreciation of existentialist philosophy may be necessary to understand Lévi-Strauss's position, the idea which has been recurrent in all his work—that cultural systems may be comparable not merely because they are palpably similar but because they represent logical transformations of a common structural theme—is one which has added an important new dimension to contemporary anthropological thinking.

When anthropologists generalize they do so on the basis of cross-cultural comparison, but the rationale of their use of comparative data seldom bears close examination. Two main styles of argument may be distinguished. On the one hand, there are theories which presuppose a psychological unity among all mankind. Similarities of culture accordingly illustrate the fact that human beings faced with similar situations will react in the same way. On the other hand, there are theories which presume the existence of social facts lying outside human control, even though they are governed by natural regularities as are the ordinary facts of physical experience. Here the point of cross-cultural comparison is to reach the autonomous world of social truth by eliminating the human variable. The present writer is inclined to share the skepticism voiced by Evans-Pritchard (1963). Cross-cultural comparison is an essential device for the exposition of anthropological argument, but it is not, and cannot be, a disguised form of scientific experiment leading to explanation. As Montesquieu once put it, "Man, as a physical being, is like other bodies, governed by invariable laws. As an intelligent being, he incessantly transgresses the laws established by God, and changes those which he himself has established" (Montesquieu [1750] 1949, p. 3).

EDMUND R. LEACH

[*For different viewpoints, see* ETHNOLOGY; EVOLUTION, INTRODUCTION *and article on* CULTURAL EVOLUTION; HISTORY, *article on* CULTURE HISTORY. *Directly related are the entries* CULTURE; DIFFUSION; FUNCTIONAL ANALYSIS; SYSTEMS ANALYSIS.]

BIBLIOGRAPHY

ACKERKNECHT, ERWIN H. 1954 On the Comparative Method in Anthropology. Pages 117–125 in R. F. Spencer (editor), *Method and Perspective in Anthropology: Papers in Honor of Wilson D. Wallis.* Minneapolis: Univ. of Minnesota Press.

BARTH, FREDRIK 1954 Father's Brother's Daughter Marriage in Kurdistan. *Southwestern Journal of Anthropology* 10:164–171.

COULT, ALLAN D.; and HABENSTEIN, ROBERT W. 1965 *Cross-tabulations of Murdock's World Ethnographic Sample.* Columbia: Univ. of Missouri Press.

Culture Element Distributions. 1937–1950 California, University of, *Anthropological Records* 1, no. 1–9, no. 3.

EGGAN, FRED 1950 *Social Organization of the Western Pueblos.* Univ. of Chicago Press.

Ethnology. → Published since 1962 under the editorship of George P. Murdock.

EVANS-PRITCHARD, E. E. (1963) 1965 The Comparative Method in Social Anthropology. L. T. Hobhouse Memorial Trust Lecture, 1963. Pages 13–36 in E. E. Evans-Pritchard, *The Position of Women in Primitive Societies and Other Essays in Social Anthropology.* London: Faber.

FORTES, MEYER 1953 The Structure of Unilineal Descent Groups. *American Anthropologist* New Series 55:17–41.

GOLDSCHMIDT, WALTER 1966 *Comparative Functionalism*. Berkeley and Los Angeles: Univ. of California Press.

HOBHOUSE, LEONARD T.; WHEELER, GERALD C.; and GINSBERG, MORRIS (1915) 1965 *The Material Culture and Social Institutions of the Simpler Peoples: An Essay in Correlation*. London School of Economics and Political Science, Monographs on Sociology, No. 3. London: Routledge.

KÖBBEN, ANORÉ J. 1952 New Ways of Presenting an Old Idea: The Statistical Method in Social Anthropology. *Journal of the Royal Anthropological Institute of Great Britain and Ireland* 82:129–146.

MALINOWSKI, BRONISLAW 1944 *A Scientific Theory of Culture and Other Essays*. Chapel Hill: Univ. of North Carolina Press.

MONTANDON, GEORGE 1934 *L'ologénèse culturelle: Traité d'ethnologie cycloculturelle et d'ergologie systématique*. Paris: Payot.

MONTESQUIEU, CHARLES DE (1750) 1949 *The Spirit of the Laws*. 2 vols. in 1. New York: Haffner. → First published in French.

MOORE, FRANK W. (editor) 1961 *Readings in Cross-cultural Methodology*. New Haven: Human Relations Area Files Press.

MURDOCK, GEORGE P. 1949 *Social Structure*. New York: Macmillan. → A paperback edition was published in 1965 by the Free Press.

POWELL, HENRY A. 1957 An Analysis of Present Day Social Structure in the Trobriand Islands. Ph.D. dissertation, Univ. of London.

RADCLIFFE-BROWN, A. R. (1931) 1948 *The Social Organization of Australian Tribes*. Glencoe, Ill.: Free Press.

RADCLIFFE-BROWN, A. R. 1951 The Comparative Method in Social Anthropology. Huxley Memorial Lecture for 1951. *Journal of the Royal Anthropological Institute of Great Britain and Ireland* 81:15–22.

SCHAPERA, I. 1953 Some Comments on Comparative Method in Social Anthropology. *American Anthropologist* New Series 55:353–362.

TYLOR, EDWARD B. (1889) 1961 On a Method of Investigating the Development of Institutions: Applied to Laws of Marriage and Descent. Pages 1–28 in Frank W. Moore (editor), *Readings in Cross-cultural Methodology*. New Haven: Human Relations Area Files Press.

YALE UNIVERSITY, INSTITUTE OF HUMAN RELATIONS (1938) 1961 *Outline of Cultural Materials*. 4th ed., rev. New Haven: Human Relations Area Files.

ANTI-SEMITISM

Anti-Semitism, literally referring to hatred of Semites but commonly understood as hatred of Jews, is a late nineteenth-century term for a phenomenon almost as old as human history. One of the earliest recorded instances of anti-Semitism occurred more than four hundred years before the birth of Christ, when a Jewish temple on an island in the Nile was wantonly destroyed by a group of Egyptian priests. The Egyptians are still at war with the Jews, or at least that portion of Jewry that inhabits the state of Israel; but the modern Egyptians are hardly alone in disliking Jews and in

believing that the Israelis are less a Middle Eastern people than an alien army of occupation. The entire Arab world is anti-Zionist, and so are Arab sympathizers in Latin America, Africa, Europe, and the United States. The Russians also dislike Zionists and/or Jews—it is not always easy to distinguish between the anti-Semite and the anti-Zionist, since they tend to behave in similar fashion. In short, despite the fact that the conscience of much of the civilized world was scarred by the Nazi murder of more than six million Jews, anti-Semitism retains its power in several countries and is everywhere a force to be reckoned with.

There are important differences, however, between modern forms of anti-Semitism and the older varieties. Modern versions, of which Nazi racism is the archetype, are both more ideological and more virulent than ancient types. The early Greek anti-Semites, for example, like all anti-Semites ever since, saw Jews as "different," but the differences they stressed were not those of the later Christian era. They could make little sense of either the theory or practice of Judaism, and what little they understood they disliked. Their own polytheism, with its numerous gods and attendant cults, festivals, feast days, and ceremonial rituals, seemed to the Greeks preferable to monotheism, which, in the Jewish version, called for fasting, days of atonement, dietary and sexual restrictions, and other chastisements. Functioning, in effect, as the Puritans of the pagan world, Jews were regarded with curiosity and barely concealed dislike. Even the great Roman historian Tacitus could not refrain from observing, in connection with the belief that the Jews worshiped Bacchus, that the "cult [of Bacchus] would be most inappropriate. Bacchus instituted gay and cheerful rites, but the Jewish ritual is preposterous and morbid." It also appeared to Tacitus that Jewish customs in general were "impious and abominable, and owe their prevalence to their [the Jews'] depravity." Jewish "prosperity," Tacitus continued, is largely due to the fact that ". . . they are obstinately loyal to each other, and always ready to show compassion, whereas they feel nothing but hatred and enmity for the rest of the world" (Tacitus, *The Histories*, vol. 2, pp. 202–208, 211–218).

Tacitus was not alone in believing that Jewish religious practices were an abomination. Plutarch, the Greek biographer, thought it possible that Jews abstained from pork because the pig was an object of veneration, whereas Strabo, the geographer, attributed such abstemiousness, along with "circumcisions and excisions," to "superstition." Apion, the most dedicated anti-Semite of the ancient world, suspected that Jews drank the blood of gentile children and also provided a novel explanation for the Jewish observance of the Sabbath. Apion wrote that after a six-day march during the exodus from Egypt the Jews "developed tumors in the groin, and that was why, after safely reaching the country now called Judaea, they rested on the seventh day, and called that day *sabbaton,* preserving the Egyptian terminology; for disease of the groin in Egypt is called *sabbo*" (Josephus, *Against Apion,* vol. 1, p. 301).

Despite these calumnies, the Greeks and Romans did not attempt to destroy Judaism root and branch; that phase of anti-Semitism began with the conversion to Christianity of the Roman emperor Constantine in 312. The first two centuries of the Christian era constitute, on the whole, a mixed period. Various edicts banned the study of Talmudic law, and under Hadrian Jewish scholars were not permitted to hold classes or meet with students. Caracalla, on the other hand, conferred full citizenship on the Jews in 212, and during the reign of Alexander Severus (222–235) the ethnic and religious character of Judaism was formally recognized. While Jews were not allowed to proselytize, they were permitted to practice their religion and live at peace with other citizens.

During the reign of Constantine (306–337) and his successors, the position of Jews in the Roman Empire was greatly altered. Christians were forbidden to convert to Judaism under penalty of death, but Jews were encouraged and at times almost forced to become Christian converts. The Theodosian and Justinian Codes of the fifth and sixth centuries excluded Jews from positions of authority. Intermarriage between Jews and Christians was prohibited, and Jews were forbidden to own Christian slaves. Social intercourse with Christians was strictly regulated. The construction of synagogues was banned, although established places of worship could be kept in repair. Notwithstanding the official church opposition to the employment of force against Jews, there were numerous anti-Jewish demonstrations and acts of violence aimed at Jews individually and collectively.

Nevertheless, Jewish life and culture survived in several areas of Europe, notably Italy, France, Visigothic Spain, and Byzantium. Despite forced conversions, massacres, and a great variety of proscriptions affecting religious practices, Jewish communities managed to survive, and in Spain, by the eleventh century, to flourish. Indeed, for almost five hundred years, culminating in the "golden age" of Jewish history from the eleventh

to the early thirteenth century, Spanish Jews under Islamic rule enjoyed freedoms and privileges unparalleled in any of the Christian countries of Europe. The blending of Jewish and Arab cultures was stimulating to both Jews and Muslims and produced discoveries of enduring significance in such fields as medicine, mathematics, physics, and astronomy. For the first time in centuries Jews were permitted to engage in a variety of careers, and in these careers many Jews made important contributions to the character and quality of life in Islamic Spain.

The position of Spanish Jewry was not shared by Jews elsewhere. Isolated in gentile communities and therefore all the more vulnerable to discriminatory acts, the Jews of France and Germany, in particular, were constantly exposed to persecution. The crusades at the end of the tenth century, marked by wholesale butchery of Jews and frequent Jewish suicides, were a clear demonstration of what Jews could expect from crusading Christians, and in this respect the crusades anticipated much that became relatively commonplace during the Middle Ages. Legal and other types of restrictions affecting Jews multiplied rapidly, especially after the Third and Fourth Lateran Councils (1179 and 1215). The Fourth Council declared flatly that Jews were outcastes with whom there was to be no social mingling, much less intermarriage. They were not to hold public office, employ Christian servants, or leave their homes during Easter week. The council decreed that since Jews were infidels, they were henceforth to wear a special badge of identification—a round patch of yellow cloth—on the upper garment.

In certain cases, however, these severe restrictions succeeded only in whetting the appetite for extreme anti-Semitism without satisfying it. England expelled the Jews in 1290, and in France, after a series of massacres, extortions from the Jewish community, and other harassments, Jews were banished in 1394. Germany designated Jews *servi camerae,* or serfs of the state, and as such they were heavily taxed and confined to the petty trades. The Spanish Jews were not expelled until 1492, but during the preceding century and a half, following the expulsion of the Arabs, the Jews were subjected to incessant persecution by the Catholic rulers of Castile and Aragon. Even the ostensible converts to Catholicism, the marranos, were not free from the tortures of the Inquisition, established in 1480 by Ferdinand and Isabella.

The intolerance of the Middle Ages, while multicausal in nature, owed more to religious fanaticism than to any other single factor. In addition to believing that persecution of Jews enjoyed divine approval, the church hierarchy suspected that Jews were responsible for various heretical tendencies, such as the Albigensian movement. Later, during the Reformation, many Catholics regarded Protestantism as a Jewish conspiracy against the church. Rank-and-file Catholics and more than a few of the clergy held the Jews responsible for the death of Jesus Christ, and large numbers of Catholics, perhaps most, were convinced that Jews engaged in bizarre religious practices, such as drinking the blood of Christian children and defiling Christian maidens on certain ceremonial occasions.

Since it was Judaism itself that was at fault, the church for many centuries would accept nothing less than the wholesale conversion of Jews to Christianity, in a word, the extirpation of Judaism as such. Jews unwilling to convert were to be treated as perpetual pariahs, and hence it was hardly unchristian for Pope Paul IV in 1555 to require that Jews wear a badge of identity to mark them forever as a people separate and inferior. He also created the ghetto by decreeing that Jews were to live apart from Christians, and he added, for good measure, a list of professions and occupations from which Jews were to be excluded.

It should hardly be construed from this, however, that the Protestant sects were more tolerant of Jews than the Roman Catholic church. Luther himself indulged in bigotry, especially after 1530, when he became convinced that Jews would not convert to Christianity in great numbers. He asked rhetorically in 1543,

What then shall we Christians do with this damned, rejected race of Jews? . . . Let me give you my honest advice. First, their synagogues or churches should be set on fire. . . . Secondly, their homes should likewise be broken down and destroyed. . . . Thirdly, they should be deprived of their prayer-books. . . . Fourthly, their rabbis must be forbidden under threat of death to teach any more. . . . Fifthly, passport and traveling privileges should be absolutely forbidden. . . . Sixthly, they ought to be stopped from usury. . . . Seventhly, let the young and strong Jews and Jewesses be given the flail, the ax, the hoe, the spade, the distaff, and spindle, and let them earn their bread by the sweat of their noses. . . . [If there is any danger, Luther counseled, of Jews doing harm to their gentile overlords] . . . let us drive them out of the country for all time . . . away with them. (In Marcus [1938] 1960, pp. 167–169)

By the end of the seventeenth century Jews had been expelled from many parts of western and central Europe, and where they were not expelled, they were, with only a few countries excepted, forced to live in ghettos, subjected to pogroms, and humiliated in countless ways. The German Jews who had migrated to Poland before 1648 were butchered by the thousands during the Cossack revolt against Polish rule. Elsewhere, while they were regulated more by edicts and less by mob violence, the laws affecting them were largely based on medieval caricatures and stereotypes. At best, they were minimally tolerated.

Nevertheless, by the end of the eighteenth century a variety of influences—political, economic, intellectual—were combining to create an era of relative toleration. On September 28, 1791, the French National Assembly that resulted from the Revolution conferred equal citizenship upon Jews, and everywhere Napoleon's armies marched local authorities were urged or required to follow the French example. England emancipated its Jews in 1860 (they had been readmitted in 1655), and Germany granted Jews equal rights in 1870. It was only in eastern Europe that the majority of Jews still lived in conditions approximating those of medieval Europe. The world's largest Jewish population was confined under Russian rule to an enormous ghetto, and there it was to remain, persecuted almost continuously, until 1917. The fortunate Jews were able to migrate to western Europe and the United States; the remainder stayed behind, pogromized by the imperial army, tsarist police, Cossacks, Poles, White Russians, and others.

The years immediately after World War I seemed to mark the dawn of a new epoch for European Jewry. The Treaty of Versailles appeared to guarantee the political, social, and cultural rights of minorities in eastern Europe. The new Polish Republic emancipated the Jews, and in 1917, the Balfour Declaration, issued by the British secretary of state for foreign affairs, announced to the world that "His Majesty's Government view with favour the establishment in Palestine of a national home for the Jewish people . . ." (Kohn 1963).

But it was more than thirty years before the national home was, in fact, established, and by that time it was too late to save most of the Jews of Europe from the Nazi holocaust. Hitler's task of extermination had been made easier, in a sense, by the frequent pogroms in Poland, Rumania, and the Ukraine during the 1920s. By 1945, as a result of Hitler's mass liquidation of the Jews, the so-called "final solution," there was no longer any important center of Jewish life in central and eastern Europe. The Jewish population of the Soviet Union, estimated to total between one and two million persons, enjoys little religious or cultural freedom. In effect, therefore, the future of

European Jewry is confined to the countries of western and southern Europe, especially the United Kingdom, France, Italy, the Netherlands, Switzerland, Belgium, and Denmark. In these countries anti-Semitism takes the form of discrimination in certain types of employment and of social snobbery.

Similar types of prejudice exist in the United States, but there is evidence that they are diminishing in intensity. The American Jewish community, numerically the world's largest with a population of more than five million, has traditionally enjoyed hospitality, although there have been times throughout American history when dislike of Jews was manifest. Peter Stuyvesant of New Amsterdam (now New York), for example, tried to exclude Jews from the Dutch colony, and two hundred years later General Ulysses S. Grant, suspecting that Jews were trading with the enemy and engaging in black market activities, endeavored to expel them from areas occupied by the Union army. The United States has occasionally heard the voice of religious anti-Semites, such as Father Coughlin, and it is familiar with the writings of literary anti-Semites, among whom the most prominent have been Henry Adams, John Jay Chapman (in his later years), and Ezra Pound. Henry Ford in the 1920s did much to spread the idea that the notorious *Protocols of the Elders of Zion* was the Jewish master plan for world conquest, and in the 1930s it was still possible for avowed anti-Semites to appear before congressional committees in opposition to the appointment of a Supreme Court justice solely on the grounds that he was a Jew.

It is beyond question, however, that American Jews have fared better than the Jews of any other country. Despite occasional outbreaks of anti-Semitism and the social and occupational discriminations affecting Jews, anti-Semitism has never been a matter of official government policy. The United States constitution states explicitly that no religious test shall ever be required for public office, and no American president has ever been a declared anti-Semite. Moreover, while no Jew has ever been nominated for the presidency, Jews have served with distinction as Supreme Court justices, governors, senators, and congressmen.

Although many first-generation and second-generation Americans have known anti-Semitism in the home, church, and school, as adults they have not taken to Jew-baiting, nor have they instituted pogroms or concentration camps. The influenza epidemic after World War I was not blamed on Jews, and the South did not attribute its defeat

in the Civil War to a Jewish conspiracy. To be sure, some professional anti-Semites have issued pamphlets "proving" that the fluoridation of water is a Jewish plot to weaken Christianity and the civil rights movement a Jewish conspiracy to "mongrelize" the white race, but it does not appear that these efforts are taken seriously by the majority of Americans. On the contrary, one notes fewer hotel and resort advertisements that include the phrase "Christians only," fewer universities that make use of the "quota" system for Jewish applicants, and fewer fraternities and sororities that refuse to admit Jewish students.

On the other hand, various studies suggest that ignorance about Jews is widespread, especially among young people, and it is far from clear that latent prejudice, as distinct from the manifest variety, has sharply diminished. According to one survey of the attitudes of high school children, "anti-Jewish prejudice of some kind and degree is found in 29 to 38 per cent of the high school students." Of the students questioned, 82 per cent overestimated the number of Jews in the United States; 28 per cent believed that Jews have too much economic power; 12 per cent thought Jews were overprivileged; and 9 per cent were of the opinion that Jews have too much political power (Anti-Defamation League of B'nai B'rith 1961, pp. 9–10).

Clearly, much that is known both about the nature of Jews and the nature of anti-Semitism has not penetrated the high school systems of the United States, and it is doubtful that education abroad has been more successful in this respect. Education must also take account of the stubborn fact that prejudice is essentially a learned response that develops at an early age out of family and neighborhood contacts; perhaps most prejudice develops between 6 and 16 years of age (Allport & Kramer 1946). Since these years are almost precisely the school years for most of the population, it would be highly desirable for the schools to devote at least as much attention to prejudice as to, say, driving lessons and home economics.

There is also much evidence that anti-Semitism, like other forms of prejudice, feeds on a variety of personality disorders. Frustration and deprivation, for example, generate hostile feelings toward Jews and other minorities (Adorno et al. 1950; Frenkel-Brunswik & Sanford 1945; Meltzer 1941). Indeed, it would appear that personality dynamics has much more to do with prejudice than the economic, cultural, or "racial" explanations usually associated with it. Thus it is possible to believe, as some anti-Semites do, that Jews are wealthy and powerful and also control radical movements, including the Communist party. The correlates of these beliefs are less with class, income, and religious backgrounds, although these are not unimportant, than with the personality structure of the believer. In a word, he *needs* to believe that Jews have all the money, or run the country, or own the newspapers. If he were deprived of this belief, which is the modern counterpart of the earlier notion that Jews drink the blood of Christian children, he would turn to another, equally false.

It remains true, however, that modern anti-Semites have fewer justifications for their prejudices than their predecessors. The notion that the Jews killed Christ and are therefore the possessors of a type of racial guilt, a notion that has inspired many a massacre and pogrom, was presumably undermined in 1965 when the fourth session of the Second Vatican Council officially . declared, "What happened to Christ in his Passion cannot be attributed to all Jews, without distinction, then alive, nor to the Jews of today" (Vatican Council . . . 1965, p. 24). The council deplored "hatred, persecutions, displays of anti-Semitism, directed against Jews at any time and by anyone" (Vatican Council . . . 1965, p. 24). Such a declaration, clearing Jews of the charge of "deicide," should do much in the future to reduce anti-Semitism everywhere, especially in the Roman Catholic countries.

The economic roots of anti-Semitism have also been exposed and at least partly destroyed in recent years. Jews have long since ceased to be thought of as exclusively moneylenders and pawnbrokers who are unable and unwilling to engage in manual labor and agricultural pursuits. The achievements of the farming kibbutzim in Israel have demonstrated that the land responds no less to Jewish than to gentile hands, and the image of the Jew as acquisitive is necessarily blurred in the acquisitive society. The belief in superior and inferior races is thoroughly discredited, and each year there are probably fewer people who believe that Jews are different from other ethnic groups in any important respect.

Nevertheless, the Jew as scapegoat has been important for almost 2,500 years, and sometime, somewhere, he may be important again. For the deprived Negro in New York's Harlem it is easy to imagine that slums and poverty are the result of exploitation by landlords and merchants who are predominantly Jewish, and the white supremacist in the southern United States has no trouble believing that Jews are responsible for the civil rights movement. Such belief systems, like the belief systems that accompany other types of prejudice, are not dislodged by simple argument, and indeed there is no simple solution for the problem of anti-Semitism. But if there is a solution at all it will take the form of efforts to promote in all humankind more maturity and rationality, more willingness to face one's own shortcomings, and more awareness of the great contributions Jews have made to civilization.

ARNOLD A. ROGOW

[*See also* JUDAISM; NATIONAL SOCIALISM; PREJUDICE; ZIONISM.]

BIBLIOGRAPHY

ADORNO, THEODOR W. et al. 1950 *The Authoritarian Personality.* American Jewish Committee, Social Studies Series No. 3. New York: Harper.

ALLPORT, GORDON W.; and KRAMER, BERNARD M. 1946 Some Roots of Prejudice. *Journal of Psychology* 22: 9–39.

ANTI-DEFAMATION LEAGUE OF B'NAI B'RITH 1961 *What the High School Students Say: A Survey of Attitudes and Knowledge About Jews and Nazism.* New York: The League.

FRENKEL-BRUNSWIK, ELSE; and SANFORD, R. NEVITT 1945 Some Personality Factors in Antisemitism. *Journal of Psychology* 20:271–291.

FREUD, SIGMUND (1934–1938) 1964 Moses and Monotheism: Three Essays. Volume 23 in *The Standard Edition of the Complete Psychological Works of Sigmund Freud.* London: Hogarth. → First published in German.

GLOCK, CHARLES Y.; and STARK, RODNEY 1966 *Christian Beliefs and Anti-Semitism.* New York: Harper.

KOHN, HANS 1963 Zionism. Pages 956–957 in *Encyclopaedia Britannica.* 14th ed. Chicago: Benton.

McWILLIAMS, CAREY 1948 *A Mask for Privilege: Anti-Semitism in America.* Boston: Little.

MARCUS, JACOB R. (1938) 1960 *The Jew in the Medieval World: A Source Book, 315–1791.* New York: Meridian.

MARGOLIS, MAX L.; and MARX, ALEXANDER (1927) 1958 *A History of the Jewish People.* New York: Meridian.

MELTZER, H. 1941 Hostility and Tolerance in Children's Nationality and Race Attitudes. *American Journal of Orthopsychiatry* 9:662–675.

MILLER, ARTHUR 1964 On Obliterating the Jews. *New Leader* 47, no. 6:6–8.

ROGOW, ARNOLD A. (editor) 1961 *The Jew in a Gentile World: An Anthology of Writings About Jews, by Non-Jews.* New York: Macmillan.

SIMMEL, ERNST (editor) 1946 *Anti-Semitism: A Social Disease.* New York: International Universities Press.

SOMBART, WERNER (1911) 1913 *The Jews and Modern Capitalism.* London: Allen & Unwin. → First published as *Die Juden und das Wirtschaftsleben.* A paperback edition was published in 1962 by Collier.

VALENTIN, HUGO (1935) 1936 *Anti-Semitism Historically and Critically Examined.* New York: Viking. → First published as *Antisemitismen i historisk och kritisk belysning.*

VATICAN COUNCIL, SECOND, SESSION 4 1965 Declaration on the Relations of the Church to Non-Christian Religions. *New York Times* October 29, p. 24, col. 5 ff.

WIRTH, LOUIS 1928 *The Ghetto.* Univ. of Chicago Press. → A paperback edition was published in 1956.

ANTITRUST LEGISLATION

Modern antitrust legislation may be said to have originated in the United States, with the Sherman Act of 1890, although government efforts to regulate the market are as old as government itself. Viewed in this larger perspective, antitrust legislation can be seen to consist of two distinct parts. The first part is a set of rules governing the behavior of firms in the market place. Any economy —capitalist, socialist, or mixed—must devise such rules to the extent that it makes use of a market. There must, for example, be a law of torts and a law of contracts. Insofar as American antitrust legislation deals with cartels and trade practices, it merely amends these two bodies of law in the interest of strengthening competition in the market place. It is this part of American antitrust legislation that has received most of the sympathetic attention of foreign observers. The British Restrictive Trade Practices Act of 1956, the German Law Against Restraint of Competition of 1957, and the cartel clause of the European Common Market Agreement probably owe something to American success in cartel suppression.

In the United States, however, antitrust legislation has done more than amend the rules of the game for businessmen. It has been employed deliberately and effectively, although often erratically, to discourage the degree of industrial concentration that a policy of laissez-faire would produce. In other countries, the complexities of legal codes sometimes contribute to this result but generally not as a matter of national policy. The American legal commitment to "trust busting," or perhaps more accurately to "trust prevention," is, as yet, unique in capitalist countries.

Authorities who support this commitment commonly base their case on one or both of two arguments. First, a policy of laissez-faire, which lets mergers go unsupervised, leads to economic waste; for the profits to be had from monopoly bring into being firms that are too large for technically efficient production. Second, economic decentralization is a good thing even though it requires the sacrifice of some economies of scale; specifically, economic decentralization helps to preserve small business activity as a way of life and contributes to the dispersion of the political power of corporate owners and managers.

Neither of these arguments has been received with much sympathy outside the United States. The assertion that a policy of laissez-faire will produce firms that are inefficiently large is unconvincing in countries whose major firms are exposed to vigorous foreign competition and, at any rate, are quite small by American standards. Foreign observers who fear the pernicious political influence of private economic concentration in their own lands are likely to favor the simple, direct remedy of public ownership over the cumbersome, indirect remedy of trust busting. Foreign observers who do not fear concentration see in antitrust policy only what Adam Smith saw in the laws against engrossing, forestalling, and regrating—a silly and perverse interference with freedom of contract.

The Sherman Act.   Section 1 (as amended) of the Sherman Act provides:

Every contract, combination in the form of trust or otherwise, or conspiracy, in restraint of trade or commerce among the several States, or with foreign nations . . . is declared illegal. . . . Every person who shall make any contract or engage in any combination or conspiracy . . . shall be deemed guilty of a misdemeanor, and, on conviction thereof, shall be punished by fine not exceeding fifty thousand dollars, or by imprisonment not exceeding one year, or by both said punishments, in the discretion of the court.

Section 2 provides:

Every person who shall monopolize, or attempt to monopolize, or combine or conspire with any other person or persons, to monopolize any part of the trade or commerce among the several States, or with foreign nations, shall be deemed guilty of a misdemeanor, and, on conviction thereof [etc.].

Given the vagueness of the above provisions, generations of judges, lawyers, and economists have puzzled over what the Sherman Act was *really* meant to accomplish. One cynical school maintains that the Congress of 1890 was merely passing a general resolution against sin; that it did not intend that litigation should ever arise under the Sherman Act. According to this school, the Republican majority, while seeking to increase import duties in 1890, became embarrassed by the charge that the tariff was "the mother of trusts" and sought to reassure the electorate by supporting an eloquent, if ambiguous, antitrust measure. Another school of thought holds that the Congress in 1890, rightly or wrongly, was seeking to stem the trend toward industrial concentration. No doubt the truth lies somewhere between these extreme interpretations of Congressional motives. Many legislators feared and resented the near monopoly positions gained by a few of the trusts, notably the Standard Oil Company, but nothing in the debates on the Sherman Act suggests that Congress anticipated its vigorous enforcement.

The historical importance of the Sherman Act

lies not in what it directed but rather in what it permitted. In effect, it represented a grant of discretionary power to the attorney general and the federal courts to deal with the emerging corporation in the American economy. Since 1890 the substance, as distinct from the form, of antitrust legislation has been supplied almost entirely by administrative initiative and court decisions. Statutory revisions of the Sherman Act have been few, infrequent, and unimportant.

A violation of the Sherman Act of 1890 may be treated as a misdemeanor and punished by fines and imprisonment, although, in fact, prison sentences are hardly ever imposed. These criminal cases are brought to the courts by the attorney general. A violation may also be treated as a civil wrong and redress sought by the attorney general through proceedings in equity. The relevant provision of the Sherman Act says only that the government may "enjoin" unlawful acts. The courts, however, have construed this provision as their authority to employ the wide range of equitable remedies that are usually lumped together as trust busting, notably dissolution of established corporations, injunctions against mergers, compulsory sale of corporate property, and decrees that restrict the types of business that a corporation may pursue. The Sherman Act also provides for enforcement through civil suits brought by private parties. The private party injured by an antitrust violation of another party may sue and if successful collect treble damages. Since 1914 he has also been able to seek an injunction that would protect him against another's unlawful course of action that might, in the future, cause him damage.

The formative period.   In the formative years of antitrust enforcement, 1891–1920, three problems especially engaged the attention of the attorney general and the courts—federal policy toward cartels, the distinction between fair and unfair trade practices, and industrial concentration. Of these problems, only the first was handled with decision and dispatch. Following passage of the Sherman Act, the attorney general moved immediately against cartels; and in the *Addyston Pipe* case (175 U.S. 211, 1899) the Supreme Court ruled that any combination of rival merchants formed for the express purpose of raising the price of their wares is illegal conspiracy within the meaning of the Sherman Act. (The case involved a cartel of six manufacturers of cast-iron pipe, which had undertaken to rig the bids on municipal government contracts.) In so ruling, the Court implicitly rejected the common-law rule that a cartel agreement is enforceable provided that the restraints on

competition imposed are reasonable, e.g., designed to hold prices at a "fair" level. With unimportant exceptions, the judicial objection to cartels was consistently reiterated and elaborated until in the *Socony-Vacuum* case (310 U.S. 150, 1940) the Supreme Court held that all efforts to restrict competition by collective action—even agreements to lower price—are illegal per se; and that it is not the business of judges to inquire into the *raison d'être* of the restraints or to balance their possible social benefits against their possible social costs.

In the areas of doubtful trade practices and industrial concentration, the evolution of federal policy was neither rapid nor consistent. This is not surprising in view of the novelty and complexity of the problems encountered in these areas. In the *E. C. Knight* case (156 U.S. 1, 1895) the attorney general halfheartedly sought to enjoin the sugar trust from acquiring four more firms but desisted when rebuffed in the Supreme Court on a technicality. A direct challenge to the presumed objects of the Sherman Act was declined by the government when three of the firms enjoined from combining to fix prices in the *Addyston Pipe* case were allowed to circumvent the decision by merging. Indeed, the government took no action at all to discourage the unprecedented wave of mergers that swept the United States in the 18 months after the condemnation of the cast-iron pipe cartel by the Circuit Court of Appeals in February 1898. Nor did federal officials for several years manifest any enthusiasm for doing legal battle with the Standard Oil Company, the trust that, at least in popular folklore, had employed every contemptible commercial practice to eliminate competition—the use of bogus independents, railroad rebates, "fighting brands," local price cutting, unwarranted lawsuits, commercial bribery, political corruption, etc.

By 1906, however, the stage had been set for the emergence of an antitrust policy that amounted to more than a harassment of cartels. A decade of serious economic inquiry, together with a generation of Populist agitation, by then had combined to destroy the faith of most lawyers, economists, and laymen in laissez-faire. Since Adam Smith's time, the case for laissez-faire—or to use the term more favored by lawyers, "freedom of contract"—had rested upon the assumption that the monopolist who succeeds in earning high profits will, in the not-so-long run, fall victim to his own success. His profits will attract new producers into his field, output will rise, and price will fall. The validity of this assumption was called into question by the spectacular success of the Standard Oil Company, which by 1906 had been holding a vastly profitable near-monopoly position in petroleum refining against all comers for thirty years. Faith in laissez-faire was further undermined by the first great merger movement in American economy (1899–1901), which in scores of industries replaced family firms with the modern corporation. In other times and places, the decline of faith in laissez-faire as a safeguard against monopoly might have produced resignation or a widespread demand for public ownership of the "basic" industries. That it did not produce this reaction in the United States of the early 1900s was, in large measure, due to the emphasis placed upon the role of "predatory" competition in discussions of the trust problem. According to this emphasis, the large firm that can manipulate markets and men has a marked "unfair" advantage over its smaller rivals; hence, the fact that a particular trust could survive and grow in the competitive struggle was not to be taken as evidence of its superior efficiency. From this reading of industrial experience, it follows that the sensible solution is an antitrust policy that curbs corporate size and enforces fair rules of the game in the business world.

The advent of antitrust policy in the United States thus marks a radical transformation in the ideology of capitalism. In the thought of nineteenth-century liberals, competition was viewed as essentially a natural process, something that would inevitably come to pass if only individuals were free to "truck, barter, and exchange one for another" without the hindrance of officious civil servants. In the philosophy of antitrust, competition is viewed as an artificial and fragile creation of legislation. (That the nineteenth-century view that made competition a natural process was probably closer to the truth is another matter; the supporter of antitrust devotes far more attention to the failures of competition than to its successes.)

The serious effort to alter the structure of the U.S. economy by antitrust action began in 1905 with the second administration of Theodore Roosevelt. The legal foundation for this ambitious undertaking had been laid in 1904 when, in the *Northern Securities* case (193 U.S. 197, 1904), the Supreme Court had compelled a holding company to dispose of the securities of two railroads. No genuine economic issues were presented by this case since the financial group, headed by J. P. Morgan, that controlled the holding company also controlled the two railroads. The decision did, however, establish the legality of the trust-busting power for use in later cases.

The government's first major effort at trust busting in the series of important cases brought be-

tween 1906 and 1920 was not wholly successful. Nevertheless, in 1911 the Supreme Court held that the Standard Oil Company of New Jersey was an illegal combination in violation of the Sherman Act and ordered it broken up. Ultimately the trust was rearranged into over thirty smaller units. Unfortunately, while the Court did not doubt that Standard Oil should be dissolved, it could not—or would not—offer a clear explanation of its action. The Standard Oil Company could have been deemed a fit subject for trust busting in 1911 because it controlled over 85 per cent of the country's petroleum refining capacity and/or because it had achieved this market share by "unfair" means. The Court was content to condemn the Rockefeller empire as an unreasonable restraint of trade without going into details.

The oligopoly problem. The successes of antitrust action between 1906 and 1920 were few but spectacular. Indeed, as examples of literal trust busting they were never to be equaled again. With a staff of only a handful of lawyers and secretaries, the Antitrust Division of the Justice Department was nevertheless able to force a notable rearrangement of corporate structure in the tobacco, explosives, farm machinery, meat-packing, transportation, and petroleum industries. These successes, however, were of the sort that could not be repeated indefinitely since they were at the expense of firms that, like the Standard Oil Company, were nearly all-powerful in their respective industries and owed their dominant market positions to mergers or objectionable trade practices. Firms that satisfied these requirements were but a tiny fraction of the business population. After the few obvious candidates for trust busting had been disposed of, it became clear that the real problem in antitrust legislation was provided not by the "bad" monopolist but rather by the "good" oligopolist, that is, the firm that has obvious market power without market domination and is content to coexist with its rivals. The good oligopolist makes his first appearance in the Supreme Court in *United States* v. *United States Steel Corp.* (251 U.S. 417, 1920).

The defendant corporation had been formed in 1901 when J. P. Morgan succeeded in amalgamating a large number of steel firms, many of which were themselves the products of recent mergers. He thereby secured control of at least 60 per cent of the country's steel-making capacity. The avowed object of the combination was more efficient steel production; but one may assume, as did the attorney general, that Morgan also perceived the monopoly profit that could be had by conducting a major portion of the steel industry as a unified operation. The presence or absence of any intent to monopolize the production of steel in 1901 was viewed by the Court as irrelevant in 1920. In its view, the crucial consideration was the failure of the corporation to secure market domination between 1901 and 1920. By 1920 the defendant corporation's share of steel-making capacity had declined to roughly 50 per cent; it was making no aggressive moves to raise this fraction again; and a majority of the justices were not convinced that it had the power to do so. Hence the Court reasonably concluded that no good purpose would be served by subjecting the corporation to dissolution. It was neither a monopolist nor the participant in an illegal cartel. Had the attorney general been able to explain the mechanics of price making in a market with few sellers, his effort in the steel case might have met with more success. But in 1920 neither the attorney general nor the professional economist had yet evolved a convincing theory of oligopoly.

Following the government's defeat in the steel case, enforcement of the antitrust laws was virtually suspended for 15 years, save for the occasional prosecution of a cartel. In the prosperity of the 1920s, few political returns were to be had from efforts at trust busting. In the first years of the great depression, the nation had more important economic issues to worry about. A knowledgeable observer surveying the American legal scene in 1936 might reasonably have concluded that the antitrust laws had, for all practical purposes, expired. He would have been quite wrong. Within the next few years, antitrust enforcement was revived with astonishing vigor. The appropriations of the Antitrust Division, which had never exceeded $300,000 in any year before 1935, reached $1.3 million in 1940 and $2.3 million in 1942. In retrospect, the main reasons for the revival are clear enough.

The restrictions imposed upon cartels by the Sherman Act had been more effective than was generally realized for many years. The merits of these restrictions became apparent during the short life of the National Industrial Recovery Administration (1933–1935), when they were virtually suspended. If, in the depths of the great depression, the cartels encouraged by the NRA were not strikingly successful in raising prices, their efforts were still politically obnoxious. Also, by the late 1930s the intellectual basis had been laid for an attack upon the good oligopolist. Thanks in large measure to the work of A. R. Burns (1936), the nature of price making in an oligopoly market was much better understood. Edward Chamberlin and Joan Robinson had called attention to the wastes of imperfect competition. The monumental, if highly uneven, investigations of the Temporary National Economic Committee had begun to cast further doubts on the efficiency of large corporations. Finally, the indispensable political base for a stronger antitrust policy was furnished by the organizations of small merchants, which had been brought into being by the hardships of the depression.

The "new" Sherman Act activity. The revival of antitrust policy implementation after 1936 is often described as the "new" Sherman Act, although no new legislation of any consequence was involved. Much of the increased effort went into the harassment of cartels on an unprecedented scale, in cases that raised no novel legal or economic issues. For the first time, private suits under the antitrust laws reached significant proportions. They were subsequently to form the greater part of antitrust litigation. Thus the Administrative Office of the United States Courts reported that 378 private suits, 21 federal criminal suits, and 42 federal civil suits were begun in 1961 under the antitrust laws. The rise of private antitrust litigation can be traced to a series of decisions, notably *Bigelow et al.* v. *RKO Pictures* (327 U.S. 251, 1946), that made damage suits much easier to win. In these decisions the courts relaxed the high standards of proof of damage that had kept their dockets virtually clear of private suits before 1936.

Some advocates of antitrust policy have viewed the rise of private litigation with considerable misgivings. The private cases mostly involve a charge of price discrimination—the practice of charging different buyers different prices for the same product—since this charge can be substantiated by the introduction of accounting data that the courts respect as tangible evidence useful for showing damage. However, in the view of most economists, price discrimination is more likely to indicate the presence of competition than an effort to destroy it. But private litigation under the antitrust laws that discourage price discrimination undoubtedly helps to preserve competitors by making it more difficult for large firms to exploit economies of scale in buying. To this extent, competitors are preserved by sacrificing the gains that competition as a process would otherwise confer.

The newness of the "new" Sherman Act lay mainly in the efforts of the attorney general, beginning with the civil suit filed against the Aluminum Company of America (Alcoa) in 1937 (302 U.S. 230), to obtain judicial approval for an ambitious trust-busting program calculated to change the face of the American economy. These efforts had two main goals, a more effective control of mergers and a removal of the legal immunity conferred on the good oligopolist by the steel decision in 1920.

The first goal has been largely, if unobtrusively, achieved—so much so that the antitrust laws now make growth by merger an unattractive proposition to most large firms. The importance of this change becomes apparent when one recalls that from 1900 through 1940 at least one-half of the growth of the 100 largest industrial firms was the product of merger. Nor is federal power over mergers any longer limited to those involving substantial shares of the market. For in *Brown Shoe Co.* v. *United States* (370 U.S. 294, 1962), the Supreme Court consented to stop a manufacturer accounting for about 4 per cent of national shoe output from acquiring a chain of retail shoe stores having less than 2 per cent of national shoe sales. By any test, the condemned acquisition could have had only a trifling effect upon the shoe industry.

The government's most energetic and spectacular efforts under the "new" Sherman Act have involved attacks on the good oligopolist. These efforts have met with but limited success. Control of the market by a single seller, monopoly in the literal sense, was condemned in the *Alcoa* case of 1945 even though the defendant's record was largely free of the mergers and intimidation of rivals that had weighed so heavily against the oil and tobacco trusts in 1911. The condemnation of market control was apparently extended to oligopoly when, in 1946, the nation's three leading manufacturers of cigarettes were convicted of violating the Sherman Act by pursuing common price policies even though the government produced no convincing evidence of collusion. In the case of *United States* v. *New York Great Atlantic & Pacific Tea Company*, filed in 1949 (CCH 1954, Trade Cases 67, 658), even the legality of size per se was placed in doubt. In this case, the country's largest grocery chain was convicted on a criminal charge of violating the Sherman Act, although at the time of the trial it had less than 10 per cent of national grocery sales.

Still, it is one thing to admonish an established enterprise with harsh words and light fines, but it is another thing to break it up. As supporters of trust busting were soon to point out, the assault on oligopoly under the "new" Sherman Act resulted in "legal victory—economic defeat." The courts were prepared to reprimand and fine large firms convicted of violating the antitrust laws as newly reinterpreted. They remained loath to carry punishment to the extent of dissolution and divestiture, which would destroy functioning economic units. The movie industry was dealt with severely in the *Paramount* case of 1948 (334 U.S. 131) and a few other sectors of the economy experienced mild trust busting. For example, in 1958 the United Fruit Company, the principal importer of bananas, was compelled to create a rival for itself from its own assets. Nevertheless, the government effort to recast the structure of the American economy by a series of civil decrees creating new firms from old has so far been largely a failure for reasons that are readily apparent. The inevitability of judicial conservatism was perhaps most succinctly explained by Judge Wyzanski in *United States* v. *United Shoe Machinery Corp.* (110 F. Supp. 295, 1953) when he wrote:

In the anti-trust field, the courts have been accorded, by common consent, an authority they have in no other branch of enacted law. . . . They would not have been given, or allowed to keep, such authority in the anti-trust field, and they would not so freely have altered from time to time the interpretation of its substantive provisions, if courts were in the habit of proceeding with the surgical ruthlessness that might commend itself to those seeking absolute assurance that there will be workable competition, and to those aiming at immediate realization of the social, political, and economic advantages of dispersal of power. (1953, p. 348)

Other legislation. While the comfortably imprecise language of the Sherman Act has been the main statutory foundation of antitrust policy, the act has several times been amended and expanded. The most ambitious attempts at revision came in 1914 with the passage of the Federal Trade Commission Act and the Clayton Act. The former established the Federal Trade Commission and charged it with the task of discouraging "unfair methods of competition" by cease-and-desist order. The latter, which is nearly as amorphous as the Sherman Act, which it purportedly clarifies, is credited by most authorities with three main objects: a more lenient legal treatment of sympathy strikes and secondary boycotts maintained by labor unions, tighter restrictions on corporate growth through mergers, and the outlawing of certain business practices that can threaten competition (notably price discrimination, exclusive dealing, and tie-in sales).

The 1914 legislation has enabled the Federal Trade Commission to share the making of antitrust policy with the Antitrust Division of the Justice Department. Until recently, however, this legislation has been so narrowly interpreted by the courts that it has given to federal officials little power that they could not reasonably have claimed under the Sherman Act. Thus the merger provision of the Clayton Act was a dead letter from the beginning because, in the view of the courts, it applied only to mergers effected by the purchase of securities. A firm wishing to evade the merger provision could do so simply by buying the physical assets of a rival firm. This loophole was not removed until the Celler Act of 1950.

The most controversial revision of the antitrust laws came with the passage of the Robinson–Patman Act in 1936. This long and complicated statute was designed to reduce the magnitude of the discounts that large firms could obtain by virtue of their power to buy in large quantities. (The Congressional supporters of this law purport to believe that these quantity discounts reflect the coercive bargaining power of the large buyer rather than any savings that the seller might realize in filling large orders.)

Some authorities contend that the Robinson–Patman Act is inconsistent with the aims of antitrust policy since it is so obviously intended to protect some businessmen from the consequences of competition. Indeed, the Supreme Court ruled in the *Nashville Milk* case of 1958 (355 U.S. 373) that certain provisions of the act cannot be used to support private damage suits under the antitrust laws. However, the protection conferred on high-cost small business is, as yet, rather limited. A seller charged with discriminating in favor of a large buyer can defend himself by showing that the challenged discounts were "made in good faith to meet an equally low price of a competitor." In any event, the Sherman and Clayton acts are rather regularly employed, especially in private damage suits, to protect small merchants from their more efficient rivals. And since, in a sense, protection of competitors is protection of competition, there is no reason to deny the claim of the Robinson–Patman Act to a place in the antitrust laws.

Various other actions of the courts and Congress have also operated to limit the force of the antitrust laws. Court decisions, notably *United Mine Workers* v. *Coronado Coal Co.* (259 U.S. 344, 1922) and *United States* v. *Hutcheson* (312 U.S. 219, 1941), have given labor unions a virtual immunity from prosecution. Cooperative market associations in agriculture have received Congressional exemption. The participation of American shipping firms in cartels is lawful, provided the United States Maritime Commission gives its consent. For rate agreements among railroads and motor carriers to be lawful, the parties concerned need only to secure the easily obtained approval of the Interstate Commerce Commission to enjoy immunity from antitrust prosecution. The McGuire Act of 1952 authorized manufacturers to set resale prices for wholesalers and retailers who handled their products, provided they did not collude with one another. And since the Webb–Pomerene Act of 1918, associations engaged solely in the export trade have enjoyed a limited exemption from the antitrust laws.

Economic consequences.   Despite the limited resources of the enforcement agencies, the exemptions given to important industries, and judicial conservatism, the economic consequences of antitrust legislation have been considerable. Above all else, antitrust legislation has prevented the emergence of strong cartels in the American economy. In fact, the practice of oligopoly, wherein price making is a matter of silent communication between rivals, is a backhanded tribute to the effectiveness of American antitrust legislation. In countries where antitrust prosecution is not feared, price making is entrusted to the more efficient device of the cartel. Again, antitrust legislation has now made growth by merger exceedingly difficult for the largest industrial firms. And several score firms now flourishing (including most of the major American oil companies) owe their creation or preservation to antitrust suits. In short, the antitrust laws have emerged as a powerful force on the side of decentralized control and decision making in the American economy. No doubt the dispersion of industrial control is purchased by the sacrifice of some economies of large scale in research and some efficiency in the use of existing industrial capacity. The magnitude of this cost, however, is virtually impossible to measure and, in view of the political popularity of antitrust policy as presently conducted, cannot be said to excite much concern.

Given the skepticism with which the case for using the antitrust laws to shape industrial organization has been received abroad, and the inherent weakness of its intellectual foundations, its nearly universal acceptance in the United States, even among professional economists, is somewhat puzzling. The explanation is probably that in an economy as nearly self-sufficient as that of the United States, it is not enough that competition exist. It must be *seen* to exist. Conceivably, an automobile industry entirely controlled by General Motors might be highly sensitive to competitive pressures in the form of competing consumer goods and foreign-produced cars. But the competitive pressures acting upon General Motors are more clearly visible in the form of its remaining domestic rivals. At present writing, the policy of using antitrust legislation to discourage economic concentration has almost no influential critics in the United States. So long as limitations on corporate size do not impose discernible handicaps on American firms in their competition with foreign rivals, this situation is unlikely to change.

DONALD J. DEWEY

[See CARTELS AND TRADE ASSOCIATIONS; INDUSTRIAL CONCENTRATION; MERGERS; MONOPOLY; OLIGOPOLY; *and also* ECONOMIES OF SCALE.]

BIBLIOGRAPHY

GENERAL WORKS

DEWEY, DONALD J. 1959 *Monopoly in Economics and Law.* Chicago: Rand McNally.

EDWARDS, CORWIN D. 1949 *Maintaining Competition: Requisites of a Governmental Policy.* New York: McGraw-Hill.

HALE, GEORGE E.; and HALE, ROSEMARY D. 1958 *Market Power: Size and Shape Under the Sherman Act.* Boston: Little.

KAYSEN, CARL; and TURNER, DONALD F. 1959 *Antitrust Policy: An Economic and Legal Analysis.* Harvard University Series on Competition in American Industry, No. 7. Cambridge, Mass.: Harvard Univ. Press.

NEALE, A. D. 1960 *The Antitrust Laws of the United States of America: A Study of Competition Enforced by Law.* National Institute of Economic and Social Research, Economic and Social Studies, No. 19. Cambridge Univ. Press.

THORELLI, HANS B. (1954) 1955 *The Federal Antitrust Policy: Origination of an American Tradition.* Baltimore: Johns Hopkins Press.

WILCOX, CLAIR (1955) 1960 *Public Policies Toward Business.* Rev. ed. Homewood, Ill.: Irwin.

EVOLUTION OF LEGAL AND ECONOMIC THOUGHT

BURNS, ARTHUR R. 1936 *The Decline of Competition: A Study of the Evolution of American Industry.* New York and London: McGraw-Hill.

CLARK, JOHN BATES; and CLARK, JOHN MAURICE (1901) 1914 *The Control of Trusts.* Rev. and enl. ed. New York: Macmillan. → John Bates Clark was the sole author of the first edition.

CLARK, JOHN D. 1931 *The Federal Trust Policy.* The Johns Hopkins University Studies in Historical and Political Science. London: Oxford Univ. Press.

DIRLAM, JOEL B.; and KAHN, ALFRED E. 1954 *Fair Competition: The Law and Economics of Antitrust Policy.* Ithaca, N.Y.: Cornell Univ. Press.

EDWARDS, CORWIN D. 1959 *The Price Discrimination Law: A Review of Experience.* Washington: Brookings Institution.

HALLE, ERNST VON 1895 *Trusts or Industrial Combinations and Coalitions in the United States.* New York and London: Macmillan.

JONES, ELIOT 1921 *The Trust Problem in the United States.* New York: Macmillan.

KEEZER, DEXTER M.; and MAY, STACY 1930 *The Public Control of Business: A Study of Anti-trust Law Enforcement, Public Interest Regulation, and Government Participation in Business.* New York and London: Harper.

LETWIN, WILLIAM L. 1965 *Law and Economic Policy in America: The Evolution of the Sherman Antitrust Act.* New York: Random House.

SIMONS, HENRY C. 1948 *Economic Policy for a Free Society.* Univ. of Chicago Press.

COMPARATIVE STUDIES

ARNDT, HELMUT (editor) 1960 *Die Konzentration in der Wirtschaft.* Berlin: Duncker & Humblot. → Published as Volume 20, numbers 1–3 of Verein für Socialpolitik, Berlin, *Schriften* New Series.

INTERNATIONAL ECONOMIC ASSOCIATION 1954 *Monopoly and Competition and Their Regulation.* Papers and Proceedings of a Conference held by the International Economic Association. Edited by Edward H. Chamberlin. New York: St. Martins.

MILLER, JOHN PERRY (editor) 1962 *Competition, Cartels and Their Regulation.* Amsterdam: North-Holland Publishing.

ANXIETY

There is no single problem of anxiety. Different theorists and different experimental investigators have tackled various aspects of a broad complex of phenomena, all of them summarized under the unifying conceptual category of anxiety. Anxiety has variously been considered as a phenomenal state of the human organism, as a physiological syndrome, and as a theoretical construct invoked to account for defensive behavior, the avoidance of noxious stimuli, and neurotic symptoms.

Historical background. The role of anxiety in the study of personality has been peculiarly a child of the twentieth century. The eighteenth-century and nineteenth-century precursors of modern psychology were first of all concerned with the rational aspects of human personality development, and it was not until the work of Alexander Bain (1859) that motivational concepts became important in speculations about complex human behavior. Thus, with the exception of such precursors of modern existential philosophy and psychology as Kierkegaard (1844), historically there was little central concern with the problem of anxiety.

However, negative, aversive, and unpleasant emotions have been the concerns of modern thinkers. Anxiety has not only been considered as the negative emotion par excellence in the theoretical writings of psychological theorists; but, even apart from its prototypical status as a negative emotion, it became generally the central emotional concept of many theoretical treatments in psychology. Anxiety *was* emotion.

On the whole, anxiety has remained the child of the psychologist, the problem of the individual. While philosophers, anthropologists, and sociologists have at various times taken the psychologist's notion of anxiety and speculated about its social and cultural antecedents, the major contributions in the area of anxiety have been those of psychologists.

The following schema briefly recapitulates the various theoretical and empirical concerns that have collectively come to be known as the problem of anxiety.

The three faces of anxiety. Three general rubrics describe various emphases within the problem of anxiety: antecedent, organismic–hypothetical, and consequent conditions. While this triad can be conceptually delimited, there are, as will be obvious, borderline problems that defy any simple categorization.

Antecedent conditions. In the first instance, there has been a continuing interest in the antecedent conditions that give rise to the anxiety phenomenon. Practically all workers in the field have, at one time or another, been concerned with the stimulus that elicits anxiety. What is it in the environment that gives rise to the experience of anxiety or to the behavior that is symptomatic of anxiety? With the notable exception of the existentialists and some psychoanalytic writers, considerations of these conditions have usually viewed anxiety as an acquired emotion, rarely found until the organism has gone through some learning experiences. As an acquired emotion, it is often distinguished from the fear aroused by a threatening or noxious event, and it is usually reserved for those learned conditions that signal or cue the impending occurrence of tissue injury or some other threat to the integrity of the organism.

Organismic conditions. The second set of conditions that is subsumed under the problem of anxiety is the hypothesized or observable state of the organism. While a theoretical purist can easily postulate the anxiety state as a hypothetical theoretical device with explanatory functions only, most notions about the phenomenon have, in addition, assumed some physiological or specifically autonomic arousal state. Those who have taken a specific position in this regard have usually assumed that the experience of anxiety is accompanied by some measurable level of sympathetic nervous system discharge. While there has been some speculation whether this discharge shows a specific pattern for the emotion of anxiety, generally it has been assumed that while the discharge may be specific to the individual it is likely not to be specific to the emotion. On the other hand, the autonomic processes involved have frequently been ignored, and, while some state of the organism has been postulated, its specific empirical referents have not necessarily been investigated. This position is particularly true of the concept of anxiety used by learning theorists in the United States. Even they, however, have at times spoken about specific proprioceptive (i.e., internal) cues associated with the anxiety state.

Consequent conditions. The consequent, experiential, or response aspects of anxiety have probably shown the widest variety of definition and emphasis. It can be assumed that the experience of anxiety falls into a general category of conditions, all of which occur consequent to some prior event or state of the organism; that is, some event must act upon receptors to be experienced. The subjective experience of anxiety is accessible only through the report of the human observer; as such, it is a behavioral, consequent event and falls into the same category as other behavioral and verbal consequences of some real or hypothetical anxiety state. One major group of anxiety theorists, the existentialists, has concerned itself primarily with these experiential correlates. In addition to what the anxious human being says about himself, the problem of anxiety deals with the effect of the various antecedent and intervening states on practically all aspects of his behavior. Apart from the effect of anxiety on neurotic or other pathological behavior, anxiety has been studied as it affects early learning, child rearing, adult acquisition of normal aversions and apprehensions, motor behavior, complex problem solving, and so forth (cf. Cofer & Appley 1964). Anxiety has also been defined in terms of expressive behavior, general level of activity, and a whole class of diagnostic behavioral and physiological symptoms.

While these three general classes of variables—antecedent, organismic, and consequent—provide a general overview of the extent of the problem of anxiety, they are, like most categories in the behavioral sciences, hardly mutually exclusive. Various conditions may at various times shift from an organismic to a consequent state, or even from a consequent to an antecedent, as, for example, when anxious behavior becomes the cue for further anxiety. Quite understandably, several writers on the problem have stressed the importance of different aspects of this triad. When the learning theorist is dealing with anxiety, he is dealing primarily with antecedent–consequent relations; when the existentialist speaks of anxiety, he is concerned primarily with the experience of anxiety and possibly with some organismic state, whereas he has relatively little concern with antecedent conditions of learning.

With these general considerations in mind, three major theoretical positions will be given a brief exposition, followed by a summary of known and stable empirical findings, a general unifying statement on the problem of anxiety, and an exposition of pathological anxiety.

Theoretical positions

Psychoanalytic theory. While much has been written about the development of, and changes in, the psychoanalytic concept of anxiety, the major position, even after several decades, remains Sigmund Freud's own set of statements. Nothing attests better to the complexity of the problem of anxiety than Freud's concern with an adequate theory of anxiety. In no other area did he change his point of view as dramatically as he did toward the origins and mechanisms of anxiety, in fact presenting two theories on the topic.

Freud's early theory of anxiety, generally stated in 1917 (Freud 1916–1917), was relatively straightforward and part of the general energy system of psychoanalytic theory. Anxiety was defined as transformed libido. The transformation occurs as a result of repression, which distorts, displaces, or generally dams up the libido associated with instinctual impulses. This transformation-of-libido or "damming-up" theory of anxiety suggests that whenever the organism is prevented from carrying out an instinctually motivated act, whether through repression or through some prevention of gratification, anxiety will ensue. Such anxiety may, of course, then serve as a motive for a symptom that in turn functions to terminate or completely prevent the subsequent occurrence of anxiety. This theory was amended in 1926 when Freud published *Inhibitions, Symptoms and Anxiety*. The new position was restated in the *New Introductory Lectures on Psychoanalysis* in 1933 and in general remained his final statement on anxiety.

The second theory reversed the relationship between repression and anxiety. Although Freud tended to maintain the possibility of both kinds of relationships, the second theory added the possibility that repression occurs because of the experience of anxiety. To Freud, this was the more important possibility. In this context, anxiety becomes a signal from the ego. Whenever real or potential danger is detected by the ego, this perception gives rise to anxiety and in turn mobilizes the defensive apparatus, including, of course, repression. Thus, because of the impending danger from unacceptable or dangerous impulses, the unpleasantness of anxiety produces the repression of the impulses, which in turn leads the organism out of danger.

Avoidance of overstimulation. It should be noted that a central concept in both of Freud's theories of anxiety is the notion of the avoidance of overstimulation. Whether libido is dammed up by not executing some instinctual act or whether the ego signals impending stimulation that cannot be adequately handled, in both cases the anxiety anticipates an impending situation for which no adequate coping mechanism is available to the organism. The ultimate unpleasantness is overstimulation, including pain, and the anxiety in both theories signals or anticipates this prototypical state. Thus, Freud derives the origin of anxiety from the prototype of overstimulation. Such a derivation is necessary at least for the second theory, which presupposes cognitive, perceptual actions on the part of the ego. Here anxiety is learned; it is acquired as a function of past experience. It is in this sense that the psychoanalytic theory of anxiety, including its several revisions, has never abandoned the first theory, which describes the development of "automatic" anxiety. In the second theory, anxiety is derived from "automatic" anxiety; in the first theory, all anxiety is "automatic."

Antecedent and organismic conditions. The origin of "automatic" anxiety is traced by Freud into the very earliest period of life, the birth trauma and the immediate period thereafter. Emphasis on the helpless infant as well as on the birth trauma as the origin of the anxiety state places him apart from Rank (1924), who relies solely on the birth trauma as the source of anxiety.

For Freud (1926), the experience of anxiety—as distinct from its antecedents or consequences or as a theoretical state—has three aspects: (1) a specific feeling of unpleasantness, (2) efferent or discharge phenomena, and (3) the organism's perception of these discharge phenomena. In other words, the perception of autonomic arousal is associated with a specific feeling of unpleasantness. As to the primitive occasions for this anxiety experience, Freud is frequently hazy. While, on the one hand, he considers the predisposition toward anxiety as a genetic mechanism ([1916–1917] 1952) at other times he considers anxiety as arising from separation from the mother, castration fears, and other early experiences. He considers the specific unpleasant experience of the anxiety state as derived from the first experience of overstimulation at the time of birth. He says that the birth experience "involves just such a concatenation of painful feelings, of discharges and excitation, and of bodily sensations, as to have become a prototype for all occasions on which life is endangered, ever after to be reproduced again in us as the dread or 'anxiety' condition" (Freud [1916–1917] 1952, p. 344). Thus, it is possible that some of the discussions that have arisen out of several interpretations of Freud's theory of anxiety have confused the specific experience of anxiety derived from the physiological make-up of the organism and the birth trauma with the conditions that produce or threaten unmanageable discharge. The conditions that produce such an anxiety state are, in addition to the birth trauma, separation or loss of the mother, with the attendant threat of overstimulation due to uncontrollable impulses and threats, and castration fears with similar consequences. Thus, where Rank places both the affect and the prototypic antecedent conditions at the period of birth, Freud lets the organism inherit or learn the affect at birth, but also adds other specific conditions that elicit it later on in early life. On this basis it is reasonable to claim, as Kubie (1941) does, "that all anxiety has as its core what Freud has called 'free floating anxiety.'" In other words, given the initial affect of anxiety that a child either genetically or experientially brings into the world, specific anxieties and fears are then situationally developed out of this basic predisposition.

In this context, the various types of fears or anxieties that Freud discusses are not different in their initial source of the affect but, rather, differ in the specific conditions that give rise to them. They are *fear,* where anxiety is directly related to a specific object; *objective anxiety (Realangst),* which is the reaction to an external danger and which is considered to be not only a useful but also a necessary function of the system; and *neurotic anxiety,* in which the anxiety is out of proportion to the real danger and frequently is related to unacceptable instinctual impulses and unconscious conflicts.

Freud's notion that anxiety is brought about when the ego receives those external or internal cues that signal helplessness or inability to cope with environmental or intrapsychic threats is mirrored in Karen Horney's position that basic anxiety is "the feeling a child has of being isolated and helpless in a potentially hostile world" (Horney 1945, p. 41). For Horney, primary anxiety is related eventually to disturbances of interpersonal relations, initially those between the child and significant adults. A similar position is taken by Harry Stack Sullivan, who relates both parental disapproval to the development of anxiety and the inadequacies, irrationalities, and confusions of the cultural pattern to its elicitation.

In summary, the psychoanalytic position not only treats anxiety as an important tool for the adequate handling of a realistically threatening environment, but it also relates anxiety to the development of neurotic behavior. The "cultural" psychoanalysts then go on to stress the social environment at large, while Freud sees the basic anxiety mechanisms in the very early mother separation and castration fears. In all cases, however, anxiety is related to the inability of the organism to cope with a situation that threatens to overwhelm him, the absence of adequate acts to deal with environmental or intrapsychic events. As Freud phrased it in one of his later formulations, "anxiety . . . seems to be a reaction to the perception of the absence of the object [e.g., goal]" (Freud [1926] 1936). With the object absent, no action is possible and helplessness, i.e., anxiety, ensues.

Learning theory.   The theoretical position taken by most representatives of modern learning or behavior theory is derived generally from the work of I. P. Pavlov and J. B. Watson. The two major positions are those of C. L. Hull and B. F. Skinner, although neither of these two men themselves have worked extensively on the problem of anxiety. Most of the work on anxiety, within the framework of learning theory, has been carried out by representatives of the Hullian school. While most of their experimental work has involved lower animals, the "conditioning" concept of anxiety has been extensively applied to complex human behavior (cf. Dollard & Miller 1950).

As Mowrer (1960) has shown, the role of anxiety for learning theory is derived mainly from the attempts to explain the nature and consequences of punishment. In the case of punishment, the application of some painful or noxious event following the performance of a response inhibits or interferes with the performance of that response on some subsequent occasion. Similarly, when an organism avoids a situation, it is, through the operation of some mediating mechanism, precluding the occurrence of a noxious or painful event. The nature of this mediating mechanism, learning theorists contend, is what is commonly called fear or anxiety.

Anxiety as an acquired drive.   The conditioning model states that a previously neutral event or stimulus (the conditioned stimulus, or *CS*), when paired with an unconditioned stimulus (*US*), which produces a noxious state such as pain, will elicit a conditioned response (*CR*) after a suitable number of pairings. This conditioned response is what is commonly called fear. In a typical experimental situation, an animal might be placed in a white box with a door leading to a black box. The floor of the white box is electrified, and the animal receives a shock (*US*) that becomes associated with the white box (*CS*). If the animal is then permitted to escape from the shock through the door to the black box, he will eventually run from the white to the black box prior to the application of shock. Learning theorists assert that the fear (*CR*) conditioned to the white box (*CS*) motivates subsequent activity. The reduction of the fear—by escape from the *CS*—thus produces avoidance of the original noxious unconditioned stimulus. Fear—or anxiety—is viewed as a secondary or acquired drive established by classical conditioning. While this basic paradigm has been extensively elaborated, it represents the basic notions about anxiety in modern learning theory.

The Skinnerian point of view has been described by Schoenfeld (1950), who argues against the notion that the organism "avoids" the unconditioned stimulus. He suggests that the organism in fact escapes from a stimulus array that consists of the conditioned stimulus *as well as* the proprioceptive and tactile stimuli, which precede the unconditioned stimulus. However, this description is not basically divergent from the more general statement that the proprioceptive and tactile stimuli are a conditioned response functioning as a drive [*see* LEARNING, *article on* AVOIDANCE LEARNING; CONFLICT, *article on* PSYCHOLOGICAL ASPECTS].

Antecedent conditions. Whether avoidance learning is achieved by the mediating effect of the conditioned fear or ascribed to conditioned aversive stimuli, the question still remains open as to the necessary characteristics of the original, unconditioned, noxious, or aversive stimulus. In one of the early statements on conditioned fear, Mowrer (1939) suggested that fear was the conditioned form of the pain response. However, it has been demonstrated that pain cannot be a necessary condition for the establishment of anxiety since individuals who are congenitally incapable of experiencing pain also show anxiety reactions. (For a summary of this argument, see Kessen & Mandler 1961.) In a more general statement about the nature of acquired drives such as fear, Miller (1951) has extended the class of unconditioned stimuli adequate for fear conditioning to essentially all noxious stimuli, and Mowrer (1960) comes close to a psychoanalytic position when he expresses essential agreement with the position that fear is a psychological warning of impending discomfort. However, work with experimental animals has failed to establish unequivocally that fear can be conditioned upon the onset of discomforting primary drives or *US*s other than those associated with painful stimuli. This failure hampers the generality of the conditioning model.

Organismic conditions. The above evidence becomes important when one considers not only the antecedent conditions for the establishment of fear, which the learning theorists relate to the conditioning paradigm, but also the nature of the mediating response (the *CR*). A variety of data (for example, Wynne & Solomon 1955) has shown that the development of the anxiety or fear state in animals depends upon an adequately functioning autonomic nervous system. Thus, within the confines of the conditioning model, those writers who have speculated upon the nature of the mediating fear or anxiety state have suggested that it presupposes some sympathetic arousal. It follows from this that fear or anxiety can be conditioned only if the unconditional stimulus also is one that produces such sympathetic or general autonomic effects. To the extent then that a learning theory position assumes emotional, autonomic responses correlated with the fear state, it also suggests that fear necessarily derives only from those primary conditions that in turn are autonomically arousing. Thus, at least as far as such writers as Mowrer are concerned, the threat of discomfort, or rise in primary drives, or overstimulation in general, can only be prototypes for anxiety if, and only if, these states in turn have autonomic components. However, this does not seem to be the case for such divergent states as hunger, thirst, and so forth.

Consequent conditions. As far as the consequences of conditioned fear are concerned, there seems to be general agreement, both theoretical and empirical, that they fall into two general classes. In the first class, fear and anxiety operate as secondary drives and exhibit all the usual properties of drives, serving as motives for the establishment of new behavior. When fear acts as a drive, new responses are reinforced by the reduction of that drive. This response-produced drive is the major emphasis that learning theory has placed on fear or anxiety. In the second class, it has also been recognized that the conditioned fear response or the *CER* (conditioned emotional response) may in a variety of situations interfere with or suppress ongoing behavior. In this sense, it is of course no different from the general anxiety concept of the psychoanalysts in that behavioral anxiety or preoccupation with anxiety may be incompatible with other behavior or thoughts required from the organism in a particular situation.

Existentialist psychology. The emergence of existentialism from a purely philosophical school to an important influence on psychology has been a phenomenon of the mid-twentieth century. What existentialist thinking has done for psychology is not so much to present it with a new theory in the tradition of well-defined deductive positions that became popular in the early part of the century, but rather to provide it with a wealth of ideas and challenges to conventional wisdom. While a variety of different positions and schools can be discerned within the movement, the problem of anxiety has remained essentially unchanged from Kierkegaard's pathbreaking formulation, published more than a hundred years ago (1844). For example, Jean-Paul Sartre's position about the problem of anxiety is, for present purposes, not noticeably at variance with it (1943). Kierkegaard's central concept of human development and human maturity was the notion of freedom. Freedom is related to man's ability to become aware of the wide range of possibility facing him in life —possibility in that sense is not statically present in his environment but created and developed by man. Freedom implies the existence and awareness of possibility.

Anxiety is intimately tied up with this existence of possibility and potential freedom. The very consideration of possibility brings with it the experience of anxiety. Whenever man considers possibilities and potential courses of action, he is faced with anxiety. Whenever the individual attempts to carry any possibility into action, anxiety is a necessary accompaniment, and growth toward freedom means the ability to experience and tolerate the anxiety that necessarily comes with the consideration of possibility. In modern terms, any choice situation involves the experience of anxiety, and thus for the existentialist position the antecedents of anxiety are, in a sense, the very existence of man in a world in which choice exists.

Kierkegaard endows even the newborn child with an unavoidable and necessary prototypical state of anxiety. However, since the child is originally in what Kierkegaard calls a "state of innocence," a state in which he is not yet aware of the specific possibilities facing him, his anxiety too is an anxiety that is general but without content. Possibility exists, but it is a possibility of action in general, not of specific choices. The peculiarly human problem of development faces the child as he becomes aware both of himself and of his environment. Possibility and actualization become specific, and anxiety appears at each point where development and individuation of the child progresses; at each point a new choice of possibilities must be faced, and anxiety must be confronted anew.

The consequences of this notion of anxiety are that as the individual develops he is continuously confronted with the unpleasant experience of anxiety and with the problem of mature development in the face of it. It is not only unavoidable as a condition of man; it is, Kierkegaard maintains, actually sought out. "Anxiety is an alien power which lays hold of an individual, and yet one cannot tear oneself away, nor has the will to do so; for one fears, but what one fears one desires. Anxiety then makes the individual impotent" (Kierkegaard [1844] 1944, p. xii). Since anxiety is unavoidable and since it must be encountered if one is to grow as a human being, all attempts at avoiding the experience of anxiety are either futile, or they result in a constricted, uncreative, and unrealistic mode of life. Only by facing the experience of anxiety can one truly become an actualized human being and face the reality of human existence.

Kierkegaard also makes a clear distinction between fear and anxiety. Fear involves a specific object that is feared and avoided, whereas anxiety is independent of the object and furthermore is a necessary attribute of all choice and possibility.

The importance of Kierkegaard, and the existentialist development in general, is not the emergence of testable scientific propositions, but rather the emphasis—found *inter alia* in some psychoanalytic writings—that anxiety may not be primarily a learned experience derived from past encounters with painful environmental events, but may be a naturally occurring initial state of the organism. Man may in fact be born with anxiety, rather than learn it through experience. While existentialism has not produced any clear definitions of anxiety, apart from appealing to an assumed common phenomenology, it has raised important questions both about the general problem of anxiety and, in the field of psychotherapy, about the proper treatment for those conditions that show pathological effects of anxiety. It is quite clear that a therapeutic attitude that considers anxiety as a normal state is radically different from an attitude that stresses the avoidance of primary and secondary traumata [see PSYCHOLOGY, *article on* EXISTENTIAL PSYCHOLOGY].

Human anxiety—empirical generalizations

Since 1950, when May remarked on the absence of the problem of human anxiety from strictly experimental concerns (1950, p. 99), literally hundreds of studies have been published, using a quantitative, experimental approach to the problem of human anxiety. Many investigations have used the concept of anxiety primarily as an explanatory rather than as a manipulated variable. These studies fall more properly under such rubrics as conflict, stress, frustration, etc. and will not be dealt with here. However, a large body of research has been devoted specifically to anxiety. This rash of experimental investigations was in the first instance instigated by the development of the so-called anxiety scales. The most widely used and influential of these is the Manifest Anxiety Scale, developed by Janet Taylor Spence (Taylor 1953).

Manifest Anxiety Scale. The Manifest Anxiety Scale was originally developed to test some of the implications of the anxiety or fear concept within the general system originated by C. L. Hull. By developing a scale that would order individuals along a continuum of anxiety, it was expected that individuals who had high anxiety scores would exhibit more general drive level than individuals with less anxiety, since anxiety is—within this theoretical position—considered to be a secondary, or acquired, drive.

The Manifest Anxiety Scale consists of 50 items from the Minnesota Multiphasic Personality Inventory, all of which are judged to be indexes of high emotionality or anxiety. Typical items are: I am easily embarrassed (if answered "true"); I do not have as many fears as my friends (if answered "false"). Experimental work with this scale bore out the primary prediction: individuals scoring high on this scale (i.e., who are highly anxious) acquire conditioned responses based on aversive unconditioned stimuli much more rapidly than individuals scoring low on the scale. This is certainly the case for eyeblink conditioning, and the evidence is in the same direction for the conditioning of the galvanic skin response. However, these predictions from drive theory do not seem to hold for nonaversive conditioning, and it has been suggested that the anxiety drive measured by the Manifest Anxiety Scale is reactive rather than chronic. In other words, an individual with high anxiety shows anxiety in situations in which there is an element of threat or even conflict, and he apparently does not react with high drive in all situations.

A further prediction from Hullian theory was that individuals with high anxiety should perform better on simple tasks than on complex ones, but that individuals with little anxiety should perform better on complex tasks. This prediction, too, has generally been borne out (Taylor 1956). Finally, even though the scale was not directly constructed to evaluate clinical levels of anxiety, it does show consistently positive correlations with clinical judgments of anxiety in both patient and normal populations.

Test Anxiety Questionnaire. Whereas the Manifest Anxiety Scale concentrated on the drive aspects of anxiety, the other widely used anxiety scale has been more specifically concerned with interfering responses generated by the anxiety state. The Test Anxiety Questionnaire was originally developed by G. Mandler and S. B. Sarason (1952). It consists of 37 graphic scales specifically concerned with the experience of anxiety in test or examination situations. The hypothesis suggested that the more an individual tends to report the occurrence of anxietylike experiences on a questionnaire, the more likely it is that these will occur in any situation that involves examination or test pressures such as potential success or failure, time pressures, and so forth. In contrast to experiments with the Manifest Anxiety Scale, studies of the Test Anxiety Questionnaire have tended to stress rather complex tasks and complex instructions to the subjects. In general, here too the predictions about the interfering nature of anxiety in complex situations have been borne out. Subjects with high anxiety do tend to show interfering or task-irrelevant responses when faced with a task that seems to imply ego involvement or potential failure.

Correlational studies of the two scales have shown a low positive relationship, but the Manifest Anxiety Scale seems to tap more general characteristics of the individual, while the Test Anxiety Questionnaire is more sensitive to situational cues, particularly those that indicate to the subject that he is being tested or examined. Both kinds of scales, however, suggest that anxietylike responses will occur when some cue indicating threat is presented, whether it be an aversive unconditioned stimulus or a test situation. In that sense, the scales are tapping personality differences in the tendency to experience anxiety to a greater or lesser degree.

Finally, J. W. Atkinson has related anxiety, as reported on the Test Anxiety Questionnaire, to a more general system of motivation by using this scale as a measure of a general motive to avoid failure (e.g., Atkinson & Litwin 1960). Attempts of this nature and the general placement of the personality dimension of anxiety within a more general system of motivation (e.g., Spence 1958) are needed to integrate the hundreds of empirical studies that have used the various anxiety scales.

One other important set of experimental studies that have specifically dealt with anxiety has been reported by Schachter (1959). These studies have shown that affiliative behavior is related to self-reported anxiety. Schachter also demonstrated that the presentation of a fear-arousing situation tended to arouse affiliative needs, such as the desire to be with others. His data suggest that stimuli unrelated to the threat may result in anxiety reduction; flight from trauma or its signals is not the only method of avoiding anxiety.

Anxiety—an integrative point of view

Certain commonalities can be found among the various theoretical views of anxiety, and all of these seem to be fairly consistent with the experiential and experimental evidence available. There is agreement that anxiety, as a mediating, experiential phenomenon, is related to the perception of impending threat, or overstimulation, or unmanageable demands and that it is accompanied by a discharge in the sympathetic nervous system. It seems also fairly well agreed that the consequences of anxiety may, in the face of an aversive event, be motivating in the sense that they make it possible for the organism to avoid the threat or danger more quickly and efficiently. Both learning theory and existential theory, surprisingly, seem to stress the importance of anxiety in making it possible for the organism to handle threatening situations, even though they might disagree about the nature of these threats. It also seems to be generally agreed that anxiety may also interfere with complex, usually cognitive, activities of the organism. There seems to be less agreement on the origin of the anxiety reaction. In psychoanalytic and learning theories the stress seems to be on some early traumatic event, while the existentialists tend to favor anxiety as a built-in characteristic of the human organism. But even here some of the psychoanalytic positions can be read as consistent with the existentialist point of view.

Some recent observations on the behavior of the newborn child and some speculations on the inadequacy of the pain experience as the foundation of all of anxiety have resulted in a series of proposals that seem to provide a broad basis for the many different theoretical conceptions. The position in question suggests that some of the psychoanalytic and existentialist assumptions about the origins of anxiety are essentially correct. There is good reason to believe that the newborn infant is, in fact, in a state of variable, spontaneous, and sometimes intense autonomic arousal. This state of arousal is correlated with a general state of infantile distress. It is certainly the case that the newborn infant shows cyclic states of distress that cannot easily be related to antecedent stimulation. It may in fact be the case that the relatively well-regulated autonomic system of the adult is a result of acquired and systematic regulation. In any case, infantile distress can be seen as the prototype of the distress that is later called anxiety, in the absence of specific environmental events, or fear, in the presence of specific stimuli. Given this general cyclical state of distress, it can also be shown that a child can be quieted by a set of environmental or organismic events that have been designated as inhibitors (Kessen & Mandler 1961). Sucking is the best-known and most intensively investigated of these inhibitors. Sucking, rocking, and other activities seem to inhibit or quiet the distress of the child. It is possible that these acts stimulate parasympathetic activity that counteracts the sympathetic discharge. It also appears that with maturation not only these apparently innate inhibitors but a whole class of secondary, probably conditioned, inhibitors also acquires this quieting or anxiety-suppressing property. On the other hand, the removal of these inhibitors or the interruption of any organized activity (Mandler 1964) appears to reinstate the general state of distress or anxiety. This view suggests that from a state of congenitally given autonomic and behavioral distress the child moves into a situation in which more and more acts and events tend to acquire the property to inhibit distress, and their removal tends to reinstate it.

Starting with Kurt Lewin's work (1935), it has been shown that interruption of well-organized behavior leads to a state of anxiety. Therefore, it is suggested that while, for the young child, there is only a limited repertoire of events and behaviors available that will inhibit or control the basic state of distress, any organized activity in the older child and in an adult will do so, and that finally any organized activity serves to ward off the state of distress. Conversely, it might be stated that whenever the organism has no well-organized behavior available to him, he is in a state of distress. Thus, whenever the organism is not able to draw upon some behavior or act that controls his environment, that is, whenever he is in a condition of helplessness, unable to control stimulation or environmental input in general, he will be in a state of anxiety.

This view is consistent with the psychoanalytic tenets on overstimulation and Freud's statement about anxiety being related to the loss of the object. When either overstimulation threatens or no object (goal) is present, the organism has no behavior available to him and cannot act; therefore he is anxious. As far as the existentialist position is concerned, the state of anxiety occurs, of course, whenever the individual has no way of coping with environmental demands; in other words, no way of confronting possibility, no way of overcoming the anxiety that goes with possibility and freedom. Finally, the noxious, painful unconditioned stimulus of learning theory typically is an event that is unmanageable, represents overstimulation, and disrupts ongoing behavior. When the organism does in fact find a way of coping with this situation by escape, this escape behavior is the way of overcoming helplessness vis-à-vis the noxious stimulus and will appear upon a signal (the conditioned stimulus) prior to the occurrence of the unconditioned stimulus.

Finally, the data on highly anxious individuals suggest that these are people who have very few mechanisms available for coping with helplessness or threat. They are in fact frequently faced with a world in which no behaviors are available for them to inhibit or avoid the threat of helplessness.

Anxiety neurosis

The most important pathological manifestation of the anxiety reaction is seen in the syndrome commonly called *anxiety neurosis*. While anxiety presumably plays a role in all neurotic disorders, this syndrome has both the overt and the subjective aspects of anxiety as its primary characteristics. The anxiety neurotic is the patient who is incapacitated by continuous and often nonspecific feelings of anxiety. Whereas anxiety in the other neuroses, particularly in the phobias, is aroused by a specific condition or set of internal or external stimuli, in the anxiety neurotic any and all external situations or thoughts may give rise to an anxiety reaction. The patient typically displays signs of apprehensiveness and fearfulness in a variety of different situations, none of which can necessarily be objectively described as threatening or aversive. While the patient may in some cases ascribe specific fearfulness to some stimulus, he will frequently find himself in situations that never before have aroused anxiety and now suddenly acquire the power to do so. Thus, while he may name a long list of thoughts or events of which he is afraid or apprehensive, he will just as frequently describe the general phenomenon of free-floating anxiety, a feeling of distress or apprehensiveness with no specific content.

Apart from the subjective feelings that accompany the general anxious state of the patient, he will usually exhibit somatic symptoms, particularly those that are in a milder form associated with the typical normal anxiety reaction. In general, he will show heightened autonomic arousal, cardiac involvement, breathing difficulties, excessive sweating, and so forth. These will frequently be accompanied by skeletal symptoms such as trembling and startle reactions. Both the intensity and the duration of the anxiety attacks may vary. They may range from a continuous feeling of uneasiness and distress to sudden, panicky attacks that may last for minutes or hours.

Since all situations are potentially cues for the anxiety reaction, the patient frequently tends to be immobilized and unable to act or plan over long periods of time.

Relatively little is known about the genesis of this pathological state, although experimental work has shown that the equivalent of the anxiety neurosis may be produced in lower animals by the presentation of unsolvable conflicts. Case histories of anxiety neurotics also generally show their backgrounds as being replete with continuous conflicts coupled with feelings of inadequacy and inferiority. Just as the experimental animal is unable to resolve the conflict between hunger and fear of shock when he has been shocked at the time and place of feeding, so the human is unable to act in the face of two conflicting motives.

For both psychoanalytic theory and learning theory, the conditions that produce the pathological anxiety reaction are seen in the inability of the patient to discriminate threatening from nonthreatening events and ideas. From a psychoanalytic point of view, infantile fears and fantasies are kept unconscious but produce an interpretation of danger in a wide variety of otherwise neutral situations. Many different stimuli reactivate childhood conflicts, and the ego, which is otherwise functioning normally, interprets as dangerous a wide variety of different situations. Another possibility is that aspects of parental behavior during early childhood training have produced the tendency to identify many different situations as dangerous.

The somewhat similar interpretation given by learning theory suggests that anxiety neurosis is the result of an overgeneralization of the original conditioned stimuli for the anxiety reaction. Whereas in the normal adult the generalization gradient in conditioning is relatively steep, the anxiety neurotic manifests a very flat generalization gradient from the original conditioned stimuli. The anxiety reaction is elicited by a wide variety of stimuli that may be only vaguely similar to the original conditioned stimulus, with verbal mediators playing an important role in generalizing to new situations. In addition, both learning theory and psychoanalytic theory suggest that the patient not only becomes afraid of the original conditioned stimulus and similar ones, but also the anxiety reaction itself becomes a conditioned stimulus for a new fear reaction, resulting in a vicious cycle of increasing anxiety eventually reaching panic levels.

Both of these positions suggest that the pathological condition of the anxiety reaction is somehow derivable from one or several early nuclear experiences. Another possibility consistent with clinical observation of anxiety neurotics relates the sources of the anxiety reaction to a generalized feeling of helplessness. The anxiety patient will practically invariably describe his subjective state as one of conflict or helplessness. He feels unable to act because he does not know how to act; he vacillates because he does not know what to do; he cannot defend one course of action as preferable to another. Conflict may arise out of the competition of two equally strong reaction tendencies; it may also derive from the fact that no one reaction tendency is, by itself, organized well enough to be executed. In other words, the inability to choose an act, the fear of facing the consequences of an act once chosen, or a general lack of confidence that any behavior could possibly be adaptive or successful may by themselves lead to anxiety. The pathological condition of the anxiety neurotic is thus related to the inability to face choices and to make choices: he is anxious because he is in conflict, and he is in conflict because he is anxious.

Finally, the genesis of the pathological anxiety reaction may not only be derived from an environment that endows a variety of thoughts and events with the label "danger" but may also be related to the individual's reaction to his physiological responses. One theory of emotion claims that the basic physiological substratum of all emotions is similar (i.e., a sympathetic nervous system reaction) and that the content of the emotion depends on cognitive or environmental factors, suggesting that a combination of physiological readiness and helplessness in view of environmental demands is basic to the problem of the anxiety neurotic (Schachter 1964; Mandler 1962). Such a position would indicate that one of the things the anxiety neurotic may not have learned is adequate labeling of his autonomic responses. In the absence of such adequate labeling or in case of hypersensitivity or hyperattention to such arousal, an individual would be much more likely to experience anxiety whenever faced with a situation in which no adequate

response is available. In this sense, the problem of the anxiety neurotic may be exactly opposite to that of the psychopath who experiences too little anxiety (Schachter 1964).

GEORGE MANDLER

[*Other relevant material may be found under* DRIVES; EMOTION; MOTIVATION; PSYCHOANALYSIS; STRESS.]

BIBLIOGRAPHY

ATKINSON, JOHN W.; and LITWIN, GEORGE H. 1960 Achievement Motive and Test Anxiety Conceived as Motive to Approach Success and Motive to Avoid Failure. *Journal of Abnormal and Social Psychology* 60:52–63.

BAIN, ALEXANDER (1859) 1899 *The Emotions and the Will.* 4th ed. London: Longmans.

CAMERON, NORMAN A. 1963 *Personality Development and Psychopathology: A Dynamic Approach.* Boston: Houghton Mifflin. → An excellent discussion of pathological anxiety states within the general framework of psychopathology.

COFER, CHARLES N.; and APPLEY, MORTIMER H. 1964 *Motivation: Theory and Research.* New York: Wiley. → A survey that places anxiety within the general framework of motivational theory and data.

DOLLARD, JOHN; and MILLER, NEAL E. 1950 *Personality and Psychotherapy: An Analysis in Terms of Learning, Thinking, and Culture.* New York: McGraw-Hill.

FREUD, SIGMUND (1916–1917) 1952 *A General Introduction to Psychoanalysis.* Authorized English translation of the rev. ed. by Joan Riviere. Garden City, N.Y.: Doubleday. → First published as *Vorlesungen zur Einführung in die Psychoanalyse.*

FREUD, SIGMUND (1926) 1936 *The Problem of Anxiety.* New York: Norton. → First published as *Hemmung, Symptom und Angst.* The British translation was published by Hogarth, London, in 1936 as *Inhibitions, Symptoms and Anxiety.* Pages cited in text refer to the American edition.

HORNEY, KAREN 1945 *Our Inner Conflicts: A Constructive Theory of Neurosis.* New York: Norton.

KESSEN, WILLIAM; and MANDLER, GEORGE 1961 Anxiety, Pain, and the Inhibition of Distress. *Psychological Review* 68:396–404.

KIERKEGAARD, SØREN A. (1844) 1957 *The Concept of Dread.* 2d ed. Princeton Univ. Press. → First published as *Begrebet angest.*

KUBIE, LAWRENCE S. 1941 A Physiological Approach to the Concept of Anxiety. *Psychosomatic Medicine* 3:263–276.

LEWIN, KURT 1935 *A Dynamic Theory of Personality: Selected Papers.* New York: McGraw-Hill.

MANDLER, GEORGE 1962 Emotion. Pages 267–343 in Roger Brown et al., *New Directions in Psychology.* New York: Holt.

MANDLER, GEORGE 1964 The Interruption of Behavior. Volume 12, pages 163–219 in David Levine (editor), *Nebraska Symposium on Motivation, 1964.* Lincoln: Univ. of Nebraska Press.

MANDLER, GEORGE; and SARASON, SEYMOUR B. 1952 A Study of Anxiety and Learning. *Journal of Abnormal and Social Psychology* 47:166–173.

MAY, ROLLO 1950 *The Meaning of Anxiety.* New York: Ronald Press. → An excellent survey and integration of the many meanings of anxiety.

MILLER, NEAL E. 1951 Learnable Drives and Rewards. Pages 435–472 in Stanley S. Stevens (editor), *Handbook of Experimental Psychology*. New York: Wiley.

MOWRER, ORVAL H. 1939 Stimulus–Response Analysis of Anxiety and Its Role as a Reinforcing Agent. *Psychological Review* 46:553–565.

MOWRER, ORVAL H. 1960 *Learning Theory and Behavior*. New York: Wiley.

RANK, OTTO (1924) 1952 *The Trauma of Birth*. New York: Brunner. → First published as *Das Trauma der Geburt*.

SARTRE, JEAN-PAUL (1943) 1956 *Being and Nothingness: An Essay on Phenomenological Ontology*. New York: Philosophical Library. → First published as *L'être et le néant, essai d'ontologie phénoménologique*.

SCHACHTER, STANLEY 1959 *The Psychology of Affiliation: Experimental Studies of the Sources of Gregariousness*. Stanford Studies in Psychology, No. 1. Stanford Univ. Press.

SCHACHTER, STANLEY; and LATANÉ, BIBB 1964 Crime, Cognition and the Autonomic Nervous System. Volume 12, pages 221–275 in David Levine (editor), *Nebraska Symposium on Motivation: 1964*. Lincoln: Univ. of Nebraska Press. → Includes two pages of comment by George Mandler.

SCHOENFELD, WILLIAM N. 1950 An Experimental Approach to Anxiety, Escape and Avoidance Behavior. Pages 70–99 in Paul H. Hoch and Joseph Zubin (editors), *Anxiety*. New York: Grune.

SPENCE, KENNETH W. 1958 A Theory of Emotionally Based Drive (D) and Its Relation to Performance in Simple Learning Situations. *American Psychologist* 13:131–141.

TAYLOR, JANET A. 1953 A Personality Scale of Manifest Anxiety. *Journal of Abnormal and Social Psychology* 48:285–290.

TAYLOR, JANET A. 1956 Drive Theory and Manifest Anxiety. *Psychological Bulletin* 53:303–320.

WYNNE, LYMAN C.; and SOLOMON, RICHARD L. 1955 Traumatic Avoidance Learning: Acquisition and Extinction in Dogs Deprived of Normal Peripheral Autonomic Function. *Genetic Psychology Monographs* 52:241–284.

APPLIED ANTHROPOLOGY
See under ANTHROPOLOGY.

APPLIED PSYCHOLOGY
See under PSYCHOLOGY.

APPORTIONMENT

Apportionment is the distribution of legislative seats among pre-existing territorial or other units entitled to representation. Although apportionment, districting, and electoral methods are interrelated, the problems involved in one are quite different from those involved in either of the other two. Districting establishes the precise geographic boundaries of a territorial constituency. The electoral system prescribes the method for electing representatives. United States constitutional practice distinguishes between apportionment and districting by vesting the two functions in different governments. The national government apportions representatives to the 50 states, but the state governments divide their respective states into congressional districts. In the United Kingdom, on the other hand, seats in the House of Commons are distributed merely by dividing the country into constituencies with special boundaries and with a relatively equal number of voters in each constituency.

History. The historical development of apportionment can be seen in the evolution of popular representation in the British House of Commons. The assignment of two members to each county and borough did not seriously violate the popular principle when the population was rather evenly distributed among these units. With the industrial revolution, however, came great shifts in the distribution of population. Many new centers of population, like Birmingham and Manchester, were either completely unrepresented or grossly underrepresented while rotten boroughs, like Old Sarum with only seven inhabitants, sent two members to the House of Commons.

Although the Reform Act of 1832 was not based on the democratic principle of apportionment according to population, 42 new parliamentary boroughs were created to provide representation for the new centers of population, the less populous boroughs were apportioned only one member rather than two, and the 56 least populous boroughs were abolished as separate parliamentary constituencies. The seats were redistributed again in 1867. The Redistribution Act of 1885 adopted the principle of the single-member constituency but allowed 27 constituencies to elect two members each. Similarly, community representation yielded to districting based on population, although only a rough arithmetic equality was achieved. A fourth redistribution act was passed in 1918 and a fifth in 1944. This last act—with amendments adopted in 1945, 1947, and 1948—abolished the multimember constituency, approached arithmetic equality with approximately 56,000 voters in each constituency, and established four separate boundary commissions (England, Wales and Monmouth, Scotland, and Northern Ireland). As a result of the recommendations made by these commissions, the Representation of the People Act of 1948 completely redrew the boundaries of the constituencies. Thus, the acts of 1832 and 1867 were apportionment measures, but the acts of 1885, 1918, and 1944 involved both apportionment and districting, and the act of 1948 involved only districting.

The units to which representation is apportioned

are usually territorial subdivisions, such as regions, provinces, states, counties, or a similar geographic unit. Canadian senators, for example, are apportioned to the five senatorial regions, members of the Canadian House of Commons to provinces, Mexican congressmen to states, and the seats in most state legislatures in the United States to counties. Representation may be apportioned, however, to functional groupings of the population. In the early parliaments of Europe, representation was apportioned to social estates (e.g., nobility, clergy, and commons). Theoretically, 70 per cent of the seats in the Cyprian House of Representatives are apportioned to the Greek community and 30 per cent to the Turkish. Similarly, representation in the Spanish Cortes and in the Portuguese Corporative Chamber is apportioned to industrial, labor, cultural, and professional associations.

Basis of apportionment. The basis of apportionment is often confused with the units to which representation is apportioned. Because representation is usually apportioned to territorial subdivisions, the literature on apportionment frequently describes two bases of representation: area and population. The territorial extent of certain sparsely populated constituencies has sometimes been offered as an excuse for establishing some districts that are less populous than others. Except for an abortive attempt in Wisconsin in 1952, actual practice in Illinois in 1955, and recent proposals in Michigan and Nebraska in 1962, no responsible group has ever seriously advocated apportionment of representation on the basis of acres, square kilometers, or any other such territorial measure. In apportionment "area" simply refers to the distribution of representation among territorial subdivisions with previously defined boundaries. In districting "area" refers to the consideration given not only to population equality but also to topography, to the boundaries of civil subdivisions, to the means of travel and communication, and to community of social, political, and economic interest.

Whereas most political scientists would give consideration to these "area" factors in *districting*, virtually all political scientists agree that population is the only legitimate basis for *apportionment* in a democratic state. They are not agreed, however, on a definition of population. If actual voters bear a constant relation to total inhabitants, citizens, and registered electors in every unit entitled to representation, it is inconsequential which of these four measures of population is used as the apportionment base. If such a uniform relation is not present, however, apportionment on any basis

other than actual voters frequently will not achieve the democratic ideal of an equal ballot for every voter. In 1962, for example, representatives were apportioned to New York and Louisiana almost exactly according to total population, but one popular vote cast for a representative in Louisiana had approximately 8½ times the weight of one cast in New York—because the number of voters per 100 inhabitants was 33 in New York but only 3.8 in Louisiana.

Apportionment patterns. Four apportionment patterns are common today.

(1) On the basis of population. Deputies in the Soviet Union, for example, are apportioned to each electoral area on the basis of one deputy for every 300,000 inhabitants, so that the total number of deputies is flexible since the ratio is fixed at 1:300,000. Most legislative bodies, however, have a fixed number of seats and a flexible ratio. Older methods for apportioning a fixed number of seats used a ratio, which was determined by dividing the total representative population by the total number of seats. The total representative population of each unit entitled to representation was then divided by the ratio to determine the number of seats to be apportioned to that unit. This method was used for apportioning United States representatives before 1911 and is still widely used for apportioning seats in American state legislatures among the several counties. Apportioning according to a ratio is not sound mathematically if the total number of seats is fixed. Mathematically sound methods assign one seat to each unit and then apportion the remaining seats among the several units according to priority numbers, which may be computed in one of five ways—smallest divisors, harmonic mean, equal proportions, major fractions, or greatest divisors—each of which is designed to apportion seats precisely according to population (Silva 1962). The major-fractions formula was used for apportioning United States representatives to the states in 1911 and 1931, whereas the equal-proportions formula was used in 1941, 1951, and 1961.

(2) On the basis of population but with weighted ratios. The Soviet constitution of 1924, for example, apportioned seats in the All Union Congress to urban areas on the basis of one deputy per 25,000 *electors*, but to rural areas on the basis of one deputy per 125,000 *inhabitants*; thus, the urban areas were probably overrepresented in relation to the rural areas. Conversely, many states in the United States apportion seats in their respective legislatures to the less populous counties on the basis of a ratio smaller than that used for

apportioning seats to the more populous counties, so that a ballot cast in a less populous county has greater weight than one cast in a more populous county.

(3) *On the basis of population but with separate representation guaranteed to the least populous units and/or with a limitation on the representation of the most populous units.* In the Fifth Republic, for example, 255 French senators are apportioned among the 90 departments of Metropolitan France roughly according to population, but each department is guaranteed 1 senator and no department has more than 22. The guarantee of separate representation to the least populous units severely limits the popular principle if the population is not rather evenly distributed among the units and if the total number of units is high in relation to the total number of seats. Until the system was invalidated by the courts, each of the 105 counties in Kansas, for example, was guaranteed 1 seat in the Kansas House, so that only 20 seats were left to be apportioned according to population. As a result, the 4 most populous counties with over 37 per cent of the state's population had only 12 per cent of the seats in the Kansas House. Such a chamber could be made more representative only by greatly increasing the number of seats, by reducing the number of counties, or by joining two or more of the less populous counties into one constituency.

(4) *On the basis of equal representation for each subordinate governmental unit regardless of population.* Various federal states—for example, Australia, Brazil, Canada, the Federal Republic of Germany, Nigeria, and the United States of America—have a bicameral federal system; one chamber is apportioned on the basis of population, whereas in the other chamber the constituent governmental units enjoy equal (or nearly equal) representation with no (or little) regard for population statistics.

Criteria for apportionment and districting. The two criteria for measuring the equity of an apportionment are: (1) the number of representative inhabitants per seat, which results from dividing a unit's representative population by that unit's number of seats (A/a), and (2) the individual representative inhabitant's share of one seat, which results from dividing his unit's number of seats by his unit's representative population (a/A). When the total number of seats is fixed, an apportionment is mathematically satisfactory if the discrepancy between the number of inhabitants per seat in *any two* units (A/a and B/b) and the discrepancy between an individual inhabitant's share

of one seat (a/A and b/B) cannot be reduced by apportioning one more seat to unit A and one less to unit B, or vice versa. Of the five modern apportionment methods, only equal proportions can be proved to meet both tests, i.e., to minimize the differences in the number of inhabitants per seat and to minimize the differences in each inhabitant's share of one seat. In practice, however, major fractions and equal proportions will almost always produce precisely the same distribution of seats.

The criteria for districting are much less precise. It is generally agreed that each constituency should be composed of contiguous and compact territory and should contain, as nearly as practicable, an equal number of representative inhabitants. Although the meaning of contiguity is relatively obvious, there is no standard measure of compactness. Nor is there any consensus on the permissible size of population differentials between constituencies. It is also agreed that representation should be based on community of interest, but no serious efforts have been made to draw the boundaries of constituencies scientifically by employing methods of area and demographic analysis, which social scientists have used successfully in determining marketing, shopping, and service districts. The imprecision of the criteria for districting has made "gerrymandering"—i.e., the creation of artificial constituencies with arbitrary boundaries that are consciously drawn for partisan advantage—a serious and unsolved problem in the United States.

The question of the multimember versus the single-member constituency is meaningless except in relation to the electoral system to be used in that constituency. The discrepancy between a political party's share of the total popular vote and its share of the seats in the chamber, the possibility of gerrymandering, and the number and alignment of political parties depend quite as much on the electoral system as on the number of representatives to be elected in the constituency. Allowing representation for a minority party *in a constituency* requires both a multimember constituency and a proportional or semiproportional electoral system so that a constituency's seats can be divided between two or more parties. The apportionment of more than three seats to a constituency with such an electoral system tends to promote a splintering and multiplication of parties. The more seats apportioned to a constituency with such an electoral system, the more precise is the proportionality between each party's share of the vote and its share of the seats, but this proportionality increases at a decreasing rate as the number of seats per constituency increases. With a block electoral system, however, a corresponding *disproportionality* increases at an increasing rate.

Where a block electoral system and the singlemember or two-member constituency have prevailed, the drive for "fair representation" has been concerned largely with apportionment and districting. In other countries, however, apportionment of the popular house has generally been, at least roughly, according to population, districting has been irrelevant, and attention has been focused on devising an electoral system that would give (or prevent giving) parliamentary representation with arithmetic precision to the various minority parties found in each multimember constituency.

RUTH C. SILVA

[*See also* ELECTIONS; LEGISLATION; REPRESENTATION.]

BIBLIOGRAPHY

ALKER, HAYWARD R. JR.; and RUSSETT, BRUCE M.   1964   On Measuring Inequality. *Behavioral Science* 9:207–218.
BUTLER, DAVID   1955   The Redistribution of Seats. *Public Administration* 33:125–147.
CANADA, PARLIAMENT, HOUSE OF COMMONS   1958   British North America Act. Volume 2, pages 1088–1104 in *Debates*. Session 1. Ottawa (Canada).
DE GRAZIA, ALFRED   1951   *Public and Republic: Political Representation in America.* New York: Knopf.
EVERETT, ROBINSON O. (editor)   1962   The Electoral Process: Part II. *Law and Contemporary Problems* 27:327–433.
GRIFFITH, ELMER C.   1907   *The Rise and Development of the Gerrymander.* Chicago: Scott, Foresman.
KRAMER, ROBERT (editor)   1952   Legislative Reapportionment. *Law and Contemporary Problems* 17:253–469.
NAGEL, STUART S.   1965   Simplified Bipartisan Computer Redistricting. *Stanford Law Review* 17:863–899.
PEASLEE, AMOS JENKINS (editor)   (1950) 1956   *Constitutions of Nations.* 3 vols., 2d ed. The Hague: Nijhoff.
SCHATTSCHNEIDER, E. E. et al.   1962   A Symposium on *Baker* v. *Carr. Yale Law Journal* 72:7–106.
SCHMECKEBIER, LAURENCE F.   1941   *Congressional Apportionment.* Institute for Government Research of the Brookings Institution, Studies in Administration, No. 40. Washington: The Institute.
SILVA, RUTH C.   1962a   Apportionment in New York. Part 1: The Legal Aspects of Reapportionment and Redistricting; *Baker* v. *Carr. Fordham Law Review* 30: 581–595.
SILVA, RUTH C.   1962b   Apportionment of the New York Assembly. *Fordham Law Review* 31:1–72.
SILVA, RUTH C.   1964   Compared Values of the Single- and the Multi-member Legislative District. *Western Political Quarterly* 17:504–516.
SILVA, RUTH C.   1964   Relation of Representation and the Party System to the Number of Seats Apportioned to a Legislative District. *Western Political Quarterly* 17:742–769.
WEAVER, JAMES B.; and HESS, SIDNEY W.   1963   A Procedure for Nonpartisan Districting: Development of Computer Techniques. *Yale Law Journal* 73:288–308.

APTITUDE TESTING

Aptitude tests constitute one of the most widely used types of psychological tests. The term "aptitude" is often used interchangeably with the term "ability."

The concept of ability.   An ability refers to a general trait of an individual that may facilitate the learning of a variety of specific skills. For example, the level of performance that a man attains in operating a turret lathe may depend on the level of his abilities of manual dexterity and motor coordination, but these abilities may be important to proficiency in other tasks as well. Thus, manual dexterity also is needed in assembling electrical components, and motor coordination is needed to fly an airplane. In our culture, verbal abilities are important in a very wide variety of tasks. The individual who has a great many highly developed abilities can become proficient at a great number of different tasks. The concept of "intelligence" really refers to a combination of certain abilities that contribute to achievement in a wide range of specific activities. The trend in aptitude testing is to provide measures of separate abilities. The identification of these separate abilities has been one of the main areas of psychological research, and it is this research that provides the basis of many aptitude tests.

Psychological tests are essentially standardized measures of a sample of an individual's behavior. Any one test samples only a limited aspect of behavior. By analogy, the chemist, by testing only a few cubic centimeters of a liquid, can infer the characteristics of the compound; the quality control engineer does not test every finished product but only a sample of them. Similarly, the psychologist may diagnose an individual's "vocabulary" from a measure based on a small number of words to which he responds, or he may infer the level of a person's "multilimb coordination" by having him make certain movements. The most important feature of this sample of behavior is that it is taken under certain controlled conditions. Performance on just any sample of words, for example, is not diagnostic of "vocabulary." For a behavior sample to qualify as a psychological test, its adequacy must be demonstrated quantitatively. (Some typical indexes for doing this will be described below.)

How abilities are identified.   Some individuals who perform well on verbal tasks (for example, those tasks requiring a large vocabulary) may do poorly on tasks requiring spatial orientation (for example, flying an airplane). Or an individual who performs well on verbal items may do poorly on numerical items. Consequently, it is obvious that there are a number of different abilities that distinguish people. But how are the great variety of abilities identified? How does the psychologist know what abilities are to be usefully considered separate from one another? The basic research technique that has been used is called *factor analysis*. A large number of tests, selected with certain hypotheses in mind, are administered to a large number of experimental subjects. Correlation coefficients among all these test performances are then computed. From these correlations, inferences are made about the common abilities needed to perform the tests. The assumption is that tests that correlate with each other measure the same ability factor, and tests that are uncorrelated measure different factors. The problem of extracting and naming these factors is somewhat complex. Examples of separate abilities that have been identified are verbal comprehension, spatial orientation, perceptual speed, and manual dexterity. Of course, this basic research also allows assessment of the kinds of tests that provide the best measures of the different ability factors.

Aptitudes and abilities.   Ability tests are usually given with the objective of making some prediction about a person's future success in some occupational activity or group of activities. The term aptitude, used in place of the term ability, has more of a predictive connotation. We could, of course, use such tests solely to attain a picture of a person's strong and weak ability traits, with no specific predictive objective. We could use such measures as variables in psychological research, for example, studies of psychological development or the relation of ability to learning. Or we may be interested in the discovery of the relation between the ability of spatial relations and the speed of learning a perceptual–motor skill. But most often these tests are used in personnel selection, vocational guidance, or for some other applied predictive purpose such as using a spatial relations test to select turret lathe operators.

Sometimes aptitude tests designed to predict success in some specific job or occupation, as would be true of a test of "clerical aptitude," actually measure combinations of different abilities (e.g., perceptual speed, numerical facility) found to be important in clerical jobs.

Achievement tests.   Aptitude tests are distinguished from achievement (or proficiency) tests, which are designed to measure degree of mastery of an area of knowledge, of a specific skill, or of a job. Thus, a final examination in a course is an achievement test used to assess student status in the course. If used to predict future performance in graduate work or in some other area, it would be called an *aptitude test*. The distinction between aptitude and achievement tests is often in terms of their use.

Ways of describing aptitude tests.   Tests may be classified in terms of the mode in which they are presented, whether they are group or individual tests, whether they are speeded, and in terms of their content. Any complete description of an aptitude test should include reference to each of these characteristics.

Mode of presenting tests.   Most tests are of the paper and pencil variety, in which the stimulus materials are presented on a printed page and the responses are made by marking a paper with a pencil. The administrative advantages of such a medium are obvious, in that many individuals can be tested at once, fewer examiners are needed, and scoring of the tests is relatively straightforward. Nonprinted tests, such as those involving apparatus, often present problems of maintenance and calibration. However, it may not be possible to assess the desired behavior by means of purely printed media. Tests of manual dexterity or multiple-limb coordination are examples of aptitude tests requiring apparatus, varying from a simple pegboard to mechanical–electronic devices. Tests for children and for illiterates frequently employ blocks and other objects, which are manipulated by the examinee.

Auditory and motion picture media have also been used in aptitude testing. For example, tests of musical aptitude are auditory, as are certain tests designed to select radiotelegraphers. The test material is presented by means of a phonograph or tape recorder. One such test was designed to measure how well individuals could estimate the relative velocity of moving objects. It is evident that this function could not have been measured by a purely printed test. However, in both these auditory and motion picture tests, the responses are, nonetheless, recorded by pencil on paper.

Group versus individual tests.   Some tests can be administered to examinees in a group; others can be administered to only one person at a time. The individual test is naturally more expensive to use in a testing program. Tests for very young children or tests requiring oral responses must be individual tests. Such tests are also used when an individual's performance must be timed accurately. Devices used to test motor abilities constitute additional examples of individual tests, although sometimes it is possible to give these in small groups.

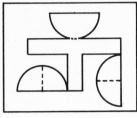
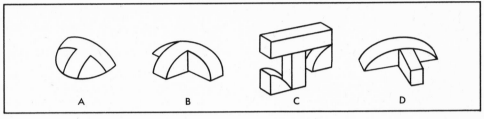

Item from a measure of spatial visualization. The examinee chooses the solid figure from which the cutout can be made.

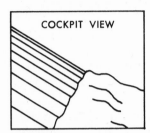
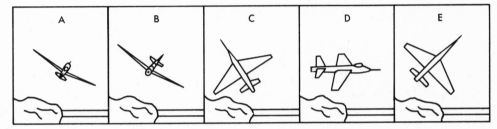

Item from a measure of spatial orientation. The examinee chooses the plane from which the cockpit view would be seen.

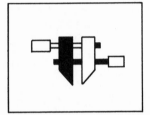
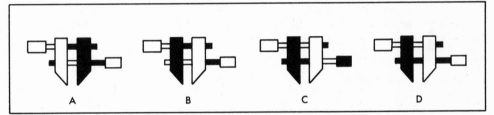

Item from a measure of perceptual speed. The examinee determines, as rapidly as possible, which figure on the right is like the figure on the left.

Three of the following groups of letters are alike in some way. Mark the one that is different.

C D E F   N O P Q   G F D H   T U V W

Write the next *two* numbers of the series.

2   5   7   12   15   17   ____   ____

−2   0   4   12   28   60   ____   ____

Items from tests requiring discovery of principles.

Figure 1 — *Examples of aptitude test items*

Sources: Adapted from Cureton & Cureton 1955; Guilford 1947; U.S. Employment Service 1946–1958.

Speeded versus nonspeeded tests. Tests differ in the emphasis placed on speed. In many functions, such as vocabulary, there is little interest in speed. Such tests are called *power tests* and have no time limits. For other functions, such as perceptual speed or finger dexterity, speed becomes an important factor in the measured behavior. *Speeded tests* may be administered by allowing all examinees a specific length of time to finish (time-limit tests), in which case the score is represented by the number of items correctly completed. Alternatively, a speeded test may require the examinee to finish a task as rapidly as possible (work-limit tests), and his score may then be expressed as the time taken to complete the test. For example, a finger dexterity test may be scored in terms of the number of seconds taken to complete a series of small screw–washer–nut assemblies.

What the tests measure. Most frequently, aptitude tests are classified in terms of what they attempt to measure. Thus, there are vocabulary tests, motor ability tests, etc. Figure 1 provides some examples of test items.

Tests containing items such as those illustrated are often grouped into standard "multiple aptitude test batteries," which provide profiles of certain separate ability test scores. Examples are the Differential Aptitude Tests (DAT), published by the Psychological Corporation, the General Aptitude Test Battery (GATB) of the U.S. Employment Service, and the Aircrew Classification Battery of the U.S. Air Force.

Characteristics of useful tests. Now that we have looked briefly at the different forms of tests, let us examine some of the basic concepts of testing. How can the usefulness of a test be evaluated?

Test construction. The process of constructing aptitude tests involves a rather technical sequence combining ingenuity of the psychologist, experimentation and data collection with suitable samples of individuals, the calculation of quantitative indexes for items and total test scores, and the application of appropriate statistical tests at various stages of test development. Some of the indexes applied in the construction phase are difficulty levels, the proportion of responses actually made to the various alternatives provided in multiple-choice tests, and the correlation of item scores with total test scores or within an independent criterion. A well-developed aptitude test goes through several cycles of these evaluations before it is even tried out as a test. The more evidence there is in the test manual for such rigorous procedure the more confidence we can have in the tests.

There are other problems that generally must be considered in evaluating test scores. Before a test is actually used, a number of conditions have to be met. There is a period of "testing the tests" to determine their applicability in particular situations. A test manual should be devised to provide information on this. Furthermore, there is the question of interpreting a test score.

Standardization. The concept of standardization refers to the establishment of uniform conditions under which the test is administered, ensuring that the particular ability of the examinee is the sole variable being measured. A great deal of care is taken to insure proper standardization of testing conditions. Thus, the examiner's manual for a particular test specifies the uniform directions to be read to everyone, the exact demonstration, the practice examples to be used, and so on. The examiner tries to keep motivation high and to minimize fatigue and distractions. If such conditions are high for one group of job applicants and not for another, the test scores may reflect motivational differences in addition to the ability differences that it is desired to measure.

Norms. A test score has no meaning by itself. The fact that Joe answered 35 words correctly on a vocabulary test or that he was able to place 40 pegs in a pegboard in two minutes gives very little information about Joe's verbal ability or finger dexterity. These scores are known as *raw scores.* In order to interpret Joe's raw score it is necessary to compare it with a distribution of scores made by a large number of other individuals, of known categories, who have taken the same test. Such distributions are called *norms.* There may be several sets of norms for a particular test, applicable to different groups of examinees. Thus, getting 75 per cent of the vocabulary items correct may turn out to be excellent when compared to norms based on high school students, but only average when compared to norms based on college graduates. If one is using a test to select engine mechanics, it is best to compare an applicant's score with norms obtained from previous applicants for this job, as well as with norms of actual mechanics.

The *mental age norm* is one in which an individual's score on an intelligence test is compared to the average score obtained by people of different ages. This, of course, is applicable mainly to children. For adults, the *percentile* norm is most frequently used. A large number of people (at least several hundred) are tested, the scores ranked, and the percentage of people falling below each score is determined. Let us suppose that an individual who gets a raw score of 35 on a test turns out to be at the 65th percentile. This tells us immediately that the person scored better than 65 per cent of the individuals in the group for which test norms were determined. A score at the 50th percentile is, by definition, the median of the distribution. The scores made by future applicants for a job may subsequently be evaluated by comparing them with the percentiles of the norm group.

Another type of norm is the *standard score.* Each individual's score can be expressed as a discrepancy from the average score of the entire group. When we divide this deviation by the standard deviation (SD) of the scores of the entire group, we have a standard score, or a score expressed in SD units. Typically, a test manual will include these standard-score equivalents as well as percentile equivalents for each raw score.

From this discussion, it is evident that a psychological test usually has no arbitrary pass–fail score.

Reliability. One of the most important characteristics of a test is its reliability. This refers to the degree to which the test measures something consistently. If a test yielded a score of 135 for an individual one day and 85 the next, we would term the test unreliable. Before psychological tests are used they are first evaluated for reliability. This is often done by the *test–retest* method, which involves giving the same test to the same individuals at two different times in an attempt to find out whether the test generally ranks individuals in about the same way each time. The statistical correlation technique is used, and the resulting correlation is called the *reliability coefficient*. Test designers try to achieve test reliabilities above .90, but often reliabilities of .80 or .70 are useful for predicting job success. Sometimes two *equivalent forms* of a test are developed; both are then given to the same individuals and the correlation determined. Sometimes a *split-half* method is used; scores on half the items are correlated with scores on the remaining half. Tests that are short often are unreliable, as are many tests that do not use objectively determined scores.

Validity.   An essential characteristic of aptitude tests is their validity. Whereas reliability refers to consistency of measurement, validity generally means the degree to which the test measures what it was designed to measure. A test may be highly reliable but still not valid. A thermometer, for example, may give consistent readings but it is certainly not a valid instrument for measuring specific gravity. Similarly, a test designed to select supervisors may be found to be highly reliable; but it will not be a valid test if scores made by new supervisors do not correlate with their later proficiency on the job.

When used for personnel selection purposes, the validity of aptitude tests is evaluated by finding the degree to which they correlate with some measure of performance on the job. The question to be answered is, Does the test given to a job applicant *predict* some aspect of his later job performance? The correlation obtained in such a determination is known as the *validity coefficient*. This is found by administering the test to unselected job applicants and later obtaining some independent measure of their performance on the job. If the validity coefficient is a substantial one, the test may be used to predict the job success of new applicants, just as it has demonstrated it can do with the original group. If the validity coefficient is low, the test is discarded as a selection instrument for this job, since it has failed to make the desired prediction of job performance.

Validity coefficients need not be very high in absolute value to make useful predictions in matching men to job requirements. A test was given to 1,000 applicants for pilot training in the Air Force. These applicants were allowed to go through training; six months later their proficiency was evaluated. It was found that scores on this ten-minute test correlated .45 with the performance of these individuals as pilots six months later. Very few of those scoring high on the test subsequently failed training, while over half of those scoring low on the test eventually failed.

Why are some tests valid and others not? The reason must be that valid tests are those that measure the kinds of abilities and skills actually needed on the job. It should be noted that tests often do not directly resemble tasks of the job, even when they are highly valid. For example, the Rotary Pursuit Test was found to have considerable validity in predicting success in pilot and bombardier training for the Army Air Force during World War II. This test requires the examinee to keep a metal stylus in contact with a target spot set toward the edge of a rotating disc. Often the examinees may have thought, "Where does the pilot (or bombardier) do anything like this?" But the reason this test is valid is not because of its resemblance to any task of these jobs, but because it samples *control precision ability*, which facilitates the learning of the jobs. (This ability factor was identified by factor analysis research.) Sometimes, in contrast, tests that appear superficially to resemble actual tasks of the job turn out to be of low validity because they fail to sample relevant abilities.

Predictive validity of the kind described above is not the only kind of validity. We may also be interested in the extent to which the test actually measures the trait we assume it measures, a somewhat different concern from the criterion it is designed to predict. This is called *construct validity*. Thus, a test assumed to be a spatial test may turn out to tap mainly the ability to understand the verbal instructions. Construct validity can be determined only experimentally, through correlation with other measures.

The selection ratio.   Another important factor affecting the success of aptitude tests in personnel selection procedures is the selection ratio. This is the ratio of those selected to those available for placement. If there are only a few openings and many applicants, the selection ratio is low; and this is the condition under which a selection program works best. For example, if only a few pilots are needed relative to the number of applicants available, one can establish a high qualifying score on the aptitude test, and there will be very few subsequent failures among those accepted. On the other hand, if practically all applicants have to be accepted to fill the vacancies, the test is not useful, regardless of its validity, since this amounts to virtual abandonment of the selection principle. If the selection ratio is kept low, validity coefficients even as low as .20 can still identify useful tests. If the selection ratio is high, higher validity is necessary.

Combining tests into a battery. Aptitude tests given in combination as multiple aptitude batteries would seem most appropriate where decisions have to be made regarding assignment of applicants to one out of several possible jobs. This kind of classification requires maximum utilization of an available manpower pool, where the same battery of tests, weighted in different combination, provides predictive indexes for each applicant for each of several jobs. Since the validity of these tests has been separately determined for each job, it may be found, for example, that tests A, D, and E predict success in job Y, while tests B, D, and C, predict success in job X. By the appropriate combinations of test scores, it is then possible to find each applicant's *aptitude index* for job X as well as for job Y. The most efficient batteries are those in which the tests have a low correlation with each other (hence, there is less duplication of abilities measured) and where the individual tests have high validity for some jobs but not for others. Thus, if a test score predicts success on job Y but not job X, a high score on this test would point to an assignment on job Y. A test that is valid for all jobs is not very useful in helping us decide the particular job for which an individual is best suited.

There are two main methods of combining scores from a test battery to make predictions of later job performance. One method is called the *successive hurdle* or *multiple-cutoff* method. With this approach, applicants are accepted or rejected on the basis of one test score at a time. In order to be selected, an applicant must score above a critical score on each test; he is disqualified by a low score on any one test.

The second approach uses *multiple correlation.* From the validity of the tests and their correlations with each other, a determination can be made of a proper weight for each test score. Using these weights as multipliers for test scores, a value of a total aptitude index can be computed for each individual. This method, then, produces a combined weighted score, which reflects the individual's performance on all the tests in a battery. The particular method chosen for combining scores depends on a number of factors in the selection situation, but both methods, which are based on aptitude information from a number of different tests, accomplish the purpose of making predictions of job success.

EDWIN A. FLEISHMAN

[*Other relevant material may be found in* ACHIEVEMENT TESTING; FACTOR ANALYSIS; INTELLIGENCE AND INTELLIGENCE TESTING; MULTIVARIATE ANALYSIS; PSYCHOMETRICS; VOCATIONAL INTEREST TESTING.]

BIBLIOGRAPHY

ADKINS, DOROTHY C. 1947 *Construction and Analysis of Achievement Tests.* Washington: Government Printing Office.

ANASTASI, ANNE (1954) 1961 *Psychological Testing.* 2d ed. New York: Macmillan.

BUROS, OSCAR K. (editor) 1959 *The Fifth Mental Measurements Yearbook.* Highland Park, N.J.: Gryphon. → See especially pages 667–721 on multiaptitude batteries.

CRONBACH, LEE J. (1949) 1960 *Essentials of Psychological Testing.* 2d ed. New York: Harper.

CRONBACH, LEE J.; and GLASER, GOLDINE C. (1957) 1965 *Psychological Tests and Personnel Decisions.* Urbana: Univ. of Illinois Press.

CURETON, EDWARD E.; and CURETON, LOUISE W. 1955 *The Multi-aptitude Test.* New York: Psychological Corp.

DVORAH, BEATRICE J. 1956 The General Aptitude Test Battery. *Personnel Guidance Journal* 35:145–154.

FLEISHMAN, EDWIN A. 1956 Psychomotor Selection Tests: Research and Application in the United States Air Force. *Personnel Psychology* 9:449–467.

FLEISHMAN, EDWIN A. (editor) 1961 *Studies in Personnel and Industrial Psychology.* Homewood, Ill.: Dorsey.

FLEISHMAN, EDWIN A. 1964 *The Structure and Measurement of Physical Fitness.* Englewood Cliffs, N.J.: Prentice-Hall.

FRENCH, JOHN W. 1951 The Description of Aptitude and Achievement Tests in Terms of Rotated Factors. *Psychometric Monographs* No. 5.

GAGNÉ, ROBERT M.; and FLEISHMAN, EDWIN A. 1959 *Psychology and Human Performance.* New York: Holt.

GHISELLI, EDWIN E. 1955 The Measurement of Occupational Aptitude. California, University of, *Publications in Psychology* 8:101–216.

GHISELLI, EDWIN E.; and BROWN, CLARENCE W. (1948) 1955 *Personnel and Industrial Psychology.* 2d ed. New York: McGraw-Hill.

GUILFORD, JOY P. (editor) 1947 *Printed Classification Tests.* U.S. Army Air Force, Aviation Psychology Program, Research Report No. 5. Washington: Government Printing Office.

GUILFORD, J. P. 1959 Three Faces of Intellect. *American Psychologist* 14:469–479.

GULLIKSEN, HAROLD 1950 *Theory of Mental Tests.* New York: Wiley.

LOEVINGER, JANE 1957 Objective Tests as Instruments of Psychological Theory. *Psychological Reports* 3:635–694.

MELTON, ARTHUR W. (editor) 1947 *Apparatus Tests.* U.S. Army Air Force, Aviation Psychology Program, Research Report No. 4. Washington: Government Printing Office.

SUPER, DONALD E.; and CRITES, J. O. (1949) 1962 *Appraising Vocational Fitness by Means of Psychological Tests.* Rev. ed. New York: Harper.

U.S. EMPLOYMENT SERVICE 1946–1958 *General Aptitude Test Battery.* Washington: Government Printing Office.

VERNON, PHILIP E. (1950) 1961 *The Structure of Human Abilities.* 2d ed. London: Methuen.

AQUINAS, THOMAS

Thomas Aquinas (1225–1274) is by common consent the greatest theologian of the Middle Ages. His work gave a new clarity and comprehensiveness to the systematization of theology, and his philosophical judgment, which was matured in the study of Aristotle, never wavered. These qualities of judgment, organization, and clarity are to be found in his discussions of social and political questions, but it is important to remember the theological context of these questions if his treatment of them is to be understood.

Nearly everything of importance that Aquinas has to say about social and political matters is to be found in the second part of his *Summa theologica*. This great work, a systematic survey of the whole field of Christian theology, is divided into three parts. The first of these is devoted to God and the creation, the second to man and his nature, and the third to Christ and the sacraments. The second part contains a long series of discussions of the end of man, the law by which he is guided to this end, and the virtues and vices which help or hinder him on his way. This part of the *Summa theologica* is thus a massive survey of human nature viewed as part of the divine plan of the universe. For convenience it is divided, in turn, into two main sections (referred to as 1, 2 and 2, 2 in what follows), which together comprise 403 questions, each arranged in the form of a series of debates between clearly contrasted positions. The problems we shall discuss occupy no more than about 20 of these questions and are thus only a small fraction of the whole work. The arrangement of the discussions required that Aquinas should summarize earlier arguments and give his judgment on one side or the other. We can only understand what he is saying if we understand both the place of these questions in his work as a whole and the tradition of discussion of which his questions and answers form a part. In what follows we shall, therefore, have to devote a good deal of attention to the background and context of the discussion.

The problems discussed by Aquinas which fall within our field are those concerned with property, trade, the just price, usury, and the political community in general, and we shall speak of them in turn.

Property. The traditional view of private property, which was still accepted in the twelfth century, ascribed its origin to human sin. The ideal community was one in which "no-one called anything his own, but they had all things common" (Acts 4.32). This view was being modified in the late twelfth century by lawyers who drew a distinction between *use*, which was private except in times of necessity, and *ownership* (*dominium*), which ought to be common. Then Aristotle's *Politics*, which was translated into Latin about 1250, introduced the medieval West to the view that private property is a necessary instrument of the good life. This view brought with it a radical transformation of the theory of property, and Aquinas was the first who combined a defense of the Aristotelian view of private property with a full discussion and criticism of traditional texts (2, 2, q. 66, art. 2). On all important points Aquinas was decisively on the side of Aristotle. He accepted the view that private property is necessary for the orderly conduct of human society. In answer to the traditional texts he asserted that the ideal of having all things common refers only to times of need; but in this connection he made the important concession that "he who is in great need may take what he needs from another's goods if he can find no-one to give them to him": such "stealing" is no sin (2, 2, q. 66, art. 7).

Aquinas' view, here as everywhere, was expressed with masterly clarity. His powerful arguments were too necessary to the rapidly developing society of the thirteenth century to meet much opposition. The last outpost of conservatism was the Franciscan order, which maintained its formal rejection of private property until 1322, when Pope John XXII revoked the arrangement whereby the Roman church held property in trust on behalf of the Franciscans. At the same time the pope declared heretical the doctrine of the absolute poverty of Christ and his disciples. In this pronouncement we may see the official disappearance of the old view of the inherent sinfulness of private property and the triumph of the view expressed by Aquinas.

Trade. There was no theory of trade in the early Middle Ages. Merchants were necessary to provide luxuries for the rich and adornments for the church, and their activities were protected accordingly. But when merchants grew in numbers, wealth, and organized power, the tide of criticism began to rise. The legal theories of the twelfth century reflected this growing aversion and fear. Gratian's authoritative collection of canon law contained texts (e.g., Luke 19.45, on the ejection of traders from the Temple) that were held to prove that no Christian ought to be a merchant. The theoretical objection to merchants (as opposed to craftsmen or farmers) arose from the fact that they bought commodities in order to sell them, unchanged, at a higher price. This was the sin of avarice, and it was held to be an almost inescapable sin in trade. The study of Aristotle yielded a further argument to an already existing hostility, since he asserted (*Politics* 1319a, 1328b) that the life of a trader was incompatible with moral excellence. As a student of Aristotle, Aquinas was much less favorable to trade than to private property. His account of the place of merchants in society (*De regno* ii, 3) is wholly inspired by Aristotle. Like Aristotle, he greatly preferred a self-sufficient to a commercial state, and he justified this preference by pointing to the risk of the failure of foreign food supplies in time of war, the corruption of manners brought about by the presence of foreigners, and the cupidity, frauds, and unwarlike dispositions induced by trade. Nevertheless, despite these dangers, merchants ought not to be entirely excluded from the state, because no state can be found that does not lack some commodities and have an excess of others. Even the perfect state, therefore, needs some merchants, but the fewer the better.

Aquinas had little more than this to say about trade in general, but (in common with other medieval authors) he presented relatively full discussions of two problems that arise from trade: the problems of the just price and of usury. This emphasis can be easily explained. As a theologian his main interest lay in distinguishing between permissible and reprehensible practices. He was not concerned with building up a theory of trade but a system of morals, and moral problems in trade chiefly arise from the sale of goods, including the sale of money, for profit, or usury. Usury in fact is only a special case of the unjust price.

The just price. The theory of the just price is a distinctively medieval contribution to economic theory, and it influenced economic thought as long as the labor theory of value was a living issue, far into the nineteenth century. But there is an important distinction between medieval theorists and modern economists: medieval theorists were not so much concerned with what does happen as with what ought to happen. Aquinas' thought on the subject follows the common medieval pattern, although his argument is immensely superior in clarity and refinement to that of most other medieval writers. He accepted the general definition of the just price, which may be stated in the form of an equation: *just price* equals *cost to seller*. This equation makes it clear that changes in demand ought to have no place in determining prices. To charge more to someone in dire need is the sin of avarice. But the meaning of the phrase "cost to seller" still remains to be determined, and it is here that Aquinas (2, 2, q. 77) introduced some refinements of considerable interest. For example, he

argued that the seller may count the personal damage he receives in parting with a cherished object as part of his cost, although he may not equally count the personal value which the buyer attaches to the same object. Further, while accepting the principle that it is sinful to buy something in order to sell it unchanged at a higher price, he argued that lapse of time between buying and selling may justify a rise in price. Aquinas devoted some attention to the new factors introduced by lapse of time: for example, labor may have been expended, or danger incurred, in moving or keeping the goods; or the goods may have improved in quality (e.g., wines), so that the seller may lose more in parting with them than he gained in acquiring them. These examples illustrate the beginnings of the analysis of the economic concept of cost, and they show how careful attention to detail could gradually turn theories that were primarily ethical in origin into descriptions of the economic process.

Usury. The problem of usury was the biggest single problem in medieval social theory. There was no area in which practice and theory were in such conspicuous conflict. Usury, whether open or concealed, was ubiquitous and necessary, but all the arguments, whether Biblical or philosophical, were against it. The arguments found in Aristotle served only to reinforce those used by Biblical commentators. The problem could not be solved, but it could be mitigated by refining the notion of usury, and Aquinas contributed several such refinements. In the first place he gave a subtle explanation of the nature of the evil of usury: it is unjust per se because it exacts the return of something that does not exist. He explained this by drawing a distinction (2, 2, q. 78, art. 1) between things that are consumed as they are used (e.g., food) and things that may be used without being consumed (e.g., a house). Only in the second case can use be separated from ownership. Money belongs to the first class. Therefore, he who sells money must sell it outright. He who exacts a price in the form of an annual payment and then demands a return of his capital is guilty of being paid twice for the same thing. No seller is entitled to receive more than an exact equivalent of what he has given up. This brings us back to the problem of the just price and to the question, "What exactly has the seller of money given up?" With his usual scrupulous regard for the facts, Aquinas agreed that the seller of money may receive damage through loss of enjoyment greater than the sum of money immediately involved. For this damage compensation is due, and this is not usury. Also, like most writers from the early thirteenth century onward, Aquinas agreed that a man who invests in a business and assumes a share of the risk is entitled to a share in the profit while retaining his rights in his capital. He fitted this into his general theory of usury by saying that, unlike the usurer, the risk sharer retains the ownership of his capital by membership in the firm. He did not seem to see that this makes a serious break in his general argument that money is a commodity which can be used only by being consumed. It was not until 1546 that this objection was developed by Charles Dumoulin in his refutation of the scholastic theory of usury.

The political community. In his general attitude to politics Aquinas displayed the same basic Aristotelianism that we find elsewhere in his social thought. The abandonment of Augustinian pessimism with regard to political society is characteristic of several writers of the twelfth and thirteenth centuries, but Aquinas gave fuller and more coherent expression to this tendency than any previous medieval writer. He accepted the argument of Aristotle's *Politics* that the state exists for the good life (1, 2, q. 92, art. 1) and that the common good is in some sense different in kind and superior to the good of the individual (1, 2, q. 90, art. 2). He saw the political community as a natural institution based on reason, which would have existed among men even if man had never sinned (1, q. 96, art. 4); and he argued that the natural end of man in political society can, in large measure at least, be achieved under a pagan ruler (2, 2, q. 10, art. 10). He went very far in accepting statements of Aristotle that have seemed to others barely consistent with a Christian view, for example, that "the perfect community is the state (*civitas*)" and that "the individual is to the perfect community as the imperfect to the perfect" (1, 2, q. 90, art. 2). But in interpreting such statements it is necessary, here as elsewhere, to remember their context. The state did not mean to Aquinas what it meant to Aristotle, still less of course what it means to us. The political community was a vaguer concept in the thirteenth century than it was in fourth-century Athens, and the "perfect community" had none of the sinister totalitarian implication of post-Hegelian theory. Nevertheless, it is undeniable that Aquinas attached less importance to individuality than he did to the good of the community. What interested him most in politics was law, and most of his discussions of political topics occur in those sections of the *Summa theologica* concerned with the relations between divine and human law and between natural and positive law. His definition of law as "an ordinance of reason, for the common good, promulgated by one who has the care of the

community" (1, 2, q. 90, art. 4) is the basis of all his political thinking. For him, the political community was at once corporate and authoritarian, rational and natural, but certainly not utilitarian or "liberal" in the modern sense.

Aquinas' great contribution to social and political thought lies in his emphasis on the importance of reason and nature in the universe. In his hands Aristotle became the main instrument for bringing the idea of natural order to its fullest development in medieval thought. A veneration for nature runs through all the work of Aquinas and explains his careful (however brief) attention to the details of social and economic life. His lucidity in exposition and moderation in argument complete his qualifications for being regarded as the Christian Aristotle.

R. W. SOUTHERN

[*For the historical context of Aquinas' work, see* ECONOMIC THOUGHT, *article on* ANCIENT AND MEDIEVAL THOUGHT, *and the biography of* ARISTOTLE.]

WORKS BY AQUINAS

Summa theologica. 22 vols. Translated by the Fathers of the English Dominican Province. London: Oates & Washbourne, 1912–1925.

Opera omnia. 25 vols. New York: Misurgia, 1948–1950.

On Kingship: To the King of Cyprus. Translated by Gerald B. Phelan. Revised with an introduction and notes by I. Th. Eschmann. Toronto: Pontifical Institute of Mediaeval Studies, 1949.

The Political Ideas of St. Thomas Aquinas: Representative Selections. Edited with an introduction by Dino Bigongiari. New York: Hafner, 1953.

Selected Political Writings. Edited with an introduction by A. P. d'Entrèves. New York: Macmillan, 1959.

SUPPLEMENTARY BIBLIOGRAPHY

BALDWIN, JOHN W. 1959 *The Medieval Theories of the Just Price: Romanists, Canonists, and Theologians in the Twelfth and the Thirteenth Centuries.* American Philosophical Society, Transactions, Vol. 49, part 4. Philadelphia: The Society.

GILBY, THOMAS 1958 *The Political Thought of Thomas Aquinas.* Univ. of Chicago Press.

NELSON, BENJAMIN N. 1949 *The Idea of Usury: From Tribal Brotherhood to Universal Otherhood.* Princeton Univ. Press.

NOONAN, JOHN T. JR. 1957 *The Scholastic Analysis of Usury.* Cambridge, Mass.: Harvard Univ. Press.

TOOKE, JOAN D. 1965 *The Just War in Aquinas and Grotius.* London: Society for Promoting Christian Knowledge.

ARBITRAGE

See SPECULATION, HEDGING, AND ARBITRAGE.

ARBITRATION

See ADJUDICATION, *article on* INTERNATIONAL ADJUDICATION; INTERNATIONAL CONFLICT RESOLUTION; LABOR RELATIONS.

ARCHEOLOGY

I

THE FIELD

In simplest terms, archeology can be defined as the anthropology of extinct cultures. It provides means of learning about mankind's ways of life for the more than 99 per cent of man's existence that lies before the earliest written records and for the vast areas of the world on which history was silent until a few centuries or a few decades ago. Archeological research, as generally practiced, shares with the rest of anthropology and the other social sciences a concern for the recurrent, patterned aspects of human behavior rather than with the isolation of the unique. It is historical in the sense that it deals with human behavior viewed through time and supplements written sources with the documentation provided by artifactual evidence from the past. During the century or so of its existence as a recognizable scholarly discipline, archeology has come more and more to apply scientific procedures to the collection and analysis of its data, even when its subject matter could be considered humanistic as well as scientific. Archeology can also be properly regarded as a set of specialized techniques for obtaining cultural data from the past, data that may be used by anthropologists, historians, art critics, economists, or any others interested in man and his activities.

This view has the advantage of eliminating the argument whether archeology is anthropology or history and allows for recognition of the varied, sometimes incompatible, purposes for which archeological data and conclusions are used. There is no reason to regard the archeology of Beazley, who analyzes Greek black-figure vases, as identical with the archeology of MacNeish, who has excavated plant remains of the earliest Mexican farmers.

The greatest significance of archeology is in the time depth with which it has supplemented anthropology's synchronic studies of societies in all parts of the world. No other reliable means is available to extend backward our knowledge of culture, since traditional histories, orally transmitted, are not only shallow in their time depth but subject to many distortions with the passage of time. Archeology has provided the data for testing a great variety of hypotheses in the realm of culture, growth, and change, which are among anthropology's major concerns. It has provided an essen-

tial check on theories of cultural evolution and is substituting fact for fancy in such matters as the origins of plant and animal domestication and the beginnings of writing, urbanization, and other crucial steps toward civilization. Although scientific archeology—in contrast to antiquarian studies and the collection of curios—is less than a century old, it has already provided a comprehensive and fairly detailed view of human activities in all parts of the world from the very beginnings of mankind (Clark 1961).

At the same time that archeology is fundamental to a scientific understanding of man, it is also a subject of tremendous popular interest, albeit too often of a superficial and sensational kind. The discovery in 1922 of the tomb of Tutankhamen, its contents still largely unlooted, was front-page news around the world, as well as a significant contribution to Egyptology. The wall paintings of Lascaux Cave, as soon as they were open to the public, attracted thousands of visitors, many of whom were willing to stand in line for hours to secure even a brief view of the murals. An archeological discovery that stirred tremendous popular interest, without any of the artistic appeal of the foregoing examples, was the excavation in Newfoundland in 1962–1963 of the first Norse settlement in the New World to be positively identified. Although popular interest in such aspects of archeology often tends to obscure the true significance of its accomplishments, it also provides a tremendous and ever-growing basis for financial support from both public and private sources. A single figure will suffice to exemplify this: in an 18-year period governmental funds of approximately $2,000,000 were provided for archeological excavation of sites threatened with destruction by dam building in the Missouri River Basin. It should not be overlooked that popular interest in archeology can sometimes support wholly nonarcheological activities, such as the extensive tomb robbing and looting of archeological sites that plague countries with abundant remains of high commercial value, such as Iran, Italy, and Mexico. This looting, whether done under the guise of archeology or frankly for profit, is carried on with no sense of scientific responsibility, although often supported indirectly by museums and individuals professing the most respectable artistic or archeological interests. Archeology, under government auspices, has sometimes become a means of awakening nationalistic pride, as it was in Italy under Mussolini. But it can also be used wisely to create public appreciation of long-neglected peoples and their cultures, as in the extensive system of archeological displays by the National Park Service of the United States or by Mexico's splendid Museo Nacional.

Nevertheless, in spite of its wide popular appeal, archeology is significant chiefly as a means of testing anthropological and other social science generalizations about cultural behavior, especially those concerned with the nature of invention, diffusion, culture change, and human ecology. Its potentialities have not by any means been fully exploited in this regard, mainly because it is only recently that archeology has achieved a sufficiently broad and detailed body of data with sufficiently firm chronological placement. Until recently emphasis has tended to be on the accumulation of data and the devising of techniques for organizing them meaningfully; and even today there are areas where first priority must go to data collecting and chronological controls.

History of archeology

The diverse origins of archeology account for its continuing dual orientation—some archeologists working most closely with natural and social scientists and regarding themselves as anthropologists concerned with the past and other archeologists working particularly within the humanities and interested chiefly in the ancient civilizations of the Old World (Daniel 1950). Archeology's roots go back to the Renaissance interest in the antiquities of Greece and Rome, an interest that emphasized the collection of works of art for their own sake and the identification of surviving relics and sites with places and events in the literature of the Greeks and Romans. To this was added in the eighteenth century an enthusiasm for a wider range of ancient relics, and, in the next century—stimulated by the romantic movement—for relics of medieval times. It became fashionable in many parts of Europe, for example, to "open" the burial mounds that were (and still are) a conspicuous part of the landscape, in search of such curiosities and grisly relics as they might contain. Excavation techniques in these investigations were generally of the crudest sort, mere casual pitting and burrowing. Nevertheless, by the 1880s in England, General Lane-Fox Pitt-Rivers had developed techniques of careful excavating and recording that remain models to the present; he substituted complete excavation for unsystematic partial digging of sites, and he shifted attention from burials to living sites, an important change that resulted in greater variety and significance of artifacts found. At about the same time, Sir Flinders Petrie, work-

ing in Egypt, developed the technique of ceramic seriation of common household vessels to reveal subtle chronological changes, and George Reisner, in Egypt and Palestine, gave added emphasis to the analysis and interpretation of natural stratification. Other archeologists of the nineteenth century, mainly in England and continental Europe, also initiated technical improvements in field work, analysis, and reporting that slowly changed antiquarianism into scientific research.

Interest in the European past was expanded and supplemented in the early 1800s by a rapid growth of interest in the Middle East, stimulated by such efforts as Napoleon's campaign in Egypt (1798–1801), in which the army was accompanied by a corps of skilled scientists and draftsmen who collected and recorded antiquities. At about the same time European diplomatic and commercial representatives in Baghdad initiated vigorous researches that led to the discovery of sophisticated civilizations that had heretofore been little more than dim legends.

The accumulation of relics of the European past gave impetus to attempts to classify them into a meaningful system, and in 1836 Thomsen, the first curator of the National Museum of Denmark, published in definitive form the scheme of three successive "ages"—stone, bronze, and iron—that he and his colleagues had developed during the preceding two decades. Although initially designed for the arrangement of specimens in museum displays, this system became the cornerstone of European, and eventually world-wide, schemes of chronology for later generations of archeologists. The division by Lubbock in 1865 (following earlier French suggestions) of the stone age into the Paleolithic and the Neolithic and the addition of such terms as Mesolithic and Chalcolithic were not profound improvements, and the convenience and popularity of the terms obscured their inadequacy. Currently, efforts are being made to establish terms referring to basic subsistence activities and settlement patterns: for example, Braidwood's "terminal food-gathering stage," "incipient agricultural stage," and "primary village farming stage."

At the same time that seventeenth-century and eighteenth-century antiquarian and romantic interests were providing one of the foundations for archeology, another line of inquiry was creating interest in man's most remote past. From the 1820s onward human skeletal remains, the bones of extinct animals, and stone objects that were eventually recognized as man-made tools were found associated with each other and in circumstances that cast increasing doubts on the orthodox belief in a single, relatively recent creation of all life forms. The controversy among geologists, biologists, theologians, antiquarians, and others finally led to the abandonment of the "catastrophic" explanation for such remains—i.e., the Biblical deluge or similar events—as the cause of the geological deposits containing these materials. Instead, uniformitarianism—the doctrine that gradual, long-continued processes of the kinds observable today accounted for such deposits—gained acceptance. Evolutionary principles developed at about the same time provided the necessary and complementary explanation of the changes observable in these deposits. The studies of geology, human paleontology, and prehistoric archeology thus grew up concurrently, all clearly part of the natural sciences and closely involved in the developing discipline of anthropology.

The relationship of archeology to history has been discussed and argued extensively and often fruitlessly. Both disciplines deal with human activities through time, but the historians' major concern is with the last four or five millennia and with Europe and the areas with which it has been most closely involved, such as the New World and the Middle East. Archeologists, on the other hand, have been steadily expanding the scope of their interests to include 1.5 million years or more of human activity and have given special attention to regions and time periods for which the written records on which historians depend are lacking. Thus in practice the two fields complement each other and only overlap in a few times and places. In their theoretical orientation they differ in that history gives much attention to individuals and to unique events, while archeology is concerned mainly with the anonymous tangible remains of human activities, from which it attempts to derive generalized conclusions as to the behavior typical of entire groups. In practice, history and archeology have operated quite independently in most of their specific investigations and have cooperated closely when they could combine data from their separate approaches and thus partially offset the limitations of each. Specifically, archeological discoveries have provided types of information on which historical records were silent or obscure, such as the domestic conveniences of the inhabitants of Pompeii and of colonial Williamsburg; and history, in its turn, has provided the means of interpreting more fully many archeological sites (see Hawkes 1954). Also, the archeological record has made possible a great extension of the chronological record of human development and the growth of civilization; a few decades ago history texts could hardly begin prior to Greece, with a brief mention of its barbaric contemporaries of Egypt and the Near East. Today a comprehensible account can begin with the simultaneous origins of man and his tools nearly two million years ago and can be world-wide in scope.

A final detail, in considering archeology's place among related disciplines, is its close dependence on ethnography. Just as historic records are invaluable to the archeologist whenever they are available, so the detailed ethnographic record of contemporary and recent peoples of the world provides the basis from which archeologists can make meaningful interpretations of their data. It is relatively easy to determine the significance of the artifacts, house patterns, food remains, etc., of a group about whose immediate descendants we have full ethnographic accounts; but without such a relationship, inferences are less sure and gross errors are possible. It is extremely fortunate for archeological interpretation that in its earlier days ethnography placed great emphasis on collecting, describing, and explaining objects of material culture.

The practice of archeology

The procedures of archeology can be identified in terms that are generally applicable to all scientific work; namely, *observation*, the numerous and complex techniques for field work; *description*, or "culture-historic integration," as Willey and Phillips have called it, including the various methods of organizing and analyzing data that are distinctive of archeology; and *explanation*, the most difficult, most important, and least certain part of the task. Although observational procedures, the means by which archeology gathers its primary data, will not be discussed here in detail, it should be noted that "field work" in archeology can range in scope from one day's work by a single archeologist with one or two volunteer helpers to the multidecade programs undertaken at large sites and involving large permanent professional staffs and scores of workmen for each "season" or "campaign." Although many elaborate techniques have been developed to meet the varied demands of archeological field work, they are all designed essentially for the dual purpose of getting out of the ground as much information as possible in the form of both objects and observations and recording this information in as complete and orderly a manner as possible. The archeologist's slow and painstaking work and his attention to details of uncertain significance are explained by the fact that the excavation of a site is also its destruction, and even if a part of a site is left undug, it is rarely feasible to return and obtain details overlooked or unrecorded the first time.

The complexity of archeological field techniques has given rise to a dilemma: many archeologists with great technical proficiency are little interested in the broader aspects of archeology, at either the descriptive or the explanatory level. Although often accepted as "professionals," they are more nearly comparable to the highly skilled medical technician than to the physician. They are indispensable in large research projects and can carry out by themselves projects of limited scope that are in turn contributory to major scholarly endeavors. In the university training of archeologists in the United States, proficiency in field techniques is left mainly to such actual field experience as they may acquire, and emphasis is on the full gamut of anthropological subfields; little attention is given to the need for more systematic training in the descriptive levels of those who might prefer careers as technicians rather than as anthropological archeologists. Both in training and in occupational terminology a clearer distinction between these two facets of research would avoid both unjustified expectations and wasted training.

Scientific description. At the descriptive level particularly and, to a lesser but growing extent at the explanatory level, archeology makes use of some concepts that are shared with either the rest of anthropology or with other fields, such as geology, as well as a number of concepts that are mainly archeological in their application. These latter concepts can conveniently be grouped as spatial, temporal, cultural, integrative, and processual.

Spatial concepts. The fundamental spatial concept of archeology is the site. The best definition, as for many of the terms discussed here, has been provided by Willey and Phillips, in their *Method and Theory in American Archaeology.* They define a site as a unit of space that is "fairly continuously covered by the remains of former occupation . . . , which may be anything from a small camp to a large city." It frequently proves, on excavation, that a site consists of several successive occupations. This offers the advantage, from the standpoint of research, that changes through time may be identified by the analysis of a separate unit of each of the superimposed strata, but it usually also introduces the disadvantage that materials from several successive occupations may be mixed by either the activities of the human occupants of the site or by subsequent natural causes and thus obscure temporal differences. Larger spatial units, such as locality, district, region, and area, are useful in

grouping similar sites or in segregating sites of decreasing degrees of similarity, but definitions for these large units have not been generally agreed on and vary with the nature of the archeological problem. The term "center" is sometimes used rather loosely to specify a site or group of sites at which cultural changes occurred and from which they spread. In the reconstruction of culture history, this concept has only limited value, except in regions that are thoroughly known. Archeology has only recently become aware of the problem of sampling and its statistical evaluation; therefore, many "centers" are probably merely the sites or groups of sites that have received the most attention thus far and with which less-known sites are necessarily compared. L. Bernabò Brea, in *Sicily Before the Greeks,* has astutely observed that "the finds plotted on a map of prehistoric Sicily reflect the distribution of research workers more than that of the various objects or sites" (1957, p. 20).

The concepts of cultural and natural areas, both defined in terms of distributions of selected items—in the one case cultural traits and in the other such aspects of the environment as plant species—have provided a widely used rough scheme for characterizing the ethnography of large regions, particularly in terms of subsistence patterns, where the coincidence is most conspicuous with features of the natural environment that are reflected in vegetation. But the boundaries of such areas have remained uncertain despite long efforts at precision, and their use as a basis for archeological generalizations has generally been unsatisfactory. In the place of these concepts, the biologists' terminology and methods, as developed for studies of plant and animal ecology, are proving more useful and, of course, move the dimensions of the analysis from merely observational to descriptive and explanatory.

Chronology. Temporal divisions are fundamental to archeology; Hawkes (1954, p. 165), for example, has said that "archeology's claim to a distinctive place among the anthropological disciplines depends to a great extent on the accuracy of the chronology for events and cultures that it can offer." In recent decades new dating techniques based on radioactive decay (carbon-14, potassium and argon) and, in a few regions, dendrochronology, have provided absolute dating, in terms of the Christian calendar and subject to only modest errors, to supplement the relative dating that has long been a cornerstone of archeology. Relative dating, through such techniques as stratigraphy, seriation, cross-dating of trade goods, and the diffusion of art styles and motifs, has made possible the establishment of numerous local sequences. Eventually, if local sequences have been determined with enough precision and detail and are reliable, they can be combined, by means of careful comparisons and the equating of closely similar segments, into regional sequences. These may cover areas as large as the Amazon Basin (1.5 million square miles) or as small as upper Egypt (less than 10,000 square miles). A very large proportion of archeologists' time and effort goes into the construction, testing, and comparing of local sequences and subsequently of regional sequences. Critical importance may be attached to artifacts, dates, and culture traits that are otherwise of minor interest; it is a constant risk of archeology to become obsessed with the continual need for chronological refinement to the exclusion of other problems of broader significance.

Sequences are frequently designated initially by numbers or letters, often preserving the identifications applied in the field as a stratigraphic deposit was recorded, with number 1 at the top, 2 below it, and so on. Eventually, small stratigraphic units are grouped into "periods," which should be (but sometimes are not) carefully constructed on the basis of definable cultural changes rather than mere arbitrary segments of a time sequence. But in nearly all sequential schemes, cultural as well as temporal terms of reference are involved, so that definition must proceed concurrently for both the cultural and the temporal units. Even though it is tempting to archeologists to characterize in wholly cultural terms what are actually temporal units, the results are a distortion of culture history. It is always wise to distinguish between the dated segments of a sequence and the successive cultural units that are eventually defined.

Cultural units. The cultural units of the archeologist must necessarily differ from those of the ethnologist; tribes, confederacies, or nations are usually unidentifiable without historic documentation. Most Americanist archeologists would agree with Willey and Phillips' opinion of the *phase* as "the practicable and intelligible unit of . . . study"; and with the definition they adapt from Kidder: "an archaeological unit possessing traits sufficiently characteristic to distinguish it from all other units similarly conceived, whether of the same or other cultures or civilizations, spatially limited to the order of magnitude of a locality or region and chronologically limited to a relatively brief interval of time" (1958, p. 22). (In practice, the time interval ranges from a few decades up to several centuries.) A number of other terms have been used with approximately the same meaning as the

phase, particularly *focus,* one of the terms of the system proposed by W. C. McKern and others in the 1930s for use in the eastern United States. A unit smaller than the phase or focus that has proved useful is the *component,* the manifestation of a phase at a single site. Differences will be found between components, but they must be minor, or else the archeologist should define a new phase to accommodate such differences. The *assemblage* is comparable in scale and refers to the whole range of artifacts used at a specific time and place. A much broader and less precise term that has had wide usage is the archeological *culture* —referring to a very widely distributed complex of culture traits or to a large number of nearly contemporaneous phases that share certain distinctive features. Unfortunately, cultures are frequently ill-defined or are characterized by a single distinctive trait (the Battle-Axe culture or the Basket-Maker culture). The term is not without its use, nevertheless, as a recognition that there are broad similarities uniting widely scattered peoples or spreading across large areas; it has been suggested that cultures correspond roughly, on an earlier and simpler level, to what are generally identified as *civilizations* at a more complex level—another term that is commonly used in both history and archeology without precise definition.

The archeological "culture" should not be confused with the term "culture" as used generally in all of anthropology, following its original definition by Tylor. This key concept of anthropology is, of course, implicit in all archeological research.

Classification. In order for the archeologist to order his primary field data, particularly the extremely numerous and often fragmentary artifacts that he collects, descriptive and analytical techniques are essential, especially systems of classification and the creation of taxonomies.

The assumption that the behavior of a group tends to occur in patterns or to repeat itself rather than being random underlies most archeological research. As a result, the tangible remains of a culture at a particular time and place will be classifiable into groups of similar objects, and descriptions of the central tendency in each group and of the range of variation within it will suffice to describe most of the objects. That is, the tools of an upper paleolithic group in Spain, the pottery of Puerto Rico in the tenth century A.D., or the houses of the Marquesas prior to European contact will, in each case, display a limited range of forms and materials. Thus, classes or groups can be defined, and an individual description of each item is superfluous. These groups are generally called *types,* and it is basic to current archeological research that their adequate definition is of major importance. Opinion is divided as to whether types can be "discovered," since they already exist in the material and must be defined in terms of an objective reality, or whether types may be "designed" in whatever way most usefully serves the investigator as a basis for useful analysis and generalization. In either case, the construction of types is a complex process requiring many trial formulations, testings, and modifications. Artifact types, once defined, however, are an indispensable tool for comparing the remains of successive occupations and of concurrent occupations over both large and small areas. They are the means of equating temporally sequences made up of otherwise dissimilar materials, as, for example, Flinders Petrie's identification of Egyptian trade with Crete and the consequent matching of synchronous points in the previously separate sequences of the two regions.

Units both larger and smaller than the type are used by archeologists. The *mode* and the *motif* both refer to individual elements or details of an artifact, and such elements may be combined in many ways, although still tending to cluster rather than to show a random distribution. A *style* is a distinctive manner of employing modes and motifs, generally in complex artifacts, and may occur in many individually separable artifact types. In general, archeology is tending toward more rigorous definitions of these concepts and thus is able to employ them in more precise areal and temporal comparisons, which in turn permit surer culture-historical reconstructions. Nevertheless, wide discrepancies still occur in the usage of such terms and in the care with which various writers define them, and uniformity in terminology is only slowly being achieved.

Archeological analysis. Another important group of archeological concepts can be termed "integrative units" and is essential in building up a cultural-historic synthesis from the initial descriptive stages of research. One of the most useful is the *horizon,* which Willey and Phillips define as "a primarily spatial continuity represented by cultural traits and assemblages whose nature and mode of occurrence permit the assumption of a broad and rapid spread" (1958, p. 33). It is usually assumed that the archeological units joined in a horizon are approximately contemporaneous. As chronology has become more precise it has sometimes been found that they form a "sloping horizon," owing to the gradual spread of a trait or cluster of traits from one region to another. Considerable effort has been devoted in the United States and Latin America to the identification of *horizon markers* or trait clusters that are sufficiently specific and short-lived, like the cylindrical tripod jars of Teotihuacán, Mexico, to make it probable that all occurrences are linked by trade or diffusion during a relatively limited span of time. Although the terms horizon and horizon marker have been little used in the Old World, the general concepts they refer to have long been familiar and in use as a major means of linking cultural manifestations over wide areas.

A companion concept, also long used and only now being carefully defined, is *tradition,* a long lasting, socially transmitted cultural form or group of forms. In practice pottery traditions, architectural traditions, and other specific and even more limited applications have proved most successful, but theoretically the concept can be applied to whole cultural traditions as well. As Willey and Phillips (1958, p. 38) have commented, "the tradition gives depth, while the horizon gives breadth, to the genetic structure of culture-historical relationships on a broad geographic scale."

For broad regional synthesis, both *period* and *stage* have often been used for major successive units. It is being recognized, however, that there is an advantage in using "period" for firmly fixed chronological subdivisions and "stage" for a segment of a historical sequence in a given (continent-wide) area, characterized by a dominating pattern of economic activity. The definition of stages in terms of economic (or social) systems depends on relatively detailed and extensive inference of these aspects of culture from the tangible remains with which archeological work begins, but it is a major step in achieving the meaningful culture-historical reconstructions that are an ultimate goal of archeology. Although not commonly employed, the concept of *climax* is also valuable in such reconstructions, to designate the maximum development or greatest intensity of a tradition or horizon or of a civilization as a whole.

In closing this brief survey of some of the more distinctive concepts employed by archeology, it should be pointed out that most of them are usually used without precise definition and that they are frequently used without specific identification and sometimes even without awareness of their use. Much archeological thinking and writing has been careless and lacking in rigor, so that conclusions have been difficult to recheck, and comparison of the work of individual investigators is impeded by differing terminologies and undefined terms. Nevertheless, in only about a century of growth as an identifiable intellectual discipline, archeology has accumulated an enormous body of carefully recorded data and sufficiently sound and far-ranging conclusions to have required the rewriting of history and permitted the exploration of some of anthropology's most significant questions, such as the degree of uniformity of cultural evolution, the relative importance of invention and diffusion for innovations, the relationships between technology and social systems, and the influence of environment on cultural form and content.

Progress toward explanation

Archeology today is changing rapidly on two fronts. First, an ever increasing number and variety of technical aids are being employed, ranging from such new devices as the proton magnetometer, for detecting underground discontinuities by means of slight variations in the magnetic field, to some of the sampling techniques and statistical tests that have long been used in other disciplines. These refinements are increasing the range and amount of data that archeologists can derive from field and laboratory work but in themselves will not change the direction or goals of archeology. A second and much more important change is the shift from the reconstruction of ever more detailed time and space frameworks, within which both old and new data can be organized, toward attempts at what Willey and Phillips call processual interpretation, which comprises the explanatory level of archeology. While this is not a wholly new approach in archeology, having been undertaken in broad terms by Childe, for example, in *What Happened in History* (1942) and urged specifically and in detail by Taylor (1948), it has had new attention in the last decade. This attention is partly a reflection of changing archeological goals but also derives from the great increase in the past two decades in the completeness and detail of both descriptive and chronological data. Without these data, the explanatory level of archeology and attempts at soundly based interpretations would have been impossible.

Social reconstruction. One of the most successful proponents of social reconstruction in the United States has been William H. Sears; the titles of two of his papers indicate the nature of the approach: "The Sociopolitical Organization of Pre-Columbian Cultures on the Gulf Coastal Plain" (1954) and "The Study of Social and Religious Systems in North American Archaeology" (1961). Sears recognizes that the accumulated data of traditional archeology are an essential prerequisite for the reconstruction of social, economic, religious, political, and ecological systems. But he also urges that

new data be collected with these broader aims clearly in mind, because excavation, recording, and analysis that are directed only toward limited descriptive or chronological goals will often miss the clues that can contribute to broader problems. He suggests (1961) that particularly valuable inferences can be derived from settlement patterns, details of ceremonial structures, burials and their accompanying artifacts, artistic representations, and evidence of specialization in artifact manufacture. To these should be added population density, evidence for the extent and nature of trade, and differential distribution of artifacts within a site. Although it is implicit in the reasoning of Sears and others that an extensive ceremonial structure or a highly differentiated economy implies a complex social and religious system, the reconstruction must actually be carried out on a far subtler basis than this. The possible significant interpretations that each line of evidence will support must be compared and contradicting and poorly supported inferences eliminated. Ethnographic analogies are often illuminating, and reconstruction is greatly aided when archeological remains are recent enough for historic records to be relevant. However, the reconstruction of social and other intangible aspects of culture is also possible for societies remote in time, with no traceable descendants, although it may have to be less certain and detailed.

Another successful application of the newer archeological techniques of social reconstruction is Deetz' *The Dynamics of Stylistic Change in Arikara Ceramics* (1965), in which a computer was programmed to determine the degree of association among some 150 stylistic attributes observable on the rim sherds of vessels from a site occupied throughout most of the eighteenth century; this in turn made it possible to determine a significant relationship between the ceramic changes through time and the historically documented shift away from the matrilocal pattern in the Arikara postmarriage residence customs. While such a study requires both protracted analysis of the ceramic data and complex calculations and would not be feasible without historic and ethnographic data on the concurrent changes in social organization, it nevertheless points the way to far more meaningful uses of archeological data and to possibilities for reconstruction of aspects of culture hitherto the subject of speculation rather than of scientifically rigorous analysis.

A comparable study, at an Arizona site occupied about A.D. 1200 and therefore without historical or ethnographic data, was carried out by William A. Longacre (1964a). He determined, by analysis of the distribution within the rooms of the site of 175 design elements occurring on potsherds, that the occupants of the village were probably divided into two localized matrilineal groups, each with its own ceremonial structure. An analysis was also made of room functions and of the pattern of burials, with significant results. Such studies exemplify the comment that the "new archeology in America is tending to be more concerned with culture process and less concerned with the descriptive content of prehistoric cultures" (Caldwell 1959, p. 304).

Ecology. Another important new development in archeology is the growing interest in ecological interpretation, that is, the analysis of archeological materials in terms of the total interrelationship between the human community and its environment. The long but superficial interest in data on subsistence (identification of plant and animal remains, with publication of mere lists of raw data) is only a small part of the larger problem of the role that the environment and human interactions with it have played in the growth of any particular culture or its successful functioning to meet human needs at a particular time. The simplistic idea of environmental "limitations" on culture is being replaced by investigation of the varying ways in which the environment may be used by a human group, depending on its technology, social organization, and value system (Butzer 1964). Awareness of the extent to which cultural activities may modify the landscape over long periods of time is also growing. Thus, not only the "economic basis" (Clark 1952) of a culture is of interest to archeologists, but also what has been aptly termed "man's role in changing the face of the earth" (International Symposium . . . 1956). An ecological approach to the study of human groups is not, of course, limited to archeology but is a trend characteristic of anthropology as a whole (Helm 1962; Leeds & Vayda 1965). There is little doubt that this approach will be further refined and strengthened and will be a valuable supplement to archeological efforts to reconstruct the social, political, and religious aspects of human actvity.

At the same time that archeology is taking these new directions, it is continuing at an increasing rate, through the support of UNESCO and many national governments, to seek familiar kinds of descriptive data through emergency programs at sites threatened with destruction by road building, dams, recreation facilities, and urban, suburban, commercial, and military construction. At the present rate at which sites are being obliterated, there

will soon be few left from which archeologists can seek the new types of data that are becoming recoverable by means of recently developed analytical techniques. It would be alarmist to predict that archeology will soon starve for lack of new raw data, but it is increasingly important that the archeologist secure from any sites he excavates the full range of data required by methodological and technical advances. Only thus can archeology continue its important role of contributing to the social sciences a body of new data for testing and verifying hypotheses and for demonstrating with time depth the nature of cultural processes.

RICHARD B. WOODBURY

[*See also* ANTHROPOLOGY, *articles on* THE FIELD *and* CULTURAL ANTHROPOLOGY; HISTORY, *articles on* CULTURE HISTORY *and* ETHNOHISTORY. *Directly related are the entries* DOMESTICATION; ECOLOGY; EVOLUTION; HUNTING AND GATHERING, *articles on* OLD WORLD PREHISTORIC SOCIETIES *and* NEW WORLD PREHISTORIC SOCIETIES; URBAN REVOLUTION. *Other relevant material may be found in the biographies of* BREUIL; CHILDE; KIDDER; KROEBER; LUBBOCK; PETRIE; PITT-RIVERS; STRONG.]

BIBLIOGRAPHY

ANTHROPOLOGICAL SOCIETY OF WASHINGTON 1955 *New Interpretations of Aboriginal-American Culture History.* 75th Anniversary Volume. Washington: The Society.

ANTHROPOLOGICAL SOCIETY OF WASHINGTON 1959 *Evolution and Anthropology: A Centennial Appraisal.* Washington: The Society.

BREA, L. BERNABÒ (1957) 1958 *Sicily Before the Greeks.* New York: Praeger.

BUTZER, KARL W. 1964 *Environment and Archeology: An Introduction to Pleistocene Geography.* Chicago: Aldine.

CALDWELL, JOSEPH R. 1959 The New American Archeology. *Science* 129:303–307.

CHANG, KWANG-CHIH 1958 Study of the Neolithic Social Grouping: Examples From the New World. *American Anthropologist* New Series 60:298–334.

CHILDE, V. GORDON (1942) 1960 *What Happened in History.* Rev. ed. Baltimore: Penguin.

CHILDE, V. GORDON 1951 *Social Evolution.* New York: Schuman.

CLARK, J. GRAHAME D. (1939) 1957 *Archaeology and Society: Reconstructing the Prehistoric Past.* 3d ed., rev. London: Methuen. → A paperback edition was published in 1960 by Methuen.

CLARK, J. GRAHAME D. 1952 *Prehistoric Europe: The Economic Basis.* London: Methuen.

CLARK, J. GRAHAME D. 1961 *World Prehistory: An Outline.* Cambridge Univ. Press.

DANIEL, GLYN E. 1950 *A Hundred Years of Archaeology.* London: Duckworth.

DEETZ, JAMES 1965 *The Dynamics of Stylistic Change in Arikara Ceramics.* Urbana: Univ. of Illinois Press.

GIMBUTAS, MARIJA 1963 European Prehistory: Neolithic to the Iron Age. Pages 69–106 in *Biennial Review of*

Anthropology: 1963. Edited by Bernard J. Siegel. Stanford (Calif.) Univ. Press.

HAWKES, CHRISTOPHER 1954 Archeological Theory and Method: Some Suggestions From the Old World. *American Anthropologist* New Series 56:155–168.

HEIZER, ROBERT F. (editor) (1949) 1958 *A Guide to Archaeological Field Methods.* 3d rev. ed. Palo Alto, Calif.: National Press. → First published as *A Manual of Archaeological Field Methods.*

HEIZER, ROBERT F. (editor) 1959 *The Archeologist at Work: A Source Book in Archaeological Method and Interpretation.* New York: Harper.

HELM, JUNE 1962 The Ecological Approach in Anthropology. *American Journal of Sociology* 67:630–639.

INTERNATIONAL SYMPOSIUM ON MAN'S ROLE IN CHANGING THE FACE OF THE EARTH, PRINCETON, N.J., *1955* 1956 *Man's Role in Changing the Face of the Earth.* Edited by William L. Thomas et al. Univ. of Chicago Press.

KRIEGER, ALEX D. 1960 Archeological Typology in Theory and Practice. Pages 141–151 in International Congress of Anthropological and Ethnological Sciences, 5th, Philadelphia, 1956, *Men and Cultures: Selected Papers.* Edited under the chairmanship of Anthony F. C. Wallace. Philadelphia: Univ. of Pennsylvania Press.

LEEDS, ANTHONY; and VAYDA, ANDREW P. (editors) 1965 *Man, Culture, and Animals: The Role of Animals in Human Ecological Adjustments.* American Association for the Advancement of Science, Publication No. 78. Washington: The Association.

LONGACRE, WILLIAM A. 1964*a* Archeology as Anthropology: A Case Study. *Science* 144:1454–1455.

LONGACRE, WILLIAM A. 1964*b* Sociological Implications of the Ceramic Analysis. Volume 2, pages 155–170 in *Chapters in the Prehistory of Eastern Arizona.* Fieldiana: Anthropology, Vol. 55. Chicago Natural History Museum.

ROUSE, IRVING 1953 The Strategy of Culture History. Pages 57–76 in International Symposium on Anthropology, New York, 1952, *Anthropology Today: An Encyclopedic Inventory.* Prepared under the chairmanship of A. L. Kroeber. Univ. of Chicago Press.

SEARS, WILLIAM H. 1954 The Sociopolitical Organization of Pre-Columbian Cultures on the Gulf Coastal Plain. *American Anthropologist* New Series 56:339–346.

SEARS, WILLIAM H. 1961 The Study of Social and Religious Systems in North American Archaeology. *Current Anthropology* 2:223–246.

SOCIETY FOR AMERICAN ARCHAEOLOGY 1956 *Seminars in Archaeology: 1955.* Assembled by Robert Wauchope. Society for American Archeology, Memoirs, No. 9. Salt Lake City, Utah: The Society.

TAYLOR, WALTER W. 1948 *A Study of Archeology.* American Anthropological Association, Memoirs, No. 69. Menasha, Wis.: American Anthropological Association.

WHEELER, ROBERT E. M. 1954 *Archaeology From the Earth.* Oxford: Clarendon. → A paperback edition was published in 1961 by Penguin.

WILLEY, GORDON R.; and PHILLIPS, PHILIP 1958 *Method and Theory in American Archaeology.* Univ. of Chicago Press.

WOODBURY, RICHARD B. 1962 New World Archaeology. Pages 79–119 in *Biennial Review of Anthropology: 1961.* Edited by Bernard J. Siegel. Stanford (Calif.) Univ. Press.

II
RESEARCH METHODS

Prehistoric archeology is concerned with the description and analysis of extinct sociocultural systems; it shares with the other subfields of anthropology the goals of understanding both the physical and cultural evolution of man.

The archeologist, of course, cannot directly observe the behavior of individuals and groups in the particular society that he is investigating. What he does observe are the physical remains of this behavior, which form the primary data of archeology. They vary from subtle differences in the color and texture of soils to artifacts of stone, bone, pottery, and any other material goods that may have been preserved. The remains of architectural features, such as houses, temples, pits, and burials, and the location and distribution of these features, are also important data for the archeologist. Viewing culture as the extrasomatic means by which humans adapt to their environment, he is interested in the nature of the environment and the particular interaction between the society and its total surroundings, both physical and social. Thus the data of archeology also include plant and animal remains, fossil pollens, and geological information that will help in reconstructing environments of the past.

Through inferential analysis, the archeologist attempts reconstruction of extinct sociocultural systems. He must place the society into a temporal framework vis-à-vis other extinct societies in his geographic region of interest in order to assess the relative rates of cultural change. This in turn permits him to compare his area with other areas of the world with respect to the nature and rate of change. In addition, he alone among social scientists is in a position to test generalizations based on the scientific observations of contemporary peoples over the past one hundred years or so against data from thousands of extinct societies.

The physical collection of archeological data involves the use of a vast number of specialized skills. The careful excavation of a prehistoric site, whether a small temporary camping spot or a large complex urban settlement, requires a vast command of skills and experience. It also demands great flexibility and the ability to innovate as the field situation demands. Without a careful and exact record, of course, the most skilled excavation is virtually useless. Thus, the archeologist must not only be proficient at excavation; he must also be a skillful and sensitive recorder, photographer, and mapper. (For a more detailed statement regarding the excavation and recording of archeological data, the interested reader is referred to any standard textbook on archeology, e.g., Hole & Heizer 1965.)

Once the data have been collected and recorded, the archeologist proceeds to analyze his material. There are two primary areas of archeological inference: chronological inference and cultural inference. Specialized methods have been developed within the field of archeology to permit these kinds of inferences to be made, but probably the greatest number of available methods have been developed in other fields of science, such as geology, physics, sociology, statistics, and biology. These methods are used by archeologists, usually in modified form. In addition, the archeologist relies increasingly on the direct aid of a number of specialists in many fields outside of his own. In order to assess the significance and implications of the contributions of these specialists, the archeologist must be somewhat versed in the basics of all these fields. But his primary task is to interpret his own data as a paleoanthropologist along with the finds of the specialists in an attempt to contribute toward the attainment of the goals of anthropology (Binford 1962).

The very nature of the data imposes severe limitations upon the archeologist. The challenge of these limits has been responsible for the development of a multitude of ingenious techniques. Every archeologist must be constantly aware of the boundaries that his data impose, but he should likewise constantly seek to bridge the boundaries through the use of sound scientific methods and judgment and, perhaps above all, imagination.

Chronological inference

Placing extinct sociocultural systems into proper temporal order is one of the primary tasks of the archeologist. This does not mean that an actual date in terms of the Christian calendar is assigned, but rather that the chronological position of a particular site or group of sites must be determined vis-à-vis other sites. This sort of dating is generally called relative dating and is accomplished by a number of techniques. The assigning of an "absolute" or calendrical date is the job of the specialist in other fields working in conjunction with the archeologist.

Probably the most important technique employed in relative dating is stratigraphy, the analysis of the natural and cultural stratification of a site or a series of sites whose occupations overlap in time. The premise of this technique is the "law of superpositioning"; the lowest stratum, house, etc., will be the earliest in a series of strata or houses overlying one another. The next earliest is the stratum above the lowest; the most recent is the topmost layer. Rarely, however, is the stratification encountered in the field that simple. Complications arise as a result of various natural factors, such as erosion, or as the result of man's activity, when, for example, he digs pits or levels areas for cultivation. The interpretation of stratification is a demanding task requiring considerable skill and experience (Hole & Heizer 1965, pp. 49–64). An excellent example of the complexity that often occurs in stratified archeological sites is reported by Haury (1957).

Repeated occupation of caves in prehistoric times produced what are perhaps the most spectacular stratified sites. An excellent example is Shanidar Cave in northern Iraq. At this site about 100,000 years are represented in the nearly fifty feet of stratified deposits. Geological depositions, habitation floors scattered with cultural materials, burials in pits, and intermittent rock falls from the roof of the cave combined to present the excavator with an extremely complex interpretive problem (Solecki 1963).

When no natural stratification can be found, the prehistorian often imposes an artificial system by excavating in arbitrary levels. Sometimes the nature of the items contained in the deposits can be used to define the strata. The kinds of items contained in the various strata are also useful in extending the chronological sequence to additional sites.

The geographical extension of an established chronology can be achieved by comparing the material obtained in a stratified site with other sites; this is called cross dating. Using this technique an archeologist can often develop a regional chronology.

An interesting example of the technique is reported by Gladwin and his associates (1937). The large and complex site of Snaketown in southern Arizona was excavated over a period of some months, and the analysis of the stratification produced a well-defined relative chronology for the region. The presence of exotic cultural items in the various strata at the site enabled the investigators to tie the relative chronology into the absolute or dated sequences known from areas farther to the north. Thus they were able to assign actual calendrical dates to the sequence at the site of Snaketown. This attempt aroused considerable controversy among southwestern archeologists, since there was some disagreement about the association and dating of the exotic cultural materials at the site. Recent work at the same site and the use of additional techniques for dating that were not available thirty years ago have supported the original Snaketown chronology (Haury 1965).

Another method for developing relative chronologies is termed seriation. The premise for this method is the supposition that stylistic phenomena tend to change at a describable rate. Styles of pottery have been most frequently used for this technique of analysis. Arranging the pottery styles in a sequence based upon stylistic similarity produces an ordering of style change through time. Once a "master chronology" for a region is worked out, the relative amounts of the various styles of pottery obtained from any site should permit the placement of that site into the relative chronology. Some archeologists feel that this method is as useful as stratigraphy for relative dating (Ford 1962; Rowe 1961), but there are problems that must be overcome before this technique will be widely used. Perhaps the most difficult aspect of this method is the problem of sampling. Frequently unexcavated sites are assigned to the master chronology on the basis of a count taken of surface materials. The collection of pottery obtained on the surface of a site need not be representative of its contents. There is the additional problem of devising a suitable method for obtaining a representative sample of the surface materials themselves.

Seriation and sequence dating are actually among the oldest methods of relative dating in archeology. Today rather sophisticated statistical tests are being devised in order to arrange stylistic phenomena into chronological sequence (Ascher & Ascher 1963; Brainerd 1951; Meighan 1959; Robinson 1951).

There are additional techniques available to the archeologist that are extremely useful in constructing relative chronologies. Among these are such methods as the chemical analysis of the fluorine content of bone to determine if specimens were deposited at approximately the same or at different times (Oakley 1963). Relative chronologies have been developed using sequences of the relative abundance of various fossil pollen types through time in many regions of the world (Dimbleby 1963; Hevly 1964a). Another technique is magnetic dating. Changes in the earth's magnetic field have produced fluctuations in the position of the earth's magnetic poles in relation to the geographical poles. Magnetic particles in baked clay "freeze" the direction of the magnetic field at the time of its firing. If the baked clay remains in place (such as in a hearth or oven), measurement of the magnetic

direction is possible. This can lead to the establishment of regional chronologies as well as provide valuable data on changes in the earth's magnetic field (Aitken 1961, pp. 121–155).

But probably the most widely known means of inferring chronology are the techniques of absolute dating available to archeology. These methods enable the specialist to assign dates to prehistoric sites in terms of the Christian calendar. The archeologist relies upon various specialists for these techniques, but the burden of interpretation and evaluation is his own.

Perhaps the most spectacular of the dating techniques is the radioactive carbon method of age determination. This technique was developed by Libby and his associates during the 1940s (Arnold & Libby 1949). The radioactive isotope of carbon (carbon-14) behaves chemically in the same manner as ordinary carbon (carbon-12). Thus, all living things as a part of their life process absorb small amounts of radioactive carbon. Any radioactive isotope decays at a constant rate, which in living matter is replaced by absorption; but at death, this replacement ceases. Knowing the rate of decay, it is possible to measure the amount of the isotope present and assign a date to a particular specimen of organic material. The radiocarbon method can currently extend dates to about seventy thousand years ago (Aitken 1961, pp. 88–120; Libby 1952; Willis 1963).

Although this technique is widely employed, there are many problems yet to be solved. There is always the possibility of contamination of a sample. Thus, the removal of an old specimen of organic material, such as wood, by use of an oily tool could drastically distort the true age. Extreme care must be exercised in collecting and cleaning datable samples. Of course, the material to be dated must be clearly associated with the materials in the stratigraphic sequence or the site to which the date will apply. There are also problems over which the archeologist has no control. If the reservoir of available radioactive carbon has not remained stable, then dating by this technique may not be reliable. There is some evidence that there has been some small-scale fluctuation in the reservoir that could produce some difficulty in arriving at accurate dates (Olson & Chatters 1965; Stuiver 1965).

Another important radioactive dating technique is the potassium–argon method, which is useful to much greater depths of time than is the radiocarbon technique. The radioactive decay of the isotope potassium-40 produces argon-40. Knowing the rate of decay and measuring the relative amounts, a date can be assigned to a specimen. This technique has been utilized in the dating of early cultural developments as well as of many geological phenomena. Perhaps the most famous example of the use of this method is the dating of the lowest bed at Olduvai Gorge in east Africa at about 1,750,000 years ago. This date pushes our estimate for the beginning of toolmaking by early man to a date twice as early as had been imagined. Recent work with this technique suggests it may be usable in the time range from about thirty thousand to more than fifteen million years ago (Evernden & Curtis 1965).

Another type of absolute dating is important in certain parts of the world. This is the technique of tree-ring dating or dendrochronology. This method was developed in the American southwest and has had its greatest use there. The method requires trees that produce annual rings which reflect well-defined growing seasons. Conifers have been most generally used. The variation in growth from year to year must be great enough to produce recognizable patterns in the rings. These patterns can then be compared to a master chronology for a region, enabling the absolute dating of some specimens of wood. Of course, in order for this technique to be used the prehistoric peoples must have made use of the proper kinds of wood, and the wood must be well enough preserved. Then, too, there are often complications, such as the reuse of roof timbers for later construction, which require careful interpretation on the part of both the archeologist and the dendrochronologist. An excellent discussion of the principles and techniques of tree-ring dating is presented by Bannister (1963).

Another dating method currently under development for use in archeological situations is thermoluminescent dating. When a crystalline substance is heated, it emits light. This is the release of energy in the form of electron displacement. The amount of light emission is proportionate to its age and its radioactive content. This property of light emission or thermoluminescence has long been a tool for research in geology. The first suggestion that the thermoluminescent glow of pottery might be used to measure its age was made by Daniels, Boyd, and Saunders (Daniels et al. 1953). Kennedy and Knopff ("Dating by Thermoluminescence" 1960) announced some success with the technique, but as yet the method has not been perfected (Aitken et al. 1963; Hall 1963). Research is currently being carried out, but the margin of error is still too great to permit its general use.

It is clear that reliable dating using this technique will be difficult to achieve, but the method is promising and will be pursued (Aitken et al. 1964; Dort et al. 1965; Fremlin & Srirath 1964).

The methods for chronological inference are many. But they must be mastered by the archeologist if he is to be able to do what many feel to be his most important job—making cultural inferences. He must be able to control the temporal dimensions of his data if he is to assess the processes of cultural change and stability. Techniques are being refined, and new ones are under development. The future archeologist will have an impressive list of techniques on which to draw if the present trends of research continue.

Cultural inference

The primary goal of prehistoric archeology is to make contributions to the larger science of anthropology. A necessary aspect of archeological research is environmental reconstruction and the analysis of the articulation of the sociocultural system and the environment.

One of the best examples of a multidisciplinary approach to this kind of problem is the major campaign undertaken by Braidwood and his associates in the uplands areas of the Near East. Their problem was to investigate the transformation from a food-collecting way of life to a food-producing way of life following the end of the Pleistocene. The focus was upon the processes of cultural change, but this required the active involvement of botanists and zoologists who worked with the critical plant and animal remains. The success of Braidwood and his colleagues is in no small way a testimony to the value of the multidisciplinary approach to paleoanthropology (Braidwood & Howe 1960). Current research by Braidwood and his students is refining our view of this critical period of cultural change (Flannery 1965). A similar approach by MacNeish (1964) has isolated comparable processes in the transformation from food collecting to food producing in the New World.

Generally, the archeologist's analysis is of the kind that permits inference regarding the behavioral aspects of the extinct society or societies with which he is working. The archeologist undertakes this analysis at several levels. His first task is to construct a problem-oriented research design formulated to investigate hypotheses of anthropological interest. He then must select the site or sites or a portion thereof to serve as his source of data. Generally this is based on his knowledge of the particular region, resulting from reconnaissance and perhaps previous excavation, and attention to statistically valid sampling procedures (Binford 1964).

The data that form the basis for later inference are gathered both from the surface and from the excavation of sites. The information the archeologist unearths consists of records of things he cannot remove from the site (such as a room or a house) and the portable specimens that are carefully labeled with their provenience.

The next task is to marshal all these data into meaningful categories and describe them. This is done by segregating the data into classes, such as ceramic containers, cutting tools, rooms, burials, and so on, and then further dividing the classes into types. When this is completed, and the occurrence of the various types and classes is tabulated along with their frequencies, one part of the descriptive analysis is finished. These data thus analyzed form the basis on which chronological inferences are often made. Many archeologists publish these sorted data in this form as site reports or monographs. These reports often serve as the basis for cultural inference and regional syntheses.

But there is another descriptive procedure that is rapidly becoming important as a necessary step in the presentation of data. This is the description of the association and covariation of all the classes and types of data recovered. It is upon these associations that some of the recent exciting inferences regarding prehistoric societies have been based. These inferences are based upon the assumption that all items that are found in an archeological site are highly patterned with respect to one another and in their placement in the site itself. This patterning is the result of the loss, breakage, abandonment, or disposal of items in a manner that should reflect the localization of specific kinds of activities in certain areas of the site, and the nature of the particular social unit performing the localized activity. Thus, the nature of variation in archeological data reflects temporal change and the different kinds of task performance by varying social groups. Inferences regarding the nature of activities and the composition of social groups are based on models generated primarily as a result of ethnographic analogy. This is why the archeologist must be well trained in general anthropology.

The use of highly sophisticated statistical tests to measure associations and covariation has only recently been possible because of the availability of high-speed data-processing equipment. In a very real sense the computer revolution has affected archeology. Archeologists are turning more and more to specialists in the fields of statistics and systems engineering for help in describing and interpreting archeological data.

To appreciate the enormousness of the task of describing archeological data, one only has to realize the staggering amount of specimens and records that result from the excavation of even a small prehistoric site. It is not unusual, for example, to recover many thousands of pieces of broken pottery, stone tools, and other cultural items from a single site. Most of these things vary in at least two dimensions. Ceramic containers vary, for instance, in their size and shape and in their color and decoration. The former variation might be a product of the particular use to which the vessel was put (large storage jars as opposed to small serving bowls), and the stylistic variation (red-painted bowls and brown jars with incised decoration) might reflect different social contexts or different uses or both. Indeed, this sort of variation might also be a product of temporal change as well.

Archeologists have long been interested in inferring aspects of social organization from their data. Recent work with the distribution of stylistic phenomena has permitted inferences regarding the nature of residence, size and composition of social groups, the division of labor, and the nature of patterns of inheritance.

Deetz (1965), using both archeological and historical data, was able to demonstrate a correlation between the clustering of stylistic attributes of pottery from a historic Arikara site and the strength of the uxorilocal residence pattern. The supporting historical data indicated that for the duration of the site's occupation, the pattern of coresident related females resulting from a strong marital residence rule gradually broke down. Deetz demonstrated a contemporaneous lessening in the degree of clustering among attributes of decoration found on the pottery (produced by women). This suggested that females coresident in one household form a "microtradition" of style that is different from other such units and that the nature of residence units might be reflected in the array of stylistic phenomena.

A somewhat similar analysis was undertaken with prehistoric data from a site in the American southwest (Longacre 1964). The distribution of 175 design attributes on pottery was analyzed at a Pueblo site dated around A.D. 1200. The study was undertaken using a multiple regression analysis that measured the covariation among the design attributes and their provenience at the site. The clustering of the stylistic phenomena taken in conjunction with the architectural pattern of the site and the highly patterned cemetery suggested the presence of at least two residence units made up of related females and in-marrying males and their offspring. These units were maintained for several generations, which indicated that inheritance of some things (rooms, access to a well-defined cemetery, and certain ceremonial activity) was in the female line.

A site in the same area dating from around A.D. 1300 was studied by Hill (1965). He employed a factor analysis in his research and was able to suggest both continuity and change in behavioral aspects compared to the earlier site. The size of the residence units had remained constant, but they were combined into larger social units. Changes such as this were related by Hill to a changing environment as analyzed by Hevly (1964b). All of these studies have aided our understanding of the evolution of culture in the southwest and have permitted generalizations about certain cultural processes (Longacre 1966).

Current research, which should shortly revolutionize our understanding of the evolution of culture, is being carried out using archeological and environmental data from sites all over the world. Sally and Lewis R. Binford are currently using factor analysis to study several Mousterian sites from the Near East and western Europe. Their preliminary results are greatly encouraging and promise to shed light on social organization, tool kits, and environmental change in the late Pleistocene. Similar research is now being carried out in various parts of North America and Middle America as well.

There are many difficulties in making cultural inferences from archeological data (Thompson 1958, pp. 1–8), but the strength of our hypotheses is increasing through the application of new techniques. Current and future research should refine and augment the methods that are now available. These should enable archeologists to make additional significant contributions to anthropological theory and, indeed, to contribute to the larger goals of the social sciences as a whole.

WILLIAM A. LONGACRE

BIBLIOGRAPHY

AITKEN, MARTIN J. 1961 *Physics and Archaeology.* New York: Interscience Publishers.

AITKEN, MARTIN J.; TITE, M. S.; and REID, J. 1963 Thermoluminescent Dating: Progress Report. *Archaeometry* 6:65–75.

AITKEN, MARTIN J.; TITE, M. S.; and REID, J. 1964 Thermoluminescent Dating of Ancient Ceramics. *Nature* 202:1032–1033.

ARNOLD, JAMES R.; and LIBBY, W. F. 1949 Age Determinations by Radiocarbon Content: Checks With Samples of Known Age. *Science* 110:678–680.

ASCHER, MARCIA; and ASCHER, ROBERT 1963 Chronological Ordering by Computer. *American Anthropologist* New Series 65:1045–1052.

BANNISTER, BRYANT 1963 Dendrochronology. Pages 162–176 in Don R. Brothwell and Eric Higgs (editors), *Science in Archaeology: A Comprehensive Survey of Progress and Research.* London: Thames & Hudson; New York: Basic Books.

BINFORD, LEWIS R. 1962 Archaeology as Anthropology. *American Antiquity* 28:217–225.

BINFORD, LEWIS R. 1964 A Consideration of Archaeological Research Design. *American Antiquity* 29:425–441.

BRAIDWOOD, ROBERT J.; and HOWE, BRUCE 1960 *Prehistoric Investigations in Iraqi Kurdistan.* Oriental Institute Studies in Ancient Oriental Civilizations, No. 31. Univ. of Chicago Press.

BRAINERD, GEORGE W. 1951 The Place of Chronological Ordering in Archaeological Analysis. *American Antiquity* 16:301–313.

DANIELS, FARRINGTON et al. 1953 Thermoluminescence as a Research Tool. *Science* 117:343–349.

Dating by Thermoluminescence. 1960 *Archaeology* 13:147–148.

DEETZ, JAMES 1965 *The Dynamics of Stylistic Change in Arikara Ceramics.* Illinois Studies in Anthropology, No. 4. Urbana: Univ. of Illinois Press.

DIMBLEBY, G. W. 1963 Pollen Analysis. Pages 139–149 in Don Brothwell and Eric Higgs (editors), *Science in Archaeology: A Comprehensive Survey of Progress and Research.* London: Thames & Hudson; New York: Basic Books.

DORT, WAKEFIELD, JR., et al. 1965 Paleotemperatures and Chronology at Archaeological Cave Site Revealed by Thermoluminescence. *Science* 150:480–481.

EVERNDEN, J. P.; and CURTIS, G. H. 1965 The Potassium–Argon Dating of Late Cenozoic Rocks in East Africa and Italy. *Current Anthropology* 6:343–385.

FLANNERY, KENT V. 1965 The Ecology of Early Food Production in Mesopotamia. *Science* 147:1247–1256.

FORD, JAMES A. 1962 *A Quantitative Method for Deriving Cultural Chronology.* Washington: Pan American Union.

FREMLIN, J. H.; and SRIRATH, S. 1964 Thermoluminescent Dating: Examples of Non-uniformity of Luminescence. *Archaeometry* 7:58–62.

GLADWIN, HAROLD S. et al. (1937) 1965 *Excavations at Snaketown.* Volume 1: Material Culture. Tucson: Univ. of Arizona Press.

HALL, E. T. 1963 Dating Pottery by Thermoluminescence. Pages 90–92 in Don Brothwell and Eric Higgs (editors), *Science in Archaeology: A Comprehensive Survey of Progress and Research.* London: Thames & Hudson; New York: Basic Books.

HAURY, EMIL W. 1957 An Alluvial Site on the San Carlos Indian Reservation, Arizona. *American Antiquity* 23:2–27.

HAURY, EMIL W. 1965 Snaketown: 1964–1965. *Kiva* 31:1–13.

HEVLY, RICHARD H. 1964a Paleoecology of Laguna Salada. Volume 2, pages 171–187 in *Chapters in the Prehistory of Eastern Arizona.* Fieldiana, Anthropology, Vol. 55. Chicago Natural History Museum.

HEVLY, RICHARD H. 1964b Pollen Analysis of Quaternary Archaeological and Lacustrine Sediments From the Colorado Plateau. Ph.D. dissertation, Univ. of Arizona, Department of Botany.

HILL, JAMES N. 1965 Changing Patterns of Social Organization in the Prehistory of Eastern Arizona. Ph.D. dissertation, Univ. of Chicago.

HOLE, FRANK; and HEIZER, ROBERT F. 1965 *An Introduction to Prehistoric Archaeology.* New York: Holt.

LIBBY, WILLARD F. (1952) 1955 *Radiocarbon Dating.* 2d ed. Univ. of Chicago Press.

LONGACRE, WILLIAM A. 1964 Archeology as Anthropology: A Case Study. *Science* 144:1454–1455.

LONGACRE, WILLIAM A. 1966 Changing Patterns of Social Integration: A Prehistoric Example From the American Southwest. *American Anthropologist* New Series 68:94–102.

MACNEISH, RICHARD S. 1964 Ancient Mesoamerican Civilization. *Science* 143:531–537.

MEIGHAN, CLEMENT W. 1959 A New Method for the Seriation of Archaeological Collections. *American Antiquity* 25:203–211.

OAKLEY, KENNETH P. 1963 Analytical Methods of Dating Bones. Pages 24–34 in Don Brothwell and Eric Higgs (editors), *Science in Archaeology: A Comprehensive Survey of Progress and Research.* London: Thames & Hudson; New York: Basic Books.

OLSON, E. A.; and CHATTERS, R. M. 1965 Meetings: Carbon-14 and Tritium Dating. *Science* 150:1488–1492.

ROBINSON, WILLIAM S. 1951 A Method for Chronologically Ordering Archaeological Deposits. *American Antiquity* 16:293–301.

ROWE, JOHN H. 1961 Stratigraphy and Seriation. *American Antiquity* 26:324–330.

SOLECKI, RALPH S. 1963 Prehistory in Shanidar Valley, Northern Iraq. *Science* 139:179–193.

STUIVER, MINZE 1965 Carbon-14 Content of 18th- and 19th-century Wood: Variations Correlated With Sunspot Activity. *Science* 149:533–535.

THOMPSON, RAYMOND H. 1958 *Modern Yucatecan Maya Pottery Making.* Memoirs of the Society for American Archaeology, No. 11. Salt Lake City, Utah: Society for American Archaeology.

WILLIS, E. H. 1963 Radiocarbon Dating. Pages 35–46 in Don Brothwell and Eric Higgs (editors), *Science in Archaeology: A Comprehensive Survey of Progress and Research.* London: Thames & Hudson; New York: Basic Books.

ARCHITECTURE

Although the word "architect" derives from the Greek phrase meaning "master builder," in practice "architecture" has gradually acquired the connotation "art of building." Today not all architects would admit that it is an art. Several of them would insist that it is an application of technology, while others would claim that it is a science. However, all would agree that the product of the discipline is real, whether it be a single building, a group of buildings, a community, or a whole city— even if the architect is concerned only with the design and conception.

The fact is that architecture started as a technique of construction, which was gradually specialized into the construction of buildings rather than the building of bridges, roads, and public works, which became the special domain of the engineer. Architecture began as a technique and was transformed into an art—sometimes completely overshadowing the technique. It began as handicraft and artisanship (the architect was the actual builder–entrepreneur), then turned to design and management. Architecture is concerned with individual houses, large composite building complexes, and even whole cities, although the latter specialization is also the province of the town planner.

Through architecture, space is compartmentalized: there is the usable interior area; the total area, that is, the shell and the means; and the external space, which is indirectly changed after the inner area has been defined. The degree to which these different kinds of space fulfill the expected requirements qualifies the degree of success of an architectural work.

Social architecture. Architecture is sometimes called a social art or social technology. This is valid in terms of the content and extent of architecture. Moreover, architecture is social in that it expresses a social trend even if that is very limited in extent. Architectural style does not represent the efforts of a single architect or of one class or even one generation but those of many persons through a number of generations, who express themselves in a way that represents all their beliefs and aspirations. For example, in ancient Greece people built timber roofs over mud-brick walls; over several centuries this particular style of construction was adapted to marble. This architecture did not have an inventor or original designer—every temple had its own master builder, who contributed minute details of refinement to an enduring style. This was a social architecture in expression and form.

Architectural needs. In every period consumers define their architectural needs in terms of quantity, volume, cost, quality, and content. In every community there is the demand for shelter; the variable occurs in the quantity and quality of shelter demanded. In the simplest effort the consumer's needs and demands coincide, as the consumer asks first of all for what is indispensable, thus automatically adjusting his needs to the possible. When incomes and technology develop, needs increase, while the previously suppressed demand starts rising; then a gap between need and demand appears. As a result the suppressed demand rises even more, and so do the needs, causing an increase of supply, and thus we have a trend toward better and higher architectural forms. As architectural needs and demands become more complex and expand into open areas, roads and public squares take on architectural significance. They then receive corresponding attention, ranging from very elementary (for example, regulations defining rights of way and heights) to very detailed (specification of the elevations, addition of works of art, and so forth).

Architectural creation. The accumulated knowledge of modern science has changed the nature of architectural creation and modified its function. Thus, that which was once a simple, natural act of covering man with shelters and helping him to survive became more and more artificial and complicated and required the mobilization of many skills and resources for its fulfillment. At the same time, the architectural solution—derived from nature in the beginning, like a cave or a hut made out of branches—became unnatural as it moved away from the simplest forms. Such an evolution had its impact on the process of creation of architectural styles. One may suppose that the outstanding builders in every community were given the most important jobs, the temple or church, the mosque or the ruler's palace, bridges or fortifications. By trial and error they learned how to produce the best; public taste was strongly influenced by the master builders and, in turn, influenced and shaped the general architectural evolution. Over a long period of time, under relatively constant external conditions, this process resulted in the creation of an architectural style. It usually took several centuries for a naturally evolving architecture to acquire its own characteristics, a specific style. The fact that in our era the distance from the natural architectural creation is increasing, together with the fact that economic, social, political, technological, and cultural conditions change so quickly, explains why we do not have our own recognizable architectural style. This lack of a distinct style creates a confusion of ideas about architecture. Today many architects try, in a completely unjustified and facile way, to create their own "styles," as if one man or group of men could overnight replace the action of a whole society over a long period of years.

Client–architect relationship. For hundreds of years the client–architect relationship was quite simple. When in need of a building, the client turned to the architect, and together they worked out an agreement for full services—from advice to design, construction, procurement of materials and labor, transport, and perhaps even financing—until the building was completed. In some way this was similar to a constituency–politician relationship. In general, the clients selected and guided their architects, who in turn led the clients within a framework of technological possibilities. Their relationship was impersonal. This situation became complicated, confused, and sometimes irrational, especially in the twentieth century, when architects were first educated in art schools and then trained in professional schools of architecture.

Specialization has been advanced to the point where, in many developed countries, members of architectural associations are not allowed to act as builders; thus they are deprived of their most important function and the ultimate justification of their profession. There is no question that the architect, in order to practice his profession properly, now needs the assistance of a great number of experts, including research specialists in the physical and social sciences.

The architect. The evolution of architectural creation and practice had its impact on the architect himself. In the early days of architectural specialization he was a mason and a builder, while the best was called a master mason, an architect. He was an artisan, known for the quality of his product in the same way as were the best painters, sculptors, decorators, and saddle, cart, and carriage makers. During the nineteenth century the process of change began that is transforming the architect-craftsman into a white-collar worker or administrator. Today most of the people actually creating what we commonly call architecture belong to the traditional class of craftsmen, while university-trained architects constitute a very small percentage of the total. The ratio of architects to population varies greatly from country to country—from the high percentages found in countries like Denmark and England, where architects are sufficiently numerous to deal with interior decoration and furniture, to the very low percentages of architects found in most of the developing countries.

Architectural evolution

In early human history local, natural architecture grew much like a plant (conditioned by the local climate and easily obtainable raw materials). Where conditions warranted (reasonable climate, enduring building materials, and the processes of civilization), the architectural plant thrived. Local architecture did not everywhere lead to great styles, but where it did, architectural efforts of the past continue to influence present-day traditions.

The buildings we have inherited from the Near Eastern civilizations of antiquity belong predominantly to religion—especially in Egypt—although there are some examples of fortifications and palaces. Regular houses, even of the wealthy families, seem always to have been built of materials that could not withstand weather and time; thus, we know only how people built for gods and kings, not how they built for themselves. Whatever we have inherited shows architecture as a monumental art and not at all as an art of everyday life.

In comparison with the previous monumental architecture, that of the Minoan period was much more human. In both enclosed and open spaces the builder's interest was not to impress humanity and serve souls and gods but to serve man in the best possible way by creating functional human spaces adjusted to the climate. Mycenaean architecture was also close to the Near Eastern tradition. We know little of the architecture of the common man in either of these periods; it may have been only a simpler expression of the architecture of palaces and fortresses, or the earlier types of buildings, constructed in less durable materials, may have continued. Classical Greek architecture is admired for its character, but also because of its use of raw materials, particularly marble. The Greek temple is perhaps the apex of the pyramid of architectural achievement. Its value also lies in the fact that it was not a monument isolated from life, but the real crown of an architecture which started with humble, timbered, mud-brick and stuccoed houses, and public buildings just one degree better than the houses, and progressed to the "agora," or central market square with its buildings, and finally, to theaters, stadiums, roads and squares, exedras, monuments, and temples. More than any other, Greek architecture was holistic, an architectural conception of the human community represented by the political unit of the city-state. The largest political unit of ancient Greece—the city-state—was so small (the average size being forty miles square) that a person standing at some height could see the entire area at once. With the acropolis at its center, the architectural composition expressed the idea of the culture.

Roman architecture differed from Greek in both content and technique. Not only did it contain greater internal differences, as between the slums of Rome and the luxurious villas and palaces; it also took big steps toward the architecture of large buildings. There were important public buildings: baths, amphitheaters, roads, bridges, and aqueducts. Brick construction played an important role, in addition to stone and marble. There still exist many examples of well-conceived and well-built Roman cities in Europe, Africa, and Asia. They do not manifest the cohesiveness of cities found in

Greece, but city-fortresses paved the way for technological advancements in later periods.

At the end of the Roman Empire and with the spread of Christianity, there were two distinct movements toward new architectural forms: one followed a path from Italy to the European mainland; the other moved eastward, back to Greece, Constantinople, and the Middle East.

The first new form—Romanesque architecture—was at the beginning a major stylistic attempt to express the new religion. The Gothic style followed and became the typical architectural expression of the long medieval period with its small, walled city, where the only hope was in God, up in the sky. The architecture of the vertical and the arch reached up, as high as possible, away from the secular world. It is not strange that such architecture was more successful in churches and cathedrals than in houses and public buildings.

It was in southern Europe with its bright light and colors that man returned to an architecture much more human in content and expression. The Renaissance started first in Italy and then spread to the rest of Europe. Although in spirit it represented a return to humanism and to ancient Greece, its direct roots came from the Italian countryside, where the peasants' houses were the prototypes of the more luxurious houses of the great landlords. When these rich men became urban dwellers—merchants or bankers—they built their cities and palaces, created their piazzas and monuments, public buildings, churches, and fortifications in a new and consistent form of architectural expression. There was continuity from the humble peasant's house to Michelangelo's Piazza del Campidoglio in Rome and to the Piazza della Signoria in Florence. As in other great periods, sculpture and painting were blended with architecture.

The Renaissance declined, and baroque style, with its sculpture and monuments, arose—an architecture of intellectual creation rather than a natural art having roots deep in the life of the people. The styles that followed, rococo and then neoclassicism and neoromanticism, widened this gap, emphasized by the *art nouveau* of the late nineteenth and early twentieth centuries.

At the southeastern end of Europe, in the eastern Mediterranean and Middle East, local architectural expressions blended with the technology of the Romans, especially in major brick constructions, and with Greek tradition. Byzantine architecture thus combined East and West and predominated for long centuries, longer perhaps than any other style we know of, until its decline in the late nineteenth century. Although this style produced great cities, palaces, and works of art, it will be remembered mainly for its churches—from the largest, like Saint Sophia in Constantinople and the monasteries of Mount Athos, to the smallest, most humble one-room churches spread over many countries in the Balkans, Greece, and the Middle East.

Special mention should be made of the Muslim–Arabic style, which, born in the Middle East, followed the road to eastern Europe; then through northern Africa and the southern coast of the Mediterranean, it entered Europe via Spain, where it produced some of the best monuments of domestic and landscape architecture.

Architectural evolution, even when studied with European emphasis, is not as simple as it may look from such a division of styles by groups and periods, because styles have seldom been confined to one place, country, or era. In general, architecture has common origins and roots. The basic elements are people, whose needs are more alike than different, and building materials—mud, bricks, stone, and timber—which behave everywhere in very much the same way. Thus, architectural expressions in early human history were similar to one another; we can speak of a universal origin of all architectural styles, based on the needs and creative potential of man. Then local, semi-isolated cultures tended to develop their own architectural expressions as local or national styles. Some styles remained of importance only in certain areas, while others, especially those with more universal characteristics (generally the simplest ones) spread over wider areas, together with the civilizations and cultures to which they belonged. For example, the ancient Greek, Roman, Muslim, and Iberian styles spread to Central and South America, and the hybrid styles of northwestern Europe were brought to North America, Africa, and Asia by the Anglo-Saxons, the French, and the Dutch. As stylistic influences diffused, they became diluted, merged into one another, and tended toward a cosmopolitan mixture.

The present and future of architecture

Today we live in an era of confusion, especially with regard to the human settlements that have become mere heaps of architectural and public works. Our villages are abandoned, and our cities gradually turn into a nightmare, where all sorts of forces, people, machines, buildings, and projects of all kinds struggle for survival and control. Architecture itself, in the original meaning of the word, is losing its importance, as the value and identity of the single building decrease with the passing of time. City inhabitants do not have the opportunity to see buildings as wholes; they know them only from the inside. Public spaces have completely lost their architectural importance. Moreover, the bulldozer tears down buildings that retain historic and aesthetic value—even relatively new buildings—whenever changes in the texture of the city demand.

In this world of change, architecture finds itself in very rapid evolution. In addition to cosmopolitanism and the decline of significant styles, other phenomena have had a great impact upon architecture. Technological innovations that permitted the construction of buildings of more than the previous limit of five or six floors were made about a century ago and spread rapidly after the invention of the elevator in 1854. In the past hundred years, industrialization and urbanization have given rise to social movements that demanded better housing for the exploding population, especially for workers in overcongested areas. Architecture has not only conquered the third dimension—height; it has also changed its content as attention has turned from the construction of monuments to the provision of services and facilities for people. A rational architecture, fostered by the great revolutionaries of our era, Gropius, Le Corbusier, Mies van der Rohe, and others, has begun to emerge. Architecture entered the second quarter of our century with new forces and has started the third one with enough momentum for the completion of this revolution.

In the meantime, the situation is not simple, and public opinion is still caught between academic and modern, between old and new. Many architects have turned toward a new eclecticism and are searching for a compromise, an easy way out, personal expression, and so on. This is far removed from the real needs of humanity, for architecture, if it is to be true to its great traditions, must cease to be merely the practice of an art form and once again become a technique that serves all the people in the best possible way.

In this tremendous effort, during this great era of change, concepts are confused. People mix the notion of new with that of progress and invent solutions, even when the traditional ones serve us best, or they tend to defend a local style rather than an international architecture, not because it might have greater values—very often it has—but just for the sake of tradition, which, if it does not serve the people any longer, should be abandoned.

However, today's greatest problem is a quantitative one. The great masses of people on earth live under unbearable conditions. We must face the real issues. The world population, and especially the urban one, is increasing at a rate not matched by architectural creation. At the same time, the full recognition that we need facilities for all has increased the dimensions of the problem. We must find the way in which architecture can catch up with changing economic and social phenomena.

Architects and all those concerned with architecture and city planning fear that a revolution may easily turn into a new academism or lose its momentum and thus stagnate. In many ways the answer lies in a return to the concepts of the past, although the materials, human and technological, are different.

The architect must find a way to bring together the knowledge and experience of the engineering industries, government, and the arts and blend them with local and international demands. In order to succeed in his new role, the architect can no longer concern himself with single buildings but rather must deal with entire settlements. He must build a *habitat,* which is a rational entity and should correspond to human dimensions. The architect must resume his traditional role as master builder, coordinator of all aspects of architectural creation, not limiting himself to the designing.

There must be the kind of architectural synthesis that will correspond to the magnitude of expanding human settlements. The architect must participate in industry, government, and centers of research and education where new notions about ways of living, the art of living, construction, and the needs of production are being developed. In this way architectural creation will be influenced at a level with which the architect is not yet acquainted but one with which he must familiarize himself if he is to achieve his purposes. In order to utilize knowledge contributed by the physical and social sciences, he must gain a much broader education than he has at present. An attempt to realize this aim is being made through the study of "ekistics," or the science of human settlements, which proposes to synthesize the economic, social, political, and administrative sciences, technology, and aesthetics into one coherent whole. The new type of human habitat can no longer be cast in the mold of the static city of the past but must be fashioned after the dynamic settlements of the present, which are spreading in all directions around pre-existing cities. Such a dynamically changing frame is bound to come into conflict with static architecture. That is why we need to build our new cities by using a basic cell that will be static but that can be repeated, thus allowing for growth. Such a cell would represent the "human community," whose dimensions would correspond both to actual human needs and to the dimensions of the city of the past. Its area should not exceed 2,000 yards square, and its population should be limited to 50,000 people. Within such communities, architecture and architectural space could retain their values without being impaired by the intrusions introduced into our urban life by fast-moving machines.

Houses and buildings must be seen in a way that allows them to be, simultaneously, individual units serving separate families or functions and also connected elements of a group that has its own internal cohesion. This may mean that a group of houses will have an internal street or square for pedestrians only, so that even if cars approach every single house, there will still be a part of the whole community that brings the residents together, around a common playground, a common garden or nursery, etc. The same principle suggests that buildings be arranged around a common courtyard or around a series of courtyards where there is no access for automobiles. This would provide a continuum of human space from room to house to courtyard, paths, gardens, and squares, a continuum big enough for the creation of real architectural space, where architecture is not limited to walls and elevations but to the broadest possible conception of space for man.

Thus, the roots of the new architecture are to be found in the entire range of architecture that preceded the nineteenth century. Such an architecture is going to be urban in character and human in content and will utilize a standardized technology. In this way architecture will become more consistent in expression and tend toward a new ecumenical form. The ecumenical qualities of architecture in the past were rooted in common responses to natural conditions; now they are reinforced by the participation of architects in what is gradually coming to be a world society.

The direction of the road toward such solutions is discernible, but the road itself is not yet open. A hard and long effort will be required of all those concerned, an effort to define the subject and a return to the proper concern of architecture: construction. Our only hope is to become good masons, so that we can expect some master masons (architects) to rise from among us. And we must try to abandon the subjective for the sake of the objective approach. If we achieve these aims, it is possible that in a few generations humanity may pass from the completely rational–utilitarian architecture—on which it must now concentrate—to a new humanistic, monumental architecture and thus a new architectural style.

C. A. Doxiadis

[*Directly related are the entries* City; Planning, social, *article on* regional and urban planning; Style. *See also the articles listed under* Art.]

BIBLIOGRAPHY

Behne, Adolf (1926) 1964 *Der moderne Zweckbau: 1923.* Berlin: Ullstein.

Boyd, Andrew C. M. 1962 *Chinese Architecture and Town Planning: 1500 B.C.–A.D. 1911.* Univ. of Chicago Press.

Branner, Robert 1961 *Gothic Architecture.* New York: Braziller.

Briggs, Martin S. 1925 *A Short History of the Building Crafts.* Oxford: Clarendon.

Briggs, Martin S. 1927 *The Architect in History.* Oxford: Clarendon.

Briggs, Martin S. 1947 *Architecture.* Oxford Univ. Press.

Cresswell, Keppel A. C. 1958 *Short Account of Early Muslim Architecture.* Baltimore: Penguin.

Disselhoff, Hans D.; and Linné, Sigvald (1960) 1962 *The Art of Ancient America: Civilizations of Central and South America.* New York: Crown. → First published in German.

Doxiadis, Constantinos A. 1963 *Architecture in Transition.* London: Hutchinson; New York: Oxford Univ. Press.

Frankl, Paul 1960 *The Gothic: Literary Sources and Interpretations Through Eight Centuries.* Princeton Univ. Press.

Futagawa, Yukio 1963 *The Roots of Japanese Architecture: A Photographic Quest.* New York: Harper.

Giedion, Sigfried (1941) 1962 *Space, Time and Architecture: The Growth of a New Tradition.* 4th ed., enl. Cambridge, Mass.: Harvard Univ. Press.

Giedion, Sigfried (1956) 1958 *Architecture, You and Me: The Diary of a Development.* Cambridge, Mass.: Harvard Univ. Press. → First published as *Architektur und Gemeinschaft: Tagebuch einer Entwicklung.*

Giedion, Sigfried 1964 *The Eternal Present: A Contribution on Constancy and Change.* Volume 2: *The Beginnings of Architecture.* New York: Pantheon.

Gropius, Walter 1955 *Scope of Total Architecture.* New York: Harper.

Hamlin, Talbot F. (1940) 1953 *Architecture Through the Ages.* Rev. ed. New York: Putnam.

Hilberseimer, Ludwig 1956 *Mies Van der Rohe.* Chicago: Theobald.

Hitchcock, Henry R. (1958) 1963 *Architecture: Nineteenth and Twentieth Centuries.* 2d ed. Baltimore: Penguin.

Hudnut, Joseph 1949 *Architecture and the Spirit of Man.* Cambridge, Mass.: Harvard Univ. Press.

[Jeanneret-Gris, Charles É.] (1923) 1959 *Towards a New Architecture,* by Le Corbusier [pseud.]. New York: Praeger. → First published in French.

[Jeanneret-Gris, Charles É.] 1929 *Une maison–un palais: "À la recherche d'une unité architecturale,"* by Le Corbusier [pseud.]. Paris: Crès.

[Jeanneret-Gris, Charles É.] 1935 *La ville radieuse: Éléments d'une doctrine d'urbanisme pour l'équipement de la civilisation machiniste,* by Le Corbusier [pseud.]. Paris: Éditions de l'Architecture d'Aujourd'hui.

Kimball, Sidney F. 1928 *American Architecture.* Indianapolis: Bobbs-Merrill.

Kubler, George; and Soria, Martin 1959 *Art and Architecture in Spain and Portugal and Their American Dominions: 1500 to 1800.* Baltimore: Penguin.

Lowry, Bates 1962 *Renaissance Architecture.* New York: Braziller.

Lynes, Russell 1963 *The Domesticated Americans.* New York: Harper.

MacDonald, William L. 1962 *Early Christian and Byzantine Architecture.* New York: Braziller.

Millon, Henry A. 1961 *Baroque and Rococo Architecture.* New York: Braziller.

Morrison, Hugh S. 1952 *Early American Architecture: From the First Colonial Settlements to the National Period.* New York: Oxford Univ. Press.

Mumford, Lewis (1924) 1955 *Sticks and Stones: A Study of American Architecture and Civilization.* 2d ed., rev. New York: Dover.

Mumford, Lewis 1961 *The City in History: Its Origins, Its Transformations, and Its Prospects.* New York: Harcourt.

Paine, Robert T.; and Soper, Alexander (1955) 1960 *The Art and Architecture of Japan.* Baltimore: Penguin.

Platz, Gustav A. (1927) 1930 *Die Baukunst der neuesten Zeit.* 2d ed. Berlin: Propyläen.

Plommer, Hugh 1956 *Ancient and Classical Architecture.* London: Longmans.

Rider, Bertha C. (1916) 1964 *Ancient Greek Houses: Their History and Development From the Neolithic Period to the Hellenistic Age.* Chicago: Argonaut. → First published as *The Greek House: Its History. . . .*

Rowland, Benjamin (1953) 1959 *The Art and Architecture of India: Buddhist, Hindu, Jain.* 2d ed. Baltimore: Penguin.

Saalman, Howard 1962 *Medieval Architecture: European Architecture, 600–1200.* New York: Braziller.

Sadler, Arthur L. (1941) 1963 *A Short History of Japanese Architecture.* Rutland, Vt.: Tuttle.

Scranton, Robert L. 1962 *Greek Architecture.* New York: Braziller.

Scully, Vincent J. 1961 *Modern Architecture: The Architecture of Democracy.* New York: Braziller.

Smith, George E. V. K. 1961 *The New Architecture of Europe: An Illustrated Guidebook and Appraisal.* Cleveland: World.

Wasmuths Lexikon der Baukunst. 5 vols. 1929–1937 Berlin: Wasmuth.

Wittkower, Rudolph (1949) 1962 *Architectural Principles in the Age of Humanism.* 3d ed., rev. London: Tiranti.

Wright, Frank Lloyd (1941) 1959 *Frank Lloyd Wright on Architecture: Selected Writings, 1894–1940.* New York: Grosset & Dunlap.

Wu, Nelson I. 1963 *Chinese and Indian Architecture: The City of Man, the Mountain of God, and the Realm of the Immortals.* New York: Braziller.

Wycherley, Richard E. (1949) 1962 *How the Greeks Built Cities.* 2d ed. London: Macmillan.

ARCHIVES

See Information storage and retrieval.

AREA

"Area" is the most inclusive generic term for any portion of the surface of the earth. A given area may be large or small, ranging from the entire earth's surface down to a single point. All areas on the earth's surface are characterized by two properties: location and content. Some may also possess a third property—organization—particularly as a corollary of function. As described by these properties, "area" may well be the most commonly used word in the geographer's lexicon.

Area as place. Area as characterized by its locational attribute is akin to the common-sense notion of place. It implies both absolute and relative measures. In absolute terms, a given area may be located on the earth's surface by reference to the graticule of parallels and meridians that cover that surface, but these are themselves in large part the products of convention. They are drawn in relation not only to the equator and the poles but also to arbitrarily chosen points from which the meridians are numbered and longitudinal distances are measured. There is no intrinsically compelling reason why any one such point should be chosen over any other. In actuality, although Greenwich is most commonly accepted as the prime meridian for mapping purposes, several others, including Paris, the island of Hierro (Ferro), and Jakarta, are also used. In this sense, the "absolute" location of a place is in itself relative, but its relativity is in terms of some arbitrarily chosen point.

Location in relative terms implies a relationship between a given area and other areas or places. Thus, Delhi is located not only *at* latitude 28°54′N. and longitude 77°13′E. but, more importantly, *in* southern Asia, *in* the north of India, *in* the west-central Indo-Gangetic plain, *on* the banks of the Jumna River, *near* the doab (interfluve) between the Indus and Ganges drainage systems, *at* the northern tip of the outliers of the Aravalli range, and a hundred miles *south* of the frontal ranges of the Himalayas. In short, all areas may be described not only in terms of some common standard reference system that is used for all places but also in terms of locational referents that vary with the individual place.

It is a fundmental axiom, then, that no two areas are alike, nor can they be. The locational referents of any one place must differ from those of every other. The uniqueness of what might be called *real* areas in terms of relative location is one of the basic facts of geographic methodology.

Area as content. The concept of area also implies enclosure, containment, content. As Hart-shorne has pointed out (Hartshorne 1939; 1959), the content and classification of area are major topics for geographic investigation. Every area is characterized by some association of phenomena within it. This is true whether the area is chosen arbitrarily or in terms of some specified criteria. Areas are unique in this sense also. No area contains the same set of characteristics as another, in the same combination, and with the same pattern of spatial distribution. However, comparison among areas in terms of a limited number of characteristics—sometimes one, often many—may result in significant generalizations concerning distributions over the surface of the earth. "Metropolitan area," for example, succinctly describes a highly complex spatial phenomenon, a gigantic localized association of people, material works, and activities that easily distinguish it from other types of areas. By definition the metropolitan area is associated with large numbers of people, high population densities, and particular types of structures and land uses. The variety among such areas presents a challenging taxonomic problem, which can be approached at either empirical or theoretical levels. Of course, such areas differ in relative location and in the sets of phenomena that they contain. Equally important, the elements that constitute these sets also possess distinctive geometric arrangements, which in turn provide a basis for further comparison and generalization. The morphology of settlement as a major field in geographic investigation is simply a variant of the focus on the content and classification of area, as is the comparative study of landscape.

Area as organization. The area concept may also refer to the ways in which activities and broadly social functions are distributed over the earth and interrelated as areal systems. The organization of area presents a problem of long-standing interest to the several social sciences and is the *raison d'être* for much contemporary geographical scholarship. It assumes some rational order in the geometry of human activity. Specifically, the concept of functional organization provides a means for comprehending the content and morphology of area.

Empirical studies suggest that men distribute themselves and their activities, particularly economic activities, according to principles that minimize randomness and maximize convenience and efficiency. The principles themselves and the ways in which they are implemented appear to differ markedly from culture to culture, and therefore from area to area, but there is considerable evidence for proposing the existence of a nested hierarchy of functionally defined areas ranging from the local to the metropolitan. As Platt (1957) and Philbrick (1957) have defined it, this hierarchy consists of groups of cell-like areal units (e.g., farms) clustered about, and tributary to, towns or central places of small size. The small-scale central places are grouped, with their theoretically circular or hexagonal hinterlands, within the tributary areas of larger towns, which, with their hinterlands, in turn appear as larger and more complex components of the hinterlands of great metropolitan areas. This hierarchy appears to exist not only as a rural–urban and interurban phenomenon but also as an intrametropolitan phenomenon as well.

In this context, the term "area" is closely related to "nodal region," sometimes also termed "focal area," an area defined by the organization of human activity about some central place. A town and its tributary area, or hinterland, form a nodal region; on a different level, so does a grain elevator and the area occupied by its suppliers; and on a lesser scale, a neighborhood grocery store and its hinterland of customers.

Such areas may be contrasted with the so-called uniform region, or "homogeneous area," which is defined in terms of the uniform distribution of some phenomenon within it. The homogeneous area may or may not reflect the characteristics of organization. A Negro ghetto in a northern American city constitutes a region of uniformity in that its population is entirely Negro; so does an area in which the major type of land use is shifting cultivation or an area covered by tropical rain forest.

Area and region. In spite of the similarities in meaning and usage between the terms "area" and "region," the two as technically employed are not necessarily equivalent. Of the two, "area" is the broader; a region, whether nodal or uniform, may be considered a special kind of area. As Hartshorne (1959, p. 131) puts it, "in using the special word 'region' rather than simply 'area' . . . even the layman implies that he regards the area called by that word as standing out in his mind, as being in some way distinct . . . the different parts of the area called a region are assumed to have in common some characteristic or association, including as a minimum a common location." In contrast, an area may be conceived of as any arbitrarily, or even randomly, chosen segment of the surface of the earth, with no specified character to it other than internal continuity and contiguity among its subareas. The delimitation of areas in the general sense presents no intellectual problem; their bounds are entirely matters of convenience. On the other hand, the delimitation of regions is one of the more demanding and fundamental problems in geographic and human ecologic research, since it involves the ascertainment of the limits to which the distinctive homology of the region extends. Solution of the regional delimitation problem thus requires specification of standards of distinctiveness among areas, as well as the development of regional models with which empirically determined regional entities can be compared and from which they can be differentiated. Since the regional concept denotes some special way of thinking about area, the term "regionalism" has evolved. Since areas are nonspecific in this respect, the word "arealism" is absent from both social-scientific and lay parlance.

Area and space. Distinctions are also appropriate between "area" and "space," although here again they are often used interchangeably both as abstract nouns and in their adjectival forms. Area as a concept is associated with bounding and content; space is not, since by definition it involves a boundless three-dimensional extent. An area, whether specifically a region or not, can be located four dimensionally: latitude, longitude, depth or height, and time. A "space," or indeed space itself, cannot, since it would then have to be defined partly, and inappropriately, in terms of itself. Also, one can conceive of, and practice, the analysis of area, meaning the analysis of the content and organization of given areas, whereas the analysis of space becomes a conceptual *reductio ad absurdum* if space is properly understood to be only the setting within which objects can be located.

The distinction has relevance also when one contemplates the adjectives "areal" and "spatial." These terms are most aptly used interchangeably at an abstract level in reference to the distribution of phenomena over the earth's surface. This use is in contrast with distributions that occur along a temporal dimension. There remains a subtle but important distinction when they are used in other ways, as in such common phrases as "spatial structure" and "spatial organization." Space itself, of course, has no character; it therefore has neither structure nor organization. "Areal structure" and "areal organization" are what is intended. Area may be characterized by organization and/or structure, and it certainly has both content and location. All phenomena, including areas, however, have a distribution through space and can be set within it. Thus, both commercial activities and the areas associated with them are distributed through space and form some sort of patterning in space. This concept has both real and theoretical significance. If one conceptually transforms space (the unbounded) into area (that is, space bounded), then the distribution of these commercial activities acquires an additional dimension, that relating to location and content.

The semantic difficulty with which the geographer and regionalist must deal is well illustrated by the concept of "spatial interaction," first introduced into the literature by Ullman (1953). On the face of it, the phrase is a contradiction in terms, since space itself cannot interact with anything, but Ullman sidesteps the difficulty by defining it as follows: "By spatial interaction I mean actual . . . *human relations between areas on the earth's' surface* [our italics], such as the reciprocal relations and flows of all kinds among industries, raw materials, markets, culture, and transportation—not static location as indicated by latitude, longitude, . . . et cetera . . ." (Ullman 1953, p. 56). Significantly, what he speaks of is interaction between areas or between phenomena in areas. Therefore, the proper term for this idea would be "areal," rather than "spatial," interaction.

Geography and areal differentiation. The distinction between concepts of area and of space represents one of the major but not necessarily irreconcilable controversies in modern geographic methodology. When Hartshorne (1939) spoke of geography as the study of areal differentiation, he meant the comparative study that will help in understanding the principles and propositions that determine associations and relations within areal units. With reference to Ullman, Hartshorne states:

Ullman has suggested that "areal differentiation" should be considered as a subconcept of geography as "spatial interaction." The suggestion seems to me to result from a misconception of the former term, if not also of the latter. Spatial interaction can only mean relations between phenomena in different places, and these phenomena, whether in place or in movement through space, form a part of the character of each area concerned. Hence the reverse is the case: variations in stationary characteristics, or forms, and variations in characteristics of movement, or functions, whether within an area or between it and another, are both included under the concept of areal variation, or differences in areas. (1959, p. 19)

In seeming contrast to this view is that of geography as a science of distributions of various types of social phenomena, or as it is sometimes termed, a "regional science" within which attention is focused not on areas but on distributional patterns in space and the processes by which these patterns come into being and relate to others. That Hartshorne (1959, p. 133), however, has long recognized the compatibility of the areal and spatial

perspectives is indicated by his statement that "the region is the areal expression of a logical generalization of process relationships, and *hence a first step in the explanation of the geography of an area* [our italics]." To some extent the apparent conflict between areal and spatial emphases may be traced to the historic dichotomy between regional and systematic geography, which, however, is passing from the methodological scene.

Area studies. Methodological distinctions have little apparent bearing on one of the ways in which "area" commonly is used, particularly in the United States—in the term "area studies." This term, especially since World War II, has come to connote interdisciplinary programs of training or research on certain parts of the world, sometimes one country, often groups of them, as exemplified by Soviet area programs, in the first case, or Sub-Saharan Africa area programs, in the second. Since the areas concerned tend to be rather clearly identified and presumably have some degree of internal cultural, economic, or political homogeneity, the term "regional studies" might seem equally appropriate, but its usage is not widespread. Significantly, however, in terms of the discussion above, the term "spatial studies" is not employed in this context.

The state area. The archetypical area in the world geographical pattern is the state, or the political territorial unit at the state level. The state or its equivalent, like all areas, is bounded, and it possesses both a location and content. Like many but not all areas, it is also characterized by a functional organization that specifically identifies the territory of a given state as a unique entity and differentiates it from all others. The areal analysis of states is one of the major components of political geography. This analysis involves the comparative study of location, content, and functional organization of states. States are also, of course, regions, whether defined in terms of the relative homogeneity of political control over territory or in terms of the semiautonomous, often nodal, ecosystem that each state possesses. Area analysis involves the identification and examination of the subsystems that compose each state and the relations among them, as well as of the interrelations among states themselves. As Lösch (1940) pointed out, moreover, political territoriality and other types of regions are not necessarily coterminous, although they often coincide in various respects. At substate levels political power may be distributed through a hierarchy of areal entities, as illustrated by the states in a federal system (see Maass 1959). On the other hand, administrative entities that are, strictly speaking, functional rather than political may cut across or further subdivide these areal entities, as in the case of Federal Reserve districts within the United States. At the same time, non-political regional units often lie uncomfortably upon, and conflict with, both politically defined and administratively defined areas, as in the case of metropolitan school districts, soil conservation districts, etc., in the United States. The problems relating to tensions arising from such areal contradictions provide a meeting ground for political scientist, planner, economist, and geographer alike.

NORTON GINSBURG

[*See also* CARTOGRAPHY; ECOLOGY; GEOGRAPHY. *Directly related are the entries* AREA STUDIES; CULTURE AREA; REGION.]

BIBLIOGRAPHY

ACKERMAN, EDWARD A. 1958 *Geography as a Fundamental Research Discipline*. Research Paper No. 53. Univ. of Chicago, Dept. of Geography.

BENNETT, WENDELL C. 1951 *Area Studies in American Universities*. New York: Social Science Research Council.

GINSBURG, NORTON S. 1959 The Regional Concept and Planning Regions. Pages 31–45 in United Nations, Department of Economic and Social Affairs, *Regional Planning*. New York: United Nations.

HARTSHORNE, RICHARD (1939) 1949 *The Nature of Geography*. Lancaster, Pa.: Association of American Geographers. → First published in Association of American Geographers, *Annals*.

HARTSHORNE, RICHARD 1959 *Perspective on the Nature of Geography*. Chicago: Rand McNally.

JAMES, PRESTON E.; and JONES, CLARENCE F. (editors) (1954) 1964 *American Geography: Inventory and Prospect*. Syracuse Univ. Press.

LÖSCH, AUGUST (1940) 1954 *The Economics of Location*. New Haven: Yale Univ. Press. → First published as *Die räumliche Ordnung der Wirtschaft*.

MAASS, ARTHUR (editor) 1959 *Area and Power: A Theory of Local Government*. Glencoe, Ill.: Free Press.

PHILBRICK, ALLEN K. 1957 Principles of Areal Functional Organization in Regional Human Geography. *Economic Geography* 33:299–336.

PLATT, ROBERT S. 1957 A Review of Regional Geography. Association of American Geographers, *Annals* 47:187–190.

ULLMAN, E. L. 1953 Human Geography and Area Research. Association of American Geographers, *Annals* 43:54–66.

AREA STUDIES

Area studies are based on a concept, are carried out with the aid of institutions called area centers, and are predicated on some measure of scholarly collaboration. The concept remains controversial; the institutions are increasing in number and vigor throughout the world; and scholars collaborate in manifold ways.

The basic concept of area studies is that the people of a definable geographical sector, acting in their society and their environment, offer an appropriate unit for scholarly attention. The concept is not a new one. Research, as distinct from speculation, demands an objective locus. When Aristotle compared the political institutions of Greek city-states and brought his conclusions to the attention of students, he engaged in activities not utterly dissimilar to those of modern area centers. Classical education, which focused on ancient Greece and Rome, may be regarded as an early form of area studies. It may even be contended that political science and perhaps other social sciences were until very recently little more than parochial studies of an area limited to western Europe and the United States, masquerading under a universal rubric.

History

During and immediately following World War II, governments discovered an alarming shortage of individuals who were seriously acquainted with the languages, cultures, and topographical characteristics of the world areas in which troops had to fight and about which important political and social decisions had to be made.

In the United States during the war, many individuals were trained in special language programs instituted by the armed forces. These programs gave intensive instruction in Japanese, Chinese, and other languages. Shortly after the war, the delicately poised hostility between East and West necessitated the development of scholarly specialization in the study of the political, economic, and social institutions of the Soviet Union. With the aid of grants from the Carnegie Corporation of New York and the Rockefeller Foundation, Columbia and Harvard universities established centers for Russian studies. The organization of these centers and the productivity of their members provided models for the study of other areas. In the late 1950s the Ford Foundation gave substantial long-term support to a number of universities for the advancement of area studies.

In Great Britain institutions such as the School for Oriental and African Studies, which had been founded in 1916 chiefly for the language training of colonial officers and others, were broadened after 1945 to include cultural and social studies. The report of the Interdepartmental Commission of Enquiry on Oriental, Slavonic, East European and African Studies (Scarbrough Report) in 1947 asked the question: "What place should be made, in the post-war life of the British people, for the study of the languages and cultures of almost all the peoples of the world which are not of Western European origin?" (Great Britain . . . 1947, p. 6). The Commission answered by stating that the existing provision for area studies "is unworthy of our country and people . . . the study of the civilisations and languages of these countries is of such great importance for this and for succeeding generations that it would be harmful to the national interest to allow the present state of affairs to continue or even to deteriorate" (Great Britain . . . 1947, p. 8). Acting on this recommendation, the British government gave support to language departments in half a dozen universities. A related report, made in 1961, on Oriental, Slavonic, east European, and African studies (Hayter Report) emphasized the expansion of area studies outside the language departments and noted that for Great Britain there were three important lessons to be learned from the development of area studies in the United States: (1) the large scale of the effort; (2) the organization of area centers; (3) the emphasis on modern studies (Great Britain . . . 1961). As a result of this report, British universities were invited to apply to the University Grants Committee for funds to assist in the establishment or development of centers for area studies—known informally as "Hayter centres." Thus, for example, the University of Hull is organizing a center for southeast Asian studies, and the University of Leeds has established a center for Chinese studies. In the United States and Great Britain, Latin America has received belated recognition; centers for Latin American studies, such as those at Cornell University and St. Antony's College, Oxford, are beginning to find private and public support.

In France a remarkable expansion of area studies took place after 1955, when the École Pratique des Hautes Études received a Rockefeller Foundation grant for the development of studies of the Far East, Russia, India, and the Muslim world. Within two years, with the aid of matching funds from the Ministry of Education and other sources, 16 new professorial chairs assigned to area programs were established in the École. Cooperation with such institutions as the École des Langues Orientales, the Musée de l'Homme, and the Foundation des Sciences Politiques was encouraged, and a new center for African studies was established at the Sorbonne.

Various forms of area centers are found in other countries as well. Since 1955 there has been a formidable development of African studies in the Soviet Union, in addition to institutes of Slavonic and Oriental research and the other area centers affiliated with the Soviet Academy of Sciences.

There is a Chinese study program in the Section of Oriental Studies of the Colegio de México, and a center for Latin American studies at the University of Rio Grande do Sul in Brazil.

Areas for study are variously delimited; the more that is known about an area, the smaller the area under institutionalized study is likely to be. For example, there is a relatively substantial amount of systematic information about Japanese society; consequently there are specialized centers for Japanese studies. But there are centers for southeast Asia as a whole, rather than for Indonesia or Thailand. The usual areas are Latin America, southeast Asia, south Asia, the Soviet Union, eastern Europe, east Asia—with a tendency toward separation of Japan and China—Africa south of the Sahara, and the Middle East, including north Africa. There are, however, other areas, such as the Caribbean islands and western Europe, that are given attention in the United States. Similarly, there are centers for American studies in European countries. The problem of dividing the world into "areas" is a continuing one, changing as the international situation creates new research needs. For example, there are 20 countries in Latin America, which differ greatly in size, language, racial composition, and other characteristics. Can such an area, having a certain geographical continuity, provide a satisfactory unit for scholarly research? Oceans used to be more readily crossed than mountain ranges and isthmuses, but since the beginning of the air age, traditional definitions of areas have shown a remarkable capacity for survival. Is the "Atlantic community" less an area, even including Turkey, than the "American states"? Do area centers that are selective within a region on the basis of former colonial connections retain utility?

Organization of area programs

Area centers are formed on the theory that collaboration is more effective than isolation in advancing knowledge about foreign areas through research, publication, and teaching. Collaboration is multiform, partly because the scholars generally hold their appointments and enjoy tenure in university departments or faculties, rather than in the area center. The majority of area courses are offered by departments or faculties and only listed by centers. However, centers may persuade departments to offer new courses or engage new faculty members; foreign scholars may give special courses as visiting lecturers at centers; and interdisciplinary seminars may be negotiated at a center's initiative.

The experience of area centers in the past 15

years demonstrates the importance of taking pains to enhance the many forms of scholarly communication. Many centers possess separate headquarters, with faculty office space, specialized libraries, and common rooms. Former students of the Russian Research Center at Harvard University recall with pleasure the interchanges afforded at the center's lunchroom, which served graduate students and faculty members together.

Area centers vary greatly in the kind of training and research offered and the degree to which programs are effectively planned and integrated. The Committee on World Area Research of the Social Science Research Council (Bennett 1951) has characterized the most desirable features of area programs: (1) intensive language instruction, including control of teaching by a linguistic scientist and scientific descriptive analysis of the language in question; (2) joint seminars, with participation by more than one faculty member; (3) group research; (4) combined study in humanities and social sciences; (5) availability of specialized materials, including newspapers, official records, maps, and other sources; (6) participation of foreign students and faculty members.

Probably the feature most difficult of realization is group research; the preparation of a substantial number of monographs may take several years, and some attempt is made at covering important subjects by publishing individual dissertations and other scholarly works. Another type of group research is that performed under contract with a governmental agency.

In addition, the integrated area centers may provide opportunities for field research and study visits by members of the faculties of centers. In 1951, when Bennett's report was written, financial support for such opportunities could rarely be found, and politics made it impossible to travel to some countries. More recently, however, greatly increased funds have become available for scholarly travel, and Russia has become hospitable to certain types of study by foreign scholars. In the United States, awards made under the Fulbright–Hayes Act, grants made by private foundations to both universities and national councils, and fellowships such as those provided by the Foreign Area Fellowship Program and the National Defense Education Act have enabled a very large proportion of students (probably the majority of those competent to complete doctoral work as area specialists) to spend at least one graduate year abroad. Such research is usually done in preparation for the doctoral dissertation. Similarly, these and other sources provide a still increasing number of opportunities

for faculty members to pursue research in a foreign country. In Great Britain and France the need for field research is equally recognized, although financial resources (especially from nongovernmental agencies) are limited.

There are only one or two area centers extant in the United States that offer the doctoral degree in "area studies." However, there are a fair number of centers or universities that confer bachelor of arts degrees in area studies, and some universities offer special intermediate degrees, such as master of international affairs, with a certificate from an area center. Doctoral degrees, however, are almost universally conferred by a department of economics, history, or other discipline. This has two fundamental advantages—maintaining high standards in disciplinary preparation, and qualifying graduates for established career patterns in teaching and the civil service.

The chief educational contribution of area centers is to add area specialization to, but not substitute it for, the regular degree requirements established in each department or faculty. An area specialist, therefore, is not a specialist in "Chinese studies" or "Latin American studies." He is first of all the recipient of a degree in a basic discipline such as geography, linguistics, one of the social sciences or arts, or possibly law or journalism. But because of his area specialization, he has passed examinations on subjects in several disciplines other than his own. He has linguistic competence appropriate to his research needs, as determined by his university's requirements, and this may mean study of more than one foreign language. He has engaged in research within his chosen foreign region or country for at least a year and often longer. If he has received his doctorate, he will have spent from one to four years more on his studies than those who are not area specialists, the length of time depending largely on the difficulty of the languages attacked.

Field research may, of course, vary greatly. For a historian, it may involve poring over records in London and Ibadan; for a political scientist it may require foreign residence for substantial periods of time and systematic interviewing; for an economist, briefer contacts for gathering of data.

The range of subjects of field research is unlimited, with the important exception that in many centers emphasis is principally, but not exclusively, on the modern period. However, even this may differ from country to country. Thus, in Paris, France, the Division des Aires Culturelles, École Pratique des Hautes Études, Centre des Recherches Historiques, VIᵉ Section, includes such titles as

Documents and Research on the Economy of Byzantine, Islamic and Slav Countries and Their Commercial Relations in the Middle Ages in its lists of publications. The line between modern and pre-modern is of course an issue in sharp dispute among scholars, some of whom assert, for example, that the contemporary Islamic world cannot be understood without an understanding of the Islamic world since the seventh century A.D.; while others say that Napoleon's invasion of Egypt is a reasonably good starting point for social scientists in the twentieth century. For some areas the great difference between classical and contemporary languages is a significant one, as in the case of India, and few scholars who are concerned with the dynamics of modern societies will take the time to learn Sanskrit, although they will probably be required to have an acquaintance with Hindi.

In effect, the range of research undertaken by students at area centers is influenced by current disciplinary fashions, by directions of concern exhibited by governmental agencies, and by problems of access to sources of data. In the case of certain European countries and Japan, during and immediately after World War II, special techniques were developed for "research at a distance"; in Hong Kong, interviewing of refugees from the Chinese mainland has become a regular practice by social scientists and others. Even in areas less formally closed, scholarly inquirers from a foreign country or different subculture, no matter how apolitical their aims and sponsorship, may have to be no less wary in the field than the local tax collectors, and even then they may run afoul of officials who suspect their motives.

There is a strong tendency for research by area specialists to be aimed principally at specific problems, such as the cause and control of inflation, changing political patterns, the modification of systems of land tenure, etc. The desire of government officials to be advised on day-to-day issues is, on the whole, resisted by social scientists, who prefer to deal painstakingly with data rather than offhandedly with hunches, but the scholars' interests in contemporary phenomena are relevant to the issues as they are faced by officials.

Although area studies in United States universities were largely created on a "know-your-enemy" basis ("With World War II came a sudden and great demand for exact information about places." Hall 1947, p. 1), an important justification has been found in the system of liberal education. More recently, acquaintance with the cultures of other peoples has been promoted as an important element of training for potential government officials concerned with the administration of programs of technical and educational assistance; this is currently an explicit justification for area studies in France. Finally, studies of foreign areas by scholars qualified by disciplinary training have received an intellectual accolade: they are becoming more and more acceptable as scientifically interesting because they offer comparative data significant for the advancement of a discipline. The post-World War II expansion of the scope of foreign policy into propaganda, education, and technical aid has created a demand for government personnel with specialized knowledge of foreign cultures and languages. Concomitantly, scholarly interest in comparative studies in the several social science disciplines has developed to such an extent that, for example, analyses of urbanization in Africa are considered as necessary as analyses of metropolitan sprawl in the United States. Political science has come to recognize studies of the bureaucracies of Burma or Mexico as being almost equal in scholarly interest to studies of the civil services of West Germany and Belgium, and as having equal theoretical relevance. Economists are beginning to be interested in the explanation of rates of inflation that Chileans and Brazilians experience and endure but which appear fantastically impractical in theories based on sober Swedish rates of growth. In this direction, scholarly respectability may happily coincide with governmental demands for world-wide comparative studies of contemporary human phenomena.

The acceptance by universities in the United States of responsibility for offering specialized training on foreign areas of a type initiated by the military services created complex sets of issues.

The first issue in the establishment of recognized area programs in United States universities was the relative importance of linguistic and social science studies. Immediately after World War II the viewpoint tended toward equating language training with area training. In practice, most of the new "area specialists" learned modern, "newspaper" Arabic or Japanese, for example, with special emphasis on one or more oral forms. Linguists developed new methods for more rapid language learning. For many of the men and women who are known as area specialists, the thorough mastery of a foreign language is not looked upon as the fundamental prerequisite for understanding a foreign culture. Language "competence" is seen, rather, as an instrument for serving various specialized requirements, for which different vocabularies and minor competences are sufficient. In an earlier day the scholarship of persons most closely qualifying as area specialists was largely philological, calligraphical, and broadly humanistic. The present generation of area specialists, in the United States at least, includes an increasingly greater proportion of social scientists and modern historians (Foreign Area Fellowship Program 1964).

It should be noted, however, that the expression "language and area studies" persists in competition with "area studies." The reason for the survival of the first term lies in the fact that language competence is often regarded as sufficient qualification for an area specialist. It is only recently, for example, that the Foreign Service Institute of the U.S. Department of State has initiated "area studies" courses in addition to its comprehensive language training.

A second and associated problem is the differences in judgment as to the relevant factors to be studied in understanding a foreign society. The issue is presented most sharply when an area center emphasizes "the modern Middle East," "contemporary China," or "postindependence Latin America." In post-Kemal Turkey how much of Byzantium remains? How deeply should Pekingologists study Confucius? These are samples of questions that continue to be debated, not without heat, by those who regard themselves as interpreters of great traditions of still-living societies and those who see little that is significant therein for the evaluation of irrigation projects, for example, or the solution of housing problems. This suggests extremes, of course, but there are many less extreme opportunities for serious difference of opinion before one reaches a middle point of accommodation and perhaps of cooperation.

A third issue is the relationship between area studies and the social sciences. The work of the historian or literary critic is relatively particularistic; it is area-bound and tradition-bound, and sometimes rather strictly so—for example, Spanish rather than Iberian. The work of the economist, at its most prestigious, is relatively universalistic, theoretical, and systematic and aims at fairly specific goals, such as maximization of gross national product. Economies are not as independent of national boundaries as are units of electrical energy, but citizens in aggregate economic behavior can be treated more collectively than can, say, novelists. It is suggested that there have been four stages in the development of relationships between area studies and the social sciences; that is to say— naming the extremes—between the gathering of data and its ordering by theoretical constructs. In the first stage, data about foreign areas were collected through field research by area specialists. A second stage saw the comparison of similar problems in different areas through the broadening of training of area specialists. In the third stage, data from several areas were used by social scientists to develop new theories and to overcome the parochial basis of much existing theory in the social sciences. In the present, fourth stage, the development of theory begins to influence the types of problems area specialists investigate and the kinds of questions they begin to ask as they undertake field research, in part because, more than ever before, the training of area specialists is becoming assimilated to the training of social scientists. This is bound to have effects on both, and we may look forward to the time when the question "What know ye of -ology who only Ruritania know?" will be a real one.

Finally, there is an issue with respect to the differential availability of funds for research. In the United States, for example, the National Science Foundation does not offer grants for research in history except the history of science. Special programs of grants for postdoctoral scholars are offered under the joint auspices of the American Council of Learned Societies and the Social Science Research Council for research on, for example, contemporary (post-1948) China and on Latin America (chiefly the period since 1830). However, scholars interested in research on earlier periods are not excluded, since they may apply in general grants programs. In addition, it should be noted that substantial support for premodern studies in a number of areas has been given to universities by private foundations and individual donors.

Future developments

Area centers are here to stay. Area centers satisfy direct governmental needs for area specialists. These needs in foreign-aid, educational, technical, and other programs and in intelligence and military services have grown in the last decade, and it is likely that they will not greatly decrease in the next. In Britain and France, with the disappearance of the colonial training services themselves, the training of area specialists in university centers and through field research becomes more essential than ever.

No less important, an intellectual commitment to research on a foreign area is becoming scientifically respected as the social sciences gradually emerge from parochialism. The increasing interest of political scientists and sociologists, for example, in comparative, cross-national empirical research bids fair to give durability to a professional, scholarly demand for area training. There is a semantic problem here: political scientists prefer to call themselves specialists in comparative politics, however enthusiastically they continue research on one area or maintain their relationship with an area center. There is also a growing demand for the study of foreign cultures and languages at educational levels lower than that for area specialists; notable is the fact that more than one-third of all colleges and universities in the United States offer at least one year's training in Russian.

The transfer of rationale for area studies from military capabilities to other capabilities, such as that for economic development or even for susceptibility to subversion, further solidifies the place of area centers in education in the humanities and social sciences.

An area-center function as yet undeveloped is that of supplementing the training of foreign students who attend universities in advanced countries. More ample collections of printed materials exist in the great libraries of Europe and the United States than in the archives of many underdeveloped countries, and scholars commanding extensive, effectively organized information can be found at principal Western universities. This inequity is, hopefully, a temporary situation; yet while it exists, certain foreign students in many fields of study may be persuaded to take advantage of it. A concomitant result might be the awakening of an appreciation on their part of the role of scholarship in the social sciences—the gathering of data and the establishment of islands of objective social analysis—as part of the very process of social and economic development.

One of the principal developments to be expected in the next decade is the establishment of new types of facilities for field research. One of these is the new Universities Service Center in Hong Kong. The Centro Latino Americano de Pesquisas em Ciências Sociais, founded in Rio de Janeiro in 1958 by UNESCO and Latin American governments, has demonstrated the possibility of collaboration. In association with local institutions, area centers can utilize diverse ways of bringing together foreign and local scholars in all countries in fruitful research collaboration.

Further, the jet airplane has made possible a quantum shift in scholarly communications. International associations in the social sciences, formed at the initiative of UNESCO, are able to hold congresses, and new national associations have been formed in Europe and elsewhere. Foreign areas are easy to reach; they presumably will become more accessible to research, particularly as an area's local scholars in history and the social sciences

increase in number. (The Institute of Economics of the University of Chile is an outstanding example in the Americas of an institution, developed by local initiative with the assistance of North American scholars, that has been hospitable to visiting scholars from other countries.) With the contracts entered into by the U.S. Agency for International Development, which provide funds for educational cooperation between local and foreign universities, special types of communication have emerged. Some private interuniversity arrangements have developed and may be expected to expand (such as those between the University of Costa Rica and the University of Kansas; the latter recently issued a publication describing the Latin American interests of some two hundred of its faculty members).

Area studies, responsive to governmental needs, embedded in university structures, increasingly acceptable as satisfying the intellectual curiosity of scholars, strongly supported by private and public funds, are likely to flourish in the visible future.

BRYCE WOOD

BIBLIOGRAPHY

AMERICAN COUNCIL ON EDUCATION 1962 *Resources for Language and Area Studies: A Report on an Inventory of the Language and Area Centers Supported by the National Defense Education Act of 1958.* Washington: The Council.

Area Studies. 1952 *International Social Science Bulletin* 4:633–699. → Now called the *International Social Science Journal.* The entire issue is devoted to area studies.

BENNETT, WENDELL C. 1951 *Area Studies in American Universities.* New York: Social Science Research Council.

BIGELOW, DONALD N.; and LEGTERS, LYMAN H. 1964 *NDEA [National Defense Education Act] Language and Area Centers: Report on the First 5 Years.* U.S. Office of Education Bulletin No. 41. Washington: Government Printing Office.

BLACK, C. E. et al. 1959 An Appraisal of Russian Studies in the United States. *American Slavic and East European Review* 18:417–441. → Now called *Slavic Review: American Quarterly of Soviet and East European Studies.*

The College and World Affairs. 1964 New York: Education and World Affairs. → Known as the "Nason Report." It supplements what is widely known as the "Morrill Committee Report," published in 1960.

COMMITTEE ON THE UNIVERSITY AND WORLD AFFAIRS 1960 *The University and World Affairs.* New York: Ford Foundation.

CONFERENCE ON THE STRENGTHENING AND INTEGRATION OF SOUTH ASIAN LANGUAGE AND AREA STUDIES, NEW YORK, *1961* 1962 *Resources for South Asian Area Studies in the United States: Report of a Conference Convened by the Committee on South Asia of the Association for Asian Studies for the United States Office of Education.* Edited by Richard D. Lambert. Philadelphia: Univ. of Pennsylvania Press.

DALLIN, ALEXANDER 1963 The Soviet Union: Political Activity. Pages 7–48 in Zbigniew K. Brzezinski (editor), *Africa and the Communist World.* Stanford (Calif.) Univ. Press.

DEMIÉVILLE, PAUL 1958 Organization of East Asian Studies in France. *Journal of Asian Studies* 18:163–181.

FISHER, HAROLD H. (editor) 1959 *American Research on Russia.* Bloomington: Indiana Univ. Press.

FOREIGN AREA FELLOWSHIP PROGRAM 1964 *Directory of Foreign Area Fellows, 1952–1963.* New York: The Program.

FRANCE, MINISTÈRE D'ÉTAT CHARGÉ DE LA RÉFORME ADMINISTRATIVE 1963 *La politique de coopération avec les pays en voie de développement.* Paris: La Documentation Française.

FREEDMAN, MAURICE 1963 A Chinese Phase in Social Anthropology. *British Journal of Sociology* 14:1–19.

GARDNER, JOHN W. 1964 *AID and the Universities: A Report to the Administrator of the Agency for International Development.* New York: Education and World Affairs.

GIBB, HAMILTON ALEXANDER R. 1963 *Area Studies Reconsidered.* Univ. of London, School of Oriental and African Studies.

GREAT BRITAIN, COMMITTEE ON MODERN LANGUAGES IN THE EDUCATIONAL SYSTEM OF GREAT BRITAIN 1918 *Modern Studies, Being the Report of the Committee on the Position of Modern Languages in the Educational System of Great Britain.* Papers by Command, Cmd. 9036. London: H.M. Stationery Office. → Known as the "Leathes Report."

GREAT BRITAIN, INTERDEPARTMENTAL COMMISSION OF ENQUIRY ON ORIENTAL, SLAVONIC, EAST EUROPEAN AND AFRICAN STUDIES (1947) 1959 *Report.* London: H.M. Stationery Office. → Known as the "Scarbrough Report."

GREAT BRITAIN, UNIVERSITY GRANTS COMMITTEE 1961 *Report of the Sub-committee on Oriental, Slavonic, East European and African Studies.* London: H.M. Stationery Office. → Known as the "Hayter Report."

GREAT BRITAIN, UNIVERSITY GRANTS COMMITTEE 1965 *Report of the Sub-committee on Latin American Studies.* London: H.M. Stationery Office. → Known as the "Parry Report."

HALL, ROBERT B. 1947 *Area Studies: With Special Reference to Their Implications for Research in the Social Sciences.* Pamphlet No. 3. New York: Social Science Research Council.

HARVARD UNIVERSITY, EAST ASIAN RESEARCH CENTER 1965 *Ten-year Report of the Director.* Cambridge, Mass.: The Center.

HARVARD UNIVERSITY, RUSSIAN RESEARCH CENTER 1958 *Ten-year Report and Current Projects, 1948–1958.* Cambridge, Mass.: The Center.

JOHNSON, WALTER 1963 *American Studies Abroad: Progress and Difficulties in Selected Countries.* Washington: U.S. Advisory Commission on International Educational and Cultural Affairs.

MOREHOUSE, WARD 1963 *The International Dimensions of Education in New York State.* Albany: State Education Department, Univ. of the State of New York.

The Non-Western World in Higher Education. 1964 *American Academy of Political and Social Science, Annals* 356:1–141. → See especially pages 2–11 on "The Leadership of the Universities," by George E. Taylor.

Organization of the Soviet Institute of Chinese Studies and Its Tasks. (1956) 1957 *Journal of Asian Studies* 16:677–678. → First published in Russian.

PARIS, ÉCOLE PRATIQUE DES HAUTES ÉTUDES, DIVISION DES AIRES CULTURELLES, SECTION DES SCIENCES ÉCONOMIQUES ET SOCIALES 1963 *Publications de la Division des Aires Culturelles.* Paris: Mouton. → Indicates the range and types of area studies currently carried on in France.

St. Antony's College, Oxford, 1950–1964. 1964 Oxford Univ. Press.

SHINKICHI, ETO 1961 Asian Studies in Japan: Recent Trends. *Journal of Asian Studies* 21:125–133.

STEWARD, JULIAN H. 1950 *Area Research: Theory and Practice.* Bulletin No. 63. New York: Social Science Research Council.

U.S. DEPARTMENT OF STATE 1964 *International Affairs Research Centers in Paris: A Directory.* Washington: Government Printing Office.

U.S. DEPARTMENT OF STATE, OFFICE OF INTELLIGENCE RESEARCH AND ANALYSIS 1954—— *Area Study Programs in American Universities.* Washington: The Department. → A serial publication.

U.S. PRESIDENT'S SCIENCE ADVISORY COMMITTEE, LIFE SCIENCES PANEL 1962 *Strengthening the Behavioral Sciences: Statement by the Behavioral Sciences Subpanel.* Washington: Government Printing Office.

WAGLEY, CHARLES (editor) 1964 *Social Science Research on Latin America: Report and Papers of a Seminar on Latin American Studies in the United States Held at Stanford, California, July 8–August 23, 1963.* New York: Columbia Univ. Press.

WAUCHOPE, ROBERT 1957 *Multi-discipline Area Research: Extracts From Reports to the President of Tulane University for the Period July 1, 1953–June 30, 1957.* Middle American Research Institute, Miscellaneous Papers, No. 10, New Orleans, La.: Tulane Univ.

ARISTOTLE

Aristotle (384–322 B.C.), the greatest systematic philosopher of ancient Greece, was born in Stagira, an outlying city near Macedonia. He spent twenty years in Plato's Academy, leaving on Plato's death in 347, and later founded his own school in the Lyceum at Athens in 335/334. Part of the interval was spent as tutor to Alexander, son of Philip, king of Macedonia. Aristotle's father had been court physician to an earlier Macedonian king. As Macedonia advanced in its conquest of Greece, Aristotle's connections with the Macedonian monarchy roused Athenian hostility. In 323, in the anti-Macedonian reaction that followed Alexander's death, Aristotle was indicted on the charge of impiety and withdrew to Chalcis, where he died the next year.

His massive surviving works range over all fields of inquiry: logic and theory of science, physics, biology, psychology, metaphysics, ethics, politics, rhetoric, and aesthetics. In most of these he laid the basis for the subsequent development of the disciplines. The scope and analytic thoroughness of his works have made them perennially influential. In the late medieval world they constituted the major available corpus of science, and Dante characterized Aristotle as "the master of those who know." A reaction against his philosophy came with the rise of modern science, but his social and humanistic writings have maintained a continuous appeal.

Aristotle's distinctive contributions to social science are (a) a methodology of inquiry that focuses on man's rationality yet stresses the continuity of man and nature rather than a basic cleavage; (b) the integration of the ethical and the social, as contrasted with the dominant modern proposals of a value-free social science and an autonomous ethics; and (c) a systematic foundation for morals, politics, and social theory, and some basic concepts for economics, law, and education.

Methodology and general outlook. Aristotle's foundation work in logic, of which the syllogism is best known, analyzes general forms of inference. His conception of systematic knowledge is rationalistic, aiming at deductive organization, with primary premises stating the essence, and theorems deriving properties. Beyond essence and property lie incidental or accidental features, and there is no science of the accidental. The distinction between essential and accidental—for example, a man is essentially rational but only accidentally white—is not offered as a relative pragmatic one, but as corresponding to types actually present in nature or reality. Basic concepts and relations in each field are grasped directly as outcomes of an inductive process. Data are furnished by accumulated observation, common opinion, and traditional generalization; and theoretical principles emerge from analytic sifting of alternative explanations.

His explanatory approach is teleological, using the model of craftsmanship: nature works like the artist, although it operates unconsciously. The scientist must therefore look for materials, structure, causal agencies, and directive goals or functions. These concepts are answers to the questions: Out of what? What is it? From where? and For the sake of what? They have been called the material, formal, efficient, and final causes, respectively. In conscious action, the final cause may lie in a purpose beyond the object analyzed, but in natural processes it is the emerging form that guides development, for example, from acorn to oak or from embryo to adult. Even in physics, Aristotle sees the fall of a stone as the striving of its earthen nature to reach its natural place at the globe's center. Order has priority over disorder in Aristotle's outlook, as a consequence of the conception of indwelling nature; he rejects the view that change is primary and that all equilibrium analysis is only approximate and falsifying. There are real structures in things; the world is a plurality of what we would today call homeostatic systems, whose groundplan may be discovered and rationally formulated through a kind of structural–functional analysis. Like the world itself, the order is neither imposed from without nor evolved, but eternal.

Matter and *form* are relative analytic concepts. Dynamically, however, matter is construed as *potentiality* for determinate development or activity and form as culminating *actuality*. Thus, man's psychic life is seen as the actualization of his organism's potentialities. The soul (*psyche*) is to the body, says Aristotle, as the power to cut is to the axe. His focus is on the total interactive situation in which man and his specialized organs, the object and its special properties, and relevant features of the medium are brought into relation in the particular activity, whether it be eating, seeing, dreaming, or thinking. His method is thus a general field approach that enables him to correlate physical and physiological study with phenomenological and behavioral study. Philosophically, he avoided the sharp dualisms of body and mind, objective and subjective, that have beset modern psychology since Descartes gave a primary metaphysical role to matter and consciousness. Aristotle's analysis of human functions culminates in a view of man as distinctively rational, able to express his nature self-consciously and attain contemplative understanding of the orderly principles of different fields.

His methodology thus served admirably for discovering existent order—whether in classifying animal species or mapping constitutions of city-states—and for seeing the development by which the normal individual reaches mature form. It does not provide a method for dealing with evolutionary development in which the new emerges out of a seedbed of constant and incidental mutation.

Ethics and politics. Aristotle's teleological approach sees man striving toward one ultimate end, which Aristotle identifies as happiness. Since the good is defined as what all men aim at, the normative is not invoked transcendentally; rather it is systematically grounded in the needs, goal seeking, and possible outcomes of human social living. While theoretical contemplation is given the crowning role as man's highest activity, most of

Aristotle's inquiry is directed to the practical good in man's social practices and relations. Ethics and politics are continuous. The one studies virtues as character formations, the other studies institutions; but both are concerned with finding ways in which the human make-up realizes fullest expression and how in less than ideal conditions this may be approximated. Aristotle's integration of the ethical and the social, of norm and fact, is thus not a failure to appreciate a much labored modern distinction but its implicit rejection, based on the assumed continuity of man and nature and an underlying teleology.

The *Politics* embodies Aristotle's conclusions from a study of the history and development of 158 constitutions, the constitution of Athens being the only one that survives. The *Politics* is more than political science. We find in it a concept of a natural order of human institutions, the projection of an ideal order, and the classification and analysis of existent sociopolitical forms and their evaluation to provide a practical program.

Although in Aristotle's own lifetime, his pupil, Alexander the Great, was building a vast empire and cosmopolitan philosophies of man were to appear, Aristotle himself expressed the conception of the older city-state. The *polis*, the organized small-city community, represents the natural fruition of man's sociality. The sophists had insisted on a dichotomy between nature and convention; Aristotle thus took his stand on the natural, rather than the conventional or contractual character of social relations. Direct participation in the constitutional processes of the *polis* is the essence of citizenship, and the megalopolitan society, with its lone isolated individuals, is contrary to nature. While in the *Ethics* Aristotle classified basic types of association in terms of the *individual* motivations of "utility," "pleasure," and "common ideals," in the *Politics* he studied the specific *social* relations: master–slave, husband–wife, parent–child, ruler–ruled. He was attentive to qualitative distinctions in the different relations rather than subsuming all political phenomena under a single concept of power or dominance–submission. The conservative potential in his natural order concept is seen in his defense of slavery and of the inferior position of women, as befitting a lower rationality, more capable of following a prescribed good than of actively understanding it.

The ideal order that Aristotle projected is an *aristocracy*, emphasizing the quality of men and apportioning rule according to merit. He regarded this not as inequality but as a proportionate type of equality, contrasting with *oligarchic* apportion-ment (according to wealth) and *democratic* apportionment (numerical or arithmetic equality). He did not expect conditions in most societies to be favorable for the ideal order, and his preponderant concern, therefore, was with the analysis and evaluation of existent forms.

The classification of constitutions is twofold: (*a*) a dichotomy between *genuine* forms, directed to the common interest, and *perverted* forms, exploitative on behalf of the ruling party; and (*b*) a numerical classification of rulers into one or few or many. This dual classification yields kingship, aristocracy, and polity (rule by numerous substantial citizens) as genuine forms and tyranny, oligarchy, and democracy as perversions on behalf of the monarchy, the wealthy, and the poor, respectively. Behind this formal classification lies an active concern with locating the vital operative differences in the character and organization of society. Thus he identified oligarchy as rule of the rich rather than merely of the few, and democracy, with its equalitarian slogans, as expressive of the interests of the poor. His examination of subtypes in each of the major divisions—for example, five varieties of kingship, five of democracy, four of oligarchy—reveals both their socioeconomic bases and the conditions under which they may be expected to function. Special detailed attention is paid to the sources of revolution, and, in an almost detached spirit, Aristotle suggested how particular forms may avoid it. A sense of inequality is seen as particularly conducive to revolution.

Aristotle took the central fact of political life in the states of his time to be the war between rich and poor. His prescription for harmony between citizens is *polity*—a kind of middle-class rule. This is congruent with his general opinion that correctness lies in the mean. In his theory of moral virtue, each virtue is construed as a mean between two vices, for example, courage is a mean between rashness and timidity, harmonizing natural feelings of fear and confidence into a stable pattern. In the *Politics*, the mean consists in balancing the opposite forces of oligarchy and democracy, so that both the arrogance of wealth and the despair of poverty may be avoided. Numerous governmental compromise devices similar to checks and balances are suggested by him. His general attitude to the democratic masses was far more favorable than might have been expected from a disciple of Plato. Aristotle did not regard the mass of men as having a dragonlike appetite that can only be repressed rather than assuaged. He saw appetite as plastic raw material for virtue or vice and men as capable of exercising considerable collective judgment on the effects of policies and the adequacy of rulers.

Aristotle's *Politics* has served as a foundation work for the whole Western tradition. It had a central influence from the thirteenth to the fifteenth century, notably in the political thought of Thomas Aquinas and subsequent Christian political thinkers and also in diverging lines such as the political Averroism of Marsilius of Padua. From the sixteenth century on, particular strands in the Aristotelian work stimulated various developments in politics: for example, his economic treatment of politics influenced Harrington in the seventeenth century; sociological elements were taken up by Montesquieu in the eighteenth century; and his concept of community influenced idealist political philosophies such as those of T. H. Green and Bosanquet in the nineteenth century. Apart from the specific content of Aristotle's work, his general concept of a natural order for man with permanent institutional forms has attracted antirelativist and antievolutionary political theorists. On the contemporary scene, it is often fused with attempted revivals of natural law.

Economic concepts. In Aristotle's discussions of household management, of the art of acquisition, and of conflicts over property forms, we find basic analyses of production, distribution, and exchange. Aristotle recognized that different modes of production yield different ways of life, and he was conscious of the limits imposed by productive processes; for example, he fantasied an automation myth, in which shuttles move of themselves, as the one condition that would render slavery unnecessary. His general preference was for the society of agricultural estates, not highly intensified commercial society. In analyzing exchange, he distinguished in effect between use value and exchange value and offered a theory of money as a conventional device for indirect exchange. This condemnation of the use of money to produce more money in usury, which he saw as an unnatural distortion of ends, had great influence on medieval views of this subject. Against Plato, he defended private property, largely for its influence on character and the promotion of responsibility; but he was ready to allow considerable social demands on private property for public purposes [*see* ECONOMIC THOUGHT, *article on* ANCIENT AND MEDIEVAL THOUGHT].

Legal concepts. Aristotle seems to have been especially interested in legal concepts. In the *Ethics,* he distinguished *distributive* justice, and the different principles of distribution in different types of constitutions, from *corrective* justice,

which restores the balance upset by man's wrongdoing. His concept of natural justice, distinguished from that of conventional regulations by its universal force, is a precursor of much subsequent natural law theory. A concept of equity is advanced to meet the complexity of particular conditions and the approximate character of legislative enactment. In the *Politics,* rule of law is preferred to rule of the legislator, chiefly as a protective device against corruption. The *Rhetoric,* essentially a handbook of training in legislative and judicial controversy, includes much on specific legal method and legal argumentation, combining psychological, ethical, logical, and stylistic materials. In this work, all the tricks of the trade are revealed, but not without a central moral focus on the public's welfare.

Education. Aristotle's moral and political writings include considerable treatment of educational themes. Moral virtues are to be developed by practice, with a master as model, rather than through intellectual learning. The process of learning culminates in the development of the facility to make moral decisions, the sensitively cultivated perceptions of men of "practical wisdom." Similarly, the propaedeutic role of laws and institutions is as strong in Aristotle's thought as it was in that of Plato or John Stuart Mill. The unfinished, last part of the *Politics* deals specifically with education. Tying his theory of education to an analysis of human psychology and the ethical theory of the good, he urges that industry be regarded as only a means to leisure and war as only a means to peace. Hence public education is primarily turned to the activities of peaceful leisure, and its goals embrace training for character, citizenship, and cultural pursuits. Cultivation of rational ability and critical judgment is pivotal. For example, Aristotle asked whether liberal education should include learning to play a musical instrument; he concluded that it should, but only up to the point necessary for acquiring sound judgment of musical performance.

ABRAHAM EDEL

[*For the historical context of Aristotle's work, see* ECONOMIC THOUGHT, *article on* ANCIENT AND MEDIEVAL THOUGHT *and the biography of* PLATO. *For discussion of the influence of his ideas, see* JUSTICE; NATURAL LAW; POLITICAL THEORY; *and the biographies of* AQUINAS; BOSANQUET; GREEN; HARRINGTON; MARSILIUS OF PADUA; MONTESQUIEU.]

WORKS BY ARISTOTLE

Works. Translated into English under the editorship of W. D. Ross. 12 vols. Oxford: Clarendon, 1908–1952.
[*Works*]. The Loeb Classical Library, Greek Authors. 17 vols.

Cambridge, Mass.: Harvard Univ. Press, 1926–1965. → Each volume entered separately. The Greek text is given with the English on facing pages.

Politics. Edited with an introduction, notes, and appendices by Ernest Barker. Oxford Univ. Press, 1946. → A paperback edition was published in 1958 by Oxford University Press.

SUPPLEMENTARY BIBLIOGRAPHY

JAEGER, WERNER W. (1923) 1948 *Aristotle: Fundamentals of the History of His Development.* 2d ed. Oxford: Clarendon. → First published in German. A paperback edition was published in 1962 by Oxford University Press. A major twentieth-century developmental study.

ORGAN, TROY W. 1949 *An Index to Aristotle in English Translation.* Princeton Univ. Press.

RANDALL, JOHN H., JR. 1960 *Aristotle.* New York: Columbia Univ. Press. → An interpretative study of Aristotle's ideas as living philosophical outlook in modern context. A paperback edition was published in 1962 by Columbia University Press.

ROSS, WILLIAM D. (1923) 1960 *Aristotle.* 5th ed., rev. London: Methuen. → The most complete study. A paperback edition was published by Meridian Books.

ARMS CONTROL

See DISARMAMENT.

ART

A number of articles in the encyclopedia deal with the arts and their relation to society. The traditional fields of art are discussed in ARCHITECTURE; DRAMA; FINE ARTS; LITERATURE; MUSIC. *There is also an article on* FILM. *Some theories of art are reviewed in* AESTHETICS; FASHION; STYLE. *For some anthropological aspects of art, see* FOLKLORE; MUSIC, *article on* ETHNOMUSICOLOGY; PRIMITIVE ART. *Material bearing on the preindustrial organization of the arts will be found in* CRAFTS. *The articles under* CREATIVITY *explore the problem of identifying the social, economic, and psychological factors that make possible outstanding achievement in the arts and sciences. Also relevant to one or more of these areas are the biographies of* BOAS; COOLEY; CROCE; DEWEY; JUNG; RANK; SAPIR; SOROKIN.

ASHLEY, WILLIAM JAMES

William James Ashley (1860–1927) was one of a group of economists (including, among others, William Cunningham, H. S. Foxwell, and W. A. S. Hewins) who at the turn of this century constituted the English school of economic history, the school which had been given its form in the 1870s and 1880s by Thorold Rogers and Arnold Toynbee. Ashley, alone of this group, also had ties with the German school of historical economists, which under the leadership of Gustav Schmoller had, from the 1870s on, posited a historical, statistical, and inductive method against the abstract, deductive method of the classical school of Ricardo.

Ashley was born in Bermondsey. His father was a journeyman hatter of modest means—a Baptist, a teetotaler, and a free trader. Ashley began his career at Oxford in 1878 as a history scholar in Balliol. There his interests were shaped under the influence of Toynbee, William Stubbs, and Sir Henry Sumner Maine. He took a First in History in 1881 and remained at Oxford for several years as a private tutor. In 1888 he was invited to occupy the chair of political economy and constitutional history at Toronto; in that same year the first part of his *An Introduction to English Economic History and Theory*, dedicated to Toynbee, was published. It proved to be a landmark in the field. In 1892 Ashley accepted an invitation from President Eliot of Harvard to fill the first chair in economic history in the world. The second part of his *Introduction*, which made an important contribution to medieval agrarian and burghal history, appeared in 1893. In 1901 Ashley returned home to become professor of commerce at the new University of Birmingham, helping to organize the first university school of commerce in the United Kingdom.

It was from the German historical economists that Ashley learned "the duty of generalization as the complement to the duty of research" (1900, p. 29). From a liberal cosmopolitanism, he was converted to the nationalist and protectionist position of his German mentors; he also adopted their social doctrine, which bore the label *Kathedersozialismus* ("socialism of the chair") and which called for state action to protect trade unions, to promote factory legislation, and to enact social reforms. Although Ashley had a better understanding of orthodox economic analysis than did the German school, he shared the latter's view of "modern economic theories," which, he declared, are "not universally true; they are true neither for the past, when the conditions they postulate did not exist, nor for the future, when, unless society becomes stationary, the conditions will have changed" (1888–1893, p. xi).

Believing that history could serve as a guide for policy, Ashley turned his attention to eighteenth-century mercantilism in essays on "The Tory Origin of Free Trade Policy" and "The Commercial Legislation of England and the American Colonies" in his *Surveys, Historic and Economic* (1900). When Joseph Chamberlain announced his neomercantilist proposals for imperial preference in 1903, Ashley and Hewins came actively to his support, especially since, along with imperialist and protectionist planks, Chamberlain had included a pension scheme reminiscent of Bismarckian social reform; orthodox economists, led by Alfred Marshall, remained loyal to free trade.

In 1912 Ashley reviewed the whole of English economic history in eight lectures delivered at Hamburg; these appeared as *The Economic Organisation of England* in 1914. In these lectures he envisioned a future society based upon the corporative theories that were being revived on the Continent; Ashley was alone among English economists in defending these theories. He saw both trusts and trade unions as inevitable parts of capitalist development and welcomed them as mitigating the evil effects of competition, which, he felt, led to crises and unemployment. He foresaw a corporation organization of both industry and labor, regulated by the state in the community interest.

Ashley's pioneering efforts in economic history had borne such fruit that, as early as 1913, he could say that "the study of specifically economic history is no longer an individual eccentricity, calling almost for an apology" (1913, p. 165). Ashley also sat on a number of governmental commissions, to which he made noteworthy contributions, and he was knighted for such services in 1917. (This governmental activity continued after his retirement from his duties at Birmingham in 1925.) In 1923 Ashley delivered the Ford lectures at Oxford, on the place of rye in the English diet. In the years that remained, he continued these researches, and the result, *The Bread of Our Forefathers*, was published posthumously, in 1928.

BERNARD SEMMEL

[*For the historical context of Ashley's work, see* ECONOMIC THOUGHT, *articles on* MERCANTILIST THOUGHT *and* THE HISTORICAL SCHOOL; *and the biographies of* CUNNINGHAM; MAINE; ROGERS; SCHMOLLER; TOYNBEE. *For discussion of the subsequent development of his ideas, see* HISTORY, *article on* ECONOMIC HISTORY.]

WORKS BY ASHLEY

(1888–1893) 1931–1936 *An Introduction to English Economic History and Theory*. 2 vols. London and New York: Longmans. → Volume 1: The Middle Ages. Volume 2: The End of the Middle Ages.

1900 *Surveys, Historic and Economic*. London and New York: Longmans. → Includes essays first published between 1889 and 1900.

(1903) 1920 *The Tariff Problem*. 4th ed. London: King.

1904 *The Progress of the German Working Classes in the Last Quarter of a Century*. London and New York: Longmans.

1913 Comparative Economic History and the English Landlord. *Economic Journal* 23:165–181.

(1914) 1949 *The Economic Organisation of England: An Outline History*. 3d ed. London and New York: Longmans.

1925 *The Christian Outlook, Being the Sermons of an Economist*. London and New York: Longmans.

1928 *The Bread of Our Forefathers: An Inquiry in Economic History*. Oxford: Clarendon.

SUPPLEMENTARY BIBLIOGRAPHY

ASHLEY, ANNE 1932 *William James Ashley: A Life*. London: King.

CLAPHAM, JOHN H. 1927 Obituary: Sir William Ashley. *Economic Journal* 37:678–683.

MACDONALD, JANET L. 1942 Sir William Ashley. Pages 20–44 in Bernadotte E. Schmitt (editor), *Some Historians of Modern Europe: Essays in Historiography by Former Students of the University of Chicago*. Univ. of Chicago Press.

SEMMEL, BERNARD 1957 Sir William Ashley as "Socialist of the Chair." *Economica* New Series 24:343–353.

ASIAN SOCIETY

The articles under this heading describe the societies of the Indian subcontinent and southeast Asia. Other Asian societies are described in CHINESE SOCIETY; JAPANESE SOCIETY; NEAR EASTERN SOCIETY; OCEANIAN SOCIETY.

Discussions of Asian philosophical, political, and religious thought will be found under BUDDHISM; CHINESE POLITICAL THOUGHT; HINDUISM; INDIAN POLITICAL THOUGHT; ISLAM; POLLUTION. *Aspects of Asian economies are discussed under* AGRICULTURE; ECONOMIC DATA; ECONOMY, DUAL; FAMINE; FOOD; LAND; LAND TENURE; PASTORALISM; PEASANTRY; PLANTATIONS. *The social structure of some of the societies of Asia is discussed in* CASTE; KINSHIP; MODERNIZATION, *article on* THE BOURGEOISIE IN MODERNIZING SOCIETIES. *For the arts of Asia, see especially* DRAMA. *See also the relevant articles under* HISTORIOGRAPHY *and the biographies of* BOGORAZ, STERNBERG, AND JOCHELSON; GRANET; MAJUMDAR; RADLOV AND BARTOL'D; SCHRIEKE; SNOUCK; WEBER, MAX.

I. SOUTH ASIA   *F. G. Bailey*
II. SOUTHEAST ASIA   *W. F. Wertheim*

I
SOUTH ASIA

The term "south Asia," which covers the countries of India, Pakistan, Ceylon, and some smaller autonomous or semiautonomous states in the Himalayas, has come into use since the partition of British India in 1947. In area and population India is by far the largest of these countries. Partly for this reason, but more because the volume of research into Indian society and culture far exceeds that on the other countries, the present account will concern mainly India.

The area as a whole, and India within the area, displays a considerable diversity. Habitats range from perennial snows in the northern mountains to tropical rain forests in the south and east, and from deserts in the northwest to areas in the east which have the heaviest rainfall in the world. The range of culture is no less great. In the remoter jungles there are still tribes who hunt and gather wild foods, and who go naked and are innocent of any civilization. Elsewhere are found centers of some of the world's most ancient civilizations, with religious and philosophical writings of a high degree of sophistication: three of the world's major religions—Hinduism, Buddhism, and Islam—are substantially represented in the area. Finally, a high degree of technical and economic complexity characteristic of modern industrial society is also to be found, especially in such major urban centers as Bombay or Calcutta.

One can only deal with such diversity by seeking principles of social organization which are common to all, or to a large part, of the population. Some of these principles are the distinctive and peculiar characteristics of south Asian society: others are more general. I intend to analyze Indian society from the point of view of the forms of social organization which are common to south Asia and to other parts of the world. For example, the caste system will be regarded not as a uniquely Indian manifestation of religious ideas about pollution but as one form of social stratification. There are several early kinds of source materials that are genetically linked with contemporary social studies.

Hinduism and Islam have both provided a wealth of religious, philosophical, and legal writings that have sociological implications. Indeed, this is one characteristic which distinguishes south Asia from the primitive areas of the world, and it is this which gives direction to both the schools of thought to be discussed here. One school sets out to link "folk" culture to this higher civilization; the other maintains that a careful study of this writing will reveal certain basic values or patterns of social thought which are distinctively Hindu (or Islamic, as the case may be) and without which we cannot understand contemporary south Asian society.

Second, there is a great volume of descriptive writing which arose out of the needs of the British administration in India and was largely done by administrators. This material is found in census reports, settlement reports, and many other kinds of documents and records. Some of this documentation is addressed to particular problems in particular areas, but there is also much written at one remove, so to speak, from the immediate administrative problems. Some of these writings are general descriptions of particular tribes (for example, the monographs by Hutton, Mills, and others on the Assam tribes), and others are encyclopedic (the various "Tribe and Caste" series). These works are valuable factual sources, although they sometimes incorporate old theoretical frameworks, for example, unilinear evolution.

There are also, third, a few but important works of theory, drawing on both the classical sources (mainly Sanskrit) and the descriptive work and concerned mostly with understanding of the caste system. Works by Hocart, Senart, and Bouglé are examples.

The present scene in the study of south Asian society was set in the decade after World War II. Between the wars and during World War II, with few exceptions, professional anthropologists who carried on research in south Asia directed their attention exclusively to tribal peoples who were to varying degrees removed from the civilizing influences of Hinduism and Islam. But the greater part of the research done in the decade of the 1950s concerned Hindu or Islamic communities and produced a number of "village studies." The results of many of these studies were summarized in outline in *Village India* (Marriott 1955) and in *India's Villages* (The Economic Weekly 1951–1954), although the editorial theme of the first collection of essays, and some contributions to the second symposium, questioned the value of studying single villages and communities.

The greater part of these village studies used the conceptual framework of social anthropology. This method has its origins in the study of what Redfield called "primitive isolates." Village studies made in India were criticized on the grounds that Indian villages are neither primitive nor isolated and that the method of structural analysis was therefore insufficient.

I think the criticism is misdirected insofar as it is aimed at the method of structural analysis. Structural analysis does not depend upon finding units which are literally and absolutely isolated. The question is rather one of determining whether or not a village (or a region, or a caste, or a particular institution) can be conceptually isolated for purposes of study, and this depends upon the intensity of social relationships within the chosen boundaries. Although relationships within villages are becoming less important than they were, over most of south Asia the village remains an important locus of social relationships. Insofar as the criticism makes the point that besides the villages there are also patterns of social organization centering upon markets, or upon descent systems of particular communities, or upon religious sects, or political parties, and that these are worthy of study, then it is valid. But it is invalid insofar as it suggests that structural analysis cannot be applied beyond the boundaries of an isolated village and that the job is better done by a type of cultural analysis.

The analysis of total cultures. Criticism of the method of structural analysis of villages was also directed to the fact that the people of these villages are not primitive but enjoy the heritage of a great civilization. Just as the villages of Ceylon or Pakistan or India are not isolated from the point of view of social relations, so also (the argument ran) they are not culturally isolated. A structural analysis of villages in these countries presents only a part of the lives of the people. A more complete analysis would be achieved by understanding the civilization they share.

The motives and intentions which give form to this method are set forth in *Peasant Society and Culture* (Redfield 1956). In its broadest aspect this method is an attempt to apprehend the world view or philosophy of life—one might almost say the mood—which characterizes and gives shape to a civilization. To grasp the totality of a culture in this way is difficult because cultures are very diverse and exhibit different levels of sophistication, and the main task then becomes that of demonstrating the connection between the different levels and showing that they are in fact a whole.

The basic concept of this approach is that of "tradition." The referent of this word is very wide and includes not only the heritage of social ideas but also particular forms of art, literature, and so forth, and particular items within these forms. Traditions exist at two levels: one, the level of those who are educated, literate, and sophisticated (the great tradition); and the other the level of the villager, a relatively primitive tradition and one preserved by word of mouth rather than in writing (the little tradition). But between these two levels there are lines of communication, so that items of village culture form part of and give shape to the great tradition (universalization), while in turn items from the great tradition become part of village culture (parochialization). These terms are used by Marriott (1955). By the use of this framework we can grasp—the argument runs—not the innumerable uncoordinated fragments of culture in the different villages but the totality of a civilization.

There are some general comments to be made concerning the actual use of this framework in research, for it seems to me to offer the possibility of two quite distinct operational schemes by which the hypotheses of universalization and parochialization may be tested. The first alternative focuses attention upon the morphology of cultural complexes or individual elements. An element or a complex which is recorded in a sacred text and is therefore part of the great tradition may be identified with an element or complex found in village rites and ceremonies by the fact that both elements possess a common attribute; or, one may work the same process from the ground upward, so to speak, by first witnessing the element in the village and later identifying it in a sacred text. The next step is to look at the other attributes which are connected with the identifying attribute at both levels and, if they differ, to try to explain why they differ. The procedure is excellently illustrated in the second part of Marriott's essay (1955). This method directs attention to the form and content of cultural elements and complexes with the aim of producing a chart of the geographical distribution of cultural elements and tracing them through what we may call the contours of society. Needless to say, the task is an immense one, and it requires a linguistic and cultural training far in excess of that possessed by most social anthropologists.

It was possibly these difficulties that caused exponents of this method to pay greater attention to the sociological problems posed by the idea of a great and a little tradition. Under this second alternative, the student focuses not so much upon the morphological similarities and differences of cultural elements as upon the fact that these elements, whatever they are, must be transmitted both upward and downward by people: indeed, both individuals and institutions may have roles which seem to have the transmission of culture as one of their most significant functions. The centers of pilgrimage are obvious examples. Yet these institutions can be structurally analyzed in terms of social roles. In south Asia the interest in civilization and tradition will no doubt govern the choice of institutions selected for study and will also produce a fuller description of the content of culture than that found in some other institutional studies. But the result is unlikely to be methodological innovation. The conceptual framework by means of which villages are studied as if they were isolated wholes is basically the tool that is also used for the sociological study of a monastery or a temple town, for these institutions too require conceptual boundaries before we can study them as social systems.

Indology. The next approach to the study of

south Asian society which I wish briefly to outline and comment upon is that of the Indologists, as exemplified by Dumont in *Contributions to Indian Sociology*. The discussion concerns India and Hinduism but is equally relevant to Islam or Buddhism.

The distinctive characteristic of this approach is that it directs our attention not so much at regular forms of social interaction but rather at the ideas which are implicit in those interactions or which are explicitly held by the actors: that is to say, it is concerned with "representations." In my opinion societies can usefully be conceived of as natural systems. The Indologists (in common with many other social anthropologists) argue that social systems are to be distinguished from natural systems because they include an element of consciousness. We cannot understand social systems (the argument runs) unless we closely analyze the motives, values, and ideas that inspire behavior. We understand a society by understanding its social philosophy, the mental constructs which the people themselves make about their social interaction, or which we can see implied in that social interaction.

Unlike primitive societies, the countries of south Asia already have a developed and sophisticated indigenous literature in social philosophy, which is itself the object of scholarly comment by historians, philologists, and others. The social anthropologists whom I have called Indologists not only take account of this literature but also make its explication one of their main objectives. One of the dangers of this approach is that the linguistic and other skills required to use this material successfully are so great that the scholar tends to leave aside material from other sources to which his Indological skills cannot be applied. The Indology, so to speak, tends to push aside, or at least to restrict, the sociology.

It would be misleading, however, to imply that commentary upon and explication of the sacred literature is the only intention of the Indologists: their aim is, in fact, much wider. Like the exponents of the "total culture" approach discussed in the previous section, they are disturbed by the somewhat fragmented picture which structural studies of Indian society have so far produced, and their aim is to portray Indian society as a unity.

This task is made easier by the definition of the word "society" as a system of ideas. In the structural approach a society is conceived of as bounded by interaction. According to the Indologists' definition, those who hold the same set of ideas about social interaction belong to the same society, although they may never interact with one another.

Thus, in respect of their different social philosophies, the Hindu, Muslim, and Christian families who are neighbors in the same village belong to different societies, while Hindus everywhere (or Muslims or Christians, as the case may be) belong to the same society. Such a conceptual framework is clearly useful for those whose main aim is to analyze the systems of ideas about society found in Hinduism, Islam, or Christianity.

From the point of view of a wider sociology, this approach has some disadvantages. There seems to me to be an important gap between a philosophy of society and an actual system of social relationships—between a system of social interaction and its "representations." By definition there is no gap when the "representations" are the constructs of the investigator, that is to say, when he is exploring the "implicit" connections between regular forms of social interaction. But when his raw material is drawn from the explicit "representations" of the people he is studying, there is certainly the possibility that these are not an accurate reflection of actual behavior, for they may well be, to name only one possibility, propagandist in intention. Propaganda too, of course, is legitimate sociological data, providing that one handles it as propaganda and not as a description of actual behavior.

These disadvantages are much increased when the investigator seeks to link behavior which he observes in the field with social philosophy found in the sacred texts of Hinduism or Islam. No doubt there are some points of contact, and it may well be that our understanding of what is distinctively Indian in the behavior of Indian party politicians or Indian capitalist entrepreneurs will be increased by a study of the social philosophy of Hinduism. At least, the hypothesis is worth investigating. But it seems to me that the understanding which we derive from this source alone will be jejune compared with the understanding which we find by observing the behavior of party politicians or capitalists elsewhere.

This leads to my second comment. The Indological approach seems likely to frustrate comparative sociology, at least in the short run. Indologists do not admit this, for their aim is first to isolate a distinctively Indian society and then to compare it with other societies. It seems to me that such a comparison is likely to be between elements which are so abstract that they give us little understanding of actual behavior. But more important is the fact that working toward a "total" picture of Hindu society or Islamic society seems to block the chance of making fruitful comparisons of particular institutions in India and elsewhere. We can illustrate, this by a brief consideration of the Indian caste system.

In structural analysis the ritual concomitants of the caste system (behavior indicating ideas about relative purity) can be described as a means of making public differences in political and economic status. All systems of social stratification seem to have ritual epiphenomena of this kind, although none so developed as the caste system in India. To this extent ritual differentiates the caste system from other forms of social stratification. But in the school of Indology, religious ideas about purity and pollution *are* the caste system, and the investigator's task is to show the systematic connection between these ideas. By doing so he may well explain what is distinctively Indian about the caste system; but it seems to me that if he does this and no more he has left in darkness the other seven-eighths of the picture—in which the caste system is a means of organizing political and economic relationships—to be understood in the comparative light of systems of stratification elsewhere.

The idiosyncrasies of Indian social philosophy are a legitimate field of investigation for a sociologist with the required linguistic and other skills. But it is also true that a knowledge of the traditional social philosophy of Hinduism (or of Islam), no matter how deep, does not of itself provide more than a minimal understanding of fragments of contemporary systems of social interaction.

An outline of south Asian society

The simplest short analysis of south Asian societies rests not upon a characteristic institution or complex of institutions but rather upon a characteristic process of change. I shall describe two institutional complexes placed on a continuum, one end of which represents a hypothetical and simplified picture of the recent past, while the other end represents what I conjecture will be the future. Any society in south Asia can be understood by placing it somewhere on this continuum and by showing how and why this society seems to be moving from one end toward the other.

In other words, one end of the continuum is represented by the simple society and the opposite end by the complex society. The criterion of simplicity is the degree to which social roles and social institutions are specialized and separated from one another according to activity. Thus, in a city in a highly industrialized state, a man may have economic relationships with one set of people, political relationships with another set, and kinship relationships with a third set; and he may conduct his religious activities with a fourth set. What happens in one type of activity may affect his relationships in another, but in each case a different set of people is involved. In a simple society, on the other hand, not only do all these activities tend to be performed with one and the same set of people, but the different roles tend to be fused into one, so that we may say that kinship is the "master principle" of one society or that the caste system is the guiding institution in another. There are other criteria as well to distinguish simple from complex societies, some connected logically and some empirically with this main distinction, which is based upon the clustering of roles. For example, simpler societies tend to have a narrower range of social relationships and to be based upon less developed economies than complex societies.

My first broad description of south Asian society is that it is changing and that the direction of change is from the simple toward the complex. I would insist that this is an empirical statement capable of verification, a matter of historical fact. But even if the historical statement is doubted, the framework still has its use as a means of classification. We could ignore the fact of change and place the different social systems in south Asia in categories, according to their respective degrees of simplicity or complexity.

This would give three very broad categories of system: tribal, village, and complex. These names are not very satisfactory, for they suggest cultural rather than social criteria, different ways of life rather than different patterns of social relationships. Furthermore, they are logical categories of social relationships, so that any given field may—and in fact does—exhibit more than one category: for example, there are Rajputs or Jats or Pathans or even Gonds, whose interactions fit into both the tribal and the village categories, and in some cases into the complex category as well. But for the moment I can speak roughly as if these were in fact population categories.

The dominant characteristic of the tribal peoples is that they are divided into groups which are all equal and none of which is ranked above or below another. The groups, in other words, are horizontally arranged, and the pattern of relationships is segmentary. This does not mean that there are no tribal chieftains, nor that a father is not the head of his family; it does mean that there is no corporate class of chieftains to be set against a corporate class of subjects. In short, *individuals* may be ranked and individual roles may be invested with authority; but the *groups* into which the population is divided—typically clans or lineages in a system of unilineal descent—are not ranked above and below one another.

Units within village society also have this segmentary pattern, but the units themselves are set in a system of institutionalized ranks. When we look at the village as a whole, the dominant characteristic is that its groups are not equal but are related to one another in activities which express superiority and inferiority: that is to say, village society is stratified, and its groups are vertically arranged.

Both village and tribal types of society fall within our category of simple, for in both there is a tendency for roles to be clustered and for relationships to be multiplex. In economic, political, and religious activities (and kinship activities too, in the case of the tribes) one man is likely to interact with the same set of people; and his role in one activity is likely to be consistent with, if not entirely fused with, his roles in other activities. Thus a relationship of brotherhood between two Kond tribesmen entails rights and duties which concern not only kinship but also politics, economics, and religion.

The complex category is more difficult to describe, beyond the bare statement that roles tend not to be clustered and that different activities are carried on with different sets of people. A positive description is difficult because our conceptual apparatus makes it far from easy to handle the institutions of a complex society in the same deft way that we have learned to deal with social institutions in simple, bounded communities. But we can at least add that while roles in complex systems tend not to be clustered, these systems are stratified, although the form of this stratification is very different from that found in the villages.

I am not here postulating a single unilinear course of necessary evolution, so that tribal people today will become village people tomorrow and in the end south Asia will be one vast complex society. But I am saying that the process of change which is to be seen everywhere in south Asia at the present time is tending to replace simple patterns of social interaction by more complex patterns: multiplex relationships are giving way to relatively single-interest relationships.

In the following sections I shall deal first with kinship in rural India as an example of the segmentary pattern of relationships which are characteristic of total tribal societies or whole castes. Second I shall describe the relationship between units in village societies; and third I shall consider change and describe the complex society which is so far only fragmentarily exemplified in south Asia.

Kin groups in rural India. In this description I assume a rule of patrilineal descent: in some parts of India other rules of descent are (or were) used —traditional Malabar is a well-known case in point. Obviously my analysis does not apply to such examples, but I insist that an analysis of the same type—one which asks the same kind of questions —could be applied.

What are these questions? First, what are the main groups into which people are divided on the basis of kinship? In this context the word "group" is strictly defined by the criterion of interaction and is not used as a loose equivalent of "category," which means a collection of persons with a similar attribute. By "the basis of kinship" I mean rules of descent and rules of marriage. Second, what functions are performed by the division of people into such groups? Through which group is property transmitted or managed? What are the rules of succession? Which group takes care of and socializes the children, and so forth? Third, having divided the people into groups, we ask the complementary question: How are these groups linked together so as to form a whole?

In general there are four levels of grouping. The largest is the tribe or the caste, and this is bounded by a rule of endogamy, across which there can be no kinship relationships. At the second level the tribe or caste is divided exhaustively into unilineal descent groups bounded by a rule of exogamy, which proscribes marriage between descendants of a common ancestor. At the third level these clans or lineages may be divided into smaller agnatic groups, joint families defined by common ownership of property and sometimes by coresidence. At the fourth level there are nuclear families consisting of a man, his wife, and their children.

Dividing the population of a caste or tribe into groups at four different levels means that every person—for simplicity let us say every adult man —has a set of rights and duties at each of these levels, as a member of a nuclear family, sometimes of a joint family, of an extended family or lineage or clan, and as a member of the caste or tribe. The first task is to show to what extent the different roles that a man possesses are consistent with one another.

In order to do this a distinction must be made between corporate groups and ego-centered groups: that is to say, from the point of view of an individual, between his unilineal kin and his kindred. Apart from the four sets of rights and duties which a man has toward those of the same descent as himself, he also has various prescribed roles toward those not of the same descent. Besides the roles of father, son, and brother (this last being widely defined to include clan or lineage brothers), a man is also a husband, son-in-law, brother-in-law, maternal uncle, father-in-law, and so forth, to people of different descent from himself.

These two kinds of roles give rise to two different kinds of groups. Descent groups are corporations in the strict sense: they exist independently of any one member and possess continuity. If one divides the population by descent—to put the point another way—there can be no overlapping: a man cannot belong to two joint families or two lineages. On the other hand, ego-centered groups are not corporations with clearly defined boundaries; they exist only with reference to an individual, and they vanish when he dies. Membership overlaps: for example, a man may belong to the ego-centered groups of his wife, his daughter-in-law, his brother, his sister, his mother's brother, and very many other individuals.

Kinship thus divides people in two ways. A rule of descent provides a "hard" division into groups which are exhaustive and clearly defined from one another. The word "hard" is also appropriate because such groups usually deal with the management and transmission of property and are likely to be in conflict with one another in various ways. But the division between such groups is rendered less sharp by ties of marriage and kin links springing from marriage between persons in different descent groups. These "soft" kinship links serve to lessen a man's commitment to his own descent group and to separate and identify him within the group of unilineal kinsmen. At the same time they are the network—perhaps web is a better metaphor—which binds the descent groups together into one caste or tribe.

Consider, for example, the relationship of husband and wife in rural areas and its connection with the joint family. She never uses his name but addresses him by teknonymy, a way of showing respect; she serves him before she has her own meal; she walks behind him, never at his side; she would not sit beside him in a public place; affection is never publicly demonstrated; men take their leisure with other men and never with their wives. Such customs seem to be saying two things: first, that the woman is subordinate, and second, that if there is a strong bond of affection between husband and wife, this bond must be concealed or even denied in the interests of the husband's other obligations, namely toward his brothers.

This is especially true when the couple live in a joint family household and the wife is under the control of her mother-in-law. It seems to be expected that this relationship will be an unhappy one; and the wife, especially when she has children of her own, may want her own kitchen and her own storeroom, and ultimately she may urge her husband to demand partition of the family land. The husband is thus faced with a direct conflict of obligation and must choose between solidarity with his brothers or separation from his brothers and a closer relationship with his wife.

Such conflicts are inevitable, and various institutions exist within a caste or a tribe for their settlement. An indication of the importance of kinship is that no person, man or woman, stands alone in a dispute. One reason why a wife can be strong in a quarrel in her husband's house, and may ultimately be able to force partition, is that she has the support and help of her own descent group. Thus, in troubles that may occur after marriage—and more especially in the often troubled negotiations leading up to marriage—the parties to the dispute are not just a man and a woman but their respective descent groups mobilized through such linking relationships as the wife's brother or the mother's brother. To resolve such troubles there are councils, often *ad hoc*, consisting of parties in the dispute and some representatives of the society at large.

We have at this point returned to the "hard" divisions, for if two brothers quarrel, then the dispute is likely to be mediated (at least in the first instance) by the remainder of the joint family; if two joint families are at odds, then the other joint families of the lineage will try to settle the conflict; and if two descent groups quarrel (as in the negotiations for a marriage), then the caste (or the tribe, as the case may be) decides the issue. The fact that other people can legitimately intervene in a quarrel brings home to both parties that they belong to one group, and in fact such regular institutionalized intervention is part of the complex of interactions that make up the lineage, or caste, or any other "hard" group.

Two further points remain to be made about this segmentary framework of horizontally arranged groups. First, the picture that I have drawn is no more than an outline, for many elaborations are possible. In particular I have not discussed the variations in relative status of wife and husband and of their respective kin groups. These variations depend very much on the amount of property that they possess and that is involved in the marriage. Roughly speaking, property is an important consideration in high castes and less important in low castes. But the very boldness of the outline is in a way appropriate, since no one can begin to understand the life of a peasant in India unless he realizes that many of the social interactions which make up his life are with kinsmen of one kind or another. The outline should be drawn heavily because kinsmen represent a major dimension of social life. Kinship institutions are important in economic life; they are also a source of protection, advice, help, and discipline. Relatives provide the security and identity which in our differentiated complex society we expect to get from the state and its agencies or from voluntary associations.

Second, the analytical framework used here has been developed less in India than in Africa. It tells us nothing which is essentially and specifically peculiar to south Asia, but it does tell us how Indian rural society is broadly organized. Our understanding of that society has, for several decades, been vitiated by undue emphasis on its more bizarre aspects. This is especially true of the caste system.

Stratification—the organic pattern. The interaction between social groups discussed in the preceding section is characteristically between units of equal rank. But where a caste system is found, such an analysis would refer to one caste in the society. As will be seen, the economic and political content of relationships between segments is very considerably modified by the fact that a large part of political and economic interaction takes place between castes and not within them. These relationships between castes are not between equals but between members of hierarchically organized units.

The most important context in which this hierarchical system operates is a village, or sometimes a cluster of villages. Assuming that a village can be treated as an isolable unit, it is possible to say categorically that any caste is divided territorially into segments. The segment that lives in one village, which in some areas is also a descent group, I call a "caste group," and I shall be concerned in this section with the relationship between the different caste groups in one village.

I have already remarked that the relationship between the segments within a caste is one of institutionalized equality. This means that the segments resemble one another in form and function and are equivalent to one another. The whole caste is no more than an aggregate of like units, and if one unit were to die out or another to be added (which happens all the time) then such an event makes no functional difference. But the totality of village relationships is not like this: it is

organic. That is to say, the units which make it up are not equivalent in function. Each has a specialized task, which it contributes to the whole, and if one unit is removed, then the totality is changed. In other words, the system of village relationships is based upon a division of labor.

Specialization of function does not logically entail a system of hierarchy, since it is possible to conceive of a division of labor between units which are ranked equally. But since the division of function in Indian rural society includes the differential allocation of power and is not confined to the production of different kinds of goods, the units in a village are differently ranked.

This ranking occurs, as one would expect in a simple society, in more than one field of activity. Thus members of one caste have roles of superiority (or inferiority, as the case may be) toward members of another caste in political, economic, and ritual activity. Also—again a characteristic of a simple society—these roles tend to be consistent, even fused, with one another. To say that X is of higher caste than Y is a statement not only about the ritual relationship between X and Y but also about their political and economic relationships.

The basis of this system of stratification is, in most parts of India, an agrarian economy, to a large extent, indeed, a subsistence economy. The basic division of labor in the field of production is threefold: those who own and manage land (usually a dominant caste); those who own no land and gain their living by labor on the land of others (often Untouchables); and those who provide specialist services—priest, herdsman, carpenter, barber, washerman, potter, scavenger, and so forth. There are no market elements in this economy, in that there is no provision for competition and no expectation that there will be bidding for terms of service. The relationship is one based rather upon status than upon contract, and it is expected to be permanent. Payment is by a fixed share of the harvest and a small fee each time the service is given; all payments are typically in kind. Furthermore, these activities lack the true specialization of a market relationship in that economic relationships are fused with other kinds of relationship. For example, the barber not only cuts hair but also has a number of ritual duties and prerogatives in the houses of those whom he serves. There are also hints of permanence in this relationship and of the absence of specialization, reflected by the terms of address: for example, the landowner and his Untouchable farm servant may address each other as "son" and "father" or "king" and "subject."

There is also a division of labor in the field of politics. The dominant caste of landowners rules the village. Sections within this group compete with one another for power. The status of the rest is, as it were, that of second-class citizens. They have access to the village council only by the grace of their patron in the dominant caste, who is also their protector. To put it another way, no caste other than the dominant caste has a full *political* existence; its members alone may enter the competition for power. The lower castes are not to be seen as political groups in opposition to the dominant caste (as would be the case in a class system). Each member of the lower castes has a political existence as a dependent either of a family in the dominant caste (in the case of the Untouchables) or of the corporate body of the dominant caste (in the case of the specialists).

This pattern of superiority and inferiority is reflected in ritual relationships between individuals in different castes. Thus there are differential degrees of purity so that, for example, food and water (in certain prescribed forms) may be exchanged between equals or may be given by a superior to an inferior. To accept these prescribed foods from a person of a different caste is to acknowledge the superiority of that caste. Furthermore, degrees of superiority are marked in a generalized fashion by differential access to places of ritual value, for example, wells or temples or the kitchen of a house. The ritual disparity is also marked in mere contact, so that a person of higher caste in some cases may be polluted by the touch of those lower in the hierarchy.

To some extent the differences in ritual purity correspond with different positions in the politico-economic hierarchy. Indeed, this must be so for the ritual observances should be regarded as public statements about politicoeconomic status. But it must be admitted at once that this correlation is exemplified only in the middle ranges of the hierarchy. The highest ritual status is held by the Brahman, who may nevertheless be poor and politically without power. The important point is that such a disparity would be regarded as normal. At the other end of the scale the Untouchable is in a corresponding, but not precisely the same, position. His ritual status too seems to have an existence of its own, apart from his politicoeconomic status, and to be more than a mere public statement of this status. If an Untouchable grows rich and powerful (as some of them do), the disparity is certainly regarded by other castes as abnormal and undesirable. A poor Brahman is part of the order of things: a rich Untouchable is not. When other castes higher in the hierarchy grow rich and powerful, their ritual standing is likely to be raised; this does not happen in the case of an Untouchable.

This is an outline of the caste system viewed as a system of interaction within a village. Its main characteristics are that its groups are ranked, are arranged in a system of organic interdependence so that no competition between caste groups is allowed for, and that different fields of activity (political, economic, and ritual) are organized by roles which are not only consistent with one another but may also be fused into a single role.

The basis of this system is the politicoeconomic hierarchy. If we are to understand village life in India, we must first close our eyes to the peculiarities of ritual interaction and see only the fact that the people of the village are either landowners or dependents and specialists. This, in general, is the framework which gives regularity to village life. The system of ritual interaction is an elaboration upon this framework and in itself has no meaning, except as a series of statements, in words or in action, about politicoeconomic relationships. I do not mean that the ritual interaction can be ignored. Far from it, for this ritual interaction is the cultural attachment which makes this politicoeconomic hierarchy peculiar to India. But I do mean that when the caste system is analyzed as a system of politicoeconomic interaction, then comparisons can be made between it and hierarchies elsewhere. The caste system is a way of organizing power relationships in the political and economic field; it defines those who are eligible to compete for power and those who must be dependents.

The process of change.   Like all systematic analyses, the picture which I have drawn of social interaction within the horizontal segmentary system in a caste or tribe and of the vertical system of organic relationships between caste groups within a village is a highly abstract one. Certain factors which are present in actual reality must be taken into account, in particular political and economic relationships extending outside the village. All villages today in India are under the control of a bureaucratic administration, and even in the past almost everywhere there has been some form of political control above the village level. The degree to which this control has in fact influenced social relationships inside the villages or between one village and another has varied immensely: at one extreme "control" was nothing more than tax raids and punitive expeditions; and at the other extreme there is, as in all the larger countries of south Asia, a government intent upon changing the structure of social, political, and economic relationships in the countryside in order to bring about a higher standard of living. Apart from these political agencies there has also been a great variety of economic institutions which directly and indirectly affect the lives of the villagers. For example, villagers may grow cash crops for world markets, or they may migrate from the villages to work in industrial enterprises.

The outside institutions have themselves changed. During the last hundred years, and with particular rapidity since the end of World War II, there has been a tendency toward more centralized and more effective government and a great expansion in the industrial and commercial capitalist economy. In order to take account of the effect on village and caste life of both outside relationships and the change in outside institutions, one must introduce a second variable—time.

In plain terms, movement along the continuum of change means that the villager acquires relationships with outsiders which he did not have before: with traders, or administrators, or politicians, and so forth. Even where the contacts are with fellow villagers they may still be new by virtue of the fact that they occur under the auspices of new institutions, for example, of a political party or in the context of a local government election. But the process does not stop there, for the new relationships bring about a change in the traditional pattern of relationships within the village or the kinship group. For example, if the son of an Untouchable farm servant is a prominent member of the local Congress party, or an official of the police, it will not be possible to treat him with formalized disdain as his father was treated. How do these changes come about?

The new relationships are typically single-interest; that is to say, they involve political activity, or economic activity, or perhaps religious belief. But the relationship upon which they impinge in the villages is a multiplex one, and by affecting one of its strands, they affect the total relationship. Multiplex relationships, characteristic of a simple society, cannot easily be maintained in the face of diversification and specialization of activities. In simplified abstract terms, this is the characteristic process of change in south Asian society.

The basis of the system described in earlier sections was an agrarian subsistence economy. In a diversified economy new ways of making a living are created, and it may happen that those who were qualified only for dependent roles in the old system (like an Untouchable or the specialist) take the lead in exploiting new opportunities. If such a man succeeds, then his new economic

status will not be consistent with his traditional ritual and political status. For example, new economic opportunities may create such anomalies as a rich Untouchable, a man of influence who desires ritual recognition of his new status.

A further basis of the system described earlier was the monopoly of force by the dominant caste of landowners. Under a close administration the power of the dominant caste may be effectively displaced by the power of the administrators and their courts, and there may be a deliberate attempt by the administration to humble the former rulers.

These are only some of the possibilities. New opportunities may be most accessible to those already rich, and the administrators may support those already in power. They may or may not bring about spatial mobility. Government may be intent upon conservation or upon reform, and different administrations may vary greatly in their effectiveness. Clearly the range of outside influences is a very wide one. On the other hand, the range of possible reactions in the village structure is a limited one.

One reaction is accommodation. Positions within the structure may be altered, but the general pattern of relationships remains the same. For example, in the system of vertical organic relationships within a village, if a group low in the hierarchy grows rich through the accident of outside relationships, it may be able to achieve social (i.e., ritual) recognition of its new status. The position of that particular group in the hierarchy changes, but the general pattern of the hierarchy does not. The system remains ranked, organic, and made up of multiplex relationships.

But for a variety of reasons, accommodation may not always be possible. There may, for example, be points of rigidity in the traditional system, as is so in the case of the Untouchables who, if they remain in the villages, find it virtually impossible to get recognition of an enhanced political and economic status. The ensuing struggle to achieve this recognition is likely to make a quite radical alteration in the structure of organic relationships within the village. First, relationships have partially ceased to be multiplex in several respects. The new wealth is achieved by relationships going outside the village. Wealth brings power, so that the Untouchables are no longer so clearly subordinated to the former dominant caste. But the ritual relationship is likely to remain disputed, inasmuch as while the Untouchables demand to be treated as social equals, the former dominant caste is likely to go on treating them as if they were still politically and economically subordinate. Political, economic, and ritual relationships can no longer be viewed as clustered into a single multiplex relationship. Second, the organic relationships of the traditional system are replaced by competitive relationships. This happens in both economic and political activities. Farm laborers break off their traditional permanent relationships with a master or a patron in the dominant caste and work for a daily wage in a system of relatively free market competition. In the political field, the aspirant group (Untouchables in the example we are considering) is likely to transform itself into a corporate group with corporate political aims. Relationships of political allegiances now run horizontally, so to speak, toward members of the same caste and not vertically, as they did before, toward masters and patrons in the dominant caste. Formerly the village was an organic system of groups ranged in an accepted pattern of superiority and inferiority: it now becomes a segmentary system of opposing and competing groups.

In discussing both accommodation and radical change, we have remained within the bounds of the village. But an essential part of this change is the slow decline of the village or the village cluster as an important center for political activity, and its replacement by arenas where competition is regulated by different institutions and where the scale of activity is usually much larger: for example, local government or state politics. To compete effectively in these fields, groups which far transcend villages and caste groups are required. How are such groups recruited?

There are two broad possibilities. The first is that traditional loyalties may be used to build up groups which compete in the new system, the most striking example in India being the use made of caste. Political allegiances grow horizontally, so to speak, first to one's fellow caste members in the same village, then to members of the same caste in other villages, and finally far beyond this to include, in some cases, members of similar castes throughout the region. The Nayar Service Society in Kerala is an example. Such groups may still be called castes, but they are operating in a system totally different from the village caste system described in the preceding section.

Political allegiances may also be created in the idiom of the new institutions, as in the case of professional associations, trade unions, or political parties. These have the advantage over organizations recruited on the basis of traditional loyalties in that they have a wider recruiting area; but they also have the corresponding disadvantage of having no existing sentiments and loyalties on which to capitalize.

In other words, there are three points on the continuum that mark the process of change characteristic of south Asian society. At the first point the people of the countryside are divided into relatively small, isolated, self-contained communities. Internally these communities are divided into parts which are organically linked with one another. At the second point, the groups are no longer so isolated. Outside relationships make it possible for erstwhile dependent categories to form political groups and compete with their masters, and the organic system of interdependent parts tends to give way to a segmentary system of competing groups. At the third point, political groupings cease to be territorially based and territorially exclusive. The tendency toward castes forming political groups in competition with one another is magnified, since caste allegiances form a useful basis for organizing political groups. But at the same time caste (or any other traditional loyalty) is only one way of organizing such groups, and it may in the end be superseded by other forms of organization. Perhaps the shortest way to describe the process of change is to say that small-scale systems of vertically organized organic groups are being replaced by large-scale horizontal systems of groups in competition with one another. In the future we may be able to look back and summarize the whole process adequately by saying that the caste system was replaced by a class system.

Prospects and opportunities

In this final section I shall discuss the contribution which research in south Asia is likely to make to the advancement of social anthropology and the study of society generally. If, in some respects, this contribution is a distinctive one, this will happen not only because of something unique and distinctive in south Asian society itself but also because of certain accidental features in the way research has developed in south Asia.

While no one can deny that the civilizations of south Asia, whether widely defined as total cultures or narrowly defined as social philosophies, are worthy and necessary objects of study, I think it is likely to prove a crippling error if *all* energies are directed into understanding "totalities" of this kind. After the heterogeneities of tribal Africa, the cultural unity of Hinduism or Islam strikes the eye (particularly if one is long-sighted enough to ignore numerous irregularities), and it is understandable that some anthropologists should have thought that these civilizations must be their first object of study; this was what distinguished their field of study from more primitive fields. But south Asia offers other, more exciting opportunities, namely, the study of social change and the chance of developing techniques for the analysis of complex societies. The process by which parochial loyalties are eroded by the demands of the nation, by which village or tribal arenas are replaced by regional and state arenas, is roughly a decade in advance of the analogous processes in sub-Saharan Africa. It is too late, even if we were so inclined, to fight a rear-guard action by proclaiming that kinship and cosmology form the subject matter of social anthropology, while the role of political parties, trade unions, and large-scale capitalist enterprise should be left in the hands of political scientists and economists.

The key to this situation is the degree to which different activities are specialized. Clearly there are levels of political and economic activity so specialized that they belong exclusively to political science and economics. But even in our own highly complex societies, there are still centers of activity where politics, economics, kinship, and religion are mingled with one another. These are the points appropriately studied by the methods of social anthropology: we replace these activities in the social matrix from which more specialized disciplines have abstracted them. The opportunity offered by south Asia is that the degree of specialization of activity is as yet much lower than in the more developed societies. We can, so to speak, grasp both the simple and the complex in one situation and by doing so, one hopes, evolve a framework of concepts which will enable us to understand both processes of change and complex patterns of social interaction. This is our opportunity. To adopt a narrower definition of the scope of social anthropology and attempt to repeat in south Asia work done in Africa, or to reach for the unattainable end of comprehending total cultures, would be to miss that opportunity.

F. G. BAILEY

[See also CASTE; HINDUISM; INDIAN POLITICAL THOUGHT; ISLAM. Other relevant material may be found in KINSHIP and SOCIAL STRUCTURE.]

BIBLIOGRAPHY

BAILEY, F. G. (1957) 1958 Caste and the Economic Frontier: A Village in Highland Orissa. New York: Humanities; Manchester (England) Univ. Press.
BAILEY, F. G. 1960 Tribe, Caste, and Nation: A Study of Political Activity and Political Change in Highland Orissa. Manchester (England) Univ. Press.
BAILEY, F. G. 1963 Closed Social Stratification in India. Archives européennes de sociologie: European Journal of Sociology 4:107–124.
BERREMAN, GERALD D. 1960 Caste in India and the United States. American Journal of Sociology 66:120–127.
BOUGLÉ, CELESTIN (1908) 1935 Essais sur le régime des castes. 3d ed. Paris: Alcan.
Contributions to Indian Sociology (Paris). → Published since 1957 under the editorship of Louis Dumont and D. Pocock.
DUMONT, LOUIS 1957 Une sous-caste de l'Inde du Sud: Organisation sociale et religion de Pramalai Kallar. Paris: Mouton.
THE ECONOMIC WEEKLY (1951–1954) 1960 India's Villages. 2d ed., rev. Edited by M. N. Srinivas. London: Asia Publishing House.
HOCART, ARTHUR M. (1938) 1950 Caste: A Comparative Study. London: Methuen. → First published in French as Les castes.
HUTTON, JOHN H. (1946) 1963 Caste in India: Its Nature, Function and Origins. 4th ed. Oxford Univ. Press.
LEACH, EDMUND R. (editor) 1960 Aspects of Caste in South India, Ceylon and North-west Pakistan. Cambridge Papers in Social Anthropology, No. 2. Cambridge Univ. Press.
MARRIOTT, McKIM (editor) 1955 Village India: Studies in the Little Community. Univ. of Chicago Press. → Also published as Memoir No. 83 of the American Anthropological Association.
MAYER, ADRIAN C. 1960 Caste and Kinship in Central India: A Village and Its Region. London: Routledge; Berkeley and Los Angeles: Univ. of California Press.
REDFIELD, ROBERT 1956 Peasant Society and Culture: An Anthropological Approach to Civilization. Univ. of Chicago Press. → A paperback edition was published in 1962, bound together with Robert Redfield's The Little Community.
SENART, ÉMILE (1896) 1930 Caste in India: The Facts and the System. London: Methuen. → First published in French.

II
SOUTHEAST ASIA

Southeast Asia includes a considerable part of the Asian continent—Burma, Thailand, the Malayan Peninsula, Cambodia, Laos, and Vietnam—and two large island groups: the Indonesian archipelago and the Philippines. In terms of population, the archipelagoes together slightly outnumber the continental countries: nearly half of the total population of southeast Asia belongs to Indonesia alone (100 million out of about 225 million). Still more striking is that nearly one-third of the total population of the area is found on an island of very moderate size: Java, with nearly seventy million inhabitants in an area of only 132,000 sq. km. The total land area of southeast Asia is 4.5 million sq. km.

These few figures may suffice to indicate one of the characteristics of the area: the extreme differences in population densities. Despite rather similar climatic conditions—described by the term "monsoon Asia" sometimes applied to this area—the distribution of the population is uneven. This may be due partly to differential soil fertility: the extremely fertile riverine valleys of the mainland and the volcanic soils of Java allow population densities unknown in rural areas in the Western world. The differences are also partly due to cultural factors, related to the prevalent type of land use. Even in early times populations that grew rice in open irrigated fields were well distinguished in cultural traits from the peoples of forest areas who practiced swidden cultivation of the slash-and-burn type.

Early civilizations

The inland states. The areas of irrigation agriculture in southeast Asia were generally those most deeply affected by Hindu civilization. Though irrigation may have been developed, particularly in Java, before contact was made with the Indian world, it is probable that Brahmins called to the princely courts of southeast Asia played an important role in the further spread of Hindu civilization, including irrigation techniques. The Dutch sociologist J. C. van Leur has put forward a hypothesis that it was Indian Brahmins who provided a sacral legitimation to ruling dynasties by furnishing mythological sanction to genealogy. At the same time they probably served these princes as chancellors, advisers in matters of government and the domestication of the rural population as well as in the construction of temples and irrigation works (van Leur 1955, pp. 103–104, 257–258). Thus, they laid the foundation for the greater southeast Asian empires based on irrigated rice-field cultivation. Within this category one could include the central Javanese kingdom of Mataram until the tenth century, the Khmer kingdom of Angkor in the area that at present constitutes Cambodia, and to a lesser extent the preponderantly mountainous Champa kingdom in the southern region of what is currently known as Annam. In the Red River basin a similar state structure emerged under Chinese influence; but in this case it was not cultural diffusion of the type carried by individual Brahmins but military conquest during the Han dynasty that laid the foundations for the bureaucratic structure. In later centuries the center of the Javanese empire temporarily shifted to eastern Java, whereas on the continent new empires emerged in the Irrawaddy and Menam delta regions.

The empires based on levies from the yields of irrigated rice fields and on socage are defined by van Leur in a Weberian term—"patrimonial bu-reaucracies." He describes these *oikos* states in the following way:

. . . mass domestication made possible by river and canal irrigation farming formed the basis for control of the population by the officialdom of the ruler. All subjects were required to render service to the authority, and that service was organized and directed bureaucratically by an administrative apparatus. The chief role of the cities was that of being royal seats—*kraton* towns, thus—in which levies in kind were brought together from the whole country, and royal storehouses in which the levies were stocked and from which the host of officials, the army, and the royal household were provided. The same system was used for lower administrative units. Large-scale planned projects of agrarian colonization were undertaken, and with the services of the subjects monumental building activities were accomplished. They were forced-labour states, socage states or liturgical states. The legal status of the agrarian population could vary from that of freeholders to that of serfs and slaves brought into the state by predatory war, purchase, or subjugation and established in agrarian colonies. (van Leur 1955, pp. 56–57)

Though a certain amount of central authority is essential for the maintenance of irrigation systems, Wittfogel's picture of these ancient Asian empires as strongly centralized units over which the prince exercised "total power" would appear to be far removed from historical reality (1957, *passim*). The very fact that the rulers had to use force time and again to keep the local lords under their control is not a sign of absolute power, but rather of weakness. Among the means tried to prevent imperial disintegration and to ensure the regular payment of tribute, Weber (1922) mentions periodic royal tours; dispatch of confidential agents; demands for "personal guarantees" (such as hostages or regular appearances at the court); attaching sons of officials to the courts as pages; putting relatives in important positions (which usually proved to be a double-edged sword), or just the reverse—appointing people of inferior class or foreigners as *min-isteriales*; brief terms of office; exclusion of public servants from seigniorages over territories where they had landed property or family connections; attaching celibates or eunuchs to the court; having officials supervised by spies or censors. None of these expedients proved to be a panacea, and imperial unity was continually threatened from within by decentralizing tendencies.

Most of the practices listed by Weber as characteristic of patrimonial states were also tried by southeast Asian rulers to check the ever-threatening centrifugal tendencies (Schrieke 1955–1957, vol. 1, pp. 184–185, and vol. 2, pp. 217–221; Vella 1955, pp. 322–331).

More difficult than a general characterization of the bureaucratic structures is a description of the basic units—the villages in the irrigated rice-growing areas of early southeast Asia. The available literary and epigraphic sources are, in general, exclusively concerned with the description of life at the courts and in monasteries. In order to get some insight into village life we must make more or less conjectural inferences from observations of later periods.

It is highly probable that the villages were largely characterized by a subsistence economy, a high proportion of the surplus being levied, through village authorities, by the bureaucratic apparatus to sustain the larger and smaller courts and the town population surrounding them. But the concept forwarded by Boeke ([1947] 1948, pp. 5, 13) of completely closed village economies in early southeast Asian societies cannot be upheld: in Java, for example, a group of neighboring villages were connected by a single market system. Moreover, the peasantry were partly dependent upon tools external to the village economy, such as imported iron plowshares.

The Marxian concept of a typically Asian mode of production—characterized by a lack of private ownership of land and the complete subjection of the individual peasant to village authority, and accounting for a basic unchangeableness of ancient Asian societies—should also be reconsidered (Chesneaux 1964, pp. 47–53). Marx's interpretation of Asian village society, based on a rather shallow range of reading, appears untenable in the light of present-day knowledge of early peasant societies in southeast Asia. The kings and their chroniclers kept up a pretense of the king's absolute ownership rights over all the lands belonging to his realm and denied any rights of the individual peasants. It is this formal interpretation that was greedily adopted by later colonial governments to substantiate their claim, as successors to the king, to domanial rights. But social reality may have substantially differed from this legal construct, as was recently demonstrated by a study of land law in Ceylon (Pieris 1956, pp. 1–22).

Though it is highly probable that the village communities in general had rather extended powers over land use and crop rotation schemes, this does not exclude the possibility that in some areas individual peasants may have enjoyed private, even hereditary, rights to definite plots of land, whereas in other areas periodic redistribution of plots may have been the normal procedure.

A rejection of Marx's concept of an "Asiatic mode of production" is not necessarily an endorse-ment of the Marxist concept of the evolution of the Western world—from slavery to feudalism to capitalism—as valid for Asian societies. There are strong indications that slavery never had the importance in southeast Asian rural economies that it had in ancient Greek–Roman civilization. Socage, not slave labor, in all probability furnished most of the manpower needed for the construction of monuments and irrigation works. This may explain why huge Hindu and Buddhist monuments are found exclusively in areas where wet-rice cultivation was prevalent, not in a center of Buddhist culture like Srivijaya (Sumatra), which was situated in a region that was characterized by swidden cultivation. One could presume that in Java the peasantry were summoned for building activities after harvest time, during the dry eastern monsoon, and that afterward they returned to their villages to till the fields. In the same way, military expeditions were undertaken by the princes of the Muslim empire of Mataram during successive years in the first decades of the seventeenth century.

The basic "unchangeableness" claimed by Marx for Asian societies "in such striking contrast with the constant dissolution and refounding of Asiatic States, and the never-ceasing changes of dynasty" (1867–1879, vol. 1, p. 394 in 1912 edition), also remains a highly debatable concept. The impression of Asian societies as static may have been conveyed by their seeming stagnancy under the impact of Western expanding capitalism in the nineteenth century; it may have been reinforced by a lack of detailed information on the social and economic history of the peoples of Asia at a time when sociological analysis was still in its beginnings. However true this may be for other parts of Asia, as far as southeast Asia was concerned there is little evidence to substantiate the validity of such a view.

There are at least two important factors that may have produced such instability and social change in the area under discussion: first, the existence of inner contradictions within the patrimonial bureaucratic structures; second, the situation of southeast Asia at a crossroad of cultural currents.

Before discussing these two factors, we should first note another aspect of southeast Asian societies that is highly relevant in facilitating social change: the great variety of social and cultural forms.

The tribal peoples. In the forest areas characterized by swidden cultivation, a way of life and political forms developed that were completely different from those found in the patrimonial bureaucratic structures. When viewing southeast Asia as a whole, however, we see certain common cultural traits expressed in similar folk beliefs and traditions. These similarities are part of a cultural heritage that derives from the times when swidden cultivation constituted the form of land use found all over the area.

Whereas the cultivators of wet-rice fields generally lived in a village community, settlements of swidden cultivators were mostly structured by genealogy, clans and tribes providing the predominant social units. Their main sites were frequently characterized by a group of permanent dwellings belonging to one tribe or to a part of it; these settlements were widespread and covered vast areas in the islands of Indonesia outside central and eastern Java and Bali, most of the Philippines until the advent of the Spanish and Portuguese, large tracts of the Malay Peninsula, and the mountainous hinterland of continental southeast Asia. The cultural diversity among these tribal peoples was probably much greater than among the settled peasants of the irrigated areas. Subsistence types and material culture also varied greatly. Rice was not necessarily the main food crop raised on the swidden; such commercial crops as pepper and spices could be grown in addition to the food crop, and both these and forest products were traded through the intermediary of tribal chiefs in exchange for salt or oil. Cattle-breeding tribes were generally distinguished by a strictly patrilineal type of family organization (Terra 1953, pp. 308–313, 442–446). Whereas the position of women in those areas of southeast Asia where wet-rice cultivation and mixed gardening were prevalent generally did not show any of the serious disabilities known from large parts of the Indian subcontinent, male authority may have been much stronger among cattle-breeding tribes.

The most striking feature of these tribal peoples, however, is that they were generally not integrated into larger political units. As political organizations the tribal units were quite often able to maintain a certain amount of independence.

The harbor principalities. In the inland states the wet-rice regions were linked with the larger and smaller court towns that were the centers of the higher and lower bureaucracies dominating these states. In addition, however, a different type of town was to be found in the southeast Asian region, spread along the seacoasts and near the river mouths: the centers of sea trade called by van Leur (1955) harbor principalities.

Van Leur demonstrated that these commercial towns cannot be compared with the Hanseatic towns of western Europe. The traders did not possess any political power and they were subordinated to princely authority. The great majority of them were small traders, living in separate quarters according to their ethnic group, each of the groups being under the command of a native chieftain appointed by princely authority. As far as their social and political structure was concerned, these harbor principalities were not essentially different from the inland court capitals, in which the royal aristocracy was dominant. The artisans and small traders were mostly foreigners, economically dependent upon the clientele of the court and, even though they may have been organized into guilds, politically subordinate to the prince.

It is true that in the harbor towns sea trade and international traffic generated a more cosmopolitan atmosphere and a greater receptivity to foreign cultural influences. But even the international trade was largely dominated by the harbor princes and their retinue, although a group of patrician merchants of foreign origin also participated in it (van Leur 1955, *passim*). Van Leur's overdrawn dichotomy between small traders—defined in his studies as peddlers—and big patrician merchants living in an aristocratic style has been criticized and refined by Meilink-Roelofsz (1962, pp. 5–12).

This domination of foreign trade provided the harbor principalities with a large portion of their revenue. It replaced as a source of income the socage-and-tithe basis of the inland states, though most of the harbor princes possessed some landed estate near the town. These estates were sometimes worked by slave labor. Many of the harbor principalities, on the other hand, profited from another type of hinterland: especially in the sparsely populated islands of Sumatra and Borneo and in the Malay Peninsula they commanded the trade with the forest areas where commercial crops were grown and forest products were gathered, and they sought to acquire these products at cheap prices through the intermediary of tribal chiefs. The political relationship with these swidden areas was, however, different from the type of dominion of the inland states over irrigated territories and their peasant populations. The harbor prince acted rather as a suzerain who dealt with a tribal chief as his vassal; no bureaucratic structure comparable to those of the inland states was to be found in the swidden areas. No food surplus of any proportion was produced nor was a manpower surplus available for the construction of public works. For menial work the harbor princes and their retinue, as well as the patrician merchants, needed slave labor imported from overseas.

The relationship between inland states and harbor principalities is an intriguing one. There is still much uncertainty about the true relationship between the inland state of early Mataram (central Java) and the powerful harbor principality of Srivijaya (Sumatra) at the time of the Sailendra dynasty (c. A.D. 800). Van Leur (1955, pp. 104–107) suggests the possibility that the dynasty ruling the Sumatran riparian sea power had temporarily exercised a kind of suzerainty over the patrimonial bureaucratic state in Java, in a way somewhat analogous to the overlordship of the *polis* Rome over its province Egypt. It is equally possible that the sovereignty over the Khmer kingdom of Cambodia, attributed by Coedès (1962, pp. 94–95) and other scholars to the Javanese kings, was in fact exercised by the rulers of Srivijaya, who were a strong sea power at that time. Benda (1962, p. 114, note 15), on the other hand, expresses his doubts that any political relationship of this kind between the two types of polity, combined in one and the same dynasty, could ever have existed. However this may be, in later years the relationship was more or less reversed. After the shift of the center of state power in Java from the central to the eastern part of the island, the kingdom of Majapahit combined patrimonial bureaucratic traits, as evidenced by the panegyric *Nagarakrtagama* (1365), with a mighty sea power extending far beyond Java and keeping some of the east Sumatran harbor principalities under subjection. The subsequent history of Java shows a continuous battle of the successive inland states against the harbor principalities along the northern coast of the island.

Cultural influences and social change. The variety of social and political structures in southeast Asia accounts for a greater amount of social change than admitted by van Leur (1955, pp. 166–169) or Schrieke (1955–1957, vol. 2, pp. 4–5), who in this respect retained the static view held by Marx and others. In any patrimonial bureaucracy there exists a basic instability, generated by an eternal tension between center and periphery—the satraps and provincial rulers in the periphery aspiring to achieve a central position by displacing the ruler. But in such a case, one could still argue, the general structure of the polity is being kept intact in spite of a fall of the ruling dynasty. A new dimension to the struggle between center and periphery is added, however, whenever the inland state at its periphery comes in contact with societies of a different order—as was the case with the harbor principalities, which provided a kind of counterpoint to the patrimonial bureaucratic structure.

As outlined before, however, other factors that could generate social change also were operative. The patrimonial structures were not immune to inner contradictions. First, there was a basic contradiction between the peasantry and the bureaucracy. The history of southeast Asia, as of China, was probably fraught with a continuous recurrence of rural unrest and jacqueries, which embodied a protest against too harsh an exploitation of the peasantry by the officials (Chesneaux 1964, p. 52). One could argue that jacqueries do not succeed in basically changing the fabric of a society, since at best they achieve a supersession of one ruler or dynasty by another, without affecting the bureaucratic structure as such. This is precisely why Marx claimed an intrinsic unchangeableness beneath all the bluster and thunder of dynastic change.

Peasant unrest in southeast Asia, however, could achieve more than a mere supersession of one master by another. There are indications that the peasantry possessed a more lasting weapon to dispose of too oppressive an exploitation. If socage service was too burdensome, the peasantry moved to other regions where the pressure was less heavy. This probably occurred in central Java when temple-building activities had been stepped up beyond the endurance of the peasantry (Schrieke 1955–1957, vol. 2, pp. 300–301) and caused a shift not only of the center of Hindu-Javanese culture and political power but also of political and religious orientations of the ruling aristocracy. In the same way, Chesneaux (1964, p. 52, note 47) suggests that the drive of Vietnamese peasants toward the south may have been caused by an excessive exploitation by the bureaucracy in the north.

The significance of the contradictions within the inland states can be fully understood only if one takes into account the tensions between royalty and clergy. Benda (1962, pp. 114–124) has clearly pointed out that the relationship between Hinduism and Buddhism in southeast Asia, which is often presented as one of accommodation and harmony, actually may have been much more strained than generally admitted. This hypothesis becomes more probable if one assumes that the universalistic appeal of Buddhism, especially Tantric Buddhism, may have won a certain following among the peasantry. Similarly, in Vietnam the Confucian scholar-gentry may have been in conflict with the Buddhist monks, who placed themselves at the helm of peasant unrest.

The picture of continuous social change achieves still greater depth from an analysis of the spread of Theravada Buddhism and Sufi Islam. As noted before, in its earlier history southeast Asia had undergone influences from India and China. About the fourteenth century new cultural currents in religious forms presented themselves to the southeast Asian societies. In Angkor the "building mania" of the god-kings had caused popular discontent, which made the peasantry susceptible to the revolutionary new faith imported from Ceylon. To quote Benda:

The innovations introduced by Theravada Buddhism were threefold. In the first place, it created a quasi-egalitarian religious community of which even the monarchs themselves became, albeit for short times and mainly symbolically, members. Secondly, it is not likely that by virtue of their example and teachings the monks could exercise a measure of restraint on the exercise of monarchical power. And, finally, the sociologically most important innovation of the new faith lay in the new monkhood which practised the principles of other-worldly simplicity and frugality, in sharp contrast to the Mahayana monks of the classical era. In spite of the close liaison between the upper ranks of the sangha [the Buddhist hierarchy] and the courts, the mass of the new monks became village "priests," permeating all aspects of peasant life and forming the undisputed center of rural education and social activities. This, I think, amounted to a revolutionary change in the religious landscape of mainland Southeast Asia, or more precisely, in the traditional balance between secular and ecclesiastic authority. The two were still, it is true, intimately connected, but they no longer represented the twin aspects of court culture only. Indeed, the new religious order had an obvious bearing on rural unrest in Theravada lands. For, as often as not it came over the centuries to be led by monks, the only spiritual and organizational leaders of the peasantry.   (1962, pp. 121–122)

The penetration of Islam into other parts of southeast Asia (Indonesia, the Malayan Peninsula, Champa, and the southern Philippines) had a somewhat different character (Johns 1961, pp. 10–23). The new faith at first found its adherents mainly among the urban traders in the harbor principalities, who discovered in the egalitarian ideology of Islam a spiritual satisfaction that was denied them under Hinduism. A situation in which a large proportion of the urban population was Islamized favored an ascent to power of Muslim rulers, either through conversion of the harbor princes under the influence of wandering ulama (Wertheim [1956] 1959, pp. 197–200) or through conquest by prominent foreign Muslims (Meilink-Roelofsz 1962, p. 6).

The Islamization of the harbor principalities, especially on the north coast of Java, sharpened their antagonism to the weakened Hinduized inland states of Java. The only way for the inland rulers to counter the impact from the coast was to embrace Islam, which provided these rulers with the

possibility of winning the allegiance of the peasantry, to which Islam also had begun to spread. The ulama, operating from their religious schools, which had replaced the former Buddhist monasteries, played an important part in this mass conversion.

Again, as with Theravada Buddhism, a more egalitarian creed had won a victory because the patrimonial bureaucratic structure, if it was to survive, was in need of striking deeper roots among the common people instead of contenting itself with mass domestication and royal charisma. This time, it was not only the upper layers that were affected by the foreign influences; by the fourteenth century these influences had reached the common people and had kindled a spark of self-reliance and human dignity.

The colonial period

Early contacts with the West. The first centuries of Western intrusion into the world of southeast Asia were not accompanied by profound structural changes within the fabric of the affected societies. Most of the Western activities and interests were in the realm of overseas trade and naval war and were therefore marginal to the life of the peasantry—the largest section of the peoples of southeast Asia. The deepest changes were brought about in the Philippines, where Roman Catholicism became dominant in most of the islands; in addition, the political units, which before the advent of the Spanish did not extend beyond the barangay (kinship group living in a settlement of village size), were integrated into a larger state structure. Even so, one could argue that until the end of the eighteenth century the Spanish did not accomplish much more than to provide the rice-growing areas with the kind of patrimonial bureaucratic superstructure that had been developed long before in Java, Angkor, and Champa under Hinduism and in the north of Vietnam under Confucianism. First the encomenderos (private persons entrusted with official power by the governor-general), and later the appointed officials, were charged with tax collection and the exaction of corvée. Monastic orders and church estates, exempted from tax liabilities, fulfilled a similar tax-collecting function in the areas allotted to them, as the Buddhist mandalas and later on Muslim pesantrens in Java, who gathered the taxes from the perdikan dessas (free villages).

Nor was the extension of Dutch power over Java in the seventeenth and eighteenth centuries accompanied with basic intrinsic change. By their overwhelming naval power, the Dutch had succeeded in establishing themselves in the Moluccas, on the north coast of Java, in Malacca, and finally in Macassar (Celebes), after having ousted first the Portuguese and then the British from the area. Despite their bourgeois origin, however, the Dutch were soon forced by their Asian environment to relinquish their bourgeois ways and to conform to the political, social, and commercial patterns of the southeast Asian harbor principalities. The East India Company's monopoly system made the existence of a free Dutch bourgeoisie impossible. The servants of the company retained the appellation of merchant or merchant in chief, but their way of living approached ever closer to that of the Eastern nobles. In Batavia, as in Indonesian harbor princedoms, the various nationalities lived in separate wards under their own chiefs. A considerable section of the population were slaves. "The Company's Batavia had become an Eastern harbour principality by the eighteenth century" (Wertheim [1956] 1959, p. 172).

As far as the rice-growing areas of central Java were concerned, the Dutch East India Company at first contented itself with exacting part of the rice surplus raised by the inland state of Mataram. In exchange, the company ousted the leading aristocracies and merchant families of the rival harbor principalities on the north coast, so much feared by the Mataram rulers; they had to take refuge in the outer islands. Later on, the company succeeded in practically subjecting the Mataram rulers, after repeated immixture into their wars of succession, and in establishing for the governor-general the status of overlord in his relationship to the divided "principalities" of central Java. Even this, however, did not produce a completely new structural phenomenon: the company, hitherto a powerful harbor principality, constituted itself as a patrimonial bureaucracy ruling over the inland state of Java and, thus, attained a position similar to that possibly achieved by Srivijaya in earlier times in relation to the inland state of early Mataram.

Economic expansion. It was not until the introduction of large-scale cultivation of commercial crops that the structure of southeast Asian societies underwent a basic change. During the eighteenth century the first steps in this direction had been taken with the introduction of forced coffee cultivation in the mountainous Preanger regencies of western Java (an area where swidden cultivation had been prevalent until that time) and with the enactment of a tobacco monopoly in the Philippines. Earlier, clove and nutmeg cultivation in the Moluccas had been subjected to strict regimenta-

tion and to enforced extirpation by the Dutch East India Company of all the trees in excess of its requirements.

The nineteenth century, however, witnessed a substantial expansion of the plantation economy. These plantations were mostly under the direct management of the colonial government at first and made use of bonded labor. The "cultivation system" in Java, from 1830 to 1860, expanded the forced cultivation of "dessert" crops, such as sugar, tea, and coffee, over large areas. Similarly, in the Philippines the cultivation of tobacco, sugar, and other crops was much expanded on government and church estates.

Private plantations expanded during the second half of the nineteenth century. Java and the Philippines led the way, but soon the plantation economy developed in other regions as well: Sumatra, the Malayan Peninsula, Cambodia, and Cochin China became important plantation centers and were run under Western management along strictly capitalistic lines. Whereas the "dessert" crops had dominated the plantation economy of Java and the Philippines, in the areas where there was still plenty of forest land available trees producing raw materials for modern industry, such as rubber and palm oil, were predominant. In addition, mining of oil, tin, and bauxite was developed in areas that had hardly been explored in former times (Borneo, Sumatra and the smaller islands east of it, and the Malayan Peninsula, including that part of it belonging to Thailand). Coal, iron, tin, zinc, phosphate, manganese, and wolfram mining was developed in Tonkin, whereas on Luzon Island vast reserves of gold, iron, and chromium ore were exploited.

The southeast Asian region thus became a typical colonial producer of raw materials for the Western industrial world and a consumer of ready-made goods, predominantly textiles. Thailand was the only country that, by playing off the imperialist powers, managed to maintain a formal independence. The social and political structure of the whole region was strongly affected by the onslaught of Western capitalism, the more so since even the cultivation of rice, the traditional food crop, was seriously affected by the new economic order: in many areas of Java rice growing was geared to a plantation economy by the introduction of a pattern of crop rotation, thus forcing the rice cultivator to become a part-time worker on the sugar plantation during the time when it was occupying his land. In Burma, on the other hand, the British colonial administration forced a system of free disposal of land and crop upon the peasantry in order to get an exportable surplus of rice in exchange for industrial products imported from the home country.

According to Furnivall (1948) both systems led equally to a disruption of the rural social order and to an impoverishment of the peasantry.

The impact of nineteenth-century and early twentieth-century Western capitalism on southeast Asian societies was profound and lasting—even in Java, where the official policy has been one intended to keep the social order intact and to preserve many native institutions, or in the Philippines, where the Spanish government for a long time tried to exclude other Western capitalists from the country and thus to shield Filipino society from foreign influences.

Changes in the state structure.   During the period of preponderantly mercantile contacts in the Philippines and Java, Asian types of bureaucracy and political relationships were largely adapted to the requirements of the Western overlords. But the expansion of commercial crop cultivation stimulated more direct forms of internal administration and the colonial government and its civil service penetrated more deeply into the rural areas.

The Dutch colonial government developed a dual system of administration. A Westernized bureaucratic apparatus was superimposed on an Indonesian infrastructure in which many patrimonial bureaucratic traits were preserved (Wertheim [1964] 1965, pp. 115–117). Until late in the nineteenth century the regents of Java were still entitled to domestic services exacted from the rural population to supplement their meager salaries and to prop the social prestige which the Dutch expected them to retain vis-à-vis the rural population. On the other hand, their involvement in commercial agriculture, as agents of Western interests, may have detracted from their traditional aura in the eyes of the rural population (Schrieke 1955–1957, vol. 1, p. 190). By the turn of the century, however, the Javanese civil servants were transformed into salaried officials. Nevertheless, on lower levels of the bureaucracy, patrimonial remnants were still prevalent. The village officials remained unsalaried even up to World War II and were remunerated indirectly by receiving a percentage from the tax revenue and by grants of land.

In the Philippines, despite a certain amount of political reform during the nineteenth century, the system of administration remained conspicuously unfit for developing commercial crop cultivation along capitalistic lines. One of the weakest points of the system was the vast extent of landed estate held by monastic orders. This land was practically free from taxation and emphasized the weak posi-

tion of the administration vis-à-vis the clergy. This was one of the main causes of the revolution of 1896. It was the Americans who, after their intervention, attempted to introduce a type of government better adapted to the requirements of a capitalistic exploitation (Corpuz 1957, pp. 5–6, 128–195).

In the regions where the British came to power, they applied the system of direct rule that they had used in India. The proclaimed British policy at the annexations of Lower Burma in 1826 and Upper Burma in 1886 ". . . was directed to the provision of a suitable code of laws, the enforcement of a moderate system of taxation, the recognition of religious and personal freedom as a fundamental principle of rule, the freedom of trade and abolition of oppressive duties, and the improvement of roads and other means of communication. Except for the final item this policy was merely negative, a policy of *laissez-faire*" (Furnivall [1948] 1956, p. 63).

Furnivall himself, however, points out that the introduction of a completely Westernized administration proved impossible or too costly and that in many respects the government had to revert to the Burmese system of payment by a commission for revenue collection. "Thus, while the European branch of the administration was becoming more centralized and mechanical, the local or Burmese branch was reverting to type, and the people were still managing their own affairs much as under their own rulers" ([1948] 1956, p. 38). Actually, therefore, in Burma under the British a dualism in the system of administration developed similar to that in Java under the Dutch.

The change of political structure, however, was not confined to the colonial sphere. Interestingly, Mindon, the ruler of the kingdom of Ava in Upper Burma, had made an effort, before the British annexation and no doubt under the impact of what had happened in Lower Burma, to reorganize and modernize his state apparatus:

He tried in particular to abolish the Myosa system of fief assignments to princes and high officials. He attempted also to end the misappropriation of moneys passing through official hands by instituting a system of designated stipends and salaries. He undertook to raise revenues for the most part from *thathameda* land-tax assessments based on a productivity index for a given area multiplied by the number of households. . . . The establishment of administrative supervisory posts checked flagrant financial abuses. . . . Unfortunately the attempts at the reform [met] with little success to eliminate feudal aspects of the Burmese administrative system. . . . (Cady 1964, p. 388)

More ambitious still were the reforms brought about by the kings of Thailand. Under King Chulalongkorn, for example, salaried officials were appointed to replace the hereditary governors. Especially after the king's younger brother, Prince Damrong, had gained influence after 1893, the provincial government was thoroughly reorganized on modern lines. Though the practical effect of many of the reforms may be doubted, the effort proves that the inefficiency of the traditional patrimonial bureaucratic system was also realized by southeast Asian rulers (Vella 1955, pp. 340–349).

The French in Indochina introduced a highly bureaucratic and centralized rule in Cochin China, but in Annam and Tonkin they retained a certain measure of indirect rule and kept the mandarinate bureaucracy, at least formally, intact. Indirect rule was also, sometimes more nominally than in fact, applied in Laos and Cambodia, in Malaya, and in large parts of the outer islands of Indonesia.

This schematic survey makes clear that, however great the divergences in political structure produced under colonial rule—each being modeled more or less in accordance with the concepts cherished by the particular colonizing power—still the economic and social realities made for a certain parallelism throughout the southeast Asian area.

Plantation society. The system of social stratification in nineteenth-century southeast Asia was strongly influenced by both the conquest of most of southeast Asia under imperialist expansion and the spread of a plantation pattern of social organization. To begin with the latter: wherever plantations were started in virgin or nearly virgin areas, such as Sumatra's east coast or Malaya, there was a clear organizational principle. The management and staff were whites; the laborers, all of them imported from elsewhere, were Asians (mostly Chinese and Javanese in Sumatra, Chinese and Indians in Malaya).

A plantation was a harsh frontier society, with rigorous discipline and a rigid code of behavior aimed at maintaining the social prestige of the white managerial group. The laborers worked under a system of indentured labor and were not free to quit or to leave the plantation. Both the planters and the coolies considered their stay at the plantation temporary and dreamed of quickly accumulating enough money to return home as well-to-do men. But only in the case of the planters was this likely to be more than a dream. Some of the Chinese and Indian workers were thrifty enough to send regularly part of their earnings home, and there were even quite a few who managed to establish themselves as independent traders in the colony and to make good in society. But for the great majority, especially for the less thrifty Javanese, there was no alternative after the expiring of the contract but to sign for another term. The management did everything in its power to prevent the coolie from quitting; playing hazard was a much-used method of getting an old-timer, whose contract had nearly expired, into debt. For the great majority of the laborers, many of whom had been cheated into signing a contract, working on a plantation meant lifelong bondage, made even harsher by the nearly exclusively male composition of the frontier society.

In later years, a larger number of female laborers from Java were employed on Sumatra's east coast plantations. Consequently, a kind of normalization occurred in the frontier society, and particularly during the rubber boom of the 1920s the regimen became, accordingly, somewhat softened. Abuses were more rigorously combated, the more so since the indentured system had come under strong criticism by the home press and political parties. But the essential traits of the plantation society were nevertheless preserved.

Still, the plantations were not established in a kind of vacuum. Even on Sumatra's east coast and in Malaya the indigenous social structure was not completely absent. For their land grants the plantation owners were dependent on the Malay sultanates—which gained in wealth, if not in prestige, among the population—because of their involvement in Western enterprise.

In areas like Java and the Philippines, where plantations were established amidst a settled population, the new institution had to be geared to traditional patterns of the surrounding rural society. The plantation managements in Java to a certain extent assumed the paternalistic ways of the native aristocracy and vied with these in style of living and forms of leisure, even after the system of bonded labor had been replaced by one of free, paid labor. In the Philippines the cultivation of commercial crops on haciendas was to an important extent in the hands of caciques, the mixed offspring of the former Malay chiefs, who used their social prestige to exact the required amount of work from their tenant-farmers, kept in peonage under the *kasama* (sharecropping) system. Thus the plantation management combined the characteristics of modern enterprise with the ways of a landed gentry. In the Philippines the cacique was at the same time landlord and magistrate.

Social stratification. The plantation society set a model for colonial society in its totality. The white colonizers superimposed themselves as a ruling caste upon the southeast Asian social body. Their status was based on ascription; their dominant position was derived from their white ancestry, even though their supremacy in military and political matters had been attained through their initial start in education and in technical and administrative matters. The nineteenth-century colonial society was molded on racial principles: belonging to the dominant white upper caste provided one with prestige and power largely independent of one's personal capabilities. A strict ritual was introduced and maintained, by force when necessary, to preserve the white caste from contacts with Asiatics on a basis of equality and to maintain the former's prestige as the dominant group.

Raymond Kennedy, who was probably the first to analyze colonial society as such in sociological terms (1945, pp. 305–346), correctly points to the great differences in colonial patterns corresponding to specific views and attitudes of the colonizing power. He indicates such national peculiarities as the British colonial code, which "draws the most rigid color line of all. . . . The entire social ritual of the colonies symbolizes the separateness of rulers and ruled. Nowhere in the colonial world are the lines of caste drawn more rigidly: in clubs, residential areas, places of public accommodation, and informal cliques. Nowhere is the taboo on intermarriage stronger and the penalty for infraction more drastic" (1945, p. 320). The Dutch suffered less from preconceptions of racial superiority and inferiority than the British and were more liberal in their attitude toward deviations from the colonial code of caste. Social relations between natives and whites were by no means free and equal, but by comparison with the British colonies the Dutch East Indies appeared as a zone of exceptional racial tolerance. Eurasians, born from a marriage of a European man with a colored woman or acknowledged by a European as his offspring in case of illegitimate birth, were legally, if not socially, assimilated into the European population. The policy of the French resembled that of the Dutch in its "relative freedom from racial prejudice" (Kennedy 1945, p. 329). The French ideal of carrying their civilization to the colonial peoples, moreover, led them to an attitude of accepting at least socially those few among the Asians who had fully assimilated French culture.

The Spanish colonizers in the Philippines did not suffer from strong racial prejudices. The Christianization of the Filipinos had furthered intermarriage, from which sprung not only the dominant landowning group of caciques but also an urban and educated intermediary class of light-colored Filipinos. The Americans, on the other hand, maintained a rather strict color line in the Philippines. It was manifested especially in the social and economic spheres. The Americans did not mix freely with Filipinos, and imposed a strong taboo on intermarriage. This social code was an obvious reflection of the racial mores of the United States, and might be characterized as a kind of "informal Jim-Crowism." It was merely understood that only under certain circumstances were Filipinos or mestizos invited to white homes, and that certain clubs and schools admitted only Americans. The caste line was not so rigid as in British colonies, but not so loose as in Dutch and French dependencies. Economic discrimination on the basis of color appeared particularly in employment practices. American firms reserved the better positions for whites, and Filipinos seldom rose above clerical jobs.   (Kennedy 1945, pp. 332–333)

Still, despite all such differences the general pattern was clearly set. However different the way the color line was drawn, the fact remains that in each instance of colonialism it existed.

The first of the universal traits of colonialism is the color line. In every dependent territory a true caste division exists, with the resident white population separated from the native masses by a social barrier that is virtually impassable. The color line, indeed, is the foundation of the entire colonial system, for on it is built the whole social, economic, and political structure. All the relationships between the racial groups are those of superordination and subordination, of superiority and inferiority.   (Kennedy 1945, p. 308)

Social reality in the different colonies was, moreover, often less varied than formal policies, as pointed out by Kennedy, would suggest. The grading of social prestige according to skin color and other characteristics pointing to one's affiliation with either racial group was to be found in most of the colonies, regardless of whether the Eurasians were included among the European group or relegated to the position of Asiatics. The specialization by Eurasians in clerical or supervisory functions, which commanded a certain social prestige as symbols of emancipation from menial tasks and familiarity with the language of the colonizing people, was typical not only in the Dutch colony and the Philippines but in British dependencies as well (Koop 1960, pp. 20, 48; Jones 1953, p. 41).

And even in independent Thailand the whites, especially under the unequal treaties, achieved a status—as foreign advisers, firm managers, or missionaries—that was not very different from their position in a colonial country. The main difference from the colonies appears to be that the "advisers" —in fact, administrators—were chosen from several countries.

On the other hand, even in the colonial countries the Western authorities could not dispense with the traditional southeast Asian social structure. Even though the "natives" were formally classified as an inferior caste, the traditional aristocracy or those who were elevated by the colonial government to an equivalent position received privileged treatment and to a certain extent were also accepted socially by the representatives of the colonial upper caste. It was also their offspring who, by enjoying better educational facilities, could aspire to positions otherwise reserved for members of the dominant caste. This was especially the case in those areas where a certain amount of indirect rule was maintained during the colonial period. Again, Thailand differs not in kind but rather in degree.

For the rest, until the end of the nineteenth century the social differentiation brought about by colonial exploitation was limited indeed. Educational facilities for the mass of the population remained very restricted; only after 1900 was a somewhat more liberal educational policy adopted, the Americans in the Philippines leading the way in this respect. The spread of a money economy into the countryside created some new types of workers, such as mechanics, tailors, cart drivers. Plantations under Western management and railway transport also required technically trained or supervisory personnel. The expanding towns opened opportunities for those who mainly from practical experience and without benefit of school training succeeded in learning a trade or a skill.

Schoolteachers and people in lower clerical jobs were also able to rise above the level of the rural and urban mass. But a peculiarity of most countries of southeast Asia under colonial rule is that up to the end of the nineteenth century there was hardly a native intermediate layer between the white upper caste, assisted by the aristocracy, and the uneducated rural masses. Not only were a large portion of the clerical jobs filled by nonnatives (in many areas Eurasians) but also the intermediate economic level—people working in trades and crafts—was largely occupied by groups coming from outside the southeast Asian area: Chinese and Indians, the latter group mostly in Burma and Malaya, the former all over the area, including independent Thailand.

Trading minorities and pluralism. In nearly virgin areas, such as east Sumatra and adjoining islands, West Borneo, Malaya, and Singapore, the Chinese settlers engaged in a wide range of economic activities. On the other hand, in the densely populated regions of Java, Tonkin, and a few other irrigated rice-field areas, they were largely relegated to commerce and crafts and remained a numerically restricted group, generally not exceeding a rather low percentage of the total population (Wertheim [1964] 1965, pp. 43–45). But even then

they played an essential role in a modernizing economy, profiting from the circumstance that in an agrarian society with an aristocratic tradition professional trade had for a long time been a scorned occupation readily left to foreigners.

New economic opportunities and the development of steamship transport brought large numbers of Chinese immigrants, who generally had to start from scratch to achieve a living in southeast Asia. In their sworn brotherhoods they developed an interesting social institution to accommodate newcomers to the new environment and to acquire a certain amount of protection. In these secret societies they created a kind of substitute for the clan organizations and guilds that dominated urban life in China. But the more well to do among the immigrant groups, some of them already living for generations in the colony, developed a more individualistic attitude to life. It was they who were nearest to what could be considered a bourgeois middle class in the Western sense.

Furnivall (1948) has developed the concept of the plural society for the colonial countries of southeast Asia to denote the strict compartmentalization of colonial society according to racial lines. Insofar as this concept suggests a juxtaposition of the different racial groups, it creates a wrong impression by neglecting the hierarchical nature of the race relationships. Another weak point in Furnivall's view is that he denies any social and cultural contacts between the different racial groups. In fact, a creolization process was very much in evidence in the colonies; in many cases the offspring of the immigrant groups (Europeans and Chinese) even adopted the native language.

Segregation is not a natural procedure in these colonies but is purposely being kept in force by the dominant group. That is why the total structure is better defined by the caste concept than by the concept of a plural society.

Urban and rural developments. The colonial type of economy produced, as one of its main concomitants, a rapid urban growth. But it was a growth of a specific and rather one-sided nature, occurring mostly near natural seaports or in delta regions and facing toward the sea as a symbol of the city's outward orientation. Philip M. Hauser (1957, pp. 86–88) has established that, with the exception of Indonesia, where there were a number of larger towns, the primary cities tended to be from five to ten times as large as the next largest city in the country. They owed their origin and growth to their function as a link between East and West, or the indigenous economy and the mother colonial power. They were likely "to be 'parasitic' in the sense that they tended to obstruct economic growth in their country of location by retarding the development of other cities in the nation, by contributing little to the development of their own hinterland, by being oriented primarily toward the contribution of services to the colonial power abroad or the colonial or indigenous élite in the great city itself" (Hauser 1957, p. 87). Industrialization was deliberately retarded by the colonial powers, and the cities were developed as seaports for the export of commercial crops and minerals and for the import of ready-made industrial goods from the West.

Moreover, the colonial setting contributed to the color caste pattern of urban settlement, with the concomitant racial segregation, which was responsible for utter ignorance and general neglect of the interests of those who lived in the native quarters.

The increasing flow of migrants was, accordingly, not so much a consequence of the pull of new opportunities for employment and the lure of attractive living conditions in the cities as of the push factor operating in the rural areas. And though most of the movement might have begun as circulation, that is, as a temporary move without losing a foothold in one's own village, in most cases it eventually led to lasting migration.

In the countryside, a certain amount of dislocation occurred as a consequence of the introduction of a money economy. Imported cheap textiles had all but abolished native handicraft. The deepening of official interference in rural affairs and the spread of governmentally managed plantations and those worked by bonded labor in behalf of monastic orders or private persons led in many cases to an increased burden of work required from the peasantry, as had the extension of statute labor for public works. New kinds of taxes were raised, and quite a number of peasants lost their land, either because of the intrusion of Western plantations, as in Java, or because of increasing rural indebtedness owing to a policy of converting both the land and its crop into commodities, as in Burma. Both landlordism and usury were on the increase, throwing a growing proportion of the population into a position of utter dependency as landless farmhands or sharecroppers.

Anticolonial stirrings. The dislocation produced a certain amount of rural unrest. But owing to a lack of politically mature leadership the discontent could express itself only in rather ineffective outbursts of rebellion, mostly under religious leadership. The messianic and millenary movements in Java led by Muslim religious teachers, who had come under the influence of Wahhabism and had no acknowledged status in Dutch colonial hierarchy; the dacoity in Burma, sometimes led by Buddhist monks, who under British overlordship had lost their leading and established position in popular education (Cady 1964, pp. 400–403); the "hundreds of bloody uprisings against Spanish oppression" in the Philippines (Jacoby [1949] 1961, p. 210)—all of these stirrings can be viewed as reactions to the intrusions from the West and as abortive attempts to restore an imaginary lost paradise.

The only really dangerous opposition to the colonial powers at the high tide of colonialism was the political opposition led by southeast Asian princes defending their independence against the foreign intruders. The nineteenth-century history of the area is a long story of battles alternating with diplomacy. The Western powers moved steadily against the native rulers, who generally tried to appeal to the religious allegiance of the peoples and to ally themselves with religious leaders—whether Muslim or Buddhist—or, in the case of Tonkin and Annam, with the mandarin bureaucrats. In the long run these princes generally were forced to yield, not only because of their relative weakness in military matters but also because of their inefficient and oppressive rule, which could hardly enlist the enthusiastic support of the rural populations under their government.

Only after a growing number of southeast Asians had mastered Western ideas, Western techniques, and Western ways of reorganization in the first decades of the twentieth century could they effectively challenge the colonial powers. Only in the Philippines, owing to the inefficient and oppressive Spanish administration and to an unusually high proportion of Filipinos of mixed parentage who had enjoyed Western education, did the first serious challenge to Western power occur just before the turn of the century.

The emancipation period

The changing stratification system. The colonial caste system was, as we have seen, preponderantly ascription based. It denied access to economic and political power and the ensuing social prestige to those who did not belong, by birth, to the upper caste. There was a basic contradiction between this principle as applied in the colony and the democratic principle as adhered to by the colonizing powers at home (with the partial exception of the United States as far as the nonwhites were concerned), according to which achievement was the only criterion for one's position within the status system.

As soon as a rapidly growing group of southeast Asians succeeded in acquiring the individual qualifications needed for social ascent, they discovered the paradox of a system that taught them new capabilities and at the same time denied them the opportunity to make full use of them. Those who had enjoyed higher education felt particularly frustrated by a colonial system that denied them access to the higher rungs of the ladder of bureaucracy, and they felt humiliated by the low esteem in which they were held in their own country.

Those who tried to climb the social ladder via private enterprise also found their way blocked by the presence of a powerful merchant class of foreign Asiatic origin, who by their greater experience, capital resources, and an established network of communications within their kinship groups were able to maintain a near-monopolistic position. This was especially the case in an area like Java, where a tradition of native trade was largely absent. In areas where the former Muslim harbor principalities had been able to maintain themselves for a long time (as in Sumatra and Borneo) small local entrepreneurs survived and took advantage of new opportunities, such as the cultivation of native rubber or coconuts on the former swidden fields.

In the first decades of the twentieth century the trend of thought was mainly individualistic; the Asian religions were affected by new rationalistic trends in the Western world. Religious reform movements, in both the Muslim and the Buddhist spheres, gave expression to an individualistic world view, trying at the same time to counter the appeal exerted on the youth by Christian missionaries (Wertheim [1964] 1965, pp. 139–140). These reform movements at the same time tended to restore a pride in native cultural values and thus could be viewed as a prelude to the growth of nationalism.

Modern organizations and nationalism. The next stage in the emancipation movements was to adopt a new principle from the Western world: the usefulness of modern organization. The impossibility of attaining their ends by individual achievement in the face of institutional barriers and other frustrations compelled the southeast Asians, whose main asset vis-à-vis the colonial powers was their number, to discover the meaning of collective action. The history of the emancipation movement can be written largely in terms of the activities of all kinds of organizations. Trade unions multiplied to emancipate the urban laborer and the plantation coolie from the excessive power of his foreign employer, who also combined forces in trusts and syndicates; traders' organizations tried to break through the monopoly of foreign groups, among whom the traditional "sworn brotherhood" type of organization also gave way to more modern ones; farmers' unions fought the oppressive power of the landlord; women's organizations aspired to emancipation from traditional male domination; youth organizations fought traditional authority. And all these movements, most of them predominantly urban centered, more or less combined into one broad nationalistic organizational frame to fight the colonial authority.

The weakening of colonial authority as a consequence of the Japanese conquest and occupation of practically the whole territory of southeast Asia (with the exception of Thailand, where, however, the Japanese influence was also strongly felt) boosted the organizational forces of the peoples of southeast Asia so as to give them a victory shortly after the war over nearly all the area.

But the victory won was still far from complete. The newly independent states of southeast Asia face many of the same problems confronting other new nations in other parts of the world.

Structural weaknesses of the new states. The first weakness relates to the role played by organizations and collectivities in the new setting. During their common anticolonial struggle the national elites were more or less unified. After independence, however, opposing organizations began to fight for supremacy within the new structure. The new societies recognized achievement as a criterion for social status in only a limited sense. Ascription by membership in a collectivity, such as the political party in power, was in many cases more effective in securing a foothold in the new bureaucracy, belonging to the "ins" or to the "outs" a much more important criterion than individual merit.

The organizations struggling for power more often than not are based on distinctions rooted in tradition, such as religion or ethnic group. Competition on an individual basis, considered a precondition for progress by nineteenth-century liberalism, is being replaced in the present world of southeast Asia by competition on a group basis, which is usually fiercer than individual competition.

Furnivall's dream that national independence would bring an end to the frictions he considered related to pluralism ([1948] 1956, p. XII) has not come true. He believed that if the racial groups concerned would develop common values, in a national setting, tensions and frictions would lessen.

In fact, however, greater cultural affinity, brought about by modern educational and economic forces, may foster communal strife by stimulating competition on a group basis (Wertheim [1964] 1965, pp. 69–70; Freedman 1960).

Group competition seriously endangers the efficiency that is so much needed in the new southeast Asian states in its neglect of the capacities of those who do not belong to the group and even by attempts to oust those against whom the group solidarity is directed—as, for example, the Indians from Burma. A schism produced by such inter-organizational competition may affect the whole society and even penetrate the countryside. Robert Jay (1963) described in detail the mounting cleavage between the pious *santris*, combining forces in Muslim organizations, and the common villagers with secular and syncretistic orientations (*abangan*), mostly under the influence of communist unions, in an area in eastern Java.

This phenomenon of mounting dissension is still more serious if it is related to the second basic problem of the new southeast Asian states, which involves their changing economy. These nations, like most Asian nations, are situated in an area where the main activities in the economic field traditionally have been conducted under the aegis of government. It is unthinkable that in these countries, where an indigenous tradition of private enterprise is all but absent, and in the largely monopolistic arena of the world economy, economic development could be achieved under a system in which private enterprise would hold pride of place (Geertz 1963a, p. 131). The new governments have each to develop a bureaucratic structure and a dynamic spirit capable of fulfilling the immense task of getting modern development under way in an economy kept backward and one-sided throughout the colonial period. These tasks, incomparably more arduous than those that had previously confronted the colonial governments, require a unified effort.

Unfortunately the formation of a modern bureaucracy finds serious obstacles in the numerous remnants of a past patrimonial bureaucratic structure (Furnivall 1958, pp. 130–132; Corpuz 1957, pp. 214–230, 243–244). The cohesive force of the urge for modern nationhood in several cases was strong enough to secure a political and military victory against the former colonial power. In many instances, however, national consciousness and the dynamic support of the national government have not been developed sufficiently to perform the Sisyphean task of economic upbuilding in peacetime. All types of particularistic loyalties, such as alle-giances to one's kin, ethnic group, or former guerrilla associates, frequently transcend the sense of a quasi-universalistic allegiance to the national state. Hence the repeated incriminations of corruption and nepotism, which in several cases are due to a conflict of loyalties still rooted in the traditional past. Neither democratic institutions adopted from the West nor military rule seems to provide a propitious atmosphere for dynamic endeavors of such a magnitude that they hold out the prospect of lasting results.

Economic backwardness and rural unrest. The most serious drawback in the development of the new states is that even though emancipation in the social and political field has made some progress, emancipation in the economic field is still in its beginnings. To do away with the remnants of the colonial economic structure appears to be much more difficult than getting rid of its concomitants in the social and political field. Industrial development in nearly all the southeast Asian countries is still very weak, except possibly in North Vietnam and to a certain extent in the Philippines and Singapore, where some progress has been made since the end of World War II. Urban centers have grown steadily, but generally they still present the unbalanced character of the colonial period, with the possible exceptions of Singapore and Hanoi. The problem of population increase is all but unmanageable in the already densely populated irrigated rice areas, including Java, parts of Luzon, and the Tonkin delta. The disguised unemployment typical of these irrigated areas also spreads to the cities, where huge numbers of migrants from the countryside have to look for employment as house servants or to cater to casual customers as small hawkers or pedicab drivers.

Despite halfhearted attempts at land reform, in most countries of southeast Asia landlordism is on the increase and rural unrest is assuming ever greater proportions. This unrest is no longer under ineffective religious leadership. The peasantry, stirred by rising expectations and unfulfilled promises during the independence struggle, is being organized according to well-devised principles of efficient political organization, though for the moment the movement is not always unified.

If Malaysia presently appears fairly prosperous and less exposed to rural unrest, it is due largely to the abundance of land and to the retarded development of the various emancipation movements in that country.

It is unfortunate that more certain knowledge of the achievements in North Vietnam, where a most interesting experiment in economic development is being made, is not widespread. It would be most interesting to know to what extent the collectivization of agriculture, combined with rapid industrialization, presents an alternative to the many abortive attempts at economic development undertaken in other densely populated countries or areas of southeast Asia.

The remnants of eminent domain. There is, finally, one more problem that touches upon the issue of emancipation. The struggle for economic emancipation may also be viewed in the light of the struggle of the peoples of southeast Asia against foreign domination, which after formal independence assumed largely an economic shape. The preponderance of British interests in Malaysia and of American interests in the Philippines and South Vietnam may still be considered a heritage of the colonial period.

These economic interests are also the main incentive for the political and military involvement of both world powers in the southeast Asian world.

Still, the real influence exerted by the Western world in southeast Asia is becoming more and more marginal, thus resembling the period of the first contacts of the Western adventurers with the southeast Asian world. It seems appropriate to remind the reader of the warning by Owen Lattimore:

. . . the European powers, and America as their partial heir, hold only a doubtful control of territories in Asia. All that they really hold is a string of bases around the rim of Asia. They have fallen back to the footholds and toeholds from which the European marauders and adventurers of the sixteenth and early seventeenth centuries began their empire building. . . . Wherever the frontier of power touches populated territory, people—which means politics—have become more important than garrisons.   (1949, pp. 45–46)

Or, if in an encyclopedia of the social sciences a quotation from a theoretical sociologist is more appropriate than one from an area specialist: "Before the end of this century, probably every vestige of European eminent-domain in Asia will have vanished. But whether it will be relinquished peaceably or will go down in blood and flame depends on whether European power-holders can adjust their ideas to the realities of to-day and to-morrow" (Ross [1920] 1938, p. 543).

W. F. WERTHEIM

[Other relevant material may be found in BUDDHISM; COLONIALISM; HINDUISM; ISLAM; MODERNIZATION.]

BIBLIOGRAPHY

BENDA, HARRY J.   1962   The Structure of Southeast Asian History: Some Preliminary Observations. *Journal of Southeast Asian History* 3, no. 1:106–138.

BOEKE, JULIUS H.   (1947) 1948   *The Interests of the Voiceless Far East: Introduction to Oriental Economics.* Rev. & enl. ed. Leiden (The Netherlands): Universitaire Pers Leiden. → First published as *Oosterse economie.*

CADY, JOHN F.   1964   *Southeast Asia: Its Historical Development.* New York: McGraw-Hill.

CHESNEAUX, JEAN   1964   Le mode de production asiatique: Quelques perspectives de recherche. *La pensée* 114:33–55. → This issue contains other important contributions and a bibliography.

COEDÈS, GEORGE   1962   *Les peuples de la péninsule Indochinoise: Histoire, civilisations.* Paris: Dunod.

CORPUZ, ONOFRE D.   1957   *The Bureaucracy in the Philippines.* Studies in Public Administration, No. 4. Manila: Univ. of the Philippines, Institute of Public Administration.

FREEDMAN, MAURICE   1960   Growth of a Plural Society in Malaya. *Pacific Affairs* 33:158–168.

FURNIVALL, JOHN S.   (1948) 1956   *Colonial Policy and Practice: A Comparative Study of Burma and Netherlands India.* New York Univ. Press.

FURNIVALL, JOHN S.   1958   *The Governance of Modern Burma.* New York: Institute of Pacific Relations, International Secretariat.

GEERTZ, CLIFFORD   1963a   *Peddlers and Princes: Social Change and Economic Modernization in Two Indonesian Towns.* Univ. of Chicago Press.

GEERTZ, CLIFFORD   1963b   *Agricultural Involution: The Process of Ecological Change in Indonesia.* Association of Asian Studies, Monographs and Papers, No. 11. Berkeley: Univ. of California Press.

GOUROU, PIERRE   (1936) 1955   *The Peasants of the Tonkin Delta: A Study of Human Geography.* 2 vols. New Haven: Human Relations Area Files. → First published as *Les paysans du delta tonkinois: Étude de géographie humaine.*

HAUSER, PHILIP M.   1957   World and Asian Urbanization in Relation to Economic Development and Social Change: Introduction to the Seminar on Urbanization in the ECAFE Region. Pages 53–95 in Joint UN/UNESCO Seminar on Urbanization in the ECAFE Region, Bangkok, 1956, *Urbanization in Asia and the Far East: Proceedings.* Calcutta: UNESCO Research Centre on the Social Implications of Industrialization in Southern Asia.

JACOBY, ERICH H.   (1949) 1961   *Agrarian Unrest in Southeast Asia.* 2d ed., rev. & enl. New York: Asia Publishing House.

JAY, ROBERT R.   1963   *Religion and Politics in Rural Central Java.* Cultural Report Series, No. 12. New Haven: Yale Univ., Southeast Asia Studies.

JOHNS, A. H.   1961   Sufism as a Category in Indonesian Literature and History. *Journal of Southeast Asian History* 2, no. 2:10–23.

JONES, STANLEY W.   1953   *Public Administration in Malaya.* London: Royal Institute of International Affairs.

KENNEDY, RAYMOND   1945   The Colonial Crisis and the Future. Pages 305–346 in Ralph Linton (editor), *The Science of Man in the World Crisis.* New York: Columbia Univ. Press.

KOOP, JOHN C.   1960   *The Eurasian Population in Burma.* Cultural Report Series, No. 6. New Haven: Yale Univ., Southeast Asia Studies.

LATTIMORE, OWEN   1949   *The Situation in Asia.* Boston: Little.

LEUR, JACOB C. VAN   1955   *Indonesian Trade and So-*

ciety: Essays in Asian Social and Economic History. The Hague: Van Hoeve.

MARX, KARL (1867–1879) 1925–1926 *Capital: A Critique of Political Economy.* 3 vols. Chicago: Kerr.

MEILINK-ROELOFSZ, MARIA A. P. 1962 *Asian Trade and European Influence in the Indonesian Archipelago Between 1500 and About 1630.* The Hague: Nijhoff.

PIERIS, RALPH 1956 *Title to Land in Kandyan Law.* Pages 1–22 in *Sir Paul Pieris: Felicitation Volume.* Colombo (Ceylon): Sir Paul Pieris Felicitation Volume Committee.

ROSS, EDWARD A. (1920) 1938 *Principles of Sociology.* 3d ed. New York: Century.

SCHRIEKE, BERTRAM J. O. 1955–1957 *Indonesian Sociological Studies: Selected Writings of B. Schrieke.* 2 vols. The Hague: Van Hoeve. → Volume 2 has a separate title: *Ruler and Realm in Early Java.*

TERRA, G. J. A. 1953 Some Sociological Aspects of Agriculture in S.E. Asia. *Indonesië* 6:297–316, 439–463.

VELLA, WALTER F. 1955 *The Impact of the West on Government in Thailand.* University of California Publications in Political Science, Vol. 4, No. 3. Berkeley: Univ. of California Press.

WEBER, MAX (1922) 1956 *Wirtschaft und Gesellschaft: Grundriss der verstehenden Soziologie.* 4th ed., 2 vols. Tübingen (Germany): Mohr.

WERTHEIM, W. F. (1956) 1959 *Indonesian Society in Transition: A Study of Social Change.* 2d ed., rev. The Hague: Van Hoeve.

WERTHEIM, W. F. (1964) 1965 *East–West Parallels: Sociological Approaches to Modern Asia.* Chicago: Quadrangle Books.

WITTFOGEL, KARL A. 1957 *Oriental Despotism: A Comparative Study of Total Power.* New Haven: Yale Univ. Press. → A paperback edition was published in 1963.

ASSIMILATION

Assimilation is a process in which persons of diverse ethnic and racial backgrounds come to interact, free of these constraints, in the life of the larger community. Wherever representatives of different racial and cultural groups live together, some individuals of subordinate status (whether or not they constitute a numerical minority) become assimilated. Complete assimilation would mean that no separate social structures based on racial or ethnic concepts remained.

Assimilation may be distinguished from *accommodation,* a process of compromise characterized by toleration, and from *acculturation,* or cultural change that is initiated by the conjunction of two or more cultural systems or the transference of individuals from their original societies and cultural settings to new sociocultural environments. Assimilation is to be distinguished also from amalgamation, or biological fusion.

Complete segregation and total assimilation of a group are opposite ends of a continuum along which may be located: varying degrees of limited desegregation; the substantial pluralism found in many communities in the United States, Canada, and Switzerland; a hypothetical integration which values structural and cultural differences, while insisting upon equal life opportunities for the members of all groups; partial assimilation (e.g., small-town Jews, who tend to be bicultural rather than marginal; see Williams 1964, pp. 303–304); individual assimilation; and group assimilation.

History of the concept. The history of the "melting pot" theory can be traced from J. Hector St. John Crèvecoeur's 1782 volume, *Letters From an American Farmer,* through Frederick Jackson Turner's thesis of 1893 concerning the fusion of immigrants in the crucible of the Western frontier into a composite American people, and Israel Zangwill's *The Melting Pot* of 1909, to Ruby Jo Reeves Kennedy's "Single or Triple Melting-pot" studies of 1944 and 1952 (see Gordon 1964, chapter 5).

As a concept in American sociology, assimilation has had various meanings. Henry Pratt Fairchild (1913, p. 396 in 1925 edition) equated assimilation with Americanization. For some scholars assimilation and acculturation are synonymous (Berry 1951, p. 217; Bierstedt [1957] 1963, p. 176). More often assimilation has *included* acculturation. According to a widely quoted point of view: "Assimilation is a process of interpenetration and fusion in which persons or groups acquire the memories, sentiments, and attitudes of other persons or groups, and, by sharing their experience and history, are incorporated with them in a common cultural life" (Park & Burgess 1921, p. 735). Park's (1926) "race relations cycle" (contacts, competition, accommodation, and eventual assimilation) has been criticized for its assumptions of the inevitability and irreversibility of the process. Vander Zanden (1963, p. 269) distinguishes *unilateral* assimilation, the process in which one group relinquishes its own beliefs and behavior patterns and takes over the culture of another, from *reciprocal* fusion, in which a third culture emerges from the blending of two or more cultures, and, also, from various intermediary levels of assimilation.

Gordon (1964, p. 71) sees the assimilation process and its subprocesses as a matter of degree, but *complete* assimilation would cover seven variables: change of cultural patterns to those of the host society; large-scale entrance into cliques, clubs, and institutions of the host society on the primary-group level; large-scale intermarriage; development of a sense of peoplehood based exclusively on the host society; absence of prejudice; absence of discrimination; and absence of value and power conflict. This conceptual scheme provides the most satisfactory criteria yet proposed for measuring assimilation and for determining to what extent it is taking place.

Variables affecting assimilation

The process of assimilation is affected by the interaction of several classes of variables: demographic, ecological, racial, structural, psychological, and cultural. There is at present no systematic comparative analysis of the variables that are most significant in different types of situations.

The importance of group size can be seen in the case of Hawaii, where there is a stronger tendency for members of the smaller ethnic and racial groups to marry outside their own groups than for those of larger groups; also, women from groups with a more balanced sex ratio outmarry to a greater extent than women from groups with a less balanced sex ratio (Cheng & Yamamura 1957, p. 81). Ecological factors have been important in the United States, where "cultural islands" created by immigrant groups often provide security but also isolate newcomers from the mainstream of American life and arouse distaste in the eyes of Old Americans. Likewise, demographic and ecological factors apparently affect the likelihood of Negro assimilation in Great Britain; Collins (1955, p. 90) attributes the more amicable interaction between Negroes and whites in London's northeast dockland, in contrast to the west and northwest dockland, in part to the size and pattern of Negro settlement in the former area.

Relative importance of racial factors. Park (1930, p. 281) held that assimilation might, in some senses and to a certain degree, be described as a function of visibility, and he attributed the Negro's lack of assimilation in the United States, during three hundred years, to physical rather than cultural traits. This oversimplified explanation has been replaced by one that stresses the interaction of racial, ecological, historical, structural, and other variables. For example, physical characteristics were an important factor, but by no means the only variable involved, in the decision made by more than 670,000 persons (Stuckert 1958) to "pass" from the Negro group to the white group in the period 1861 to 1960. Other variables of importance in "passing" are age and socioeconomic status; people who are well established in the Negro community and older people seldom pass socially and completely. However, color continues to be an important factor; for example, a study of Chicago's Negro community shows that color affects choice of marriage partners, recruitment into the professions, social relations, and other aspects of life (Wilson 1960, p. 171). Recent studies have shown that color and social class are not the only variables affecting the differential assimilation of Negroes. In a study of New Orleans Negroes, primary role identifications occasioned by conditioning in one of four "social worlds" (the middle class, the matriarchy, the male gang, the isolated family, and a residual group of the culturally marginal) were found to play a larger part in the self-conceptions and the experiences of individuals than any identification with the Negro race in general (Rohrer & Edmonson 1960, pp. 51–55, 71–74, 80–83).

For overseas students in London, finding a room depends largely on color: approximately 70 per cent of the landladies were unwilling to accept colored students and, in the case of very dark Africans or West Indians, the figure was 85 per cent (Senior 1957, p. 306). By virtue of sharing halls of residence and dining rooms, as well as having more opportunities for participation in university societies, the social life of colored students is fuller in Oxford and Cambridge than in London (*Coloured Immigrants* . . . 1960, pp. 79–80).

Assimilation in Latin America. When slavery was abolished in Brazil toward the end of the nineteenth century, the population increased and changed in composition with the influx of more than a million Italians, thousands of Polish and German settlers, and many Portuguese, Spanish, and Syrian immigrants. These nationalities continued to migrate to Brazil in the twentieth century, together with some 200,000 Japanese, who have multiplied to about 500,000 persons. Most of those entering the middle sectors of the economy have been of European origin; but mestizos, mulattoes, and Negroes in substantial numbers also have found opportunities to improve their status. Persons of dark color are not barred from assimilation into the national society, but the *preto*'s attempts to advance are made more difficult because he lacks one determinant of status—light color. Some of the residents of German, Italian, and Japanese colonies have not been assimilated into Luso-Brazilian life, in part because of language differences and their physical separation from other Brazilians (see Smith [1946] 1963, p. 62; James [1942] 1959, p. 522; Johnson 1958, p. 4). The interaction of cultural and ecological factors in the process of assimilation can also be seen in the conditions for accepting "recognized Indians" into the national societies of Latin America: learning to speak the national language (Spanish or Portuguese) fluently; adopting European-type clothing; and moving from a recognized

Indian community to a city or town that is regarded as national in its culture (Gillin 1960, pp. 19–20).

Ideology and culture. Psychological variables play an important role in the process of assimilation. For example, Banton emphasizes that much of British conduct toward colored people and Jews is a form of avoidance of strangers that is found in nearly all societies, adding that if groups are to be respected they must to some extent be exclusive (Banton 1959, pp. 112–113, 181–182). On the part of newcomers, aspirations and responses to settlement in Britain vary considerably. Asians constitute an accommodating group trying to live alongside the local community, while west Africans and West Indians seek acceptance within the community (Banton 1959, pp. 182–183).

Attention should be called to attitudinal factors that have retarded assimilation in specific historical situations, particularly the belief that the members of one or another racial or ethnic group are unassimilable. Practices and policies of segregation, mass expulsion, and even genocide have been rationalized on the ground that some groups are unassimilable because of their innate inferiority. For example, the Nazi "racial" policies were based on the doctrine of the unassimilability of the Jews. South Africa's policy of apartheid derives from the belief that differences between Europeans and Africans require social, political, and economic separation to permit each group to attain its fullest development. In the United States, a recrudescence of the belief in the innate inferiority of the Negro and, consequently, the necessity of opposing steps toward integration characterized the "race and reason" movement in the early 1960s (Comas 1961). The French colonial policy of "assimilationism" during the first half of the twentieth century was supported, like the continuing colonial policy of the Portuguese (Herskovits 1962, pp. 288–289), by the belief that for a long time only a select few among a non-Western people are capable of being absorbed into the metropolitan system.

In contrast to the policy of forced separation of racial and cultural minorities, antipathy toward minority groups has also taken the form of forced assimilation. In 1917 the communists promised freedom for the customs and institutions of Russia's numerous cultural and national minorities; Stalin was instrumental in formulating the policy of separating statehood from nationality, and cultural autonomy was permitted within the framework of Soviet economics and politics. However, since 1940 the reinstitution of some aspects of the tsarist policy of Russification has dispersed some minorities. Jews have been labeled "cosmopoli-

tans," and since 1957 a campaign against the remaining aspects of Jewish communal life has been carried on. The goal of this program appears to be the "total assimilation" of Jews (Goldhagen 1960, pp. 42–43).

Opposition to assimilation also may be shown by members of a minority group. In the United States the Old Order Amish and numerous other religio-ethnic groupings have sought to preserve their separateness and distinctiveness (Williams 1964, pp. 302–303). Among Negro Americans a small but militant group known as the Black Muslims is virtually alone in not seeking complete assimilation. Black nationalists perceive white society as united in rejecting Negroes as full citizens. Thus, feelings of alienation and powerlessness cause these persons to reject American society and culture, and the leaders of the movement strive to develop an awareness of group identity among the urban masses of Negroes (Essien-Udom 1962, pp. 54–59, 325–329; Lincoln 1961, chapter 2). Among the group's objectives are the establishment of a Negro homeland and a postapocalyptic Black Nation, goals that are only vaguely defined. Another new nationalist movement in North America calls for a revision of the relationship between French and English Canadians: Some French Canadians envision the "separation of the State, not Province, of Quebec from Canada; if not separation, then a new constitution giving Quebec a special status" (Hughes 1963, p. 884). The history of these and many other minorities in the New World is discussed by Wagley and Harris (1958, pp. 285–289), who analyze the different strategies for working toward the opposite goals of assimilation and pluralism.

Assimilation of immigrants in Israel. The interaction of structural, cultural, and psychological variables is clearly seen in the assimilation of immigrants to Israel (Eisenstadt 1954). The basic motivation of settlers during the mandatory period (1920–1948) was rooted in the decline of traditional Jewish society amidst the modern, universalistic societies. Their aims were mainly solidary and cultural rather than adaptive and instrumental. Unlike many who came during the mass migration to Israel after 1948, the earlier immigrants, in general, showed a relatively strong predisposition to change and a lack of adherence to the social patterns of their countries of origin.

The new immigrants came from four main types of communities. The *traditional* sector (Yemenite Jews and some north African Jews) was characterized by a relatively high degree of social autonomy and orientation toward particularist Jewish values and traditions and a cultural view of the out-group that was mainly negative. In contrast, the *insecure transitional* sector, made up of large parts of urban north African Jewish communities and most of the central and eastern European communities, showed a very low degree of social autonomy and relatively strong aspirations toward entrance into the Gentile society. The *secure transitional* sector, composed of Jewish communities settled within and approved by Gentile society (Serbian and Bulgarian Jewries in Eisenstadt's sample), was marked by a small degree of social autonomy, strong primary identification with the general community, and acceptance of their Jewishness by the Gentile community as a subsystem within the general social structure. They had immigrated as a result of general upheavals; there was no question of deportation. In the sector consisting of *ex-inmates of DP camps*, their experience in those places overshadowed other social traditions. Among these new immigrants a positive predisposition to change was found mostly in the traditional sector and the secure transitional sector, while a negative predisposition occurred mostly in the other two sectors.

Among the structural factors that had a strong bearing on the incorporation of newcomers into Israeli life were the various bureaucratic agencies that defined the immigrant's initial situation and, later, the army and the educational system, which took the lead in transmitting universal roles and the common orientation of the absorbing society. Finally, the values and roles of the immigrants were transformed through mobility of groups and individuals in the larger society and through leadership selection and development [*see* REFUGEES].

Chinese and Japanese Americans. Ecological, racial, cultural, and structural variables have affected the assimilation of the Chinese in the United States. In earlier years, racial–cultural barriers threw Chinese-American young people back upon their own group. However, wars and depressions gradually weakened the economic and social structures of Chinatowns and helped to bring about a redistribution of their populations. As the process of acculturation has continued, upward mobility has increased. Moreover, as persons of Chinese ancestry become more acculturated, intermarriage will increase; evidence of the increased tolerance of white–Mongoloid marriages is seen in the growing number of marriages between American servicemen and Japanese or Korean wives (Lee 1960, p. 251).

Although the economic integration of Japanese Americans has steadily increased, assimilation in

other respects has been slower, except for those whose education and broad interests have made possible contacts in the larger community. The interaction of psychological, cultural, and structural factors in the assimilative process is shown in a study of Japanese Americans in Chicago. The compatibility of the Japanese and the American middle classes, in terms of their value systems and personality structures (Caudill 1952, p. 29), will facilitate the acculturation, as well as the eventual assimilation, of Japanese Americans.

Studies of intermarriage

Interrelationships among ecological, demographic, racial, and cultural variables are revealed in studies of marriages among American Catholics. Considerably higher percentages of intermarriage occur in middle, upper, and suburban rental areas than in lower or in mixed lower and middle areas. With the exception of groups characterized by marked color differences, the rate of assimilation tends to be correlated inversely with the group's size.

Surveys taken in the 1930s revealed that approximately 6 per cent of Jewish families in the United States were intermarried; in 1957 the federal government's survey of religious composition showed that 7.2 per cent of all Jewish families had a non-Jewish partner. Marriage licenses in Iowa in 1953 showed that 31 per cent of the Jewish marriages were mixed. A 1960 survey of the Jewish population in Washington, D.C., indicated an intermarriage rate of 12.2 per cent, and the intermarriage rate in 1959 in San Francisco was 17.2 per cent. According to Rosenthal (1960, p. 288), if the national intermarriage rate of 7.2 per cent found in 1957 is accepted and if it is assumed that the Iowa and San Francisco rates are simply regional variations, Jews may be justified in concluding that the current "survival" formula (a modicum of Jewish education; voluntary segregation; and residence in a high-status area) is adequate for group preservation. Kennedy (1963) calls the high degree of endogamy in the Jewish group "selective assimilation" and emphasizes that the important point on the intermarriage of Jews is not the fact that it is increasing, but the very slight extent to which it has increased.

It should be pointed out, however, that available data on the intermarriages of Jews and non-Jews in the United States are minimal figures, because they do not include the cases where the spouse was converted to the religion of the other prior to marriage. Furthermore, certain developments in contemporary life contribute to the further individual assimilation of Jews. Of the Jewish population between the ages of 18 and 25 years, 62 per cent are attending colleges or graduate schools, as compared with 22 per cent in their parents' generation (Fishman 1963, p. 147). Moreover, two-thirds of American Jews live in suburban counties of metropolitan areas, and this dispersion of Jewish urban concentration may have marked effects on attempts at Jewish retentionism. For example, Cahnman (1963, pp. 179–180) reports that the intermarriage rate of Jews tends to be higher in high-status neighborhoods and among college graduates.

Popular belief holds that Negroes in the United States desire to marry white persons, but in a Chicago study (Bogue & Dizard 1964, p. 7) almost no respondents, including middle-class Negroes living in mixed neighborhoods, said they would encourage their child to marry a white person. Despite this lack of desire for intermarriage, at least on a conscious level, increasing desegregation and integration will inevitably raise the rate of Negro–white marriage.

In southeast Asia structural separation and cultural differences prevent intermarriage from promoting further group assimilation. The indigenous women who marry Chinese in Indonesia contribute Chinese children to a Chinese subsociety, but they do not form a bridge from one subsociety to another. Likewise, although intermediate social and cultural types have been produced by intermarriage in Thailand and Indochina, a Chinese subsociety has continued in these countries (Freedman 1955, p. 411).

Assimilation of American Negroes

Although the incorporation of minority peoples into American life over time presents a mixed picture, the general trend has been toward greater integration and assimilation of these groups. Some indications of this change with respect to Negroes are cited here (for more complete information see Simpson & Yinger 1965). Slight gains in employment opportunities have been made during the postwar period, but these have been offset to some extent by higher rates of unemployment among Negroes as compared with whites. The average Negro family's income, as a percentage of the average white family's income, has fluctuated during the 1950s and 1960s, but Negroes now receive approximately 5 per cent of the gross national income, as compared with less than 1 per cent in 1935. The proportion of Negro pupils in the 17 southern and border states and the District of Co-

lumbia attending biracial schools rose from 6 per cent in May 1960 to 10.8 per cent in the fall of 1964. Although only 2 per cent of all the Negro public school children in the 11 southern states were attending school with whites in 1964, the number of these pupils almost doubled in the fall of that year. At that time slightly over half of the 513 colleges and universities in the 11 southern states accepted both white and Negro students. By the early 1960s discriminatory policies on the admission of Negroes to medical schools had declined greatly, and a marked improvement had occurred in the availability of internships and residencies, mostly in white hospitals.

Negro voting registration in the South increased from an estimated 70,000 in the 1920s to more than 1.5 million in 1964. Between 1943 and 1958 virtually complete integration was achieved in the armed forces of the United States. One-third of the Negro Roman Catholics in the United States attend racially mixed churches. However, integration in Protestant churches is increasing slowly; presently from 10 to 15 per cent of the "white" Protestant churches in the North and West are interracial to some degree, but not more than 2 per cent of Negro Protestants attend interracial churches. Widespread segregation in housing remains a key factor in the total Negro–white situation, especially as it relates to the problem of school segregation; in some areas housing segregation has increased as an unanticipated consequence of publicly assisted urban-renewal programs. In the period 1945–1965 resistance to Negro–white intermarriage remained at a very high level, while resistance to all other types of intermarriage (interfaith, international, and interracial) declined.

In addition to legislation, litigation, and intergroup education aimed at increasing integration, a significant development in the 1960s is the "Negro revolt" (Simpson & Yinger 1965, pp. 533–535), which has actually included persons of diverse racial, religious, and cultural backgrounds. The emergence of organized protest groups and skilled leaders who are capable of articulate and determined opposition to patterns of segregation is important among the factors facilitating assimilation.

Future prospects. Among the practical consequences of a greater degree of integration in American economic life is the likelihood that business and professional people in racial and ethnic groups who have benefited economically from segregation will be forced to take a more active part in the attack on discrimination. An example is the picketing of the American Medical Association by young Negro physicians because of the inclusion of an increasing number of Negro patients in insurance schemes that give them access to clinics or hospitals that are not open to Negro physicians (Hughes 1963, p. 886). Reduction of discrimination in places of public accommodation undermines the protected economic position of the older Negro middle class. Within another generation, or sooner, increases in intermarriage and individual assimilation rates will force organizations that depend upon ethnic group support to consider the problems of membership, funds, and program.

If the ultimate test of complete assimilation is large-scale intermarriage, that state will not be reached in the United States in the near future. Changes will occur in the relations between members of diverse racial and ethnic groups, but these changes will consist mainly in a closer approximation to equal educational and economic opportunities, increased political participation, and an acceleration of desegregation in schools and places of public accommodation. The rate of integration will vary from region to region and from one social institution to another and will be affected by the general trend of events domestically and internationally. As desegregation and integration increase, it is inevitable that assimilation will be furthered.

GEORGE EATON SIMPSON

[*See also* ACCULTURATION; CONSTITUTIONAL LAW, *article on* CIVIL RIGHTS; ETHNIC GROUPS; MINORITIES; PREJUDICE; RACE; RACE RELATIONS; SEGREGATION; *and the biographies of* FRAZIER; HERSKOVITS; PARK; TURNER.]

BIBLIOGRAPHY

The Statistical Summary *of school desegregation, issued annually by the Southern Education Reporting Service (SERS), Nashville, Tennessee, is the best source on educational desegregation in the United States. SERS publishes bimonthly the* Southern Education Report, *containing information on educational developments, with emphasis on programs for the education of the culturally disadvantaged in the 17 Southern and border states and the District of Columbia. The Southern Regional Council, Atlanta, Georgia, issues reports from time to time on various aspects of race relations in the South. The annual reports and other publications of the United States Commission on Civil Rights are valuable.* Phylon, The Journal of Negro Education, *and* Crisis *publish useful articles on changing race relations.*

The most comprehensive work on American Negroes is Simpson & Yinger 1965. Attention is given in this book to other minorities, but the major emphasis is on the Negro. Pettigrew 1964 and Broom & Glenn 1965 are good briefer books.

BANTON, MICHAEL (1959) 1960 *White and Coloured: The Behaviour of British People Toward Coloured Immigrants.* New Brunswick, N.J.: Rutgers Univ. Press.

BERRY, BREWTON (1951) 1965 *Race and Ethnic Rela-* *tions.* 3d ed. Boston: Houghton Mifflin. → First published as *Race Relations: The Interaction of Ethnic and Racial Groups.*

BIERSTEDT, ROBERT (1957) 1963 *The Social Order.* 2d ed. New York: McGraw-Hill.

BOGUE, DONALD J.; and DIZARD, JAN E. 1964 Race, Ethnic Prejudice, and Discrimination as Viewed by Subordinate and Superordinate Groups. Unpublished manuscript. Univ. of Chicago, Community and Family Study Center.

BROOM, LEONARD; and GLENN, NORVAL D. 1965 *The Transformation of the Negro American.* New York: Harper.

CAHNMAN, WERNER J. 1963 Intermarriage Against the Background of American Democracy. Pages 173–195 in Werner J. Cahnman (editor), *Intermarriage and Jewish Life: A Symposium.* Conference on Intermarriage and Jewish Life, New York, 1960. New York: Herzl Press.

CAUDILL, WILLIAM 1952 *Japanese-American Personality and Acculturation.* Genetic Psychology Monographs, Vol. 45, 1st half. Provincetown, Mass.: Journal Press.

CHENG, C. K.; and YAMAMURA, DOUGLAS S. 1957 Interracial Marriage and Divorce in Hawaii. *Social Forces* 36:77–84.

CLARK, KENNETH B. 1965 *Dark Ghetto: Dilemmas of Social Power.* New York: Harper & Row.

COLLINS, SYDNEY 1955 The British-born Coloured. *Sociological Review* New Series 3:77–92.

Coloured Immigrants in Britain. By J. A. G. Griffith et al. 1960 London and New York: Oxford Univ. Press.

COMAS, JUAN 1961 "Scientific" Racism Again? *Current Anthropology* 2:303–340. → A review of recent instances of "scientific" racism, with critical comment.

Crisis. → Published since 1910 by the National Association for the Advancement of Colored People.

EISENSTADT, SHMUEL N. (1954) 1955 *The Absorption of Immigrants.* Glencoe, Ill.: Free Press.

Essien-Udom, E. U. 1962 *Black Nationalism: A Search for an Identity in America.* Univ. of Chicago Press. → A sociological analysis of the Black Muslim movement.

FAIRCHILD, HENRY P. (1913) 1933 *Immigration: A World Movement and Its American Significance.* Rev. ed. New York: Macmillan.

FISHMAN, JOSHUA A. 1963 Moving to the Suburbs: Its Possible Impact on the Role of the Jewish Minority in American Community Life. *Phylon* 24:146–153.

FREEDMAN, MAURICE 1955 The Chinese in Southeast Asia. Pages 388–411 in Andrew W. Lind (editor), *Race Relations in World Perspective.* Honolulu: Univ. of Hawaii Press.

GILLIN, JOHN P. 1960 Some Signposts for Policy. Pages 14–62 in Richard N. Adams et al., *Social Change in Latin America Today: Its Implications for United States Policy.* New York: Harper.

GOLDHAGEN, ERICH 1960 Communism and Anti-Semitism. *Problems of Communism* 9:35–43.

GORDON, MILTON M. 1964 *Assimilation in American Life: The Role of Race, Religion, and National Origin.* New York: Oxford Univ. Press.

HERSKOVITS, MELVILLE J. 1962 *The Human Factor in Changing Africa.* New York: Knopf.

HUGHES, EVERETT C. 1963 Race Relations and the Sociological Imagination. *American Sociological Review* 28:879–890.

JAMES, PRESTON E. (1942) 1959 *Latin America.* 3d ed. New York: Odyssey.

JOHNSON, JOHN J. 1958 *Political Change in Latin America: The Emergence of the Middle Sectors.* Stanford (Calif.) Univ. Press.

Journal of Negro Education. → Published since 1932 by Howard University, Bureau of Educational Research.

KENNEDY, RUBY J. R. 1963 What Has Social Science to Say About Intermarriage? Pages 19–37 in Werner J. Cahnman (editor), *Intermarriage and Jewish Life: A Symposium.* Conference on Intermarriage and Jewish Life, New York, 1960. New York: Herzl Press.

LEE, ROSE HUM 1960 *The Chinese in the United States of America.* Hong Kong Univ. Press; New York: Oxford Univ. Press.

LINCOLN, CHARLES ERIC 1961 *The Black Muslims in America.* Boston: Beacon. → A paperback edition was published in 1962 by Beacon Press.

PARK, ROBERT E. 1926 Our Racial Frontier on the Pacific. *Survey* 66:192–196.

PARK, ROBERT E. 1930 Assimilation, Social. Volume 2, pages 281–283 in *Encyclopaedia of the Social Sciences.* New York: Macmillan.

PARK, ROBERT E.; and BURGESS, ERNEST W. (1921) 1929 *Introduction to the Science of Sociology.* 2d ed. Univ. of Chicago Press.

PETTIGREW, THOMAS F. 1964 *A Profile of the Negro American.* Princeton, N.J.: Van Nostrand.

Phylon. → Published since 1940 by Atlanta University.

ROHRER, JOHN H.; and EDMONSON, MUNRO S. (editors) 1960 *The Eighth Generation: Cultures and Personalities of New Orleans Negroes.* New York: Harper.

ROSENTHAL, ERICH 1960 Acculturation Without Assimilation: The Jewish Community of Chicago, Illinois. *American Journal of Sociology* 66:275–288.

ROSENTHAL, ERICH 1963 Studies of Jewish Intermarriage in the United States. Volume 64, pages 3–53 in *American Jewish Year Book.* New York: The American Jewish Committee.

SENIOR, CLARENCE 1957 Race Relations and Labor Supply in Great Britain. *Social Problems* 4:302–312.

SIMPSON, GEORGE E.; and YINGER, J. MILTON 1965 *Racial and Cultural Minorities: An Analysis of Prejudice and Discrimination.* 3d ed., rev. New York: Harper. → The first edition was published in 1953.

SMITH, T. LYNN (1946) 1963 *Brazil: People and Institutions.* Baton Rouge: Louisiana State Univ. Press.

Statistical Summary. → Issued annually by the Southern Educational Reporting Service, Nashville, Tennessee. The best source on educational desegregation.

STUCKERT, ROBERT P. 1958 The African Ancestry of the White American Population. *Ohio Journal of Science* 58:155–160.

VANDER ZANDEN, JAMES W. 1963 *American Minority Relations: The Sociology of Race and Ethnic Groups.* New York: Ronald Press.

WAGLEY, CHARLES; and HARRIS, MARVIN 1958 *Minorities in the New World.* New York: Columbia Univ. Press. → A comparative analysis of six minority groups.

WILLIAMS, ROBIN M. JR. 1964 *Strangers Next Door: Ethnic Relations in American Communities.* Englewood Cliffs, N.J.: Prentice-Hall.

WILSON, JAMES Q. 1960 *Negro Politics: The Search for Leadership.* Glencoe, Ill.: Free Press.

YINGER, J. MILTON; and SIMPSON, GEORGE E. 1956 The Integration of Americans of Mexican, Puerto Rican, and Oriental Descent. American Academy of Political and Social Science, *Annals* 304:124–131.

ASSOCIATION, STATISTICS OF

See under STATISTICS, DESCRIPTIVE.

ASSOCIATIONISM

See GESTALT THEORY *and the biography of* HARTLEY.

ASSOCIATIONS

See CARTELS AND TRADE ASSOCIATIONS; COOPERATIVES; LABOR UNIONS; ORGANIZATIONS; VOLUNTARY ASSOCIATIONS.

ATOMIC WAR

See LIMITED WAR; NUCLEAR WAR.

ATTENTION

The contemporary approach to attention has been strongly influenced by neurophysiological research on the attention, or arousal, systems of the brain (Lindsley 1960). Attention as behavior is associated with the responses of these systems and also with the neuromuscular responses that govern the orientation of the eyes, ears, and other sensory surfaces of the body. This midcentury emphasis on response processes is a considerable departure from the classical view, as expressed by Titchener (1908) or William James (1890, chapter 11), that attention is an aspect of the structure of consciousness.

Some categories from the classical approach continue to be important. For example, *prior entry,* the notion that "the object of attention comes into consciousness more quickly than objects we are not attending to" (Titchener 1908, p. 251), is the basis for the common use of response latency as a measure of attentiveness. Similarly, Wundt's position (see Titchener 1908, p. 263) that attention is discontinuous and intermittent foreshadowed modern models of attention that emphasize discrete processes (e.g., Broadbent 1958). However, the classical approach as a whole was unsuccessful, because it could not generate clear and productive paradigms for research on attention. Thus, a major textbook introduced its conventional coverage of this topic with the admission that "the status of attention in systematic psychology has been uncertain and dubious for a long time" (Woodworth & Schlosberg [1938] 1954, p. 72). The successful neurophysiological analysis mentioned earlier, and the new behavioral approaches described below, have revived interest in attention as a major topic in the behavioral sciences.

There is some tendency to equate the capacity

for sustained attention or for encompassing a broad field in one's "attention span" with the biological evolution of complex behavior. It is well to keep in mind when considering this position that the attention systems of the brain that have been well identified, the brain stem and thalamic reticular systems, are phylogenetically among the most primitive systems in the vertebrate central nervous system. Some aspects of attentive behavior should therefore depend on very primitive functions that occur over a wide range of vertebrates. The progressive evolution of attention may occur through the appearance of mechanisms that permit the organism to choose whether to observe *A* or *B* in the external environment or even to observe the internal environment instead by attending to "stored" memories [see FANTASY].

In the laboratory, attentiveness is usually studied in relation to discrimination or detection performance. For such studies it is useful to redefine attentiveness as the emission of observing responses that act to select an effective signal from among the available sensory stimuli. The nature of the observing response as a single unit of behavior is discussed in the next section. The section entitled "Vigilance" deals with the properties of relatively large numbers of observing responses emitted over a period of time.

The observing response

Three rather different approaches to observing responses are current in the mid-1960s: (1) as a response in classical conditioning; (2) as a directly measurable response in instrumental conditioning; and (3) as a theoretical construct for the analysis of discrimination performance.

Observing and classical conditioning. The first and oldest approach to observing responses, developed in the context of Pavlovian classical conditioning, is concerned with the orienting reflex [see STIMULATION DRIVES]. This "reflex" is part of the unconditioned response to a novel stimulus, and the crucial point is that the response pattern follows essentially all *novel* stimuli. It is therefore not the unconditioned response to a specific stimulus. The complete orienting-reflex pattern includes neural, muscular, and autonomic components. These are measured by electroencephalographic (EEG) effects, such as alpha-blocking; by limb, head, ear, and eye orientations; and by changes in pupillary diameter, in galvanic skin responses, and in heart rate. The response is extinguished under repeated presentation of the stimulus. However, slight changes in the stimuli will evoke the response again.

The physiological analysis of the orienting reflex relates it to the reticular activating system at brain-stem and thalamic levels. Much of the research on the orienting reflex, which originated in the Soviet Union, is described in the English translation of Sokolov's *Perception and the Conditioned Reflex* (1958; see also Berlyne 1960).

The Western equivalent of the orienting reflex is the arousal response, defined physiologically as a replacement of high-amplitude slow waves in the EEG by low-amplitude fast waves (Lindsley 1960, p. 1563). Alpha-blocking is a good example of such arousal; it occurs in resting subjects who exhibit good alpha waves in their EEG (10 per second high-amplitude sinusoidal waves) and is manifested by the complete disappearance of alpha when a visual signal is presented. Alpha-blocking and other arousal effects are associated with excitatory and inhibitory systems in the reticular formation of the brain.

The arousal systems are also involved in the enhancement and suppression of cortical evoked responses and of motor responses to peripheral stimulation (Lindsley 1960, p. 1586). They may therefore be thought of as systems that "gate" incoming information by enhancing or attenuating incoming signals. In this sense, these systems permit one to consider observing responses as being of varying intensity.

Observing and instrumental conditioning. Western psychologists usually understand the observing response in terms of the instrumental conditioning paradigm. The response occurs prior to perception and is instrumental in permitting perception to occur.

Attempts at direct measurement of observing as an instrumental response have often used eye movements and visual signals. Such studies (see Carmichael & Dearborn 1947) assume, essentially, that shifts of attention can be equated with changes in eye fixation. Perception is diminished during a saccadic eye movement, and the "blind" period may last for from 5 to 40 milliseconds, depending on the arc covered by the eye. The duration of a typical eye fixation, in reading, for example, is of the order of 200 to 400 milliseconds. To the extent that attention mechanisms act in parallel with eye orientations, they would act within those time limits [see VISION, *article on* EYE MOVEMENTS].

The problem with this approach is that paying attention *cannot* be equated in a simple way with eye fixations. This is illustrated in a study by Baker on eye movements during a vigilance task with easily detected signals (1963, p. 151). Baker found that of 100 missed signals 99 occurred despite the fact that his observers' eyes were fixated directly upon the display. His subjects were looking without seeing, a familiar phenomenon in everyday life. In studies concerned with the direction, rather than the level, of attention it is much easier to base conclusions on eye-movement data. For example, Berlyne (1960, pp. 98–100) found that eye orientations were biased toward more complex and novel visual stimuli, and in that case it was proper to infer that attention was biased in the same way.

If a discrete measurable movement is necessary in order to receive a stimulus, that movement is, by definition, an observing response. Butler's well-known studies of curiosity in monkeys (see Berlyne 1960, p. 154) are based on a window-opening response that fits this paradigm. Butler showed that his monkeys emitted observing responses, that is, opened the window, with the only obvious reinforcement of being able to look out at objects in their environment. Significantly, the monkeys responded differently to different objects, which implies that the observing response was reinforced more by some objects than by others.

In a carefully designed experiment with human observers, which also fits this paradigm, Atkinson (1961) was able to show that the observers would select one of two possible observing responses with a predictable probability depending on the reinforcement schedule. His work is of additional interest because of his use of a mathematical model of discrimination learning in which the observing response is treated as one of a chain of responses in the discrimination process.

An application of this kind of technique by Holland (1958) to the analysis of human vigilance involved a switch operation to illuminate a display on which signals were presented. The observer had to operate the switch very rapidly if any visual information was to be obtained from the display. Holland was able to show that the signals acted as reinforcements for the observing responses in the same way that food pellets can reinforce bar pressing in operant conditioning. It is important to note that Holland's results can be obtained only if the response switch is hard to operate. This implies that a "cost" must be associated with an observing response if it is to be used in conditioning situations (see Jerison & Pickett 1963, pp. 220–222).

Observing as a theoretical construct. Approaches in which the observing response is defined by its theoretical role have the important function of making precise statements about the appropriate dimensions for the analysis of attention. Broadbent (1958) has developed an influential theory in which the observing response is considered as a filtering process that acts to select a message from among the stimuli reaching the senses for a "final common path" in perception. The problems raised by Broadbent and discussed more recently by Sanders (1963) raise a number of issues that are not presently resolved. Is attention a single-channel or multichannel operation? Is it a continuous or a discrete process? Present evidence favors the position that it is a discrete, single-channel process, and this view, in turn, raises additional questions. What is the duration of an act of attention? Is there a significant switching time required to shift attention from one point to another?

Questions such as these are being attacked in experiments performed during the middle 1960s. As an example, a study by Schmidt and Kristofferson (1963) suggests a duration for a "moment" of attention on the order of fifty milliseconds and assumes instantaneous switching. Studies based on Broadbent's filter theory have also appeared, which contribute to the analysis of the duration of an observing response, or, to use Sanders' term, a "selective act." It seems clear that the minimum duration is less than 250 milliseconds, but the details of the mechanism of the observing response, the more precise specification of the duration, and the understanding of the sequence of events in selective attention remain incompletely solved research problems.

If one visualizes the observing response as the opening or closing of a shutter of variable size to admit a sensory message, then spatial as well as temporal aspects of the response are important. Swets (1964, chapter 29) reports experiments on the detectability of pure tones when the observer is uncertain about their pitch. Performance was found to depend on central factors as well as on the frequency analysis at the level of the sense cells predicted by auditory theory. The central factors are equivalent to the shutter size or shape. One of the interesting points that Swets makes is that several different types of shutters may be available to the observer. One shutter may be tuned to a single band of frequencies, another to several bands. The available data are consistent with the notion that the observer selects among the shutters to satisfy his preferred strategy for observing in a particular task.

Significant advances have been made by each approach to observing responses. In the case of the orienting reflex and arousal, very important qualitative and some quantitative results have related behavioral to neurophysiological levels of analysis. In addition to providing a description of the activity of the organism in the alerted condition, this approach provides the means for measuring the intensity of observing. The approach emphasizing the direct measurement of observing as an instrumental response has suggested that such a response can be reinforced by signals and other stimuli, that it involves a "cost" to the organism, and that it is subject to conditioning and extinction. The indirect analysis of observing as a theoretical construct has raised precise questions and may eventually yield equally precise answers about temporal and other properties of the observing response, such as its switching time, its fixation time, and the selectivity of its filtering action.

Vigilance

The "vigilance" situation is a useful experimental approach to attention as a continuing activity involving populations of freely emitted observing responses. It deals with the performance of observers during prolonged vigils at tasks requiring the detection of occasionally presented signals. The signals, though weak, are readily detectable by an alert observer, and a failure to report a signal may be ascribed to a failure of attention. In this situation the observer emits many observing responses, and their characteristics are analyzed by sampling them at the moment when a signal is presented. The probability that an observing response will be emitted under given conditions is estimated by the ratio of detections to signals under those conditions.

In a vigilance task an observer watches a display, such as a meter or a cathode-ray tube, and observes a recurring nonsignal stimulus. A specified change in the stimulus is a "signal," and the observer's task is merely to report the signals when they occur. One of the early vigilance tasks, designed to simulate a radar display, was N. H. Mackworth's (1950) "clock test," in which the stimuli were steps of a clock hand and a long step was the signal. Other tasks have used displays with a continuous nonsignal stimulus (e.g., steady light) and clearly defined signals (e.g., onset of flickering). In most research on this topic observers worked alone and without interruption for an hour or more on a task such as Mackworth's, but the basic effects can be obtained with a variety of displays.

Important research findings. The most important results of research on vigilance can be summarized under three headings: the decrement function, display parameters, and subject parameters. More detailed expositions of those results are available in several surveys of the literature (e.g., Jerison & Pickett 1963; Leplat 1962;

Schmidtke & Micko 1964) and in the symposium on vigilance edited by Buckner and McGrath (1963).

The decrement function. The central result in vigilance studies is that although detection performance is nearly perfect at the beginning of a long vigil, it drops rapidly and appears to reach a plateau after 15 minutes or so. The problem in analysis has been to account for the decrement and for the plateau level, and this has been done by manipulating display parameters and subject parameters.

Display parameters. There is evidence (Jerison 1965) that the decrement may occur only if observing responses are elicited at a high rate, either by presenting nonsignal stimuli very frequently or by entirely omitting a cue about when to observe. When the decrement occurs, the level of the plateau varies with signal intensity, signal duration, and the conditional probability of a signal, given a nonsignal stimulus. The performance function with respect to visual signals is altered if there is uncertainty about both the spatial and the temporal positions of the signal. If there is spatial uncertainty, a demand is placed on the observer to search, or scan, the display, and patterns of search behavior can be "biased" toward higher probability regions by presenting signals with different probabilities at different positions on the display. Performance requiring search as well as attentiveness is also affected by "natural" scanning patterns, which tend to be biased toward contour lines, edges, and toward the center of a display.

Subject parameters. Performance on vigilance tasks is affected by cognitive, social, and individual-difference variables. Knowledge of results improves performance, as does the presence of a peer or an authority figure. Performance tends to be fairly stable within subjects, with test–retest reliabilities on the order of .80. Individual differences are very marked; an experiment based on 20 observers will typically have several who detect all the signals and some who miss 70 or 80 per cent of them. False alarms (errors of commission) tend to be restricted to a fraction of the subject population.

Theoretical analysis of vigilance. Theories of vigilance as of 1961 have been reviewed by Frankmann and Adams (1962). Since that time a clear theoretical advance has occurred with the application of decision theory to the problem. When the application is to decisions about whether or not to report a signal, then vigilance is a special case of signal-detectability theory (Swets 1964). Among those who attempt such an application, Jane Mackworth and Maurice Taylor (1963) consider the major vigilance effects as producing changes in the detectability index, d', of the signal, whereas Broadbent and Gregory (1963) consider the effects in terms of changes of criterion, β, toward increasing severity as a vigil progresses. Both d' and β are precisely defined variables in signal-detectability theory.

Decision-theory models are parsimonious, because they permit a unified analysis of expectancy effects associated with signal probability and of motivational effects associated with the importance of observing, detecting, and reporting signals. These effects may be analyzed separately and also combined in a single measure, the "expected value" of a response.

Jerison and Pickett (1963) have suggested that the decision-theory approach may be applied to the emission of observing responses rather than detection-indicating responses. They assume that the decision whether or not to observe depends on the utility of observing and on the probability that observing will be reinforced by a signal. The approach stresses a role for the ease or difficulty of paying attention and for the amount and kind of reinforcement for paying attention. Knowledge of results, for example, may affect the utility of observing by removing ambiguity about whether or not a signal, that is, a reinforcement or payoff, has been delivered. All theories of vigilance (e.g., Baker 1963) are concerned with the role of expectancy; a decision-theory approach provides a quantitative definition for expectancy as the a priori conditional probability of a signal given a stimulus (see Broadbent in Buckner & McGrath 1963, p. 166).

The basic problems in contemporary studies of attention are to describe and analyze the observing response as a physiological and psychophysical event or sequence of events and to show its relationship to other behavior. Great successes have been achieved in the resolution of the first problem by the discovery and analysis of the attention systems of the brain. Important, though less dramatic, advances have occurred in the more purely behavioral areas. The spatial and temporal parameters of the observing response are being studied within behavioral theories, such as Broadbent's filter theory (1958) and the theory of signal detectability (Swets 1964). The conditions under which observing responses are emitted are also analyzed within a decision-theory framework (Jerison & Pickett 1963), and additional insights are suggested by the research paradigms of operant conditioning (Holland 1958) and by the mathematical models of discrimination learning (Atkinson 1961).

At mid-century, attention is a rejuvenated topic in psychology. "Organs" of attention have been discovered in the brain, and physiological and behavioral methods have been developed that are yielding new and clearer insights into the mechanisms of attention.

HARRY J. JERISON

[*Directly related are the entries* HEARING; NERVOUS SYSTEM; SENSES; VISION. *Additional relevant material may be found in* DECISION THEORY; LEARNING, *articles on* CLASSICAL CONDITIONING *and* DISCRIMINATION LEARNING.]

BIBLIOGRAPHY

ATKINSON, RICHARD C. 1961 The Observing Response in Discrimination Learning. *Journal of Experimental Psychology* 62:253–262.

BAKER, C. H. 1963 Further Toward a Theory of Vigilance. Pages 127–170 in Donald N. Buckner and James J. McGrath (editors), *Vigilance: A Symposium*. New York: McGraw-Hill.

BERLYNE, D. E. 1960 *Conflict, Arousal, and Curiosity*. New York: McGraw-Hill.

BROADBENT, DONALD E. 1958 *Perception and Communication*. Oxford: Pergamon Press.

BROADBENT, DONALD E.; and GREGORY, MARGARET 1963 Vigilance Considered as a Statistical Decision. *British Journal of Psychology* 54:309–323.

BUCKNER, DONALD N.; and MCGRATH, JAMES J. (editors) 1963 *Vigilance: A Symposium*. New York: McGraw-Hill.

CARMICHAEL, LEONARD; and DEARBORN, WALTER F. 1947 *Reading and Visual Fatigue*. Boston: Houghton Mifflin.

FRANKMANN, JUDITH P.; and ADAMS, JACK A. 1962 Theories of Vigilance. *Psychological Bulletin* 59:257–272.

HAIDER, MANFRED; SPONG, P.; and LINDSLEY, D. B. 1964 Attention, Vigilance, and Cortical Evoked Potentials in Humans. *Science* New Series 145:180–182.

HOLLAND, JAMES G. 1958 Human Vigilance. *Science* New Series 128:61–67.

JAMES, WILLIAM (1890) 1962 *The Principles of Psychology*. New York: Smith.

JERISON, HARRY J. 1965 Human and Animal Vigilance. *Perceptual and Motor Skills* 21:580–582.

JERISON, HARRY J.; and PICKETT, RONALD M. 1963 Vigilance: A Review and Re-evaluation. *Human Factors* 5:211–238.

LEPLAT, JACQUES 1962 Travaux de surveillance et d'inspection: Bibliographie commentée de quelques recherches expérimentales. *Bulletin du Centre d'Études et Recherches Psychotechniques* 11:155–175.

LINDSLEY, DONALD B. 1960 Attention, Consciousness, Sleep and Wakefulness. Volume 3, pages 1553–1593 in American Physiological Society, *Handbook of Physiology*. Section 1: Neurophysiology. Edited by H. W. Magoun et al. Baltimore: Williams & Wilkins.

MACKWORTH, JANE F.; and TAYLOR, MAURICE M. 1963 The d' Measure of Signal Detectability in Vigilance-like Situations. *Canadian Journal of Psychology* 17:302–325.

MACKWORTH, N. H. 1950 *Researches on the Measure-*

ment of Human Performance. Medical Research Council Special Report, No. 268. London: H.M. Stationery Office.

SANDERS, ANDRIES F. 1963 *The Selective Process in the Functional Visual Field.* Assen (Netherlands): Van Gorcum.

SCHMIDT, MARIANNE W.; and KRISTOFFERSON, ALFRED B. 1963 Discrimination of Successiveness: A Test of a Model of Attention. *Science* New Series 139:112–113.

SCHMIDTKE, HEINZ; and MICKO, CHRISTOPH 1964 *Untersuchungen über die Reaktionszeit bei Dauerbeobachtung.* Forschungsberichte des Landes Nordrhein-Westfalen, No. 1360. Cologne and Opladen (Germany): Westdeutscher Verlag.

SOKOLOV, EVGENII N. (1958) 1963 *Perception and the Conditioned Reflex.* New York: Macmillan. → First published as *Vospriiatie i uslovnyi refleks.*

SWETS, JOHN A. (editor) 1964 *Signal Detection and Recognition by Human Observers: Contemporary Readings.* New York: Wiley.

TITCHENER, EDWARD B. 1908 *Lectures on the Elementary Psychology of Feeling and Attention.* New York: Macmillan.

WOODWORTH, ROBERT S. (1938) 1954 *Experimental Psychology.* Rev. ed. by Robert S. Woodworth and Harold Schlosberg. New York: Holt.

ATTITUDES

General considerations of attitude structures, their development, and their measurement are discussed under this heading. For discussion of similar concepts see GENERAL WILL; IDEOLOGY; NORMS; PUBLIC OPINION; VALUES. *Attitudinal development is described in* ADOLESCENCE; AGING; DEVELOPMENTAL PSYCHOLOGY; INFANCY; LEARNING THEORY; MORAL DEVELOPMENT; PERSONALITY; SOCIALIZATION. *Specific configurations of attitudes are discussed in* BODY IMAGE; CONFORMITY; CONSENSUS; INTERNATIONAL RELATIONS, *article on* PSYCHOLOGICAL ASPECTS; PERSONALITY, POLITICAL; PREJUDICE; SELF CONCEPT; STEREOTYPES; SYSTEMS ANALYSIS, *article on* PSYCHOLOGICAL SYSTEMS. *Methods of inducing attitude change are described in* BRAINWASHING; COMMUNICATION, MASS; COMMUNICATION, POLITICAL; EDUCATION, *article on* EDUCATION AND SOCIETY; GROUPS, *articles on* GROUP FORMATION *and* GROUP BEHAVIOR; HYPNOSIS; PERSUASION; PROPAGANDA; SUGGESTION. *Methods of assessing attitudes are discussed in* INTERVIEWING, *article on* SOCIAL RESEARCH; SURVEY ANALYSIS. *Major theoretical positions are described in* COGNITIVE THEORY; FIELD THEORY; GESTALT THEORY. *Also relevant are the biographies of* ALLPORT; HOVLAND; MCDOUGALL; STOUFFER; THURSTONE.

I
THE NATURE OF ATTITUDES

The concept of attitude is not only indispensable to social psychology, as Allport has pointed out in his classic article (1935), but also to the psychology of personality. The purpose of this article is to consider its relevance for the two fields by describing the structure and function of attitudes within the total personality and the various ways in which attitudes may lead to or determine social behavior.

Allport traces three points of origin of the modern concept of attitude: (1) the experimental psychology of the late nineteenth century, which, in its laboratory investigations of reaction time, perception, memory, judgment, thought and volition, employed such conceptual precursors to attitude as muscular set, task-attitude, *Aufgabe,* mental and motor attitudes, *Einstellung,* and determining tendencies; (2) psychoanalysis, which emphasized the dynamic and unconscious bases of attitudes; and (3) sociology, wherein attitudes came to be recognized as the psychological representations of societal and cultural influence. The sociological study of the Polish peasant by Thomas and Znaniecki (1918) is generally credited with being the first to propose that the study of social attitudes is the central task of social psychology, and it was the first to give systematic priority to this concept.

But it was not until the decade of the 1940s, which began with the publication of Erich Fromm's *Escape From Freedom* (1941) and ended with *The Authoritarian Personality* (Adorno et al. 1950), that the relevance of social attitudes for personality theory became widely recognized.

Despite the central position of attitudes in social psychology and personality, the concept has been plagued with a good deal of ambiguity. As the student pores over and ponders the many definitions of attitude to be found in the literature, he finds it difficult to grasp in precisely what ways they are conceptually similar to, or different from, one another. Even more important, it is difficult to assess what difference these variations in conceptual definitions make. Most of the definitions of attitude seem to be more or less interchangeable insofar as attitude measurement and hypothesis testing are concerned.

Two critics have gone so far as to suggest that the attitude concept be discarded. Doob (1947) argues that while attitude is a socially useful concept, it has no systematic status as a scientific construct and therefore should be replaced with such learning theory constructs as afferent-habit strength, efferent-habit strength, drive, anticipatory and mediating responses, etc. Blumer (1955), writing from a sociological standpoint, recommends abandoning the concept because it is ambiguous, thereby blocking the development of a body of sound social-psychological theory; it is difficult to ascertain what data to include as part of an attitude and what to exclude; and it lacks an empirical reference and hence cannot be used effectively as a unit of analysis either in personality organization or in the study of social action.

Such views are, however, in the minority; and it is safe to predict that the concept of attitude will, despite its ambiguity, remain with us for many years to come. This writer is of the opinion that the confused status of the concept can best be corrected not by abandoning it but by subjecting it to continued critical analysis with the aim of giving it a more precise conceptual and operational meaning.

Definition of attitude

What exactly is an attitude? A favorite way to proceed is to present first several definitions of attitude found in the literature and then after commenting on their common elements present one's own with the hope that it is a distillation of the essence of these other definitions. Rather than burdening the reader with such an approach, this writer will start out with his own definition and, in elaborating upon it, comment on the ways in which it is similar and dissimilar to other conceptions of the nature of attitudes. *An attitude is a relatively enduring organization of beliefs around an object or situation predisposing one to respond in some preferential manner.*

Relatively enduring. Some predispositions are momentary ones, in which case they are not called attitudes. While such concepts as set, or *Einstellung,* are typically employed in referring to a momentary predisposition, the concept of attitude is typically reserved for more enduring, persistent organizations of predispositions. It is not possible to pin down more precisely the difference between temporary and enduring predispositions except to say that a minimum requirement might be test–retest consistency or reliability of measurement. One rarely asks about the reliability of an experimentally induced set, but one always asks about the reliability of an attitude questionnaire. "Attitudes are particularly enduring sets formed by past experiences" (Asch 1952, p. 585).

While there may well be a possible hereditary basis for attitudes, as Allport (1950) suggests, all writers are agreed that attitudes are acquired through the principles of learning, whatever these are or may turn out to be. Along with Sherif and Cantril (1945–1946), and Chein (1948), the issue of what attitudes are is seen here to be altogether independent of how they are learned.

An organization of beliefs. Virtually all theorists agree that an attitude is not a basic, irreducible element within the personality but represents a cluster or syndrome of two or more interrelated elements. In the above definition, the elements are beliefs (or cognitions, or expectancies, or hypotheses).

Definition of belief. A belief is any simple proposition, conscious or unconscious, inferred from what a person says or does, capable of being preceded by the phrase "I believe that. . . ." The content of a belief may *describe* an object or situation as true or false; *evaluate* it as good or bad; or *advocate* a certain course of action as desirable or undesirable. Whether or not the content of a belief is to describe, evaluate, or advocate action, or to do all three, all beliefs are predispositions to action; and an attitude is thus a set of interrelated predispositions to action organized around an object or situation.

Each belief within an attitude organization is conceived to have three components:

(1) A *cognitive* component, because it represents a person's knowledge, held with varying degrees of certitude, about what is true or false, good or bad, desirable or undesirable.

(2) An *affective* component, because under suitable conditions the belief is capable of arousing affect of varying intensity centering (*a*) around the object of the belief, or (*b*) around other objects (individuals or groups) taking a positive or negative position with respect to the object of belief, or (*c*) around the belief itself, when its validity is seriously questioned, as in an argument.

(3) A *behavioral* component, because the belief, being a response predisposition of varying threshold, must lead to some action when it is suitably activated. The kind of action it leads to is dictated strictly by the content of the belief. Thus, even a belief that merely describes is a predisposition to action under appropriate conditions. Consider, for example, my belief that Columbus discovered America in 1492. The behavioral component of this predisposition may remain unactivated until the day I leaf through two history books to decide which one to buy for my young son. One gives the date as 1492 and the other as 1482. My belief will predispose me, other things being equal, to choose the one giving the 1492 date. I am pro the 1492 book, and con the 1482 book.

Harding et al. (1954) have pointed out that the

relationship between these three components is so close that it makes little difference which ones are used to rank individuals with respect to their attitudes toward specific ethnic groups. In experimental research, one component of a belief is difficult, if not impossible, to isolate and to manipulate independently of a second component. Rosenberg (1960), for example, has tried to alter experimentally the affective component of a belief under hypnosis in order to determine its effect on the cognitive component. Such an approach assumes that the independent variable can be manipulated without manipulating the dependent variable at the same time. It is equally likely, however, that the effect on the dependent variable is not a consequence but a concomitant of the experimental manipulation of the independent variable.

Rosenberg's research is only one of many carried out in recent years in which such concepts as balance, harmony, symmetry, congruity, and dissonance play an important theoretical role. All such notions share the common assumption that man strives to maintain consistency between the cognitive, affective, and behavioral components within a single belief, between two or more related beliefs, between all the beliefs entering into an attitude organization, and between all the beliefs and attitudes entering into a total system of beliefs.

Beliefs and attitudes. The conception of an attitude as an organization of beliefs is consistent with Krech and Crutchfield's view that all attitudes incorporate beliefs but not all beliefs are necessarily a part of attitudes. But the definition does not promulgate one widely held distinction between belief and attitude, namely that beliefs have only a cognitive component while attitudes have both cognitive and affective components, a distinction made by Krech and Crutchfield (1948, p. 153).

There are several grounds for objecting to such a conceptual distinction between belief and attitude. First, Osgood, Suci, and Tannenbaum (1957), as well as many others, have shown that virtually any concept is factorially loaded on an evaluative dimension, the dimension that, as Katz and Stotland state, operationally differentiates the concept of attitude from that of belief (1959, p. 428). In this connection, it is interesting to note that the distinction Krech and Crutchfield drew between belief and attitude in 1948 no longer appears in their more recent work (Krech, Crutchfield, & Ballachey 1962); and in discussing the cognitive component of attitudes, they emphasize mainly the "evaluative beliefs."

Second, any belief considered singly, representing as it does a predisposition to respond in a preferential way with respect to the object of the belief, can thus be said to have an affective, as well as a cognitive, component. This affective component will not become manifest under all conditions (every single time a prejudiced white Southerner sees a Negro) but only when the belief is somehow challenged by the attitude object or by someone else (a Negro asks to be served in a segregated restaurant) or when the preferential action toward which one is predisposed is somehow blocked (a travel agent violates a belief by routing a passenger from New York to Chicago via London). The reason we do not speak of pro or con in the case of many beliefs (e.g., the shape of the earth) is that such beliefs, enjoying universal consensus, do not come up in a controversial way, with everyone preferring the same "pro-round" response. Thus, the affective component of such predispositions is typically not activated. But the affective component must be assumed to be there, and if and when such a belief becomes a matter of controversy, it will become activated. Thus, there was a time centuries ago when most people believed the earth was flat. When this "pro-flat" belief was challenged by the "pro-rounds" the response was undoubtedly far from affectively neutral. Any taken-for-granted belief, however impersonal, has the property of generating affective reactions when its validity is challenged, if for no other reason than that it raises questions about the person's ability to appraise reality correctly. We care about the correctness of our beliefs; truth is good and falsity is bad.

Third, it is not necessary to assume that the positive or negative affect associated with a belief or attitude is necessarily directed toward the object of the belief or attitude. As already noted, the affect may also be directed toward other objects—individuals or groups who agree with us or oppose us with respect to the object—or it may arise from our efforts to preserve the validity of the belief itself.

On the basis of the preceding considerations, an attitude is defined simply as an organization of interrelated beliefs around a common focus. The attitude has cognitive and affective properties by virtue of the fact that the several beliefs constituting it have cognitive and affective properties that interact and reinforce one another.

The concept of organization. There are a number of structural dimensions frequently employed to describe the organization of several parts within a whole. These dimensions can, with more or less equal ease, be employed to describe the organization of the several beliefs contained within an attitude, of several attitudes within a more inclusive attitude system, or to describe the organization of all of man's beliefs, attitudes, and values within his total cognitive system.

Differentiation refers to the degree of articulation of the various parts within a whole, and the greater the number of parts the greater the degree of differentiation. A concept used more or less synonymously with differentiation is *complexity*, or *multiplexity*. Degree of differentiation is an index of the total amount of correct and incorrect information or knowledge possessed about the focus of the attitude. In a paranoid system, an attitude may be highly differentiated but is not necessarily correct. Smith, Bruner, and White (1956), therefore, distinguish between degree of differentiation, a phenomenological concept, and its objective counterpart, degree of *informational support*.

Cognitive organization also implies a cognitive *integration* of whatever parts are differentiated; there is an appreciation of similarities as well as of differences between parts. We speak of *isolation* or *segregation* or *compartmentalization* of parts within a psychological whole whenever two or more parts within a whole are not functionally integrated, or are not seen to be interrelated with one another, or when their contradictory nature is not perceived. Levinson (Adorno et al. 1950), for example, describes the isolated structure of anti-Semitic attitudes: the Jew is believed to be seclusive, but also intrusive; the Jew is believed to be a capitalist, but also a communist.

Another organizational variable is *centrality*. The parts are conceived to be arranged along a central–peripheral dimension wherein the more central parts are conceived as being more salient or important, more resistant to change, and, if changed, as exerting relatively greater effects on other parts.

Organization in terms of *time perspective* refers to the extent to which the whole or the part is viewed in terms of the historical past, present, or future and the interrelations between past, present, and future. A time perspective may be broad or narrow. An attitude may have a narrow time perspective in the sense that the beliefs constituting it are oriented primarily in terms of either the historical past, or present, or future.

Specificity or *generality* refers to the extent to which one can predict one belief from a knowledge of another within an attitude organization (e.g., from a belief about desegregating the Negro in education to a belief about desegregating the Negro in housing) or one attitude from another (from attitude toward the Jew to attitude toward the Negro) or nonverbal behavior from the verbal expression of a belief or attitude. It is assumed that the specificity–generality of behavior is a function of the degree of differentiation, integration, and isolation of one belief from another and of one attitude from another.

Breadth or *narrowness* of an attitude or a system of beliefs refers not to the number of parts within a whole but to category width or to the total range, or spectrum, of relevant social reality that is actually represented within the whole. An attitude toward Russia, for example, may be broad (e.g., covering many facets of Russian life) but relatively poorly differentiated, or it may be narrow (e.g., covering only political freedom in Russia) and at the same time highly differentiated.

Focus on an object or a situation.   In the first case, we refer to an attitude object, which may be concrete or abstract (a person, a group, an institution, an issue). In the second case, we have in mind a specific situation (an ongoing event or activity) around which a person organizes a set of interrelated beliefs about how to behave.

Neglect of "attitudes-toward-situations." Attitude theorists have generally been more interested in the theory and measurement of attitudes toward objects, across situations, than in the theory and measurement of attitudes toward situations, across objects. We have, for example, scales that measure attitude toward the Negro, the church, labor, and socialism. We do not have scales that measure attitudes toward such situations as managing or eating in a restaurant, being a passenger or driver of a bus, buying or selling real estate. As a result, the study of attitudes-toward-situations has become more or less split off from the study of attitudes-toward-objects. And to account for the characteristic ways that people behave with respect to specific social situations, altogether new concepts are introduced, personality psychologists typically preferring *trait* concepts and social psychologists typically preferring *role* concepts and such additional concepts as group norm, definition of the situation, and social structure.

The splitting off of attitude-toward-situation from attitude-toward-object has, in the writer's opinion, severely retarded the growth of attitude theory. For one thing, it has resulted in a failure to appreciate that an attitude object is always encountered within some situation, about which we also have an organized attitude. It has resulted in unsophisticated attempts to predict behavior on the basis of a single attitude-toward-object, ignoring the equally relevant attitude-toward-situation. And it has resulted in unjustified interpretations and conclusions, to the effect that there is often an inconsistency between attitudes and behavior, or a lack of dependence of behavior on attitudes.

A more detailed consideration of the relation between attitudes and behavior is reserved for a later section.

Interrelated predispositions to respond.   Not all writers are agreed that attitudes are predispositions (or preparations, or states of readiness) to respond. Horowitz (1944) sees an attitude as "a response rather than a set to respond." Doob (1947), analyzing an attitude from the standpoint of behavior theory, sees it as an implicit response. Most writers, however, seem to agree that an attitude is a predisposition of some sort, although there seems to be some difference of opinion about what kind of predisposition it is: predisposition to respond; predisposition to evaluate; predisposition toward an evaluative response; or predisposition to experience, to be motivated, and to act. In the present formulation, we prefer simply "predisposition to respond," with the understanding that a response may be either a verbal expression of an opinion or some form of nonverbal behavior. And, following Campbell (1963), attitudes are acquired behavioral dispositions differing from other behavioral dispositions, such as habit, motive, trace, and cell assembly, in that they also represent a person's knowledge or view of the world.

The present formulation differs from other dispositional formulations in one important respect. An attitude, representing as it does an organization of beliefs, is not a single predisposition but a set of interrelated predispositions focused on an attitude object or situation. Not all of these predispositions need necessarily become activated by an attitude object or situation. Which ones are activated depends on the particular situation within which a particular attitude object is encountered. For example, a prejudiced white person's encountering a Negro on a bus in a city with a history of segregation will not necessarily activate the same predispositions as his encountering a Negro on a bus in Paris and consequently will not necessarily lead to the same response toward the attitude object.

Another way in which the present formulation differs from other formulations is that all attitudes are here assumed to be "agendas for action" or to have a behavioral component because all the beliefs constituting them, regardless of whether they describe, evaluate, or advocate, represent predispositions which, when activated, will lead to a response. This formulation differs from that of Chein (1948), Smith, Bruner, and White (1956), and Katz and Stotland (1959), who all hold that an attitude may or may not have a behavioral compo-

nent. "For example," Katz and Stotland write, "one may regard impressionistic art as desirable but not go to a museum of modern art, read about impressionism, or acquire prints of impressionistic paintings. An individual who has an attitude with a behavioral component, on the other hand, has some degree of impulsion to do something to or about the object" (p. 429).

This writer would suggest that such an attitude toward art must also have a behavioral component, because the individual holding it must have made some response from which this attitude was inferred. Perhaps he had *said* something about it in a particular situation; perhaps he had *looked* admiringly at an impressionistic painting when visiting a friend; perhaps he was impelled to *argue* about it. If he had said or done absolutely nothing about it, it is difficult to see how anyone could have inferred that he possessed this attitude. A predisposition that does not lead to some response cannot be detected.

Leads to a preferential response.   While everyone agrees that an attitude leads to a preferential (or discriminatory) response, the basis for the preferential response is not clear. Is a positive or negative preference due to the fact that the attitude object or situation is affectively liked or disliked, or because it is cognitively evaluated as good or bad? In most discussions on attitude, it is assumed that the two dimensions—affection and evaluation—are more or less synonymous. Katz and Stotland (1959), for example, define attitude as a "predisposition to evaluate," include the cognitive and affective elements under evaluation, and operationally define evaluation in terms of verbal statements of goodness–badness. Osgood, Suci, and Tannenbaum (1957) define attitude as synonymous with the evaluation dimension of the semantic space. Krech, Crutchfield, and Ballachey (1962), while they distinguish the affective component from evaluative beliefs (which are included under the cognitive component), seem to assume implicitly that affection and evaluation generally go together to produce a favorable or unfavorable attitude.

Affective and evaluative components.   The conceptual difficulty arises from the fact that the two dimensions of *like–dislike* and *goodness–badness* do not necessarily go together. When speaking of the pro–con dimension, often said to be *the* defining characteristic of attitude, we do not know whether the preferential response of approach or avoidance is due to the fact that it is liked or disliked, or because it is seen to be good or bad. It is possible to like something bad and to dislike something good. A person may believe, for example, that T. S. Eliot's poetry is good but still not like it; that a particular medicine is good but dislike the way it tastes. Conversely, a person may believe cigarette smoking is bad but enjoy it. Clearly, there is no necessary one-to-one relation between affect and evaluation. Whether or not the preferential response will be positive or negative will therefore depend on the relative strength of one's evaluative beliefs and of one's positive or negative feelings. A person will make a pro response to an object toward which he harbors negative feelings if he believes the object to be sufficiently good for him.

The definition, therefore, emphasizes that an attitude predisposes one to make a preferential response and avoids the implication that the response itself is either affective or evaluative. It may, and usually does, involve both positive and negative; or it may be a resolution of opposing forces between affection and evaluation. Accurate prediction of the preferential response therefore requires a separate assessment of affective and evaluative predispositions underlying the response.

Objects of preferential response.   Toward what may the preferential response be directed? As already mentioned, an attitude predisposes one to respond preferentially not only to the attitude object or situation but also to other objects—individuals and groups who agree with, or oppose, us with respect to the attitude. A favorable or unfavorable attitude toward a presidential candidate, for example, not only predisposes us to respond preferentially to such a candidate on Election Day but also toward all others who take an attitudinal position with respect to such a candidate. Finally, the preferential response may be directed toward the maintenance or preservation of the attitude itself. A person with a particular attitude is predisposed to selectively perceive, recognize, judge, interpret, learn, forget, recall, and think in ways congruent with his attitude; and such selective responses, while mediated by an attitude, are not necessarily responses directed toward the attitude object or situation itself.

A final point is that all three types of responses —toward attitude objects, toward other objects, and toward the maintenance of the attitude itself —may be expected to be positively intercorrelated because they are all mediated by the same attitude.

Attitude differentiated from other concepts

A major source of conceptual confusion arises from the fact that there is considerable disagreement over how the concept of attitude should be distinguished from closely related concepts. Allport (1935) points out that attitudes have a wide range of usage. This writer ventures to suggest that this broad usage can and must be remedied. What follows is an attempt to differentiate among various concepts that come up in discussions of attitude, in the hope of giving each of them a more precise meaning.

Belief system.   A belief system represents the total universe of a person's beliefs about the physical world, the social world, and the self. It is conceived as being organized along several dimensions (Rokeach 1960), and additional dimensions can be added as required by further analysis or empirical research. A belief system can further be analyzed in terms of subsystems of varying breadth or narrowness. An attitude is one type of subsystem of beliefs, organized around an object or situation that is, in turn, embedded within a larger subsystem, etc.

Ideology.   The concept of belief system is broader than ideology, containing preideological, as well as ideological, beliefs. An ideology is an organization of beliefs and attitudes—religious, political, or philosophical in nature—that is more or less institutionalized or shared with others, deriving from external authority.

Value.   The concept of value has at least three distinct meanings. To Thomas and Znaniecki value is a sociological concept, a natural object that has, in fact, acquired social meaning and, consequently, "is or may be an object of activity" (1918, p. 21). To Campbell (1963) and many others, a value is synonymous with attitude because the attitude object has *valence.* To yet many others, a value is seen to be more basic than an attitude, often underlying it.

In this writer's conception, a value is a type of belief, centrally located within one's total belief system, about how one ought, or ought not, to behave, or about some end state of existence worth, or not worth, attaining. Values are thus abstract ideals, positive or negative, not tied to any specific attitude object or situation, representing a person's beliefs about ideal modes of conduct and ideal terminal goals—what Lovejoy (1950) calls generalized adjectival and terminal values. Some examples of ideal modes of conduct are to seek truth and beauty, to be clean and orderly, to behave with sincerity, justice, reason, compassion, humility, respect, honor, and loyalty. Some examples of ideal goals or end states are security, happiness, freedom, equality, ecstasy, fame, power, and states of grace and salvation. A person's values, like all beliefs, may be consciously conceived or unconsciously held, and must be inferred from what a person says or does.

A grown person probably has tens of thousands of beliefs, hundreds of attitudes, but only dozens of values. A value system is a hierarchical organization—a rank ordering—of ideals or values in terms of importance. To one person, truth, beauty, and freedom may be at the top of the list, and thrift, order, and cleanliness at the bottom; to another person, the order may be reversed. The Allport–Vernon–Lindzey Scale of Values (1931) enables one to measure the relative order of importance of six classes of values: theoretical, social, political, religious, aesthetic, and economic.

The relation between attitudes and values will be considered further in the section "Functions of an attitude."

Opinion.   An opinion is defined here as a verbal expression of some belief, attitude, or value. Which underlying belief, attitude, or value the opinion reflects is a matter of inference. There are all kinds of reasons why a particular verbal expression cannot necessarily be taken at face value. A person may be unable or unwilling to reveal to himself or to others his real beliefs, attitudes, or values. He may need to conceal from himself, for example, his idealization of power and transform it, by a process of rationalization, into ideals of charity and responsibility. In the literature, a distinction is often made between public and private attitudes, and similar distinctions could also be made between public and private beliefs and values. An opinion typically represents a public belief, attitude, or value, but it may come closer to private ones when verbally expressed under increasing conditions of privacy.

Faith, delusion, and stereotype.   Faith refers to one or more beliefs a person accepts as true, good, or desirable, regardless of social consensus or objective evidence, which are perceived as irrelevant. A delusion is a belief held on faith judged by an external observer to have no objective basis and which is, in fact, wrong. A stereotype is a socially shared belief that describes and/or evaluates an attitude object in an oversimplified or undifferentiated manner. In contrast to a delusion, a person's stereotype is judged by an external observer to contain an element of truth in it, but it is not qualified by other beliefs about the attitude object.

Sentiment.   The concept of sentiment, which has had a long history, seems to have fallen into general disuse in the past decade or two. Most writers (e.g., Murray & Morgan 1945) agree that sentiment is more or less synonymous with attitude. Asch (1952), however, seems to talk of sentiments as if they are closer to what we have here called values. Insofar as operational definition and measurement are concerned, sentiment and attitude seem indistinguishable.

Attitudes and behavior

A preferential response toward an attitude object cannot occur in a vacuum. It must necessarily be elicited within the context of some social situation, about which, as already noted, we also have attitudes. It is perhaps helpful to conceive of any particular attitude object as the *figure* and the situation in which it is encountered as the *ground*. How a person will behave with respect to an object within a situation will therefore depend, on the one hand, on the particular beliefs or predispositions activated by the attitude object and, on the other hand, by the beliefs or predispositions activated by the situation. We thus postulate that a person's social behavior must always be mediated by at least two types of attitudes—one activated by the object, the other activated by the situation.

If one focuses only on attitude-toward-object one is bound to observe some inconsistency between attitude and behavior, or, at least, a lack of dependence of behavior on attitude. Most frequently mentioned as evidence in this connection are such studies as those by La Piere (1934) and by Kutner et al. (1952), in which there were found to be marked discrepancies among restaurant and hotel owners between their verbal expressions of discrimination toward Chinese and Negroes via letter or phone and their nondiscriminatory face-to-face behavior. One possible explanation of such apparent inconsistency is suggested by the present analysis: the investigators did not obtain all the relevant attitudinal information needed to make accurate predictions. The subjects not only had attitudes toward Chinese and Negroes but, being managers of an ongoing business, also had attitudes about how to conduct such a business properly. The investigator's methods, however, are typically focused on obtaining data relevant to attitude-toward-object and are generally insensitive toward attitude-toward-situation.

One may thus readily agree with Krech, Crutchfield, and Ballachey when they say that behavior is determined by a number of attitudes, wants, and situational conditions rather than by a single attitude (1962). Their additional statement that "attitude test scores alone are usually not enough to predict behavior" (p. 163) does not necessarily follow from the preceding. As already suggested, a "situational condition" can psychologically be reformulated as "attitude-toward-situation" and assessed by methods similar to those employed in assessing attitude-toward-object. Unfortunately, however, only the latter kind of attitude has thus far been the focus of operational definition and measurement, even though attitudes have typically been more broadly defined as predispositions toward situations as well as toward objects.

However, it is not enough merely to assess in advance the two kinds of attitudes discussed. It is also necessary to recognize that attitude-toward-object and attitude-toward-situation will cognitively interact with one another and will have differing degrees of importance with respect to one another, thereby resulting in behavior that will be differentially influenced by the two sets of attitudes. In one case, an attitude object may activate relatively more powerful beliefs than those activated by the situation, thereby accounting for the generality of behavior with respect to an attitude object; or, the situation may activate the more powerful beliefs, thereby accounting for the specificity of behavior with respect to an attitude object. Campbell (1963) has shown that the threshold of discrimination toward Chinese seeking reservations for overnight lodging and restaurants is without exception lower —there is more discrimination—in non-face-to-face situations. He has similarly shown that the threshold of discrimination toward Negro miners by white miners is always lower in town than in the mines (Minard 1952). In pointing to "different situational thresholds," Campbell is not only explaining away the apparent inconsistency between attitude and behavior, or between one behavior and another, but he is also suggesting that certain situations consistently activate discriminatory behavior with respect to a specific attitude object more than do other situations.

In the context of this discussion, one may fruitfully raise again Blumer's criticism (1955). The state of present attitude theory is such that there are no rigorous criteria available for ascertaining when we are dealing with one attitude or with more than one attitude. We speak, for example, of *an* attitude toward the Negro, but also of *an* attitude toward desegregation of the Negro in education. In line with the present analysis, we would prefer to say that the way we feel toward desegregation of the Negro in the school involves the activation of at least two attitudes, one concerning the Negro, the other concerning a particular educational situation.

Functions of an attitude

Does an attitude possess drive-producing properties, or do motives come from sources other than the attitude itself? This issue has provoked much debate in the literature and for lack of space will

not be discussed here except to say that the controversy does not seem to have led to any empirical research. It is at present a moot point, as Chein (1948) points out.

In the past few decades, there has, nevertheless, been a slow but steady advance toward increasingly more comprehensive formulations regarding the functions of an attitude. Beginning with Freud (1930), and followed by such thinkers as Lasswell (1930), Fromm (1941), Maslow (1943), and culminating in *The Authoritarian Personality* (Adorno et al. 1950), the proposition that attitudes serve mainly irrational, ego-defensive functions became widely accepted. Students of personality and culture and of sociology further emphasized the adjustive function of attitudes—the adjustment of primitive and modern man to their specific cultures and subcultures. And influenced by these ideas, as well as by gestalt psychology and by more recent developments in psychoanalytic ego psychology (which stressed the autonomous nature of an ego freed from the service of id and superego), Sarnoff and Katz (1954) and Smith, Bruner, and White (1956) were among the first to explicitly recognize the positive functions that attitudes also serve. This was shortly followed by several additional refinements, leading to Katz's most recent formulation (1960, p. 170) of four functions of attitudes: (1) instrumental, adjustive, or utilitarian; (2) ego-defensive; (3) value-expression; and (4) provision of knowledge based upon the individual's need to give adequate structure to his universe.

These four functions are not regarded as operating in isolation from one another. A particular attitude may simultaneously serve several or all of these functions. This writer, in describing the function of belief systems, speaks of the need to "understand the world insofar as possible, and to defend against it insofar as necessary" (1960, p. 400). Maslow (1963) speaks of two simultaneous functions—the need to know and fear of knowing.

There is no reason to assume, however, that Katz's four functions are unique to attitudes. These are also the functions of single beliefs (e.g., belief in the existence of a Creator) and of organizations of beliefs broader than attitudes—variously referred to by such terms as ideology, belief system, *Weltanschauung*, philosophy of life, etc.

While the conceptual isolation of these four functions is a distinct step forward, we have not yet advanced sufficiently in our theories and methods to determine by objective procedures precisely which functions a particular attitude serves for a particular person and to what degree. The objective assessment of function becomes even more formidable when it is recognized that a particular function may be judged present when viewed from an inside, phenomenological standpoint but absent when viewed from an outside, objective standpoint. In this writer's research with three chronic paranoid schizophrenics (1964), it was found that various delusional beliefs served not only last-ditch, ego-defensive functions but also knowledge functions. Delusions represent a search for meaning, giving the person holding them the illusion of understanding even though they are grotesque, ego-defensive distortions of reality.

An attitude can be likened to a miniature theory in science, having similar functions and similar virtues and vices. An attitude, like a theory, is a frame of reference, saves time, organizes knowledge, has implications for the real world, and changes in the face of new evidence. A theory, like an attitude, is a prejudgment, may be selective and biased, may support the *status quo*, may arouse affect when challenged, and may resist change in the face of new evidence. An attitude, in short, may act, in varying degrees, like a good theory or a bad theory, and depending on what kind of a theory an attitude acts like, may serve one function better than another.

Value-expressive function as superordinate. A final point concerns the relation between the value-expressive function and the remaining three functions. Does not the knowledge function also refer to a person's central values concerning truth, understanding, and the search for meaning; and does it not also serve self-expression, self-development, and self-realization? In the same way, the adjustive function can be said to involve such values as security, achievement, competence, success, and loyalty to in-group. And the ego-defensive function may be reflected in the excessive glorification of such phenomenologically perceived positive values as neatness and cleanliness, thrift, honor, chivalry, and sexual and racial purity, or may be reflected in the excessive condemnation of such negative values as lust, intemperance, subversion, waste and extravagance, and racial mongrelization.

It is thus possible to conceive of the value-expressive function as superordinate to all other functions and to suggest that all of a person's beliefs and attitudes may be in the service of, or instrumental to, the satisfaction of one and another pre-existing, often conflicting, values: adjustive values, ego-defensive values, and knowledge and other self-realizing values.

And the function that seems to be served by all the values within one's value system is the enhancement of what McDougall (1908) has aptly called the master of all sentiment, the sentiment of self-regard.

Summary

To summarize this article, the following more extended definition of attitude is offered: An attitude is a relatively enduring organization of inter-related beliefs that describe, evaluate, and advocate action with respect to an object or situation, with each belief having cognitive, affective, and behavioral components. Each one of these beliefs is a predisposition that when suitably activated results in some preferential response toward the attitude object or situation, or toward others who take a position with respect to the attitude object or situation, or toward the maintenance or preservation of the attitude itself. Since an attitude object must always be encountered within some situation about which we also have an attitude, a minimum condition for social behavior is the activation of at least two interacting attitudes, one concerning the attitude object and the other concerning the situation.

MILTON ROKEACH

[*Directly related are the entries* PUBLIC OPINION; VALUES. *Other relevant material may be found in* COGNITIVE THEORY; CONCEPT FORMATION; GESTALT THEORY; SYSTEMS ANALYSIS, *article on* PSYCHOLOGICAL SYSTEMS.]

BIBLIOGRAPHY

ADORNO, THEODOR W. et al. 1950 *The Authoritarian Personality: Studies in Prejudice.* American Jewish Committee, Social Studies Series, No. 3. New York: Harper.

ALLPORT, GORDON W. 1935 Attitudes. Pages 798–844 in Carl Murchison (editor), *A Handbook of Social Psychology.* Worcester, Mass.: Clark Univ. Press.

ALLPORT, GORDON W. 1950 Prejudice: A Problem in Psychological and Social Causation. *Journal of Social Issues* Supplement Series, No. 4.

ALLPORT, GORDON W.; VERNON, PHILIP E.; and LINDZEY, GARDNER (1931) 1960 *A Study of Values.* 3d ed. Boston: Houghton Mifflin.

ASCH, SOLOMON E. (1952) 1959 *Social Psychology.* Englewood Cliffs, N.J.: Prentice-Hall.

BLUMER, HERBERT 1955 Attitudes and the Social Act. *Social Problems* 3:59–64.

CAMPBELL, DONALD T. 1963 Social Attitudes and Other Acquired Behavioral Dispositions. Volume 6, pages 94–172 in Sigmund Koch (editor), *Psychology: A Study of a Science.* New York: McGraw-Hill.

CHEIN, ISIDOR 1948 Behavior Theory and the Behavior of Attitudes: Some Critical Comments. *Psychological Review* 55:175–188.

DOOB, LEONARD W. 1947 The Behavior of Attitudes. *Psychological Review* 54:135–156.

FREUD, SIGMUND (1930) 1958 *Civilization and Its Discontents.* Garden City, N.Y.: Doubleday. → First published as *Das Unbehagen in der Kultur.*

FROMM, ERICH (1941) 1960 *Escape From Freedom.* New York: Holt.

HARDING, JOHN et al. 1954 Prejudice and Ethnic Relations. Volume 2, pages 1021–1061 in Gardner Lindzey (editor), *Handbook of Social Psychology.* Cambridge, Mass.: Addison-Wesley.

HOROWITZ, EUGENE L. 1944 Race Attitudes. Pages 139–247 in Otto Klineberg (editor), *Characteristics of the American Negro.* New York: Harper.

KATZ, DANIEL L. 1960 The Functional Approach to the Study of Attitudes. *Public Opinion Quarterly* 24:163–204.

KATZ, DANIEL L.; and STOTLAND, EZRA 1959 A Preliminary Statement to a Theory of Attitude Structure and Change. Volume 3, pages 423–475 in Sigmund Koch (editor), *Psychology: A Study of a Science.* New York: McGraw-Hill.

KRECH, DAVID; and CRUTCHFIELD, RICHARD 1948 *Theory and Problems of Social Psychology.* New York: McGraw-Hill.

KRECH, DAVID; CRUTCHFIELD, RICHARD; and BALLACHEY, EGERTON L. 1962 *Individual in Society: A Textbook of Social Psychology.* New York: McGraw-Hill.

KUTNER, BERNARD; WILKINS, CAROL; and YARROW, PENNY R. 1952 Verbal Attitudes and Overt Behavior Involving Racial Prejudice. *Journal of Abnormal and Social Psychology* 47:649–652.

LA PIERE, RICHARD T. 1934 Attitudes vs. Actions. *Social Forces* 13:230–237.

LASSWELL, HAROLD D. (1930) 1960 *Psychopathology and Politics.* New ed., with afterthoughts by the author. New York: Viking.

LOVEJOY, ARTHUR O. 1950 Terminal and Adjectival Values. *Journal of Philosophy* 47:593–608.

McDOUGALL, WILLIAM (1908) 1936 *An Introduction to Social Psychology.* 23d ed., enl. London: Methuen. → A paperback edition was published in 1960 by Barnes and Noble.

MASLOW, A. H. 1943 The Authoritarian Character Structure. *Journal of Social Psychology* 18:401–411.

MASLOW, A. H. 1963 The Need to Know and the Fear of Knowing. *Journal of General Psychology* 68:111–125.

MINARD, RALPH D. 1952 Race Relationships in the Pocahontas Coal Field. *Journal of Social Issues* 8:29–44.

MURRAY, HENRY A.; and MORGAN, CHRISTIANA D. 1945 A Clinical Study of Sentiments. *Genetic Psychology Monographs* 32:3–149, 153–311.

OSGOOD, CHARLES E.; SUCI, G. J.; and TANNENBAUM, P. H. (1957) 1961 *The Measurement of Meaning.* Urbana: Univ. of Illinois Press.

ROKEACH, MILTON 1960 *The Open and Closed Mind: Investigations Into the Nature of Belief Systems and Personality Systems.* New York: Basic Books.

ROKEACH, MILTON 1964 *The Three Christs of Ypsilanti.* New York: Knopf.

ROSENBERG, MILTON J. 1960 A Structural Theory of Attitude Dynamics. *Public Opinion Quarterly* 24:319–340.

SARNOFF, IRVING; and KATZ, DANIEL 1954 The Motivational Basis of Attitude Change. *Journal of Abnormal and Social Psychology* 49:115–124.

SHERIF, MUZAFER; and CANTRIL, HADLEY 1945–1946 The Psychology of Attitudes. *Psychological Review* 52:295–319; 53:1–24.

SMITH, MAHLON B.; BRUNER, JEROME S.; and WHITE, ROBERT W. 1956 *Opinions and Personality.* New York: Wiley.

THOMAS, WILLIAM I.; and ZNANIECKI, FLORIAN (1918) 1958 *The Polish Peasant in Europe and America.* Vol. 1. 2d ed. New York: Dover.

II
ATTITUDE CHANGE

Interpreted broadly, the topic of attitude change is not only a focal preoccupation of theory and research in social psychology; it embraces phenomena and problems that equally concern students of personality, of culture, of political affairs, and of consumer preferences. The molding of public opinion by propaganda and through processes of persuasion is a matter of attitude change, but so also are the development or reduction of prejudice and the socialization of the child to adhere to the sentiments and values of his culture. Even the modification of interpersonal feelings and expectations during the course of personal acquaintance or in psychotherapy is a matter of attitude change.

Scope and brief history

The concept of attitude, although variously defined, is most commonly employed to designate inferred *dispositions*, attributed to an individual, according to which his thoughts, feelings, and perhaps action tendencies are organized with respect to a psychological object. The topic of attitude change thus embraces the conditions under which such dispositions are initially formed and subsequently modified in the course of a person's transactions with his physical, social, and informational environment. It includes changes both in relatively superficial and specific matters of "opinion" and in deep-seated sentiments or "cathexes" that are properly regarded as constitutive of personality, changes that occur in the natural course of maturation and experience as well as those that result from exposure to deliberate persuasion or propaganda.

Although the scope of the topic is thus embarrassingly broad, substantial research has been brought to bear upon it only along a much narrower front. When attitudes became the central focus of social psychology in the 1920s and 1930s (Allport 1935; Murphy et al. 1937) and techniques had been worked out for their measurement by pencil-and-paper tests, social psychologists came to investigate under this rubric favorable or unfavorable orientations toward consensually defined social objects and issues (war, the church, ethnic groups, etc.), leaving to specialists in personality research the conceptualization and study of man's deeper and more idiosyncratic attachments. The approach characteristic of this early period was mainly descriptive and correlational, with little sustained attention to the conditions under which attitudes are formed and modified and little effort toward linking the psychology of attitudes with more general explanatory principles.

Four developments in the 1930s and 1940s radically changed the complexion of the field, making problems of attitude change salient and for the first time justifying the claim that in attitudes—previously a matter of academic but quite untheoretical preoccupation—social psychology finds one of its most important and fertile topics.

Sample surveys and polling. A major influence on social psychology has been the development of the technology of sample surveys and survey analysis—public opinion polling. The new survey research institutes, equipped to conduct and analyze door-to-door interviews with the general public, escaped the restricted world of the earlier questionnaire studies carried out with readily accessible college student respondents. When repeated surveys asked the same questions, trend data on opinion change brought to the fore the problem of how events and exposure to mass communications influence opinions. With the invention of the "panel" technique of survey design and analysis, involving repeated interviews with the same respondents, the persuasive impact of mass communications on ordinary publics became the subject of fruitful research. The study of voting behavior, in particular, by these methods produced findings relevant to attitude change.

Small-group research. A second important trend brought social realities under experimental scrutiny, in the tradition of research on small-group dynamics begun by Kurt Lewin and his students (Lewin 1939–1947; Festinger 1950). Conceptual equipment and experimental techniques became available for treating systematically the social influences on attitudes and behavior to which people are exposed by virtue of their memberships and participation in groups. The interrelations between these first two trends—survey research and small-group research—are examined by E. Katz and Lazarsfeld (1955).

Psychoanalytic formulations. Meanwhile psychoanalytic conceptions were gaining favor among American psychologists, revolutionizing their approach to personality research. Following pathways suggested earlier by Harold Lasswell, the authors of *The Authoritarian Personality* (Adorno et al. 1950) illustrated in depth, for the special case of anti-Semitism as well as general ethnic prejudice, how attitudes may be an integral part of the defensive postures that people assume against the consequences of deep-seated inner conflict. From this perspective, the psychology of attitude formation and change became an integral part of the study of personality dynamics.

Experimental studies of communication. The fourth formative development was the concerted deployment of experimental method in the study of conditions governing the effects of persuasive communication begun during World War II and continued in the postwar years by Carl Hovland and his associates (Hovland, Lumsdaine, & Sheffield 1949; Hovland, Janis, & Kelley 1953). Planning their experiments within a broadly mapped conception of the process of communication, which accommodated hypotheses arising from a variety of theoretical contexts, these investigators demonstrated the power of carefully designed experimentation to identify the main and interactive effects on attitudes of numerous characteristics of the source and content of communications and of audiences.

By mid-century, the effect of these developments was to make attitude change not only a field of active investigation, via both controlled experimentation and the correlational methods of the sampling survey and panel, but also an arena in which theoretical approaches of general and social psychology were being elaborated and applied. The focus on predictive hypotheses concerning change now made such theories relevant, as they had not been in the earlier, descriptive phase of attitude research.

Before we turn to examine the major theoretical treatments of attitude change, the ensuing section reviews current conceptualizations of the origin and development of attitudes.

Formation and development of attitudes

In an influential early formulation, Allport (1935, pp. 810–812) listed four conditions for the formation of attitudes: the *integration* of numerous specific responses within an organized structure; the *differentiation* of more specific action patterns and conceptual systems from primordial, nonspecific attitudes of approach and withdrawal; *trauma,* involving "a compulsive organization of the mental field following a single intense emotional experience"; and the adoption of attitudes by imitation of parents, teachers, or peers. These categories can readily be applied to describing the development of particular attitudes, but it is clear that they are descriptive rather than explanatory and are neither logically coordinate nor mutually exclusive. They variously emphasize different aspects of attitudinal learning, such as its gradualness or suddenness, the emotional intensity of the learning experience, and the informational basis on which attitudes are acquired.

Regarding attitudes as a special case of the more general category *acquired behavioral dispositions,* Campbell (1963, pp. 107–111) focuses on the problem of informational basis and proposes six different ways of acquiring the information upon which such dispositions are based: blind trial-and-error, general perception, perception of others' responses, perception of the outcomes of others' explorations, verbal instructions relevant to behavior, and verbal instructions about objects' characteristics. Although these represent varying degrees of efficiency, Campbell argues that dispositions acquired by these different modes are psychologically equivalent and that the several modes combine additively to result in stronger dispositions. However, solid evidence for the equivalence of the several modes is lacking.

Theorizing about the modes and processes by which attitudes are acquired should rest upon an extensive "natural history" of the development of attitudes, based on longitudinal and cross-sectional research that would sample a variety of content domains. The research needed for such a natural history largely remains to be done. There have been no long-term longitudinal investigations tracing the development and change of attitudes in the same individuals over substantial segments of the life cycle. Newcomb has contributed two classic short-term longitudinal studies: one (1943) following changes in students' liberalism–conservatism over their college years and another (1961) investigating the development and change of interpersonal attitudes among members of a specially assembled college living group. Cross-sectional research comparing the attitudes of different age groups has focused heavily on the single domain of ethnic prejudice (see Allport 1954; Harding et al. 1954), with some attention also to the development of political attitudes (Hyman 1959).

In both these domains, there is evidence supporting Allport's conception of differentiation as characterizing the early stages of attitude development in childhood. The evident manifestations of prejudice in childhood involve diffuse rejection of the out-group and its symbols; only later is the culturally prescribed content of prejudice elaborated. Similarly, American children learn early to identify with their family's political affiliation; more specific attitudes on political issues come only later. Scattered evidence suggests that with increasing maturity, attitudes may become more highly integrated in the sense of showing more internal consistency. But age trends in the organization of attitudes urgently require study, across different topics and different social and cultural groups.

Theoretical approaches to attitude change

Although the natural history of attitude development remains largely to be written, the processes underlying attitude change have nonetheless become the subject of active experimental inquiry. In part, inquiry has been directed toward formulating and refining empirical generalizations about factors that influence attitudes. (Representative findings are reviewed by Janis & Smith 1965.) To a major extent, however, inquiry has been guided by theoretical orientations imported from other areas of psychology.

Although the possibility that attitudes have innate components cannot be excluded (see, for instance, Hebb & Thompson 1954, p. 549 on innate fear of the strange), the primary contribution of learning to the formation and development of attitudes is beyond question. Theories of learning are thus exploited for their bearing on the conditions of attitude change. Attitudes also embody the results of information processing and in turn affect the way that a person conceives and judges aspects of his world. Theories of the cognitive processes are therefore a second source of hypotheses about attitude change. As organized dispositions toward psychological objects, moreover, attitudes are important components of personality. To the extent that the personality has properties of a dynamic system, a person's attitudes should develop and change under the influence of the roles that they play in personality adjustments and transactions. A third group of theoretical orientations to attitude change thus have their roots in personality theory.

Since the major types of theoretical orientation to the study of attitude change are addressed to different questions and concerned with different variables, they cannot be regarded as mutually exclusive or even as seriously competitive. A comprehensive view of attitude change might require an integration drawn from all of them. Such an integration has not been forthcoming, however, and the *Zeitgeist* of recent theoretically oriented research has tended to seek progress in increasingly precise and formalized models of component processes.

Learning theories. Although the study of attitude change has not been a major proving ground for the learning theories that flourished in recent American psychology, each of the major variants of learning theory has been applied to it. Thus for Skinner (1957) and his followers, who dissolve the dispositional concept of attitude into overt verbal behaviors, attitude change becomes a matter of the shaping of verbal behavior under the control of schedules of reinforcement. Clark Hull's learning theory has been applied to the psychology of attitudes by Doob (1947). Empirical evidence is available (e.g., Scott 1957) supporting the prediction from reinforcement theory that people tend to adopt, as their own, attitudinal positions that they have been asked to espouse publicly in experiments, when their performance has been accompanied by reward. Establishment of attitudes by the procedures of classical Pavlovian conditioning has also been demonstrated (Staats & Staats 1958).

But the mere demonstration that attitudes *can* be established and modified according to learning principles does not lead very far in research. The more important contribution of learning theory to the understanding of attitude change has come from investigators who have taken its relevance for granted and applied its categories of stimulus–response analysis, reinforcement, generalization, and conflict to empirically derived problems of persuasive communication and attitude change. Such an approach was characteristic of the Yale studies under the leadership of Carl Hovland, which also drew with catholicity on other theoretical traditions. Thus, in one study of the effects of fear-arousing appeals in persuasive communication, the lesser effectiveness of strongly threatening appeals is interpreted in terms of the learning of interfering responses (incompatible with acceptance of the communicator's recommendations) to reduce the induced state of anxiety (Hovland, Janis, & Kelley 1953, pp. 77–89). No test of a specific deduction from learning theory is involved; rather, the categories of learning theory serve heuristically to set the terms of the empirical problem and to suggest lines of interpretation that give direction to subsequent investigation.

Cognitive approaches.   The theoretical controversies of the generation of American psychology between 1930 and 1950 pitted the cognitive orientation derived from gestalt psychology against the predominant stimulus–response learning theories of American behaviorism. These controversies carried over into the social psychology of attitude change, particularly with respect to interpretation of the processes of social influence involved in the traditional topic of prestige suggestion. People tend to evaluate objects, such as slogans or literary passages, more highly when they are attributed to a highly valued, prestigious source than when they are attributed to a source toward which their existing attitudes are less favorable. Is this influence of the source to be interpreted in essentially associative terms, in which the positive or negative affect aroused by the source adheres to the message on the model of classical conditioning? Or, as Asch (1952, pp. 387–417) argued eloquently from a gestalt orientation, does attribution serve rather to provide a new context of meaning that

induces changes in the cognitive object, about which changed evaluative judgments and accompanying affect are then appropriate? [*See* Cognitive theory; Gestalt theory.]

At least two issues appear to have been confounded in the controversy. One has to do with the priority of cognitive as compared with affective factors in attitude change. Do people change their feelings about an object because they have come to see it differently, or do they change their beliefs about it to fit prior alterations in their feelings? The evidence now seems clear that both sorts of processes occur; what may be primary is a tendency to bring beliefs and feelings into congruence (Rosenberg 1960). The second issue also seems rather dated from present perspectives: Are the processes of influence to be interpreted in associative or meaningful terms? Recent elaborations of associative theory, in their emphasis on central mediational processes intervening between stimulus and response, tend to converge with the older cognitive theories. Heat has dissipated from controversy as theorists socialized to feel at home with stimulus–response or with cognitive terminologies come to see their differences as more a matter of linguistic preferences and conceptual strategy and less a question of truth versus falsity (see Campbell 1963, pp. 112–135).

Contemporary cognitive approaches to attitude change have therefore lost the polemical cast that used to characterize cognitive theory when it was a minority systematic position in opposition to behavioristic psychology. Concern has shifted from system building to the clarification of particular aspects of attitude change. Here a minor theme draws upon the psychology of judgment; a major one postulates trends toward cognitive consistency or balance as underlying attitude change.

Judgmental processes and attitude change.   As inferred dispositions, attitudes are customarily measured by eliciting acts of judgment: agreement or disagreement with standard statements of opinion. Much of the behavior to which attitudes give rise is mediated by further acts of judgment that involve the placement of the issue or object in an evaluative framework and its asignment to a category. Concepts and principles drawn from the general psychology of judgment should therefore throw light on the processes of attitude change. Sherif and Hovland (1961) and Sherif et al. (1965) have made promising beginnings toward bringing about this rapprochement.

As applied to the context of persuasive communication, their thinking may be simplified as follows: A person's attitude on a controversial issue may be coordinated to the range of discriminable opinion positions that he finds acceptable. The person's *latitude of acceptance* will typically be narrower than the accompanying *latitude of rejection* when he is highly ego-involved with the issue or when his position is extreme. In responding to a persuasive communication that advocates some position on the issue, he places it on a subjective pro–con scale of favorability with respect to the issue. The effects of the communication on the recipient will depend heavily on the distance between the recipient's stand and the position advocated by the communication as he locates it in his scale of judgment. The same objective differences in the positions of two communications may be perceived very differently by different individuals, depending on the nature of their judgment scales, which in turn are determined by such factors as their familiarity with the issue and the extremity of their own positions. Maximal persuasive effects are to be expected when the position advocated in the communication falls near the boundary of the recipient's latitude of acceptance; under these conditions the recipient is likely to minimize its judged distance from his own position (*assimilation effect*) and to be open to its influence. When the position of the communication falls within his latitude of rejection, he is likely to exaggerate its judged distance from his own stand (*contrast effect*) and to resist influence. On issues characterized by low ego-involvement, where latitudes of acceptance are correspondingly great, the persuasive effect may be a positive function of the distance between the recipient's stand and the position advocated, within relatively broad limits.

This schematic summary may suggest the promise of reconceptualizing attitudinal processes in terms of the psychology of judgment. At present, the promise has yet to be realized. Major areas of theoretical ambiguity remain to be clarified, and the data that have thus far been brought to bear are not fully consistent.

Helson's theory of adaptation level—a zone of neutrality on the stimulus continuum that is established as a weighted mean of focal and background stimuli and of the residues of previous stimulation—represents an alternative conceptualization of judgmental processes that is founded in extensive psychophysical research. In principle, it should be applicable to the analysis of attitude change. In the hands of Helson and his co-workers (Helson 1964, pp. 609–630), however, its application has thus far been so broadly analogical that it has contributed little to bringing attitude change in conceptual contact with fundamental processes of judgment. What emerges is the assertion that ex-

pressions of attitude are a joint function of the presenting stimulus, of the social context and its pressures ("background factors"), and of personality ("residual factors")—hardly a novel formulation.

Consistency or balance theories.   Since the mid-1950s, the most active front in the study of attitude change has centered on a group of related theories that seek to come to grips with the dynamics of attitude change via formulations of the interplay between the person's postulated tendency toward consistency in specified aspects of his beliefs and attitudes and the incoming information with which he is confronted. The idea of a trend toward psychological consistency is an old one. What is new in the recent attention that it has received is the combination of theoretical formalization and experimental ingenuity to test inferences that go beyond the earlier common sense. The theories to be considered vary greatly in scope and ambition, but none of them purports to offer a general account of attitude change.

Heider's theory of balance.   The phenomenologically oriented theorist Heider (1946; 1958, pp. 200–209) initiated the recent emphasis on trends toward consistency with a treatment of the seemingly very narrow problem involved in identifying states of balance and "imbalance" in the cognitive field of an experiencing person p, as he entertains specified relationships with another person o, and with some attitudinal object x. Relations of two kinds are considered: the *sentiment* (or attitude) relation of liking or disliking and the *unit* relation involved in perceiving persons or objects as belonging together in a specially close way. Both types of relations when they exist may be positive or negative (degrees of relationship are not considered). The relations in a p-o-x triad are balanced when all three relations are positive or when two of the relations are negative and one is positive. Imbalance occurs when two of the relations are positive and one is negative.

Heider gives as an example of imbalance the following triad: p worships o (liking, positive); o tells a lie (positive unit relation between o and x); p disapproves of lying (negative relation of dislike between p and x). Were p to come to dislike o, the triad would come into balance. Other routes by which p could re-establish balance would be to sever the unit relation between p and x ("it isn't typical of o to lie") or to dissolve the experienced unity of o by introducing a cognitive differentiation that segregates the aspect of o as liar (disliked) from the rest of o (liked)—both differentiated aspects now entering into balanced triads. According to the theory, balanced states are stable; imbalanced states are unstable. Heider postulates a general trend to re-establish balance when it is disturbed by the registration of new information; but his formulation is intuitive and qualitative, containing no basis for predicting the route by which balance will be attained.

Newcomb's theory. The relations with which Heider is concerned obtain within the cognitive field of an experiencing subject *p*. Newcomb (1961), who like Heider has been interested in the relationships between attitudes and interpersonal attraction, offers a slightly modified version of the conditions under which *p-o-x* relations are *subjectively* balanced or imbalanced. (He also uses a different notation.) On the additional assumptions that reciprocated attractions between persons are more rewarding than nonreciprocated ones and that accurate perceptions of the attitudes of *o*'s toward *x*'s will in the long run be more rewarding to each *p* than inaccurate ones, Newcomb goes on to derive the prediction that as interpersonal relations stabilize in established social groups they will approximate conditions of *objective* balance in which, for example, people who share agreement on important issues and feel the same way about other people also come to like each other. His study of *The Acquaintance Process* in specially convened student living groups provides evidence of strong trends toward subjective balance from the beginning, with increasing trends toward objective balance developing over time. Newcomb thus extends Heider's principle of balance from the private worlds of phenomenology to the objective world of interpersonal relations.

Theory of cognitive consistency. In a provocative recent venture, Rosenberg and Abelson (1960) introduced a degree of formalization and extended the principle of balance from the restricted scope of *p-o-x* relations to encompass more general conditions of consistency within and between cognitions about an emotionally significant issue.

Rosenberg and Abelson posit a hierarchy of responses to imbalance in a cognitive structure, such that imbalance is resolved by that route that involves the minimal number of changes in the relations and signs of cognitive elements. But the tendency to reduce imbalance is not the only factor that determines how persons go about the resolution of cognitive discrepancies: there is also a tendency, independent of the striving for consistency, for the individual to prefer solutions that maximize his potential hedonic gain.

This model has yet to undergo much testing in research and will undoubtedly have only a short life in its present form. It is nevertheless worth consideration as exemplifying one of the directions in which trends toward consistency are currently being explored in accounting for attitude change. Its virtues of flexibility and generality are in contrast to those of specificity and quantification presented by Osgood and Tannenbaum's congruity model (1955), which generates precise predictions of shifts in the evaluation of both subject (e.g., "Eisenhower") and object (e.g., "communism") when assertions join them in positive (e.g., "praises") or negative (e.g., "condemns") associative linkage.

Festinger's cognitive dissonance theory. Of all the versions in which the consistency principle has appeared, Festinger's theory of cognitive dissonance has attracted the most active investigation in the late 1950s and early 1960s (Festinger 1957; Brehm & Cohen 1962). Any two cognitive elements—beliefs or bits of knowledge—may be *consonant, dissonant,* or *irrelevant* to one another. Dissonance occurs when one element follows psychologically from the contrary of the other. The total amount of dissonance that a person experiences is a function of the importance of the elements in a dissonant relationship and of the proportion of relevant relations that are dissonant. There is a tendency for the person to attempt to reduce dissonance when it arises: states of dissonance have motivational properties. Dissonance may be reduced in three major ways: by changing one or more of the elements involved in dissonant relations, by adding new cognitive elements that are consonant with already existing cognitions, and by decreasing the importance of the dissonant elements. A general tendency for cognitions to be brought into correspondence with impinging reality is assumed.

Although this capsule statement sounds like a very general consistency theory, the ingenious program of experimentation that Festinger and his followers have carried out has been primarily concerned with a much more restricted sphere of consistency or inconsistency—that between a person's cognitions of what he has done and his awareness of grounds for not having done it. Typical cases arise after a person makes a decision or when he has been induced to comply with a distasteful request. In the first instance, decisions are supposed to be followed by residual dissonance between awareness of the decision and awareness of the reasons supporting the alternative course of action that was rejected. The attempt to reduce such dissonance may lead the person to seek out informational or social support for the decision that he has taken.

The second case, that of "forced compliance," involves dissonance between the person's awareness of the compliant act to which he has irrevocably committed himself and his cognition of the grounds for not having wanted to do it. One way of reducing the dissonance is to change his private attitude or preference in the direction of consonance with the compliant behavior. Here is the basis for some of the "nonobvious" predictions from the confirmation of which Festinger claims strong support for his theory. Thus, when a person is induced by bribe or threat to voice opinions contrary to those that he privately holds, the weaker the inducement, the *more* likely he is to change his private views in a direction that brings them into accord with the ones that he has been induced to express. So long as the positive or negative inducement is sufficient to bring about compliance, the greater the inducement, the more disproportional the grounds for compliance, and therefore the less the dissonance and the less the motivation for attitude change to reduce it.

Clearly there is a wide discrepancy between the apparent generality of the theory and the rather special character of the experiments that have tested it. Brehm and Cohen (1962, pp. 299–300), in their comprehensive review of the evidence bearing on dissonance theory, seek to plug the gap in part by pointing out that where the antecedents of behavior have been a major concern of other theories, dissonance theory is concerned, at least in part, with the *consequences* of behavior. They go on to suggest that *commitment* may be necessary before the psychologically consonant or dissonant status of particular cognitive elements can be determined. They reformulate the core assertion of the theory to state that "a person will try to justify a commitment to the extent that there is information discrepant with that commitment" (Brehm & Cohen 1962, p. 300)—a significant and important statement, but one much narrower in scope than Festinger's original propositions.

In spite of the large amount of research recently stimulated by Festinger's theory, most of which purports to confirm it, the status of the theory is still far from clear. The experiments tend to be open to alternative interpretations. The experimental manipulations by which commitment is brought about as a precondition for the arousal of dissonance have not been critically scrutinized and may be important. To a considerable extent, experimental ingenuity has substituted for theoretical explicitness: experimentally, for example, alternative routes for the reduction of dissonance have been eliminated to leave attitude change as the predicted outcome, but the theory has little to say about which of the possible ways of reducing dissonance a person will employ. Where predictions from learning theories of reinforcement and conflict are pitted against predictions based on dissonance theory, as in some recent studies, the outcomes do not consistently support dissonance theory. The conjecture may be ventured that, in the long run, dissonance theory will turn out to have made sense of certain paradoxical feed-back effects of a person's behavior upon his attitudes but to have said little that is important about the main themes governing the formation of attitudes and the direction of behavior. Or it may become incorporated in a more comprehensive theory that deals with these themes. The lure of the paradoxical "nonobvious prediction" can deflect attention from the main story, which may be "obvious" but needs to be formulated and specified.

Approaches based on theories of personality. Learning theories have their sources in rigorous experimentation with lower species and college sophomores; judgmental theories still bear the marks of the psychophysical laboratory; other cognitive theories find their models in rigorous research on perceptual processes; but personality theories trace their origin to the clinic and consulting room. The atmosphere is entirely different. Rigor and precision are likely to be sacrificed in favor of relevance to human experience and problems. Whether the gain justifies the loss is a major issue that divides modern psychology.

Psychoanalysis. Among personality theories, psychoanalysis shows most strongly the characteristic virtues and vices of clinical origins. A generally psychoanalytic, but not doctrinaire, perspective was brought to bear upon the sources of prejudiced attitudes in *The Authoritarian Personality* (Adorno et al. 1950). This suggestively rich, influential, but technically vulnerable study portrayed the prejudiced person as using his attitudes to maintain a rigid and precarious defensive posture, bolstering his self-esteem by identifying with the strong and rejecting the weak, resolving his own uncertainties and keeping his unacceptable impulses in check (while giving them covert expression) by cleaving moralistically to a world of clear-cut alternatives, a world in which the safe areas of conventional respectability seem bounded by unknown dangers and conspiracies. This study did not deal directly with attitude change, but the implications were clear: to the extent that prejudiced attitudes are so grounded, there is little to be hoped from rational persuasion. The expression of prejudice can be controlled by firm authority; its dynamic roots perhaps excised by psychotherapy; and its occasion avoided by wiser child rearing. In present perspective this is a one-sided picture, even for this least rational of attitudes.

Like learning theory, psychoanalytic theory has suggested concepts, categories, and hypotheses to investigators of attitude change whose principal research directives have arisen from the phenomena being studied. Such influence is particularly apparent in the work of Janis (e.g., 1959), whose treatment of decisional conflicts represents an important alternative to Festinger's.

Self theories.   Approaches to personality that emphasize self, self-image, and identity have not given rise to formal theories of attitude change. That such theories might well be developed is suggested by the widespread and loose evocation of the term "ego-involvement" (Sherif & Cantril 1947) as a determinant of resistance to change in attitudes. Also suggestive is Rokeach's (1960) treatment of belief systems, in which he contrasts a central region of primitive beliefs about self and world with a peripheral region comprising the variety of beliefs that a person receives on authority. More directly relevant are the accounts of attitude change under the conditions of extreme coercive persuasion that characterized the so-called brainwashing or thought reform conducted by the Chinese Communists (Lifton 1961; Schein et al. 1961). In cases where deep-seated convictions were substantially shaken and relatively profound changes of attitude brought about, we hear of references to "death and rebirth" being employed. To unfreeze attitudes that have become central constituents of the self, the sense of identity itself is attacked; guilt is evoked, confessed, and expiated. Somewhat similar processes have been described for the transformation of a young layman into a monk (Erikson 1958) or of a recruit into an officer (Smith 1949). The seeming significance and human cogency of the phenomena touched upon in these descriptions raise doubts about the extent to which the theory of attitude change may have been impoverished by too close confinement to the pallid topics and mild pressures of the laboratory. There are striking similarities between the processes of attitude change in self-involving life settings and in psychotherapy (Frank 1961).

Functional approaches to attitude change.   Not tied to any single theory of personality, a group of recent approaches to the development and change of attitudes is nevertheless oriented to the personality as an empirical system. These functional approaches attempt a relatively comprehensive account of the functions that a person's opinions and attitudes serve in the ongoing economy of personality, on the assumption that knowledge of the motivational basis of attitudes should point to the conditions under which change can be expected. From the functional standpoint, the vigorous resistance with which persuasive efforts are commonly met suggests that people have a strong interest in maintaining their attitudes with as little change as possible.

Smith, Bruner, and White (1956), on the basis of an intensive clinical study, offer a classification in terms of three broad functions served by opinions and attitudes: (1) *object appraisal,* (2) *social adjustment,* and (3) *externalization.* Any persistent attitude is likely to serve all three functions to some extent, but there is considerable variation from issue to issue and from person to person with respect to the function that predominates.

Object appraisal.   The first function involves scanning and appraising the input of information from the external world for its relevance to the person's motives, goals, values, and interests, thus giving rise to selective self-exposure and attention to information. A person's stock of *existing* beliefs and opinions simplifies his task of scanning by providing him with already evaluated categories to which incoming information can be fitted. When object appraisal predominates, attitudes should be malleable, in response to rational presentations of information that lead the person to reappraise the bearing of reality factors on his interests and enterprises. Even in this case some resistance may be expected, since relatively stable categories are an advantage to a person in coordinating an effective way of coping with the too unstable world.

Social adjustment.   The part played by a person's opinions in facilitating, disrupting, or simply maintaining his relations with significant others is termed social adjustment. Since attitudes may be organized in response to motivated nonconformity, as well as to conformist motives, a better term for this function might be the *mediation of self–other relations.* In contrast with object appraisal, in which informational input about the object of the attitude is the crucial formant and source of change, here the strategic information pertains to how other people regard the object. This information engages his motives to affiliate and identify himself with them or to detach himself and oppose them. The influence of reference groups on a person's attitudes is classified here.

Externalization.   The final class of functions, more broadly phrased as externalization and ego defense, involves response to an external object or event in a way that is colored by a person's unresolved inner problems. The attitude taken toward external facts is an overt symbolic substitute for covert attitudes taken in the inner struggle. This function has been emphasized by psychoanalysis to the exclusion of the others, and, of course, it is the function that is one-sidedly stressed in *The Authoritarian Personality* (Adorno et al. 1950). Attitudes so motivated are unlikely to be influenced by rationally presented information, but they may respond to authoritative reassurances that allay anxiety, to changes brought about in self-insight, or to the uncovering processes that go on in psychoanalytic therapy.

A closely related classification of four functions is provided by Katz (1960; see also Katz & Stotland 1959), who develops the implications of each for conditions of attitude change.

Such functional classifications must be regarded as devices of heuristic convenience, not as theories that are true or false. But the hypotheses about attitude change for which they provide a framework are being tested in empirical research. Here difficulties in assessing motivation combine with those inherent in the study of attitudes to make clear-cut results difficult to obtain.

Some concluding remarks

This essay has focused on theoretical approaches to the study of attitude change; but the research on which this spate of theories, models, and approaches is grounded is not entirely in good order, and a few cautionary remarks are appropriate in conclusion.

The recent rapid flow of research has not represented, in a way that is adequate for the healthy development of theory, the full range of phenomena implied by the customary definitions of attitude. We have noted the relative dearth of naturalistic descriptive studies. When the relevant variables and relationships are yet to be discerned, premature leaping into rigidly designed experimentation may be costly. The too frequent failure of apparently well-designed studies to stand up to replication should be a warning. Reasons of efficiency have also led to the restriction of experimental studies of change to relatively superficial attitudes and beliefs in regard to which exposure to brief communications might be expected to have measurable effects. Similar reasons have led to a concentration on short-term effects instead of the more important long-term ones.

The integration of attitude research with the study of personality structure and processes is largely still incomplete. By and large, the investigators who study personality change, as in psychotherapy, are different from those who are interested in attitude change; they conceive of their problems within different frameworks and theorize about them in different terms.

More strictly technical aspects of research on attitude change should also cause concern. The care expended by psychometricians on the refinement of sophisticated scaling models for the measurement of attitudes has largely been lost to the experimentalist, who is fastidious about experimental design but slipshod in his techniques of measurement. Although perhaps more serious from the perspective of fostering the specification and development of theory, investigators and theorists alike have been entirely too cavalier in referring to attitude change without specifying the *aspect* of attitude—belief, feeling, or action tendency—in which change is predicted and measured. It often seems as though any stray feature of opinion in which change can readily be produced will do for experimentation. Moreover, researchers would do well to return to the safeguards employed by Hovland, Lumsdaine, and Sheffield (1949) against the contamination of results by the expectations of guinea pig subjects who know that they are under study.

For all these strictures, research on attitude change has made immense strides in recent decades. Knowledge in this field should be advanced and consolidated if current trends in research toward theoretical and experimental virtuosity are balanced by equal concern with representativeness and fidelity to the phenomena.

M. Brewster Smith

[*Directly related are the entries* Brainwashing; Education; Persuasion; Propaganda. *Other relevant material may be found in* Cognitive theory; Communication; Gestalt theory; Learning theory; Mental disorders, treatment of; Prejudice; Psychoanalysis; Self concept; Socialization.]

BIBLIOGRAPHY

Adorno, Theodor W. et al. 1950 *The Authoritarian Personality.* American Jewish Committee, Social Studies Series, No. 3. New York: Harper.

Allport, Gordon W. 1935 Attitudes. Pages 798–844 in Carl Murchison (editor), *A Handbook of Social Psychology.* Worcester, Mass.: Clark Univ. Press.

Allport, Gordon W. 1954 *The Nature of Prejudice.* Cambridge, Mass.: Addison-Wesley. → An abridged paperback edition was published in 1958 by Doubleday.

Asch, Solomon E. (1952) 1959 *Social Psychology.* Englewood Cliffs, N.J.: Prentice-Hall.

Brehm, Jack W.; and Cohen, Arthur R. 1962 *Explorations in Cognitive Dissonance.* New York: Wiley.

Campbell, Donald T. 1963 Social Attitudes and Other Acquired Behavioral Dispositions. Pages 94–172 in

Sigmund Koch (editor), *Psychology: A Study of a Science*. Volume 6: Investigations of Man as Socius: Their Place in Psychology and the Social Sciences. New York: McGraw-Hill.

COHEN, ARTHUR R. 1964 *Attitude Change and Social Influence*. New York and London: Basic Books.

DOOB, LEONARD 1947 The Behavior of Attitudes. *Psychological Review* 54:135–156.

ERIKSON, ERIK H. (1958) 1962 *Young Man Luther: A Study in Psychoanalysis and History*. Austin Riggs Monograph No. 4. New York: Norton.

FESTINGER, LEON 1950 Informal Social Communication. *Psychological Review* 57:271–282.

FESTINGER, LEON 1957 *A Theory of Cognitive Dissonance*. Evanston, Ill.: Row, Peterson.

FRANK, JEROME D. 1961 *Persuasion and Healing: A Comparative Study of Psychotherapy*. Baltimore: Johns Hopkins Press.

HARDING, JOHN S. et al. 1954 Prejudice and Ethnic Relations. Volume 2, pages 1021–1061 in Gardner Lindzey (editor), *Handbook of Social Psychology*. Cambridge, Mass.: Addison-Wesley.

HEBB, D. O.; and THOMPSON, W. R. 1954 The Social Significance of Animal Studies. Volume 1, pages 532–561 in Gardner Lindzey (editor), *Handbook of Social Psychology*. Cambridge, Mass.: Addison-Wesley.

HEIDER, FRITZ 1946 Attitudes and Cognitive Organization. *Journal of Psychology* 21:107–112.

HEIDER, FRITZ 1958 *The Psychology of Interpersonal Relations*. New York: Wiley.

HELSON, HARRY 1964 *Adaptation-level Theory: An Experimental and Systematic Approach to Behavior*. New York: Harper.

HOVLAND, CARL I.; JANIS, IRVING L.; and KELLEY, HAROLD H. 1953 *Communication and Persuasion: Psychological Studies of Opinion Change*. New Haven: Yale Univ. Press.

HOVLAND, CARL I.; LUMSDAINE, ARTHUR A.; and SHEFFIELD, FREDERICK D. 1949 *Experiments on Mass Communication*. Studies in Social Psychology in World War II, Vol. 3. Princeton Univ. Press; Oxford Univ. Press.

HYMAN, HERBERT H. 1959 *Political Socialization: A Study in the Psychology of Political Behavior*. Glencoe, Ill.: Free Press.

JANIS, IRVING L. 1959 Motivational Factors in the Resolution of Decisional Conflicts. Volume 7, pages 198–231 in Marshall R. Jones (editor), *Nebraska Symposium on Motivation*. Lincoln: Univ. of Nebraska Press.

JANIS, IRVING L.; and SMITH, M. BREWSTER 1965 Effects of Education and Persuasion on National and International Images. Pages 190–235 in Herbert C. Kelman (editor), *International Behavior: A Social-psychological Analysis*. New York: Holt.

KATZ, DANIEL 1960 The Functional Approach to the Study of Attitudes. *Public Opinion Quarterly* 24:163–204.

KATZ, DANIEL; and STOTLAND, EZRA 1959 A Preliminary Statement to a Theory of Attitude Structure and Change. Pages 423–475 in Sigmund Koch (editor), *Psychology: A Study of a Science*. Volume 3: Formulations of the Person and the Social Context. New York: McGraw-Hill.

KATZ, ELIHU; and LAZARSFELD, PAUL F. 1955 *Personal Influence: The Part Played by People in the Flow of Mass Communications*. Glencoe, Ill.: Free Press.

LEWIN, KURT (1939–1947) 1963 *Field Theory in Social Science: Selected Theoretical Papers*. Edited by Dorwin Cartwright. London: Tavistock.

LIFTON, ROBERT J. 1961 *Thought Reform and the Psychology of Totalism: A Study of "Brainwashing" in China*. New York: Norton.

MURPHY, GARDNER; MURPHY, L. B.; and NEWCOMB, T. M. 1937 *Experimental Social Psychology*. Rev. ed. New York: Harper. → See especially pages 889–1046 on "Social Attitudes and Their Measurement." G. Murphy and L. B. Murphy were the authors of the first edition published in 1931.

NEWCOMB, THEODORE M. (1943) 1957 *Personality and Social Change: Attitude Formation in a Student Community*. New York: Dryden.

NEWCOMB, THEODORE M. 1961 *The Acquaintance Process*. New York: Holt.

OSGOOD, CHARLES E.; and TANNENBAUM, PERCY H. 1955 The Principle of Congruity in the Prediction of Attitude Change. *Psychological Review* 62:42–55.

ROKEACH, MILTON 1960 *The Open and Closed Mind: Investigations Into the Nature of Belief Systems and Personality Systems*. New York: Basic Books.

ROSENBERG, MILTON J. 1960 An Analysis of Affective–Cognitive Consistency. Pages 15–64 in *Attitude Organization and Change: An Analysis of Consistency Among Attitude Components*. Yale Studies in Attitude and Communication, Vol. 3. New Haven: Yale Univ. Press.

ROSENBERG, MILTON J.; and ABELSON, ROBERT P. 1960 An Analysis of Cognitive Balancing. Pages 112–163 in Milton J. Rosenberg et al., *Attitude Organization and Change*. Yale Studies in Attitude and Communication, Vol. 3. New Haven: Yale Univ. Press.

SCHEIN, EDGAR H.; SCHNEIER, I.; and BARKER, C. H. 1961 *Coercive Persuasion: A Socio-psychological Analysis of "Brainwashing" of American Civilian Prisoners by the Chinese Communists*. New York: Norton.

SCOTT, WILLIAM A. 1957 Attitude Change Through Reward of Verbal Behavior. *Journal of Abnormal and Social Psychology* 55:72–75.

SHERIF, CAROLYN W.; SHERIF, MUZAFER; and NEBERGALL, ROGER E. 1965 *Attitude and Attitude Change: The Social Judgment–Involvement Approach*. London: Rube.

SHERIF, MUZAFER; and CANTRIL, HADLEY 1947 *The Psychology of Ego-involvements, Social Attitudes and Identifications*. New York: Wiley; London: Chapman & Hall.

SHERIF, MUZAFER; and HOVLAND, CARL I. 1961 *Social Judgment: Assimilation and Contrast Effects in Communication and Attitude Change*. Yale Studies in Attitude and Communication, Vol. 4. New Haven: Yale Univ. Press.

SKINNER, BURRHUS F. 1957 *Verbal Behavior*. New York: Appleton.

SMITH, M. BREWSTER 1949 Untitled Memorandum. Pages 389–390 in Samuel A. Stouffer et al. *The American Soldier*. Volume 1: Adjustment During Army Life. Princeton Univ. Press.

SMITH, M. BREWSTER; BRUNER, JEROME S.; and WHITE, R. W. 1956 *Opinions and Personality*. New York: Wiley.

STAATS, ARTHUR W.; and STAATS, CAROLYN K. 1958 Attitudes Established by Classical Conditioning. *Journal of Abnormal and Social Psychology* 57:37–40.

ATTRIBUTES, STATISTICS OF

See COUNTED DATA; STATISTICS, DESCRIPTIVE; SURVEY ANALYSIS; *and the biography of* YULE.

AUDIENCES
See Communication, mass; Drama; Film.

AUGUSTINE

Aurelius Augustine (354–430), bishop of Hippo Regius (now Bona) in Africa, is by common consent the greatest name in political philosophy between Cicero and Thomas Aquinas. He was the first thinker to attempt the elaboration of a systematic Christian philosophy of society; he set the stage for the great controversy over the relation between church and state that was to be the central preoccupation of political philosophers throughout the ensuing centuries; and it has been claimed for him, variously, that he is the keystone of a supposed "bridge" that leads from classical political philosophy (much of which he certainly knew at first hand) to modern political philosophy, that he is the founder of the philosophy of history, and that he is one of the remote sources of that emphasis upon "the individual" and "individuality" that some authorities deem to be characteristic of the intellectual tradition of the West. His thought is known to us primarily through two books, *The Confessions,* written in the years 397–401, and *The City of God,* which he began in the year 413 and completed in 425. Augustine was, *inter alia,* a teacher of rhetoric, an ecclesiastical administrator who greatly influenced the history of the Roman Catholic church in Africa, a theologian, and the founder of the "rule" observed even today by many Catholic religious orders.

There are several major doctrines commonly associated with Augustine's name. (1) Man, in his quest for knowledge of the highest good (which he is duty-bound to achieve) and of the greatest evil (which he is duty-bound to shun), can find infallible guidance only in sacred Scriptures. (2) Man must, therefore, cultivate the "sacred science," which bases itself upon principles revealed to man by God and treats the subject matters of the several philosophical sciences (such as ethics, politics, and history) with an eye to those principles. (3) While the ancient philosophers rightly held that the life of politics is not the best life (Plato) and that man must pursue a way of life more divine than human (Aristotle), they could not, in the absence of sacred science, define the goal of the best life or discover the path that leads to it; concretely, the higher truth toward which they were groping is the truth that man owes absolute allegiance to no earthly society. (4) Man's proper goal and the path he must follow are laid down by the holy laws that God gave to the people of Israel, by the Old Testament prophets, and in accordance with the latter's prophecies, by Jesus Christ and the church Jesus founded; the man who follows that path follows God. (5) Both history and politics achieve a higher unity and acquire new and valid meaning when considered in the context of the principles of sacred science.

The Confessions, an autobiography, is superficially an account of Augustine's conversion to Christianity and of his subsequent spiritual struggles and ordeals. Many critics, indeed, have read it as merely the record of a single individual's progress from bad to good and from unbelief to belief. More penetrating critics have seen in it a history, epic in conception and execution, of a representative man's struggle to find a foothold that will enable him to contemplate reality from the point of view of the Divine. Confession, Augustine argued in Book x, i–iv, is less a profession of faith than a mode of discovery; and in Book x, v ff., he contended that the individual can, through the faculty of memory, become conscious of his own existence in history and thus of himself as the subject of history. Some scholars hold that Augustine's act of self-awareness constitutes a major turning point in the intellectual and spiritual history of Western man.

Augustine's contributions to political philosophy may be considered under two categories: "the two visible societies" and "the two invisible cities."

The two visible societies. Although previous political philosophers had taught that the problems of politics necessarily transcend political philosophy and must be dealt with on the metaphysical or even the religious level and that political authority must therefore be confined within certain bounds, Augustine was the first political philosopher to pose the problem of the limits of political philosophy in the now familiar terms of two "spheres": the secular, that is, the state, and the religious, or the church, each a distinct "society" and each beneficent. Augustine, echoing Aristotle, defined the state as the rule of free men over free men; it is rendered necessary by the "order of nature" and properly concerns itself with "just dealing" and "good manners." He did not, as some interpreters suggest, attribute the existence of the state as such to "sin" and "guilt"; rather, sin and guilt, which take the form of "ambition" and "proud sovereignty," explain only one kind of state, namely, the state whose characteristic is not rule of free men by free men through deliberation (which is the rule prescribed both by nature and by God) but rule by masters through coercive authority.

Augustine thus enunciated ideas that are genuine landmarks in the development of antiauthoritarian political philosophy in the West.

The two invisible cities. History, for Augustine, is the unfolding relation between the "earthly city," the abode of all men dominated by self-love, and the "heavenly city," made up of men dominated by the love of God. The history of the former is "profane history," an account of man's actual political life; the history of the latter is "salvation history," that is, an account of man's relatedness to God. Armed with these two concepts—which must not be confused with those of church and state—Augustine attempted (*a*) a total critique of pagan political order, especially the Roman Empire, which he deemed bad in principle because wrongly related to God and divine law, and (*b*) the outlines of a Christian philosophy of right order and of the conditions under which man's history becomes meaningful.

To do justice to Augustine's theory of the state and to his indictment of the pagan empire one must understand the visible societies against the background of the invisible cities. Despite what some commentators have said, Augustine was not a detractor of the state but taught rather that the citizens of the heavenly city have a duty to work within the state on behalf of the rule of free men and so against the ambition and pride that are its typical vices; only the "blessed" can move the state toward its proper end, which is the temporal common good; any attempt, like that of the empire, to develop within the state the virtues necessary to that end without reference to God and divine law, is foredoomed to failure; the virtues it develops, because pursued not for God's sake, but their own, are in fact vices. The state, then, far from being simply evil, is more or less good to the extent that it is penetrated—through the ministrations of the second visible society, the church—by the heavenly city. The critical problem for political philosophy thus became with Augustine (and continued to be through many centuries) that of the relation between church and state.

The meaning of history, Augustine argued, is not to be found within history itself, since historical events are, as such, empty of inner significance; it is to be found rather in the eruption into history of transhistorical purpose. The history of the earthly city is a history of sin, death, and human failure; that of the heavenly city, beginning with Adam, is a record of meaningful growth and development down through the centuries to the time of Christ, whose redemptive ministry initiates a final, nondevelopmental historical epoch, to end with the Second Coming of Christ. Augustine repudiated the hitherto regnant notions of historical inevitability and of historical development as "cyclical" and taught that while God "foreknows" some events and while there is a Divine Providence at work in history, historical events are nevertheless caused by free decisions made by man in the context of Divine Governance. If Western man typically thinks of himself as living in a historical present, between a past made by the free decisions of his forbears and a future for whose shape he and other men are responsible—that is, in historical time—Augustine has certainly been one of his great teachers.

WILLMOORE KENDALL

[*Related to Augustine's work are* POLITICAL THEORY; STATE; *and the biographies of* AQUINAS; ARISTOTLE; PLATO.]

WORKS BY AUGUSTINE

Basic Writings of Saint Augustine. 2 vols., edited with an introduction and notes by Whitney J. Oates. New York: Random House, 1948. → Volume 1: *The Confessions; Twelve Treaties.* Volume 2: *The City of God; On the Trinity.*

Introduction to St. Augustine: The City of God, *Being Selections From the* De civitate Dei, *Including Most of the XIX*th *Book, With Text.* Translated and with a running commentary by A. H. Barrow. London: Faber, 1950.

The Works of Aurelius Augustine. 15 vols., edited by Marcus Dods. Edinburgh: Clark, 1872–1934.

WORKS ABOUT AUGUSTINE

ANDRESEN, CARL (editor) 1962 *Zum Augustin-Gespräch der Gegenwart.* Darmstadt (Germany): Wissenschaftliche Buchgesellschaft. → See especially the bibliography on pages 459–583.

BURLEIGH, JOHN H. S. 1949 The City of God: *A Study of St. Augustine's Philosophy.* London: Nisbet.

CALLAHAN, JOHN F. 1948 *Four Views of Time in Ancient Philosophy.* Cambridge, Mass.: Harvard Univ. Press.

CHROUST, ANTON-HERMANN 1950 St. Augustine's Philosophical Theory of Law. *Notre Dame Lawyer* 25:285–315.

DEANE, HERBERT A. 1963 *The Political and Social Ideas of St. Augustine.* New York: Columbia Univ. Press.

FIGGIS, JOHN N. 1921 *The Political Aspects of St. Augustine's* City of God. London: Longmans.

FRIBERG, HANS D. 1944 *Love and Justice in Political Theory: A Study of Augustine's Definition of the Commonwealth.* Univ. of Chicago Press.

GARRETT, THOMAS M. 1956 St. Augustine and the Nature of Society. *New Scholasticism* 30:16–36.

GILSON, ÉTIENNE H. (1931) 1960 *The Christian Philosophy of St. Augustine.* Translated by L. E. M. Lynch. New York: Random House. → First published as *Introduction à l'étude de Saint Augustin.*

GUARDINI, ROMANO (1935) 1960 *The Conversion of Augustine.* Westminster, Md.: Newman. → First published as *Die Bekehrung des heiligen Aurelius Augustinus.*

HEARNSHAW, FOSSEY J. C.; and CARLYLE, A. J. (1923) 1950 St. Augustine and *The City of God.* Pages 34–

52 in Fossey J. C. Hearnshaw (editor), *The Social and Political Ideas of Some Great Mediaeval Thinkers.* New York: Barnes & Noble.

LADNER, GERHART B.   1953   The History of Ideas in the Christian Middle Ages From the Fathers to Dante in American and Canadian Publications of the Years 1940–1952. *Traditio* 9:439–514.

LADNER, GERHART B.   1959   *The Idea of Reform: Its Impact on Christian Thought and Action in the Age of the Fathers.* Cambridge, Mass.: Harvard Univ. Press. → See especially pages 153–283 on "St. Augustine and the Difference Between the Reform Ideas of the Christian East and West."

McCoy, CHARLES N. R.   1963   *The Structure of Political Thought: A Study in the History of Political Ideas.* New York: McGraw-Hill. → See especially pages 99–131 on "Christianity and Political Philosophy: The Relation of Church and State."

MARSHALL, ROBERT T.   1952   *Studies in the Political and Socio-religious Terminology of the* De civitate Dei. Washington: Catholic Univ. of America Press.

MILLAR, MOORHOUSE F. X.   1930   The Significance of St. Augustine's Criticism of Cicero's Definition of the State. Volume 1, pages 99–109 in *Philosophia perennis: Abhandlungen zu ihrer Vergangheit und Gegenwart.* Edited by Fritz-Joachim von Rintelen. Regensburg (Germany): Habbel.

AUSPITZ, RUDOLF, AND LIEBEN, RICHARD

The work of Rudolf Auspitz (1837–1906) and Richard Lieben (1842–1919) constitutes the sole mathematical contribution of the early Austrian school. As a matter of fact, *Untersuchungen über die Theorie des Preises* (1889) must be considered the most important early mathematical work in economics in German, after the signal contribution of von Thünen.

The authors of this pioneering work were practical men of affairs from the Jewish upper middle class of the Austro-Hungarian Empire (Winter 1927). Auspitz was a sugar magnate and a member of parliament, Lieben the head of a well-known banking house. Their general position in society and their great analytical power in economics suggest a comparison with Ricardo (Hutchison [1953] 1962, p. 189).

Auspitz and Lieben's main contribution to price analysis is in the field of partial equilibrium. (General equilibrium is treated in an appendix.) They utilize total and marginal (but not average) curves, and most of the discussion is in terms of diagrams. They must be considered independent originators of the concept of indifference curves. They also utilize the concept of consumers' surplus. Like Jevons, they have the idea of disutility of labor.

In their discussion of production they indicate certain dynamic problems connected with the holding of stocks, expectations, and speculation. Their discussion of monopoly and of market situations between free competition and monopoly suggests the theory of Pareto and much later developments in the field of imperfect or monopolistic competition.

Their work was sharply criticized by Menger (1871) and never exercised much influence within the Austrian school proper, which was fiercely antimathematical. But contemporary mathematical economists like Pareto (1892), Edgeworth (1889), and Irving Fisher (1892) were deeply influenced by the work of Auspitz and Lieben. Auspitz and Lieben also had an interesting discussion with Walras about the merits and limitations of partial analysis (Walras 1890; [1874–1877], pp. 483–487 in the 1900 edition). This method is similar to that of Marshall (1879).

One of the greatest later Austrian economists has explicitly recognized their merit (Schumpeter 1954, p. 844). The judgment of a contemporary British historian of economic doctrines is: ". . . No work of our period, not even Marshall's or Pareto's, contains a greater number of precise and original contributions to the pure analysis of the individual consumer and firm, and to the clarification of the main assumptions on which this analysis has since been seen to rest" (Hutchison [1953] 1962, p. 189).

GERHARD TINTNER

[*For the historical context of Auspitz and Lieben's work, see the biography* JEVONS. *For discussion of their ideas, see* ECONOMIC EQUILIBRIUM; UTILITY; *and the biographies* EDGEWORTH; FISHER, IRVING; PARETO; WALRAS.]

WORKS BY AUSPITZ AND LIEBEN

1889   *Untersuchungen über die Theorie des Preises.* Leipzig: Duncker & Humblot. By Auspitz and Lieben.

1890   Die klassische Werttheorie und die Theorie vom Grenznutzen. *Jahrbücher für Nationalökonomie und Statistik* 55:288–293. By Auspitz.

1894   Der letzte Maasstab des Güterwertes und die mathematische Methode. *Zeitschrift für Volkswirtschaft, Sozialpolitik und Verwaltung* 3:489–511. By Auspitz.

1908   Die mehrfachen Schnittpunkte zwischen der Angebots- und der Nachfragekurve. *Zeitschrift für Volkswirtschaft, Sozialpolitik und Verwaltung* 17:607–616. By Lieben.

SUPPLEMENTARY BIBLIOGRAPHY

EDGEWORTH, FRANCIS Y.   1889   On the Application of Mathematics to Political Economy. *Journal of the Royal Statistical Society* 52:538–576.

FISHER, IRVING   (1892) 1961   *Mathematical Investigations in the Theory of Value and Prices.* New Haven: Yale Univ. Press; New York: Kelley.

HUTCHISON, TERENCE W.   (1953) 1962   *A Review of Economic Doctrines, 1870–1929.* Oxford: Clarendon.

Marshall, Alfred (1879) 1930 *The Pure Theory of Foreign Trade* and *The Pure Theory of Domestic Values*. Series of Reprints of Scarce Tracts in Economic and Political Science, No. 1. London School of Economics and Political Science.

Menger, Karl (1871) 1950 *Principles of Economics*. 2d ed. Translated and edited by J. Dingwall and B. F. Hoselitz. Glencoe, Ill.: Free Press. → First published as *Grundsätze der Volkswirtschaftslehre*.

Pareto, Vilfredo 1892 La teoria dei prezzi dei signori Auspitz e Lieben e le osservazioni del professor Walras. *Giornale degli economisti: Rivista mensile degli interessi italiani* 4:201–239.

Schumpeter, Joseph A. 1930 Rudolf Auspitz. Volume 2, page 317 in *Encyclopaedia of the Social Sciences*. New York: Macmillan.

Schumpeter, Joseph A. (1954) 1960 *History of Economic Analysis*. Edited by E. B. Schumpeter. New York: Oxford Univ. Press.

Walras, Léon (1874–1877) 1954 *Elements of Pure Economics; or, the Theory of Social Wealth*. Translated by William Jaffé. Homewood, Ill.: Irwin; London: Allen & Unwin. → First published in French as *Éléments d'économie politique pure*.

Walras, Léon 1890 Observations sur le principe de la théorie du prix de MM. Auspitz et Lieben. *Revue d'économie politique* 4:320–323.

Weinberger, Otto 1931 Rudolf Auspitz und Richard Lieben: Ein Beitrag zur Geschichte der mathematischen Methode in der Volkswirtschaftslehre. *Zeitschrift für die gesamte Staatswissenschaft* 91:457–492.

Weinberger, Otto 1933 Richard Lieben. Volume 9, pages 451–452 in *Encyclopaedia of the Social Sciences*. New York: Macmillan.

Weinberger, Otto 1935 Rudolf Auspitz. Volume 8, pages 37–44 in *Neue österreichische Biographie, 1815–1918*. Vienna: Amalthea Verlag.

Winter, Josefine 1927 *Fünfzig Jahre eines Wiener Hauses*. Vienna: Braumüller.

AUSTIN, JOHN

John Austin, jurist, whose works *The Province of Jurisprudence Determined* (1832) and *Lectures on Jurisprudence: Or, the Philosophy of Positive Law* (published posthumously in 1863) exerted a profound and lasting influence on the development of jurisprudence and legal studies in England and in most English-speaking countries, was born in 1790, the eldest son of an East Anglian miller. After six years of service in the army, he practiced at the English bar, and on the foundation of the University of London in 1826 he became its first professor of jurisprudence. In 1833, discouraged by his dwindling audiences, he resigned his professorship and lived in retirement until his death in 1859.

Austin was a convinced utilitarian and a close friend and pupil of Jeremy Bentham, although he did not share Bentham's political radicalism. Much of his work consists in the lucid exposition, illustration, and elaboration of Bentham's ideas in a form more comprehensible and palatable to English lawyers than Bentham's own writings. Hobbes and Hume were important, although secondary, influences on Austin's theory of law and society, and he derived from his study of Roman and pandect law important ideas concerning the analysis, classification, and systematization of legal notions.

Austin's doctrines may best be viewed as the advocacy of three principal theses, which collectively make his work a prime example of what is now known as legal positivism. The first of these theses concerns the definition of law, the second the relationship between law and morals, and the third the nature and scope of a form of legal study which he termed "general jurisprudence."

Definition of law. Austin defined law as a species of command distinguished by the fact that it enjoins or prohibits courses of action rather than single actions and is "set" or given to the members of a society by the sovereign. A legal system is therefore a collection of laws emanating from the same sovereign. Much of *The Province of Jurisprudence Determined* is devoted to the precise expositions of the terms used in this definition. For Austin, a command is an expression of desire that another person act or abstain from some action, accompanied by a threat of evil (a sanction) in the event of disobedience. A sovereign is the person or persons to whom the bulk of a given society is in a habit of obedience but who himself renders no such obedience to anyone. Austin considered that in every civil society where law exists such a sovereign is to be found: in Great Britain the sovereign body consists of the crown, members of the House of Lords, and the electorate; and in the United States the sovereign is the aggregate body of the electorates of all the states. Austin allowed that a command might be either explicit, as in the case of legislation, or "tacit," i.e., inferred from the fact that the sovereign permits laws that were introduced by an earlier sovereign or are of customary origin to be enforced by his subordinates. It follows, however, from Austin's definition of law that neither international law nor customary law may properly be called law prior to enforcement in particular cases.

Relation between law and morals. Though Austin knew that the development of law had in fact been profoundly influenced by morals and that many legal rules conformed to or reproduced the requirements of morality, he insisted, in opposition to theories of natural law, that there is no necessary or conceptual connection between law and morals and said that the tendency to confuse law and morals is "one most prolific source of jargon, darkness and perplexity." Hence a legal rule, however morally iniquitous, is still valid if it is enacted in due form. Austin did not think that men were morally bound to obey all valid laws, although they should always consider, before disobeying a law, whether in all the circumstances disobedience would produce worse consequences than obedience.

Within the sphere of morality Austin distinguished between "positive morality"—i.e., the actually accepted or conventional morality of a particular social group—and the "laws of God," of which utility (the greatest happiness of the greatest number) is the "index." These "laws of God" are the supreme test of the rules of both positive law and positive morality, the standards determining not what they are, but what they ought to be. "Positive morality" was used by Austin to embrace all man-made rules of human conduct except positive law and includes, besides moral rules in the ordinary sense, codes of manners as well as international law.

The form of utilitarianism which Austin advocated is today known as "rule utilitarianism," which makes utility the test not of the rightness or wrongness of particular actions but of general rules, an action being right if it conforms to the requirement of rules that pass the test of utility.

Scope and nature of jurisprudence. Austin distinguished, as did Bentham in different terminology, between the science of legislation, concerned with the criticism and reform of law, and the science of jurisprudence, concerned with the exposition, analysis, and orderly arrangement of systems of law. He believed that there are fundamental distinctions and notions common to all mature systems of law and that general jurisprudence is concerned with their clarification and analysis. They include such distinctions as those between written and unwritten law and between torts and crimes and such notions as rights, obligations, injuries, persons, things, and acts. General jurisprudence is exclusively an analytical study concerned neither with the history nor with the evaluation of law, but solely with the clarification of meanings. Such a value-free analytical study is today usually referred to as analytical jurisprudence.

The influence of Austin's work was small during his lifetime, although his writings were much admired by members of the Benthamite circle, including John Stuart Mill, Sir George Cornewall Lewis, and Sir Samuel Romilly. But after the posthumous publication of the whole of his work, his

ideas came to dominate English jurisprudence, which for long remained primarily analytical in character. Austin's influence in the United States has been less considerable, although it can be distinctly traced in the works of John Chipman Gray and Oliver Wendell Holmes. On the continent of Europe, Austin's work was until recently recognized only by a few positivist thinkers, such as Karl Bergbohm in Germany, Ernest Roguin in France, and Hans Kelsen, whose "pure theory" of law has many similarities to Austin's doctrine.

Criticisms of Austin's works have ranged very widely. His definition of law has been attacked on the ground that in spite of obvious analogies between criminal statutes and commands, there are many sorts of law that are distorted by assimilation to a command. His conception of the sovereign has been criticized as a misrepresentation of the structure of anything but a very simple form of society, and especially inapplicable to those societies whose supreme legislature is subject to legal limitations imposed by a constitution. Austin's insistence on the separation of law and morals has been criticized, notably in the United States, for obscuring the true character of the judicial process that is exhibited at those points where judges have a creative choice left open to them by legal rules and therefore have recourse to standards of morality and justice. Similarly, his insistence on the importance of a purely analytical jurisprudence has been criticized as an example of the vicious abstraction of law from its social setting and function, characteristic of English lawyers. Austin has even been criticized for encouraging subservience to tyranny and an uncritical attitude to bad laws. Some, but not all, of these criticisms are well founded. Their debate has usually advanced the understanding of law as a form of social control, and it is a great merit of Austin's lucid and penetrating work to have provoked it.

H. L. A. HART

[*For the historical context of Austin's work, see* PLURALISM; SOVEREIGNTY; *and the biographies of* BENTHAM; HOBBES; HUME. *For discussion of the subsequent development of Austin's ideas, see* JURISPRUDENCE; POLITICAL GROUP ANALYSIS; POLITICAL THEORY; PUBLIC LAW; *and the biographies of* HOLMES; KELSEN; MILL.]

WORKS BY AUSTIN

(1832–1863) 1954 *The Province of Jurisprudence Determined* and *The Uses of the Study of Jurisprudence.* London: Weidenfeld & Nicolson. → Two books bound together.

(1863) 1911 *Lectures on Jurisprudence: Or, the Philosophy of Positive Law.* 5th ed., rev. 2 vols. London: Murray.

SUPPLEMENTARY BIBLIOGRAPHY

AGNELLI, ARDUINO 1959 *John Austin alle origini del positivismo giuridico.* Istituto di Scienze Politiche dell' Università di Torino, Pubblicazioni, Vol. 7. Turin (Italy): Edizioni Giappichelli.

HART, H. L. A. 1961 *The Concept of Law.* Oxford: Clarendon. → See especially Chapters 1–3.

MAINE, HENRY S. (1875) 1897 *Lectures on the Early History of Institutions.* 7th ed. London: Murray. → See especially Chapter 12 on "Sovereignty" and Chapter 13 on "Sovereignty and Empire."

MANNING, C. A. W. 1933 Austin To-day: Or, *The Province of Jurisprudence* Re-examined. Pages 180–226 in London School of Economic and Political Science, *Modern Theories of Law.* Oxford Univ. Press.

MILL, JOHN STUART (1863) 1874 Austin on Jurisprudence. Volume 4, pages 157–226 in John Stuart Mill, *Dissertations and Discussions: Political, Philosophical, and Historical.* New York: Holt.

MORISON, W. L. 1958 Some Myth About Positivism. *Yale Law Journal* 68:212–233.

AUSTRIAN SCHOOL

See under ECONOMIC THOUGHT.

AUTHORITARIANISM

See DICTATORSHIP; PERSONALITY, POLITICAL.

AUTHORITY

The concept of authority, like the related concepts with which it is frequently associated—power, influence, and leadership—is used in a variety of ways in political philosophy and the social sciences. In part, the diversity stems from the ubiquity of the phenomenon. Whether it be defined as (1) a *property* of a person or office, especially the right to issue orders; (2) a *relationship* between two offices, one superior and the other subordinate, such that both incumbents perceive the relationship as legitimate; (3) a *quality* of a communication by virtue of which it is accepted; or (4) countless variations on one or more of these logical forms of definition, the phenomenon of authority is basic to human behavior. One philosopher, Bertrand de Jouvenel, has put it more strongly: "The phenomenon called 'authority' is at once more ancient and more fundamental than the phenomenon called 'state'; the natural ascendancy of some men over others is the principle of all human organisations and all human advances" ([1955] 1957, p. xiii). In any event, the problem of political authority, as distinct from the quest for a precise definition of the concept, is at least as old as government itself. Since the emergence of the social sciences, authority has been a subject of research in a variety of empirical settings: the family (parental authority); small groups (informal authority or leadership); intermediate organizations, such as schools, churches, armies, industrial and governmental bureaucracies (organizational and bureaucratic authority); and society-wide or inclusive organizations ranging from the most primitive tribal society to the modern nation–state and international organization (political authority). To what extent these are different kinds of authority remains an open question. Definitive answers must await more research on their interrelationships: for example, how attitudes toward parental authority condition subsequent attitudes toward civic participation and how the dominant style of political rule affects the ways in which authority is exercised in primary and intermediate organizations.

Development of the concept

The implications of man's involvement in the state, i.e., his obligations as a citizen, are given their classic statement in Plato's famous dialogues, *Apology* and *Crito.* The trial and conviction of Socrates poses the basic problem of political authority. What is man's relationship to the state? Is he obliged to obey an unjust law? For Socrates, the contractual relationship with his state, entered into by every citizen upon reaching adulthood, provides only limited alternatives to complete obedience, even to the point of death. On the one hand, the citizen may argue, persuade others, or attempt to change the law. On the other hand, he may abandon his citizenship and leave the country. (The existence of these two alternatives is still crucial in distinguishing between democratic and totalitarian states.) Unsuccessful in the first alternative and unwilling to adopt the second alternative, Socrates accepts the verdict of his trial as legitimate and drinks the fatal hemlock.

The justification of political authority, the location of sovereignty, the balancing of freedom and authority, the requirements of political obligation —these have been core questions for political philosophy from Plato and Aristotle to the present. Yet these great thinkers, their most important successors (Augustine, Aquinas, Machiavelli, Hobbes, Locke, Rousseau), and particularly twentieth-century social scientists have not been concerned solely with questions of what ought to be. They have also addressed themselves to questions of what is—how authority and power are in fact distributed in society. To the extent that these political philosophers and social scientists have arrived at different conclusions, they have often been led to use these concepts in different ways.

Perhaps the seminal treatment of the concept of authority in the twentieth century is that of Max

Weber (1922). He distinguishes between three pure types of authority—(1) legal–rational, (2) traditional, and (3) charismatic—according to the kind of claim to legitimacy typically made by each. In the last two cases the obligation is to a person, the traditional chief or the heroic or messianic leader. Legal authority is more restricted in scope; obedience is owed to the legally established impersonal network of positions ([1922] 1957, pp. 325–328). Weber's treatment of legal–rational authority, which distinguishes between, but does not elaborate on, authority inherent in office and authority based on technical knowledge, provides the basic framework for most contemporary analyses of bureaucracy (Peabody 1962). His treatment of charismatic authority, or more precisely, charismatic leadership (Bierstedt 1954, pp. 71–72), has been followed up in studies of national political leadership (Lipset 1963; Neumann 1942; Pye 1962).

But social scientists are by no means agreed on how the concept of authority should be used. For example, Michels, in the *Encyclopaedia of the Social Sciences* (1930, p. 319) defines authority as "the capacity, innate or acquired, for exercising ascendancy over a group." However, Bierstedt (1954, pp. 67–81) takes issue with each of these points. Authority is not a capacity; it is a relationship. Furthermore, it is neither innate, nor a matter of exercising ascendancy. Bierstedt argues that Michels has confused authority with competence. Yet both agree as to the close relationship between authority and power. For Michels, authority "is a manifestation of power" (1930, p. 319); for Bierstedt, "authority becomes a power phenomenon. . . . it is sanctioned power, institutionalized power" (1954, pp. 79–80).

Contemporary uses

The use of authority by contemporary political scientists is no more free from dispute. Thus, Lasswell and Kaplan, in a widely quoted definition paralleling Bierstedt's, define authority as "formal power" (1950, p. 133). However, Friedrich (1963, chapters 9–13; p. 207, n. 15; p. 226, n. 20) explicitly rejects this definition by Lasswell and Kaplan, and defines authority as "the quality of a communication," which is "capable of reasoned elaboration" (1958, pp. 35–36; 1963, pp. 218, 224). They are also in disagreement as to whether power or influence is the more inclusive term: Lasswell and Kaplan arguing that "power is a form of influence" (1950, p. 85); Friedrich maintaining that "influence is a kind of power, indirect and unstructured" (1963, p. 199, p. 207, n. 15). It seems of limited value to pursue a definition of authority as a special case of power or influence (the genus-and-differentia form). Social scientists have not as yet been able to formulate a precise and widely accepted operational definition of power. These concepts, even if given operational definition, would appear to open up more difficulties than they resolve.

Several conclusions emerge from a review of these various attempts at definition and explication. First, what clearly distinguishes authority from coercion, force, and power on the one hand, and leadership, persuasion, and influence on the other hand, is *legitimacy*. Superiors feel that they have a right to issue commands; subordinates perceive an obligation to obey. If the character of the communication is questioned, then authority is diminished and the bond that holds the participants together is in danger of being severed. Authority is strongest when subordinates anticipate the commands of superiors even before they are voiced. Second, authority is exercised most characteristically within a network of clearly defined hierarchical roles: parent–child, teacher–pupil, employer–employee, ruler–ruled. These authority relations are institutionalized: duties and obligations are specified, behavior is reasonably predictable, and the relations continue over time. In a system of well-established authority, men of great ability are less in demand. Charisma is transformed through routinization; the entrepreneur is replaced by the bureaucrat. Finally, most social scientists agree that authority is but one of several resources available to incumbents of formal positions. The policeman may initially depend upon authority symbolized by his uniform and badge to lend legitimacy to his orders. But if his authority fails and persuasion is not successful, then he must resort to the threat or use of physical force, or even firearms, in order to bring about compliance. In cases in which one criminal is joined by others, the policeman can call upon other policemen, the governor, the national guard, and, if need be, the supreme commander and the army. In the final analysis, it is this nesting of authority, and the possibility of tapping greater and greater resources, that explains why criminals get arrested despite their failure to consent to a policeman's authority. A head of state is dependent upon a similar nesting of authority. His legitimacy must be acknowledged not just by citizens but, more importantly, also by those who control other valued resources: his immediate staff, his cabinet, military leaders, and, in the long run, the political and administrative apparatus of the entire society.

Research and problem areas

The usefulness of authority as a general analytical concept in the social sciences would seem to be dependent on further research directed at answering the following questions:

(1) *What is the impact of the dominant style of political authority in a given country on the ways in which authority is exercised in the many different primary groups and intermediate organizations making up the society?* Societies may be characterized by the congruency or diffused and fragmented nature of their multiple layers of authority patterns. Little is known about the way in which the dominant style of political authority—totalitarian, autocratic, constitutional elitism, mass democratic, or some combination of these—structures the attitudes and practices in the primary and intermediate groups and organizations in society. Bendix's pioneering study of the impact of four different cultures—Russia under the czars, Engand in the process of industrialization, America during the first four decades of the twentieth century, and East Germany after World War II—on management–worker ideologies is suggestive of the kind of research that is needed (1956). From a related orientation, Eckstein (1961, pp. 6–12) hypothesizes that the stability of a government is related to the congruency of its style of authority with the other authority patterns of society. The leadership practices of British political parties and the British cabinet structure are put forward as an example of high congruence. The experiences of the Weimar Republic, where democracy was largely confined to the level of parliamentary government, illustrate the opposite case (pp. 17–21).

Studies of totalitarian dictatorships—Hitler's Germany, Mussolini's Italy, and Russia under Stalin—stress the creation of a vacuum between the elite and mass and a resulting disintegration of communication affecting all traditional authority patterns. ". . . the bonds of confidence in social relationships are corroded by the terror and propaganda. . . . The confidence which ordinarily binds the manager of a plant to his subordinates, members of a university faculty to each other and to their students, lawyer to client, doctor to patient, and even parents to children as well as brothers to sisters is disrupted" (Friedrich & Brzezinski 1956, p. 166). Although the basic pattern of authority may be quite different, the totalitarian government also seeks congruency, a stability imposed from above. The objective is a system of authority in which parents are totally responsible for their children's behavior, as is the party secretary for the cell, the chairman for the collective, and the central leadership for the whole of the Soviet Union (Mead 1951).

(2) *How are attitudes and behavior shaped in infancy, childhood, and adolescence so as to affect the degree and kind of subsequent political participation and attitudes toward political authority?* The second problem area, political socialization, is shaped by but also affects the first. The training of the young—character building, education, instruction in citizenship—has obvious consequences for adult political behavior. At least in the United States, the single best predictor of a child's choice of a political party is his parents' party preference. Much of the literature on the development of personality, authoritarianism, and voting preferences testifies to the importance of attitudes formed in the early years of life as a conditioner of later, mature civic activity (Hyman 1959). While the survey literature of the United States abounds with evidence of an adult cynicism toward politics and the low or ambivalent status of politicians, these attitudes are not apparent among young school children (Greenstein 1960). Family tradition, the extent to which a family is politicized, does, however, have a substantial impact upon an individual's orientation toward politics and political authority, influencing the degree, kind, and direction of his political participation. Cross-national studies of political socialization are still relatively rare (Hess 1963).

(3) *What are the strengths and bases of support of differing forms of political authority at the local and national level and between governmental institutions as diverse as the chief executive, the bureaucracy, the legislature, and the courts?* Easton (1953) has equated the study of politics with the analysis of "the authoritative allocation of values." Much of the community power literature has focused on how choices are made between competing values, who makes them, and once made, why citizens accept them as "authoritative." While many of the early sociological analyses of community power stress the importance of a business elite, more recent studies by political scientists emphasize the integrative role played by public officials. Banfield (1961) found that the mayor of Chicago was able to provide a degree of informal centralization through party organization of what would otherwise be a fragmented formal authority resulting from multiple and overlapping governmental jurisdictions. Dahl (1961) and his associates traced a historical shift in political influence in New Haven, Connecticut, from oligarchy to pluralism, through the intensive analysis of three key decision

areas: political nominations, public education, and urban redevelopment. What coordination and continuity exist in a system characterized by dispersed inequality of resources is largely brought about by elected officials, particularly the mayor of New Haven.

Numerous studies of the multiple centers of authority and power in modern industrial states have been undertaken—the executive, the legislature, the courts, the bureaucracy, political parties, and interest groups. However, social scientists are only beginning to understand what takes place when conflict erupts between competing centers of authority, such as that which characterized the promulgation of the United States Supreme Court decisions in the school integration cases. Neustadt's analysis of how a president makes his extensive formal and legal powers work for him should facilitate comparisons with other national heads of state. The problem of implementing authority is common to all: "how to be on top in fact as well as name" (Neustadt 1960, p. vii).

One of the advantages that democratic forms of government have over more autocratic or totalitarian forms is that conflict and tensions are decentralized and dispersed. Successions from one administration to another or one regime to the next provide a critical test. As Friedrich and Brzezinski note in their study of totalitarian dictatorships, succession "exposes a regime's authority to its greatest strain, since the passing away of the ruler calls not only his, but the system's, authority into question" (1956, p. 54). This strain, while not without its frictions, is considerably reduced in a democracy.

(4) *How does political authority vary from culture to culture and from traditional to modern societies in terms of each of these three problem areas?* Ultimately, clarification of concepts and the development of generalizations about authority patterns must come from cross-cultural comparative analysis. Single-nation studies, for example, Benedict's study of Japan (1946) and Mead's analysis of Soviet attitudes toward authority (1951), have set the stage. A basic norm of Japanese culture is "taking one's proper station," a norm that is learned and meticulously observed in the family and later extended to the wider fields of economic life and government. Benedict outlines at some length the extensive system of hierarchical obligations and their reciprocals in Japan (1946, p. 116). Ward (1963) traces the development of democratic and pluralistic tendencies leading to the dilution and modification of the oligarchic pattern of rule in Japan.

Mead portrays a contrasting, if not always internally consistent, theory of Soviet leadership. Each party member is enjoined to be a model for those beneath him, but those below are urged not to take their cues from their immediate superiors but instead to model their behavior after the top leader, Lenin, Stalin, Khrushchev, and their successors (Mead 1951, pp. 68–69). The Soviet industrial worker "is expected to respond, not with a careful delimited measured response to the particular demands of his job, but with total devotion and spontaneity" (p. 35). After experimenting with the belief that the socialist society would assume full responsibility for the upbringing of children, the Soviet government shifted to encouragement of the growth of the close-knit family and strong parental authority.

By utilizing comparative case studies of policy making in the United States and the Soviet Union, Brzezinski and Huntington have substantially advanced our understanding of political authority and politics in the two systems (1964).

Research stimulated by the Social Science Research Council's Committee on Comparative Politics has begun to break through the limitations of single-nation studies and to reap the benefits of systematic theory, cross-national analysis, and the use of survey research techniques applied simultaneously to a number of countries. Almond and Verba (1963) compare the political cultures of five nations, the United States, Great Britain, Germany, Italy, and Mexico, basing their analysis upon stratified, multistage probability samples of about one thousand respondents in each country. They distinguish three pure types of political cultures—parochial, subject, and participant—as well as various combinations of these types. Several implications of each main type in shaping attitudes toward political authority are immediately apparent. The political cultures of African tribal societies and autonomous local communities described by Coleman (Almond & Coleman 1960, pp. 254–256) are clearly *parochial* in orientation. Political roles are not specialized. Diffuse political, social, economic, and religious roles are combined in headmanship or chieftainship. Members of the society expect little in the way of change or progress. In the *subject* political culture, the citizen "is aware of specialized governmental authority; he is affectively oriented to it, perhaps taking pride in it, perhaps disliking it; and he evaluates it either as legitimate or as not" (Almond & Verba 1963, p. 19). But the relationship is essentially passive. In the third type of political culture, the *participative* culture, individual members are oriented to both the input and output aspects of the political system. They endorse the norm of active participation in governmental decision making, although they may vary greatly in the degree to which they themselves are involved. As Pye (1962) points out in his study of national character and political attitudes in Burma, perhaps the top priority problems in emerging nations are the quest for new collective as well as individual identities, the inculcation of a sense of national loyalty, and the development of a propensity to obey the regulations of central governmental authority.

The diverse uses of authority as a political concept have been illustrated. The ambiguity of everyday language, the mixture of fact and value implicit in the term, the omnipresence of the phenomenon in all cultures, and the multiple approaches to the study of authority by social scientists from a great range of disciplines—all these factors have contributed to the confusion often accompanying the use of the concept. Yet, precisely because relative superordination and subordination are so fundamental at the family, group, organizational, and national levels, authority remains an almost indispensable general analytical concept.

ROBERT L. PEABODY

[See also LEGITIMACY; POLITICAL THEORY; POWER. Other relevant material may be found under LEADERSHIP.]

BIBLIOGRAPHY

ALMOND, GABRIEL A.; and COLEMAN, JAMES S. (editors) 1960   The Politics of the Developing Areas. Princeton Univ. Press.

ALMOND, GABRIEL A.; and VERBA, SIDNEY 1963   The Civic Culture: Political Attitudes and Democracy in Five Nations. Princeton Univ. Press.

BANFIELD, EDWARD C. 1961   Political Influence. Glencoe, Ill.: Free Press.

BENDIX, REINHARD 1956   Work and Authority in Industry: Ideologies of Management in the Course of Industrialization. New York: Wiley. → A paperback edition was published in 1963 by Harper.

BENEDICT, RUTH 1946   The Chrysanthemum and the Sword: Patterns of Japanese Culture. Boston: Houghton Mifflin.

BIERSTEDT, ROBERT (1954) 1964   The Problem of Authority. Pages 67–81 in Morroe Berger et al. (editors), Freedom and Control in Modern Society. New York: Octagon Books.

BRZEZINSKI, ZBIGNIEW; and HUNTINGTON, SAMUEL P. 1964   Political Power: USA/USSR. New York: Viking.

DAHL, ROBERT A. (1961) 1963   Who Governs?: Democracy and Power in an American City. New Haven: Yale Univ. Press.

DE GRAZIA, SEBASTIAN 1959   What Authority Is Not. American Political Science Review 53:321–331.

EASTON, DAVID 1953   The Political System: An Inquiry into the State of Political Science. New York: Knopf.

ECKSTEIN, HARRY 1961   A Theory of Stable Democracy. Center of International Studies Research Monograph No. 10. Princeton Univ., Woodrow Wilson School of Public and International Affairs.

FRIEDRICH, CARL J. (editor) 1958   Authority. American Society of Political and Legal Philosophy, Nomos, Vol. 1. Cambridge, Mass.: Harvard Univ. Press.

FRIEDRICH, CARL J. 1963   Man and His Government: An Empirical Theory of Politics. New York: McGraw-Hill.

FRIEDRICH, CARL J.; and BRZEZINSKI, ZBIGNIEW K. (1956) 1966   Totalitarian Dictatorship and Autocracy. 2d ed. rev. Cambridge, Mass.: Harvard Univ. Press. → A paperback edition was published by Praeger in 1961.

GREENSTEIN, FRED I. 1960   The Benevolent Leader: Children's Images of Political Authority. American Political Science Review 54:934–943.

HESS, ROBERT D. 1963   The Socialization of Attitudes Toward Political Authority: Some Cross-national Comparisons. International Social Science Journal 15:542–559.

HYMAN, HERBERT H. 1959   Political Socialization: A Study in the Psychology of Political Behavior. Glencoe, Ill.: Free Press.

JOUVENEL, BERTRAND DE (1955) 1957   Sovereignty: An Inquiry Into the Political Good. Univ. of Chicago Press. → First published in French as De la souveraineté: À la recherche du bien politique.

LASSWELL, HAROLD D.; and KAPLAN, ABRAHAM 1950   Power and Society: A Framework for Political Inquiry. Yale Law School Studies, Vol. 2. New Haven: Yale Univ. Press. → A paperback edition was published in 1963 by the Yale University Press.

LIPSET, SEYMOUR M. 1963   The First New Nation: The United States in Historical and Comparative Perspective. New York: Basic Books.

MEAD, MARGARET 1951   Soviet Attitudes Toward Authority: An Interdisciplinary Approach to Problems of Soviet Character. New York: McGraw-Hill.

MICHELS, ROBERTO 1930   Authority. Volume 2, pages 319–321 in Encyclopaedia of the Social Sciences. New York: Macmillan.

MILLER, WALTER B. 1955   Two Concepts of Authority. American Anthropologist New Series 57:271–289.

NEUMANN, FRANZ L. (1942) 1963   Behemoth: The Structure and Practice of National Socialism, 1933–1944. 2d ed. New York: Octagon Books.

NEUSTADT, RICHARD E. 1960   Presidential Power: The Politics of Leadership. New York: Wiley.

PEABODY, ROBERT L. 1964   Organizational Authority: Superior–Subordinate Relationships in Three Public Service Organizations. New York: Atherton.

PEABODY, ROBERT L. 1962   Perceptions of Organizational Authority: A Comparative Analysis. Administrative Science Quarterly 6:463–482.

PYE, LUCIAN W. 1962   Politics, Personality, and Nation Building: Burma's Search for Identity. New Haven: Yale Univ. Press.

WARD, ROBERT E. 1963   Political Modernization and Political Culture in Japan. World Politics 15:569–596.

WEBER, MAX (1922) 1957   The Theory of Social and Economic Organization. Edited by Talcott Parsons. New York: Oxford Univ. Press. → First published in German as Part 1 of Wirtschaft und Gesellschaft.

AUTISM

See MENTAL DISORDERS, article on CHILDHOOD MENTAL DISORDERS.

AUTOCRACY

In political writing, "autocracy" suggests a government or polity in which a single governor has or claims unlimited power. The word "autocrat" has been used infrequently by social scientists, who have preferred to refer to the unlimited or unrestricted governor as a dictator or a despot. Although interest in the problems of autocracy has recently been revived by communism and Nazism, the theory of autocracy has received too little attention from contemporary writers. The features and the background of "totalitarian autocracy" have been described, but these descriptions have usually depended upon such undefined and imprecise concepts as "unlimited or unrestricted power," "irresponsibility," and "not subject to rules."

An abstract concept. Autocracy is an abstract concept that corresponds to no past or present government. Its meaning depends upon a logical extension of certain governmental tendencies, and when this meaning is stated and explained, it should provide a standard to which all governments can be compared and ranked according to the degree of power possessed by their most powerful members. This ability to compare actual governments to the hypothetical concept of autocracy should help the student of politics understand the reasons why governments exhibit greater or lesser concentrations of power.

If we take "autocracy" to mean government dominated by a single governor, its definition depends upon a definition of government. Although there has never been agreement upon a definition of government, it appears acceptable to postulate that the function of governing implies the intentional affecting of human activity, and that all governors are able to affect some activities by the use, or threatened use, of physical coercion. When the autocrat is said to have "unlimited power," it is implied that this is power to affect human activity, but not necessarily by any specific methods.

Power and authority. Although the word "power" has several different meanings, when we speak of the autocrat's power we refer to his ability or potential to affect human activity, rather than to his actual effects upon it. An understanding of this potential depends upon an understanding of the two ways—to be called "control" and "influence"— in which one person can affect the activity of another. When a person influences another's activity, he evokes a response that is freely performed; when he controls it, he acts so that the respondent has no alternative reaction.

Every governor is able to influence and able to control, and his total power is a combination of these two abilities—his ability to persuade, for example, combined with his ability to imprison. The power to control is greater than the power to influence, because it is more likely that an exercise of control will elicit the response that the governor desires. The likelihood of obtaining such responses is an index of the governor's power. His ability to use physical coercion gives him power to control, and the use of coercion is in fact his principal method of control. The governor's total power increases as more human activities and more human beings become subject to his coercive power, exercised either through law or arbitrarily and at random.

Writers on autocracy have not always distinguished the governor's actual power from his authority or right to a certain amount of power. Dictionaries define an autocrat as "a governor with absolute power" or "a monarch ruling with unlimited authority," but these definitions are incompatible. A man is an authority when other people believe he has a special ability to do what is correct; hence a governor's authority depends upon the acceptance of his subjects. This dependence on their belief that he has a special ability to govern sets a limit to his actual power. The Russian tsar's "unlimited right to govern" was based on, and thus limited by, the Russian people's belief in his competence to rule in conformity with their conception of government. The possession of authority will add to the power of a relatively weak governor, but it will also hinder the indefinite increase of his power.

The extent of the autocrat's power. The activities under the control of the autocrat are those of his subjects, and they can include not only overt bodily actions but beliefs, thoughts, and values as well. The degree of a governor's power depends upon both the number and the importance of the activities he can control. The governor who is able to control basic beliefs and actions, such as those associated with love and religion, is more powerful than the governor who controls superficial activities, such as styles of clothing and modes of locomotion.

The unlimited power of the autocrat implies that he is independent of his fellow governors as well as of his subjects. Autocracies are absolute governments, that is, they are governments with complete power over their subjects. There are, however, other absolute governments consisting of a multiplicity of men all dependent for their power upon one another. An autocrat cannot allow anyone else to have any power whatever; he must depend on no one, and thus he must be able to dispense at any time with any of his subordinates. All absolute governments tend to develop toward autocracy, and the less the principal governor depends upon his subordinates, the more closely he approaches the status of an autocrat.

The autocrat's methods.   In order to obtain and maintain complete power over his subjects and governmental associates, the autocrat must follow a rather inflexible course of action. He cannot have the power to control every activity of every person unless he constantly exercises it; he can never rest without allowing his power to become circumscribed. His ability to control his subjects' economic behavior, for example, can easily become restricted without continual use, because an extended period of unaffected production and distribution generates habits and expectations that become difficult or even impossible to control. Prolonged regularity in any aspect of his subjects' lives is the principal impediment to the governor's power over them. Such regularity provides the basis of what is called "constitutionalism."

The autocrat must not only be in continuous action, but his actions must be both necessary and sufficient to bring about his subjects' reactions. His power is exercised when his action is sufficient to evoke a certain response, but his power is not increased unless his action is also necessary for the response—that is, unless the response would not have occurred in its absence. When, for example, a governor forbids his subjects to embrace a religion that is repugnant to them, his only effect may be to reinforce the regularity of their lives. This reinforcement may then prevent his gaining the power to control them in other areas against their will.

If the autocrat is constantly to affect everyone in a way that admits of no alternative responses, he must act as arbitrarily as possible. The necessity for arbitrariness can be seen most clearly in his relationship with the few governmental associates whose minimum cooperation is indispensable to him. To maintain his undiluted power over them, he must never allow them to have any stable relationships among themselves or between them and any segment of the governed. To prevent such stabilization, he must make sure that none of them stands in a stable relationship to him, and he can accomplish this only by behaving toward all of them as arbitrarily as he can. For a single governor to monopolize power, he must constantly control everyone else in a completely unpredictable way.

The autocrat is always in action, and no one can anticipate how he will act.

The circumstances of autocracy.   The social circumstances required for the existence of autocracy can be inferred from the preceding account of the nature of the autocrat's power and the techniques necessary to gain and hold it. The social circumstances underlying autocracy are those that prevent stability and regularity among the governed. These conditions first create the division between governors and governed that results in absolutism. The tendency of absolutism to develop into autocracy becomes more marked as social conditions become more disrupted; the less stability there is among the governed, the more instability there is likely to be among the governors. If the governors share a single idea of authority, for example, it will be more difficult for an autocrat to rise above them.

There are several basic causes of intense social irregularity and instability. A stable pattern of interactions, expectations, and recognized obligations is difficult to establish among a culturally heterogeneous population, and the difficulty increases with the size of the population. When life is a continuous struggle for food, a community of interests and values strong enough to check great governmental power is unlikely to develop. The chances for such a community are equally small when the people's livelihood depends upon a few men who monopolize control of natural resources or employment. The ignorance and superstition that often accompany these conditions further impede communication among the governed and thus contribute to the social fragmentation.

A people that has stable beliefs about natural, supernatural, and human affairs possesses a barrier to excessive governmental power. The belief that the community is responsible to God or to its ancestors, for example, provides a standard for government and thus limits governmental power. The conscience of the chief or the king, normally a product of the beliefs of the whole society, creates a similar limitation. When people are dominated by a sense of fatalism anything is considered possible, and the governor is bound by no expectations of regularity and consistency; indeed, the opposite expectations may prevail.

Periods of economic and social disruption are conducive to the sense of insecurity that encourages increases in the government's power to control. Revolution and warfare have always been favorable to the rise of absolutist governments and autocratic governors. It is no accident that the twentieth century—with its wars, delicate economic system, loss of faith in transcendent standards, and advanced organizational forms and techniques of coercion—has produced, in the leaders of its great totalitarian regimes, governors who have come very close to the abstract concept of the autocrat.

C. W. CASSINELLI

[*See also* DICTATORSHIP; POWER; TOTALITARIANISM.]

BIBLIOGRAPHY

ARENDT, HANNAH 1951 *The Origins of Totalitarianism.* New York: Harcourt. → Part 3 contains information on the methods and circumstances of communism and Nazism.
CASSINELLI, C. W. 1966 *Free Activities and Interpersonal Relations.* The Hague: Nijhoff. → For concepts of control, influence, power, authority, and governing, see especially Chapters 3, 4, and 5.
FRIEDRICH, CARL J.; and BRZEZINSKI, ZBIGNIEW K. (1956) 1965 *Totalitarian Dictatorship and Autocracy.* 2d ed., rev. Cambridge, Mass.: Harvard Univ. Press.
MOORE, BARRINGTON JR. 1954 *Terror and Progress— USSR: Some Sources of Change and Stability in the Soviet Dictatorship.* Harvard University Russian Research Center Studies, No. 12. Cambridge, Mass.: Harvard Univ. Press. → For the methods of Soviet communism, see especially Chapter 1.
OPPENHEIM, FELIX E. 1961 *Dimensions of Freedom: An Analysis.* New York: St. Martins; London: Macmillan.
PYE, LUCIAN W. 1962 *Politics, Personality, and Nation Building: Burma's Search for Identity.* New Haven: Yale Univ. Press.
WITTFOGEL, KARL A. 1957 *Oriental Despotism: A Comparative Study of Total Power.* New Haven: Yale Univ. Press. → See especially Chapters 4 and 5 on autocracy and absolutism. A paperback edition was published in 1963.

AUTOMATION

Periods of acceleration in the rate of technological change and the resulting improvements in the productivity of the labor force have generally coincided with re-examinations of the impact of technology upon the economy. During the 1950s and 1960s new techniques in production—referred to as automation—have rekindled interest in the relation between technological change and the characteristics of the labor force. The questions asked currently are no different from those asked during previous periods of rapid technological progress: Is the rapid increase in productivity predominantly due to the new techniques? Do the new techniques place different demands upon workers, affect working conditions drastically, require different skills and education, etc.? In this light, the impact of automation on the U.S. labor force may be an interesting case study of the adaptation of workers and the economy to change.

A description of automation. In popular literature any form of mechanization that improves the productivity of labor has been tagged automation. The introduction of the mechanical cotton picker, the big combine, the forklift, and many other machines that displace labor are all described as automation. The assembly line—first used in the automobile industry in 1913—has also been frequently cited as an example of automation.

Technical writers try to distinguish automation from other changes in production techniques by defining it as a special case of technological change and limiting the term to two kinds of production processes: those which utilize the automatic, or feedback, principle, in which a control mechanism triggers the operation after taking into account what has happened before; and those in which a number of discrete production steps are consolidated into a single process through the use of machinery—a technique also known as "Detroit automation." Unlike the old-fashioned assembly-line technique, in which a part was moved from one manned work station to another, Detroit automation consists of moving parts from one machine to another, while automatic adjustments are made in the positioning of the tools that shape them. For instance, a precast aluminum block is inserted into one end of the machine, and a finished automobile engine is spewed out on the other. Some who have examined the organization of production processes in detail have classified as automation any production technique more advanced than that generally used in a particular industry at a particular time.

Confusion about the character of automation arises when technologies that have some, but not all, of the characteristics of the automatic process are called automation. For instance, machine-directors, which activate and control the movement of machine tools and permit the shaping of complicated parts without human assistance, have often been cited as examples of automation. If such operations are to be classed as automation, is there any reason to exclude a screw-making machine from this category, just because it produces a less complicated shape?

The most careful attempt at defining automation was made by James R. Bright (1958), who gave up and instead divided technology in the production process into 17 levels of sophistication. The simplest technologies, according to Bright, involve the use of human labor only or human labor and hand tools; the more complicated do not require human interference in the selection and identification of the appropriate action; the most sophisticated correct performance during the operation or after the operation is completed, or they even anticipate required action and automatically make adjustments to provide for it (Bright 1958, pp. 41–46).

Most manufacturing operations—even those dubbed automation—consist of series of work stations, where mechanization has progressed to different levels of sophistication. For instance, a seamless-pipe mill described by Walker (1957) as an example of the automatic factory consisted of a series of analog, pneumatic, and mechanical devices ingeniously combined to speed the movement of steel through the pipe-making process. The new production line cut the requirements for workers from 20 men to 9 men and increased output four times.

The ultimate in automation is the closed-loop process, a method of operation that requires no human interference from the time the raw material is inserted into the machine to the time the finished product is stored or stacked at the end of the production line (for a lucid general discussion, see Macmillan 1956). In the middle 1960s few closed-loop processes were in operation. Even in the case of oil refineries, which have been heavily instrumented and automated since the 1950s, the rhythm of the process is under human control in most refineries. An attempt to schedule the refinery process by computer is still in the experimental stage.

Since the end of World War II considerable changes in techniques of production have taken place. Most plants acquired more efficient and faster machines; these changes could very well be classified as more intensive mechanization. Other plants substantially changed the method of organization of production; these changes may be put under the heading of automation. The innovations generally fell into five categories: assembly of parts, generally through automatic insertion of one part into another; material movement from one location to another, especially between machines; consolidation of control activities into one panel; mechanization of testing and inspection; and data processing through the use of computers.

Automation in record handling or data processing deserves special mention because it falls outside the conventional scope of automation. Since the 1950s electronic computers have replaced and supplemented the use of mechanical devices in manipulating Hollerith cards. This change in technology has resulted in a dramatic decline in computing cost per operation and has given business increasing flexibility in the manipulation of

and access to various records. Computer operations are under the control of a program that utilizes the "feedback" principle: the sequence of operations is determined by the outcome of a previous operation.

The scope of automation. Without agreement on a definition of automation, it is difficult to delineate its scope. Nevertheless, it may be worthwhile to cite some statistics that indicate the extent of the acceptance of automatic techniques.

New ideas about the organization of production processes appear to have permeated most business organizations. A survey conducted by the McGraw-Hill Company in the middle 1960s (*Universe . . . 1964*) indicated that some automatic control and measurement devices and data-handling systems were used by 21,000 out of 32,000 manufacturing establishments employing over 100 persons. Nearly nine out of ten petroleum, instrument, computer, or control equipment plants reported using these devices. Two-thirds of equipment, machinery, and metal-working plants also were using control systems. Undoubtedly, the sophistication of the control systems must have varied from plant to plant, but their prevalence is surprisingly high.

Another survey conducted by McGraw-Hill queries businessmen annually about investment decisions. In 1963 this survey indicated that nearly $7 billion, or 18 per cent of the gross investment in manufacturing (and roughly one-third of investment in machinery), was being spent on equipment that respondents considered either automatic or advanced. Expenditures on automatic or advanced equipment accounted for 11 per cent of the gross investment of manufacturing in 1955 and, according to the survey, are still increasing; businessmen were planning to spend $8 billion on this type of equipment in 1964 and in succeeding years. The share of investment devoted to automation varied considerably from industry to industry. In the forefront were communications, transportation, electrical machinery, steel, and automobile manufacturers (McGraw-Hill, Department of Economics 1963).

These two surveys give only an inkling of the scope of automation. The definition of control systems in the first survey is not rigorous, and the response to a question about what constitutes advanced types of machinery cannot help but be subjective. Probably some control systems used in the plants are no more complicated than circuit breakers. Similarly, an industry that became mechanized or automated in the early 1950s may be reporting automated plants as conventional, while a backward industry may be reporting more intensively mechanized plants as advanced. Two conclusions can be drawn from the results of these surveys: that automation, to some degree, is common to most manufacturing establishments in the United States and that its tempo is increasing rapidly.

The impression persists that automatic techniques have spread widely, but not very deeply, in the production process. There are a number of roadblocks to the adoption of automatic techniques. First, because of technological difficulties, it often requires vast resources and is risky. Thus, automation is generally—though not always—adopted by enterprises that are bigger than average. The management of smaller enterprises may not have the foresight or be willing to risk the resources to adapt modern technologies to their needs. Even more important, a small enterprise may not have long enough runs of a similar product to justify economically an automated process. Most automated processes are inflexible and are expensive to re-engineer and change, especially those which deal with noncontinuous processes. In certain areas, such as data processing, technology favors the larger firm. The cost per throughput of larger machines is much lower than that of smaller machines, and only large companies can afford large machines. Set-up costs—in this case, programming—are proportional to the complexity of the job, not its volume. The cost per data-processing unit of work is much less for large companies that have many repetitive jobs.

Second, automation—especially Detroit automation—requires that raw materials of a uniform quality be fed into the production line. Minor adjustments of a machine tool because of excessive hardness of steel cannot be made as easily by machines as they can be by humans. In most manufacturing industries, automation is feasible only when precise techniques of measurement are developed and the nomenclature and quality of parts are standardized.

To summarize, some features of automatic production are common to many U.S. manufacturing enterprises. The spread of these features is retarded by certain characteristics of automatic processes, namely, the risk associated with violent change, the inflexibility of the production methods, and the need for raw materials of uniform quality.

Automation and productivity

Side by side with efforts at automation, there occur improvements in mechanization, changes in organization, product improvements, and other changes that can materially affect the productivity of workers. Since automatic processes affect only a small part of the production effort of a given enterprise, one way to assess the effect of automation on productivity is to compare a period when the technology was not available with the present time. Another way of estimating the effect of automation is to examine the productivity trends of industries in which automatic methods of production have been widely adopted and to contrast them with other industries in which they have not.

Neither of these approaches will measure the effect of automation upon productivity with certainty. For instance, changes in output per production man-hour for manufacturing in the United States have fluctuated between a small improvement of 0.7 per cent per annum in the first decade of this century to a high of 4.6 per cent in the 1919–1929 period. During the great depression the rate of improvement in production per man-hour fell to 1.9 per cent. From 1948 to 1961 the average rate of increase in productivity per man-hour was 3.9 per cent (for these and other relevant figures, see U.S. Bureau of the Census 1965c, p. 236, Table No. 318). Preliminary estimates for the early 1960s, which are subject to considerable revision, place the increase in productivity at somewhere near 4.0 per cent. These figures tend to indicate that the impact of the new technologies developed since the end of the war is not unprecedented and that it may be likened to what the assembly line, the endless-chain drives, and individual drives (substituted for overhead drives for machinery) did for the manufacturing industry in the 1920s.

Also, without minimizing the impact of automation (defined in its narrower terms), it is important to realize that other mechanization techniques have not yet fully permeated the economy and that considerable improvements in productivity can occur, as they have in past decades, merely through further mechanization. A recent study by the U.S. Bureau of Labor Statistics (1964b) examined technological trends in 36 major American industries. It characterized the prospects of the U.S. economy as follows: 10 industries were likely to have their productivity affected by devices that principally partook of the mechanization process; 10 more, by automation processes; and the remaining 16, by a combination of the two. This survey indicates that there is still considerable room for improvement in productivity by mechanizing the handling of raw materials and finished products, the installation of more up-to-date and faster conventional equipment, and rationalization of existing production processes. It also points to the improvements in productivity that can come about from better scheduling of labor with the help of computers, the impact of electronic data processing on the front office, and the integration of the production process through a marriage of control and instrument devices with existing production techniques.

Another way of trying to estimate the impact of automation on productivity is to examine technological developments in industries where output per employee increased faster than the average in the recent past. For instance, productivity per employee in the 1950–1960 period grew faster than 4 per cent in the following industries: agriculture, coal mining, motor vehicle manufacturing, aircraft and aerospace industries, textiles, chemicals, petroleum manufacturing, radio and television (in mass communication), telephone, air transportation, and electric and gas and steam plants (Jaffe 1963). For many of these industries, better mechanization, improved organization, or the introduction of new products, rather than feedback or Detroit automation, must be credited with the productivity increase; in this category fall agriculture, coal mining, textiles, radio and television, and air transportation. Other industries, such as motor vehicle manufacturing, aircraft and aerospace, chemicals, and petroleum, probably owe their increases in productivity to the techniques that fall under the heading of automation. The telephone industry and utilities, which have high rates of productivity increase, probably take their place in between the other two categories; part of the improvement in productivity in these industries is due to an improvement in organization or the introduction of new products, such as bigger generators in electric utilities or message-switching equipment in telephones; and part is due to automation of the billing procedure, the use of computers for the dispatch of power, and the routing of telephone calls.

Employment and changes in productivity. The impact of changes in production techniques upon employment has varied considerably from industry to industry. In some industries, such as chemicals and aerospace, remarkable increases in productivity have been paralleled by employment increases. In others, such as automobile manufacturing or meat packing, the productivity increases—remarkable or just average—reduced the number of available jobs. In general, industries for which the demand increased faster than average had larger than average productivity increases, and the impact of productivity upon employment, with the exception of such industries as coal mining, did not

result in as much dislocation as might have been the case (for more detailed analysis of these trends, see Jaffe 1963, p. 1601).

One can find numerous references to the impact of automation or productivity on the number of jobs available in the United States (see, for instance, Clague 1961; Killingsworth 1963). Most of these statements are made in a static context; it is assumed that a given level of production would be achieved with or without an increase in productivity. The difference between the labor force required in the current year to produce the current output and that which would have been required to produce the same output in any previous year with a lower productivity has often been described as the impact of automation on the job market. This shortsighted point of view assumes that investment, wages, and consumption are in no way affected by the productivity of the labor force. In actual fact, if productivity were to remain static, it is quite likely that the volume of investment goods purchased would decline, wages would stay constant or fall, and consumption would be at a different level.

Automation and rapid technological change should be looked upon in the broader context of how they affect income distribution, the demand for new investment, and so on, and hence how they affect the level at which the economy will stabilize. The consistently high unemployment rates experienced by the United States in the late 1950s and early 1960s raise doubts about the ability of our society to adapt easily to rapid technological change. These doubts are not new and were voiced often during the 1930s, although no systematic effort was made to analyze them in order to explain underemployment.

Under what circumstances can technological change cause underemployment? The most obvious circumstance would be technological unemployment, that is, when workers used in old-fashioned production processes are thrown out of jobs and cannot readjust to the requirements of the new production processes. There is little evidence that this is the case to any greater degree in the 1960s than previously. Most firms manage to retrain some of their employees for new production processes, getting along with fewer employees as they increase production. Workers who lose jobs are no less mobile than workers thrown out of jobs in previous periods of U.S. history (Gallaway 1963). Unemployment rates during the early 1960s, either by industry or by occupations, do not appear to have been affected by technological change

(Gordon 1964). Although there is no consensus on the reasons for unemployment, a considerable number of social scientists have blamed inadequate demand [see EMPLOYMENT AND UNEMPLOYMENT].

Inadequate demand can be brought about by technological change if either investment or consumption is affected unfavorably. For instance, if a highly automated plant costs no more (and sometimes costs less) than a conventional plant, there can be overwhelming reasons for substituting a little capital for a lot of labor and thus depressing the level of investment. In those instances where a shift can be made from mechanical technologies to pneumatic processes in moving materials, or when mechanical or manual methods of metal cutting or inspection can be replaced by electronic technology, the cost advantages are overwhelmingly on the side of sophisticated technical processes. Hence the demand for investment per production unit may decline. Unless the industry scraps old producers' goods at an accelerated rate and replaces them with new equipment more rapidly than heretofore (and there are a number of institutional reasons why this is not done, in addition to the very economic reason that variable costs of the old process should be larger than the variable and fixed costs of the new process), the total demand for investment in the economy may not rise fast enough to equal savings. Hence unemployment ensues.

The balance between savings and investment may not be restored because: prices may not be reduced to reflect the savings in the production process; and technological changes may affect the job content drastically, making job-evaluation standards increasingly subjective and resulting in wage setting based on historical standards rather than on competitive considerations. Even if—and especially if—bargaining for wages in technologically advanced industries results in a proportional or greater than proportional sharing of benefits with labor, we may move to a bipolar society that consists of a shrinking number of steadily employed workers with high incomes and a large mass of workers with less steady jobs and low incomes.

This is not the place to go into a detailed and rigorous discussion of the conditions that may result in rising employment. Suffice it to say here that technological change has, even before this most recent period, restricted the number of production jobs or, for that matter, the total number of jobs in manufacturing. For instance, the same number of workers was employed in manufacturing in the United States in 1919 as in 1939—about 10.5 million persons. Between 1948 and 1960 employment in that sector increased by only one million, that is, from 15.5 to 16.5 million (U.S. Bureau of the Census 1965b, p. 220, Table No. 305). During some periods in U.S. history, increases in productivity have been sufficient to satisfy the increased demand for manufactured goods. Whenever this occurs, jobs for a growing labor force must be found in other sectors of the economy.

Besides the over-all increases or decreases in employment that result from technological change, automation or new technological breakthroughs may affect the distribution of workers within an enterprise. In the past decades we have observed a decrease in the share of production workers in total employment and an increase in overhead staffs in most industries. This shift has given increasing concern to the unions, who do not control the loyalty of the front office, and it has also given considerable grounds to wits who have ascribed this tendency to "Parkinson's law" (for which, see Parkinson 1957).

Two opposing tendencies have contributed to the growth of overhead staffs. First, the increased mechanization and automation in the factory have reduced the number of persons on the factory floor. Under these circumstances, the proportion of persons in the front office, per unit produced, would increase even if their number remained constant. Second, the mechanization of conventional front office jobs, which has tended to decrease the number of office people, has been offset by a more important secondary effect: it has encouraged the centralization of record-keeping functions. Clerical functions on the production floor have been pulled into the front office. Currently, the jobs of assistant foreman, record keeper, and parts clerk are becoming less common on the factory floor. Even the foreman's job is being threatened, as scheduling, an important foreman's prerogative, is done increasingly by computer (for these and related trends see, for instance, U.S. Bureau of Labor Statistics 1962 and the other case studies in the same series).

Skills and education

There is considerable divergence of opinion on the subject of skills required for jobs in industries that are being automated. A number of ex-cathedra statements have been made to the effect that skill requirements in industries with advanced technologies are much higher than those in technologically conventional industries. Succor for these views can be found in two areas. First, the average skill level of workers in the United States has increased in every decade since the beginning of the century. In other words, clerical occupations have grown faster than skilled ones, the skilled faster than the semiskilled, and semiskilled faster than unskilled occupations. In the 1950s the absolute number of unskilled workers in the U.S. labor force declined (U.S. Bureau of the Census 1965a, p. 228, Table No. 313). Second, there is some evidence that the growth of skilled occupations is more prevalent in industries with high increases in productivity per employee than in those with low productivity (unpublished research by the present writer).

Detailed studies of employment in plants with automatic processes have indicated that the new skills are not comparable with the old ones (see, for instance, Bright 1958, pp. 176–191). Generally these new skills can be acquired, and the jobs staffed, by workers with backgrounds equivalent to those of semiskilled operators. In the increasingly important maintenance area, where growing numbers of automated-factory workers are being employed, the weight of empirical evidence favors those scholars who believe that job requirements are at the semiskilled level.

The whole controversy about skills has a hollow ring. The majority of companies that have radically altered their production processes have had considerable success in retraining workers for the new jobs. This retraining was generally done under their own auspices and in a relatively short time. The crucial point is that the new jobs had very few of the characteristics of the old ones. In automated processes the production worker's role consists of monitoring, information handling, and adjusting and maintaining of machinery. The principal challenge of the job is to coordinate the rhythm of the production process under his control with that of other members of the team responsible for other areas of the process. In most instances, the work is likely to require manual dexterity and judgment but is not very tiring physically. Workers have often complained of the strains brought about by these conditions.

These strains are different in degree, but not in kind, from those imposed by the continuous assembly line, inasmuch as each operation depends upon the successful completion of a previous operation. The decreased size of work teams and the increasing physical isolation of workers have often been mentioned as sources of dissatisfaction by workers transferred to automatic processes (Walker 1957; Mann & Hoffman 1960). New working conditions requiring less physical labor and more mental exertion are often not highly regarded by workers who prefer physical labor. On the other hand, the prestige of working in a new plant goes a long way to offset this resentment. Studies of the change-over to automatic processes have uncovered a great deal of apprehension before and during the change-over but have come to the conclusion that workers were equally or more satisfied with new working conditions after the end of the shakedown period (see Faunce et al. 1962 for a review of some relevant case studies).

Automatic processes have been resented by older workers, supervisors, and workers with a high status in the old process. Older workers have had psychological difficulties in adjusting themselves to new working conditions and have often been reluctant to give up old skills acquired over the years. Supervisors, in those cases where the number of subordinates has been reduced, have often strongly resented the introduction of the new equipment. They have been apprehensive about their own status. Furthermore, especially with front office automation, supervisors have lost some leeway in scheduling of work, deciding the format of the work, and so on. For instance, bills have to be rendered in a certain form in a mechanized office. Partial payments must also be arranged according to instructions of a central methods staff. Among white-collar workers another area of stress has been the introduction of shift work. Clerical workers are being increasingly used on second and third shifts to keep computers busy.

The effect of front office automation upon management has been studied least of all. A number of observers have claimed that some middle-management jobs have been eliminated by computers (Melitz 1961; Uris 1963). These jobs were generally of a routine supervisory nature but were often the road used for promotion to management. It is very likely that front office automation will affect the promotion route to management drastically, forcing large corporations to rely more on the promotion of professionals to management jobs. So far its effect has been very slight (Whisler 1965). Except for shifting some of the power fulcrums to areas that produce the increased volume of "facts," management has not changed its practices substantially. One of the reasons for this slow adaptation has been the difficulty of retrieving facts for management decisions on an exception basis. The introduction by most computer manufacturers of products that make such retrieval possible will affect management practices drastically if some way is found to quantify essentially intuitive processes, which are the basis for most management decisions.

Upgrading the average level of skills among production workers is not central to automation or automatic processes and sometimes is not relevant to it. Time and again unskilled jobs are eliminated because of decisions that have nothing to do with automation, thus resulting in a rise in the average skill level. For instance, many unskilled jobs are being eliminated in the area of material handling, sometimes through the introduction of mechanical devices such as the forklift. In other cases, since automated processes are self-contained and reduce the waste and dirt attendant on the manufacturing operation, a number of in-plant service jobs are being eliminated.

The above discussion indicates that the skills and rhythms of work necessary to automatic processes may be acquired, without any drastic upheaval, by workers currently employed in industry. This has serious implications for the educational requirements of the workers of tomorrow. In the less than full employment situation of the late 1950s and early 1960s, workers who had not completed high school had considerable difficulty in finding new job openings. This fact led to the unwarranted conclusion that the new jobs opening up in the economy required at least a high school education. Actually, an examination of labor mobility between jobs shows that a large number of workers move from the unskilled to the semiskilled category, and from the semiskilled to the skilled category, without the benefit of a high school diploma (see the tabulations on educational attainment of the U.S. population for 1960, in U.S. Bureau of the Census 1963). It is much more likely that under conditions of less than full employment employers choose to hire the best-educated applicants, without regard for the educational requirements for the job. An examination of the educational achievement of new entrants in the labor force in the decade of the 1950s bears out this conclusion (unpublished research by A. J. Jaffe and the present writer). Perhaps it would be better to justify the increased emphasis on education in a highly productive society on the basis of what that society can afford, rather than what it needs.

Reactions to rapid technological change

Rapid technological change, whether it be automation or not, does produce certain dislocations in the economy. We have seen that in the United States in the late 1950s and early 1960s it caused employment to grow more slowly than the number of people who were seeking jobs. Under these circumstances it is only natural for labor unions to be greatly concerned about the rate of introduction of innovations and the effect of these innovations on job opportunities for their members.

The ability of unions to negotiate the rate at which innovations may be introduced by management depends on the past scope of their contracts (for a review, see U.S. Bureau of Labor Statistics 1964a). With few exceptions, unions have been ineffective in retarding the adoption of labor-saving practices. In a number of industries, such as railroads, steel, and that of the longshoremen, where in an earlier period management lost the right to make work assignments, changes in working conditions were less easy to impose than in such industries as automobile manufacturing, meat packing, and textiles, where these rights were reserved by management. In the first category mechanization or automation was delayed; and when it was finally adopted, management had to pay a healthy price for union agreement. For instance, the West Coast longshoremen required management to deposit $29 million in trust, during the five and a half years following October 1960, to "buy out" rights to abrogate the most restrictive work rules. The money was to be used for annual wage guarantees, early retirement, and death benefits.

Some unions have negotiated separation payments for workers who may be laid off because of technological change. Others have tried to protect job security by negotiating job rights that would extend to the company as a whole, rather than to a given plant. Still others, faced with the prospect of shrinking numbers of jobs, have attempted to minimize layoffs by including provisions in union contracts to encourage retirement of workers at age 60 instead of age 65. Less effective union-negotiated contracts provide for a 90-day notification before a plant shutdown, and, in at least one instance, the union negotiated for the establishment of a fund to study the problems of laid-off workers (Kennedy 1962).

The increasing concern for facilitating the mobility of the labor force has prompted a government committee to recommend the vesting of pension funds to workers, thus allowing an employee to transfer his pension fund from one employer to another as he changes jobs. Other government efforts to promote mobility, such as job retraining, have had equally little impact on the labor force.

Unless specific job openings exist, it is difficult to know what skills to impart to workers. The most promising way of attacking unemployment—the resettlement of workers from depressed areas—has not become a major tool of U.S. manpower policy, although it has been favorably received in such economically advanced countries as Sweden.

All economic changes are painful for the less skilled, older, and minority-group workers—especially Negroes; this is the conclusion of a survey of the impact of industrial dislocation upon workers from 1929 to 1962 (Haber et al. 1963). The ability of workers to adjust to the change depends upon the health of the economy at the time the disruption hits them. The implication of these findings is obvious: adjustments to rapid technological change can best be aided by action that stabilizes the economy at a high level of employment.

This conclusion runs counter to the belief of a number of social scientists who claim that minimum wages and union-set wage levels play a large part in causing unemployment. Members of this school of thought believe that the substitution of capital for labor has been accelerated by wage levels artificially pegged too high. Empirical studies of the reasons for mechanization indicate that other factors play an extremely important part in this process (see, for instance, Bright 1958, chapter 5; Erbe 1962; Clayton 1962; and contrast U.S. Office of Manpower 1965). In some instances plants have been automated because it was not feasible to integrate production on a larger scale in any other way. In other instances new technologies, which were not capital intensive (i.e., did not require more capital investment per worker), reduced the labor content of the process so much that a small decline in real wages would have had no influence in arresting the change-over. The influence of small changes in wage levels on employment needs better empirical justification before it is given much weight.

In any discussion of technological change or automation, it is essential to keep in mind that the techniques of production are only one of many factors that influence the size and composition of the labor force. Dictates of taste, as well as government policy, probably have far more important effects upon the labor force composition. For instance, the preference of U.S. consumers for slimmer television chassis encouraged manufacturers to substitute printed circuits for wiring and incidentally eliminated many skilled jobs. Also, between 1950 and 1960 professional, technical, and kindred workers in the labor force increased by

2.4 million. In 1960, the 7.2 million professionals accounted for 11.3 per cent of the labor force, as compared to 4.9 million in 1950, or 8.3 per cent of the labor force (U.S. Bureau of the Census 1965a, p. 228, Table No. 313). These figures could imply that modern production processes demand much more professional participation. Actually, some 60 per cent of this increase occurred in industries that are not considered to be market-oriented, such as education and welfare, and in defense-oriented industries, such as aerospace, the electronic industries, and communications.

Automation, which is a subset of technological change, has probably accelerated the increase in productivity of the working force. It has probably been less instrumental in changing the skill composition of workers than has popularly been believed. Many of the problems that have been associated with it are due to the inability of the economy to adjust to rapid technological change.

The future impact of automation

The spread of automation has coincided with a general acceleration of mechanization; together, the two processes have raised the productivity of the labor force. It is not easy to delimit the future impact of automation on the productivity of the economy. In areas where it can be applied, increases in the productivity of the labor force have often been spectacular. On the other hand, such increases in productivity are not unprecedented: similar increases occurred with the introduction of the assembly line, for example, in motorcar manufacturing. The future impact of automation is hence dependent on the number of areas to which it will spread.

The prospects of a utopia, or a Calvinist hell, where work will become redundant, are not likely to face Western society in the near future. Historically, periods of increases in productivity have been followed by periods of stagnation in the rate of increase in productivity. Especially in the United States, where more and more demand is concentrated in the service area, which has been untouched by automation, the prospects are not good for general idleness as a way of life.

Automation is also unlikely to revolutionize the structure of society. Less has been heard about the ascendance of the technocrats during the current upsurge in productivity than during the 1930s. The innovators and the participants in new production processes appear not to have gained much status or power. New occupations, which generally enjoy a high status, have lost standing faster than ever before. In 1958, when computers were first introduced on a large scale, programmers were required to have a graduate degree in mathematics. Six years later, many programmers had nothing more than a high school education, and their status in the business hierarchy is continuously declining.

The big challenge to the U.S. and other Western economies is to bring out cheaply, through automation or otherwise, new products that will tempt the consumer's jaded taste. These new products, in turn, will stimulate investment. In European countries, where increases in productivity have been equally spectacular, no underemployment problem has occurred; the population's unsated demand for consumer durables has kept economic activity at an extremely high level. In the United States this demand was satisfied in preceding decades, and policies to stimulate aggregate demand were not adopted early enough. Further rapid increases in productivity as a result of wider application of automation techniques can benefit our society if economic policies are all shaped so as to permit demand to increase in step with productivity.

JOSEPH N. FROOMKIN

[*See also* EMPLOYMENT AND UNEMPLOYMENT; INDUSTRIAL RELATIONS, *article on* THE SOCIOLOGY OF WORK; LABOR FORCE; LEISURE; PRODUCTIVITY; TECHNOLOGY; WORKERS.]

BIBLIOGRAPHY

Automation is often discussed under the more general headings "technological change" and "productivity." Most of the relevant literature in English has originated in the United States, where several government bodies have published hearings, compilations of readings, and statistical surveys in the area, as well as a number of special studies and reports. The most comprehensive of these so far are U.S. Congress, Senate 1964 *and* U.S. Bureau of Labor Statistics 1962–1964. *The* U.S. President's Commission on Automation 1966 *was not available to the present writer.*

Of the large body of academic research and writing, the most valuable works are those based on case studies of individual companies. Outstanding examples are Walker 1957; Bright 1958; Mann & Hoffman 1960. Michigan State University . . . 1958–1961 *is a valuable bibliography. Symposia that accurately reflect academic thinking on automation are* Automation 1962 *and* American Assembly 1962.

Most journalistic or business analyses limit themselves to case studies of a single process or industry. Many articles of this kind, of varied interest to social scientists, have been published in Automation; Computers and Automation; Control Engineering; Datamation; Fortune; *and* Productivity Measurement Review. *Somewhat more comprehensive studies of particular industries have been undertaken by the U.S. Department of Labor, Bureau of Labor Statistics, whose current lists of publications should be regularly consulted. Many of these and other comparable studies are listed in* U.S. Bureau of Labor Statistics 1963, *which is also useful for its systematic listing of the most commonly discussed topics relating to automation.*

Outside the United States, automation is most often treated in the broader context of technological change. In Europe, references to automation can be found in current lists of publications of the Organization for Economic Cooperation and Development. In the U.S.S.R., case studies of automated processes frequently appear in Ekonomicheskaia gazeta. Two recent Soviet books deserve some attention: Veinberg 1964, *which deals with the labor force implications of automation; and* Kats 1964, *which is a more general study of productivity.* Conference on Labor Productivity . . . 1964 *is an illuminating exchange of views between Eastern and Western economists on concepts of productivity.*

AMERICAN ASSEMBLY 1962 *Automation and Technical Change.* Edited by John T. Dunlop. Englewood Cliffs, N.J.: Prentice-Hall.

Automation. Edited by Charles C. Killingsworth. 1962 American Academy of Political and Social Science, *Annals* Special Issue No. 340.

Automation: The Magazine of Automatic Production Operations. → Published since 1954.

BEAUMONT, RICHARD A.; and HELFGOTT, ROY B. 1964 *Management, Automation and People.* New York: Industrial Relations Counselors.

BRIGHT, JAMES R. 1958 *Automation and Management.* Boston: Harvard Univ., Graduate School of Business Administration, Division of Research.

CLAGUE, EWAN 1961 Social and Economic Aspects of Automation. *Monthly Labor Review* 84, no. 9:957–960.

CLAYTON, CURTIS T. 1962 Automatic Ships—Only Hope for the U.S. Merchant Marine? *Control Engineering* 9:73–76.

Computers and Automation. → Published since 1951.

CONFERENCE ON LABOR PRODUCTIVITY, CADENABBIA, ITALY, 1961 1964 *Labor Productivity.* Edited by John T. Dunlop and Vasilii P. Diatchenko. New York: McGraw-Hill.

Control Engineering: Instrumentation and Automatic Control Systems. → Published since 1954.

Datamation: The Automatic Handling of Information. → Published since 1957.

Ekonomicheskaia gazeta. → Published since 1956.

ERBE, J. RAYMOND 1962 Electrical Equipment for Automation of the Blast Furnace. *Blast Furnace and Steel Plant* [1962] July:641–652.

FAUNCE, WILLIAM A.; HARDIN, EINAR; and JACOBSON, EUGENE H. 1962 Automation and the Employee. American Academy of Political and Social Science, *Annals* 68:60–68.

Fortune. → Published since 1930.

GALLAWAY, L. E. 1963 Labor Mobility, Resource Allocation and Structural Unemployment. *American Economic Review* 53:694–716.

GORDON, R. A. 1964 Has Structural Unemployment Worsened? *Industrial Relations* 3:53–77.

HABER, WILLIAM et al. 1963 *The Impact of Technological Change: The American Experience.* Kalamazoo, Mich.: Upjohn Institute for Employment Research.

JAFFE, A. J. 1963 [Prepared Statement.] Part 5, page 1601 in U.S. Congress, Senate, Committee on Labor and Public Welfare, *Nation's Manpower Revolution.* Hearings before the Subcommittee on Employment and Manpower, 88th Congress, 1st Session. Washington: Government Printing Office.

KATS, A. I. 1964 *Proizvoditel'nost' truda v S.S.S.R. i glavnykh kapitalisticheskikh stranakh* (Work Productivity in the Soviet Union and in the Main Capitalistic Countries). Moscow: Ekonomika.

KENNEDY, THOMAS 1962 *Automation Funds and Displaced Workers.* Boston: Harvard Univ., Graduate School of Business Administration, Division of Research.

KILLINGSWORTH, CHARLES C. 1963 [Testimony.] Part 5, pages 1475–1479 in U.S. Congress, Senate, Committee on Labor and Public Welfare, *Nation's Manpower Revolution.* Hearings before the Subcommittee on Employment and Manpower, 88th Congress, 1st Session. Washington: Government Printing Office.

McGRAW-HILL, DEPARTMENT OF ECONOMICS, *Annual Survey of Investment Decisions.* → Published annually in mimeographed form for a limited distribution.

MACMILLAN, ROBERT H. 1956 *Automation: Friend or Foe?* Cambridge Univ. Press.

MANN, FLOYD C.; and HOFFMAN, L. RICHARD 1960 *Automation and the Worker: A Study of Social Change in Power Plants.* New York: Holt.

MELITZ, P. W. 1961 Impact of Electronic Data Processing on Managers. *Advanced Management* 26:4–6.

MICHAEL, DONALD N. 1965 *The Next Generation: The Prospects Ahead for the Youth of Today and Tomorrow.* New York: Random House.

MICHIGAN STATE UNIVERSITY OF AGRICULTURE AND APPLIED SCIENCE, LABOR AND INDUSTRIAL RELATIONS CENTER 1958–1961 *Economic and Social Implications of Automation.* Vols. 1–2. East Lansing, Mich.: The Center. → Volume 1: *A Bibliographic Review,* by G. Cheek, 1958. Volume 2: *An Annotated Bibliography: Literature, 1957–1960,* by E. Hardin, W. B. Eddy, and S. E. Deutsch, 1961.

PARKINSON, CYRIL NORTHCOTE 1957 *Parkinson's Law, and Other Studies in Administration.* Boston: Houghton Mifflin. → A satire on bureaucracy in which it is maintained, *inter alia,* that paperwork increases, rather than decreases, in proportion to the size of the administrative and clerical staff.

Productivity Measurement Review. → Published since 1955 in English and French.

SALTER, W. E. G. 1960 *Productivity and Technical Change.* Cambridge Univ. Press.

SOLOW, ROBERT M. 1964 *The Nature and Sources of Unemployment in the United States.* Stockholm: Almqvist & Wiksell.

U.S. BUREAU OF LABOR STATISTICS 1962 *Impact of Technological Change and Automation in the Pulp and Paper Industry.* Bulletin No. 1347. Washington: Government Printing Office.

U.S. BUREAU OF LABOR STATISTICS 1962–1964 *Implications of Automation and Other Technological Developments: A Selected Annotated Bibliography.* Washington: Government Printing Office.

U.S. BUREAU OF LABOR STATISTICS 1963 *Implications of Automation and Other Technological Developments: A Selected Annotated Bibliography.* Bulletin No. 1319-1. Washington: Government Printing Office.

U.S. BUREAU OF LABOR STATISTICS 1964a *Recent Collective Bargaining and Technological Change.* Report No. 266. Washington: Government Printing Office.

U.S. BUREAU OF LABOR STATISTICS 1964b *Technological Trends in 36 Major American Industries.* A study prepared for the President's Committee on Labor–Management Policy. Washington: Government Printing Office.

U.S. BUREAU OF THE CENSUS 1963 *U.S. Census of Population: 1960; Subject Reports: Occupation by Industry.* Final Report PC(2)-7C. Washington: Government Printing Office.

U.S. BUREAU OF THE CENSUS 1965a Employed Persons, by Sex and Major Occupation Group: 1950 to 1965. Table No. 313. Page 228 in U.S. Bureau of the Census, *Statistical Abstracts of the United States: 1965.* Washington: The Bureau.

U.S. BUREAU OF THE CENSUS 1965b Employees in Nonagricultural Establishments—Annual Averages, by Industry: 1940 to 1965. Table No. 305. Page 220 in U.S. Bureau of the Census, *Statistical Abstracts of the United States: 1965.* Washington: The Bureau.

U.S. BUREAU OF THE CENSUS 1965c Indexes of Real Product per Man-hour for the Private Economy 1947 to 1964. Table No. 318. Page 236 in U.S. Bureau of the Census, *Statistical Abstracts of the United States: 1965.* Washington: The Bureau.

U.S. CONGRESS, JOINT COMMITTEE ON THE ECONOMIC REPORT 1955 *Automation and Technological Change.* Report of the Sub-committee on Economic Stabilization. Washington: Government Printing Office.

U.S. CONGRESS, SENATE, COMMITTEE ON LABOR AND PUBLIC WELFARE 1963–1964 *Nation's Manpower Revolution.* Hearings before the Sub-committee on Employment and Manpower, 10 vols. Washington: Government Printing Office.

U.S. CONGRESS, SENATE, COMMITTEE ON LABOR AND PUBLIC WELFARE 1964 *Selected Readings in Employment and Manpower.* 6 vols. Compiled for the Subcommittee on Employment and Manpower. Washington: Government Printing Office.

U.S. NATIONAL RESOURCES COMMITTEE 1937 *Technological Trends and National Policy, Including the Social Implications of New Inventions.* Washington: Government Printing Office.

U.S. NATIONAL SCIENCE FOUNDATION, OFFICE OF SPECIAL STUDIES 1959— *Current Projects on Economic and Social Implications of Science and Technology.* Washington: Government Printing Office.

U.S. OFFICE OF MANPOWER, AUTOMATION AND TRAINING 1965 *Management Decision to Automate.* Washington: The Office. → Contains eight case studies adapted from a report with the same title by Richard S. Roberts, Jr.

Universe of Control System Design and Use in U.S. Manufacturing Plants. 1964 New York: McGraw-Hill. → A research report from *Control Engineering.*

URIS, AUREN 1963 Middle Management and Technological Change: Abstract. *Management Review* 52, October:55–58.

VEINBERG, ADOLF M. 1964 *Vliianie tekhnicheskogo progressa na kharakter truda* (The Influence of Technical Progress on the Character of Work). Moscow: Ekonomika.

WALKER, CHARLES R. 1957 *Toward the Automatic Factory: A Case Study of Men and Machines.* New Haven: Yale Univ. Press.

WHISLER, THOMAS L. 1965 The Management and the Computer. *Journal of Accountancy* 60:27–32.

AVERAGES

See STATISTICS, DESCRIPTIVE, *article on* LOCATION AND DISPERSION.

AVERAGES, LAW OF

See PROBABILITY.

AVOIDANCE LEARNING

See under LEARNING.

B

BABBAGE, CHARLES

Charles Babbage (1792–1871), English mathematician, did pioneering work on calculating machines and in operations research and was active in winning public support for science. A man far ahead of his time, he was generally recognized only long after his death. However, his work strikingly anticipated certain key developments in modern thought. The great electronic computers, whose uses have multiplied enormously since they were developed in the mid-twentieth century, are based on principles first stated by Babbage.

His dream was to mechanize the abstract operations of mathematics for use in industry. His first idea was that of the "difference engine," a machine for integrating difference equations, which formed mathematical tables by interpolation and set them directly into type. Babbage pointed out the advantages such a machine would have for the government in preparing its lengthy tables for navigation and astronomy. With the enthusiastic approval of the Royal and Astronomical societies, the government of England agreed to grant funds for the construction of such a machine. Work proceeded for about eight years but stopped abruptly after a dispute between Babbage and his chief engineer. Shortly thereafter Babbage thought of another machine, the "analytical engine," built on an entirely new principle—internal programming—and wholly superseding and transcending the difference engine. Babbage explained his new idea to the first lord of the Treasury and asked for an official decision on whether to continue and complete the original difference engine or to suspend work on it until the analytical engine was further developed.

The government had already spent £17,000 on the difference engine, and Babbage had contributed a large amount from his private fortune. After years of correspondence with various government officials, Babbage was advised that the prime minister, Sir Robert Peel, had decided the government must abandon the project because of the expense involved.

Babbage continued to work on his analytical engine. The machine he envisioned (which he called "the Engine eating its own tail") was one that could change its operations in accordance with the results of its own calculations. The machine could make judgments by comparing numbers and then, acting on the result of its comparisons, could proceed along lines not specified in advance by its instructions. These notions are acknowledged as the backbone of modern digital computers. Bound by the technology of his time, Babbage had to translate his great idea into wholly mechanical form, using a mass of intricate clockwork in pewter, brass, and steel, with punched cards modeled on those of the Jacquard loom.

After some years of work on his analytical engine, Babbage decided to design a second difference engine, which would incorporate the improvements suggested by his work on the analytical engine. He again asked for government support but was again refused. Babbage completed only small bits of a working engine and did not publish any detailed descriptions of them other than the informal ones in the autobiography he wrote as a disappointed old man, *Passages From the Life of a Philosopher* (1864). After his death one of his sons, Major Henry P. Babbage, compiled and published a book including papers both by Babbage himself and by his contemporaries, entitled *Babbage's Calculating Engines*.

While working on his engines, Babbage became deeply involved in the problems of establishing and maintaining in his machine shop and drafting room the new standards of precision that his designs demanded. Under his direction the machinists he employed developed tools and methods far ahead of contemporary practice; these developments alone might have justified the government's expenditures. Babbage also invented a scheme of mechanical symbols that could make clear the action of all the complicated moving parts of his machinery. The detailed drawings of his engines were models for their day.

The son of a banker in Devon, who later left him a considerable fortune, Charles Babbage was educated mostly at home, with mathematics his favorite subject. At Cambridge University his closest friends were John Herschel (later the astronomer royal) and George Peacock (later the dean of Ely); with them Babbage solemnly entered into a compact to "do their best to leave the world wiser than they found it." They began their mission by translating Sylvestre Lacroix's *An Elementary Treatise on the Differential and Integral Calculus* and founding the Analytical Society, whose purpose was to put "English mathematicians on an equal basis with their continental rivals." Babbage published a variety of mathematical papers after receiving his M.A. from Cambridge in 1817. His interest in mathematics led directly to a concern for accurate and readable mathematical tables. A chance conversation with Herschel, while the two were checking a table of calculations done for the Astronomical Society (which they had recently helped to found), led Babbage to his dream of a machine for calculating mathematical tables, a dream that was to become the obsession of his life.

Although he never abandoned the pursuit of his engines, his great curiosity and enthusiasm led him onto many other paths. The problems he encountered in the construction of his own machines aroused his interest in the general problems of manufacturing. After a tour of factories throughout England and the Continent, Babbage wrote his most popular book, *On the Economy of Machinery and Manufactures* (1832). The book included a detailed description and classification of the tools and machinery he had observed, together with a discussion of the "economical processes of manufacturing." A pioneer work in the field that, one hundred years later, we call operations research, the *Economy* is still good reading.

In addition to pure and applied mathematics, Babbage wrote papers on physics and geology, astronomy and biology. He even ventured into the fields of archeology and apologetics and wrote one of the first clear popular accounts of the theory of life insurance. He also enjoyed making suggestions for practical inventions of all kinds, ranging from the cowcatcher on a railway locomotive to a system of flashing signals for lighthouses.

An enthusiastic conference man, Babbage was an active member of learned societies all over the world. He was instrumental, with Herschel, in founding the Royal Astronomical Society in 1820, the British Association for the Advancement of Science (BAAS) in 1831, and the Statistical Society in 1834. For years Babbage led an assault on the decline of science in England, attacked the neglect of science in the universities, and urged government support of scientists. He pointed out that only men with private fortunes could pursue abstract science and that "scientific knowledge today hardly exists among the higher classes." The chief target of his book *Reflections on the Decline of Science in England* (1830) was the Royal Society, to which he had been elected while still at Cambridge. He attacked the autocratic misrule of the society by a social clique and pointed out that only a small proportion of the society's members ever contributed papers to its *Transactions*. His book received a good deal of support from other members, and within the next twenty years the Royal Society did succeed in reorganizing itself in response to their criticisms. In an appendix to the *Decline of Science*, Babbage reprinted without comment an account of "an annual Congress of German naturalists meeting in each successive year in some great town." This account probably inspired the first meeting of the BAAS in 1831, with Babbage taking a leading part in shaping its constitution.

Babbage was deeply committed to the belief that careful analysis, mathematical procedures, and statistical calculations—using high-speed computation—could be reliable guides in practical and productive life. This conviction, combined with the wide range of his organizational and scientific interests, gives him still a wonderful modernity.

PHILIP MORRISON AND EMILY MORRISON

[*For discussion of the subsequent development of Babbage's ideas, see* COMPUTATION *and* CYBERNETICS.]

WORKS BY BABBAGE

1830 *Reflections on the Decline of Science in England, and on Some of Its Causes.* London: Fellowes.

(1832) 1841 *On the Economy of Machinery and Manufactures.* 4th ed. enl. London: Knight.

1864 *Passages From the Life of a Philosopher.* London: Longmans.

Babbage's Calculating Engines: Being a Collection of Papers Relating to Them; Their History and Construction. Edited by Henry P. Babbage. London: Spon. 1889.

Charles Babbage and His Calculating Engines: Selected Writings by Charles Babbage and Others. Edited with an introduction by Philip and Emily Morrison. New York: Dover. 1961.

SUPPLEMENTARY BIBLIOGRAPHY

BOWDEN, BERTRAM V. (editor) (1953) 1957 *Faster Than Thought: A Symposium on Digital Computing Machines.* London: Pitman.

MULLETT, CHARLES F. 1948 Charles Babbage: A Scientific Gadfly. *Scientific Monthly* 67:361–371.

BACHOFEN, JOHANN JAKOB

Johann Jakob Bachofen (1815–1887) was a Swiss jurist, student of Greco–Roman antiquity, and anthropologist.

Bachofen came from a prominent Basel family that, from the early eighteenth century, had amassed great wealth in the silk industry. This wealth rendered Bachofen financially independent. After graduating from the Gymnasium, in 1834, he studied at the universities of Basel, Berlin, and Göttingen; his interests lay in the classics and in jurisprudence. While Bachofen was at Berlin, Friedrich von Savigny focused his interest on Roman law, and the doctoral dissertation he submitted to the University of Basel was in this field (1840). He concluded his studies with a two years' stay in Paris and in England. When he was only 27, he was appointed full professor of the history of Roman law at Basel, from which position he resigned two years later, in 1844, to have more time for his own research. From 1842 to 1866 he also held an appointment as a judge.

Bachofen wrote two monographs on legal history, which were published in 1843, and these were followed by his major works on Roman civil law, (1847 and 1848). In spite of the recognition these works received from his professional colleagues, Bachofen abandoned the field of jurisprudence. His decision to do so was not a sudden one. While examining some ancient tombs in Italy during a trip in 1842–1843, he was struck by a new approach to the understanding of the innermost nature of ancient culture: interpretation of the symbolism of tombs. From then on he was fascinated by tombs, which for him conveyed a "truly universal doctrine." His studies of mythology and symbolism led him far beyond a concern with the ancient world to important insights into the ways of primitive man, primitive law, and primitive religion.

This new vision found no written expression until his books on law had been completed. A sec-

ond trip to Italy in 1848–1849 and another to Italy and Greece in 1851–1852 deepened Bachofen's insights, which he presented in a series of books published between 1850 and 1870. In 1851 there appeared the monograph *Die Geschichte der Römer* ("History of the Romans"), which Bachofen wrote with F. D. Gerlach. *Versuch über Gräbersymbolik der Alten* ("Essay on the Tomb Symbolism of the Ancients"; see 1841–1890, vol. 4) followed in 1859, *Das Mutterrecht* ("Mother-right"; see 1841–1890, vols. 2–3) in 1861, *Die Unsterblichkeitslehre der orphischen Theologie* ("The Doctrine of Immortality in Orphic Theology"; see 1841–1890, vol. 7) in 1867, *Die Sage von Tanaquil* ("The Legend of Tanaquil"; see 1841–1890, vol. 6) in 1870, and there were several shorter monographs.

Bachofen's fame is based on his *Mutterrecht*, one of the books on which modern social anthropology is based. It is the first scientific history of the family as a social institution. Bachofen was the first to challenge seriously the long-established conviction that the monogamous patriarchal family was a datum of nature; instead, he asserted that mother-right had preceded father-right in the evolution of human institutions.

While the *Mutterrecht* is ostensibly universal in scope, Bachofen's evidence is derived largely from his reading of the Greek and Roman classics; he had not yet incorporated the epoch-making scientific discoveries of the nineteenth century into his work. Indeed, it was not known that Bachofen actually did extensive ethnological research until recently, when his unpublished manuscripts were examined in connection with the publication of his *Gesammelte Werke*, a large project undertaken in the 1940s. It appears that Bachofen's work on the *Mutterrecht* was only the beginning of his ethnological explorations. In 1869 he decided to revise the *Mutterrecht* to encompass the entire earth, and in the next fifteen years proceeded to familiarize himself with nearly all known cultures. He also studied the works of such theorists as McLennan, Tylor, Lubbock, Bastian, and Lewis H. Morgan and exchanged views with them. He had sufficient flexibility to incorporate McLennan's and Morgan's research findings on the institution of kinship into his own system. Indeed, after 1872, Morgan's influence on Bachofen increased constantly; contrary to common opinion, however, Morgan neither adopted nor developed Bachofen's ideas and only referred to them in his *Ancient Society* (1877) and in later works.

In 1873 Bachofen turned his attention to the avunculate in particular. His monographs written between 1873 and 1877 on the avunculate in the classical, Germanic, and Indian worlds, as well as a work on *Schwestersohnsrecht nach den Über-lieferungen Indiens* ("The Avunculate According to Indian Records"), written between 1878 and 1880, have been partly reconstructed from unpublished manuscripts; a small portion of this material was published in the *Antiquarische Briefe* . . . (see 1841–1890, vol. 8).

Bachofen's relationship with A. Giraud-Teulon of Geneva is very important for the understanding of this later period of his work. Their friendship developed into a sort of scientific symbiosis, so that in Giraud-Teulon's *Les origines de la famille* (1874) one may find a systematic outline of Bachofen's sociological conceptions. Again, when Bachofen in 1881 abandoned his work on a comprehensive account of a modified version of his system (because the first volume of *Antiquarische Briefe* had been received with uncomprehending silence), Giraud-Teulon wrote *Les origines du mariage et de la famille* (1884) and conveyed the essentials of Bachofen's sociological ideas. Only the encouragement of J. Kohler, one of the founders of the discipline of comparative law, induced Bachofen to publish the second volume of the *Antiquarische Briefe*.

Bachofen's contemporaries could judge him only on the basis of his published work. While philologists rejected his work because from their point of view it lacked both theoretical rigor and accuracy, ethnologists immediately appreciated the importance of his discovery of matriarchy. To the end of the nineteenth century most sociologists accepted the pioneer formulations of the *Mutterrecht*, a countermovement setting in only with E. A. Westermarck's sweeping critique. In other than social scientific circles, Bachofen and L. H. Morgan became known, oddly enough, as two of the principal witnesses in support of the communist theory of society—largely because communist theorists so interpreted them. A comprehensive assessment of his contributions is only now becoming possible, with the preparation of a critical edition of his *Gesammelte Werke* by Karl Meuli.

JOHANNES DÖRMANN

[*For the historical context of Bachofen's work, see the biographies of* BASTIAN; LUBBOCK; MCLENNAN; MORGAN, L. H.; TYLOR. *For discussion of the subsequent development of his ideas, see* KINSHIP.]

WORKS BY BACHOFEN

1840   *De romanorum judiciis civilibus, de legis actionibus, de formulis et de condictione dissertatio historico-dogmatica.* Göttingen (Germany): Dieterich.

(1841–1890) 1943—   *Gesammelte Werke.* Edited by Karl Meuli. Vols. 1—. Basel (Switzerland): Schwabe. →

Volume 1: *Antrittsrede; Politische Betrachtungen über das Staatsleben des römischen Volkes; Beiträge zur Geschichte der Römer; Politische Aufsätze zur Zeitgeschichte,* (1841–1863) 1943. Volumes 2–3: *Das Mutterrecht,* (1861) 1948. Volume 4: *Versuch über die Gräbersymbolik der Alten,* (1859) 1954. Volume 6: *Die Sage von Tanaquil,* (1870) 1951. Volume 7: *Die Unsterblichkeitslehre der orphischen Theologie,* (1867) 1958; *Römische Grablampen,* (1890) 1958. Volume 8: *Antiquarische Briefe,* (1880–1886) 1966. The published volumes of a projected ten-volume publication. The volumes contain new and important evaluations of Bachofen's writings by various authors.

1843a   *Die Lex Voconia und die mit ihr zusammenhängenden Rechtsinstitute: Eine rechtshistorische Abhandlung.* Basel (Switzerland): Schweighauser.

1843b   *Das Nexum, die Nexi und die Lex Petillia.* Basel (Switzerland): Neukirch.

1843c   Zur Lehre von der civilen Berechnung der Zeit. *Zeitschrift für Civilrecht und Prozess* 18:38–80.

1847   *Das römische Pfandrecht.* Volume 1. Basel (Switzerland): Schweighauser.

1848   *Ausgewählte Lehren des römischen Civilrechts; Das vellejanische Senatusconsult; Die Veräusserungsverbote und Beschränkungen; Die testamentarische Adoption; Das Manitipationstestament; Die Erbschaftssteuer.* Bonn: Marcus.

1851   GERLACH, FRANZ D.; and BACHOFEN, JOHANN J. *Die Geschichte der Römer.* Basel (Switzerland): Bahnmaier.

SUPPLEMENTARY BIBLIOGRAPHY

BAEUMLER, ALFRED 1965 *Das mythische Weltalter: Bachofens romantische Deutung des Altertums.* Munich (Germany): Beck.

BERNOULLI, C. A. 1924 *Johann Jakob Bachofen und das Natursymbol: Ein Würdigungsversuch.* Basel (Switzerland): Schwabe.

DÖRMANN, JOHANNES 1965 War Johann Jakob Bachofen Evolutionist? *Anthropos* 60:1–48.

GIRAUD-TEULON, ALEXIS 1874 *Les origines de la famille: Questions sur les antécédents des sociétés patriarcales.* Geneva: Cherbuliéz.

GIRAUD-TEULON, ALEXIS 1884 *Les origines du mariage et de la famille.* Geneva: Cherbuliéz.

KOHLER, JOSEPH 1889 Johann Jakob Bachofen. *Zeitschrift für vergleichende Rechtswissenschaft* 8:148–155.

SCHMIDT, GEORG 1929 *Johann Jakob Bachofens Geschichtsphilosophie.* Munich (Germany): Beck.

BACON, FRANCIS

Francis Bacon, Viscount St. Albans, English statesman and philosopher, was born in 1561. His father, a leading official in Queen Elizabeth's government, had Bacon educated at Cambridge and Gray's Inn. At the university he soon began to develop the impatience with traditional philosophy that was to run through his writings; at the Inn of Court he learned what he always called "my profession." The law was to be the career that eventually took him to high political office, and it was also one of the objects of his schemes for reform.

Reform was the constant preoccupation of Bacon's life. Apart from his love of luxury and ostentation, the chief reason he sought political power was his conviction that his plans could be implemented only with governmental support. For over forty years he prepared a succession of memoranda and dedications of books for his monarchs, asking them to overhaul almost every element of English society, from agriculture to education. His most cherished and comprehensive project, the "Great Instauration" of science, designed to relieve man's estate, required a marshaling of effort that, so he believed, only the crown was capable of organizing. Despite many excellent connections (his uncle, Lord Burghley, was Elizabeth's chief minister), over two decades of futile office seeking passed before Bacon was appointed solicitor general to James I in 1607, then attorney general in 1613, lord keeper in 1617, and finally lord chancellor in 1618. But when he was impeached and disgraced in 1621, largely as a result of the efforts of his archrival, Sir Edward Coke, in the House of Commons, his short political career proved to have been in vain, and his attempts to return to favor during the remaining five years of his life were to no avail. Even in a position of considerable influence, as lord chancellor, Bacon was unable to persuade the king, in whose power and wisdom he trusted completely, to support the reforms he proposed. James reputedly found the *Novum organum* to be "like the peace of God, that passeth all understanding."

Various historians of Stuart England, including S. R. Gardiner (1885, pp. 812–813), have suggested that the execution of Bacon's program might have averted the English Civil War; but in the long run the lord chancellor's fame has rested on his vision for the future of mankind, not on his recommendations for immediate political action, which his contemporaries ignored. Less than twenty years after his death he became the inspiration for an entire generation of scientists and social reformers in England, and thereafter his reputation, despite attacks, was secure. It has been pointed out that Bacon himself was a poor scientist; that he missed completely the significance of the conceptual and mathematical breakthroughs achieved by contemporaries such as Gilbert, Galileo, and Harvey; and that his much vaunted inductive method was neither original nor particularly helpful to scientific advance. It has also been shown that he owed a great debt, usually unacknowledged, to some of the very traditions and thinkers he attacked. Men such as Palissy, Telesio, Cardano, and Campanella, who advocated observation and experience and questioned accepted attitudes; the hopeful

view of the future held by Leroy and others; Ramus' criticism of Aristotelian logic and method; and the wish to control nature expressed by alchemists and practitioners of magic—all had a profound influence on Bacon's ideas. And yet he was able to combine these various elements of late sixteenth-century thought into a distinct and personal message. As he himself rightly saw, he was not really a "combatant," a participator in the philosophical inquiries of his day. Rather he was a "trumpeter," calling men to action, urging them to turn "with united forces against the Nature of Things, to storm and occupy her castles and strongholds, and extend the bounds of human empire, as far as God Almighty . . . may permit" (*De augmentis scientiarum* [1623] in *The Works of Francis Bacon*, vol. 9, p. 14).

Man's dominion over nature; the resultant amelioration of his lot on earth; and the improvement of the educational, administrative, legal, and religious institutions into which his society is organized—these were the goals toward which Bacon's writings and propaganda were directed. It is difficult to consider him a philosopher in the literal sense, because all his concerns were so intensely practical. Wisdom on its own was of little interest. Only if it had some obvious material value was it worth achieving. Bacon completely separated divine from secular learning, and concerning the latter category he wrote, "Human knowledge and human power meet in one." "Truth . . . and utility are here the very same things." Man's highest ambition in temporal matters should be "to establish and extend the power and dominion of the human race itself over the universe." But he cautioned, "the empire of man over things depends wholly on the arts and sciences. For we cannot command nature except by obeying her" (*Novum organum* [1620] in *The Works*, vol. 8, pp. 67, 157, 162–163).

It was crucial, therefore, to supply mankind with a method of inquiry into nature that would ensure practical and productive results. Method thus came to be Bacon's chief interest, receiving more attention in his writings than any other subject. At an early age he grew disillusioned with the investigations of traditional philosophy, and he repeatedly attacked Greek, scholastic, and Renaissance thinkers for not producing "any magnitude of works." Impelled by profound humanitarian concerns and a deeply Christian sense of charity, he denounced his predecessors and their unquestioning adherents for failing to improve life on earth. While faith helped man to recover the innocence he had lost at the Fall, science should help him to recover the dominion over nature he had lost at the same time.

It was no less than a sin for a philosopher to ignore this ultimate purpose of his work, and so Bacon condemned all earlier methods of inquiry for this one overwhelming failure. But if he were to pose as the prophet of an advancement of learning, he had to furnish mankind with an approach to knowledge whose efficacy and fruitfulness were guaranteed.

It has often been assumed by his detractors (e.g., Cohen 1926) that Bacon's "method" consisted simply of a recommendation to return to nature: careful and exhaustive observation, followed by a painstaking process of induction, which led very slowly to absolutely certain generalizations. In essence, this was indeed the antidote he proposed for the vague hypotheses and abstractions of previous philosophers; but it was only one-half of his program. The other half, the organization of the effort of inquiry, was equally important and just as much a part of his over-all "method." For Bacon wanted to control the social and psychological influences that stimulated scientific advance as carefully as he wanted to control the procedures used by individual scientists. Thus, when he explained why learning had progressed so little in past ages, he concentrated on the cultural, political, and other defects of the unproductive societies. The Greeks, for example, had been too close to their myths and had lacked the awareness of history and a sense of the difference of other nations necessary for an interest in the study of nature. Conversely, a great age could be created by social forces, such as proper governmental encouragement, exemplified by the policies of the Roman emperors from Nerva to Commodus. Bacon's famous doctrine of the four idols that hinder intellectual advance—"Idols of the Tribe," errors caused by human nature; "Idols of the Cave," errors caused by personal idiosyncrasies; "Idols of the Market Place," errors caused by misleading words; and "Idols of the Theatre," errors caused by the wish to create philosophical systems (*Novum organum* [1620] in *The Works*, vol. 8, aphorisms XXXVIII–LXIX)—outlined the principal psychological, cultural, and linguistic pressures that interfere with man's reason. Knowledge was held back not only by the inherent shortcomings of the human mind but also by the effects of one's physical needs, background, and environment. When Bacon surveyed the reasons for stagnation of learning in his day (*Advancement of Learning* [1605] in *The Works*, vol. 8, pp. 383–520; vol. 9, pp. 13–357), he stressed the inadequacies of institutions, patronage, education, and society as a whole, rather than the mistakes of individual thinkers. Certainly scien-

tists would have to adopt a better approach to nature, but this would have to be accompanied by a complete reorganization of the scholarly community. He wanted to see rewards for inventors, drastic revisions of university curricula, more frequent exchanges between scholars, and an expansion of the physical resources available to researchers, such as libraries. His description of Salomon's House, a college of scientists in his ideal state (*New Atlantis* [1627] in *The Works*, vol. 5, pp. 347–413), suggested that only with careful planning could constant progress be assured.

In Salomon's House laboratories were established for every possible type of experiment or investigation. Constant contact with foreign advances was maintained by a special group of traveling scholars, and each stage of scientific research, arranged according to Bacon's inductive process, was carefully organized and assigned to those whose talents were suitable for each level of inquiry. Unhampered and undistracted, the scientists would undertake a steady stream of experiments, seek practical applications for their discoveries, and reach higher and higher generalizations. As Bacon himself admitted, he was hoping "to level men's wits." Having dwelt at length on the weakness and proclivity to error of the human mind, he wished to reduce reliance on "individual excellence." But it is misleading to conclude that Bacon saw no place for genius or considered one researcher as good as another. His wish was to place genius within a precise structure so that it could have maximum effect. The brilliant mind, instead of working in lone and purposeless splendor, must be harnessed to a well-coordinated effort. Each researcher would work according to his abilities in the framework of a program that remorselessly increased man's dominion over nature. Bacon allowed his optimism to get the better of his remarkable foresight only when he suggested that the final encyclopedia containing all natural science would be merely a few times larger than Pliny's *Natural History*.

Nearly all of Bacon's writings discussed reforms of one kind or another. He wanted to simplify and codify England's legal system in order to eliminate litigiousness, delays, and uncertainties in the law. Because of the obviously practical value of technology and the mechanical arts, he hoped to raise their status. He suggested the relief of poor economic conditions and a re-evaluation of relations between king and Parliament in order to prevent political troubles. He also had a solution—peaceful colonization—for the perennial problem of Ireland. It has been shown (Crane 1923) that even in his later literary works, the last two editions of his *Essays* (first published in 1597, enlarged in 1612 and again in 1625) he kept his long-term aims in mind. He wrote on subjects such as anger and sedition because of the insufficiency of studies of human nature and "civil knowledge." One of his greatest hopes was that eventually research would enable man to control his passions, and the *Essays* gave him the opportunity to make preliminary investigations that would eventually form part of a complete body of knowledge about the mind. In political science and ethics he admired, with reservations, the realism of Machiavelli; but studies of history, which could teach man so much, he found woefully inadequate, particularly in the case of intellectual history. He envisioned vast projects to remedy these deficiencies, and his *History of the Reign of King Henry VII* ([1622] in *The Works*, vol. 11) was intended as part of a complete history of England. Medicine, too, occupied his interest; he believed that like all sciences, it had to be systematized if it was to progress toward its ultimate goal, the prolongation of life.

Bacon's writings ranged over so many topics—from ethics to teratology—because he believed in an essential unity of all the sciences. Methods of inquiry should be the same in all subjects, starting with observations of fact and moving slowly to careful generalizations. The highest study of all, which he called the prime philosophy, would contain generalizations about the entirety of knowledge, and he wanted researchers in different disciplines to be in contact so that they could learn from one another. When in 1592 he wrote, "I have taken all of knowledge to be my province," he was stressing the basic unity of science, which enabled him to study many widely separated fields. But the very breadth of his vision, combined with an active public life, forced him to leave most of his work unfinished. Only fragments of his sweeping program for the Great Instauration ever came to be written. Its most complete section, the *Novum organum*, where Bacon outlined the shortcomings of past science and expounded his inductive method, consisted of aphorisms that he himself said served to "invite men to enquire farther" (*Advancement of Learning* [1605] in *The Works*, vol. 8).

Nonetheless, the indifference he faced in his lifetime soon gave way to widespread admiration. William Harvey's gibe that he wrote "philosophy like a Lord Chancellor" may have pinpointed Bacon's mediocrity as a scientist—he knew too little to appreciate the vital importance of hypotheses and mathematics—but it also hinted at Bacon's unique position in the thought of his century. He

has been called a statesman and strategist of science, and he was indeed primarily an organizer and a prophet, not a notable discoverer. Although much respect was later accorded to his general stress on experiment and induction, the reverence he inspired was due mainly to his vision of science as an organized, collaborative, and fruitful inquiry. Leibniz acknowledged his importance, even though he felt that Bacon's ignorance of mathematics put him outside the course of actual scientific development. Descartes, too, despite a radically different view of scientific thought, paid homage to the lord chancellor. And during the English Civil War, the man who had been ignored by his contemporaries suddenly became a hero not only to revolutionaries who wanted to reform society but also to the scientists, such as Boyle, who were to found the Royal Society of London in 1662 in a deliberate attempt to put his program into practice. Other scientific academies throughout Europe followed suit, and in the realm of philosophy Hobbes, Locke, the eighteenth-century encyclopedists, and Bentham joined the many who reflected his influence. In his advocacy of a systematic organization of learning, a skeptical attitude toward knowledge, a humanitarian goal for science, and a study of society and the mind as well as nature, Bacon heralded the beginning of a new era in man's conception of himself and his universe.

THEODORE K. RABB

[*For discussion of the subsequent development of Bacon's ideas, see the articles under* SCIENCE *and the biographies of* BENTHAM; DESCARTES; HOBBES; LOCKE.]

WORKS BY BACON

The Works of Francis Bacon. Collected and edited by James Spedding, Robert Leslie Ellis, and Douglas Denon Heath. 15 vols. New York: Hurd & Houghton, 1863–1872. → Volumes 1–7: *Philosophical Works.* Volumes 8–10: *Translation of the* Philosophical Works. Volumes 11–15: *Literary and Professional Works.* The *Essays* are contained in Volume 12.

WORKS ABOUT BACON

ANDERSON, FULTON H. 1948 *The Philosophy of Francis Bacon.* Univ. of Chicago Press. → A major work that has influenced all subsequent studies.

ANDERSON, FULTON H. 1962 *Francis Bacon: His Career and His Thought.* Los Angeles: Univ. of California Press. → The best concise biography.

BERTOLINO, ALBERTO 1929 *Bacone e l'economia.* Siena (Italy): Circolo Giuridico della R. Università.

BOCK, HELLMUT 1937 *Staat und Gesellschaft bei Francis Bacon: Ein Beitrag zur politischen Ideologie der Tudorzeit.* Berlin: Junker & Dünnhaupt.

BROAD, C. D. 1926 *The Philosophy of Francis Bacon: An Address Delivered at Cambridge.* Cambridge Univ. Press. → An excellent brief exposition of Bacon's classification of knowledge.

COHEN, MORRIS R. 1926 The Myth About Bacon and the Inductive Method. *Scientific Monthly* 23:504–508.

CRANE, RONALD S. 1923 The Relation of Bacon's *Essays* to His Program for the Advancement of Learning. Pages 87–105 in *Schelling Anniversary Papers*. New York: Century.

FARRINGTON, BENJAMIN 1949 *Francis Bacon: Philosopher of Industrial Science*. New York: Schuman. → A pioneering study of the social aims of Bacon's thought. A paperback edition was published in 1961 by Collier.

FARRINGTON, BENJAMIN 1964 *The Philosophy of Francis Bacon: An Essay on Its Development From 1603 to 1609*. Liverpool (England) Univ. Press.

GARDINER, SAMUEL RAWSON 1885 Francis Bacon. Volume 1, pages 800–821 in *Dictionary of National Biography*. London: Smith & Elder.

HILL, CHRISTOPHER 1965 *Intellectual Origins of the English Revolution*. Oxford: Clarendon. → See Chapter 3, on Bacon's milieu.

JONES, RICHARD F. (1936) 1961 *Ancients and Moderns: A Study of the Rise of the Scientific Movement in Seventeenth-century England*. 2d ed. St. Louis, Mo.: Washington Univ. Press.

KOCHER, PAUL H. 1957 Francis Bacon on the Science of Jurisprudence. *Journal of the History of Ideas* 18:3–26.

MACAULAY, THOMAS B. (1837) 1898 Lord Bacon. Volume 8, pages 496–647 in Thomas Macaulay, *Works of Lord Macaulay*. London: Longmans.

McRAE, ROBERT 1957 The Unity of the Sciences: Bacon, Descartes, and Leibniz. *Journal of the History of Ideas* 18:27–48.

MERTON, ROBERT K. 1961 Singletons and Multiples in Scientific Discovery: A Chapter in the Sociology of Science. American Philosophical Society, *Proceedings* 105:470–486. → A paper delivered at a celebration of the 400th anniversary of Bacon's birth; sees Bacon as making contributions to the sociology of science.

ORSINI, NAPOLEONE 1936 *Bacone e Machiavelli*. Genoa (Italy): Orfini.

PRIOR, MOODY E. 1954 Bacon's Man of Science. *Journal of the History of Ideas* 15:348–370.

ROSSI, PAOLO 1957 *Francesco Bacone: Dalla magia alla scienza*. Bari (Italy): Laterza. → Reveals Bacon's debt to magic and other contemporary traditions. Together with Anderson and Farrington, Rossi has brought about a complete revaluation of Bacon's significance.

WHITAKER, VICTOR K. 1962 *Francis Bacon's Intellectual Milieu*. Los Angeles: Univ. of California, William Andrew Clark Memorial Library.

BAGEHOT, WALTER

I

ECONOMIC CONTRIBUTIONS

Walter Bagehot (1826–1877) was one of the last and best of nineteenth-century England's special breed of versatile men of letters. His literary output was phenomenal, not only for volume and quality, but also for the breadth of its subject matter. He wrote regularly on financial and economic matters with a penetrating knowledge of the inner workings of business affairs, and he was similarly incisive as a student of government and as a literary critic and author of biographical sketches and character studies. His literary style was clean and deft and has lost little of its power and attractiveness over the past hundred years.

Bagehot's father, Thomas Watson Bagehot, and his mother, Edith Stuckey Bagehot, both came from families of prominent Somerset merchants, and Stuckey's Bank, in which Thomas Bagehot was a senior officer, was one of the leading banks of the west country. Bagehot was educated at the Langport Grammar School and Bristol College. In 1842 he entered University College, London, where he received his B.A. with first-class honors in 1846 and his M.A. in 1848, winning the university's Gold Medal for Moral and Intellectual Philosophy. He subsequently read for the bar and was admitted, but he did not practice, deciding instead to enter the family banking business.

In 1857 he became acquainted with James Wilson, founder and editor of the remarkable London weekly newspaper *The Economist,* and this led to marriage and a career. He married Eliza, the eldest of Wilson's six daughters, the following year and was designated director of *The Economist* in 1859, when Wilson left for India on a mission to reform that country's finances. Upon Wilson's death, in 1861, Bagehot was offered his post on the Indian viceroy's council but declined it, primarily for family reasons (his mother, to whom he was devoted, suffered from intermittent fits of insanity), and instead became editor of *The Economist.* This was his chief occupation until his death, in 1877, although he continued to be active in the management of Stuckey's Bank as well.

As a schoolboy he seems to have been a rather intense grind. He held aloof from his fellows and was almost universally disliked by them. Yet his adult contemporaries have uniformly represented him as a friendly, easy, and charming man. He was, perhaps, extraordinarily precocious as a youth and reached the full maturity of his powers while he was still quite young. His first publications in economics were remarkable performances for a man of 22, and his later works, although excellent, are not really superior to his first.

Bagehot had a strong desire to enter politics (as a Liberal), but he was unsuccessful in all four of his attempts to secure nomination or election. He was unable to make a strong appeal as a public speaker, and his unwillingness to corrupt voters told against him in close elections. It is indicative of his character that he did not become embittered by these failures but rather developed a deeper and even more objective understanding of the political process. He may indeed have had more influence on government policy as an independent commentator than he would have had as a member of Parliament or even a minister. He was able to occupy the delicate position of both critic and friend of ministers. He was held in high esteem, often made privy to governmental confidences, and his advice was sought. Gladstone is supposed to have referred to him as "a kind of spare Chancellor of Exchequer." He is credited with the invention of the treasury bill as a governmental borrowing instrument in 1876, in response to a request for advice by the Disraeli government. Undoubtedly his intimate relations with those in high positions, both in government and in finance, were of great importance in enabling him to develop *The Economist* into the unique institution of economic information and comment it became during his editorship.

Central banking theory.   Although a strong advocate of free trade, Bagehot was not a doctrinaire believer in laissez-faire. In his first published article (1848) he laid down the boundaries of the laissez-faire argument with a perception that stands up well even today, and in particular he criticized his future father-in-law, James Wilson, for applying the principle of laissez-faire to money. Bagehot believed that currency should be created by a government monopoly and that the monetary system should be deliberately managed. These ideas were the foundation of his most important contribution to economics, his theory of central banking, which he advanced first in articles in *The Economist* and later in a book that became a classic, *Lombard Street* (1873).

Lombard Street developed two major arguments about central banking. First, it is an institutional fact that British banks, by holding part of their cash reserves in larger and more central banks, produced a pyramid of cash reserves, and that the Bank of England had consequently come to be the holder of the central reserves of the whole system. Second, it is a psychological fact that a banking panic can be broken only by providing people with as much liquidity as they feel they require. From these facts Bagehot drew the conclusion, at that time unorthodox, that the Bank of England was not merely *primus inter pares* in the banking system, but a special bank with special responsibilities. Bagehot pointed out that in times of crisis the Bank had in fact not acted as if it were merely an ordinary private bank. It had attempted to support other banks that were in difficulty, but it had

acted hesitantly and, given the psychology of the liquidity crisis, had thus more often done harm than good. Bagehot concluded that the Bank of England should explicitly acknowledge its central position in the financial system as custodian of the final reserve and lender of last resort; that the Bank of England should increase its reserve to an amount that would inspire full confidence; that the bank rate should be used to regulate external currency drains; and most important of all, that the Bank of England should undertake to lend freely at all times so as to erase all doubt about the availability of bank accommodation. Bagehot's propositions were accepted immediately by Jevons, Cairnes, and many other economists, but it took another twenty years before the City and the Bank of England were convinced of their merit.

Views on political economy.   Despite his great success as an economic journalist and adviser, Walter Bagehot was eager, in later life, to make a contribution to economic science that would be of permanent importance. Unaware of how significant and enduring his journalistic efforts would in fact prove to be, he was strongly motivated to carve his name in the harder stone of economic theory. He projected a large treatise covering many facets of economic theory, including an examination of its methodology and studies of the great economists of the past. His death at the age of 51 left this ambition unfulfilled, but a volume containing such papers as those he had drafted for this treatise was published posthumously under the title *Economic Studies* in 1880.

Although he thought highly of contemporary "English political economy," Bagehot regarded it as suffering from three main limitations. It was not, as was often claimed, universally applicable to all societies; second, its proponents were too content with abstract presentations and did not provide sufficient concrete illustrations; third, there was too little effort at empirical verification of economic propositions.

Bagehot regarded the first of these deficiencies as the most important and its theme is to be found reiterated often in his writings. "English political economy" was, according to Bagehot, an analysis of a monetary economy that was organized through the mechanism of competitive markets and powered by the motivations of private gain. Such an analysis was, in Bagehot's view, applicable only to a highly developed money-exchange economy, like that of England. In other societies, where the basic postulates of the analysis, i.e., the easy mobility of labor and capital, were not to be found, the analysis was inadequate. The new anthropological findings of his time, added to his own strong view of the importance of cultural and psychological factors in economic and political behavior, reinforced his belief that such fundamental differences existed between societies that a universally applicable science of economics was impossible. This view emerges most concretely in his study of labor and capital mobility but more profoundly in his monetary writings: a monetary-exchange economy was for Bagehot not merely an extension or elaboration of a barter-exchange economy but a reflection of basic differences of culture and social psychology.

General economic ideas. Bagehot's economic thought was founded largely on three general ideas: (1) the existence of a fundamental difference between a monetary economy and a non-monetary one; (2) the interconnectedness of all economic processes; and (3) the importance of psychological and sociological elements in the analysis of economic behavior. Virtually all his economic writings make use of one or more of these ideas, and his lasting contributions are traceable to his skill in using such ideas as instruments for penetrating complex economic phenomena.

H. S. GORDON

[*For discussion of the subsequent development of Bagehot's economic ideas, see* BANKING, CENTRAL.]

BIBLIOGRAPHY

The bibliography for this article is combined with the bibliography of the article that follows.

II
POLITICAL CONTRIBUTIONS

Walter Bagehot was not only an economic journalist and theorist but a general social scientist whose ideas cut across the disciplines of politics, psychology, and sociology. He thus belongs to the line of European thinkers that extends from Edmund Burke in the eighteenth century and Alexis de Tocqueville and John Stuart Mill in the nineteenth to Max Weber and Graham Wallas in the early twentieth.

Bagehot's strength, manifested very early in his "Letters on the French *coup d'état* of 1851" (1852), lay in his grasp of the interconnectedness between political and economic institutions and the national character. His reports from Paris (for the *Inquirer*, a Unitarian journal) undercut the assumption, common to the British of his day, that there are principles of representative parliamentary government that are valid everywhere and at all times, just as his later economic studies challenged the

assumption of universal economic principles. In his political ideas, as in his economic thought, he was an institutionalist, concerned both with penetrating beyond the outward forms and traditional justifications of social behavior and with discovering what factors shape going institutions within a social system. He had been deeply influenced by the ethnologist J. C. Pritchard and by Sir Henry Maine's *Ancient Law* and had developed a more detached anthropological viewpoint than most of his contemporaries. His detachment often made his writings appear iconoclastic and even flippant to his more staid readers.

His analysis of Louis Napoleon's *coup d'état* was based on his conception of a kind of congruence between the French national character and French political institutions. Instead of attacking Louis Napoleon for his dictatorial methods and for his liquidation of what might have become a viable democratic regime—as Tocqueville did in discussing the same coup (in his *Souvenirs* and in his notable letter to the editor of *The Times*, December 11, 1851)—Bagehot quoted a description of the French as *des machines nerveuses*. He asked rhetorically: "Can their excitable, volatile, superficial, over-logical, uncompromising character be managed and manipulated as to fit them for entering on a practically uncontrolled system of Parliamentary Government?" ([1852] 1965, p. 433). While his English readers reacted to the Catholicism of the French only with mistrust, Bagehot sought instead to understand the relationship between French religion and French politics. Again, rather than condemning Louis Napoleon's repression of the French newspapers, Bagehot interpreted this as the necessary action of a strong leader trying to tame the volatile and absolutist elements in the French character. His delight in paradox led him to say (in the third letter) that "the most essential mental quality for a free people, whose liberty is to be progressive, permanent and on a large scale . . . is much *stupidity*" ([1852] 1965, p. 403). This was his way of referring to the pragmatic bent of the British national character and its refusal to accept absolute categories or values, as against the ideological bent of the French, along with their "excessive sensibility to present impressions" which contrasts with British obstinacy. Thus, what Bagehot was reaching for, expressed in more recent terminology, was a political sociology and psychology based on the convergence of culture and personality structure, of the functional and institutional with the behavioral. He was more successful, however, in dealing with patterns of national psychology than with patterns of culture.

His favorite medium for analysis of national psychology was the journalistic essay on historical, political, and literary figures. A few examples are Gibbon, Shelley, Arthur Hugh Clough (who influenced him greatly at University College, London), Bolingbroke, Peel, and Disraeli. These were published in various magazines, including the *Prospective Review*, the *National Review*, which he founded and edited together with his close friend Richard H. Hutton, and finally and increasingly in *The Economist*, to which as editor he gave that stamp of a far-ranging and penetrating journal which it still retains.

The underlying theme of his essays on political figures is that great leadership comes from a leader's ability to establish a responsive relationship with an electorate. An aristocrat at heart, Bagehot himself recoiled from the truckling courtship of the mass. This attitude may help account for his failure to get himself elected to the House of Commons: he made a number of attempts, failed several times to be adopted as a candidate, and when he did stand was twice defeated. He lacked both oratorical ability and the common touch, and his wit and flair for epigram were more disabling than helpful.

Yet Bagehot did have a feeling for the nuances of the changes in social stratification that formed the shifting base of the suffrage demands. In a widely read pamphlet he proposed a limited reform of the suffrage, extending the franchise on a property basis to towns with a population over 75,000, thus reaching the new working classes. He expressed in his writings the deep fears held by the propertied, educated middle class of being overwhelmed by new waves of working-class voters. To these fears, which he rationalized by the contention that property is at least a rough measure of political intelligence, he added the social Darwinist view that the evolutionary process should not be distorted by excessive concern for the unfit. In governing England, he wrote, "the true principle is, that every person has a right to *so much political power as he can exercise without impeding any other person who would fitly exercise such power*" ([1859] 1965, p. 314). Resigned to the Second Reform Act of 1867, which he had opposed, he turned his attention to adjusting the new electorate to its responsibilities—first, by a lifting of its living standards (which he called comfort) and second, by education. Instead of "Register! Register! Register!" he suggested, "The cry should now be, 'Educate! Educate! Educate!'"

The passage of the Second Reform Act coincided with the publication of Bagehot's first, and what

has proved to be his most influential, book, *The English Constitution* (1865–1867). In it Bagehot pierced the rhetoric that commonly obscured the authentic workings of the English constitution and found inside the parliamentary monarchy a functioning republic, if not a democracy. The book explained the realities of British government not only to the new English voting classes but to the whole world. More recently, it has become relevant to the problems facing the small elites of the newly formed African and Asian nations; they may also find significant what Bagehot wrote some ten years later, in an essay on Lord Althorp: "The characteristic danger of great nations . . . is that they may at last fail from not comprehending the great institutions they have created" ([1876*b*] 1965, p. 150).

Instead of accepting the traditional analysis that power is divided between king and Commons and Lords, he drew a new dividing line between the "dignified" element of the government (the parliamentary monarchy and its trappings) and the "effective" element (the functioning cabinet). His discussion of the dignified element is both anthropological and psychological; he described the enthrallment of the people by the fanfare and plumage of the monarchy much as an ethnologist might describe the enthrallment of savages by the magical investment of a shaman. Underlying this deference to the dignified element he saw the social structure and aspirations of Victorian England: the dominant bourgeoisie hankered for entrance into the aristocracy, and both in rural England and among the emerging working class the monarch represented a needed continuous tradition. What Bagehot discovered about the English monarchy was what Gibbon had discovered about religion in imperial Rome: both were politically useful. Bagehot saw England as the classic case of the "deferential nation," where parliamentary institutions worked because a response to what we may call political theater (not only coronations but also elections and orations) had been built, as it were, into the popular mind.

The "effective" element of the English constitution was lodged in the cabinet, which Bagehot described as "a board of control chosen by the legislature, out of persons whom it trusts and knows, to rule the nation . . . , a combining committee—a *hyphen* which joins, a *buckle* which fastens, the legislative part of the State to the executive part of the State" ([1865–1867] 1964, pp. 67–68). He rejected sharply the idea that British government was based on the separation of powers, on a system of checks and balances between the three organs of government, and pointed out that what made a cabinet government work was that the cabinet embodied a fusion rather than a separation of powers. This was the hidden republic inside the monarchy. The hidden republic worked just because it was flexible enough to overcome the formal separation of powers.

In a sense, Bagehot's book, written just after the end of the American Civil War, was a comparative study of presidential and cabinet government. He found cabinet government far superior to presidential government. Although Bagehot had never visited the United States, he had strong notions about it (notions that were less insightful than those of Tocqueville or James Bryce, who had studied the country at first hand). Bagehot felt that the American system was too rigid: it was cramped by the division between states' rights and federal power, which created a perennial centrifugal force, and by the separation of the powers of the three branches of government, which resulted in constant deadlocks. The only merit of the American system—that of having a chief executive—the British had also in the form of a prime minister: "We have in England an elective first magistrate as truly as the Americans have an elective first magistrate" ([1865–1867] 1964, p. 66). What Bagehot did not realize was that some of the difficulties he diagnosed would disappear as the United States changed from a checks and balances government to a presidential form of government; nor did he take account, as Tocqueville did, of the positive effect on the political process of the American common voter's participation in voluntary associations.

Immediately after the publication of *The English Constitution* in book form (originally, it had been presented in installments in the *Fortnightly Review*), Bagehot started a new work (also serialized in the same journal). This was *Physics and Politics* (1872), in which the first term was a metonymy for science and the second for the study of society. Starting from the recent writings on evolution and natural selection, he set as his problem the question of how human societies had developed from the earliest primitive human life. Much of his material was drawn from the writings of anthropologists—Lubbock, McLennan, Maine—but his use of the material was highly original [see Lubbock; McLennan; Maine]. What he shaped in the book, with subtlety and force, was a social psychology of political development, which stressed the role of unconscious habit (reflex action), custom, war, innovation, and imitation. In the fashion characteristic of books based on evolutionary theories, this work traces mankind through three stages: the

"preliminary age," before any developed polity emerged; the "fighting age," when the desired end was social cohesion, when war was the means employed to achieve it, and when local and family loyalties were transformed through the "cake of custom," which had the sanction of law; and the "age of discussion," when the cake of custom has been broken by the innovating forces of the mind and men can make free choices between varying views and policies and fuse order and innovation into an "animated moderation."

This book, his most seminal, although not his most influential, was Bagehot's last work in general social science; afterward he turned increasingly to economics. What made his writing on social theory so remarkable was his lack of pomposity in a pompous age, his candor in an age of cant, and his tough-minded facing of political and social reality in an age of moralism.

Max Lerner

[*For the historical context of Bagehot's work, see* Constitutions and constitutionalism; Democracy; National character; Parliamentary government; *and the biographies of* Burke; Mill; Tocqueville.]

WORKS BY BAGEHOT

ECONOMIC WORKS

(1848) 1915   The Currency Monopoly. Volume 8, pages 146–187 in *The Works and Life of Walter Bagehot*. London: Longmans.

(1873) 1927   *Lombard Street: A Description of the Money Market.* New ed. Edited by Hartley Withers. London: Murray. → A paperback edition was published in 1962 by Irwin.

(1876a) 1885   *The Postulates of English Political Economy.* Preface by Alfred Marshall. New York and London: Putnam. → Originally published in the *Fortnightly Review* and republished with some other material in *Economic Studies.* The 1885 edition is an inexpensive students' edition, published at the instigation of Alfred Marshall.

(1880) 1895   *Economic Studies.* New ed. Edited by R. H. Hutton. London: Longmans. → Published posthumously. Reprinted in 1953 by Academic Reprints (Stanford, Calif.).

POLITICAL WORKS

(1852) 1965   Letters on the French *coup d'état* of 1851. Pages 381–436 in *Bagehot's Historical Essays.* Garden City, N.Y.: Anchor.

(1852–1877) 1965   *Bagehot's Historical Essays.* Edited with an introduction by Norman St. John-Stevas. Garden City, N.Y.: Anchor.

(1859) 1965   Parliamentary Reform. Pages 296–347 in *Bagehot's Historical Essays.* Garden City, N.Y.: Anchor.

(1865–1867) 1964   *The English Constitution.* London: Watts. → First published in the *Fortnightly Review.*

(1872) 1956   *Physics and Politics: Or Thoughts on the Application of the Principles of "Natural Selection" and "Inheritance" to Political Society.* Boston: Beacon.

(1876b) 1965   Lord Althorp and the Reform Act of 1832.

Pages 147–179 in *Bagehot's Historical Essays*. Garden City, N.Y.: Anchor.

COLLECTED WORKS

The Works of Walter Bagehot: With Memoirs by R. H. Hutton. 5 vols. Edited by Forrest Morgan. Hartford, Conn.: Travelers Insurance Co., 1889. → Includes Bagehot's principal economic works, but no articles from *The Economist*. The editor has taken some liberties with Bagehot's original text.

The Works and Life of Walter Bagehot. 10 vols. Edited by Emilie I. Barrington. London: Longmans, 1915. → Includes the principal economic works but virtually no economic articles from *The Economist*. Volume 10 contains the *Life of Walter Bagehot* by Emilie I. Barrington.

The Collected Works of Walter Bagehot: The Literary Essays. 2 vols. Edited by Norman St. John-Stevas. Cambridge, Mass.: Harvard Univ. Press, 1966. → Projected volumes are: Volume 3: *Historical Essays*. Volumes 4–5: *Political Essays*. Volumes 6–7: *Economic Essays*. Volume 8: *Letters and Miscellany*.

SUPPLEMENTARY BIBLIOGRAPHY

BARNES, HENRY A. 1921–1922 Some Typical Contributions of English Sociology to Political Theory. *American Journal of Sociology* 27:289–324, 442–485, 573–587, 737–757; 28:49–66, 179–204.

BAUMANN, ARTHUR A. (1916) 1927 *The Last Victorians*. London: Benn. → See especially pages 165–183 on "Walter Bagehot."

BRIGGS, ASA (1954) 1955 *Victorian People: A Reassessment of Persons and Themes, 1851–1867*. Univ. of Chicago Press. → A paperback edition was published in 1963 by Harper.

BRINTON, CLARENCE CRANE (1933) 1949 *English Political Thought in the Nineteenth Century*. Cambridge, Mass.: Harvard Univ. Press. → A paperback edition was published in 1965 by Harper.

BUCHAN, ALASTAIR 1959 *The Spare Chancellor: The Life of Walter Bagehot*. London: Chatto & Windus.

DEXTER, BYRON 1945 Bagehot and the Fresh Eye. *Foreign Affairs* 24: 108–118.

DRIVER, C. H. (1933) 1950 Walter Bagehot and the Social Psychologists. Pages 194–221 in Fossey J. C. Hearnshaw (editor), *The Social and Political Ideas of Some Representative Thinkers of the Victorian Age*. New York: Barnes & Noble.

EASTON, DAVID 1949 Walter Bagehot and Liberal Realism. *American Political Science Review* 43:17–37.

GIFFEN, ROBERT 1880 Bagehot as an Economist. *Fortnightly* 33:549–567.

HALSTED, JOHN B. 1958 Walter Bagehot on Toleration. *Journal of the History of Ideas* 19:119–128.

HEARNSHAW, F. J. C. (editor) 1933 The Social and Political Ideas of Some Representative Thinkers of the Victorian Age. London: Harrap.

HIRST, FRANCIS W. (1943) 1944 Walter Bagehot. Pages 64–72 in The Economist, London, *The Economist, 1843–1943: A Centenary Volume*. Oxford Univ. Press.

HOUGHTON, WALTER E. 1957 *The Victorian Frame of Mind: 1830–1870*. New Haven: Yale Univ. Press.

IRVINE, WILLIAM 1939 *Walter Bagehot*. London: Longmans.

KEYNES, J. M. 1915 The Works of Bagehot. *Economic Journal* 25:369–375.

LERNER, MAX 1939 Walter Bagehot: A Credible Victorian. Pages 305–314 in Max Lerner, *Ideas Are Weapons: The History and Uses of Ideas*. New York: Viking.

MURRAY, ROBERT H. 1929 Bagehot's Seminal Mind. Volume 2, pages 220–273 in Robert H. Murray, *Studies in the English Social and Political Thinkers of the Nineteenth Century*. Cambridge: Heffer.

READ, HERBERT E. (1938) 1956 Bagehot. Pages 299–314 in Herbert E. Read, *The Nature of Literature*. New York: Horizon. → First published as *Collected Essays in Literary Criticism*.

ST. JOHN-STEVAS, NORMAN 1959 *Walter Bagehot: A Study of His Life and Thought Together With a Selection From His Political Writings*. Bloomington: Indiana Univ. Press.

STEPHEN, LESLIE (1899) 1907 Walter Bagehot. Volume 3, pages 155–187 in Leslie Stephen, *Studies of a Biographer*. New York: Putnam.

WILSON, WOODROW (1895) 1965 A Literary Politician. Pages 69–103 in Woodrow Wilson, *Mere Literature, and Other Essays*. Port Washington, N.Y.: Kennikat. → First published in Volume 76 of the *Atlantic Monthly*.

WILSON, WOODROW 1898 A Wit and a Seer. *Atlantic Monthly* 82:527–540.

YOUNG, GEORGE M. 1948 The Greatest Victorian. Pages 237–243 in George M. Young, *Today and Yesterday: Collected Essays and Addresses*. London: Hart-Davis.

BAIN, ALEXANDER

Alexander Bain (1818–1903) is remembered primarily as an associationist and physiological psychologist, and his contributions to social and differential psychology have perhaps been unduly neglected. Bain's father was an ex-soldier turned weaver, whose earnings progressively diminished as his eight children grew up. Bain himself left school and began to work at the age of 11; indeed, he assisted his siblings financially for a considerable portion of his life. He felt handicapped in competition with his economically more fortunate peers and, not surprisingly, developed lifelong dyspepsia and a tendency toward merciless criticism of the shortcomings of others. Certain of his personal characteristics clearly affected his career: his sincerity led to religious nonconformity, and this delayed his academic advancement (he became professor of logic and rhetoric at the University of Aberdeen in 1860, after several abortive candidacies for other chairs); his perseverance gave rise to a thoroughness of method, a comprehensive erudition, and a large volume of production (over ninety published works); and his propensity to dominate his fellows culminated in his appointment as rector of the University of Aberdeen for three terms (1884, pp. 175–200).

The Senses and the Intellect (1855) and *The Emotions and the Will* (1859) are Bain's best-known works. Together they dealt with all aspects of psychology and were used as textbooks until nearly the end of the nineteenth century, even after

James Ward's attack on associationism in the *Encyclopaedia Britannica* (1886, vol. 20, pp. 37–85). In these books Bain consistently applied the principle that "the time has now come when many of the striking discoveries of Physiologists relative to the nervous system should find a recognized place in the Science of Mind" (1855, preface, p. iii in 1874 edition).

Although these works suffered because Bain frequently juxtaposed, rather than integrated, psychology and physiology, their shortcomings should not obscure some of their original features. One of these was Bain's characterization of then current theories of consciousness as "shifting quicksands." Integrating the emotional and intellectual aspects of consciousness, he related it to physiological events: "The clear, distinctive discrimination that we obtain of different things that strike us, which is the very foundation of an intellectual development, is originally bred from cerebral shocks, not improperly styled surprises" (1859, p. 619 in 1865 edition). Also unusual for its time was Bain's behaviorally oriented theory of belief. Belief, he asserted, "has no meaning, except in reference to our actions—no mere conception that does not directly or indirectly implicate our voluntary exertions, can ever amount to the state in question" (1859, p. 568 in 1865 edition). Bain's analysis of spontaneity was original, and it anticipated later behaviorism in some respects, although it did include a major mistake: the analysis was based on the notion of initial general activity that becomes specified through reward and punishment, so that feelings become linked with actions (1859, pp. 328–329, 339 in 1865 edition). Bain thought that spontaneous activity was "at the outset independent of any stimulus from without" (1859, p. 327 in 1865 edition), but more recent work has shown that he failed to distinguish "without" from "within."

In *The Emotions and the Will*, and in earlier, forgotten works, Bain put forward a pioneer social psychology that has received little attention. It dealt with sympathy, social conformity, and interpersonal behavior. Bain analyzed sympathy more clearly than had his predecessors (e.g., Adam Smith and Thomas Brown); he characterized it as one's assumption of the mental state of another by the development of the bodily states one attributes to the other by virtue of his behavior (1859, p. 215 in 1865 edition). An understanding of social conformity is sought, according to Bain, through the study of moral habits. This study produces a distinction between disinterested action and conscience (these being matters of psychology), on the one hand, and ultimate moral standards, on the other (*Mental and Moral Science* [1868] 1872, p. 344; and *Dissertations on Leading Philosophical Topics* 1903). Bain treated interpersonal behavior principally by showing how sympathy leads to cohesion in social groups ("The Human Mind" [1849] 1858, pp. 337–352) and how egotistic feelings develop into the need for "social alliance" (1872, p. 250).

Bain made other insufficiently appreciated contributions. Thus, in "On Toys" (1842), he set forth the view that the manipulation of toys is important for revealing aptitudes and interests and for developing skills. In his book *Education as a Science* (1879), he developed a detailed rationale for relating punishment to individual differences and reflected carefully on the severity of punishment that was possible without damage to the individual. *On the Study of Character* (1861) contained suggestions on testing that were well in advance of his time; moreover, as he reported in his *Autobiography* (1904, p. 132), he had begun thinking about the subject even earlier. In the *Autobiography* and in his *Logic* (1870) he recast, acutely and critically, Comte's classification of the sciences.

As the author of texts that were not replaced until those of Stout and James appeared and as the founder of *Mind* (in 1876), Bain's place in psychology remains secure.

J. A. CARDNO

[*For the historical context of Bain's work, see the biographies of* HARTLEY *and* LOCKE; *for discussion of the subsequent development of his ideas, see* CONFORMITY; EMOTION; LEARNING, *article on* REINFORCEMENT; PUNISHMENT; SOCIAL PSYCHOLOGY; SYMPATHY AND EMPATHY.]

WORKS BY BAIN

1842　On Toys. *Westminster Review* 37:97–121.

(1849) 1858　The Human Mind. Volume 2, pages 337–352 in *Chamber's Information for the People.* London and Edinburgh: Chambers.

1850　Animal Instincts and Intelligence. Volume 6, number 82, pages 1–32 in *Chambers' Papers for the People.* Edinburgh: Chambers.

(1855) 1894　*The Senses and the Intellect.* 4th ed. New York: Appleton.

(1859) 1899　*The Emotions and the Will.* 4th ed. London: Longmans.

1861　*On the Study of Character: Including an Estimate of Phrenology.* London: Parker.

(1868) 1872　*Mental and Moral Science.* London: Longmans.

(1870) 1889　*Logic.* New ed., rev. New York: Appleton.

(1872) 1879　*Mind and Body: The Theories of Their Relation.* New York: Appleton.

1879　*Education as a Science.* New York: Appleton.

1884　*Practical Essays.* New York: Appleton.

1903　*Dissertations on Leading Philosophical Topics.* London: Longmans.

1904　*Autobiography.* London: Longmans.

WORKS ABOUT BAIN

BORING, EDWIN G. (1929) 1950 Alexander Bain. Pages 233–240 in Edwin G. Boring, *A History of Experimental Psychology.* New York: Appleton.

CARDNO, JAMES A. 1955 Bain and Physiological Psychology. *Australian Journal of Psychology* 7:108–120.

CARDNO, JAMES A. 1956 Bain as a Social Psychologist. *Australian Journal of Psychology* 8:66–76.

CARDNO, JAMES A. 1963 Bain and Individual Differences. *Aberdeen University Review* 40:124–132.

DAVIDSON, WILLIAM L. 1904 Professor Bain's Philosophy. *Mind* New Series 13:161–179.

WATSON, ROBERT I. 1963 Alexander Bain. Pages 196–200 in Robert I. Watson, *The Great Psychologists: From Aristotle to Freud.* Philadelphia: Lippincott.

SUPPLEMENTARY BIBLIOGRAPHY

BRETT, GEORGE S. (1912–1921) 1962 *Brett's History of Psychology.* Rev. ed. London: Allen & Unwin; New York: Macmillan. → See especially pages 456–465 on "Classification of Mental Activities."

MILL, JAMES 1869 *Analysis of the Phenomena of the Human Mind.* 2 vols. London: Longmans. → Contains critical notes by Alexander Bain.

MURPHY, GARDNER (1929) 1949 *Historical Introduction to Modern Psychology.* Rev. ed. New York: Harcourt. → See especially Chapter 7 on "British Psychology in the Mid-nineteenth Century."

WARD, JAMES 1886 Psychology. Volume 20, pages 37–85 in *Encyclopaedia Britannica.* 9th ed. Edinburgh: Black.

WARREN, HOWARD C. 1921 *A History of the Association Psychology.* New York: Scribner. → See especially pages 104–109 on "Alexander Bain's Conception of Association"; pages 109–115 on "Bain's Derivation of Mental Phenomena"; and pages 115–117 on "Culmination of Pure Associationism."

BAKUNIN, MIKHAIL A.

Mikhail A. Bakunin (1814–1876), professional revolutionary and anarchist theorist, was the oldest son of a provincial Russian nobleman who was influenced by European culture and who at one time had liberal leanings. Revolting against parental authority, Bakunin early abandoned his military career and enrolled in Moscow University, where, together with Vissarion Belinski and Alexander Herzen, he became one of the leaders of the newly emerging intelligentsia. He went to the University of Berlin to study philosophy, but he quickly became dissatisfied with the tedious conservatism of German academic life. During the years 1843 to 1848, he wandered through Europe, meeting such European radicals as Wilhelm Weitling, Proudhon, and Marx, and absorbing their ideas.

Bakunin hailed the outbreak of the revolutions of 1848 with feverish enthusiasm, racing first to Paris and then to central Europe where he played an important role in the Slav Congress, which met at Prague in June 1848. Captured in an abortive uprising at Dresden in May 1849, he was successively imprisoned, tried, and sentenced by Saxon and Austrian justice before, finally in 1851, being turned over to the Russian authorities, who consigned him, without a semblance of trial, to the gloomy depths of the Fortress of St. Peter and St. Paul. Exiled to Siberia in 1857, by grace of the new tsar, Alexander II, he escaped four years later and made his way to London, where he collaborated with his friends Herzen and Nikolai Ogarev in the publication of the *Bell.* After an unsuccessful attempt to lead an expedition of volunteers to Poland during the insurrection of 1863, he transferred the seat of his operations to Italy, founding there the most formidable of his many revolutionary organizations, the International Alliance of Social Democracy. Bakunin lived to participate in two more uprisings, both of them abortive: that of Lyon in 1870 and that of Bologna in 1874. But the most notable and lasting feature of the activity of his later years was his conflict with Marx within the First International, which ended in the disintegration of that organization and the secession of the anarchists.

Most writers agree that Bakunin's anarchism was not so much a theory as a psychological necessity. As E. H. Carr has observed, "The call of revolution was in his blood, as some men feel the call of sea or hills" (1937, p. 148). Consequently, Bakuninism suggests an outlook, a temperament, and a revolutionary tactic, rather than a system of ideas. Bakunin's ideological odyssey (for that is how his tumultuous spiritual development must be thought of) can best be divided into three parts: a first, apolitical, stage lasting until 1841, in which he confined himself to a conservative and romantic interpretation of German idealistic philosophy; a second, Pan-Slav phase lasting from 1847 to 1863, during which he saw the key to European revolution in the disintegration of the Hapsburg empire and its replacement by a free federation of Slavic peoples; and a final, anarchist, period.

The political philosophy of Bakunin's later years is a paean to destruction: all political, social, and religious institutions must be destroyed, the goal being a free federation of independent associations in which all would have equal rights and equal privileges, including that of secession. The means for the attainment of this anarchist utopia would be a universal rebellion of the lower orders of society, led by a secret group of conspirators bound together by an iron discipline and subject to a single will.

The determination of Bakunin's influence is a far from easy task. As a theorist of society, he had little to say that was not said first and better by

Proudhon and Marx. His collected writings are a mass of fragments, abounding in shrewd insights and powerful passages of polemic, but lacking in the kind of sustained and precise analysis necessary for a social thinker of the first order. As a revolutionary and as an organizer, he is noted mainly for the indefatigability of his revolutionary ardor and for the imagination with which he dreamed up conspiratorial societies that never came into existence. Yet his importance in the history of nineteenth-century social movements is not to be questioned. A personality of almost superhuman proportions, Bakunin had a rare ability to inspire men. Through his lieutenants, James Guillaume, Elie and Elisée Reclus, Carlo Cafiero, and Giuseppe Fanelli, he shaped the working-class movements of Italy, Spain, and Russia, and, to some degree at least, those of France and Switzerland.

Bakunin's political legacy is more ambiguous. No man ever pushed the principles of individualism and individual liberty further. But it has been pointed out increasingly in recent years (in particular by Carr 1937; Pyziur 1955; and Hepner 1950) that if Bakunin's ends point toward freedom, his means—the revolutionary party—lead to totalitarianism. And it is indisputable that in his desire for a bloody revolution of the masses, led by a small, select group of professional revolutionaries, men without roots or conscience, he was a distant forerunner of the Bolshevik, fascist, and national socialist revolutions of the twentieth century.

ROBERT WOHL

[*For the historical context of Bakunin's work, see the biographies* MARX; PROUDHON. *For discussions of the subsequent development of his ideas, see* ANARCHISM; RADICALISM; REVOLUTION.]

WORKS BY BAKUNIN

No complete edition of Bakunin's works is yet available. For selective editions in French (1895–1913), German (1921–1924), and Russian (1934–1936), see below.

1895–1913   *Oeuvres.* 6 vols. Paris: Stock.
1896   *Correspondance de Michel Bakounine; Lettres à Herzen et à Ogaroff.* Paris: Perrin. → First published as *Pis'ma M. A. Bakunina.*
(1921) 1932   *Confession.* Paris: Rieder. → First published as *Ipoved' i pis'mo Aleksandru* II.
1921–1924   *Gesammelte Werke.* 3 vols. Berlin: Der Syndikalist.
1934–1936   *Sobranie sochinenii i pisem* (Selected Works and Correspondence). 4 vols. Moscow: Izd. Vsesoiuznogo Obschestva Politkatorzhan i Ssyl'noposelentsev.
1953   *The Political Philosophy of Bakunin: Scientific Anarchism.* Compiled and edited by G. P. Maximoff. Glencoe, Ill.: Free Press. → Contains a biographical sketch of Bakunin by Max Netteau. A paperback edition was published in 1964.

1961   *Michel Bakounine et l'Italie, 1871–1872.* Edited by A. Lehning, A. Y. C. Rüter, and P. Schreibert. Archives Bakounine, Volume I. Leiden (Netherlands): Brill. → The first volume of a projected series of Bakunin's unpublished works.

SUPPLEMENTARY BIBLIOGRAPHY

CARR, EDWARD H.   (1937) 1961   *Michael Bakunin.* New York: Vintage.
HEPNER, BENOÎT-P.   1950   *Bakounine et le panslavisme révolutionnaire.* Paris: Rivière.
KENAFICK, K. J.   1948   *Michael Bakunin and Karl Marx.* Melbourne and London: Freedom Press.
KORNILOV, A. N.   1917   *Molodye gody Mikhaila Bakunina* (The Youthful Years of Mikhail Bakunin). Moscow: Sabashnikov.
KORNILOV, A. N.   1925   *Gody stranstvii Mikhaila Bakunina* (The Wandering Years of Mikhail Bakunin). Leningrad: Gosudarstvennoe Izdatelstvo.
LAMPERT, EVGENII   1957   *Studies in Rebellion.* London: Routledge.
PYZIUR, EUGENE   1955   *The Doctrine of Anarchism of Michael A. Bakunin.* Milwaukee, Wis.: Marquette Univ. Press.
STEKLOV, Y. M.   1926–1927   *Mikhail Aleksandrovich Bakunin, ego zhizn' i deiatelnost, 1814–1876* (Mikhail Aleksandrovich Bakunin, His Life and Activities, 1814–1876). 4 vols., 2d rev. ed. Moscow: Izdatelstvo Kommunisticheskoi Akademii.
VENTURI, FRANCO   1952   *Il populismo russo.* 2 vols. Turin (Italy): Einaudi.

BALANCE OF PAYMENTS

See under INTERNATIONAL MONETARY ECONOMICS.

BALANCE OF POWER

The concept of the balance of power is indispensable to the understanding of international relations, despite the very different meanings and uses of the notion and the equally divergent assessments of the political realities to which it refers.

Some authors apply the term "balance of power" to any *distribution* of power among states, whether it be one of relative equilibrium or even one of disequilibrium—for instance, a situation in which one state has a preponderance of power in a certain area. When the independence of some states appears threatened by the moves of one or several of the others, the former states try to prevent the latter from imposing their domination either in the form of hegemony or in that of a regional or even a world empire. In this connection, the term "balance of power" has been used (*a*) to refer to a *policy* on the part of states that deliberately aims at preventing the preponderance of any one state and at maintaining an approximate equilibrium of power among the major rivals and (*b*) to designate a *system* of international politics in which the pattern of relations among the actors tends to curb the ambitions or the opportunities of the chief rivals and to preserve an approximate equilibrium of power among them. In this article the concept will be limited to the meanings listed above under (*a*) and (*b*) and to that distribution of power which can legitimately be called balanced.

Conditions. A balance of power may exist whenever there are at least two major actors in the international competition. The term "balance of power" referring to a *system* designates a pattern of relations among more than two major units, i.e., a multipolar system. However, even in a bipolar world, such as the one in which we have lived since 1945 or Greece in the fifth century B.C. as described by Thucydides, it is perfectly conceivable that one power—the one that is on the defensive and tries to prevent the adversary from establishing its preponderance—should pursue a balance-of-power *policy* in order to checkmate its rival; if it is successful, the *distribution* of power thus obtained may once again be called a balance.

When there are more than two major powers, a balance-of-power *system* may appear, even if the main actors do not have as a policy goal the establishment or maintenance of equilibrium; the system may emerge because of political circumstances rather than as the product of statesmen's intentions and choices. Among these circumstances are:

(*a*) a relative equilibrium of power among the major units;

(*b*) a frontier at which those units can expand and at which their occasional clashes are likely to be less dangerous than clashes in the core area of international politics;

(*c*) domestic regimes in which the state's control over the political allegiance and economic activities of the citizens is not exclusive;

(*d*) relative technological stability, especially in the area of military technology;

(*e*) the possibility of a common conception of international legitimacy.

Even though each unit may not have as an explicit goal the maintenance of the system, such a conception allows for a kind of common language in the manipulation of the system and usually presupposes a modicum of similarity among regimes and among beliefs concerning the nature and role of the state. These conditions of relative homogeneity were met to some extent among the Greek and Italian city-states, as well as in the European state system from 1648 to 1789 and from 1815 to 1914.

Methods. The methods used by states which lead to or preserve a balanced distribution of power are not the same in a bipolar system and in a multipolar one.

In a bipolar system the chief contenders are concerned primarily with the development of rival networks of alliances, with the preservation of unity within their respective camps, and with gaining support from the uncommitted states. In a multipolar system the balance of power is maintained among the main units either peacefully or through the use of force. The peaceful methods consist of rewards for good, i.e., moderate, behavior (for instance, in the form of compensations) and of threats of punishment in case of bad behavior (facing the troublemaker with the prospect of being stopped by an overwhelming coalition if he pushes too far). The use of force includes the resort to wars of two different sorts: "stalemating" wars, in which a coalition of powers tries to stop the alliance of those states that seek to modify the *status quo*, and "imbalance" wars, in which the troublemaker has to confront a coalition of all or most of the other major units, for instance, the War of the Grand Alliance, 1688–1697, in which Louis XIV had to face such an alignment. Britain, from the sixteenth century to the early twentieth, often played the part of the "balancer," i.e., a state sufficiently aloof from the competition of Continental powers to intervene only when a troublemaker threatened to disrupt the balance by his actions and in such a way as to throw its weight to the side of those threatened by him.

It can be seen that a balance-of-power system, in contrast with a bipolar one, presupposes among its chief actors (*a*) flexibility of alignments, i.e., the willingness to make alliances with almost anyone in case of need—in particular in order to stop a troublemaker—without any concern for the domestic regime or ideology of the ally and the willingness to abandon or break such alliances whenever the initial circumstances have changed, and (*b*) an acceptance of international hierarchy, i.e., the refusal to envisage such permanent hostility among the major actors that the recruitment of clienteles of allies among the smaller states would become imperative and the consideration of occasional common interests of the major states impossible.

Effects. International competition is fundamentally uncertain: the ends pursued by states are multiple, often intangible, and frequently contradictory; the power at their disposal is not measurable, nor is it the measure of foreign policy.

Consequently, any configuration of power that can be called balanced is necessarily unstable.

Such instability is, of course, much greater in a bipolar system, in which any sudden advance—geographical or technological—of one of the contenders may destroy the precarious equilibrium. A multipolar balance-of-power system is only comparatively stable. First, the system may be endangered by changes in the conditions listed above: the balance-of-power system of the nineteenth century was gradually weakened by the rise of nationalism; one should never forget that a system is the outcome of a great number of circumstances beyond its own control. Second, the mechanism itself has flaws. Since no power is always sure in advance that it will be stopped by the others if it pushes ahead, this uncertainty of calculations and alignments leads to wars that can be called disturbances *in* the system, caused by the more ambitious actors. To these must be added the disturbances caused *for* the maintenance of the system by the powers that try to stop a troublemaker. A balance-of-power system is not necessarily a peaceful one. Nor does it necessarily protect the independence of small states, as was shown by the partitions of Poland in the eighteenth century. Nor does it necessarily satisfy the big powers: their policies frequently aim at aggrandizement rather than *status quo*, at superiority rather than balance; the frustration of their ambitions by the very success of the balancing mechanism may lead them to destroy the system, either deliberately or through actions incompatible with the maintenance of the system (such as the formation of rigid alliances on the eve of 1914).

However, the real merit of the multipolar balance-of-power system lies elsewhere: it does not eliminate war or international inequities but tends to moderate them. Wars started and gains made by troublemakers may be stopped by other states: the wages of sin, so to speak, will be small. Wars waged to preserve the system are fought for limited goals and with limited means. The very "cynicism" of a diplomacy that envisages no permanent commitments contributes to such moderation. The balance-of-power system has its own sanctions—political rather than moral or legal—but even the "delinquent," once he has agreed to play again according to the rules, is allowed to return to the fold. The limitation of ends and means that the system enforces and the recognition of the major units' common interests, which is both a condition and a consequence of the system's operation, permit the development of international law on a basis of reciprocity. Balance-of-power systems thus appear as the golden ages of the skillful diplomat and the complacent international lawyer; they are the ages when power is managed in the most civilized manner and the sword, which is of the essence of world politics, is either sheathed or used to warn and to wound rather than to kill.

History.   The concept of the balance of power has been discussed in all the situations in which there were a number of independent units competing for power. There is almost no mention of this concept during the Roman Empire and the Middle Ages, but Thucydides referred to it and so did Italian writers of the Renaissance. Later, a number of British thinkers analyzed the balance of power as a means of preserving moderation in international politics and as a goal for British policy: Francis Bacon, Lord Bolingbroke, and David Hume showed an acute awareness of the advantages of such a system, of the delicacy of its operations, and of Britain's special position. Two kinds of critics of power politics countered with attacks against the balance of power. Thinkers, such as Rousseau and Kant, for whom the imperative of peace—i.e., an end to international anarchy—was supreme denounced the balance as an immoral sport of kings and a mere continuation of what Hobbes called the state of war. Thinkers, such as Richard Cobden, who thought that industrial and commercial developments would unite the peoples of the world attacked balance-of-power thinking as an obstacle to progress. This somewhat paradoxical hostility of political and economic liberals to a system that tends to moderate violence culminated in Woodrow Wilson's repudiation of the balance of power and in his appeal for a "community of power" to replace it.

The establishment of the League of Nations was an attempt at substituting collective security—i.e., a system in which all states commit themselves to the repression of individual resorts to force—for the old system in which the individual state's use of force was considered legal and in which other states joined in order to stop a troublemaker only if they felt that this was in their interest at the moment. The interwar period was marked both by the failure of collective security and by the absence of any balance-of-power system. In a heterogeneous world, some of the major states remained in isolation and the defenders of the *status quo* failed to stop the aggressors. [See COLLECTIVE SECURITY.]

Assessment.   After World War II, controversies among writers resumed. At one end, some remained faithful to the ideal of collective security and carried on the liberal critique of the balance of power. At the other extreme, Hans Morgenthau (1948) described the balance as the necessary outcome of the inevitable struggle for power and prescribed it as a desirable policy for the United States. In the middle, a growing number of scholars have preferred to abandon advocacy for analysis and to dispel confusion by sorting out the various meanings and uses of the concept, by studying the historical circumstances of past balance-of-power systems, and by trying to see to what extent the concept remains useful in the new conditions of the nuclear age.

Most of the transformations that are, or may be, necessary stem not from bipolarity—a phenomenon that is neither new nor final—but from the invention of thermonuclear weapons.

If we consider the *distribution* of power, we find that there is a need to distinguish the new "balance of terror" from the old balance of power. The latter consisted of an approximately even distribution of capabilities that included actually mobilized military forces, military potential, and economic and human resources; it involved primarily the power to defend and to seize territory. The balance of terror is based on readily available thermonuclear forces; it exists even if the rival quantities are unevenly matched as long as each side has enough of these forces to inflict unacceptable reprisals, for this balance involves the power to deter or to destroy.

If by balance of power we mean a *policy*, nuclear weapons have complicated the making of such a policy for their possessors. On the one hand, calculations of power have become even more uncertain because of a galloping technology and the fortunate lack of experience in thermonuclear strategy. On the other hand, one may argue that the power to deter and destroy no longer entails the need to control large areas of territory and to line up numerous allies; indeed, allies whose protection may require risking the destruction of the nuclear protector may well be more a nuisance than an asset. However, a state that would possess only thermonuclear weapons might find itself locked in the dilemma of "holocaust or humiliation" in every crisis. Moreover, the very prudence shown by nuclear powers and the trend toward the invulnerability of the nuclear forces of the chief contenders tend to restore the importance of the classical ingredients of power.

If we look at the post-1945 *system*, we find that the superpowers are increasingly reluctant to use large levels of force in their confrontation for fear of escalation. We find also that the residual risk of all-out war, which nuclear weapons create despite the trend toward invulnerability, may still be exploited in some important areas to redress an imbalance in nonnuclear forces. Thus, thermonuclear weapons tend to inject into a basically unstable and revolutionary bipolar system an element of moderation; if we reserve the term "balance-of-power systems" for multipolar moderate ones, the present bipolar one may deserve to be called a "balance-of-terror system." Whether this element of moderation would survive in a world in which the number of nuclear powers multiplied is far from clear.

The achievement of a balance of power in the sense of an even distribution or of a successful policy has also been affected by developments only indirectly connected with nuclear weapons or quite independent of them. The basic units are not only the states but also new entities, such as the emerging European community and a host of international organizations, which are stakes, as well as forces, in the competition. Both the ideological and revolutionary character of postwar world politics and the resort by the superpowers to forms of action other than the military forces that are too dangerous necessitate the inclusion of new elements of power and influence in the calculations of states. Hence the idea of a "multiple equilibrium." This suggests that in a system that now embraces the whole world and performs functions previously excluded from the once much more limited realm of world politics, assessments of power become progressively more complicated. The balance of power (as distribution and policy) used to be essential because war provided the minute of truth in the tests of states. Today, a balance is essential primarily in order to prevent war. As a result, the minute of truth is postponed, and all the intangible components of power and all the uses of power short of massive coercion gain in importance—elements and uses that are very widely distributed and hard to evaluate. Today's international system is bipolar at the level of the balance of terror, polycentric as a result of the decline in the actual use of large-scale force, and incipiently multipolar as a result of nuclear proliferation. But as long as the competition continues and the risk of war persists, i.e., as long as there is no mutation in world society, the distribution of military power (both nuclear and traditional) may well remain crucial.

STANLEY HOFFMANN

[*See also* INTERNATIONAL POLITICS; POWER TRANSITION; SYSTEMS ANALYSIS, *article on* INTERNATIONAL SYSTEMS. *Other relevant material may be found in* INTERNATIONAL RELATIONS *and* NATIONAL INTEREST.]

BIBLIOGRAPHY

ARON, RAYMOND 1962 *Paix et guerre entre les nations.* Paris: Calmann-Lévy.

ARON, RAYMOND (1963) 1965 *The Great Debate: Theories of Nuclear Strategy.* Garden City, N.Y.: Doubleday. → First published as *Le grand débat: Initiation à la stratégie atomique.*

CLAUDE, INIS L. JR. 1962 *Power and International Relations.* New York: Random House.

DUPUIS, CHARLES 1909 *Le principe d'équilibre et le concert européen de la paix de Westphalie à l'acte d'Algésiras.* Paris: Perrin.

FRIEDRICH, CARL J. 1938 *Foreign Policy in the Making: The Search for a New Balance of Power.* New York: Norton.

GULICK, EDWARD V. 1955 *Europe's Classical Balance of Power: A Case History of the Theory and Practice of One of the Great Concepts of European Statecraft.* Ithaca, N.Y.: Cornell Univ. Press.

HAAS, ERNST B. 1953a The Balance of Power as a Guide to Policy-making. *World Politics* 15:370–398.

HAAS, ERNST B. 1953b The Balance of Power: Prescription, Concept, or Propaganda? *World Politics* 5:442–477.

HAAS, ERNST B. 1964 *Beyond the Nation-state: Functionism and International Organization.* Stanford (Calif.) Univ. Press.

HINSLEY, FRANCIS H. 1963 *Power and the Pursuit of Peace: Theory and Practice in the History of Relations Between States.* Cambridge Univ. Press.

HOFFMANN, STANLEY 1965 *The State of War.* New York: Praeger.

HUME, DAVID (1742) 1953 *Of the Balance of Power.* Pages 185–192 in David Hume, *Theory of Politics.* Edited by Frederick Watkins. Austin: Univ. of Texas Press.

KAPLAN, MORTON 1957 *System and Process in International Politics.* New York: Wiley.

KISSINGER, HENRY A. (1957) 1964 *A World Restored.* New York: Grosset & Dunlap.

LISKA, GEORGE 1957 *International Equilibrium: A Theoretical Essay on the Politics and Organization of Security.* Cambridge, Mass.: Harvard Univ. Press.

MORGENTHAU, HANS J. (1948) 1962 *Politics Among Nations: The Struggle for Power and Peace.* New York: Knopf.

ORGANSKI, A. F. K. 1958 *World Politics.* New York: Knopf.

SEABURY, PAUL (editor) 1965 *Balance of Power.* San Francisco: Chandler.

SNYDER, GLENN H. 1961 *Deterrence and Defense: Toward a Theory of National Security.* Princeton (N.J.) Univ. Press.

TAYLOR, ALAN J. P. 1954 *The Struggle for Mastery in Europe, 1848–1918.* New York and London: Oxford Univ. Press.

VAGTS, ALFRED 1948 The Balance of Power: Growth of an Idea. *World Politics* 1:82–101.

WALTZ, KENNETH N. 1964 The Stability of a Bipolar World. *Dædalus* 93:881–909.

WOLFERS, ARNOLD 1962 *Discord and Collaboration: Essays on International Politics.* Baltimore: Johns Hopkins Press.

BALDWIN, JAMES MARK

James Mark Baldwin (1861–1934), American psychologist, was prominent in the newly scientific American psychology between 1890 and 1910. In general, he may be said to have been a philosophical psychologist who preferred writing and speculation to experimentation—despite the fact that during his career he equipped three different psychological laboratories. He was a brilliant, erudite, and facile writer, but his thinking was involved and his prose, although precise, was not lucid.

Baldwin was born in Columbia, South Carolina, on January 12, 1861, to a family with Northern sympathies. At the age of 18 he entered a preparatory school in Salem, New Jersey, and three years later went to Princeton University, where he acquired an interest in philosophy. He was graduated with an A.B. in 1884. Upon graduation he won a fellowship for European study and spent a year studying with Wilhelm Wundt at Leipzig and Friedrich Paulsen at Berlin. Those were the days when philosophers were excited about the discovery of a new field of philosophy—experimental psychology. They did not realize how far apart in personal values are the rational and empirical modes of intellectual endeavor. Wundt was at heart a philosopher, a pioneer in the new psychology but not basically a laboratory man; Baldwin was ruled by a similar temperamental bias.

Baldwin returned from Europe to teach German and French at Princeton, but he took a course at the theological seminary and thought of the ministry for a while. From 1887 to 1889 he was professor of philosophy at Lake Forest. Baldwin had not liked the theological dogmatism he found at Princeton and turned definitely toward psychology, undertaking in his first book, the *Handbook of Psychology; Senses and Intellect* (1889), to correct the lack of texts in the new psychology. William James's *Principles of Psychology* was still a year away, and John Dewey's later greatness was not yet apparent in his *Psychology* of 1886, so there was only G. T. Ladd's big *Physiological Psychology* available. At the end of Baldwin's stay at Lake Forest, Princeton awarded him the PH.D. for a dissertation in which he undertook—at the unwavering insistence of President James McCosh, a Presbyterian—to refute materialism.

From Lake Forest, Baldwin went as professor of psychology to Toronto, where he was provided with a small grant with which to start a psychological laboratory, the first on Commonwealth soil. There he published the second volume of his *Handbook,* the account of *Feeling and Will* (1891).

In 1893 he returned to Princeton, where he spent ten years as Stuart professor of psychology. For the second time, he established a psychological laboratory, but his personal laboratory was the nursery of his two daughters, aged four and two. His many observations of these two girls were the basis of his claim to be a pioneer in developmental child psychology.

Evolution had by then taken American intellectuals by storm, and Baldwin, like G. Stanley Hall but with much greater sophistication, became an American exponent of evolution and functionalism in psychology. He published *Mental Development in the Child and the Race* (1895) and *Social and Ethical Interpretations in Mental Development* (1897). These books were followed by *Development and Evolution* (1902a) and by the three volumes of his *Genetic Logic* (1906–1911), in which he undertook to expound the nature of thought and meaning in developmental terms. In evolutionary theory, he is perhaps best known for his doctrine of organic selection, the view that the establishment of variation in an organism is helped by the adaptation of the organism, a conception that slants the Darwinian theory slightly toward the Lamarckian. Baldwin founded laboratories but did not use them, and this stream of highly speculative theorizing with but slim empirical base prejudiced most American experimental psychologists against him.

While he was at Princeton, Baldwin performed two important services for psychology. In 1894 he founded with J. McK. Cattell the *Psychological Review* and its two adjuncts, the *Psychological Index* and the *Psychological Monographs*. In 1901 and 1902 he published two huge volumes of the *Dictionary of Philosophy and Psychology*, which he had edited and which was later supplemented by Benjamin Rand's great bibliographical volume.

Baldwin went in 1903 to Johns Hopkins, where he rescued from oblivion G. Stanley Hall's old laboratory. Here the first two volumes of *Genetic Logic* were written. Baldwin was developing other interests, however. He traveled frequently; while in Mexico City he advised on the organization of the university. He liked Mexico and Paris, and after five years at Johns Hopkins he spent 1909–1913 at the National University of Mexico where, among other activities, he finished *Genetic Logic*.

In 1913 he moved to Paris, where he spent the rest of his life. He saw World War I as a moral issue and through the years of American neutrality sought American support for the Allies. He was already a member of the Institut de France, and his work for France during the war brought him

further recognition; but his contributions to psychology and his version of its philosophy were done. His reminiscences and letters were published in 1926, and he died in Paris on November 8, 1934.

Edwin G. Boring

[*Other relevant material may be found in* Developmental psychology *and the biographies of* Hall *and* Wundt.]

WORKS BY BALDWIN

1889–1891 *Handbook of Psychology.* 2 vols. New York: Holt. → Volume 1: *Senses and Intellect*, 1889. Volume 2: *Feeling and Will*, 1891.

1893 *Elements of Psychology.* New York: Holt. → A condensation of *Handbook of Psychology.*

(1895) 1906 *Mental Development in the Child and the Race: Methods and Processes.* 3d ed., rev. New York and London: Macmillan.

(1897) 1906 *Social and Ethical Interpretations in Mental Development: A Study in Social Psychology.* 4th ed., rev. & enl. New York: Macmillan.

(1898) 1915 *The Story of the Mind.* New York: Appleton. → An elementary text.

(1901–1905) 1960 Baldwin, James Mark (editor). *Dictionary of Philosophy and Psychology.* 3 vols. New ed., with corrections. Gloucester, Mass.: Peter Smith. → Volume 1, A–L, 1901. Volume 2, L–Z, 1902. Volumes 1 and 2 were edited by J. M. Baldwin. Volume 3, Bibliography, 1905, was compiled by Benjamin Rand.

1902a *Development and Evolution, Including Psychophysical Evolution, Evolution by Orthoplasy, and the Theory of Genetic Modes.* New York: Macmillan.

1902b *Fragments in Philosophy and Science, Being Collected Essays and Addresses.* New York: Scribner.

1906–1911 *Thought and Things: A Study of the Development and Meaning of Thought; or Genetic Logic.* 3 vols. New York: Macmillan; London: Sonnenschein. → Volume 1: *Functional Logic, or Genetic Theory of Knowledge*, 1906. Volume 2: *Experimental Logic, or Genetic Theory of Thought*, 1908. Volume 3: *Interest and Art, Being Real Logic and Genetic Epistemology*, 1911.

1909 *Darwin and the Humanities.* Baltimore: Review Pub.

(1910) 1911 *The Individual and Society; or Psychology and Sociology.* Boston: Badger. → First published in French.

1913a *French and American Ideals.* London: Sherratt & Hughes. → Reprinted from *Sociological Review*, April 1913.

1913b *History of Psychology: A Sketch and an Interpretation.* 2 vols. London: Watts.

(1915a) 1916 *France and the War, as Seen by an American.* New York: Appleton. → Published in France and England in 1915.

1915b *Genetic Theory of Reality.* New York and London: Putnam.

1916a *American Neutrality: Its Cause and Cure.* New York and London: Putnam.

1916b *The Super-state and the "Eternal Values."* London and New York: Oxford Univ. Press.

1926 *Between Two Wars: 1861–1921, Being Memories, Opinions and Letters Received.* 2 vols. Boston: Stratford.

WORKS ABOUT BALDWIN

Baldwin, James M. 1930 *Autobiography.* Volume 1, pages 1–30 in Carl Murchison (editor), *A History of*

Psychology in Autobiography. Worcester, Mass.: Clark Univ. Press; Oxford Univ. Press.

BORING, EDWIN G. (1929) 1950 *A History of Experimental Psychology.* 2d ed. New York: Appleton. → See pages 528–532 and 547 ff. on Baldwin.

URBAN, W. M. 1935 James Mark Baldwin: Co-editor, *Psychological Review,* 1894–1909. *Psychological Review* 42:303–306.

WASHBURN, M. F. 1935 James Mark Baldwin: 1861–1934. *American Journal of Psychology* 47:168–169.

BANDELIER, ADOLPH

Adolph Francis Alphonse Bandelier (1840–1914) was an American anthropologist and documentary historian whose field was the Indian cultures of the southwestern United States, Mexico, and the Andean highlands. He was born in Berne, Switzerland, but his family emigrated to the United States in 1848 and settled in Highland, Illinois. As a young man in Highland he engaged in business enterprises, which he disliked exceedingly; his spare time was passionately devoted to the study of the Spanish documentary history of Mexico. In 1873 he met Lewis H. Morgan and became Morgan's ardent disciple. To support Morgan's thesis that Aztec society was essentially like that of the democratic Iroquois, Bandelier published three heavily documented papers in the annual reports of the Peabody Museum: "On the Art of War and Mode of Warfare of the Ancient Mexicans" (1877), "On the Distribution and Tenure of Lands and the Customs With Respect to Inheritance Among the Ancient Mexicans" (1878), and "On the Social Organization and Mode of Government of the Ancient Mexicans" (1879).

In 1880, Bandelier left the world of business and thereafter devoted himself to scholarship. That year he went to New Mexico, where, with the exception of 14 months during which he made an archeological tour of Mexico, he remained until 1892, engaging in archeological, ethnological, and documentary studies of the region. His principal works of this period were *Final Report of Investigations Among the Indians of the Southwestern United States* (1890–1892) and an ethnological novel, *The Delight Makers* (1890). In 1892 he went to Peru and Bolivia, where he made archeological, ethnological, and documentary studies; *The Islands of Titicaca and Koati* (1910) was the principal publication of this period. After his return to New York, in 1903, he was successively associated with the American Museum of Natural History, Columbia University, the Hispanic Society of America, and the Carnegie Institution of Washington. He went to Spain in 1913 to continue his documentary researches on the Pueblo Indians and died in Seville, where he was buried.

Bandelier's studies of the Indians of the Southwest are still of value to the scholar today, although they are not easy to use. His reports on his researches in Peru and Bolivia are also substantial. His three monographs on the ancient Mexicans, however, possess little more than historical significance; although these studies were undertaken in order to substantiate Morgan's thesis of Pan-American Indian democracy, the data contained in them invalidate that thesis.

LESLIE A. WHITE

[*For the historical context of Bandelier's work, see* INDIANS, NORTH AMERICAN, *and the biography of* MORGAN, LEWIS HENRY.]

WORKS BY BANDELIER

1877 On the Art of War and Mode of Warfare of the Ancient Mexicans. Volume 2, pages 95–161 in Harvard University, Peabody Museum of American Archaeology and Ethnology, *Annual Report,* 10th. Cambridge, Mass.: The Museum. → Also published as a separate pamphlet.

1878 On the Distribution and Tenure of Lands and the Customs With Respect to Inheritance Among the Ancient Mexicans. Volume 2, pages 385–448 in Harvard University, Peabody Museum of American Archaeology and Ethnology, *Annual Report,* 11th. Cambridge, Mass.: The Museum.

1879 On the Social Organization and Mode of Government of the Ancient Mexicans. Volume 2, pages 557–699 in Harvard University, Peabody Museum of American Archaeology and Ethnology, *Annual Report,* 12th. Cambridge, Mass.: The Museum. → Also published as a separate pamphlet.

(1890) 1954 *The Delight Makers.* New York: Dodd.

1890–1892 *Final Report of Investigations Among the Indians of the Southwestern United States, Carried on Mainly in the Years From 1880 to 1885.* 2 vols. Papers of the Archaeological Institute of America, American Series, Nos. 3 and 4. Cambridge, Mass.: Wilson.

1910 *The Islands of Titicaca and Koati.* New York: Hispanic Society of America.

1940 *Pioneers in American Anthropology: The Bandelier–Morgan Letters, 1873–1883.* 2 vols. Albuquerque: Univ. of New Mexico Press.

1960 *Correspondencia de Adolfo F. Bandelier.* Serie Historia, No. 4. Mexico City: Instituto Nacional de Antropología e Historia.

WORKS ABOUT BANDELIER

HODGE, F. W. 1932 Biographical Sketch and Bibliography of Adolphe Francis Alphonse Bandelier. *New Mexico Historical Review* 7:353–370.

KIDDER, A. V. 1928 Adolph F. Bandelier. Volume 1, pages 571–572 in *Dictionary of American Biography.* New York: Scribner.

BANKING

A bank deals in money and money substitutes; it also provides a range of financial services. In a formal sense, it borrows or receives "deposits" from firms, individuals, and (sometimes) governments and, on the basis of these resources, either makes "loans" to others or purchases securities, which are listed as "investments." In general, it covers its expenses and earns its profits by borrowing at one rate of interest and lending at a higher rate. In addition, commissions may be charged for services rendered.

A bank is under an obligation to repay its customers' balances either on demand or whenever the amounts credited to them become due. For this reason, a bank must hold some cash (which for this purpose may include balances at a bankers' bank, such as a central bank) and keep a further proportion of its assets in forms that can readily be converted into cash. It is only in this way that confidence in the banking system can be maintained. In its turn, confidence is the basis of "credit." Provided its promises are always honored (for example, to convert notes into gold or deposit balances into cash), a bank can "create credit" for use by its customers—either by issuing additional notes or by making new loans (which in turn become new deposits). A bank is able to do this because the public believes the bank can and will without question honor these promises, which will then be accepted at their face value and circulate as money. As long as they remain outstanding, these promises continue to constitute claims against that bank and can be transferred by means of checks or other instruments from one party to another. In essence, this is what is known as "deposit banking." With some variations, it is the accepted basis of commercial banking as practiced in the modern world. Indeed, deposit banking cannot be said to exist as long as the assets held by a bank consist only of cash lodged by depositors. Once the accounts of banks begin to show more deposits than cash, part of these deposits must represent loans that have been made by a banker to his customers, that is, deposits created by the banking system.

Origins

Although no adequate documentation exists prior to the thirteenth century, banking is known to have a longer history. However, many of the early "banks" dealt primarily in coin and bullion, much of their business being concerned with money-changing and the supply of lawful foreign and domestic coin of the correct weight and fineness. A second and important group consisted of merchant-bankers who dealt not only in goods but also in bills of exchange, which provided for the remittance of money and the payment of accounts at a distance, without shipping actual coin. This was possible because many of these merchants had an international business and held assets at a number of points on the trading routes of medieval Europe. For a consideration, a merchant would be prepared to accept instructions to pay out money through an agent elsewhere to a named party, the amount of the bill of exchange to be debited by the agent to the merchant-banker's account. In addition to the consideration paid, the merchant-banker would also hope to make a profit from the exchange of one currency for another. Since there was the possibility of loss, any profit or gain was not regarded as usurious. There were also techniques for making concealed loans by supplying foreign exchange at a distance but deferring payment for it until a later date. The interest charge was camouflaged by fluctuations in the rate of exchange between the date of ordering goods and the date of payment for them.

The acceptance of deposits was another early banking activity. These might relate either to the deposit of money or valuables merely for safekeeping or for purposes of transfer to another party or to the deposit of money in current account. A balance in current account might also represent the proceeds of a loan granted by the banker. Indeed, by oral agreement between the parties, recorded in the banker's journal, a loan might be granted merely by allowing a customer to overdraw his account. In all these instances, a banker was held liable to meet on demand the claims of his depositors.

Deposit banking. By the seventeenth century English bankers had begun to develop a deposit-banking business, and the techniques evolved there and in Scotland were in due course to prove highly influential elsewhere. As men of wealth and reputation, the London goldsmiths already kept money and other valuables in safe custody for customers. They also dealt in bullion and foreign exchange and this led to their acquiring and sorting coin for profit. In order to attract coin for sorting, they offered to pay a rate of interest and, in this way, began to supplant as deposit bankers their great rivals the "money scriveners." These were notaries who had come to specialize in bringing together borrowers and lenders and had themselves been accepting deposits.

It was soon discovered that when merchants deposited money with a goldsmith or scrivener they tended, as a group, to maintain their deposits at a fairly steady level; the goldsmith was able to "depend upon a course of Trade whereby Money comes in as fast as it is taken out." In addition, customers preferred to leave their surplus money with the goldsmith and to hold only enough for their everyday needs. Hence, there was likely to be a fund of idle cash that could be lent out at interest to those who could use such money to advantage.

Invention of the check. There had also grown up a practice whereby the customer could arrange for the transfer to another party of part of his credit balance with his banker by addressing to him an order to this effect. This was the origin of the modern check (the earliest known example in England is dated 1670). It was but a short step from making a loan in specie to permitting customers to borrow by issuing checks. One technique was to debit a loan account with the full amount borrowed and immediately to credit an equivalent amount to a current account against which checks could be drawn. Alternatively, the customer might be permitted to overdraw his account. In the former case, interest was charged on the full amount placed to the debit of the loan account; in the latter, interest was charged only on the amount actually borrowed. But, in both cases, the customer was permitted to borrow by issuing checks in payment for goods or services. The checks represented claims against the bank, which had a corresponding claim against its customer.

Bank notes. Another means whereby a bank could create claims against itself was by issuing notes. If the volume of notes so issued exceeded the amount of specie or bullion held, additional money would have been created. The amount that was issued depended on the banker's calculation of the possible demand from his customers for specie; the public would accept such notes only because of the banker's known integrity. The evidence suggests that in London the goldsmith bankers were developing the use of the bank note at about the same time as the check, although the first bank notes in Europe were issued in 1661 by the Bank of Stockholm (later to become the Bank of Sweden). Some commercial banks are still permitted to issue their own notes, but most such issues have now been taken over by the central bank.

Bank credit. In Britain the check proved to be such a convenient means of payment that gradually the public came to prefer the use of checks for the larger part of their monetary transactions, using coin (and, later, notes) for the smaller kinds of payments. In consequence of this development, the banks grew bold and accorded their borrowers the right to draw checks far in excess of the amount of cash actually held. In other words, the banks were then creating "money"—claims that were generally accepted as means of payment. This money came to be known as "bank money" or "credit." If bank notes are excluded, this money consists of figures in bank ledgers and is money only because of confidence in the ability of the banks to honor their liabilities when called upon to do so.

When a check is drawn and passed to another party in payment for goods or services, the check will usually be paid into another bank account, although certain checks may be cashed by direct presentation. If the check has been drawn by a borrower (and assuming that the overdraft technique is employed), the mere act of drawing and passing the check will create a loan as soon as the check is paid by the borrower's banker. Because every loan so made tends to return to the banking system as a deposit, deposits will tend, for the system as a whole, to increase (and to decrease) approximately to the same extent as loans. If the money lent has been debited to a loan account and the amount of the loan has been credited to the customer's current account, a deposit will be created immediately.

Negotiable instruments. In England, where the mercantile courts had greater scope than on the Continent, one of the most important factors in promoting the development of banking was the legal recognition of the negotiability of credit instruments. When orders of payment were first introduced in Europe they were certainly nonnegotiable, but in England many such orders were drawn in terms similar to those of a bill of exchange and, when the doctrine of negotiability had been established and accepted by the Courts of Common Law, the check was explicitly defined as a bill of exchange and recognized as a negotiable instrument. This helps to explain some of the differences between banking arrangements in Continental Europe and in Britain, as well as in countries influenced by British traditions. In particular, Continental limitations on the negotiability of an order of payment stood in the way of the extension of deposit banking based on the check that became such a feature of British development in the eighteenth and early nineteenth centuries. Meanwhile, Continental countries were developing a system of *Giro* payments, whereby transfers were effected on the basis of written instructions to debit the *Giro* account of the payer and to credit that of the payee.

Despite the above differences, the various banking systems have many similarities. This may be attributed to the fact that all banks trade in a type of "commodity" (money and money substitutes) that has particular characteristics. Thus, in all banking institutions (with the partial exception of those in the U.S.S.R. and those based on the same system), there is some emphasis on the need for liquidity (or the ease with which assets can be converted into cash without substantial loss) and on margins of safety in lending. Even where certain of the commercial banks are state owned (for example, in Australia, Egypt, France, and India), this has remained true.

Structure of banking systems

It is more interesting, therefore, to establish why banking systems in the several countries do differ from one another, sometimes in quite material respects. The problems that face banks are much the same the world over but there is considerable variety in the solutions that are put forward to resolve them. Hence, it is in the details of organization and technique that one tends to find the differences. Yet there is a tendency for the differences to become less pronounced because of growing efficiency in international communication and the disposition to emulate practices that have proved successful elsewhere. Those differences that survive are largely the result of influences deriving from the economic and sociopolitical environment. These similarities and differences can be discussed in terms of: (*a*) the structure of commercial banking systems; and (*b*) the varying emphases in the types of business that are done by banks in different countries.

Although one must be careful not to oversimplify, it is possible to classify banking structures as falling within one or another of certain broad categories. For example, "unit banking" still describes fairly accurately the commercial banking arrangements that obtain over large areas in the United States, which has nearly fourteen thousand banks and not very many more bank branches. In a number of other countries it is more usual to find a small number of commercial banks, each of which operates a highly developed network of bank branches. In England and Wales, for example, only 11 banks (5 much larger than the rest) do nearly all the domestic banking business through more than 11,500 branches and agencies. Between these two extremes, there are many instances of "hybrid" systems, where the services of banks that are national in scope are supplemented by those that restrict their activities to either a region or a locality. Examples of such banking systems would be those of France and India. Although these hybrid systems are slowly changing their

character (banks are tending to become fewer in number and individually larger, often with networks of branches), so far they have remained different enough from the two other main types of banking systems to warrant separate classification.

Unit banking—the United States. Over large areas of the United States, bank organization is still passing through a phase of structural development that many other countries went through some decades ago. This is not to deny that there has been much experimentation in the evolution of the American banking system, but its development has been subject to constraints that have certainly influenced the path that was chosen. For example, the United States has a federal form of government with a constitution that permits both federal and state legislatures to pass laws to regulate banking. A bank can, therefore, be subject to the banking laws of its own state as well as to those passed by the federal Congress. Some states permit branch banking (sometimes subject to restrictions); others prohibit it. Of itself, this has cut across any integrating forces operating on a nationwide basis. Thus the constitutional arrangements, reinforced by the political influence of small local bankers, provided the legal framework that encouraged the establishment and retention of a large number of unit banks. It must be emphasized that it was not federalism as such but the division of powers within the federation that constituted the barrier to concentration. In Australia, which also has a federal constitution, the federal government has exclusive power to legislate for all banking except that conducted by banks owned by a state government and operating within the state, and for the most part the laws relating to banks have been applied nationally. As it happens, there have been no legal impediments to the spread of branch banking in Australia, and this system is in fact well developed.

The initial establishment of a large number of banks in the United States was due to the scarcity of capital in relation to profitable opportunities for investment as the frontiers of settlement were pushed rapidly westward by the early pioneers. To satisfy the heavy demand for loans and for a medium of exchange, banks sprang up across the country. At this time, too, communications between the frontiers of settlement and the established centers of commerce and finance were still undeveloped. It was only with the coming of the railroads that east–west traffic expanded at all rapidly. Steady territorial expansion also converted the United States into a country of immense distances; there was an obvious need for a large number of banks to serve the diverse and rapidly expanding demands of a growing and constantly migrating population.

As long as communications remained imperfect, therefore, it is not difficult to explain the existence of large numbers of competing institutions. But why the subsequent failure of bank mergers or amalgamations to produce a concentration of financial resources in the hands of large banking units serving local needs through a network of branches? The retention of a primarily unit-banking system long after the barriers of distance had been broken down can be attributed in part to the federal constitution; disinclination to change was further strengthened by the widespread distrust of monopoly and the deep-rooted fear that a "money trust" might develop. There was wide acceptance of a political philosophy that emphasized the virtues of individualism and free competition. Moreover, restrictions on branching, bank mergers, and holding companies were a feature of both the state and federal banking laws. However, in parts of the United States bank branches are already numerous (especially in California, where branching is state-wide; also in New York, although there the area covered by a branch network is restricted) and, despite regulation, a large number of bank mergers have been approved.

Branch banking—Britain. The demand for larger banking units is generally a concomitant of economic growth, with which may often be associated a rapid increase in population and its aggregation in industrial centers. A prior condition not only of growth but also of the integration of an economy and its financial institutions (without which larger units could scarcely emerge) is the development of adequate transport facilities and communications. Without efficient communications, banks could not clear checks drawn on other banks and effect their remittances easily and quickly. Branch banking is not necessarily a function of growth, but in England it was associated with it. Again, good communications were a prerequisite, in order to control branches at a distance. The Scots, for example, who from the establishment of the Bank of Scotland in 1695 favored the establishment of branches, were not initially very successful—primarily because of poor communications and the difficulty of moving adequate supplies of coin. It was not until after the Napoleonic Wars that these banks began to expand their branches with vigor. The banks then sought to overcome their difficulties by appointing as "agents" to take charge of their branches local men of standing and repute, for whom banking was

often merely a sideline. Only much later, as communications improved, was responsibility for authorizing advances gradually shifted from the "agent" to the head office.

By the 1830s in England, the stream of industrial progress was running fast and already the size of the business unit was growing. A large number of small private banks were proving inadequate to meet the needs of an industrial structure no longer capable of financing itself. Bigger industrial units required financial units with greater resources, whether for lending or in the form of the more extensive connections essential to the provision of an increasing range of services. Small banks, unable to stand the strain of these enlarged demands, often became overextended and failed. This was the economic basis for the growth in bank size that was encouraged by legislation, beginning in 1826, permitting joint-stock ownership. The more widely spread proprietary, less exposed to the vagaries of human frailty, was a much more important influence on growth than limited liability, which at first—and until after the failure of the City of Glasgow Bank in 1878—was regarded with some suspicion.

Although most of the early joint-stock banks tended for some time to remain localized in their business, joint-stock ownership, latterly with limited liability, furnished the basis for the subsequent growth of the English banks in both resources and geographic coverage. These developments, which assisted in attracting deposits and in spreading the banking risk over a wider range of industries and areas, were undoubtedly encouraged by the competitive spirit and desire for personal power. They were greatly accelerated by the bank amalgamation movement that began during the nineteenth century and came to fruition during the first two decades of the twentieth century, giving Britain substantially the kind of banking system that it has today.

Hybrid banking. Different again from the unit banking of the United States and the primarily branch-banking systems of, for example, Britain, Australia, Canada, New Zealand, and South Africa are the hybrid banking systems. These are characterized by a small number of banks with branches throughout the country that hold the larger part of total deposits; the balance of deposits are lodged in a relatively large number of small banks. Although there are differences of degree and the long-term trend would seem to be toward concentrating bank deposits in fewer institutions, it has been found in many instances (for example, in France, Germany, Italy, the Netherlands, and

India) that the number of the small banks decreases rather slowly. In Japan, where there is a small number of large city banks with branch networks and a larger number of local banks, there was a small increase in the total following World War II and then virtual stability.

It is pertinent to inquire why the decrease should be slow and what obstacles exist to impede integration. Their precise character will vary from country to country; only a few examples can be offered here. These will be drawn from France and India. Frenchmen, for example, are individualists; this is reflected in the large number of small businesses that still exist and in the continuing demand for the small banking unit that can provide a more individual and personal service than the larger bank. Again, particularism is still strong in some parts of France; this manifests itself in support for local institutions. Moreover, the local banker can often attract business simply because of his special knowledge of the local industries and people; this enables him to accept risks that the big banks will decline. Also, in the past, the larger institutions in France preferred to open their own branches in new areas rather than to absorb local and regional banks.

In a less developed country like India, where a relatively large number of small banks still exists, there are other kinds of impediments. India is primarily an agricultural country, with an economic and social structure based largely on villages. These are often separated by both distance and poor communications. Integration of banking, based as it is on the spread of new ideas and institutions, is also impeded by the great barriers of ignorance and illiteracy; some degree of literacy is an obvious prerequisite for operating a bank account. In addition, there are the barriers of language and caste, as well as the difficulties that arise from joint family ownership (for example, when providing security for a bank loan). Again, habits of thrift are not easy to inculcate until incomes can be lifted sufficiently to provide a margin for saving. Hence the still strong preference for the indigenous banker with his flexible methods, and even for the moneylender. Both have existed for centuries. The indigenous banker, who is also a merchant, offers genuine banking services—accepting deposits (when available) and remitting funds; making loans quickly and with a minimum of formality; and, by means of the *hundi* (an indigenous credit instrument in promissory note form), financing a significant, if decreasing, part of India's domestic trade and commerce.

It is hoped that the moneylender in India will gradually be displaced, however, by the development of a network of rural credit cooperatives, although in some areas progress has been very slow. In addition, as an act of policy and over a period of years, a progressively larger number of "pioneer" bank branches have been opened in rural areas, initially by the semipublic Imperial Bank of India and more recently by its nationalized successor, the State Bank of India. Meanwhile, many of the smaller banks that tend to serve the persons or concerns that initially sponsored them have begun to disappear.

Norway provides an interesting example of the effects on banking structure of physical geography. Almost everywhere the country is mountainous, and overland transport (especially in winter) is often difficult. Although airlines and telecommunications are beginning to knit the country together more effectively, it will be some time before improved communications can break down the particularisms that favor the continued existence of the local banks.

Yet in all these countries there is already evidence of much integration as a result of the steady growth in the size of branch networks, as well as in the share of total business done by the more important banks. Regional and local banks have been absorbed, a process that has been quickened by the need for larger resources than can be mustered by the smaller banks. In France, regional and some local banks have become associated with an institution in the capital. In India small banks have amalgamated on a regional basis, usually with the active encouragement of the Reserve Bank of India, which has hoped thereby to impart a greater degree of strength and stability to the Indian banking system. India has also encouraged the progressive extension of "pioneer branches," a technique that has also been employed in Pakistan. In all these countries (as in the United States) there is widespread use of bank correspondents. Indeed, when banking systems are either of a unit or hybrid type, institutions must carry a rather higher proportion of total funds as balances with correspondents than do branch-banking institutions, in order to compensate the correspondent for providing a range of services that otherwise could be supplied only by setting up a local branch.

Types of banking business

It remains to inquire into the degree to which there are variations in the types of business done by commercial banks in different countries and to establish the reasons for such differences. The essential characteristics of banking business can be most readily understood within the framework of a simple balance sheet.

The main liabilities are *capital* (including reserve accounts) and *deposits*—domestic and foreign—whether of corporations, firms, private individuals, other banks, or (sometimes) governments; whether repayable on demand (that is, sight or current accounts) or after the lapse of a period of time (time, term, or fixed deposits, but also including on occasion savings deposits).

The most important assets items are: *cash,* (which may be in the form of credit balances with other banks—for example, with the central bank or with correspondents); *liquid assets,* such as money at call and short notice, day-to-day money, short-term government paper (for example, Treasury bills and notes), and commercial bills of exchange, all of which may be readily converted into cash without risk of substantial loss; *investments* or *securities* (medium-term and long-term government securities, including those of local authorities such as states, provinces, or municipalities; also, in certain countries, participations and shares in industrial concerns); *advances and loans* to customers of all kinds, but primarily those in trade and industry, including in some countries term and mortgage loans (discounts, that is, discounted commercial bills of exchange, may sometimes be shown here, instead of under *liquid assets*); and *premises, furniture, and fittings* (usually written down to quite nominal figures).

A bank balance sheet must also include an item to cover contingent liabilities (for example, on bills of exchange whether "accepted" or endorsed by the bank); this will be exactly balanced by a "contra" item on the other side, representing the customer's obligation to the bank (for which the bank might also have taken security). Virtually all banks of any size nowadays provide acceptance credits (sometimes called bankers' acceptances), primarily to finance external trade. As the acceptor of a bill, a bank lends its name and reputation to it and thereby ensures the readier discount of paper that might otherwise have been difficult to place. A bank endorsement may serve a similar purpose.

Bank deposits. Deposit banks, as their name suggests, operate largely on the basis of their deposits. These consist of borrowed money (and therefore liabilities), but insofar as an increase in deposits provides a banker with additional cash (an asset), this increase in cash will supplement his loanable resources. Capital and reserve accounts, which are the other important liability

item, now serve primarily as the ultimate cover against losses (for example, on loans and investments). But they usually represent only a small part of the total liabilities of deposit banks. In the United States, the capital accounts are also significant as they provide the statutory basis of a bank's lending limit to the individual borrower. However, those institutions concerned with investment banking (for example, the French *banques d'affaires*), a proportion of whose loans and industrial investment is likely to be long-term and therefore less liquid, must necessarily depend to a rather greater extent on their own capital resources.

For the banking system as a whole, an increase in deposits may arise in two ways: (*a*) if the banks increase their loans they will either transfer the money borrowed to a current account and create a new deposit directly or they will accord the borrower a limit up to which he may draw checks, which when they are deposited by third parties create a new deposit; or (*b*) the growth in deposits may stem from enlarged government expenditure financed by the central bank—claims on the government equivalent to cash will be paid into the commercial banks as deposits and their ownership thereby transferred from their initial recipients to the banks themselves. In the first case, as bank deposits increase, there is a related increase in the potential liability to pay out cash; in the second, the increase in deposits with the commercial banks will be accompanied by a corresponding increase in bank holdings of money claims equivalent to cash.

For the individual bank, an increase in its loans may result in a direct increase in deposits, either by transfer to a current account (as above) or by transfer to another customer of the same bank. Again, there will be an increase in the potential liability to pay out cash. But an increase in loans by another bank (including central bank loans to the government) may result in increased deposits with the first bank matched by a corresponding claim to cash (or its equivalent). Thus, the individual bank can generally expect that an increase in deposits will result in some net acquisition of cash or in a corresponding claim for receipt of cash from a third party. It is in this sense that an accretion to deposits provides the basis for further bank lending.

Except in countries where banks may still be small and insecure, the banks as a whole can usually depend on current account debits being offset very largely by the related credits, although an individual bank may from time to time experience marked fluctuations in its deposit totals. Further inertia may be added to the deposit structure by accepting money contractually for a fixed term or repayable only subject to notice. Nevertheless, at the banker's discretion, funds may in fact be withdrawn prior to due date. Alternatively, a bank may lend against the security of such a deposit. Overdependence on foreign deposits, which tend to be more volatile than those of domestic origin, may have the opposite effect, since rumors from a distance are apt to prompt precipitate action.

Indeed, at all times, confidence in the banks is the true basis of stability. This is greatly enhanced where there exists a central bank prepared to act as "lender of last resort." Deposit insurance (as in the United States and India) is another means of maintaining confidence as it protects the small depositor against loss in the event of a bank failure. This was also the ostensible purpose of the "nationalization" of bank deposits in Argentina from 1946 to 1957. The recipient bank acted merely as the agent of the government-owned and government-controlled central bank, all bank deposits being guaranteed by the state.

Cash and liquidity requirements. The essence of the banker–customer relationship is the banker's undertaking to provide his customers with cash on demand or after an agreed period of notice. Hence the necessity to hold a cash reserve and to maintain a "safe" ratio of cash to deposits. This ratio may be established by convention (as in England) or by statute (as in the United States and elsewhere). In either case, the choice has been based on experience. However, where a minimum cash ratio is imposed by law a bank's assets will in fact be impounded and, in the absence of any revision of the required ratio, be unavailable to meet sudden demands for cash by the bank's customers. Indeed, the necessity to provide some day-to-day flexibility is one reason why required ratios are often based on the averaged cash holdings of an institution over a legally specified period.

One of the first bankers to publicize the importance of maintaining an adequate proportion of deposits in cash (or other liquid form) was George Rae; this was in 1875. Whatever the amount of cash held (short of covering demand deposits 100 per cent), no bank could meet depositors' claims in their entirety if all customers were to exercise fully their rights to demand cash. If that were a common phenomenon, it would not be possible to base banking on the receipt of deposits. But for the most part the public is prepared to leave its surplus funds on deposit with the banks, confident that their money will be repaid as required. Nevertheless, there are occasions when unexpected demands for cash may exceed what might reasonably have been anticipated. A banker must, in consequence, always hold part of his assets in cash and a proportion of the remainder in assets that without significant loss can be quickly converted into cash. In theory, even his less liquid assets should be self-liquidating within a reasonable time.

While no banker can safely ignore the necessity to maintain adequate reserves of liquid assets, some tend to emphasize instead the desirability of limiting the sum of loans and investments to a certain percentage of deposits (say, to 70 per cent). They would feel "uncomfortable" if their loan–deposit ratio were to run for any length of time at too high a level; investments are often regarded as something of a residual. But whichever ratio were adopted as a guide to action would matter little, since the effects would be much the same.

There are three main ways in which a bank's assets may be mobilized: (*a*) loans may be "callable" (repayment may be demanded immediately or at short notice); (*b*) securities may be sold in an organized market; or (*c*) paper representing investments or loans may be discounted at the central bank or submitted as security for an advance. However, any precipitate calling in of loans would so disrupt the delicate nexus of debtor–creditor relations as to exaggerate the loss of confidence liable to occasion a run on the banks. So would heavy selling of marketable assets, with sharply falling prices and consequent losses. Ready cash may be obtainable only at a high price. Either the banks must maintain cash reserves and liquid assets at a high level, or there must exist a "lender of last resort" (for example, a central bank) able and willing (albeit subject to conditions) to provide the banks with cash, when required, in exchange for or against the security of eligible assets. In either event, liquid assets (including cash) are an essential component of the bank balance sheet, and, indeed, in some countries the commercial banks may be required to maintain a minimum liquid asset ratio. This is common, for example, in western European countries and also applies in effect to the English, Australian, and Canadian banks. In Asia, the requirement is usually limited to cash reserve ratios only, although Malaysia is an exception. A minimum liquid assets ratio has also been prescribed for commercial banks by several of the new African central banks (for example, in Ghana and Nigeria) and in Jamaica.

At the same time, a central bank resorts to such requirements nowadays less as a means of maintaining appropriate levels of commercial bank liquidity than as a technique for influencing directly the lending potential of the banks.

Bank investments.   The commercial banks rightly regard their investments (often consisting largely of medium-term government securities, but also sometimes including industrial shares and participations) as rather less liquid than money-market assets (such as call money and treasury bills). Nevertheless, by staggering their maturities, they are able to ensure that a portion of their holdings is regularly approaching redemption, thereby constituting a secondary liquid reserve. Following redemption at maturity, the banks usually reinvest all or most of this money by purchasing longer-term securities that in due course themselves become increasingly shorter-term. (In Britain, the average maturity of a bank investment portfolio is about five years; it is usually rather less in the United States.) But selling before maturity is also quite common—in order to vary the spread of maturities, or to restore a bank's liquidity, or to expand loans. Because market conditions may be variable and longer maturity dates give less opportunity to avoid loss by holding securities to maturity, banks tend for balance-sheet purposes to "write down" the value of their investments (and other assets) and thereby to create "hidden reserves." The essential difference between money-market assets and bank investments is that as a rule the liquidity of investments depends primarily on marketability (although sometimes it depends on the readiness of the government or its agent to exchange its own securities for cash), whereas the liquidity of money-market assets depends partly on marketability and partly on eligibility at the central bank. For this reason, money-market assets are more liquid.

Long-term finance.   Where special investment banks exist (like the French *banques d'affaires,* although these also undertake a sizable deposit banking business, especially for firms in which they hold shares or any other kind of capital interest), or where the commercial banks are accustomed to finance long-term industrial developments (as in West Germany), it is no more than ordinary business prudence both to operate on the basis of relatively large capital funds (plus long-term deposits) and to value the relevant investments most conservatively. The risk of error and therefore of loss tends to increase with the period of the commitment, which after the initial technical investigation may begin as an interim credit to be converted later into a participation. Since one of the functions of these banks (which frequently organize themselves in consortiums or syndicates) is to "nurse" investments until a venture is well established, it may be necessary to hold such participations for long periods. Then, if in the bank's judgment market conditions are deemed favorable, the original investment can be converted into marketable securities by arranging an issue of shares to the public. Nevertheless, even assuming the ultimate success of the issue, a bank may on occasion be obliged to hold such shares for long periods before being able to liquidate the bulk of its holdings and begin the process all over again. In fact, a *banque d'affaires* will often retain a sufficient percentage of a firm's shares to ensure a degree of continuing control.

In contrast with Continental tradition, the long-term provision of industrial finance is usually referred in the countries of the British Commonwealth (including the United Kingdom) to specialist institutions, with the commercial banks providing part of the necessary capital. Except in the United States, where the banks are active competitors for this business, installment credit (hire-purchase finance) is also provided in most countries largely by specialist houses. In Japan, the long-term financial needs of industry are met partly by special industrial banks (which supplement their capital with the proceeds of debenture issues) and partly by the ordinary commercial banks (on the basis of the large volume of time deposits they attract).

Since World War II, term lending has been systematically developed in the United States, largely for the purpose of financing industrial re-equipment and growth. This policy owes its origin to the poor loan demand of the 1930s, when the banks sought to induce additional borrowing, especially at times when stock markets were unfavorable for new issues, by offering finance for a period of years. These loans, the majority of which have an effective maximum maturity of little more than five years, are subject to a formal agreement between the customer and (usually) a group of lending banks, sometimes in cooperation with other institutions, such as insurance companies. More recently, banks in several other countries (including Britain and Australia) have instituted term loans to finance exports and capital expenditure, both in industry and in agriculture.

Loans and advances.   Yet even in countries where commercial banks do lend long-term to industry, it is the self-liquidating loans and advances that constitute the core (and often the most profitable part) of earning assets. Traditionally, much of this accommodation is of the "seed-time to harvest" kind, that is, provision of working capital, although there may be some temporary financing of fixed capital development pending arrangements to raise long-term finance elsewhere. Overdrafts, whereby a borrower may overdraw his account (or go into debit) up to an agreed limit, are the common means of bank lending in the United Kingdom and in a number of other countries. In theory they are temporary but usually renewable annually or repayable after due and reasonable notice has been given; in practice they may run on for long periods, depending on the character of the business being financed. The advance is reduced or repaid when credits are paid into the account, and recreated when new checks are drawn. The "cash credit" employed in India and Pakistan to finance the holding of stocks is similar. Even in countries where the overdraft predominates (for example, in Britain and the Netherlands), the method of debiting a loan account for credit to a current account may sometimes be used; checks are drawn on the current account, with interest payable on the whole amount of the loan (itself usually for a fixed period) instead of only on the amount actually overdrawn.

Elsewhere (for example, on the Continent and in the United States and Japan), bank finance is often made available short-term on the basis of discountable paper—commercial bills or promissory notes, often subject to a line of credit similar to an overdraft limit. This accommodation is also self-liquidating as it matures, although such paper may be renewable at the discretion of the lender. If eligible for rediscount at the central bank, it becomes virtually a liquid asset, unlike a bank advance or loan. Under both systems, finance may be made available with or without formal security, depending on the reputation and financial strength of the borrower. In many countries the customer may seek finance (and other services) from a number of banks (to protect their own interests these institutions will usually freely exchange information about joint credit risks), but in Britain and in the Netherlands the tendency is for all but the largest concerns to use the services of a single institution to meet the bulk of their banking needs.

Nonbank financial intermediaries

Finally, we must consider the relations between the commercial banks and other types of financial intermediary that undertake quasi-banking business. In the days of "cloakroom" banking (lending out mainly such money as had in fact been deposited in cash), banks were not in any important sense "creators of money," except to the extent of their note issues. In a similar way, installment credit (or hire-purchase) finance companies, mortgage banks, and building societies (or savings and loan associations) in effect lend out only what they receive and, since money deposited with them usually and with little delay finds its way back to the banks themselves, the existence of such intermediaries cannot seriously affect the level of bank deposits. Other institutions, such as local governmental and other authorities, collect savings to spend; these, again, reappear in bank accounts. Yet, although they may not "create money" in the same way as the commercial banks, nonbank financial intermediaries can be the means of activating otherwise idle balances (accumulated from savings in earlier periods) and can thereby add to the intensity of the use made of monetary assets. In large measure what they do is merely gather savings together and direct these (by lending them) into the hands of those who will use them. In this event they lend no more than savers decide to place with them from their current income receipts. Only to the limited extent that these intermediaries invest in government securities may deposits be lost to the banking system, just as when commercial undertakings buy treasury bills. However, during times of credit restriction, when bank lending has been significantly curtailed, the nonbank financial intermediaries have been able to increase their share of the types of loans also made by the banks. In that way they seriously compete with the latter for business that once lost is difficult to regain. In addition, the competition for new loan business has certainly been intensified by the growth of lending institutions other than banks, and in a number of countries banks have been forced either to acquire capital interests in finance companies or themselves to develop installment credit or hire-purchase business.

J. S. G. Wilson

[*See also* Banking, central; Financial intermediaries; Money.]

BIBLIOGRAPHY

American Bankers Association 1962 *The Commercial Banking Industry.* A monograph prepared for the Commission on Money and Credit. Englewood Cliffs, N.J.: Prentice-Hall.

Beckhart, Benjamin H. (editor) 1954 *Banking Systems.* New York: Columbia Univ. Press.

Commission on Money and Credit 1961 *Money and Credit: Their Influence on Jobs, Prices and Growth.* Englewood Cliffs, N.J.: Prentice-Hall.

Crick, W. F. (editor) 1965 *Commonwealth Banking Systems.* Oxford: Clarendon.

DIAMOND, WILLIAM 1957 *Development Banks*. Published for the International Bank for Reconstruction and Development, Economic Development Institute. Baltimore: Johns Hopkins Press.

GREAT BRITAIN, COMMITTEE ON FINANCE AND INDUSTRY 1931a *Report*. Papers by Command, Cmd. 3897. London: H.M. Stationery Office. → Commonly known as the Macmillan Report.

GREAT BRITAIN, COMMITTEE ON FINANCE AND INDUSTRY 1931b *Minutes of Evidence Taken Before the Committee*. Vol. 1. London: H.M. Stationery Office.

GREAT BRITAIN, COMMITTEE ON THE WORKING OF THE MONETARY SYSTEM 1959 *Report*. Papers by Command, Cmd. 827. London: H.M. Stationery Office. → Commonly known as the Radcliffe Report.

GREAT BRITAIN, COMMITTEE ON THE WORKING OF THE MONETARY SYSTEM 1960a *Minutes of Evidence*. London: H.M. Stationery Office.

GREAT BRITAIN, COMMITTEE ON THE WORKING OF THE MONETARY SYSTEM 1960b *Principal Memoranda of Evidence*. 3 vols. London: H.M. Stationery Office.

JACOBY, NEIL H.; and SAULNIER, R. J. 1947 *Business Finance and Banking*. National Bureau of Economic Research, Financial Research Program. Princeton Univ. Press.

PLUMPTRE, ARTHUR F. W. 1940 *Central Banking in the British Dominions*. Toronto Univ. Press; Oxford Univ. Press.

RESERVE BANK OF INDIA, COMMITTEE OF DIRECTION OF THE ALL-INDIA RURAL CREDIT SURVEY 1954 *All-India Rural Credit Survey*. Bombay. → Volume 1: *The Survey Report*. Parts 1 and 2. Volume 2: *The General Report*. Volume 3: *The Technical Report*.

SAYERS, RICHARD S. (editor) 1952 *Banking in the British Commonwealth*. Oxford: Clarendon.

SAYERS, RICHARD S. (editor) 1962 *Banking in Western Europe*. Oxford: Clarendon.

[U.S.] BOARD OF GOVERNORS OF THE FEDERAL RESERVE SYSTEM 1941 *Banking Studies*. Baltimore: Waverly.